What Has a **Pointed Head** and Eats Lizards?

WRITTEN BY **Robert Kanner**
ILLUSTRATED BY **Russ Daff**

dingles&company New Jersey

FOR ANGELA RODGERS

First Printing

Published by dingles&company
P.O. Box 508
Sea Girt, New Jersey 08750

LIBRARY OF CONGRESS CATALOG CARD NUMBER
2007904350

ISBN
978-1-59646-832-0

Printed in the United States of America

The Uncover & Discover series is based on the original concept of Judy Mazzeo Zocchi.

ART DIRECTION & DESIGN
Rizco Design

EDITORIAL CONSULTANT
Andrea Curley

PROJECT MANAGER
Lisa Aldorasi

EDUCATIONAL CONSULTANTS
Melissa Oster and Margaret Bergin

CREATIVE DIRECTOR
Barbie Lambert

PRE-PRESS
Pixel Graphics

WEBSITE
www.dingles.com

E-MAIL
info@dingles.com

The **Uncover & Discover** series encourages children to inquire, investigate, and use their imagination in an interactive and entertaining manner. This series helps to sharpen their powers of observation, improve reading and writing skills, and apply knowledge across the curriculum.

Uncover each one and see you can when you're

clue one by
what dinosaur
discover
done!

My pointed **head** is the smallest part of my body. It's only 3 inches long!

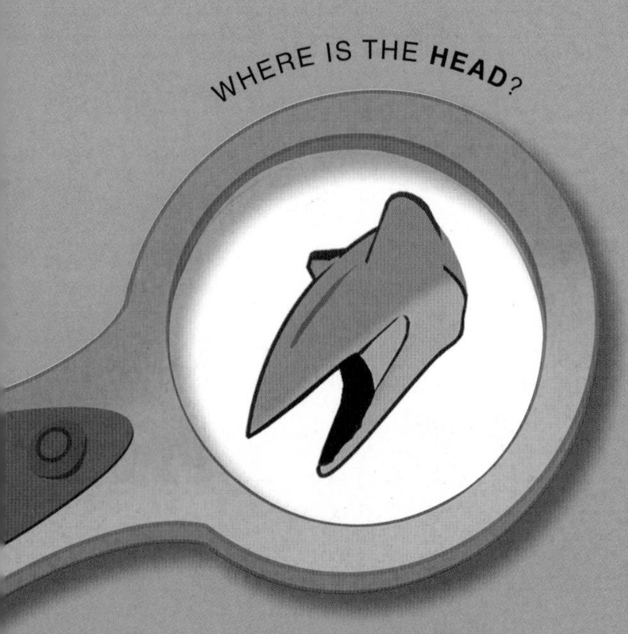

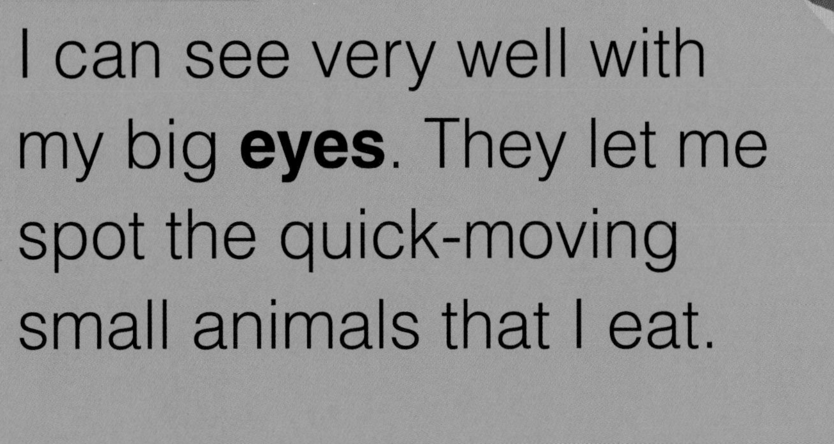

I can see very well with my big **eyes**. They let me spot the quick-moving small animals that I eat.

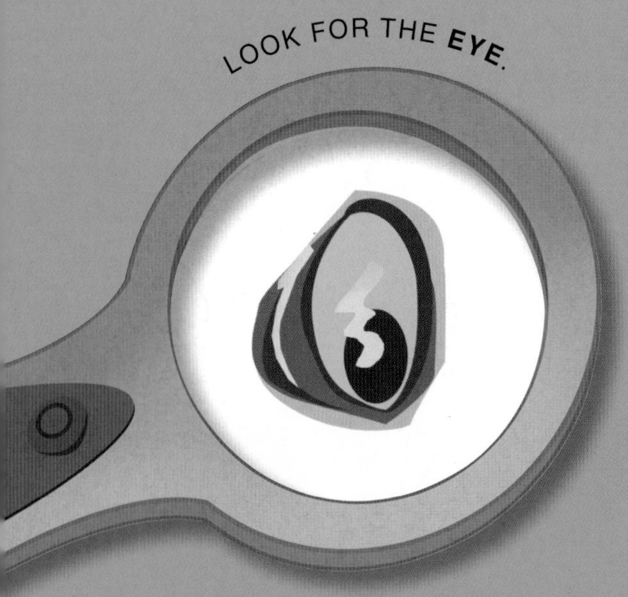

LOOK FOR THE **EYE**.

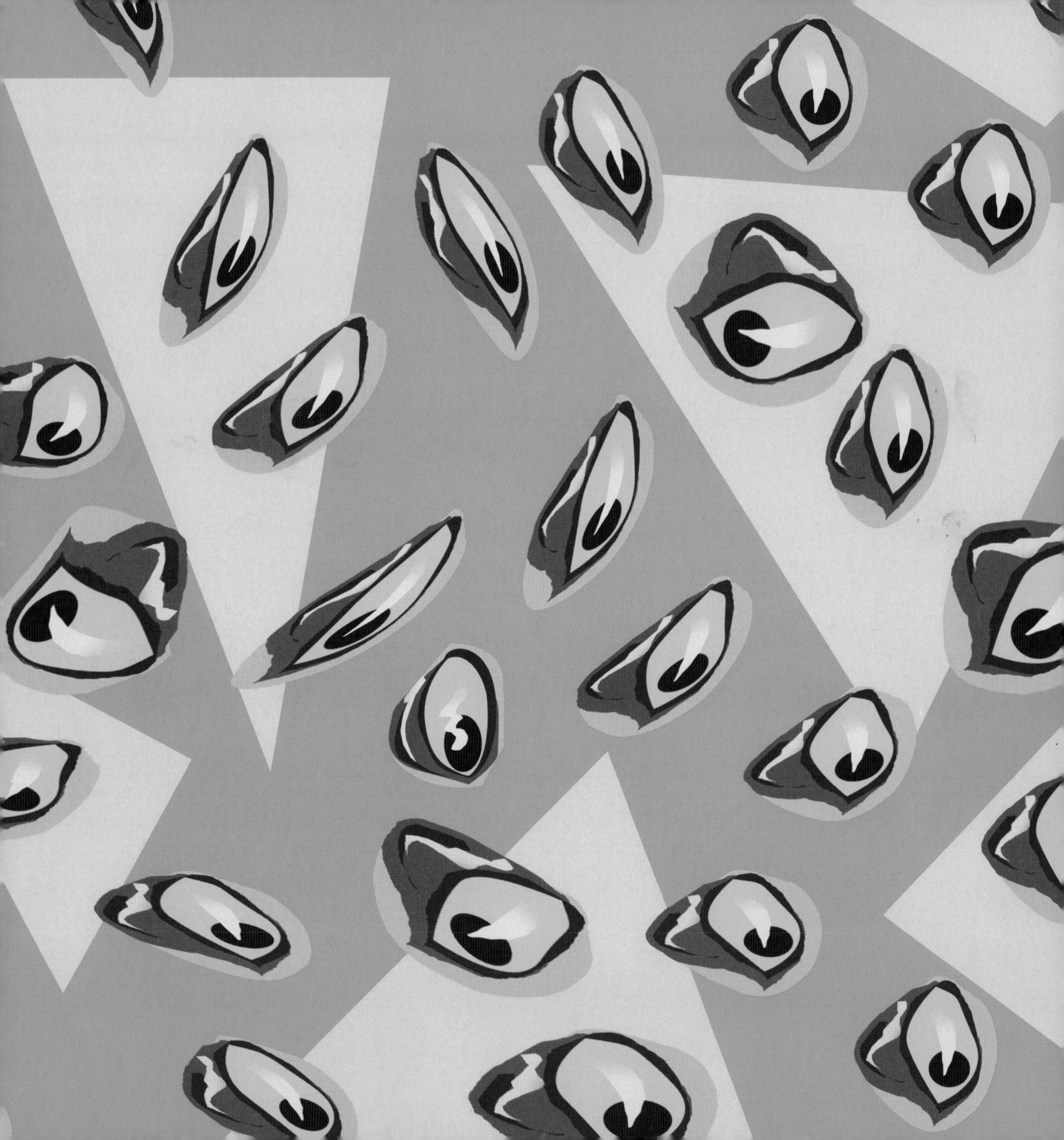

My long, stretchy **neck** allows my head to reach the ground so I can catch the fast animals.

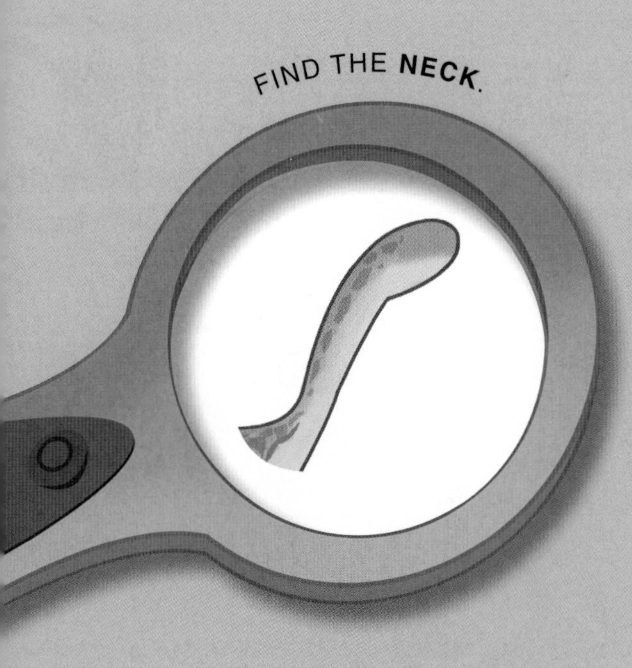

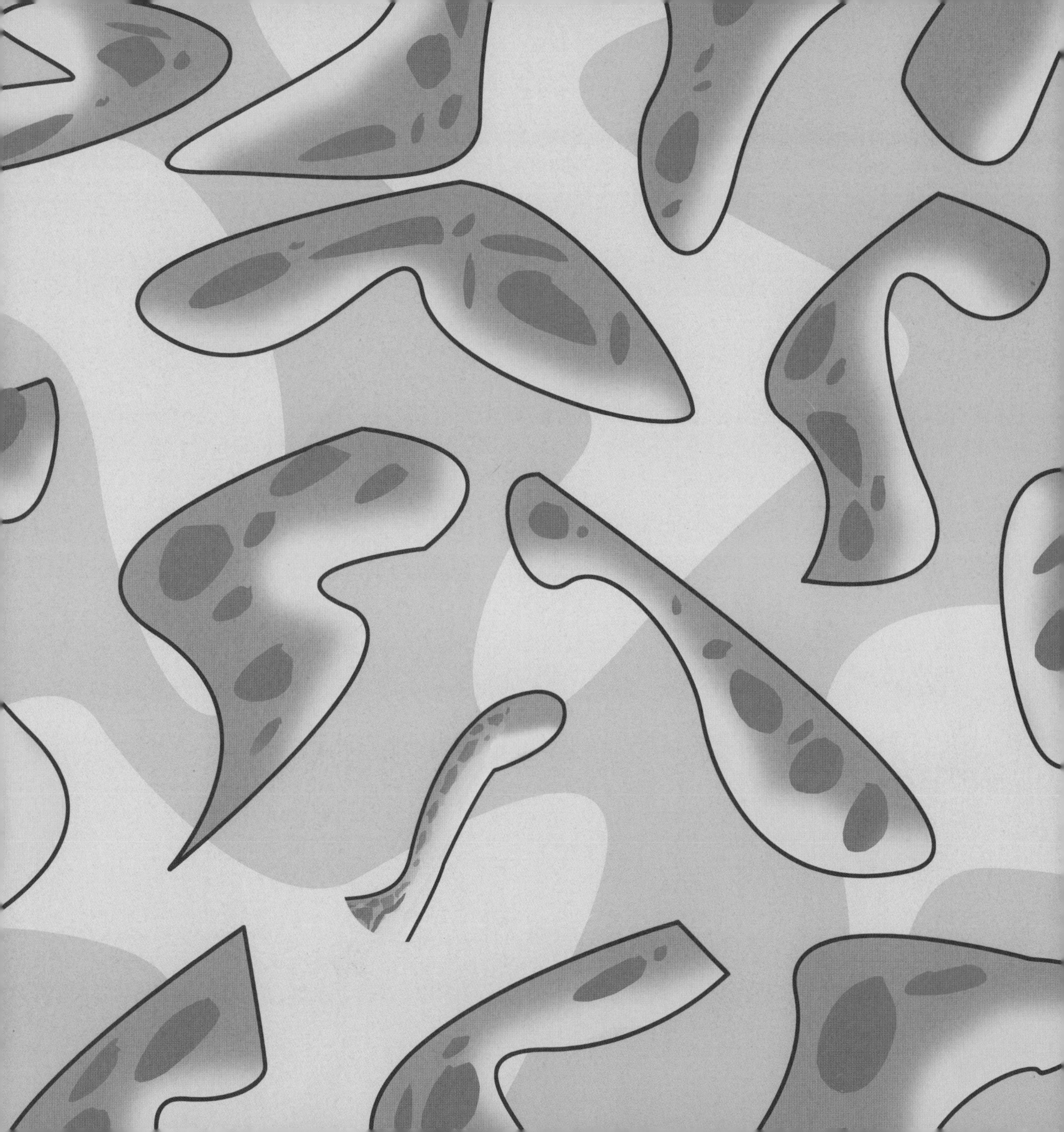

I like to eat small animals such as **lizards** and insects.

I use my sharp **teeth** to chew my food.

I have two clawed **fingers** on each of my hands. I use them to dig into insect nests and to rip apart my food.

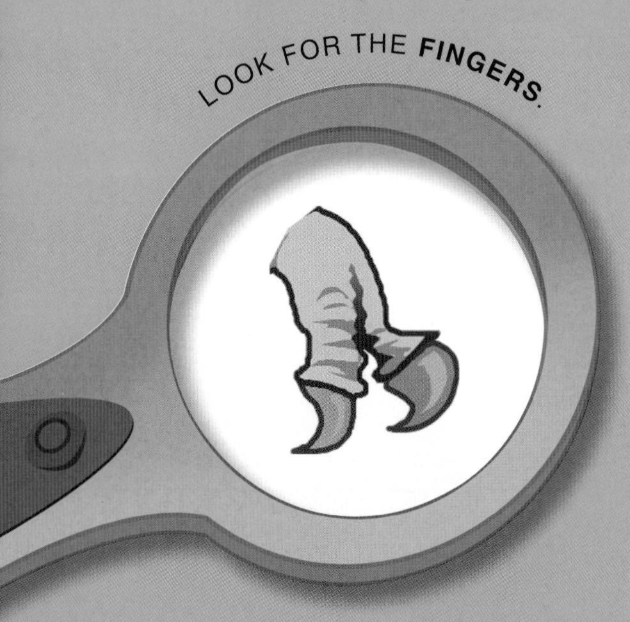

My **arms** are very short, so I walk or run upright on my legs.

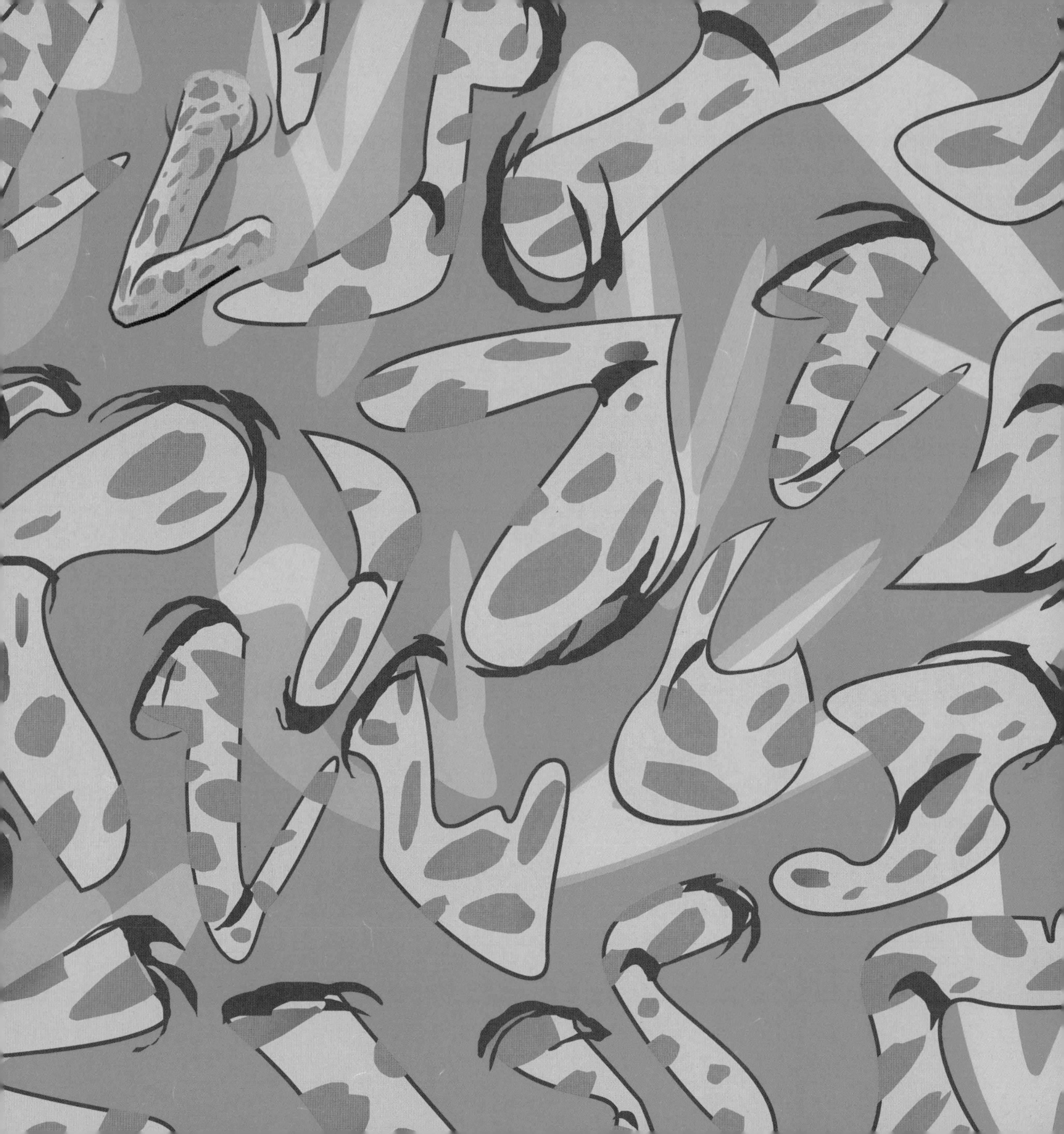

I can run fast on two long, thin **legs** to get away from enemies.

My long **feet** help stop me from falling over when I run.

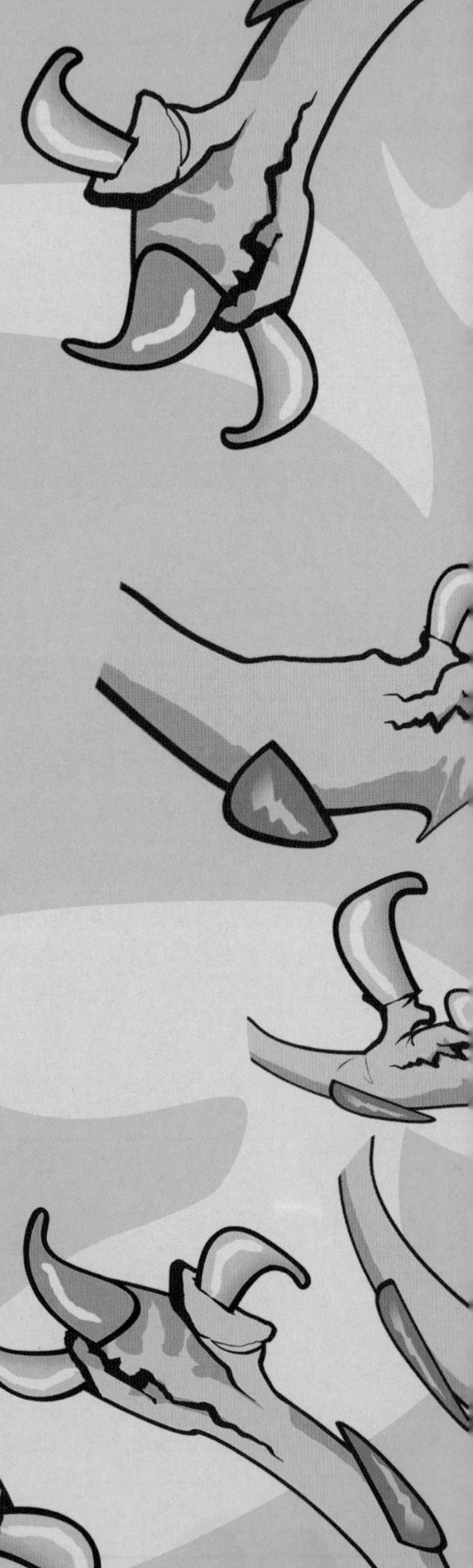

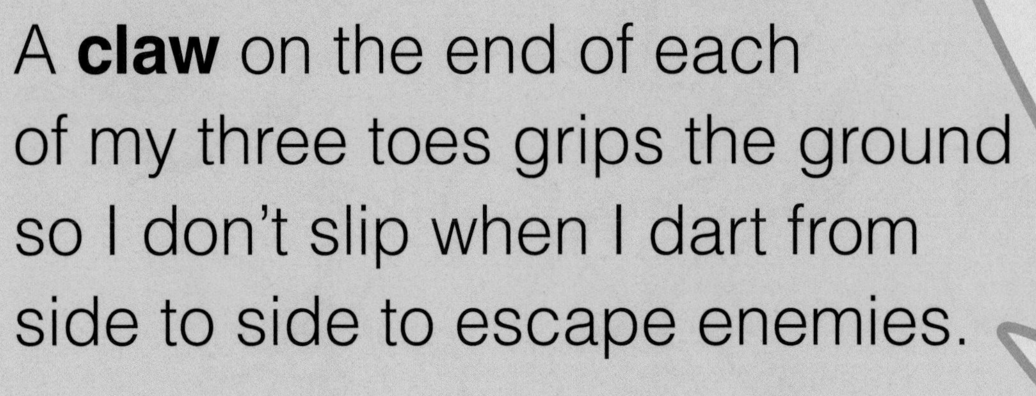

A **claw** on the end of each of my three toes grips the ground so I don't slip when I dart from side to side to escape enemies.

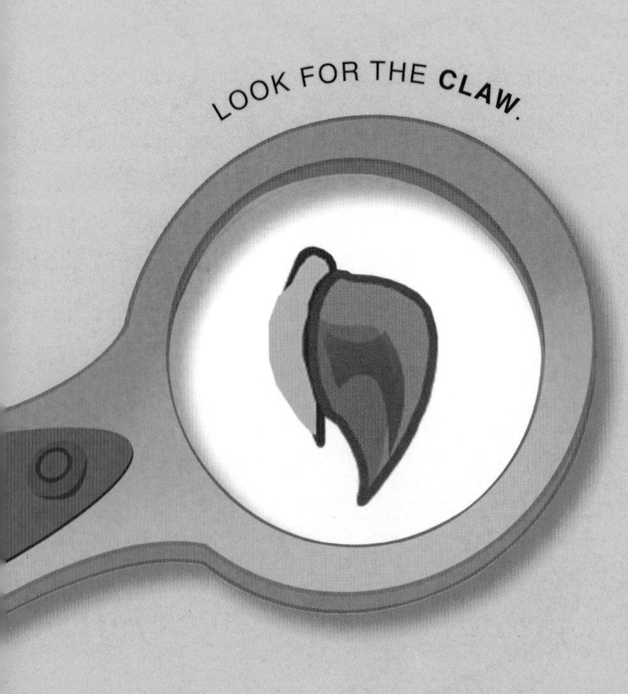

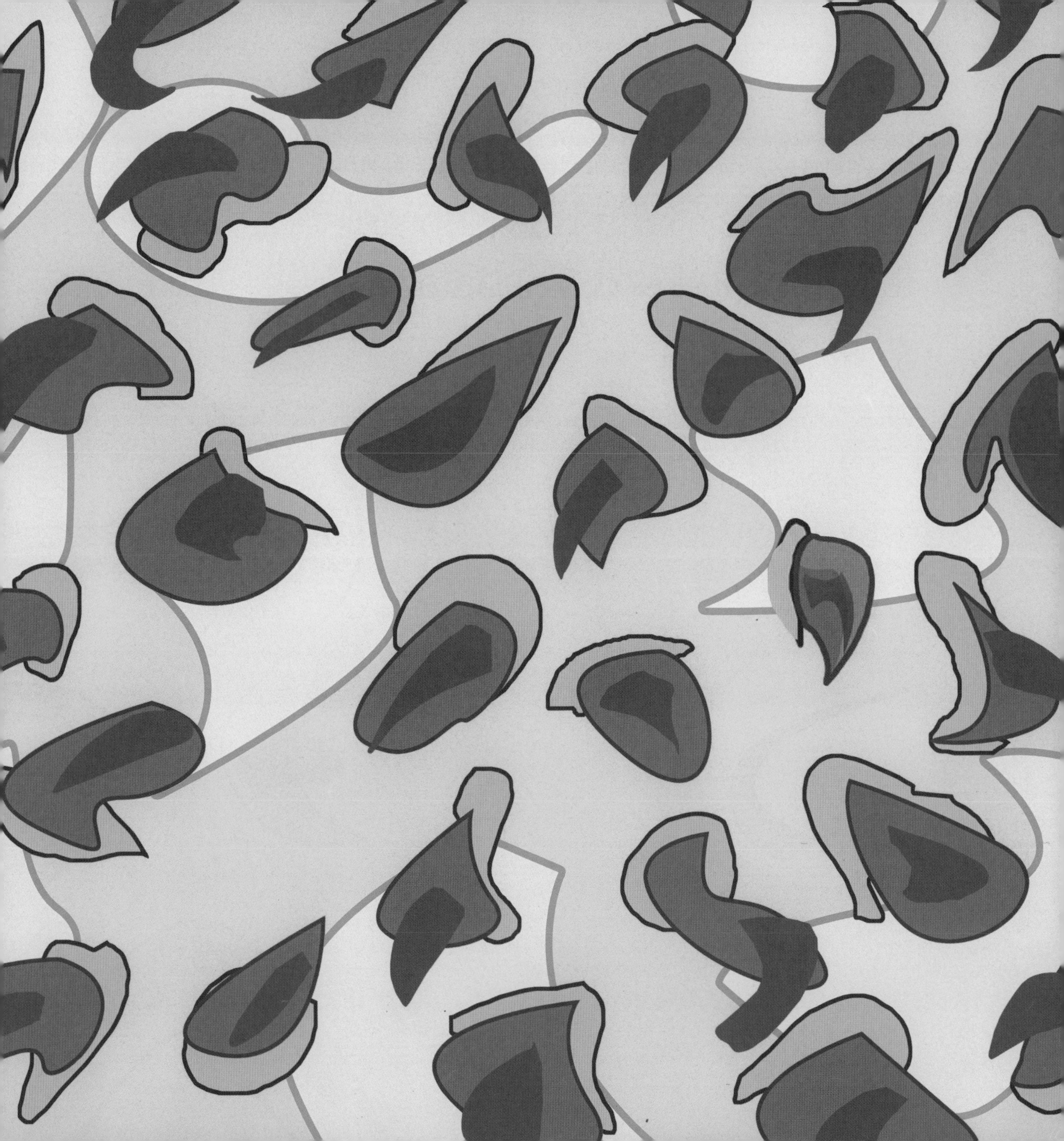

My stiff **tail** is longer than my head, neck, and body combined. It helps me keep my balance when I run fast.

FIND THE **TAIL**.

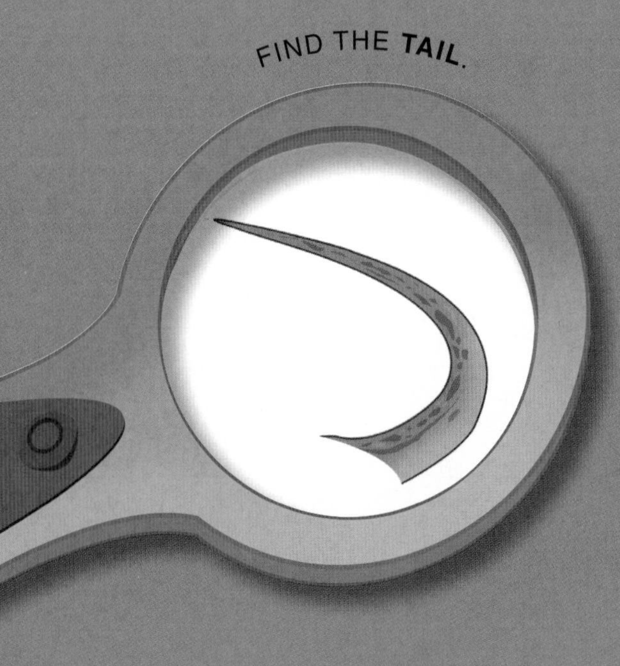

There are a lot of plants, **ferns**, and trees where I live.

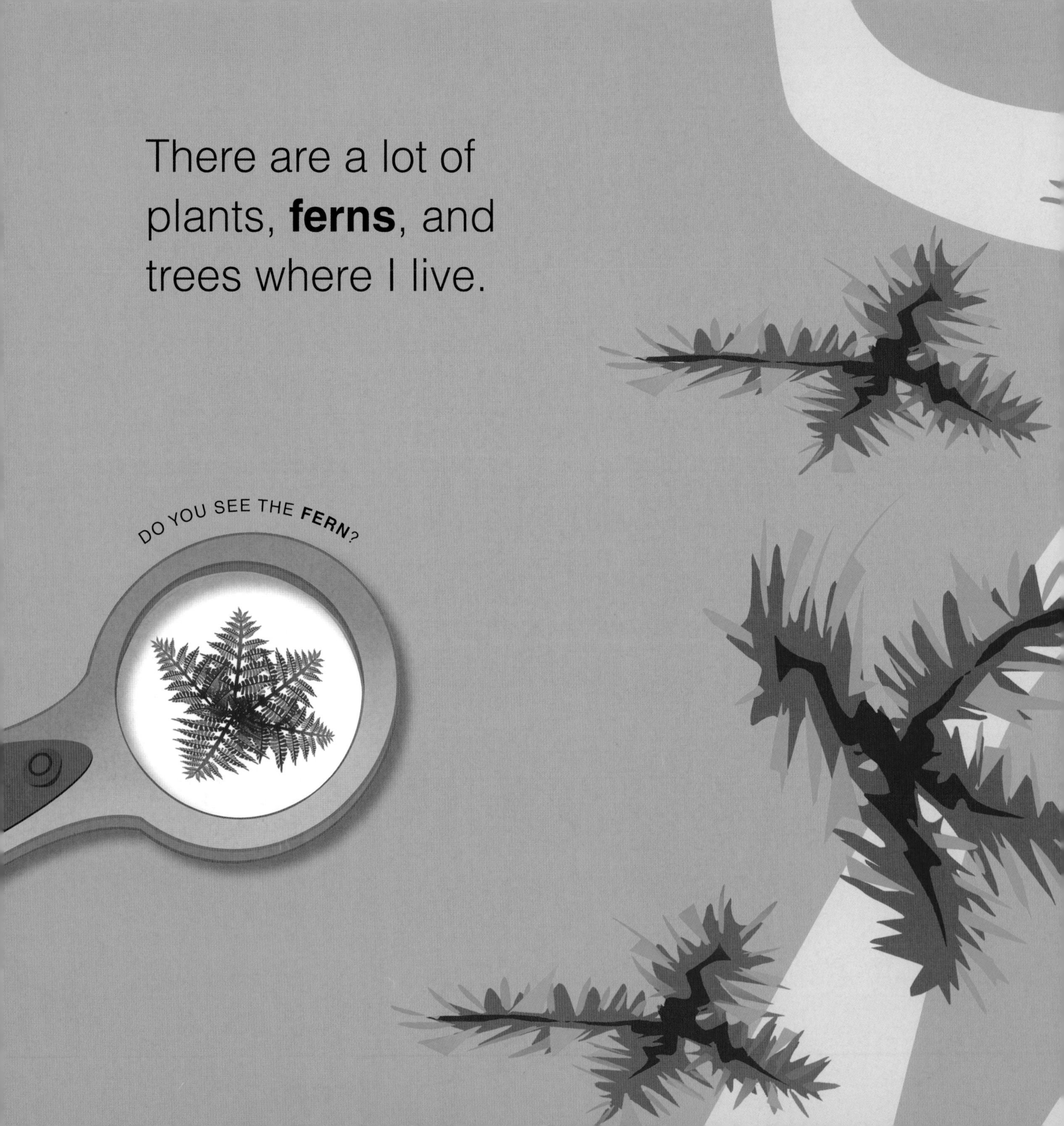

You have uncovered the clues. **Have you guessed what I am?**

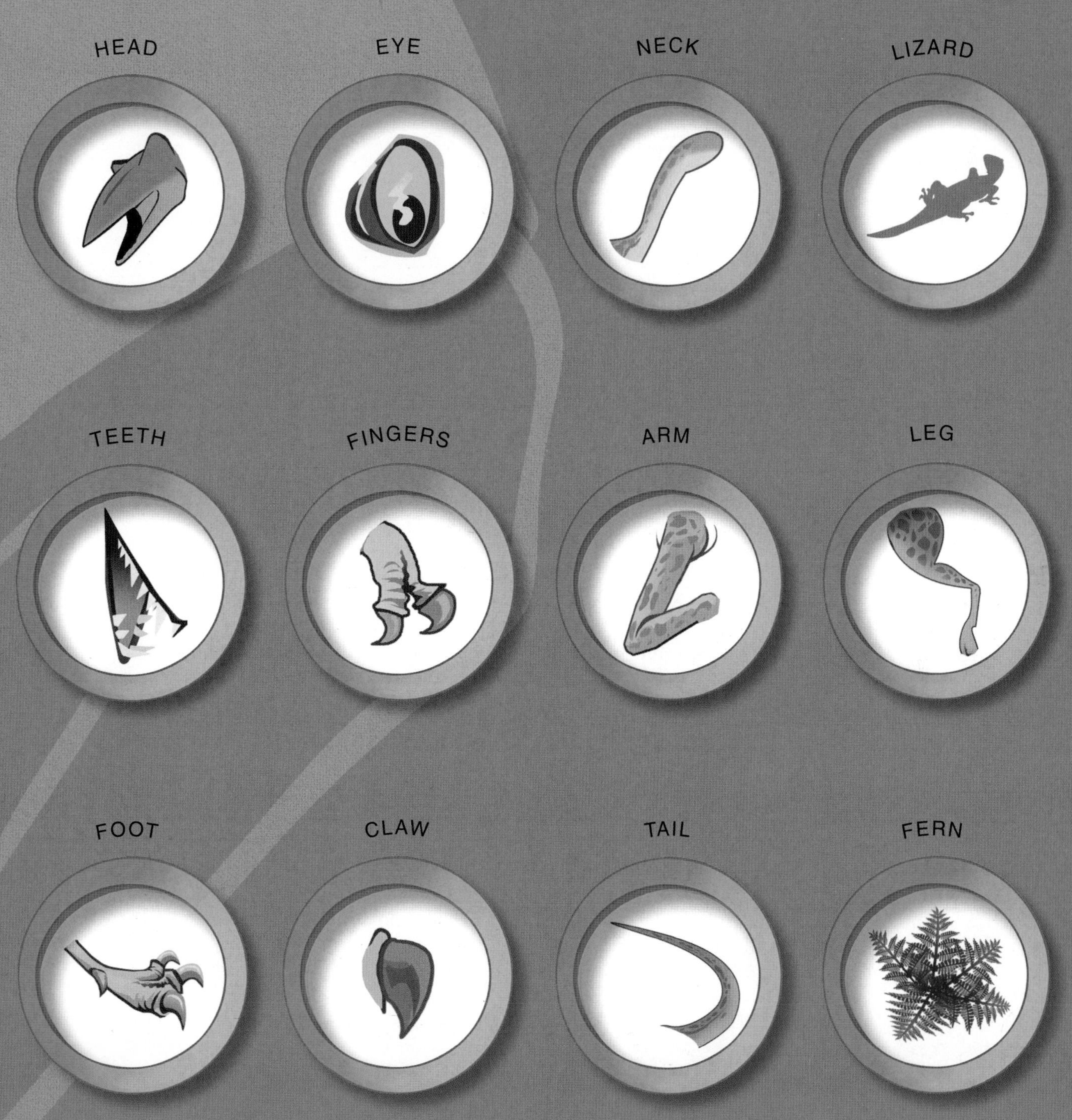
HEAD
EYE
NECK
LIZARD
TEETH
FINGERS
ARM
LEG
FOOT
CLAW
TAIL
FERN

If not, here are more clues.

1. I am a prehistoric reptile that lives on the land.
2. I am one of the smallest of a group of dinosaurs that walk on two legs. Like the others in my group, I am a fast runner and have short arms, a long, stiff tail, and sharp teeth.
3. I am about 3 feet long and 10 inches tall (about the size of a large house cat).
4. I weigh about 6 pounds (about the same as a chicken).

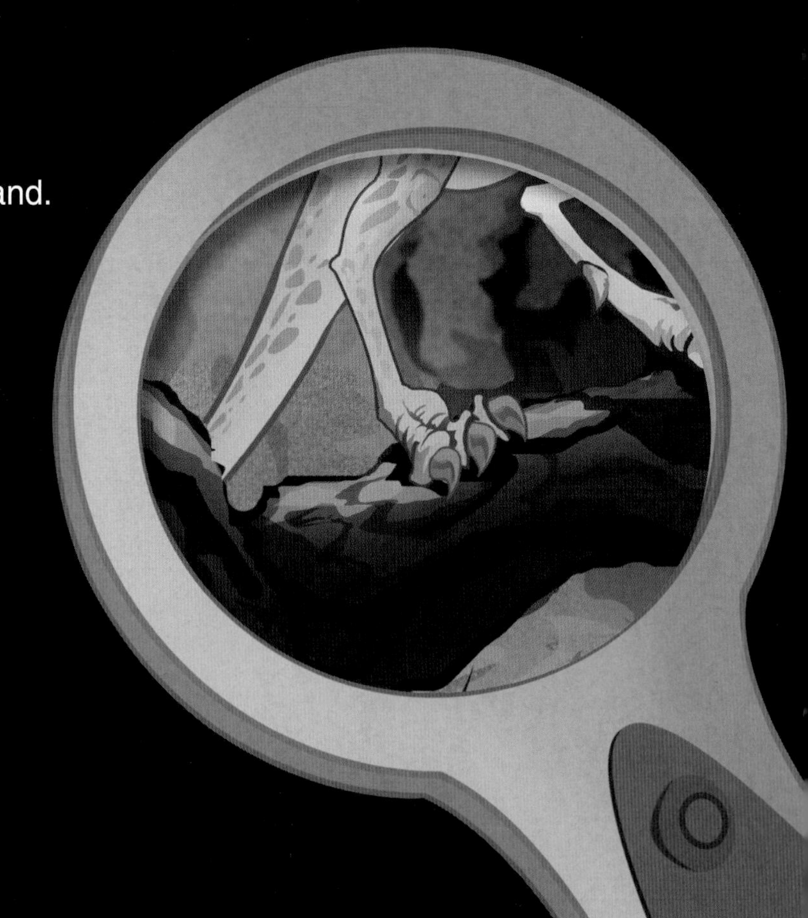

5. I'm small but have long legs with light bones. That's why I can run up to 25 miles per hour, about the same speed that an elephant runs!

6. I was hatched from an egg.

7. I live on an island that's warm and dry.

8. I am a carnivore, which means I am a meat eater.

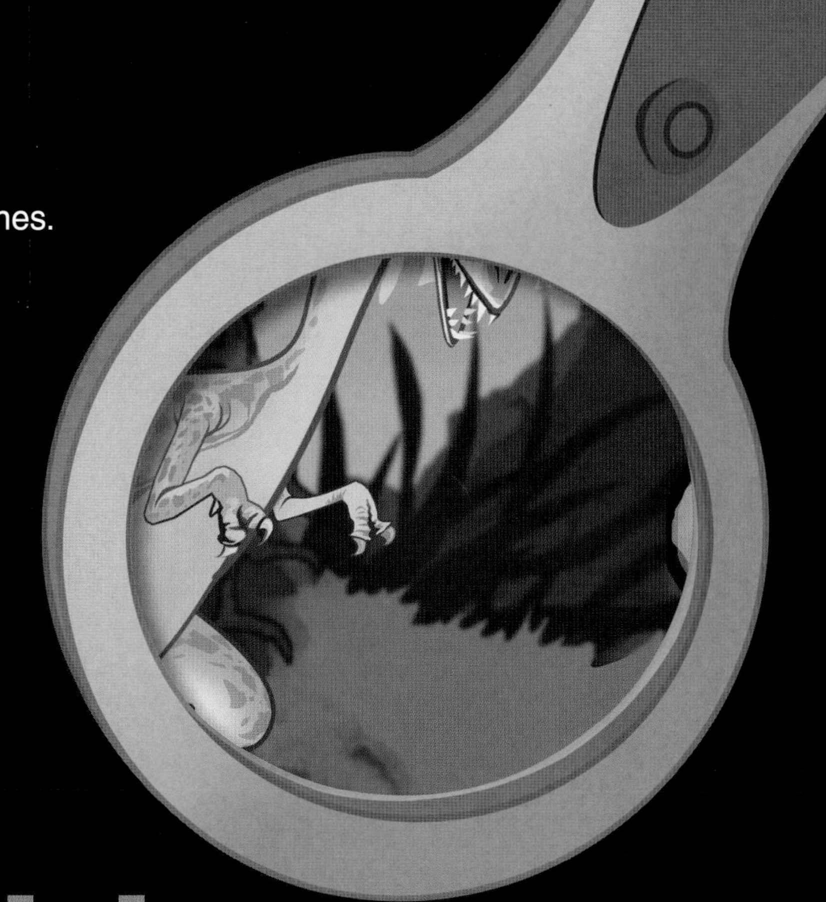

Now add them up and you'll see...

I'm a
Compsognathus
and you
discovered me!

Do you want to know more about me?

Here are some *Compsognathus* fun facts.

1. *Compsognathus* (komp-sog-NAY-thus) means "elegant jaw." The name comes from the way the jaw was placed in the dinosaur's long, slender skull.

2. *Compsognathus* lived during the late Jurassic period, about 155 to 145 million years ago. During this period the one huge landmass on Earth had separated into continents. This is the period when dinosaurs such as gigantic plant eaters and smaller meat eaters roamed the land.

3. Only three fossil skeletons of *Compsognathus* have been found. The first was a nearly complete skeleton; the other two were partial skeletons.

4. Scientists think that *Compsognathus* was a meat eater because they discovered the fossilized remains of a fast-running lizard inside the tiny dinosaur's stomach.

5. Scientists believe that *Compsognathus* was the biggest land meat eater on the islands where it lived. It probably ate large insects, small mammals, and lizards.

6. *Compsognathus* had unusually short arms for an animal of its size. This birdlike feature is one reason scientists began to think that dinosaurs may be ancestors of birds.

7. The first *Compsognathus* fossil was discovered by Dr. Siegfried Oberndorfer. He found it in Bavaria, a region of Germany, in the late1850s. The fossil was named by Johann Wagner, a paleontologist (a scientist who learns about prehistoric life-forms by studying fossils), in 1861.

Who, **What**, Where, When, Why, and How

USE THE QUESTIONS who, what, where, when, why, and how to help the child apply knowledge and process the information in the book. Encourage him or her to investigate, inquire, and imagine.

In the Book…

DO YOU KNOW WHO discovered the first *Compsognathus* fossil?

DO YOU KNOW WHAT the featured dinosaur in the book is?

DO YOU KNOW WHERE the first *Compsognathus* fossil was discovered?

DO YOU KNOW WHEN *Compsognathus* lived?

DO YOU KNOW WHY scientists think *Compsognathus* was a meat eater?

DO YOU KNOW HOW much *Compsognathus* weighed?

In Your Life...

Compsognathus hatched from an egg. What modern-day animals hatch from eggs?

Cross-Curricular Extensions

Math

Compsognathus could run 25 miles per hour. If *Compsognathus* was chasing a lizard that was running 12 miles an hour, how much faster could *Compsognathus* run than the lizard?

Science

Compsognathus was a carnivore. What is a carnivore? What do you think a carnivore would have eaten during the time that *Compsognathus* lived?

Social Studies

Compsognathus lived in what is now part of Germany and France. On which continent are these two countries located?

You have uncovered the clues and discovered *Compsognathus*.

ASSIGNMENT
Compsognathus lived on islands. Use your imagination and write a story about living on an island in prehistoric times.

INCLUDE IN YOUR STORY
Who else lives on the island?
What do you like or dislike about living on the island?
Where is your island located?
When did you arrive on the island?
Why are you living on the island?
How do you get food to eat?

WRITE
Enjoy the writing process while you take what you have imagined and create your story.

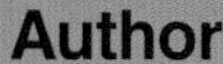

Author

Robert Kanner is part of the writing team for the Uncover & Discover series as well as the Global Adventures and Holiday Happenings series. An extensive career in the film and television business includes work as a film acquisition executive at the Walt Disney Company, a story editor for a children's television series, and an independent family-film producer. He holds a bachelor's degree in psychology from the University of Buffalo and lives in the Hollywood Hills, California, with Tom and Miss Murphy May.

Illustrator

Since graduating from Falmouth School of Art in 1993, **Russ Daff** has enjoyed a varied career. For eight years he worked on numerous projects in the computer games industry, producing titles for Sony PlayStation and PC formats. While designing a wide range of characters and environments for these games, he developed a strong sense of visual impact that he later utilized in his illustration and comic work. Russ now concentrates on his illustration and cartooning full-time. When he is not working, he enjoys painting, writing cartoon stories, and playing bass guitar. He lives in Cambridge, England.

EXPERIENCE Human Development

THIRTEENTH EDITION

Diane E. PAPALIA

Gabriela MARTORELL

EXPERIENCE HUMAN DEVELOPMENT: THIRTEENTH EDITION

Published by McGraw-Hill Education, 2 Penn Plaza, New York, NY 10121.

Some ancillaries, including electronic and print components, may not be available to customers outside the United States.

This book is printed on acid-free paper.

2 3 4 5 6 7 8 9 0 CTP/CTP 1 0 9 8 7

ISBN 978-1-259-25162-7
MHID 1-259-25162-4

www.mhhe.com

about the authors

Diane E. Papalia As a professor, Diane E. Papalia taught thousands of undergraduates at the University of Wisconsin–Madison. She received her bachelor's degree, majoring in psychology, from Vassar College and both her master's degree in child development and family relations and her PhD in life-span developmental psychology from West Virginia University. She has published numerous articles in such professional journals as *Human Development, International Journal of Aging and Human Development, Sex Roles, Journal of Experimental Child Psychology,* and *Journal of Gerontology.* Most of these papers have dealt with her major research focus, cognitive development from childhood through old age. She is especially interested in intelligence in old age and factors that contribute to the maintenance of intellectual functioning in late adulthood. She is a Fellow in the Gerontological Society of America. She is the coauthor of *Human Development,* now in its eleventh edition, with Sally Wendkos Olds and Ruth Duskin Feldman; of *Adult Development and Aging,* now in its third edition, with Harvey L. Sterns, Ruth Duskin Feldman, and Cameron J. Camp; and of *Child Development: A Topical Approach* with Dana Gross and Ruth Duskin Feldman.

Gabriela Alicia Martorell was born in Seattle, Washington, but moved as a toddler to Guatemala. At eight, she moved back to the United States and lived in Northern California until leaving for her undergraduate training at University of California, Davis. After obtaining her BS in Psychology, she earned her PhD in Developmental and Evolutionary Psychology at University of California, Santa Barbara. Since that time, she has served a number of learning institutions including Portland State University, Norfolk State University, and her current full-time position at Virginia Wesleyan College. Gabi has taught graduate and undergraduate courses in introductory psychology, research methods, life-span human development, infant development, child development, adolescent development, adulthood and aging, cultural issues in psychology, evolutionary psychology, developmental psychopathology, and community-based learning courses in Early Childhood Education and Adult Development and Aging. She is committed to teaching, mentoring, and advising. She is currently conducting research on attachment processes in immigrant Latino/a adolescents that was funded by the Virginia Foundation for Independent Colleges, and is Co-Investigator for a National Science Foundation grant focused on student retention and success in science, technology, engineering, and math. She lives in Virginia with her husband Michael, daughters Amalia and Clara, and two dogs.

To Charles Robert Zappa,
with love.

To Susy and Rey,
my parents, especially for putting up with me
during my teenage years.

brief contents

contents

part 3 Early Childhood

part 5 Adolescence

chapter 11

chapter 12

part 6 Emerging and Young Adulthood

part 7 Middle Adulthood

part 9 The End of Life

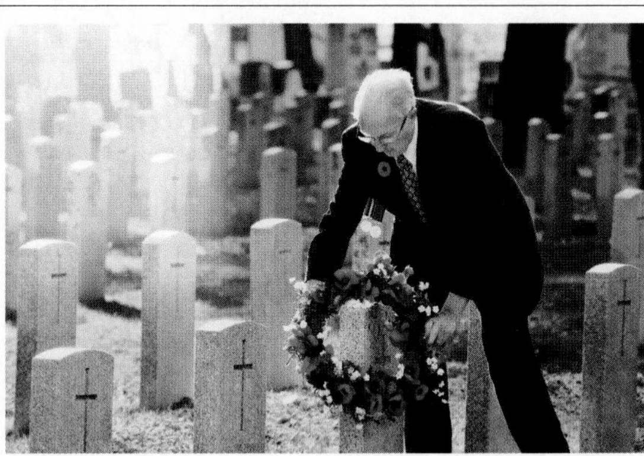

preface

EXPERIENCE THE Human Side

Experience Human Development helps students experience the human side of development by exposing them to culture and diversity, immersing them in practical application, and helping them study smarter through personalized learning and reporting.

Experience Human Development takes a practical approach to research and recognizes that just as people develop in their own way, your students also learn in their own ways. With our adaptive, personalized learning program, LearnSmart, students are guided toward success on their terms. With integrated resources like Milestones of Child Development, Milestones: Transitions, and short author tutorials on some of the most challenging learning objectives, *Experience Human Development* makes a difference for your students.

Better Data, Smarter Revision, Improved Results

Here's how it used to be: The revision process for a new edition typically began with asking several dozen instructors what they would change and what they would keep. Also, experts in the field were asked to provide comments that point out new material to add and dated material to remove. Using all these reviews, authors would revise the material. But now, a new tool has revolutionized that paradigm. LearnSmart, a tool powered by McGraw-Hill Connect Lifespan Development, is the adaptive learning system that provides students with an individualized assessment of their own progress. McGraw-Hill authors have access to real student data from this tool to create their revisions.

- **Student Data**

  This student data is anonymously collected from the many students who use LearnSmart. Because virtually every text paragraph is tied to several questions that students answer while using LearnSmart, empirical data showing the specific concepts with which students have the most difficulty is easily pinpointed.

# of Development

This student data from LearnSmart is in the form of a *heat map,* which graphically illustrates "hot spots" in the text that cause students the most difficulty. Using these hot spots, McGraw-Hill authors can refine the wording and content in the new edition to make these areas clearer than before.

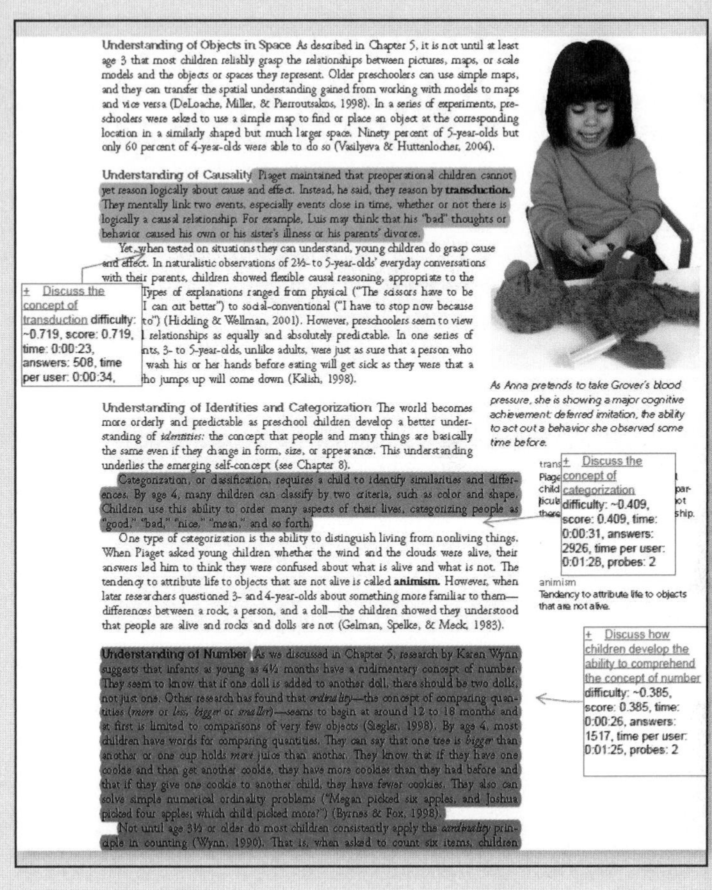

Understanding of Objects in Space As described in Chapter 5, it is not until at least age 3 that most children reliably grasp the relationships between pictures, maps, or scale models and the objects or spaces they represent. Older preschoolers can use simple maps, and they can transfer the spatial understanding gained from working with models to maps and vice versa (DeLoache, Miller, & Pierroutsakos, 1998). In a series of experiments, preschoolers were asked to use a simple map to find or place an object at the corresponding location in a similarly shaped but much larger space. Ninety percent of 5-year-olds but only 60 percent of 4-year-olds were able to do so (Vasilyeva & Huttenlocher, 2004).

Understanding of Causality Piaget maintained that preoperational children cannot yet reason logically about cause and effect. Instead, he said, they reason by **transduction.** They mentally link two events, especially events close in time, whether or not there is logically a causal relationship. For example, Luis may think that his "bad" thoughts or behavior caused his own or his sister's illness or his parents' divorce.

Yet, when tested on situations they can understand, young children do grasp cause and effect. In naturalistic observations of 2½- to 5-year-olds' everyday conversations with their parents, children showed flexible causal reasoning, appropriate to the Types of explanations ranged from physical ("The scissors have to be I can cut better") to social-conventional ("I have to stop now because to") (Hickling & Wellman, 2001). However, preschoolers seem to view relationships as equally and absolutely predictable. In one series of nts, 3- to 5-year-olds, unlike adults, were just as sure that a person who wash his or her hands before eating will get sick as they were that a ho jumps up will come down (Kalish, 1998).

\+ Discuss the concept of transduction difficulty: ~0.719, score: 0.719, time: 0:00:23, answers: 508, time per user: 0:00:34,

As Anna pretends to take Grover's blood pressure, she is showing a major cognitive achievement: deferred imitation, the ability to act out a behavior she observed some time before.

Understanding of Identities and Categorization The world becomes more orderly and predictable as preschool children develop a better understanding of *identities:* the concept that people and many things are basically the same even if they change in form, size, or appearance. This understanding underlies the emerging self-concept (see Chapter 8).

Categorization, or classification, requires a child to identify similarities and differences. By age 4, many children can classify by two criteria, such as color and shape. Children use this ability to order many aspects of their lives, categorizing people as "good," "bad," "nice," "mean," and so forth.

\+ Discuss the concept of categorization difficulty: ~0.409, score: 0.409, time: 0:00:31, answers: 2926, time per user: 0:01:28, probes: 2

One type of categorization is the ability to distinguish living from nonliving things. When Piaget asked young children whether the wind and the clouds were alive, their answers led him to think they were confused about what is alive and what is not. The tendency to attribute life to objects that are not alive is called **animism.** However, when later researchers questioned 3- and 4-year-olds about something more familiar to them—differences between a rock, a person, and a doll—the children showed they understood that people are alive and rocks and dolls are not (Gelman, Spelke, & Meck, 1983).

animism
Tendency to attribute life to objects that are not alive.

Understanding of Number As we discussed in Chapter 5, research by Karen Wynn suggests that infants as young as 4½ months have a rudimentary concept of number. They seem to know that if one doll is added to another doll, there should be two dolls, not just one. Other research has found that *ordinality*—the concept of comparing quantities (*more* or *less, bigger* or *smaller*)—seems to begin at around 12 to 18 months and at first is limited to comparisons of very few objects (Siegler, 1998). By age 4, most children have words for comparing quantities. They can say that one tree is *bigger* than another or one cup holds *more* juice than another. They know that if they have one cookie and then get another cookie, they have more cookies than they had before and that if they give one cookie to another child, they have fewer cookies. They also can solve simple numerical ordinality problems ("Megan picked six apples, and Joshua picked four apples; which child picked more?") (Byrnes & Fox, 1998).

Not until age 3½ or older do most children consistently apply the *cardinality* principle in counting (Wynn, 1990). That is, when asked to count six items, children

\+ Discuss how children develop the ability to comprehend the concept of number difficulty: ~0.385, score: 0.385, time: 0:00:26, answers: 1517, time per user: 0:01:25, probes: 2

- **LearnSmart**

  Powered by McGraw-Hill Connect® Lifespan Development, LearnSmart is our response to today's student. LearnSmart is designed to maximize productivity and efficiency in learning, helping students "know what they know" while helping them learn what they don't know. In fact, instructors using LearnSmart are reporting that their students' performance is improving by a letter grade or more. Through this unique tool, instructors have the ability to identify struggling students quickly and easily, *before* the first exam.

Regardless of individual study habits, preparation, and approaches to the course, students will find that *Experience Human Development* connects with them on a personal, individual basis and provides a road map for real success in the course.

- **SmartBook**

  Fueled by LearnSmart, SmartBook™ creates a personalized reading experience by highlighting the most impactful concepts a student needs to learn at that moment in time. This ensures that every minute spent with SmartBook is returned to the student as the most value-added minute possible. The reading experience continuously adapts by highlighting content based on what the student knows and doesn't know. Real-time reports quickly identify the concepts that require more attention from individual students—or the entire class. SmartBook detects the content a student is most likely to forget and brings it back to improve long-term knowledge retention.

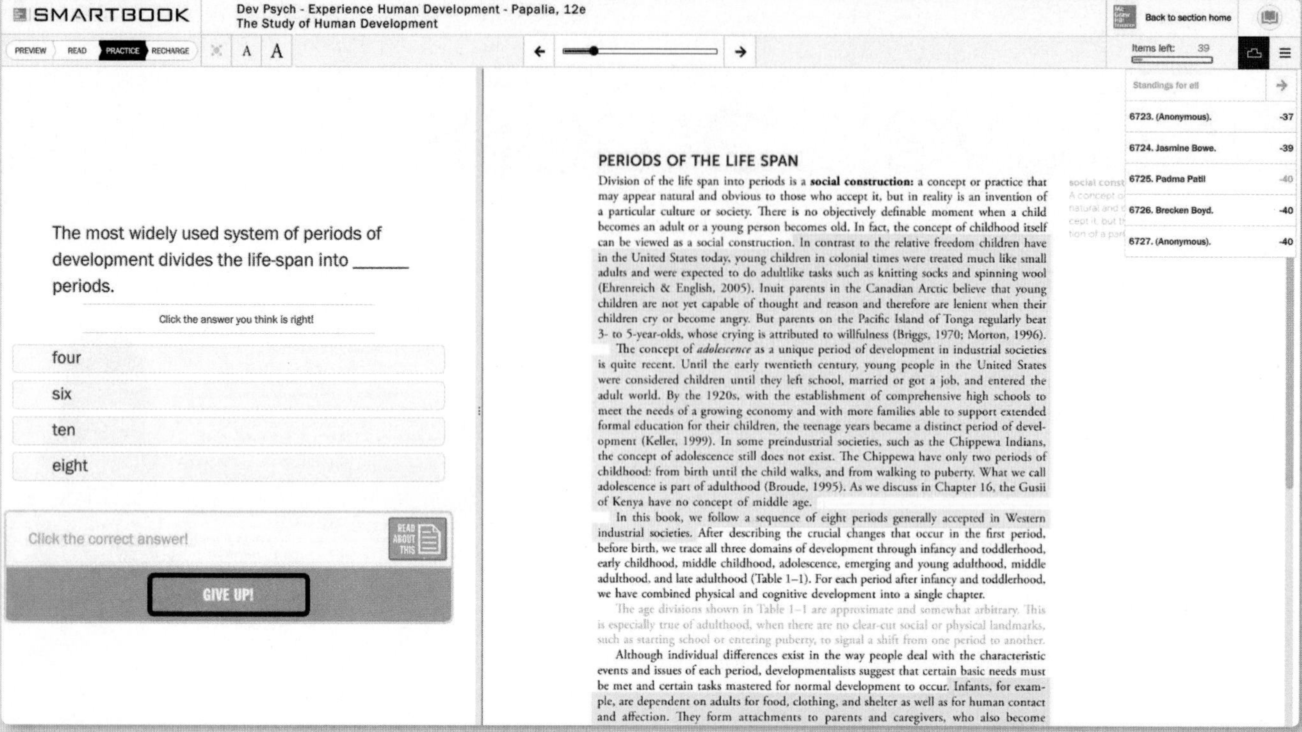

SMARTBOOK
Dev Psych - Experience Human Development - Papalia, 12e
The Study of Human Development
Back to section home
PREVIEW READ PRACTICE RECHARGE
A A
Items left: 39
Standings for all
6723. (Anonymous). -37
6724. Jasmine Bowe. -39
6725. Padma Patil -40
6726. Brecken Boyd. -40
6727. (Anonymous). -40
The most widely used system of periods of development divides the life-span into ______ periods.
Click the answer you think is right!
four
six
ten
eight
Click the correct answer!
READ ABOUT THIS
GIVE UP!
PERIODS OF THE LIFE SPAN
Division of the life span into periods is a **social construction:** a concept or practice that may appear natural and obvious to those who accept it, but in reality is an invention of a particular culture or society. There is no objectively definable moment when a child becomes an adult or a young person becomes old. In fact, the concept of childhood itself can be viewed as a social construction. In contrast to the relative freedom children have in the United States today, young children in colonial times were treated much like small adults and were expected to do adultlike tasks such as knitting socks and spinning wool (Ehrenreich & English, 2005). Inuit parents in the Canadian Arctic believe that young children are not yet capable of thought and reason and therefore are lenient when their children cry or become angry. But parents on the Pacific Island of Tonga regularly beat 3- to 5-year-olds, whose crying is attributed to willfulness (Briggs, 1970; Morton, 1996).
The concept of *adolescence* as a unique period of development in industrial societies is quite recent. Until the early twentieth century, young people in the United States were considered children until they left school, married or got a job, and entered the adult world. By the 1920s, with the establishment of comprehensive high schools to meet the needs of a growing economy and with more families able to support extended formal education for their children, the teenage years became a distinct period of development (Keller, 1999). In some preindustrial societies, such as the Chippewa Indians, the concept of adolescence still does not exist. The Chippewa have only two periods of childhood: from birth until the child walks, and from walking to puberty. What we call adolescence is part of adulthood (Broude, 1995). As we discuss in Chapter 16, the Gusii of Kenya have no concept of middle age.
In this book, we follow a sequence of eight periods generally accepted in Western industrial societies. After describing the crucial changes that occur in the first period, before birth, we trace all three domains of development through infancy and toddlerhood, early childhood, middle childhood, adolescence, emerging and young adulthood, middle adulthood, and late adulthood (Table 1–1). For each period after infancy and toddlerhood, we have combined physical and cognitive development into a single chapter.
The age divisions shown in Table 1–1 are approximate and somewhat arbitrary. This is especially true of adulthood, when there are no clear-cut social or physical landmarks, such as starting school or entering puberty, to signal a shift from one period to another.
Although individual differences exist in the way people deal with the characteristic events and issues of each period, developmentalists suggest that certain basic needs must be met and certain tasks mastered for normal development to occur. Infants, for example, are dependent on adults for food, clothing, and shelter as well as for human contact and affection. They form attachments to parents and caregivers, who also become

- **StudySmart**

Experience Human Development, Thirteenth Edition was designed to help students study smarter. "StudySmart" icons appear throughout each chapter alerting students to potential "hot spots," or challenging concepts. These concepts were identified through data collected anonymously from thousands of students using LearnSmart, and when paired with SmartBook, provide students a powerful learning experience. StudySmart icons also direct instructors to digital activities in Connect Lifespan Development that can be assigned for reinforcement and engagement.

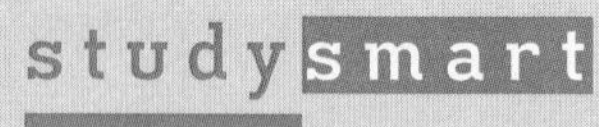

Operant Conditioning

In addition, students will find other "StudySmart" icons in the margin focusing on a specific challenging concept such as "Operant Conditioning." These guide students to assignable and assessable digital activities that are part of Connect Lifespan Development. This means instructors and students can determine how well they understand that concept prior to taking the high-stakes test.

Real People, Real World, Real Life

Many of the Connect StudySmart icons guide students to McGraw-Hill's Milestones, another opportunity to enhance learning.

McGraw Hill's Milestones is a powerful tool that allows students to experience life as it unfolds, from infancy through late adulthood. This tool consists of two essential components that work together to capture key changes throughout the life span—**Milestones of Child Development** and **Milestones: Transitions.**

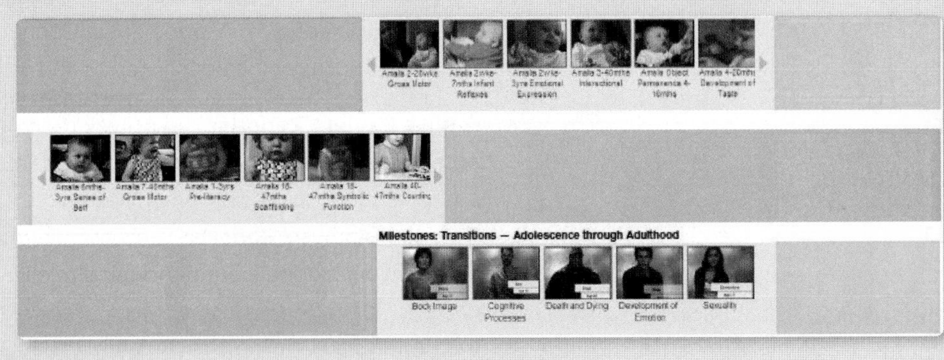

In **Milestones of Child Development,** students track the early stages of physical, social, and emotional development. By watching one child over time or comparing various children, Milestones provides a unique, experiential learning environment that can only be achieved by watching real human development as it happens—all in pre-, transitional, and post-milestone segments.

In **Milestones: Transitions,** students meet a series of people—from teenagers to individuals in late adulthood—to hear individual perspectives on changes that occur throughout the life span. Through a series of interviews, students are given the opportunity to think critically while exploring the differences in attitudes on everything from body image to changes in emotion, sexuality, cognitive processes, and death and dying.

We continue to emphasize *Experience Human Development* hallmarks of research, and culture. In addition to updating the research base of each chapter, "Research in Action" features provide an in-depth examination of research topics such as Chapter Six's material about how postpartum depression affects early development. Stressing the cultural development, the "Window on the World" features explore cultural and socioeconomic issues.

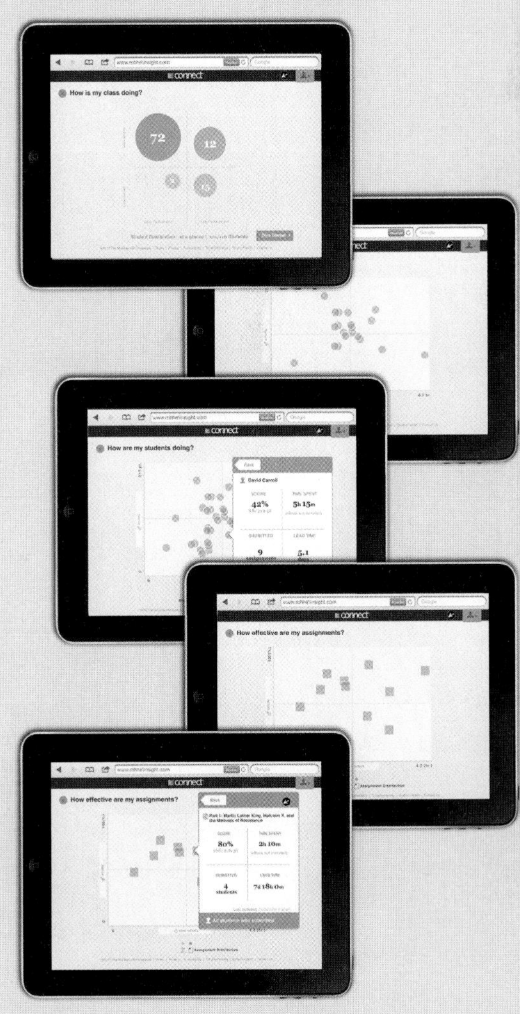

Personalized Grading, On the Go, Made Easier

connect INSIGHT

The first and only analytics tool of its kind, Connect Insight™ is a series of visual data displays—each framed by an intuitive question—that provide at-a-glance information regarding how your class is doing.

- **Intuitive:** You receive an instant, at-a-glance view of student performance matched with student activity.
- **Dynamic:** Connect Insight puts real-time analytics in your hands so you can take action early and keep struggling students from falling behind.
- **Mobile:** Connect Insight travels from office to classroom, available on demand wherever and whenever it's needed.

Whether a class is face-to-face, hybrid, or entirely online, *Experience Human Development* provides the tools needed to reduce the amount of time and energy that instructors must expend to administer their course. Easy-to-use course management in Connect Lifespan Development allows instructors to spend less time administering and more time teaching.

- **At-Risk Student Reports:** The At-Risk report provides instructors with one-click access to a dashboard that identifies students who are at risk of dropping out of a course due to low engagement levels.
- **Category Analysis Reports:** The Category Analysis report is the place to find out how your students are performing relative to specific learning objectives and goals.
- **Item Analysis Reports:** The Item Analysis report is the best way to get a bird's-eye view of a single assignment. You'll be able to tell if students are improving or if the concepts are something you want to spend additional time on in class.
- **Student Performance Reports:** The Student Performance report helps you search for a specific student in your class and focus on that student's progress across your assignments.
- **Assignment Results and Statistics Reports:** The Assignment Results report shows your entire class's performance across all of your assignments. Assignment Statistics reports will give you quick data on each assignment including the mean score, high score, and low scores, as well as the number of times it was submitted.

chapter-by-chapter changes

This is a chapter-by-chapter list of topics that are new to this edition or have been substantially revised or updated.

1 The Study of Human Development

- Streamlined introduction to chapter
- Updated research on school lunch program
- Revised section on studying the life span
- Expanded section on human development today
- Updated information about minority children in the United States
- Updated information on poverty and ethnicity
- Updated information on global poverty

2 Theory and Research

- Clarified material on what a theory is
- Expanded material on early philosophical foundations of psychology and nature of active and reactive development
- Revised section on mechanistic and organismic views of psychology
- Expanded material about Freud's ideas
- Added example of how Erikson's stages feed into each other
- Revised information on assimilation, accommodation, and equilibrium
- Revised material on neo-Piagetian approaches
- Clarified example of the exosystem
- Revised ethology section and provided example
- Revised evolutionary psychology section
- Expanded material about qualitative and quantitative research and the scientific method
- Provided new example of experimental design
- Revised section on laboratory, field, and natural experiments
- Revised section on developmental research designs
- Revised ethics material

3 Forming a New Life

- Rewrote introduction to chapter
- Revised and updated material on multiple births
- Clarified information on the human genome
- Revised information on dominant and recessive genes
- Revised information on polygenic inheritance
- Revised section on genotype and phenotype
- Revised material on incomplete dominance
- Revised information on sex-linked inheritance
- Expanded and revised section on heritability
- Added a simile for canalization
- Added example of nonshared environmental influences

4 Birth and Physical Development during the First Three Years

- Updated maternal and infant mortality rates
- Expanded material on stages of labor
- Revised section on electronic fetal monitoring
- Expanded information on fontanels and neonate skull
- Added information on the functioning of body systems in neonates
- Revised distinction between low-birth-weight and small-for-date infants
- Updated material on interventions for preterm delivery
- Updated statistics on stillbirth in the United States
- Updated statistics on worldwide neonatal mortality rates
- Provided new examples of cephalocaudal and proximodistal development
- Added information on the functions of the different lobes of the brain
- Revised material on neuronal pruning
- Expanded information on plasticity
- Expanded and revised material on ecological systems and dynamic systems theories of motor development

5 Cognitive Development during the First Three Years

- Revised description of operant conditioning
- Expanded material on the use of conditioning techniques in the study of infant memory
- Revised description of intelligent behavior
- Expanded description of developmental tests
- Expanded material on the influence of parental responsiveness
- Revised section on early intervention
- Revised material on imitative abilities
- Expanded description of pictorial competence
- Expanded description of scale error and the dual representation hypothesis
- Expanded and revised description of habituation and dishabituation
- Added example of how visual preference is used in infant habituation research
- Revised material describing how habituation can be used to investigate visual recognition
- Added example on the development of causality
- Revised description of the violation of expectations paradigm and how it can be used to investigate object permanence
- Revised material on conceptual understanding and perceptual awareness
- Expanded definition of implicit memory
- Expanded definition and added example for working memory
- Added material about the early sensitization of infants to their native language
- Expanded definition of phonemes and phonological rules and provided examples of both
- Added example of syntax
- Expanded descriptions of underextension and overextension
- Revised material on overregularization
- Revised and added example to the learning theoretical approach to language acquisition
- Revised section on child-directed speech

6 Psychosocial Development during the First Three Years

- Added example of an emotional response
- Revised definition of social cognition
- Revised introduction to temperament
- Expanded example of a slow-to-warm-up child
- Revised and expanded description of stability of temperament
- Expanded material on behavior inhibition
- Revised information on Erikson's approach and expanded section on trust versus mistrust
- Expanded and revised description of the attachment categories
- Expanded description of internal working mothers and maternal sensitivity and responsiveness
- Expanded description of interactional synchrony and mutual regulation
- Added example of social referencing
- Revised description of the development of conscience
- Expanded description of situational and committed compliance
- Updated statistics on maternal employment and early child care
- Updated statistics on child abuse
- Expanded description of nonorganic failure to thrive
- Expanded description of who abusers are

7 Physical and Cognitive Development in Early Childhood

- Expanded and revised section on brain development
- Expanded information on organized sports
- Revised and updated information on left-handedness
- Updated statistics on undernutrition and food security
- Updated and revised worldwide child mortality information and statistics
- Updated information on homelessness
- Revised introduction to the Piagetian approach
- Expanded section on symbolic function, deferred imitation, and pretend play
- Revised material on understanding causality
- Revised research description of egocentrism
- Expanded conservation material
- Revised description of how early social cognition is linked to theory of mind
- Revised and added examples for basic processes, capacities, and systems in memory
- Added example of recall memory
- Added examples of episodic and generic memories
- Revised and added examples for influences on memory retention
- Revised information on scaffolding and the zone of proximal development
- Added example of fast mapping
- Revised descriptions of grammar and syntax
- Added example for pragmatics
- Revised definition of emergent literacy
- Revised and expanded material on compensatory preschool programs
- Expanded material on the child in kindergarten

8 Psychosocial Development in Early Childhood

- Revised example of self-definition
- Revised and expanded developmental changes in self-esteem
- Revised section on emotional understanding
- Added example of initiative
- Revised introduction to gender differences
- Revised and updated critique of evolutionary approach to gender differences
- Added information on father influences on gender development
- Added supporting research on cultural influences

9 Physical and Cognitive Development in Middle Childhood

- Updated statistics on typical height and weight
- Revised and expanded material on brain development
- Revised information on rough-and-tumble play
- Updated overweight and obesity statistics
- Expanded spatial relationships and causality material and added example
- Revised categorization material and added example
- Expanded inductive and deductive reasoning
- Revised conservation material
- Revised link between culture and mathematical reasoning
- Revised link between egocentrism and moral reasoning
- Added example for link between attention, memory, and planning
- Revised description of executive functioning
- Added example of selective attention
- Revised working memory material
- Expanded description of metamemory
- Provided example of a mnemonic strategy and expanded description
- Explained link between working memory and conservation tasks
- Added definition of psychometrics
- Revised material on culture and IQ
- Revised section on Sternberg's triarchic theory
- Added information about scaffolding to dynamic tests of intelligence
- Expanded definition of syntax
- Revised and expanded section on reading and writing
- Expanded description of metacognition
- Added example of self-efficacy
- Revised introduction to special needs
- Expanded definition of inclusion programs
- Revised and expanded description of convergent and divergent thinking

10 Psychosocial Development in Middle Childhood

- Expanded definition of self-concept
- Revised and expanded section on industry versus inferiority
- Revised description of emotion regulation and included examples
- Revised information on the influence of family conflict
- Expanded definition of coregulation
- Updated statistics on children living in poverty
- Updated statistics on family structure, including living arrangements and father-absent homes
- Revised section on custody, visitation, and co-parenting
- Updated statistics on one-parent families, step families, gay families, and adoptive families
- Expanded section on sociometric popularity
- Revised section on levels of friendship in school-age children
- Expanded example and description of hostile attributional biases
- Added research critiquing arguments for the link between video games and aggression
- Expanded description of resilience and added example

11 Physical and Cognitive Development in Adolescence

- Expanded definition of adolescence as a social construction
- Revised section on adolescence as a time of opportunity and risk
- Revised section on puberty
- Expanded and revised section on family influences on pubertal timing
- Expanded and revised section on the adolescent brain
- Revised introduction to physical and mental health
- Updated statistics on sleep needs and problems
- Updated statistics on the use of alcohol, marijuana, tobacco, and other drugs
- Included recent trends on the use of prescription drugs
- Revised section on alcohol use and included binge drinking as a key term
- Updated statistics on depression and on suicide rates in adolescence
- Revised definition of formal operations and hypothetical-deductive reasoning
- Revised evaluation of Piaget's approach
- Expanded and added example to language development
- Expanded Kohlberg's theory of moral reasoning
- Revised critique of Kohlberg's theory and added an example
- Revised description to Gilligan's theory of moral development
- Revised material on prosocial moral reasoning and added an example
- Updated statistics on high school graduation rates
- Added examples of self-efficacy
- Revised information on brain differences by gender
- Updated statistics on high school dropout rates

12 Psychosocial Development in Adolescence

- Revised and expanded material on moratorium, identity development, and fidelity
- Revised definitions of crisis and commitment
- Expanded and revised material on Marcia's stages of identity formation
- Revised material on gender differences in identity formation
- Revised material on ethnic factors in identity formation
- Added example of cultural socialization
- Updated statistics on sexual activity, contraceptive usage, sexually transmitted infections, and teenage pregnancy
- Revised material on teen pregnancy prevention
- Revised introduction to relationships section
- Added examples of individuation
- Added example of a behavioral control technique
- Revised material on authoritative parenting
- Expanded information on parental monitoring
- Expanded information on the influence of family conflict
- Revised and expanded material on maternal employment
- Revised and expanded information on sibling relationships
- Revised introduction to antisocial behavior and juvenile delinquency
- Revised material on authoritative parenting and its impact on the influence of deviant peers
- Revised material on the youth violence epidemic
- Revised definition of collective efficacy

13 Physical and Cognitive Development in Emerging and Young Adulthood

- Revised definition of emerging adulthood
- Revised and expanded genetic influences on health
- Updated worldwide trends in obesity
- Updated guidelines for suggested exercise and physical activity per week
- Clarified association between SES, minority status, and health
- Included information on same sex marriage and its impact on health insurance coverage
- Updated statistics on drug use and abuse
- Revised introduction to cognition in adulthood
- Revised information on reflective thinking
- Revised and expanded section on postformal thought
- Added examples to all stages of Schaie's life-span model of cognitive development
- Revised material on Sternberg's model of intelligence
- Revised section on Kohlberg's model of moral reasoning
- Revised section on gender and moral reasoning
- Updated statistics on college attendance
- Included information on massive open online courses (MOOCs)
- Revised information on the effect of college on intellectual development
- Updated statistics on expected lifetime earnings by educational level

14 Psychosocial Development in Emerging and Young Adulthood

- Expanded introduction to identity development
- Added examples to stages of recentering
- Expanded introduction to normative stage models
- Expanded and revised section on intimacy versus isolation
- Expanded section on trait models of personality
- Revised material on personality change in adulthood
- Expanded evaluation of five-factor model of personality
- Revised section on friendship
- Added examples of passion and commitment to section on love
- Updated statistics on single adults
- Revised material on gay and lesbian adults and added current information on same-sex marriage
- Updated statistics on political affiliation, religion, age, and support for same-sex marriage
- Updated statistics on first marriages in the United States
- Updated statistics on parenthood and unwed mothers
- Expanded introduction to parenthood
- Revised information on paternal involvement in child care
- Revised section on parenthood and marital satisfaction
- Revised material on dual-income families

15 Physical and Cognitive Development in Middle Adulthood

- Revised introduction to middle age
- Revised sensory and psychomotor functioning
- Revised and expanded material on basal metabolic functioning
- Revised and expanded section on the brain at midlife
- Revised description of menopausal transition
- Revised material on symptoms of menopause
- Revised information on male sexual functioning and erectile dysfunction
- Revised and expanded section on behavioral influences on health
- Included information on the Affordable Care Act in section on socioeconomic status and health
- Revised and expanded section on race/ethnicity and health
- Revised description of hormone therapy for menopause
- Revised information on stress in middle age
- Revised section on mental health
- Revised and expanded section on how stress affects health
- Revised material on the Seattle Longitudinal Study
- Revised and expanded description of fluid and crystallized intelligence and added metaphor
- Revised and expanded description of encapsulation
- Revised and expanded section on characteristics of creative achievers
- Revised and expanded section on work and cognitive development

16 Psychosocial Development in Middle Adulthood

- Revised section on trait models of personality
- Revised and expanded sections on generativity versus stagnation
- Revised and expanded section on timing of events and the social clock
- Added examples to and expanded introduction to midlife crises
- Revised material on midlife review
- Revised and expanded material on identity assimilation, identity accommodation, and identity balance
- Expanded description of narrative psychology
- Revised and expanded descriptions of multiple dimensions of well-being
- Revised material on marital capital
- Revised section on marital status, well-being, and health
- Added example of kinkeeping
- Revised description of and added example for filial maturity

17 Physical and Cognitive Development in Late Adulthood

- Updated statistics for and revised introduction to the graying of the population
- Revised and expanded definition of geriatrics and gerontology
- Updated statistics on life expectancy in the United States
- Updated statistics on regional and racial/ethnic differences in life expectancy
- Revised introduction to why people age
- Revised and expanded section on genetic programming theories of death
- Revised and expanded section on variable rate theories of death
- Revised definition of survival curves
- Expanded definition of reserve capacity and added metaphor
- Expanded and revised description of age-related macular degeneration
- Expanded material on periodontal disease
- Added example of dementia
- Revised information on factors that influence development of dementia
- Added metaphor for cognitive declines
- Revised material on cognitive abilities and mortality
- Expanded material on and added examples for sensory and working memory
- Revised material on semantic memory
- Expanded material on and added examples for procedural memory
- Revised and expanded material on the effects of aging on speech and memory
- Expanded definition of wisdom

18 Psychosocial Development in Late Adulthood

- Revised and added example to cognitive appraisal model
- Revised section on coping strategies
- Revised section on disengagement theory versus activity theory
- Revised and added examples to continuity theory
- Revised and expanded information on selective optimization with compensation
- Updated statistics on the finances of older people
- Updated statistics on living arrangements
- Revised section on the importance of social relationships
- Updated statistics on widowhood
- Updated statistics on single life
- Revised section on sibling relationships

19 Dealing with Death and Bereavement

- Expanded and added example to description of palliative care
- Updated statistics on near death experiences
- Expanded description of bereavement
- Revised and updated information on ambiguous loss
- Added recent examples of ethics of right-to-die cases and advance directives
- Revised information on passive euthanasia
- Added material to introduction on advance directives
- Updated statistics on the effect of Oregon's assisted-suicide law

integrated instructor resources

The password-protected Online Learning Center for *Experience Human Development,* Thirteenth Edition, contains valuable tools for instructors to use in the classroom. This site includes chapter-by-chapter Instructor's Manual, Test Bank files, and PowerPoint presentations.

- **Instructor's Manual**—The instructor's manual includes classroom activities available to both new and experienced instructors. Among the featured resources are teaching outlines, suggested lecture topics, and classroom discussions and activities. The manual is available in electronic format, for convenient access, editing, and printing.
- **Test Bank**—Each chapter's test bank holds approximately 100 questions that are designed to test factual, conceptual, and practice-based understanding. The test bank is compatible with **EZTest,** McGraw-Hill's **Computerized Test Bank** program.
- **PowerPoint Presentations**—These slides cover the key points of each chapter and include charts and graphs from the text. The PowerPoint presentations serve as an organization and navigation tool integrated with examples and activities from an expert instructor. The slides can be used as is or modified to meet your needs.

EXPERIENCE

Human Development

part 1

ABOUT HUMAN DEVELOPMENT

chapter 1

The Study of Human Development

outline

Human Development: An Ever-Evolving Field

The Study of Human Development: Basic Concepts

Influences on Development

The Life-Span Developmental Approach

learning objectives

Describe human development and how its study has evolved.

Describe the domains and periods of human development.

Give examples of the influences that make one person different from another.

Discuss the principles of the life-span perspective.

did you know?

- In some societies there is no concept of adolescence or middle age?
- Many scholars today agree that race is not a concept that can be defended on a biological basis?
- More than 16 million U.S. children live in poverty and are at risk for health, cognitive, emotional, and behavioral problems?

In this chapter we describe how the field of human development has itself developed. We identify aspects of development and show how they interrelate. We summarize major developments during each period of life. We look at influences on development and the contexts in which each occurs.

There is nothing permanent except change.

—Heraclitus, *fragment* (sixth century BCE)

Human Development: An Ever-Evolving Field

From the moment of conception, human beings begin a process of change that will continue throughout life. A single cell develops into a living, breathing, walking, talking person who moves through an ever-changing world, both being influenced by and influencing it. Babies grow and become children, who grow and become adults. Although we are all individuals and follow our own unique trajectory, we share a species heritage, many common experiences, and broad patterns of development. Those patterns of development are explored throughout this book.

The field of **human development** focuses on the scientific study of the systematic processes of change and stability in people. Developmental scientists (or developmentalists)—individuals engaged in the professional study of human development—look at ways in which people change from conception through maturity as well as at characteristics that remain fairly stable. Which characteristics are most likely to endure? Which are likely to change, and why? These are among the questions developmental scientists seek to answer.

human development
Scientific study of processes of change and stability throughout the human life span.

The work of developmentalists can have a dramatic impact on people's lives. Research findings often have applications to child rearing, education, health, and social policy. For example, research has shown that students who go to school hungry have poorer grades and more emotional and behavioral problems than their classmates, and that this effect is most striking in students from deprived environments. When breakfast programs are implemented, students show academic gains, an effect driven partly by improved nutrition and partly by the decrease in absences that generally accompanies such programs (Hoyland, Dye, & Lawton, 2009). Research showing that the adolescent brain is still immature has prompted suggestions that adolescents accused of crimes be exempt from the death penalty. An understanding of adult development can help people understand and deal with life transitions: a woman returning to work after maternity leave, a person making a career change, a widower dealing with loss, someone coping with a terminal illness.

Developmental psychologists have helped identify key achievements in development across childhood. Many parenting Web sites include lists of these milestones to help parents track their children's growth.

STUDYING THE LIFE SPAN

When the field of developmental psychology emerged as a scientific discipline, most researchers focused their energies on infant and child development. Growth and development are more obvious during these times given the rapid pace of change. As the field matured, however, it became clear that development included more than infancy and childhood. Now researchers consider **life-span development** to be from "womb to tomb," comprising the entire human life span from conception to death. Moreover, they acknowledge that development can be either positive (e.g., becoming toilet trained or enrolling in a college course after retirement) or negative (e.g., once again wetting the bed after a traumatic event or isolating yourself after retirement). For these reasons, events such as the timing of parenthood, maternal employment, and marital satisfaction are now also studied as part of developmental psychology.

life-span development
Concept of human development as a lifelong process, which can be studied scientifically.

HUMAN DEVELOPMENT TODAY

As the field of human development itself developed, its goals came to include description, explanation, prediction, and intervention. For example, to *describe* when most

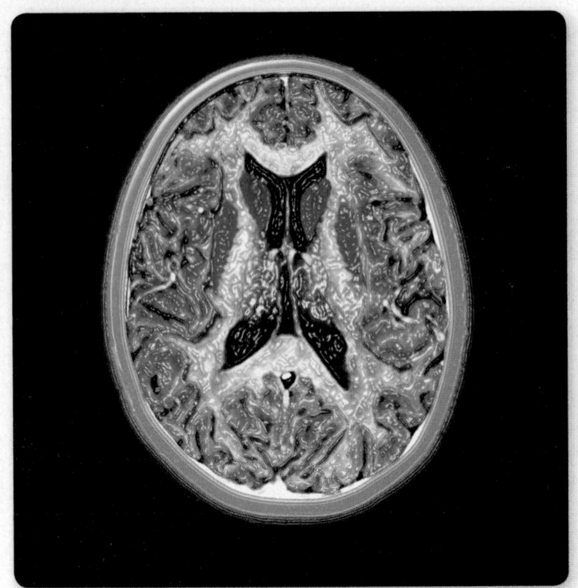

Brain imaging techniques, such as functional magnetic resonance imaging (fMRI), positron emission tomography (PET), and electroencephalogram (EEG), are used to map out where certain thought processes take place within the structure of the brain.

children say their first word or how large their vocabulary is at a certain age, developmental scientists observe large groups of children and establish norms, or averages, for behavior at various ages. They then attempt to *explain* how children acquire language and why some children learn to speak later than usual. This knowledge may make it possible to *predict* future behavior, such as the likelihood that a child will have serious speech problems. Finally, an understanding of how language develops may be used to *intervene* in development, for example, by giving a child speech therapy.

The scientific study of human development is ever evolving. The questions that developmental scientists try to answer, the methods they use, and the explanations they propose are more sophisticated and more varied than they were even five years ago. These shifts reflect progress in understanding as new investigations build on or challenge those that went before. They also reflect advances in technology. Scientists now have access to sensitive instruments that measure eye movement, heart rate, and muscle tension. They are able to use digital technology that allows them to analyze how mothers and babies communicate. Advances in brain imaging make it possible to probe the mysteries of temperament or to compare a normally aging brain with the brain of a person with dementia.

Development is messy. It's complex and multifaceted and shaped by interacting arcs of influence. Thus development is best understood with input from a variety of theoretical and research orientations and is most appropriately studied using multiple disciplines. Not surprisingly, the study of development has been interdisciplinary almost from the start (Parke, 2004b). Students of human development draw collaboratively from a wide range of disciplines, including psychology, psychiatry, sociology, anthropology, biology, genetics, family science, education, history, and medicine. This book includes findings from research in all these fields.

checkpoint can **you** . . .

- Give examples of practical applications of research on human development?
- Identify four goals of the scientific study of human development?
- Name at least six disciplines involved in the study of human development?

The Study of Human Development: Basic Concepts

Developmentalists study processes of change and stability in all domains, or aspects, of development throughout all periods of the life span.

DOMAINS OF DEVELOPMENT

Developmental scientists study three major *domains,* or aspects, of the self: physical, cognitive, and psychosocial. Growth of the body and brain, sensory capacities, motor skills, and health are parts of **physical development.** Learning, attention, memory, language, thinking, reasoning, and creativity make up **cognitive development.** Emotions, personality, and social relationships are aspects of **psychosocial development.**

Although in this book we talk separately about physical, cognitive, and psychosocial development, these domains are interrelated: each aspect of development affects the others. For example, physical development affects cognitive and psychosocial development. A child with frequent ear infections may develop language more slowly than a child without this physical problem. During puberty, dramatic physical and hormonal changes affect the developing sense of self. In contrast, physical changes in the brains of some older adults may lead to intellectual and personality deterioration.

physical development
Growth of body and brain, including patterns of change in sensory capacities, motor skills, and health.

cognitive development
Pattern of change in mental abilities, such as learning, attention, memory, language, thinking, reasoning, and creativity.

psychosocial development
Pattern of change in emotions, personality, and social relationships.

Similarly, cognitive advances and declines are related to physical and psychosocial development. A child who is precocious in language development may bring about positive reactions in others and thus gain in self-worth. Memory development reflects gains or losses in physical connections in the brain. An adult who has trouble remembering people's names may feel shy in social situations.

These children are engaging in all three domains of development: sensory perception (physical development), learning (cognitive development), and social relationships building (psychosocial development).

And finally, psychosocial development can affect cognitive and physical functioning. Indeed, without meaningful social connections, physical and mental health suffers. Motivation and self-confidence are important contributors to school success, whereas negative emotions such as anxiety can impair performance. Researchers even have identified possible links between a conscientious personality and length of life.

Although for simplicity's sake we look separately at physical, cognitive, and psychosocial development, development is a unified process. Throughout the text, links among the three major domains of development are highlighted.

study**smart**

Domains of Development

PERIODS OF THE LIFE SPAN

Division of the life span into periods is a **social construction:** a concept or practice that is an invention of a particular culture or society. There is no objectively definable moment when a child becomes an adult or a young person becomes old. Because the concept of childhood is a social construction, the form it takes varies across cultures. In contrast to the relative freedom children have in the United States today, young children in colonial times were expected to do adultlike tasks such as knitting socks and spinning wool (Ehrenreich & English, 2005). Inuit parents in the Canadian Arctic believe that young children are not yet capable of thought and reason and therefore are lenient when their children cry or become angry. But parents on the Pacific Island of Tonga regularly beat 3- to 5-year-olds, whose crying is attributed to willfulness (Briggs, 1970; Morton, 1996).

social construction
A concept or practice that may appear natural and obvious to those who accept it, but that in reality is an invention of a particular culture or society.

A similar construction involves *adolescence,* which is a recent concept that emerged as society became more industrialized. Until the early twentieth century, young people in the United States were considered children until they left school, married or got a job, and entered the adult world. By the 1920s, with the establishment of comprehensive high schools to meet the needs of a growing economy and with more families able to support extended formal education for their children, the teenage years became a distinct period of development (Keller, 1999). In some preindustrial societies, such as the Chippewa Indians, the concept of adolescence still does not exist. The Chippewa have only two periods of childhood: from birth until the child walks, and from walking to puberty. What we call adolescence is part of adulthood (Broude, 1995).

In this book, we follow a sequence of eight periods generally accepted in Western industrial societies. After describing the crucial changes that occur in the first period, before birth, we trace all three domains of development through infancy and toddlerhood, early childhood, middle childhood, adolescence, emerging and young adulthood, middle adulthood, and late adulthood (Table 1). For each period after infancy and toddlerhood, we have combined physical and cognitive development into a single chapter.

The interactions between domains of development can be conceptualized as a giant spiderweb where one thread of development is affected by what is going on in the rest of the web. A vibration experienced in one area is experienced by the whole web.

The age divisions shown in Table 1 are approximate and somewhat arbitrary. This is especially true of adulthood, when there are no clear-cut social or physical landmarks, such as starting school or entering puberty, to signal a shift from one period to another.

TABLE 1 Typical Major Developments in Eight Periods of Human Development			
Age Period	**Physical Developments**	**Cognitive Developments**	**Psychosocial Developments**
Prenatal Period (conception to birth)	Conception occurs by normal fertilization or other means. The genetic endowment interacts with environmental influences from the start. Basic body structures and organs form; brain growth spurt begins. Physical growth is the most rapid in the life span. Vulnerability to environmental influences is great.	Abilities to learn and remember and to respond to sensory stimuli are developing.	Fetus responds to mother's voice and develops a preference for it.
Infancy and Toddlerhood (birth to age 3)	All senses and body systems operate at birth to varying degrees. The brain grows in complexity and is highly sensitive to environmental influence. Physical growth and development of motor skills are rapid.	Abilities to learn and remember are present, even in early weeks. Use of symbols and ability to solve problems develop by end of second year. Comprehension and use of language develop rapidly.	Attachments to parents and others form. Self-awareness develops. Shift from dependence toward autonomy occurs. Interest in other children increases.
Early Childhood (ages 3 to 6)	Growth is steady; appearance becomes more slender and proportions more adultlike. Appetite diminishes, and sleep problems are common. Handedness appears; fine and gross motor skills and strength improve.	Thinking is somewhat egocentric, but understanding of other people's perspectives grows. Cognitive immaturity results in some illogical ideas about the world. Memory and language improve. Intelligence becomes more predictable. Preschool experience is common, and kindergarten experience is more so.	Self-concept and understanding of emotions become more complex; self-esteem is global. Independence, initiative, and self-control increase. Gender identity develops. Play becomes more imaginative, more elaborate, and usually more social. Altruism, aggression, and fearfulness are common. Family is still the focus of social life, but other children become more important.
Middle Childhood (ages 6 to 11)	Growth slows. Strength and athletic skills improve. Respiratory illnesses are common, but health is generally better than at any other time in the life span.	Egocentrism diminishes. Children begin to think logically but concretely. Memory and language skills increase. Cognitive gains permit children to benefit from formal schooling. Some children show special educational needs and strengths.	Self-concept becomes more complex, affecting self-esteem. Coregulation reflects gradual shift in control from parents to child. Peers assume central importance.

TABLE 1 Typical Major Developments in Eight Periods of Human Development

Age Period	Physical Developments	Cognitive Developments	Psychosocial Developments
Adolescence (ages 11 to about 20)	Physical growth and other changes are rapid and profound. Reproductive maturity occurs. Major health risks arise from behavioral issues, such as eating disorders and drug abuse.	Ability to think abstractly and use scientific reasoning develops. Immature thinking persists in some attitudes and behaviors. Education focuses on preparation for college or vocation.	Search for identity, including sexual identity, becomes central. Relationships with parents are generally good. Peer group may exert a positive or negative influence.
Emerging and Young Adulthood (ages 20 to 40)	Physical condition peaks, then declines slightly. Lifestyle choices influence health.	Thought and moral judgments become more complex. Educational and occupational choices are made, sometimes after period of exploration.	Personality traits and styles become relatively stable, but changes in personality may be influenced by life stages and events. Intimate relationships and personal lifestyles are established but may not be lasting. Most people marry, and most become parents.
Middle Adulthood (ages 40 to 65)	Slow deterioration of sensory abilities, health, stamina, and strength may begin, but individual differences are wide. Women experience menopause.	Mental abilities peak; expertise and practical problem-solving skills are high. Creative output may decline but improve in quality. For some, career success and earning powers peak; for others, burnout or career change may occur.	Sense of identity continues to develop; midlife transition may occur. Dual responsibilities of caring for children and parents may cause stress. Launching of children leaves empty nest.
Late Adulthood (age 65 and over)	Most people are healthy and active, although health and physical abilities generally decline. Slowing of reaction time affects some aspects of functioning.	Most people are mentally alert. Although intelligence and memory may deteriorate in some areas, most people find ways to compensate.	Retirement from workforce may occur and may offer new options for use of time. People develop more flexible strategies to cope with personal losses and impending death. Relationships with family and close friends can provide important support. Search for meaning in life assumes central importance.

Although individual differences exist in the way people deal with the characteristic events and issues of each period, developmentalists suggest that certain basic needs must be met and certain tasks mastered for normal development to occur. Infants, for example, are dependent on adults for food, clothing, and shelter as well as for human contact and affection. They form attachments to parents and caregivers, who also become attached to them. With the development of speech and self-locomotion, toddlers become more self-reliant; they need to assert their autonomy but also need parents to set limits on their behavior. During early childhood, children gain more self-control and become more interested in other children. During middle childhood, control over behavior gradually shifts from parent to child, and the peer group becomes increasingly important. A central task of adolescence is the search for identity—personal, sexual, and occupational. As adolescents become physically mature, they deal with conflicting needs and emotions as they prepare to leave the parental nest.

checkpoint can **you** . . .

- Identify the three domains of development and give examples of how they are interrelated?
- Name eight periods of human development and list several key issues or tasks of each period?

During emerging adulthood, an exploratory period in the early to midtwenties, many people are not yet ready to settle down to the typical tasks of young adulthood: establishing independent lifestyles, occupations, and families. By the 30s, most adults have successfully fulfilled those tasks. During middle adulthood, some decline in physical capabilities is likely. At the same time, many middle-aged people find excitement and challenge in life changes—launching new careers and adult children—while some face the need to care for elderly parents. In late adulthood, people need to cope with losses in their faculties, the loss of loved ones, and preparations for death. If they retire, they must deal with the loss of work-based relationships but may get increased pleasure out of friendships, family, volunteer work, and the opportunity to explore previously neglected interests. Many older people become more introspective, searching out the meaning of their lives.

Influences on Development

individual differences
Differences in characteristics, influences, or developmental outcomes.

What makes each person unique? Although students of development are interested in the universal processes of development experienced by all normal human beings, they also study **individual differences** in characteristics, influences, and developmental outcomes. People differ in gender, height, weight, and body build; in health and energy level; in intelligence; and in temperament, personality, and emotional reactions. The contexts of their lives differ too: the homes, communities, and societies they live in, the relationships they have, the schools they go to (or whether they go to school at all), and how they spend their free time. Every person has a unique developmental trajectory, an individual path to follow. One challenge in developmental psychology is to identify the universal influences on development, and then apply those to understanding individual differences in developmental trajectories.

HEREDITY, ENVIRONMENT, AND MATURATION

heredity
Inborn traits or characteristics inherited from the biological parents.

environment
Totality of nonhereditary, or experiential, influences on development.

Some influences on development originate primarily with **heredity:** inborn traits or characteristics inherited from the biological parents. Other influences come largely from the **environment:** the world outside the self, beginning in the womb, and the learning that comes from experience. Which of these two factors has more impact on development? The issue of the relative importance of *nature* (heredity) and *nurture* (environmental influences both before and after birth) historically generated intense debate.

Today scientists have found ways to measure more precisely the roles of heredity and environment in the development of specific traits within a population. When we look at a particular person, however, research with regard to almost all characteristics points to a blend of inheritance and experience. Thus, even though intelligence is strongly influenced by heredity, parental stimulation, education, peer influence, and other variables also affect it. Contemporary theorists and researchers are more interested in finding ways to explain how nature and nurture work together than in arguing about which factor is more important.

maturation
Unfolding of a natural sequence of physical and behavioral changes.

Many typical changes of infancy and early childhood, such as the abilities to walk and talk, are tied to **maturation** of the body and brain—the unfolding of a natural sequence of physical changes and behavior patterns. As children grow into adolescents and then into adults, individual differences in innate characteristics and life experience play a greater role. Throughout life, however, maturation continues to influence certain biological processes, such as brain development.

Even in processes that all people undergo, rates and timing of development vary. Throughout this book, we talk about average ages for the occurrence of certain events: the first word, the first step, the first menstruation or nocturnal emission, the development of logical thought, and menopause. But these ages are *merely* averages, and there is wide variation among people with respect to these norms. Only when deviation from the average is extreme should we consider development exceptionally advanced or delayed.

To understand development, then, we need to look at the *inherited* characteristics that give each person a start in life. We also need to consider the many *environmental* factors that affect development, especially such major contexts as family, neighborhood, socioeconomic status, race/ethnicity, and culture. We need to consider how heredity and environment interact. We need to understand which developments are primarily maturational and which are not. We need to look at influences that affect many or most people at a certain age or a certain time in history and also at those that affect only certain individuals. Finally, we need to look at how timing can accentuate the impact of certain influences.

To get a callus, you have to have "callus-making" genes of some sort, but the environmental input of repeated friction on your skin is also required or a callus would never form. So are calluses more nature or more nurture?

CONTEXTS OF DEVELOPMENT

Human beings are social beings. From the beginning they develop within a social and historical context. For an infant, the immediate context normally is the family, but the family in turn is subject to the wider and ever-changing influences of neighborhood, community, and society.

study smart

Nature/Nurture

Family The **nuclear family** is a household unit consisting of one or two parents and their children, whether biological, adopted, or stepchildren. Historically, the two-parent nuclear family has been the normative family unit in the United States and other Western societies. However, instead of the large, rural family in which parents and children worked side by side on the family farm, we now see smaller, urban families in which both parents work outside the home and children spend much of their time in school or child care. The increased incidence of divorce also has affected the nuclear family. Children of divorced parents may live with one or the other parent or may move back and forth between them. The household may include a stepparent and stepsiblings or a parent's live-in partner. There are increasing numbers of single and childless adults, unmarried parents, and gay and lesbian households (Dye, 2010; Hernandez, 2004; Teachman, Tedrow, & Crowder, 2000).

nuclear family
Two-generational kinship, economic, and household unit consisting of one or two parents and their biological children, adopted children, or stepchildren.

extended family
Multigenerational kinship network of parents, children, and other relatives, sometimes living together in an extended-family household.

In many societies in Asia, Africa, and Latin America and among some U.S. families that trace their lineage to those countries, the **extended family**—a

An extended-family household might include grandparents, aunts, and cousins.

multigenerational network of grandparents, aunts, uncles, cousins, and more distant relatives—is the traditional family form. Many people live in *extended-family households*, where they have daily contact with kin. Adults often share breadwinning and child-raising responsibilities, and older children are responsible for younger brothers and sisters.

Today the extended-family household is becoming slightly less typical in many developing countries due to industrialization and migration to urban centers (Kinsella & Phillips, 2005). Meanwhile, in the United States, economic pressures, housing shortages, and out-of-wedlock childbearing have helped to fuel a trend toward three- and even four-generational family households. In 2009, almost 17 percent of households could be characterized as multigenerational (Pew Research Center, 2011).

Multigenerational households have become more common in recent years for a variety of reasons. First, both men and women are marrying at later ages, and thus remaining at home for longer than was previously typical. This has become particularly common with recent downturns in the U.S. economy. Second, there has been an influx of immigrant populations since 1970, and these immigrants are more likely than native-born families to seek out multigenerational homes for reasons of practicality as well as preference. Indeed, even among nonimmigrants, race and ethnicity play a part. Latinos, African Americans, and Asians are all more likely to live in multigenerational families than are whites. In addition, people are living longer, and elderly parents may sometimes benefit from inclusion in their children's households (Pew Research Center, 2010b).

socioeconomic status (SES)
Combination of economic and social factors describing an individual or family, including income, education, and occupation.

Socioeconomic Status and Neighborhood A family's **socioeconomic status (SES)** is based on family income and the educational and occupational levels of the adults in the household. Throughout this book, we examine many studies that relate SES to developmental processes (such as mothers' verbal interactions with their children) and to developmental outcomes (such as health and cognitive performance). SES affects these processes and outcomes indirectly, through such related factors as the kinds of homes and neighborhoods people live in and the quality of nutrition, medical care, and schooling available to them.

When we are immersed in a culture, it is difficult to see how much of what we do is affected by it. For example, there are regional differences in the United States regarding what soft drinks are called. The term "pop" is most common in the Midwest, Great Plains, and Northwest, "coke" is commonly used in the South and New Mexico, and "soda" is primarily used in California and bordering states.

More than 1.2 billion people lived on less than $1.25 a day in 2008. Although this is a large number, it has fallen by approximately 25 percent in the last 30 years, most notably in China and India, which account for the majority of change in poverty levels (Figure 1; Olinto, Beegle, Sobrado, & Uematsu, 2013). The expanding global economy is one of the major factors contributing to the overall decrease in poverty (United Nations, 2009).

In the United States, where poverty thresholds depend on family size and composition, more than 16 million children—21.9 percent of all children under age 18—live in poverty, and 7.41 million children—almost 7 percent—are in extreme poverty (Children's Defense Fund, 2012; DeNavas-Walt, Proctor, & Smith, 2012).* Virtually all progress made with respect to child poverty since 1974 was wiped out by the current recession (Foundation for Child Development, 2010).

Poverty, especially if it is long-lasting, can be harmful to the physical, cognitive, and psychosocial well-being of children and families. Poor children are more likely than other children to have emotional or behavioral problems, and their cognitive potential and school performance suffer more (Evans, 2004). The harm done by poverty may be indirect, through its impact on parents' emotional state and parenting practices and on the home environment they create. Threats to well-being multiply if, as often happens, several **risk factors**—conditions that increase the likelihood of a negative outcome—are present.

risk factors
Conditions that increase the likelihood of a negative developmental outcome.

The composition of a neighborhood affects children as well. Living in a poor neighborhood with large numbers of unemployed people makes it less likely that effective social support will be available (Black & Krishnakumar, 1998). Still, positive development can occur despite serious risk factors. Consider the Pulitzer Prize–winning author

*A family of four was considered extremely poor in 2012 if their household income was below half of the official poverty line (Children's Defense Fund, 2012).

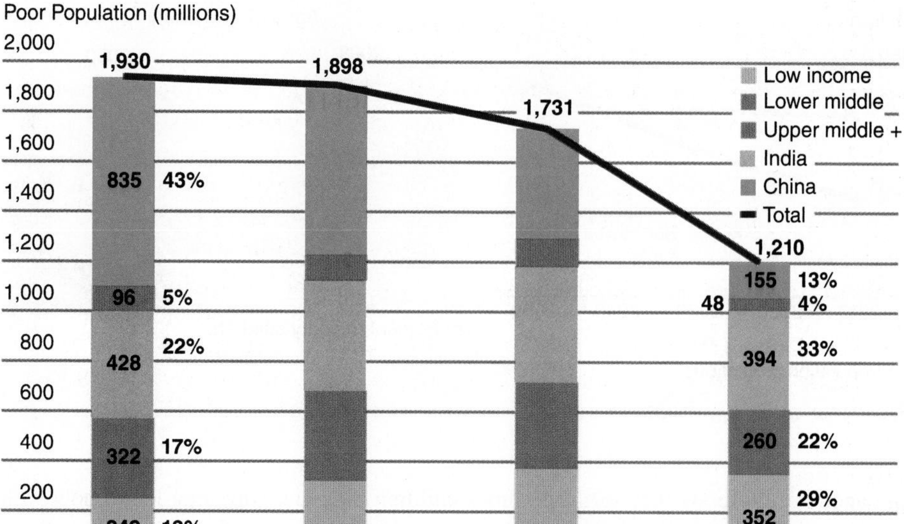

Source: Olinto, Beegle, Sobrado, & Uematsu, 2013.

FIGURE 1
People Living in Poverty, 1981–2010

Maya Angelou, the country singer Shania Twain, and former U.S. president Abraham Lincoln, all of whom grew up in poverty (Kim-Cohen, Moffitt, Caspi, & Taylor, 2004).

Affluence doesn't necessarily protect children from risk. Some children in affluent families face pressure to achieve and are often left on their own by busy parents. Such children have high rates of substance abuse, anxiety, and depression (Luthar & Latendresse, 2005). Although poor families are often less positive about their neighborhoods and feel less safe in them, a number of strengths can be found within the immediate family context. Parents report being just as close with their children, they attend church with their families just as often, they feel just as safe at home and school, and they eat meals together as a family more often than wealthier families. It may be that the scientific community has focused too strongly on the negative effects of poverty and not paid enough attention to the strengths and resiliencies found in lower SES homes (Valladares & Moore, 2009).

People in the United States are far more likely to self-disclose personal information than are people in Japan. Why might this be? The freer social structure in the United States might be one reason. When you can make and break friends easily, you need to cement social bonds as much as possible.

Schug, Yuki, & Maddux, 2010

Culture and Race/Ethnicity **Culture** refers to a society's or group's total way of life, including its customs, traditions, laws, knowledge, beliefs, values, language, and physical products, from tools to artworks—all of the behavior and attitudes that are learned, shared, and transmitted among members of a social group. Culture is constantly changing, often through contact with other cultures. Today cultural contact has been enhanced by computers and telecommunications. E-mail, texting, and social media sites offer almost instantaneous communication across the globe, and digital services such as iTunes give people around the world easy access to one another's music and movies.

culture
A society's or group's total way of life, including customs, traditions, beliefs, values, language, and physical products—all learned behavior, passed on from parents to children.

ethnic group
A group united by ancestry, race, religion, language, or national origins, which contribute to a sense of shared identity.

An **ethnic group** consists of people united by a distinctive culture, ancestry, religion, language, or national origin, all of which contribute to a sense of shared identity and shared attitudes, beliefs, and values. By 2050, due to rising immigration and high birthrates among immigrant families, ethnic minorities in the United States are expected to become the majority. In fact, in 2008, roughly a third of all children and nearly half of children under the age of 5 were from a minority group (U.S. Census Bureau, 2008a, 2009d). It is predicted that by 2050, 62 percent of the nation's children will be members of what are now minority groups, and the proportion of Hispanic or Latino/a children—39 percent—will surpass the 38 percent who will be non-Hispanic white (U.S. Census Bureau, 2008a; Figure 2). Already, nearly one-fourth of U.S. kindergarteners and one-fifth of all kindergarten through 12th grade students are Hispanic (U.S. Census Bureau, 2009b, 2009c).

Ethnic and cultural patterns affect development by their influence on the composition of a household, its economic and social resources, the way its members act toward

FIGURE 2

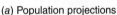

Population Projections for Non-Hispanic White and Minority Groups, 2010–2050

(a) According to Census Bureau projections, racial/ethnic minorities will reach 54 percent of the U.S. population, exceeding the proportion of non-Hispanic white people by 2050. (b) Also by 2050, "minority" children under age 18 are expected to make up 62 percent of the child population.

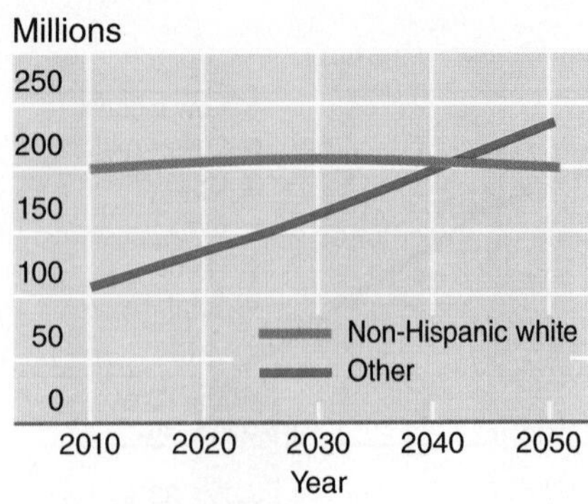

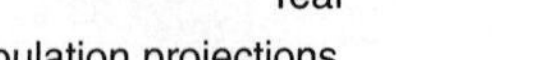

(*a*) Population projections

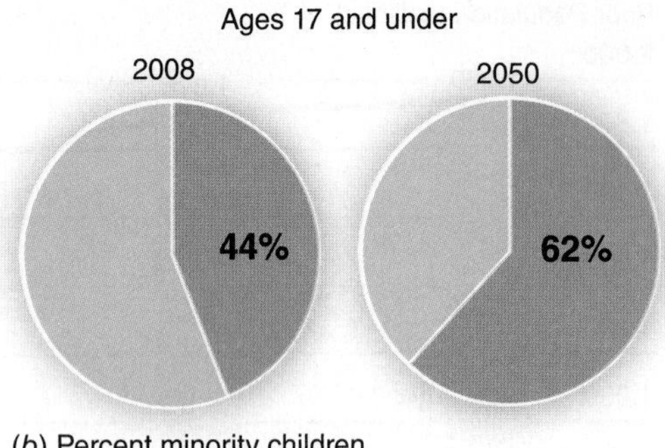

(*b*) Percent minority children

Source: U.S. Census Bureau, 2008a.

one another, the foods they eat, the games children play, the way they learn, how well they do in school, the occupations adults engage in, and the way family members think and perceive the world (Parke, 2004b). For example, children of immigrants in the United States are nearly twice as likely as native-born children to live with extended families and are less likely to have mothers who work outside the home (Shields & Behrman, 2004).

The United States has always been a nation of immigrants and ethnic groups, but the primary ethnic origins of the immigrant population have shifted from Europe and Canada to Asia and Latin America (Hernandez, 2004). In 2007, more than 20 percent of the population were immigrants or children of immigrants (Box 1). More immigrants came from Mexico, 40 percent, than from any other country, and the remaining 60 percent came from nations in the Caribbean, East and West Asia, Australia, Central and South America, Indochina, the former Soviet Union, and Africa.

The existence of Marcia and Millie Biggs, who as fraternal twins share approximately 50 percent of their genes, calls into question the concept of race as a biological construct.

Wide diversity exists within broad ethnic groups. The European-descended "white majority" consists of many distinct ethnicities—German, Belgian, Irish, French, Italian, and so on. Cuban Americans, Puerto Ricans, and Mexican Americans—all Hispanic Americans—have different histories and cultures and may be of African, European, Native American, or mixed descent (Johnson et al., 2003; Sternberg, Grigorenko, & Kidd, 2005). African Americans from the rural South differ from those of Caribbean ancestry. Asian Americans hail from a variety of countries with distinct cultures, from modern industrial Japan to communist China to the remote mountains of Nepal, where many people still practice their ancient way of life. Native Americans consist of hundreds of recognized nations, tribes, bands, and villages (Lin & Kelsey, 2000).

The term *race,* historically and popularly viewed as an identifiable biological category, is more accurately defined as a social construct. There is no clear scientific consensus on its definition, and it is impossible to measure reliably (Helms, Jernigan, & Mascher, 2005; Smedley & Smedley, 2005). Human genetic variation occurs along a broad continuum, and 90 percent of such variation occurs *within* rather than among socially defined races (Bonham, Warshauer-Baker, & Collins, 2005; Ossorio & Duster, 2005). Nevertheless, race as a social category remains a

window on the world

CHILDREN OF IMMIGRANT FAMILIES

The United States has always been a nation of immigrants and ethnic groups, but the primary ethnic origins of the immigrant population have shifted from Europe and Canada—the homelands of 97 percent of immigrants in 1910—to Latin America, the Caribbean, Asia, and Africa, which now account for 88 percent of all immigrants.

Nearly one-fourth (24 percent) of U.S. children lived in immigrant families in 2007. Faster growing than any other group of children in the country, they are the leading edge of the coming shift of racial and ethnic minorities to majority status. Whereas earlier waves of immigrants were almost entirely white and Christian, more than one-third (37 percent) of children in immigrant families have nonwhite parents. Many of these families are Confucian, Buddhist, Hindu, Jewish, Muslim, Shinto, Sikh, Taoist, or Zoroastrian, and, although predominantly Spanish-speaking, they speak a wide variety of languages.

Immigrant families are widely dispersed. Children in immigrant families account for at least 10 percent of all children in 27 states and the District of Columbia, but they are most highly concentrated in California, Texas, New York, Florida, and Illinois, which together are home to 64 percent of children of immigrants.

More immigrants come from Mexico (40 percent) than from any other country (Hernandez & Macartney, 2008). An estimated 5 million Mexican-born children or children of Mexican-born parents live in the United States. Many of these parents work at low-paying jobs in the food service, maintenance, construction, farming, and manufacturing industries, earning less than $20,000 a year full time. With anti-immigrant sentiment rising, undocumented parents live in constant fear of losing their job (if they can find one) and of being deported (Children in North America Project, 2008). Nearly half of all children in immigrant families (47.9 percent) live in poverty (Hernandez, Denton, & Macartney, 2007), and many do not have health insurance despite being eligible, even though most of the parents work hard to support their families.

Most children of immigrants live with two married or cohabiting parents, but these children are nearly twice as likely as other children to live in extended-family households with grandparents, other relatives, and even nonrelatives, often in overcrowded housing. Children in immigrant families are more than 3 times as likely as those in native families to have fathers who have not finished high school (40 percent as compared to 12 percent). Immigrant parents often have high educational aspirations for their children but may lack the knowledge and experience to help their children succeed in school.

A little-known fact is that almost 1 in 4 children in immigrant families (24 percent) has one parent born in the United States, and nearly half (48 percent) have a parent who is a naturalized citizen. More than 2 out of 3 (68 percent) have parents who have lived in the United States for 10 years or more, and nearly 4 out of 5 (79 percent) of the children were born in the United States. In fact, nearly 2 out of 3 (63 percent) children living with undocumented parents are themselves natural-born citizens.

As immigration fuels dramatic changes in the U.S. population, developmental issues affecting children in immigrant families will become increasingly important subjects for research.

Source: Unless otherwise cited, the source is Hernandez, Denton, & Macartney (2007).

Are you (or any members of your family) immigrants or children of immigrants? If so, what factors helped or hindered your (or their) adjustment to life in the United States? How do you imagine life may be different for children of immigrants 40 years from now?

factor in research because it makes a difference in "how individuals are treated, where they live, their employment opportunities, the quality of their health care, and whether [they] can fully participate" in their society (Smedley & Smedley, 2005, p. 23).

Categories of culture, race, and ethnicity are fluid, "continuously shaped and redefined by social and political forces" (Fisher et al., 2002, p. 1026). Geographic dispersion and intermarriage together with adaptation to varying local conditions have produced a great heterogeneity of physical and cultural characteristics within populations

ethnic gloss
Overgeneralization about an ethnic or cultural group that obscures differences within the group.

(Smedley & Smedley, 2005). Thus, President Barack Obama, who has a black, African father and a white, American mother, falls into more than one racial/ethnic category and may identify more strongly with one or another at different times (Hitlin, Brown, & Elder, 2006). A term such as *black* or *Hispanic* can be an **ethnic gloss**—an overgeneralization that obscures or blurs such variations.

checkpoint can you . . .

- Give examples of the influences of family and neighborhood composition, socioeconomic status, culture, race/ethnicity, and historical context?

The Historical Context At one time developmentalists paid little attention to the historical context—the time in which people live. Then, as early longitudinal studies of childhood extended into the adult years, investigators began to focus on how certain experiences, tied to time and place, affect the course of people's lives. Today, the historical context is an important part of the study of development.

NORMATIVE AND NONNORMATIVE INFLUENCES

normative
Characteristic of an event that occurs in a similar way for most people in a group.

historical generation
A group of people strongly influenced by a major historical event during their formative period.

cohort
A group of people born at about the same time.

nonnormative
Characteristic of an unusual event that happens to a particular person or a typical event that happens at an unusual time of life.

To understand similarities and differences in development, we need to look at two types of **normative** influences: biological or environmental events that affect many or most people in a society in similar ways and events that touch only certain individuals (Baltes & Smith, 2004).

Normative age-graded influences are highly similar for people in a particular age group. The timing of biological events is fairly predictable within a normal range. For example, people don't experience puberty at age 35 or menopause at 12.

Normative history-graded influences are significant events (such as the Great Depression or World War II) that shape the behavior and attitudes of a **historical generation:** a group of people who experience the event at a formative time in their lives. For example, the generations that came of age during the Depression and World War II tend to show a strong sense of social interdependence and trust that has declined among more recent generations (Rogler, 2002). Depending on when and where they live, entire generations may feel the impact of famines, nuclear explosions, or terrorist attacks. In Western countries, medical advances as well as improvements in nutrition and sanitation have dramatically reduced infant and child mortality. As children grow up today, they are influenced by computers, digital television, the Internet, and other technological developments. Social changes, such as the increase in employed mothers and the increase in single-parent households, have greatly altered family life.

> *Media exposure provides a normative influence on children today, and toddlers are now skillful at using iPhone apps developed specifically for them. How might this shape their development?*
>
> Stout, 2010

A historical generation is not the same as an age **cohort:** a group of people born at about the same time. A historical generation may contain more than one cohort, but cohorts are part of a historical generation only if they experience major, shaping historical events at a formative point in their lives (Rogler, 2002).

Nonnormative influences are unusual events that have a major impact on *individual* lives because they disturb the expected sequence of the life cycle. They are either typical events that happen at an atypical time of life (such as the death of a parent when a child is young) or atypical events (such as surviving a plane crash). Some of these influences are largely beyond a person's control and may present rare opportunities or severe challenges that the person perceives as turning points. On the other hand, people sometimes help create their own nonnormative life events—say, by deciding to have a baby in their midfifties or taking up a risky hobby such as skydiving—and thus participate actively in their own development. Taken together, the three types

Widespread use of computers is a normative history-graded influence on children's development, which did not exist in earlier generations.

Newborn ducklings followed and became attached to the first moving object they saw, which happened to be ethologist Konrad Lorenz. Lorenz called this behavior imprinting.

of influences—normative age-graded, normative history-graded, and nonnormative—contribute to the complexity of human development as well as to the challenges people experience in trying to build their lives.

checkpoint can you . . .

- Give examples of normative age-graded, normative history-graded, and nonnormative influences?

TIMING OF INFLUENCES: CRITICAL OR SENSITIVE PERIODS

In a well-known study, Konrad Lorenz (1957), an Austrian zoologist, showed that newly hatched ducklings will instinctively follow the first moving object they see, whether it is a member of their species or not. This phenomenon is called **imprinting,** and Lorenz believed that it was automatic and irreversible. Usually, this instinctive bond is with the mother; when the natural course of events is disturbed, however, other attachments, such as the one to Lorenz, or none at all can form. Imprinting, said Lorenz, is the result of a *predisposition toward learning:* the readiness of an organism's nervous system to acquire certain information during a brief *critical period* in early life.

imprinting
Instinctive form of learning in which, during a critical period in early development, a young animal forms an attachment to the first moving object it sees, usually the mother.

A **critical period** is a specific time when a given event, or its absence, has a specific impact on development. If a necessary event does not occur during a critical period of maturation, normal development will not occur; and the resulting abnormal patterns may be irreversible (Kuhl, Conboy, Padden, Nelson, & Pruitt, 2005). However, the length of a critical period is not absolutely fixed; if ducklings' rearing conditions are varied to slow their growth, the usual critical period for imprinting can be extended, and imprinting itself may even be reversed (Bruer, 2001).

critical period
Specific time when a given event or its absence has a specific impact on development.

Do human beings experience critical periods, as ducklings do? If a woman receives X-rays, takes certain drugs, or contracts certain diseases at certain times during pregnancy, the fetus may show specific ill effects, depending on the nature of the insult, its timing, and characteristics of the fetus itself. If a muscle problem interfering with the ability to focus both eyes on the same object is not corrected within a critical period early in childhood, depth perception probably will not develop (Bushnell & Boudreau, 1993).

However, the concept of critical periods in humans is controversial. Because many aspects of development, even in the physical domain, have been found to show **plasticity,** or modifiability of performance, it may be more useful to think about **sensitive periods,** when a developing person is especially responsive to certain kinds of experiences (Bruer, 2001).

plasticity
Range of modifiability of performance.

sensitive periods
Times in development when a person is particularly open to certain kinds of experiences.

There is growing evidence that plasticity is not just a general characteristic of development that applies to all members of a species, but that there are individual differences in plasticity of responses to environmental events as well. It appears as if some children—especially those with difficult temperaments, those who are highly reactive, and those with particular gene variants—may be more profoundly affected by childhood experiences, whether positive or negative, than other children (Belsky & Pluess, 2009). This new research suggests that characteristics generally assumed to be negative—such as a difficult or reactive temperament—can be adaptive (positive) when the environment is supportive of development. For example, one study found that children who were highly reactive to environmental events showed, as expected,

A new study suggests that seeking out dangerous activities may be influenced by our genes. Specifically, a mutation in genes that code for dopa[…] appears to be related to risk-taking behaviors.

Derringer et al., 2011

research in action

IS THERE A CRITICAL PERIOD FOR LANGUAGE ACQUISITION?

2

In 1967 Eric Lenneberg (1967, 1969) proposed a critical period for language acquisition beginning in early infancy and ending around puberty. Lenneberg argued that it would be difficult, if not impossible, for a child who had not yet acquired language by the onset of puberty to do so after that age.

In 1970, a 13-year-old girl called Genie offered the opportunity for a test of Lenneberg's hypothesis (Curtiss, 1977; Fromkin, Krashen, Curtiss, Rigler, & Rigler, 1974; Pines, 1981; Rymer, 1993). The victim of an abusive father, she had been confined for nearly 12 years to a small room in her parents' home, tied to a potty chair and cut off from normal human contact. When found, she recognized only her name and the word "sorry." Could Genie be taught to speak, or was it too late? The National Institutes of Mental Health (NIMH) funded a study to provide intensive testing and language training for Genie.

Genie's progress during the study both supported and challenged the idea of a critical period for language acquisition. She learned some simple words and could string them together into primitive sentences. But "her speech remained, for the most part, like a somewhat garbled telegram" (Pines, 1981, p. 29). Her mother regained custody, cut her off from the NIMH researchers, and then eventually sent her into the foster care system. A series of abusive foster homes rendered Genie silent once more.

What explains Genie's initial progress and her inability to sustain it? Her understanding of her name and the single word "sorry" may mean that her language-learning mechanisms had been triggered early in the critical period, allowing later learning to occur. The timing of the NIMH language training and her ability to learn some simple words at age 13 may indicate that she was still in the critical period, though near its end. On the other hand, her extreme abuse and neglect may have retarded her development so much that she could not be considered a true test of the critical period concept (Curtiss, 1977).

Genie's case dramatizes the difficulty of acquiring language after the early years of life, but because of the complicating factors, it does not permit conclusive judgments about whether such acquisition is possible. Some researchers consider the prepubertal years a sensitive rather than critical period for learning language (Newport, Bavelier, & Neville, 2001; Schumann, 1997). Brain imaging research has found that even if the parts of the brain best suited to language processing are damaged early in childhood, nearly normal language development can continue as other parts of the brain take over (Boatman et al., 1999; Hertz-Pannier et al., 2002; M. H. Johnson, 1998). In fact, shifts in brain organization and utilization occur throughout the course of normal language learning (M. H. Johnson, 1998; Neville & Bavelier, 1998).

If either a critical or a sensitive period for language learning exists, what explains it? Do the brain's mechanisms for acquiring language decay as the brain matures? That would seem strange, as other cognitive abilities improve. An alternative hypothesis is that this very increase in cognitive sophistication interferes with an adolescent's or adult's ability to learn a language. Young children acquire language in small chunks that can be digested readily. Older learners, when they first begin learning a language, tend to absorb a great deal at once and then may have trouble analyzing and interpreting it (Newport, 1991).

Have you had difficulty learning a new language as an adult? If so, does this explanation help you understand why?

---

heckpoint
can you . . .

Contrast critical and sensitive eriods and give examples?

negative responses such as aggression and behavior problems when faced with stressors such as marital conflict in their families. Surprisingly, however, when the levels of family adversity were low, highly reactive children showed even more adaptive profiles than children low in reactivity. These highly reactive children were more prosocial, more engaged in school, and showed lower levels of externalizing symptoms (Obradovic et al., 2010). Research such as this clearly points to a need to reconceptualize the nature of plasticity in early development with an eye toward examining issues of resilience as well as risk. Box 2 discusses how the concepts of critical and sensitive periods apply to language development.

The Life-Span Developmental Approach

Paul B. Baltes (1936–2006) and his colleagues (1987; Baltes & Smith, 2004; Baltes, Lindenberger, & Staudinger, 1998; Staudinger & Bluck, 2001) have identified seven key principles of a life-span developmental approach that sum up many of the concepts discussed in this chapter. Together these principles serve as a widely accepted conceptual framework for the study of life-span development:

1. *Development is lifelong.* Development is a lifelong process of change. Each period of the life span is affected by what happened before and will affect what is to come. Each period has unique characteristics and value. No period is more or less important than any other.
2. *Development is multidimensional.* It occurs along multiple interacting dimensions—biological, psychological, and social—each of which may develop at varying rates.
3. *Development is multidirectional.* As people gain in one area, they may lose in another, sometimes at the same time. Children grow mostly in one direction—up—both in size and in abilities. Then the balance gradually shifts. Adolescents typically gain in physical abilities, but their facility in learning a new language typically declines. Some abilities, such as vocabulary, often continue to increase throughout most of adulthood; others, such as the ability to solve unfamiliar problems, may diminish; but some new attributes, such as wisdom, may increase with age.
4. *Relative influences of biology and culture shift over the life span.* The process of development is influenced by both biology and culture, but the balance between these influences changes. Biological abilities, such as sensory acuity and muscular strength and coordination, weaken with age, but cultural supports, such as education, relationships, and technologically age-friendly environments, may help compensate.
5. *Development involves changing resource allocations.* Individuals choose to invest their resources of time, energy, talent, money, and social support in varying ways. Resources may be used for growth (for example, learning to play an instrument or improving one's skill), for maintenance or recovery (practicing to maintain or regain proficiency), or for dealing with loss when maintenance and recovery are not possible. The allocation of resources to these three functions changes throughout life as the total available pool of resources decreases. In childhood and young adulthood, the bulk of resources typically goes to growth; in old age, to regulation of loss. In midlife, the allocation is more evenly balanced among the three functions.
6. *Development shows plasticity.* Many abilities, such as memory, strength, and endurance, can be improved significantly with training and practice, even late in life. However, even in children, plasticity has limits that depend in part on the various influences on development. One of the tasks of developmental research is to discover to what extent particular kinds of development can be modified at various ages.
7. *Development is influenced by the historical and cultural context.* Each person develops within multiple contexts—circumstances or conditions defined in part by maturation and in part by time and place. Human beings not only influence but also are influenced by their historical-cultural context. As we discuss throughout this book, developmental scientists have found significant cohort differences, for example, in intellectual functioning, in women's midlife emotional development, and in the flexibility of personality in old age.

▷ Summarize the seven principles of the life-span developmental approach?

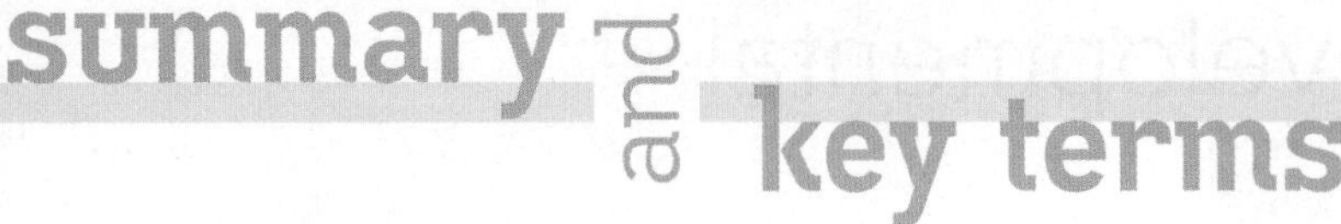

Human Development: An Ever-Evolving Field

- Human development is the scientific study of processes of change and stability.
- Developmental research has important applications in various fields.
- As researchers have become interested in following development through adulthood, life-span development has become a field of study.
- The study of human development seeks to describe, explain, predict, and, when appropriate, intervene in development.
- Students of human development draw on such disciplines as psychology, psychiatry, sociology, anthropology, biology, genetics, family science, education, history, philosophy, and medicine.
- Methods of studying human development are still evolving, making use of advanced technologies.

human development
life-span development

The Study of Human Development: Basic Concepts

- Developmental scientists study change and stability in all domains of development throughout the life span.
- The three major domains of development are physical, cognitive, and psychosocial. Each affects the others.
- The concept of periods of development is a social construction. In this book, the life span is divided into eight periods: prenatal, infancy and toddlerhood, early childhood, middle childhood, adolescence, emerging and young adulthood, middle adulthood, and late adulthood. In each period, people have characteristic developmental needs and tasks.

physical development
cognitive development
psychosocial development
social construction

Influences on Development

- Influences on development come from both heredity and environment. Many typical changes during childhood are related to maturation. Individual differences tend to increase with age.
- In some societies, the nuclear family predominates; in others, the extended family.
- Socioeconomic status (SES) affects developmental processes and outcomes through the quality of home and neighborhood environments, nutrition, medical care, and schooling. Multiple risk factors increase the likelihood of poor outcomes.
- Important environmental influences stem from culture, race/ethnicity, and historical context. Race is viewed by most scholars as a social construction.
- Influences may be normative (age-graded or history-graded) or nonnormative.
- There is evidence of critical or sensitive periods for certain kinds of early development.

individual differences
heredity
environment
maturation
nuclear family
extended family
socioeconomic status (SES)
risk factors
culture
ethnic group
ethnic gloss
normative
historical generation
cohort
nonnormative
imprinting
critical period
plasticity
sensitive periods

The Life-Span Developmental Approach

- The principles of the life-span developmental approach include the propositions that (1) development is lifelong, (2) development is multidimensional, (3) development is multidirectional, (4) the relative influences of biology and culture shift over the life span, (5) development involves changing resource allocations, (6) development shows plasticity, and (7) development is influenced by the historical and cultural context.

chapter 2 Theory and Research

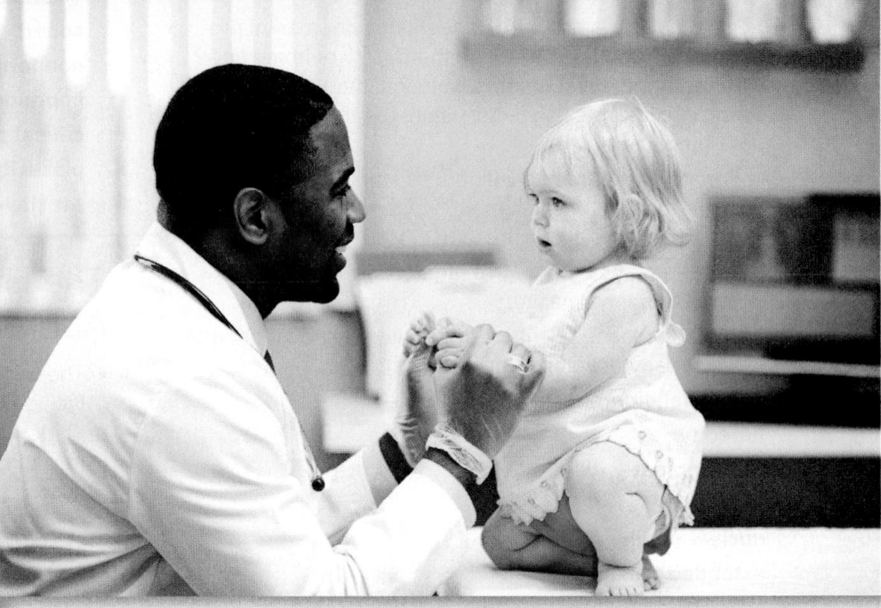

outline

learning objectives

Describe the purpose of a theory in research and two theoretical issues on which developmental scientists differ.

Summarize the main theories of human development.

Describe the methods developmental researchers use to collect data and the advantages and disadvantages of each.

Explain ethical guidelines for researchers who study people.

did you know?

- Theories are never "set in stone"; they are always open to change as a result of new findings?
- Cross-cultural research enables us to learn which aspects of development are universal and which are culturally influenced?
- The results of laboratory experiments may be less applicable than experiments carried out in a home, school, or public setting?

In this chapter we present an overview both of major theories of human development and of research methods used to study it. We explore important issues and theoretical perspectives that underlie much research in human development, and we look at how researchers gather and assess information. Ethical issues that may arise in research on humans are also addressed.

The most exciting phrase to hear in science, the one that heralds new discoveries, is not "Eureka" but "That's funny. . . ."

—Isaac Asimov

Basic Theoretical Issues

A scientific **theory** of development is a set of logically related concepts or statements that seek to describe and explain development and to predict the kinds of behavior that might occur under certain conditions. Theories organize and explain *data,* the information gathered by research. As painstaking research adds, bit by bit, to the body of knowledge, theoretical concepts help us make sense of, and see connections between, isolated pieces of data.

theory
Coherent set of logically related concepts that seeks to organize, explain, and predict data.

hypotheses
Possible explanations for phenomena, used to predict the outcome of research.

Theory and research are interwoven strands in the seamless fabric of scientific study. Theories inspire further research and predict its results. They do this by generating **hypotheses,** explanations or predictions that can be tested by further research. Research can indicate whether a theory is accurate in its predictions but cannot conclusively show a theory to be true. Theories can be disproved but never proved, and they change to incorporate new findings. Sometimes research supports a hypothesis and the theory on which it was based. At other times, scientists must modify their theories to account for unexpected data. Research findings often suggest additional hypotheses to be examined and provide direction for dealing with practical issues.

People generally think theories are less well supported than laws, but in scientific terms the opposite is true. Laws are observations without explanations. Theories, by contrast, are observations and explanations. So theories have more support, not less.

Developmental science cannot be completely objective. Theories and research about human behavior are products of human individuals, whose inquiries and interpretations are inevitably influenced by their own values and experience. In striving for objectivity, researchers must scrutinize how they and their colleagues conduct their work, the assumptions on which it is based, and how they arrive at their conclusions. For example, early developmentalists assumed that human psychology was the same in every culture. However, as the science of psychology progressed, it became clear that cultural differences existed and mattered. Theories of development had to be changed to accommodate these findings.

Throughout this book, we examine many, often conflicting theories. In assessing them, it is important to keep in mind that they reflect the outlooks of the human beings who originated them. The way theorists explain development depends in part on their assumptions about two basic issues: (1) whether people are active or reactive in their own development, and (2) whether development is continuous or occurs in stages. A third issue is whether development is more influenced by heredity or by environment.

checkpoint
can you . . .

- **Explain the relationships among theories, hypotheses, and research?**

ISSUE 1: IS DEVELOPMENT ACTIVE OR REACTIVE?

Psychology is an outgrowth of philosophy in many ways, and philosophers have frequently grappled with questions of psychology and development. Exactly how does the child learn? What happens during that process?

There have been a variety of perspectives. For example, the eighteenth-century English philosopher John Locke held that a young child is a *tabula rasa*—a "blank slate"—upon which society writes. How the child developed, in either positive or negative ways, depended entirely on experiences. In contrast, the French philosopher Jean Jacques Rousseau believed that children are born "noble savages" who develop

Remember Calvin and Hobbes *comic strips? The names of the two primary characters were drawn from other philosophers who speculated on our essential nature.*

These issues are also applicable in the real world. For instance, if you believe in the worth of programs like Head Start, that implies you believe in the power of environmental influences. If you think such programs are not worth the financial investment, that implies you feel heredity is more important. Which do you believe?

according to their own positive natural tendencies if not corrupted by society. This debate remains important today, although in modern terms we speak of heredity and environmental influences.

Additional philosophical debates about development, and the same basic issues philosophers argued about, are reflected in the psychological theories of today. In this section we address the debate about active and reactive development. Psychologists who believe in reactive development conceptualize the developing child as a hungry sponge that soaks up experiences and is shaped by this input over time. Psychologists who believe in active development argue that people create experiences for themselves and are motivated to learn about the world around them. Things aren't just happening to them, they are involved in making their world what it is.

mechanistic model
Model that views human development as a series of predictable responses to stimuli.

Mechanistic and Organismic Models of Development

Mechanistic Model The debate over Locke's and Rousseau's philosophies led to two contrasting models, or images, of development: *mechanistic* and *organismic*. Locke's view was the forerunner of the **mechanistic model.** In this model, people are like machines that react to environmental input (Pepper, 1942, 1961).

Machines do not operate of their own will; they react automatically to physical forces or inputs. Fill a car with gas, turn the ignition key, press the accelerator, and the car will move. In the mechanistic view, human behavior is much the same: it results from the operation of biological parts in response to external or internal stimuli. If we know enough about how the human "machine" is put together and about the forces acting on it, we can predict what the person will do.

Mechanistic researchers want to identify the factors that make people behave as they do. For example, to explain why some college students drink too much alcohol, a mechanistic theorist might look for environmental influences, such as advertising and whether the student's friends are heavy drinkers.

organismic model
Model that views human development as internally initiated by an active organism and as occurring in a sequence of qualitatively different stages.

Organismic Model Rousseau was the precursor of the **organismic model.** This model sees people as active, growing organisms that set their own development in motion (Pepper, 1942, 1961). They initiate events; they do not just react. Thus the driving force for change is internal. Environmental influences do not *cause* development, though they can speed or slow it.

Because human behavior is viewed as an organic whole, it cannot be predicted by breaking it down into simple responses to environmental stimulation. An organismic theorist, in studying why some students drink too much, look at what kinds of situations they choose to participate in, and with whom. Do they choose friends who prefer to party or to study?

For organicists, development has an underlying, orderly structure, though it may not be obvious from moment to moment. As a fertilized egg cell develops into an embryo and then into a fetus, it goes through a series of changes not overtly predictable from what came before. Swellings on the head become eyes, ears, mouth, and nose. The brain begins to coordinate breathing, digestion, and elimination. Sex organs form. Similarly, organicists describe development after birth as a progressive sequence of stages, moving toward full maturation.

Quantitative change is like counting apples; there are fewer or more apples, but they are all apples. Qualitative change is like comparing apples and oranges.

ISSUE 2: IS DEVELOPMENT CONTINUOUS OR DISCONTINUOUS?

The mechanistic and organismic models also differ on the second issue: is development *continuous,* that is, gradual and incremental, or *discontinuous,* that is, abrupt or uneven? Mechanist theorists see development as continuous: as occurring in small incremental stages (Figure 1a). Development is always governed by the same processes and involves the gradual refinement and extension of early skills into later abilities, allowing one to make predictions about future characteristics on the basis of past performance. This type of change is known as **quantitative change**—a change in number or amount, such as height, weight, or vocabulary size. A primary characteristic of quantitative change is

quantitative change
Changes in number or amount, such as in height, weight, size of vocabulary, or frequency of communication.

(a)

(b)

FIGURE 1
Quantitative and Qualitative Change

A major difference among developmental theories is (a) whether it proceeds continuously, as learning theorists and information-processing theorists propose, or (b) whether development occurs in distinct stages, as Freud, Erikson, and Piaget maintained.

that you are measuring fundamentally the same thing over time, even if there might be more or less of it.

Organismic theorists see development as discontinuous; as marked by the emergence of new phenomena that could not be easily predicted on the basis of past functioning. Development at different points in the life span is, in this view, fundamentally different in nature. It is a change in kind, structure, or organization, not just in number. This type of change is known as **qualitative change.**

qualitative change
Discontinuous changes in kind, structure, or organization.

Be careful here. If you Google "quantitative" and "qualitative," you are likely to find Web pages that focus on qualitative and quantitative statistics, not change. Although these are related concepts, they are not quite the same thing.

Organismic theorists are proponents of *stage theories* in which development is seen as occurring in a series of distinct stages, like stair steps (Figure 1b). At each stage, what is going on is fundamentally different from previous stages. Moreover, stages build upon each other. Stages cannot be skipped, and development only proceeds in a positive direction. It is believed that these processes are universal and account for the development of all humans everywhere, although the particular timing may vary a bit.

studysmart

Quantitative and Qualitative Changes

checkpoint
can **you** . . .

- Discuss two issues regarding human development?
- Contrast the mechanistic and organismic models?
- Compare quantitative and qualitative change?

Theoretical Perspectives

Theories can generally be characterized as either mechanistic or organismic, and as describing change as either continuous or discontinuous, even if those beliefs are not directly stated. But all developmental theories have implicit assumptions that underlie their approach. These assumptions influence the questions researchers ask, the methods they use, and the ways they interpret data. To evaluate and interpret research, it is important to recognize the theoretical perspective on which it is based.

Five major perspectives underlie much influential theory and research on human development: (1) psychoanalytic, which focuses on unconscious emotions and drives; (2) learning, which studies observable behavior; (3) cognitive, which analyzes thought processes; (4) contextual, which emphasizes the impact of the historical, social, and cultural context; and (5) evolutionary/sociobiological, which considers evolutionary and biological underpinnings of behavior. Following is a general overview of the basic propositions, methods, and causal emphasis of each of these perspectives and some leading theorists within each perspective. These are summarized in Table 1.

studysmart

Theoretical Perspectives

studysmart

Application of Theories

PERSPECTIVE 1: PSYCHOANALYTIC

Sigmund Freud (1856–1939) was a Viennese physician who had a profound effect on the field of psychology. He was the originator of the **psychoanalytic perspective** and

psychoanalytic perspective
View of human development as shaped by unconscious forces that motivate human behavior.

TABLE 1 Five Perspectives on Human Development

Perspective	Important Theories	Basic Propositions	Stage-Oriented	Causal Emphasis	Active/ Reactive Individual
Psycho-analytic	Freud's psychosexual theory	Behavior is controlled by powerful unconscious urges.	Yes	Innate factors modified by experience	Reactive
	Erikson's psychosocial theory	Personality is influenced by society and develops through a series of crises.		Interaction of innate and experiential factors	Active
Learning	Behaviorism, or traditional learning theory (Pavlov, Skinner, Watson)	People are responders; the environment controls behavior.	No	Experience	Reactive
	Social learning (social cognitive) theory (Bandura)	Children learn in a social context by observing and imitating models; they are active contributors to learning.		Experience modified by innate factors	Active and reactive
Cognitive	Piaget's cognitive-stage theory	Qualitative changes in thought occur between infancy and adolescence. Children are active initiators of development.	Yes	Interaction of innate and experiential factors	Active
	Vygotsky's sociocultural theory	Social interaction is central to cognitive development.	No	Experience	
	Information-processing theory	Human beings are processors of symbols.	No	Interaction of innate and experiential factors	
Contextual	Bronfenbrenner's biecological theory	Development occurs through interaction between a developing person and five surrounding, interlocking contextual systems of influences, from microsystem to chronosystem.	No	Interaction of innate and experiential factors	Active
Evolutionary/ sociobiological	Evolutionary psychology; Bowlby's attachment theory	Human beings are the product of adaptive processes; evolutionary and biological bases for behavior and predisposition toward learning are important.	No	Interaction of innate and experiential factors	Active and reactive (theorists vary)

believed in reactive development, as well as qualitative changes over time. Freud proposed that humans were born with a series of innate, biologically based drives such as hunger, sex, and aggression. He thought people were motivated to satisfy their urges, and that much of development involved learning how to do so in socially acceptable ways. In addition, Freud believed that early experiences shaped later functioning, and he drew attention to childhood as an important precursor to adult behavior. Freud also promoted the idea that there was a vast, hidden reserve to our psyche, and what we consciously know about and experience is only the small tip of the iceberg of who we are. Following is a summary of Freud's theory of psychosexual development. Other theorists, including Erik H. Erikson, whom we discuss next, have expanded and modified Freud's theory.

Although this is not originally what it stood for, an easy way to remember what the id wants is by remembering "instinctual desires."

Sigmund Freud: Psychosexual Development Freud (1953, 1964a, 1964b) believed that people are born with biological drives that must be redirected to make it possible to live in society. He proposed three hypothetical parts of the personality: the *id,* the *ego,* and the *superego.* Newborns are governed by the *id,* which operates under the *pleasure principle*—the drive to seek immediate satisfaction of their needs and desires. When gratification is delayed, as it is when infants have to wait to be fed, they begin to see themselves as separate from the outside world. The *ego,* which represents reason, develops gradually during the first year or so of life and operates under the *reality principle.* The ego's aim is to find realistic ways to gratify the id that are acceptable to the *superego,* which develops at about age 5 or 6. The *superego* includes the conscience and incorporates socially approved "shoulds" and "should nots" into the child's value system. The superego is highly demanding; if its standards are not met, a child may feel guilty and anxious. The ego mediates between the impulses of the id and the demands of the superego.

studysmart

Psychoanalytic Perspective

Freud proposed that personality forms through unconscious childhood conflicts between the inborn urges of the id and the requirements of civilized life. These conflicts occur in a sequence of five stages of **psychosexual development** (Table 2), in which sensual pleasure shifts from one body zone to another—from the mouth to the anus and then to the genitals. At each stage, the behavior that is the chief source of gratification (or frustration) changes—from feeding to elimination and eventually to sexual activity.

psychosexual development
In Freudian theory, an unvarying sequence of stages of childhood personality development in which gratification shifts from the mouth to the anus and then to the genitals.

Freud considered the first three stages to be crucial for personality development. According to Freud, if children receive too little or too much gratification in any of these stages, they are at risk of *fixation,* an arrest in development that can show up in adult personality. Babies whose needs are not met during the *oral stage,* when feeding is the main source of pleasure, may grow up to become nail-biters or smokers. A person who, as a toddler, had too-strict toilet training may be fixated at the *anal stage,* and be obsessively clean, rigidly tied to schedules and routines, or defiantly messy.

According to Freud, a key event in psychosexual development occurs in the *phallic stage* of early childhood. Boys develop sexual attachment to their mothers, and girls to their fathers, and they have aggressive urges toward the same-sex parent, whom they regard as a rival. Freud called these developments the *Oedipus* and *Electra complexes.*

Children eventually resolve their anxiety over these feelings by identifying with the same-sex parent and move into the *latency stage* of middle childhood, a period of relative emotional calm and intellectual and social exploration. They redirect their sexual energies into other pursuits, such as schoolwork, relationships, and hobbies.

The *genital stage,* the final stage, lasts throughout adulthood. The sexual urges repressed during latency now resurface to flow in socially approved channels, which Freud defined as heterosexual relations with persons outside the family of origin.

Sigmund Freud developed an original theory of psychosexual development. His daughter, Anna, shown here, followed in his footsteps and constructed her own theories of personality development.

Freud's theory made historic contributions and inspired a whole generation of followers, some of whom took psychoanalytic theory in new directions. Many of Freud's ideas now are widely considered obsolete or are impossible to investigate scientifically. Psychoanalysts today reject his narrow emphasis on sexual and aggressive drives to the exclusion of other motives. Nevertheless, several of his central themes have "stood the test of time" (Westen, 1998, p. 334). Freud made us aware of the importance of unconscious thoughts, feelings, and motivations; the role of childhood experiences in forming personality; the ambivalence of emotional responses, the role of mental representations of the self and others in the establishment of intimate relationships; and the

TABLE 2 Developmental Stages According to Various Theories

Psychosexual Stages (Freud)	Psychosocial Stages (Erikson)	Cognitive Stages (Piaget)
Oral (birth to 12–18 months). Baby's chief source of pleasure involves mouth-oriented activities (sucking and feeding).	*Basic trust versus mistrust (birth to 12–18 months).* Baby develops sense of whether world is a good and safe place. Virtue: hope.	*Sensorimotor (birth to 2 years).* Infant gradually becomes able to organize activities in relation to the environment through sensory and motor activity.
Anal (12–18 months to 3 years). Child derives sensual gratification from withholding and expelling feces. Zone of gratification is anal region, and toilet training is important activity.	*Autonomy versus shame and doubt (12–18 months to 3 years).* Child develops a balance of independence and self-sufficiency over shame and doubt. Virtue: will.	*Preoperational (2 to 7 years).* Child develops a representational system and uses symbols to represent people, places, and events. Language and imaginative play are important manifestations of this stage. Thinking is still not logical.
Phallic (3 to 6 years). Child becomes attached to parent of the other sex and later identifies with same-sex parent. Superego develops. Zone of gratification shifts to genital region.	*Initiative versus guilt (3 to 6 years).* Child develops initiative when trying out new activities and is not overwhelmed by guilt. Virtue: purpose.	
Latency (6 years to puberty). Time of relative calm between more turbulent stages.	*Industry versus inferiority (6 years to puberty).* Child must learn skills of the culture or face feelings of incompetence. Virtue: skill.	*Concrete operations (7 to 11 years).* Child can solve problems logically if they are focused on the here and now but cannot think abstractly.
Genital (puberty through adulthood). Reemergence of sexual impulses of phallic stage, channeled into mature adult sexuality.	*Identity versus identity confusion (puberty to young adulthood).* Adolescent must determine own sense of self ("Who am I?") or experience confusion about roles. Virtue: fidelity. *Intimacy versus isolation (young adulthood).* Person seeks to make commitments to others; if unsuccessful, may suffer from isolation and self-absorption. Virtue: love. *Generativity versus stagnation (middle adulthood).* Mature adult is concerned with establishing and guiding the next generation or else feels personal impoverishment. Virtue: care. *Integrity versus despair (late adulthood).* Older adult achieves acceptance of own life, allowing acceptance of death, or else despairs over inability to relive life. Virtue: wisdom.	*Formal operations (11 years through adulthood).* Person can think abstractly, deal with hypothetical situations, and think about possibilities.

Note: All ages are approximate.

checkpoint can you . . .

- Identify the chief focus of the psychoanalytic perspective?
- Name Freud's five stages of development and three parts of the personality?

path of normal development from an immature, dependent state to a mature, interdependent state. In all these ways, Freud left an indelible mark on psychoanalysis and developmental psychology (Gedo, 2001; Westen, 1998).

We need to remember that Freud based his theories about normal development not on a population of average children, but on a clientele of Victorian upper-middle-class adults, mostly women, in therapy. His concentration on the influences of sexual urges and early experience did not take into account other, and later, influences on personality—including the influences of society and culture, which many heirs to the Freudian tradition, such as Erik Erikson, stress.

Erik Erikson: Psychosocial Development Erik Erikson (1902–1994) modified and extended Freudian theory by emphasizing the influence of society on the developing personality. Erikson also was a pioneer in taking a life-span perspective. Note that both theorists, as they proposed stage theories, believed in qualitative change.

Erikson's (1950, 1982; Erikson, Erikson, & Kivnick, 1986) theory of **psychosocial development** covers eight stages across the life span (refer to Table 2), which we discuss in the appropriate chapters throughout this book. Each stage involves what Erikson originally called a *crisis* in personality*—a major psychosocial challenge that is particularly important at that time and will remain an issue to some degree throughout the rest of life. These issues must be satisfactorily resolved for healthy ego development.

Each stage requires balancing a positive and a negative tendency. The positive quality should dominate, but some degree of the negative quality is needed as well for optimal development. The critical theme of infancy, for example, is *basic trust versus basic mistrust.* People need to trust the world and the people in it. However, they also need some mistrust to protect themselves from danger. The successful outcome of each stage is the development of a particular *virtue,* or strength—in this case, the virtue of *hope.*

Successful resolution of each crisis puts the person in a particularly good position to address the next crisis, a process that occurs iteratively across the life span. So, for example, a child who successfully develops a sense of trust in infancy would be well prepared for the development of a sense of autonomy—the second psychosocial challenge—in toddlerhood. After all, if you feel that others have your back, you are more likely to try to develop your skills knowing that they will be there to comfort you if you fail.

Erikson's theory is important because of its emphasis on social and cultural influences and on development beyond adolescence.

psychosocial development
In Erikson's eight-stage theory, the socially and culturally influenced process of development of the ego, or self.

The psychoanalyst Erik H. Erikson emphasized societal influences on personality.

checkpoint can **you . . .**

- Tell two ways that Erikson's theory differs from Freud's?

PERSPECTIVE 2: LEARNING

The **learning perspective** maintains that development results from *learning,* a long-lasting change in behavior based on experience or adaptation to the environment. Learning theorists seek to discover objective laws that govern changes in observable behavior and see development as continuous.

Learning theorists have helped to make the study of human development more scientific. Their terms are defined precisely, and their focus on observable behaviors means that theories can be tested in the laboratory. Two important learning theories are *behaviorism* and *social learning theory.*

learning perspective
View of human development that holds that changes in behavior result from experience or from adaptation to the environment.

Behaviorism **Behaviorism** is a mechanistic theory that describes observed behavior as a predictable response to experience. Behaviorists consider development as reactive and continuous. They hold that human beings at all ages learn about the world the same way other organisms do: by reacting to conditions or aspects of their environment that they find pleasing, painful, or threatening. Behavioral research focuses on *associative learning,* in which a mental link is formed between two events. Two kinds of associative learning are *classical conditioning* and *operant conditioning.*

behaviorism
Learning theory that emphasizes the predictable role of environment in causing observable behavior.

Classical Conditioning The Russian physiologist Ivan Pavlov (1849–1936) devised experiments in which dogs learned to salivate at the sound of a bell that rang at feeding time. These experiments were the foundation for **classical conditioning,** in which

classical conditioning
Learning based on associating a stimulus that does not ordinarily elicit a response with another stimulus that does elicit the response.

*Erikson broadened the concept of "crisis" and later referred instead to conflicting or competing tendencies.

Pavlov was originally studying salivary enzymes in dogs. He put a plate of meat in front of them so he could collect their saliva. He made his breakthrough discovery when he realized that the dogs were salivating before the meat was presented to them.

a response (in this case, salivation) to a stimulus (the bell) is evoked after repeated association with a stimulus that normally elicits the response (food).

The American behaviorist John B. Watson (1878–1958) applied such stimulus-response theories to children, claiming that he could mold any infant in any way he chose. In one of the earliest and most famous demonstrations of classical conditioning in human beings (Watson & Rayner, 1920), he taught an 11-month-old baby known as "Little Albert" to fear furry white objects.

In this study, Albert was exposed to a loud noise when he started to stroke the rat. The noise frightened him, and he began to cry. After repeated pairings of the rat with the loud noise, Albert whimpered with fear when he saw the rat. Albert also started showing fear responses to white rabbits and cats, and the beards of elderly men. The study, although unethical, demonstrated that fear could be conditioned.

McDonalds' habit of putting playgrounds in some of their restaurants is in part an attempt to condition children into forming positive associations with McDonalds.

Classical conditioning occurs throughout life. Food likes and dislikes may be a result of conditioned learning. Fear responses to objects like a car or a dog may be the result of an accident or a bad experience.

Operant Conditioning Angel lies in his crib. When he starts to babble ("ma-ma-ma"), his mother smiles and repeats the syllables. Angel learns that his behavior (babbling) can produce a desirable consequence (loving attention from a parent); and so he keeps babbling to attract his mother's attention. An originally accidental behavior (babbling) has become a conditioned response.

operant conditioning
Learning based on association of behavior with its consequences.

reinforcement
The process by which a behavior is strengthened, increasing the likelihood that the behavior will be repeated.

punishment
The process by which a behavior is weakened, decreasing the likelihood of repetition.

This type of learning is called **operant conditioning** because the individual learns from the consequences of "operating" on the environment. Unlike classical conditioning, operant conditioning involves voluntary behavior, such as Angel's babbling and involves the consequences rather than the predictors of behavior.

You can think of classical conditioning as the before—what happens to provoke a response. And operant conditioning as the after—what happens after a response occurs that shapes the likelihood of it happening again.

The American psychologist B. F. Skinner (1904–1990), who formulated the principles of operant conditioning, argued that an organism—animal or human—will tend to repeat a response that has been reinforced by desirable consequences and will suppress a response that has been punished. Thus **reinforcement** is the process by which a behavior is strengthened, *increasing* the likelihood that the behavior will be repeated. In Angel's case, his mother's attention reinforces his babbling. **Punishment** is the process by which a behavior is weakened, *decreasing* the likelihood of repetition. If Angel's mother frowned when he babbled, he would be less likely to babble again.

Classical and Operant Conditioning

Operant Conditioning

Reinforcement is most effective when it immediately follows a behavior. If a response is no longer reinforced, it will eventually be *extinguished,* that is, return to its original (baseline) level. If, after a while, no one repeats Angel's babbling, he may babble less often than if his babbles still brought reinforcement.

Behavior modification therapy is a form of operant conditioning used to eliminate undesirable behavior, such as temper tantrums, or to instill desirable behavior, such as putting away toys after play. For example, every time a child puts toys away, she or he gets a reward, such as praise or a treat or new toy. Behavior modification is particularly effective among children with special needs, such as those with mental or emotional disabilities. However, Skinnerian psychology is limited in application because it does not adequately address individual differences, cultural and social influences, or biologically influenced behavioral patterns.

social learning theory
Theory that behaviors are learned by observing and imitating models. Also called *social cognitive theory.*

Social Learning (Social Cognitive) Theory The American psychologist Albert Bandura (b. 1925) developed many of the principles of **social learning theory.** Whereas behaviorists see the environment as the chief impetus for development, Bandura (1977, 1989; Bandura & Walters, 1963) suggests that the impetus for development is bidirectional. Bandura called this concept **reciprocal determinism**—the person acts on the world as the world acts on the person.

Classic social learning theory maintains that people learn appropriate social behavior chiefly by observing and imitating models—that is, by watching other people. This process is called **observational learning,** or *modeling.* People tend to choose models who are prestigious, who control resources, or who are rewarded for what they do—in other words, those whose behavior is perceived as valued in their culture. Note that this is an active process. Imitation of models is a key element in how children learn a language, deal with aggression, develop a moral sense, and learn gender-appropriate behaviors. Observational learning can occur even if a person does not imitate the observed behavior.

Bandura's (1989) updated version of social learning theory is *social cognitive theory.* The change of name reflects a greater emphasis on cognitive processes as central to development. Cognitive processes are at work as people observe models, learn *chunks* of behavior, and mentally put the chunks together into complex new behavior patterns. Rita, for example, imitates the toes-out walk of her dance teacher but models her dance steps after those of Carmen, a slightly more advanced student. Even so, she develops her own style of dancing by putting her observations together into a new pattern.

Through feedback on their behavior, children gradually form standards for judging their actions and become more selective in choosing models who demonstrate those standards. They also begin to develop a sense of **self-efficacy,** the confidence that they have what it takes to succeed.

According to Skinner's principles, a punishment, such as this child's time-out, reduces the likelihood that a behavior will be repeated.

PERSPECTIVE 3: COGNITIVE

The **cognitive perspective** focuses on thought processes and the behavior that reflects those processes. This perspective encompasses both organismic and mechanistically influenced theories. It includes the cognitive-stage theory of Piaget and Vygotsky's sociocultural theory of cognitive development. It also includes the information-processing approach and neo-Piagetian theories, which combine elements of information-processing theory and Piagetian theory.

Jean Piaget's Cognitive-Stage Theory Our understanding of how children think owes a great deal to the work of the Swiss theoretician Jean Piaget (1896–1980). Piaget's **cognitive-stage theory** was the forerunner of today's "cognitive revolution" with its emphasis on mental processes. Piaget viewed development organismically, as the product of children's efforts to understand and act on their world. He also believed that development was discontinuous, so his theory describes development as occurring in stages.

Piaget's *clinical method* combined observation with flexible questioning. By asking children questions, he realized that children of the same ages made similar types of errors in logic. So, for example, he discovered that a typical 4-year-old believed that pennies or flowers were more numerous when arranged in a line than when heaped or piled up. From his observations of his own and other children, Piaget created a comprehensive theory of cognitive development.

Piaget suggested that cognitive development begins with an inborn ability to adapt to the environment. By rooting for a nipple, feeling a pebble, or exploring the boundaries

checkpoint
can **you** . . .

- Identify the chief concerns of the learning perspective?
- Tell how classical conditioning and operant conditioning differ?
- Contrast reinforcement and punishment?
- Compare behaviorism and social learning theory?

reciprocal determinism
Bandura's term for bidirectional forces that affect development.

observational learning
Learning through watching the behavior of others.

self-efficacy
Sense of one's capability to master challenges and achieve goals.

cognitive perspective
View that thought processes are central to development.

cognitive-stage theory
Piaget's theory that children's cognitive development advances in a series of four stages involving qualitatively distinct types of mental operations.

organization
Piaget's term for the creation of categories or systems of knowledge.

schemes
Piaget's term for organized patterns of thought and behavior used in particular situations.

adaptation
Piaget's term for adjustment to new information about the environment, achieved through processes of assimilation and accommodation.

assimilation
Piaget's term for incorporation of new information into an existing cognitive structure.

accommodation
Piaget's term for changes in a cognitive structure to include new information.

equilibration
Piaget's term for the tendency to seek a stable balance among cognitive elements; achieved through a balance between assimilation and accommodation.

Jean Piaget studied children's cognitive development by observing and talking with them in many settings, asking questions to find out how their minds worked.

of a room, young children develop a more accurate picture of their surroundings and greater competence in dealing with them. This cognitive growth occurs through three interrelated processes: *organization, adaptation,* and *equilibration.*

Organization is the tendency to create categories, such as birds, by observing the characteristics that individual members of a category, such as sparrows and cardinals, have in common. According to Piaget, people create increasingly complex cognitive structures called **schemes,** ways of organizing information about the world that govern the way the child thinks and behaves in a particular situation. As children acquire more information, their schemes become more and more complex. Take sucking, for example. A newborn infant has a simple scheme for sucking but soon develops varied schemes for how to suck at the breast, a bottle, or a thumb. The infant may have to open her mouth wider, or turn her head to the side, or suck with varying strength. Schemes are originally concrete in nature (e.g., how to suck on objects) and become increasingly abstract over time (e.g., what a dog is).

Adaptation is Piaget's term for how children handle new information in light of what they already know. Adaptation occurs through two complementary processes: (1) **assimilation,** taking in new information and incorporating it into existing cognitive structures, and (2) **accommodation,** adjusting one's cognitive structures to fit the new information.

Organization/Schemes/Piaget

How does the shift from assimilation to accommodation occur? Piaget argued that children strive for **equilibration** between their cognitive structures and new experiences. In other words, children want what they understand of the world to match what they observe around them. When children's understanding of the world does not match what they are experiencing, they find themselves in a state of disequilibrium. Disequilibrium can be thought of as an uncomfortable motivational state, and it pushes children into accommodation. For example, a child knows what birds are and sees a plane for the first time. The child labels the plane a "bird" (assimilation). Over time the child notes differences between planes and birds, which makes her somewhat uneasy (disequilibrium) and motivates her to change her understanding (accommodation) and provide a new label for the plane. She then is at equilibrium. Thus assimilation and accommodation work together to produce equilibrium. Throughout life, the quest for equilibrium is the driving force behind cognitive growth.

Assimilation and Accommodation

Piaget described cognitive development as occurring in four universal, qualitatively different stages (listed in Table 2). From infancy through adolescence, mental operations evolve from learning based on simple sensory and motor activity to logical, abstract thought.

checkpoint can **you . . .**

- **List three interrelated principles that bring about cognitive growth, according to Piaget, and give an example of each?**

Piaget's observations have yielded much information and some surprising insights. Piaget has shown us that children's minds are not miniature adult minds. Knowing how children think makes it easier for parents and teachers to understand and teach them. Piaget's theory has provided rough benchmarks for what to expect of children at various ages and has helped educators design curricula appropriate to varying levels of development.

Piaget wrote his first scientific paper at the age of 10, on the sighting of an albino sparrow.

Yet Piaget seems to have seriously underestimated the abilities of infants and children. Some contemporary psychologists question his distinct stages, pointing instead to evidence that cognitive development is more gradual and continuous (Courage & Howe, 2002). Further, cross-cultural research indicates that performance on formal reasoning tasks is as much a function of culture as it is of development; people from industrialized societies who have participated in a formal educational system show better performance on those tasks (Buck-Morss, 1975). Last, research on adults suggests that Piaget's focus on formal logic as the climax of cognitive development is too narrow. It does not account for the emergence of such mature abilities as practical problem solving, wisdom, and the capacity to deal with ambiguous situations.

According to Lev Vygotsky, children learn through social interaction.

Lev Vygotsky's Sociocultural Theory The Russian psychologist Lev Semenovich Vygotsky (1896–1934) focused on the social and cultural processes that guide children's cognitive development. Vygotsky's (1978) **sociocultural theory,** like Piaget's theory, stresses children's active engagement with their environment; but, whereas Piaget described the solo mind taking in and interpreting information about the world, Vygotsky saw cognitive growth as a *collaborative* process. People, said Vygotsky, learn through social interaction. They acquire cognitive skills as part of their induction into a way of life. Shared activities help children internalize their society's modes of thinking and behaving. Vygotsky placed special emphasis on *language,* not merely as an expression of knowledge and thought but as an essential tool for learning and thinking about the world.

According to Vygotsky, adults or more advanced peers must help direct and organize a child's learning before the child can master and internalize it. This guidance is most effective in helping children cross the **zone of proximal development (ZPD),** the gap between what they are already able to do by themselves and what they can accomplish with assistance. Sensitive and effective instruction, then, should be aimed at the ZPD and increase in complexity as the child's abilities improve. Responsibility for directing learning gradually shifts to the child, such as when an adult teaches a child to float: the adult first supports the child in the water and then lets go gradually as the child's body relaxes into a horizontal position.

sociocultural theory
Vygotsky's theory of how contextual factors affect children's development.

zone of proximal development (ZPD)
Vygotsky's term for the difference between what a child can do alone and what the child can do with help.

scaffolding
Temporary support to help a child master a task.

Some followers of Vygotsky (Wood, 1980; Wood, Bruner, & Ross, 1976) have applied the metaphor of *scaffolds*—the temporary platforms on which construction workers stand—to this way of teaching. **Scaffolding** is the temporary support that parents, teachers, or others give a child in doing a task until the child can do it alone.

Vygotsky believed that play often occurs in the ZPD, pushing children's abilities to their limit. For example, if you ask a child to pretend to be a statue, that child is likely to be able to remain motionless longer than if you ask the child just not to move. The child knows the "rules" of being a statue, and those rules provide scaffolding.

study smart

Scaffolding

Vygotsky's theory has important implications for education and for cognitive testing. Tests that focus on a child's potential for learning provide a valuable alternative to standard intelligence tests that assess what the child has already learned; and many children may benefit from the sort of expert guidance Vygotsky prescribes. Moreover, Vygotsky's ideas have successfully been implemented in preschool children's curricula and show great promise for promoting the development of self-regulation, which affects later academic achievement (Barnett et al., 2008).

The Information-Processing Approach The **information-processing approach** seeks to explain cognitive development by analyzing the processes involved in making sense of incoming information and performing tasks effectively: such processes as attention, memory, planning strategies, decision making, and goal setting. The information-processing approach is not a single theory but a framework that supports a wide range of theories and research.

information-processing approach
Approach to the study of cognitive development by observing and analyzing the mental processes involved in perceiving and handling information.

Some information-processing theorists compare the brain to a computer: there are certain inputs (such as sensory impressions) and certain outputs (such as behaviors). Information-processing theorists are interested in what happens in the middle. Why does the same input sometimes result in different outputs? In large part, information-processing researchers use observational data to *infer* what goes on between a stimulus and a response. For example, they may ask a person to recall a list of words and then observe any difference in performance if the person repeats the list over and over before being asked to recall the words or is kept from doing so. Through such studies, some information-processing researchers have developed *computational models* or flowcharts that analyze the specific steps people go through in gathering, storing, retrieving, and using information.

checkpoint
can **you** . . .

- Explain how Vygotsky's theory differs from Piaget's and how it applies to educational teaching and testing?
- Describe what information-processing researchers do, and tell three ways in which such research can be applied?

Like Piaget, information-processing theorists see people as active thinkers about their world. Unlike Piaget, they generally do *not* speak in terms of stages of development. Instead, they view development as continuous and incremental. They note age-related increases in the speed, complexity, and efficiency of mental processing and in the amount and variety of material that can be stored in memory.

The information-processing approach has practical applications. By assessing certain aspects of infant information processing, researchers are able to estimate an infant's later intelligence. It enables parents and teachers to help children learn by making them more aware of their mental processes and of strategies to enhance them. Psychologists often use information-processing models to test, diagnose, and treat learning problems.

PERSPECTIVE 4: CONTEXTUAL

contextual perspective
View of human development that sees the individual as inseparable from the social context.

bioecological theory
Bronfenbrenner's approach to understanding processes and contexts of human development that identifies five levels of environmental influence.

According to the **contextual perspective,** development can be understood only in its social context. Contextualists see the individual, not as a separate entity interacting with the environment, but as an inseparable part of it. (Vygotsky's sociocultural theory, which we discussed as part of the cognitive perspective, also can be classified as contextual.)

The American psychologist Urie Bronfenbrenner's (1917–2005) **bioecological theory** (1979, 1986, 1994; Bronfenbrenner & Morris, 1998) identifies five levels of environmental influence, ranging from very intimate to very broad: *microsystem, mesosystem, exosystem, macrosystem,* and *chronosystem* (Figure 2). To understand the complexity of influences on development, we must see a person within the context of these multiple environments.

A *microsystem* is the everyday environment of home, school, work, or neighborhood, including face-to-face relationships with spouse, children, parents, friends, classmates, teachers, employers, or colleagues. How does a new baby affect the parents' lives? How do male professors' attitudes affect a young woman's performance in college?

The *mesosystem* is the interlocking of various microsystems. It may include linkages between home and school (such as parent-teacher conferences) or between the family and the peer group (such as relationships that develop among families of children in a neighborhood play group). For example, a parent's bad day at work might affect interactions with a child later that evening in a negative way. Despite never having actually gone to the workplace, the child is still affected by it.

The mesosystem focuses on interactions between microsystems, but the *exosystem* consists of interactions between a microsystem and an outside system or institution. Though the effects are indirect, they can still have a profound impact on a child. For example, different countries have policies on what type, if any, of maternal or paternal leave accommodations are available for new parents. Whether or not a parent has the option to stay home with a newborn is a substantial influence on development. Thus governmental policies trickle down and can affect a child's day-to-day experiences.

The *macrosystem* consists of overarching cultural patterns, such as dominant beliefs, ideologies, and economic and political systems. How is an individual affected by living in a capitalist or socialist society?

Finally, the *chronosystem* adds the dimension of time: change or constancy in the person and the environment. Time marches on, and, as it does, changes occur. These

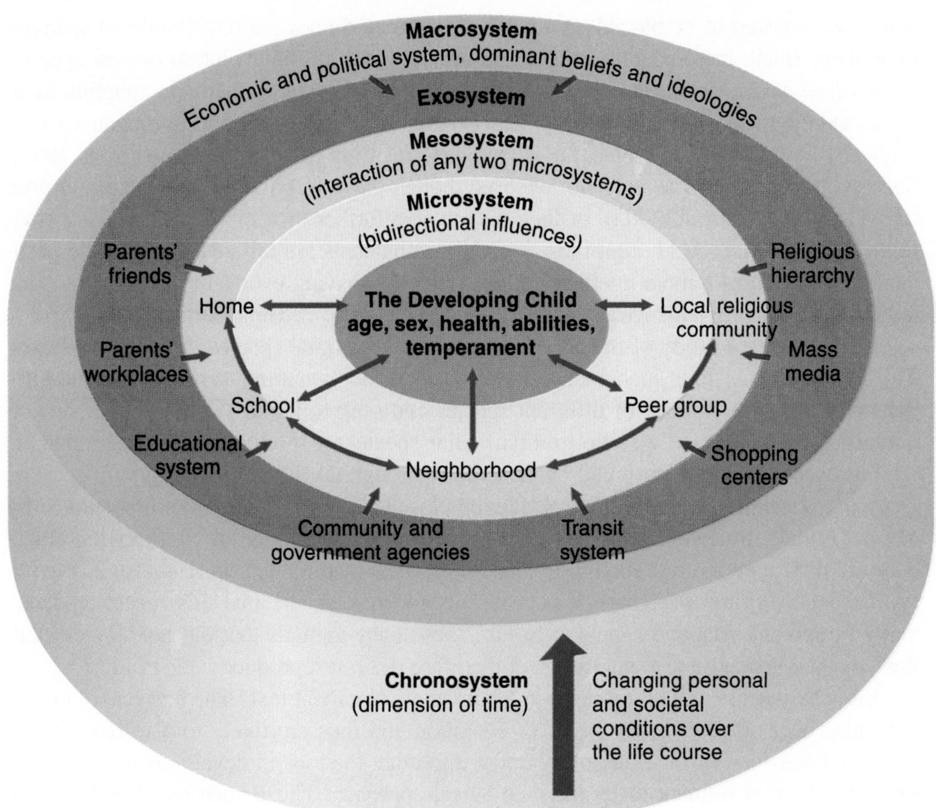

FIGURE 2

Bronfenbrenner's Bioecological Theory

Concentric circles show five levels of environmental influence on the individual, from the most intimate environment (the microsystem) to the broadest (the chronosystem)—all within the perpendicular dimension of time.

can include changes in family composition, place of residence, or parents' employment, as well as larger events such as wars, ideology, political system, and economic cycles.

According to Bronfenbrenner, a person is not merely an outcome of development but is also a shaper of it. People affect their development through their biological and psychological characteristics, talents and skills, disabilities, and temperament.

By looking at systems that affect individuals in and beyond the family, this bioecological approach helps us to see the variety of influences on development. The contextual perspective also reminds us that findings about the development of people in one culture or in one group within a culture (such as white, middle-class Americans) may not apply equally to people in other societies or cultural groups.

An economic cycle is the fluctuation between growth (expansion) and contraction (recession). Just as people, economies also seem to have a life cycle, although the time line of the changes is not easily predictable.

checkpoint can **you** . . .

- State the chief assumptions of the contextual perspective?
- Differentiate Bronfenbrenner's five levels of contextual influence?

PERSPECTIVE 5: EVOLUTIONARY/SOCIOBIOLOGICAL

The **evolutionary/sociobiological perspective** proposed by E. O. Wilson (1975) focuses on evolutionary and biological bases of behavior. Influenced by Darwin's theory of evolution, it draws on findings of anthropology, ecology, genetics, ethology, and evolutionary psychology to explain the adaptive, or survival, value of behavior for an individual or species.

evolutionary/sociobiological perspective
View of human development that focuses on evolutionary and biological bases of behavior.

According to Darwin, species have developed through the related processes of *survival of the fittest* and *natural selection*. Individuals with heritable traits *fitted* (better adapted) to their environments survive and reproduce more than those that are less fitted (less well adapted). Thus, through differential reproduction success, individuals with more adaptive characteristics pass on their traits to future generations at higher levels than individuals who are less adaptively fit. In this way, adaptive characteristics, ultimately coded in their

The peak of morning sickness is in the first trimester, which corresponds to the formation of nearly all the major body structures. So the mother is least likely to consume potentially damaging foods during the most sensitive time period.

Flaxman & Sherman, 2000

ethology
Study of distinctive adaptive behaviors of species of animals that have evolved to increase survival of the species.

These parts of our mind can be thought of as similar to apps on an iPhone—useful for specific, constrained functions. Just like in your phone, there's a mind app for almost all important human functions.

evolutionary psychology
Application of Darwinian principles of natural selection and survival of the fittest to individual behavior.

checkpoint can you . . .

- Identify the chief focus of the evolutionary/sociobiological perspective and explain how Darwin's theory of evolution underlies this perspective?
- Tell what kinds of topics ethologists and evolutionary psychologists study?

genes, are selected to be passed on, and the less adapted ones die out. Over vast spans of time, these small, incremental changes add up and result in the evolution of new species.

Evolved mechanisms are behaviors that developed to solve problems in adapting to an earlier environment. For example, sudden aversion to certain foods during pregnancy may originally have evolved to protect the vulnerable fetus from toxic substances (Profet, 1992). Such evolved mechanisms may survive even though they no longer serve a useful purpose (Bjorklund & Pellegrini, 2002), or they may evolve further in response to changing environmental conditions. Although most evolved mechanisms are tailored to a specific problem, others, such as human intelligence, are viewed as having evolved to help people face a wide range of problems (MacDonald, 1998; MacDonald & Hershberger, 2005).

Ethology is the study of the adaptive behaviors of animal species in natural contexts. The assumption is that such behaviors evolved through natural selection. Ethologists generally compare animals of different species and seek to identify which behaviors are universal and which are specific to a particular species or modifiable by experience.

For example, one widespread characteristic throughout the animal kingdom is called *proximity-seeking*, or, more casually, "staying close to mommy." This was first studied by Konrad Lorenz in newborn ducklings, who imprint on and follow the first moving object they see until they are old enough to survive on their own. Other animals also engage in similar behavior, and over time it became clear to researchers that this innate tendency was an important adaptive behavior. In fact, those baby animals that did not stay close to their mothers tended not to survive, and therefore did not reproduce later in life.

But why discuss animal research in a human development text? The answer is humans have also been subject to the forces of evolution and thus are likely to also have innate adaptive behaviors. In fact, one of the most important theories in developmental psychology was strongly influenced by the ethological approach. The British psychologist John Bowlby (1969) drew upon his knowledge of proximity-seeking behavior in animals of different species as he formed his ideas about attachment in humans. He viewed infants' attachment to a caregiver as a mechanism that evolved to protect them from predators.

A related extension of the ethological approach can be found in **evolutionary psychology.** Ethologists focus on cross-species comparisons, whereas evolutionary psychologists focus on humans and apply Darwinian principles to human behavior. Evolutionary psychologists believe that just as we have a heart specialized as a pump, lungs specialized for air exchange, and thumbs specialized for grasping, we also have aspects of our human psychology specialized for solving adaptive problems. According to this theory, people unconsciously strive to perpetuate their genetic legacy. They do so by seeking to maximize their chances of having offspring who will survive to reproduce and pass down their characteristics.

It is important to note that an evolutionary perspective does not reduce human behavior to the effects of genes seeking to reproduce themselves despite arguing that ultimately the transmission of genes is what drives many evolved behaviors. Evolutionary psychologists place great weight on the environment to which humans must adapt and the flexibility of the human mind.

A SHIFTING BALANCE

One of the strengths of the scientific method is that as new data emerges, and as our understanding evolves, theories shift and change. Most of the early pioneers in the field, including Freud, Erikson, and Piaget, favored organismic, or stage, approaches. The mechanistic view gained support during the 1960s with the popularity of learning theories. Today much attention is focused on the biological and evolutionary bases of behavior.

Moreover, instead of looking for broad stages, developmental scientists seek to discover what specific kinds of behavior show continuity and what processes are involved in each. Rather than abrupt changes, a close examination of Piaget's stages of cognitive development, for example, reveals gradual, sometimes almost imperceptible, advances that add up to a qualitative shift. Similarly, most infants do not learn to walk overnight, but rather by a series of tentative movements that gradually become more self-assured. Even when observable behavior seems to change suddenly, the biological or neurological processes that underlie that behavioral change may be continuous (Courage & Howe, 2002).

Instead of debating active versus reactive development, investigators often find that influences are *bidirectional:* people change their world even as it changes them. A baby girl born with a cheerful disposition is likely to get positive responses from adults, which strengthen her trust that her smiles will be rewarded and motivate her to smile more. A manager who offers constructive criticism and emotional support to his subordinates is likely to elicit greater efforts to produce. Improved productivity, in turn, is likely to encourage him to keep using this managerial style.

Theories of human development grow out of, and are tested by, research. Research questions and methods often reflect a researcher's particular theoretical orientation. For example, in trying to understand how a child develops a sense of right and wrong, a behaviorist would examine the way the parents respond to the child's behavior: what kinds of behavior they punish or praise. A social learning theorist would focus on imitation of moral examples, possibly in stories or in movies. An information-processing researcher might do a task analysis to identify the steps a child goes through in determining the range of moral options available and then in deciding which option to pursue. An evolutionary psychologist might be interested in universal aspects of moral development that serve adaptive purposes and in how they affect social behavior.

With the vital connection between theory and research in mind, let's look at the methods developmental researchers use.

Research Methods

Researchers in human development work within two methodological traditions: quantitative and qualitative. Each of these traditions has different goals and different ways of seeing and interpreting reality and emphasizes different means of collecting and analyzing data.

QUANTITATIVE AND QUALITATIVE RESEARCH

Generally, when most people think of scientific research, they are thinking of what is called *quantitative research.* **Quantitative research** deals with objectively measurable, numerical data that can answer questions such as "how much?" or "how many?" and that is amenable to statistical analysis. For example, quantitative researchers might study the fear and anxiety children feel before surgery by asking them to answer questions, using a numerical scale, about how fearful or anxious they are. These data could then be compared to data for children not facing surgery to determine whether a statistically significant difference exists between the two groups.

quantitative research
Research that deals with objectively measurable data.

Quantitative research on human development is based on the **scientific method,** which has traditionally characterized most scientific inquiry. Its usual steps are:

scientific method
System of established principles and processes of scientific inquiry, which includes identifying a problem to be studied, formulating a hypothesis to be tested by research, collecting data, analyzing the data, forming tentative conclusions, and disseminating findings.

1. *Identification of a problem* to be studied, often on the basis of a theory or of previous research;
2. *Formulation of hypotheses* to be tested by research;
3. *Collection of data;*
4. *Statistical analysis of the data* to determine whether they support the hypothesis;
5. *Formation of tentative conclusions;* and
6. *Dissemination of findings* so other observers can check, learn from, analyze, repeat, and build on the results.

The Scientific Method

Qualitative research, in contrast, focuses on the how and why of behavior. It more commonly involves nonnumerical (verbal or pictorial) descriptions of participants' subjective understanding, feelings, or beliefs about their experiences. Qualitative researchers might study the same subject areas as quantitative researchers, but their perspective informs both how they collect data and how they interpret it. For example, if qualitative

qualitative research
Research that focuses on nonnumerical data, such as subjective experiences, feelings, or beliefs.

researchers were to study children's emotional state prior to surgery, they might do so with unstructured interviews or by asking children to draw their perceptions of the upcoming event. Whereas the goal in quantitative research is to generate hypotheses from previous research and empirically test them, the goal in qualitative research is to understand the "story" of the event. Qualitative research is more flexible and informal, and these researchers might be more interested in gathering and exploring large amounts of data to see what hypotheses emerge than in running statistical analyses on numerical data.

The selection of quantitative or qualitative methods may depend on the purpose of the study, how much is already known about the topic, and the researcher's theoretical orientation. Quantitative research often is done in controlled laboratory settings; qualitative research typically is conducted in everyday settings, such as the home or school. Quantitative investigators seek to remain detached from study participants so as not to influence the results; qualitative investigators may get to know participants to better understand why they think, feel, and act as they do, and it is assumed they are interpreting the results through the lens of their own experiences and characteristics.

sample
Group of participants chosen to represent the entire population under study.

random selection
Selection of a sample in such a way that each person in a population has an equal and independent chance of being chosen.

SAMPLING

Because studying an entire *population* (a group to whom the findings may apply) is usually too costly and time-consuming, investigators select a **sample,** a smaller group within the population. To be sure that the results of quantitative research are true generally, the sample should adequately represent the population under study—that is, it should show relevant characteristics in the same proportions as in the entire population. Otherwise the results cannot properly be *generalized,* or applied to the population as a whole.

Often quantitative researchers seek to achieve representativeness through **random selection,** in which each person in a population has an equal and independent chance of being chosen. The result of random selection is a *random sample.* If we wanted to study the effects of an educational program, for example, one way to select a random sample of students would be to put all of their names into a large bowl, stir it, and then draw out a certain number of names. A random sample, especially a large one, is likely to represent the population well. Unfortunately, a random sample of a large population is often difficult to obtain. Instead, many studies use samples selected for convenience or accessibility (for example, children born in a particular hospital or patients in a particular nursing home). The findings of such studies may not apply to the population as a whole.

In qualitative research, samples tend to be focused rather than random. Participants may be chosen for their ability to communicate the nature of a certain experience, such as how it feels to go through puberty or menopause. A carefully selected qualitative sample may have a fair degree of generalizability.

checkpoint
can you . . .

- Compare quantitative and qualitative research and give an example of each?
- Summarize the six steps in the scientific method and tell why each is important?
- Explain the purpose of random selection and tell how it can be achieved?

There is no one "best way" of collecting data; rather, each technique has costs and benefits associated with it.

FORMS OF DATA COLLECTION

Common ways of gathering data (Table 3) include *self-reports* (verbal or visual reports by study participants), *observation* of participants in laboratory or natural settings, and *behavioral* or *performance measures.* Researchers may use one or more of these data collection techniques in any research design. Qualitative research tends to rely on self-reports, often in the form of in-depth, open-ended interviews or visual techniques (such as asking participants to draw their impressions of an experience), and on observation in natural settings. Quantitative research typically uses standardized, structured methods involving numerical measurements of behavior or performance.

Let's look more closely at several common methods of data collection.

Self-Reports: Diaries, Visual Techniques, Interviews, and Questionnaires The simplest form of self-report is a *diary* or log. Adolescents may be asked, for example, to record what they eat each day or the times when they feel depressed. In studying young children, *parental self-reports*—diaries, journals, interviews, or questionnaires—are commonly used, often together with other methods, such as videotaping or recording.

TABLE 3 Major Methods of Data Collection

Type	Main Characteristics	Advantages	Disadvantages
Self-report: diary, visual reports, interview, or questionnaire	Participants are asked about some aspect of their lives; questioning may be highly structured or more flexible; self-report may be verbal or visual.	Can provide firsthand information about a person's life, attitudes, or opinions. Visual techniques (e.g., drawing, mapping, graphing) avoid need for verbal skills.	Participant may not remember information accurately or may distort responses in a socially desirable way; how question is asked or by whom may affect answer.
Naturalistic observation	People are observed in their normal setting, with no attempt to manipulate behavior.	Provides good description of behavior; does not subject people to unnatural settings that may distort behavior.	Lack of control; observer bias.
Laboratory observation	Participants are observed in the laboratory, with no attempt to manipulate behavior.	Provides good descriptions; offers greater control than naturalistic observation because all participants are observed under same controlled conditions.	Observer bias; controlled situation can be artificial.
Behavioral and performance measures	Participants are tested on abilities, skills, knowledge, competencies, or physical responses.	Provides objectively measurable information; avoids subjective distortions.	Cannot measure attitudes or other nonbehavioral phenomena; results may be affected by extraneous factors.

Visual representation techniques—asking participants to draw or paint or to provide maps or graphs that illuminate their experience—can avoid reliance on verbal skills.

In a face-to-face or telephone *interview,* researchers ask questions about attitudes, opinions, or behavior. In a *structured* interview, each participant is asked the same set of questions. An *open-ended* interview is more flexible; the interviewer can vary the topics and order of questions and can ask follow-up questions based on the responses. To reach more people and to protect their privacy, researchers sometimes distribute a printed or online *questionnaire,* which participants fill out and return.

By questioning a large number of people, investigators can get a broad picture—at least of what the respondents *say* they believe or do or did. However, people willing to participate in interviews or fill out questionnaires may not accurately represent the population as a whole. Furthermore, heavy reliance on self-reports may be unwise because people may not have thought about what they feel and think or honestly may not know. They may forget when and how events took place or may consciously or unconsciously distort their replies to fit what is considered socially desirable.

How a question is asked, and by whom, can affect the answer. When questioned about potentially risky or socially disapproved behavior, such as sexual habits and drug use, respondents may be more candid in responding to a computerized survey than to a paper-and-pencil survey (Turner et al., 1998).

Which interview technique do you think would yield more reliable results—structured or open-ended?

One of the problems with the results of Cosmo *magazine polls is that they are not a random sample. The data come from "people who answer* Cosmo *magazine polls," a select group of individuals.*

Naturalistic and Laboratory Observation Observation takes two forms: *naturalistic observation* and *laboratory observation*. In **naturalistic observation,** researchers look at people in real-life settings. The researchers do not try to alter behavior or the environment; they simply record what they see. In **laboratory observation,** researchers observe and record behavior in a controlled environment, such as a laboratory. By observing all participants under the same conditions, investigators can more clearly identify any differences in behavior not attributable to the environment.

Both kinds of observation can provide valuable descriptions of behavior, but they have limitations. For one, they do not explain *why* people behave as they do, though

naturalistic observation
Research method in which behavior is studied in natural settings without intervention or manipulation.

laboratory observation
Research method in which all participants are observed under the same controlled conditions.

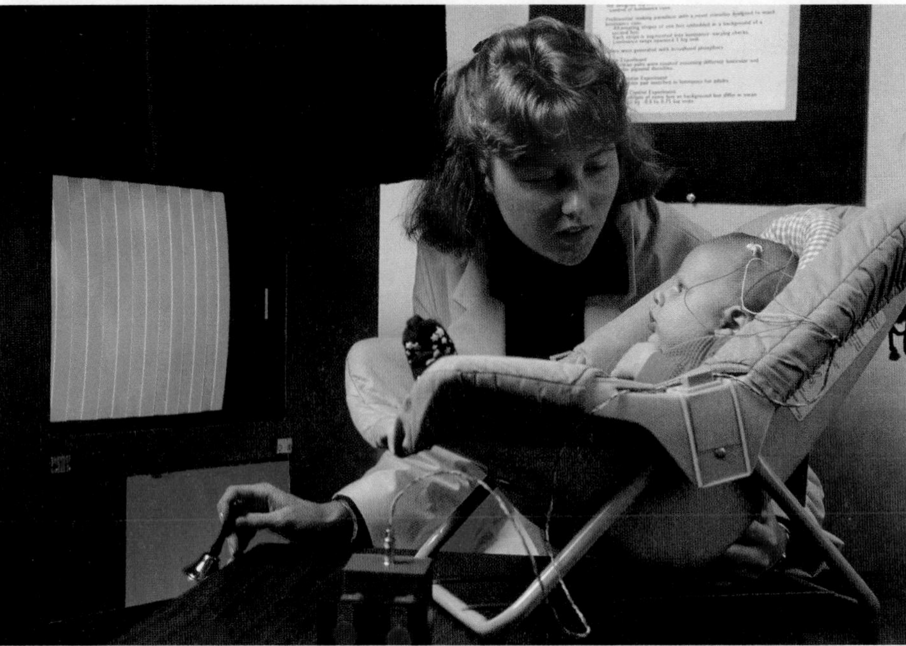

A baby under laboratory observation may or may not behave the same way as in a naturalistic setting, such as at home, but both kinds of observation can provide valuable information.

the observers may suggest interpretations. Then, too, an observer's presence can alter behavior. When people know they are being watched, they may act differently. Finally, there is a risk of *observer bias:* the researcher's tendency to interpret data to fit expectations or to emphasize some aspects and minimize others.

Behavioral and Performance Measures For quantitative research, investigators typically use more objective measures of behavior or performance instead of, or in addition to, self-reports or observation. Tests and other behavioral and neuropsychological measures may be used to assess abilities, skills, knowledge, competencies, or physiological responses, such as heart rate and brain activity. Although these measures are less subjective than self-reports or personal observation, such factors as fatigue and self-confidence can affect results.

Observation doesn't work terribly well for very rare events either. Suppose you wanted to do research on heroic rescues and decided to wait by a bridge to observe whether anyone helps when people try to commit suicide by jumping off. How long would you be waiting?

Some written tests, such as intelligence tests, compare performance with that of other test-takers. Such tests can be meaningful and useful only if they are both *valid* (the tests measure the abilities they claim to measure) and *reliable* (the results are reasonably consistent from one time to another). To avoid bias, tests must be *standardized,* that is, given and scored by the same methods and criteria for all test-takers.

When measuring a characteristic such as intelligence, it is important to define exactly what is to be measured in a way that other researchers will understand so they can repeat the experiment and comment on the results. For this purpose, researchers use an **operational definition**—a definition stated solely in terms of the operations used to measure a phenomenon. Intelligence, for example, can be defined as the ability to achieve a certain score on a test covering logical relationships, memory, and vocabulary recognition. Some people may disagree with this definition, but no one can reasonably claim that it is not clear.

operational definition
Definition stated solely in terms of the operations or procedures used to produce or measure a phenomenon.

cognitive neuroscience
Study of links between neural processes and cognitive abilities.

For most of the history of psychology, theorists and researchers studied cognitive processes apart from the physical structures of the brain in which these processes occur. Now, sophisticated imaging instruments, such as functional magnetic resonance imaging (fMRI) and positron emission tomography (PET), make it possible to see the brain in action, and the new field of **cognitive neuroscience** is linking our understanding of cognitive functioning with what happens in the brain.

studysmart

Validity/Reliability

EVALUATING QUANTITATIVE AND QUALITATIVE RESEARCH

In comparison with quantitative research based on the scientific method, qualitative research has both strengths and limitations. On the positive side, qualitative research can examine a question in great depth and detail, and the research framework can readily be revised in the light of new data. Findings of qualitative research can be a rich source of insights into attitudes and behavior. The interactive relationship between investigators and participants can humanize the research process and reveal information that would not emerge under the more impersonal conditions of quantitative research. On the other hand, qualitative research tends to be less rigorous and more subject to bias than quantitative research. Because samples are often small and usually not random, results are less generalizable and replicable than the results of quantitative research. The large volume of data makes analysis and interpretation time-consuming, and the quality of the findings and conclusions depends greatly on the skills of the researcher (Mathie & Carnozzi, 2005).

Yet the line between these methodologies is not necessarily clear-cut. Qualitative data may be analyzed quantitatively—for example, by statistical analysis of interview transcripts or videotaped observations to see how many times certain themes or behaviors occur. Conversely, quantitative data may be illuminated by qualitative research—for example, by interviews designed to examine the motivations and attitudes of children who make high scores on achievement tests (Yoshikawa, Weisner, Kalil, & Way, 2008).

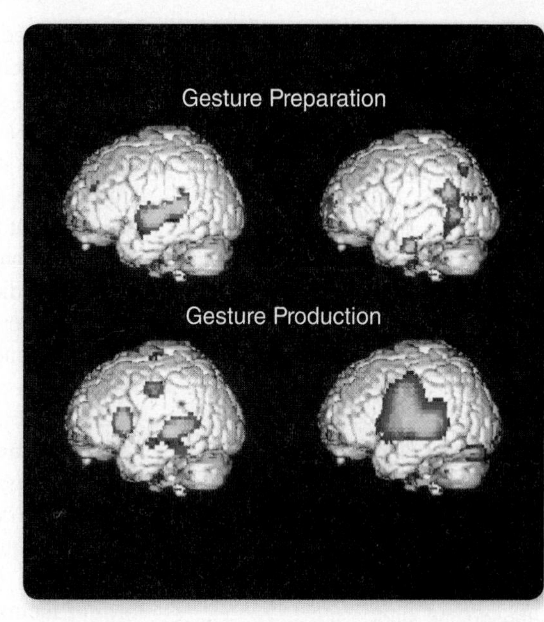

Researchers can analyze an fMRI (functional magnetic resonance imaging) brain scan taken during an activity or task to observe the link between cognitive activity and what happens in the brain. The regions shown in red are activated when thinking about making a gesture (preparation) and then in performing it (production).

BASIC RESEARCH DESIGNS

A research design is a plan for conducting a scientific investigation: what questions are to be answered, how participants are to be selected, how data are to be collected and interpreted, and how valid conclusions can be drawn. Four basic designs used in developmental research are *case studies, ethnographic studies, correlational studies,* and *experiments.* The first two designs are qualitative; the last two are quantitative. Each design has advantages and drawbacks, and each is appropriate for certain kinds of research problems (Table 4).

TABLE 4 Basic Research Designs

Type	Main Characteristics	Advantages	Disadvantages
Case study	In-depth study of single individual.	Flexibility; provides detailed picture of one person's behavior and development; can generate hypotheses.	May not generalize to others; conclusions not directly testable; cannot establish cause and effect.
Ethnographic study	In-depth study of a culture or subculture.	Can help overcome culturally based biases in theory and research; can test universality of developmental phenomena.	Subject to observer bias.
Correlational study	Attempt to find positive or negative relationship between variables.	Enables prediction of one variable on basis of another; can suggest hypotheses about causal relationships.	Cannot establish cause and effect.
Experiment	Controlled procedure in which an experimenter controls the independent variable to determine its effect on the dependent variable; may be conducted in the laboratory or field.	Establishes cause-and-effect relationships; is highly controlled and can be repeated by another investigator; degree of control greatest in the laboratory experiment.	Findings, especially when derived from laboratory experiments, may not generalize to situations outside the laboratory.

case study
Study of a single subject, such as an individual or family.

The Rorschach Inkblot test asks you to say what you see in an inkblot. Presumably, what you see reveals truths about your personality and functioning. The problem? It is notoriously unreliable. What good is a test if you cannot get a straight answer about what it means?

Case Studies A **case study** is a study of an individual. Some theories, such as Freud's, grew out of clinical case studies, which included careful observation and interpretation of what patients said and did. Case studies also may use behavioral or physiological measures and biographical, autobiographical, or documentary materials. Case studies are particularly useful when studying something relatively rare, when it simply is not possible to find a large enough group of people with the characteristic in question to conduct a traditional laboratory study. Case studies offer useful, in-depth information. They can explore sources of behavior and can test treatments, and they suggest directions for further research.

Case studies do have shortcomings, however. Using case studies, we can learn much about the development of a single person, but not how the information applies to people in general. Furthermore, case studies cannot explain behavior with certainty or make strong causal statements because there is no way to test their conclusions.

ethnographic study
In-depth study of a culture, which uses a combination of methods including participant observation.

participant observation
Research method in which the observer lives with the people or participates in the activity being observed.

Ethnographic Studies An **ethnographic study** seeks to describe the pattern of relationships, customs, beliefs, technology, arts, and traditions that make up a society's way of life. In a way, it is like a case study of a culture. Ethnographic research can be qualitative, quantitative, or both. It uses a combination of methods, including informal, unstructured interviewing and **participant observation.** Participant observation is a form of naturalistic observation in which researchers live or participate in the societies or smaller groups they observe, as anthropologists often do for long periods of time.

Because of ethnographers' involvement in the events or societies they are observing, their findings are especially open to observer bias. On the positive side, ethnographic research can help overcome cultural biases in theory and research (Box 1). Ethnography demonstrates the error of assuming that principles developed from research in Western cultures are universally applicable.

correlational study
Research design intended to discover whether a statistical relationship between variables exists.

Correlational Studies A **correlational study** seeks to determine whether a *correlation,* or statistical relationship, exists between *variables,* phenomena that change or vary among people or can be varied for purposes of research. Correlations are expressed in terms of direction (positive or negative) and magnitude (degree). Two variables that are correlated *positively* increase or decrease together. Studies show a positive, or direct, correlation between televised violence and aggression. That is, children who watch more violent television tend to fight more than children who watch less violent television. Two variables have a *negative,* or inverse, correlation if, as one increases, the other decreases. Studies show a negative correlation between amount of schooling and the risk of developing dementia (mental deterioration) due to Alzheimer's disease in old age. In other words, the less education, the more dementia (Katzman, 1993).

Correlations

Correlations are reported as numbers ranging from −1.0 (a perfect negative relationship) to +1.0 (a perfect positive relationship). Perfect correlations are rare. The closer a correlation comes to +1.0 or −1.0, the stronger the relationship, either positive or negative. A correlation of zero means that the variables have no relationship.

Correlations enable us to predict one variable in relation to another. On the basis of the positive correlation between watching televised violence and aggression, we can predict that children who watch violent shows are more likely to get into fights than children who do *not* watch such shows. The greater the magnitude of the correlation between the two variables, the greater the ability to predict one from the other.

A correlation of +/− 1.0 means you are measuring the same thing in different ways. For example, inches and centimeters are perfectly correlated.

Although strong correlations suggest possible cause-and-effect relationships, these are merely hypotheses and need to be examined and tested critically. We cannot be sure from a positive correlation between televised violence and aggressiveness that watching televised violence *causes* aggression; we can conclude only that the two variables are related. It is possible that the causation goes the other way: aggressive behavior may lead children to watch more violent programs. Or a third variable—perhaps an inborn predisposition toward aggressiveness or a violent living environment—may cause a child *both* to watch violent programs and to act aggressively. Similarly, we cannot be sure that schooling protects against dementia; it may be that another variable, such as socioeconomic status, might explain both lower levels of schooling and higher levels of dementia. The only way to

window on the world

PURPOSES OF CROSS-CULTURAL RESEARCH

When David, a European American child, was asked to identify the missing detail in a picture of a face with no mouth, he said, "The mouth." But Ari, an Asian immigrant child in Israel, said that the body was missing. Since art in his culture does not present a head as a complete picture, he thought the absence of a body was more important than the omission of "a mere detail like the mouth" (Anastasi, 1988, p. 360).

By looking at children from different cultural groups, researchers can learn in what ways development is universal (and thus intrinsic to the human condition) and in what ways it is culturally determined. For example, children everywhere learn to speak in the same sequence, advancing from cooing and babbling to single words and then to simple combinations of words. The words vary from culture to culture, but toddlers around the world put them together in the same ways to form sentences. Such findings suggest that the capacity for learning language is universal and inborn.

On the other hand, culture seems to exert a surprisingly large influence on early motor development. African babies, whose parents often prop them in a sitting position and bounce them on their feet, tend to sit and walk earlier than U.S. babies (Rogoff & Morelli, 1989). The society in which children grow up also influences the skills they learn. In the United States, children learn to read, write, and, increasingly, to operate computers. In rural Nepal, they learn how to drive water buffalo and find their way along mountain paths.

One important reason to conduct research among different cultural groups is to recognize biases in traditional Western theories and research that often go unquestioned until they are shown to be a product of cultural influences. Because so much research in child development has focused on Western industrialized societies, typical development in these societies may be seen as the norm, or standard of behavior. Measuring against this "norm" leads to narrow—and often wrong—ideas about development. Pushed to its extreme, this belief can cause the development of children in other ethnic and cultural groups to be seen as deviant (Rogoff & Morelli, 1989).

Barriers exist to our understanding of cultural differences, particularly those involving minority subcultures. As with David and Ari in our opening example, a question or task may have different conceptual meanings for different cultural groups. Sometimes the barriers are linguistic. In a study of children's understanding of kinship relations among the Zinacanta people of Chiapas, Mexico (Greenfield & Childs, 1978), instead of asking "How many brothers do you have?" the researchers—knowing that the Zinacantas have separate terms for older and younger siblings—asked, "What is the name of your older brother?" Using the same question across cultures might have obscured, rather than revealed, cultural differences and similarities (Parke, 2004b).

Results of observational studies of ethnic or cultural groups may be affected by the ethnicity of the researchers. For example, in one study European American observers noted more conflict and restrictiveness in African American mother-daughter relationships than African American observers noted (Gonzales, Cauce, & Mason, 1996).

In this book we discuss several influential theories developed from research in Western societies that do not hold up when tested on people from other cultures—theories about gender roles, abstract thinking, moral reasoning, and other aspects of human development. Throughout this book, we consistently look at children in cultures and subcultures other than the dominant one in the United States to show how closely development is tied to society and culture and to add to our understanding of normal development in many settings. In so doing, however, we need to keep in mind the pitfalls involved in cross-cultural comparisons.

Can you think of a situation in which you made an incorrect assumption about a person because you were unfamiliar with her or his cultural background?

show with certainty that one variable causes another is through experimentation—a method that, when studying human beings, is not always possible for practical or ethical reasons.

experiment
Rigorously controlled, replicable procedure in which the researcher manipulates variables to assess the effect of one on the other.

Experiments An **experiment** is a controlled procedure in which the experimenter manipulates variables to learn how one affects another. Scientific experiments must be conducted and reported in such a way that another experimenter can *replicate* them, that is, repeat them in exactly the same way with different participants to verify the results and conclusions.

The number of churches in a town is highly correlated with the number of liquor bottles found in the garbage cans of the town. But it would be inappropriate to conclude that religion drives people to drink. Rather, a third variable—population size—explains this relationship. We always need to include critical thinking in our observations.

experimental group
In an experiment, the group receiving the treatment under study.

control group
In an experiment, a group of people, similar to those in the experimental group, who do not receive the treatment under study.

Groups and Variables A common way to conduct an experiment is to divide the participants into two kinds of groups. An **experimental group** consists of people who are to be exposed to the experimental manipulation or *treatment*—the phenomenon the researcher wants to study. Afterward, the effect of the treatment will be measured one or more times to find out what changes, if any, it caused. A **control group** consists of people who are similar to the experimental group but do not receive the experimental treatment or may receive a different treatment. An experiment may include one or more of each type of group. If the experimenter wants to compare the effects of different treatments (say, of two methods of teaching), the overall sample may be divided into *treatment groups,* each of which receives one of the treatments under study. To ensure objectivity, some experiments, particularly in medical research, use *double-blind* procedures, in which neither participants nor experimenters know who is receiving the treatment and who is instead receiving an inert *placebo.*

One team of researchers wanted to find out if 11-month-old infants could be trained to focus their attention (Wass, Porayska-Pomsta, & Johnson, 2011). The researchers brought 42 infants to their laboratory and had them participate in a variety of tasks. Half of the infants were given about an hour of attentional training. This training required babies to use sustained gaze to make a fun event happen on a computer. For example, if babies fixated on an elephant, the elephant became animated. If the babies looked away, the elephant stopped moving. The other group of children were shown television clips and animations, but were not trained. At the end of 2 weeks, the babies were tested on a series of cognitive tasks. Babies who underwent the training performed better on the tasks than did the babies who were not trained. It is reasonable to conclude, then, that the attentional training improved the babies' performance on the tasks as it was the only thing varied between the two groups.

Sometimes placebos (pills with no active ingredients) are used for pain management. Pain is a perception, but it generally involves damage to the body. So would you say the placebo is affecting our bodies or our minds? What's the difference?

In this experiment, the type of activity (training versus watching television) was the *independent variable,* and the children's test performance the *dependent variable*. An **independent variable** is something over which the experimenter has direct control. A **dependent variable** is something that may or may not change as a result of changes in the independent variable; in other words, it *depends* on the independent variable. In an experiment, a researcher manipulates the independent variable to see how changes in it will affect the dependent variable. The hypothesis for a study states how a researcher thinks the independent variable affects the dependent variable.

independent variable
In an experiment, the condition over which the experimenter has direct control.

dependent variable
In an experiment, the condition that may or may not change as a result of changes in the independent variable.

random assignment
Assignment of participants in an experiment to groups in such a way that each person has an equal chance of being placed in any group.

Random Assignment If an experiment finds a significant difference in the performance of the experimental and control groups, how do we know that the cause was the independent variable? For example, in the attentional training experiment, how can we be sure that the training and not some other factor (such as intelligence) caused the difference in test performance of the two groups? The best way to control for effects of such extraneous factors is **random assignment:** assigning the participants to groups in such a way that each person has an equal chance of being placed in any group. (Random assignment differs from random selection, which determines who gets into the full sample.)

If assignment is random and the sample is large enough, differences in such factors as age, gender, and ethnicity will be evenly distributed so that the groups initially are as alike as possible in every respect except for the variable to be tested. Otherwise, unintended differences between the groups might *confound,* or contaminate, the results, and any conclusions drawn from the experiment would have to be viewed with suspicion. To control for confounds, the experimenter must make sure that everything except the independent variable is held constant during the course of the experiment. For example, in the attentional training study, children in the experimental and control groups must spend the same amount of time on their different tasks. When participants in an experiment are randomly assigned to treatment groups and conditions other than the independent variable are carefully controlled, the experimenter can be reasonably confident that a causal relationship has (or has not) been established. In other words, any differences found between groups can be attributed to the action of the independent variable (in this case, training) and not some other factor.

Of course, with respect to some variables we might want to study, such as age, gender, and race/ethnicity, random assignment is not possible. We cannot assign Terry to be 5 years old and Brett to be 10, or one to be a boy and the other a girl. When studying such a variable—for example, whether boys or girls are stronger in certain abilities—researchers can strengthen the validity of their conclusions by randomly selecting participants and by trying to make sure that they are statistically equivalent in other ways that might make a difference in the study.

Dependent variables are also known as "end measures" because their values are used to check whether you are right at the end of the study.

Laboratory, Field, and Natural Experiments There are various ways to conduct research, and one essential distinction is between laboratory, field, and natural experiments. A laboratory experiment is best for determining cause and effect; it generally consists of asking participants to visit a laboratory where they are subject to conditions manipulated by the experimenter. The attentional training experiment described earlier was a laboratory study. The tight control of a laboratory study allows researchers to be more certain that their independent variable caused change in their dependent variable; however, because of the artificiality of the laboratory experience, the results may be less generalizable to real life. People may not act as they typically would.

A field experiment is a controlled study conducted in an everyday setting, such as a home or school. Variables can still be manipulated, so causal claims can still be investigated. Because the experiments occur in the real world, there is more confidence that the behaviors that are seen are generalizable to natural behaviors. However, researchers have less control over events that may occur—the real world is often messy, and things do not always go as planned.

Research conducted on Katrina survivors that compared them to people in other cities who were similar on many measures, except for the experience of living through the traumatic events of the hurricane, is an example of a quasi-experimental design.

When, for practical or ethical reasons, it is impossible to conduct a true experiment, a *natural experiment,* also called a *quasi-experiment,* may provide a way of studying certain events. A natural experiment compares people who have been accidentally "assigned" to separate groups by circumstances of life—one group who were exposed, say, to famine or HIV or superior education, and another group who were not. A natural experiment, despite its name, is actually a correlational study because controlled manipulation of variables and random assignment to treatment groups are not possible.

One natural experiment looked at what happened when a casino opened on an Indian reservation in North Carolina, raising the income of tribal members (Costello, Compton, Keeler, & Angold, 2003). The study found a decline in behavioral disorders among children in these families as compared with children in the same area whose families did not receive increased income. Still, because it was correlational, the study could not prove that the increased income actually *caused* improvements in mental health.

Controlled experiments have two important advantages over other research designs: they can establish cause-and-effect relationships, and they permit replication. However, such experiments can be too artificial and too narrowly focused. In recent decades, many researchers have concentrated less on laboratory experimentation or have supplemented it with a wider array of methods.

checkpoint can you . . .

- Compare the uses and drawbacks of case studies, ethnographic studies, correlational studies, and experiments?
- Explain why only a controlled experiment can establish causal relationships?
- Distinguish among laboratory, field, and natural experiments and tell what kinds of research seem most suitable to each?
- Compare the advantages and disadvantages of various forms of data collection?

DEVELOPMENTAL RESEARCH DESIGNS

One of the primary goals of developmental research is to study change over time, and developmental psychologists have developed a variety of methods to do so. The two most common research strategies are *cross-sectional* and *longitudinal studies* (Figure 3). A **cross-sectional study** most clearly illustrates similarities or differences among people of different ages; a **longitudinal study** tracks people over time and focuses on individual change with age. Both designs have pros and cons. A third type of study, a **sequential study,** combines the two approaches to minimize the drawbacks of the separate approaches.

cross-sectional study
Study designed to assess age-related differences, in which people of different ages are assessed on one occasion.

longitudinal study
Study designed to assess age changes in a sample over time.

sequential study
Study design that combines cross-sectional and longitudinal techniques.

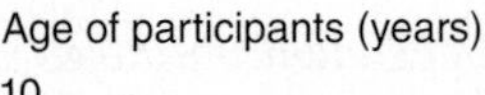

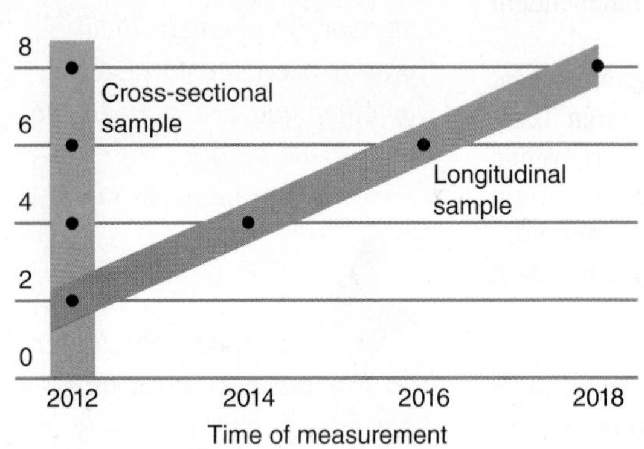

FIGURE 3

Developmental Research Designs

In the cross-sectional study, groups of 2-, 4-, 6-, and 8-year-olds were tested in 2012 to obtain data about age-related differences. In the longitudinal study, a sample of children were first measured in 2012, when they were 2 years old; follow-up testing is done when the children are 4, 6, and 8, to measure age-related changes. Note: Dots indicate times of measurement.

Cross-Sectional, Longitudinal, and Sequential Studies In a cross-sectional study, children of different ages are assessed at one point in time. Generally, the children are matched on other important characteristics and their ages are varied. For example, in one cross-sectional study, researchers presented 193 boys and girls between the ages of 7 months and 5 years with pairs of objects. The children were invited to reach for one of the objects, which were identical with the exception that one object was always pink, and the other was either green, blue, yellow, or orange. The researchers found that girls showed no preference for pink objects until age 2, when they began to reach for the pink object more frequently. The girls increasingly preferred the pink object as they aged. By age 4, girls chose the pink object almost 80 percent more frequently than the other colors. Boys, however, showed a different pattern. Like girls, they initially showed no preference for pink over the other colors. Starting at about 2 years of age, however, they became less and less likely to choose the pink object. By age 5, they chose the pink object only about 20 percent of the time. The researchers concluded that girls' preference for the color pink was learned over time, and they theorized that it was related to the acquisition of knowledge about gender (LoBue & DeLoache, 2011).

Can we draw this conclusion with certainty? The problem with cross-sectional studies is that we cannot know whether the 5-year-olds' preference for certain colors when they were under the age of 2 years was the same as that of the current babies in the study. We cannot be certain that this is a developmental change rather than merely a difference in formative experiences for the two age groups. For example, if a popular television program that targets children over the age of 2 and that strongly promotes gender stereotypes had been introduced in the year previous to the study, the older children might show color preferences as a result of watching the show and not because of an increased understanding of gender. Although it may appear to be a change related to age, it might instead be the result of television programming.

The only way to know whether change occurs with age is to conduct a longitudinal study of a particular person or group. In a longitudinal study, researchers study the same person or group of people over time, sometimes years apart.

The Oakland Growth Study was a groundbreaking longitudinal study of the physical, intellectual, and social development of 167 fifth and sixth graders in Oakland, California. The study began at the outset of the Great Depression of the 1930s. The children were followed intensively until the age of 18 or 19, and then on five occasions during their adult years. The data collected included interviews, health assessments, personality inventories, and fact-sheet questionnaires. The researchers found that the societal disruption of the Great Depression seemed to negatively affect family processes and child development. Just as with cross-sectional designs, there is a caveat. Because individual people are studied over time, researchers have access to each person's specific individual trajectory. This is rich and valuable data because it can show each person's development over time. However, the results from one cohort might not apply to a study of a different cohort. For example, the results of a study on children born in the 1920s, such as the Oakland Growth Study, might not apply to children born in the 1990s. Therefore, care must be taken in the interpretation of longitudinal research.

Attrition is not random; it is almost always biased in some fashion. For example, the people most likely to drop out of a study are those with the most chaotic lifestyles. The people still in the study at its conclusion might look really good, but it could be because the people who were not doing well are gone.

In attempting to determine the best research design, neither cross-sectional nor longitudinal design is superior. Rather, both designs have strengths and weaknesses (Table 5). For example, cross-sectional design is fast—we don't have to wait 30 years for results. This also makes it a more economical choice. Moreover, because participants are assessed only once, we don't have to consider attrition (people dropping out of the study) or repeated testing (which can produce practice effects). But cross-sectional design uses group averages, so individual differences and trajectories may be obscured. More important, the results can be affected by the differing experiences of people born at different times, as previously explained.

TABLE 5 Cross-Sectional, Longitudinal, and Sequential Research: Pros and Cons

Type of Study	Procedure	Advantages	Disadvantages
Cross-sectional	Data are collected on people of different ages at the same time.	Can show similarities and differences among age groups; speedy, economical; presents no problem of attrition or repeated testing.	Cannot establish age effects; masks individual differences; can be confounded by cohort effects.
Longitudinal	Data are collected on same person or persons over a period of time.	Can show age-related change or continuity; avoids confounding age with cohort effects.	Is time-consuming, expensive; presents problems of attrition, bias in sample, and effects of repeated testing; results may be valid only for cohort tested or sample studied.
Sequential	Data are collected on successive cross-sectional or longitudinal samples.	Can avoid drawbacks of both cross-sectional and longitudinal designs.	Requires large amount of time and effort and analysis of very complex data.

Longitudinal research shows a different and complementary set of strengths and weaknesses. Because the same people are studied repeatedly over time, researchers can track individual patterns of continuity and change. This makes longitudinal studies more time-consuming and expensive than cross-sectional studies. In addition, repeated testing of participants can result in practice effects. For example, your performance on an intelligence test might get better over time from practice rather than from any increase in intelligence. Attrition can be problematic in longitudinal research as well because it tends to be non-random, which can introduce a positive bias to the study. Those who stay with the study tend to be above average in intelligence and socioeconomic status, and those who drop out tend to have more chaotic lives and worse overall outcomes. Moreover, practical issues, such as turnover in research personnel, loss of funding, or the development of new measures or methodologies, can introduce potential problems with data collection.

Researchers are attempting to overcome the drawbacks of longitudinal and cross-sectional design with the design of sequential studies. Sequential designs track people of different ages (like cross-sectional designs) over time (like longitudinal designs). The combination of cross-sectional and longitudinal designs (as shown in Figure 4) allows researchers to separate age-related changes from cohort effects, and provides a more complete picture of development than would be possible with either design alone. The major drawbacks of sequential studies relate to time, effort, and complexity. Sequential designs require large numbers of participants and collection and analysis of huge amounts of data over a period of years. Interpreting these findings and conclusions can demand a high degree of sophistication.

checkpoint can **you** . . .

- List advantages and disadvantages of longitudinal, cross-sectional, and sequential research?

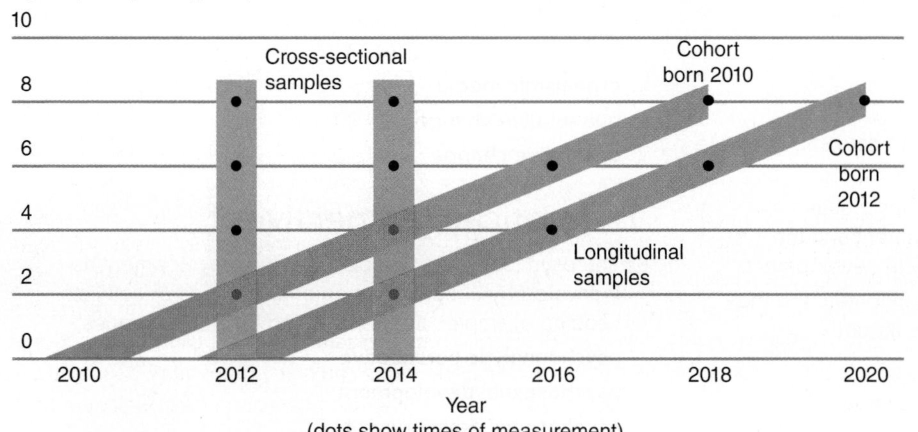

FIGURE 4
A Sequential Design

Two successive cross-sectional groups of 2-, 4-, 6-, and 8-year-olds were tested in 2012 and 2014. Also, a longitudinal study of a group of children first measured in 2012, when they were 2 years old, is followed by a similar longitudinal study of another group of children who were 2 years old in 2014.

Ethics of Research

Should research that might harm its participants ever be undertaken? How can we balance the possible benefits against the risk of mental, emotional, or physical injury to individuals?

Objections to the study of "Little Albert" (described earlier in this chapter) as well as several other early studies gave rise to today's more stringent ethical standards. Institutional review boards at colleges, universities, and other institutions review proposed research from an ethical standpoint. Guidelines of the American Psychological Association (APA, 2002) cover such issues as *informed consent* (consent freely given with full knowledge of what the research entails), *avoidance of deception*, protection of participants from *harm and loss of dignity*, guarantees of *privacy and confidentiality*, the *right to decline or withdraw* from an experiment at any time, and the responsibility of investigators to *correct any undesirable effects*, such as anxiety or shame.

In resolving ethical dilemmas, researchers should be guided by three principles. The first is *beneficence*, which is the obligation to maximize potential benefits to participants and to minimize potential harm. For example, suppose you are a researcher studying the effect of failure on self-esteem. If you are going to deceive some of your participants by telling them they failed on a laboratory task, what steps will you take to mitigate any potential harm you might cause them? The second principle is *respect* for participants' autonomy and protection of those who are unable to exercise their own judgment. For example, if you are conducting research with toddlers, and a 2-year-old refuses to participate, should you force the child to participate? What is the appropriate action in this case? The third principle is *justice*, which, in this case, is the inclusion of diverse groups together with sensitivity to any special impact the research may have on them. For example, it may be important that your study includes an appropriate and representative selection of diverse people. If this is the case, have you developed culturally appropriate materials and methods to use?

Should informed consent involve telling participants about what your hypotheses for your research are? Why or why not?

Developmental psychologists must be particularly careful as their research frequently involves vulnerable individuals, such as infants or children. In response, the Society for Research in Child Development (2007) has developed standards for age-appropriate treatment of children in research, covering such principles as avoidance of physical or psychological harm, obtaining the child's assent as well as a parent's or guardian's informed consent, and responsibility to follow up on any information that could jeopardize the child's well-being. For example, infants' and very young children's ability to cope with the stress of the research situation may hinge on the presence of a parent or trusted caregiver, a familiar setting and procedure, and familiar objects.

checkpoint can you . . .

- List at least three ethical issues affecting rights of research participants?
- Identify three principles that should govern inclusion of participants in research?

summary and key terms

Basic Theoretical Issues

- A theory is used to organize and explain data and generate hypotheses that can be tested by research.
- Developmental theories differ on two basic issues: the active or reactive character of development and the existence of continuity or discontinuity in development.
- Two contrasting models of human development are the mechanistic model and the organismic model.

theory
hypotheses
mechanistic model
organismic model
quantitative change
qualitative change

Theoretical Perspectives

- The psychoanalytic perspective sees development as motivated by unconscious emotional drives or conflicts. Leading examples are Freud's and Erikson's theories.

psychoanalytic perspective
psychosexual development
psychosocial development

- The learning perspective views development as a result of learning based on experience. Leading examples are Watson's and Skinner's behaviorism and Bandura's social learning (social cognitive) theory.

  learning perspective
  behaviorism
  classical conditioning
  operant conditioning
  reinforcement
  punishment
  social learning theory
  reciprocal determinism
  observational learning
  self-efficacy

- The cognitive perspective is concerned with thought processes. Leading examples are Piaget's cognitive-stage theory, Vygotsky's sociocultural theory, and the information-processing approach.

  cognitive perspective
  cognitive-stage theory
  organization
  schemes
  adaptation
  assimilation
  accommodation
  equilibration
  sociocultural theory
  zone of proximal development (ZPD)
  scaffolding
  information-processing approach

- The contextual perspective focuses on the individual in a social context. A leading example is Bronfenbrenner's bioecological theory.

  contextual perspective
  bioecological theory

- The evolutionary/sociobiological perspective, represented by E. O. Wilson and influenced by Darwin's theory of evolution, focuses on the adaptiveness, or survival value, of behavior. A leading example is Bowlby's attachment theory.

  evolutionary/sociobiological perspective
  ethology
  evolutionary psychology

Research Methods

- Research can be either quantitative or qualitative, or both.
- To arrive at sound conclusions, quantitative researchers use the scientific method.
- Random selection of a research sample can ensure generalizability.
- Three forms of data collection are self-reports, observation, and behavioral and performance measures.

  quantitative research
  scientific method
  qualitative research
  sample
  random selection
  naturalistic observation
  laboratory observation
  operational definitions
  cognitive neuroscience

- A design is a plan for conducting research. Two qualitative designs used in developmental research are the case study and the ethnographic study. Cross-cultural research can indicate whether certain aspects of development are universal or culturally influenced.
- Two quantitative designs are the correlational study and the experiment. Only experiments can firmly establish causal relationships.
- Experiments must be rigorously controlled to be valid and replicable. Random assignment of participants can ensure validity.
- Laboratory experiments are easiest to control and replicate, but findings of field experiments may be more generalizable. Natural experiments may be useful in situations in which true experiments would be impractical or unethical.
- The two most common designs used to study age-related development are cross-sectional and longitudinal. Cross-sectional studies assess age differences; longitudinal studies describe continuity or change in the same participants. The sequential study is intended to overcome the weaknesses of the other two designs.

  case study
  ethnographic study
  participant observation
  correlational study
  experiment
  experimental group
  control group
  independent variable
  dependent variable
  random assignment
  cross-sectional study
  longitudinal study
  sequential study

Ethics of Research

- Researchers seek to resolve ethical issues on the basis of principles of beneficence, respect, and justice.
- Ethical issues in research include the rights of participants to informed consent, avoidance of deception, protection from harm and loss of dignity and self-esteem, and guarantees of privacy and confidentiality.
- Standards for protection of children used in research cover such principles as parental informed consent and protection from harm or jeopardy to the child's well-being.

part 2
BEGINNINGS

Forming a New Life

outline

Conceiving New Life

Mechanisms of Heredity

Nature and Nurture: Influences of Heredity and Environment

Prenatal Development

Monitoring and Promoting Prenatal Development

learning objectives

Explain how conception occurs and what causes multiple births.

Describe the mechanisms of heredity in normal and abnormal human development.

Explain how heredity and environment interact in human development.

Describe prenatal development, including environmental influences.

Discuss the importance of high-quality prenatal care.

did you know?

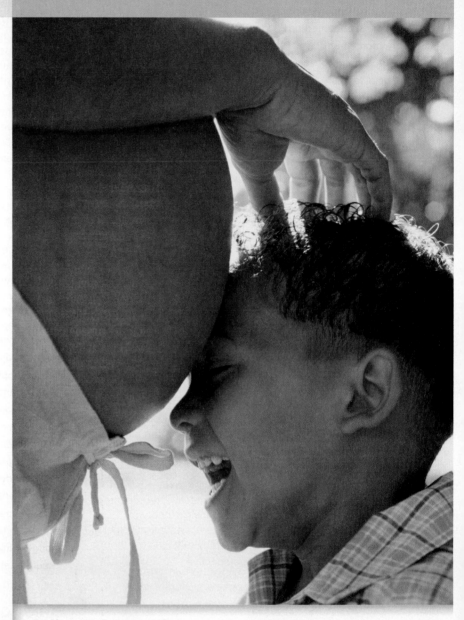

- Fetuses can learn and remember while in the womb, and they respond to their mother's voice?
- Drinking or using drugs during pregnancy can do permanent damage to an unborn child?
- Prenatal care should begin *before* conception?

We describe how conception normally occurs, how the mechanisms of heredity operate, and how biological inheritance interacts with environmental influences within and outside the womb. We trace the course of prenatal development, describe influences on it, and discuss ways to monitor it.

Genes and family may determine the foundation of the house, but time and place determine its form.

—Jerome Kagan, as quoted in *Childhood,* Robert H. Wozniak (1991)

Conceiving New Life

Most people think of development as beginning on the day of birth, when the new child—squalling and thrashing—is introduced to the world. However, development starts earlier. It starts at conception, as sperm and egg meet and an entirely new individual is created from parental genomes. Development continues as the fertilized egg grows and differentiates and edges closer to independent life outside the womb. And it persists in the dance between nature and nurture that shapes the unique individual that is the product of these processes. This chapter is about that story.

HOW FERTILIZATION TAKES PLACE

Tania wanted to have a baby. She carefully watched the calendar, counting the days after each menstrual period to take advantage of her "fertile window," the time during which conception is possible. When after 2 months Tania had not yet achieved her pregnancy, she wondered what possibly might have gone wrong. What Tania didn't realize is that although a woman is usually fertile between the 6th and 21st days of the menstrual cycle, the timing of the fertile window can be highly unpredictable (Wilcox, Dunson, & Baird, 2000). Although conception is far more likely at certain times, she may be able to conceive at any time during the month. Concurrently, even though conception is more likely during certain parts of the month, it may not always occur during that time.

fertilization
Union of sperm and ovum to produce a zygote; also called *conception.*

zygote
One-celled organism resulting from fertilization.

Fertilization, or *conception,* is the process by which sperm and ovum—the male and female *gametes,* or sex cells—combine to create a single cell called a **zygote,** which then duplicates itself again and again by cell division to produce all the cells that make up a baby. But conception is not as simple as it sounds. Several independent events need to coincide to conceive a child, and not all conceptions end in birth.

At birth, a girl is believed to have about 2 million immature ova in her two ovaries, each ovum in its own *follicle,* or small sac. In a sexually mature woman, *ovulation*—rupture of a mature follicle in either ovary and expulsion of its ovum—occurs about once every 28 days until menopause. The ovum is swept along through one of the fallopian tubes by the *cilia,* tiny hair cells, toward the uterus, or womb.

Sperm are produced in the testicles (testes), or reproductive glands, of a mature male at a rate of several hundred million a day and are ejaculated in the semen at sexual climax. Deposited in the vagina, they try to swim through the *cervix,* the opening of the uterus, and into the fallopian tubes; but only a tiny fraction make it that far.

Fertilization normally occurs while the ovum is passing through the fallopian tube. If fertilization does not occur, the ovum and any sperm cells in the woman's body die. The sperm are absorbed by the woman's white blood cells, and the ovum passes through the uterus and exits through the vagina.

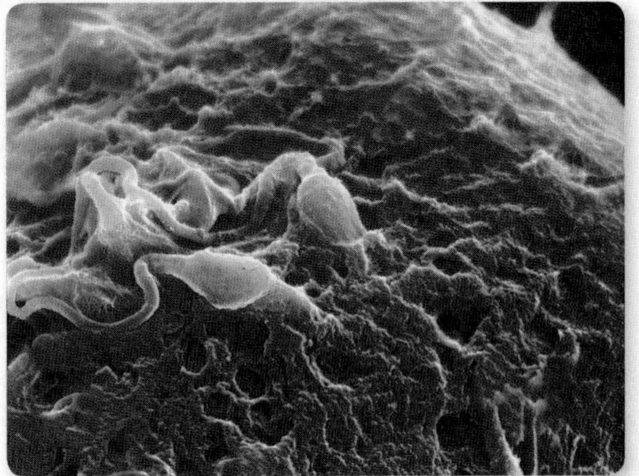

This color-enhanced scanning electron micrograph (SEM) shows two sperm (orange) attracted to an ovum's blue surface. A sperm's long tail enables it to swim through the cervix and up the fallopian tube. The sperm's rounded head releases enzymes that help it penetrate the ovum's thick surface and fertilize the ovum by fusing with its nucleus.

WHAT CAUSES MULTIPLE BIRTHS?

Multiple births happen in two ways. Although twins are the most common variation, triplets, quadruplets, and other multiple births are possible.

dizygotic twins
Twins conceived by the union of two different ova (or a single ovum that has split) with two different sperm cells; also called *fraternal twins*; they are no more alike genetically than any other siblings.

Dizygotic twins, or fraternal twins, are the result of two separate eggs being fertilized by two different sperm to form two unique individuals. Genetically, they are like siblings who inhabit the same womb at the same time, and they can be the same or different sex. Dizygotic twins tend to run in families and are the result of multiple eggs being released at one time. This tendency may have a genetic basis and seems to be passed down from a woman's mother (Martin & Montgomery, 2002; National Center for Health Statistics [NCHS], 1999). When dizygotic twins skip generations, it is normally because a mother of dizygotic twins has only sons to whom she cannot pass on the tendency (NCHS, 1999).

monozygotic twins
Twins resulting from the division of a single zygote after fertilization; also called *identical twins*; they are genetically similar.

Monozygotic twins are the result of a far different process. They result from the cleaving of one fertilized egg and are generally genetically identical. They can still differ outwardly, however, because people are the result of the interaction between genes and environmental influences. For example, in one condition that affects only monozygotic twins (twin-to-twin transfusion syndrome), the blood vessels of the placenta form abnormally, and the placenta is shared unequally between the twins. One twin receives a smaller share of nutrients than does the other. Mortality is high, but if both twins survive, one twin will be significantly larger than the other at birth despite being genetically identical.

Moreover, environmental differences add up over time. The differences between identical twins generally magnify as twins grow older. So, for example, 3-year-old monozygotic twins appear more similar than 30-year-old monozygotic twins. These differences may result from chemical modifications in a person's genome shortly after conception or may be due to later experiences or environmental factors, such as exposure to smoke or other pollutants (Fraga et al., 2005). This process, known as *epigenesis*, is discussed later in this chapter.

The rate of monozygotic twins (about 4 per 1,000 live births) appears to be constant at all times and places, but the rate of dizygotic twins, the more common type, varies (Martin & Montgomery, 2002; NCHS, 1999). For example, West African and African American women are more likely to have dizygotic twins than Caucasian women, who, in turn, are more likely to have them than Chinese or Japanese women (Martin & Montgomery, 2002).

The incidence of multiple births in the United States has grown rapidly since 1980. By 2009 the twin birthrate had risen by 76 percent, from 18.9 to 33.3 twins per 1,000 live births (Martin, Hamilton, & Osterman, 2012). Two related factors in the rise in multiple births are (1) the trend toward delayed childbearing and (2) the increased use of fertility drugs, which spur ovulation, and of assisted reproductive techniques such as in vitro fertilization, which tend to be used by older women (Martin, Kirmeyer, et al., 2009).

The explosion of multiple births, especially triplets and higher multiples, is of concern because such births, which often result from assisted reproduction, are associated with increased risks: pregnancy complications, premature delivery, low-birth-weight infants, and disability or death of the infant (Hoyert, Mathews, et al., 2006; Martin, Kirmeyer, et al., 2009). Perhaps because of such concerns, the proportion of assisted reproduction procedures involving three or more embryos has declined, and the birthrate for triplets and higher multiples, which had quadrupled during the 1980s and 1990s, has since taken a downturn (Martin, Kirmeyer, et al., 2009).

checkpoint
can you . . .

- Explain how and when fertilization normally takes place?
- Distinguish between and explain monozygotic and dizygotic twins?
- Give reasons for the increase in multiple births in the United States?

Mechanisms of Heredity

The science of genetics is the study of *heredity:* the genetic transmission of heritable characteristics from parents to offspring. When ovum and sperm unite, they endow the baby-to-be with a genetic makeup that influences a wide range of characteristics from color of eyes and hair to health, intellect, and personality.

THE GENETIC CODE

The "stuff" of heredity is a chemical called **deoxyribonucleic acid (DNA).** The double-helix structure of a DNA molecule resembles a long, spiraling ladder whose steps are made of pairs of chemical units called *bases* (Figure 1). The bases—adenine (A), thymine (T), cytosine (C), and guanine (G)—are the "letters" of the **genetic code,** which cellular machinery "reads."

Chromosomes are coils of DNA that consist of smaller segments called **genes,** the functional units of heredity. Each gene is located in a definite position on its chromosome and contains thousands of bases. The sequence of bases in a gene tells the cell how to make the proteins that enable it to carry out specific functions. The complete sequence of genes in the human body constitutes the **human genome.** Of course, every human has a unique genome. The human genome is not meant to be a recipe for making a particular human. Rather, the human genome is a reference point, or representative genome, that shows the location of all human genes.

A useful analogy is to consider the DNA of an individual as a series of books in a library. Until those books are "read" by an enzyme called RNA polymerase, and transcribed into a readable copy of messenger RNA (m-RNA), the knowledge contained within the books is not actualized. And what books will be pulled down from the shelf and read is in part determined by environmental factors that turn genes on and off at different points in development (Champagne & Mashoodh, 2009).

Every cell in the normal human body except the sex cells (sperm and ova) has 23 pairs of chromosomes—46 in all. Through a type of cell division called *meiosis,* which the sex cells undergo when they are developing, each sex cell ends up with only 23 chromosomes—one from each pair. When sperm and ovum fuse at conception, they produce a zygote with 46 chromosomes, 23 from the father and 23 from the mother (Figure 2).

At conception, then, the single-celled zygote has all the biological information needed to guide its development into a unique individual. Through *mitosis,* a process by which the non–sex cells divide in half over and over again, the DNA replicates itself, so that each newly formed cell has the same DNA structure as all the others. Each cell division creates a genetic duplicate of the original cell, with the same hereditary information. Sometimes a mistake in copying is made, and a **mutation** may result. Mutations are permanent alterations in genetic material. When development is normal, each cell (except the sex cells) continues to have 46 chromosomes identical to those in the original zygote. As the cells divide, they differentiate, specializing in a variety of complex bodily functions that enable the child to grow and develop.

Genes spring into action when conditions call for the information they can provide. Genetic action that triggers the growth of body and brain is often regulated by hormonal levels—both in the mother and in the developing baby—that are affected by such environmental conditions as

DNA is the genetic material in all living cells. It consists of four chemical units, called bases. These bases are the letters of the DNA alphabet. A (adenine) pairs with T (thymine) and C (cytosine) pairs with G (guanine). There are 3 billion base pairs in human DNA.

Letters of the DNA alphabet

T = Thymine
A = Adenine
G = Guanine
C = Cytosine

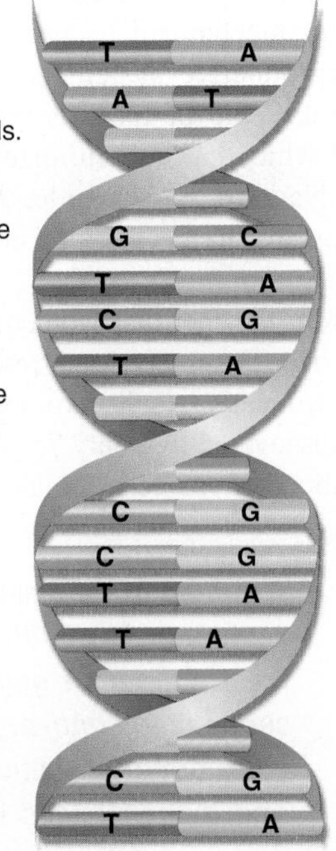

FIGURE 1
DNA: The Genetic Code

Source: Ritter, 1999.

New research indicates that a single gene—Pax6—is responsible for regulating human brain development.

Zhang et al., 2010

deoxyribonucleic acid (DNA)
Chemical that carries inherited instructions for the development of all cellular forms of life.

genetic code
Sequence of bases within the DNA molecule; governs the formation of proteins that determine the structure and functions of living cells.

chromosomes
Coils of DNA that consist of genes.

genes
Small segments of DNA located in definite positions on particular chromosomes; functional units of heredity.

human genome
Complete sequence of genes in the human body.

study**smart**

The Genetic Code

mutation
Permanent alterations in genes or chromosomes that may produce harmful characteristics.

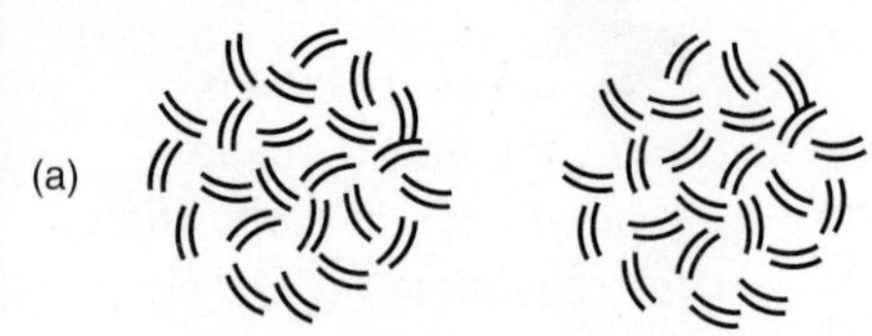

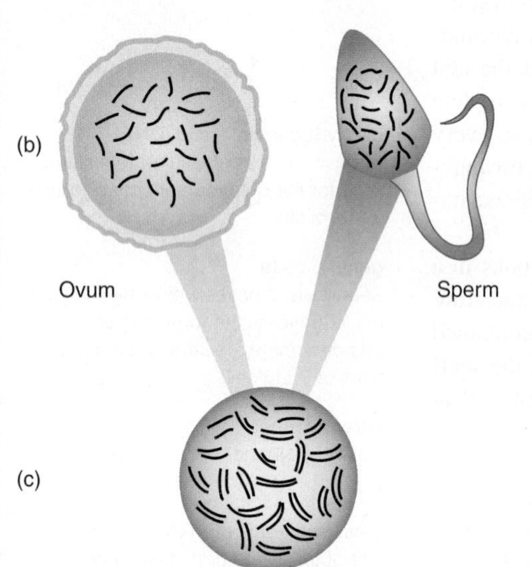

FIGURE 2
Hereditary Composition of the Zygote

(a) Body cells of women and men contain 23 pairs of chromosomes, which carry the genes, the basic units of inheritance. (b) Each sex cell (ovum and sperm) has only 23 single chromosomes because of a special kind of cell division (meiosis). (c) At fertilization, the 23 chromosomes from the sperm join the 23 from the ovum so that the zygote receives 46 chromosomes, or 23 pairs.

nutrition and stress. Thus, from the start, heredity and environment are interrelated.

WHAT DETERMINES SEX?

In many villages in Nepal, it is common for a man whose wife has borne no male babies to take a second wife. In some societies, a woman's failure to produce sons is justification for divorce. The irony of these customs is that it is the father's sperm that genetically determines a child's sex.

At the moment of conception, the 23 chromosomes from the sperm and the 23 from the ovum form 23 pairs. Twenty-two pairs are **autosomes,** chromosomes that are not related to sexual expression. The twenty-third pair are **sex chromosomes**—one from the father and one from the mother—that govern the baby's sex.

Sex chromosomes are either *X chromosomes* or *Y chromosomes.* The sex chromosome of every ovum is an X chromosome, but the sperm may contain either an X or a Y chromosome. The Y chromosome contains the gene for maleness, called the *SRY* gene. When an ovum (X) is fertilized by an X-carrying sperm, the zygote formed is XX, a genetic female. When an ovum (X) is fertilized by a Y-carrying sperm, the resulting zygote is XY, a genetic male (Figure 3).

Initially, the embryo's rudimentary reproductive system appears almost identical in males and in females. About 6 to 8 weeks after conception, male embryos normally start producing the male hormone testosterone. Exposure of a genetically male embryo to steady, high levels of testosterone ordinarily results in the development of a male body with male sexual organs. However, the process is not automatic. Research with mice has found that hormones must first signal the SRY gene, which then triggers cell differentiation and formation of the testes. Without this signaling, a genetically male mouse will develop genitals that appear female rather than male (Hughes, 2004; Meeks, Weiss, & Jameson, 2003; Nef et al., 2003). It is likely that a similar mechanism occurs in human males. The development of the female reproductive system is equally complex and depends on a number of variants. One of these is the signaling molecule called *Wnt-4,* a variant form of which can masculinize a genetically female fetus (Biason-Lauber, Konrad, Navratil, & Schoenle, 2004; Hughes, 2004). Thus sexual differentiation appears to be a more complex process than simple genetic determination.

Further complexities arise from the fact that women have two X chromosomes, whereas men have only one. For many years researchers believed that the duplicate genes on one of a woman's two X chromosomes are inactive, or turned off. Recently, however, researchers discovered that only 75 percent of the genes on the extra X chromosome are inactive. About 15 percent remain active, and 10 percent are active in some women but not in others (Carrel & Willard, 2005). This variability in gene activity could help explain gender differences both in normal traits and in disorders linked to the X chromosome, which are discussed later in this chapter. The extra X chromosome also may help explain why women are generally healthier and longer lived than men: harmful changes in a gene on one X chromosome may be offset by a backup copy on the other X chromosome (Migeon, 2006).

The human genome was first sequenced in 2006. More recently, the Neandertal genome was also sequenced, and analysis of the commonalities between Neandertal and human genes suggests that we engaged in limited interbreeding. In other words, some of their genes live on in us.

Green et al., 2010

checkpoint
can **you** . . .

- Describe the structure of DNA and its role in the inheritance of characteristics?
- Distinguish between meiosis and mitosis?
- Explain why the sperm normally determines a baby's sex and discuss possible complicating factors?

PATTERNS OF GENETIC TRANSMISSION

During the 1860s, Gregor Mendel, an Austrian monk, crossbred pea plants that produced only yellow seeds with pea plants that produced only green seeds. The resulting hybrid plants produced only yellow seeds, meaning, he said, that yellow was *dominant* over green. Yet when he bred the yellow-seeded hybrids with each other, only 75 percent of their offspring had yellow seeds, and the other 25 percent had green seeds. This showed, Mendel said, that a hereditary characteristic (in this case, the color green) can be *recessive;* that is, be carried by an organism that does not express, or show, it.

Mendel also tried breeding for two traits at once. Crossing pea plants that produced round yellow seeds with plants that produced wrinkled green seeds, he found that color and shape were independent of each other. Mendel thus showed that hereditary traits are transmitted separately.

Today we know that the genetic picture in humans is far more complex than Mendel imagined. Although some human traits, such as the presence of facial dimples, are inherited via simple dominant transmission, most human traits fall along a continuous spectrum and result from the actions of many genes in concert. Nonetheless, Mendel's groundbreaking work laid the foundations for our modern understanding of genetics.

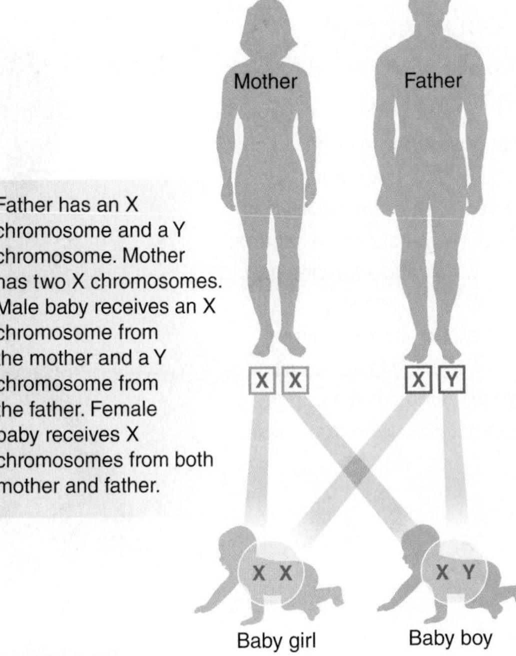
Mother
Father
Father has an X chromosome and a Y chromosome. Mother has two X chromosomes. Male baby receives an X chromosome from the mother and a Y chromosome from the father. Female baby receives X chromosomes from both mother and father.
X X
X Y
X X
X Y
Baby girl
Baby boy

FIGURE 3
Genetic Determination of Sex

Because all babies receive an X chromosome from the mother, sex is determined by whether an X or a Y chromosome is received from the father.

Dominant and Recessive Inheritance Do you have dimples? If so, you probably inherited them through *dominant inheritance*. If your parents have dimples but you do not, *recessive inheritance* occurred. How do these two types of inheritance work?

Genes that can produce alternative expressions of a characteristic (such as the presence or absence of dimples) are called **alleles.** Alleles are alternate versions of the same gene. Every person receives one maternal and one paternal allele for any given trait. When both alleles are the same, the person is **homozygous** for the characteristic; when they are different, the person is **heterozygous.** In **dominant inheritance,** the dominant allele is always expressed, or shows up as a trait in that person. The person will look the same whether or not he or she is heterozygous or homozygous because the recessive allele doesn't show. For the trait to be expressed in **recessive inheritance,** the person must have two recessive alleles, one from each parent. If a recessive trait is expressed, that person cannot have a dominant allele.

Let's take the presence of dimples as an example. Dimples are a dominant trait, so you will have dimples if you receive at least one copy (D) from either parent. If you inherited one allele for dimples from each parent (Figure 4), you are homozygous for this trait and have one or more dimples. If you receive one copy of the dimpling allele (D) and one copy of an allele for lack of dimples (d), you are heterozygous. In both cases, your expressed characteristic is that you have dimples. The only situation in which you would not have dimples is if you received two recessive copies (d), one from each parent.

Relatively few traits are determined in this simple fashion. Most traits result from **polygenic inheritance,** the interaction of several genes. For example, there is not an "intelligence" gene that determines whether or not you are smart. Rather, a large number of genes work in concert to determine your intellectual potential. Like intelligence, most individual variations in complex behaviors or traits are governed by the additive influences of many genes with small

Hetero *means different and* homo *means the same, just as when we speak of heterosexual and homosexual orientations. Heterozygous individuals have two different alleles, homozygous individuals have two of the same allele.*

autosomes
In humans, the 22 pairs of chromosomes not related to sexual expression.

sex chromosomes
Pair of chromosomes that determines sex: XX in the normal human female, XY in the normal human male.

alleles
Two or more alternative forms of a gene that occupy the same position on paired chromosomes and affect the same trait.

homozygous
Possessing two identical alleles for a trait.

heterozygous
Possessing differing alleles for a trait.

dominant inheritance
Pattern of inheritance in which, when a child receives different alleles, only the dominant one is expressed.

recessive inheritance
Pattern of inheritance in which a child receives identical recessive alleles, resulting in expression of a nondominant trait.

polygenic inheritance
Pattern of inheritance in which multiple genes at different sites on chromosomes affect a complex trait.

FIGURE 4
Dominant and Recessive Inheritance

Because of dominant inheritance, the same observable phenotype (in this case, dimples) can result from two different genotypes (DD and Dd). A phenotype expressing a recessive characteristic (such as no dimples) must have a homozygous genotype (dd).

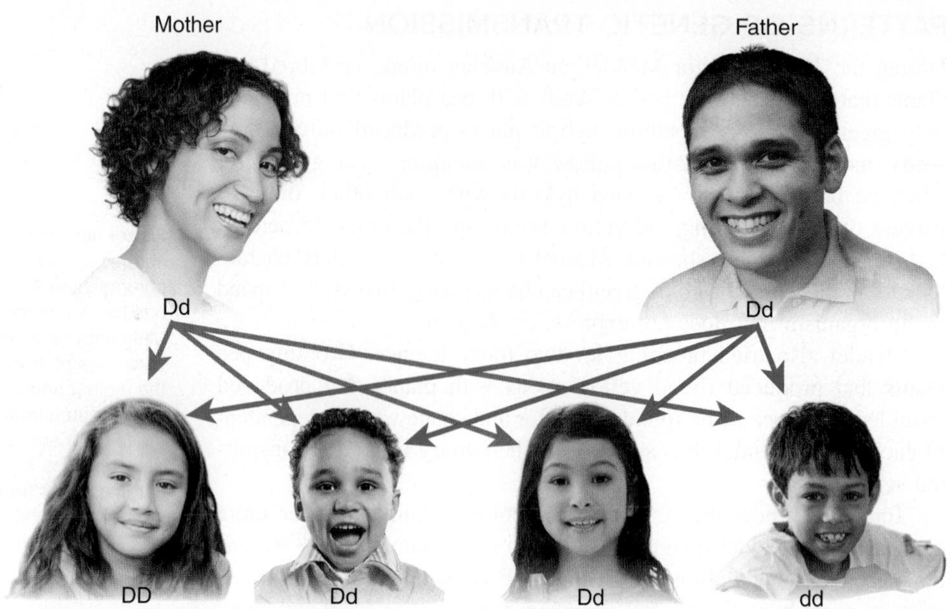

Dimples are unusual in that they are inherited through simple dominant transmission. Most traits are influenced by multiple genes, often in combination with other factors.

but identifiable effects. In other words, they are polygenic. Although single genes often determine abnormal traits, there is no single gene that by itself significantly accounts for individual differences in any complex normal behavior.

Genotypes and Phenotypes: Multifactorial Transmission If you have dimples, that is part of your **phenotype,** the observable characteristics through which your **genotype,** or underlying genetic makeup, is expressed. The phenotype is the product of the genotype and any relevant environmental influences. The difference between genotype and phenotype helps explain why a clone (a genetic copy of an individual) or even an identical twin can never be an exact duplicate of another person.

As Figure 4 illustrates, people with different genotypes may exhibit the same phenotype. For example, a child who is homozygous for a dominant dimples allele will have dimples, but so will a child who is heterozygous for that same allele. Because it is dominant, the dimples are expressed, and the recessive nondimpling allele is hidden.

Furthermore, the hidden alleles can float around undetected for generations and then be expressed if both parents carry a hidden copy. For example, if you are heterozygous for dimples, and you find a mate who is also heterozygous for dimples, approximately one-fourth of your children should not have dimples. Each child has a 25 percent chance to inherit both of the recessive alleles, and thus express the recessive trait (a lack of dimples). Note that any dimpled children might be either homozygous (25 percent chance) or heterozygous (50 percent chance) for this trait. Because the dominant trait is always expressed, all that you would know, upon seeing a dimpled child, is that the child had to have at least one dimpling allele.

Dimples have a strong genetic base; but experience modifies the expression of the genotype for most traits—a phenomenon called **multifactorial transmission.** Multifactorial transmission illustrates the action of nature and nurture influences and how they

phenotype
Observable characteristics of a person.

genotype
Genetic makeup of a person, containing both expressed and unexpressed characteristics.

Your genotype is the recipe for making you. Your phenotype is how you actually turn out.

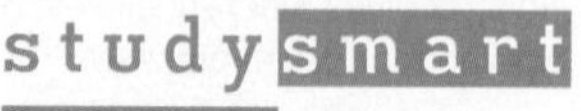

Genotype and Phenotype

multifactorial transmission
Combination of genetic and environmental factors to produce certain complex traits.

mutually and reciprocally affect outcomes. Imagine that Steven has inherited musical talent. If his family nurtures his talent and he practices regularly, he may become a skilled musician. However, if he is not encouraged and not motivated to play music, his genotype for musical ability may not be expressed (or may be expressed to a lesser extent) in his phenotype. Some physical characteristics (including height and weight) and most psychological characteristics (such as intelligence and musical ability) are products of multifactorial transmission. Many disorders arise when an inherited predisposition (an abnormal variant of a normal gene) interacts with an environmental factor, either before or after birth. Attention-deficit/hyperactivity disorder (ADHD) is one of several behavioral disorders thought to be transmitted multifactorially (Price, Simonoff, Waldman, Asherson, & Plomin, 2001).

Later in this chapter we discuss in more detail how environmental influences work together with the genetic endowment to influence development.

Rainbow, on the left, nuzzles her clone, Cc, on the right. They are genetically identical, but have different appearances and personalities.

Epigenesis: Environmental Influence on Gene Expression Until recently, most scientists believed that the genes a child inherits were firmly established during fetal development, though their effects on behavior could be modified by experience. Now, mounting evidence suggests that gene expression itself is controlled by a third component, a mechanism that regulates the functioning of genes within a cell without affecting the structure of the cell's DNA. Genes are turned off or on as they are needed by the developing body or when triggered by the environment. This phenomenon is called **epigenesis,** or *epigenetics*. Far from being fixed once and for all, epigenetic activity is affected by a continual bidirectional interplay with nongenetic influences (Gottlieb, 2007; Mayo Foundation for Medical Education and Research, 2009; Rutter, 2007). In other words, the environment can influence when and which genes turn on and off.

epigenesis
Mechanism that turns genes on or off and determines functions of body cells.

Epigenesis (meaning "on, or above, the genome") refers to chemical molecules (or "tags") attached to a gene that alter the way a cell "reads" the gene's DNA. If we think of the human genome as a computer, we can visualize this epigenetic framework as the software that tells the DNA when to work. Because every cell in the body inherits the same DNA sequence, the function of the chemical tags is to differentiate various types of body cells, such as brain cells, skin cells, and liver cells. In this way, genes for the types of cells that are needed are turned on, and genes for unneeded cells are left off.

Cloned cats illustrate how development is not merely genetic. Despite having identical genetic material, cloned cats may have differently colored fur as a result of environmental influences. In other words, epigenetic changes alter their phenotype without altering their genotype.

Epigenetic changes can occur throughout life in response to environmental factors such as nutrition, smoking, sleep habits, stress, and physical activity (Fraga et al., 2005). Epigenetics may contribute to such common ailments as cancer, diabetes, and heart disease. It may explain why one monozygotic twin is susceptible to a disease such as schizophrenia whereas the other twin is not, and why some twins get the same disease but at different ages (Fraga et al., 2005; Wong, Gottesman, & Petronis, 2005). Environmental influences can also be social in nature. For example, social isolation can lead to a variety of health vulnerabilities including cardiovascular disease, decreased immune responses, and an increased risk of inflammation-related diseases (Cole, 2009).

Cells are particularly susceptible to epigenetic modification during critical periods such as puberty and pregnancy (Mayo Foundation for Medical Education and Research, 2009; Rakyan & Beck, 2006). Furthermore, epigenetic modifications, especially those that occur early in life, may be heritable. Studies of human sperm cells found age-related epigenetic variations capable of being passed on to future generations (Rakyan & Beck, 2006). Thus good health and nutritional practices throughout a woman's reproductive years may help ensure the health of her future children and grandchildren.

One example of epigenesis is *genome,* or *genetic, imprinting*. Imprinting is the differential expression of certain genetic traits, depending on whether the trait has been inherited from the mother or the father. In imprinted gene pairs, genetic information inherited from the parent of one sex is activated, but genetic information from the other parent is suppressed. Imprinted genes play an important role in regulating fetal growth and development. When a normal pattern of imprinting is disrupted, abnormal fetal growth or congenital growth disorders may result (Hitchins & Moore, 2002).

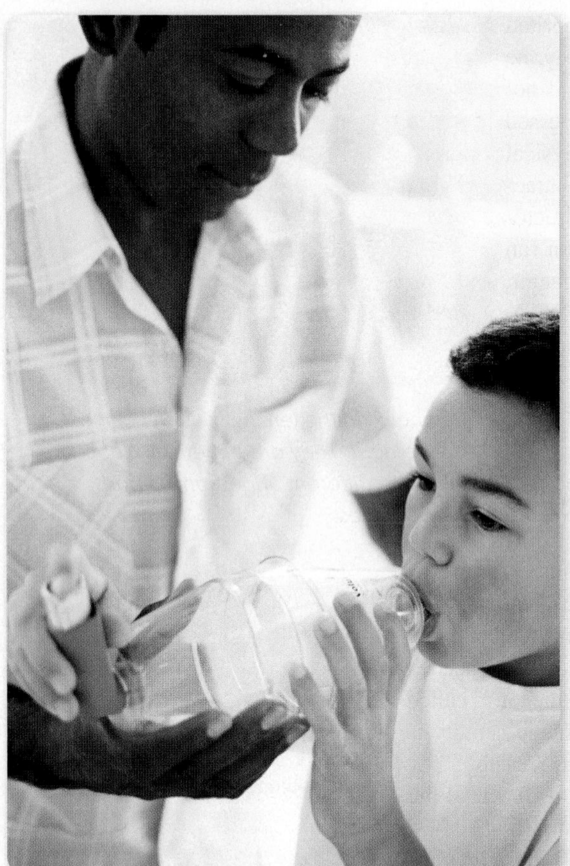

Problems in genome imprinting may explain why a child with an asthmatic mother is more likely to develop asthma than a child with an asthmatic father.

Disturbances in genome imprinting may explain why the child of a diabetic father but not of a diabetic mother is likely to develop diabetes and why the opposite is true for asthma (Day, 1993). Imprinting problems also may explain why children who inherit Huntington's disease from their fathers are far more likely to be affected at an early age than children who inherit it from their mothers (Sapienza, 1990), and why children who receive a certain allele from their mothers are more likely to have autism than those who receive that allele from their fathers (Ingram et al., 2000).

GENETIC AND CHROMOSOMAL ABNORMALITIES

Most birth disorders are fairly rare (Table 1), affecting only about 3 percent of live births (Waknine, 2006). Nevertheless, they are the leading cause of infant death in the United States, accounting for 19.5 percent of all deaths in the first year in 2007 (Xu et al., 2010). The most prevalent defects are cleft lip or cleft palate, followed by Down syndrome. Other serious malformations involve the eye, the face, the mouth, or the circulatory, gastronomical, or musculoskeletal systems (Centers for Disease Control and Prevention [CDC], 2006b).

Not all genetic or chromosomal abnormalities are apparent at birth. Symptoms of Tay-Sachs disease (a fatal degenerative disease of the central nervous system common in Jews of eastern European ancestry) and sickle-cell anemia (a blood disorder most common among African Americans) may not appear until at least age 6 months; cystic fibrosis (a condition, especially common in children of northern European descent, in which excess mucus accumulates in the lungs and digestive tract), not until age 4; and glaucoma (a disease in which fluid pressure builds up in the eye) and Huntington's disease (a progressive degeneration of the nervous system), usually not until middle age.

It is in genetic defects and diseases that we see most clearly the operation of dominant and recessive transmission, and also of a variation, *sex-linked inheritance,* discussed in a subsequent section.

checkpoint can you...

- **Tell how dominant inheritance and recessive inheritance work, and why most normal traits are not the products of simple dominant or recessive transmission?**
- **Explain how epigenesis and genome imprinting occur, and give examples?**

Dominant or Recessive Inheritance of Defects Most of the time, normal genes are dominant over those carrying abnormal traits, but sometimes the gene for an abnormal trait is dominant. When one parent has one dominant abnormal gene and one recessive normal gene and the other parent has two recessive normal genes, each of their children has a 50-50 chance of inheriting the abnormal gene. Among the 1,800 disorders known to be transmitted by dominant inheritance are achondroplasia (a type of dwarfism) and Huntington's disease. Defects transmitted by dominant inheritance are less likely to be lethal at an early age than those transmitted by recessive inheritance because any affected children would be likely to die before reproducing. Therefore, that gene would not be passed on to the next generation and would soon disappear from the population.

Recessive defects are expressed only if the child is homozygous for that gene; in other words, a child must inherit a copy of the recessive gene from each parent. Because recessive genes are not expressed if the parent is heterozygous for that trait, it may not always be apparent that a child is at risk for receiving two alleles of a recessive gene. Defects transmitted by recessive genes tend to be lethal at an earlier age, in contrast to those transmitted by dominant genes, because recessive genes can be transmitted by heterozygous carriers who do not themselves have the disorder. Thus they are able to reproduce and pass the genes down to the next generation.

incomplete dominance
Pattern of inheritance in which a child receives two different alleles, resulting in partial expression of a trait.

In **incomplete dominance,** a trait is not fully expressed. Normally the presence of a dominant/recessive gene pair results in the full expression of the dominant gene and the masking of the recessive gene. In incomplete dominance, the resulting phenotype is a combination of both genes. For example, people with only one sickle-cell allele and one

TABLE 1 Some Birth Defects

Problem	Characteristics of Condition	Who Is at Risk	What Can Be Done
Alpha$_1$ antitrypsin deficiency	Enzyme deficiency that can lead to cirrhosis of the liver in early infancy and emphysema and degenerative lung disease in middle age.	1 in 1,000 white births	No treatment.
Alpha thalassemia	Severe anemia that reduces ability of the blood to carry oxygen; nearly all affected infants are stillborn or die soon after birth.	Primarily families of Malaysian, African, and Southeast Asian descent	Frequent blood transfusions.
Beta thalassemia (Cooley's anemia)	Severe anemia resulting in weakness, fatigue, and frequent illness; usually fatal in adolescence or young adulthood.	Primarily families of Mediterranean descent	Frequent blood transfusions.
Cystic fibrosis	Overproduction of mucus, which collects in the lung and digestive tract; children do not grow normally and usually do not live beyond age 30; the most common inherited *lethal* defect among white people.	1 in 2,000 white births	Daily physical therapy to loosen mucus; antibiotics for lung infections; enzymes to improve digestion; gene therapy (in experimental stage).
Duchenne muscular dystrophy	Fatal disease usually found in males, marked by muscle weakness; minor mental retardation is common; respiratory failure and death usually occur in young adulthood.	1 in 3,000 to 5,000 male births	No treatment.
Hemophilia	Excessive bleeding, usually affecting males; in its most severe form, can lead to crippling arthritis in adulthood.	1 in 10,000 families with a history of hemophilia	Frequent transfusions of blood with clotting factors.
NEURAL-TUBE DEFECTS			
Anencephaly	Absence of brain tissues; infants are stillborn or die soon after birth.	1 in 1,000	No treatment.
Spina bifida	Incompletely closed spinal canal, resulting in muscle weakness or paralysis and loss of bladder and bowel control; often accompanied by hydrocephalus, an accumulation of spinal fluid in the brain, which can lead to mental retardation.	1 in 1,000	Surgery to close spinal canal prevents further injury; shunt placed in brain drains excess fluid and prevents mental retardation.
Phenylketonuria (PKU)	Metabolic disorder resulting in mental retardation.	1 in 15,000 births	Special diet begun in first few weeks of life can prevent mental retardation.
Polycystic kidney disease	*Infantile form:* enlarged kidneys, leading to respiratory problems and congestive heart failure. *Adult form:* kidney pain, kidney stones, and hypertension resulting in chronic kidney failure.	1 in 1,000	Kidney transplants.
Sickle-cell anemia	Deformed, fragile red blood cells that can clog the blood vessels, depriving the body of oxygen; symptoms include severe pain, stunted growth, frequent infections, leg ulcers, gallstones, susceptibility to pneumonia, and stroke.	1 in 500 African Americans	Painkillers, transfusions for anemia and to prevent stroke, antibiotics for infections.
Tay-Sachs disease	Degenerative disease of the brain and nerve cells, resulting in death before age 5.	Historically found mainly in Eastern European Jews	No treatment.

Source: Adapted from AAP Committee on Genetics, 1996; NIH Consensus Development Panel, 2001; Tisdale, 1988, pp. 68–69.

FIGURE 5
Sex-Linked Inheritance

In the most common form, the female sex chromosome of an unaffected mother carries one recessive abnormal gene and one dominant normal one (X). The father has one normal male X and Y chromosome complement.
The odds for each *male* child are 50-50:
1. 50% risk of inheriting the abnormal X and the disorder
2. 50% chance of inheriting normal X and Y chromosomes
The odds for each *female* child are 50-50:
1. 50% chance of inheriting one abnormal X, to be a carrier like mother
2. 50% chance of inheriting no abnormal genes
Carrier mother
Normal father
X X
X Y
X Y
X X
X Y
X X
Normal male
Normal female
Affected male
Carrier female
Possible hereditary results

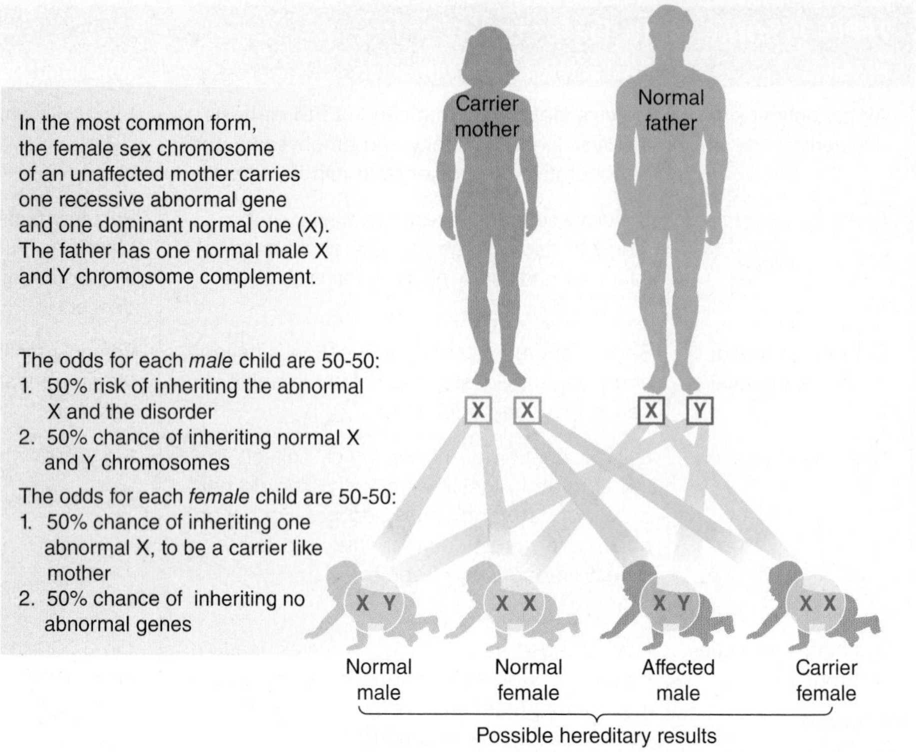

normal allele do not have sickle-cell anemia with its distinctive, abnormally shaped blood cells. Their blood cells are not the typical round shape either. They are an intermediate shape, which shows that the sickle-cell gene for these people is incompletely dominant.

sex-linked inheritance
Pattern of inheritance in which certain characteristics carried on the X chromosome inherited from the mother are transmitted differently to her male and female offspring.

Sex-Linked Inheritance of Defects In **sex-linked inheritance** (Figure 5), certain recessive disorders affect male and female children differently. This is due to the fact that males are XY and females are XX. In humans, the Y chromosome is smaller and carries far fewer genes than the X chromosome. One outcome of this is that males receive only one copy of any gene that happens to be carried on the sex chromosomes, whereas females receive two copies. So, if a woman has a "bad" copy of a particular gene, she has a backup copy. However, if a male has a "bad" copy of a particular gene, that gene will be expressed.

Heterozygote females who carry one "bad" copy of a recessive gene and one "good" one are called carriers. If such a woman has children with an unaffected male (a man who has a "good" copy of the gene), she has a 50 percent chance of passing the disorder on to any sons they might have. If they have a son (who is XY by virtue of being male), the father contributed a Y chromosome, and the mother contributed the X chromosome. Because she has one "good" copy and one "bad" copy, either outcome is equally likely. Daughters (who are XX by virtue of being female) may be protected because the father will pass on his "good" copy to daughters, so the girls have a 50 percent chance either of being completely unaffected or of carrying a hidden recessive copy of the gene.

Children with Turner syndrome are always girls. Because so little information is carried on the Y chromosome, an embryo with only a Y chromosome and no X chromosome is not viable. Alternatively, an embryo with an X chromosome, but no Y, often is.

Sex-linked recessive disorders are more common in males than in females. For example, red-green color blindness, hemophilia (a disorder in which blood does not clot when it should), and Duchenne muscular dystrophy (a disorder that results in muscle degeneration and eventually death) are all more common in males, and all result from genes located on the X chromosome. Occasionally, a female does inherit a sex-linked condition. For this to happen, the father must have a "bad" copy, and the mother must also be a carrier or herself have the condition.

Chromosomal Abnormalities Chromosomal abnormalities typically occur because of errors in cell division, resulting in an extra or missing chromosome. For example, Klinefelter syndrome is caused by an extra female sex chromosome (shown by the pattern XXY). Turner syndrome results from a missing sex chromosome (XO). The

TABLE 2 Sex Chromosome Abnormalities

Pattern/Name	Typical Characteristics*	Incidence	Treatment
XYY	Male; tall stature; tendency toward low IQ, especially verbal.	1 in 1,000 male births	No special treatment.
XXX (triple X)	Female; normal appearance, menstrual irregularities, learning disorders, mental retardation.	1 in 1,000 female births	Special education.
XXY (Klinefelter)	Male; sterility, underdeveloped secondary sex characteristics, small testes, learning disorders.	1 in 1,000 male births	Hormone therapy, special education.
XO (Turner)	Female; short stature, webbed neck, impaired spatial abilities, no menstruation, infertility, underdeveloped sex organs, incomplete development of secondary sex characteristics.	1 in 1,500 to 2,500 female births	Hormone therapy, special education.
Fragile X	Minor-to-severe mental retardation; symptoms, which are more severe in males, include delayed speech and motor development, speech impairments, and hyperactivity; the most common *inherited* form of mental retardation.	1 in 1,200 male births; 1 in 2,000 female births	Educational and behavioral therapies when needed.

*Not every affected person has every characteristic.

likelihood of errors increase in offspring of women age 35 or older. Characteristics of the most common sex chromosome disorders are shown in Table 2.

Down syndrome, the most common chromosomal abnormality, accounts for about 40 percent of all cases of moderate-to-severe mental retardation (Pennington, Moon, Edgin, Stedron, & Nadel, 2003). The condition is also called *trisomy-21* because it is characterized in more than 90 percent of cases by an extra 21st chromosome. The most obvious physical characteristic associated with the disorder is a downward-sloping skin fold at the inner corners of the eyes.

Another common sign of Down syndrome involves the lines that palm readers use to tell your fortune. In children with Down syndrome, there is a single horizontal line across the palm.

Down syndrome
Chromosomal disorder characterized by moderate-to-severe mental retardation and by such physical signs as a downward-sloping skin fold at the inner corners of the eyes. Also called *trisomy-21.*

Approximately 1 in every 700 babies born alive has Down syndrome. Although the risk of having a child with Down syndrome rises with age (Society for Neuroscience, 2008), because of the higher birthrates of younger women, more young mothers have children with Down syndrome (National Institute of Child Health and Development, 2008). Nonetheless, the increased tendency to delay childrearing seems to be resulting in a complementary increase in the number of children born with Down syndrome. Between 1979 and 2003, there has been a 31 percent increase in live births of children with Down syndrome (Shin et al., 2009), presumably because of higher rates of older mothers.

The brains of children with Down syndrome appear nearly normal at birth but shrink in volume by young adulthood, particularly in the hippocampal area and prefrontal cortex, resulting in cognitive dysfunction, and in the cerebellum, leading to problems with motor coordination and balance (Davis, 2008; Pennington et al., 2003). With early intervention, however, the prognosis for these children is brighter than was once thought. Children with Down syndrome, like other children with disabilities, tend to benefit cognitively, socially, and emotionally when placed in regular classrooms rather than in special schools (Davis, 2008) and when provided with regular, intensive therapies designed to help them achieve important skills. As adults, many live in small group homes and support themselves; they tend to do well in structured job situations. More than 70 percent of people with Down syndrome live into their 60s, but they are at elevated risk of early death from various causes, including

Although Down syndrome is a major cause of mental retardation, people with this chromosomal abnormality can live productive lives.

leukemia, cancer, Alzheimer's disease, and cardiovascular disease (Bittles, Bower, Hussain, & Glasson, 2006; Hayes & Batshaw, 1993; Hill et al., 2003).

GENETIC COUNSELING AND TESTING

When Alicia became pregnant after 5 years of marriage, she and her husband, Eduardo, were overjoyed. They turned their study into a nursery and eagerly looked forward to bringing the baby home. But the baby never entered that brightly decorated nursery. He was born dead, a victim of Edwards syndrome, a condition in which a child is born with an extra 18th chromosome and suffers from a variety of birth defects, including abnormalities in the heart, kidneys, gastrointestinal system, and brain. The couple, heartbroken, were afraid to try again. They still wanted a baby but feared that they might not be able to conceive a normal child.

genetic counseling
Clinical service that advises prospective parents of their probable risk of having children with hereditary defects.

Genetic counseling can help prospective parents like Alicia and Eduardo assess their risk of bearing children with genetic or chromosomal defects. People who have already had a child with a genetic defect, who have a family history of hereditary illness, who suffer from conditions known or suspected to be inherited, or who come from ethnic groups at higher-than-average risk of passing on genes for certain diseases can get information about their likelihood of producing affected children.

Geneticists have made great contributions to avoidance of birth defects. For example, genetic testing has virtually eliminated Tay-Sachs disease in the Jewish population. Similarly, screening and counseling of women of childbearing age from Mediterranean countries, where beta thalassemia (refer to Table 1) is common, has brought a decline in births of affected babies and greater knowledge of the risks of being a carrier (Cao, Rosatelli, Monni, & Galanello, 2002).

checkpoint can you . . .

- Explain the operation of dominant inheritance, recessive inheritance, incomplete dominance, sex-linked inheritance, and mutations in transmission of birth defects?
- Tell three ways chromosomal disorders occur?
- Explain the purposes of genetic counseling?

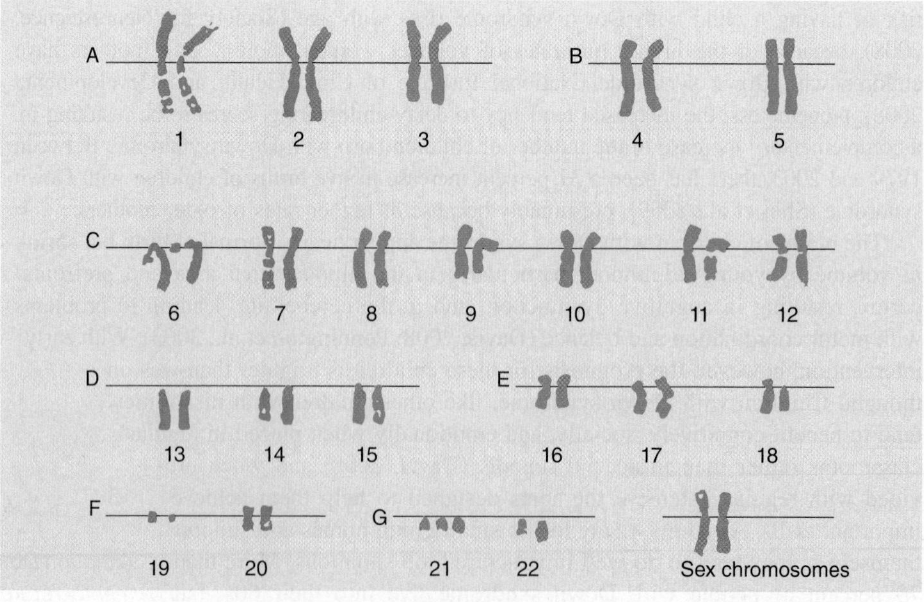

A genetic counselor takes a family history and gives the prospective parents and any biological children physical examinations. Laboratory investigations of blood, skin, urine, or fingerprints may be performed. Chromosomes from body tissues may be analyzed and photographed, and the photographs enlarged and arranged according to size and structure on a chart called a *karyotype*. This chart can show chromosomal abnormalities and can indicate whether a person who appears normal might transmit genetic defects to a child (Figure 6). The counselor tries to help clients understand the mathematical risk of a particular condition, explains its implications, and presents information about alternative courses of action.

FIGURE 6
Karyotype of a Female with Down Syndrome

A karyotype is a photograph that shows the chromosomes when they are separated and aligned for cell division. We know that this is a karyotype of a person with Down syndrome because there are three chromosomes instead of the usual two on pair 21. Because pair 23 consists of two Xs, we know that this is the karyotype of a female.

A 1 2 3 B 4 5
C 6 7 8 9 10 11 12
D 13 14 15 E 16 17 18
F 19 20 G 21 22 Sex chromosomes

Source: Babu & Hirschhorn, 1992; March of Dimes Birth Defects Foundation, 1987.

GENETIC TESTING

Scientists have now completed mapping of the human genome, which is estimated to contain between 20,000 and 25,000 genes (International Human Genome Sequencing Consortium, 2004). The mapping of the human genome has greatly advanced our ability to identify which genes affect specific traits or behaviors. *Genomics,* the scientific study of the functions and interactions of the various genes, has untold implications for *medical genetics,* the application of genetic information to therapeutic purposes (McKusick, 2001; Patenaude, Guttmacher, & Collins, 2002). Scientists are increasingly able to identify genes that cause, trigger, or increase susceptibility to particular disorders. Already, more than 1,000 genetic tests are available from clinical testing laboratories (U.S. Department of Energy Office of Science, 2008a). Genetic screening of newborns is saving lives and preventing mental retardation by permitting early identification and treatment of such disorders as sickle-cell anemia and phenylketonuria (PKU) (Holtzman, Murphy, Watson, & Barr, 1997; Khoury, McCabe, & McCabe, 2003). However, for the most part decoding the genome has not resulted in improvements in health and the development of medical treatments. Given that the causes of disease are almost always complex and interactive, the identification of single mutations has not been as useful as once was hoped.

Additionally, genetic testing involves ethical and political issues related to privacy and fair use of genetic information. Although medical data are supposed to be confidential, some courts have ruled that blood relatives have a legitimate claim to information about a patient's genetic health risks that may affect them, even though such disclosures violate confidentiality (Clayton, 2003).

A major concern, particularly regarding commercial tests aimed at currently healthy people, is *genetic determinism:* the misconception that a person with a gene for a disease is bound to get the disease. All such testing can tell us is the *likelihood* that a person will contract a disease. Most diseases involve a complex combination of genes or depend in part on lifestyle or other environmental factors. Until recently, federal and state laws failed to provide adequate protection, and fear of discrimination and social stigmatization kept many people from having genetic tests recommended by their doctors (Clayton, 2003; Khoury et al., 2003; U.S. Department of Energy Office of Science, 2008a). The federal Genetic Information Nondiscrimination Act , signed in 2008, prohibits discrimination based on genetic testing (Wexler, 2008).

The psychological impact of test results is also troubling. Predictions are imperfect; a false positive result may cause needless anxiety, and a false negative result may lull a person into complacency. A panel of experts has recommended against genetic testing for diseases for which there is no known cure (Institute of Medicine [IOM], 1993). Further concerns, especially with home testing kits being marketed directly to the public, are the possibilities of error and of misinterpretation of test results (U.S. Department of Energy Office of Science, 2008a).

A particularly chilling prospect is that genetic testing could be misused to justify sterilization of people with "undesirable" genes or abortion of a normal fetus with the "wrong" genetic makeup (Plomin & Rutter, 1998). Gene therapy has the potential for similar abuse. Should it be used to make a short child taller or a chubby child thinner? To improve an unborn baby's appearance or intelligence? The path from therapeutic correction of defects to genetic engineering for cosmetic or functional purposes may well be a slippery slope, leading to a society in which some parents could afford to provide the "best" genes for their children and others could not (Rifkin, 1998).

Genetic testing opens the door to *gene therapy,* an experimental technique for repairing or replacing defective genes or regulating the extent to which a gene is turned on or off. Though early gene therapy experiments did not produce good results, more recently gene therapy was used to improve immune function in nine Italian infants and children with severe combined immunodeficiency (SCID). None of these children contracted leukemia, though seven had other serious side effects; and all were alive after 2 to 8 years (Aluti et al., 2009). The success of this research may open the way to the development of safe methods for treatment of a variety of genetic disorders, including hemophilia, muscular dystrophy, and neurodegenerative conditions (Kohn & Candotti, 2009). Gene therapy has been used successfully to treat congenital blindness, advanced melanoma (skin cancer), and myeloid blood disorders (Bainbridge et al., 2008; Morgan et al., 2006; Ott et al., 2006; U.S. Department of Energy Office of Science, 2008b).

Genetic testing has the potential to revolutionize medical practice. It is important to ensure that the benefits outweigh the risks.

Would you want to know that you had a gene predisposing you to lung cancer? To Alzheimer's disease? Would you want your child to be tested for these genes?

Today researchers are rapidly identifying genes that contribute to many serious diseases and disorders, as well as those that influence normal traits. Their work is likely to lead to widespread genetic testing to reveal genetic profiles—a prospect that involves dangers as well as benefits (Box 1).

Nature and Nurture: Influences of Heredity and Environment

The relative importance of heredity and environment was a major issue among early psychologists and the general public. Today it has become clear that, although certain rare physical disorders are virtually 100 percent inherited, phenotypes for most normal traits, such as those having to do with intelligence and personality, are subject to a complex array of hereditary and environmental forces. Let's see how scientists study and explain the influences of heredity and environment and how these two forces work together.

behavioral genetics
Quantitative study of relative hereditary and environmental influences on behavior.

heritability
Statistical estimate of contribution of heredity to individual differences in a specific trait within a given population.

concordant
Term describing tendency of twins to share the same trait or disorder.

STUDYING HEREDITY AND ENVIRONMENT

One approach to the study of heredity and environment is quantitative: it seeks to measure *how much* heredity and environment influence particular traits. This is the traditional goal of the science of **behavioral genetics**.

Measuring Heritability Behavioral geneticists have developed a means of estimating how much of a trait is due to genetics and how much is the result of environmental influences by using a concept known as **heritability.** Every trait is a consequence of genes and environment. By looking at groups of people with known genetic relationships, and assessing whether or not they are **concordant,** meaning *the same,* on a given trait, behavioral geneticists can estimate the relative influence of genes and environment.

Keep in mind that a high heritability estimate does not mean that a trait cannot be influenced by environment. If the environment changes, the heritability estimate may change as well.

For example, we may wish to know what the relative influences of genes and environment are for homosexuality. One way to estimate this is to look at large groups of monozygotic and dizygotic twins and calculate how concordant they are on the trait. In other words, if one twin is homosexual, what are the chances the other twin is as well? Remember that monozygotic twins generally share 100 percent of their genes, whereas dizygotic twins share approximately 50 percent. If genes are implicated in homosexuality, the concordance rates for monozygotic twins should be higher than that of those for dizygotic twins because they share more genes. If genes don't matter, the concordance rate should be the same for both types of twins. By the same token, if the environment exerts a large influence on a trait, people who live together should be more similar on traits than people who do not live together, and those who live apart should be less similar. By comparing concordance rates of family members of known genetic relatedness and in either the same or different environments, we can determine the relative influences of genes versus environment. Twin and adoption studies support a moderate to high hereditary basis for many normal and abnormal characteristics (McGuffin, Riles, & Plomin, 2001).

In what ways are you like your mother and in what ways like your father? How are you similar and dissimilar to your siblings? Which differences would you guess come chiefly from heredity and which from environment? Can you see possible effects of both?

There are multiple variations of this basic approach. For example, immediate family members might be compared to more distant relatives, adopted children might be compared to their biological and adopted parents, or twins adopted by two different families might be compared to twins raised in the same family—but the essential logic is the same. If we know, on average, how many genes people share by virtue of knowing their genetic relationship, and whether or not they are raised together or apart, we can measure how similar they are on traits and work backward to determine the relative environmental influence.

Monozygotic twins separated at birth are sought by researchers who want to study the impact of genes on personality. These twins, adopted by different families and not reunited until age 31, both became firefighters. Was this a coincidence, or did it reflect the influence of heredity?

Heritability is expressed as a percentage ranging from 0.0 to 1.0: the higher the number, the greater the heritability of a trait. A heritability estimate of 1.0 indicates that genes are 100 percent responsible for variances in the trait within the population. A heritability estimate of 0.0 percent would indicate the environment shaped a trait exclusively. Note that heritability does not refer to the influences that shaped any one particular person because those influences are virtually impossible to separate. Nor does heritability tell us how traits develop. It merely indicates the statistical extent to which genes contribute to a trait at a certain time within a given population.

Behavioral geneticists recognize that the effects of genetic influences, especially on behavioral traits, are rarely inevitable: even in a trait strongly influenced by heredity, the environment can have substantial impact (Rutter, 2002). In fact, environmental interventions sometimes can overcome genetically "determined" conditions. For example, a special diet begun soon after birth often can prevent mental retardation in children with the genetic disease phenylketonuria (PKU) (Widaman, 2009; refer to Table 1).

checkpoint can **you** . . .

- **State the basic assumption underlying studies of behavioral genetics and how it applies to family studies, twin studies, and adoption studies?**

HOW HEREDITY AND ENVIRONMENT WORK TOGETHER

Today many developmental scientists have come to regard a solely quantitative approach to the study of heredity and environment as simplistic. They see these two forces as fundamentally intertwined. Instead of looking at genes and experience as operating directly on an organism, they see both as part of a complex *developmental system* (Gottlieb, 1991, 1997; Lickliter & Honeycutt, 2003). From conception on, throughout life, a combination of constitutional factors (related to biological and psychological makeup) and social, economic, and cultural factors help shape development. The more advantageous these circumstances and the experiences to which they give rise, the greater is the likelihood of optimum development.

Let's consider several ways in which inheritance and experience work together.

Reaction Range Many characteristics vary, within limits, under varying hereditary or environmental conditions. The concept of *reaction range* can help us visualize how this happens.

Reaction range refers to a range of potential expressions of a hereditary trait. Body size, for example, depends largely on biological processes, which are genetically regulated. Even so, a range of sizes is possible, depending on environmental opportunities and constraints and a person's behavior. In societies in which nutrition has dramatically improved, an entire generation has grown up to tower over the generation before. The

reaction range
Potential variability, depending on environmental conditions, in the expression of a hereditary trait.

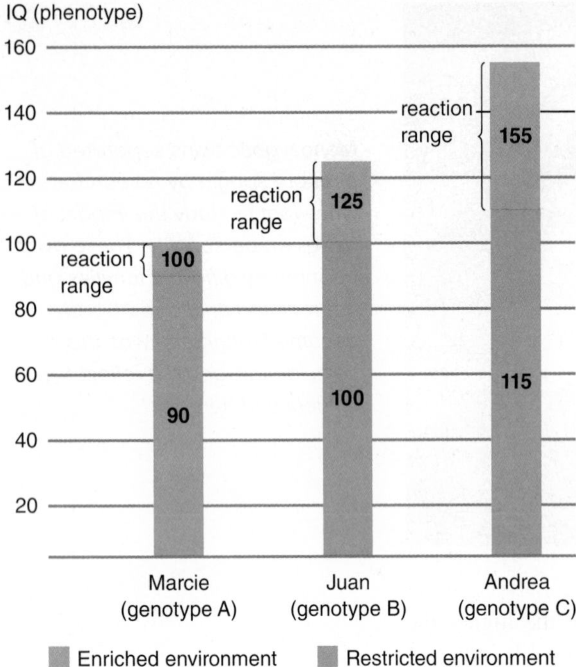

FIGURE 7

Intelligence and Reaction Range

Children with different genotypes for intelligence will show varying reaction ranges when exposed to a restricted (blue portion of bar) or enriched (entire bar) environment.

better-fed children share their parents' genes but have responded to a healthier world. Once a society's average diet becomes adequate for more than one generation, however, children tend to grow to heights similar to their parents'. Ultimately, height has genetic limits; we don't see people who are only 1 foot tall or who are 10 feet tall.

Heredity can influence whether a reaction range is wide or narrow. For example, a child born with a defect producing mild cognitive limitations is more able to respond to a favorable environment than a child born with more severe limitations. Likewise, a child with greater native intelligence is likely to benefit more from an enriched home and school environment than a child with normal intelligence (Figure 7).

Canalization Some traits have an extremely narrow range of reaction. The metaphor of **canalization** illustrates how heredity restricts the range of development for some traits. After a heavy storm, the rainwater that has fallen on a pavement has to go somewhere. If the street has potholes, the water will fill them. If deep canals have been dug along the edges of the street, the water will flow into the canals. Highly canalized traits, such as eye color, are analogous to the deep canals. They are strongly programmed by genes, and there is little opportunity for variance in their expression. Because of the deep, genetically dug channel, it would take an extreme change in environment to alter their course.

canalization
Limitation on variance of expression of certain inherited characteristics.

Behaviors that depend largely on maturation seem to appear when a child is ready. Typical babies follow a predictable sequence of motor development: crawling, walking, and running, in that order, at certain approximate ages. This sequence is said to be canalized, in that children will follow this same blueprint irrespective of many variations in the environment. Many highly canalized traits tend to be those necessary for survival. In the case of very important traits such as these, natural selection has designed them to develop in a predictable and reliable way within a variety of environments and a multitude of influences. They are too important to be left to chance.

Cognition and personality are not highly canalized. They are more subject to variations in experience: the kinds of families children grow up in, the schools they attend, and the people they encounter. Consider reading. Before children can learn to read, they must reach a certain level of cognitive, language, and perceptual skills. No 2-year-old could read this sentence, no matter how enriched the infant's home life might be. Environment plays a large part in reading skills development. Parents who play letter and word games and who read to their children are likely to have children who learn to read earlier than if these skills are not encouraged or reinforced.

In humans, walking and talking are essential to adult functioning. Not surprisingly, these are highly canalized.

Scientists have begun to recognize that a usual or typical *experience,* too, can dig canals, or channels for development (Gottlieb, 1991). For example, infants who hear only the sounds peculiar to their native language soon lose the ability to perceive sounds characteristic of other languages. Throughout this book you will find many examples of how socioeconomic status, neighborhood conditions, and educational opportunity can powerfully shape developmental outcomes, from the pace and complexity of language development to the likelihood of early sexual activity and antisocial behavior.

genotype-environment interaction
The portion of phenotypic variation that results from the reactions of genetically different individuals to similar environmental conditions.

Genotype-Environment Interaction **Genotype-environment interaction** usually refers to the effects of similar environmental conditions on genetically different individuals, and a discussion of these interactions is a way to conceptualize and talk about the different ways nature and nurture interact. To take a familiar example, many children are exposed to pollen and dust, but those with a genetic predisposition are more likely to develop allergic reactions. Interactions can work the other way as well: genetically similar children often develop differently depending on their home environments (Collins et al., 2000). A child born with a difficult temperament may develop adjustment problems in one family and thrive in another, depending largely on parental handling. Thus it is the interaction of hereditary and environmental factors, not just one or the other, that produces certain outcomes.

> *One of the environmental factors that has been identified as protective against severe allergies in children is early exposure to animals.*
>
> Wegienka et al., 2011

study smart

Genotype-Environment Correlations

Genotype-Environment Correlation Because genes influence a person's exposure to particular environments, the environment often reinforces genetic differences (Rutter, 2007). That is, certain genetic and environmental influences tend to act in the same direction. This is called **genotype-environment correlation,** or *genotype-environment covariance,* and it works in three ways to strengthen the phenotypic expression of a genotypic tendency (Bergeman & Plomin, 1989; Scarr, 1992; Scarr & McCartney, 1983). The first two ways are common among younger children, the third among older children, adolescents, and adults.

genotype-environment correlation
Tendency of certain genetic and environmental influences to reinforce each other; may be passive, reactive (evocative), or active. Also called *genotype-environment covariance.*

- *Passive correlations:* Parents, who provide the genes that predispose a child toward a trait, also tend to provide an environment that encourages the development of that trait. For example, a musical parent is likely to create a home environment in which music is heard regularly, to give a child music lessons, and to take the child to musical events. If the child inherited the parent's musical talent, the child's musicality will reflect a combination of genetic and environmental influences. This type of correlation is called *passive* because the child does not control it. The child has inherited the environment, as well as genes that might make that child particularly well-suited to respond to those particular environmental influences. Passive correlations are most applicable to young children, whose parents have a great deal of control over their early experiences. Additionally, passive correlations function only when a child is living with a biologically related parent.
- *Reactive, or evocative, correlations:* Children with differing genetic makeups evoke different reactions from others. For example, parents who are not musically inclined may make a special effort to provide musical experiences for a child who shows interest and ability in music. This response, in turn, strengthens the child's genetic inclination toward music. This type of correlation is called *reactive* because the other people react to the child's genetic makeup.
- *Active correlations:* As children get older and have more freedom to choose their own activities and environments, they *actively* select or create experiences consistent with their genetic tendencies. A shy child is more likely than an outgoing child to spend time in solitary pursuits. An adolescent with a talent for music will probably seek out musical friends, take music classes, and go to concerts if such opportunities are available. This tendency to seek out environments compatible with one's genotype is called **niche-picking;** it helps explain why identical twins reared apart tend to have similar characteristics.

> *The easiest way to remember what passive correlations are is to recall that, when you are living with your biological parents, you are inheriting both genes and environments from them. Sometimes those two complement each other precisely because they came from the same source.*

> *Another way to think of evocative correlations is to remember that children evoke, or pull out, certain responses from others.*

niche-picking
Tendency of a person, especially after early childhood, to seek out environments compatible with his or her genotype.

What Makes Siblings So Different? The Nonshared Environment Although two children in the same family may bear a striking physical resemblance, siblings can differ greatly in intellect and especially in personality (Plomin & Daniels, 2011). One reason may be genetic differences, which lead children to need different kinds of stimulation or to respond differently to a similar home environment. For example, one child may be more affected by family discord than another (Horowitz et al., 2010). In addition, studies in behavioral genetics suggest that many of the experiences that strongly affect

An adolescent with musical abilities may seek out musical friends and might even start up a band. This is an example of niche-picking.

development vary for different children in a family (McGuffin et al., 2001; Plomin & Daniels, 1987; Plomin & DeFries, 1999).

These **nonshared environmental effects** result from the unique environment in which each child in a family grows up. Children in a family have a shared environment—the home they live in, the people in it, and the activities a family jointly engage in—but they also, even if they are twins, have experiences that are not shared by their brothers and sisters. Parents and siblings may treat each child differently. Certain events, such as illnesses and accidents, and experiences outside the home affect one child and not another. For example, if you are the oldest child in a family, one of your early influences was the ability to have your parents' undivided attention. A secondborn or later child is not born into that same environment. Later siblings must share their parents' attention. Therefore, despite being in the same family, the influences are not identical. Indeed, some behavioral geneticists have concluded that although heredity accounts for most of the similarity between siblings, the nonshared environment accounts for most of the difference (McClearn et al., 1997; Plomin, 1996, 2004; Plomin & Daniels, 1987; Plomin & DeFries, 1999; Plomin, Owen, & McGuffin, 1994). However, methodological challenges and additional empirical evidence point to the more moderate conclusion that nonshared environmental effects do not greatly outweigh shared ones; rather, there seems to be a balance between the two (Rutter, 2002).

Genotype-environment correlations may play an important role in the nonshared environment. Children's genetic differences may lead parents and siblings to react to them differently and treat them differently, and genes may influence how children perceive and respond to that treatment and what its outcome will be. Children also mold their environments by the choices they make—what they do and with whom—and their genetic makeup influences these choices. A child who has inherited artistic talent may spend a great deal of time creating "masterpieces" in solitude, whereas a sibling who is athletically inclined spends more time playing ball with others. Thus, not only will the children's abilities (in, say, painting or soccer) develop differently, but their social lives will be different as well. These differences tend to be accentuated as children grow older and have more experiences outside the family (Bouchard, 1994; Plomin, 1996; Plomin et al., 1994; Scarr, 1992).

The old nature-nurture puzzle is far from resolved; we know now that the problem is more complex than previously thought. A variety of research designs can continue to augment and refine our understanding of the forces affecting development.

nonshared environmental effects
The unique environment in which each child grows up, consisting of distinctive influences or influences that affect one child differently than another.

checkpoint can you...

- Explain and give at least one example of reaction range or norm of reaction, canalization, and genotype-environment reaction?
- Differentiate the three types of genotype-environment correlation?
- List three kinds of influences that contribute to nonshared environmental effects?

SOME CHARACTERISTICS INFLUENCED BY HEREDITY AND ENVIRONMENT

Keeping in mind the complexity of unraveling the influences of heredity and environment, let's look at what is known about their roles in producing certain characteristics.

Physical and Physiological Traits Not only do monozygotic twins generally look alike, but they also are more concordant than dizygotic twins in their risk for such medical disorders as high blood pressure, heart disease, stroke, rheumatoid arthritis, peptic ulcers, and epilepsy (Brass, Isaacsohn, Merikangas, & Robinette, 1992; Plomin et al., 1994). Life span, too, seems to be influenced by genes (Hjelmborg et al., 2006).

Obesity is measured by body mass index, or BMI (comparison of weight to height). Until recently, a child who was at or above the 95th percentile for his or her age and sex was said to be overweight. However, new guidelines now define children between the 85th and 95th percentiles as overweight, and those above the 95 percentile as obese (Ogden, Carroll, Curtin, Lamb, & Flegal, 2010). Another criterion, used primarily for adults, is percentage of body fat: 25 percent or more for men and 30 percent or more

obesity
Extreme overweight in relation to age, sex, height, and body type as defined by having a body mass index at or above the 95th percentile.

for women. Obesity is a multifactorial condition; twin studies, adoption studies, and other research suggest that 40 to 70 percent of the risk is genetic, but environmental influences also contribute to it (Chen et al., 2004). More than 430 genes or chromosome regions are associated with obesity (Nirmala, Reddy, & Reddy, 2008; Snyder et al., 2004).

Although generally the genetic influences for obesity are presumed to work together with environmental influences such as diet and exercise, there may be people with certain genetic profiles that make the attainment and maintenance of a healthy body more challenging. For example, a recent study suggests that a small subset of obese people suffer from a deletion of approximately 30 genes and that all of the people with this deletion are obese (Bochukova et al., 2009).

The risk of obesity is 2 to 3 times higher for a child with a family history of obesity, especially severe obesity (Nirmala et al., 2008). However, this increased risk is not solely genetic. The kind and amount of food eaten in a particular home or in a particular social or ethnic group and the amount of exercise that is encouraged can increase or decrease the likelihood that a child will become overweight. The rise in the prevalence of obesity in Western countries seems to result from the interaction of a genetic predisposition with overeating, supersized portions, and inadequate exercise (Arner, 2000).

In March 2013, New York City planned to institute a ban on large sodas and sugary drinks to combat obesity. A New York state judge struck the ruling down, arguing that the board of health had overstepped its authority. Advocates of the ban argue such steps are needed to curb obesity; opponents argue people should be allowed to buy what they like. What's more important—public health or individual liberties?

Intelligence Heredity exerts a strong influence on general intelligence (as measured by intelligence tests) and, to a lesser extent, on specific abilities such as memory, verbal ability, and spatial ability. Intelligence is a polygenic trait; it is influenced by the additive effects of large numbers of genes working together. Intelligence also depends in part on brain size and structure, which are under strong genetic influence (Toga & Thompson, 2005). Experience counts too; as Figure 7 shows, an enriched or impoverished environment can substantially affect the development and expression of innate ability (Neisser et al., 1996). Environmental influence is greater, and heritability lower, among poor families than among more economically privileged families. Parents' educational levels have a similar effect (Posthuma & de Geus, 2006; Toga & Thompson, 2005).

Indirect evidence of the role of heredity in intelligence comes from adoption and twin studies. Adopted children's IQs are consistently closer to the IQs of their biological mothers than to those of their adoptive parents and siblings, and monozygotic twins are more alike in intelligence than dizygotic twins (Petrill et al., 2004; Plomin & DeFries, 1999).

The genetic influence, which is primarily responsible for stability in cognitive performance, increases with age. This increase probably is a result of niche-picking. The shared family environment seems to have a dominant influence on young children but almost no influence on adolescents, who are more apt to find their own niche by actively selecting environments compatible with their hereditary abilities and related interests. The *non*shared environment, in contrast, is influential throughout life and is primarily responsible for changes in cognitive performance (Bouchard, 2004; Petrill et al., 2004; Toga & Thompson, 2005).

Personality and Psychopathology Scientists have identified genes directly linked with specific aspects of personality such as a trait called neuroticism, which may contribute to depression and anxiety (Lesch et al., 1996). Heritability of personality traits appears to be between 40 and 50 percent, and there is little evidence of shared environmental influence (Bouchard, 2004).

Temperament, an aspect of personality, is a person's characteristic way of approaching and reacting to situations. It appears to be largely inborn and is often consistent over the years, though it may respond to special experiences or parental handling (A. Thomas & Chess, 1984; A. Thomas, Chess, & Birch, 1968). Siblings—both twins and nontwins—tend to be similar in temperament. An

Another trait influenced by genetics is religiosity. Behavioral genetics research suggests that the tendency to believe strongly in a religion is moderately heritable; that is, at about the same level as intelligence.

Waller et al., 1990

temperament
Characteristic disposition, or style of approaching and reacting to situations.

This shy 3-year-old boy may "just be in a phase," or his shyness may be an inborn aspect of his temperament.

observational study of 7-year-old siblings (50 pairs of adoptive siblings and 50 pairs of siblings by birth) found significant genetic influences on the temperamental characteristics of activity, sociability, and emotionality (Schmitz, Saudino, Plomin, Fulker, & DeFries, 1996). An observational study of 294 twin pairs (about half monozygotic and half dizygotic) found significant genetic influences on behavior regulation (Gagne & Saudino, 2010).

There is evidence for a strong hereditary influence on such mental disorders as schizophrenia, autism, alcoholism, and depression. All tend to run in families and to show greater concordance between monozygotic twins than between dizygotic twins. However, heredity alone does not produce such disorders; an inherited tendency can be triggered by environmental factors.

schizophrenia
Mental disorder marked by loss of contact with reality; symptoms include hallucinations and delusions.

Schizophrenia is a neurological disorder that affects about 1 percent of the U.S. population each year (Society for Neuroscience, 2008); it is characterized by loss of contact with reality; hallucinations and delusions; loss of coherent, logical thought; and inappropriate emotionality. Estimates of heritability are as high as 85 percent (McGuffin, Owen, & Farmer, 1995; Picker, 2005). However, monozygotic twins are not always concordant for schizophrenia, perhaps due to epigenesis (Fraga et al., 2005; H. Wong et al., 2005).

A wide array of rare gene mutations, some of which involve missing or duplicated segments of DNA, may increase susceptibility to schizophrenia (P.-L. Chen et al., 2009; Vrijenhoek et al., 2008; Walsh et al., 2008). Researchers also have looked at possible nongenetic influences, such as a series of neurological insults in fetal life (Picker, 2005; Rapoport, Addington, & Frangou, 2005); exposure to influenza or the mother's loss of a close relative in the first trimester of pregnancy (Brown, Begg, et al., 2004; Khashan et al., 2008); or maternal rubella or respiratory infections in the second and third trimesters. Infants born in urban areas or in late winter or early spring appear to be at increased risk, as are those whose mothers experienced obstetric complications or who were poor or severely deprived as a result of war or famine (Picker, 2005). Studies in the Netherlands, Finland, and China have found a link between fetal malnutrition and schizophrenia (St. Clair et al., 2005; Susser & Lin, 1992; Wahlbeck, Forsen, Osmond, Barker, & Eriksson, 2001). Advanced paternal age is a risk factor for schizophrenia. In several large population-based studies, the risk of the disorder was heightened when the father was age 30 or older (Byrne, Agerbo, Ewald, Eaton, & Mortenson, 2003; Malaspina et al., 2001; Sipos et al., 2004). (Autism, depression, and alcoholism are discussed later in this book.)

checkpoint
can you . . .

- Assess the evidence for genetic and environmental influences on physical and physiological traits, intelligence, temperament, and schizophrenia?

Prenatal Development

For many women, the first clear (though not necessarily reliable) sign of pregnancy is a missed menstrual period. But even before that first missed period, a pregnant woman's body undergoes subtle but noticeable changes. Table 3 lists early signs and symptoms of pregnancy. Although these signs are not unique to pregnancy, a woman who experiences one or more of them may wish to take a home pregnancy test or to seek medical confirmation that she is pregnant.

Pregnancy tests identify the presence of human chorionic gonadotropin, which, under normal circumstances, is only produced by embroyos and fetuses. So there are no false positives. A pregnancy might not be viable, but a positive pregnancy test tells a women a conception has occurred.

gestation
Period of development between conception and birth.

gestational age
Age of an unborn baby, usually dated from the first day of an expectant mother's last menstrual cycle.

During **gestation,** the period between conception and birth, an unborn child undergoes dramatic processes of development. The normal range of gestation is between 37 and 41 weeks (Martin, Hamilton, et al., 2009). **Gestational age** is usually dated from the first day of an expectant mother's last menstrual cycle.

In this section we trace the course of gestation, or prenatal development,

TABLE 3 Early Signs and Symptoms of Pregnancy

Physical Change	Causes and Timing
Tender, swollen breasts or nipples	Increased production of the female hormones estrogen and progesterone stimulates breast growth to prepare for producing milk (most noticeable in a first pregnancy).
Fatigue; need to take extra naps	Woman's heart is pumping harder and faster to produce extra blood to carry nutrients to the fetus. Stepped-up production of hormones takes extra effort. Progesterone depresses central nervous system and may cause sleepiness. Concerns about pregnancy may sap energy.
Slight bleeding or cramping	*Implantation bleeding* may occur about 10 to 14 days after fertilization when fertilized ovum attaches to lining of uterus. Many women also have cramps (similar to menstrual cramps) as the uterus begins to enlarge.
Food cravings	Hormonal changes may alter food preferences, especially during first trimester, when hormones have greatest impact.
Nausea with or without vomiting	Rising levels of estrogen produced by placenta and fetus cause stomach to empty more slowly. Also, heightened sense of smell may trigger nausea in response to certain odors, such as coffee, meat, dairy products, or spicy foods. *Morning sickness* may begin as early as 2 weeks after conception, but usually around 4 to 8 weeks, and may occur at any time of day.
Frequent urination	Enlarging uterus during first trimester exerts pressure on the bladder.
Frequent, mild headaches	Increased blood circulation caused by hormonal changes may bring these on.
Constipation	Increase in progesterone may slow digestion, so food passes more slowly through intestinal tract.
Mood swings	Flood of hormones early in pregnancy can produce emotional highs and lows.
Faintness and dizziness	Lightheaded feeling may be triggered by blood vessel dilation and low blood pressure or by low blood sugar.
Raised basal body temperature	Basal body temperature (taken first thing in the morning) normally rises soon after ovulation each month and then drops during menstruation. When menstruation ceases, temperature remains elevated.

Source: Mayo Clinic, 2005.

and discuss environmental factors that can affect the developing person-to-be. In the next section, we assess techniques for determining whether development is proceeding normally and explain the importance of prenatal care.

STAGES OF PRENATAL DEVELOPMENT

Prenatal development takes place in three stages: *germinal, embryonic,* and *fetal.* (Table 4 gives a month-by-month description.) During these three stages of gestation, the original single-celled zygote grows into an *embryo* and then a *fetus.*

Stages of Prenatal Development

Both before and after birth, development proceeds according to two fundamental principles: growth and motor development occur from the top down and from the center of the body outward. The embryo's head and trunk develop before the limbs, and the arms and legs before the fingers and toes.

Germinal Stage (Fertilization to 2 Weeks) During the **germinal stage,** from fertilization to about 2 weeks of gestational age, the zygote divides, becomes more complex, and is implanted in the wall of the uterus.

germinal stage
First 2 weeks of prenatal development, characterized by rapid cell division, blastocyst formation, and implantation in the wall of the uterus.

Within 36 hours after fertilization, the zygote enters a period of rapid cell division and duplication (mitosis). Seventy-two hours after fertilization, it has divided first into 16 and then into 32 cells; a day later it has 64 cells. While the fertilized ovum is dividing, it is also making its way through the fallopian tube to the uterus, a journey of 3 or 4 days. Its form changes into a *blastocyst,* a fluid-filled sphere, which floats freely in the uterus until the sixth day after fertilization, when it begins to implant itself in the uterine wall. Only about 10 to 20 percent of fertilized ova complete the task of **implantation** and continue to develop. Where the egg implants will determine the placement of the placenta.

implantation
The attachment of the blastocyst to the uterine wall, occurring at about day 6.

TABLE 4 Prenatal Development

Month	Description
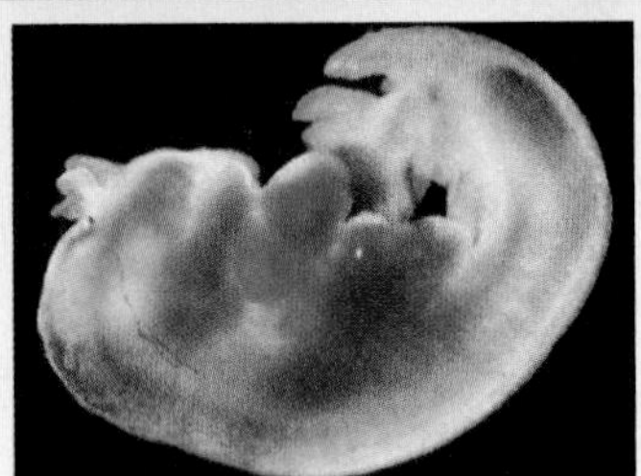 *1 month*	During the first month, growth is more rapid than at any other time during prenatal or postnatal life; the embryo reaches a size 10,000 times greater than the zygote. By the end of the first month, it measures about ½ inch in length. Blood flows through its veins and arteries, which are very small. It has a minuscule heart, beating 65 times a minute. It already has the beginning of a brain, kidneys, liver, and digestive tract. The umbilical cord, its lifeline to the mother, is working. By looking very closely through a microscope, it is possible to see the swellings on the head that will eventually become eyes, ears, mouth, and nose. Its sex cannot yet be detected.
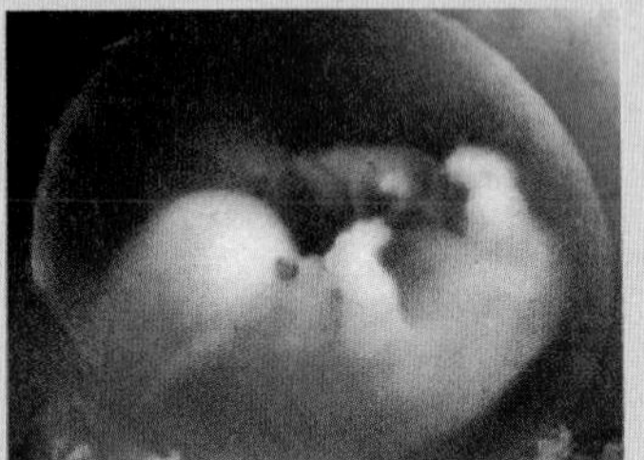 *7 weeks*	By the end of the second month, the embryo becomes a fetus. It is less than 1 inch long and weighs only ⅓ ounce. Its head is half its total body length. Facial parts are clearly developed, with tongue and teeth buds. The arms have hands, fingers, and thumbs, and the legs have knees, ankles, feet, and toes. The fetus has a thin covering of skin and can make handprints and footprints. Bone cells appear at about 8 weeks. Brain impulses coordinate the function of the organ system. Sex organs are developing; the heartbeat is steady. The stomach produces digestive juices; the liver, blood cells. The kidneys remove uric acid from the blood. The skin is now sensitive enough to react to tactile stimulation.
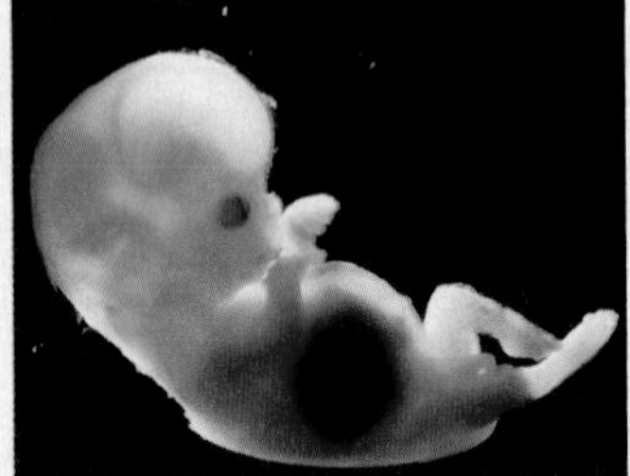 *3 months*	By the end of the third month, the fetus weighs about 1 ounce and measures about 3 inches in length. It has fingernails, toenails, eyelids (still closed), vocal cords, lips, and a prominent nose. Its head is still large—about one-third its total length—and its forehead is high. Sex can easily be detected. The organ systems are functioning, and so the fetus may now breathe, swallow amniotic fluid into the lungs and expel it, and occasionally urinate. Its ribs and vertebrae have turned into cartilage. The fetus can now make a variety of specialized responses: it can move its legs, feet, thumbs, and head; its mouth can open and close and swallow. If its eyelids are touched, it squints; if its palm is touched, it makes a partial fist; if its lip is touched, it will suck; and if the sole of the foot is stroked, the toes will fan out. These reflexes will be present at birth but will disappear during the first months of life.
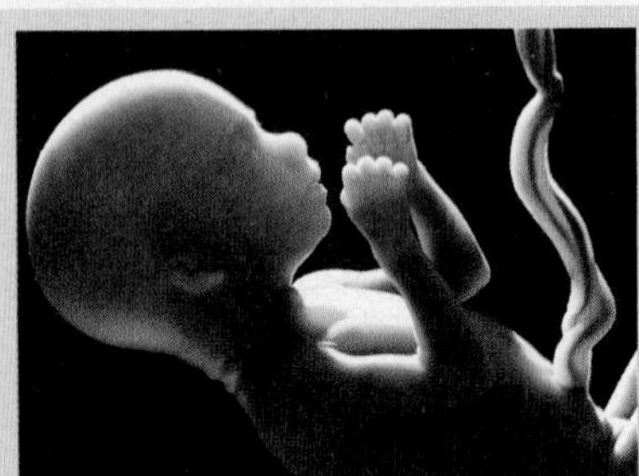 *4 months*	The body is catching up to the head, which is now only one-fourth the total body length, the same proportion it will be at birth. The fetus now measures 8 to 10 inches and weighs about 6 ounces. The umbilical cord is as long as the fetus and will continue to grow with it. The placenta is now fully developed. The mother may be able to feel the fetus kicking, a movement known as *quickening,* which some societies and religious groups consider the beginning of human life. The reflex activities that appeared in the third month are now brisker because of increased muscular development.
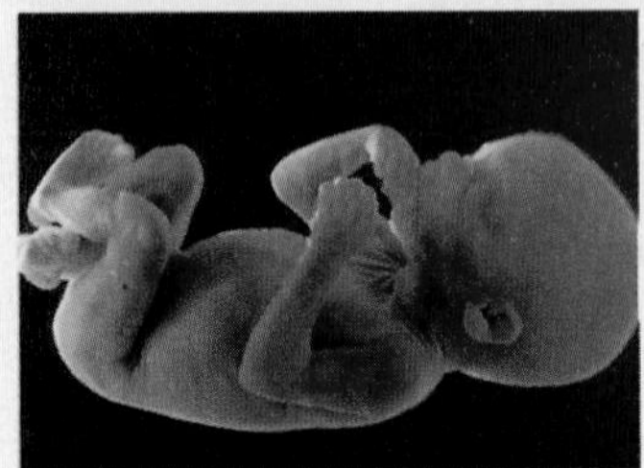 *5 months*	The fetus, now weighing about 12 ounces to 1 pound and measuring about 1 foot, begins to show signs of an individual personality. It has definite sleep-wake patterns, has a favorite position in the uterus (called its *lie*), and becomes more active—kicking, stretching, squirming, and even hiccuping. By putting an ear to the mother's abdomen, it is possible to hear the fetal heartbeat. The sweat and sebaceous glands are functioning. The respiratory system is not yet adequate to sustain life outside the womb; a baby born at this time does not usually survive. Coarse hair has begun to grow for eyebrows and eyelashes, fine hair is on the head, and a woolly hair called *lanugo* covers the body.

TABLE 4 Prenatal Development

Month	Description
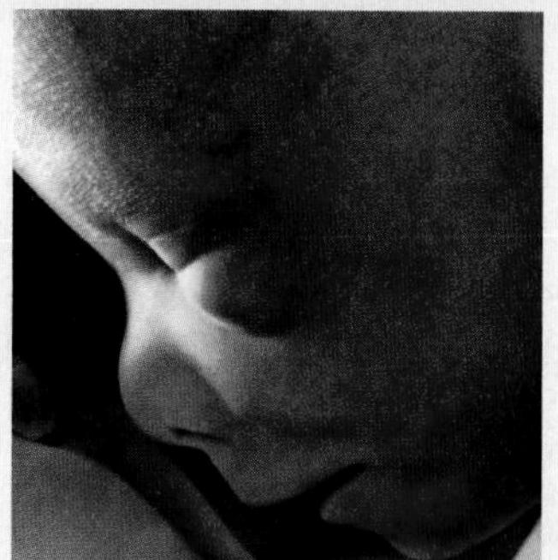 6 months	The rate of fetal growth has slowed a little—by the end of the sixth month, the fetus is about 14 inches long and weighs 1¼ pounds. It has fat pads under the skin; the eyes are complete, opening, closing, and looking in all directions. It can hear, and it can make a fist with a strong grip. A fetus born early in the sixth month has only a slight chance of survival because the breathing apparatus has not matured. However, medical advances have made survival increasingly likely.
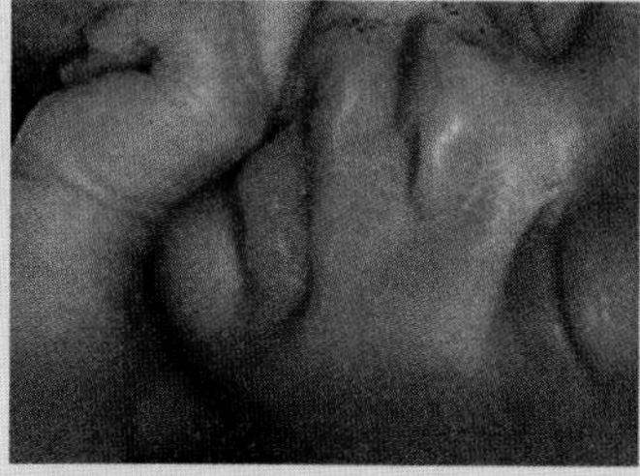 7 months	By the end of the seventh month, the fetus, about 16 inches long and weighing 3 to 5 pounds, now has fully developed reflex patterns. It cries, breathes, and swallows, and it may suck its thumb. The lanugo may disappear at about this time, or it may remain until shortly after birth. Head hair may continue to grow. The chances that a fetus weighing at least 3½ pounds will survive are fairly good, provided it receives intensive medical attention. It will probably need to be kept in an isolette until a weight of 5 pounds is attained.
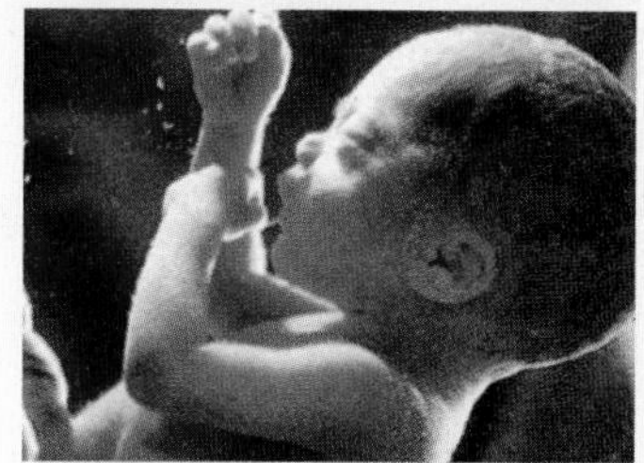 8 months	The 8-month-old fetus is 18 to 20 inches long and weighs between 5 and 7 pounds. Its living quarters are becoming cramped, and so its movements are curtailed. During this month and the next, a layer of fat is developing over the fetus's entire body, which will enable it to adjust to varying temperatures outside the womb.
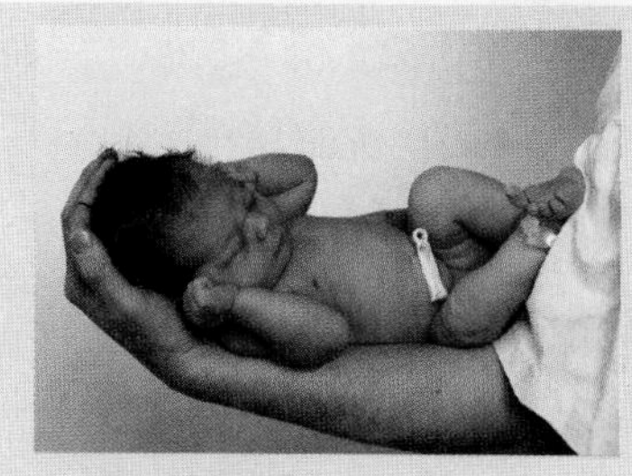 9 months–newborn	About a week before birth, the fetus stops growing, having reached an average weight of about 7½ pounds and a length of about 20 inches, with boys tending to be a little longer and heavier than girls. Fat pads continue to form, the organ systems are operating more efficiently, the heart rate increases, and more wastes are expelled through the umbilical cord. The reddish color of the skin is fading. At birth, the fetus will have been in the womb for about 266 days, though gestational age is usually estimated at 280 days because most doctors date the pregnancy from the mother's last menstrual period.

Note: Even in these early stages, individuals differ. The figures and descriptions given here represent averages.

Before implantation, as cell differentiation begins, some cells around the edge of the blastocyst cluster on one side to form the *embryonic disk,* a thickened cell mass from which the embryo begins to develop. This mass will differentiate into three layers. The *ectoderm,* the upper layer, will become the outer layer of skin, the nails, hair, teeth, sensory organs, and the nervous system, including the brain and spinal cord. The *endoderm,* the inner layer, will become the digestive system, liver, pancreas, salivary glands, and respiratory system. The *mesoderm,* the middle layer, will develop and differentiate into the inner layer of skin, muscles, skeleton, and excretory and circulatory systems.

Other parts of the blastocyst begin to develop into organs that will nurture and protect development in the womb: the *amniotic cavity,* or *amniotic sac,* with its outer layers, the *amnion* and *chorion;* the *placenta;* and the *umbilical cord.* The *amniotic sac* is a fluid-filled membrane that encases the developing embryo, protecting it and giving it room to move and grow. The *placenta* allows oxygen, nourishment, and wastes to pass between mother and embryo. It is connected to the embryo by the *umbilical cord.* Nutrients from the mother pass from her blood to the embryonic blood vessels, which carry them, via the umbilical cord, to the embryo. In turn, embryonic blood vessels in the umbilical cord carry embryonic wastes to the placenta, where they can be eliminated by maternal blood vessels. The mother's and embryo's circulatory systems are not directly linked; instead, this exchange occurs by diffusion across the blood vessel walls. The placenta also helps to combat internal infection and gives the unborn child immunity to various diseases. It produces the hormones that support pregnancy, prepare the mother's breasts for lactation, and eventually stimulate the uterine contractions that will expel the baby from the mother's body.

embryonic stage
Second stage of gestation (2 to 8 weeks), characterized by rapid growth and development of major body systems and organs.

spontaneous abortion
Natural expulsion from the uterus of an embryo that cannot survive outside the womb; also called *miscarriage.*

Embryonic Stage (2 to 8 Weeks) During the **embryonic stage,** from about 2 to 8 weeks, the organs and major body systems—respiratory, digestive, and nervous—develop rapidly. This process is known as *organogenesis.* This is a critical period, when the embryo is most vulnerable to destructive influences in the prenatal environment (Figure 8). Any organ system or structure that is still developing at the time of exposure is most likely to be affected. Because of this, defects that occur later in pregnancy are likely to be less serious as the major organ systems and physical structures of the body are complete. Brain growth and development begins during the embryonic stage and continues after birth and beyond.

The most severely defective embryos usually do not survive beyond the first *trimester,* or 3-month period, of pregnancy. A **spontaneous abortion,** commonly called a

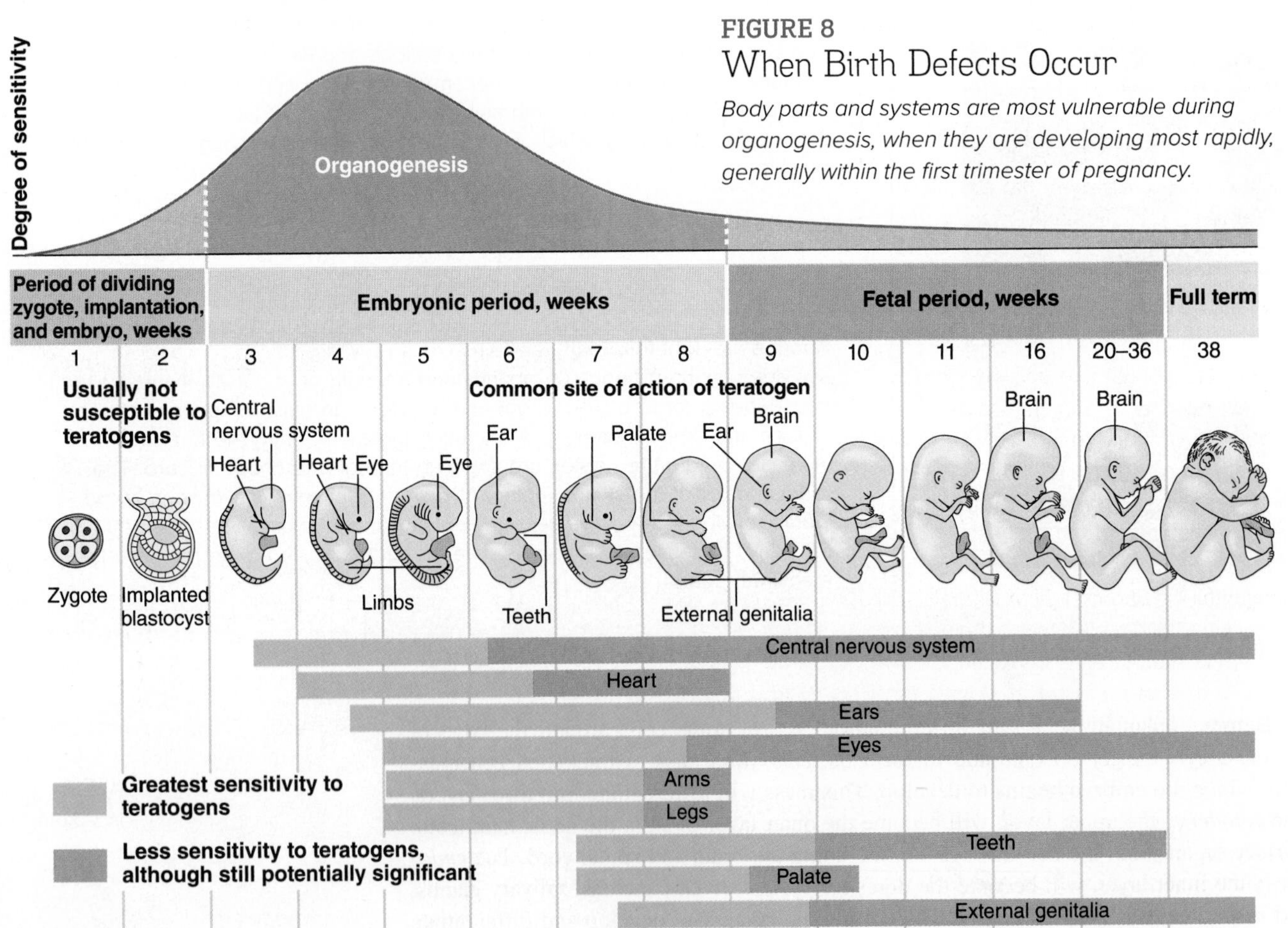

FIGURE 8
When Birth Defects Occur
Body parts and systems are most vulnerable during organogenesis, when they are developing most rapidly, generally within the first trimester of pregnancy.

miscarriage, is the expulsion from the uterus of an embryo or fetus that is unable to survive outside the womb. A miscarriage that occurs after 20 weeks of gestation is generally characterized as a stillbirth. As many as 1 in 4 recognized pregnancies end in miscarriage, and the actual figure may be as high as 1 in 2 because many spontaneous abortions take place before the woman realizes she is pregnant. Estimates are that this results in approximately 1 million fetal deaths each year in the United States alone (MacDorman & Kirmeyer, 2009). About 3 out of 4 miscarriages occur during the first trimester (Neville, n.d.). Most miscarriages result from abnormal pregnancies; about 50 to 70 percent involve chromosomal abnormalities (Hogge, 2003). Smoking, drinking alcohol, and drug use increase the risks of miscarriage (American College of Obstetricians and Gynecologists, 2002). Miscarriages are more common in African American, Native American, and Alaskan native women, in both young and older (greater than 35 years of age) mothers, and more likely to occur in pregnancies involving twins or higher order multiples (MacDorman & Kirmeyer, 2009).

Males are more likely than females to be spontaneously aborted or to be *stillborn* (dead at or after the 20th week of gestation). Thus, although about 125 males are conceived for every 100 females—a fact that has been attributed to the greater mobility of sperm carrying the smaller Y chromosome—only about 105 boys are born for every 100 girls. Males' greater vulnerability continues after birth: more die early in life, and at every age they are more susceptible to many disorders. As a result, there are only about 96 males for every 100 females in the United States (Martin, Hamilton, et al., 2009; Spraggins, 2003).

checkpoint can **you** . . .

- **Describe how a zygote becomes and embryo, and explain why defects and miscarriages most often occur during the embryonic stage?**

Fetal Stage (8 Weeks to Birth) The appearance of the first bone cells at about 8 weeks signals the beginning of the **fetal stage,** the final stage of gestation. During this period, the fetus grows rapidly to about 20 times its previous length, and organs and body systems become more complex. Right up to birth, "finishing touches" such as fingernails, toenails, and eyelids continue to develop.

fetal stage
Final stage of gestation (from 8 weeks to birth), characterized by increased differentiation of body parts and greatly enlarged body size.

ultrasound
Prenatal medical procedure using high-frequency sound waves to detect the outline of a fetus and its movements, so as to determine whether a pregnancy is progressing normally.

Fetuses are not passive passengers in their mothers' wombs. They breathe, kick, turn, flex their bodies, do somersaults, squint, swallow, make fists, hiccup, and suck their thumbs. The flexible membranes of the uterine walls and amniotic sac, which surround the protective buffer of amniotic fluid, permit and stimulate limited movement. Fetuses also can feel pain, but it is highly unlikely that they do so before the third trimester (Lee et al., 2005).

Scientists can observe fetal movement through **ultrasound,** the use of high-frequency sound waves to detect the outline of the fetus. Other instruments can monitor heart rate, changes in activity level, states of sleep and wakefulness, and cardiac reactivity.

The movements and activity level of fetuses show marked individual differences, and their heart rates vary in regularity and speed. Male fetuses, regardless of size, are more active and tend to move more vigorously than female fetuses throughout gestation (Almli, Ball, & Wheeler, 2001). Thus infant boys' tendency to be more active than girls may be at least partly inborn (DiPietro, Hodgson, Costigan, Hilton, & Johnson, 1996; DiPietro et al., 2002).

Obesity can affect the quality of an ultrasound. Normally, the sound waves bounce off the fetus floating in the amnion, a process that is disrupted in the presence of high levels of abdominal body fat.

Beginning at about the 12th week of gestation, the fetus swallows and inhales some of the amniotic fluid in which it floats. The amniotic fluid contains substances that cross the placenta from the mother's bloodstream and enter the fetus's bloodstream. Partaking of these substances may stimulate the budding senses of taste and smell and may contribute to the development of organs needed for breathing and digestion (Mennella & Beauchamp, 1996; Smotherman & Robinson, 1996). Mature taste cells appear at about 14 weeks of gestation. The olfactory system, which controls the sense of smell, also is well developed before birth (Bartoshuk & Beauchamp, 1994; Mennella & Beauchamp, 1996; Savage, Fisher, & Birch, 2007).

In one study, babies recognized the Dr. Suess book read to them by their mother daily during the last trimester of pregnancy, even when the book was read by a different person.

DeCasper & Spence, 1986

Fetuses respond to the mother's voice and heartbeat and the vibrations of her body, suggesting that they can hear and feel. Hungry infants, no matter on which side they are held, turn toward the breast in the direction from which they hear the mother's voice (Noirot & Algeria, 1983, cited in Rovee-Collier, 1996). Thus familiarity with the mother's voice may have an evolutionary survival function: to help newborns locate the source of food. Responses to sound and vibration seem to begin at 26 weeks of gestation, increase, and

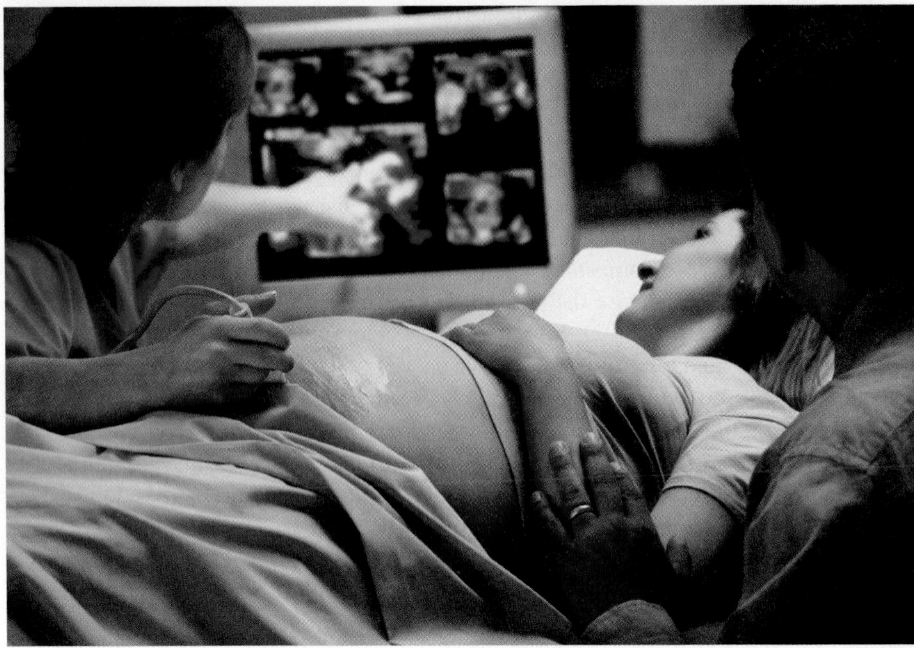

Ultrasound, the procedure this woman is undergoing, is a diagnostic tool that presents an immediate image of the fetus in the womb. High-frequency sound waves directed at the woman's abdomen reveal the fetus's outline and movements. Ultrasound is widely used to monitor fetal development and to detect abnormalities.

then reach a plateau at about 32 weeks (Kisilevsky & Haines, 2010; Kisilevsky, Muir, & Low, 1992). In addition, fetuses nearing full term show the basic ability to recognize the voice of their mother and of their native language (Kisilevsky et al., 2009).

Fetuses seem to learn and remember. In one experiment, 3-day-old infants sucked more on a nipple that activated a recording of a story their mother had frequently read aloud during the last 6 weeks of pregnancy than they did on nipples that activated recordings of two other stories. Apparently, the infants recognized the pattern of sound they had heard in the womb. A control group, whose mothers had not recited a story before birth, responded equally to all three recordings (DeCasper & Spence, 1986). Similar experiments have found that newborns age 2 to 4 days prefer musical and speech sequences heard before birth. They also prefer their mother's voice to those of other women, female voices to male voices, and their mother's native language to another language (DeCasper & Spence, 1986; Fifer & Moon, 1995; Kisilevsky et al., 2003; Lecanuet, Granier-Deferre, & Busnel, 1995). Moreover, they not only remember and recognize voices, they also have some limited ability to reproduce them. In one study, newborn infants used distinctly different intonation patterns in their cries that mirrored aspects of their mothers' native language (Mampe, Friederici, Christophe, & Wermke, 2009).

study smart

Prenatal

How do we know that these preferences develop before rather than after birth? When 60 fetuses heard a female voice reading, their heart rate increased if the voice was their mothers' and decreased if it was a stranger's (Kisilevsky et al., 2003). In another study, newborns were given the choice of sucking to turn on a recording of the mother's voice or a filtered version of her voice as it might sound in the womb. The newborns sucked more often to turn on the filtered version, suggesting that fetuses develop a preference for the kinds of sounds they hear before birth (Fifer & Moon, 1995; Moon & Fifer, 1990). Current estimates suggest that fetal memory begins to function at approximately 30 weeks gestational age, when fetuses are able to hold information in memory for 10 minutes. By 34 weeks, they are able to remember information for a period of 1 month (Dirix et al., 2009).

checkpoint can you...

- **List several changes that occur during the fetal stage?**
- **Discuss findings about fetal activity, sensory development, and memory?**

ENVIRONMENTAL INFLUENCES: MATERNAL FACTORS

Because the prenatal environment is the mother's body, virtually everything that influences her well-being, from her diet to her moods, may alter her unborn child's environment and affect its growth.

A **teratogen** is an environmental agent, such as a virus, a drug, or radiation, that can interfere with normal prenatal development. However, not all environmental hazards are equally risky for all fetuses. An event, substance, or process may be teratogenic for some fetuses but have little or no effect on others. Sometimes vulnerability may depend on a gene either in the fetus or in the mother. For example, fetuses with a particular variant of a growth gene, called *transforming growth factor alpha,* have greater risk than other fetuses of developing a cleft palate if the mother smokes while pregnant (Zeiger, Beaty, & Liang, 2005). The timing of exposure, dose, duration, and interaction with other teratogenic factors also may make a difference.

teratogen
Environmental agent, such as a virus, a drug, or radiation, that can interfere with normal prenatal development and cause developmental abnormalities.

Nutrition and Maternal Weight Pregnant women typically need 300 to 500 additional calories a day, including extra protein. Women of normal weight and body build who gain 16 to 40 pounds are less likely to have birth complications or to bear babies whose weight at birth is dangerously low or overly high. Yet about one-third of U.S. mothers gain more or less than the recommended amount (Martin et al., 2009). Either too much or too little weight gain can be risky. If a woman does not gain enough, her baby may suffer growth retardation in the womb, be born prematurely, experience distress during labor and delivery, or die at or near birth. Some research has shown that maternal calorie restriction during pregnancy might put children at risk for later obesity, perhaps by setting their metabolism to be thrifty (Caballero, 2006). A woman who gains too much weight risks having a large baby that needs to be delivered by induced labor or cesarean section (Chu et al., 2008; Martin, Hamilton, et al., 2009).

Desirable weight gain depends on body mass index (BMI) before pregnancy. Women who are overweight or obese before becoming pregnant or in the early months of pregnancy tend to have longer deliveries, to need more health care services (Chu et al., 2008), and to bear infants with birth defects (Gilboa et al., 2009; Stothard, Tennant, Bell, & Rankin, 2009). Obesity also increases the risk of other complications of pregnancy, including miscarriage, difficulty inducing labor, and a greater likelihood of cesarean delivery (Brousseau, 2006; Chu et al., 2008). Current recommendations are that women who are underweight should gain 28 to 40 pounds, normal weight women should gain 25 to 35 pounds, and obese women should gain only 11 to 20 pounds (Rasmussen, Yaktine, & Institute of Medicine and National Research Council, 2009).

What an expectant mother eats is also important. For example, newborns whose mothers ate fish high in DHA, an omega-3 fatty acid found in Atlantic salmon and tuna, showed more mature sleep patterns (a sign of advanced brain development) than infants whose mothers' blood had lower levels of DHA (Cheruku, Montgomery-Downs, Farkas, Thoman, & Lammi-Keefe, 2002; Colombo et al., 2004).

Babies whose mothers drink large amounts of carrot juice in the last trimester are more likely to like carrots.

Mennella, Jagnow, & Beauchamp, 2001

Folic acid, or folate (a B vitamin), is critical in a pregnant woman's diet. For some time, China had the highest incidence in the world of babies born with anencephaly and spina bifida (refer to Table 1). In the 1980s researchers linked this high incidence with the timing of the babies' conception. Traditionally, Chinese couples marry in January or February and try to conceive as soon as possible. Thus their pregnancies often begin in the winter, when rural women have little access to fresh fruits and vegetables, important sources of folic acid.

After medical detective work established the lack of folic acid as a cause of anencephaly and spina bifida, China embarked on a massive program to give folic acid supplements to prospective mothers. The result was a large reduction in the prevalence of these defects (Berry et al., 1999). Addition of folic acid to enriched grain products has been mandatory in the United States since 1998, reducing the incidence of these defects (Honein, Paulozzi, Mathews, Erickson, & Wong, 2001). It is estimated that if all women took 5 milligrams of folic acid each day before pregnancy and during the first trimester, an estimated 85 percent of neural-tube defects could be prevented (Wald, 2004).

Milder folic acid deficiencies in pregnant mothers can result in less severe, but still troubling problems. For example, low folate levels during pregnancy have been associated with later attention-deficit/hyperactivity in 7- to 9-year-old children (Schlotz et al., 2009).

Malnutrition Prenatal malnutrition may have long-range effects. In rural Gambia, in western Africa, people born during the *hungry season,* when foods from the previous harvest are depleted, are 10 times more likely to die in early adulthood than people born during other parts of the year (Moore et al., 1997). In studies done in the United Kingdom, children whose mothers had low vitamin D levels late in pregnancy had low bone mineral content at age 9, potentially increasing their risk of osteoporosis in later life (Javaid et al., 2006). And, as reported earlier, several studies have revealed a link between fetal undernutrition and schizophrenia.

It is important to identify malnutrition early in pregnancy so it can be treated. Malnourished women who take dietary supplements while pregnant tend to have bigger, healthier, more active, and more visually alert infants (J. L. Brown, 1987; Vuori et al., 1979); and women with low zinc levels who take daily zinc supplements are less likely to have babies with low birth weight and small head circumference (Hess & King, 2009). In a large-scale randomized study of low-income households in 347 Mexican communities, women who took nutrient-fortified dietary supplements while pregnant or lactating tended to have infants who grew more rapidly and were less likely to be anemic (Rivera et al., 2004).

Thalidomide, which causes severe birth defects, had been tested for safety in rats, and that research did not suggest there would be problems. Although animal research can be a useful tool, it must be interpreted carefully because results may not generalize across species.

Physical Activity and Strenuous Work Among the Ifaluk people of the western Caroline Islands, women are advised to refrain from harvesting crops during the first 7 months of pregnancy, when the developing fetus is thought to be weak, but to resume manual labor during the last 2 months to encourage a speedy delivery (Le, 2000). Actually, moderate exercise any time during pregnancy does not seem to endanger the fetuses of healthy women (Committee on Obstetric Practice, 2002; Riemann & Kanstrup Hansen, 2000). Regular exercise prevents constipation and improves respiration, circulation, muscle tone, and skin elasticity, all of which contribute to a more comfortable pregnancy and an easier, safer delivery (Committee on Obstetric Practice, 2002). Employment during pregnancy generally entails no special hazards. However, strenuous working conditions, occupational fatigue, and long working hours may be associated with a greater risk of premature birth (Bell, Zimmerman, & Diehr, 2008; Luke et al., 1995).

The American Congress of Obstetricians and Gynecologists (2002) recommends that women in low-risk pregnancies be guided by their own abilities and stamina. The safest course seems to be for pregnant women to exercise moderately, not pushing themselves and not raising their heart rate above 150, and, as with any exercise, to taper off at the end of each session rather than stop abruptly.

Drug Intake Practically everything an expectant mother takes in makes its way to the uterus. Drugs may cross the placenta, just as oxygen, carbon dioxide, and water do. Vulnerability is greatest in the first few months of gestation, when development is most rapid.

What are the effects of the use of specific drugs during pregnancy? Let's look first at medical drugs; then at alcohol, nicotine, and caffeine; and finally at three illegal drugs: marijuana, cocaine, and methamphetamine.

Medical Drugs It once was thought that the placenta protected the fetus against drugs the mother took during pregnancy—until the early 1960s, when a tranquilizer called *thalidomide* was banned after it was found to have caused stunted or missing limbs, severe facial deformities, and defective organs in some 12,000 babies. The thalidomide disaster sensitized medical professionals and the public to the potential dangers of taking drugs while pregnant.

Among the medical drugs that may be harmful during pregnancy are the antibiotic tetracycline; certain barbiturates, opiates, and other central nervous system depressants; several hormones, including diethylstilbestrol (DES) and androgens; certain anticancer drugs, such as methotrexate; Accutane, a drug often prescribed for severe acne; drugs used to treat epilepsy; and several antipsychotic drugs (Briggs, Freeman, & Yaffe, 2012; Einarson & Boskovic, 2009; Koren, Pastuszak, & Ito, 1998). Angiotensin-converting enzyme (ACE) inhibitors and nonsteroidal anti-inflammatory drugs (NSAIDs), such as naproxen and ibuprofen, have been linked to birth defects when taken anytime from the first trimester on (Cooper et al., 2006; Ofori, Oraichi, Blais, Rey, & Berard, 2006). In addition, certain antipsychotic drugs used to manage severe psychiatric disorders may have serious potential effects on the fetus, including withdrawal symptoms at birth (AAP Committee on Drugs, 2000). The American Academy of Pediatrics (AAP) Committee on Drugs (2001) recommends that *no* medication be taken by a pregnant or breast-feeding woman unless it is essential for her health or her child's (Koren et al., 1998) and that care be taken in choosing the safest drug available. For example, although certain types of antibiotics (collectively known as "sulfa drugs") are associated with an increased risk of birth defects, many of the commonly used antibiotics such as penicillin and erythromycin do not seem to result in any elevation of risk (Crider et al., 2009).

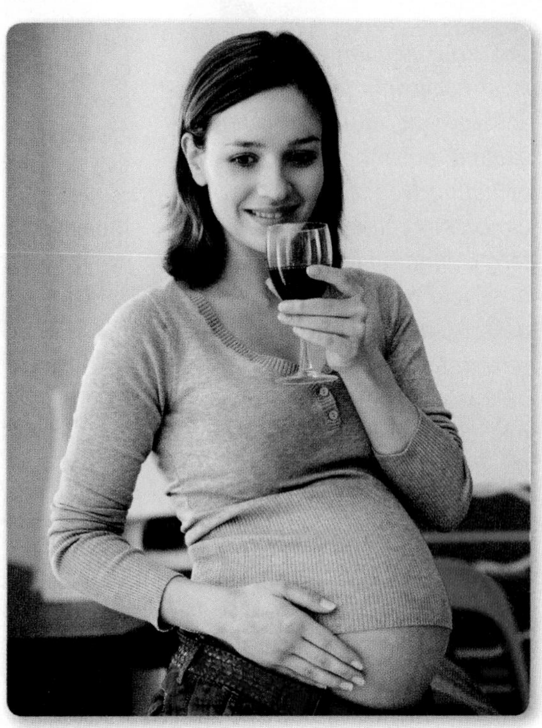

A mother who drinks during pregnancy risks having a child born with fetal alcohol syndrome.

Alcohol Prenatal alcohol exposure is the most common cause of mental retardation and the leading preventable cause of birth defects in the United States. **Fetal alcohol syndrome (FAS)** is characterized by a combination of retarded growth, face and body malformations, and disorders of the central nervous system. FAS and other less severe alcohol-related conditions are estimated to occur in nearly 1 in every 100 births (Sokol, Delaney-Black, & Nordstrom, 2003).

Even small amounts of social drinking may harm a fetus (Sokol et al., 2003), and the more the mother drinks, the greater the effect. Moderate or heavy drinking during pregnancy seems to disturb an infant's neurological and behavioral functioning, and this may affect early social interaction with the mother, which is vital to emotional development (Hannigan & Armant, 2000; Nugent, Lester, Greene, Wieczorek-Deering, & Mahony, 1996). Heavy drinkers who continue to drink after becoming pregnant are likely to have babies with reduced skull and brain growth as compared with babies of nondrinking women or expectant mothers who stop drinking (Handmaker et al., 2006).

fetal alcohol syndrome (FAS)
Combination of mental, motor, and developmental abnormalities affecting the offspring of some women who drink heavily during pregnancy.

FAS-related problems can include, in infancy, reduced responsiveness to stimuli, slow reaction time, and reduced visual acuity (sharpness of vision) (Carter et al., 2005; Sokol et al., 2003) and, throughout childhood, short attention span, distractibility, restlessness, hyperactivity, learning disabilities, memory deficits, and mood disorders (Sokol et al., 2003) as well as aggressiveness and problem behavior (Sood et al., 2001). Prenatal alcohol exposure is a risk factor for development of drinking problems and alcohol disorders in young adulthood (Alati et al., 2006; Baer, Sampson, Barr, Connor, & Streissguth, 2003).

Some FAS problems recede after birth; but others, such as retardation, behavioral and learning problems, and hyperactivity, tend to persist. Enriching these children's education or general environment does not always enhance their cognitive development (Kerns, Don, Mateer, & Streissguth, 1997; Spohr, Willms, & Steinhausen, 1993; Streissguth et al., 1991; Strömland & Hellström, 1996), but recent interventions targeted at cognitive skills in children with FAS are showing promise (Paley & O'Connor, 2011). Children with FAS may be less likely to develop behavioral and mental health problems if they are diagnosed early and are reared in stable, nurturing environments (Streissguth et al., 2004).

Because it would be unethical to conduct the kind of randomized, experimental research that would answer the question, we cannot determine what "safe" levels of drinking are.

Nicotine Maternal smoking during pregnancy has been identified as the single most important factor in low birth weight in developed countries (DiFranza, Aligne, & Weitzman, 2004). Women who smoke during pregnancy are more than 1½ times as likely as nonsmokers to bear low-birth-weight babies (weighing less than 5½ pounds at birth). Even light smoking (fewer than five cigarettes a day) is associated with a greater risk of low birth weight (Hoyert, Mathews, et al., 2006; Martin, Hamilton, et al., 2005; Shankaran et al., 2004).

Tobacco use during pregnancy also brings increased risks of miscarriage, growth retardation, stillbirth, small head circumference, sudden infant death, colic (uncontrollable, extended crying for no apparent reason) in early infancy, hyperkinetic disorder (excessive movement), and long-term respiratory, neurological, cognitive, attentional, and behavioral problems (AAP Committee on Substance Abuse, 2001; DiFranza et al., 2004;

The drug Accutane is most commonly used for severe acne, although it has multiple other applications, including treatment of some cancers. Accutane is highly teratogenic and can cause a variety of severe birth defects, including mental retardation, facial abnormalities, and hearing and vision problems. Should the use of Accutane be permitted for women of childbearing age? What safeguards should be required?

Froehlich et al., 2009; Hoyert, Mathews, et al., 2006; Linnet et al., 2005; Martin, Hamilton, et al., 2007; Shah, Sullivan, & Carter, 2006; Smith et al., 2006). The effects of prenatal exposure to secondhand smoke on development tend to be worse when children also experience socioeconomic hardship during the first 2 years of life (Rauh et al., 2004), when they are exposed to additional teratogens such as lead (Froehlich et al., 2009), or deprived of necessary nutrients such as folic acid (Mook-Kanamori et al., 2010) at the same time. Moreover, some fetuses' genotypes are more robust. In one study, fetuses with a specific genotype for an enzyme involved in the metabolism of tobacco smoke were protected against the negative effects of *moderate* rates of maternal smoking. However, children with this genetic profile born to mothers who were heavy smokers did show negative effects of exposure (Price, Grosser, Plomin, & Jaffee, 2010).

Caffeine Can the caffeine a pregnant woman consumes in coffee, tea, cola, or chocolate cause trouble for her fetus? For the most part, results have been mixed. It does seem clear that caffeine is *not* a teratogen for human babies (Christian & Brent, 2001). A controlled study of 1,205 new mothers and their babies showed no effect of reported caffeine use on low birth weight, premature birth, or retarded fetal growth (Santos, Victora, Huttly, & Carvalhal, 1998). On the other hand, in a controlled study of 1,063 pregnant women, those who consumed at least two cups of regular coffee or five cans of caffeinated soda daily had twice the risk of miscarriage as those who consumed no caffeine (Weng, Odouli, & Li, 2008). Four or more cups of coffee a day during pregnancy may increase the risk of sudden death in infancy (Ford et al., 1998).

Marijuana, Cocaine, and Methamphetamine Studies of marijuana use by pregnant women are sparse. However, some evidence suggests that heavy marijuana use can lead to birth defects, low birth weight, withdrawal-like symptoms (excessive crying and tremors) at birth, and increased risk of attention disorders and learning problems later in life (March of Dimes Birth Defects Foundation, 2004b). In two longitudinal studies, prenatal use of marijuana was associated with impaired attention, impulsivity, and difficulty in use of visual and perceptual skills after age 3, suggesting that the drug may affect functioning of the brain's frontal lobes (Fried & Smith, 2001).

Another way of saying this is that many of the effects of prenatal cocaine exposure are indirect rather than direct consequences. This is similar to the fact that maternal heroin addiction is related to greater risk of being HIV positive. It's not that the heroin directly causes HIV infection, it's that heroin is related to lifestyle issues that can cause infection.

Cocaine use during pregnancy has been associated with spontaneous abortion, delayed growth, premature labor, low birth weight, small head size, birth defects, and impaired neurological development (Bunikowski et al., 1998; Chiriboga, Brust, Bateman, & Hauser, 1999; Macmillan et al., 2001; March of Dimes Birth Defects Foundation, 2004a; Scher, Richardson, & Day, 2000; Shankaran et al., 2004). In some studies, cocaine-exposed newborns show acute withdrawal symptoms and sleep disturbances (O'Brien & Jeffery, 2002). In a more recent study, high prenatal cocaine exposure was associated with childhood behavior problems, independent of the effects of alcohol and tobacco exposure (Bada et al., 2007). So great has been the concern about prenatal cocaine exposure that some states have taken criminal action against expectant mothers suspected of using cocaine. Other studies, however, have found no specific connection between prenatal cocaine exposure and physical, motor, cognitive, emotional, or behavioral deficits that could not also be attributed to other risk factors, such as low birth weight; exposure to tobacco, alcohol, or marijuana; or a poor home environment (Frank, Augustyn, Knight, Pell, & Zuckerman, 2001; Messinger et al., 2004; Singer et al., 2004).

Methamphetamine use among pregnant women is an increasing concern in the United States. In a study of 1,618 infants, 84 were found to have been exposed to methamphetamine. The methamphetamine-exposed infants were more likely to have low birth weight and to be small for their gestational age than the remainder of the sample. This finding suggests that prenatal methamphetamine exposure is associated with fetal growth restriction (Smith et al., 2006). Additionally, prenatal exposure to methamphetamines has been implicated in fetal brain damage to areas of the brain involved in learning, memory, and control (Roussotte et al., 2011). Methamphetamine-exposed children also have less white matter in their brains, a finding that has implications for the developmental delays commonly found in such children (Cloak, Ernst, Fujii, Hedemark, & Chang, 2009).

Early treatment for alcohol, nicotine, and other substance abuse can greatly improve health outcomes. Among 2,073 women enrolled in an early prenatal care program, risks of stillbirth, preterm delivery, low birth weight, and placental separation from the uterus were no higher than for a control group of 46,553 women with no evidence of substance abuse, whereas risks for 156 untreated substance abusers were dramatically higher (Goler, Armstrong, Taillac, & Osejo, 2008).

Does society's interest in protecting unborn children justify coercive measure against pregnant women who ingest harmful substances?

Maternal Illnesses Both prospective parents should try to prevent all infections—common colds, flu, urinary tract and vaginal infections, as well as sexually transmitted diseases. If the mother does contract an infection, she should have it treated promptly.

Acquired immune deficiency syndrome (AIDS) is a disease caused by the human immunodeficiency virus (HIV), which undermines functioning of the immune system. If an expectant mother has the virus in her blood, *perinatal transmission* may occur: the virus may cross over to the fetus's bloodstream through the placenta during pregnancy, labor, or delivery or, after birth, through breast milk.

acquired immune deficiency syndrome (AIDS)
Viral disease that undermines effective functioning of the immune system.

The biggest risk factor for perinatal HIV transmission is a mother who is unaware she has HIV. In the United States, new pediatric AIDS cases have declined steadily since 1992 due to routine testing and treatment of pregnant women and newborn babies and to advances in the prevention, detection, and treatment of HIV infection in infants. As a result, the estimated rate of perinatal HIV infection is now less than 2 percent. The risk of transmission also can be reduced by choosing cesarean delivery, especially when a woman has not received antiretroviral therapy, and by promotion of alternatives to breast-feeding among high-risk women (CDC, 2006a).

Rubella (German measles), if contracted by a woman before her 11th week of pregnancy, is almost certain to cause deafness and heart defects in her baby. Chances of catching rubella during pregnancy have been greatly reduced in Europe and the United States since the late 1960s, when a vaccine was developed that is now routinely administered to infants and children. Efforts in less developed countries to provide rubella vaccinations resulted in a decrease of reported rubella cases of more than 80 percent from 2000 to 2009 (Reef et al., 2011).

Because some parents are reluctant to vaccinate their children, rates of measles and whopping cough in the United States are now on the rise.

An infection called *toxoplasmosis,* caused by a parasite harbored in the bodies of cattle, sheep, and pigs and in the intestinal tracts of cats, typically produces either no symptoms or symptoms like those of the common cold. In an expectant woman, however, especially in the second and third trimesters of pregnancy, it can cause fetal brain damage, severely impaired eyesight or blindness, seizures, miscarriage, stillbirth, or death of the baby. If the baby survives, there may be later problems, including eye infections, hearing loss, and learning disabilities. Treatment with antiparasitic drugs during the first year of life can reduce brain and eye damage (McLeod et al., 2006). To avoid infection, expectant mothers should not eat raw or very rare meat, should wash hands and all work surfaces after touching raw meat, should peel or thoroughly wash raw fruits and vegetables, and should not dig in a garden where cat feces may be buried. Women who have a cat should have it checked for the disease, should not feed it raw meat, and, if possible, should have someone else empty the litter box (March of Dimes Foundation, 2002).

Your veterinarian can run an easy blood test on your cat to scan for the presence of the parasite. Alternatively, your blood can be tested for antibodies to toxoplasmosis. If you were previously exposed, you are in the clear.

Offspring of mothers with diabetes are 3 to 4 times more likely than offspring of other women to develop a wide range of birth defects (Correa et al., 2008). Women with diabetes need to be sure their blood glucose levels are under control *before* becoming pregnant (Li, Chase, Jung, Smith, & Loeken, 2005). Use of multivitamin supplements during the 3 months before conception and the first 3 months of pregnancy can help reduce the risk of diabetes-associated birth defects (Correa, Botto, Liu, Mulinare, & Erickson, 2003).

Maternal Anxiety, Stress, and Depression Some tension and worry during pregnancy are normal and do not necessarily increase risks of birth complications, such as low birth weight (Littleton, Breitkopf, & Berenson, 2006). Moderate maternal anxiety may even spur organization of the developing brain. In one study, newborns whose mothers experienced moderate levels of both positive and negative stress showed signs of accelerated neurological development (DiPietro et al., 2010), and these gains may persist over time. In a series of studies, 2-year-olds whose mothers had shown moderate anxiety midway through pregnancy scored higher on measures of motor and mental development than did age-mates whose mothers had not shown anxiety during pregnancy (DiPietro, 2004; DiPietro, Novak, Costigan, Atella, & Reusing, 2006).

stress
Physical or psychological demands on a person or organism.

On the other hand, a mother's self-reported **stress** and anxiety during pregnancy has been associated with more active and irritable temperament in newborns (DiPietro et al., 2010), inattentiveness during a developmental assessment in 8-month-olds (Huizink, Robles de Medina, Mulder, Visser, & Buitelaar, 2002), and negative emotionality or behavioral disorders in early childhood (Martin, Noyes, Wisenbaker, & Huttunen, 2000; O'Connor, Heron, Golding, Beveridge, & Glover, 2002). Additionally, chronic stress can result in preterm delivery, perhaps through the action of elevated levels of stress hormones (which are implicated in the onset of labor) or the resulting dampened immune functioning, which makes women more vulnerable to inflammatory diseases and infection that can also trigger labor (Schetter, 2009). Also, major stress during the 24th to 28th weeks of pregnancy has been implicated in autism (Beversdorf et al., 2001).

Depression may have similar negative effects on development. In one study of British children, children of mothers who had been depressed during pregnancy showed elevated levels of violent and antisocial behaviors in adolescence, even when family environment, continued maternal depression, and prenatal nicotine and alcohol exposure were controlled for (Hay, Pawlby, Waters, Perra, & Sharp, 2010). However, the depressed mothers were themselves more likely than the general population to have been involved in similar antisocial acts during their own adolescence, suggesting that passive genotype-environment correlations need to be taken into account.

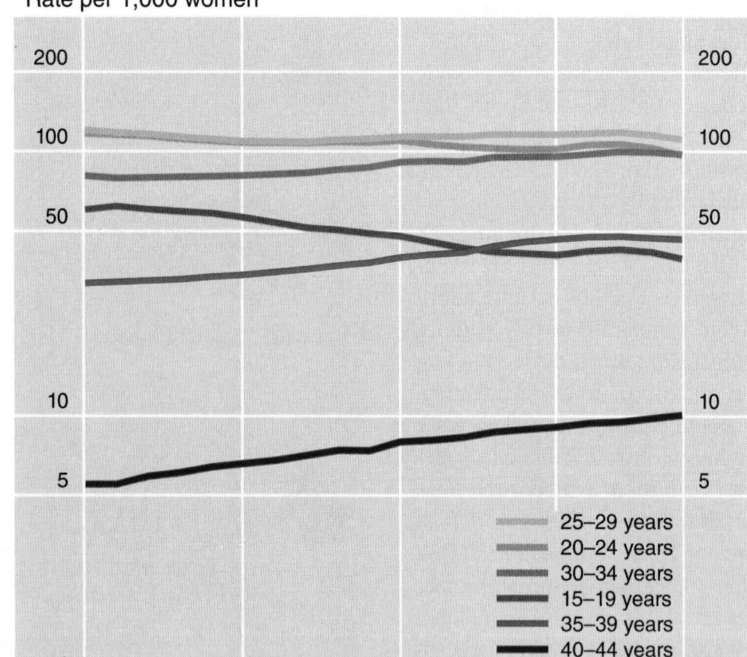

FIGURE 9

U.S. Rate of First Births, by Age of Mother

From 1990 to 2009 the proportion of first births to women aged 35 years and over increased nearly 8 times. In 2009, about 10.1 in 1,000 first births were to women aged 40–44 years and over compared with a rate of 7.4 in 1,000 first births in 1999.

Source: Martin, Hamilton, Ventura, et al., 2011.

Maternal Age On December 30, 2006, in Barcelona, Spain, Maria del Carmen Bousada became the oldest woman on record to give birth. She had become pregnant after in vitro fertilization and delivered twins by cesarean section about a week before her 67th birthday. In August and November, 2008, two Indian women who claimed to be 70, Omkari Panwar and Rajo Devi, apparently topped that record, also giving birth after IVF. However, these women's ages could not be confirmed because they had no birth certificates.

Birthrates of U.S. women in their 30s and 40s are at their highest levels since the 1960s, in part due to multiple births associated with fertility treatments—an example of a history-graded influence. The number of births to women in their early 40s more than doubled between 1990 and 2009, and reached its highest level since 1967 (Figure 9). Births to women ages 50 to 54 have increased an average of 15 percent each year since 1997 (Martin et al., 2010).

Although most risks to the infant's health are not much greater than for babies born to younger mothers, the chance of miscarriage or stillbirth rises with maternal age. In fact, the risk of miscarriage reaches 90 percent for women age 45 or older (Heffner, 2004). Women 30 to 35 are more likely to suffer complications due to diabetes, high blood pressure, or severe bleeding. There is also higher risk of premature delivery, retarded fetal growth, birth defects, and chromosomal abnormalities, such as Down syndrome. However, due to widespread screening among older expectant mothers, fewer malformed babies are born nowadays (Cunningham & Leveno, 1995; Heffner, 2004).

Adolescent mothers tend to have premature or underweight babies—perhaps because a young girl's still-growing body consumes vital nutrients the fetus needs (Martin, Hamilton, et al., 2007). These newborns are at heightened risk of death in the first month, disabilities, or health problems.

Outside Environmental Hazards Air pollution, chemicals, radiation, extremes of heat and humidity, and other environmental hazards can affect prenatal development. Pregnant women who regularly breathe air that contains high levels of fine combustion-related particles are more likely to bear infants who are premature or undersized (Parker, Woodruff, Basu, & Schoendorf, 2005) or have chromosomal abnormalities (Bocskay et al., 2005). Exposure to high concentrations of disinfection by-products is associated with low birth weight and slowed fetal growth (Hinckley, Bachand, & Reif, 2005). Women who work with chemicals used in manufacturing semiconductor chips have about twice the rate of miscarriage as other female workers (Markoff, 1992), and women exposed to DDT tend to have more preterm births (Longnecker, Klebanoff, Zhou, & Brock, 2001). Two insecticides, chlorpyrifos and diazinon, apparently cause stunting of prenatal growth (Whyatt et al., 2004). Research in the United Kingdom found a 33 percent increase in risk of nongenetic birth defects among families who were living within 2 miles of hazardous waste sites (Vrijheld et al., 2002).

Fetal exposure to low levels of environmental toxins, such as lead, mercury, and dioxin, as well as nicotine and ethanol, may help explain the sharp rise in asthma, allergies, and autoimmune disorders such as lupus (Dietert, 2005). Both maternal exposure to the hydrocarbons and the children's asthma symptoms were associated with epigenetic changes in the gene ACSL3, which affects the lungs (Perera et al., 2009). Childhood cancers, including leukemia, have been linked to pregnant mothers' drinking chemically contaminated groundwater (Boyles, 2002) and use of home pesticides (Menegaux et al., 2006). Infants exposed prenatally even to low levels of lead, especially during the third trimester, tend to show IQ deficits during childhood (Schnaas et al., 2006).

Women who have routine dental X-rays during pregnancy triple their risk of having full-term, low-birth-weight babies (Hujoel, Bollen, Noonan, & del Aguila, 2004). In utero exposure to radiation 8 through 15 weeks after fertilization has been linked to mental retardation, small head size, chromosomal malformations, Down syndrome, seizures, and poor performance on IQ tests and in school (Yamazaki & Schull, 1990).

From the 1920s to the 1970s, a shoe-fitting machine that enabled customers to view their X-rayed feet within shoes was a common gimmick in shoe stores. Now that we know how damaging X-rays are for both adults and children, these machines are no longer in use.

ENVIRONMENTAL INFLUENCES: PATERNAL FACTORS

A man's exposure to lead, marijuana or tobacco smoke, large amounts of alcohol or radiation, DES, pesticides, or high ozone levels may result in abnormal or poor-quality sperm (Sokol et al., 2006; Swan et al., 2003). Offspring of male workers at a British nuclear processing plant were at elevated risk of being born dead (Parker, Pearce, Dickinson, Aitkin, & Craft, 1999). Babies whose fathers had diagnostic X-rays within the year prior to conception or had high lead exposure at work tended to have low birth weight and slowed fetal growth (Chen & Wang, 2006; Lin, Hwang, Marshall, & Marion, 1998; Shea, Little, & the ALSPAC Study Team, 1997).

Men who smoke have an increased likelihood of transmitting genetic abnormalities (AAP Committee on Substance Abuse, 2001). A pregnant woman's exposure to the father's secondhand smoke has been linked with low birth weight, infant respiratory infections, sudden infant death, and cancer in childhood and adulthood (Ji et al., 1997; D. H. Rubin, Krasilnikoff, Leventhal, Weile, & Berget, 1986; Sandler, Everson, Wilcox, & Browder, 1985; Wakefield, Reid, Roberts, Mullins, & Gillies, 1998). In a study of 214 nonsmoking mothers in New York City, exposure to *both* paternal smoking and urban air pollution resulted in a 7 percent reduction in birth weight and a 3 percent reduction in head circumference (Perera et al., 2004).

Older fathers may be a significant source of birth defects due to damaged or deteriorated sperm. Birthrates for fathers ages 30 to 49 have risen substantially since 1980

checkpoint
can **you** . . .

- **Summarize recommendations for an expectant mother's diet?**
- **Discuss effects on the developing fetus of a parent's use of medical drugs, alcohol, tobacco, caffeine, marijuana, cocaine, and methamphetamine?**
- **Assess the risks of maternal illnesses, anxiety, stress, and advanced age on pregnancy?**

(Martin et al., 2009). Advancing paternal age is associated with increases in the risk of several rare conditions, including dwarfism (Wyrobek et al., 2006). Advanced age of the father also may be a factor in a disproportionate number of cases of schizophrenia (Byrne et al., 2003; Malaspina et al., 2001), bipolar disorder (Frans et al., 2008), and autism and related disorders (Reichenberg et al., 2006; Tsuchiya et al., 2008).

Monitoring and Promoting Prenatal Development

Not long ago, almost the only decision parents had to make about their babies before birth was the decision to conceive; most of what happened in the intervening months was beyond their control. Now scientists have developed an array of tools to assess an unborn baby's progress and well-being and even to intervene to correct some abnormal conditions (Table 5).

study**smart**

Fetal Development

Progress is being made in the use of noninvasive procedures, such as ultrasound and blood tests, to detect chromosomal abnormalities. In one study, a combination of three noninvasive tests conducted at 11 weeks of gestation predicted the presence of Down syndrome with 87 percent accuracy. When the 11-week tests were followed by further noninvasive testing early in the second trimester, accuracy reached 96 percent (Malone et al., 2005). Contrary to previous findings, amniocentesis and chorionic villus sampling, which can be used earlier in pregnancy, carry only a slightly higher miscarriage risk than these noninvasive procedures (Caughey, Hopkins, & Norton, 2006; Eddleman et al., 2006).

Screening for defects and diseases is only one important reason for early prenatal care. Early, high-quality prenatal care, which includes educational, social, and nutritional services, can help prevent maternal or infant death and other birth complications. It can provide first-time mothers with information about pregnancy, childbirth, and infant care. Poor women who get prenatal care benefit by being put in touch with other needed services, and they are more likely to get medical care for their infants after birth (Shiono & Behrman, 1995).

DISPARITIES IN PRENATAL CARE

In the United States prenatal care is widespread, but not universal as in many European countries; and it lacks uniform national standards and guaranteed financial coverage. Use of early prenatal care (during the first 3 months of pregnancy) rose modestly between 1990 and 2003 but then plateaued and declined slightly in 2006, possibly due to changes in welfare and Medicaid policies (Martin et al., 2009).

Historically, rates of low birth weight and premature birth continue to rise. Why? One answer is the increasing number of multiple births, which often are early births, with heightened risk of death within the first year. However, new data suggest that this increase may have finally peaked, as rates of premature delivery declined for the second straight year in a row from 2006 to 2008 (Martin, Osterman, & Sutton, 2010).

A second answer is that the benefits of prenatal care are not evenly distributed. Although usage of prenatal care has grown, especially among ethnic groups that have tended not to receive early care, the women most at risk of bearing low-birth-weight babies—teenage and unmarried women, those with little education, and some minority women—are still least likely to receive it (Martin et al., 2006; National Center for Health Statistics [NCHS], 2005; USDHHS, 1996a). In 2006, as in earlier years, non-Hispanic black and Hispanic women were more than twice as likely as non-Hispanic white women to receive late or no care (Martin et al., 2009).

Can you suggest ways to induce more pregnant women to seek early prenatal or preconception care?

A related concern is an ethnic disparity in fetal and postbirth mortality. After adjusting for such risk factors as SES, overweight, smoking, hypertension, and diabetes, the chances of perinatal death (death between 20 weeks' gestation and 1 week after birth) remain 3.4 times higher for blacks, 1.5 times higher for Hispanics, and 1.9 times higher for other minorities than for whites (Healy et al., 2006).

TABLE 5 Prenatal Assessment Techniques

Technique	Description	Uses and Advantages	Risks and Notes
Ultrasound (sonogram), sonoembryology	High-frequency sound waves directed at the mother's abdomen produce a picture of fetus in uterus. Sonoembryology uses high-frequency transvaginal probes and digital image processing to produce a picture of embryo in uterus.	Monitor fetal growth, movement, position, and form; assess amniotic fluid volume; judge gestational age; detect multiple pregnancies. Detect major structural abnormalities or death of a fetus. Guide amniocentesis and chorionic villus sampling. Help diagnose sex-linked disorders. Sonoembryology can detect unusual defects during embryonic stage.	Done routinely in many places. Can be used for sex-screening of unborn babies.
Embryoscopy, fetoscopy	Tiny viewing scope is inserted in woman's abdomen to view embryo or fetus. Can assist in diagnosis of nonchromosomal genetic disorders.	Can guide fetal blood transfusions and bone marrow transplants.	Riskier than other prenatal diagnostic procedures.
Amniocentesis	Sample of amniotic fluid is withdrawn under guidance of ultrasound and analyzed. Most commonly used procedure to obtain fetal cells for testing.	Can detect chromosomal disorders and certain genetic or multifactorial defects; more than 99 percent accuracy rate. Usually performed in women ages 35 and over; recommended if prospective parents are known carriers of Tay-Sachs disease or sickle-cell anemia or have family history of Down syndrome, spina bifida, or muscular dystrophy. Can help diagnose sex-linked disorders.	Normally not performed before 15 weeks' gestation. Results usually take 1 to 2 weeks. Small (0.5–1%) added risk of fetal loss or injury; early amniocentesis (at 11 to 13 weeks' gestation) is riskier and not recommended. Can be used for sex-screening of unborn babies.
Chorionic villus sampling (CVS)	Tissues from hairlike chorionic villi (projections of membrane surrounding fetus) are removed from placenta and analyzed.	Early diagnosis of birth defects and disorders. Can be performed between 10 and 12 weeks' gestation; yields highly accurate results within a week.	Should not be performed before 10 weeks' gestation. Some studies suggest 1–4% more risk of fetal loss than with amniocentesis.
Preimplantation genetic diagnosis	After in vitro fertilization, a sample cell is removed from the blastocyst and analyzed.	Can avoid transmission of genetic defects or predispositions known to run in the family; a defective blastocyst is *not* implanted in uterus.	No known risks.
Umbilical cord sampling (cordocentesis, or fetal blood sampling)	Needle guided by ultrasound is inserted into blood vessels of umbilical cord.	Allows direct access to fetal DNA for diagnostic measures, including assessment of blood disorders and infections, and therapeutic measures such as blood transfusions.	Fetal loss or miscarriage is reported in 1–2% of cases; increases risk of bleeding from umbilical cord and fetal distress.
Maternal blood test	A sample of the prospective mother's blood is tested for alpha fetoprotein.	May indicate defects in formation of brain or spinal cord (anencephaly or spina bifida); also can predict Down syndrome and other abnormalities. Permits monitoring of pregnancies at risk for low birth weight or stillbirth.	No known risks, but false negatives are possible. Ultrasound and/or amniocentesis needed to confirm suspected conditions.

Sources: Chodirker et al., 2001; Cicero, Curcio, Papageorghiou, Sonek, & Nicolaides, 2001; Cunniff & the Committee on Genetics, 2004; Kurjak, Kupesic, Matijevic, Kos, & Marton, 1999; Verlinsky et al., 2002.

THE NEED FOR PRECONCEPTION CARE

A more fundamental answer is that even early prenatal care is insufficient. Care should begin *before* pregnancy to identify preventable risks. The CDC (2006c) has issued comprehensive, research-based guidelines for *preconception care* for all women of childbearing age. Such care should include the following:

- *Physical examinations* and the taking of medical and family histories
- *Vaccinations* for rubella and hepatitis B
- *Risk screening* for genetic disorders and infectious diseases such as STDs
- *Counseling* women to avoid smoking and alcohol, maintain a healthy body weight, and take folic acid supplements

Interventions should be provided where risks are indicated and also between pregnancies for women who have had poor pregnancy outcomes in the past.

The CDC (2006c) urges all adults to create a reproductive life plan so as to focus attention on reproductive health, avoid unintended pregnancies, and improve pregnancy outcomes. The CDC also calls for increased health insurance for low-income women to make sure they have access to preventive care.

Good preconception and prenatal care can give every child the best possible chance for entering the world in good condition to meet the challenges of life outside the womb.

checkpoint can **you** . . .

- **Describe seven techniques for identifying defects or disorders prenatally?**
- **Discuss possible reasons for disparities in utilization of prenatal care?**
- **Tell why early, high-quality prenatal care is important and why preconception care is needed?**

summary and key terms

Conceiving New Life

- Fertilization, the union of an ovum and a sperm, results in the formation of a one-celled zygote, which then duplicates itself by cell division.
- Multiple births can occur either by the fertilization of two ova (or one ovum that has split) or by the splitting of one fertilized ovum. Higher multiple births result from either one of these processes or a combination of the two.
- Dizygotic (fraternal) twins have different genetic makeups and may be of different sexes. Although monozygotic (identical) twins typically have much the same genetic makeup, they may differ in temperament or other respects.

fertilization
zygote
dizygotic twins
monozygotic twins

Mechanisms of Heredity

- The basic functional units of heredity are the genes, which are made of deoxyribonucleic acid (DNA). DNA carries the biochemical instructions, or genetic code, that governs the development of cell functions. Each gene is located by function in a definite position on a particular chromosome. The complete sequence of genes in the human body is called the *human genome.*

deoxyribonucleic acid (DNA)
genetic code
chromosomes
genes
human genome
mutations

- At conception, each normal human being receives 23 chromosomes from the mother and 23 from the father. These form 23 pairs of chromosomes—22 pairs of autosomes and 1 pair of sex chromosomes. A child who receives an X chromosome from each parent is genetically female. A child who receives a Y chromosome from the father is genetically male.
- The simplest patterns of genetic transmission are dominant and recessive inheritance. When a pair of alleles are the same, a person is homozygous for the trait; when they are different, the person is heterozygous.

autosomes
sex chromosomes
alleles
homozygous
heterozygous
dominant inheritance
recessive inheritance

- Most normal human characteristics are the result of polygenic or multifactorial transmission. Except for most monozygotic twins, each child inherits a unique genotype. Dominant inheritance and multifactorial transmission explain why a person's phenotype does not always express the underlying genotype.

- The epigenetic framework controls the functions of particular genes; it can be affected by environmental factors.

  polygenic inheritance

  phenotype

  genotype

  multifactorial transmission

  epigenesis

- Birth defects and diseases may result from simple dominant, recessive, or sex-linked inheritance, from mutations, or from genome imprinting. Chromosomal abnormalities also can cause birth defects.
- Through genetic counseling, prospective parents can receive information about the mathematical odds of bearing children with certain defects.
- Genetic testing involves risks as well as benefits.

  incomplete dominance

  sex-linked inheritance

  Down syndrome

  genetic counseling

Nature and Nurture: Influences of Heredity and Environment

- Research in behavioral genetics is based on the assumption that the relative influences of heredity and environment within a population can be measured statistically. If heredity is an important influence on a trait, genetically closer persons will be more similar in that trait. Family studies, adoption studies, and studies of twins enable researchers to measure the heritability of specific traits.
- The concepts of reaction range, canalization, genotype-environment interaction, genotype-environment correlation (or covariance), and niche-picking describe ways in which heredity and environment work together.
- Siblings tend to be more different than alike in intelligence and personality. According to some behavioral geneticists, heredity accounts for most of the similarity, and nonshared environmental effects account for most of the difference.

  behavioral genetics

  heritability

  concordant

  reaction range

  canalization

  genotype-environment interaction

  genotype-environment correlation

  niche-picking

  nonshared environmental effects

- Obesity, longevity, intelligence, temperament, and other aspects of personality are influenced by both heredity and environment.
- Schizophrenia is a highly heritable neurological disorder that also is environmentally influenced.

  obesity

  temperament

  schizophrenia

Prenatal Development

- Prenatal development occurs in three stages of gestation: the germinal, embryonic, and fetal stages.
- Severely defective embryos often are spontaneously aborted during the first trimester of pregnancy.
- As fetuses grow, they move less, but more vigorously. Swallowing amniotic fluid, which contains substances from the mother's body, stimulates taste and smell. Fetuses seem able to hear, exercise sensory discrimination, learn, and remember.

  gestation

  gestational age

  germinal stage

  implantation

  embryonic stage

  spontaneous abortion

  fetal stage

  ultrasound

- The developing organism can be greatly affected by its prenatal environment. The likelihood of a birth defect may depend on the timing and intensity of an environmental event and its interaction with genetic factors.
- Important environmental influences involving the mother include nutrition, smoking, intake of alcohol or other drugs, transmission of maternal illnesses or infections, maternal stress, anxiety, or depression, maternal age and physical activity, and external environmental hazards, such as chemicals and radiation. External influences also may affect the father's sperm.

  teratogen

  fetal alcohol syndrome (FAS)

  acquired immune deficiency syndrome (AIDS)

  stress

Monitoring and Promoting Prenatal Development

- Ultrasound, sonoembryology amniocentesis, chorionic villus sampling, fetoscopy, preimplantation genetic diagnosis, umbilical cord sampling, and maternal blood tests can be used to determine whether an unborn baby is developing normally.
- Early, high-quality prenatal care is essential for healthy development. It can lead to detection of defects and disorders and, especially if begun early and targeted to the needs of at-risk women, may help reduce maternal and infant death, low birth weight, and other birth complications.
- Racial/ethnic disparities in prenatal care may be a factor in disparities in low birth weight and perinatal death.
- Preconception care for every woman of childbearing age would reduce unintended pregnancies and increase the chances of good pregnancy outcomes.

chapter 4

Birth and Physical Development during the First Three Years

outline

Childbirth and Culture: How Birthing Has Changed

The Birth Process

The Newborn Baby

Complications of Childbirth

Survival and Health

Early Physical Development

Motor Development

learning objectives

Specify how childbirth has changed in developed countries.

Describe the birth process.

Describe the adjustment of a healthy newborn and the techniques for assessing its health.

Explain potential complications of childbirth and the prospects for infants with complicated births.

Identify factors affecting infants' chances for survival and health.

Discuss the patterns of physical growth and development in infancy.

Describe infants' motor development.

did you **know**?

- The cesarean rate in the United States is among the highest in the world?
- In the industrialized world, smoking during pregnancy is the leading factor in low birth weight?
- Cultural practices, such as how much freedom babies have to move about, can affect the age at which they begin to walk?

In this chapter we describe how babies come into the world, how newborn babies look, and how their body systems work. We discuss ways to safeguard their life and health and observe their rapid early physical development. We see how infants become busy, active toddlers and how caregivers can foster healthy growth and development.

A 2-year-old is kind of like having a blender, but without a top on it.

—**Jerry Seinfeld**

Childbirth and Culture: How Birthing Has Changed

Prior to the twentieth century, childbirth in Europe and in the United States was a female social ritual.* The woman, surrounded by female relatives and neighbors, sat up in her bed or perhaps in the stable, modestly draped in a sheet; if she wished, she might stand, walk around, or squat over a birth stool. The midwife who presided over the event had no formal training; she offered "advice, massages, potions, irrigations, and talismans" (Fontanel & d'Harcourt, 1997, p. 28). After the baby emerged, the midwife cut and tied the umbilical cord and cleaned and examined the newborn. Within a few hours or days, a peasant mother would be back at work in the fields; a more affluent woman could rest for several weeks.

Childbirth in those times was "a struggle with death" for both mother and baby (Fontanel & d'Harcourt, 1997, p. 34). In seventeenth- and eighteenth-century France, a woman had a 1 in 10 chance of dying while or shortly after giving birth. Thousands of babies were stillborn, and 1 out of 4 who were born alive died during their first year.

Childbirth can still be a dangerous endeavor in some developing countries in sub-Saharan Africa and South Asia. There, 60 million women deliver at home each year without the benefit of skilled care, and until recently more than 500,000 women and 4 million newborns died in or shortly after childbirth (Sines, Syed, Wall, & Worley, 2007). There are promising trends in maternal mortality though. Estimates suggest that maternal mortality dropped to approximately 287,000 in 2010, representing a 47 percent decline from 1990 (World Health Organization, 2012).

After the turn of the twentieth century, childbirth began to be professionalized in the United States, at least in urban settings. The growing use of maternity hospitals led to somewhat safer, more antiseptic conditions for childbirth. This served to reduce mortality for women, and the new field of obstetrics grew. In 1900, only 5 percent of U.S. deliveries occurred in hospitals; by 1920, in some cities 65 percent did (Scholten, 1985). A similar trend took place in Europe. Most recently, in the United States 98.7 percent of babies are born in hospitals, and 86.1 percent of births are attended by physicians (Martin, Hamilton, Ventura, Osterman, & Mathews, 2013).

The dramatic reductions in risks surrounding pregnancy and childbirth in industrialized countries are largely due to the availability of antibiotics, blood transfusions, safe anesthesia, improved hygiene, and drugs for inducing labor. In addition, improvements in prenatal assessment and care make it far more likely that a baby will be born healthy. Mortality rates for both mothers and children have decreased dramatically as noted in Figures 1 and 2.

However, the "medicalization" of childbirth has had social and emotional costs (Fontanel & d'Harcourt, 1997). Today a small but growing percentage of women in developed countries are going back to the intimate, personal experience of home birth (MacDorman, Menacker, & Declercq, 2010). Home births usually are attended by a trained nurse-midwife, with the resources of medical science close at hand. Arrangements may be made with a physician and a nearby hospital in case an emergency arises.

The Guinness Book of World Records reports that the highest number of births from one woman is held by a Russian woman who, from 1725 to 1765, gave birth to 16 sets of twins, 7 sets of triplets, and 4 sets of quadruplets over the course of 29 pregnancies.

*This discussion is based on Eccles (1982), Fontanel and d'Harcourt (1997), Gélis (1991), and Scholten (1985).

FIGURE 1

U.S. Maternal Mortality Rates, 1915–2003

Since 1915 the maternal mortality rate in the United States has dropped from 607.9 deaths per 100,000 live births for the birth registration area to 12.1 deaths per 100,000 live births in 2003.

Prior to 1933, data for birth registration states only. Line breaks are shown between successive *International Classification of Diseases* revisions.

Source: National Center for Health Statistics, 2007; S. L. Clark, 2012.

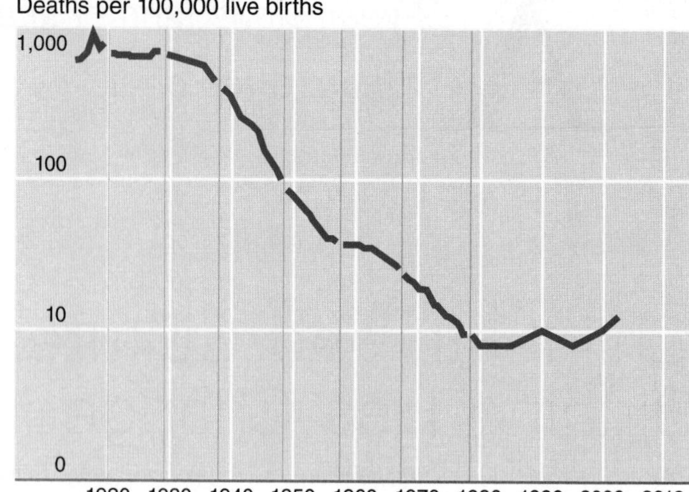

Some studies suggest that planned home births with speedy transfer to a hospital available in case of need can be as safe as hospital births for low-risk deliveries attended by skilled, certified midwives or nurse-midwives (American College of Nurse-Midwives, 2005). In fact, there are some suggestions that, at least for healthy pregnancies and planned home births, the risk of problems in childbirth might actually be lower than in a hospital (MacDorman et al., 2010). However, the American College of Obstetricians and Gynecologists (ACOG, 2008) and the American Medical Association (AMA House of Delegates, 2008) oppose home births, maintaining that complications can arise suddenly, even in low-risk pregnancies, and hospitals or accredited birthing centers are best equipped to respond to such emergencies.

Today hospitals are finding ways to humanize childbirth. Labor and delivery may take place in a comfortable birthing room, under soft lights, with the father or partner present as a coach and older siblings invited to visit after the birth. Rooming-in policies allow a baby to stay in the mother's room much or all of the time so that mothers can feed their newborns when they are hungry rather than when an arbitrary schedule allows. By "demedicalizing the experience of childbirth, hospitals are seeking to establish—or reestablish—an environment in which tenderness, security, and emotion carry as much weight as medical techniques" (Fontanel & d'Harcourt, 1997, p. 57).

checkpoint can **you . . .**

- Identify two ways childbirth has changed in developed countries and tell why it is less risky than it once was?
- Compare advantages of various settings for childbirth?

FIGURE 2

U.S. Infant Mortality Rates, 1940–2006

The U.S. infant mortality rate has decreased from 47.0 infant deaths per 1,000 live births in 1940 to 6.7 in 2006. During the same period, the neonatal rate decreased 85 percent, from 28.8 to 4.5 deaths per 1,000 live births, and the postneonatal rate decreased 88 percent from 18.3 to 2.2 deaths per 1,000 live births.

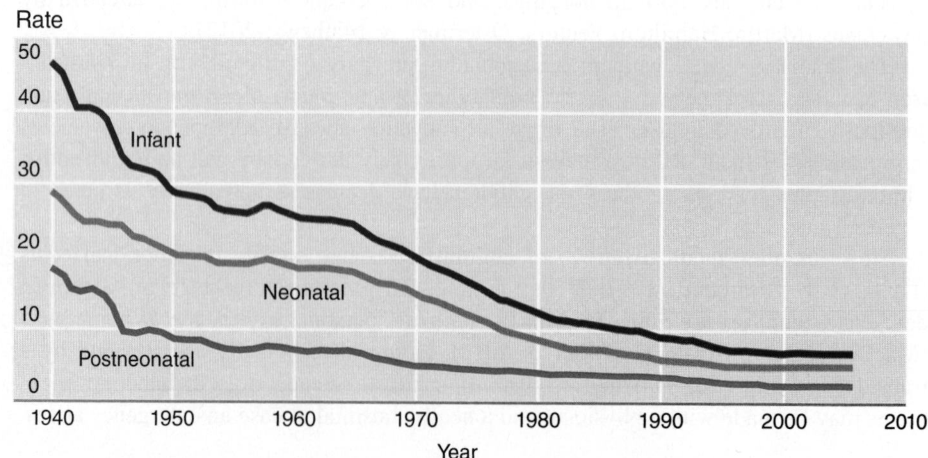

Source: Heron et al., 2009.

The Birth Process

Labor is an apt term for the process of giving birth. Birth is hard work for both mother and baby. What brings on labor is a series of uterine, cervical, and other changes called **parturition.** Parturition is the act or process of giving birth, and it typically begins about 2 weeks before delivery, when sharply rising estrogen levels stimulate the uterus to contract and the cervix to become more flexible.

parturition
The act or process of giving birth.

The uterine contractions that expel the fetus begin—typically about 266 days after conception—as a tightening of the uterus. A woman may have felt false contractions (known as *Braxton-Hicks contractions*) at times during the final months of pregnancy, or even as early as the second trimester, when the muscles of the uterus tighten for up to 2 minutes. In comparison with the relatively mild and irregular Braxton-Hicks contractions, real labor contractions are more frequent, rhythmic, and painful, and they increase in frequency and intensity.

STAGES OF CHILDBIRTH

Labor takes place in three overlapping stages (Figure 3).

Stage 1: Dilation of the Cervix The first stage, dilation of the cervix, is the longest, typically lasting 12 to 14 hours for a woman having her first child. In subsequent births, the first stage tends to be shorter. During this stage, regular and increasingly frequent uterine contractions—15 to 20 minutes apart at first—cause the cervix to shorten and dilate, or widen, in preparation for delivery. Toward the end of the first stage, contractions occur every 2 to 5 minutes. This stage lasts until the cervix is fully open (10 centimeters, or about 4 inches) so the baby can descend into the birth canal.

Stage 2: Descent and Emergence of the Baby The second stage, descent and emergence of the baby, typically lasts up to an hour or two. It begins when the baby's head begins to move through the cervix into the vaginal canal, and it ends when the baby emerges completely from the mother's body. If this stage lasts longer than 2 hours, signaling that the baby may need help, a doctor may grasp the baby's head with forceps or, more often, use vacuum extraction with a suction cup to pull the baby out of the mother's body. At the end of this stage, the baby is born but is still attached to the placenta in the mother's body by the umbilical cord, which must be cut and clamped.

FIGURE 3

The Three Stages of Childbirth

(a) During the first stage of labor, a series of increasingly stronger contractions dilates the cervix, the opening to the mother's womb. (b) During the second stage, the baby's head moves down the birth canal and emerges from the vagina. (c) During the brief third stage, the placenta and umbilical cord are expelled from the womb. Then the cord is cut.

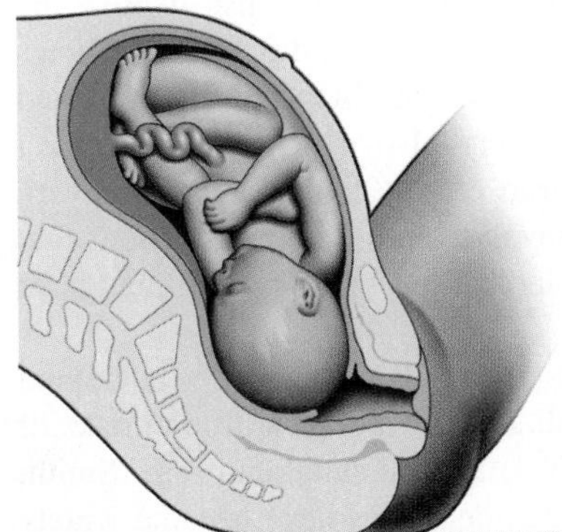

Stage one: Baby positions itself

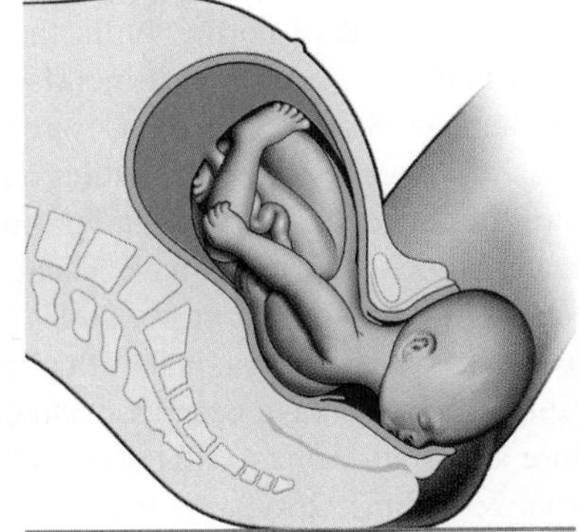

Stage two: Baby begins to emerge

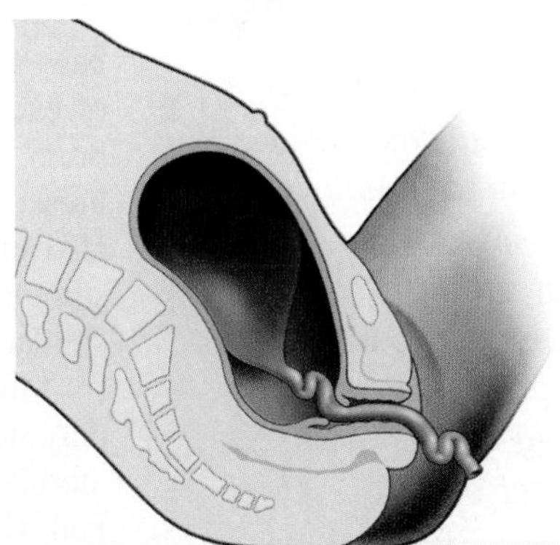

Stage three: Placenta is expelled

Stage 3: Expulsion of the Placenta The third stage, expulsion of the placenta, lasts between 10 minutes and 1 hour. During this stage, the placenta and the remainder of the umbilical cord are expelled from the mother.

ELECTRONIC FETAL MONITORING

electronic fetal monitoring Mechanical monitoring of fetal heartbeat during labor and delivery.

Most births have a happy outcome, but labor and delivery are nonetheless risky. To lessen these risks, technologies have been developed to monitor the fetus prior to delivery. **Electronic fetal monitoring** can be used to track the fetus's heartbeat during labor and delivery and to indicate how the fetal heart is responding to the stress of uterine contractions. Monitoring is most commonly done with the use of sensors attached to the woman's midsection and held in place with an electric belt. The sensors monitor heart rate and alert medical personnel of potentially problematic changes. The procedure was used in 89 percent of live births in the United States in 2004 (Chen, Chauhan, Ananth, Vintzileos, & Abuhamad, 2013).

Electronic fetal monitoring can provide valuable information in high-risk deliveries. However, monitoring can have drawbacks if it is used routinely in low-risk pregnancies. It is costly; it restricts the mother's movements during labor; and, most important, it has an extremely high false-positive rate, suggesting that fetuses are in trouble when they are not. Such warnings may prompt doctors to deliver by the riskier cesarean method rather than vaginally (Banta & Thacker, 2001; Nelson, Dambrosia, Ting, & Grether, 1996).

VAGINAL VERSUS CESAREAN DELIVERY

cesarean delivery Delivery of a baby by surgical removal from the uterus.

The usual method of childbirth, previously described, is *vaginal delivery*. Alternatively, **cesarean delivery** can be used to surgically remove the baby from the uterus through an incision in the mother's abdomen. In 2008, a record-high 32.2 percent of U.S. births were by cesarean delivery, a 56 percent increase since 1996 (Martin, Hamilton, et al., 2010). Use of this procedure also increased in European countries during the 1990s, and despite a modest decrease in 2008 to 30 percent, cesarean birthrates in the United States are among the highest in the world (Gibbons et al., 2010).

The operation is commonly performed when labor progresses too slowly, when the fetus seems to be in trouble, or when the mother is bleeding vaginally. Often a cesarean is needed when the fetus is in the breech position (feet or buttocks first) or in the transverse position (lying crosswise in the uterus) or when the head is too big to pass through the mother's pelvis.

The increase in cesarean rates is attributed largely to rising proportions of older first-time mothers, who tend to have multiple births, and of very premature infants (Martin, Hamilton, et al., 2010) for whom cesarean delivery significantly reduces the risk of dying during the 1st month of life (Malloy, 2008). Physicians' fear of malpractice suits and women's preferences also may play a part in the choice of cesarean deliveries (Ecker & Frigoletto, 2007; Martin, Hamilton, et al., 2009), as may the increased revenue hospitals generate when a woman has a cesarean rather than a vaginal birth.

Cesarean deliveries carry risks of serious complications for the mother, such as bleeding, infection, damage to pelvic organs, and postoperative pain, and heighten risks of problems in future pregnancies (Ecker & Frigoletto, 2007). They also deprive the baby of important benefits of normal birth: the surge of hormones that clear the lungs of excess fluid, mobilize stored fuel to nourish cells, and send blood to the heart and brain (Lagercrantz & Slotkin, 1986). Cesarean delivery also may negatively affect breast-feeding, which can influence bonding (Zanardo et al., 2010). Vaginal delivery also stimulates the release of oxytocin, a hormone involved in uterine contractions that stimulates maternal behavior in animals. There are indications that oxytocin may have similar effects in humans (Swain et al., 2008).

Oxytocin is involved in a variety of positive social interactions outside of the maternal relationship as well. For example, nasal sprays of oxytocin can help people who are low in social competence accurately read the emotions of others.

Bartz, 2010

Most physicians warn that a vaginal birth after cesarean (VBAC) should be attempted only with caution. VBACs have been associated with greater (though still low) risks of uterine rupture and brain damage (Landon et al., 2004) as well as infant death (Smith, Pell, Cameron, & Dobbie, 2002). As the risks of such deliveries have become widely known, the rate of VBACs among U.S. women has fallen by 67 percent since 1996

(Hoyert, Mathews, et al., 2006). Today, if a woman has had a cesarean delivery, chances are about 92 percent that any subsequent deliveries will be by cesarean (MacDorman, Declercq, & Menacker, 2011).

Because the risks of a VBAC are still quite low, a recent NIH (2010b) Consensus Development Conference has concluded that a trial of labor is a reasonable option for women who have had a previous low transverse uterine incision. In addition, in 2010 the American Congress of Obstetricians and Gynecologists issued new guidelines with the goal of expanding the pool of women eligible for VBAC. For example, a trial of labor is now recommended for twin pregnancies, as well as for women who have had more than one cesarean (Grady, 2010).

MEDICATED VERSUS NONMEDICATED DELIVERY

For centuries, pain was considered an unavoidable part of giving birth. Then, in the mid-nineteenth century, sedation with ether or chloroform became common practice as more births took place in hospitals (Fontanel & d'Harcourt, 1997).

During the twentieth century, several alternative methods of **natural childbirth** or **prepared childbirth** were developed. These methods minimize or eliminate the use of drugs that may pose risks for babies and enable both parents to participate fully in a natural, empowering experience.

natural childbirth
Method of childbirth that seeks to prevent pain by eliminating the mother's fear through education about the physiology of reproduction and training in breathing and relaxation during delivery.

prepared childbirth
Method of childbirth that uses instruction, breathing exercises, and social support to induce controlled physical responses to uterine contractions and reduce fear and pain.

The Lamaze method, introduced by the French obstetrician Fernand Lamaze in the late 1950s, acknowledges that labor is painful and teaches expectant mothers to work actively with their bodies through controlled breathing. The woman learns to relax her muscles as a conditioned response to the voice of her coach (usually the prospective father or a friend), who attends classes with her, takes part in the delivery, and helps with the exercises. Using the LeBoyer method, introduced in the 1970s, a woman gives birth in a quiet room under low lights to reduce stress, and the newborn is gently massaged to ease crying. Another technique, developed by the French physician Michael Odent, is submersion of the laboring mother in a soothing pool of water. Other methods use mental imagery, massage, gentle pushing, and deep breathing. Perhaps most extreme is the Bradley method, which rejects all obstetrical procedures and other medical interventions.

Today, improvements in medicated delivery have led many mothers to choose pain relief, sometimes along with natural methods. A woman may be given local (vaginal) anesthesia, also called a *pudendal block,* usually during the second stage of labor or if forceps are used. Or she can receive an *analgesic* (painkiller), which reduces the perception of pain by depressing the activity of the central nervous system. However, analgesics may slow labor, cause maternal complications, and make the baby less alert after birth.

study smart

Medicated versus Nonmedicated Delivery

Approximately 60 percent of women in labor have regional *(epidural or spinal)* injections (Eltzschig, Lieberman, & Camann, 2003). Regional anesthesia, which is injected into a space in the spinal cord between the vertebrae in the lumbar (lower) region, blocks the nerve pathways that would carry the sensation of pain to the brain. Epidurals given early can shorten labor with no added risk of needing cesarean delivery (C. A. Wong et al., 2005).

doula
An experienced mentor who furnishes emotional support and information for a woman during labor.

With any of these forms of anesthesia, a woman can see and participate in the birth process and can hold her newborn immediately afterward. All of these drugs, however, pass through the placenta and enter the fetal blood supply and tissues and thus may pose some danger to the baby.

Pain relief should not be the only consideration in a decision about whether a woman should have anesthesia. More important to her satisfaction with the childbirth experience may be her involvement in decision making, her relationship with the professionals caring for her, and her expectations about labor. Social and cultural attitudes and customs may play a part (Eltzschig et al., 2003). A woman and her doctor should discuss the various options early in pregnancy, but her choices may change once labor is under way.

In many traditional cultures, childbearing women are attended by a **doula,** an experienced mentor, coach, and helper who can furnish emotional support and information and can stay at a woman's bedside throughout labor. In 11 randomized, controlled studies, women attended by doulas had shorter labor, less anesthesia, and fewer cesarean deliveries than women not attended by doulas (Hodnett, Gates, Hofmeyr, & Sakala, 2005).

checkpoint can **you . . .**

- Describe the three stages of vaginal childbirth?
- Discuss reasons for the sharp increase in cesarean births?
- Compare medicated delivery with alternative methods of childbirth?

A doula, or experienced helper, stays at a woman's bedside throughout labor and provides emotional support. Research has found that women attended by doulas tend to have shorter labor and easier deliveries.

The Newborn Baby

neonatal period
First 4 weeks of life, a time of transition from intrauterine dependency to independent existence.

The **neonatal period,** the first 4 weeks of life, is a time of transition from the uterus, where a fetus is supported entirely by the mother, to an independent existence. What are the physical characteristics of newborn babies, and how are they equipped for this crucial transition?

SIZE AND APPEARANCE

neonate
Newborn baby, up to 4 weeks old.

An average **neonate,** or newborn, in the United States is about 20 inches long and weighs about 7½ pounds. At birth, 95 percent of full-term babies weigh between 5½ and 10 pounds and are between 18 and 22 inches long. Boys tend to be slightly longer and heavier than girls, and a firstborn child is likely to weigh less at birth than laterborns. In their first few days, neonates lose as much as 10 percent of their body weight, primarily because of a loss of fluids. They begin to gain weight again at about the 5th day and are generally back to birth weight by the 10th to the 14th day.

New babies have distinctive features, including a large head (one-fourth the body length) and a receding chin (which makes it easier to nurse). Newborn infants also have areas on their heads known as *fontanels* where the bones of the skull do not meet. Many people refer to these holes as soft spots. Fontanels are covered by a tough membrane that allows for flexibility in shape, which eases the passage of the neonate through the vaginal canal. In fact, many vaginally delivered newborns have a misshaped skull for a few weeks after birth as a result of squeezing through the vaginal canal. Over time, the skull rounds out again to a more typical form. In the first 18 months of life, the plates of the skull gradually fuse together.

Many newborns have a pinkish cast; their skin is so thin that it barely covers the capillaries through which blood flows. During the first few days, some neonates are very hairy because some of the *lanugo,* a fuzzy prenatal hair, has not yet fallen off. Almost all new babies are covered with *vernix caseosa* ("cheesy varnish"), an oily protection against infection that dries within the first few days.

"Witch's milk," a secretion that sometimes leaks from the swollen breasts of newborn boys and girls around the 3rd day of life, was believed during the Middle Ages to have special healing powers. Like the whitish or blood-tinged vaginal discharge of some newborn girls, this fluid emission results from high levels of the hormone estrogen, which is secreted by the placenta just before birth and goes away within a few days or weeks. A newborn, especially if premature, also may have swollen genitals.

In 1914, President Woodrow Wilson proclaimed Mother's Day a national holiday.

Gifted children tend to weigh more at birth.

Data suggest that "Cool Caps," designed to lower the temperature of the brain of babies suffering from anoxia, may slow or prevent brain damage by reducing the brain's energy needs.

Gluckman et al., 2005

BODY SYSTEMS

Before birth, blood circulation, respiration, nourishment, elimination of waste, and temperature regulation are accomplished through the mother's body. All these systems, with the exception of the lungs, are functioning to some degree by the time a full-term birth occurs, but the mother's own body systems are still involved and the fetus is not yet an independent entity. After birth, all of the baby's systems and functions must operate on their own. Most of the work of this transition occurs during the first 4 to 6 hours after delivery (Ferber & Makhoul, 2004).

During pregnancy, the fetus and mother have separate circulatory systems and heartbeats. The fetus gets oxygen through the umbilical cord, which carries used blood to the placenta and returns a fresh supply. Once born, a neonate must take over this function fully. Moreover, a newborn needs more oxygen than before. Most babies start to breathe as soon as they are exposed to air. The heartbeat at first is fast and irregular, and blood pressure does not stabilize until about 10 days after birth. If a neonate does not begin breathing within about 5 minutes, the baby may suffer permanent brain injury caused by **anoxia,** lack of oxygen, or *hypoxia,* a reduced oxygen supply. Because infants' lungs have only one-tenth as many air sacs as adults' do, infants (especially those born prematurely) are susceptible to respiratory problems. Anoxia or hypoxia may occur during delivery (though rarely so) as a result of repeated compression of the placenta and umbilical cord with each contraction. This form of *birth trauma* can leave permanent brain damage, causing mental retardation, behavior problems, or even death.

anoxia
Lack of oxygen, which may cause brain damage.

neonatal jaundice
Condition, in many newborn babies, caused by immaturity of liver and evidenced by yellowish appearance; can cause brain damage if not treated promptly.

In the uterus, the fetus relies on the umbilical cord to bring food from the mother and to carry fetal body wastes away. At birth, babies instinctively suck to take in milk, and their own gastrointestinal secretions digest it. During the first few days infants secrete *meconium,* a stringy, greenish-black waste matter formed in the fetal intestinal tract. When the bowels and bladder are full, the sphincter muscles open automatically; a baby will not be able to control these muscles for many months.

The layers of fat that develop during the last 2 months of fetal life help healthy full-term infants to keep their body temperature constant after birth despite changes in air temperature. Newborn babies also maintain body temperature by increasing their activity when air temperature drops.

Three or four days after birth, about half of all babies (and a larger proportion of babies born prematurely) develop **neonatal jaundice:** their skin and eyeballs look yellow. This kind of jaundice is caused by the immaturity of the liver. Usually it is not serious, does not need treatment, and has no long-term effects. However, severe jaundice that is not monitored and treated promptly may result in brain damage.

checkpoint
can **you . . .**

- Describe the normal size and appearance of a newborn, and list several changes that occur within the first few days?
- Compare five fetal and neonatal body systems?
- Identify two dangerous conditions that can appear soon after birth?

MEDICAL AND BEHAVIORAL ASSESSMENT

The first few minutes, days, and weeks after birth are crucial for development. It is important to know as soon as possible whether a baby has any problem that needs special care.

Apgar scale
Standard measurement of a newborn's condition; it assesses appearance, pulse, grimace, activity, and respiration.

The Apgar scale is popular because it's easy to remember and requires no fancy medical equipment, making it useful to quickly assess the health of a newborn.

The Apgar Scale One minute after delivery, and then again 5 minutes after birth, most babies are assessed using the **Apgar scale** (Table 1). Its name, after its developer, Dr. Virginia Apgar (1953), helps us remember its five subtests: *a*ppearance (color), *p*ulse (heart rate), *g*rimace (reflex irritability), *a*ctivity (muscle tone), and *r*espiration (breathing). The newborn is rated 0, 1, or 2 on each measure, for a maximum score of 10. A 5-minute score of 7 to 10—achieved by 98.4 percent of babies born in the United States—indicates that the baby is in good to excellent condition (Martin, Hamilton, et al., 2009). A score below 5–7 means the baby needs help to establish breathing; a score below 4 means the baby needs immediate lifesaving treatment. If resuscitation is successful, bringing the baby's score to 4 or more at 10 minutes, no long-term damage is likely to result (AAP Committee on Fetus and Newborn & American College of Obstetricians and Gynecologists Committee on Obstetric Practice, 1996).

Brazelton Neonatal Behavioral Assessment Scale (NBAS)
Neurological and behavioral test to measure neonate's responses to the environment.

Assessing Neurological Status: The Brazelton Scale The **Brazelton Neonatal Behavioral Assessment Scale (NBAS)** is a neurological and behavioral test to measure a neonate's responses to the environment. It is used to help parents, health care providers, and researchers assess neonates' responsiveness to their physical and social environment, to identify strengths and possible vulnerabilities in neurological functioning, and to predict future development. The test, suitable for infants up to 2 months old, is named for its designer, Dr. T. Berry Brazelton (1973, 1984; Brazelton & Nugent, 1995, 2011). It assesses *motor organization,* as shown by such behaviors as activity level and the ability to bring a hand to the mouth; *reflexes; state changes,* such as irritability, excitability, and ability to quiet down after being upset; *attention and interactive capacities,* as shown by general alertness and response to visual and auditory stimuli; and indications of *central nervous system instability,* such as tremors and changes in skin color. The NBAS takes about 30 minutes, and scores are based on a baby's best performance.

Neonatal Screening for Medical Conditions Children who inherit the enzyme disorder phenylketonuria, or PKU, will become mentally retarded unless they are fed a special diet beginning in the first 3 to 6 weeks of life (National Institute of Child Health and Human Development, 2010). Screening tests administered soon after birth often can discover this and other correctable defects.

TABLE 1 Apgar Scale

Sign*	0	1	2
Appearance (color)	Blue, pale	Body pink, extremities blue	Entirely pink
Pulse (heart rate)	Absent	Slow (below 100)	Rapid (over 100)
Grimace (reflex irritability)	No response	Grimace	Coughing, sneezing, crying
Activity (muscle tone)	Limp	Weak, inactive	Strong, active
Respiration (breathing)	Absent	Irregular, slow	Good, crying

*Each sign is rated in terms of absence or presence from 0 to 2; highest overall score is 10.

Source: Adapted from Apgar, V. (1953). A proposal for a new method of evaluation of the newborn infant. *Current Researches in Anesthesia and Analgesia,* 32(4), 260–267.

Routine screening of all newborn babies for such rare conditions as PKU (1 case in 15,000 births), congenital hypothyroidism (1 in 3,600 to 5,000), galactosemia (1 in 60,000 to 80,000), and other, even rarer, disorders is expensive. Yet the cost of testing thousands of newborns to detect one case of a rare disease may be less than the cost of caring for one mentally retarded person for a lifetime. Now, with more sophisticated blood tests, a single blood specimen can be screened for 20 or more disorders, so about half of all states as well as many developed countries have expanded their mandatory screening programs (Howell, 2006).

checkpoint
can **you**...

- Discuss the uses of the Apgar scale and the Brazelton scale?
- Weigh arguments for and against routine screening for rare disorders?

STATES OF AROUSAL

Are you an early bird or a night owl? Do you get particularly sleepy or alert at certain points of the day? When do you get hungry? These tendencies are likely related to your own internal clock. This clock regulates your states of arousal and activity over the course of a day. Babies also have an internal clock that regulates their daily cycles of eating, sleeping, and elimination and perhaps even their moods. These periodic cycles of wakefulness, sleep, and activity, which govern an infant's **state of arousal,** or degree of alertness (Table 2), seem to be inborn and highly individual. Changes in state are coordinated by multiple areas of the brain and are accompanied by changes in the functioning of virtually all body systems (Ingersoll & Thoman, 1999; Scher, Epstein, & Tirosh, 2004).

state of arousal
An infant's physiological and behavioral status at a given moment in the periodic daily cycle of wakefulness, sleep, and activity.

Most new babies sleep about 75 percent of their time—up to 18 hours a day—but wake up every 3 to 4 hours, day and night, for feeding (Ferber & Makhoul, 2004).

study**smart**

Sleep

TABLE 2 States of Arousal in Infancy

State	Eyes	Breathing	Movements	Responsiveness
Regular sleep	Closed; no eye movement	Regular and slow	None, except for sudden, generalized startles	Cannot be aroused by mild stimuli.
Irregular sleep	Closed; occasional rapid eye movements	Irregular	Muscles twitch, but no major movements	Sounds or light bring smiles or grimaces in sleep.
Drowsiness	Open or closed	Irregular	Somewhat active	May smile, startle, suck, or have erections in response to stimuli.
Alert inactivity	Open	Even	Quiet; may move head, limbs, and trunk while looking around	An interesting environment (with people or things to watch) may initiate or maintain this state.
Waking activity and crying	Open	Irregular	Much activity	External stimuli (such as hunger, cold, pain, being restrained, or being laid down) bring about more activity, perhaps starting with soft whimpering and gentle movements and turning into a rhythmic crescendo of crying or kicking, or perhaps beginning and enduring as uncoordinated thrashing and spasmodic screeching.

Source: Adapted from information in Prechtl & Beintema, 1964; P. H. Wolff, 1966.

In addition to daily sleep cycles, our bodies experience other ones. For example, we experience regular nasal dominance cycles: one nostril is dominant, and this switches on a regular basis over the course of the day.

Eccles, 1978

study smart

Swaddling

Newborns' sleep alternates between quiet (regular) and active (irregular) sleep. Active sleep is probably the equivalent of rapid eye movement (REM) sleep, which in adults is associated with dreaming. Active sleep appears rhythmically in cycles of about 1 hour and accounts for up to 50 percent of a newborn's total sleep time. The amount of REM sleep declines to less than 30 percent of daily sleep time by age 3 and continues to decrease steadily throughout life (Hoban, 2004).

Beginning in their first month, nighttime sleep periods gradually lengthen as babies grow more wakeful in the daytime and need less sleep overall. Some infants begin to sleep through the night as early as 3 months. By 6 months, an infant typically sleeps for 6 hours straight at night, but brief nighttime waking is normal even during late infancy and toddlerhood. A 2-year-old typically sleeps about 13 hours a day, including a single nap, usually in the afternoon (Hoban, 2004).

Babies' sleep rhythms and schedules vary across cultures. Among the Micronesian Truk and the Canadian Hare peoples, babies and children have no regular sleep schedules; they fall asleep whenever they feel tired. Some U.S. parents try to time the evening feeding to encourage nighttime sleep. Mothers in rural Kenya allow their babies to nurse as they please, and their 4-month-olds continue to sleep only 4 hours at a stretch (Broude, 1995). In many predominantly Asian countries, bedtimes are later and total sleep time is shorter than in predominantly Caucasian countries (Mindell et al., 2010).

checkpoint can **you**...

- Explain how states of arousal reflect neurological status, and discuss variations in newborns' states?
- Tell how sleep patterns change, and how cultural practices can affect these patterns?

Complications of Childbirth

Although the great majority of births result in normal, healthy babies, some, sadly, do not. Some are born prematurely or very small, some remain in the womb too long, and some are born dead or die soon after birth. Let's look at these potential complications of birth and how they can be avoided or treated so as to maximize the chances of favorable outcomes.

LOW BIRTH WEIGHT

low-birth-weight babies
Weight of less than 5½ pounds (2,500 grams) at birth because of prematurity or being small-for-date.

preterm (premature) infants
Infants born before completing the 37th week of gestation.

small-for-date (small-for-gestational-age) infants
Infants whose birth weight is less than that of 90 percent of babies of the same gestational age, as a result of slow fetal growth.

Low-birth-weight babies (LBW) are those neonates born weighing less than 2,500 grams (5 pounds) at birth. There are two types of LBW babies: those born early and those born small. Typical gestation is 40 weeks, and babies born before the 37th week of gestation are known as **preterm (premature) infants.** Being born early is closely associated, as might be expected, with being smaller than a full-term infant (Figure 4). More than 43 percent of preterm infants are of low birth weight, as compared with only about 3 percent of full-term infants (Martin et al., 2009). Some babies, known as **small-for-date (small-for-gestational-age) infants,** are born at or around their due dates, but are smaller than would be expected. These babies weigh less than 90 percent of babies of the same gestational age. They are small, not because they were born early and did not have a chance to finish putting on weight, but for other reasons, most commonly inadequate prenatal nutrition, which slows fetal growth.

An estimated 15 percent of all infants worldwide are born with low birth weight, and the percentages are far greater in less economically developed countries (UNICEF, 2008b). The true extent of low birth weight may be much higher because as many as 3 out of 4 newborns in the developing world are not weighed. Low birth weight in developing regions stems primarily from the mother's poor health and nutrition. In the industrialized world, smoking during pregnancy is the leading factor in low birth weight (UNICEF & WHO, 2004).

In the United States, 8.3 percent of infants born in 2006 were low-birth-weight babies—the highest percentage in four decades. In the same year, 12.8 percent of U.S. infants were preterm, 36 percent more than in the early 1980s. Much of the rise in low-birth-weight and preterm births is likely due to delayed childbearing, multiple births, and use of fertility drugs and induced and cesarean deliveries; but low birth weight and prematurity also have increased among single births (Martin,

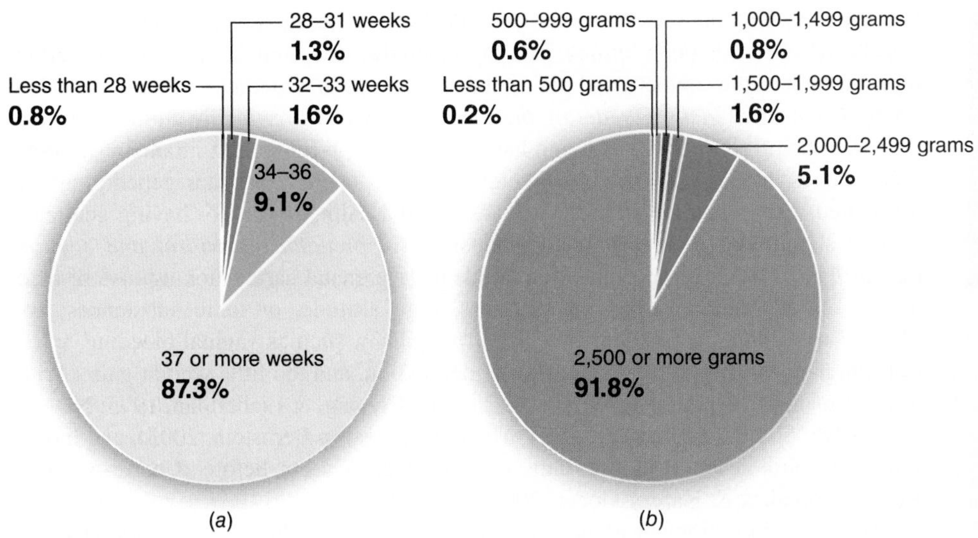

Source: Adapted from Mathews & MacDorman, 2008, figures 2 & 3.

FIGURE 4
Birth Complications, United States, 2005

Percentages of live births that were (a) preterm (less than 37 weeks gestation) or (b) low birth weight (less than 2,500 grams). Low-birth-weight babies can be preterm or small-for-date, or both.

Hamilton, et al., 2009). Despite these issues, however, there is hope. Following steady increases in preterm births from the 1980s on, rates declined in both 2007 and 2008, the first 2-year decline in over three decades (Martin, Osterman, & Sutton, 2010).

From 1990 to 2006, there has been a 20 percent increase in late preterm birth. Late preterm infants, delivered between 34 and 36 weeks' gestation, tend to weigh more and to fare better than those born earlier in gestation; but in comparison with full-term babies, they too are at greater risk of early death or adverse effects (Martin, Hamilton, et al., 2009; Mathews & MacDorman, 2008) such as respiratory distress, hospitalization, and brain injuries. The reason for the rate increase may be the increased use of labor inductions and cesarean delivery prior to the full 40 weeks of normal gestational age (Martin, Kirmeyer, Osterman, & Shepherd, 2009).

Birth weight and length of gestation are the two most important predictors of an infant's survival and health (Mathews & MacDorman, 2008). Together they constitute the second leading cause of death in infancy in the United States after birth defects and the leading cause during the neonatal period (Kung, Hoyert, Xu, & Murphy, 2008). Preterm birth is involved in nearly half of neurological birth defects, such as cerebral palsy, and more than one-third of infant deaths; altogether, low-birth-weight infants account for more than two-thirds of infant deaths. Internationally, low birth weight is an underlying factor in 60 to 80 percent of neonatal deaths worldwide (UNICEF, 2008b).

The United States has been more successful than any other country in saving low-birth-weight babies, but the rate of such births to U.S. women remains higher than in some European and Asian nations (MacDorman & Mathews, 2009; UNICEF & WHO, 2004). Preventing preterm births would greatly increase the number of babies who survive the first year of life. In the last decade, some countries have halved deaths attributed to preterm delivery, most notably with training and the provision of equipment and supplies. For example, even low-tech changes such as ensuring appropriate warmth, support for breast-feeding, and training in basic care for infections and breathing problems can reduce mortality rates (March of Dimes, 2012).

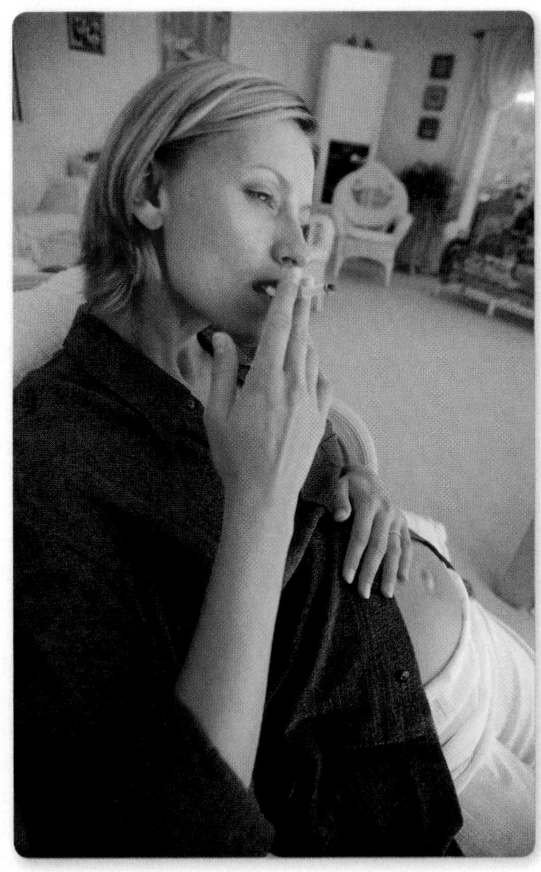

A girl under age 17 who smokes while pregnant has two risk factors for bearing a low-birth-weight baby.

Who Is Likely to Have a Low-Birth-Weight Baby? Factors increasing the likelihood that a woman will have an underweight baby include

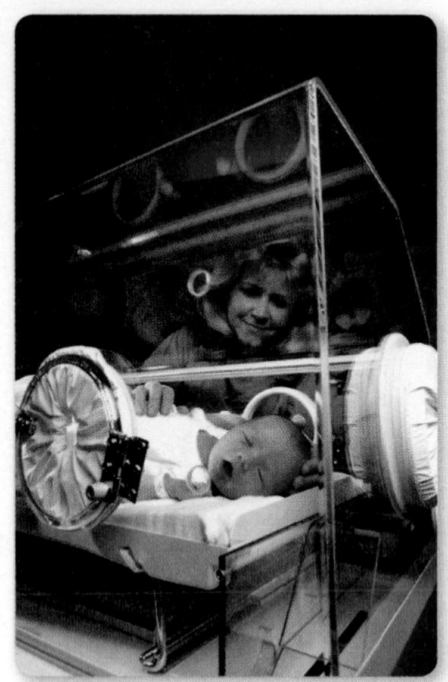

The antiseptic, temperature-controlled crib, or isolette, in which this premature baby lies has holes through which the infant can be examined, touched, and massaged. Frequent human contact helps low-birth-weight infants thrive.

(1) *demographic and socioeconomic factors,* such as being African American, under age 17 or over 40, poor, unmarried, or undereducated, and being born in certain regions, such as the southern and plains states (Thompson, Goodman, Chang, & Stukel, 2005); (2) *medical factors predating the pregnancy,* such as having no children or more than four, being short or thin, having had previous low-birth-weight infants or multiple miscarriages, having had low birth weight oneself, having particular genetic variants associated with higher risk (National Institutes of Health, 2010a), or having genital or urinary abnormalities or chronic hypertension; (3) *prenatal behavioral and environmental factors,* such as poor nutrition, inadequate prenatal care, smoking, use of alcohol or other drugs, or exposure to stress, high altitude, or toxic substances; and (4) *medical conditions associated with the pregnancy,* such as vaginal bleeding, infections, high or low blood pressure, anemia, depression, and too little weight gain (Arias, MacDorman, Strobino, & Guyer, 2003; Chomitz, Cheung, & Lieberman, 1995; Nathanielsz, 1995; Shiono & Behrman, 1995; Yonkers, quoted in Bernstein, 2003), and having last given birth fewer than 6 months or more than 5 years before (Conde-Agudelo, Rosas-Bermúdez, & Kafury-Goeta, 2006).

The high proportion (11.85 percent) of low-birth-weight babies in the non-Hispanic black population—more than twice as high as among white and Hispanic babies (Martin, Hamilton, et al., 2009)—is a major factor in the high mortality rates of black babies (Martin, Hamilton, et al., 2007; MacDorman & Mathews, 2008). Reasons for the greater prevalence of low birth weight, preterm births, and infant mortality among African American babies include (1) health behaviors and SES; (2) higher levels of stress in African American women; (3) greater susceptibility to stress; (4) the impact of racism, which may contribute to or exacerbate stress; and (5) ethnic differences in stress-related body processes, such as blood pressure and immune reactions (Giscombé & Lobel, 2005).

Immediate Treatment and Outcomes The most pressing fear regarding very small babies is that they will die in infancy. Because their immune systems are not fully developed, they are especially vulnerable to infection, which has been linked to slowed growth and developmental delays (Stoll et al., 2004). Also, these infants' nervous systems may be too immature for them to perform functions basic to survival, such as sucking, so they may need to be fed intravenously (through the veins). Feeding them breast milk can help prevent infection (AAP Section on Breastfeeding, 2005). Moreover, because they do not have enough fat to insulate them and to generate heat, it is hard for them to stay warm.

A low-birth-weight or at-risk preterm baby may be placed in an *isolette* (an antiseptic, temperature-controlled crib) and fed through tubes. To counteract the sensory impoverishment of life in an isolette, hospital workers and parents are encouraged to give these small babies special handling. Gentle massage seems to foster growth, weight gain, motor activity, alertness, and behavioral organization, as assessed by the Brazelton NBAS (T. Field, Diego, & Hernandez-Reif, 2007).

kangaroo care
Method of skin-to-skin contact in which a newborn is laid face down between the mother's breasts for an hour or so at a time after birth.

Kangaroo care, a method of skin-to-skin contact in which a newborn is laid face down between the mother's breasts for an hour or so at a time after birth, can help preemies—and full-term infants—make the adjustment from fetal life to the jumble of sensory stimuli in the outside world. This soothing maternal contact seems to reduce stress on the central nervous system and help with self-regulation of sleep and activity (Ferber & Makhoul, 2004).

Respiratory distress syndrome is common in preterm babies who lack an adequate amount of an essential lung-coating substance called *surfactant,* which keeps air sacs from collapsing. These babies may breathe irregularly or stop breathing altogether. Administering surfactant to high-risk preterm newborns has dramatically increased survival rates since 1994 (Martin, Hamilton, et al., 2005; Msall, 2004; Stoelhorst et al., 2005) as well as neurological and developmental status at 18 to 22 months (Vohr, Wright, Poole, & McDonald for the NICHD Neonatal Research Network Follow-up Study, 2005). Since 2000 the percentage of *extremely-low-birth-weight* infants (about

1 to 2 pounds at birth) who survived without neurological impairment has increased further (Wilson-Costello et al., 2007).

Long-Term Outcomes Even if low-birth-weight babies survive the dangerous early days, their future is in question. For example, both preterm and small-for-gestational-age infants may be at increased risk of adult-onset diabetes, and small-for-gestational-age infants appear to be at increased risk of cardiovascular disease (Hofman et al., 2004; Sperling, 2004). Moreover, preterm birth leads to heightened risk of death throughout childhood, diminished reproductive rates in adulthood, and, for women, increased risk of bearing preterm infants themselves (Swamy, Ostbye, & Skjaerven, 2008). In addition, the shorter the period of gestation, the greater the likelihood of cerebral palsy, mental retardation, autistic disorders, and low educational and job-related income levels (Moster, Lie, & Markestad, 2008).

A brain lipid called Docosahexaenoic acid (DHA) is not adequately developed in infants born before 33 weeks' gestation and can lead to impaired mental development. In a longitudinal study of infants born before that gestational age, girls, but not boys, who received compensating high doses of fatty acids through breast milk or infant formula until what would have been full term showed better mental development at 18 months than premature girls who had been fed a low-DHA diet (Makrides et al., 2009).

In longitudinal studies of extremely low-birth-weight infants (about 1 to 2 pounds at birth) and infants born before 26 weeks of gestation, the survivors tend to be smaller than full-term children and more likely to have neurological, sensory, cognitive, educational, and behavioral problems (Anderson, Doyle, & the Victorian Infant Collaborative Study Group, 2003; Mikkola et al., 2005; Samara, Marlow, & Wolke for the EPICure Study Group, 2008). In a study of children born in the United Kingdom and Ireland in 1995, those born at or before 25 weeks of gestation—especially boys—were about 5 times more likely to show serious behavior problems at age 6 than a control group who had not been born preterm, possibly because early separation from the mother affects the developing brain (Samara et al., 2008).

The less low-birth-weight children weigh at birth, the lower their IQs and achievement test scores tend to be and the more likely they are to require special education or to repeat a grade (Saigal, Hoult, Streiner, Stoskopf, & Rosenbaum, 2000). Cognitive deficits, especially in memory and processing speed, have been noted among very-low-birth-weight babies (2 to 3½ pounds at birth) by age 5 or 6 months, continuing through childhood (Rose, Feldman, & Jankowski, 2002) and into adulthood (Fearon et al., 2004; Hardy, Kuh, Langenberg, & Wadsworth, 2003). Very-low-birth-weight children and adolescents also tend to have more behavioral and mental health problems than those born at normal weight (Hack et al., 2004) as well as impaired motor development both in the 1st year of life and throughout childhood and adolescence (de Kieviet, Piek, Aarnousde-Moens, & Oosterlaan, 2009).

On the other hand, in a prospective longitudinal study of 166 extremely-low-birth-weight babies in Ontario, Canada, where health care is universal, a significant majority overcame earlier difficulties to become functioning young adults—finishing high school, working, and living independently, and many of them pursuing postsecondary education. These children were predominantly white and in two-parent families, about half of them of high SES (Saigal et al., 2006). Birth weight alone, then, does not necessarily determine the outcome. Environmental factors make a difference, as we discuss in a subsequent section.

CAN A SUPPORTIVE ENVIRONMENT OVERCOME EFFECTS OF BIRTH COMPLICATIONS?

For nearly five decades, Emmy E. Werner (1987, 1995; Werner & Smith, 2001) and a team of pediatricians, psychologists, public health workers, and social workers have followed 698 children, born in 1955 on the Hawaiian island of Kauai, from gestation

Thanks to their own resilience, many children who live in less than ideal circumstances, such as this child in war-torn Afghanistan, can develop into self-confident, successful adults.

to middle adulthood. The researchers interviewed the mothers-to-be, monitored their pregnancies, and interviewed them again when the children were ages 1, 2, and 10. They observed the children at home, gave them aptitude, achievement, and personality tests in elementary and high school, and obtained progress reports from their teachers. The young people themselves were interviewed periodically after they reached adulthood.

Although they are fragile and must be handled carefully, low-birth-weight babies who are cuddled and held gain weight and are released from the hospital faster.

The physical and psychological development of children who had suffered low birth weight or other birth complications were seriously impaired *only* when the children grew up in persistently poor environmental circumstances. Unless the early damage was so serious as to require institutionalization, those children who had a stable and enriching environment did well (E. E. Werner, 1985, 1987). In fact, they had fewer language, perceptual, emotional, and school problems than did children who had *not* experienced unusual stress at birth but who had received little intellectual stimulation or emotional support at home (E. E. Werner, 1989; E. Werner et al., 1968). The children who had been exposed to *both* birth-related problems and later stressful experiences had the worst health and the most delayed development (E. E. Werner, 1987).

Most remarkable is the resilience of children who escaped damage despite *multiple* sources of stress. Even when birth complications were combined with chronic poverty, family discord, divorce, or parents who were mentally ill, many children came through relatively unscathed. Of the 276 children who at age 2 had been identified as having four or more risk factors, two-thirds developed serious learning or behavior problems by age 10 or, by age 18, had become pregnant, gotten in trouble with the law, or become emotionally disturbed. Yet by age 30, one-third of these highly at-risk children had managed to become "competent, confident, and caring adults" (E. E. Werner, 1995, p. 82). Of the full sample, about half of those on whom the researchers were able to obtain follow-up data successfully weathered the age-30 and age-40 transitions. Women tended to be better adapted than men (E. Werner & Smith, 2001).

protective factors
Influences that reduce the impact of potentially negative influences and tend to predict positive outcomes.

Protective factors, which tended to reduce the impact of early stress, fell into three categories: (1) individual attributes, such as energy, sociability, and intelligence; (2) affectionate ties with at least one supportive family member; and (3) rewards at school, work, or place of worship that provide a sense of meaning and control over one's life (E. E. Werner, 1987). Although the home environment seemed to have the most marked effect in childhood, in adulthood the individuals' own qualities made a greater difference (E. E. Werner, 1995).

This study underlines the need to look at development in context. It shows how biological and environmental influences interact, making resiliency possible even in babies born with serious complications.

checkpoint can **you**...

- Name three protective factors identified by the Kauai study?

POSTMATURITY

When people think about birth complications, they generally think about issues related to being born too early or too small. However, babies can also be negatively affected by staying too long in the womb. In fact, nearly 6 percent of pregnant women in the United States have not gone into labor after 42 or more weeks' gestation (Martin, Hamilton, et al., 2009). At that point, a baby is considered **postmature.** Postmature babies tend to be long and thin because they have kept growing in the womb but have had an insufficient blood supply toward the end of gestation. Possibly because the placenta has aged and become less efficient, it may provide less oxygen. The baby's greater size also complicates labor; the mother has to deliver a baby the size of a normal 1-month-old.

postmature
A fetus not yet born as of 2 weeks after the due date or 42 weeks after the mother's last menstrual period.

Because postmature fetuses are at risk of brain damage or even death, doctors sometimes induce labor or perform cesarean deliveries. The increasing use of both of these techniques probably explains a decline in postterm births in recent years (Martin, Hamilton, et al., 2006).

STILLBIRTH

Still birth, the sudden death of a fetus at or after the 20th week of gestation, is a tragic union of opposites—birth and death. Sometimes fetal death is diagnosed prenatally; in other cases, the baby's death is discovered during labor or delivery.

stillbirth
Death of a fetus at or after the 20th week of gestation.

Worldwide, about 3.2 million fetuses were stillborn annually (Lawn et al., 2010). In the United States the incidence of stillbirth has fallen steadily since 1990, mainly due to a decline in third-trimester deaths. Still, there were almost 26,000 stillbirths in the United States in 2006, a number representing 6.05 fetal deaths for every 1,000 live births (MacDorman, Kirmeyer, & Wilson, 2012). Boys are more likely to be stillborn than girls, non-Hispanic black fetuses are more likely to be stillborn than fetuses of other racial/ethnic groups, and twins and higher multiples are more likely to be stillborn than singletons. Use of assisted reproductive technologies may increase the risk of stillbirth (MacDorman & Kirmeyer, 2009).

Although the cause of stillbirth is often not clear, many stillborn fetuses are small for gestational age, indicating malnourishment in the womb (MacDorman & Kirmeyer, 2009; Surkan, Stephansson, Dickman, & Cnattingius, 2004). The reduction in stillbirths may be due to electronic fetal monitoring, ultrasound, and other measures to identify fetuses at risk for restricted growth. Fetuses believed to have problems can have prenatal surgery in the womb to correct congenital problems or be delivered prematurely (Goldenberg, Kirby, & Culhane, 2004; Goldenberg & Rouse, 1998).

A stillbirth is what family therapist Pauline Boss (2007) calls an *ambiguous loss,* one that leaves the bereaved parents with more questions than answers. The bereaved parents may ask themselves, "Why did our baby die? Did I contribute to the death? Should we have another baby? Will this happen again? Could I endure it?" Although the stillborn baby is physically absent, "the baby's psychological presence continues for the rest of the family members' lives" (Cacciatore, DeFrain, & Jones, 2008, p. 4). A mother may express shame over her body's failure to produce a live, healthy baby and may wonder whether her husband blames her. Siblings may show such physical symptoms as insomnia, lack of appetite or overeating, regression in development, anxiety, irritability, anger, apathy, nervous tics, muscle tension, emotional outbursts, and tearfulness (Cacciatore et al., 2008).

checkpoint
can **you**...

- Discuss the risk factors, treatment, and outcomes for low-birth-weight babies?
- Explain the risks attending postmaturity?
- Discuss trends and risk factors for stillbirth?

Survival and Health

Infancy and toddlerhood are risky times of life. How many babies die during the first year, and why? What can be done to prevent dangerous or debilitating childhood diseases? How can we ensure that infants and toddlers live, grow, and develop as they should?

REDUCING INFANT MORTALITY

Great strides have been made in protecting the lives of new babies, but these advances are not evenly distributed. In 2012, there were 6.6 million worldwide infant deaths. Nearly 3 million of those babies died in their first month of life, and half of those deaths occurred in the first 24 hours of life. The vast majority of these early deaths are in developing countries, especially in South Asia and West and Central Africa (World Health Organization, 2013; Figure 5).

The chief causes of neonatal death worldwide, accounting for 86 percent of all neonatal deaths, are severe infections, including sepsis or pneumonia, tetanus, and diarrhea (36 percent); preterm delivery (27 percent); and asphyxia (difficulty breathing)

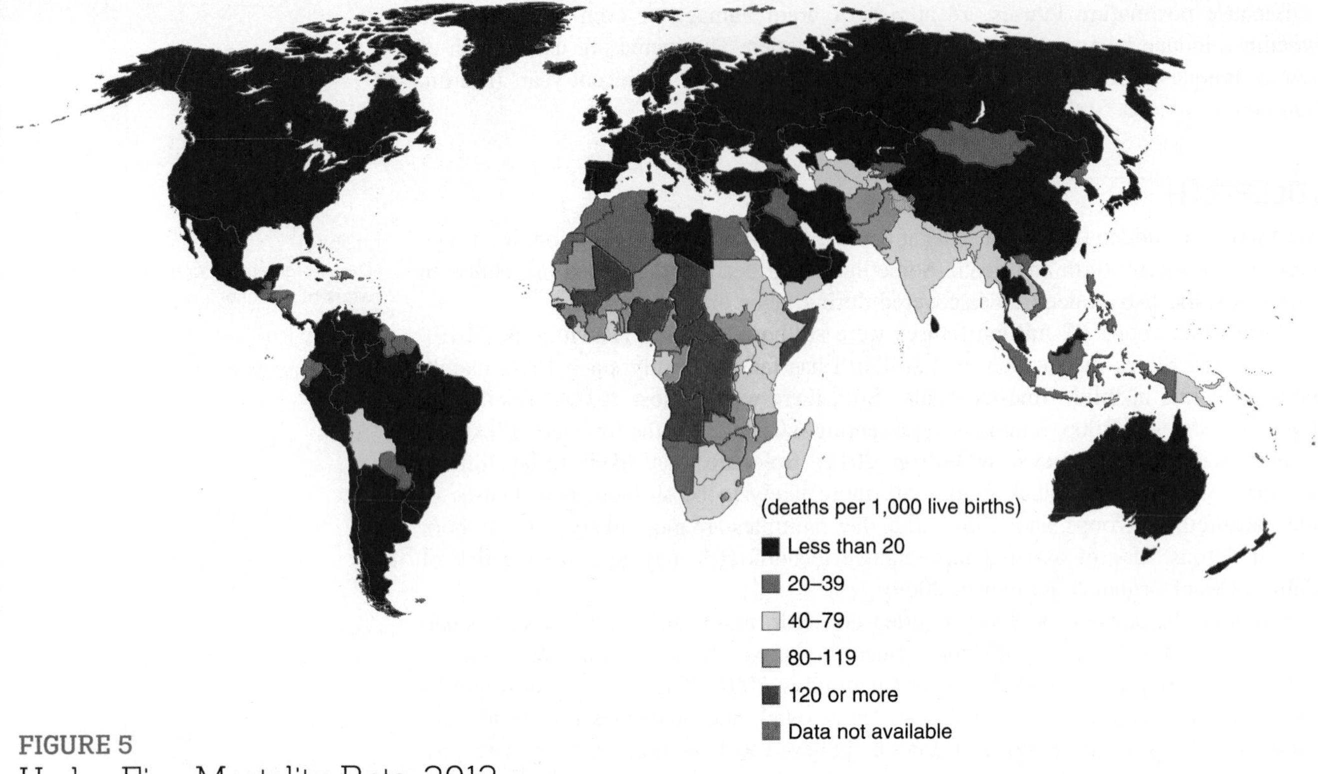

FIGURE 5

Under-Five Mortality Rate, 2012

Most neonatal deaths occur in sub-Saharan Africa and Asia.

Source: WHO, 2013.

at birth (23 percent) (UNICEF, 2008b). Many of these deaths are preventable, resulting from a combination of poverty, poor maternal health and nutrition, infection, and inadequate medical care (Lawn et al., 2005; UNICEF, 2008b). About two-thirds of maternal deaths from complications of childbirth occur during the immediate postnatal period, and infants whose mothers have died are more likely to die than infants whose mothers remain alive (Sines et al., 2007; UNICEF, 2007, 2008b). Community-based postnatal care for mothers and babies in the first few days after birth might save many of these lives.

infant mortality rate
Proportion of babies born alive who die within the 1st year.

In the United States, the **infant mortality rate**—the proportion of babies who die within the first year—has fallen almost continuously since the beginning of the twentieth century, when 100 infants died for every 1,000 born alive. However, the rate plateaued from 2000 to 2006, when 6.7 infants died for every 1,000 live births (Mathews & McDorman, 2010). More than half of U.S. infant deaths take place in the first week of life, and about two-thirds occur during the neonatal period (Heron et al., 2009).

Birth defects are the leading cause of infant deaths in the United States, followed by disorders related to prematurity or low birth weight, sudden infant death syndrome (SIDS), maternal complications of pregnancy, and complications of the placenta, umbilical cord, and membranes (Heron et al., 2009). In 2005, more than two-thirds of all deaths in infancy were of preterm babies, and more than half were of very preterm infants. In that same year, only 0.8 percent of U.S. infants were born weighing less than 1,000 grams (about 2 pounds), but they represented nearly half (48.2 percent) of all infant deaths (Mathews & MacDorman, 2008).

The overall improvement in U.S. infant mortality rates since 1990 is attributable largely to prevention of SIDS (discussed in the next section) as well as to effective treatment for respiratory distress and medical advances in keeping very small babies alive (Arias et al., 2003). Still, mainly because of the prevalence of preterm births and low birth weight, U.S. babies have less chance of reaching their 1st birthday than do babies in many other developed countries (MacDorman & Mathews, 2009). The U.S. infant mortality rate in 2008 was higher than in 44 countries worldwide (U.S. Census Bureau, 2009a; Figure 6).

Racial/Ethnic Disparities in Infant Mortality Although infant mortality has declined for all races and ethnic groups in the United States, large disparities remain. Black babies are nearly 2½ times as likely to die in their 1st year as white and Hispanic babies (Figure 7). This disparity largely reflects the greater prevalence of low birth weight and SIDS among African Americans. Infant mortality among American Indians and Alaska Natives is about 1½ times that among white babies, mainly due to SIDS and fetal alcohol syndrome (American Public Health Association, 2004; Mathews & MacDorman, 2008).

Intragroup variations are often overlooked. Within the Hispanic population, Puerto Rican infants are more than twice as likely to die as Cuban infants (Kung et al., 2008). Asian Americans, overall, are least likely to die in infancy, but Hawaiian infants are more than 3 times as likely to die as Chinese American babies (NCHS, 2006).

Racial or ethnic disparities in access to and quality of health care for minority children (Flores, Olson, & Tomany-Korman, 2005) may help account for differences in infant mortality, but behavioral factors such as obesity, smoking, and alcohol consumption also play a part. Because causes and risk factors for infant mortality vary among ethnic groups, efforts to further reduce infant deaths need to focus on factors specific to each ethnic group (Hesso & Fuentes, 2005).

	Infant mortality rate
Hong Kong	1.8
Sweden	2.4
Japan	2.8
Finland	3.0
Norway	3.1
Singapore	3.1
Czech Republic	3.4
Greece	3.8
Portugal	3.8
Spain	3.8
France	3.9
Germany	3.9
Ireland	4.0
Austria	4.2
Switzerland	4.2
Denmark	4.4
Israel	4.4
Italy	4.6
Korea	4.6
Netherlands	4.9
Australia	5.0
New Zealand	5.1
Cuba	5.3
United Kingdom	5.3
United States	6.8

FIGURE 6

Infant Mortality Rates in Industrialized Countries

Despite dramatic improvements, the United States has a higher infant mortality rate than 24 other industrialized nations, largely because of its diverse population, health disparities for disadvantaged groups, and its high percentage of low-birth-weight infants, especially among African American infants.

Source: United Nations Statistics Division, 2007.

Sudden Infant Death Syndrome (SIDS) **Sudden infant death syndrome (SIDS),** sometimes called *crib death*, is the sudden death of an infant under age 1 in which the cause of death remains unexplained after a thorough investigation that includes an autopsy. SIDS is the leading cause of postneonatal infant death in the United States (Anderson & Smith, 2005). It peaks between 2 and 3 months and is most common among African American and American Indian/Alaska Native babies; boy babies; those born preterm; and those whose mothers are young and received late or no prenatal care (AAP Task Force on Sudden Infant Death Syndrome, 2005).

SIDS most likely results from a combination of factors. An underlying biological defect may make some infants vulnerable during a critical period to certain contributing or triggering experiences, such as prenatal exposure to smoke—one of the major identified risk factors. In the absence of any risk factors, SIDS is rare. Babies who die from SIDS frequently have multiple risk factors (Ostfeld, Esposity, Perl, & Hegyl, 2010).

At least six gene mutations affecting the heart have been linked to SIDS cases (Ackerman et al., 2001; Cronk et al., 2006; Tester et al., 2006). Nearly 10 percent of victims have mutations or variations in genes associated with irregular heart rhythms (Arnestad et al., 2007; Wang et al., 2007). A gene variant that appears in 1 out of 9 African Americans may help explain the greater incidence of SIDS among black babies (Plant et al., 2006; Weese-Mayer et al., 2004).

sudden infant death syndrome (SIDS)
Sudden and unexplained death of an apparently healthy infant.

An important clue has emerged from the discovery of defects in the brain stem, which regulates breathing, heartbeat, body temperature, and arousal (Paterson et al., 2006). These defects may prevent SIDS babies who are sleeping face down or on their sides from waking or turning their heads when they breathe stale air containing carbon dioxide trapped under their blankets (AAP Task Force on Infant Sleep Position and Sudden Infant Death Syndrome, 2000; Panigrahy et al., 2000). Similarly, babies who have low levels of serotonin may not awaken under conditions of oxygen deprivation and carbon dioxide buildup and are thus at greater risk as well (Duncan et al., 2010). Sleeping with a fan, which circulates the air, has been associated with a 72 percent reduction in SIDS risk (Coleman-Phox, Odouli, & De-Kun, 2008).

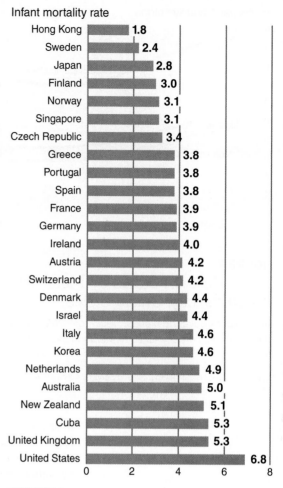

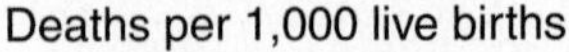

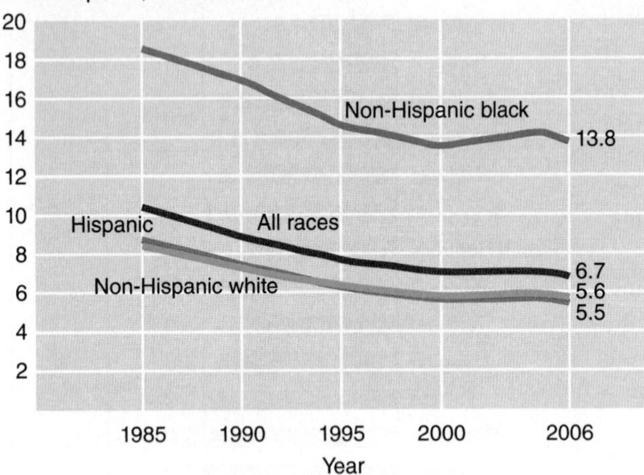

FIGURE 7

Infant Mortality Rates by Maternal Race/Ethnicity, United States

Black babies have the highest death rates. Mortality rates of black infants are 2.4 times higher than those of white infants.

Source: USDHHS, Health Resources and Services Administration, Maternal and Child Health Bureau, 2008.

Research strongly supports a relationship between SIDS and sleeping on the stomach. SIDS rates declined in the United States by 53 percent between 1992 and 2001 (AAP Task Force on Sudden Infant Death Syndrome, 2005) and in some other countries by as much as 70 percent following recommendations that healthy babies be laid down to sleep on their backs (Dwyer, Ponsonby, Blizzard, Newman, & Cochrane, 1995; Hunt, 1996; Skadberg et al., 1998; Willinger, Hoffman, & Hartford, 1994).

Doctors recommend that infants *not* sleep on soft surfaces, such as pillows, quilts, or sheepskin, or under loose covers, which, especially when the infant is face down, may increase the risk of overheating or rebreathing (breathing the infant's own exhaled carbon dioxide) (AAP Task Force on Sudden Infant Death Syndrome, 2005). The risk of SIDS is increased 20-fold when infants sleep in adult beds, on sofas or chairs, or on other surfaces not designed for infants (Scheers, Rutherford, & Kemp, 2003). Studies associate use of pacifiers with lower risk of SIDS. Contrary to popular reports, studies show no connection between immunizations and SIDS (AAP Task Force on Sudden Infant Death Syndrome, 2005; Hauck et al., 2003; Hauck, Omojokun, & Siadaty, 2005; Mitchell, Blair, & L'Hoir, 2006).

Deaths from Injuries Unintentional injuries are the fifth leading cause of death in infancy in the United States (Heron et al., 2009) and the third leading cause of death after the first 4 weeks, following SIDS and birth defects (Anderson & Smith, 2005). Infants have the second highest death rate from unintentional injuries among children and adolescents, exceeded only by 15- to 19-year-olds. About two-thirds of injury deaths in the 1st year of life are by suffocation. Among children ages 1 to 4, traffic accidents are the leading cause of unintentional injury deaths, followed by drowning and burns. Falls are by far the major cause of nonfatal injuries in both infancy (52 percent) and toddlerhood (43 percent). Boys of all ages are more likely to be injured and to die from their injuries than girls (Borse et al., 2008). Black infants are 2½ times as likely to die of injuries as white infants and more than 3 times as likely to be victims of homicide (Tomashek, Hsia, & Iyasu, 2003).

The back-to-sleep campaign is a great example of a successful public health campaign. However, it comes with unexpected consequences. Because babies spend less time trying to push up on their arms to see the world, several motor milestones (such as rolling over) are now delayed relative to where they used to be.

Davis, Moon, Sachs, & Ottolini, 1998

checkpoint
can you . . .

- Summarize trends in infant mortality and injury deaths, and give reasons for racial/ethnic disparities?
- Discuss risk factors for, causes of, and prevention of sudden infant death syndrome?

About 90 percent of all injury deaths in infancy are due to one of four causes: suffocation, motor vehicle traffic, drowning, and residential fires or burns (Pressley et al., 2007). Many of these accidental injuries occur at home. Some injuries reported as accidental may actually be inflicted by caregivers unable to cope with a crying baby.

IMMUNIZATION FOR BETTER HEALTH

Such once-familiar and sometimes fatal childhood illnesses as measles, pertussis (whooping cough), and polio are now largely preventable, thanks to the development of vaccines that mobilize the body's natural defenses. Unfortunately, many children still are not adequately protected.

Worldwide, more than 78 percent of children now receive routine vaccinations during their 1st year (UNICEF, 2007). Still, during 2002, 2.5 million vaccine-preventable deaths occurred among children under 5 years old, nearly 2 million of them in Africa and Southeast Asia. A Global Immunization Vision Strategy for 2006–2015 seeks to extend routine vaccinations to every eligible person (Department of Immunization, Vaccines, and Biologicals, WHO; United Nations Children's Fund; Global Immunization Division, National Center for Immunization and Respiratory Diseases; & McMorrow, 2006).

The 1998 article by Dr. Andrew Wakefield that first linked autism and vaccines was retracted in February of 2010 by The Lancet *amid allegations of bias and unethical conduct by Dr. Wakefield.*

In the United States, thanks to a nationwide immunization initiative, 77.4 percent of 19- to 35-month-olds in all racial/ethnic groups had completed a recommended series of childhood vaccinations* in 2007, a record high, and at least 90 percent had received most of the recommended vaccines (Darling, Kolasa, & Wooten, 2008). Still, many children, especially poor children, lack one or more of the required shots, and there are regional differences in coverage (Darling et al., 2008).

Some parents hesitate to immunize their children because of speculation that certain vaccines—particularly the diphtheria-pertussis-tetanus (DPT) and measles-mumps-rubella (MMR) vaccines—may cause autism or other neurodevelopmental disorders, but the preponderance of evidence suggests no reason for this concern (Hornig et al., 2008; see Box 2). With nearly 8 percent of children who are eligible for vaccination left unprotected against measles, recent outbreaks of the disease have occurred in certain communities (Darling et al., 2008).

Another parental worry is that infants receive too many vaccines for their immune system to handle safely. Actually, the opposite is true. Multiple vaccines fortify the immune system against a variety of bacteria and viruses and reduce related infections (Offit et al., 2002).

The rates of infectious diseases have plummeted in the United States thanks to widespread immunization, but many children in low-income urban areas are not properly immunized.

checkpoint
can **you**...

- **Explain why full immunization of all infants and preschoolers is important?**

Early Physical Development

Fortunately, most infants survive, develop normally, and grow up healthy. What principles govern their development? What are the typical growth patterns of body and brain? How do babies' needs for nourishment and sleep change? How do their sensory and motor abilities develop?

PRINCIPLES OF DEVELOPMENT

As before birth, physical growth and development follow the *cephalocaudal principle* and the *proximodistal principle*.

According to the **cephalocaudal principle,** growth occurs from the top down. Because the brain grows rapidly before birth, a newborn baby's head is disproportionately large. The head becomes proportionately smaller as the child grows in height and the lower parts of the body develop (Figure 8). Sensory and motor development proceed according to the same principle: infants learn to use the upper parts of the body before the lower parts. So, for example, a baby learns to use her arms for grasping prior to learning to use her legs for walking, and holds her head up before she can sit unaided.

cephalocaudal principle
Principle that development proceeds in a head-to-tail direction, that is, that upper parts of the body develop before lower parts of the trunk.

According to the **proximodistal principle** (inner to outer), growth and motor development proceed from the center of the body outward. In the womb, the head and trunk

proximodistal principle
Principle that development proceeds from within to without, that is, that parts of the body near the center develop before the extremities.

*The series consists of four doses of diphtheria, tetanus, and pertussis vaccines; three doses of polio vaccines; one or more doses of measles, mumps, and rubella vaccine; three doses of Haemophilus influenza type b vaccine; three doses of hepatitis B vaccine; and one or more doses of varicella, or chicken-pox, vaccine (Darling et al., 2008).

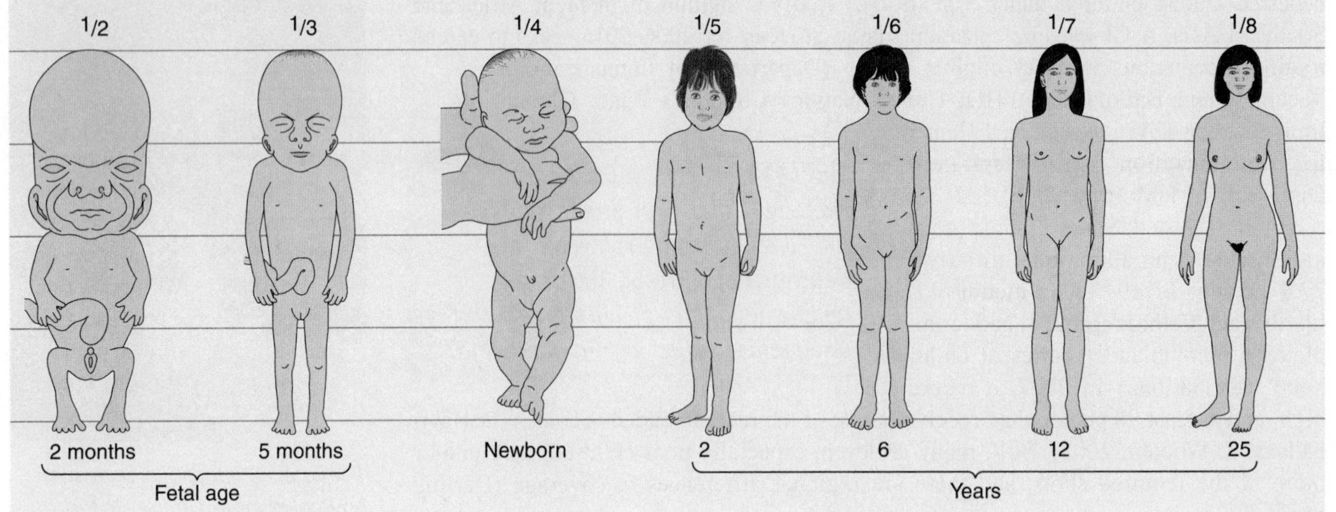

FIGURE 8
Changes in Proportions of the Human Body during Growth

The most striking change is that the head becomes smaller relative to the rest of the body. The fractions indicate head size as a proportion of total body length at several ages. More subtle is the stability of the trunk proportion (from neck to crotch). The increasing leg proportion is almost exactly the reverse of the decreasing head proportion.

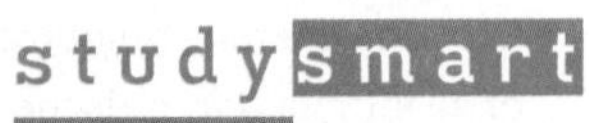

Cephalocaudal and Proximodistal Principles of Growth

develop before the arms and legs, then the hands and feet, and then the fingers and toes. During infancy and early childhood, the limbs continue to grow faster than the hands and feet. Babies learn to use the parts of their bodies closest to the center of their body before they learn to use the outermost parts. For example, babies first learn to control their arms when reaching, then use their hands in a scooping motion, then finally learn to use their thumb and pointer finger in a pincer grip.

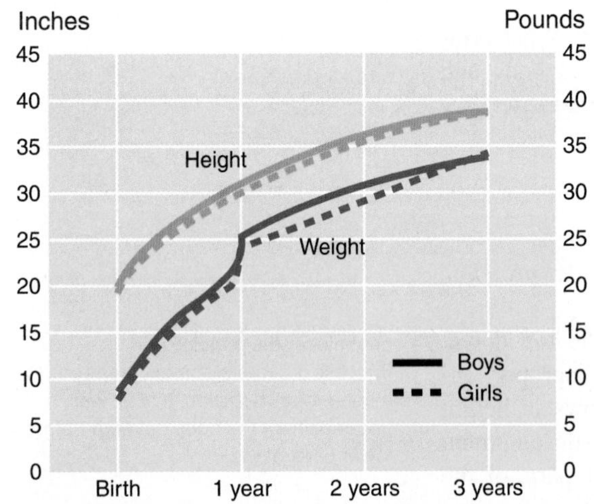

FIGURE 9
Growth in Height and Weight during Infancy and Toddlerhood

Babies grow most rapidly in both height and weight during the first few months of life and then taper off somewhat by age 3. Baby boys are slightly larger, on average, than baby girls.

Note: Curves shown are for the 50th percentiles for each sex.

GROWTH PATTERNS

Children grow faster during the first 3 years, especially during the first few months, than they ever will again (Figure 9). By 5 months, the average U.S. baby boy's birth weight has doubled to nearly 16 pounds, and, by 1 year, has more than tripled to exceed 25 pounds. This rapid growth rate tapers off during the 2nd and 3rd years. A boy typically gains about 5½ pounds by his second birthday and 3 more pounds by his third, when he tips the scales at almost 34 pounds. A boy's height typically increases by 10 inches during the 1st year (making the average 1-year-old boy about 30 inches tall), by 5 inches during the 2nd year (so that the average 2-year-old boy is about 3 feet tall), and by 2½ inches during the 3rd year (to approach 39 inches). Girls follow a similar pattern but are slightly smaller at most ages (Kuczmarski et al., 2000; McDowell et al., 2008). As a baby grows into a toddler, body shape and proportions change too; a 3-year-old typically is slender compared with a chubby, potbellied 1-year-old.

The genes an infant inherits have a strong influence on whether the child will be tall or short, thin or stocky, or somewhere in between. This genetic influence interacts with such environmental influences as nutrition and living conditions. For example, Japanese American children are taller and weigh more than children the same age in Japan, probably because of dietary differences (Broude, 1995). Today children in many developed countries are growing taller and maturing at an earlier age than children did a century ago, probably because of better nutrition, improved sanitation and medical care, and the decrease in child labor.

Teething usually begins around 3 or 4 months, when infants begin grabbing almost everything in sight to put into their mouths; but the first tooth may not actually arrive until sometime between 5 and 9 months, or even later. By the 1st birthday, babies generally have 6 to 8 teeth; by age 2½, they have a mouthful of 20.

checkpoint can you . . .

- Summarize typical patterns of physical growth and change during the first 3 years?
- Identify factors that affect growth?

NUTRITION

Proper nutrition is essential to healthy growth. Feeding needs change rapidly during the first 3 years of life.

Breast or Bottle? Feeding a baby is an emotional as well as a physical act. Warm contact with the mother's body fosters emotional linkage between mother and baby. Such bonding can take place through either breast-feeding or bottle-feeding and through many other caregiving activities, most of which can be performed by fathers as well as mothers. The quality of the relationship between parent and child and the provision of abundant affection and cuddling may be at least as important as the feeding method.

study smart

Nutritional Benefits of Breast-Feeding

Nutritionally speaking, however, breast-feeding is almost always best for infants—and mothers (Table 3). The American Academy of Pediatrics Section on Breastfeeding (2005) recommends that babies be *exclusively* breast-fed for 6 months. Breast-feeding should begin immediately after birth and should continue for at least 1 year, longer if mother and baby wish. A recent study on the benefits of breast-feeding has determined that if 90 percent of U.S. mothers complied with the AAP's recommendation to breast-feed for 6 months, it could potentially prevent 911 infant deaths and save the United States $13 billion annually (Bartick & Reinhold, 2010). The only acceptable alternative to breast milk is an iron-fortified formula that is based on either cow's milk or soy protein and contains supplemental vitamins and minerals. Infants weaned during the 1st year should receive iron-fortified formula. At 1 year, babies can switch to cow's milk (AAP Section on Breastfeeding, 2005).

On average, an ounce of breast milk has about 22 calories in it.

Kellymom Breast Feeding and Parenting, 2006

TABLE 3 Benefits of Breast-Feeding over Formula-Feeding

BREAST-FED BABIES . . .

- Are less likely to contract infectious illnesses such as diarrhea, respiratory infections, otitis media (an infection of the middle ear), and staphylococcal, bacterial, and urinary tract infections.
- Have a lower risk of SIDS and of postneonatal death.
- Have less risk of inflammatory bowel disease.
- Have better visual acuity, neurological development, and long-term cardiovascular health, including cholesterol levels.
- Are less likely to develop obesity, asthma, eczema, diabetes, lymphoma, childhood leukemia, and Hodgkin's disease.
- Are less likely to show language and motor delays.
- Score higher on cognitive tests at school age and into young adulthood.
- Have fewer cavities and are less likely to need braces.

BREAST-FEEDING MOTHERS . . .

- Enjoy quicker recovery from childbirth with less risk of postpartum bleeding.
- Are more likely to return to their prepregnancy weight and less likely to develop long-term obesity.
- Have reduced risk of anemia and almost no risk of repeat pregnancy while breast-feeding.
- Report feeling more confident and less anxious.
- Are less likely to develop osteoporosis or ovarian and premenopausal breast cancer.

Sources: AAP Section on Breastfeeding, 2005; Black, Morris, & Bryce, 2003; Chen & Rogan, 2004; Dee, Li, Lee, & Grummer-Strawn, 2007; Kramer et al., 2008; Lanting, Fidler, Huisman, Touwen, & Boersma, 1994; Mortensen, Michaelson, Sanders, & Reinisch, 2002; Owen, Whincup, Odoki, Gilg, & Cook, 2002; Singhal, Cole, Fewtrell, & Lucas, 2004; United States Breastfeeding Committee, 2002.

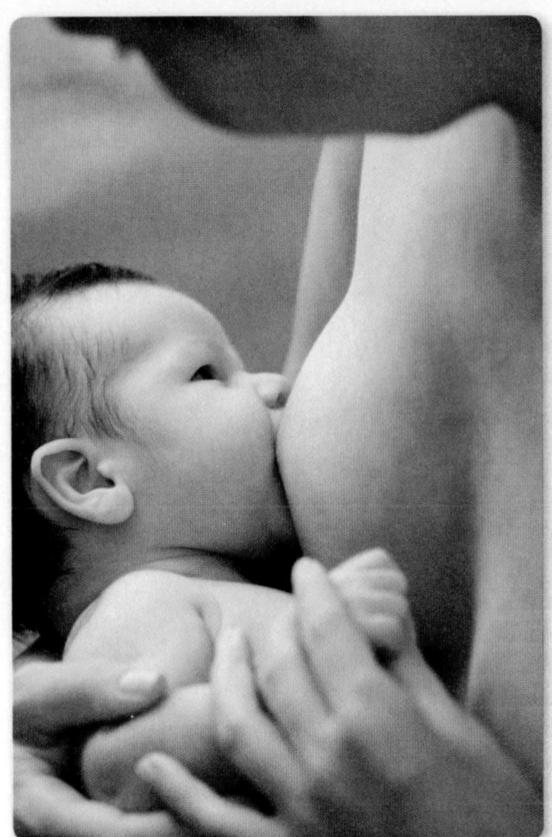

Breast milk can be called the "ultimate health food" because it offers so many benefits to babies—physical, cognitive, and emotional.

Since 1991, some 16,000 hospitals and birthing centers worldwide have been designated as "Baby-Friendly" under a United Nations initiative for encouraging institutional support of breast-feeding. These institutions offer new mothers rooming-in, tell them of the benefits of breast-feeding, help them start nursing within 1 hour of birth, show them how to maintain lactation, encourage on-demand feeding, give infants nothing but breast milk unless medically necessary, and establish ongoing breast-feeding support groups. Breast-feeding in U.S. hospitals and elsewhere greatly increased after the program went into effect, and mothers were more likely to continue nursing (Kramer et al., 2001; Labarere et al., 2005; Merewood, Mehta, Chamberlain, Philipp, & Bauchner, 2005).

Increases in breast-feeding in the United States are most notable in socioeconomic groups that historically have been less likely to breast-feed: black women, teenage women, poor women, working women, and those with no more than high school education, but many of these women do not continue breast-feeding. Postpartum maternity leave, flexible scheduling, the ability to take relatively frequent and extended breaks at work to pump milk, privacy for nursing mothers at work and at school, as well as education about the benefits of breast-feeding and availability of breast pumping facilities might increase its prevalence in these groups (Guendelman et al., 2009; Ryan, Wenjun, & Acosta, 2002; Taveras et al., 2003).

Breast-feeding is inadvisable if a mother is infected with the AIDS virus or any other infectious illness, if she has untreated active tuberculosis, if she has been exposed to radiation, or if she is taking any drug that would not be safe for the baby (AAP Section on Breastfeeding, 2005). The risk of transmitting HIV infection to an infant continues as long as an infected mother breast-feeds (Breastfeeding and HIV International Transmission Study Group, 2004). However, by receiving treatment with nevirapine or with both nevirapine and zidovudine during the first 14 weeks of life, HIV-infected breast-feeding mothers can significantly reduce this risk (Kumwenda et al., 2008).

Other Nutritional Concerns Contrary to recommendations for earlier generations, healthy babies should consume *nothing* but breast milk or iron-fortified formula for the first 6 months. Pediatric experts recommend that iron-enriched solid foods—usually beginning with cereals—be introduced gradually during the second half of the 1st year. At this time, too, water may be introduced (AAP Section on Breastfeeding, 2005). Unfortunately, many parents do not follow these guidelines. According to random telephone interviews with parents and caregivers of more than 3,000 U.S. infants and toddlers, 29 percent of infants are given solid food before 4 months, 17 percent drink juice before 6 months, and 20 percent drink cow's milk before 12 months. Furthermore, like older children and adults, many infants and toddlers eat too much and eat the wrong kinds of food. From 7 to 24 months, the median food intake is 20 to 30 percent above normal daily requirements (Fox, Pac, Devaney, & Jankowski, 2004). By 19 to 24 months, French fries become the most commonly consumed vegetable. More than 30 percent of children this age eat no fruit, but 60 percent eat baked desserts, 20 percent candy, and 44 percent sweetened beverages each day (American Heart Association [AHA] et al., 2006).

In many low-income communities around the world, malnutrition in early life is widespread—and often fatal. Malnutrition is implicated in more than half of deaths of children globally, and many children are irreversibly damaged by age 2 (World Bank, 2006). Undernourished children who survive their first 5 years are at high risk for stunted growth and poor health and functioning throughout life. In a longitudinal study of a nutritional program in 347 poor rural communities of Mexico, infants who received fortified nutrition supplements—along with nutrition education, health care, and financial assistance for the family—showed better growth and lower rates of anemia than a control group of infants not yet assigned to the program (Rivera et al., 2004).

Being overweight has increased in infancy as in all age groups in the United States. In 2000–2001, 5.9 percent of U.S. infants up to 6 months old were obese, meaning that their weight for height was in the 95th percentile for age and gender, up from 3.4 percent in 1980. An additional 11.1 percent were overweight (in the 85th percentile), up from 7 percent in 1980 (Kim et al., 2006). Rapid weight gain during the first 4 to 6 months is associated with future risk of overweight (AHA et al., 2006).

Two factors seem to influence most strongly the chances that an overweight child will become an obese adult: whether the child has an obese parent and the age of the child. Before age 3, parental obesity is a stronger predictor of a child's obesity as an adult than is the child's own weight. Having one obese parent increases the odds of obesity in adulthood by 3 to 1, and if both parents are obese, the odds increase to more than 10 to 1 (AAP Committee on Nutrition, 2003). Among 70 children followed, there was little difference in weight and body composition at age 2 between children with overweight mothers and children with lean mothers, but by age 4, those with overweight mothers tended to weigh more and, by age 6, also had more body fat than those with lean mothers (Berkowitz, Stallings, Maislin, & Stunkard, 2005). Thus a 1- or 2-year-old who has an obese parent—or especially two obese parents—may be a candidate for preventive efforts.

A child under age 3 with an obese parent is likely to become obese as an adult, regardless of the child's own weight.

THE BRAIN AND REFLEX BEHAVIOR

What makes newborns respond to a nipple? What tells them to start the sucking movements that allow them to control their intake of fluids? These are functions of the **central nervous system**—the brain and *spinal cord* (a bundle of nerves running through the backbone)—and of a growing peripheral network of nerves extending to every part of the body. Through this network, sensory messages travel to the brain, and motor commands travel back.

checkpoint can **you**...

- Summarize pediatric recommendations regarding early feeding and the introduction of cow's milk, solid foods, and fruit juices?
- Discuss the dangers of early malnutrition?
- Cite factors that contribute to obesity in later life?

central nervous system
Brain and spinal cord.

Building the Brain The growth of the brain is a lifelong process fundamental to physical, cognitive, and emotional development. Through various brain imaging tools, researchers are gaining a clearer picture of how brain growth occurs (Box 1).

The brain at birth is only about one-fourth to one-third of its eventual adult volume (Toga, Thompson, & Sowell, 2006). By age 6, it is almost adult size, but specific parts of the brain continue to grow and develop functionally into adulthood. The brain's growth occurs in fits and starts called *brain growth spurts*. Different parts of the brain grow more rapidly at different times.

Mothers' brains have been shown to increase in size after childbirth in key areas regulating motivation, emotional processing, sensory integration, reasoning, and judgment. Researchers suspect the experience of holding and cuddling a newborn infant triggers this effect, and that it helps mothers be more effective in their interactions with infants.

Kinsley & Meyer, 2010

Major Parts of the Brain Beginning about 3 weeks after conception, the brain gradually develops from a long hollow tube into a spherical mass of cells (Figure 10). By birth, the growth spurt of the spinal cord and *brain stem* (the part of the brain responsible for such basic bodily functions as breathing, heart rate, body temperature, and the sleep-wake cycle)

research in action

LESSONS FROM NEUROSCIENCE

Although we have known for some time that early experiences can have a profound effect on who we are and who we become, neuroscience and behavioral research is beginning to illuminate the specific ways in which our brain development itself is shaped by such processes. On the basis of decades of scientific inquiry, the National Symposium on Early Childhood Science and Policy issued a series of brief summaries encapsulating basic concepts in early brain development. They specify five basic concepts about early brain development:

1. *Brains are built over time, from the bottom up.* Brains do not emerge fully formed in adulthood. Rather, their construction begins in the fetal period and continues at an incredibly rapid pace through early childhood. Our brains are constructed out of the millions of influences and interactions all of us go through in our lives. And our abilities come online in a prescribed and organized fashion: first sensation and perception, then language and cognitive functions.
2. *The interactive influence of genes and experience shape the developing brain.* Although the nature-nurture debate certainly predates the existence of the field of psychology, research in early brain development has highlighted the importance of the social environment in shaping the physical structure of the brain. Babies are immersed in a social world that may either be rich and varied and warm, and thus support their growing brains; or stark and harsh and cold, constraining their development in potentially permanent ways.
3. *The brain's capacity for change decreases with age.* Our brains remain plastic and capable of change throughout the life span, but this flexibility is more pronounced early in life. The environment has a more profound effect on brain development early in life than later in life.
4. *Cognitive, emotional, and social capacities are inextricably intertwined throughout the life course.* When we learn about the brain, we often differentiate the areas of the brain and their specific functions, but the reality is that our brains are complex, interrelated, dynamic organs that work as an integrated whole. There is no "left brain" and "right brain"; there is only one brain. All areas of our development are likewise related. For example, without feeling safe and loved, babies are less likely to explore their environment, limiting their ability to learn about the world.
5. *Toxic stress damages developing brain architecture, which can lead to lifelong problems in learning, behavior, and physical and mental health.* Our bodies are well adapted to dealing with time-limited stressors, but we are not made to handle chronic stress effectively. Long-term stress is very damaging to our bodies as a whole and can have especially strong effects on a young brain. Unfortunately, many children are exposed to toxic levels of stress through such factors as poverty, abuse or neglect, and parental mental illness.

How do findings such as these translate into action in the real world? The National Symposium on Early Childhood Science and Policy has used these basic concepts to develop a series of recommendations for interventions in early childhood. First, the work on plasticity suggests that the earlier the intervention, the more effective it will be. Second, all areas of development must be considered in concert. For example, an intervention focused solely on cognitive development is not likely to be effective if social and emotional factors are ignored. Third, babies need an attachment relationship with a caring and dependable adult. Ideally that relationship would be found within the home, but services that provide such relationships outside the home are also beneficial. Finally, early intervention should have a close focus on stress and how chronic stress might be alleviated in the very young.

In view of what is known about the plasticity of the infant brain, should every baby have access to an appropriately stimulating environment? If so, how can this goal be accomplished?

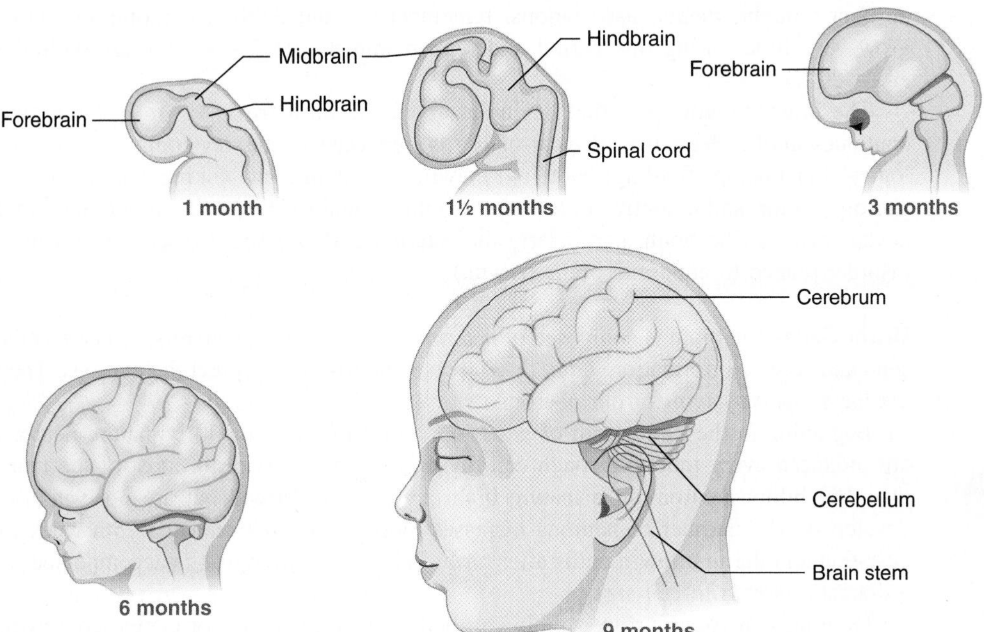

Source: Adapted from Cowan, 1979.

FIGURE 10

Brain Development during Gestation

Fetal nervous system development begins at about 3 weeks. At 1 month, major regions of the brain appear: the forebrain, midbrain, and hindbrain. As the brain grows, the front part expands to form the cerebrum, the seat of conscious brain activity. The cerebellum grows most rapidly during the 1st year of life.

has nearly run its course. The *cerebellum* (the part of the brain that maintains balance and motor coordination) grows fastest during the 1st year of life (Casaer, 1993; Knickmeyer et al., 2008).

The *cerebrum,* the largest part of the brain, is divided into right and left halves, or hemispheres, each with specialized functions. This specialization of the hemispheres is called **lateralization.** The left hemisphere is mainly concerned with language and logical thinking, the right hemisphere with visual and spatial functions such as map reading and drawing. Joining the two hemispheres is a tough band of tissue called the *corpus callosum,* which allows them to share information and coordinate commands. The corpus callosum grows dramatically during childhood, reaching adult size by about age 10. Each cerebral hemisphere has four lobes or sections, which control different functions. They include the *occipital, parietal, temporal,* and *frontal lobes* (Figure 11). The occipital lobe is the smallest of the four lobes and is primarily concerned with visual processing. The parietal lobe is involved with integrating sensory information from the body. It helps us move our bodies through space and manipulate objects in our world. The temporal lobe helps us interpret smells and sounds and is involved in memory. The frontal lobes, the newest region of the brain, are involved with a variety of higher-order processes, such as goal setting, inhibition, reasoning, planning, and problem solving. The regions of the *cerebral cortex* (the outer surface of the cerebrum) that govern vision, hearing, and other sensory information grow rapidly in the first few months after birth and are mature by age 6 months, but the areas of the frontal cortex responsible for

study smart

Four Lobes of the Brain

lateralization
Tendency of each of the brain's hemispheres to have specialized functions.

FIGURE 11

The Human Brain

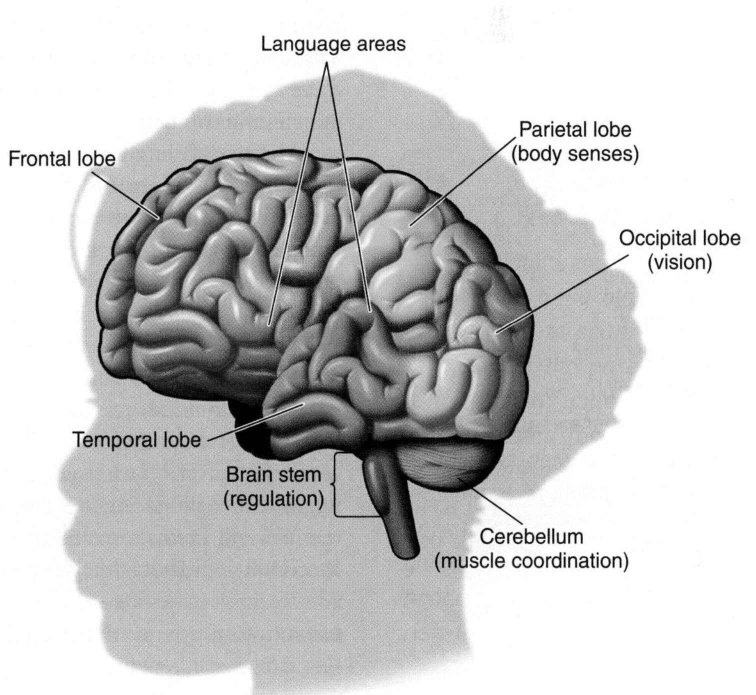

abstract thought, mental associations, remembering, and deliberate motor responses grow very little during this period and remain immature for several years (Gilmore et al., 2007).

The brain growth spurt that begins at about the third trimester of gestation and continues until at least the 4th year of life is important to the development of neurological functioning. Smiling, babbling, crawling, walking, and talking—all the major sensory, motor, and cognitive milestones of infancy and toddlerhood—reflect the rapid development of the brain, particularly the cerebral cortex. (Box 2 discusses autism, a disorder related to abnormal brain growth.)

neurons
Nerve cells.

Brain Cells The brain is composed of *neurons* and *glial cells*. **Neurons,** or nerve cells, send and receive information. *Glia,* or glial cells, nourish and protect the neurons. They are the support system for our neurons.

Beginning in the 2nd month of gestation, an estimated 250,000 immature neurons are produced every minute through cell division (mitosis). At birth, most of the more than 100 billion neurons in a mature brain are already formed but are not yet fully developed. The number of neurons increases most rapidly between the 25th week of gestation and the first few months after birth. This cell proliferation is accompanied by a dramatic growth in cell size.

As an analogy, think of this as a sports team. Integration *involves all members of the team learning to work together in a coordinated fashion.* Differentiation *involves each team member taking on a specific position to play.*

Originally the neurons are simply cell bodies with a nucleus, or center, composed of deoxyribonucleic acid (DNA), which contains the cell's genetic programming. As the brain grows, these rudimentary cells migrate to various parts of the brain (Bystron, Rakic, Molnar, & Blakemore, 2006). Most of the neurons in the cortex are in place by 20 weeks of gestation, and its structure becomes fairly well-defined during the next 12 weeks.

Once in place, the neurons sprout *axons* and *dendrites*—narrow, branching, fiberlike extensions. Axons send signals to other neurons, and dendrites receive incoming messages from them, through *synapses,* tiny gaps, which are bridged with the help of chemicals called *neurotransmitters* that are released by the neurons. Eventually, a particular neuron may have anywhere from 5,000 to 100,000 synaptic connections.

integration
Process by which neurons coordinate the activities of muscle groups.

differentiation
Process by which cells acquire specialized structures and functions.

The multiplication of dendrites and synaptic connections, especially during the last 2½ months of gestation and the first 6 months to 2 years of life, accounts for much of the brain's growth and permits the emergence of new perceptual, cognitive, and motor abilities. As the neurons multiply, migrate to their assigned locations, and develop connections, they undergo the complementary processes of *integration* and *differentiation.* Through **integration,** the neurons that control various groups of muscles coordinate their activities. Through **differentiation,** each neuron takes on a specific, specialized structure and function.

Myelin is made primarily of fat. As breast milk is designed to be ideal for a baby's nutrition, it contains relatively high but healthy levels of this essential ingredient.

At first the brain produces many more neurons and synapses than it needs. The large number of excess neurons provided by this early proliferation give the brain flexibility—with more connections available than will ever be needed, many potential paths are open for the growing brain. As early experience shapes the brain, the paths are selected, and unused paths are pruned away. This process involves **cell death,** which may sound negative but is a way to calibrate the developing brain to the local environment and help it work more efficiently. This process begins during the prenatal period and continues after birth.

cell death
In brain development, normal elimination of excess brain cells to achieve more efficient functioning.

Only about half the neurons originally produced survive and function in adulthood (Society for Neuroscience, 2008). Yet, even as unneeded neurons die out, others may continue to form during adult life (Gould, Reeves, Graziano, & Gross, 1999). Meanwhile, connections among cortical cells continue to strengthen and to become more reliable and precise, enabling more flexible and more advanced motor and cognitive functioning (Society for Neuroscience, 2008).

myelination
Process of coating neural pathways with a fatty substance called myelin, which enables faster communication between cells.

Myelination Much of the credit for efficiency of neural communication goes to the glia that coat the neural pathways with a fatty substance called *myelin.* This process of **myelination** enables signals to travel faster and more smoothly.

research in action

THE AUTISM "EPIDEMIC"

Autism is a severe disorder of brain functioning characterized by lack of normal social interaction, impaired communication, repetitive movements, and a highly restricted range of activities and interests. Autism may involve a lack of coordination between different regions of the brain needed for complex tasks (Just, Cherkassky, Keller, Kana, & Minshew, 2007). Postmortem studies have found fewer neurons in the amygdala in the brains of people who had autism (Schumann & Amaral, 2006). People with autism also show deficits in executive function and theory of mind (Zelazo & Müller, 2002).

Asperger syndrome is a related but less severe disorder. Children with Asperger syndrome usually function at a higher level than children with autism. They have large vocabularies and stilted speech patterns, are often awkward and poorly coordinated, and may have restricted interests. Their odd or eccentric behavior makes social contacts difficult (National Institute of Neurological Disorders and Stroke, 2007).

Perhaps due to increased awareness and more accurate diagnosis, the reported prevalence of these conditions has increased markedly since the mid-1970s. Approximately 1 in 68 children are diagnosed with autism and related disorders annually, and 4 out of 5 are boys (Centers for Disease Control and Prevention, 2009b, 2014; Markel, 2007; Myers, Johnson, & Council on Children with Disabilities, 2007). The greater prevalence of autism in boys has been attributed to a number of factors, among them (1) boys' larger brain size and the larger-than-average brains of autistic children (Gilmore et al., 2007) and (2) boys' natural strength in systematizing and the propensity of autistic children to systematize (Baron-Cohen, 2005). These findings support the idea of autism as an extreme version of the male brain.

Autism and related disorders appear to have a strong genetic basis (Constantino, 2003; Ramoz et al., 2004; Rodier, 2000). An international team of researchers has identified one gene and pinpointed the location of another that may contribute to autism (Szatmari et al., 2007). Deletions and duplications of gene copies at chromosome 16 may account for a small number of cases (Eichler & Zimmerman, 2008; R. B. Weiss et al., 2008). Other research suggests that high levels of fetal testosterone in utero may contribute to difficulties in social relationships, a key feature in autism (Knickmeyer, Baron-Cohen, Raggatt, & Taylor, 2005).

Environmental factors may sometimes trigger an inherited tendency toward autism (Rodier, 2000). Many parents blamed thimerosal, a preservative used in vaccines, for the increased incidence of autism. The Centers for Disease Control and Prevention (2004), on the basis of multiple studies on thimerosal and its effects, has found no conclusive link between the preservative and autism. Later research also has failed to find a relationship between childhood vaccination and autism (Baird et al., 2008; Thompson et al., 2007). Other factors, such as complications of pregnancy, advanced parental age, first births, threatened fetal loss, epidural anesthesia, induced labor, and cesarean delivery are associated with higher incidence of autism (Glasson et al., 2004; Juul-Dam, Townsend, & Courchesne, 2001; Reichenberg et al., 2006).

Studies have found that children who do not respond to their name by age 12 months or who show deficits in communicative and cognitive skills at 16 months are likely to develop an autism-related disorder or developmental delay (Nadig et al., 2007; Stone, McMahon, Yoder, & Walden, 2007). Studies like these offer promise for early detection and treatment at a time when the brain is most plastic and systems related to communication are beginning to develop (Dawson, 2007).

Very early signs of possible autism or related disorders include the following (Johnson, Myers, & the Council on Children with Disabilities, 2007):

- No joyful gazing at a parent or caregiver
- No back-and-forth babbling between infant and parent (beginning about age 5 months)
- Not recognizing a parent's voice
- Failure to make eye contact
- Delayed onset of babbling (past 9 months)
- No or few gestures, such as waving or pointing
- Repetitive movements with objects
- No single words by 16 months
- No babbling, pointing, or other communicative gestures by 1 year
- No two-word phrases by 2 years
- Loss of language skills at any age

Though no cure is available, substantial improvement may occur with early interventions that help the child develop independence and personal responsibility; speech and language therapy; and instruction in social skills, along with medical management as necessary (Myers, Johnson, & Council on Children with Disabilities, 2007).

Have you ever known anyone with autism? If so, in what ways did that person's behavior seem unusual?

Myelination begins about halfway through gestation in some parts of the brain and continues into adulthood in others. The pathways related to the sense of touch—the first sense to develop—are myelinated by birth. Myelination of visual pathways, which are slower to mature, begins at birth and continues during the first 5 months of life. Pathways related to hearing may begin to be myelinated as early as the 5th month of gestation, but the process is not complete until about age 4. The parts of the cortex that control attention and memory are not fully myelinated until young adulthood. Myelination of the *hippocampus,* a structure deep in the temporal lobe that plays a key role in memory, continues to increase until at least age 70 (Benes, Turtle, Khan, & Farol, 1994).

Myelination of sensory and motor pathways before birth in the spinal cord and after birth in the cerebral cortex may account for the appearance and disappearance of early reflexes, a sign of neurological organization and health.

reflex behaviors
Automatic, involuntary, innate responses to stimulation.

Early Reflexes When your pupils contract as you turn toward a bright light, they are acting involuntarily. Such an automatic, innate response to stimulation is called a **reflex behavior.** Reflex behaviors are controlled by the lower brain centers that govern other involuntary processes, such as breathing and heart rate.

Human infants have an estimated 27 major reflexes, many of which are present at birth or soon after (Gabbard, 1996; Table 4). *Primitive reflexes,* such as sucking, rooting for the nipple, and the Moro reflex (a response to being startled or beginning to fall), are related to instinctive needs for survival and protection or may support the early connection to the caregiver. Some primitive reflexes may be part of humanity's evolutionary legacy. One example is the grasping reflex, which enables infant monkeys to hold on to their mothers' fur. Human infants show a similar reflex wherein they tightly grasp any object placed in their palm, a holdover from our ancestral past.

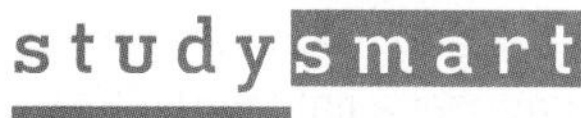

Reflexes

As the higher brain centers become active during the first 2 to 4 months, infants begin to show *postural reflexes:* reactions to changes in position or balance. For example, infants who are tilted downward extend their arms in the parachute reflex, an instinctive attempt to break a fall. *Locomotor reflexes,* such as the walking and swimming reflexes, resemble voluntary movements that do not appear until months after the reflexes have disappeared.

Most of the early reflexes disappear during the first 6 to 12 months. Reflexes that continue to serve protective functions—such as blinking, yawning, coughing, gagging, sneezing, shivering, and dilation of the pupils in the dark—remain. Disappearance of unneeded reflexes on schedule is a sign that motor pathways in the cortex have been partially myelinated, enabling a shift to voluntary behavior. Thus we can evaluate a baby's neurological development by seeing whether certain reflexes are present or absent.

checkpoint can **you**...

- Describe early brain development?
- Explain the functions of reflex behaviors and why some drop out?

Molding the Brain: The Role of Experience Although the brain's early development is genetically directed, it is continually modified by environmental experience. The physical architecture of our brain is a reflection of the experiences we have had throughout our life. Our brains are not static; rather, they are living, changeable organs that respond to environmental influences. The technical term for this malleability of the brain is **plasticity.** Plasticity may be an evolutionary mechanism to enable adaptation to environmental change (Pascual-Leone, Amedi, Fregni, & Merabet, 2005; Toga et al., 2006).

plasticity
Modifiability, or "molding," of the brain through experience.

Plasticity enables learning. Individual differences in intelligence may reflect differences in the brain's ability to develop neural connections in response to experience (Garlick, 2003). Early experience can have lasting effects on the capacity of the central nervous system to learn and store information (Society for Neuroscience, 2008).

There are two sides to every coin: just as plasticity allows learning in response to appropriate environmental input, it can also lead to damage in the case of harmful input. During the formative period of early life when the brain is most plastic, the brain is

TABLE 4 Early Human Reflexes

Reflex	Stimulation	Baby's Behavior	Typical Age of Appearance	Typical Age of Disappearance
Moro	Baby is dropped or hears loud noise.	Extends legs, arms, and fingers, arches back, draws back head.	7th month of gestation	3 months
Darwinian (grasping)	Palm of baby's hand is stroked.	Makes strong fist; can be raised to standing position if both fists are closed around a stick.	7th month of gestation	4 months
Tonic neck	Baby is laid down on back.	Turns head to one side, assumes fencer position, extends arm and leg on preferred side, flexes opposite limbs.	7th month of gestation	5 months
Babkin	Both of baby's palms are stroked at once.	Mouth opens, eyes close, neck flexes, head tilts forward.	Birth	3 months
Babinski	Sole of baby's foot is stroked.	Toes fan out; foot twists in.	Birth	4 months
Rooting	Baby's cheek or lower lip is stroked with finger or nipple.	Head turns; mouth opens; sucking movements begin.	Birth	9 months
Walking	Baby is held under arms, with bare feet touching flat surface.	Makes steplike motions that look like well-coordinated walking.	1 month	4 months
Swimming	Baby is put into water face down.	Makes well-coordinated swimming movements.	1 month	4 months

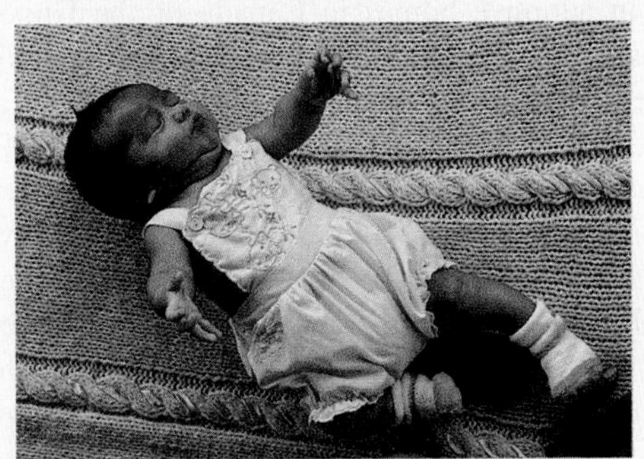
Moro reflex

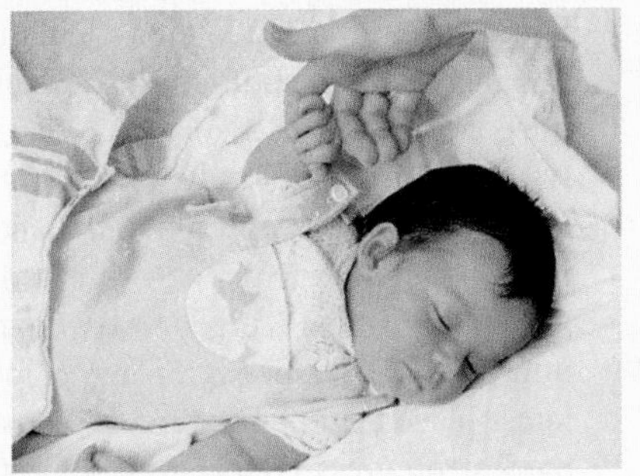
Darwinian reflex

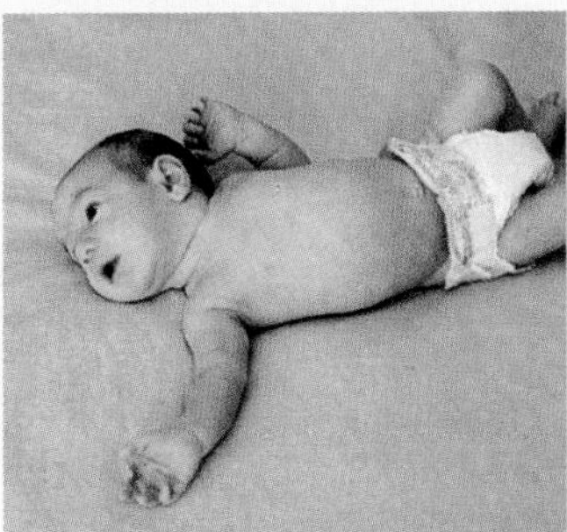
Tonic neck reflex

Babinski reflex

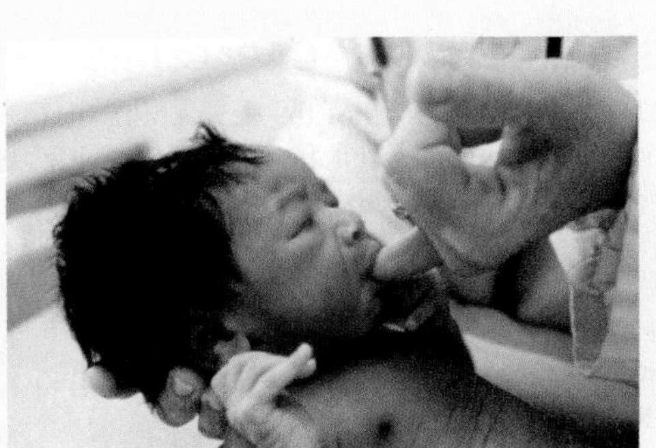
Rooting reflex

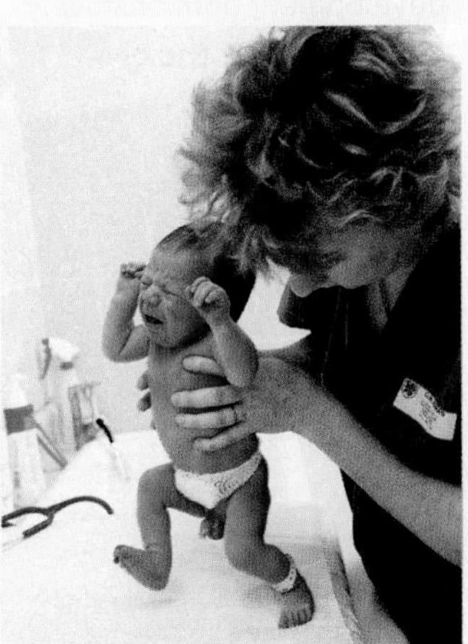
Walking reflex

especially vulnerable. Exposure to hazardous drugs, environmental toxins, or maternal stress before or after birth can threaten the developing brain, and malnutrition can interfere with normal cognitive growth. Early abuse or sensory impoverishment can leave an imprint on the brain as it adapts to the environment in which the developing child must live, delaying neural development or affecting brain structure (AAP, Stirling, and the Committee on Child Abuse and Neglect and Section on Adoption and Foster Care; American Academy of Child and Adolescent Psychiatry, Amaya-Jackson; & National Center for Child Traumatic Stress, Amaya-Jackson, 2008). Other research suggests that lack of environmental input may inhibit the normal process of cell death and the streamlining of neural connections, resulting in smaller head size and reduced brain activity (C. A. Nelson, 2008).

By the same token, enriched experience can spur brain development (Society for Neuroscience, 2008) and even make up for past deprivation (J. E. Black, 1998). Animals raised in toy-filled cages sprout more axons, dendrites, and synapses than animals raised in bare cages (Society for Neuroscience, 2008). Plasticity continues throughout life as neurons change in size and shape in response to environmental experience (Rutter, 2002). Such findings have sparked successful efforts to stimulate the brain development of premature infants (Als et al., 2004) and children with Down syndrome and to help victims of brain damage recover function.

Ethical constraints prevent controlled experiments on the effects of environmental deprivation on human infants. However, the discovery of thousands of infants and young children raised in overcrowded Romanian orphanages offered a natural experiment (Ames, 1997; Becket et al., 2006). These abandoned children appeared to be starving, passive, and emotionless. They had spent much of their time lying quietly in their cribs or beds with nothing to look at. Most of the 2- and 3-year-olds did not walk or talk, and the older children played aimlessly. PET scans of their brains showed extreme inactivity in the temporal lobes, which regulate emotion and receive sensory input.

Some of these children were placed in adoptive homes in Canada or the United Kingdom. Age of adoption, length of previous institutionalization, and the specific features of the institutional experience were key factors in the children's prospects for improvement (C. A. Nelson, 2008; Rutter, O'Connor, & the ERA Study Team, 2004). In one longitudinal study, for example, Romanian children who had been removed from institutions *before* age 6 months and adopted by English families showed no cognitive impairment by age 11 as compared with a control group of English children adopted within the United Kingdom. By contrast, the average IQs of Romanian children adopted into English families *after* age 6 months were 15 points lower. At ages 6 and 11, the latest-placed adoptees were the most cognitively impaired, though this group did show modest progress (Beckett et al., 2006). Apparently, then, it may take very early environmental stimulation to fully overcome the effects of extreme deprivation. These findings suggest that high-quality foster care may partly overcome the adverse effects of early institutionalization on the processing of socioemotional information (Moulson, Fox, Zeanah, & Nelson, 2009).

checkpoint can **you**...

- Discuss how early experience can affect brain growth and development both positively and negatively, and give examples?

EARLY SENSORY CAPACITIES

The rearward regions of the developing brain, which control sensory information, grow rapidly during the first few months of life, enabling newborn infants to make fairly good sense of what they touch, see, smell, taste, and hear (Gilmore et al., 2007).

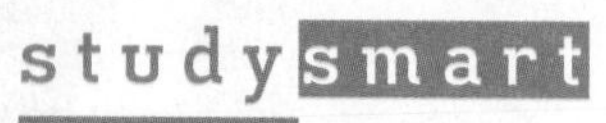

Taste, Sound, Visual Acuity

Touch and Pain Touch is the first sense to develop, and for the first several months it is the most mature sensory system. When a newborn's cheek is stroked near the mouth, the baby responds by trying to find a nipple, an evolved survival mechanism (Rakison, 2005).

In the past, physicians performing surgery (such as circumcision) on newborn babies often used no anesthesia because of a mistaken belief that neonates cannot feel pain or feel it only briefly. Actually, there is evidence that the capacity for pain perception may emerge during the third trimester of pregnancy (Lee et al., 2005). Newborns can and do feel pain, and they become more sensitive to it during the next few days. The American Academy of Pediatrics and Canadian Paediatric Society (2000) now maintain that prolonged or severe pain can do long-term harm to newborns and that pain relief during surgery is essential.

Smell and Taste The senses of smell and taste also begin to develop in the womb. A preference for pleasant odors seems to be learned in utero and during the first few days after birth, and the odors transmitted through the mother's breast milk may further contribute to this learning (Bartoshuk & Beauchamp, 1994). This attraction to the fragrance of the mother's milk may be another evolutionary survival mechanism (Rakison, 2005).

Certain taste preferences seem to be largely innate (Bartoshuk & Beauchamp, 1994). Newborns prefer sweet tastes to sour, bitter, or salty tastes (Haith, 1986). An inborn sweet tooth may help a baby adapt to life outside the womb, as breast milk is quite sweet (Harris, 1997; Ventura & Mennella, 2011). Newborns' rejection of bitter tastes is probably another survival mechanism, as many bitter substances are toxic (Bartoshuk & Beauchamp, 1994; Beauchamp & Mennella, 2009).

Taste preferences developed in infancy may last into early childhood. In one study, 4- and 5-year-olds who, as infants, had been fed different types of formula had differing food preferences (Mennella & Beauchamp, 2002). Exposure to the flavors of healthy foods through breast-feeding may improve acceptance of healthy foods after weaning and later in life (AHA et al., 2006).

Hearing Hearing, too, is functional before birth; fetuses respond to sounds and seem to learn to recognize them. From an evolutionary perspective, early recognition of voices and language heard in the womb may lay the foundation for the relationship with the mother, which is critical to early survival (Rakison, 2005).

Auditory discrimination develops rapidly after birth. Three-day-old infants can tell new speech sounds from those they have heard before (L. R. Brody, Zelazo, & Chaika, 1984). In addition, infants as young as 2 days old were able to recognize a word they heard up to a day earlier (Swain, Zelano, & Clifton, 1993). At 1 month, babies can distinguish sounds as close as *ba* and *pa* (Eimas, Siqueland, Jusczyk, & Vigorito, 1971).

Because hearing is a key to language development, hearing impairments should be identified as early as possible. Hearing loss occurs in 1 to 3 of 1,000 live births (Gaffney, Gamble, Costa, Holstrum, & Boyle, 2003).

Sight Vision is the least developed sense at birth, perhaps because there is so little to see in the womb. From an evolutionary developmental perspective, the other senses, as we have pointed out, are more directly related to a newborn's survival. Visual perception and the ability to use visual information—identifying caregivers, finding food, and avoiding dangers—become more important as infants become more alert and active (Rakison, 2005).

The eyes of newborns are smaller than those of adults, the retinal structures are incomplete, and the optic nerve is underdeveloped. A neonate's eyes focus best from about 1 foot away—just about the typical distance from the face of a person holding a newborn. Newborns blink at bright lights. Their field of peripheral vision is very narrow; it more than doubles between 2 and 10 weeks and is well developed by 3 months (Maurer & Lewis, 1979; E. Tronick, 1972). The ability to follow a moving target also develops rapidly in the first months, as does color perception (Haith, 1986).

Visual acuity at birth is approximately 20/400 but improves rapidly, reaching the 20/20 level by about 8 months (Kellman & Arterberry, 1998; Kellman & Banks, 1998). *Binocular vision*—the use of both eyes to focus, enabling perception of depth and distance—usually does not develop until 4 or 5 months (Bushnell & Boudreau, 1993). Early screening is essential to detect any problems that may interfere with vision (AAP Committee on Practice and Ambulatory Medicine and Section on Opthalmology, 1996, 2002).

checkpoint can **you**...

- Give evidence for early development of the senses?
- Tell how breast-feeding plays a part in the development of smell and taste?
- List three ways in which newborns' vision is underdeveloped?

Motor Development

Babies do not have to be taught such basic motor skills as grasping, crawling, and walking. They just need room to move and freedom to see what they can do. When the central nervous system, muscles, and bones are ready and the environment offers the right opportunities for exploration and practice, babies keep surprising the adults around them with new abilities.

MILESTONES OF MOTOR DEVELOPMENT

systems of action
Increasingly complex combinations of motor skills, which permit a wider or more precise range of movement and more control of the environment.

Motor development is marked by a series of milestones: achievements that develop systematically, each newly mastered ability preparing a baby to tackle the next. Babies first learn simple skills and then combine them into increasingly complex **systems of action,** which permit a wider or more precise range of movement and more effective control of the environment. In developing the precision grip, for example, an infant first tries to pick things up with the whole hand, fingers closing against the palm. Later the baby masters the *pincer grasp,* in which thumb and index finger meet at the tips to form a circle, making it possible to pick up tiny objects. In learning to walk, an infant gains control of separate movements of the arms, legs, and feet before putting these movements together to take that momentous first step.

Denver Developmental Screening Test
Screening test given to children 1 month to 6 years old to determine whether they are developing normally.

gross motor skills
Physical skills that involve the large muscles.

fine motor skills
Physical skills that involve the small muscles and eye-hand coordination.

The **Denver Developmental Screening Test** (Frankenburg, Dodds, Fandal, Kazuk, & Cohrs, 1975) is used to chart progress between ages 1 month and 6 years and to identify children who are not developing normally. The test measures **gross motor skills** (those using large muscles), such as rolling over and catching a ball, and **fine motor skills** (using small muscles), such as grasping a rattle and copying a circle. It also assesses language development (for example, knowing the definitions of words) and personality and social development (such as smiling spontaneously and dressing without help). The newest edition, the Denver II Scale (Frankenburg et al., 1992), includes revised norms. Table 5 provides some examples.

When we talk about what the "average" baby can do, we refer to the 50 percent Denver norms, but normality covers a wide range: about half of babies master these skills before the ages given, and about half afterward. Also, the Denver norms were developed with reference to a Western population and are not necessarily valid when assessing children from other cultures.

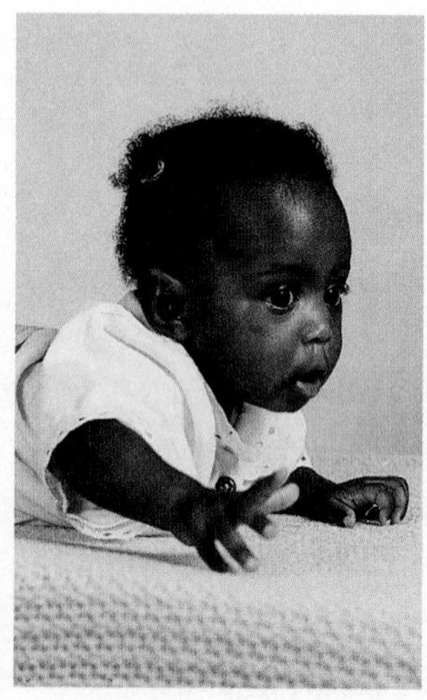

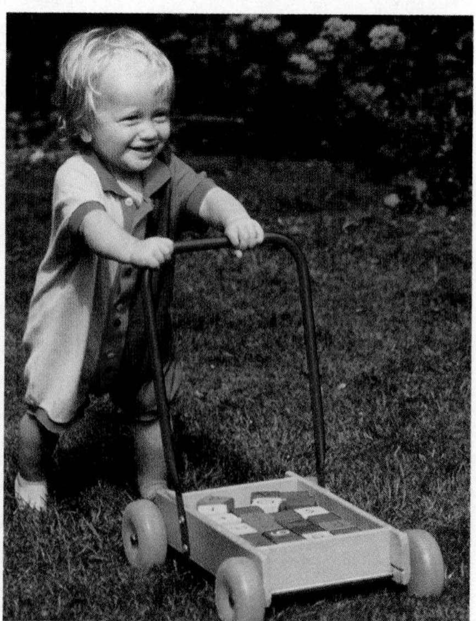

Lifting and holding up the head from a prone position, crawling along the floor to reach something enticing, such as a furry cat's tail, and walking well enough to push a wagon full of blocks are important early milestones of motor development.

TABLE 5 Milestones of Motor Development

Skill	50 Percent	90 Percent
Rolling over	3.2 months	5.4 months
Grasping rattle	3.3 months	3.9 months
Sitting without support	5.9 months	6.8 months
Standing while holding on	7.2 months	8.5 months
Grasping with thumb and finger	8.2 months	10.2 months
Standing alone well	11.5 months	13.7 months
Walking well	12.3 months	14.9 months
Building tower of two cubes	14.8 months	20.6 months
Walking up steps	16.6 months	21.6 months
Jumping in place	23.8 months	2.4 years
Copying circle	3.4 years	4.0 years

Note: This table shows the approximate ages when 50 percent and 90 percent of children can perform each skill, according to the Denver Training Manual II.

Source: Adapted from Frankenburg et al., 1992.

As we trace typical progress in head control, hand control, and locomotion, notice how these developments follow the cephalocaudal (head to tail) and proximodistal (inner to outer) principles outlined earlier. Note, too, that although boy babies tend to be a little bigger and more active than girl babies, there are no gender differences in infants' motor development (Mondschein, Adolph, & Tamis-LeMonda, 2000).

For the first 6 months of life, babies show a slight preference for turning their heads to the right rather than the left. Researchers have suggested that our adult propensity to kiss with our heads tilted to the right—as approximately 64 percent of adults do—is a reemergence of this early bias.

Gunturkun, 2003

Head Control At birth, most infants can turn their heads from side to side while lying on their backs. When lying chest down, many can lift their heads enough to turn them. Within the first 2 to 3 months, they lift their heads higher and higher—sometimes to the point where they lose their balance and roll over on their backs. By 4 months, almost all infants can keep their heads erect while being held or supported in a sitting position.

Hand Control Babies are born with a grasping reflex. If the palm of an infant's hand is stroked, the hand closes tightly. At about 3½ months, most infants can grasp an object of moderate size, such as a rattle, but have trouble holding a small object. Next, they begin to grasp objects with one hand and transfer them to the other, and then to hold (but not pick up) small objects. Sometime between 7 and 11 months, their hands become coordinated enough to pick up a tiny object, such as a pea, using the pincer grasp. By 15 months, the average baby can build a tower of two cubes. A few months after the 3rd birthday, the average toddler can copy a circle fairly well.

Although we tend to think of crawling as a milestone of development, it is not universal. Some babies move directly from sitting or scooting to walking, and bypass crawling altogether.

Locomotion After 3 months, the average infant begins to roll over deliberately (rather than accidentally, as before)—first from front to back and then from back to front. The average baby can sit without support by 6 months and can assume a sitting position without help by about 8½ months.

Between 6 and 10 months, most babies begin to get around under their own power by means of creeping or crawling. This new achievement of *self-locomotion* has striking cognitive and psychosocial ramifications (Bertenthal & Campos, 1987; Bertenthal, Campos, & Barrett, 1984; Bertenthal, Campos, & Kermoian, 1994; J. Campos,

Bertenthal, & Benson, 1980; Karasik, Tamis-LeMonda, & Adolph, 2011). Crawling infants become more sensitive to where objects are, how big they are, whether they can be moved, and how they look. Crawling helps babies learn to judge distances and perceive depth. They learn to look to caregivers for clues as to whether a situation is secure or frightening—a skill known as *social referencing* (Hertenstein & Campos, 2004).

By holding onto a helping hand or a piece of furniture, the average baby can stand at a little past age 7 months. The average baby can let go and stand alone well at about 11½ months.

All these developments lead up to the major motor achievement of infancy: walking. Humans begin to walk later than other species, possibly because babies' heavy heads and short legs make balance difficult. For some months before they can stand without support, babies practice cruising while holding onto furniture. Soon after they can stand alone well most infants take their first unaided steps. Within a few weeks, shortly after the first birthday, the average child is walking fairly well and thus achieves the status of toddler.

During the 2nd year, children begin to climb stairs one at a time, putting one foot after another on the same step; later they will alternate feet. Walking down stairs comes later. Also in their 2nd year, toddlers run and jump. By age 3½, most children can balance briefly on one foot and begin to hop.

MOTOR DEVELOPMENT AND PERCEPTION

Sensory perception enables infants to learn about themselves and their environment so they can make better judgments about how to navigate in it. Motor experience, together with awareness of their changing bodies, sharpens and modifies their perceptual understanding of what is likely to happen if they move in a certain way. This bidirectional connection between perception and action, mediated by the developing brain, gives infants much useful information about themselves and their world (Adolph & Eppler, 2002).

Sensory and motor activity seem fairly well coordinated from birth (Bertenthal & Clifton, 1998; von Hofsten, 2004). Infants begin reaching for and grasping objects at about 4 to 5 months; by 5½ months they can adapt their reach to moving or spinning objects (Wentworth, Benson, & Haith, 2000). Piaget and other researchers long maintained that reaching depended on **visual guidance:** the use of the eyes to guide the movement of the hands (or other parts of the body). Now, research has found that infants in that age group can use other sensory cues to reach for an object. They can locate an unseen rattle by its sound, and they can reach for a glowing object in the dark, even though they cannot see their hands (Clifton, Muir, Ashmead, & Clarkson, 1993; McCall & Clifton, 1999). They even can reach for an object based only on their memory of its location (McCarty, Clifton, Ashmead, Lee, & Goubet, 2001). Slightly older infants, ages 5 to 7½ months, can grasp a moving, fluorescent object in the dark—a feat that requires awareness, not only of how their own hands move but also of the object's path and speed, so as to anticipate the likely point of contact (Robin, Berthier, & Clifton, 1996).

visual guidance
Use of the eyes to guide movements of the hands or other parts of the body.

Depth perception, the ability to perceive objects and surfaces in three dimensions, depends on several kinds of cues that affect the image of an object on the retina of the eye. These cues involve not only binocular coordination but also motor control (Bushnell & Boudreau, 1993). *Kinetic cues* are produced by movement of the object or the observer, or both. To find out whether an object is moving, a baby might hold his or her head still for a moment, an ability that is well established by about 3 months.

depth perception
Ability to perceive objects and surfaces three-dimensionally.

Sometime between 5 and 7 months, after babies can reach for and grasp objects, they develop **haptic perception,** the ability to acquire information through touch, for example, by handling objects rather than by simply looking at them. Haptic perception enables babies to respond to such cues as relative size and differences in texture and shading (Bushnell & Boudreau, 1993).

haptic perception
Ability to acquire information about properties of objects, such as size, weight, and texture, by handling them.

ELEANOR AND JAMES GIBSON'S ECOLOGICAL THEORY OF PERCEPTION

Depth perception has implications when it comes to the development of self-propelled motion, which for most children involves learning how to crawl. In a classic experiment by Richard Walk and Eleanor Gibson (1961), 6-month-old babies were seated on top of a plexiglass tabletop laid over two ledges. Between the ledges was an apparent drop. This illusory drop was made more prominent by using both low light to minimize any reflection from the plexiglass and a bright checkerboard patterned cloth. From the far side of the table, the infants' mothers then beckoned their children. To the babies, it appeared that their mothers were asking them to crawl over a **visual cliff**—a steep drop down to the floor. Walk and Gibson wanted to know if babies would willingly crawl over the deep end of the visual cliff when urged to do so by their mothers.

Walk and Gibson were investigating the factors that helped babies decide whether to move across a ledge or slope, and experiments such as these were pivotal in the development of Eleanor Gibson and James J. Gibson's **ecological theory of perception** (E. J. Gibson, 1969; J. J. Gibson, 1979; Gibson & Pick, 2000). In this approach, locomotor development depends on infants' increasing sensitivity to the interaction between their changing physical characteristics and new and varied characteristics of their environment. Babies' bodies continually change with age—their weight, center of gravity, muscular strength, and abilities. And each new environment provides a new challenge for babies to master. For example, sometimes a baby might have to make her way down a slight incline, and other times might have to navigate stairs. Instead of relying on solutions that previously worked, with experience babies learn to continually gauge their abilities and adjust their movements to meet the demands of their current environment.

This process of "learning to learn" (Adolph, 2008, p. 214) is an outcome of both perception and action. It involves visual and manual exploration, testing alternatives, and flexible problem solving. What worked at one time may not work now, and what worked in one environment may not work well in another. For example, when faced with steep downward slopes, infants who have just begun to crawl or walk seem unaware of the limits of their abilities and are more likely to plunge recklessly down steep slopes. Infants who have been crawling for some time are better at judging slopes and know how far they can push their limits without losing their balance. They also explore the slope before attempting it (Adolph, 2000, 2008; Adolph & Eppler, 2002; Adolph, Vereijken, & Shrout, 2003). For example, they may gauge the steepness with their hands first, or turn around to go down backward as if they are going down stairs. They have learned how to learn about the slope through their everyday experiences.

This is not a stage approach, and thus does not imply that locomotion develops in functionally related, universal stages. Rather, the baby is somewhat like a small scientist testing out new ideas in each situation. According to Gibson, "each problem space has its own set of information-generating behaviors and its own learning curve" (Adolph, 2008, p. 214). So, for example, babies who learn how far they can reach for a toy across a gap while in a sitting position without tumbling over must acquire this knowledge anew for situations

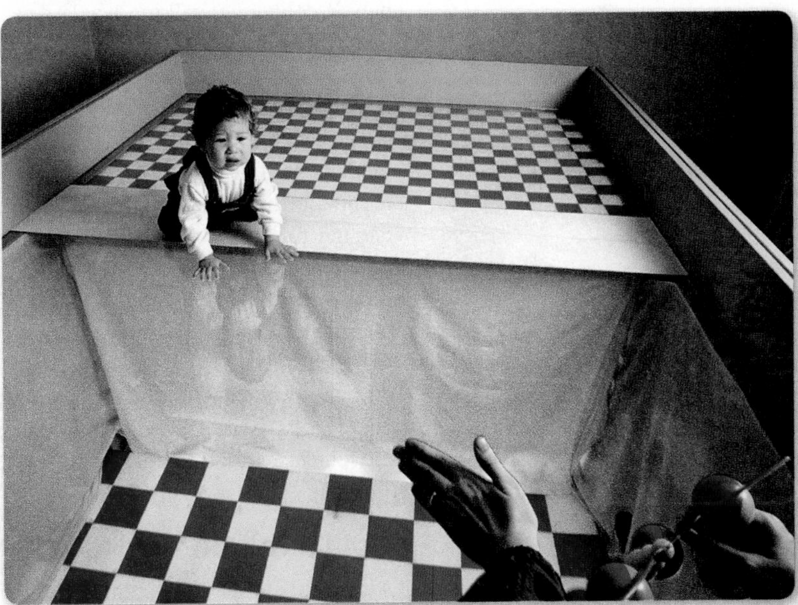

No matter how enticing a mother's arms are, this baby is staying away from them. As young as she is, she can perceive depth and wants to avoid falling off what looks like a cliff.

study smart

Ecological vs. Systems Views of Motor Development

visual cliff
Apparatus designed to give an illusion of depth and used to assess depth perception in infants.

ecological theory of perception
Theory developed by Eleanor and James Gibson, which describes developing motor and perceptual abilities as interdependent parts of a functional system that guides behavior in varying contexts.

involving crawling. Likewise, when crawling babies who have mastered slopes begin to walk, they have to learn to cope with slopes all over again (Adolph & Eppler, 2002).

HOW MOTOR DEVELOPMENT OCCURS: THELEN'S DYNAMIC SYSTEMS THEORY

study smart

Bipedal Posture and Dynamic Systems Theory

Traditionally, motor development was thought to be genetically determined and largely automatic. Presumably, the maturing brain would produce a predetermined set of motor abilities at the appropriate point in development. Today many developmental psychologists consider this view too simplistic. Instead, motor development is considered to be a continuous process of interaction between the baby and the environment (Thelen, 1995; Smith & Thelen, 2003).

dynamic systems theory (DST) Esther Thelen's theory, which holds that motor development is a dynamic process of active coordination of multiple systems within the infant in relation to the environment.

Ester Thelen, in her influential **dynamic systems theory (DST),** argued that "behavior emerges in the moment from the self-organization of multiple components" (Spencer et al., 2006, p. 1523). Infant and environment form an interconnected, dynamic system. Opportunities and constraints presented by the infant's physical characteristics, motivation, energy level, motor strength, and position in the environment at a particular moment in time affect whether and how an infant achieves a goal. Ultimately, a solution emerges as the baby explores various combinations of movements and assembles those that most efficiently contribute to that end. Furthermore, the solution must be flexible and subject to modification in changing circumstances. Rather than being solely in charge of it, the maturing brain is but one component of a dynamic process. Indeed, no one factor determines the pace of development, and no predetermined timetable specifies when a particular skill will emerge. Rather, normal babies tend to develop the same skills in the same order because they are built approximately the same way and have similar challenges and needs. However, because these factors can vary from baby to baby, this approach also allows for variability in the timeline of individual development.

Thelen used the walking reflex to illustrate her approach. When neonates are held upright with their feet touching a surface, they spontaneously make coordinated stepping movements. This behavior usually disappears by the 4th month. Not until the latter part of the 1st year, when a baby is getting ready to walk, do the movements appear again. The traditional explanation focused on cortical control, and the belief was that an older baby's deliberate walking was a new skill masterminded by the developing brain. However, this explanation did not make sense to Thelen. She wondered why the stepping reflex—which used the same series of movements that would become walking—should stop, particularly as other early behaviors, such as kicking, persisted. The answer, she suggested, might be found by considering other relevant variables that could affect movement. For example, babies' legs become thicker and heavier during the early months of life, but the large leg muscles used to control movements are not yet strong enough to handle the increased weight (Thelen & Fisher, 1982, 1983). In support of this hypothesis, when infants who had stopped stepping were held in warm water, stepping reappeared. Presumably, the water helped support their legs and lessened the pull of gravity on their muscles, allowing them to once again demonstrate the skill. Their ability to produce the movement had not changed—only the physical and environmental conditions that inhibited or promoted it. Maturation alone cannot explain such an observation, said Thelen. These same systems of dynamic influences affect all motor movements, from reaching for a rattle to sitting independently to learning to walk.

Some observers have suggested that babies from the Yucatan develop motor skills later than American babies because they are swaddled. However, Navajo babies, like this one, are also swaddled for most of the day, and they begin to walk at about the same time as other American babies, suggesting a hereditary explanation.

CULTURAL INFLUENCES ON MOTOR DEVELOPMENT

Although motor development follows a virtually universal sequence, its *pace* does respond to certain cultural factors. According to some research, African babies tend to be more advanced than U.S. and European infants in sitting, walking, and running. In Uganda, for example, babies typically walk at 10 months, as compared with 12 months in the United States and 15 months in France. Such differences may, in part, be related to ethnic differences in temperament (H. Kaplan & Dove, 1987) or may reflect a culture's child-rearing practices (Gardiner & Kosmitzki, 2005).

Some cultures actively encourage early development of motor skills. In many African and West Indian cultures in which infants show advanced motor development, adults use special *handling routines*, such as bouncing and stepping exercises, to strengthen babies' muscles. In one study, Jamaican infants, whose mothers used such handling routines daily, sat, crawled, and walked earlier than English infants, whose mothers gave them no such special handling (Hopkins & Westra, 1988, 1990).

On the other hand, some cultures discourage early motor development. Children of the Ache in eastern Paraguay do not begin to walk until age 18 to 20 months (H. Kaplan & Dove, 1987). Ache mothers pull their babies back to their laps when the infants begin to crawl away. The Ache mothers closely supervise their babies to protect them from the hazards of nomadic life. Yet, as 8- to 10-year-olds, Ache children climb tall trees, chop branches, and play in ways that enhance their motor skills (H. Kaplan & Dove, 1987). Normal development, then, need not follow the same timetable to reach the same destination.

checkpoint can **you** . . .

- Trace a typical infant's progress in head control, hand control, and locomotion, according to the Denver norms?
- Discuss how maturation, perception, and cultural influences relate to early motor development?
- Compare the Gibsons' ecological theory of perception and Thelen's dynamic systems theory?

summary and key terms

Childbirth and Culture: How Birthing Has Changed

- In Europe and the United States, childbirth before the twentieth century was not much different from childbirth in some developing countries today. Birth was a female ritual that occurred at home and was attended by a midwife. Pain relief was minimal, and risks for mother and baby were high.
- The development of the science of obstetrics professionalized childbirth. Births took place in hospitals and were attended by physicians. Medical advances dramatically improved safety.
- Today, delivery at home or in birth centers attended by midwives can be a relatively safe alternative to physician-attended hospital delivery for women with normal, low-risk pregnancies.

The Birth Process

- Birth normally occurs after a preparatory period of parturition.
- The birth process consists of three stages: (1) dilation of the cervix, (2) descent and emergence of the baby, and (3) expulsion of the umbilical cord and the placenta.
- Electronic fetal monitoring can detect signs of fetal distress, especially in high-risk births.
- About 32 percent of births in the United States are by cesarean delivery.
- Alternative methods of childbirth can minimize the need for painkilling drugs and maximize parents' active involvement.
- Modern epidurals can give effective pain relief with smaller doses of medication than in the past.
- The presence of a doula can provide physical benefits as well as emotional support.

parturition
electronic fetal monitoring
cesarean delivery
natural childbirth
prepared childbirth
doula

The Newborn Baby

- The neonatal period is a time of transition from intrauterine to extrauterine life.
- At birth, the circulatory, respiratory, digestive, elimination, and temperature regulation systems become independent of the mother's. If a newborn cannot start breathing within about 5 minutes, brain injury may occur.
- Newborns have a strong sucking reflex and secrete meconium from the intestinal tract. They are commonly subject to neonatal jaundice due to immaturity of the liver.
- At 1 minute and 5 minutes after birth, a neonate's Apgar score can indicate how well he or she is adjusting to extrauterine life. The Brazelton Neonatal Behavioral Assessment Scale can assess responses to the environment and predict future development.
- Neonatal screening is done for certain rare conditions, such as PKU and congenital hypothyroidism.
- A newborn's state of arousal is governed by periodic cycles of wakefulness, sleep, and activity. Sleep takes up the major, but a diminishing, amount of a neonate's time. By about 6 months babies do most of their sleeping at night.
- Cultural customs affect sleep patterns.

neonatal period
neonate
anoxia
neonatal jaundice
Apgar scale
Brazelton Neonatal Behavioral Assessment Scale (NBAS)
state of arousal

Complications of Childbirth

- Complications of childbirth include low birth weight, postmature birth, and stillbirth.
- Low-birth-weight babies may be either preterm (premature) or small-for-gestational-age. Low birth weight is a major factor in infant mortality and can cause long-term physical and cognitive problems. Very-low-birth-weight babies have a less promising prognosis than those who weigh more.
- A supportive postnatal environment and other protective factors often can improve the outcome for babies suffering from birth complications.

low-birth-weight babies
preterm (premature) infants
small-for-date (small-for-gestational-age) infants
kangaroo care
protective factors
postmature
stillbirth

Survival and Health

- The vast majority of infant deaths occur in developing countries. Postnatal care can reduce infant mortality.
- Although infant mortality has diminished in the United States, it is still disturbingly high, especially among African American babies. Birth defects are the leading cause of death in infancy, followed by disorders related to prematurity and low birth weight, sudden infant death syndrome (SIDS), maternal complications of pregnancy, and complications of the placenta, umbilical cord, and membranes.
- Sudden infant death syndrome (SIDS) is the leading cause of postneonatal death in the United States. SIDS rates have declined markedly following recommendations to lay babies on their backs to sleep.
- Vaccine-preventable diseases have declined as rates of immunization have improved, but many preschoolers are not fully protected.

infant mortality rate
sudden infant death syndrome (SIDS)

Early Physical Development

- Normal physical growth and sensory and motor development proceed according to the cephalocaudal and proximodistal principles.
- A child's body grows most dramatically during the 1st year of life; growth proceeds at a rapid but diminishing rate throughout the first 3 years.
- Breast-feeding offers many health advantages and sensory and cognitive benefits and, if possible, should be done exclusively for at least the first 6 months.
- Overweight babies are not at special risk of becoming obese adults unless they have obese parents.
- The central nervous system controls sensorimotor activity. Lateralization enables each hemisphere of the brain to specialize in different functions.
- The brain grows most rapidly during the months before and immediately after birth as neurons migrate to their assigned locations, form synaptic connections, and undergo integration and differentiation. Cell death and myelination improve the efficiency of the nervous system.
- Reflex behaviors—primitive, locomotor, and postural—are indications of neurological status. Most early reflexes drop out during the 1st year as voluntary, cortical control develops.
- Especially during the early period of rapid growth, environmental experience can influence brain development positively or negatively.
- Sensory capacities, present from birth and even in the womb, develop rapidly in the first months of life. Very young infants show pronounced abilities to discriminate between stimuli.
- Touch is the first sense to develop and mature. Newborns are sensitive to pain. Smell, taste, and hearing also begin to develop in the womb.
- Vision is the least well-developed sense at birth. Peripheral vision, color perception, acuteness of focus, binocular vision, and the ability to follow a moving object with the eyes all develop within the first few months.

cephalocaudal principle
proximodistal principle
central nervous system
lateralization
neurons
integration
differentiation
cell death
myelination
reflex behaviors
plasticity

Motor Development

- Motor skills develop in a certain sequence, which may depend largely on maturation but also on context, experience, and motivation. Simple skills combine into increasingly complex systems.
- Self-locomotion brings about changes in all domains of development.
- Perception is intimately related to motor development. Depth perception and haptic perception develop in the first half of the 1st year.
- According to Gibson's ecological theory, sensory perception and motor activity are coordinated from birth, helping infants figure out how to navigate in their environment.
- Thelen's dynamic systems theory holds that infants develop motor skills, not by maturation alone but by active coordination of multiple systems of action within a changing environment.
- Cultural practices may influence the pace of early motor development.

systems of action
Denver Developmental Screening Test
gross motor skills
fine motor skills
visual guidance
depth perception
haptic perception
visual cliff
ecological theory of perception
dynamic systems theory (DST)

chapter 5

Cognitive Development during the First Three Years

outline

Studying Cognitive Development: Six Approaches

Behaviorist Approach: Basic Mechanics of Learning

Psychometric Approach: Developmental and Intelligence Testing

Piagetian Approach: The Sensorimotor Stage

Information-Processing Approach: Perceptions and Representations

Cognitive Neuroscience Approach: The Brain's Cognitive Structures

Social-Contextual Approach: Learning from Interactions with Caregivers

Language Development

learning objectives

Identify six approaches to the study of cognitive development.

Describe how infants learn and remember.

Discuss infant assessment measures and the prediction of intelligence.

Summarize and evaluate Piaget's theory of cognitive development.

Explain how infants process information and begin to understand the characteristics of the physical world.

Describe the development of language in infancy.

did you **know**?

- Brain growth spurts coincide with changes in cognitive behavior?
- Newborns as young as 2 days prefer new sights to familiar sights?
- Infants and toddlers who are read to frequently learn to read earlier?

In this chapter we look at infants' and toddlers' cognitive abilities from a variety of perspectives: behaviorist, psychometric, Piagetian, information processing, cognitive neuroscientific, and social-contextual. We trace the early development of language.

> You cannot write for children. They're much too complicated. You can only write books that are of interest to them.
>
> —Maurice Sendak, *Boston Globe*, January 4, 1987

Studying Cognitive Development: Six Approaches

How do babies learn to solve problems? When does memory develop? What accounts for individual differences in cognitive abilities? Can we predict how smart a baby will be in the future? These questions have long intrigued developmental scientists, many of whom have taken one of six approaches to their study:

- The **behaviorist approach** studies the basic *mechanics* of learning. Behaviorists are concerned with how behavior changes in response to experience.
- The **psychometric approach** measures *quantitative differences* in abilities that make up intelligence by using tests that indicate or predict these abilities.
- The **Piagetian approach** looks at changes, or stages, in the *quality* of cognitive functioning. It is concerned with how the mind structures its activities and adapts to the environment.
- The **information-processing approach** focuses on perception, learning, memory, and problem solving. It aims to discover how children process information from the time they encounter it until they use it.
- The **cognitive neuroscience approach** seeks to identify what brain structures are involved in specific aspects of cognition.
- The **social-contextual approach** examines the effects of environmental aspects of the learning process, particularly the role of parents and other caregivers.

behaviorist approach
Approach to the study of cognitive development that is concerned with basic mechanics of learning.

psychometric approach
Approach to the study of cognitive development that seeks to measure intelligence quantitatively.

Piagetian approach
Approach to the study of cognitive development that describes qualitative stages in cognitive functioning.

information-processing approach
Approach to the study of cognitive development that analyzes processes involved in perceiving and handling information.

cognitive neuroscience approach
Approach to the study of cognitive development that links brain processes with cognitive ones.

social-contextual approach
Approach to the study of cognitive development that focuses on environmental influences, particularly parents and other caregivers.

Behaviorist Approach: Basic Mechanics of Learning

Babies are born with the ability to see, hear, smell, taste, and touch, and they have some ability to remember what they learn. Learning theorists are interested in mechanisms of learning. Here we examine both *classical* and *operant conditioning*, and then focus on *habituation.*

CLASSICAL AND OPERANT CONDITIONING

Eager to capture Anna's memorable moments, her father took pictures of her smiling, crawling, and showing off her other achievements. Whenever the flash went off, Anna blinked. One evening Anna saw her father hold the camera up to his eye—and she

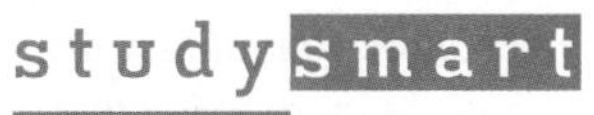

Positive and Negative Reinforcement and Punishment

blinked *before* the flash. She had learned to associate the camera with the bright light, so that the sight of the camera alone activated her blinking reflex.

classical conditioning Learning based on associating a stimulus that does not ordinarily elicit a response with another stimulus that does elicit the response.

Anna's blinking at the sight of the camera is an example of **classical conditioning,** in which a person learns to make a reflex, or involuntary, response (in this case, blinking) to a stimulus (the camera) that originally did not bring about the response. Classical conditioning enables infants to anticipate an event before it happens. Classically conditioned learning will become *extinct,* or fade, if it is not reinforced by repeated association. Thus, if Anna frequently saw the camera without the flash, she eventually would stop blinking at the sight of the camera alone.

operant conditioning Learning based on association of behavior with its consequences.

Whereas classical conditioning focuses on the prediction of events (a flash) based on their associates (a camera), **operant conditioning** focuses on the consequences of behaviors and how they affect the likelihood of that behavior occurring again. Specifically, behaviors may be reinforced and become more likely to occur, or they may be punished and become less likely to occur. For example, a baby may learn that when she babbles her parents respond with smiles and attention, and she may increase this behavior to receive even more smiles and attention. In other words, she has been reinforced for her babbling. By contrast, a baby may see that when she throws her food her parents tend to frown and speak sharply to her. To avoid this punishment, she might learn not to throw her food.

INFANT MEMORY

Can you remember anything that happened to you before you were about 2 years old? Chances are you can't. Developmental scientists have proposed various explanations for this common phenomenon. Piaget (1969) argued that early events are not retained in memory because the brain is not yet developed enough to store them. Freud, by contrast, believed early memories are stored but often are repressed because they are emotionally distressing. Other researchers (Nelson, 2005) take an evolutionary developmental approach and argue that abilities develop as they become useful for adapting to the environment.

Why do we experience infantile amnesia? Part of the reason is that early procedural knowledge (e.g., how to hold a pencil) and perceptual knowledge (e.g., what an apple tastes like) are not the same as the later explicit, language-based memories used by adults (e.g., what you did last Sunday). Infancy is a time of great change, and retention of those early experiences is not likely to be useful for long.

Luckily, we can use operant conditioning techniques to "ask" infants questions about what they remember, so we need not rely on retrospective accounts of adults. For example, Carolyn Rovee-Collier (1999) and her associates (1996) brought 2- to 6-month-old infants in to their laboratory and attached a string between one of their ankles and a mobile. The babies soon learned that when they kicked their leg, the mobile moved. As this was reinforcing to them, the number of kicks increased. When they were later brought in to the same laboratory, they repeated the kicking even though their ankle was no longer attached to the mobile. The fact that they kicked more than other infants who had not been conditioned in this fashion showed that the recognition of the mobiles triggered a memory of their initial experience with them. Similar research has been conducted with older infants and toddlers, and in this way researchers have been able to determine that the length of time a conditioned response lasts increases with age. At 2 months of age, the typical infant can remember a conditioned response for 2 days; 18-month-olds can remember it for 13 weeks (Hartshorn et al., 1998; Rovee-Collier, 1999; Rovee-Collier et al., 1996).

An Indian snake charmer's son plays with a snake his father has trained, showing that fear of snakes is usually a learned, not instinctive, response. Children can be conditioned to fear animals that are associated with unpleasant or frightening experiences.

Young infants do have the capacity to remember events, but this memory is less robust than for older children. Infant

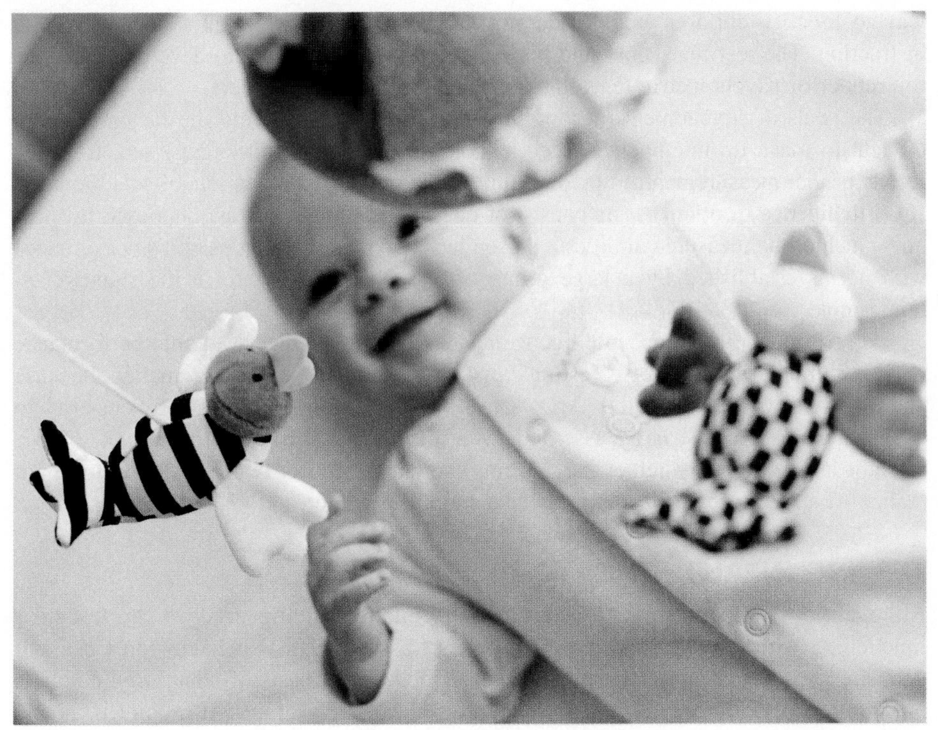

Operant conditioning techniques can help us "ask" babies what they remember. Babies 2 to 6 months old who are conditioned to kick in order to activate a mobile remember this skill even if the mobile is removed for up to 2 weeks. When the mobile is returned, the baby starts kicking as soon as he sees it.

memory appears to be linked specifically to the original cues encoded during conditioning. For example, 2- to 6-month-olds trained to press a lever to make a train go around a track repeated the learned behavior only when they saw the original train. But by 9 to 12 months, infants and toddlers could generalize their memory and press the lever to make a different train move if no more than 2 weeks had gone by since the conditioning. By the same token, 3-, 9-, and 12-month-olds could recognize a mobile or train in a different setting than the one in which they were trained. However, after a long delay, they were no longer able to do so (Rovee-Collier, 1999).

Research using operant conditioning techniques has illustrated that infants' memory processes may not differ fundamentally from those of older children and adults except that their retention time is shorter and memory is more dependent on encoding cues. Moreover, studies have found that just as with adults, memory can be aided by reminders. Brief, nonverbal exposure to the original stimulus can sustain a memory from early infancy through age 1½ to 2 years (Rovee-Collier, 1999).

checkpoint can **you**...

- Compare six important approaches to the study of cognitive development and identify their goals?
- Give examples of classical and operant conditioning, and discuss what operant conditioning studies have found about infant memory?

Psychometric Approach: Developmental and Intelligence Testing

Although there is no clear scientific consensus on a definition of intelligence, most professionals agree on some basic criteria. Intelligence enables people to acquire, remember, and use knowledge; to understand concepts and relationships; and to solve everyday problems. Moreover, **intelligent behavior** is presumed to be goal oriented, meaning it exists for the purposes of attaining a goal. It is also presumed to be adaptive in that it helps an organism adjust to the varying circumstances of life.

intelligent behavior
Behavior that is goal-oriented and adaptive to circumstances and conditions of life.

The modern intelligence testing movement began in the early twentieth century, when school administrators in Paris asked the psychologist Alfred Binet to devise a

Piaget, whom you will read about in a few pages, first became interested in children's cognition while working on this project. Put to work standardizing reasoning tasks for the intelligence tests, he became more interested in the logical errors children made than in their correct answers to the questions.

IQ (intelligence quotient) tests
Psychometric tests that seek to measure intelligence by comparing a test-taker's performance with standardized norms.

The Bayley Scales

Only two of the Bayley Scales items correlate to later IQ: speed of habituation (how quickly they get bored by items) and preference for novelty (whether or not they like new stimuli). More on this later.

Bayley Scales of Infant and Toddler Development
Standardized test of infants' and toddlers' mental and motor development.

Home Observation for Measurement of the Environment (HOME)
Instrument to measure the influence of the home environment on children's cognitive growth.

way to identify children who could not handle academic work and needed special instruction. The test that Binet and his colleague, Theodore Simon, developed was the forerunner of psychometric tests that score intelligence by numbers.

The goals of psychometric testing are to measure quantitatively the factors that are thought to make up intelligence (such as comprehension and reasoning) and, from the results of that measurement, to predict future performance (such as school achievement). **IQ (intelligence quotient) tests** consist of questions or tasks that are supposed to show how much of the measured abilities a person has by comparing that person's performance with norms established by a large group of test-takers who were in the standardization sample.

For school-age children, intelligence test scores can predict academic performance fairly accurately and reliably. Testing infants and toddlers is another matter. Because babies cannot tell us what they know and how they think, the most obvious way to gauge their intelligence is by assessing what they can do. But if they do not grasp a rattle, it is hard to tell whether they do not know how, do not feel like doing it, do not realize what is expected of them, or have simply lost interest.

TESTING INFANTS AND TODDLERS

Although it is virtually impossible to measure infants' intelligence, we can test their functioning with development tests. These tests assess infants' behavior on tasks and compare their performance with norms established on the basis of what large numbers of infants and toddlers can do at particular ages. So, for example, if a child is unable to perform a task that the "average baby" can do by a particular age, that child may be delayed in that area. By contrast, a baby can also be ahead of the curve by performing better than her same-age peers.

The **Bayley Scales of Infant and Toddler Development** (Bayley, 1969, 1993, 2005) is a developmental test designed to assess children from 1 month to 3½ years. Scores on the Bayley-III indicate a child's competencies in each of five developmental areas: *cognitive, language, motor, social-emotional,* and *adaptive behavior.* An optional *behavior rating scale* can be completed by the examiner, in part on the basis of information from the child's caregiver. Separate scores, called *developmental quotients* (DQs), are calculated for each scale. DQs are most commonly used for early detection of emotional disturbances and sensory, neurological, and environmental deficits and can help parents and professionals plan for a child's needs.

ASSESSING THE IMPACT OF THE EARLY HOME ENVIRONMENT

Intelligence was once thought to be fixed at birth, but we now know that it is influenced by both inheritance and experience. Early brain stimulation is a key to future cognitive development. What characteristics of the early home environment may influence measured intelligence and other measures of cognitive development?

Using the **Home Observation for Measurement of the Environment (HOME)** (R. H. Bradley, 1989; Caldwell & Bradley, 1984), trained observers interview the primary caregiver and rate on a yes-or-no checklist the intellectual stimulation and support observed in a child's home. HOME scores are significantly correlated with measures of cognitive development (Totsika & Sylva, 2004).

One important factor that HOME assesses is parental responsiveness. HOME gives credit to the parent of an infant or toddler for caressing or kissing the child during an examiner's visit. Researchers pay particular attention to this because longitudinal research has illustrated the importance of parental responsiveness. Parental responsiveness at 6 months has been positively correlated with IQ, achievement test scores, and classroom behavior at 13 years of age (Bradley, Corwyn, Burchinal et al., 2001).

Other important variables that have been identified with the HOME inventory include the number of books in the home, the presence of playthings that encourage the development of concepts, and parents' involvement in children's play. In an analysis of HOME assessments of 29,264 U.S. children, learning stimulation was consistently associated with kindergarten achievement scores, language competence, and motor and social development (Bradley, Corwyn, Burchinal et al., 2001).

Of course, some HOME items may be less culturally relevant in non-Western than in Western families (Bradley, Corwyn, McAdoo et al., 2001). Also, we cannot be sure on the basis of correlational findings that parental responsiveness or an enriched home environment increases a child's intelligence. All we can say is that these factors are associated with high intelligence. Intelligent, well-educated parents may be more likely to provide a positive, stimulating home environment as well as genes for high intelligence.

Other research has identified seven aspects of the early home environment that help prepare children for school. These seven conditions are (1) encouraging exploration of the environment; (2) mentoring in basic cognitive and social skills; (3) celebrating developmental advances; (4) guidance in practicing and extending skills; (5) protection from inappropriate disapproval, teasing, and punishment; (6) communicating richly and responsively; and (7) guiding and limiting behavior. The consistent presence of all seven conditions early in life is "causally linked to many areas of brain functioning and cognitive development" (C. T. Ramey & S. L. Ramey, 2003, p. 4). Table 1 lists specific suggestions to help babies develop cognitive competence.

The Home Observation for Measurement of the Environment gives positive ratings to parents who praise their children and are attentive to their questions.

EARLY INTERVENTION

Early intervention is a systematic process of planning and providing therapeutic and educational services for families that need help in meeting infants', toddlers', and preschool children's developmental needs. Such programs are expensive, and assessment research is typically required to justify continued funding.

early intervention
Systematic process of providing services to help families meet young children's developmental needs.

A large number of research programs have sought to determine the effectiveness of intervention programs. For example, both Project CARE (Wasik, Ramey, Bryant, & Sparling, 1990) and the Abcedarian (ABC) Project (Campbell, Ramey, Pungello, Sparling, & Miller-Johnson, 2002) have been investigated with randomly assigned, controlled experimental designs. These programs involved a total of 174 at-risk babies who participated in the research from age 6 weeks through 5 years. In each project, an experimental group was enrolled in Partners for Learning, a full-day, year-round early childhood education program at a university child development center. Control groups received pediatric and social work services, but they were not enrolled in Partners for Learning (Ramey & Ramey, 2003).

In both projects, the children who received the early intervention showed a widening advantage over the control groups in developmental test scores between 12 and 18 months, and performed equal to or better than the average for the general population. By age 3, the average IQ in the Abcedarian experimental group was 101 and in the CASE experimental group it was 105. By contrast, the control groups had average IQs of 84 and 93, respectively (Ramey & Ramey, 1998b).

Studies have shown that early educational intervention can help offset environmental risks.

TABLE 1 Fostering Competence

Findings from studies using the HOME scales and from neurological studies and other research suggest the following guidelines for fostering infants' and toddlers' cognitive development:

- In the early months, *provide sensory stimulation* but avoid overstimulation and distracting noises.
- As babies grow older, *create an environment that fosters learning*—one that includes books, interesting objects (which do not have to be expensive toys), and a place to play.
- *Respond to babies' signals.* This establishes a sense of trust that the world is a friendly place and gives babies a sense of control over their lives.
- *Give babies the power to effect changes,* through toys that can be shaken, molded, or moved. Help a baby discover that turning a doorknob opens a door, flicking a light switch turns on a light, and opening a faucet produces running water for a bath.
- *Give babies freedom to explore.* Do not confine them regularly during the day in a crib, jump seat, or small room and only for short periods in a playpen. Baby-proof the environment and let them go!
- *Talk to babies.* They will not pick up language from listening to the radio or television; they need interaction with adults.
- In talking to or playing with babies, *enter into whatever they are interested in* at the moment instead of trying to redirect their attention to something else.
- *Arrange opportunities to learn basic skills,* such as labeling, comparing, and sorting objects (say, by size or color), putting items in sequence, and observing the consequences of actions.
- *Applaud new skills and help babies practice and expand them.* Stay nearby but do not hover.
- *Read to babies in a warm, caring atmosphere from an early age.* Reading aloud and talking about the stories develop preliteracy skills.
- *Use punishment sparingly.* Do not punish or ridicule results of normal trial-and-error exploration.

Sources: R. R. Bradley & Caldwell, 1982; R. R. Bradley, Caldwell, & Rock, 1988; R. H. Bradley et al., 1989; C. T. Ramey & Ramey, 1998a, 1998b; S. L. Ramey & Ramey, 1992; Staso, quoted in Blakeslee, 1997; J. H. Stevens & Bakeman, 1985; B. L. White, 1971; B. L. White, Kaban, & Attanucci, 1979.

checkpoint
can you . . .

- Tell why developmental tests are sometimes given to infants and toddlers?
- Identify aspects of the early home environment that may influence cognitive development?
- Discuss the value of early intervention?

These findings, and others like them, show that early educational intervention can help offset environmental risks and provide significant benefits even if the striking early gains that are often seen do not persist. The most effective early interventions are those that (1) start early and continue throughout the preschool years; (2) are highly time-intensive (that is, occupy more hours in a day or more days in a week, month, or year); (3) are center-based, providing direct educational experiences, not just parental training; (4) take a comprehensive approach, including health, family counseling, and social services; and (5) are tailored to individual differences and needs. As occurred in the two North Carolina projects, initial gains tend to diminish without sufficient ongoing environmental support (Brooks-Gunn, 2003; Ramey & Ramey, 1998a).

Prevention is when you intervene before a problem exists, often on the basis of known risk factors. Intervention is when you intervene to help with an existing problem.

Piagetian Approach: The Sensorimotor Stage

sensorimotor stage
Piaget's first stage in cognitive development, in which infants learn through senses and motor activity.

The first of Piaget's four stages of cognitive development is the **sensorimotor stage.** During this stage (birth to approximately age 2), infants learn about themselves and their world through their developing sensory and motor activity. Babies change from creatures who respond primarily through reflexes and random behavior into goal-oriented toddlers.

SUBSTAGES OF THE SENSORIMOTOR STAGE

The sensorimotor stage consists of six substages (Table 2) that flow from one to another as a baby's **schemes,** organized patterns of thought and behavior, become more elaborate. During the first five substages, babies learn to coordinate input from their senses and organize their activities in relation to their environment. During the sixth substage, they progress to using symbols and concepts to solve simple problems.

Much of this early cognitive growth comes about through **circular reactions,** in which an infant learns to reproduce events originally discovered by chance. Initially, an activity such as sucking produces an enjoyable sensation that the baby wants to repeat. The repetition again produces pleasure, which motivates the baby to do it yet again (Figure 1). The originally chance behavior has been consolidated into a new scheme.

schemes
Piaget's term for organized patterns of thought and behavior used in particular situations.

circular reactions
Piaget's term for processes by which an infant learns to reproduce desired occurrences originally discovered by chance.

TABLE 2 Substages of Piaget's Sensorimotor Stage of Cognitive Development*

Substage	Ages	Description	Behavior
1. Use of reflexes	Birth to 1 month	Infants exercise their inborn reflexes and gain some control over them. They do not coordinate information from their senses. They do not grasp an object they are looking at.	Dorri begins sucking when her mother's breast is in her mouth.
2. Primary circular reactions	1 to 4 months	Infants repeat pleasurable behaviors that first occur by chance (such as thumb sucking). Activities focus on the infant's body rather than the effects of the behavior on the environment. Infants make first acquired adaptations; that is, they suck different objects differently. They begin to coordinate sensory information and grasp objects.	When given a bottle, Dylan, who is usually breast-fed, is able to adjust his sucking to the rubber nipple.
3. Secondary circular reactions	4 to 8 months	Infants become more interested in the environment; they repeat actions that bring interesting results (such as shaking a rattle) and prolong interesting experiences. Actions are intentional but not initially goal directed.	Alejandro pushes pieces of dry cereal over the edge of his high chair tray one at a time and watches each piece as it falls to the floor.
4. Coordination of secondary schemes	8 to 12 months	Behavior is more deliberate and purposeful (intentional) as infants coordinate previously learned schemes (such as looking at and grasping a rattle) and use previously learned behaviors to attain their goals (such as crawling across the room to get a desired toy). They can anticipate events.	Anica pushes the button on her musical nursery rhyme book, and "Twinkle, Twinkle, Little Star" plays. She pushes this button over and over again, choosing it instead of the buttons for the other songs.
5. Tertiary circular reactions	12 to 18 months	Toddlers show curiosity and experimentation; they purposefully vary their actions to see results (for example, by shaking different rattles to hear their sounds). They actively explore their world to determine what is novel about an object, event, or situation. They try out new activities and use trial and error in solving problems.	When Bjorn's big sister holds his favorite board book up to his crib bars, he reaches for it. His first efforts to bring the book into his crib fail because the book is too wide. Soon, Bjorn turns the book sideways, pulls it in, and hugs it, delighted with his success.
6. Mental combinations	18 to 24 months	Because toddlers can mentally represent events, they are no longer confined to trial and error to solve problems. Symbolic thought enables toddlers to begin to think about events and anticipate their consequences without always resorting to action. Toddlers begin to demonstrate insight. They can use symbols, such as gestures and words, and can pretend.	Jenny plays with her shape box, searching carefully for the right hole for each shape before trying—and succeeding.

*Infants show enormous cognitive growth during Piaget's sensorimotor stage, as they learn about the world through their senses and their motor activities. Note their progress in problem solving and the coordination of sensory information. All ages are approximate.

FIGURE 1

Primary, Secondary, and Tertiary Circular Reactions

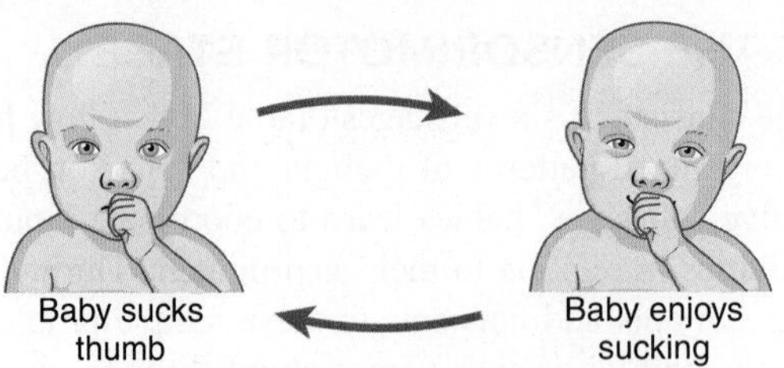

(a) Primary circular reaction: Action and response both involve infant's own body (1 to 4 months).

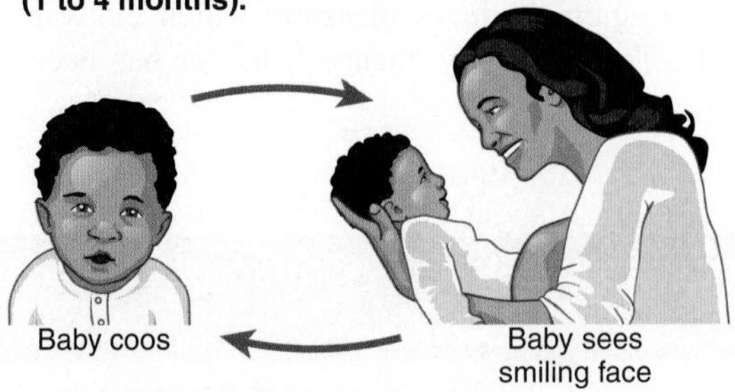

(b) Secondary circular reaction: Action gets a response from another person or object, leading to baby's repeating original action (4 to 8 months).

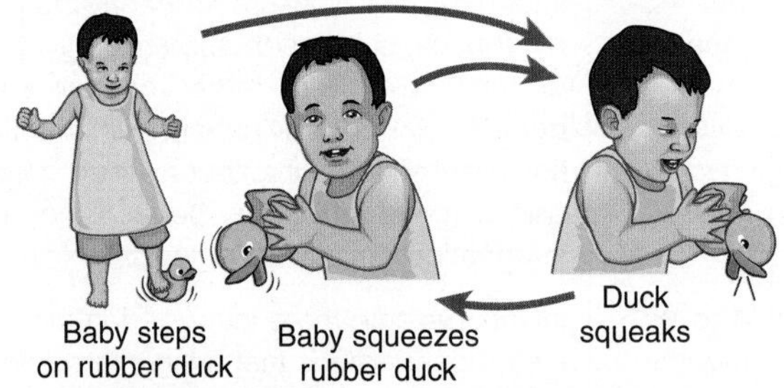

(c) Tertiary circular reaction: Action gets one pleasing result, leading baby to perform similar actions to get similar results (12 to 18 months).

study smart

Piaget's 6 Substages of Sensorimotor Stage and Schemes/Organization

In the *first substage* (birth to about 1 month), neonates practice their reflexes, engaging in a behavior even when its normal stimulus is not present. For example, newborns suck reflexively when their lips are touched. But they soon learn to find the nipple even when they are not touched, and they suck at times when they are not hungry. Infants thus modify and extend the scheme for sucking.

In the *second substage* (about 1 to 4 months), babies learn to repeat purposely a pleasant bodily sensation first achieved by chance (say, sucking their thumbs, as in Figure 1a). Also, they begin to turn toward sounds, showing the ability to coordinate different kinds of sensory information (vision and hearing).

The *third substage* (about 4 to 8 months) coincides with a new interest in manipulating objects and learning about their properties. Babies intentionally repeat an action not merely for its own sake, as in the second substage, but to get results *beyond the infant's own body.* For example, a baby this age might repeatedly shake a rattle to hear the noise.

By the time infants reach the *fourth substage* (about 8 to 12 months), they have learned to generalize from past experience to solve new problems. They modify and coordinate previous schemes, such as the schemes for crawling, pushing, and grabbing, to find one that works. This substage marks the development of complex, goal-directed behavior.

In the *fifth substage* (about 12 to 18 months), babies begin to experiment with new behavior to see what will happen. They now engage in *tertiary circular reactions,* varying an action to get a similar result, rather than merely repeating pleasing behavior they have accidentally discovered. For example, a toddler may squeeze a rubber duck that squeaked when stepped on, to see whether it will squeak again (as shown in Figure 1c). For the first time, children show originality in problem solving. By trial and error, they try out behaviors until they find the best way to attain a goal.

The *sixth substage* (about 18 months to 2 years) is a transition to the preoperational stage of early childhood. **Representational ability**—the ability to mentally represent objects and actions in memory, largely through symbols such as words, numbers, and mental pictures—frees toddlers from immediate experience. They can pretend, and their representational ability affects the sophistication of their pretending (Bornstein, Haynes, O'Reilly, & Painter, 1996). They can think about actions before taking them. They no longer have to go through laborious trial and error to solve problems—they can try out solutions in their mind.

During these six substages, infants develop the abilities to think and remember. They also develop knowledge about aspects of the physical world, such as objects and spatial relationships. Researchers inspired by Piaget have found that some of these developments conform fairly closely to his observations, but other developments, including representational ability, may occur earlier than Piaget claimed. (Table 3 compares Piaget's views on these and other topics with more current findings; refer to this table as you read on.)

representational ability
Piaget's term for capacity to store mental images or symbols of objects and events.

checkpoint
can **you**...

- Summarize major developments during the six substages of the sensorimotor stage?
- Explain how primary, secondary, and tertiary circular reactions work?
- Tell why the development of representational ability is important?

DO IMITATIVE ABILITIES DEVELOP EARLIER THAN PIAGET THOUGHT?

One-year-old Clara watches carefully as her older sister brushes her hair. When her sister puts the brush down, Clara carefully picks it up and tries to brush her hair. Although she gets it wrong, brushing with the flat end rather than the bristles, Clara nonetheless has learned something about the function of the object she saw her older sister holding.

TABLE 3 Key Developments of the Sensorimotor Stage

Concept or Skill	Piaget's View	More Recent Findings
Imitation	Invisible imitation develops around 9 months; deferred imitation begins after development of mental representations in the sixth substage (18–24 months).	Controversial studies have found invisible imitation of facial expressions in newborns and deferred imitation as early as 6 weeks. Deferred imitation of complex activities seems to exist as early as 6 months.
Object permanence	Develops gradually between the third and sixth substage.	Infants as young as 3½ months (second substage) seem to show object knowledge, though interpretation of findings is in dispute.
Symbolic development	Depends on representational thinking, which develops in the sixth substage (18–24 months).	Understanding that pictures stand for something else occurs at about 19 months. Children under 3 tend to have difficulty interpreting scale models.
Categorization	Depends on representational thinking, which develops during the sixth substage (18–24 months).	Infants as young as 3 months seem to recognize perceptual categories; by the end of the first year they can categorize by function.
Causality	Develops slowly between 4–6 months and 1 year, based on an infant's discovery, first of effects of own actions and then of effects of outside forces.	Some evidence suggests early awareness of specific causal events in the physical world, but general understanding of causality may be slower to develop.
Number	Depends on use of symbols, which begins in the sixth substage (18–24 months).	Infants as young as 5 months may recognize and mentally manipulate small numbers, but interpretation of findings is in dispute.

Imitation is an important means of learning, and it becomes increasingly valuable late in the first year of life as babies try out new skills (Nelson, 2005). Piaget noted this behavior in his own observations, and maintained that **visible imitation**—imitation that uses body parts such as hands or feet that babies can see—develops first and is then followed by **invisible imitation**—imitation that involves parts of the body that babies cannot see—at 9 months.

visible imitation
Imitation with parts of one's body that one can see.

invisible imitation
Imitation with parts of one's body that one cannot see.

However, it appears that imitative abilities may have earlier roots than Piaget thought. For instance, studies have shown that babies less than 72 hours old can imitate adults by opening their mouths and sticking out their tongues (Meltzoff & Moore, 1989), although this ability does seem to disappear by about 2 months of age (Bjorklund & Pellegrini, 2000).

Researchers have proposed a variety of explanations for this behavior. Some researchers argue that early imitative behavior is the basis for later social cognition (Meltzoff, 2007). In this view, babies are presumed to have an evolved "like me" mechanism that underlies their later ability to understand their social interaction. Before a child can model others' thoughts and minds, they model their behaviors, and this early physical imitation leads to a later understanding of mental states. Researchers have also argued that infants have an innate predisposition to imitate human faces that may serve the evolutionary purpose of communication with a caregiver (Rakison, 2005). Finally, some researchers have argued that the tongue thrust may simply be exploratory behavior aroused by the sight of an adult tongue—or of some other, narrow, pointed object approaching an infant's mouth (Kagan, 2008). If so, the use of the word *imitation* to describe young infants' behavior in this situation may be misleading.

deferred imitation
Piaget's term for reproduction of an observed behavior after the passage of time by calling up a stored symbol of it.

Piaget also believed that children under 18 months could not engage in **deferred imitation.** Deferred imitation is the reproduction of an observed behavior after the passage of time. As the behavior is no longer happening, deferred imitation requires that a stored symbol of the action be recalled. Piaget argued that young children could not engage in deferred imitation because they lacked the ability to retain mental representations.

However, even babies as young as 6 weeks appear to be able to imitate an adult's facial movements after a 24-hour delay, as long as they are in the presence of the same adult. This finding suggests that even very young babies can retain a mental representation of simple events, at least for relatively short periods of time (Meltzoff & Moore, 1994). Deferred imitation abilities become more sophisticated with age. Deferred imitation of novel or complex events seems to begin by about 6 to 9 months (Bauer, 2002). Note that the findings on deferred imitation agree with those on operant conditioning (Rovee-Collier, 1999), and both sets of data suggest that infants are capable of remembering after a delay.

elicited imitation
Research method in which infants or toddlers are induced to imitate a specific series of actions they have seen but not necessarily done before.

In **elicited imitation,** infants and toddlers are induced to imitate a specific series of actions they have seen, but not done before. For example, more than 40 percent of 9-month-olds can reproduce a simple two-step procedure, such as dropping a toy car down a vertical chute and then pushing a car with a rod to make it roll to the end of a track and turn on a light. Moreover, they can do this after a delay of 1 month on the basis of only the initial demonstration and explanation and without further training (Bauer, 2002; Bauer, Wiebe, Carver, Waters, & Nelson, 2003). It may be that how well they perform on this task is tied to how well they consolidate the memory into long-term storage. Brain scans of infants looking at photos of the procedure a week after the initial session indicate that the memory traces of infants who later performed well on the task were more robust than scans of those who did not do as well (Bauer et al., 2003). Four factors seem to determine young children's long-term recall: (1) the number of times a sequence of events has been experienced, (2) whether the child actively participates or merely observes, (3) whether the child is given verbal reminders of the experience, and (4) whether the sequence of events occurs in a logical, causal order (Bauer, Wenner, Dropik, & Wewerka, 2000).

DEVELOPMENT OF KNOWLEDGE ABOUT OBJECTS AND SYMBOLS

The ability to perceive the size and shape of objects and to discern their movements may be an early evolved mechanism for avoidance of predators (Rakison, 2005). The *object concept*—the idea that objects have their own independent existence, characteristics, and locations in space—is a later *cognitive* development fundamental to an orderly view of physical reality. The object concept is the basis for children's awareness that they themselves exist apart from objects and other people. It is essential to understanding a world full of objects and events.

This little girl seems to be showing some concept of object permanence by searching for an object that is partially hidden. The age when object permanence begins to develop is in dispute.

When Does Object Permanence Develop? One aspect of the object concept is **object permanence,** the realization that an object or person continues to exist when out of sight.

Object permanence develops gradually during the sensorimotor stage. At first, infants appear to have no such concept. By the third substage, from about 4 to 8 months, they will look for something they have dropped; but, if they cannot see it, they act as if it no longer exists. In the fourth substage, about 8 to 12 months, they will look for an object in a place where they first found it after seeing it hidden, even if they later saw it being moved to another place; this is known as the A-not-B error. In the fifth substage, 12 to 18 months, they will search for an object in the *last* place they saw it hidden. However, they will not search for it in a place where they did *not* see it hidden. By the sixth substage, 18 to 24 months, object permanence is fully achieved; toddlers will look for an object even if they did not see it hidden.

object permanence
Piaget's term for the understanding that a person or object still exists when out of sight.

Esther Thelen's dynamic systems theory proposes that the decision where to search for a hidden object is not about what babies *know,* but about what they *do,* and why. One factor is how much time has elapsed between the infant's seeing the object hidden in a new place and the infant's reaching for it. If the elapsed time is brief, the infant is more likely to reach for the object in the new location. When the time interval is longer, however, the memory of having previously found the object in the old place inclines the infant to search there again, and that inclination grows stronger the more times the infant has found it there (Smith & Thelen, 2003; Spencer et al., 2006).

Other research suggests that babies may fail to search for hidden objects because they cannot yet carry out a two-step sequence of actions, such as lifting the cover of a box before grasping the object. When given repeated opportunities, during a period of 1 to 3 months, to explore, manipulate, and learn about such a task, infants at 6 to 12 months can succeed (Bojczyk & Corbetta, 2004).

Methods based only on infants' looking behavior eliminate the need for any motor activity and thus can be used at very early ages. As we discuss later in this chapter, research using information-processing methodology suggests that infants as young as 3 or 4 months seem not only to have a sense of object permanence but also to understand causality and categorization, to have a rudimentary concept of number, and to know other principles governing the physical world.

Symbolic Development, Pictorial Competence, and Understanding of Scale Much of the knowledge people acquire about their world is gained through *symbols,* intentional representations of reality. Learning to interpret symbols is an essential task of childhood. One aspect of symbolic development is the growth of *pictorial competence,* the ability to understand the nature of pictures (DeLoache, Pierroutsakos, & Uttal, 2003). For example, think of how suns are represented in children's books. Generally they are drawn as a yellow circle with radiating spires. A child who understands that this simple graphic stands in for the ball of light in the sky has attained some degree of pictorial competence.

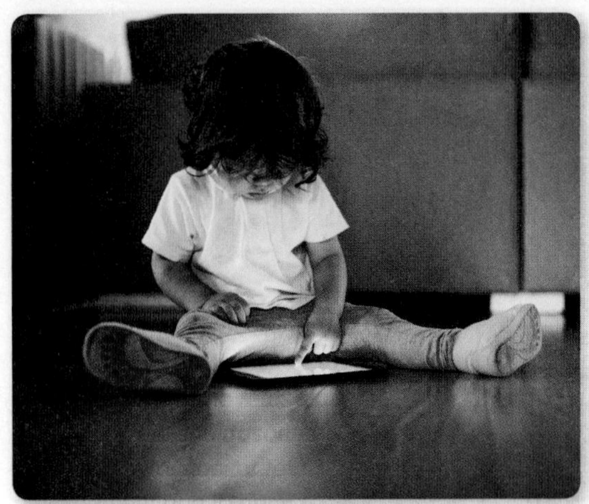

Eighteen- to 36-month-olds were observed trying to slide down tiny slides, sit in dollhouse chairs, and squeeze into miniature cars after similar child-sized objects were removed from their playroom.

Until about 15 months, infants use their hands to explore pictures as if they were objects—rubbing, patting, or attempting to lift a depicted object off the page. By about 19 months children are able to point at a picture of an object while saying its name, demonstrating an understanding that a picture is a symbol of something else (DeLoache, Pierroutsakos, & Uttal, 2003). By age 2, children understand that a picture is *both* an object and a symbol (Preissler & Bloom, 2007).

Although toddlers may spend a good deal of time watching television, at first they seem unaware that what they are seeing is a representation of reality (Troseth, Saylor, & Archer, 2006). In one series of experiments, 2- and 2½-year-olds watched a video of an adult hiding an object in an adjoining room. When taken to the room, the 2½-year-olds found the hidden object easily, but 2-year-olds could not. Yet the younger children did find the object if they had watched through a window as it was being hidden (Troseth & DeLoache, 1998). Apparently, what the 2-year-olds lacked was representational understanding of screen images. Similarly, 2-year-olds who were told face-to-face where to find a hidden toy were able to do so, whereas age-mates who were told the same information from a person on video could not find the toy (Troseth et al., 2006).

Have you ever seen toddlers try to put on a hat that is too small for their head, or sit in a chair much too tiny to hold them? This is known as a *scale error*—a momentary misperception of the relative sizes of objects. In one study, 18- to 36-month-olds were first allowed to interact with play objects that fit their body size, such as a toy car to ride in, a chair to sit in, or a plastic slide to slide down. Then the life-size objects were replaced with miniature replicas. The children were then videotaped trying to slide down tiny slides, sit in dollhouse chairs, and squeeze their bodies into miniature cars. Why would they treat the objects as if they were full size?

The researchers suggested that these actions might in part be based on a lack of impulse control—the children wanted to play with the objects so badly that they ignored perceptual information about size. However, toddlers might also be exhibiting faulty communication between immature brain systems that ordinarily work together during interactions with familiar objects. One brain system enables the child to recognize and categorize an object ("That's a chair") and to plan what to do with it ("I'm going to sit in it"). A separate system may be involved in perceiving the size of the object and using visual information to control actions pertaining to it ("It's big enough to sit in"). When communication between these areas breaks down, children momentarily, and amusingly, treat the objects as if they were full size (DeLoache, Uttal, & Rosengreen, 2004).

dual representation hypothesis
Proposal that children under age 3 have difficulty grasping spatial relationships because of the need to keep more than one mental representation in mind at the same time.

The **dual representation hypothesis** offers yet another proposed explanation for scale errors. An object such as a toy chair has two potential representations. The chair is both an object in its own right, as well as a symbol for a class of things ("chairs"). According to this hypothesis, it is difficult for toddlers to simultaneously mentally represent both the actual object and the symbolic nature of what it stands for. In other words, they can either focus on the particular chair they are faced with ("This is a miniature chair") or the symbol and what it represents ("Chairs are for sitting in"), and so they may confuse the two (DeLoache, 2006; DeLoache et al., 2003).

EVALUATING PIAGET'S SENSORIMOTOR STAGE

According to Piaget, the journey from reflex behavior to the beginnings of thought is a long, slow one. For a year and a half or so, babies learn only from their senses and movements; not until the last half of the 2nd year do they make the breakthrough to conceptual thought. However, research using simplified tasks and modern tools suggests that limitations Piaget saw in infants' early cognitive abilities, such as object permanence, may instead have reflected immature linguistic and motor skills. The answers that Piaget received were as much a function of the ways in which he asked the questions as they were a reflection of the actual abilities of young children.

In terms of describing what children do under certain circumstances, and the basic progression of skills, Piaget was correct. However, infants and toddlers are more cognitively competent than Piaget imagined. This does not mean that infants come into the world with minds fully formed. As Piaget observed, immature forms of cognition precede more mature forms. However, Piaget may have been mistaken in his emphasis on motor experience as the primary engine of cognitive growth. Infants' perceptions are far ahead of their motor abilities, and today's methods enable researchers to make observations and inferences about those perceptions, as we discuss it in the next section.

checkpoint can **you . . .**

- Explain why Piaget may have underestimated some of infants' cognitive abilities, and discuss the implications of more recent research?

Information-Processing Approach: Perceptions and Representations

Information-processing researchers analyze the separate parts of a complex task to figure out what abilities are necessary for each part of the task and at what age these abilities develop. Information-processing researchers also measure, and draw inferences from, what infants pay attention to, and for how long.

HABITUATION

At about 6 weeks, Stefan lies peacefully in his crib near a window, sucking a pacifier. It is a cloudy day, but suddenly the sun breaks through, and an angular shaft of light appears on the end of the crib. Stefan stops sucking for a few moments, staring at the pattern of light and shade. Then he looks away and starts sucking again.

We don't know what was going on in Stefan's mind when he saw the shaft of light, but we can tell by his sucking and looking behavior at what point he began paying attention and when he stopped. Much information-processing research with infants is based on **habituation,** a type of learning in which repeated or continuous exposure to a stimulus, such as the shaft of light, reduces attention to that stimulus. In other words, familiarity breeds loss of interest.

habituation
Type of learning in which familiarity with a stimulus reduces, slows, or stops a response.

When doing research with babies, researchers need to figure out how to ask questions in ways that babies can answer. Natural behaviors such as those performed by Stefan give researchers a means by which to do this. Habituation is a type of learning in which repeated or continuous exposure to a stimulus (such as a shaft of light) reduces attention to that stimulus (such as looking away). It can be compared to boredom, and the rate of habituation (how quickly infants look away) can be used to ask infants how interesting they think various objects are.

Habituation

Researchers study habituation in newborns by repeatedly presenting a stimulus such as a sound or visual pattern, and then monitoring responses such as heart rate, sucking, eye movements, and brain activity. A baby who has been sucking typically stops or sucks less vigorously when a stimulus is first presented in order to pay attention to the stimulus. After the stimulus loses its novelty, the infant generally resumes sucking vigorously. This indicates that habituation has occurred. If a new sight or sound is presented, the baby's attention is generally captured once again, and the baby will reorient toward the interesting stimulus and once again sucking slows. This response to a new stimulus is called **dishabituation.**

dishabituation
Increase in responsiveness after presentation of a new stimulus.

Researchers gauge the efficiency of infants' information processing by measuring how quickly babies habituate to familiar stimuli, how fast their attention recovers when they are exposed to new stimuli, and how much time they spend looking at the new and the old. Liking to look at new things and habituating to them quickly correlates with later signs of cognitive development, such as a preference for complexity, rapid exploration of the environment, sophisticated play, quick problem solving, and the ability to match pictures. In fact, as we will see, speed of habituation and other information-processing abilities show promise as predictors of intelligence (Fagan, Holland, & Wheeler, 2007).

VISUAL AND AUDITORY PERCEPTUAL AND PROCESSING ABILITIES

visual preference
Tendency of infants to spend more time looking at one sight than another.

The tendency to spend more time looking at one sight rather than another is known as **visual preference.** Researchers can use this natural tendency to ask babies which of two objects they prefer. For example, if babies given a choice between looking at a curved or straight line spend more time focused on the curved line, the implication is that babies like curved lines more than straight lines. With this technique, researchers have determined that babies less than 2 days old prefer curved lines to straight lines, complex patterns to simple patterns, three-dimensional objects to two-dimensional objects, pictures of faces or facelike configurations, to pictures of other things, and new sights to familiar sights (Fantz, 1963, 1964, 1965; Fantz, Fagen, & Miranda, 1975; Fantz & Nevis, 1967; Turati, Simion, Milani, & Umilta, 2002). The tendency to prefer new sights to familiar ones is called *novelty preference.*

The finding that babies like to look at new things afforded researchers with yet another tool with which to ask them questions. Babies can be shown a stimulus and be allowed to habituate to it. Then they can be concurrently presented with the familiar stimulus, as well as an additional novel stimulus, and their visual preference can be measured. If the baby spends longer looking at the novel stimulus, that suggests that the baby recognizes the familiar stimulus. In other words, because the novel stimulus is new and babies like new things, it is more interesting and thus warrants a better look than the previously seen, more boring, stimulus. This behavior demonstrates **visual recognition memory,** an ability that depends on the capacity to form and refer to mental representations (P. R. Zelazo, Kearsley, & Stack, 1995).

visual recognition memory
Ability to distinguish a familiar visual stimulus from an unfamiliar one when shown both at the same time.

Contrary to Piaget's view, such studies suggest that a rudimentary representational ability exists at birth or very soon after and quickly becomes more efficient. Individual differences in efficiency of information processing reflect the speed with which infants form and refer to such mental images. When shown two sights at the same time, infants who quickly shift attention from one to another tend to have better recognition memory and stronger novelty preference than infants who take longer looks at a single sight (Jankowski, Rose, & Feldman, 2001).

Speed of processing increases rapidly during infants' 1st year. It continues to increase during the 2nd and 3rd years, as toddlers become better able to distinguish new information from information they have already processed (Rose, Jankowski, & Feldman, 2002; P. R. Zelazo et al., 1995).

Auditory discrimination studies also are based on attentional preference. Such studies have found that newborns can tell sounds they have already heard from those they have not. In one study, infants who heard a certain speech sound one day after birth appeared to remember that sound 24 hours later, as shown by a reduced tendency to turn their heads toward the sound and even a tendency to turn away (Swain, Zelazo, & Clifton, 1993).

Piaget held that the senses are unconnected at birth and are only gradually integrated through experience. If so, this integration begins almost immediately. The fact that neonates will look at a source of sound shows that they associate hearing and sight. A more sophisticated ability is **cross-modal transfer,** the ability to use information gained from one sense to guide another—as when a person negotiates a dark room by feeling for the location of familiar objects. In one study, 1-month-olds showed that they could transfer information gained from sucking (touch) to vision. When the infants saw a rigid object (a hard plastic cylinder) and a flexible one (a wet sponge) being manipulated by a pair of hands, the infants looked longer at the object they had just sucked (Gibson & Walker, 1984).

cross-modal transfer
Ability to use information gained by one sense to guide another.

Researchers also study how attention itself develops. From birth to about 2 months, the amount of time infants typically gaze at a new sight increases. Between about 2 and 9 months, looking time shortens as infants learn to scan objects more efficiently and shift attention. Later in the 1st year and into the 2nd, when sustaining attention becomes more voluntary and task-oriented, looking time plateaus or increases (Colombo, 2002; Colombo et al., 2004).

Failure to engage in joint attention is an early warning sign of autism.

The capacity for *joint attention*—which is of fundamental importance to social interaction, language acquisition, and the understanding of others' intentions and mental states—develops between 10 and 12 months, when babies follow an adults' gaze by looking or pointing in the same direction (Brooks & Meltzoff, 2002, 2005). Young children who follow an adults' gaze at 10 or 11 months have a larger vocabulary at 18 months and 2 years than those who do not, especially if they spontaneously point at the object as well (Brooks & Meltzoff, 2005, 2008).

Watching television may impede attentional development. The more hours children spend viewing television at ages 1 and 3, the more likely they are to have attentional problems by age 7 (Christakis, Zimmerman, DiGiuseppe, & McCarty, 2004). Children who watch at least 3 hours a day score lower on cognitive measures at age 6 than children who spend less time watching television (Zimmerman & Christakis, 2005). However, the association between television viewing and attentional problems may exist only for those children who watch excessive amounts of television (Foster & Watkins, 2010). The question of whether infants and toddlers watch too much television is explored in Box 1.

checkpoint can **you** . . .

- Summarize the information-processing approach to the study of cognitive development?
- Explain how habituation measures the efficiency of infants' information processing?
- Identify several early perceptual and processing abilities that serve as predictors of intelligence?

INFORMATION PROCESSING AS A PREDICTOR OF INTELLIGENCE

Because of a weak correlation between infants' scores on developmental tests such as the Bayley Scales and their later IQ, many psychologists assumed that the cognitive functioning of infants had little in common with that of older children and adults—in other words, that there was a discontinuity in cognitive development. However, when researchers assess how infants and toddlers process information, some aspects of mental development seem to be fairly continuous from birth (Courage & Howe, 2002). Children who, from the start, are efficient at taking in and interpreting sensory information score well on later intelligence tests.

By age 4, girls are generally convinced they are smarter than boys; it takes boys approximately 3 to 4 more years to come to the same conclusion.

Shepherd, 2010

Habituation and attention-recovery abilities from 6 months to 1 year are moderately useful in predicting childhood IQ. So is visual recognition memory. In one study, a combination of visual recognition memory at 7 months and cross-modal transfer at 1 year predicted IQ at age 11 and also showed a modest relationship to processing speed and memory at that age (Rose & Feldman, 1995, 1997).

Visual reaction time and *visual anticipation* can be measured by the *visual expectation paradigm.* In this research design, a series of computer-generated pictures briefly appears, some on the right and some on the left side of an infant's peripheral visual field. The same sequence of pictures is repeated several times. The infant's eye movements are measured to see how quickly his or her gaze shifts to a picture that has just appeared (visual reaction time) or to the place where the infant expects the next picture to appear (visual anticipation). These measurements are thought to indicate attentiveness and processing speed, as well as the tendency to form expectations on the basis of experience. In a longitudinal study, visual reaction time and visual anticipation at 3½ months correlated with IQ at age 4 (Dougherty & Haith, 1997).

All in all, there is much evidence that the abilities infants use to process sensory information are related to the cognitive abilities intelligence tests measure. Still, we need to be cautious in interpreting these findings. For one thing, the predictability of childhood IQ from measures of habituation and recognition memory is only modest. Furthermore, predictions based on information-processing measures alone do not take

research in action

DO INFANTS AND TODDLERS WATCH TOO MUCH TELEVISION?

Six-month-old Caitlin bounces up and down, claps, and laughs out loud as the bright images of her Baby Einstein DVD flash across the screen. Caitlin has been watching Baby Einstein since she was 5 weeks old.

Caitlin is neither precocious nor unusual. According to a random survey of 1,000 parents of preschoolers (Zimmerman, Christakis, & Meltzoff, 2007), by 3 months of age, 40 percent of U.S. infants watch an hour of television, DVDs, or videos every day. By age 2, 90 percent of U.S. children watch television an average of 1½ hours a day. Another national survey (Vandewater et al., 2007) found that 68 percent of children age 2 and under watched television daily, and almost one-fifth of these children had televisions in their bedrooms. Many of these very young children watch alone despite evidence that parental involvement and participation increase the positive impact of educational shows.

During the past 10 years an avalanche of media geared to infants and toddlers has become commercially available. Television shows now aim at children as young as 12 months; computer games have been developed with special keyboards for infants as young as 9 months; and developers provide a constant stream of apps for smart phones and tablet computers.

This increased screen time flies in the face of recommendations by the American Academy of Pediatrics Committee on Public Education (2001) that children under age 2 be discouraged from watching television at all. Instead, the committee recommends they engage in activities that promote brain development, such as talking, playing, singing, and reading with parents. In one survey (Rideout, Vandewater, & Wartella, 2003), children under age 2 spent more than twice as much time watching television as they spent being read to (see figure). "Heavy watchers" were less likely to learn to read by age 6.

In view of the potential developmental risks, why do parents expose their infants and toddlers to television and other visual media? One reason is the belief that media is educational (Zimmerman et al., 2007). Yet in a prospective longitudinal study, time spent watching television between birth and age 2 did not improve language or visual motor skills at age 3 (Schmidt, Rich, Rifas-Shiman, Oken, & Taveras, 2009). And, in another study focused on deliberately exposing children to an educational DVD that highlighted target vocabulary words, 12- to 18-month-old children did not show any significant differences in comparison to a control groups not exposed to the educational video (DeLoache et al., 2010).

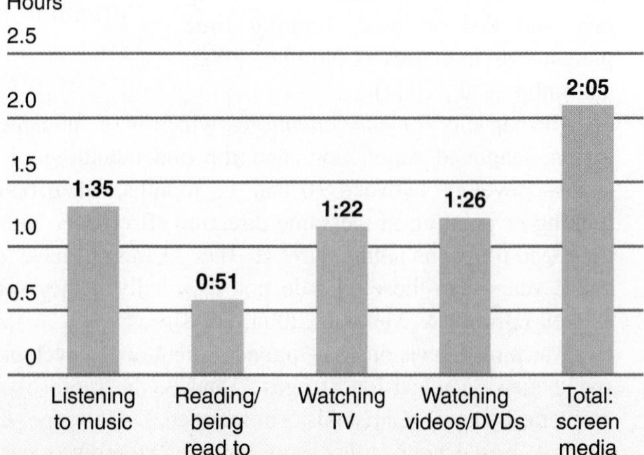

Average amount of time children under 2 spend on media and other activities in a typical day, according to mothers' reports.
Note: These data include only children who participate in these activities.
Source: Rideout et al., 2003.

Other reasons parents give for exposing infants to media are the belief that viewing is enjoyable or relaxing for the child and the use of media as an electronic babysitter (Zimmerman et al., 2007). In one national survey almost one-fifth of the children age 2 and under who watched television daily had televisions in their bedrooms. The two most common reasons for this practice were to free the family television for other family members and to keep the child occupied (Vandewater et al., 2007).

What effect does constant media use have on neurological and cognitive development? Does it stimulate aggressive behavior? Does having a television in the bedroom interfere with sleep? Do video and computer games help visual and spatial skills or risk eyestrain and ergonomic problems? There is already evidence that background media interfere with toddlers' concentration on play (Anderson & Pempek, 2005), but further study is needed to determine how heavy exposure to television affects infants' and toddlers' development. One thing is clear: time spent on media takes away time from exploratory play and from interaction with family members, both of which are developmentally important activities.

At what age would you let a baby watch television or a videotape or play a computer game, and what restrictions, if any, would you place on such activities?

into account the influence of environmental factors. For example, maternal responsiveness in early infancy seems to play a part in the link between early attentional abilities and cognitive abilities later in childhood (Bornstein & Tamis-LeMonda, 1994) and even at age 18 (Sigman, Cohen, & Beckwith, 1997).

INFORMATION PROCESSING AND THE DEVELOPMENT OF PIAGETIAN ABILITIES

As we discussed earlier in the chapter, there is evidence that several of the cognitive abilities Piaget described as developing toward the end of the sensorimotor stage seem to arise much earlier. Here we consider categorization, causality, object permanence, and number, all of which depend on formation of mental representations (refer to Table 3).

Categorization Adults can understand that plants and animals are both living things. Furthermore, they can understand that some animals are pets, that among those pets are cats and dogs, and that a chihuahua is a type of dog. These nested relationships are known as *categories*. Dividing the world into meaningful categories is vital to thinking about objects or concepts and their relationships. It is the foundation of language, reasoning, problem solving, and memory; without it, the world would seem chaotic and meaningless.

According to Piaget, the ability to group things into categories does not appear until around 18 months. Yet, by looking longer at items in a new category, even 3-month-olds seem to know, for example, that a dog is not a cat (French, Mareschal, Mermillod, & Quinn, 2004). Indeed, brain imaging has found that basic components of the neural structures needed to support categorization are functional within the first 6 months of life (Quinn, Westerlund, & Nelson, 2006). Infants at first seem to categorize on the basis of *perceptual* features, such as shape, color, and pattern; but by 12 to 14 months their categories become *conceptual,* based on real-world knowledge, particularly of function (Mandler, 1998, 2007). In one series of experiments, 10- and 11-month-olds recognized that chairs with zebra-striped upholstery belong in the category of furniture, not animals (Pauen, 2002). As time goes on, these broad concepts become more specific. For example, 2-year-olds recognize particular categories, such as "car" and "airplane," within the overall category of "vehicles" (Mandler, 2007).

In the 2nd year, language becomes a factor in the ability to categorize. In one study, 14-month-olds who understood more words were more flexible in their categorizing than those with smaller understood vocabularies; they categorized objects by more than one criterion, such as material as well as shape (Ellis & Oakes, 2006).

Causality Eight-month-old Aviva accidentally squeezes her toy duck and it quacks. Startled, she drops it, and then, staring at it intently, she squeezes it again. She laughs when the duck once again quacks, and looks up at her mother with a wide smile. Aviva is beginning to understand causality—the principle that one event (squeezing) causes another (quacking). Piaget maintained that this understanding develops slowly during infants' 1st year. At about 4 to 6 months, as infants become able to grasp objects, they begin to recognize that they can act on their environment. However, according to Piaget, infants do not yet know that causes must come before effects; and not until close to 1 year do they realize that forces outside of themselves can make things happen.

However, information-processing studies suggest that an understanding of causality may emerge earlier, when infants have gained experience in observing how and when objects move (Saxe & Carey, 2006). Infants 6½ months old seem to see a difference between events that are the immediate cause of other events (such as a brick striking a second brick, which is then pushed out of position) and events that occur with no apparent cause (such as a brick moving away from another brick without having been struck

by it) (Leslie, 1982, 1984, 1995). Some researchers attribute the growth of causal understanding to a gradual improvement in information-processing skills. As infants accumulate more information about how objects behave, they are better able to see causality as a general principle operating in a variety of situations (Cohen & Amsel, 1998; Cohen, Chaput, & Cashon, 2002).

Research also has explored infants' expectations about hidden causes. In one experiment, 10- to 12-month-olds looked longer when a human hand emerged from the opposite side of a lighted stage onto which a beanbag had been thrown than when the hand emerged from the same side as the beanbag, suggesting that the infants understood that the hand probably had thrown the beanbag. The infants did *not* have the same reaction when a toy train rather than a hand appeared or when the thrown object was a self-propelled puppet (Saxe, Tenenbaum, & Carey, 2005). In another set of experiments, infants as young as 7 months used the motion of a beanbag to infer the position of a hand, but not of a toy block (Saxe, Tzelnic, & Carey, 2007). Thus 7-month-olds appear to know that (1) an object incapable of self-motion must have a causal agent to set it in motion, (2) a hand is a more likely causal agent than a toy train or block, and (3) the existence and position of an unseen causal agent can be inferred from the motion of an inanimate object. In addition, 7-month-olds who had begun to crawl recognized self-propulsion of objects, but noncrawling 7-month-olds did not. This finding suggests that infants' ability to identify self-propelled motion is linked to the development of self-locomotion, which gives them new ways of understanding objects in their world (Cicchino & Rakison, 2008).

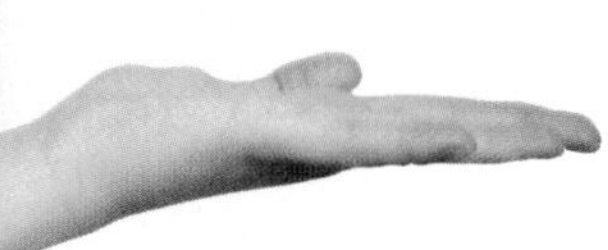

Seven-month-old babies appear to understand that an object incapable of self-motion, such as a beanbag, must be set in motion by a causal agent, such as a hand.

Object Permanence When Piaget investigated object permanence, he used infants' motor responses to gauge whether or not infants understood that a hidden object still existed. Their failure to reach for the hidden object was interpreted to mean they did not. However, it was possible that infants understood object permanence but could not demonstrate this knowledge with motor activity. At that time, infant development research methodologies were more limited and a better means of investigation did not exist. However, once researchers developed the basic habituation and visual preference paradigms described earlier, they could ask babies the question in a different way, using what has since become known as the violation-of-expectations paradigm.

violation-of-expectations
Research method in which dishabituation to a stimulus that conflicts with experience is taken as evidence that an infant recognizes the new stimulus as surprising.

Violation-of-expectations begins with a familiarization phase in which infants see an event happen normally. After the infant becomes bored and has habituated to this procedure, the event is changed in a way that conflicts with—or violates—normal expectations. If the baby looks longer at this changed event, researchers assume the additional interest shown by the baby implies that the baby is surprised.

For example, in one experiment, infants as young as 3½ months were first shown an animation of a carrot moving back and forth behind a screen (Hespos & Baillargeon, 2008). The center of the screen was notched, and a tall carrot should have shown momentarily as it moved in front of the notch, as shown in Figure 2. In the "possible" event, the carrot could be seen as it passed in front of the notch. In the "impossible" event, the carrot would appear at one side, never show in the middle, and then emerge out the opposite side. Infants showed surprise by looking longer at the "impossible" event, indicating that the "impossible" event violated their expectations.

This procedure was important to the study of object permanence because for babies to be surprised by the carrot's failure to show, they needed to be able to remember that the carrot continued to exist. Such studies suggest that at least a rudimentary form of object permanence may be present in the early months of life.

Number The violation-of-expectations paradigm can also be used to ask babies questions about their understanding of number. Karen Wynn (1992) tested whether 5-month-old babies can add and subtract small numbers of objects. The infants watched as Mickey Mouse dolls were placed behind a screen, and a doll was either added or taken away. The screen then was lifted to reveal either the number of dolls that should have been there or a different number of dolls. Babies looked longer at surprising "wrong"

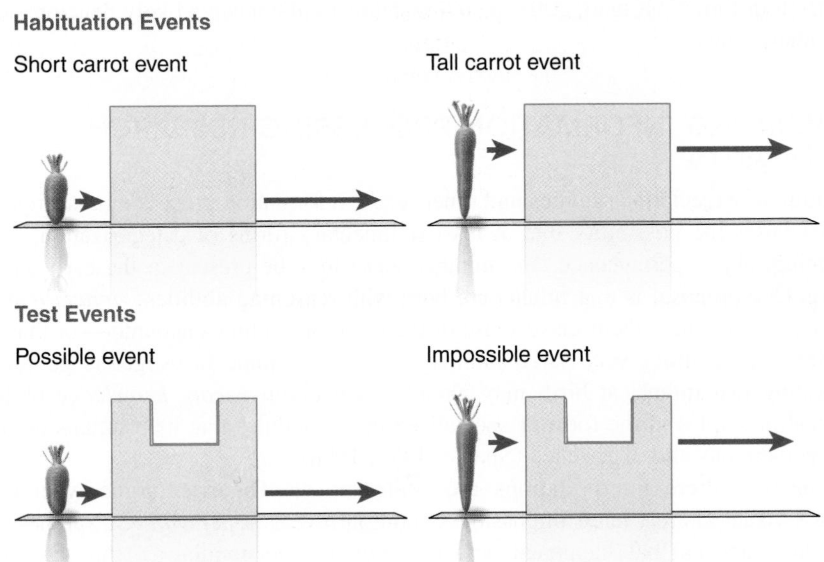

FIGURE 2

How Early Do Infants Show Object Permanence?

In this experiment, 3½-month-olds watched a short carrot and then a tall carrot slide along a track, disappear behind a screen, and then reappear. After they became accustomed to seeing these events, the opaque screen was replaced by a screen with a large notch at the top. The short carrot did not appear in the notch when passing behind the screen; the tall carrot, which should have appeared in the notch, also did not. The babies looked longer at the tall than at the short carrot event, suggesting that they were surprised that the tall carrot did not appear in the notch.

Source: Baillargeon & DeVos, 1991.

answers than at expected "right" ones, suggesting that they had mentally computed the right answers. This understanding of number seems to begin long before Piaget's sixth substage.

Wynn interpreted this research as suggesting that numerical concepts are inborn. However, skeptics point out that the infants in these studies were already 5 and 6 months old. Furthermore, the infants might simply have been responding *perceptually* to the puzzling presence of a doll they saw removed from behind the screen or the absence of a doll they saw placed there (Cohen & Marks, 2002; Haith, 1998; Haith & Benson, 1998). Other researchers suggest that, although infants do seem to discriminate visually between sets of, say, two and three objects, they may merely notice differences in the overall contours, area, or collective mass of sets of objects rather than compare the number of objects in the sets (Mix, Huttenlocher, & Levine, 2002).

In response to such criticisms, McCrink and Wynn (2004) designed an experiment to find out whether 9-month-olds can add and subtract numbers too large for mere perceptual discrimination. The infants saw five abstract objects go behind an opaque square. Five more objects then appeared and went behind the square. The infants looked longer when the screen dropped to reveal five objects than when it revealed 10. The authors concluded that "humans possess an early system that supports numerical combination and manipulation" (p. 780). Again, however, this finding does not establish whether numerical concepts are present at birth or whether they are qualitatively similar to the number concepts of later childhood. As one prominent developmental scientist wrote, "Attributing number concepts to infants simply because they can discriminate among arrays containing different numbers of elements is analogous to attributing a number competence to pigeons who can be taught to peck at a key

Babies may use a rudimentary understanding of probability in figuring out other people's preferences. For example, if they see a person pick a blue toy out of a box filled primarily with red toys, they will assume that person likes blue toys. If a person picks a blue toy out of a box filled with equal amounts of red and blue toys, they are less likely to assume there was a preference for blue toys. In a way, they are performing a statistical analysis of the likelihood of each act, and basing their assumptions on that.

Kushnir, Xu, & Wellman, 2010

exactly four times" (Kagan, 2008, p. 1613). Numerical concepts likely develop slowly over many years.

EVALUATING INFORMATION-PROCESSING RESEARCH ON INFANTS

Violation-of-expectations studies and other recent information processing research with infants raises the possibility that at least rudimentary forms of categorization, causal reasoning, object permanence, and number sense may be present in the early months of life. One proposal is that infants are born with reasoning abilities—*innate learning mechanisms* that help them make sense of the information they encounter—or that they acquire these abilities very early (Baillargeon, 1994). Some investigators go further, suggesting that infants at birth may already have intuitive *core knowledge* of basic physical principles in the form of specialized brain modules that help infants organize their perceptions and experience (Spelke, 1994, 1998).

However, these interpretations are controversial. Theorists argue whether an infant's visual interest in an impossible condition reveals a *perceptual* awareness that something unusual has happened or a *conceptual* understanding of the way things work. For instance, if an infant looks longer at one scene than another, it may be because the infant can perceptually discriminate between the two. In other words, the two scenes look different from each other, and because infants like to look at new things, they gaze longer at the "impossible" condition. Alternatively, it's possible that an infant, in becoming accustomed to a habituation event, has developed an expectation about what should happen that is then violated by the surprising event. In other words, they look longer because their concept of what should have happened was challenged (Goubet & Clifton, 1998; Haith, 1998; Haith & Benson, 1998; Kagan, 2008; Mandler, 1998; Munakata, 2001; Munakata, McClelland, Johnson, & Siegler, 1997). Defenders of violation-of-expectations research insist that a conceptual interpretation best accounts for the findings (Baillargeon, 1999; Spelke, 1998). However, critics say, we must be careful about overestimating infants' cognitive abilities from data that may have simpler explanations or may represent only partial achievement of mature abilities (Kagan, 2008).

checkpoint
can **you** . . .

- Discuss three areas in which information-processing research challenges Piaget's account of development?
- Describe the violation-of-expectations research method, tell how and why it is used, and list some criticisms of it?

Cognitive Neuroscience Approach: The Brain's Cognitive Structures

Current brain research bears out Piaget's assumption that neurological maturation is a major factor in cognitive development. Brain growth spurts (periods of rapid growth and development) coincide with changes in cognitive behavior similar to those Piaget described (Fischer, 2008; Fischer & Rose, 1994, 1995).

Some researchers have used brain scans to determine which brain structures are tied to cognitive functions and to chart developmental changes. These brain scans provide physical evidence of the location of two separate long-term memory systems—*implicit* and *explicit*—that acquire and store different kinds of information (Squire, 1992; Vargha-Khadem et al., 1997). **Implicit memory** refers to remembering that occurs without effort or even conscious awareness, for example, knowing how to tie your shoe or throw a ball. It most commonly pertains to habits and skills. Implicit memory seems to develop early and is demonstrated by such actions as an infant's kicking on seeing a familiar mobile (Nelson, 2005). **Explicit memory,** also called *declarative memory,* is conscious or intentional recollection, usually of facts, names, events, or other things that can be stated or declared. Delayed imitation of complex behaviors is evidence that declarative memory is developing in late infancy and toddlerhood.

implicit memory
Unconscious recall, generally of habits and skills; sometimes called *procedural memory.*

explicit memory
Intentional and conscious memory, generally of facts, names, and events.

In early infancy, when the structures responsible for memory storage are not fully formed, memories are relatively fleeting. The maturing of the *hippocampus,* a structure deep in the temporal lobes, along with the development of cortical structures coordinated by the hippocampal formation make longer-lasting memories possible (Bauer, 2002; Bauer et al., 2000, 2003).

The *prefrontal cortex* (the large portion of the frontal lobe directly behind the forehead) is believed to control many aspects of cognition. This part of the brain develops more slowly than any other (Diamond, 2002; M. H. Johnson, 1998). During the second half of the 1st year, the prefrontal cortex and associated circuitry develop the capacity for **working memory.** Working memory is short-term storage of information the brain is actively processing, or working on. For example, when you try to figure out how much an item on sale will cost at the register, you are using working memory to make the calculations. Working memory can be overwhelmed, as when someone speaking to you while you try to calculate the sale price interrupts this process.

Working memory appears relatively late in development and may be responsible for the slow development of object permanence, which seems to be seated in a rearward area of the prefrontal cortex (Nelson, 1995). By 12 months, this region may be developed enough to permit an infant to avoid the A-not-B error by controlling the impulse to search in a place where the object previously was found (Bell & Fox, 1992; Diamond, 1991).

Although memory systems continue to develop beyond infancy, the early emergence of the brain's memory structures underlines the importance of environmental stimulation from the first months of life. Social-contextual theorists and researchers pay particular attention to the impact of environmental influences.

study smart

Implicit and Explicit Memory

working memory
Short-term storage of information being actively processed.

checkpoint can **you** . . .

- Identify the brain structures apparently involved in explicit, implicit, and working memory, and mention a task made possible by each?

Social-Contextual Approach: Learning from Interactions with Caregivers

Researchers influenced by Vygotsky's sociocultural theory study how the cultural context affects early social interactions that may promote cognitive competence. **Guided participation** refers to mutual interactions with adults that help structure children's activities and bridge the gap between a child's understanding and an adult's. This concept was inspired by Vygotsky's view of learning as a collaborative process. Guided participation often occurs in shared play and in ordinary, everyday activities in which children learn informally the skills, knowledge, and values important in their culture.

In one cross-cultural study (Göncü, Mistry, & Mosier, 2000; Rogoff, Mistry, Göncü, & Mosier, 1993), researchers visited the homes of 14 children 1 to 2 years old in each of four culturally different places: a Mayan town in Guatemala, a tribal village in India, and middle-class urban neighborhoods in Salt Lake City and Turkey. The investigators interviewed caregivers about their child-rearing practices and watched them help the toddlers learn to dress themselves and to play with unfamiliar toys.

Cultural differences affected the types of guided participation the researchers observed. In the Guatemalan town and the Indian village where children saw their mothers at work, the children customarily played alone or with older siblings while the mother worked nearby. After initial demonstration and instruction, mostly nonverbal, in, for example, how to tie shoes, the children took over, while the parent or other caregiver remained available to help. The U.S. toddlers, who had full-time caregivers, interacted with adults in the context of child's play rather than work or social worlds. Caregivers managed and motivated children's learning with praise and excitement. Turkish families, who were in transition from a rural to an urban way of life, showed a pattern somewhere in between.

The cultural context influences the way caregivers contribute to cognitive development. Direct adult involvement in children's play and learning may be better adapted to a middle-class urban community, in which parents or caregivers have more time,

guided participation
Adult's participation in a child's activity that helps to structure it and bring the child's understanding of it closer to the adult's.

Rogoff points out that despite the varied ways in which children learn, they all learn what they need to learn to be effective adults in that culture. She argues there is no "one best way"; rather, there are multiple, equally valid ways of learning.

checkpoint can **you** . . .

- Give an example of how cultural patterns affect caregivers' contributions to toddlers' learning?

greater verbal skills, and possibly more interest in children's play and learning, than to a rural community in a developing country, in which children frequently observe and participate in adults' work activities (Rogoff et al., 1993).

Language Development

language
Communication system based on words and grammar.

Language is a communication system based on words and grammar. Once children know words, they can use them to represent objects and actions. They can reflect on people, places, and things; and they can communicate their needs, feelings, and ideas in order to exert more control over their lives.

In this section, we look first at a typical sequence of milestones in language development (Table 4) and at some characteristics of early speech. Then we consider how

TABLE 4 Language Milestones from Birth to 3 Years

Age in Months	Development
Birth	Can perceive speech, cry, make some response to sound.
1½ to 3	Coos and laughs.
3	Plays with speech sounds.
5 to 6	Recognizes frequently heard sound patterns.
6 to 7	Recognizes all phonemes of native language.
6 to 10	Babbles in strings of consonants and vowels.
9	Uses gestures to communicate and plays gesture games.
9 to 10	Intentionally imitates sounds.
9 to 12	Uses a few social gestures.
10 to 12	No longer can discriminate sounds not in own language.
10 to 14	Says first word (usually a label for something).
10 to 18	Says single words.
12 to 13	Understands symbolic function of naming; passive vocabulary grows.
13	Uses more elaborate gestures.
14	Uses symbolic gesturing.
16 to 24	Learns many new words, expanding expressive vocabulary rapidly from about 50 words to as many as 400; uses verbs and adjectives.
18 to 24	Says first sentence (two words).
20	Uses fewer gestures; names more things.
20 to 22	Has comprehension spurt.
24	Uses many two-word phrases; no longer babbles; wants to talk.
30	Learns new words almost every day; speaks in combinations of three or more words; makes grammatical mistakes.
36	Says up to 1,000 words, 80 percent intelligible; makes some mistakes in syntax.

Source: Bates, O'Connell, & Shore, 1987; Capute, Shapiro, & Palmer, 1987; Kuhl, 2004; Lalonde & Werker, 1995; Lenneberg, 1969. Newman, 2005.

babies acquire language, how brain growth is linked to language development, and how parents and other caregivers contribute to it.

SEQUENCE OF EARLY LANGUAGE DEVELOPMENT

Before babies can use words, they make their needs and feelings known through sounds that progress from crying to cooing and babbling, then to accidental imitation, and then deliberate imitation. These sounds are known as **prelinguistic speech.** Infants also grow in the ability to recognize and understand speech sounds and to use meaningful gestures. Babies typically say their first word around the end of the 1st year, and toddlers begin speaking in sentences about 8 months to a year later.

prelinguistic speech
Forerunner of linguistic speech; utterance of sounds that are not words. Includes crying, cooing, babbling, and accidental and deliberate imitation of sounds without understanding their meaning.

Early Vocalization *Crying* is a newborn's first means of communication. Different pitches, patterns, and intensities signal hunger, sleepiness, or anger (Lester & Boukydis, 1985). Adults find crying aversive for a reason—it motivates them to find the source of the problem and fix it. Thus crying has great adaptive value.

Between 6 weeks and 3 months, babies start *cooing* when they are happy—squealing, gurgling, and making vowel sounds like "ahhh." *Babbling*—repeating consonant-vowel strings, such as "ma-ma-ma-ma"—occurs between ages 6 and 10 months and is often mistaken for a baby's first word. Babbling, although initially nonsensical, becomes more wordlike over time.

Imitation is key to early language development. First, infants *accidentally* imitate language sounds and then imitate themselves making these sounds. Generally, they are reinforced by their parents' positive responses, and thus encouraged to produce such sounds more and more over time. Then, at about 9 to 10 months, infants *deliberately* imitate sounds without understanding them. Once they have a repertoire of sounds, they string them together in prelinguistic speech patterns that sound like language but seem to have no meaning. Finally, after infants become familiar with the sounds of words and phrases, they begin to attach meanings to them (Fernald, Perfors, & Marchman, 2006; Jusczyk & Hohne, 1997).

Sometimes making a particular sound results in a tongue position more or less suited toward making another sound. So, for example, "da" is easier to say for a baby than "bi." When you look at the most common kinship terms across cultures, they almost all use some variation of "ba," "pa," "da," and "ma." These are, not coincidentally, the easiest sounds for babies to make.

Perceiving Language Sounds and Structure Imitation of language sounds requires the ability to perceive subtle differences between sounds. Infants' brains seem to be preset to discriminate basic linguistic units, perceive linguistic patterns, and categorize them as similar or different (Kuhl, 2004).

This process of sound discrimination apparently begins in the womb. In one experiment, the heart rates of fetuses in the 35th week of gestation slowed when a tape recording of a rhyme the mother had spoken frequently was played near her abdomen. The fetal heart rate did not slow for a different rhyme another pregnant woman had spoken. Because the voice on the tape was not the mother's, the fetuses apparently were responding to the linguistic sounds they had heard the mother use. This finding suggests that hearing the "mother tongue" before birth may pretune an infant's ears to pick up its sounds (DeCasper, Lecanuet, Busnel, Granier-Deferre, & Maugeais, 1994). In fact, newborn babies even cry with an "accent" as a result of early experiences with sound. In French, words tend to have a pattern of rising intonation, whereas in German the converse is true. Newborn French and German babies show this same pattern in their cries, presumably as a consequence of hearing language in the womb (Mampe, Friederici, Christophe, & Wemke, 2009). This process continues in the 1st year of life as infants become rapidly sensitized to their native language.

Phonemes are the smallest units of sound in speech. For example, the word *dog* has three phonemes: the *d,* the *o,* and the *g* sound. Every language has its own unique phonology, or system of sounds, that are used in the production of speech. At first, infants can discriminate the sounds of any language. In time, however, the ongoing process of pattern perception and categorization commits the brain's neural networks to further learning of the patterns of the infant's native language and constrains future learning of nonnative language patterns (Kuhl & Rivera-Gaxiola, 2008). This exposure can either occur prenatally or postnatally. If a mother speaks two languages regularly during pregnancy, her newborn baby will recognize both languages and be more interested in listening to speakers in the languages he or she was previously exposed to. Even more important, the baby will show differential responses to both languages, suggesting that even newborns have some understanding that two language systems are involved, and that they are sensitive not just to the overall sounds but to the patterns and rhythms that distinguish the two languages (Byers-Heinlein, Burns, & Werker, 2010). By 6 to 7 months, hearing babies have learned to recognize the approximately 40 *phonemes,* or basic sounds, of their native language and to adjust to slight differences in the way different speakers form those sounds (Kuhl, Williams, Lacerda, Stevens, & Lindblom, 1992). The ability to discriminate native-language sounds at this age predicts individual differences in language abilities during the 2nd year (Tsao, Liu, & Kuhl, 2004), whereas nonnative sound discrimination does not (Kuhl et al., 2005).

Starting as early as 6 months for vowels and by 10 months for consonants, recognition of native phonetic sounds significantly increases, while discrimination of nonnative sounds declines. By the end of the 1st year, babies lose their sensitivity to sounds that are not part of the language or languages they usually hear spoken (Kuhl & Rivera-Gaxiola, 2008). Deaf babies undergo a similar restrictive process with regard to recognition of signs (Kuhl & Rivera-Gaxiola, 2008). Presumably, this increased sensitivity to native sounds or gestures helps the child more efficiently acquire language. Indeed, babies who lack early exposure to this patterning feature of language—whether spoken or signed—during a critical or sensitive period are unlikely to acquire language normally (Kuhl, 2004; Kuhl et al., 2005).

How does this change occur? One hypothesis, for which there is evidence from behavioral studies and brain imaging, is that infants mentally compute the relative frequency of particular phonetic sequences in their language and learn to ignore sequences they infrequently hear (Kuhl, 2004). Another hypothesis, also supported by behavioral and brain imaging studies, is that early language experience modifies the neural structure of the brain, facilitating rapid progress toward detection of word patterns in the native language while suppressing attention to nonnative patterns that would slow native language learning. These early pattern-detection skills predict continuity of language development. In one study, toddlers who at 7½ months had shown better neural discrimination of native phonemes were more advanced in word production and sentence complexity at 24 months and at 30 months than toddlers who, at 7½ months, had been better able to discriminate phonetic contrasts in other nonnative languages (Kuhl & Rivera-Gaxiola, 2008).

One way in which this structure is reflected is in babies' babbling. One-year-olds babble in their native language. In other words, their babbling follows the phonological rules of their language.

In addition to learning what the phonemes in their language are, babies also learn the rules for how they fit together. For example, in English, the sound combination in "kib" is acceptable, although "kib" is not a word. However, the nonsense word "bnik" breaks the phonological rules in English as a "b" and an "n" are not typically found next to each other within the same word. Between 6 and 12 months, babies begin to become aware of the phonological rules of their language. Research with infants supports this, and suggests that they may have a mechanism for discerning abstract rules of sentence structure (Marcus, Vijayan, Rao, & Vishton, 1999; Saffran, Pollak, Seibel, & Shkolnik, 2007).

Gestures Before babies can speak, they point (Liszkowski, Carpenter, & Tomasello, 2008). Pointing is important to language acquisition and serves several functions. At 11 months, Maika pointed to her cup to show that she wanted it. She also pointed to a dog chasing his tail, using the gesture to communicate with her mother about an interesting sight. At 12 months, she pointed at a pen her brother had dropped and was looking for. Pointing helps regulate joint interactions and does not need to be taught to neurotypical children.

Babies generally start pointing with their entire hand, and then move to using their pointer finger.

By 12 months, Maika learned some *conventional social gestures:* waving bye-bye, nodding her head to mean "yes," and shaking her head to signify "no." By about 13 months, she used more elaborate *representational gestures;* for example, she would hold an empty cup to her mouth to show that she wanted a drink or hold up her arms to show that she wanted to be picked up.

Symbolic gestures, such as blowing to mean "hot" or sniffing to mean "flower," often emerge around the same time that babies say their first words, and they function much like words. Both hearing and deaf babies use such gestures in much the same ways (Goldin-Meadow, 2007). By using them, babies show an understanding that symbols can refer to specific objects, events, desires, and conditions. Gestures usually appear before children have a vocabulary of 25 words and drop out when children learn the word for the idea they were gesturing and can say it instead (Lock, Young, Service, & Chandler, 1990).

Toddlers often combine gestures with words. Gesture-word combinations serve as a signal that a child is about to begin using multiword sentences (Goldin-Meadow, 2007).

This toddler is communicating with his father by pointing at something that catches his eye. Gesturing seems to come naturally to young children and may be an important part of language learning.

First Words The average baby says a first word sometime between 10 and 14 months, initiating **linguistic speech**—verbal expression that conveys meaning. At first, an infant's total verbal repertoire is likely to be "mama" or "dada." Or it may be a simple syllable that has more than one meaning depending on the context in which the child utters it. "Da" may mean "I want that," "I want to go out," or "Where's Daddy?" A word like this, in which an entire sentence is expressed with one word, is called a **holophrase.**

Long before infants can connect sounds to meanings, they learn to recognize sound patterns they hear frequently, such as their name. Infants 5 months old listen longer to their name than to other names (Newman, 2005). Infants at 8 months or younger start learning the forms of words by discerning such perceptual cues as syllables that usually occur together (such as *ba* and *by*) and store these possible word forms in memory. They also notice pronunciation, stress placed on syllables, and changes in pitch. This early auditory learning lays the foundation for vocabulary growth (Swingley, 2008).

linguistic speech
Verbal expression designed to convey meaning.

holophrase
Single word that conveys a complete thought.

study smart

Language Development: 10–18 Months

Babies understand many words before they can use them. Six-month-olds look longer at a video of their mothers when they hear the word "mommy" and of their fathers when they hear "daddy" (Tincoff & Jusczyk, 1999). By 13 months, most children understand that a word stands for a specific thing or event, and they can quickly learn the meaning of a new word (Woodward, Markman, & Fitzsimmons, 1994).

Between 10 months and 2 years, the process by which babies learn words gradually changes from simple association to following social cues. At 10 months, infants associate a name they hear with an object they find interesting whether or not the name is the correct one for that object. At 12 months, they begin to pay attention to cues from adults, such as looking or pointing at an object while saying its name. However, they still learn names only for interesting objects and ignore uninteresting ones. By 18 to 24 months, children follow social cues in learning names, regardless of the intrinsic interest of the objects (Golinkoff & Hirsh-Pasek, 2006; Pruden, Hirsh-Pasek, Golinkoff, & Hennon, 2006). Pointing is one of the primary scaffolds for learning word meaning. At 24 months, children quickly recognize names of familiar objects in the absence of visual cues (Swingley & Fernald, 2002).

Receptive vocabulary—what infants understand—continues to grow as verbal comprehension gradually becomes faster and more accurate and efficient (Fernald et al., 2006). Generally, infants have a far greater receptive vocabulary than an expressive—or spoken—vocabulary. By 18 months, 3 out of 4 children can understand 150 words and can say 50 of them (Kuhl, 2004). Children with larger vocabularies and quicker reaction times can recognize spoken words from just the first part of the word. For example,

If you want to help a toddler learn color words, label the object you are referring to, then name the color.

Dye, 2010

when they hear "daw" or "ki," they will point to a picture of a dog or kitten (Fernald, Swingley, & Pinto, 2001). This early language learning is closely related to later cognitive development. In a longitudinal study, children's speed of recognition of spoken words and vocabulary size at 25 months predicted linguistic and cognitive skills at 8 years (Marchman & Fernald, 2008).

Addition of new words to the *expressive* (spoken) *vocabulary* is slow at first. Then, sometime between 16 and 24 months, a "naming explosion" may occur (Ganger & Brent, 2004). Within a few months, many toddlers go from saying about 50 words to saying several hundred (Courage & Howe, 2002). Rapid gains in spoken vocabulary reflect increases in speed and accuracy of word recognition during the 2nd year (Fernald et al., 2006) as well as an understanding that things belong in categories (Courage & Howe, 2002).

Nouns seem to be the easiest type of word to learn. In a cross-cultural study, Spanish, Dutch, French, Hebrew, Italian, Korean, and U.S. parents all reported that their 20-month-old children knew more nouns than any other class of words (Bornstein et al., 2004). At 24 to 36 months, children can figure out the meaning of unfamiliar adjectives from context or from the nouns they modify (Mintz, 2005).

First Sentences The next important linguistic breakthrough comes when a toddler puts two words together to express one idea ("Dolly fall"). Generally, children do this between 18 and 24 months. However, this age range varies greatly. Although prelinguistic speech (such as babbling) is fairly closely tied to chronological age, linguistic speech is not. Most children who begin talking fairly late catch up eventually—and many make up for lost time by talking nonstop to anyone who will listen!

telegraphic speech
Early form of sentence use consisting of only a few essential words.

A child's first sentences typically deal with everyday events, things, people, or activities (Braine, 1976; Rice, 1989; Slobin, 1973). Children typically use **telegraphic speech,** consisting of only a few essential words. When Rita says, "Damma deep," she seems to mean, "Grandma is sweeping the floor." Children's use of telegraphic speech, and the form it takes, varies, depending on the language being learned (Braine, 1976; Slobin, 1983). Word order generally conforms to what a child hears; Rita does not say, "Deep Damma," when she sees her grandmother sweeping.

syntax
Rules for forming sentences in a particular language.

Sometime between 20 and 30 months, children show increasing competence in **syntax,** the fundamental rules for putting sentences together in their language. Syntax is why a sentence like "man bites dog" differs from "dog bites man," and it allows us to understand and produce an infinite number of utterances. They become somewhat more comfortable with articles (*a, the*), prepositions (*in, on*), conjunctions (*and, but*), plurals, verb endings, past tense, and forms of the verb *to be* (*am, are, is*). They also become increasingly aware of the communicative purpose of speech and of whether their words are being understood (Dunham, Dunham, & O'Keefe, 2000; Shwe & Markman, 1997)—a sign of growing sensitivity to the mental lives of others. By age 3, speech is fluent, longer, and more complex. Although children often omit parts of speech, they get their meaning across well.

The term telegraphic speech *is derived from the fact that telegrams charged by the word. To save money, people would eliminate all but the essential components of speech in much the same way that babies use only the words best able to communicate their intent.*

CHARACTERISTICS OF EARLY SPEECH

Early speech has a character all its own, no matter what language a child is speaking (Slobin, 1971, 1990). As we have seen, young children *simplify.* They use telegraphic speech to say just enough to get their meaning across ("No drink milk!").

Young children *understand grammatical relationships they cannot yet express.* At first, Nina may understand that a dog is chasing a cat, but she cannot string together enough words to express the complete action. Her sentence comes out as "Puppy chase" rather than "Puppy chase kitty."

Children also make mistakes with respect to what category a word describes by either underextending or overextending word meaning. When they *underextend word meanings,* they use words in too narrow of a category. Lisa's uncle gave her a toy car, which the 13-month-old called her "koo-ka." Then her father came home with a gift, saying, "Look, Lisa, here's a little car for you." Lisa shook her head. "Koo-ka," she said, and ran and got the one from her uncle. To her, *that* car—and *only* that car—was a little car, and it took some time before she called any other toy cars by the same name. Lisa was underextending the word *car* by restricting it to a single object.

Alternatively, children also *overextend word meanings* by using words in too broad of a category. At 14 months, Amir jumped in excitement at the sight of a gray-haired man on the television screen and shouted, "Gampa!" Amir was overgeneralizing, or overextending, a word; he thought that because his grandfather had gray hair, all gray-haired men could be called "Grandpa." As children develop a larger vocabulary and get feedback from adults on the appropriateness of what they say, they overextend less. ("No, honey, that man looks a little like Grandpa, but he's somebody else's grandpa, not yours.")

Young children *overregularize rules.* Overregularization is a language error, but it nonetheless illustrates children's growing knowledge of syntax. It occurs when children inappropriately apply a syntactical rule. For instance, when children say sentences such as "Daddy goed to the store" or "I drawed that," they are applying the English language rule "add *–ed* to a verb to make it past tense." It takes a while for children to learn the rule as well as the exceptions to it. For example, children commonly use the exceptions to the rule first. They generally learn these by rote for phrases they commonly hear ("Daddy went to the store"). Then they learn the rule and use that to fill in the blanks when they can't recall the exception ("Daddy goed to the store"). By early school age, as they become more proficient in language, they memorize the exceptions and begin to apply them, once again saying the phrase correctly ("Daddy went to the store").

English is generally considered to be a challenging second language to learn. Part of the reason for this is that English has so many exceptions to the rules.

checkpoint can **you** . . .

- Trace a typical sequence of milestones in early language development?
- Describe five ways in which early speech differs from adult speech?

CLASSIC THEORIES OF LANGUAGE ACQUISITION: THE NATURE-NURTURE DEBATE

Is linguistic ability learned or inborn? In the 1950s, a debate raged between two schools of thought: one led by B. F. Skinner, the foremost proponent of learning theory, the other by the linguist Noam Chomsky.

Skinner (1957) maintained that language learning, like other learning, is based on experience and learned associations. According to classic learning theory, children learn language through the processes of operant conditioning. At first, babies utter sounds at random. Caregivers reinforce the sounds that happen to resemble adult speech. Infants then repeat these reinforced sounds, and language is gradually shaped. Social learning theorists extended this early model to account for imitation. According to social learning theory, babies imitate the sounds they hear adults make and, again, are reinforced for doing so.

For example, Lila, while babbling to herself, inadvertently says "da." Her parents hear her and provide her with smiles, attention, and praise for this sound. Lila is thus reinforced and continues to say "da." Eventually, her parents no longer provide as much reinforcement for the sound. But then Lila happens to say "dada," perhaps by imitating her parents. Now her parents once again reward her lavishly. Again, their praise eventually tapers off, and now the word is only reinforced when her father is present. Over time, her parents' selective reinforcement of closer and closer approximations to speech in the right context results in the shaping of language.

Observation, imitation, and reinforcement do contribute to language development, but, as Chomsky (1957) persuasively argued, they cannot fully explain it. For one thing, word combinations and nuances are so numerous and so complex that they cannot all be acquired by specific imitation and reinforcement. In addition, caregivers often reinforce utterances that are not strictly grammatical, as long as they make sense ("Gampa go bye-bye"). Adult speech itself is an unreliable model to imitate, as it is often ungrammatical and contains false starts, unfinished sentences, and slips of the tongue. Also,

Is linguistic ability learned or inborn? Though inborn language capacity may underlie this baby's ability to speak, when this mother repeats the sounds her baby makes, she is reinforcing the likelihood the baby will repeat those sounds—highlighting the influences of both nature and nurture.

learning theory does not account for children's imaginative ways of saying things they have never heard, such as when 2-year-old Anna said she didn't want to go to sleep yet because she wasn't "yawny."

Chomsky's view is called **nativism.** Unlike Skinner's learning theory, nativism emphasizes the active role of the learner. Chomsky (1957, 1972, 1995) proposed that the human brain has an innate capacity for acquiring language; babies learn to talk as naturally as they learn to walk. He suggested that an inborn **language acquisition device (LAD)** programs children's brains to analyze the language they hear and to figure out its rules.

nativism
Theory that human beings have an inborn capacity for language acquisition.

language acquisition device (LAD)
In Chomsky's terminology, an inborn mechanism that enables children to infer linguistic rules from the language they hear.

Support for the nativist position comes from newborns' ability to differentiate similar sounds, suggesting that they are born with perceptual "tuning rods" that pick up characteristics of speech. Nativists point out that almost all children master their native language in the same age-related sequence without formal teaching. Furthermore, the brains of human beings, the only animals with fully developed language, contain a structure that is larger on one side than on the other, suggesting that an inborn mechanism for sound and language processing may be localized in the larger hemisphere—the left for most people (Gannon, Holloway, Broadfield, & Braun, 1998). Still, the nativist approach does not explain precisely how such a mechanism operates. It does not tell us why some children acquire language more rapidly and efficiently than others, why children differ in linguistic skill and fluency, or why (as we'll see) speech development appears to depend on having someone to talk with, not merely on hearing spoken language.

Just as deaf babies hand-babble, deaf parents engage in baby-talk (aka motherese or parentese) with gestures.

Deaf babies seem to learn sign language in much the same fashion and in the same sequence as hearing infants learn speech. Just as hearing babies of hearing parents imitate vocal utterances, deaf babies of deaf parents seem to imitate the sign language they see their parents using, first stringing together meaningless motions and then repeating them over and over in what has been called *hand-babbling.* As parents reinforce these gestures, the babies attach meaning to them (Petitto & Marentette, 1991; Petitto, Holowka, Sergio, & Ostry, 2001).

Learning theory does not explain the correspondence between the ages at which linguistic advances in both hearing and nonhearing babies typically occur (Petitto & Kovelman, 2003). Deaf babies begin hand-babbling between ages 7 and 10 months, about the age when hearing infants begin voice-babbling (Petitto, Holowka et al., 2001). Deaf babies also begin to use sentences in sign language at about the same time that hearing babies begin to speak in sentences (Meier, 1991). These observations suggest that an inborn language capacity may underlie the acquisition of both spoken and signed language and that advances in both kinds of language are tied to brain maturation.

Most developmental scientists today maintain that language acquisition, like most other aspects of development, depends on an intertwining of nature and nurture. Children, whether hearing or deaf, probably have an inborn capacity to acquire language, which may be activated or constrained by experience.

checkpoint
can you . . .

- Summarize how learning theory and nativism seek to explain language acquisition and point out strengths and weaknesses of each theory?
- Discuss implications of how deaf babies acquire language?

INFLUENCES ON EARLY LANGUAGE DEVELOPMENT

What determines how quickly and how well children learn to understand and use language? Research has focused on both neurological and environmental influences.

Brain Development The tremendous brain growth during the early months and years is closely linked with language development. A newborn's cries are controlled by the *brain stem* and *pons,* the most primitive parts of the brain and the earliest to develop. Repetitive babbling may emerge with the maturation of parts of the *motor cortex,* which control movements of the face and larynx. A brain imaging study points to the emergence of a link between the brain's phonetic perception and motor systems as early as 6 months—a connection that strengthens by 6 to 12 months (Imada et al., 2006). The development of language actively affects brain networks, committing them to the recognition of native language sounds only (Kuhl, 2004; Kuhl et al., 2005). In other words, language exposure helps shape the developing brain, and then the developing brain helps the infant learn language.

Brain scans, which measure changes in electrical potential at particular brain sites during cognitive activity, confirm the sequence of vocabulary development outlined earlier in this chapter. In toddlers with large vocabularies, brain activation tends to focus on the left temporal and parietal lobes, whereas in toddlers with smaller vocabularies, brain activation is more scattered (Kuhl & Rivera-Gaxiola, 2008). Cortical regions associated with language continue to develop until at least the late preschool years or beyond—some even until adulthood.

In about 98 percent of people, the left hemisphere is dominant for language, though the right hemisphere participates as well (Knecht et al., 2000). Studies of babbling babies show that the mouth opens more on the right side than on the left. The left hemisphere of the brain controls activity on the right side of the body, and lateralization of linguistic functions apparently begins to take place very early in life (Holowka & Petitto, 2002).

Social Interaction: The Role of Parents and Caregivers Language is a social act. It requires interaction. Language takes not only the necessary biological machinery and cognitive capacity but also interaction with a live communicative partner. Children who grow up without normal social contact, such as children with autism or children who are linguistically isolated, do not develop language normally. Neither do children who are exposed to language only through television. In a laboratory experiment, native Mandarin speakers read to and played with 9-month-old infants regularly for 4 to 6 weeks. Behavioral tests and brain scans up to 1 month after the final session showed that the infants had learned—and retained—Mandarin syllables not used in English. By contrast, a control group who had been exposed to the same Mandarin speech through televised or audio-only tutors did no better than another control group who had heard only English (Kuhl & Rivera-Gaxiola, 2008). As Bronfenbrenner's bioecological model would predict, the age of parents or caregivers, the way they interact with and talk with an infant, the child's birth order, child care experience, and, later, schooling, peers, and television exposure all affect the pace and course of language acquisition. So does the wider culture. The milestones of language development described in this chapter are typical of Western, middle-class children who are spoken to directly. They are not necessarily typical in all cultures, nor at all socioeconomic levels (Hoff, 2006).

Prelinguistic Period At the babbling stage, adults help an infant advance toward true speech by repeating the sounds the baby makes and rewarding her efforts. The baby finds this imitation engaging and soon joins in the game, repeating the sounds back. Parents' imitation of babies' sounds affects the amount of infant vocalization (Goldstein, King, & West, 2003) and the pace of language learning (Hardy-Brown & Plomin, 1985; Schmitt, Simpson, & Friend, 2011). It also helps babies experience the social aspect of speech

Playing peek-a-boo involves turn-taking, which is what also happens within conversations and most social interactions.

Children in bilingual homes often use elements of both languages, but this doesn't mean they confuse the two languages.

(Kuhl, 2004). As early as 4 months, babies in a game of peekaboo show sensitivity to the structure of social exchange with an adult (Rochat, Querido, & Striano, 1999).

Vocabulary Development How can parents facilitate language development in their children? When babies begin to talk, parents or caregivers can boost vocabulary development by repeating their first words and pronouncing them correctly. Joint attention leads to more rapid vocabulary development (Hoff, 2006). In one longitudinal study, mothers' responsiveness to 9-month-olds' and, even more so, to 13-month-olds' vocalization and play predicted the timing of language milestones, such as first spoken words and sentences (Tamis-LeMonda, Bornstein, & Baumwell, 2001). This is not surprising; a shared understanding and focus on an event or object coupled with maternal labeling is an extremely supportive framework for language acquisition.

A strong relationship exists between the frequency of specific words in mothers' speech and the order in which children learn these words (Brent & Siskind, 2001; Huttenlocher, Haight, Bryk, Seltzer, & Lyons, 1991) as well as between mothers' talkativeness and the size of toddlers' vocabularies (Huttenlocher, 1998; Schmitt et al., 2011). Mothers with higher socioeconomic status tend to use richer vocabularies and longer utterances, and their 2-year-olds have larger spoken vocabularies—as much as 8 times as large as those of low-SES children the same age (Hoff, 2003; C. T. Ramey & Ramey, 2003). By age 3, vocabularies of low-income children vary greatly, depending in large part on the diversity of word types they have heard their mothers use (Pan, Rowe, Singer, & Snow, 2005).

However, parental sensitivity and responsiveness may count even more than the number of words a mother uses. In a yearlong study of 290 low-income families of 2-year-olds, both parents' sensitivity, positive regard for the child, and the cognitive stimulation they provided during play predicted the child's receptive vocabulary and cognitive development at ages 2 and 3 (Tamis-LeMonda, Shannon, Cabrera, & Lamb, 2004).

In households where more than one language is spoken, babies achieve similar milestones in each language on the same schedule as children who hear only one language (Petitto, Katerelos, et al., 2001; Petitto & Kovelman, 2003). However, children learning two languages tend to have smaller vocabularies in each language than children learning only one language (Hoff, 2006). Bilingual children often use elements of both languages, sometimes in the same utterance—a phenomenon called **code mixing** (Petitto & Kovelman, 2003). In Montreal, children as young as 2 in dual-language households differentiate between the two languages, using French with a predominantly French-speaking father and English with a predominantly English-speaking mother (Genesee, Nicoladis, & Paradis, 1995). This ability to shift from one language to another is called **code switching.**

code mixing
Use of elements of two languages, sometimes in the same utterance, by young children in households where both languages are spoken.

code switching
Changing one's speech to match the situation, as in people who are bilingual.

Child-Directed Speech You do not have to be a parent to speak *parentese.* If, when you talk to an infant or toddler, you speak slowly in a sing-song, high-pitched voice with exaggerated ups and downs, simplify your speech, exaggerate vowel sounds, and use short words and sentences and much repetition, you are engaging in **child-directed speech (CDS),** sometimes called *parentese, motherese,* or *baby talk.* Most adults and

child-directed speech (CDS)
Form of speech often used in talking to babies or toddlers; includes slow, simplified speech, a high-pitched tone, exaggerated vowel sounds, short words and sentences, and much repetition; also called *parentese* or *motherese.*

When babies hear CDS, their heart rate slows, a physiological state that is consistent with orienting toward and absorbing information.

even children do it naturally, and other babyish stimuli, such as puppies or kittens, also can elicit it. Such baby talk has been documented in many languages and cultures, suggesting it is universal in nature and serves a function. In one observational study, mothers in the United States, Russia, and Sweden were taped speaking to their 2- to 5-month-old infants. Whether the mothers were speaking English, Russian, or Swedish, they produced more exaggerated vowel sounds when talking to the infants than when talking to other adults. At 20 weeks, the babies' babbling contained distinct vowels that reflected phonetic differences in their mothers' speech (Kuhl et al., 1997).

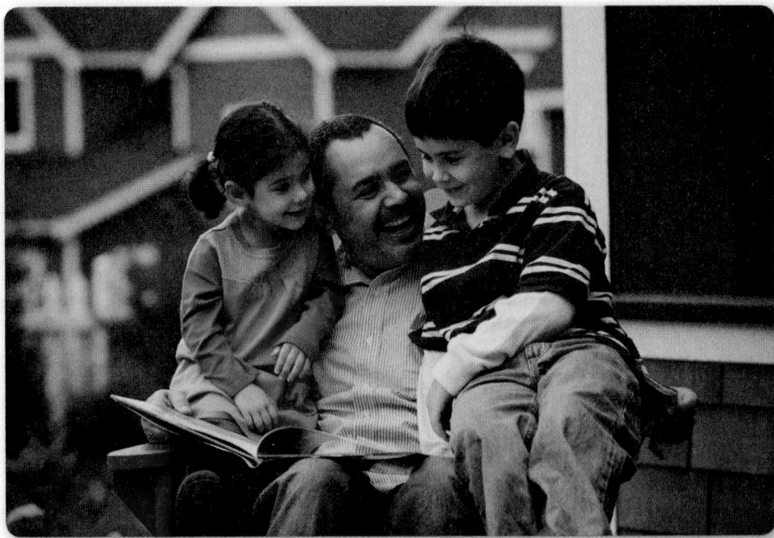

By reading aloud to their young children and asking questions about the pictures in the book, parents help their children build language skills and learn how letters look and sound.

Many researchers believe that CDS helps infants learn their native language or at least pick it up faster by exaggerating and directing attention to the distinguishing features of speech sounds (Kuhl et al., 2005). Moreover, infants are "captured" attentionally by the sound and find it highly engaging, resulting in more rapid learning (Fernauld, 1985). It is clear that infants themselves prefer to hear simplified speech. This preference is clear before 1 month and does not seem to depend on any specific experience (Cooper & Aslin, 1990; Kuhl et al., 1997; Werker, Pegg, & McLeod, 1994).

PREPARING FOR LITERACY: THE BENEFITS OF READING ALOUD

Most babies love to be read to. The frequency with which caregivers read to them can influence how well children speak and eventually how well and how soon they develop **literacy**—the ability to read and write. In a study of 2,581 low-income families, about half of the mothers reported reading daily to their preschool children between 14 months and 3 years. Children who had been read to daily had better cognitive and language skills at age 3 (Raikes et al., 2006). And their emerging language abilities have repercussions for school readiness and later academic achievement. A recent study of almost 700 twin pairs found that those children who developed language sooner were better prepared to enter school. Moreover, early language ability is affected more by home environment than genetics, suggesting that intervention programs targeting variables in the home (like encouraging parents to read to their children) might be highly effective (Forget-Dubois, Dionne, Lemelin, Perusse, Tremblay, & Boivin, 2009).

literacy
Ability to read and write.

The way parents or caregivers read to children makes a difference. Adults tend to have one of three styles of reading to children: the describer style, comprehender style, and performance-oriented style. A *describer* focuses on describing what is going on in the pictures and inviting the child to do so ("What are the Mom and Dad having for breakfast?"). A *comprehender* encourages the child to look more deeply at the meaning of a story and to make inferences and predictions ("What do you think the lion will do now?"). A *performance-oriented* reader reads the story straight through, introducing the main themes beforehand and asking questions afterward. An adult's read-aloud style is best tailored to the needs and skills of the child. In an experimental study of 50 four-year-olds in Dunedin, New Zealand, the describer style resulted in the greatest overall benefits for vocabulary and print skills, but the performance-oriented style was more beneficial for children who started out with large vocabularies (Reese & Cox, 1999).

Social interaction in reading aloud, play, and other daily activities is a key to much of childhood development. Children call forth responses from the people around them and, in turn, react to those responses.

checkpoint can you . . .

- Name areas of the brain involved in early language development, and tell the function of each?
- Explain the importance of social interaction, and give at least three examples of how parents or caregivers help babies learn to talk?
- Assess the arguments for and against the value of child-directed speech (CDS)?
- Tell why reading aloud to children at an early age is beneficial, and describe an effective way of doing so?

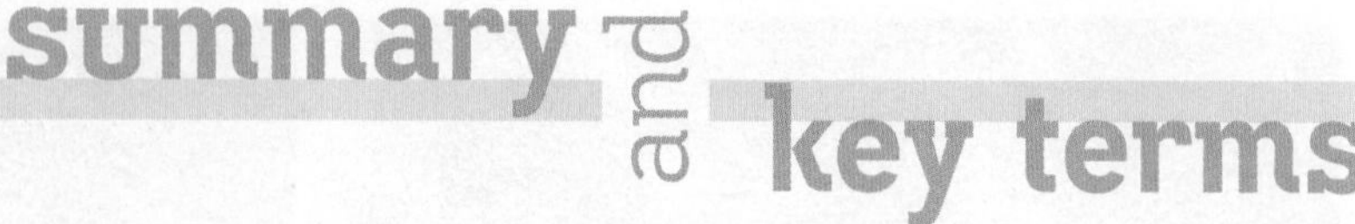

summary and key terms

Studying Cognitive Development: Six Approaches

- Six approaches to the study of cognitive development are behaviorist, psychometric, Piagetian, information-processing, cognitive neuroscience, and social-contextual.
- All of these approaches can shed light on how early cognition develops.

behaviorist approach
psychometric approach
Piagetian approach
information-processing approach
cognitive neuroscience approach
social-contextual approach

Behaviorist Approach: Basic Mechanics of Learning

- Two simple types of learning that behaviorists study are classical conditioning and operant conditioning.
- Rovee-Collier's research suggests that infants' memory processes are much like those of adults, though this conclusion has been questioned. Infants' memories can be jogged by periodic reminders.

classical conditioning
operant conditioning

Psychometric Approach: Developmental and Intelligence Testing

- Psychometric tests measure factors presumed to make up intelligence.
- Developmental tests, such as the Bayley Scales of Infant and Toddler Development, can indicate current functioning but are generally poor predictors of later intelligence.
- The home environment may affect measured intelligence.
- If the home environment does not provide the necessary conditions that pave the way for cognitive competence, early intervention may be needed.

intelligent behavior
IQ (intelligence quotient) tests
Bayley Scales of Infant and Toddler Development
Home Observation for Measurement of the Environment (HOME)
early intervention

Piagetian Approach: The Sensorimotor Stage

- During Piaget's sensorimotor stage, infants' schemes become more elaborate. They progress from primary to secondary to tertiary circular reactions and finally to the development of representational ability, which makes possible deferred imitation, pretending, and problem solving.
- Object permanence develops gradually, according to Piaget, and is not fully operational until 18 to 24 months.
- Research suggests that a number of abilities, including imitation and object permanence, develop earlier than Piaget described.

sensorimotor stage
schemes
circular reactions
representational ability
invisible imitation
visible imitation
deferred imitation
elicited imitation
object permanence
dual representation hypothesis

Information-Processing Approach: Perceptions and Representations

- Information-processing researchers measure mental processes through habituation and other signs of visual and perceptual abilities. Contrary to Piaget's ideas, such research suggests that representational ability is present virtually from birth.
- Indicators of the efficiency of infants' information processing, such as speed of habituation, tend to predict later intelligence.
- Information-processing research techniques such as habituation, novelty preference, and the violation-of-expectations method have yielded evidence that infants as young as 3 to 6 months may have a rudimentary grasp of such Piagetian abilities as categorization, causality, object permanence, a sense of number, and an ability to reason about characteristics of the physical world. Some researchers suggest that infants may have innate learning mechanisms for acquiring such knowledge. However, the meaning of these findings is in dispute.

habituation
dishabituation
visual preference
visual recognition memory
cross-modal transfer
violation-of-expectations

Cognitive Neuroscience Approach: The Brain's Cognitive Structures

- Explicit memory and implicit memory are located in different brain structures.
- Working memory emerges between 6 and 12 months of age.
- Neurological developments help explain the emergence of Piagetian skills and memory abilities.

implicit memory
explicit memory
working memory

Social-Contextual Approach: Learning from Interactions with Caregivers

- Social interactions with adults contribute to cognitive competence through shared activities that help children learn skills, knowledge, and values important in their culture.

guided participation

Language Development

- The acquisition of language is an important aspect of cognitive development.
- Prelinguistic speech includes crying, cooing, babbling, and imitating language sounds. By 6 months, babies have learned the basic sounds of their language and have begun to link sound with meaning. Perception of categories of sounds in the native language may commit the neural circuitry to further learning in that language only.
- Before they say their first word, babies use gestures.
- The first word typically comes sometime between 10 and 14 months, initiating linguistic speech. For many toddlers, a naming explosion occurs sometime between 16 and 24 months.
- The first brief sentences generally come between 18 and 24 months. By age 3, syntax and communicative abilities are fairly well developed.
- Early speech is characterized by oversimplification, underextending and overextending word meanings, and overregularizing rules.
- Two classic theoretical views about how children acquire language are learning theory and nativism. Today, most developmental scientists hold that an inborn capacity to learn language may be activated or constrained by experience.
- Influences on language development include neural maturation and social interaction.
- Family characteristics, such as socioeconomic status, adult language use, and maternal responsiveness, affect a child's vocabulary development.
- Children who hear two languages at home generally learn both at the same rate as children who hear only one language, and they can use each language in appropriate circumstances.
- Child-directed speech (CDS) seems to have cognitive, emotional, and social benefits, and infants show a preference for it. However, some researchers dispute its value.
- Reading aloud to a child from an early age helps pave the way for literacy.

language
prelinguistic speech
linguistic speech
holophrase
telegraphic speech
syntax
nativism
language acquisition device (LAD)
code mixing
code switching
child-directed speech (CDS)
literacy

chapter 6

Psychosocial Development during the First Three Years

outline

Foundations of Psychosocial Development

Developmental Issues in Infancy

Developmental Issues in Toddlerhood

Contact with Other Children

Children of Working Parents

Maltreatment: Abuse and Neglect

learning objectives

Discuss the development of emotions and personality in infancy.

Describe infants' social relationships with caregivers, including attachment.

Discuss the emerging sense of self, autonomy, and moral development in toddlerhood.

Explain how social contexts influence early development.

Explain child maltreatment and its effects.

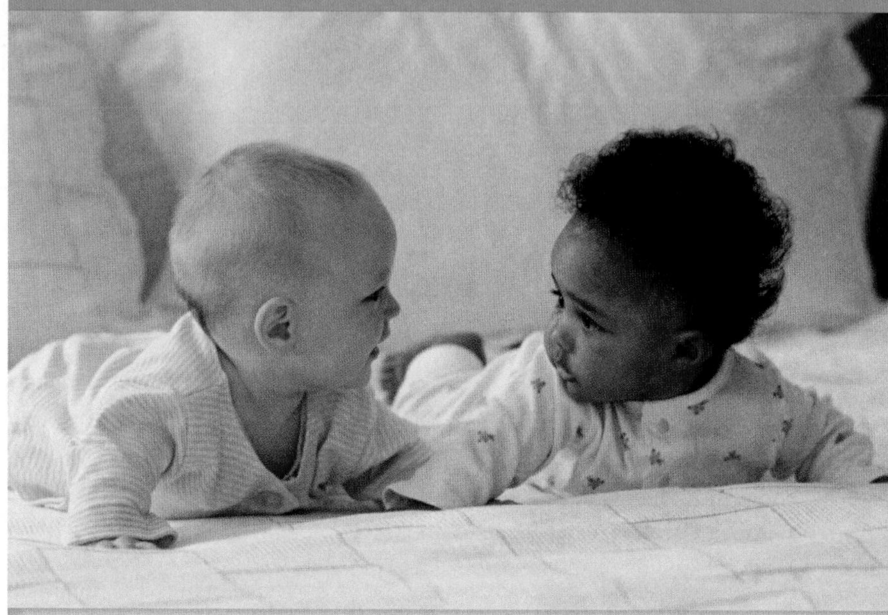

did you **know**?

- Pride, shame, and guilt are among the last emotions to develop?
- Conflict with siblings or playmates can help toddlers learn to negotiate and resolve disputes?
- The impact of parental employment and early child care is much less than that of family characteristics, such as a mother's sensitivity to her child?

In this chapter, we examine foundations of psychosocial development and consider Erikson's views about the development of trust and autonomy. We look at relationships with caregivers, the emerging sense of self, and the foundations of conscience. We explore relationships with siblings and other children and consider the impact of parental employment and early child care. Finally, we discuss child maltreatment and what can be done to protect children from harm.

Play is the highest form of research.

—Albert Einstein

Foundations of Psychosocial Development

Although babies share common patterns of development, each, from the start, shows a distinct **personality:** the relatively consistent blend of emotions, temperament, thought, and behavior that makes each person unique. One baby may usually be cheerful; another easily upset. One toddler plays happily with other children; another prefers to play alone. Such characteristic ways of feeling, thinking, and acting, which reflect both inborn and environmental influences, affect the way children respond to others and adapt to their world. From infancy on, personality development is intertwined with social relationships; this combination is called *psychosocial development.* See Table 1 for highlights of psychosocial development during the first 3 years.

personality
The relatively consistent blend of emotions, temperament, thought, and behavior that makes a person unique.

In our exploration of psychosocial development, we first look at emotions, which shape responses to the world. Then we focus on temperament, an early building block of personality. Finally, we discuss an infant's earliest social experiences in the family and how parents can influence behavioral differences between girls and boys.

EMOTIONS

Recall the last time you were scared during a horror movie. Your heart was probably racing, and you may have breathed more heavily. It's likely your eyes were fixed on

TABLE 1 Highlights of Infants' and Toddlers' Psychosocial Development, Birth to 36 Months

Approximate Age, Months	Characteristics
0–3	Infants are open to stimulation. They begin to show interest and curiosity, and they smile readily at people.
3–6	Infants can anticipate what is about to happen and experience disappointment when it does not. They show this by becoming angry or acting warily. They smile, coo, and laugh often. This is a time of social awakening and early reciprocal exchanges between the baby and the caregiver.
6–9	Infants play social games and try to get responses from people. They talk to, touch, and cajole other babies to get them to respond. They express more differentiated emotions, showing joy, fear, anger, and surprise.
9–12	Infants are intensely preoccupied with their principal caregiver, may become afraid of strangers, and act subdued in new situations. By 1 year, they communicate emotions more clearly, showing moods, ambivalence, and gradations of feeling.
12–18	Toddlers explore their environment, using the people they are most attached to as a secure base. As they master the environment, they become more confident and more eager to assert themselves.
18–36	Toddlers sometimes become anxious because they now realize how much they are separating from their caregivers. They work out their awareness of their limitations in fantasy and in play and by identifying with adults.

Source: Adapted from Sroufe, 1979.

the screen and you were focused closely on the action unfolding in front of you. If someone were to grab you suddenly, you probably would have been startled. You were feeling the emotion of fear. **Emotions** such as fear are subjective reactions to experience that are associated with physiological and behavioral changes. A person's characteristic pattern of emotional reactions begins to develop during infancy and is a basic element of personality. People differ in how often and how strongly they feel a particular emotion, in the kinds of events that may produce it, in the physical manifestations they show, and in how they act as a result. Culture, too, influences the way people feel about a situation and the way they show their emotions. Some Asian cultures, which stress social harmony, discourage expressions of anger but place much importance on shame. The opposite is often true in American culture, which stresses self-expression, self-assertion, and self-esteem (Cole, Bruschi, & Tamang, 2002).

emotions
Subjective reactions to experience that are associated with physiological and behavioral changes.

studysmart

Emotional Exploration

First Signs of Emotion Newborns plainly show when they are unhappy. They let out piercing cries, flail their arms and legs, and stiffen their bodies. It is harder to tell when they are happy. During the 1st month, they become quiet at the sound of a human voice or when they are picked up. They may smile when their hands are moved together to play pat-a-cake. As time goes by, infants respond more to people—smiling, cooing, reaching out, and eventually going to them.

These early signals or clues to babies' feelings are important indicators of development. When babies want or need something, they cry; when they feel sociable, they smile or laugh. When their messages bring a response, their sense of connection with other people grows. Their sense of control over their world grows, too, as they see that their cries bring help and comfort and that their smiles and laughter elicit smiles and laughter in return. They become more able to participate actively in regulating their states of arousal and their emotional life.

Crying Crying is the most powerful way infants can communicate their needs. There are four patterns of crying (Wolff, 1969): the basic *hunger cry* (a rhythmic cry, which is not always associated with hunger); the *angry cry* (a variation of the rhythmic cry, in which excess air is forced through the vocal cords); the *pain cry* (a sudden onset of loud crying without preliminary moaning, sometimes followed by holding the breath); and the *frustration cry* (two or three drawn-out cries, with no prolonged breath-holding) (Wood & Gustafson, 2001). As children age, they begin to realize that crying serves a communicative function. By 5 months of age, babies have learned to monitor their caregivers' expressions, and if ignored will first cry harder in an attempt to get attention, and then stop crying if their attempt is unsuccessful (Goldstein, Schwade & Bornstein, 2009).

Crying is the most powerful way, and sometimes the only way, that babies can communicate their needs. Parents may soon learn to recognize whether their baby is crying because of hunger, anger, frustration, or pain.

Some parents worry that constantly picking up a crying baby will spoil the infant. However, this is not the case, especially when levels of distress are high. For example, if parents wait until cries of distress escalate to shrieks of rage, it may become more difficult to soothe the baby; and such a pattern, if experienced repeatedly, may interfere with an infant's developing ability to regulate, or manage, his or her own emotional state (R. A. Thompson, 1991, 2011). Indeed, mothers' rapid and sensitive response to crying is associated with later social competence and positive adjustment, regardless of whether or not babies cry frequently or rarely (Leerkes, Blankson, & O'Brien, 2009). Ideally, the most developmentally sound approach may be to *prevent* distress, making soothing unnecessary.

When a healthy baby cries for more than 3 hours a day, 3 days a week, for more than 3 weeks with no apparent cause for the distress, the reason is usually colic.

Smiling and Laughing The earliest faint smiles occur spontaneously soon after birth, apparently as a result of subcortical nervous system activity. These involuntary smiles frequently appear during periods of REM sleep. Through 1 month of age, smiles are often elicited by high-pitched tones when an infant is drowsy. During the 2nd month, as visual recognition develops, babies smile more at visual stimuli, such as faces they know (Sroufe, 1997).

These early smiles are sometimes known as "windy grins" because they can occur in response to gas.

Social smiling, when newborn infants gaze at their parents and smile at them, develops during the 2nd month of life. Social smiling signals the infant's active, positive participation in the relationship. Laughter is a smile-linked vocalization that becomes more common between 4 and 12 months (Salkind, 2005).

Through 6 months of age, infant smiles reflect an emotional exchange with a partner. As babies grow older, they become more actively engaged in mirthful exchanges. A 6-month-old may giggle in response to the mother making unusual sounds or appearing with a towel over her face; a 10-month-old may laughingly try to put the towel back on her face when it falls off. This change reflects cognitive development: by laughing at the unexpected, babies show that they know what to expect; by turning the tables, they show awareness that they can make things happen (Sroufe, 1997).

By 12 to 15 months, infants are intentionally communicating to the partner about objects. **Anticipatory smiling**—in which infants smile at an object and then gaze at an adult while continuing to smile—may be the first step. Anticipatory smiling rises sharply between 8 and 10 months and seems to be among the first types of communication in which the infant refers to an object or experience.

When Do Emotions Appear? Emotional development is an orderly process; complex emotions unfold from simpler ones. According to one model (Lewis, 1997; Figure 1),

study smart

Social Smile

social smiling
Beginning in the 2nd month, newborn infants gaze at their parents and smile at them, signaling positive participation in the relationship.

anticipatory smiling
Infant smiles at an object and then gazes at an adult while still smiling.

checkpoint can you . . .

- Explain the significance of patterns of crying, smiling, and laughing?

Embarrassment
Envy
Empathy

From 15 to 24 months

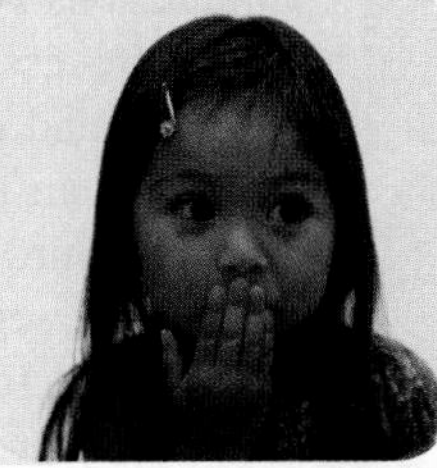

Embarrassment
Pride
Shame
Guilt

From 2 1/2 to 3 years

Source: Adapted from Lewis, 1997.

FIGURE 1
Differentiation of Emotions during the First 3 Years

The primary, or basic, emotions emerge during the first 6 months or so; the self-conscious emotions develop beginning in the 2nd year, as a result of the emergence of self-awareness together with accumulation of knowledge about societal standards. Note: There are two kinds of embarrassment. The earlier kind does not involve evaluation of behavior and may simply be a response to being singled out as the object of attention. Evaluative embarrassment, which emerges during the 3rd year, is a mild form of shame.

babies show signs of contentment, interest, and distress soon after birth. These are diffuse, reflexive, mostly physiological responses to sensory stimulation or internal processes. During the next 6 months or so, these early emotional states differentiate into true emotions: joy, surprise, sadness, disgust, and then anger and fear—reactions to events that have meaning for the infant. As we discuss in a subsequent section, the emergence of these basic, or primary, emotions is related to neurological maturation.

Self-awareness and an understanding that others can think things that you know are not true is also related to another developmental milestone: lying. Although we do not generally think of it as such, lying is actually a profound developmental achievement.

self-conscious emotions
Emotions, such as embarrassment, empathy, and envy, that depend on self-awareness.

self-awareness
Realization that one's existence and functioning are separate from those of other people and things.

self-evaluative emotions
Emotions, such as pride, shame, and guilt, that depend on both self-awareness and knowledge of socially accepted standards of behavior.

Self-conscious emotions, such as embarrassment, empathy, and envy, arise only after children have developed **self-awareness:** the cognitive understanding that they have a recognizable identity, separate and different from the rest of their world. This consciousness of self seems to emerge between 15 and 24 months. Self-awareness is necessary before children can be aware of being the focus of attention, identify with what other "selves" are feeling, or wish they had what someone else has.

By about age 3, having acquired self-awareness plus a good deal of knowledge about their society's accepted standards, rules, and goals, children become better able to evaluate their own thoughts, plans, desires, and behavior against what is considered socially appropriate. Only then can they demonstrate the **self-evaluative emotions** of pride, guilt, and shame (Lewis, 1995, 1997, 1998, 2007).

Brain Growth and Emotional Development The development of the brain after birth is closely connected with changes in emotional life: emotional experiences are affected by brain development and can have long-lasting effects on the structure of the brain (Mlot, 1998; Sroufe, 1997).

Four major shifts in brain organization roughly correspond to changes in emotional processing (Schore, 1994; Sroufe, 1997). During the first 3 months, differentiation of basic emotions begins as the *cerebral cortex* becomes functional, bringing cognitive perceptions into play. REM sleep and reflexive behavior, including the spontaneous neonatal smile, diminish.

The second shift occurs around 9 or 10 months, when the *frontal lobes* begin to interact with the *limbic system,* a seat of emotional reactions. At the same time, limbic structures such as the *hippocampus* become larger and more adultlike. Connections between the frontal cortex and the *hypothalamus* and limbic system, which process sensory information, may facilitate the relationship between the cognitive and emotional spheres. As these connections become denser and more elaborate, an infant can experience and interpret emotions at the same time.

The third shift takes place during the 2nd year, when infants develop self-awareness, self-conscious emotions, and a greater capacity for regulating their emotions and activities. These changes, which coincide with greater physical mobility and exploratory behavior, may be related to myelination of the frontal lobes.

The fourth shift occurs around age 3, when hormonal changes in the autonomic (involuntary) nervous system coincide with the emergence of evaluative emotions. Underlying the development of such emotions as shame may be a shift away from dominance by the *sympathetic system,* the part of the autonomic system that prepares the body for action, as the *parasympathetic system,* the part of the autonomic system that is involved in excretion and sexual excitation, matures.

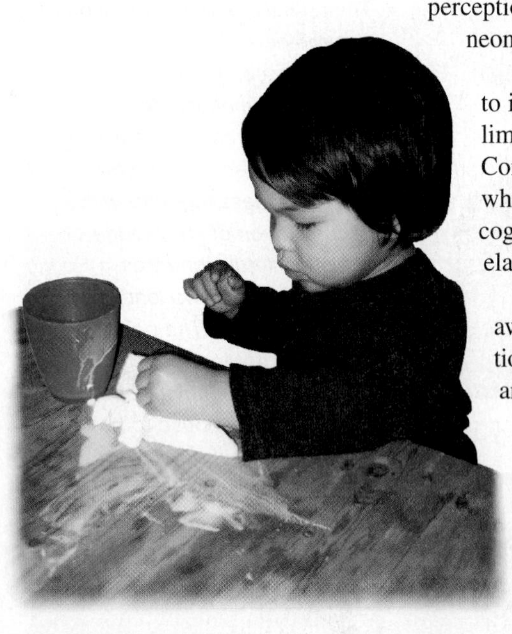
Children who do not live up to behavioral standards may feel guilty and try to make amends by cleaning up after they've spilled. Guilt is thought to develop between ages 2½ and 3.

Altruistic Helping, Empathy, and Social Cognition A guest of 18-month-old Alex's father—a person Alex had never seen before—dropped his pen on the floor, and it rolled under a cabinet, where the guest couldn't quite reach it. Alex, being small enough, crawled under the cabinet, retrieved the pen, and gave it to the guest. By acting out of concern for a stranger with no expectation of reward, Alex showed **altruistic behavior** (Warneken & Tomasello, 2006).

altruistic behavior
Activity intended to help another person with no expectation of reward.

Altruistic behavior seems to come naturally to toddlers. Well before the 2nd birthday, children often help others, share belongings and food, and offer comfort (Warneken & Tomasello, 2008; Zahn-Waxler, Radke-Yarrow, Wagner, & Chapman, 1992). However, the environment also influences how much altruism babies engage in. In one study, 18-month-old toddlers who were shown a picture of two dolls facing each other were more likely to spontaneously help an adult than toddlers of the same age who were shown a picture of two dolls facing away from each other. Presumably, seeing two dolls facing each other triggered their natural inclination to help (Over & Carpenter, 2009).

In another experiment, when the researcher was having trouble reaching a goal, 18-month-olds helped in 6 out of 10 situations. They did not help when the researcher did not appear to be having trouble, for example, when he deliberately dropped a pen. Zahn-Waxler and colleagues (1992) concluded that such behavior may reflect **empathy,** the ability to imagine how another person might feel in a particular situation. The roots of empathy can be seen in early infancy. Two- to 3-month-olds react to others' emotional expressions (Tomasello, 2007). Six-month-olds engage in *social evaluation,* valuing someone on the basis of that person's treatment of others (Hamlin, Wynn, & Bloom, 2007).

empathy
Ability to put oneself in another person's place and feel what the other person feels.

Research in neurobiology has recently identified special brain cells called *mirror neurons,* which may underlie empathy and altruism. **Mirror neurons,** located in several parts of the brain, fire when a person does something but also when he or she observes someone else doing the same thing. By "mirroring" the activities and motivations of others, they allow a person to see the world from someone else's point of view (Iacoboni, 2008; Iacoboni & Mazziotta, 2007; Oberman & Ramachandran, 2007).

> *Young children often engage in what is known as overimitation, closely copying all actions they see an adult do, even if some of those actions are clearly irrelevant or impractical. Chimps, by contrast, will skip steps that don't accomplish anything. Researchers think our universal propensity to overimitate may be tied to the depth and complexity of our culture.*
>
> Nielsen & Tomaselli, 2010

mirror neurons
Neurons that fire when a person does something or observes someone else doing the same thing.

Empathy also depends on **social cognition,** the ways in which we process information about other people. Part of social cognition involves the ability to understand that others have mental states and to gauge their feelings and intentions. Research suggests that social cognition begins in the 1st year of life. In one study, 9-month-olds (but not 6-month-olds) reacted differently to a person who was unwilling to give them a toy than to a person who tried to give them a toy but accidentally dropped it. This finding suggests that the older infants had gained some understanding of another person's intentions (Behne, Carpenter, Call, & Tomasello, 2005).

social cognition
The ability to understand that others have mental states and to gauge their feelings and actions.

checkpoint can you . . .

- **Trace a typical sequence of emergence of the basic, self-conscious, and evaluative emotions, and explain its connection with cognitive and neurological development?**

TEMPERAMENT

From the very first day of life, all babies are unique. Some babies are fussy; others are happy and placid. Some are active, kicking and squirming restlessly at the slightest provocation; some lay calmly. Some babies like meeting new people; some shrink from contact.

Psychologists call these early individual differences **temperament.** Temperament can be defined as an early-appearing, biologically based tendency to respond to the environment in predictable ways. Temperament affects how children approach and react to the outside world, as well as how they regulate their mental, emotional, and behavioral functioning (Rothbart, Ahadi, & Evans, 2000; Rueda & Rothbart, 2009). Temperament is closely linked to emotional responses to the environment, and many responses, such as smiles or cries, are emotional in nature. However, unlike emotions such as fear, excitement, and boredom, which come and go, temperament is relatively consistent and

temperament
Characteristic disposition or style of approaching and reacting to situations.

enduring. Individual differences in temperament, which are thought to derive from a person's basic biological makeup, form the core of the developing personality.

Studying Temperamental Patterns: The New York Longitudinal Study To better appreciate how temperament affects behavior, let's look at three sisters. Amy, the eldest, was a cheerful, calm baby who ate, slept, and eliminated at regular times. She greeted each day and most people with a smile, and the only sign that she was awake during the night was the tinkle of the musical toy in her crib. When Brooke, the middle sister, woke up, she would open her mouth to cry before she even opened her eyes. She slept and ate little and irregularly; she laughed and cried loudly, often bursting into tantrums; and she had to be convinced that new people and new experiences were not threatening before she would have anything to do with them. The youngest sister, Christina, was midway in her responses. She was wary of new situations but would eventually warm up. For example, if she went on a playdate to a new friend's house, she would at first hide behind her mother's legs, shyly peeking out. However, within half an hour, she would be happily chattering away and playing with her new friend.

study**smart**

Temperament

Amy, Brooke, and Christina exemplify the three main types of temperament found by the New York Longitudinal Study (NYLS). In this pioneering study on temperament, researchers followed 133 infants into adulthood. The researchers looked at how active the children were; how regular their hunger, sleep, and bowel habits were; how readily they accepted new people and situations; how they adapted to changes in routine; how sensitive they were to sensory stimuli; whether their mood tended to be joyful or unhappy; and whether they persisted at tasks (A. Thomas, Chess, & Birch, 1968).

The researchers were able to place most of the children in the study into one of three categories (Table 2).

- Forty percent were **"easy" children** like Amy: generally happy, rhythmic in biological functioning, and accepting of new experiences.
- Ten percent were what the researchers called **"difficult" children** like Brooke: more irritable and harder to please, irregular in biological rhythms, and more intense in expressing emotion.
- Fifteen percent were **"slow-to-warm-up" children** like Christina: mild but slow to adapt to new people and situations (A. Thomas & Chess, 1977, 1984).

"easy" children
Children with a generally happy temperament, regular biological rhythms, and a readiness to accept new experiences.

"difficult" children
Children with irritable temperament, irregular biological rhythms, and intense emotional responses.

"slow-to-warm-up" children
Children whose temperament is generally mild but who are hesitant about accepting new experiences.

TABLE 2 Three Temperamental Patterns (according to the New York Longitudinal Study)

"Easy" Child	"Difficult" Child	"Slow-to-Warm-Up" Child
Has moods of mild to moderate intensity, usually positive.	Displays intense and frequently negative moods; cries often and loudly; also laughs loudly.	Has mildly intense reactions, both positive and negative.
Responds well to novelty and change.	Responds poorly to novelty and change.	Responds slowly to novelty and change.
Quickly develops regular sleep and feeding schedules.	Sleeps and eats irregularly.	Sleeps and eats more regularly than the difficult child, less regularly than the easy child.
Takes to new foods easily. Smiles at strangers. Adapts easily to new situations. Accepts most frustrations with little fuss.	Accepts new foods slowly. Is suspicious of strangers. Adapts slowly to new situations. Reacts to frustration with tantrums.	Shows mildly negative initial response to new stimuli (a first encounter with a new food, person, place, or situation).
Adapts quickly to new routines and rules of new games.	Adjusts slowly to new routines.	Gradually develops liking for new stimuli after repeated, unpressured exposures.

Source: Adapted from Thomas, A., and S. Chess, "Genesis and evolution of behavioral disorders: From infancy to early adult life." Reprinted with permission from the *American Journal of Psychiatry*, 141, © 1984, pp. 1–9. Copyright © 1984 by the American Psychiatric Association. Reproduced with permission.

Some children (including 35 percent of the NYLS sample) do not fit neatly into any of these three categories. A baby may eat and sleep regularly but be afraid of strangers. Another child may warm up slowly to new foods but adapt quickly to new babysitters (A. Thomas & Chess, 1984). A child may laugh intensely but not show intense frustration, and a child with rhythmic toilet habits may show irregular sleeping patterns (Rothbart et al., 2000). All these variations are normal.

The way you ask a question often influences the answers you find. The researchers in this study based their data on parental reports—what the parents said about their children—so it is not surprising that the most salient dimensions that emerged were the relative difficulty or easiness of the children.

How Stable Is Temperament? Newborn babies show different patterns of sleeping, fussing, and activity, and these differences tend to persist to some degree (Korner, 1996). Studies using the Infant Behavior Questionnaire (IBQ), a parental report instrument, have found strong links between infant temperament and childhood personality at age 7 (Rothbart, Ahadi, Hershey, & Fisher, 2001). Other researchers, using temperament types similar to those of the NYLS, have found that temperament at age 3 closely predicts aspects of personality at ages 18 and 21 (Caspi, 2000; Newman, Caspi, Moffitt, & Silva, 1997).

That temperament is relatively stable speaks to the underlying biological influences on temperament. Temperament appears to be largely inborn, probably hereditary (Braungart, Plomin, DeFries, & Fulker, 1992; Emde et al., 1992; Schmitz et al., Saudino, Plomin, Fulker, & DeFries, 1996; Thomas & Chess, 1984), so it is not surprising that we find stability in temperament over time. That does not mean, however, that temperament is fully formed at birth. Temperament develops as various emotions and self-regulatory capacities appear (Rothbart et al., 2000) and can change in response to parental treatment and other life experiences (Belsky, Fish, & Isabella, 1991; Kagan & Snidman, 2004).

For example, temperament is affected by culturally influenced child-raising practices. Infants in Malaysia tend to be less adaptable, more wary of new experiences, and more readily responsive to stimuli than U.S. babies. This may be because Malay parents do not often expose young children to situations that require adaptability, and they encourage infants to be acutely aware of sensations, such as the need for a diaper change (Banks, 1989).

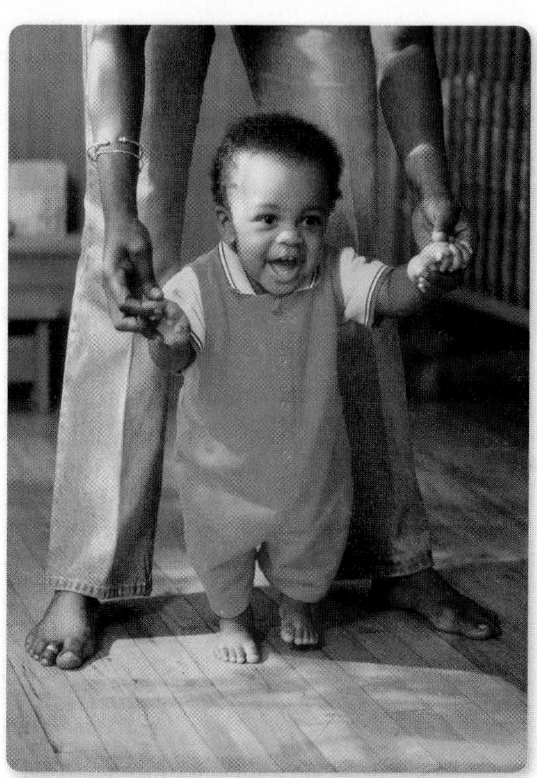

Tyrell's ready smile and excitement about new experiences, such as walking, are signs of an easy temperament.

Temperament and Adjustment: Goodness of Fit According to the NYLS, the key to healthy adjustment is **goodness of fit**—the match between a child's temperament and the environmental demands and constraints the child must deal with. If a very active child is expected to sit still for long periods, if a slow-to-warm-up child is constantly pushed into new situations, or if a persistent child is constantly taken away from absorbing projects, tensions may occur. Infants with difficult temperaments may be more susceptible to the quality of parenting than infants with easy or slow-to-warm-up temperaments and may need more emotional support (Belsky, 1997, 2005; Stright, Gallagher, & Kelley, 2008). Caregivers who recognize that a child acts in a certain way, not out of willfulness, laziness, or spite but because of inborn temperament, may be less likely to feel guilty, anxious, or hostile. They can anticipate the child's reactions and help the child adapt—for example, by giving early warnings of the need to stop an activity or by gradually introducing a child to new situations.

goodness of fit
Appropriateness of environmental demands and constraints to a child's temperament.

There is a relationship between what a parent says a baby will be like before a child is born and what a parent later says about that child as an infant. In particular, the perceptions of a child as difficult precede the birth of that child. What might explain this finding?

Pauli-Pott, Mertesacker, Bade, Haverkock, & Beckman, 2003

Shyness and Boldness: Influences of Biology and Culture As we have explained, temperament has a biological basis. One biologically based individual difference that has been identified is *behavioral inhibition.* Behavioral inhibition has to do with how boldly or cautiously a child approaches unfamiliar objects and situations, and it is associated with certain biological characteristics (Kagan & Snidman, 2004).

Behavioral inhibition is most clearly seen when babies are presented with novel stimuli. When babies high in behavioral inhibition were presented with a new stimulus, they became overly aroused, pumping their arms and legs vigorously and sometimes arching their backs. This feeling of being overaroused eventually became unpleasant for them, and most cried. Approximately 20 percent of babies respond in this way. Babies low in behavioral inhibition, however, respond quite differently. When presented with a new stimulus, these babies are relaxed. They show little distress or motor activity, and often calmly stare at new stimuli, sometimes smiling at it. About 40 percent of babies respond in this manner. These differences between babies are theorized to be the result of an underlying difference in physiology. The researchers suggested that inhibited children may be born with an unusually excitable amygdala. The amygdala detects and reacts to unfamiliar events, and, in the case of behaviorally inhibited children, responds vigorously and easily to most novel events (Kagan & Snidman, 2004).

Infants who were identified as inhibited or uninhibited seemed to maintain these patterns to some degree during childhood (Kagan, 1997; Kagan & Snidman, 2004), along with specific differences in physiological characteristics. Inhibited children were more likely to have a thin body build, narrow face, and blue eyes, whereas uninhibited children were taller, heavier, and more often brown-eyed. In addition, inhibited children showed higher and less variable heart rates than uninhibited children, and the pupils of their eyes dilated more (Arcus & Kagan, 1995). It may be that the genes that contribute to reactivity and inhibited or uninhibited behavior also influence these physiological traits (Kagan & Snidman, 2004).

checkpoint
can **you** . . .

- Describe the three patterns of temperament identified by the New York Longitudinal Study?
- Assess evidence for the stability of temperament?
- Explain the importance of goodness of fit?
- Discuss evidence of biological influences on shyness and boldness?

However, experience can moderate or accentuate early tendencies. Male toddlers who were inclined to be fearful and shy were more likely to outgrow their inhibition if parents did not completely shield them from new situations and instead supported them during anxiety-provoking situations (Park, Belsky, Putnam, & Crnic, 1997). In other research, when mothers responded neutrally to infants who were behaviorally inhibited, the inhibition tended to remain stable or increase (Fox, Hane, & Pine, 2007). Other environmental influences, such as birth order, race/ethnicity, culture, relationships with teachers and peers, and unpredictable events also can reinforce or soften a child's original temperament bias (Kagan & Snidman, 2004).

EARLIEST SOCIAL EXPERIENCES: THE INFANT IN THE FAMILY

Infant care practices and patterns of interaction vary greatly around the world. In Bali, infants are believed to be ancestors reborn or gods brought to life in human form and thus must be treated with utmost dignity and respect. The Beng of West Africa think young babies can understand all languages, whereas people in the Micronesian atoll of Ifaluk believe babies cannot understand language at all, and therefore adults do not speak to them (DeLoache & Gottlieb, 2000).

In some societies, infants have multiple caregivers. Among the Efe people of central Africa, infants typically receive care from five or more people in a given hour and are routinely breast-fed by other women and the mother (Tronick, Morelli, & Ivey, 1992). Among the Gusii in western Kenya, where infant mortality is high, parents keep their infants close to them, respond quickly when they cry, and feed them on demand (LeVine, 1994). The same is true of Aka hunter-gatherers in central Africa, who move around frequently in small, tightly knit groups marked by extensive sharing, cooperation, and concern about danger. However, Ngandu farmers in the same region, who tend to live farther apart and to stay in one place for long periods of time, are more likely to leave their infants alone and to let them fuss or cry, smile, vocalize, or play (Hewlett, Lamb, Shannon, Leyendecker, & Schölmerich, 1998).

As we discuss patterns of adult-infant interaction, we need to keep in mind that many of these patterns are culture-based. Moreover, it is important to recognize the wide diversity in family systems, even within the United States, where the number of nontraditional families, such as those headed by single parents and gay and lesbian couples, has increased in recent years. With that caution in mind, let's look first at the roles of the mother and father—how they care for and play with their babies, and how their influence begins to shape personality differences between boys and girls. Later in this chapter, we look more deeply at relationships with parents and then at interactions with siblings.

When infant monkeys could choose whether to go to a wire "mother" or a warm, soft, terry-cloth "mother," they spent more time clinging to the cloth mother, even if their food came from the wire mother.

The Mother's Role In a series of pioneering experiments by Harry Harlow and his colleagues, rhesus monkeys were separated from their mothers 6 to 12 hours after birth. The infant monkeys were put into cages with one of two kinds of surrogate "mothers": a plain cylindrical wire-mesh form or a form covered with terry cloth. Some monkeys were fed from bottles connected to the wire mothers; others were fed by the warm, cuddly cloth mothers. When the monkeys were allowed to spend time with either kind of mother, they all spent more time clinging to the cloth surrogates, even if they were being fed only by the wire surrogates. In an unfamiliar room, the babies "raised" by cloth surrogates showed more natural interest in exploring than those "raised" by wire surrogates.

Apparently, the monkeys also remembered the cloth surrogates better. After a year's separation, the "cloth-raised" monkeys eagerly ran to embrace the terry-cloth forms, whereas the "wire-raised" monkeys showed no interest in the wire forms (Harlow & Zimmerman, 1959). None of the monkeys in either group grew up normally, however (Harlow & Harlow, 1962), and none were able to nurture their own offspring (Suomi & Harlow, 1972).

It is hardly surprising that a dummy mother would not provide the same kinds of stimulation and opportunities for positive development as a live mother. These experiments show that feeding is not the only, or even the most important, thing babies get from their mothers. Mothering includes the comfort of close bodily contact and, at least in monkeys, the satisfaction of an innate need to cling.

Human infants also have needs that must be satisfied if they are to grow up normally. One of these needs is for a mother who responds warmly and promptly to the infant. Later in this chapter we discuss how responsiveness contributes to the mutual attachment between infants and mothers that develops during infancy, with far-reaching effects on psychosocial and cognitive development.

The Father's Role The fathering role is in many ways a social construction (Doherty, Kouneski, & Erickson, 1998), having different meanings in different cultures. The role may be taken or shared by someone other than the biological father: the mother's brother, as in Botswana; or a grandfather, as in Vietnam (Engle & Breaux, 1998; Richardson, 1995; Townsend, 1997). In some societies fathers are more involved in their young children's lives—economically, emotionally, and in time spent—than in others. In many parts of the world, what it means to be a father has changed dramatically and continues to change (Engle & Breaux, 1998).

There are suggestions that involved fathers show decreasing testosterone and increasing estradiol over the course of their partner's pregnancy, theorized to be in the service of preparing new dads for parenting and nurturant behaviors.

Berg & Wynne-Edwards, 2001

Among the Huhot of Inner Mongolia, fathers traditionally are responsible for economic support and discipline and mothers for nurturing (Jankowiak, 1992). Men almost never hold infants. Fathers interact more with toddlers but

As more mothers work outside the home, fathers in the United States are taking on more child care responsibilities and in some cases are the primary caregivers.

perform child care duties only if the mother is absent. However, urbanization and maternal employment are changing these attitudes. Fathers—especially college-educated fathers—now seek more intimate relationships with children, especially sons (Engle & Breaux, 1998).

Among the Aka of central Africa, in contrast with the Huhot, "fathers provide more direct infant care than fathers in any other known society" (Hewlett, 1992, p. 169). In Aka families, husbands and wives frequently cooperate in subsistence tasks and other activities (Hewlett, 1992). Thus the father's involvement in child care is part and parcel of his overall role in the family.

In the United States, fathers' involvement in caregiving has greatly increased as more mothers have begun to work outside the home and as concepts of fathering have changed (Cabrera et al., 2000; Casper, 1997; Pleck, 1997). A father's frequent and positive involvement with his child, from infancy on, is directly related to the child's well-being and physical, cognitive, and social development (Cabrera et al., 2000; Kelley, Smith, Green, Berndt, & Rogers, 1998; Shannon, Tamis-LeMonda, London, & Cabrera, 2002).

GENDER: HOW DIFFERENT ARE BABY BOYS AND GIRLS?

Identifying as male or female affects how people look, how they move their bodies, and how they work, dress, and play. It influences what they think about themselves and what others think of them. All these characteristics—and more—are included in the word **gender:** what it means to be male or female.

gender
Significance of being male or female.

Gender Differences in Infants and Toddlers Measurable differences between baby boys and baby girls are few, at least in U.S. samples. Boys are a bit longer and heavier and may be slightly stronger but are physically more vulnerable from conception on. Beginning prenatally boys are more active than girls. Girls are less reactive to stress and more likely to survive infancy (Davis & Emory, 1995; Keenan & Shaw, 1997). Boys' brains at birth are about 10 percent larger than girls' brains, a difference that continues into adulthood (Gilmore et al., 2007). On the other hand, the two sexes are equally sensitive to touch and tend to teethe, sit up, and walk at about the same ages (Maccoby, 1980). They also achieve other motor milestones of infancy at about the same times.

One of the earliest *behavioral* differences between boys and girls, appearing between ages 1 and 2, is in preferences for toys and play activities and for playmates of the same sex (Campbell, Shirley, Heywood, & Crook, 2000; Serbin, Poulin-Dubois, Colburne, Sen, & Eichstedt, 2001). Boys as young as 17 months tend to play more aggressively than girls (Baillargeon et al., 2007). Between ages 2 and 3, boys and girls tend to say more words pertaining to their own sex (such as "tractor" versus "necklace") than to the other sex (Stennes, Burch, Sen, & Bauer, 2005).

Psychologists have found evidence that infants begin to perceive differences between males and females long before their behavior is gender-differentiated and even before they can talk. Habituation studies have found that 6-month-olds respond differently to male and female voices. By 9 to 12 months, infants can tell the difference between male and female faces, apparently on the basis of hair and clothing. At approximately 19 months, children start to use gender labels such as "mommies" and "daddies" to describe people in their social world, and those children who begin to use such labels earlier generally show earlier gender-typed play as well (Zosuls et al., 2009). During the 2nd year, infants begin to associate gender-typical toys such as dolls with a face of the correct gender (Martin, Ruble, & Szkrybalo, 2002).

How Parents Shape Gender Differences Parents in the United States tend to *think* baby boys and girls are more different than they actually are. For example, despite identical performance, mothers of 11-month-old infants expect sons to crawl more effectively than daughters (Mondschein et al., 2000).

gender-typing
Socialization process by which children, at an early age, learn appropriate gender roles.

U.S. parents begin to influence boys' and girls' personalities very early. Fathers, especially, promote **gender-typing,** the process by which children learn behavior that their culture considers appropriate for each sex (Bronstein, 1988). Fathers treat boys and girls more differently than mothers do, even during the 1st year (M. E. Snow, Jacklin, & Maccoby, 1983). During the 2nd year, fathers talk more and spend more time with sons than with daughters (Lamb, 1981). Mothers talk more, and more supportively, to daughters than to sons (Leaper, Anderson, & Sanders, 1998), and girls at this age tend to be more talkative than boys (Leaper & Smith, 2004). Fathers of toddlers play more roughly with sons and show more sensitivity to daughters (Kelley et al., 1998).

However, a highly physical style of play, characteristic of many fathers in the United States, is not typical of fathers in all cultures. Swedish and German fathers usually do not play with their babies this way (Lamb, Frodi, Frodi, & Hwang, 1982; Parke, Grossman, & Tinsley, 1981). African Aka fathers (Hewlett, 1987) and those in New Delhi, India, also tend to play gently with small children (Roopnarine, Hooper, Ahmeduzzaman, & Pollack, 1993; Roopnarine, Talokder, Jain, Josh, & Srivastav, 1992).

checkpoint can **you**...

- Give examples of cultural differences in infant care?
- Compare the roles of fathers and mothers in meeting infants' needs?
- Discuss gender differences in infants and toddlers and how parents influence gender-typing?

Developmental Issues in Infancy

How does a dependent newborn, with a limited emotional repertoire and pressing physical needs, become a child with complex feelings and the abilities to understand and control them? Much of this development revolves around relationships with caregivers.

Research showed that mothers who took their babies to baby sign-language classes were more stressed than mothers who did not. Given that length of time spent in classes was not related to increased stress, the researchers concluded that the classes did not cause stress. What is an alternative explanation for the finding?

Howlett, Kirk, & Pine, 2010

DEVELOPING TRUST

Human babies are dependent on others for food, protection, and nurturance for a far longer period than the young of most mammals. According to Erikson, this extended period results in the first stage of psychosocial development being centered on forming a sense of trust.

Erikson (1950) argued that at each stage in the life span, we are faced with a challenge and a complementary risk. As babies, our first challenge involves forming a **basic sense of trust versus mistrust.** If we are successful, we develop a sense of the reliability of people and objects in our world. We feel safe and loved. The risk, however, is that, instead, we develop a sense of mistrust and feel that those around us cannot be counted on in times of need.

basic sense of trust versus mistrust Erikson's first stage in psychosocial development, in which infants develop a sense of the reliability of people and objects.

The stage begins in infancy and continues until about 18 months. Ideally, babies develop a balance between trust (which lets them form intimate relationships) and mistrust (which enables them to protect themselves). If trust predominates, as it should, children develop hope and the belief that they can fulfill their needs and obtain their desires (Erikson, 1982). If mistrust predominates, children view the world as unfriendly and unpredictable and have trouble forming quality relationships.

study smart

Trust and Autonomy

The critical element in developing trust is sensitive, responsive, consistent caregiving. Erikson saw the feeding situation as the setting for establishing the right mix of trust and mistrust. Can the baby count on being fed when hungry, and can the baby therefore trust the mother as a representative of the world? Trust enables an infant to let the mother out of sight "because she has become an inner certainty as well as an outer predictability" (Erikson, 1950, p. 247).

checkpoint can **you**...

- Explain the importance of basic trust and identify the critical element in its development?

DEVELOPING ATTACHMENTS

When Ahmed's mother is near, he looks at her, smiles at her, babbles to her, and crawls after her. When she leaves, he cries; when she comes back, he squeals with joy. When he is frightened or unhappy, he clings to her. Ahmed has formed his first attachment to another person.

study smart

Emotions and Attachment

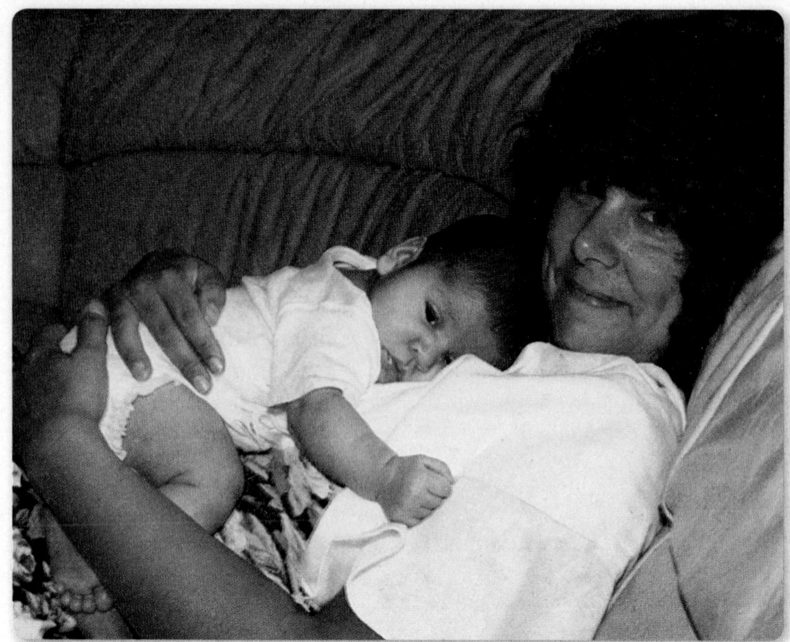

Both Anna and Diane contribute to the attachment between them by the way they act toward each other. The way the baby molds herself to her mother's body shows her trust and reinforces Diane's feelings for her child, which she displays through sensitivity to Anna's needs.

Attachment is a reciprocal, enduring emotional tie between an infant and a caregiver, each of whom contributes to the quality of the relationship. From an evolutionary point of view, attachments have adaptive value for babies, ensuring that their psychosocial as well as physical needs will be met (MacDonald, 1998). According to ethological theory, infants and parents are biologically predisposed to become attached to each other, and attachment promotes a baby's survival.

Studying Patterns of Attachment The study of attachment owes much to the ethologist John Bowlby (1951), a pioneer in the study of bonding in animals. From his knowledge of Harlow's seminal work with rhesus monkeys demonstrating the importance of contact comfort rather than food and from observations of disturbed children in a London psychoanalytic clinic, Bowlby became convinced of the importance of the mother-baby bond and warned against separating mother and baby without providing good substitute care. Mary Ainsworth, a student of Bowlby's in the early 1950s, went on to study attachment in African babies in Uganda through naturalistic observation in their homes (Ainsworth, 1967). Ainsworth later devised the **Strange Situation,** a now-classic, laboratory-based technique designed to assess attachment patterns between an infant and an adult. Typically, the adult is the mother (though other adults have taken part as well), and the infant is 10 to 24 months old.

attachment
Reciprocal, enduring tie between two people—especially between infant and caregiver—each of whom contributes to the quality of the relationship.

Strange Situation
Laboratory technique used to study infant attachment.

The Strange Situation consists of a sequence of episodes and takes less than half an hour. The episodes are designed to trigger the emergence of attachment-related behaviors. During that time, the mother twice leaves the baby in an unfamiliar room, the first time with a stranger. The second time she leaves the baby alone, and the stranger comes back before the mother does. The mother then encourages the baby to explore and play again and gives comfort if the baby seems to need it (Ainsworth, Blehar, Waters, & Wall, 1978). Of particular concern is the baby's response each time the mother returns.

When Ainsworth and her colleagues observed 1-year-olds in the Strange Situation and at home, they found three main patterns of attachment. These are *secure attachment* (the most common category, into which about 60 to 75 percent of low-risk North American babies fall) and two forms of anxious, or insecure, attachment: *avoidant* (15 to 25 percent) and *ambivalent,* or *resistant* (10 to 15 percent) (Vondra & Barnett, 1999).

secure attachment
Pattern in which an infant cries or protests when the primary caregiver leaves and actively seeks out the caregiver on his or her return.

avoidant attachment
Pattern in which an infant rarely cries when separated from the primary caregiver and avoids contact on his or her return.

ambivalent (resistant) attachment
Pattern in which an infant becomes anxious before the primary caregiver leaves, is extremely upset during his or her absence, and both seeks and resists contact on his or her return.

Babies with **secure attachment** are flexible and resilient in the face of stress. They sometimes cry when a caregiver leaves, but they quickly obtain the comfort they need once the caregiver returns. Some babies with secure attachment are comfortable being left with a stranger for a short period of time; however, they clearly indicate they prefer the caregiver to the stranger in the reunion episode, often smiling at, greeting, or approaching the caregiver. Babies with **avoidant attachment,** by contrast, are outwardly unaffected by a caregiver leaving or returning. They generally continue to play in the room, and frequently interact with the stranger. However, upon the caregiver's return, they ignore or reject the caregiver, sometimes deliberately turning away. Avoidantly attached babies tend to show little emotion, either positive or negative. Babies who exhibit **ambivalent (resistant) attachment** are generally anxious even before the caregiver leaves, sometimes approaching the caregiver for comfort when the stranger looks at or approaches them for interaction. They are extremely reactive to the caregiver's departure from the room and generally become very upset. Upon the caregiver's return, these babies tend to remain upset for long periods of time, kicking, screaming, refusing to be distracted with toys, and sometimes arching back and away from contact. They show a mix of proximity-seeking and angry behaviors and are very difficult to settle.

A baby's attachment style is best determined by how a mother soothes an upset child rather than by how that child acts when she is not around.

Note that in all of these cases what the baby does during the caregiver's absence is not diagnostic of attachment categorization. What is diagnostic is what the babies do when the caregiver *returns.* The important component is the attachment relationship and how the babies use a caregiver to obtain comfort *while* in his or her presence.

These three attachment *patterns* are universal in all cultures in which they have been studied—cultures as different as those in Africa, China, and Israel—though the percentage of infants in each category varies (van IJzendoorn & Kroonenberg, 1988; van IJzendoorn & Sagi, 1999). Generally, however, secure attachment is the largest category (van IJzendoorn & Sagi, 1999).

Other research (Main & Solomon, 1986) identified a fourth pattern, **disorganized-disoriented attachment.** Babies with the disorganized pattern seem to lack a cohesive strategy to deal with the stress of the Strange Situation. Instead, they show contradictory, repetitive, or misdirected behaviors (such as seeking closeness to the stranger instead of the mother or showing a fear response upon the caregiver's entry). They seem confused and afraid (Carlson, 1998; van IJzendoorn, Schuengel, & Bakermans-Kranenburg, 1999).

disorganized-disoriented attachment Pattern in which an infant, after separation from the primary caregiver, shows contradictory, repetitious, or misdirected behaviors on his or her return.

Disorganized attachment is thought to occur in at least 10 percent of low-risk infants (Vondra & Barnett, 1999). It is most prevalent in babies with mothers who are insensitive, intrusive, or abusive; who are fearful or frightening and thus leave the infant with no one to alleviate the fear the mother arouses; or who have suffered unresolved loss or have unresolved feelings about their childhood attachment to their own parents. The likelihood of disorganized attachment increases in the presence of multiple risk factors, such as maternal insensitivity plus marital discord plus parenting stress. Disorganized attachment is a reliable predictor of later behavioral and adjustment problems (Bernier & Meins, 2008; Carlson, 1998; van IJzendoorn et al., 1999).

Some infants seem to be more susceptible to disorganized attachment than others. Some manage to form organized attachments despite atypical parenting, while others who are *not* exposed to atypical parenting form disorganized attachments (Bernier & Meins, 2008). One explanation might be a *gene-environment interaction.* Studies have identified a variant of the DRD4 gene as a possible risk factor for disorganized attachment, and the risk increases nearly 19-fold when the mother has an unresolved loss (Gervai et al., 2005; Lakatos et al., 2000, 2002; van IJzendoorn & Bakermans-Kranenburg, 2006). Another explanation might be a *gene-environment correlation.* The infant's inborn characteristics may place unusually stressful demands on a parent and thus elicit parenting behaviors that promote disorganized attachment (Bernier & Meins, 2008).

How Attachment Is Established By the time babies are 1 year old, they have established a characteristic style of attachment. According to Bowlby, attachment styles are the result of repeated interactions with a caregiver. For example, if every time a baby cries the mother responds quickly and sensitively to that bid for comfort, over time the baby comes to expect it. By contrast, if a mother responds inconsistently to crying, babies form a very different set of expectations regarding the likely responses of the mother to their cries.

Bowlby called these sets of expectations working models and theorized that these early working models became the blueprint for the dynamics of that relationship. As long as the mother continues to act the same way, the model holds up. If her behavior changes—not just once or twice but repeatedly—the baby may revise the model, and security of attachment may change. Because the working model emerges as a result of interactions between both partners in the relationship, babies can have different working models (and attachment styles) with different people.

A baby's working model of attachment is related to Erikson's concept of basic trust. Secure attachment reflects trust; insecure attachment, mistrust. Securely attached babies have learned to trust not only their caregivers but also their own ability to get

Sensitive mothering is related to another important developmental achievement, at least in the eyes of parents. Mothers who respond sensitively to their infants end up with babies who fall asleep faster, sleep longer, and wake less often.

Teti, Bo-Ram, Mayer, & Countermine, 2010

what they need. Not surprisingly, mothers of securely attached infants and toddlers tend to be sensitive and responsive (Ainsworth et al., 1978; Braungart-Rieker, Garwood, Powers, & Wang, 2001; De Wolff & van IJzendoorn, 1997; Isabella, 1993; NICHD Early Child Care Research Network, 1997). Equally important are mutual interaction, stimulation, a positive attitude, warmth and acceptance, and emotional support (De Wolff & van IJzendoorn, 1997; Lundy, 2003).

Alternative Methods of Attachment Study Although much research on attachment has been based on the Strange Situation, some investigators have questioned its validity. The Strange Situation *is* strange; it takes place in a laboratory, and adults follow a script rather than behaving naturally. Also, the Strange Situation may be less valid in some non-Western cultures (Miyake, Chen, & Campos, 1985).

To address these concerns, researchers have devised methods to study children in natural settings. The Waters and Deane (1985) Attachment Q-set (AQS) has mothers or other home observers sort a set of descriptive words or phrases ("cries a lot"; "tends to cling") into categories ranging from most to least characteristic of the child and then compare these descriptions with expert descriptions of the prototypical secure child.

In a study using the AQS, mothers in China, Colombia, Germany, Israel, Japan, Norway, and the United States described their children as behaving more like than unlike the "most secure child." Furthermore, the mothers' descriptions of "secure-base" behavior were about as similar across cultures as within a culture. These findings suggest that the tendency to use the mother as a secure base is universal, though it may take somewhat varied forms (Posada et al., 1995).

Neurobiological studies may offer another way to study attachment. Functional MRIs given to Japanese mothers showed that certain areas of a mother's brain were activated at the sight of her own infant smiling or crying but not at the sight of other infants showing similar behaviors, suggesting that attachment may have a neurological basis (Noriuchi, Kikuchi, & Senoo, 2008.)

The Role of Temperament How much does temperament influence attachment and in what ways? In a study of 6- to 12-month-olds and their families, both a mother's sensitivity and her baby's temperament influenced attachment patterns (Seifer, Schiller, Sameroff, Resnick, & Riordan, 1996). Neurological or physiological conditions may underlie temperamental differences in attachment. For example, variability in an infant's heart rate is associated with irritability, and heart rate seems to vary more in insecurely attached infants (Izard, Porges, Simons, Haynes, & Cohen, 1991).

A baby's temperament may have not only a direct impact on attachment but also an indirect impact through its effect on the parents. In a series of studies in the Netherlands (van den Boom, 1989, 1994), 15-day-old infants classified as irritable were much more likely than nonirritable infants to be insecurely (usually avoidantly) attached at 1 year. However, irritable infants whose mothers received home visits with instruction on how to soothe their babies were as likely to be rated as securely attached as the nonirritable infants. Thus irritability on an infant's part may prevent the development of secure attachment, but not if the mother has the skills to cope with the baby's temperament (Rothbart et al., 2000). Goodness of fit between parent and child may well be a key to understanding security of attachment.

stranger anxiety
Wariness of strange people and places, shown by some infants during the second half of the 1st year.

separation anxiety
Distress shown by someone, typically an infant, when a familiar caregiver leaves.

Stranger Anxiety and Separation Anxiety Chloe used to be a friendly baby, smiling at strangers and going to them, continuing to coo happily as long as someone—anyone—was around. Now, at 8 months, she turns away when a new person approaches and howls when her parents try to leave her with a babysitter. Chloe is experiencing both **stranger anxiety,** wariness of a person she does not know, and **separation anxiety,** distress when a familiar caregiver leaves her.

Babies rarely react negatively to strangers before age 6 months but commonly do so by 8 or 9 months (Sroufe, 1997). This change may reflect cognitive development. Chloe's stranger anxiety involves memory for faces, the ability to compare the stranger's appearance with her mother's, and perhaps the recollection of situations in which she has been left with a stranger. If Chloe is allowed to get used to the stranger gradually in a familiar setting, she may react more positively (Lewis, 1997; Sroufe, 1997).

Separation anxiety may be due not so much to the separation itself as to the quality of substitute care. When substitute caregivers are warm and responsive and play with 9-month-olds *before* they cry, the babies cry less than when they are with less responsive caregivers (Gunnar, Larson, Hertsgaard, Harris, & Brodersen, 1992).

Stability of care is also important. Pioneering work by René Spitz (1945, 1946) on institutionalized children emphasizes the need for substitute care to be as close as possible to good mothering. Research has underlined the value of continuity and consistency in caregiving, so children can form early emotional bonds with their caregivers.

Babies, at least when they are themselves down on the ground, respond more negatively to tall strangers than to short strangers.

Weinraub, 1978

Long-Term Effects of Attachment As attachment theory proposes, security of attachment seems to affect emotional, social, and cognitive competence, presumably through the action of internal working models (Sroufe, Coffino, & Carlson, 2010). The more secure a child's attachment to a nurturing adult, the more likely that the child will develop good relationships with others.

If children, as infants, had a secure base and could count on parents' or caregivers' responsiveness, they are apt to feel confident enough to be actively engaged in their world (Jacobsen & Hofmann, 1997). For example, in a study of 70 fifteen-month-olds, those who were securely attached to their mothers showed less stress in adapting to child care than did insecurely attached toddlers (Ahnert, Gunnar, Lamb, & Barthel, 2004).

Securely attached toddlers tend to have larger, more varied vocabularies than those who are insecurely attached (Meins, 1998). They have more positive interactions with peers, and their friendly overtures are more likely to be accepted (Fagot, 1997). Insecurely attached toddlers tend to show more negative emotions (fear, distress, and anger), whereas securely attached children are more joyful (Kochanska, 2001).

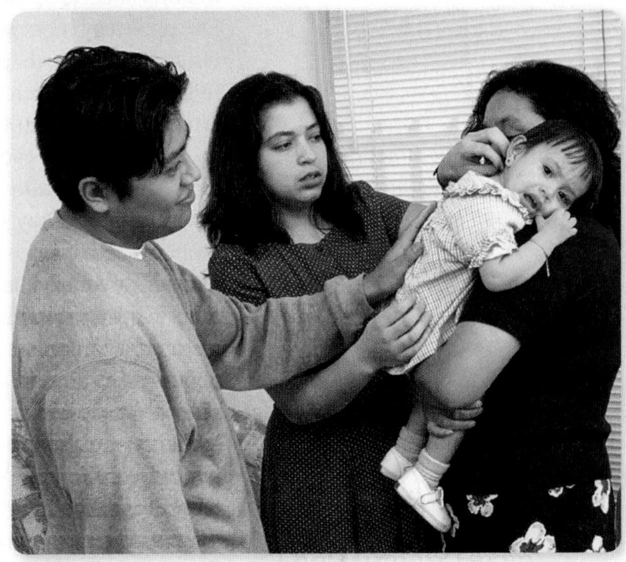

Little Maria is showing separation anxiety about her parents' leaving her with a babysitter. Separation anxiety is common among 6- to 12-month-old babies.

Between ages 3 and 5, securely attached children are likely to be more curious, competent, empathic, resilient, and self-confident, to get along better with other children, and to form closer friendships than children who were insecurely attached as infants (Arend, Gove, & Sroufe, 1979; Elicker, Englund, & Sroufe, 1992; Jacobson & Wille, 1986; Waters, Wippman, & Sroufe, 1979; Youngblade & Belsky, 1992). They interact more positively with parents, preschool teachers, and peers; are better able to resolve conflicts; and tend to have a more positive self-image (Elicker et al., 1992; Verschueren, Marcoen, & Schoefs, 1996; Sroufe, Egeland, Carlson, & Collins, 2005). In middle childhood and adolescence, securely attached children (at least in Western cultures, where most studies have been done) tend to have the closest, most stable friendships (Schneider, Atkinson, & Tardif, 2001; Sroufe, Carlson, & Shulman, 1993) and to be socially well adjusted (Jaffari-Bimmel, Juffer, van IJzendoorn, Bakermans-Kranenberg, & Mooijaart, 2006). Secure attachment in infancy also influences the quality of attachment to a romantic partner in young adulthood (Simpson, Collins, Tran, & Haydon, 2007).

Insecurely attached children, in contrast, often are more likely to have inhibitions and negative emotions in toddlerhood, hostility toward other children at age 5, and dependency during the school years (Calkins & Fox, 1992; Fearon, Bakersmans-Kranenburg, van Ijzendoorn, Lapsley, & Roisman, 2010; Kochanska, 2001; Lyons-Ruth, Alpern, & Repacholi, 1993; Sroufe, Carlson, & Shulman, 1993). They also are more likely to show evidence of externalizing behaviors such as aggression and conduct problems. This appears to be more true for boys, for clinically referred children, and when the attachment assessments are based on observational data. Effects for avoidant and resistant (ambivalent) attachment were small, whereas results for disorganized attachment were quite large (Fearon et al., 2010). Indeed, those with disorganized attachment tend to have behavior problems at all levels of schooling and psychiatric disorders at age 17 (Carlson, 1998).

Intergenerational Transmission of Attachment Patterns The *Adult Attachment Interview* (AAI) (George, Kaplan, & Main, 1985; Main, 1995; Main, Kaplan, & Cassidy, 1985) asks adults to recall and interpret feelings and experiences related to their childhood attachments. Studies using the AAI have found that the way adults recall early experiences with parents or caregivers is related to their emotional well-being and may influence the way they respond to their own children (Adam, Gunnar, & Tanaka, 2004; Dozier, Stovall, Albus, & Bates, 2001; Pesonen, Raïkkönen, Keltikangas-Järvinen, Strandberg, & Järvenpää, 2003). A mother who was securely attached to *her* mother or who understands why she was insecurely attached can accurately recognize the baby's attachment behaviors, respond encouragingly, and help the baby form a secure attachment to her (Bretherton, 1990). Mothers who are preoccupied with their past attachment relationships tend to show anger and intrusiveness in interactions with their children. Depressed mothers who dismiss memories of their past attachments tend to be cold and unresponsive to their children (Adam et al., 2004). Parents' attachment history also influences their perceptions of their baby's temperament, and those perceptions may affect the parent-child relationship (Pesonen et al., 2003).

Fortunately, a cycle of insecure attachment can be broken. In one study, 54 first-time Dutch mothers who were classified by the AAI as insecurely attached received home visits in which they either were given video feedback to enhance sensitive parenting or participated in discussions of their childhood experiences in relation to their current caregiving. After the interventions, these mothers were more sensitive than a control group who had not received the visits. Maternal gains in sensitivity to children's needs most strongly affected the security of infants with highly reactive (negatively emotional) temperaments (Klein-Velderman, Bakermans-Kranenburg, Juffer, & van IJzendoorn, 2006).

checkpoint can **you**...

- Describe four patterns of attachment?
- Discuss how attachment is established, including the role of the baby's temperament?
- Discuss factors affecting stranger anxiety and separation anxiety?
- Describe long-term behavioral influences of attachment patterns and intergenerational transmission of attachment?

EMOTIONAL COMMUNICATION WITH CAREGIVERS: MUTUAL REGULATION

At 1 month, Max gazes attentively at his mother's face. At 2 months, when his mother smiles at him and rubs his tummy, he smiles back. By 3 months, Max smiles first, inviting his mother to play (Lavelli & Fogel, 2005).

Infants are communicating beings; they have a strong drive to interact with others. The ability of both infant and caregiver to respond appropriately and sensitively to each other's mental and emotional states is known as **mutual regulation.** Infants take an active part in mutual regulation by sending behavioral signals, like Max's smiles, that influence the way caregivers behave toward them. Typically, interaction moves back and forth between well-regulated states and poorly regulated states. For example, when a baby's goals are met, the baby tends to be joyful, or at least interested (Tronick, 1989). However, when a mother or caregiver is not synchronous in her interaction with the baby—for example, if an invitation to play is ignored or an adult is overly intrusive—the baby can become frustrated or sad. In fact, even very young infants can perceive emotions expressed by others and vary their behavior accordingly to repair the interaction (Legerstee & Varghese, 2001; Montague & Walker-Andrews, 2001). From this process, babies learn how to send signals and what to do when their signals are not effective. Not surprisingly, there are links to later social behaviors. Children whose mothers were high in interactional synchrony when young are more likely later to be better at regulating their behavior, to comply with parental requests, to have higher IQ, to use more words referencing mental states (such as "think"), and to have fewer behavioral problems (Feldman, 2007). It may be that mutual regulation processes help them learn to read others' behavior and to respond appropriately. Box 1 discusses how a mother's depression may contribute to developmental problems in her baby.

mutual regulation
Process by which infant and caregiver communicate emotional states to each other and respond appropriately.

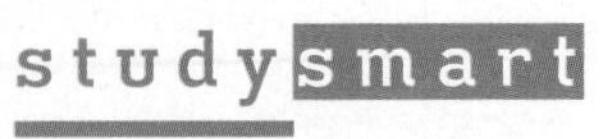

Interactional Synchrony

research in action

HOW POSTPARTUM DEPRESSION AFFECTS EARLY DEVELOPMENT

Reading emotional signals lets mothers assess and meet babies' needs and helps babies respond to the mother's behavior toward them. What happens when that communication system seriously breaks down, and can anything be done about it?

Much media attention has been focused on the issue of postpartum depression. Such celebrities as Brooke Shields and Marie Osmond have shared stories of their personal battles with this distressing condition.

Postpartum depression—major or minor depression occurring within 4 weeks of giving birth—affects about 14.5 percent of new mothers (Wisner, Chambers, & Sit, 2006). A dramatic drop in estrogen and progesterone following childbirth may trigger depression. Depression also may be brought on by the significant emotional and lifestyle changes new mothers face. First-time mothers are at especially high risk (Munk-Olsen, Laursen, Pedersen, Mors, & Mortensen, 2006).

Unless treated promptly, postpartum depression may affect the way a mother interacts with her baby, with detrimental effects on the child's cognitive and emotional development (Gjerdingen, 2003). Depressed mothers are less sensitive to their infants than nondepressed mothers, and their interactions with their babies are generally less positive (NICHD Early Child Care Research Network, 1999b). Depressed mothers are less likely to interpret and respond to an infant's cries (Donovan, Leavitt, & Walsh, 1998).

Babies of depressed mothers may give up on sending emotional signals and learn that they have no power to draw responses from other people, that their mothers are unreliable, and that the world is untrustworthy. They also may become depressed themselves (Ashman & Dawson, 2002; Gelfand & Teti, 1995; Teti, Gelfand, Messinger, & Isabella, 1995), whether due to a failure of mutual regulation, an inherited predisposition to depression, or exposure to hormonal or other biochemical influences in the prenatal environment. It may be that a combination of genetic, prenatal, and environmental factors puts infants of depressed mothers at risk. A bidirectional influence may be at work; an infant who does not respond normally may further depress the mother, and her unresponsiveness may in turn further depress the infant (T. Field, 1995, 1998a, 1998c; Lundy et al., 1999). Depressed mothers who are able to maintain good interactions with their infants tend to nurture better emotional regulation in their children than do other depressed mothers (Field, Diego, Hernandez-Reif, Schanberg, & Kuhn, 2003). Interactions with a nondepressed adult can help infants compensate for the effects of depressed mothering (T. Field, 1995, 1998a, 1998c).

Infants of depressed mothers tend to show unusual patterns of brain activity, similar to the mothers' patterns. Within 24 hours of birth, they show relatively less activity in the left frontal region of the brain, which seems to be specialized for approach emotions such as joy and anger, and more activity in the right frontal region, which controls *withdrawal* emotions, such as distress and disgust (G. Dawson et al., 1992, 1999; T. Field, 1998a, 1998c; T. Field, Fox, Pickens, Nawrocki, & Soutollo, 1995; N. A. Jones, Field, Fox, Lundy, & Davalos, 1997). Newborns of depressed mothers also tend to have higher levels of stress hormones (Lundy et al., 1999), lower scores on the Brazelton Neonatal Behavior Assessment Scale, and lower vagal tone, which is associated with attention and learning (T. Field, 1998a, 1998c; N. A. Jones et al., 1998). These findings suggest that a woman's depression during pregnancy may contribute to her newborn's neurological and behavioral functioning.

Children with depressed mothers tend to be insecurely attached (Gelfand & Teti, 1995; Teti et al., 1995). They are likely to grow poorly, to perform poorly on cognitive and linguistic measures, and to have behavior problems (T. Field, 1998a, 1998c; T. M. Field et al., 1985; Gelfand & Teti, 1995; NICHD Early Child Care Research Network, 1999b; Zuckerman & Beardslee, 1987). As toddlers these children tend to have trouble suppressing frustration and tension (Cole, Barrett, & Zahn-Waxler, 1992; Seiner & Gelfand, 1995), and in early adolescence they are at risk for violent behavior (Hay, 2003).

Antidepressant drugs such as Zoloft (a selective serotonin reuptake inhibitor) and nortriptyline (a tricyclic) appear to be safe and effective for treating postpartum depression (Wisner et al., 2006). Other techniques that may help improve a depressed mother's mood include listening to music, visual imagery, aerobics, yoga, relaxation, and massage therapy (T. Field, 1995, 1998a, 1998c). Massage also can help depressed babies (T. Field, 1998a, 1998b; T. Field et al., 1996), possibly through effects on neurological activity (N. A. Jones et al., 1997). In one study, such mood-brightening measures—plus social, educational, and vocational rehabilitation for the mother and day care for the infant—improved their interaction behavior. The infants showed faster growth and had fewer pediatric problems, more normal biochemical values, and better developmental test scores than a control group (T. Field, 1998a, 1998b).

Can you suggest ways to help depressed mothers and babies, other than those mentioned here?

SOCIAL REFERENCING

Ann toddles warily toward the new playground and stops at the entrance, staring at the laughing, screaming children scaling the bright structure. Unsure of herself, she turns toward her mother and makes eye contact. Her mother smiles at her, and Ann, emboldened by her mother's response, walks in and starts to climb the structure. When babies look at their caregivers on encountering an ambiguous event, they are engaging in **social referencing,** seeking emotional information to guide behavior. In social referencing, one person forms an understanding of how to act in an ambiguous, confusing, or unfamiliar situation by seeking and interpreting another person's perception of it.

social referencing
Understanding an ambiguous situation by seeking another person's perception of it.

Research provides experimental evidence of social referencing at 12 months (Moses, Baldwin, Rosicky, & Tidball, 2001). When exposed to jiggling or vibrating toys fastened to the floor or ceiling, both 12- and 18-month-olds moved closer to or farther from the toys depending on the experimenters' expressed emotional reactions ("Yecch!" or "Nice!"). In one pair of studies, 12-month-olds (but not 10-month-olds) adjusted their behavior toward certain unfamiliar objects according to nonvocal emotional signals given by an actress on a television screen (Mumme & Fernald, 2003). In another pair of experiments (Hertenstein & Campos, 2004), whether 14-month-olds touched plastic creatures that dropped within their reach was related to the positive or negative emotions they had seen an adult express about the same objects an hour before. Eleven-month-olds responded to such emotional cues only if the delay was very brief (3 minutes). As children age, social referencing becomes less dependent on facial expression and more dependent on language. Children between the ages of 4 and 5 years are more likely to trust information that comes from their mother than from a stranger (Corriveau et al., 2009).

checkpoint
can **you** . . .

- Describe how mutual regulation works and explain its importance?
- Give examples of how infants seem to use social referencing?

Social referencing, and the ability to retain information gained from it, may play a role in such key developments of toddlerhood as the rise of self-conscious emotions (embarrassment and pride), the development of a sense of self, and the processes of *socialization* and *internalization,* to which we turn in the next section of this chapter.

Developmental Issues in Toddlerhood

study smart
Sense of Self

At about halfway between their 1st and 2nd birthdays, babies become toddlers. This transformation can be seen not only in such physical and cognitive skills as walking and talking, but in the ways children express their personalities and interact with others.

Let's look at three psychological issues that toddlers—and their caregivers—have to deal with: the emerging *sense of self;* the growth of *autonomy,* or self-determination; and *socialization,* or *internalization of behavioral standards.*

THE EMERGING SENSE OF SELF

The **self-concept** is our image of ourselves—our total picture of our abilities and traits. It describes what we know and feel about ourselves and guides our actions (Harter, 1996). Children incorporate into their self-image the picture that others reflect back to them.

self-concept
Sense of self; descriptive and evaluative mental picture of one's abilities and traits.

When and how does the self-concept develop? From a jumble of seemingly isolated experiences (say, from one breast-feeding session to another), infants begin to extract consistent patterns that form rudimentary concepts of self and other. Depending on what kind of care the infant receives and how she or he responds, pleasant or unpleasant emotions become connected with experiences that play an important part in the growing concept of the self (Harter, 1998).

autonomy versus shame and doubt
Erikson's second stage in psychosocial development, in which children achieve a balance between self-determination and control by others.

By at least 3 months of age, infants pay attention to their mirror image (Courage & Howe, 2002); 4- to 9-month-olds show more interest in images of others than of themselves (Rochat & Striano, 2002). This early *perceptual* discrimination may be the foundation of the *conceptual* self-awareness that develops between 15 and 18 months. Between 4 and 10 months, when infants learn to reach, grasp, and make things happen, they experience a sense of personal *agency,* the realization that they can control external events. At about this time infants develop *self-coherence,* the sense of being a physical whole with boundaries separate from the rest of the world. These developments occur in interaction with caregivers in games such as peekaboo, in which the infant becomes increasingly aware of the difference between self and other.

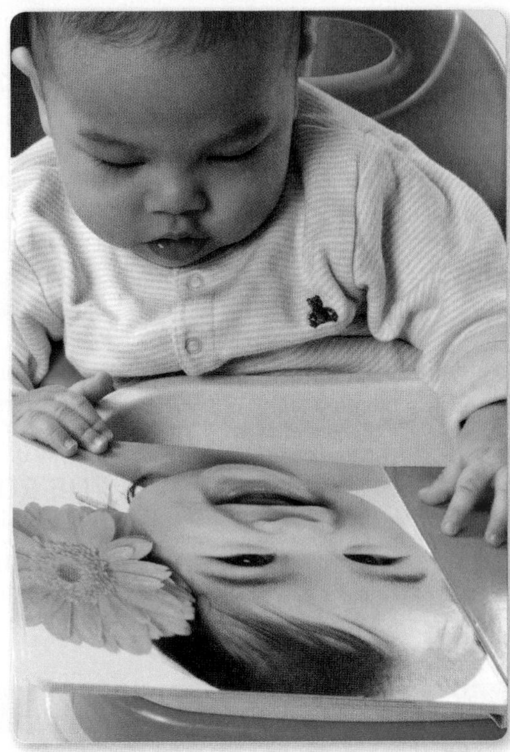

Four- to 9-month-olds show more interest in images of others than in images of themselves.

The emergence of *self-awareness*—conscious knowledge of the self as a distinct, identifiable being—builds on this dawning of perceptual distinction between self and others. Self-awareness can be tested by studying whether an infant recognizes his or her own image. In a classic line of research, investigators dabbed rouge on the noses of 6- to 24-month-olds and sat them in front of a mirror. Three-fourths of 18-month-olds and all 24-month-olds touched their red noses more often than before, whereas babies younger than 15 months never did. This behavior suggests that these toddlers had self-awareness. They knew they did not normally have red noses and recognized the image in the mirror as their own (Lewis, 1997; Lewis & Brooks, 1974). In a later study, 18- and 24-month-olds were about as likely to touch a sticker on their leg, which was visible only in a mirror, as one on their face (Nielsen, Suddendorf, & Slaughter, 2006). Once children can recognize themselves, they show a preference for looking at their own video image over an image of another child the same age (Nielsen, Dissanayake, & Kashima, 2003).

By 20 to 24 months, toddlers begin to use first-person pronouns, another sign of self-awareness (Lewis, 1997). Between 19 and 30 months they begin to apply descriptive terms ("big" or "little"; "straight hair" or "curly hair") and evaluative terms ("good," "pretty," or "strong") to themselves. The rapid development of language enables children to think and talk about the self and to incorporate parents' verbal descriptions ("What a hard worker!" "What a big boy!") into their emerging self-image (Stipek, Gralinski, & Kopp, 1990). Similarly, toddlers of this age demonstrate self-understanding through acknowledging objects that belong to them and those that belong to others (Fasig, 2000).

Dabbing rouge on children's noses is known as the Rouge Task, and research has shown that dolphins, chimpanzees, and elephants also share our ability for self-recognition.

DEVELOPMENT OF AUTONOMY

As children mature, they are driven to seek independence from the very adults to whom they have become attached. "Me do!" is the byword as toddlers use their developing muscles and minds to try to do everything on their own—not only to walk, but to feed and dress themselves and to explore their world.

Learning to control your temper is a form of self-control.

Erikson (1950) identified the period from about 18 months to 3 years as the second stage in personality development, **autonomy versus shame and doubt,** which is marked by a shift from external control to self-control. Having come through infancy with a sense of basic trust in the world and an awakening self-awareness, toddlers begin to substitute their own judgment for their caregivers'. The virtue that emerges during this stage is *will.* Toilet training is an important step toward autonomy and self-control; so is language. As children are better able to make their wishes known, they become more powerful. Because unlimited freedom is neither safe nor healthy, said Erikson, shame and doubt have a necessary place. Toddlers need adults to set appropriate limits, and shame and doubt help them recognize the need for those limits.

checkpoint
can you . . .

- Trace the early development of the self-concept?
- Describe the conflict of autonomy versus shame and doubt and explain why the terrible twos is considered a normal phenomenon?

In the United States, toddlers often enjoy testing the notions that they are individuals, that they have some control over their world, and that they have new, exciting powers. They are driven to try out their own ideas, exercise their own preferences, and make their own decisions. This drive often shows itself in the form of *negativism,* the tendency to shout, "No!" just for the sake of resisting authority. Almost all U.S. children show negativism to some degree; it usually begins before age 2, tends to peak at about 3½ to 4, and declines by age 6. Caregivers who view children's expressions of self-will as a normal, healthy striving for independence, not as stubbornness, can help them learn self-control, contribute to their sense of competence, and avoid excessive conflict. Table 3 gives specific, research-based suggestions for dealing with the terrible twos.

Many U.S. parents might be surprised to hear that the terrible twos are not universal. In some developing countries, the transition from infancy to early childhood is relatively smooth and harmonious (Mosier & Rogoff, 2003; Box 2).

THE ROOTS OF MORAL DEVELOPMENT: SOCIALIZATION AND INTERNALIZATION

socialization
Development of habits, skills, values, and motives shared by responsible, productive members of a society.

Socialization is the process by which children develop habits, skills, values, and motives that make them responsible, productive members of society. Compliance with

TABLE 3 Dealing with the Terrible Twos

The following research-based guidelines can help parents of toddlers discourage negativism and encourage socially acceptable behavior.

- *Be flexible.* Learn the child's natural rhythms and special likes and dislikes.
- *Think of yourself as a safe harbor,* with safe limits, from which a child can set out and discover the world and to which the child can keep coming back for support.
- *Make your home child-friendly.* Fill it with unbreakable objects that are safe to explore.
- *Avoid physical punishment.* It is often ineffective and may even lead a toddler to do more damage.
- *Offer a choice*—even a limited one—to give the child some control. ("Would you like to have your bath now or after we read a book?")
- *Be consistent* in enforcing necessary requests.
- *Don't interrupt an activity unless absolutely necessary.* Try to wait until the child's attention has shifted.
- *If you must interrupt, give warning.* ("We have to leave the playground soon.")
- *Suggest alternative activities* when behavior becomes objectionable. (When Ashley is throwing sand in Keiko's face, say, "Oh, look! Nobody's on the swings now. Let's go over and I'll give you a good push!")
- *Suggest; don't command.* Accompany requests with smiles or hugs, not criticism, threats, or physical restraint.
- *Link requests with pleasurable activities.* ("It's time to stop playing so that you can go to the store with me.")
- *Remind the child of what you expect:* "When we go to this playground, we *never* go outside the gate."
- *Wait a few moments before repeating a request* when a child doesn't comply immediately.
- *Use a "time-out" to end conflicts.* In a nonpunitive way, remove either yourself or the child from a situation.
- *Expect less self-control during times of stress* (illness, divorce, the birth of a sibling, or a move to a new home).
- *Expect it to be harder for toddlers to comply with "dos" than with "don'ts."* "Clean up your room" takes more effort than "Don't write on the furniture."
- *Keep the atmosphere as positive as possible.* Make your child *want* to cooperate.

Sources: Haswell, Hock, & Wenar, 1981; Kochanska & Aksan, 1995; Kopp, 1982; Kuczynski & Kochanska, 1995; Power & Chapieski, 1986.

window on the world

ARE STRUGGLES WITH TODDLERS NECESSARY?

Are the terrible twos a normal phase in child development? Many Western parents and psychologists think so. Actually, though, the terrible twos do not appear to be universal.

In Zinacantan, Mexico, toddlers do not typically become demanding and resistant to parental control. Instead, toddlerhood in Zinacantan is a time when children move from being mama's babies toward being "mother's helpers," responsible children who tend a new baby and help with household tasks (Edwards, 1994). A similar developmental pattern seems to occur in Mazahua families in Mexico and among Mayan families in San Pedro, Guatemala. San Pedro parents "do not report a particular age when they expect children to become especially contrary or negative" (Mosier & Rogoff, 2003, p. 1058).

One arena in which issues of autonomy and control appear in Western cultures is in sibling conflicts over toys and the way children respond to parental handling of these conflicts. To explore these issues, a cross-cultural study compared 16 San Pedro families with 16 middle-class European American families in Salt Lake City. All of the families had toddlers 14 to 20 months old and older siblings 3 to 5 years old. The researchers interviewed each mother about her child-raising practices. They then handed the mother a series of attractive objects (such as dolls and puppets) and, in the presence of the older sibling, asked the mother to help the toddler operate them, with no instructions about the older child. Researchers found striking differences in the way siblings interacted in the two cultures and in the way the mothers viewed and handled sibling conflict.

Whereas older siblings in Salt Lake City often tried to take and play with the objects, this did not generally happen in San Pedro. Instead, the older San Pedro children would offer to help their younger siblings, or the two children would play with the toys together. When there was a conflict over possession of the toys, the San Pedro mothers favored the toddlers 94 percent of the time, even taking an object away from the older child if the younger child wanted it; and the older siblings tended to go along, willingly handing the objects to the toddlers or letting them have the objects from the start. In contrast, in more than one-third of the interactions in Salt Lake City, the mothers tried to treat both children equally, negotiating with them or suggesting that they take turns or share. These observations were consistent with reports of mothers in both cultures as to how they handled such issues at home. San Pedro children are given a privileged position until age 3; then they are expected to willingly cooperate with social expectations.

What explains these cultural contrasts? A clue emerged when the mothers were asked at what age children can be held responsible for their actions. Most of the Salt Lake mothers maintained that their toddlers understood the consequences of touching prohibited objects; several said this understanding arises as early as 7 months. Yet all but one of the San Pedro mothers placed the age of understanding social consequences of actions much later—between 2 and 3 years. The Salt Lake mothers regarded their toddlers as capable of intentional misbehavior and punished their toddlers for it; most San Pedro mothers did not. All of the Salt Lake preschoolers (toddlers and their siblings) were under direct caregiver supervision; 11 of the 16 San Pedro preschoolers were on their own much of the time and had more mature household responsibilities.

The researchers suggest that the terrible twos may be a phase specific to societies that place individual freedom before the needs of the group. Ethnographic research suggests that, in societies that place higher value on group needs, freedom of choice does exist, but it goes hand in hand with interdependence, responsibility, and expectations of cooperation. Salt Lake parents seem to believe that responsible behavior develops gradually from engaging in fair competition and negotiations. San Pedro parents seem to believe that responsible behavior develops rapidly when children are old enough to understand the need to respect others' desires as well as their own.

From your experience or observation of toddlers, which of the two ways of handling sibling conflict would you expect to be more effective?

2

internalization
During socialization, process by which children accept societal standards of conduct as their own.

parental expectations can be seen as a first step toward compliance with societal standards. Socialization rests on **internalization** of these standards. Children who are successfully socialized no longer obey rules or commands merely to get rewards or avoid punishment; rather, they have internalized those standards and made them their own (Grusec & Goodnow, 1994; Kochanska, 2002; Kochanska & Aksan, 1995; Kochanska, Tjebkes, & Forman, 1998). They obey societal or parental dictates, not because they are afraid of getting in trouble but because they themselves believe them to be right and true.

Developing Self-Regulation Laticia, age 2, is about to poke her finger into an electric outlet. In her child-proofed apartment, the sockets are covered, but not here in her grandmother's home. When Laticia hears her father shout, "No!" the toddler pulls her arm back. The next time she goes near an outlet, she starts to poke her finger, hesitates, and then says, "No." She has stopped herself from doing something she remembers she is not supposed to do. She is beginning to show **self-regulation:** control of her behavior to conform to a caregiver's demands or expectations of her, even when the caregiver is not present.

self-regulation
A child's independent control of behavior to conform to understood social expectations.

Self-regulation is the foundation of socialization, and it links all domains of development—physical, cognitive, emotional, and social. Until Laticia was physically able to get around on her own, electric outlets posed no hazard. To stop herself from poking her finger into an outlet requires that she consciously remember and understand what her father told her. Cognitive awareness, however, is not enough; restraining herself also requires emotional control. By reading their parents' emotional responses to their behavior, children continually absorb information about what conduct their parents approve of. As children process, store, and act on this information, their desire to please their parents leads them to do as they know their parents want them to, whether or not the parents are there to see. Moreover, the quality of their relationship with their parents affects this emerging skill. Maternal sensitivity, parents' tendency to use mental terms when talking to the child, and support of the child's autonomous behavior are all important influences on self-regulation (Bernier, Carlson, & Whipple, 2010).

Before they can control their own behavior, children may need to be able to regulate, or control, their *attentional processes* and to modulate negative emotions (Eisenberg, 2000). Attentional regulation enables children to develop willpower and cope with frustration (Sethi, Mischel, Aber, Shoda, & Rodriguez, 2000). For example, control of attentional processes might allow a child to distract herself enough that she manages not to steal the cookies temptingly cooling on the counter.

The growth of self-regulation parallels the development of the self-conscious and evaluative emotions, such as empathy, shame, and guilt (Lewis, 1995, 1997, 1998). It requires the ability to wait for gratification. It is correlated with measures of conscience development, such as resisting temptation and making amends for wrongdoing (Eisenberg, 2000). In most children, the full development of self-regulation takes at least 3 years (Kopp, 1982).

Origins of Conscience: Committed Compliance Young children cooperate with parental dictates because they know they are supposed to. Although this self-regulation is important, the goal of parenting is often internalization of parental mores. Parents want their children to do the right thing and to avoid doing the wrong thing because the children truly believe it for themselves. In other words, the eventual goal is development of a **conscience,** which involves both the ability to refrain from certain acts as well as to feel emotional discomfort if they fail to do so.

conscience
Internal standards of behavior, which usually control one's conduct and produce emotional discomfort when violated.

Grazyna Kochanska and her colleagues looked for the origins of conscience in a longitudinal study of a group of toddlers and mothers in Iowa. Researchers studied 103 children ages 26 to 41 months and their mothers playing together with toys for 2 to 3 hours, both at home and in a homelike laboratory setting (Kochanska & Aksan, 1995).

After a free-play period, a mother would give her child 15 minutes to put away the toys. The laboratory had a special shelf with other, unusually attractive toys, such as a bubble gum machine, a walkie-talkie, and a music box. The child was told not to touch anything on that shelf. After about an hour, the experimenter asked the mother to go into an adjoining room, leaving the child alone with the toys. A few minutes later, a woman entered, played with several of the forbidden toys, and then left the child alone again for 8 minutes.

Some children could put the toys away as long as their parents were there to remind them. These children showed what is called **situational compliance.** They needed the extra assistance provided by their parents' reminder and prompts to complete the task. In a different situation that did not include those reminders, these children might fail to put the toys away. However, other children seemed to have internalized their parents' requests more fully. These children showed **committed compliance**—that is, they were committed to following requests and could do so without their parents' direct intervention (Kochanska, Coy, & Murray, 2001).

situational compliance
Kochanska's term for obedience of a parent's orders only in the presence of signs of ongoing parental control.

committed compliance
Kochanska's term for wholehearted obedience of a parent's orders without reminders or lapses.

receptive cooperation
Kochanska's term for eager willingness to cooperate harmoniously with a parent in daily interactions, including routines, chores, hygiene, and play.

The roots of committed compliance go back to infancy. Committed compliers, most typically girls, tend to be those who, at 8 to 10 months, could refrain from touching when told, "No!" Committed compliance tends to increase with age, whereas situational compliance decreases (Kochanska, Tjebkes, & Forman, 1998). Mothers of committed compliers, as contrasted with mothers of situational compliers, tend to rely on gentle guidance rather than force, threats, or other forms of negative control (Eisenberg, 2000; Kochanska & Aksan, 1995; Kochanska, Friesenborg, Lange, & Martel, 2004).

Receptive cooperation goes beyond committed compliance. It is a child's eager willingness to cooperate harmoniously with a parent, not only in disciplinary situations, but in a variety of daily interactions, including routines, chores, hygiene, and play. Receptive cooperation enables a child to be an active partner in socialization. In a longitudinal study of 101 children, begun at 7 months of age, those who were prone to anger, who received unresponsive parenting, or who were insecurely attached at 15 months also tended to be low in receptive cooperation. Children who were securely attached and whose mothers had been responsive to the child during infancy tended to be high in receptive cooperation (Kochanska, Aksan, & Carlson, 2005).

One new development in the parenting domain is the influence of instantly and always available technology. Research by Sherry Turkle of the Massachusetts Institute of Technology suggests that young children are increasingly experiencing hurt feelings as a result of competition with computers and smart phones.

Turkle, 2011

Factors in the Success of Socialization The way parents go about the job of socializing a child and the quality of the parent-child relationship may help predict how hard or easy socialization will be. However, not all children respond in the same way. For example, a temperamentally fearful toddler may respond better to gentle reminders than to strong admonitions, whereas a more bold toddler may require more assertive parenting (Kochanska, Aksan, & Joy, 2007).

Secure attachment and a warm, mutually responsive, parent-child relationship seem to foster committed compliance and conscience development. From the child's 2nd year until early school age, researchers observed more than 200 mothers and children in lengthy, naturalistic interactions: caregiving routines, preparing and eating meals, playing, relaxing, and doing household chores. Children who were judged to have mutually responsive relationships with their mothers tended to show *moral emotions* such as guilt and empathy; *moral conduct* in the face of strong temptation to break rules or violate standards of behavior; and *moral cognition,* as judged by their response to hypothetical, age-appropriate moral dilemmas (Kochanska, 2002).

Constructive conflict over a child's misbehavior—conflict that involves negotiation, reasoning, and resolution—can help children develop moral understanding by enabling them to see another point of view. In one observational study, 2½-year-olds whose mothers gave clear explanations for their requests, compromised, or bargained with the child were better able to resist temptation at age 3 than children whose mothers had threatened, teased, insisted, or given in. Discussion of emotions in conflict situations ("How would you feel if . . .") also led to conscience development, probably by fostering the development of moral emotions (Laible & Thompson, 2002).

checkpoint
can **you . . .**

- Tell when and how self-regulation develops and how it contributes to socialization?
- Distinguish among committed compliance, situational compliance, and receptive cooperation?
- Discuss how temperament, attachment, and parenting practices affect socialization?

Contact with Other Children

Although parents exert a major influence on children's lives, relationships with other children—both in the home and out of it—also are important from infancy on.

SIBLINGS

Sibling relationships play a distinct role in socialization. Sibling conflicts can become a vehicle for understanding social relationships (Ram & Ross, 2001). Lessons and skills learned from interactions with siblings carry over to relationships outside the home (Brody, 1998; Ji-Yeon, McHale, Crouter, & Osgood, 2007).

In many non-Western cultures, it is common to see older siblings caring for younger siblings.

Babies usually become attached to their older brothers and sisters. Although rivalry may be present, so is affection. The more securely attached siblings are to their parents, the better they get along with each other (Teti & Ablard, 1989).

Nevertheless, as babies begin to move around and become more assertive, they inevitably come into conflict with siblings—at least in U.S. culture. Sibling conflict increases dramatically after the younger child reaches 18 months (Vandell & Bailey, 1992). During the next few months, younger siblings begin to participate more fully in family interactions and become more involved in family disputes. As they do, they become more aware of others' intentions and feelings. They begin to recognize what kind of behavior will upset or annoy an older brother or sister and what behavior is considered "naughty" or "good" (Dunn & Munn, 1985; Recchia & Howe, 2009).

As this cognitive and social understanding grows, sibling conflict tends to become more constructive, and the younger sibling participates in attempts to reconcile. Constructive conflict with siblings helps children recognize each other's needs, wishes, and point of view, and it helps them learn how to fight, disagree, and compromise within the context of a safe, stable relationship (Kramer, 2010; Vandell & Bailey, 1992).

SOCIABILITY WITH NONSIBLINGS

Infants and—even more so—toddlers show interest in people outside the home, particularly people their own size. During the first few months, they look, smile, and coo at other babies (T. M. Field, 1978). From about 6 to 12 months, they increasingly smile at, touch, and babble to them (Hay, Pedersen, & Nash, 1982). At about 1 year, when the biggest items on their agenda are learning to walk and to manipulate objects, babies pay less attention to other people (T. M. Field & Roopnarine, 1982). This stage does not last long, though. From about 1½ years to almost 3, children show growing interest in what other children do and an increasing understanding of how to deal with them (Eckerman, Davis, & Didow, 1989).

Toddlers learn by imitating one another. Games such as follow-the-leader help toddlers connect with other children and pave the way for more complex games during the preschool years (Eckerman et al., 1989). Imitation of each other's actions leads to more frequent verbal communication (such as "You go in playhouse," or "Look at me"), which helps peers coordinate joint activity (Eckerman & Didow, 1996). Cooperative activity develops during the 2nd and 3rd years as social understanding grows (Brownell, Ramani, & Zerwas, 2006). As with siblings, conflict also can have a purpose: helping children learn how to negotiate and resolve disputes (Kramer, 2010).

Some children, of course, are more sociable than others, reflecting such temperamental traits as their usual mood, readiness to accept new people, and ability to adapt to change. Sociability is also influenced by experience; babies who spend time with other babies, as in child care, become sociable earlier than those who spend almost all their time at home.

checkpoint
can you . . .

- Explain how sibling relationships play a part in socialization?
- Describe changes in sibling interactions during toddlerhood?
- Trace changes in sociability during the first 3 years, and state two influences on it?

Children of Working Parents

Parents' work determines more than the family's financial resources. Much of adults' time, effort, and emotional involvement goes into their occupations. How do their work and their child care arrangements affect infants and toddlers? Most research on this subject pertains to mothers' work.

EFFECTS OF MATERNAL EMPLOYMENT

More than half (55.8 percent) of mothers of infants in their 1st year of life and 54 percent of women with children under age 3 were in the labor force in 2011, a dramatic increase since 1975 (U.S. Bureau of Labor Statistics, 2008a, 2012; Figure 2).

How does early maternal employment affect children? Longitudinal data on 900 European American children from the National Institute of Child Health and Human Development (NICHD) Study of Early Child Care showed negative effects on cognitive development at 15 months to 3 years when mothers worked 30 or more hours a week by a child's 9th month. However, maternal sensitivity, a high-quality home environment, and high-quality child care lessened these negative effects (Brooks-Gunn, Han, & Waldfogel, 2002).

Similarly, among 6,114 children from the National Longitudinal Survey of Youth (NLSY), those whose mothers worked full-time in the 1st year after giving birth were more likely to show negative cognitive and behavioral outcomes at ages 3 to 8 than children whose mothers worked part-time or not at all during their 1st year. However, children in disadvantaged families showed fewer negative cognitive effects than children in more advantaged families (Hill, Waldfogel, Brooks-Gunn, & Han, 2005).

Although parents may feel guilty about how much time they spend with their children given the conflicting modern demands of work and family, research suggests that they actually spend more time with their kids than previous generations did. How do parents fit it in? Apparently, moms spend less time cooking and cleaning, and dads spend less time at the office.

Ramey & Ramey, 2010

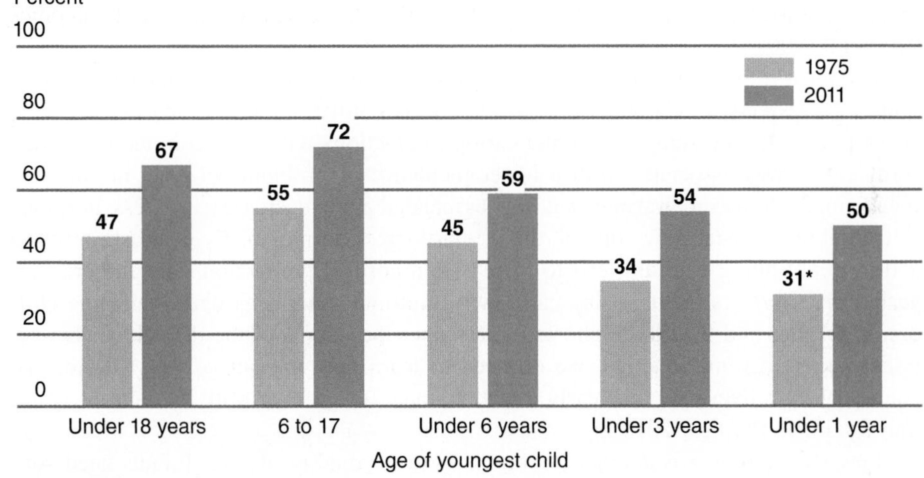

FIGURE 2

Labor Force Participation Rates of Mothers with Own Children, 1975 and 2011

Labor force participation by mothers of children of all ages has increased dramatically in the past three decades. In 1975, fewer than half of all mothers were working or looking for work. In 2011, about 7 out of 10 mothers were labor force participants. Participation rates in 2011 ranged from 50 percent for mothers whose youngest child was under 1 year old to 72 percent for mothers whose youngest child was age 6 to 17.

Sources: Data from Hayghe, 1986; U.S. Bureau of Labor Statistics, 2012.

In 2009, full-time child care costs for a year exceeded average yearly college tuition and fees in 40 states.

National Association of Child Care Resource and Referral Agencies (NACCRRA), 2010

EARLY CHILD CARE

One factor in the impact of a mother's working outside the home is the type of substitute care a child receives. More than 50 percent of the 11.3 million children not yet in kindergarten whose mothers were employed received care from relatives: 30 percent from grandparents, 25 percent from their fathers, and 11 percent from other relatives. More than 30 percent were in organized day care or preschools. With nonrelative care averaging $129 a week (U.S. Census Bureau, 2008b), affordability and quality of care are pressing issues.

Factors Having an Impact on Child Care The impact of early child care may depend on the type, amount, quality, and stability of care as well as the family's income and the age at which children start receiving nonmaternal care. By 9 months, about 50 percent of U.S. infants are in some kind of regular nonparental child care arrangement, and 86 percent of these infants enter child care before they reach 6 months. More than 50 percent of these babies are in child care more than 30 hours a week (NCES, 2005a).

Temperament and gender of the child make a difference (Crockenberg, 2003). Shy children in child care experience greater stress, as shown by cortisol levels, than sociable children (Watamura, Donzella, Alwin, & Gunnar, 2003), and insecurely attached children experience greater stress than securely attached children when introduced to full-time child care (Ahnert et al., 2004). Boys are more vulnerable to stress, in child care and elsewhere, than are girls (Crockenberg, 2003).

A critical factor in determining the effects of child care is the quality of care a child receives. Quality of care can be measured by *structural characteristics,* such as staff training and the ratio of children to caregivers; and by *process characteristics,* such as the warmth, sensitivity, and responsiveness of caregivers and the developmental appropriateness of activities. Structural quality and process quality may be related; in one study, well-trained caregivers and low child-staff ratios were associated with higher process quality, which, in turn, was associated with better cognitive and social outcomes (Marshall, 2004).

The most important element in quality of care is the caregiver. Stimulating interactions with responsive adults are crucial to early cognitive, linguistic, and psychosocial development. In one study, warm and caring interactions with staff at home-based day care centers was associated with a lower incidence of problem behavior in children. Interestingly, however, warmth was *not* associated with decreases in stress hormone activation (as measured by cortisol, the primary stress hormone). By contrast, intrusive and overcontrolling care did lead to increases in cortisol production. The authors suggested that overly structured day cares with multiple transitions overwhelm the children's abilities and lead to heightened stress over the course of the day. However, this is not necessarily maladaptive. We all need to learn how to manage stress during the course of our lives, so this early practice may not be harmful (Gunnar, Kryzer, Van Ryzin, & Phillips, 2010).

Low staff turnover is another important factor in quality of care. Infants need consistent caregiving in order to develop trust and secure attachments (Burchinal, Roberts, Nabors, & Bryant, 1996; Shonkoff & Phillips, 2000). Stability of care facilitates coordination between parents and child care providers, which may help protect against any negative effects of long hours of care (Ahnert & Lamb, 2003). Table 4 provides guidelines for selecting a high-quality child care facility.

The NICHD Study: Isolating Child Care Effects Because child care is an integral part of what Bronfenbrenner calls a child's bioecological system, it is difficult to measure its influence alone. The most comprehensive attempt to separate child care effects from the effects of other factors, such as family characteristics, the child's characteristics, and the care the child receives at home, is a study sponsored by the National Institute of Child Health and Human Development (NICHD).

TABLE 4 Checklist for Choosing a Good Child Care Facility

• Is the facility licensed? Does it meet minimum state standards for health, fire, and safety? (Many centers and home care facilities are not licensed or regulated.)
• Is the facility clean and safe? Does it have adequate indoor and outdoor space?
• Does the facility have small groups, a high adult-to-child ratio, and a stable, competent, highly involved staff?
• Are caregivers trained in child development?
• Are caregivers warm, affectionate, accepting, responsive, and sensitive? Are they authoritative but not too restrictive, and neither too controlling nor merely custodial?
• Does the program promote good health habits?
• Does it provide a balance between structured activities and free play? Are activities age appropriate?
• Do the children have access to educational toys and materials that stimulate mastery of cognitive and communicative skills at a child's own pace?
• Does the program nurture self-confidence, curiosity, creativity, and self-discipline?
• Does it encourage children to ask questions, solve problems, express feelings and opinions, and make decisions?
• Does it foster self-esteem, respect for others, and social skills?
• Does it help parents improve their child-rearing skills?
• Does it promote cooperation with public and private schools and the community?

Sources: American Academy of Pediatrics (AAP), 1986; Belsky, 1984; Clarke-Stewart, 1987; NICHD Early Child Care Research Network, 1996; Olds, 1989; Scarr, 1998.

This longitudinal study of 1,364 children and their families began in 1991 across the United States, shortly after the children's birth. The sample was socioeconomically, educationally, and ethnically diverse. Most infants entered nonmaternal care before 4 months and received, on average, 33 hours of care each week. Child care arrangements varied widely in type and quality. Researchers measured the children's social, emotional, cognitive, and physical development at frequent intervals from age 1 month through ninth grade.

The study showed that the amount and quality of care children received as well as the type and stability of care influenced specific aspects of development. Long days in child care were associated with stress for 3- and 4-year-olds (Belsky et al., 2007; NICHD Early Child Care Research Network, 2003). And the 15 percent of 2- and 3-year-olds who experienced more than one regular child care arrangement were at increased risk of behavior problems and were less likely to help and share (Morrissey, 2009). However, this was not the entire story. Although it was true that, overall, child care was associated with a small increase in externalizing behaviors, good child care quality and small peer group size were important positive influences.

Moreover, children in child care centers with low child-staff ratios, small group sizes, and trained, sensitive, responsive caregivers who provided positive interactions and language stimulation scored higher on tests of language comprehension, cognition, and readiness for school than did children in lower-quality care. Their mothers also reported fewer behavior problems (NICHD Early Child Care Research Network, 1999a, 2000, 2002). Children who had received higher-quality care before entering kindergarten had better vocabulary scores in fifth grade than children who had received lower-quality care (Belsky et al., 2007).

However, factors related to child care were less influential than family characteristics, such as income, the home environment, the amount of mental stimulation the mother provided, and the mother's sensitivity to her child. These characteristics strongly predicted developmental outcomes, regardless of how much time children spent in outside care (Belsky et al., 2007; Marshall, 2004; NICHD Early Child Care Research Network, 1998a, 1998b, 2000, 2003).

It should not be surprising that what look like effects of child care often may be related to family characteristics. After all, stable families with favorable home environments are more able and therefore more likely to place their children in high-quality care.

Did the effects of early child care persist across time? Follow-up studies conducted when the children were 15 years of age suggest that some may have, although effects were small. In general, higher-quality care was associated with increases in cognitive skills, academic achievement, and fewer problem behaviors. Unfortunately, child care also was related to increases in risk-taking behaviors and impulsivity. As before, the magnitude of positive effects was strongest for children in the highest-quality day cares. This suggests that future work should be on increasing day care quality from average to high, rather than from low quality to average (Vandell et al., 2010). Similar findings emerged from a large-scale meta-analyses of more than 69 studies spanning five decades. In this study, maternal employment during infancy and early childhood was associated with higher levels of academic achievement and lower levels of internalizing behaviors, and these findings were most striking for single mothers and for mothers on public assistance (Lucas-Thompson, Goldberg, & Prause, 2010).

checkpoint can **you . . .**

- Evaluate the impact of a mother's employment on her baby's well-being?
- List at least five criteria for good child care?
- Compare the impact of child care and of family characteristics on emotional, social, and cognitive development?

To sum up, a number of large-scale studies give high-quality child care good marks overall, especially for its impact on cognitive development and interaction with peers. Some observers say that the areas of concern the study pinpointed—stress levels in infants and toddlers and possible behavior problems related to amounts of care and multiple caregiving arrangements—might be counteracted by activities that enhance children's attachment to caregivers and peers, emphasize child-initiated learning and internalized motivation, and focus on group social development (Maccoby & Lewis, 2003).

Maltreatment: Abuse and Neglect

Although most parents are loving and nurturing, some cannot or will not take proper care of their children, and some deliberately harm them. *Maltreatment,* whether perpetrated by parents or others, is deliberate or avoidable endangerment of a child.

Maltreatment can take several specific forms, and the same child can be a victim of more than one type (USDHHS, Administration on Children, Youth and Families, 2008). These types include the following:

- **Physical abuse,** injury to the body through punching, beating, kicking, or burning
- **Neglect,** failure to meet a child's basic needs, such as food, clothing, medical care, protection, and supervision
- **Sexual abuse,** any sexual activity involving a child and an older person
- **Emotional maltreatment,** including rejection, terrorization, isolation, exploitation, degradation, ridicule, or failure to provide emotional support, love, and affection

physical abuse
Action taken deliberately to endanger another person, involving potential bodily injury.

neglect
Failure to meet a dependent's basic needs.

sexual abuse
Physically or psychologically harmful sexual activity or any sexual activity involving a child and an older person.

emotional maltreatment
Rejection, terrorization, isolation, exploitation, degradation, ridicule, or failure to provide emotional support, love, and affection; or other action or inaction that may cause behavioral, cognitive, emotional, or mental disorders.

State and local child protective service agencies received an estimated 3.4 million referrals for alleged maltreatment of 6.2 million children in 2011 and substantiated an estimated 681,000 cases. In what may be a glimmer of hope, this number represents a slight decrease over the previous 5 years. Almost 79 percent of children identified as maltreated were neglected, 17.6 percent were physically abused, and 9.1 percent were sexually abused. Younger children are more likely to be victims of abuse than older children, particularly those under the age of 3 years. An estimated

1,545 children died of maltreatment, and the actual number may well have been considerably higher (USDHHS, Administration on Children, Youth, and Families, 2012).

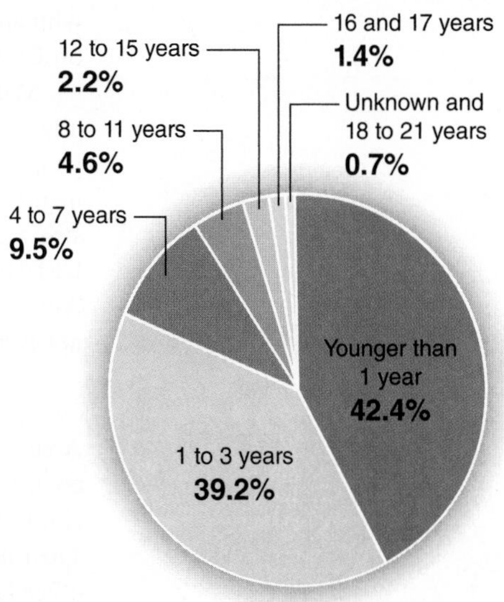

FIGURE 3
Deaths from Maltreatment by Age, 2011

More than three-quarters of fatalities are children younger than age 3.

Source: Child Welfare Information Gateway, 2013.

MALTREATMENT IN INFANCY AND TODDLERHOOD

Children are abused and neglected at all ages, but the highest rates of victimization and of death from maltreatment are for age 3 and younger (Child Welfare Information Gateway, 2008; USDHHS, Administration on Children, Youth and Families, 2012; Figure 3).

Babies need to form attachments to others as much as they need their basic survival needs taken care of. Babies who do not receive nurturance and affection or who are neglected sometimes suffer from **nonorganic failure to thrive,** slowed or arrested physical growth with no known medical cause, accompanied by poor developmental and emotional functioning. Symptoms may include lack of appropriate weight gain, irritability, excessive sleepiness and fatigue, avoidance of eye contact, lack of smiling or vocalizing, and delayed motor development. In short, they neither grow nor develop normally despite a lack of underlying physical or medical causes. Failure to thrive can result from a combination of inadequate nutrition, difficulties in breast-feeding, improper formula preparation or feeding techniques, and disturbed interactions with parents. Poverty is the greatest single risk factor for failure to thrive worldwide. Infants whose mother or primary caregiver is depressed, abuses alcohol or other substances, is under severe stress, or does not show warmth or affection toward the baby also are at heightened risk (Block, Krebs, the Committee on Child Abuse and Neglect, & the Committee on Nutrition, 2005; Lucile Packard Children's Hospital at Stanford, 2009).

nonorganic failure to thrive
Slowed or arrested physical growth with no known medical cause, accompanied by poor developmental and emotional functioning.

shaken baby syndrome
Form of maltreatment in which shaking an infant or toddler can cause brain damage, paralysis, or death.

Shaken baby syndrome is a form of maltreatment found mainly in children under 2 years old, most often in infants. Because the baby has weak neck muscles and a large, heavy head, shaking makes the brain bounce back and forth inside the skull. This causes bruising, bleeding, and swelling and can lead to permanent and severe brain damage, paralysis, and even death (AAP, 2000; National Institute of Neurological Disorders and Stroke [NINDS], 2006). The damage is typically worse if the baby is thrown into bed or against a wall. Head trauma is the leading cause of death in child abuse cases in the United States (Dowshen, Crowley, & Palusci, 2004). About 20 percent of shaken babies die within a few days. Survivors may be left with a wide range of disabilities from learning and behavioral disorders to neurological injuries, paralysis or blindness, or a permanent vegetative state (King, McKay, Sirnick, & The Canadian Shaken Baby Study Group, 2003; National Center on Shaken Baby Syndrome, 2000; NINDS, 2006).

CONTRIBUTING FACTORS: AN ECOLOGICAL VIEW

As Bronfenbrenner's bioecological theory would suggest, abuse and neglect are not caused by one thing. The causes of abuse are not in the individual, nor are they in the family, nor are they in the wider social and cultural environment. The causes are in *all* those places, and to understand why it happens, we need to consider *all* the contributing factors.

Characteristics of Abusive and Neglectful Parents and Families Oftentimes, abusive adults appear to be just like everyone else; there is no identifying behavior or characteristic that determines who will or will not abuse a child. In more than 8 out of 10 cases of maltreatment, the perpetrators are the child's parents, usually the mother; and 78.5 percent of these cases involve neglect. About 6 percent of perpetrators are other relatives, and 4.4 percent are unmarried partners of parents. Three out of 4 perpetrators who are family friends and neighbors commit sexual abuse (USDHHS, Administration on Children, Youth, and Families, 2012).

Maltreatment by parents is a symptom of extreme disturbance in child rearing, usually aggravated by other family problems, such as poverty, lack of education, alcoholism, depression, or antisocial behavior. A disproportionate number of abused and neglected children are in large, poor, or single-parent families, which tend to be under stress and to have trouble meeting children's needs (Sedlak & Broadhurst, 1996; USDHHS, 2004). Yet what pushes one parent over the edge, another may take in stride. Although many neglect cases occur in very poor families, most low-income parents do not neglect their children.

The likelihood that a child will be physically abused has less do with the child's own characteristics and more to do with the household environment (Jaffee et al., 2004). Abuse may begin when a parent who is already anxious, depressed, or hostile tries to control a child physically but loses self-control and ends up shaking or beating the child. Parents who abuse children tend to have marital problems and to fight physically. Their households are often disorganized, and they experience more stressful events than other families.

Abuse and neglect sometimes occur in the same families (USDHHS, Administration on Children, Youth, and Families, 2006). Such families tend to have no one to turn to in times of stress and no one to see what is happening (Dubowitz, 1999). Substance abuse is a factor in at least one-third of cases of abuse and neglect (USDHHS, 1999a). Sexual abuse often occurs along with other family disturbances such as physical abuse, emotional maltreatment, substance abuse, and family violence (Kellogg & the Committee on Child Abuse and Neglect, 2005).

Community Characteristics and Cultural Values Child abuse is a systems issue, and we cannot ignore the contribution of the local environment on maltreatment. What makes one low-income neighborhood a place where children are highly likely to be maltreated and another, matched for ethnic population and income levels, safer? In one inner-city Chicago neighborhood, the proportion of children who died from maltreatment (1 death for every 2,541 children) was about twice the proportion in another inner-city neighborhood. In the high-abuse community, criminal activity was rampant, and facilities for community programs were dreary. In the low-abuse neighborhood, people described their community as a poor but decent place to live. They painted a picture of a neighborhood with robust social support networks, well-known community services, and strong political leadership. In a community like this, maltreatment is less likely to occur (Garbarino & Kostelny, 1993).

Two cultural factors associated with child abuse are societal violence and physical punishment of children. In countries where violent crime is infrequent and children are rarely spanked, such as Japan, China, and Tahiti, child abuse is rare (Celis, 1990). In the United States, homicide, domestic violence, and rape are common, and many states still permit corporal punishment in schools. According to a representative sampling, more than 9 out of 10 parents of preschoolers and about half of parents of school-age children report using physical punishment at home (Straus & Stewart, 1999).

HELPING FAMILIES IN TROUBLE

State and local child protective service agencies investigate reports of maltreatment. After making a determination of maltreatment, they determine what steps, if any, need to be taken and marshal community resources to help. Agency staff may try to help the family resolve their problems or arrange for alternative care for children who cannot safely remain at home (USDHHS, Administration on Children, Youth, and Families, 2012). Services for children who have been abused and their parents include shelters, education in parenting skills, and therapy. However, availability of services is often limited (Burns et al., 2004).

When authorities remove children from their homes, the usual alternative is foster care. Foster care removes a child from immediate danger, but it is often unstable, further alienates the child from the family, and may turn out to be another abusive situation. Often a child's basic health and educational needs are not met (David and Lucile Packard Foundation, 2004; National Research Council [NRC], 1993b).

In part because of a scarcity of traditional foster homes and an increasing caseload, a growing proportion of placements are in kinship foster care, under the care of grandparents or other family members (Berrick, 1998; Geen, 2004). Although most foster children who leave the system are reunited with their families, about 28 percent reenter foster care within the next 10 years (Wulczyn, 2004). Children who have been in foster care are more likely than other children to become homeless, to commit crimes, and to become teenage mothers (David and Lucile Packard Foundation, 2004).

LONG-TERM EFFECTS OF MALTREATMENT

Consequences of maltreatment may be physical, emotional, cognitive, and social, and these types of consequences are often interrelated. A physical blow to a child's head can cause brain damage resulting in cognitive delays and emotional and social problems. Similarly, severe neglect or unloving parents can have traumatic effects on the developing brain (Fries et al., 2005). In one study, neglected children were more likely than either abused children or those who were not maltreated to misread emotional signals on faces (Sullivan, Bennett, Carpenter, & Lewis, 2007).

Long-term consequences of maltreatment may include poor physical, mental, and emotional health; impaired brain development (Glaser, 2000); cognitive, language, and academic difficulties; problems in attachment and social relationships (National Clearinghouse on Child Abuse and Neglect Information [NCCANI], 2004); memory problems (Brunson et al., 2005), and, in adolescence, heightened risks of poor academic achievement, delinquency, teenage pregnancy, alcohol and drug use, and suicide (Dube et al., 2001, 2003; Lansford et al., 2002; NCCANI, 2004). An estimated one-third of adults who were abused and neglected in childhood victimize their own children (NCCANI, 2004).

What are the long-term consequences of sexual abuse? In a study that followed 68 sexually abused children for 5 years, these children showed more disturbed behavior, had lower self-esteem, and were more depressed, anxious, or unhappy than a control group (Swanston, Tebbutt, O'Toole, & Oates, 1997). Sexually abused children may become sexually active at an early age (Fiscella, Kitzman, Cole, Sidora, & Olds, 1998). Adults who were sexually abused as children tend to be anxious, depressed, angry, or hostile; to mistrust people; to feel isolated and stigmatized; to be sexually maladjusted (Browne & Finkelhor, 1986); and to abuse alcohol or drugs (NRC, 1993b; USDHHS, 1999a).

Why do some abused children grow up to become antisocial or abusive, while others do not? One possible difference is genetic; some genotypes may be more resistant to trauma than others (Caspi et al., 2002; Jaffee et al., 2005). Research with rhesus monkeys suggests another answer. When baby monkeys endured high rates of maternal rejection and abuse in the 1st month of life, their brains produced less serotonin, a brain chemical. Low levels of serotonin are associated with anxiety, depression, and impulsive aggression in humans as well as in monkeys. Abused female monkeys who became abusive mothers had less serotonin in their brains than abused females who did not become abusive mothers. This finding suggests that treatment with drugs that increase serotonin levels early in life may prevent an abused child from growing up to abuse her own children (Maestripieri et al., 2006).

Many maltreated children show remarkable resilience. Optimism, self-esteem, intelligence, creativity, humor, and independence are protective factors, as is the social support of a caring adult (NCCANI, 2004). The topic of resilience is so important in development that it is researched extensively.

There are short-term risks as well. Even preschool children can experience episodes of clinical depression, although it may look a bit different than it does in adults. For example, depressed preschool children may have episodes of normal functioning interspersed with periods of sadness or irritation throughout the day.

checkpoint
can you . . .

- Define four types of child abuse and neglect?
- Discuss the incidence of maltreatment and explain why it is hard to measure?
- Identify contributing factors to maltreatment having to do with the family, the community, and the culture?
- Cite ways to prevent or stop maltreatment and help its victims?
- Give examples of long-term effects of child abuse and neglect and factors that promote resilience?

summary and key terms

Foundations of Psychosocial Development

- Emotional development is orderly; complex emotions seem to develop from earlier, simpler ones.
- Crying, smiling, and laughing are early signs of emotion. Other indices are facial expressions, motor activity, body language, and physiological changes.
- Brain development is closely linked with emotional development.
- Self-conscious and self-evaluative emotions arise after the development of self-awareness.

personality
emotions
social smiling
anticipatory smiling
self-conscious emotions
self-awareness
self-evaluative emotions
altruistic behavior
empathy
mirror neurons
social cognition

- Many children seem to fall into one of three categories of temperament: "easy," "difficult," and "slow-to-warm-up."
- Temperamental patterns appear to be largely inborn and to have a biological basis. They are generally stable but can be modified by experience.
- Goodness of fit between a child's temperament and environmental demands aids adjustment.
- Cross-cultural differences in temperament may reflect child-raising practices.

temperament
"easy" children
"difficult" children
"slow-to-warm-up" children
goodness of fit

- Child-raising practices and caregiving roles vary around the world.
- Infants have strong needs for maternal closeness, warmth, and responsiveness as well as physical care.
- Fatherhood is a social construction. Fathering roles differ in various cultures.
- Although significant gender differences typically do not appear until after infancy, U.S. fathers, especially, promote early gender-typing.

gender
gender-typing

Developmental Issues in Infancy

- According to Erikson, infants in the first 18 months are in the first stage of personality development, basic sense of trust versus mistrust. Sensitive, responsive, consistent caregiving is the key to successful resolution of this conflict.
- Research based on the Strange Situation has found four patterns of attachment: secure, avoidant, ambivalent (resistant), and disorganized-disoriented.
- Newer instruments measure attachment in natural settings and in cross-cultural research.
- Attachment patterns may depend on a baby's temperament as well as on the quality of parenting and may have long-term implications for development.
- Stranger anxiety and separation anxiety may arise during the second half of the 1st year and appear to be related to temperament and circumstances.
- A parent's memories of childhood attachment can influence his or her own child's attachment.
- Mutual regulation enables babies to play an active part in regulating their emotional states.
- A mother's depression, especially if severe or chronic, may have serious consequences for her infant's development.
- Social referencing has been observed by 12 months.

basic sense of trust versus mistrust
attachment
Strange Situation
secure attachment
avoidant attachment
ambivalent (resistant) attachment
disorganized-disoriented attachment
stranger anxiety
separation anxiety
mutual regulation
social referencing

Developmental Issues in Toddlerhood

- The sense of self arises between 4 and 10 months, as infants begin to perceive a difference between self and others and to experience a sense of agency and self-coherence.
- The self-concept builds on this perceptual sense of self and develops between 15 and 24 months with the emergence of self-awareness and self-recognition.
- Erikson's second stage concerns autonomy versus shame and doubt. In U.S. culture, negativism is a normal manifestation of the shift from external control to self-control.

- Socialization, which rests on internalization of societally approved standards, begins with the development of self-regulation.
- A precursor of conscience is committed compliance to a caregiver's demands; toddlers who show committed compliance tend to internalize adult rules more readily than those who show situational compliance. Children who show receptive cooperation can be active partners in their socialization.
- Parenting practices, a child's temperament, the quality of the parent-child relationship, and cultural and socioeconomic factors may affect the ease and success of socialization.

self-concept
autonomy versus shame and doubt
socialization
internalization
self-regulation
conscience
committed compliance
situational compliance
receptive cooperation

Contact with Other Children

- Sibling relationships play a distinct role in socialization; what children learn from relations with siblings carries over to relationships outside the home.
- Between ages 1½ and 3 years, children tend to show more interest in other children and an increasing understanding of how to deal with them.

Children of Working Parents

- In general, mothers' workforce participation during a child's first 3 years seems to have little impact on development, but cognitive development may suffer when a mother works 30 or more hours a week by her child's 9th month.
- Substitute child care varies in quality. The most important element in quality of care is the caregiver.
- Although quality, quantity, stability, and type of care influence psychosocial and cognitive development, the influence of family characteristics seems greater overall.

Maltreatment: Abuse and Neglect

- Forms of maltreatment are physical abuse, neglect, sexual abuse, and emotional maltreatment.
- Most victims of maltreatment are infants and toddlers. Some die due to failure to thrive. Others are victims of shaken baby syndrome.
- Characteristics of the abuser or neglecter, the family, the community, and the larger culture all contribute to child abuse and neglect.
- Maltreatment can interfere with physical, cognitive, emotional, and social development, and its effects can continue into adulthood. Still, many maltreated children show remarkable resilience.
- Preventing or stopping maltreatment may require multifaceted, coordinated community efforts.

physical abuse
neglect
sexual abuse
emotional maltreatment
nonorganic failure to thrive
shaken baby syndrome

part 3

EARLY CHILDHOOD

chapter 7

Physical and Cognitive Development in Early Childhood

outline

learning objectives

Identify physical changes in early childhood.

Describe three views of the cognitive changes that occur in early childhood.

Summarize how language develops in early childhood.

Evaluate different approaches to early childhood education.

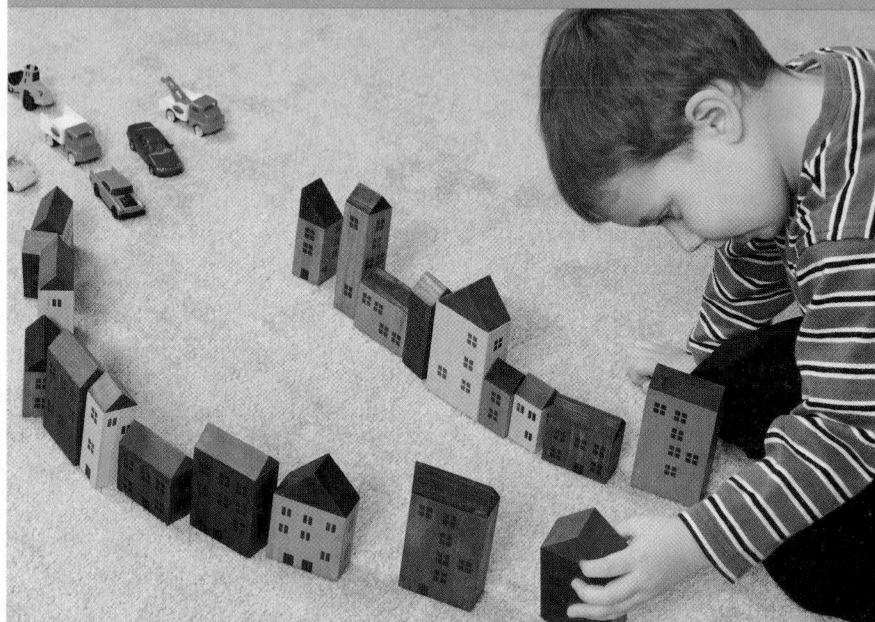

did you know?

- The leading cause of death in early childhood in the United States is accidents?
- The way parents talk with a child about a shared memory can affect how well the child will remember it?
- When children talk to themselves, they may be trying to solve a problem by thinking out loud?

In this chapter we look at physical and cognitive development from ages 3 to 6. Children grow more slowly than before, but make enormous progress in muscle development and coordination. We trace their advances in the abilities to think, speak, and remember and consider several health concerns. We end with a discussion of early childhood education.

Truly wonderful, the mind of a child is.

—Yoda, ***Star Wars Episode II, Attack of the Clones***

PHYSICAL DEVELOPMENT

Aspects of Physical Development

In early childhood, children slim down and shoot up. They need less sleep than before and are more likely to develop sleep problems. They improve in running, hopping, skipping, jumping, and throwing balls. They also become better at tying shoelaces, drawing with crayons, and pouring cereal; and they begin to show a preference for using either the right or left hand.

BODILY GROWTH AND CHANGE

Children grow rapidly between ages 3 and 6, but less quickly than before. At about 3, children normally begin to lose their babyish roundness and take on the slender, athletic appearance of childhood. As abdominal muscles develop, the toddler potbelly tightens. The trunk, arms, and legs grow longer. The head is still relatively large, but the other parts of the body continue to catch up as body proportions steadily become more adultlike.

studysmart

Patterns of Growth

The pencil mark on the wall shows Eve's height is 38 inches from the floor, and this "average" 3-year-old now weighs about 34 pounds. Her twin brother, Isaac, like most boys this age, is a little taller and heavier and has more muscle per pound of body weight, whereas Eve, like most girls, has more fatty tissue. Both boys and girls typically grow about 2 to 3 inches a year during early childhood and gain approximately 4 to 6 pounds annually (Table 1). Boys' slight edge in height and weight continues until the growth spurt of puberty.

Muscular and skeletal growth progresses, making children stronger. Cartilage turns to bone at a faster rate than before, and bones become harder, giving the child a firmer shape and protecting the internal organs. These changes, coordinated by the still-maturing brain and nervous system, promote the development of a wide range of

TABLE 1 Physical Growth, Ages 3 to 6 (50th percentile*)

	HEIGHT (INCHES)		WEIGHT (POUNDS)	
Age	Boys	Girls	Boys	Girls
3	38.7	38.6	33.8	34.2
4	42.1	41.4	39.8	38.6
5	45.1	44	46.3	43.3
6	47.6	46.6	52.2	48.8

*Fifty percent of children in each category are above this height or weight level, and 50 percent are below it.

Source: McDowell, Fryar, Ogden, & Flegal, 2008; data from *Anthropometric Reference Data for Children and Adults: United States, 2003–2006*, National Health Statistics Report, No. 10, October 22, 2008.

FIGURE 1

Typical Sleep Requirements in Childhood

Preschoolers get all or almost all their sleep in one long nighttime period. The number of hours of sleep steadily decreases throughout childhood, but individual children may need more or fewer hours than shown here.

Source: Ferber, 1985; similar data in Iglowstein, Jenni, Molinari, & Largo, 2003. Reprinted with the permission of Fireside, a Division of Simon & Schuster, Inc., from *Solve Your Child's Sleep Problems*, New Revised & Expanded by Richard Ferber, M.D.

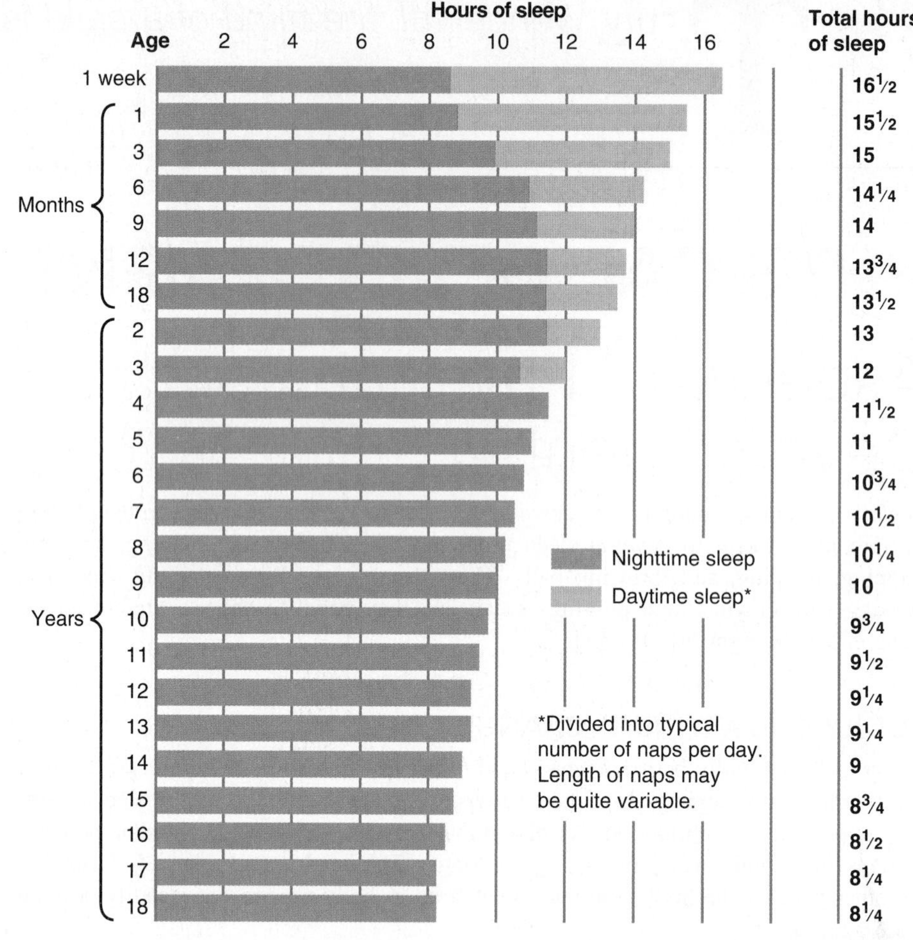

checkpoint can **you**...

- Describe typical physical changes between ages 3 and 6, and compare boys' and girls' growth?

It is best to try not to wake a sleepwalking child but rather to gently guide the child back to bed.

motor skills. The increased capacities of the respiratory and circulatory systems build physical stamina and, along with the developing immune system, keep children healthier.

SLEEP PATTERNS AND PROBLEMS

Sleep patterns change throughout the growing-up years (Figure 1), and early childhood has its own distinct rhythms. Most U.S. children average about 11 hours of sleep at night by age 5 and give up daytime naps (Hoban, 2004). In some other cultures the timing of sleep may vary. Among the Gusii of Kenya, the Javanese in Indonesia, and the Zuni in New Mexico, young children have no regular bedtime and are allowed to stay up until they are sleepy. Among the Canadian Hare, 3-year-olds don't take naps but are put to sleep right after dinner and sleep as long as they wish in the morning (Broude, 1995).

About 1 in 10 U.S. parents or caregivers of preschoolers say their child has a sleep problem, such as frequent night waking or talking while asleep (National Sleep Foundation, 2004). Sleep disturbances may be caused by accidental activation of the brain's motor control system (Hobson & Silvestri, 1999) or by incomplete arousal from a deep sleep (Hoban, 2004) or may be triggered by disordered breathing or restless leg movements (Guilleminault, Palombini, Pelayo, & Chervin, 2003). These disturbances tend to run in families (Hoban, 2004) and are often associated with separation anxiety (Petit, Touchette, Tremblay, Boivin, & Montplaisir, 2007).

TABLE 2 Encouraging Good Sleep Habits

HELPING CHILDREN GO TO SLEEP
• Establish a regular, unrushed bedtime routine—about 20 minutes of quiet activities, such as reading a story, singing lullabies, or having quiet conversation.
• Allow no scary or loud television shows.
• Avoid highly stimulating, active play before bedtime.
• Keep a small night-light on if it makes the child feel more comfortable.
• Don't feed or rock a child at bedtime.
• Stay calm but don't yield to requests for "just one more" story, one more drink of water, or one more bathroom trip.
• Offer rewards for good bedtime behavior, such as stickers on a chart or simple praise.
• Try sending the child to bed a little later. Sending a child to bed too early is a common reason for sleep problems.
HELPING CHILDREN GO BACK TO SLEEP
• If a child gets up during the night, take him or her back to bed. Speak calmly, but be pleasantly firm and consistent.
• After a nightmare, reassure a frightened child and occasionally check in on the child. If frightening dreams persist for more than 6 weeks, consult a doctor.
• After night terrors, do not wake the child. If the child wakes, don't ask any questions. Just let the child go back to sleep.
• Help the child get enough sleep on a regular schedule; overtired or stressed children are more prone to night terrors.
• Walk or carry a sleepwalking child back to bed. Childproof your home with gates at the top of stairs and at windows and with bells on the child's bedroom door, so as to know when she or he is out of bed.

Sources: American Academy of Child and Adolescent Psychiatry (AACAP), 1997; American Academy of Pediatrics (AAP), 1992; L. A. Adams & Rickert, 1989; Graziano & Mooney, 1982.

In most cases sleep disturbances are only occasional and usually are outgrown. (Table 2 gives suggestions for helping children go—or go back—to sleep.) Persistent sleep problems may indicate an emotional, physiological, or neurological condition that needs to be examined.

A child who experiences a *sleep* (or *night*) *terror* appears to awaken abruptly early in the night from a deep sleep in a state of agitation. The child may scream and sit up in bed, breathing rapidly and staring or thrashing about. Yet he is not really awake, quiets down quickly, and the next morning remembers nothing about the episode. Sleep terrors are quite common (Petit et al., 2007). They occur mostly between ages 3 and 13 (Laberge, Tremblay, Vitaro, & Montplaisir, 2000) and affect boys more often than girls (AACAP, 1997; Hobson & Silvestri, 1999).

Parents often view extended bed-wetting as deliberate, but generally it is not. It is a developmental issue, and no number of sticker charts or punishments will help a child outgrow enuresis until he or she is developmentally ready.

Walking and talking during sleep are fairly common in early childhood (Petit et al., 2007). Although sleepwalking itself is harmless, sleepwalkers may be in danger of hurting themselves. Still, it is best not to interrupt sleepwalking or night terrors, as interruptions may confuse and further frighten the child (Hoban, 2004; Vgontzas & Kales, 1999).

Nightmares are also common (Petit, Touchette, Tremblay, Boivin, & Montplaisir, 2007). They are often brought on by staying up too late, eating a heavy meal close to bedtime, or overexcitement, perhaps seeing a terrifying movie, or hearing a frightening bedtime story (Vgontzas & Kales, 1999). An occasional bad dream is no cause for alarm, but frequent or persistent nightmares may signal excessive stress (Hoban, 2004).

Most children stay dry, day and night, by ages 3 to 5; but **enuresis**—repeated, involuntary urination at night by children old enough to be expected to have bladder control—is not unusual. About 10 to 15 percent of 5-year-olds, more commonly boys, wet the bed regularly, perhaps while sleeping deeply. More than half outgrow the condition by age 8 without special help (Community Paediatrics Committee, 2005).

enuresis
Repeated urination in clothing or in bed.

Children (and their parents) need to be reassured that enuresis is common and not serious. The child is not to blame and should not be punished. Enuresis that persists beyond ages 8 to 10 may be a sign of poor self-concept or other psychological problems (Community Paediatrics Committee, 2005).

BRAIN DEVELOPMENT

During the first few years of life, brain development is rapid and profound. At about 3 years of age, the brain is approximately 90 percent of adult weight (Gabbard, 1996). From ages 3 to 6, the most rapid brain growth occurs in the frontal areas that regulate planning and goal setting. Synapses connecting neighboring neurons continue to form during this time, and the density of synapses in the prefrontal cortex peaks at age 4 (Lenroot & Giedd, 2006). In addition, myelin (a fatty substance that coats the axons of nerve fibers and accelerates neural conduction) continues to form, and the myelination of pathways for hearing is completed (Benes, Turtle, Khan, & Farol, 1994). By age 6, the brain has attained about 95 percent of its peak volume. Two normally functioning children of the same age, however, could have as much as a 50 percent difference in brain volume (Lenroot & Giedd, 2006). From ages 6 to 11, rapid brain growth occurs in areas that support associative thinking, language, and spatial relations (P. M. Thompson et al., 2000).

checkpoint
can **you**...

- Identify five common sleep problems and give recommendations for handling them?

The *corpus callosum* is a thick band of nerve fibers that connects both hemispheres of the brain and allows them to communicate with each other. It continues to be myelinized until the age of 15, allowing more rapid and efficient integration between hemispheres (Toga, Thompson, & Sowell, 2006) and improved coordination of the senses, attention and arousal, and speech and hearing (Lenroot & Giedd, 2006).

MOTOR SKILLS

Development of the sensory and motor areas of the cerebral cortex permits better coordination between what children want to do and what they can do. Preschool children make great advances in **gross motor skills,** such as running and jumping, which involve the large muscles (Table 3). Because their bones and muscles are stronger and their lung capacity is greater, they can run, jump, and climb farther and faster.

gross motor skills
Physical skills that involve the large muscles.

Children vary in adeptness, depending on their genetic endowment and their opportunities to learn and practice motor skills. Only 20 percent of 4-year-olds can throw a ball well, and only 30 percent can catch well (AAP Committee on Sports Medicine and Fitness, 1992). Most children under age 6 are generally not ready to take part in any organized sport. If the demands of a sport exceed the child's physical and motor capabilities, it can result in feelings of frustration on the part of the child (AAP Committee on Sports Medicine and Fitness & Committee on School Health, 2001). Physical development flourishes best in active, unstructured free play.

TABLE 3 Gross Motor Skills in Early Childhood

3-Year-Olds	4-Year-Olds	5-Year-Olds
Cannot turn or stop suddenly or quickly	Have more effective control of stopping, starting, and turning	Can start, turn, and stop effectively in games
Can jump a distance of 15 to 24 inches	Can jump a distance of 24 to 33 inches	Can make a running jump of 28 to 36 inches
Can ascend a stairway unaided, alternating feet	Can descend a long stairway alternating feet, if supported	Can descend a long stairway unaided, alternating feet
Can hop, using largely an irregular series of jumps with some variations added	Can hop four to six steps on one foot	Can easily hop a distance of 16 feet

Source: Corbin, 1973.

Children make significant advances in motor skills during the preschool years. As they develop physically, they are better able to make their bodies do what they want. Large-muscle development lets them ride a tricycle or kick a ball; increasing eye-hand coordination helps them use scissors or chopsticks. Children with disabilities can do many activities with the aid of special devices.

Fine motor skills, such as buttoning shirts and drawing pictures, involve eye-hand and small-muscle coordination. Gains in these skills allow young children to take more responsibility for their personal care.

As they develop motor skills, preschoolers continually merge abilities they already have with those they are acquiring to produce more complex capabilities. Such combinations of skills are known as **systems of action.**

fine motor skills
Physical skills that involve the small muscles and eye-hand coordination.

systems of action
Increasingly complex combinations of skills, which permit a wider or more precise range of movement and more control of the environment.

handedness
Preference for using a particular hand.

Handedness **Handedness,** the preference for using one hand over the other, is usually evident by about age 3. Because the left hemisphere of the brain, which controls the right side of the body, is usually dominant, most people favor their right side. In people whose brains are more functionally symmetrical, the right hemisphere tends to dominate, making them left-handed. Handedness is not always clear-cut; not everybody prefers one hand for every task. Boys are more likely to be left-handed than are girls. For every 100 left-handed girls there are 123 left-handed boys (Papadatou-Pastou, Martin, Munafo, & Jones, 2008).

Is handedness genetic or learned? Some researchers argue for genetic explanations, citing, for example, gene variants that make it more likely a child will be left-handed (Klar, 1996). Others argue that environmental influences are likely to be key given that such factors as low birth weight and difficult deliveries are associated with left-handedness (Alibeik & Angaji, 2010). One large study of more than 30,000 adults indicated that twins and triplets were more likely to be left-handed than singletons, suggesting that prenatal environment may be an influence (Vuoksimaa, Koskenvuo, Rose, & Kaprio, 2009). As further evidence, twins are generally not concordant for left-handedness, suggesting that genetics has less to do with handedness than environment (Vuoksimaa et al., 2009; Medland et al., 2009).

Graphical Representation/
Symbolic Function

Artistic Development In a landmark study of children's art, Rhoda Kellogg (1970) examined more than 1 million drawings by children, half of them under age 6. She discovered what she believed to be a universal progression of changes, reflecting maturation of the brain as well as of the muscles (Figure 2). She found that 2-year-olds *scribble*—not randomly but in patterns, such as vertical and zigzag lines. By age 3, children draw *shapes*—circles, squares, rectangles, triangles, crosses, and Xs—and then begin combining the shapes into more complex *designs*. The *pictorial* stage typically begins between ages 4 and 5. The switch from abstract form and design to depicting real objects marks a fundamental

FIGURE 2
Artistic Development in Early Childhood

There is a great difference between the very simple shapes shown in (a) and the detailed pictorial drawings in (e).

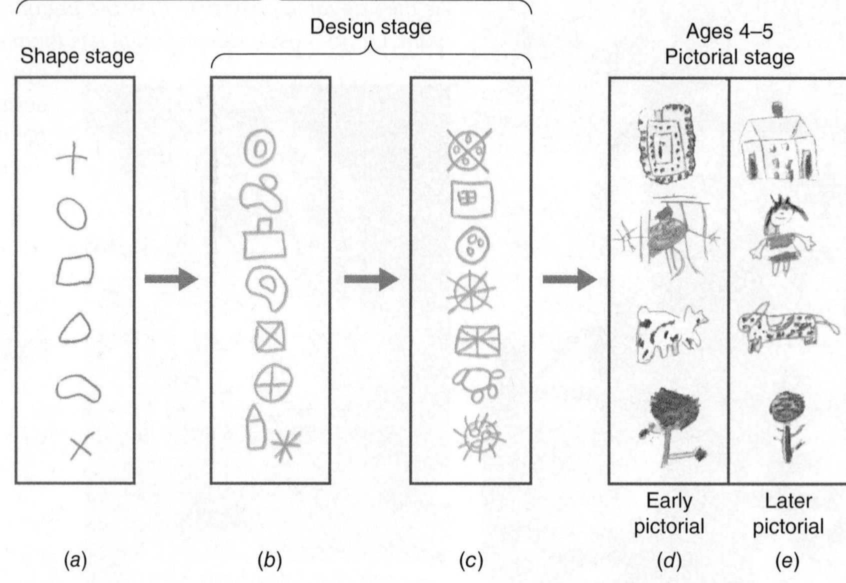

Source: Kellogg, 1970.

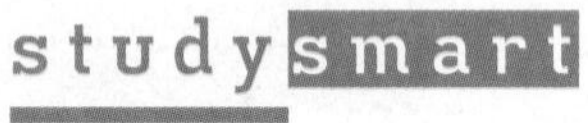

Artistic Development

change in the purpose of children's drawing, reflecting the cognitive development of representational ability.

In Kellogg's view, this developmental sequence occurs by processes internal to the child; the less adult involvement the better. By asking children what their drawings are meant to represent, Kellogg warned, adults may encourage greater pictorial accuracy but stifle the energy and freedom children typically show in their early efforts.

Drawings from children's early pictorial stage show energy and freedom, according to Kellogg; those from the later pictorial stage show care and accuracy. Why do you think these changes occur?

This individualistic model is dominant in the United States, but it is not the only model. Vygotsky, for example, saw the development of drawing skills as occurring in the context of social interactions (Braswell, 2006). Children pick up the features of adult drawing that are within their zone of proximal development (ZPD). Children also learn by looking at and talking about each other's drawings (Braswell, 2006).

Furthermore, the patterns Kellogg described in children's drawings are not universal. Cross-cultural variations exist, for example, in the way children make a person or an animal. Finally, Kellogg's view that adult intervention has a negative influence on children's drawing, although widely shared by many U.S. educators, is also culture-bound. Chinese parents, for example, provide art instruction or models for their children; and Chinese children tend to be more advanced artistically than U.S. children (Braswell, 2006).

checkpoint
can **you**...

- Summarize changes in the brain during childhood and discuss their possible effects?
- Distinguish between gross motor skills and fine motor skills, and give examples of each type that improve during early childhood?
- Tell how brain functioning is related to motor skills and handedness?
- Evaluate Kellogg's findings on young children's drawing skills in light of other research?

Health and Safety

Because of widespread immunization, many of what once were the major diseases of childhood are much less common in Western industrialized countries. In the developing world, however, such vaccine-preventable diseases as measles, pertussis (whooping cough), and tetanus still take a large toll. Even in technologically advanced societies, this is a less healthy time for some children than for others.

PREVENTING OBESITY

Obesity *is* a serious problem among U.S. preschoolers. In 2003–2006, more than 12 percent of 2- to 5-year-olds had a body mass index (BMI) at or above the 95th percentile for their age, and about 12 percent more were at or above the 85th percentile (Ogden, Carroll, & Flegal, 2008). The greatest increase in prevalence of overweight is among children in low-income families (Ritchie et al., 2001), cutting across all ethnic groups (AAP Committee on Nutrition, 2003).

Worldwide, an estimated 22 million children under age 5 are obese (Belizzi, 2002). As junk food spreads through the developing world, as many as 20 to 25 percent of 4-year-olds in some countries, such as Egypt, Morocco, and Zambia, are obese—a larger proportion than are malnourished.

A tendency toward obesity can be hereditary, but the main factors driving the obesity epidemic are environmental (AAP, 2004). Excessive weight gain hinges on caloric intake and lack of exercise (AAP Committee on Nutrition, 2003).

Prevention of obesity in the early years is critical (AAP Committee on Nutrition, 2003; Quattrin, Liu, Shaw, Shine, & Chiang, 2005). Overweight children tend to become obese adults (AAP Committee on Nutrition, 2003; Whitaker, Wright, Pepe, Seidel, & Dietz, 1997), and excess body mass is a threat to health. Thus early childhood is a good time to treat overweight, when a child's diet is still subject to parental influence or control (Quattrin et al., 2005).

Much television advertising aimed at young children fosters poor nutrition and weight gain by promoting fats and sugars rather than proteins and whole foods. How might parents counteract these pressures?

A key to preventing obesity may be to make sure older preschoolers are served appropriate portions—and not to force them to clean their plates (Rolls, Engell, & Birch, 2000). Data collected on approximately 8,550 preschool children suggest that three factors are critical in the prevention of obesity: (1) regularly eating an evening meal together as a family, (2) getting adequate amounts of sleep, and (3) watching less than 2 hours of television a day (Anderson & Whitaker, 2010). Too little physical activity is an important factor in obesity as well. In a longitudinal study of 8,158 U.S. children, each additional hour of TV watching above 2 hours increased the likelihood of obesity at age 30 by 7 percent, presumably because each additional hour watching television replaced an hour of physical activity (Viner & Cole, 2005).

An obese child might have trouble keeping up with peers—physically and socially. Obesity among young children has increased.

In 2008, Pixar films released Wall-E, an animated science fiction film in which humans were depicted as obese and sedentary, floating in a mechanized environment. Where do you think humans are headed if we do not change our ways? Could this view of humanity ever become a reality?

UNDERNUTRITION

Undernutrition is an underlying cause in more than half of all deaths before age 5 (Bryce, Boschi-Pinto, Shibuya, Black, & the WHO Child Health Epidemiology Reference Group, 2005). South Asia has the highest level of undernutrition; 33 percent of children under age 5 in South Asia are moderately or severely underweight as compared to 22 percent in West and Central Africa, 3 percent in Latin America and the Caribbean, and 15 percent of young children worldwide (UNICEF, 2013). Even in the United States, 17 percent of children under age 18 lived in food-insecure households in 2007 (Federal Interagency Forum on Child and Family Statistics, 2007). Box 1 has more information about food security.

In view of childhood undernutrition's apparent long-term effects on physical, social, and cognitive development, what can and should be done to combat it?

Because undernourished children usually live in extremely deprived circumstances, the specific effects of poor nutrition may be hard to determine. However, taken together, these deprivations may negatively affect not only growth and physical well-being but cognitive and psychosocial development

research in action

FOOD SECURITY

Most families in the United States are food secure—they have dependable access to enough food to support healthy living. Sadly, a growing number of families must deal with the challenges of insufficient food supplies for their households. Food insecurity is experienced when (1) the availability of future food is uncertain, (2) the amount and kind of food required for a healthy lifestyle is insufficient, or (3) individuals must resort to socially unacceptable ways to acquire food (NRC, 2006).

In a recent study, the U.S. Agriculture Department found that more than 36 million people suffered from "very low food security," a figure representing 12 percent of all Americans. The number in the worst-off category suffering the greatest hunger levels has risen 40 percent since 2000, and the prevalence of food insecurity for households with children is about twice that for households without children (Nord, Andrews, & Carlson, 2008).

Families with insufficient resources to provide food for the entire household usually try to protect children from disrupted eating and reduced food intake. Even so, 691,000 children went hungry in 2007, a 50 percent increase over 2006 (Nord et al., 2008). With the challenging economic conditions currently facing the United States, it is highly likely this figure will continue to rise.

Not surprisingly, food insecurity adversely affects children's health, cognitive abilities, and socioemotional well-being. The quality of food consumed is affected along with the quantity. As food budgets shrink, the first items to drop out of the diet are usually healthy foods such as whole grains, lean meats, dairy products, vegetables, and fruit. Energy-rich starches, sweets, and fats, which are often nutrient-poor, typically offer the cheapest way to fill hungry stomachs (Drewnowski & Eichelsdoerfer, 2009). Relative moderate levels of food insecurity and lower-quality diet have been linked to poor health, decreased learning capabilities, lowered motivation levels, and increased anxiety and depression.

Food security status of U.S. households, 2011

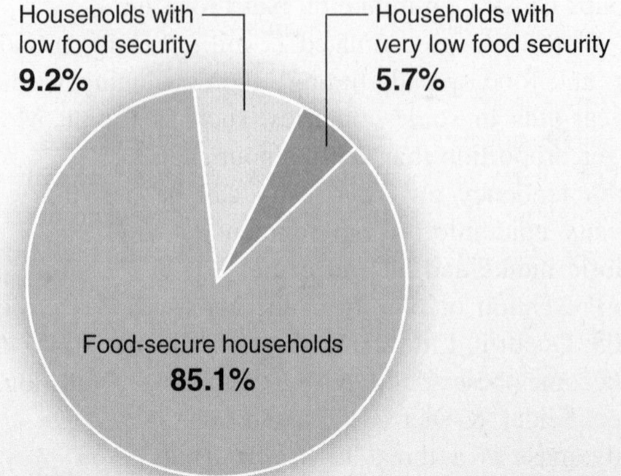

Food-insecure households include low and very low food security.
Source: Data from U.S. Department of Agriculture Economic Research Service, 2011.

In some developing nations, famine is widespread and severe malnutrition prevalent. In the United States the effects of hunger are generally less severe, in part because federal nutrition programs provide assistance to low-income families. What programs are you aware of? What are the benefits (and drawbacks) of these types of programs?

as well (Alaimo, Olson, & Frongillo, 2001). Moreover, effects of undernutrition may be long lasting. Among 1,559 children born on the island of Mauritius in a single year, those who were undernourished at age 3 had poorer verbal and spatial abilities, reading skills, scholastic ability, and neuropsychological performance than their peers at age 11 (Liu, Raine, Venables, Dalais, & Mednick, 2003).

Studies suggest effects of undernutrition on growth can be lessened with improved diet (Engle et al., 2007; Lewit & Kerrebrock, 1997), but the most effective treatments go beyond physical care. A longitudinal study (Grantham-McGregor, Powell, Walker, Chang, & Fletcher, 1994) followed two groups of Jamaican children who had been hospitalized for severe undernourishment in infancy or toddlerhood.

Health care paraprofessionals played with an experimental group in the hospital and, after discharge, visited them at home every week for 3 years, showing the mothers how to make toys and encouraging them to interact with their children. Three years after the program stopped, the experimental group's IQs were well above those of a control group who had received only standard medical care. Furthermore, the IQs of the experimental group remained higher than those of the control group as much as 14 years after leaving the hospital.

Early education may help counter the effects of undernourishment. In another Mauritian study, 3- to 5-year-olds received nutritional supplements and medical examinations and were placed in special preschools with small classes. At age 17, these children had lower rates of antisocial behavior and mental health problems than a control group (Raine, Mellingen, Lui, Venables, & Mednick, 2003).

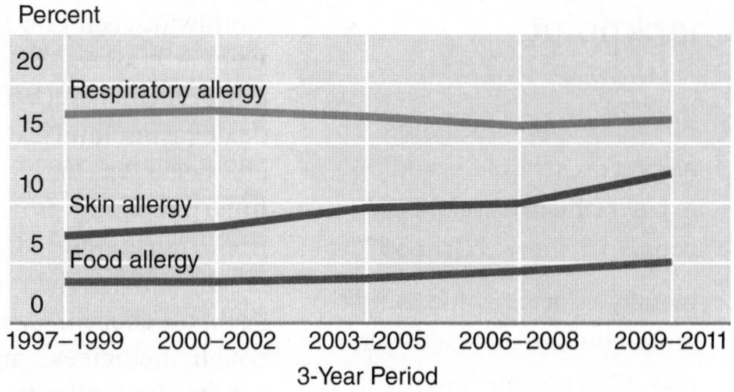

FIGURE 3

U.S. Children under Age 18 with a Reported Allergic Condition in Previous 12 Months, 1997–2011

Recent data show that skin and food allergies have increased among children birth to 17 years old.

Source: CDC/NCHS, Health Data Interactive, National Health Interview Survey.

FOOD ALLERGIES

A food allergy is an abnormal immune system response to a specific food. Reactions can range from tingling in the mouth and hives to more serious, life-threatening reactions like shortness of breath and even death. Ninety percent of food allergies can be attributed to eight foods; milk, eggs, peanuts, tree nuts, fish, soy, wheat, and shellfish (Boyce et al., 2010). Food allergies are more prevalent in children than adults, and most children will outgrow their allergies (Branum & Lukacs, 2008). In 2007, about 5 out of every 100 children suffered from some type of food allergy (Jackson, Howie, & Akinbami, 2013).

Research on children under age 18 has demonstrated an increase in the prevalence of skin and food allergies over the past 10 years. There is no clear pattern to this increase, and it exists equally for boys and girls and across different races and ethnicities (Branum & Lukacs, 2009; Jackson et al., 2013; Figure 3). Changes in diet, how foods are processed, and decreased vitamin D based upon less exposure to the sun have all been suggested as contributors to the increase in allergy rates. A theory that society is too clean and that children's immune systems are less mature because they are not exposed to enough dirt and germs has also been explored. Additionally, better awareness by doctors and parents might factor into the reported increases. Although possible explanations abound, not enough evidence exists to pinpoint a cause.

In 2010, ABC released a mini-series called Jamie Oliver's Food Revolution. *Many people were shocked at his demonstration of how far removed the children featured in his program were from real food. In a striking segment, first graders were unable to identify fresh tomatoes, cauliflower, mushrooms, eggplant, or potatoes.*

DEATHS AND ACCIDENTAL INJURIES

More than 7 out of 10 deaths of children under age 5 occur in poor, rural regions of sub-Saharan Africa and South Asia, where nutrition is inadequate, water is unsafe, and sanitary facilities are lacking (Black et al., 2003; Bryce et al., 2005). Box 2 discusses children's chances of surviving the first 5 years of life the world over.

In the United States, deaths in childhood are relatively few compared with deaths in adulthood, and accidents are the leading cause of death after infancy throughout childhood and adolescence (Heron et al., 2009). More than 800,000 children die

checkpoint
can **you** . . .

- Summarize obesity trends among preschoolers, and explain why overweight is a concern in early childhood?
- Identify effects related to undernutrition and factors that may influence the long-term outcome?
- Compare the health status of young children in developed and developing countries?
- Tell where and how young children are most likely to be injured?

worldwide each year from burns, drowning, car crashes, falls, poisonings, and other accidents (WHO, 2008). Most deaths from injuries among preschoolers occur in the home—often from fires, drowning in bathtubs, suffocation, poisoning, or falls (Nagaraja et al., 2005). Everyday medications, such as aspirin, acetaminophen, and cough medicines, and even vitamins can be dangerous to inquisitive young children.

The typical symbol used for poison now is "Mr. Yuk"—a grimacing, green cartoon face sticking his tongue out. This graphic was put into use when researchers and public health agencies realized the traditional skull and crossbones, rather than indicating danger to young children, intrigued and interested them in the contents of containers.

U.S. laws requiring the use of car seats, childproof caps on medicine bottles and other dangerous household products, regulation of product safety, mandatory helmets for bicycle riders, and safe storage of medicines have improved child safety.

HEALTH IN CONTEXT: ENVIRONMENTAL INFLUENCES

Why do some children have more illnesses or injuries than others? Some children seem genetically predisposed toward certain medical conditions. In addition, environmental factors play major roles.

Socioeconomic Status and Race/Ethnicity The lower a family's SES, the greater a child's risks of illness, injury, and death (Chen, Matthews, & Boyce, 2002). Poor children are more likely than other children to have chronic conditions and activity limitations, to lack health insurance, and to have unmet medical and dental needs. However, the general health of poor children has been improving; between 1984 and 2003, the percentage of poor children in very good or excellent health rose from 62 percent to 71 percent, as compared with 86 percent to 89 percent for nonpoor children over the same time period (Federal Interagency Forum on Child and Family Statistics, 2005, 2007).

Medicaid, a government program that provides medical assistance to eligible low-income persons and families, has been a safety net for many poor children since 1965. However, it has not reached millions of children whose families earn too much to qualify but too little to afford private insurance. In 1997 the federal government created the State Children's Health Insurance Program (SCHIP) to help states extend health care coverage to uninsured children in poor and near-poor families. Now known simply as CHIP, legislation passed in 2009 expanded the program and extended the coverage from 7 million to 11 million children (Centers for Medicare & Medicaid Services, 2009). Even with that expansion, there were about 9 million uninsured children in the United States (Devoe, Ray, Krois, & Carlson, 2010). The passage of the Affordable Care Act of 2010 may result in changes to these numbers. Among the provisions are the expansion of benefits to many previously ineligible poor families, elimination of pre-existing condition coverage exclusions, oral and vision coverage for children, and initiatives to prevent and address childhood obesity.

Access to quality health care is a particular problem among black and Latino children, especially those who are poor or near poor (Flores et al., 2005). According to the Children's Defense Fund (2008), 1 in 5 Latino children and 1 in 8 black children are uninsured compared with a rate of 1 in 13 for white children. Language and cultural barriers and the need for more Latino care providers may help explain some of these disparities (Flores et al., 2002). Even Asian American children, who tend to be in better health than non-Hispanic white children, are less likely to access and use health care, perhaps because of similar barriers (NCHS, 2005; Yu, Huang, & Singh, 2004).

window on the world

SURVIVING THE FIRST FIVE YEARS OF LIFE

The chances of a child's living to his or her fifth birthday have doubled during the past four decades, but survival depends to a great extent on where the child lives. Worldwide, more than 17 million children under age 5 died in 1970. Today this number has dropped to 8.8 million each year (UNICEF, 2009).

International efforts to improve child health focus on the first 5 years because nearly 90 percent of deaths of children under age 15 occur during those years. Fully 98 percent of child deaths occur in poor, rural regions of developing countries, where nutrition is inadequate, water is unsafe, and sanitary facilities are lacking (UNICEF, 2009).

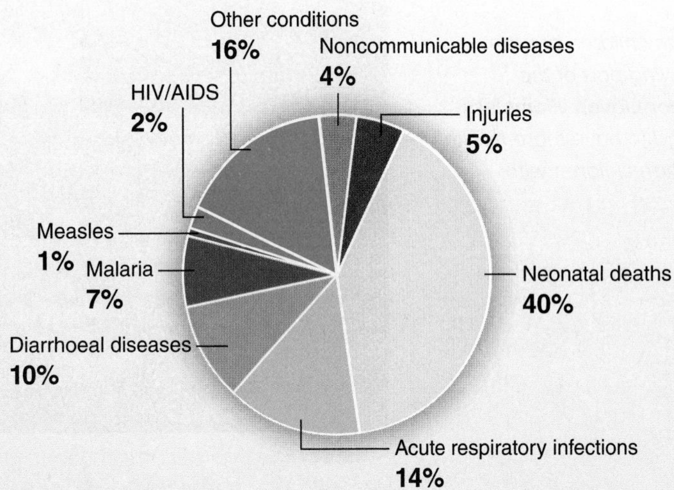

Major causes of death in children younger than 5 and in neonates (yearly average, 2010).
Source: WHO, 2010.

Worldwide, four major causes of death, accounting for 54 percent of deaths in children younger than age 5, are communicable diseases: pneumonia, diarrhea, malaria, and neonatal sepsis. In more than half of these deaths, undernutrition is an underlying cause (Bryce et al., 2005).

More advanced developing countries of the eastern Mediterranean region, Latin America, and Asia are experiencing a shift toward the pattern in more developed countries, where child deaths are most likely to be caused by complications of birth. More than 60 countries have reduced their mortality rate for children under age 5 by 50 percent (United Nations Childrens' Fund, 2007). In general, the strongest improvement has occurred in rich industrialized nations and in those developing countries where child mortality was already relatively low (WHO, 2003).

In some African countries, HIV/AIDS is responsible for as many as 60 percent of child deaths. Fourteen African countries saw *more* young children die in 2002 than in 1990. On the other hand, eight countries in the region, among them Gabon, Gambia, and Ghana, have reduced child mortality by more than 50 percent since 1970 (WHO, 2003).

In Latin America, the most dramatic reductions in child mortality have taken place in Chile, Costa Rica, and Cuba, where child deaths have dropped more than 80 percent since 1970. In contrast, Haitian children still die at a rate of 133 per 1,000, almost double the rate in Bolivia, which has the next worst mortality record in the Americas (WHO, 2003).

With the exception of China, India, Pakistan, and Nepal, boys are more likely to die than girls. In China, where families traditionally prefer boys, young girls have a 33 percent greater risk of dying—often, it has been reported, through abandonment, infanticide (Carmichael, 2004; Hudson & den Boer, 2004; Lee, 2004), or benign neglect.

What might be done to produce more rapid and more evenly distributed improvements in child mortality throughout the world?

Homelessness Homelessness results from complex circumstances that force people to choose between food, shelter, and other basic needs (National Coalition for the Homeless, 2009). Since the 1980s, as affordable rental housing has become scarce and poverty has spread, homelessness has increased dramatically in the United States. An

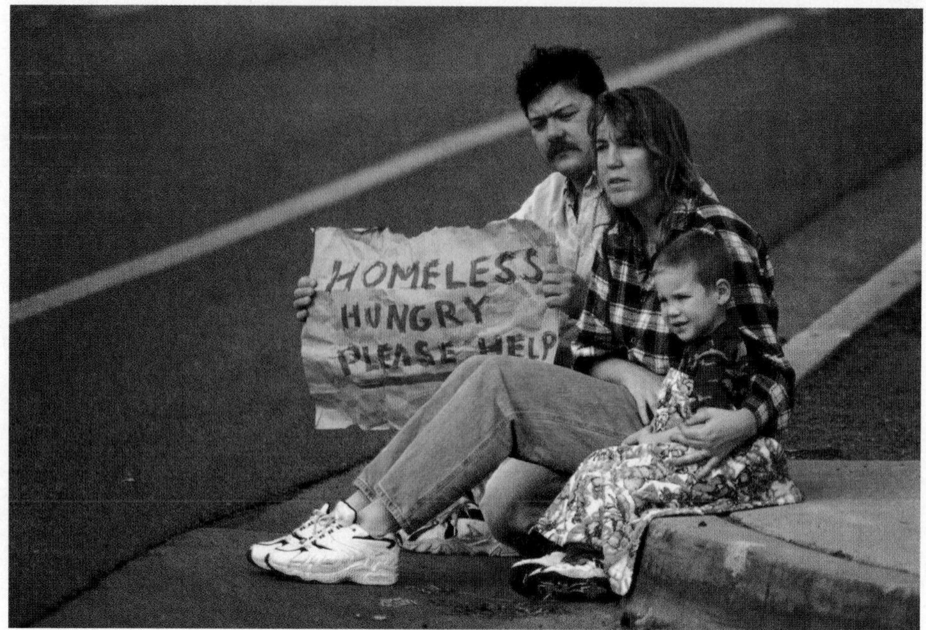

Families with children are the fastest-growing part of the homeless population. Homeless children tend to have more health problems than children with homes.

estimated 1.35 million children experience homelessness each year (National Coalition for the Homeless, 2009).

Families now make up 33 percent of the homeless population, and the proportion is higher in rural areas (National Coalition for the Homeless, 2009). In fact, with the economic downturn in the late 2000s, the number of homeless children has increased to about 1 in every 45 children (America's Youngest Outcasts, 2011). Many homeless families are headed by single mothers in their 20s (Park, Metraux, & Culhane, 2010).

Many homeless children spend their early years in unstable, insecure, and often unsanitary environments. They may be cut off from ready access to medical care and schooling. These children suffer more physical health problems than poor children who have homes, and they are more likely to die in infancy. Homeless children also tend to suffer from depression and anxiety and to have academic and behavior problems (CDF, 2004; National Coalition for the Homeless, 2006; Weinreb et al., 2002). In large cities that have provided safe housing for poor and homeless families in stable neighborhoods, the children's behavior and school performance improved greatly (CDF, 2004).

checkpoint
can **you** . . .

- Discuss environmental influences that endanger children's health and development?

Exposure to Smoking, Air Pollution, Pesticides, and Lead Parental smoking is a preventable cause of childhood illness and death. The potential damage caused by exposure to tobacco is greatest during the early years of life (DiFranza et al., 2004), when children's bodies are still developing. Children exposed to parental smoke are at increased risk of respiratory infections such as bronchitis and pneumonia, ear problems, worsened asthma, and slowed lung growth (Office on Smoking and Health, 2006).

Air pollution is associated with increased risks of death and of chronic respiratory disease. Environmental contaminants also may play a role in certain childhood cancers, neurological disorders, attention-deficit/hyperactivity disorder, and mental retardation (Goldman et al., 2004; Woodruff et al., 2004). In 2006, 60 percent of U.S. children up to age 17 lived in counties that failed to meet one or more national air quality standards (Federal Interagency Forum for Child and Family Statistics, 2008).

Children are more vulnerable than adults to chronic pesticide damage (Goldman et al., 2004). There is some, though not definitive, evidence that low-dose pesticide exposure may affect the developing brain (Weiss, Amler, & Amler, 2004). Pesticide exposure is greater among children in agricultural and inner-city families (Dilworth-Bart & Moore, 2006).

Children can get elevated concentrations of lead from contaminated food or water, from airborne industrial wastes, or from inhaling dust or playing with paint chips in places where there is peeling lead-based paint. Lead poisoning can interfere with cognitive development and can lead to irreversible neurological and behavioral problems (AAP Committee on Environmental Health, 2005; Federal Interagency Forum for Child and Family Statistics, 2007). Very high levels of blood lead concentration may cause headaches, abdominal pain, loss of appetite, agitation, or lethargy and eventually vomiting, stupor, and convulsions (AAP Committee on Environmental Health, 2005). Yet all these effects are completely preventable.

Children's median blood lead levels have dropped by 89 percent in the United States compared to 1976–1980 levels due to laws mandating removal of lead from gasoline and paints and reducing smokestack emissions (Federal Interagency Forum for Child and Family Statistics, 2005). Still, about 25 percent of U.S. children live in households with deteriorating lead paint (AAP Committee on Environmental Health, 2005).

COGNITIVE DEVELOPMENT

Piagetian Approach: The Preoperational Child

In Jean Piaget's theory, infants learn about the world via their senses and motor activity during the sensorimotor stage. Now, we turn our attention to Piaget's second stage, the **preoperational stage.** Lasting from approximately ages 2 to 7, it is characterized by an expansion in the use of symbolic thought. This is most clearly illustrated with the advent of our most profound system of symbolic representation—language. Although children show increasing facility with language, they are not yet ready to engage in logical mental operations. Let's look at some advances and some immature aspects of preoperational thought (Table 4 and Table 5) and at recent research, some of which challenges Piaget's conclusions.

preoperational stage
In Piaget's theory, the second major stage of cognitive development, in which symbolic thought expands but children cannot yet use logic.

ADVANCES OF PREOPERATIONAL THOUGHT

Advances in symbolic thought are accompanied by a growing understanding of space, causality, identities, categorization, and number. Some of these understandings have roots in infancy and toddlerhood; others begin to develop in early childhood but are not fully achieved until middle childhood.

The Symbolic Function "I want ice cream!" announces Kerstin, age 4, trudging indoors from the hot, dusty backyard. She has not seen or smelled or tasted anything that triggered this desire—no open freezer door, no television commercial, no bowl of sweet ice cream temptingly sitting on the counter waiting to be eaten. Rather, she has called up the concept from her memories.

Children with imaginary friends have better storytelling skills

Trionfi & Reese, 2009

Being able to think about something in the absence of sensory or motor cues

TABLE 4 Cognitive Advances during Early Childhood

Advance	Significance	Example
Use of symbols	Children do not need to be in sensorimotor contact with an object, person, or event in order to think about it.	Simon asks his mother about the elephants they saw on their trip to the circus several months earlier.
	Children can imagine that objects or people have properties other than those they actually have.	Rolf pretends that a slice of apple is a vacuum cleaner "vrooming" across the kitchen table.
Understanding of identities	Children are aware that superficial alterations do not change the nature of things.	Antonio knows that his teacher is dressed up as a pirate but is still his teacher underneath the costume.
Understanding of cause and effect	Children realize that events have causes.	Seeing a ball roll from behind a wall, Aneko looks behind the wall for the person who kicked the ball.
Ability to classify	Children organize objects, people, and events into meaningful categories.	Rosa sorts the pinecones she collected on a nature walk into two piles: "big" and "little."
Understanding of number	Children can count and deal with quantities.	Lindsay shares some candy with her friends, counting to make sure that each girl gets the same amount.
Empathy	Children become more able to imagine how others might feel.	Emilio tries to comfort his friend when he sees that his friend is upset.
Theory of mind	Children become more aware of mental activity and the functioning of the mind.	Blanca wants to save some cookies for herself, so she hides them from her brother in a pasta box. She knows her cookies will be safe there because her brother will not look in a place where he doesn't expect to find cookies.

TABLE 5 Immature Aspects of Preoperational Thought (According to Piaget)

Limitation	Description	Example
Centration: inability to decenter	Children focus on one aspect of a situation and neglect others.	Jacob teases his younger sister that he has more juice than she does because his juice box has been poured into a tall, skinny glass, but hers has been poured into a short, wide glass.
Irreversibility	Children fail to understand that some operations or actions can be reversed, restoring the original situation.	Jacob does not realize that the juice in each glass can be poured back into the juice box from which it came, contradicting his claim that he has more than his sister.
Focus on states rather than transformations	Children fail to understand the significance of the transformation between states.	In the conservation task, Jacob does not understand that transforming the shape of a liquid (pouring it from one container into another) does not change the amount.
Transductive reasoning	Children do not use deductive or inductive reasoning; instead they jump from one particular to another and see cause where none exists.	Luis was mean to his sister. Then she got sick. Luis concludes that he made his sister sick.
Egocentrism	Children assume everyone else thinks, perceives, and feels as they do.	Kara doesn't realize that she needs to turn a book around so that her father can see the picture she is asking him to explain to her. Instead, she holds the book directly in front of her, where only she can see it.
Animism	Children attribute life to objects not alive.	Amanda says that spring is trying to come but winter is saying, "I won't go! I won't go!"
Inability to distinguish appearance from reality	Children confuse what is real with outward appearance.	Courtney is confused by a sponge made to look like a rock. She states that it looks like a rock and it really is a rock.

characterizes the **symbolic function.** Children who have attained symbolic function can use symbols, or mental representations, such as words, numbers, or images to which a person has attached meaning. This is a vital achievement because without symbols people could not communicate verbally, make change, read maps, or treasure photos of distant loved ones. Having symbols for things helps children remember and think about them without having them physically present.

Preschool children show symbolic function in a variety of ways. For example, *deferred imitation,* in which children imitate an action at some point after having observed it, becomes more robust after 18 months. Deferred imitation is related to symbolic function because it requires the child to have kept a mental representation of an observed action. A child must pull a representation out of memory in order to repeat it. Another marker of symbolic function is **pretend play.** In pretend play, also called *fantasy play, dramatic play,* or *imaginary play,* children use an object to represent something else. For example, a child may hold up a remote control to her ear while pretending to talk on a telephone. The remote control is a symbol for the telephone she has seen her mother use. By far the most extensive use of the symbolic function is language. Language, at its heart, is a system of symbols. For example, the word "key" is a symbol for the class of objects used to open doors. When we see the emergence of language in young children, we have a wide and clear window into their increasing use of the symbolic function.

symbolic function
Piaget's term for ability to use mental representations (words, numbers, or images) to which a child has attached meaning.

pretend play
Play involving imaginary people and situations; also called *fantasy play, dramatic play,* or *imaginative play.*

transduction
Piaget's term for a preoperational child's tendency to mentally link particular phenomena, whether or not there is logically a causal relationship.

Understanding of Objects in Space In addition to their growing ability to use the symbolic function, children also begin to be able to understand the symbols that describe physical spaces, although this process is slow. It is not until at least age 3 that most children reliably grasp the relationships between pictures, maps, or scale models and the objects or spaces they represent. Older preschoolers can use simple maps, and they can transfer the spatial understanding gained from working with models to maps and vice versa (DeLoache, Miller, & Pierroutsakos, 1998; Sharon & DeLoache, 2003). In a series of experiments, preschoolers were asked to use a simple map to find or place an object at the corresponding location in a similarly shaped but much larger space. Ninety percent of 5-year-olds but only 60 percent of 4-year-olds were able to do so (Vasilyeva & Huttenlocher, 2004).

Understanding of Causality Piaget maintained that preoperational children cannot yet reason logically about cause and effect. Instead, he said, they reason by **transduction.** They mentally link two events, especially events close in time, whether or not there is logically a causal relationship. For example, Luis may think that his "bad" thoughts or behavior caused his own or his sister's illness or his parents' divorce.

Piaget was incorrect in believing that young children could not understand causality. When tested in situations that are appropriate to their overall level of cognitive development, young children do grasp cause and effect. In naturalistic observations of 2½- to 5-year-olds' everyday conversations with their parents, children showed flexible causal reasoning, appropriate to the subject. Types of explanations ranged from physical ("The scissors have to be clean so I can cut better") to social-conventional ("I have to stop now because you said to") (Hickling & Wellman, 2001).

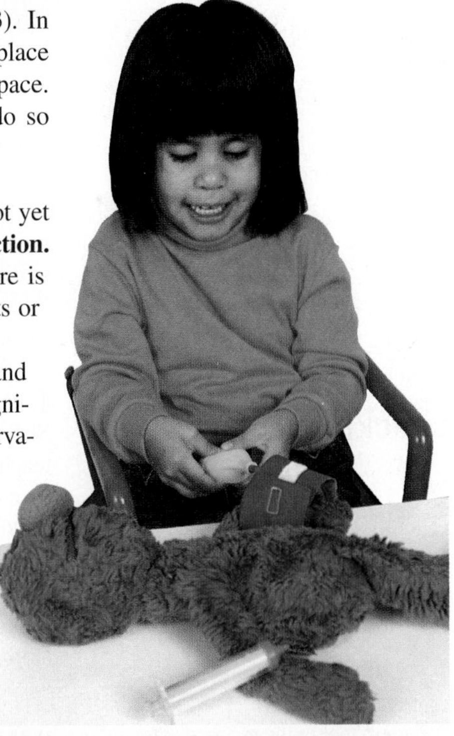
As Anna pretends to take Grover's blood pressure, she is showing a major cognitive achievement: deferred imitation, the ability to act out a behavior she observed some time before.

Understanding of Identities and Categorization The world becomes more orderly and predictable as preschool children develop a better understanding of *identities:* the concept that people and many things are basically the same even if they change in outward form, size, or appearance. For example, putting on a wig does not make a person a different person; rather, it is just a surface change in appearance. This understanding underlies the emerging self-concept, and many of the processes involved in understanding the identity of others are mirrored in the understanding of one's own identity.

Categorization, or classification, requires a child to identify similarities and differences. By age 4, many children can classify by two criteria, such as color and shape. Children use this ability to order many aspects of their lives, categorizing people as "good," "bad," "nice," "mean," and so forth.

One type of categorization is the ability to distinguish living from nonliving things. When Piaget asked young children whether the wind and the clouds were alive, their answers led him to think they were confused about what is alive and what is not. The tendency to attribute life to objects that are not alive is called **animism.** However, when later researchers questioned 3- and 4-year-olds about something more familiar to them—differences between a rock, a person, and a doll—the children showed they understood that people are alive and rocks and dolls are not (Gelman, Spelke, & Meck, 1983; Jipson & Gelman, 2007). In general, it appears that children attribute animism to items that share characteristics with living things: things that move, make sounds, or have lifelike features such as eyes.

animism
Tendency to attribute life to objects that are not alive.

Understanding of Number Research by Karen Wynn suggests that infants as young as 4½ months have a rudimentary concept of number. They seem to know that if one doll is added to another doll, there should be two dolls, not just one. Other research has found that *ordinality*—the concept of comparing quantities (*more* or *less, bigger* or *smaller*)—seems to begin at around 9 to 11 months (Brannon, 2002; Siegler, 1998). By age 4, most children have words for comparing quantities. They can say that one tree is *bigger* than another or one cup holds *more* juice than another. They also can solve simple numerical ordinality problems ("Megan picked six apples, and Joshua picked four apples; which child picked more?") (Byrnes & Fox, 1998).

study**smart**

Piaget's Preoperational Stages

Not until age 3½ or older do most children consistently apply the *cardinality* principle in counting (Sarnecka & Carey, 2007; Wynn, 1990). That is, when asked to count six items, children younger than 3½ tend to recite the number-names (one through six) but not to say how many items there are altogether (six). However, there is some evidence that children as young as 2½ use cardinality in practical situations, such as checking to make sure which plate has more cookies on it (Gelman, 2006). By age 5, most children can count to 20 or more and know the relative sizes of the numbers 1 through 10 (Siegler, 1998). Children intuitively devise strategies for adding by counting on their fingers or by using other objects (Naito & Miura, 2001).

study**smart**

Counting

By the time they enter elementary school, most children have developed basic *number sense* (Jordan, Kaplan, Oláh, & Locuniak, 2006). This basic level of number skills includes *counting, number knowledge* (ordinality), *number transformations* (simple addition and subtraction), *estimation* ("Is this group of dots more or less than 5?"), and recognition of *number patterns* (2 plus 2 equals 4, and so does 3 plus 1).

SES and preschool experience affect how rapidly children advance in math. By age 4, children from middle-income families have markedly better number skills than low-SES children, and their initial advantage tends to continue. Children whose preschool teachers do a lot of "math talk" (such as asking children to help count days on a calendar) tend to make greater gains (Klibanoff, Levine, Huttenlocher, Vasilyeva, & Hedges, 2006). Also, playing number board games with children enhances their numerical knowledge and can help low-income children catch up to their middle-income peers (Siegler, 2009). Numerical competence is important; how well children understand numbers in kindergarten predicts their academic performance in math through 3rd grade (Jordan, Kaplan, Raminemi, & Locuniak, 2009).

checkpoint
can **you**...

- **Summarize findings about preschool children's understanding of symbols, space, causality, identities, categorization, and number?**

IMMATURE ASPECTS OF PREOPERATIONAL THOUGHT

One of the main characteristics of preoperational thought is **centration:** the tendency to focus on one aspect of a situation and neglect others. According to Piaget, preschoolers come to illogical conclusions because they cannot **decenter**—think about several aspects of a situation at one time. Centration can limit young children's thinking about both social and physical relationships.

centration
In Piaget's theory, the tendency of preoperational children to focus on one aspect of a situation and neglect others.

decenter
In Piaget's terminology, to think simultaneously about several aspects of a situation.

Egocentrism **Egocentrism** is a form of centration. According to Piaget, young children center so much on their own point of view that they cannot take in another's. Three-year-olds are not as egocentric as newborn babies, but, said Piaget, they still think the universe centers on them. Egocentrism may help explain why young children sometimes have trouble separating reality from what goes on inside their own heads and why they may show confusion about what causes what. When Luis believes that his "bad thoughts" have made his sister sick, or that he caused his parents' marital troubles, he is thinking egocentrically.

To study egocentrism, Piaget designed the *three-mountain task* (Figure 4). A child sits facing a table that holds three large mounds. A doll is placed on a chair at the opposite side of the table. The investigator asks the child how the "mountains" would look to the doll. Piaget found that young children could only describe the mountains from their own perspective. Piaget saw this as evidence that preoperational children cannot imagine a different point of view (Piaget & Inhelder, 1967).

However, posing the problem in a different way can yield different results. In one study, a child was given instructions to select one object from a set of objects by an experimenter who could only see some of the objects. The researchers found that children as young as 3 were able to take the experimenter's perspective. For example, two of the objects were rubber ducks. In one condition, the experimenter could only see one of the rubber ducks. When the child heard the instructions to retrieve the rubber duck, the child more often selected the rubber duck that the experimenter could see even though the child could see both (Nilsen & Graham, 2009).

Why were these children able to take another person's point of view when those doing the mountain task were not? It may be because the "rubber duck" task calls for thinking in more familiar, less abstract, and less complex ways. Most children do not look at mountains and do not think about what other people might see when looking at one, but most preschoolers do know something about passing objects to others. Thus young children may show egocentrism primarily in situations beyond their immediate experience.

egocentrism
Piaget's term for inability to consider another person's point of view; a characteristic of young children's thought.

conservation
Piaget's term for awareness that two objects that are equal according to a certain measure remain equal in the face of perceptual alteration so long as nothing has been added to or taken away from either object.

irreversibility
Piaget's term for a preoperational child's failure to understand that an operation can go in two or more directions.

Conservation Tasks

Conservation Another classic example of centration is the failure to understand **conservation,** the fact that two things that are equal remain so if their appearance is altered, as long as nothing is added or taken away. Piaget found that children do not fully grasp this principle until the stage of concrete operations and that they develop different kinds of conservation at different ages. Table 6 shows how various dimensions of conservation have been tested.

In one type of conservation task, conservation of liquid, 5-year-old Justin is shown two identical clear glasses, each short and wide and each holding the same amount of water. Justin is asked, "Is the amount of water in the two glasses equal?" When he agrees, the researcher pours the water in one glass into a third glass, a tall, thin one. Justin is now asked, "Do both glasses contain the same amount of water? Or does one contain more? Why?" In early childhood—even after watching the water being poured out of one of the short, fat glasses into a tall, thin glass or even after pouring it himself—Justin will say that either the taller glass or the wider one contains more water.

Why do children make this error? Their responses are influenced by two immature aspects of thought: centration and **irreversibility.** Centration involves focusing on one dimension while ignoring the other. Preoperational children cannot consider height and width at the same time as

FIGURE 4
Piaget's Three-Mountain Task
A preoperational child is unable to describe the mountains from the doll's point of view—an indication of egocentrism, according to Piaget.

TABLE 6 Tests of Various Kinds of Conservation

Conservation Task	What Child Is Shown*	Transformation	Question for Child	Preoperational Child's Usual Answers
Number	Two equal, parallel rows of candies	Space the candies in one row farther apart.	"Are there the same number of candies in each row or does one row have more?"	"The longer one has more."
Length	Two parallel sticks of the same length	Move one stick to the right.	"Are both sticks the same size or is one longer?"	"The one on the right (or left) is longer."
Liquid	Two identical glasses holding equal amounts of liquid	Pour liquid from one glass into a taller, narrower glass.	"Do both glasses have the same amount of liquid or does one have more?"	"The taller one has more."
Matter (mass)	Two balls of clay of the same size	Roll one ball into a sausage shape.	"Do both pieces have the same amount of clay or does one have more?"	"The sausage has more."
Weight	Two balls of clay of the same weight	Roll one ball into a sausage shape.	"Do both weigh the same or does one weigh more?"	"The sausage weighs more."
Area	Two toy rabbits, two pieces of cardboard (representing grassy fields), with blocks or toys (representing barns on the fields); same number of "barns" on each board	Rearrange the blocks on one piece of board.	"Does each rabbit have the same amount of grass to eat or does one have more?"	"The one with the blocks close together has more to eat."
Volume	Two glasses of water with two equal-sized balls of clay in them	Roll one ball into a sausage shape.	"If we put the sausage back in the glass, will the water be the same height in each glass, or will one be higher?"	"The water in the glass with the sausage will be higher."

*Child then acknowledges that both items are equal.

checkpoint
can **you** . . .

- Tell how centration limits preoperational thought?
- Discuss research that challenges Piaget's views on egocentrism in early childhood?

they cannot *decenter,* or consider multiple attributes of an object or situation. In addition, children are limited by irreversibility: failure to understand that an action can go in two or more directions. Because their thinking is concrete, preoperational children cannot mentally reverse the action and realize that the original state of the water can be restored by pouring it back into the other glass, and thus it must be the same. Preoperational children commonly think as if they were watching a slide show with a series of static frames: they *focus on successive states,* said Piaget, and do not recognize the transformation from one state to another.

DO YOUNG CHILDREN HAVE THEORIES OF MIND?

theory of mind
Awareness and understanding of mental processes.

Theory of mind is the awareness of the broad range of human mental states—beliefs, intents, desires, dreams, and so forth—and the understanding that others have their own distinctive beliefs, desires, and intentions. Having a theory of mind allows us to understand and predict the behavior of others and makes the social world understandable.

> *We can see how important theory of mind is when we see what happens when it is broken, as in autism. Researchers believe that the failure to adequately develop theory of mind is one of the fundamental deficits found in this disorder.*
>
> Baron-Cohen, Leslie, & Frith, 1985

Piaget (1929) was the first scholar to investigate children's theory of mind. He asked children such questions as "Where do dreams come from?" and "What do you think with?" On the basis of the answers, he concluded that children younger than 6 cannot distinguish between thoughts or dreams and real physical entities and have no theory of mind. However, more recent research indicates that between ages 2 and 5, children's knowledge about mental processes grows dramatically (Flavell et al., 1995; Wellman, Cross, & Watson, 2001).

Again, methodology seems to have made the difference. Piaget's questions were abstract, and he expected children to be able to put their understanding into words. Contemporary researchers observe children in everyday activities or give them concrete examples. In this way, we have learned, for example, that 3-year-olds can tell the difference between a boy who has a cookie and a boy who is thinking about a cookie, and they know which boy can touch, share, and eat it (Astington, 1993). Let's look at several aspects of theory of mind.

Knowledge about Thinking and Mental States Between ages 3 and 5, children come to understand that thinking goes on inside the mind; that it can deal with either real or imaginary things; that someone can be thinking of one thing while doing or looking at something else; that a person whose eyes and ears are covered can think about objects; that someone who looks pensive is probably thinking; and that thinking is different from seeing, talking, touching, and knowing (Flavell, 2000; Flavell et al., 1995).

However, preschoolers generally believe that mental activity starts and stops. Not until middle childhood do children know that the mind is continuously active (Flavell, 1993, 2000; Flavell et al., 1995). Preschoolers also have little or no awareness that they or other people think in words, or "talk to themselves in their heads," or that they think while they are looking, listening, reading, or talking (Flavell, Green, Flavell, & Grossman, 1997). Preschoolers typically believe they can dream about anything they wish. Not until about age 11, however, do children fully realize that they cannot control their dreams (Woolley & Boerger, 2002).

The recognition that others have mental states accompanies the decline of egocentrism and the development of empathy (Povinelli & Giambrone, 2001). By age 3, children realize that if someone gets what he wants he will be happy, and if not, he will be sad (Wellman & Woolley, 1990). Four-year-olds begin to understand that people have differing beliefs about the world—true or mistaken—and that these beliefs affect their actions.

False Beliefs and Deception The understanding that people can hold false beliefs flows from the realization that people hold mental representations of reality, which can sometimes be wrong. Although infants as young as 13 months can illustrate some understanding of the mental states of others if asked in an appropriate manner (Scott & Baillargeon, 2009), it is not until about 4 years of age that children consistently pass false belief tasks (Flavell et al., 1995).

Three-year-olds' failure to recognize false beliefs may stem from egocentric thinking. At that age, children tend to believe that everyone else knows what they know and believes what they do, and they have trouble understanding that their own beliefs can be false (Lillard & Curenton, 1999). Four-year-olds understand that people who see or hear different versions of the same event may come away with different beliefs. Not until about age 6, however, do children realize that two people who see or hear the *same* thing may interpret it differently (Pillow & Henrichon, 1996).

Deception is an effort to plant a false belief in someone else's mind. Some studies have found that children become capable of deception as early as age 2 or 3; others, at 4 or 5. The difference may have to do with the means of deception children are expected to use. In a series of experiments, 3-year-olds were asked whether they would like to play a trick on an experimenter by giving a false clue about which of two boxes a ball had been hidden in. The children were better able to carry out the deception when asked to put a picture of the ball on the wrong box, or to point to that box with an arrow, than when they pointed with their fingers, which children this age are accustomed to doing truthfully (Carlson, Moses, & Hix, 1998).

Distinguishing between Appearance and Reality According to Piaget, not until about age 5 or 6 do children begin to understand the distinction between what *seems* to be and what *is*. Much research bears him out, though some studies have found this ability beginning to emerge before age 4.

In one classic series of experiments (Flavell, Green, & Flavell, 1986), 3-year-olds seemed to confuse appearance and reality in a variety of tests. For example, when the children put on special sunglasses that made milk look green, they said the milk *was* green, even though they had just seen white milk. However, 3-year-olds' difficulty in distinguishing appearance from reality may itself be more apparent than real. When children were asked questions about the uses of such objects as a candle wrapped like a crayon, only 3 out of 10 answered correctly. But when asked to respond with actions rather than words ("I want a candle to put on a birthday cake"), 9 out of 10 handed the experimenter the crayonlike candle (Sapp, Lee, & Muir, 2000).

Distinguishing between Fantasy and Reality Sometime between 18 months and 3 years, children learn to distinguish between real and imagined events. Three-year-olds know the difference between a real dog and a dog in a dream, and between something invisible (such as air) and something imaginary. They can pretend and can tell when someone else is pretending (Flavell, 2000). By 3, and, in some cases, by age 2, they know that pretense is intentional; they can tell the difference between trying to do something and pretending to do the same thing (Rakoczy, Tomasello, & Striano, 2004).

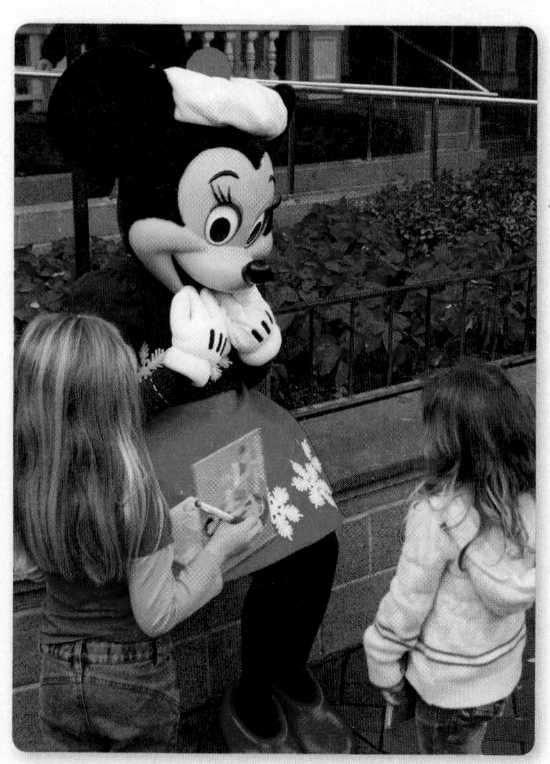

Is it really Minnie Mouse? These children aren't quite sure. The ability to distinguish fantasy from reality develops by age 3, but 4- to-6-year-olds may imagine that a fantasy figure is real.

Magical thinking in children ages 3 and older does *not* seem to stem from confusion between fantasy and reality. Often magical thinking is a way to explain events that do not seem to have obvious realistic explanations (usually because children lack knowledge about them), or simply to indulge in the pleasures of pretending—as with a belief in imaginary companions. Children, like adults, generally are aware of the magical nature of fantasy figures but are more willing to entertain the possibility that they may be real (Woolley, 1997). Magical thinking tends to decline near the end of the preschool period (Woolley, Phelps, Davis, & Mandell, 1999).

Influences on Individual Differences in Theory-of-Mind Development Some children develop theory-of-mind abilities earlier than others. In part, this development reflects brain maturation and general improvements in cognition. What other influences explain these individual differences?

Infant social attention has been closely linked to theory of mind development (Wellman & Liu, 2004). In a recent study, 45 children were evaluated as infants and then again as 4-year-olds. Measures of infant social attention significantly predicted later theory of mind. The fact that those infants who were better at paying attention later showed more facility with theory of mind tasks suggests there is continuity in social cognition and that skills build on each other over time (Wellman, Lopez-Duran, LaBounty, & Hamilton, 2008).

Social competence and language development also contribute to an understanding of thoughts and emotions (Cassidy, Werner, Rourke, Zubernis, & Balaraman, 2003). Children whose teachers and peers rate them high on social skills are better able to recognize false beliefs, to distinguish between real and pretend emotion, and to take another person's point of view. These children also tend to have strong language skills (Cassidy et al., 2003; Watson, Nixon, Wilson, & Capage, 1999). The *kind* of talk a young child hears at home may affect the child's understanding of mental states. A mother's reference to others' thoughts and knowledge is a consistent predictor of a child's later mental state language. Empathy usually arises earlier in children whose families talk a lot about feelings and causality (Dunn, 1991, 2006; Dunn, Brown, Slomkowski, Tesla, & Youngblade, 1991).

Young infants are extremely interested in other people's eyes. What relationship might this have to theory of mind? What type of social information does eye gazing convey?

Families that encourage pretend play stimulate the development of theory-of-mind skills. As children play roles, they try to assume others' perspectives. Talking with children about how the characters in a story feel helps them develop social understanding (Lillard & Curenton, 1999).

Bilingual children, who speak and hear more than one language at home, do somewhat better than children with only one language on certain theory-of-mind tasks (Bialystok & Senman, 2004; Goetz, 2003). Bilingual children know that an object or idea can be represented linguistically in more than one way, and this knowledge may help them see that different people may have different perspectives. Bilingual children also recognize the need to match their language to that of their partner, and this recognition may make them more aware of others' mental states. Finally, bilingual children tend to have better attentional control, which may enable them to focus on what is true or real rather than on what only seems to be so (Bialystok & Senman, 2004; Goetz, 2003).

Brain development is also necessary for theory of mind. In particular, neural activity in the prefrontal cortex has been identified as important. In one study, children who were able to correctly reason about the mental states of characters in animated scenarios showed brain wave activation in their left frontal cortex, much as the adults in the study did. However, those children who were not able to correctly pass the task did not (Liu, Sabbagh, Gehring, & Wellman, 2009).

An incomplete or ineffective theory of mind may be a sign of a cognitive or developmental impairment. Individuals with this type of impairment have a hard time understanding things from any other perspective than their own. Thus they have difficulty determining the intentions of others, lack understanding of how their behavior affects others, and have a difficult time with social reciprocity. Research suggests that children with autism do not employ a theory of mind and that these children have particular difficulties with tasks requiring them to understand another person's mental state (Baron-Cohen, Leslie, & Frith, 1985).

checkpoint can you . . .

- Give examples of research that challenges Piaget's views on young children's cognitive limitations?
- Describe changes between ages 3 and 6 in children's knowledge about the way their minds work, and identify influences on that development?

Information-Processing Approach: Memory Development

During early childhood, children improve in attention and in the speed and efficiency with which they process information; and they begin to form long-lasting memories. Still, young children do not remember as well as older ones. For one thing, young children tend to focus on exact details of an event, which are easily forgotten, whereas older children and adults generally concentrate on the gist of what happened. Also, young children, because of their lesser knowledge of the world, may fail to notice important aspects of a situation, such as when and where it occurred, which could help jog their memory.

BASIC PROCESSES AND CAPACITIES

encoding
Process by which information is prepared for long-term storage and later retrieval.

storage
Retention of information in memory for future use.

retrieval
Process by which information is accessed or recalled from memory storage.

sensory memory
Initial, brief, temporary storage of sensory information.

working memory
Short-term storage of information being actively processed.

executive function
Conscious control of thoughts, emotions, and actions to accomplish goals or solve problems.

long-term memory
Storage of virtually unlimited capacity that holds information for long periods.

central executive
In Baddeley's model, element of working memory that controls the processing of information.

Information-processing theorists focus on the processes that affect cognition. According to this view, memory can be described as a filing system that has three steps, or processes: *encoding, storage,* and *retrieval.* **Encoding** is like putting information in a folder to be filed in memory; it attaches a "code" or "label" to the information so it will be easier to find when needed. For example, if you were asked to list "things that are red," you might list apples, stop signs, and hearts. Presumably, all these items were tagged in memory with the concept "red" when they were originally encoded. This code is what now enables you to access these seemingly disparate objects. **Storage** is putting the folder away in the filing cabinet. It is where the information is kept. When the information is needed, you access storage, and through the process of **retrieval,** you search for the file and take it out.

The way the brain stores information is believed to be universal, although the efficiency of the system varies from one person to another (Siegler, 1998). Information processing models depict the brain as containing three types of storage: *sensory memory, working memory,* and *long-term memory.* **Sensory memory** is a temporary storehouse for incoming sensory information. For example, the light trail that is visible when a sparkler is moved quickly on a dark night illustrates visual sensory memory. Sensory memory shows little change from infancy on (Siegler, 1998). However, without processing (encoding), sensory memories fade quickly.

Information being encoded or retrieved is kept in **working memory,** a short-term storehouse for information a person is actively working on, trying to understand, remember, or think about. Brain imaging studies have found that working memory is located partly in the prefrontal cortex, the large portion of the frontal lobe directly behind the forehead (Nelson et al., 2000). Working memory has a limited capacity. Researchers can assess the capacity of working memory by asking children to recall a series of scrambled digits (for example, 2-8-3-7-5-1 if they heard 1-5-7-3-8-2). The capacity of working memory—the number of digits a child can recall—increases rapidly (Cowan, Nugent, Elliott, Ponomarev, & Saults, 1999). At age 4, children typically remember only two digits; at 12 they typically remember six (Zelazo, Müller, Frye, & Marcovitch, 2003). The growth of working memory may permit the development of **executive function,** the conscious control of thoughts, emotions, and actions to accomplish goals or to solve problems. Executive function enables children to plan and carry out goal-directed mental activity. It probably emerges around the end of an infant's 1st year and develops in spurts with age. Changes in executive function between ages 2 and 5 enable children to make up and use complex rules for solving problems (Zelazo et al., 2003; Zelazo & Müller, 2002).

> *By the age of 3 or 4, children differentiate between fictional cartoon worlds. So, if Barney were to show up on Sesame Street, they would be extremely surprised.*
>
> Skolnick Weisberg & Bloom, 2009

Long-term memory is a storehouse of virtually unlimited capacity that holds information for long periods of time. Presumably, this information is transferred from working memory if it is deemed important enough. But who decides its importance? According to a widely used model, a **central executive** controls processing operations in working memory (Baddeley, 1998, 2001). The central executive orders information encoded for transfer to long-term memory. The central executive also retrieves information from long-term memory for further processing. The central executive can temporarily expand the capacity of working memory by moving information into two separate subsidiary systems while the central executive is occupied with other tasks. One of these subsidiary systems holds verbal information (as in the digit task), and the other holds visual-spatial images.

RECOGNITION AND RECALL

recall
Ability to reproduce material from memory.

recognition
Ability to identify a previously encountered stimulus.

Recognition and *recall* are types of retrieval. **Recall** is the ability to reproduce knowledge from memory (for example, describing a lost mitten at the lost-and-found desk). **Recognition** is the ability to identify something encountered before (for example, to pick out a missing mitten from a lost-and-found box). Preschool children, like all age groups, do better on recognition than on recall, but both abilities improve with age. The more familiar children are with an item, the better they can recall it.

Young children often fail to use strategies for remembering—even strategies they already know—unless reminded. This tendency not to generate efficient strategies may reflect lack of awareness of how a strategy would be useful (Sophian, Wood, & Vong, 1995). Older children tend to become more efficient in the spontaneous use of memory strategies.

checkpoint can **you . . .**

- Identify three processes and three storehouses of memory?
- Compare recognition and recall?

FORMING AND RETAINING CHILDHOOD MEMORIES

Memory of experiences in early childhood is rarely deliberate: young children simply remember events that made a strong impression. Most of these early conscious memories seem to be short-lived. One investigator has distinguished three types of childhood memory that serve different functions: *generic, episodic,* and *autobiographical* (Nelson, 1993).

generic memory
Memory that produces scripts of familiar routines to guide behavior.

script
General remembered outline of a familiar, repeated event, used to guide behavior.

episodic memory
Long-term memory of specific experiences or events, linked to time and place.

autobiographical memory
Memory of specific events in one's life.

Generic memory, which begins at about age 2, produces a **script,** or general outline of a familiar, repeated event, such as riding the bus to preschool or having lunch at Grandma's house. It helps a child know what to expect and how to act.

Episodic memory refers to awareness of having experienced a particular event at a specific time and place. Given a young child's limited memory capacity, episodic memories are temporary. Unless they recur several times (in which case they are transferred to generic memory), they last for a few weeks or months and then fade (Nelson, 2005). For example, getting vaccinated at the pediatrician's office might originally be an episodic memory—a child might remember the particular event. Over time and repeated visits, a child might form a generic memory of the doctor's office being a place where shots are administered.

Autobiographical memory, a type of episodic memory, refers to memories of distinctive experiences that form a person's life history. Not everything in episodic memory becomes part of autobiographical memory—only those memories that have a special, personal meaning to the child (Fivush & Nelson, 2004). Autobiographical memory generally emerges between ages 3 and 4 (Nelson, 2005).

A suggested explanation for the relatively slow arrival of autobiographical memory is that children cannot store in memory events pertaining to their own lives until they develop a concept of self (Howe, 2003; Nelson & Fivush, 2004). Also critical is the emergence of language, which enables children to share memories and organize them into personal narratives (Fivush & Nelson, 2004; Nelson & Fivush, 2004; Nelson, 2005).

"Remember when we all played in the snow together last winter?" Young children are most likely to remember unique events and may recall details from a special trip for a year or longer.

Influences on Memory Retention Why do some memories last longer and remain clearer than others? One important factor is the uniqueness of the event. When events are rare or unusual, children seem to remember them better. In addition, events with emotional impact seem to be remembered better (Powell & Thomson, 1996), although some evidence suggests attention is focused on central aspects of the situation rather than on peripheral details (Levine & Edelstein, 2009). So, for example, if you were frightened by a scary film, you might show enhanced memory for events in the film but forget if you bought candy or who you went with. Still another factor is children's active participation. Preschoolers tend to remember things they did better than things they merely saw (Murachver, Pipe, Gordon, Owens, & Fivush, 1996). Self-awareness matters as well. In one experiment, self-awareness at age 2 was predictive of the ability to retell stories more accurately at age 3 (Reese & Newcombe, 2007).

social interaction model
Model, based on Vygotsky's sociocultural theory, that proposes children construct autobiographical memories through conversation with adults about shared events.

Finally, and most important, the way adults talk with a child about experiences strongly affects autobiographical memory (Cleveland & Reese, 2005; Fivush & Haden, 2006; McGuigan & Salmon, 2004). Why might this be the case? The **social interaction model,** based on Vygotsky's sociocultural approach, provides a rationale. Theorists argue that children collaboratively construct autobiographical memories with parents or other adults as they talk about shared events. Adults initiate and guide these conversations and provide children with models of the narrative structure of memory, placing the past events in a coherent and meaningful framework (Fivush & Haden, 2006). For example, think of a mother and child sitting down and leafing through a photo album together. As they go through the book, the mother is likely to guide the child's recollection of events. "See, this is when we went to Grandma's house. Remember how we all played together in the living room, and you did that puzzle? That was fun, wasn't it?" Children will tend to remember those events that are frequently rehearsed with parents via conversations about past events.

Parents differ with respect to how they talk about past events (Fivush & Haden, 2006). When a child gets stuck, adults with a *low elaborative style* repeat their own previous statements or questions. Such a parent might ask, "Do you remember how we traveled to Florida?" and then, receiving no answer, ask, "How did we get there? We went in the ________." A parent with a *high elaborative style* would ask a question that elicits more information: "Did we go by car or by plane?" In one study, children at ages 2 and 3 whose mothers had been trained to use highly elaborative techniques in talking with their children recalled richer memories than children of untrained mothers (Reese & Newcombe, 2007). Mothers tend to talk more elaboratively with girls than with boys. This finding may explain why women tend to have detailed, vivid recollections of childhood experiences from an earlier age than men do (Fivush & Haden, 2006).

Elaborative talk promotes autogiographical memory by providing verbal labels for aspects of an event and giving it an orderly, comprehensible structure (Nelson & Fivush, 2004). In reminiscing about past events, children learn to interpret those events and the thoughts and emotions connected with them. They build a sense of self as continuous in time, and they learn that their own perspective on an experience may differ from another person's perspective on the same experience (Fivush & Haden, 2006).

The relationship between elaborative, parent-guided reminiscing and children's autobiographical memory has been replicated widely across cultures. However, mothers in middle-class Western cultures tend to be more elaborative than mothers in non-Western cultures (Fivush & Haden, 2006). In reminiscing with 3-year-olds, U.S. mothers might say, "Do you remember when you went swimming at Nana's? What did you do that was really neat?" Chinese mothers tend to ask leading questions, leaving little for the child to add ("What did you play at the place of skiing? Sat on the ice ship, right?") (Nelson & Fivush, 2004).

checkpoint
can **you** . . .

- Identify three types of early memories and four factors that affect retention?
- Discuss how social interaction and culture influence memory?

Intelligence: Psychometric and Vygotskian Approaches

One factor that may affect the strength of early cognitive skills is intelligence. Although the definition of intelligence is controversial, most psychologists agree that intelligence involves the ability to learn from situations, adapt to new experiences, and manipulate abstract concepts. Let's look at two ways intelligence is measured—through traditional psychometric tests and through newer tests of cognitive potential and then at influences on children's performance.

TRADITIONAL PSYCHOMETRIC MEASURES

Three- to 5-year-old children are more proficient with language than younger children, so intelligence tests for this age group can include more verbal items. These tests, beginning at age 5, tend to be fairly reliable in predicting measured intelligence and school success later in childhood. The two most commonly used individual tests for preschoolers are the Stanford-Binet Intelligence Scales and the Wechsler Preschool and Primary Scale of Intelligence.

The **Stanford-Binet Intelligence Scales** are used for ages 2 and up and take 45 to 60 minutes. The child is asked to define words, string beads, build with blocks, identify the missing parts of a picture, trace mazes, and show an understanding of numbers. The child's score is supposed to measure fluid reasoning (the ability to solve abstract or novel problems), knowledge, quantitative reasoning, visual-spatial processing, and working memory. The fifth edition, revised in 2003, includes nonverbal methods of testing all five of these dimensions of cognition and permits comparisons of verbal and nonverbal performance. In addition to providing a full-scale IQ, the Stanford-Binet yields separate measures of verbal and nonverbal IQ plus composite scores spanning the five cognitive dimensions.

Stanford-Binet Intelligence Scales
Individual intelligence tests for ages 2 and up used to measure fluid reasoning, knowledge, quantitative reasoning, visual-spatial processing, and working memory.

The **Wechsler Preschool and Primary Scale of Intelligence, Revised (WPPSI-IV)** is an individual test taking 30 to 60 minutes. It has separate levels for ages 2½ to 4 and 4 to 7 and yields verbal, performance, and combined scores. It includes subtests designed to measure both verbal and nonverbal fluid reasoning, receptive versus expressive vocabulary, and processing speed. Both the Stanford-Binet and the WPPSI-IV have been restandardized on samples of children representing the population of preschool-age children in the United States. The WPPSI-IV also has been validated for special populations, such as children with intellectual disabilities, developmental delays, language disorders, and autistic disorders.

Wechsler Preschool and Primary Scale of Intelligence, Revised (WPPSI-IV)
Individual intelligence test for children ages 2½ to 7 that yields verbal and performance scores as well as a combined score.

INFLUENCES ON MEASURED INTELLIGENCE

A common misconception is that IQ scores represent a fixed quantity of inborn intelligence. In reality, an IQ score is simply a measure of how well a child can do certain tasks at a certain time in comparison with other children of the same age. Indeed, test scores of children in many industrialized countries have risen steadily since testing began, forcing test developers to raise standardized norms (Flynn, 1984, 1987). This trend was thought to reflect better nutrition, exposure to educational television, preschools, better-educated parents, smaller families in which each child receives more attention, and a wide variety of mentally demanding games, as well as changes in the tests themselves. However, in tests of Norwegian and Danish army recruits, the trend has slowed and even reversed since the 1970s and 1980s, perhaps because such influences have reached a saturation point (Sundet, Barlaug, & Torjussen, 2004; Teasdale & Owen, 2008).

The degree to which family environment influences a child's intelligence is in question. We do not know how much of parents' influence on intelligence comes from their genetic contribution and how much from the fact that they provide a child's earliest environment for learning. Twin and adoption studies suggest that family life has its strongest influence in early childhood, and this influence diminishes greatly by adolescence (Bouchard & McGue, 2003; McGue, 1997; Neisser et al., 1996).

The correlation between socioeconomic status and IQ is well documented (Neisser et al., 1996; Strenze, 2007). Family income is associated with cognitive development and achievement in the preschool years and beyond. Family economic circumstances can exert a powerful influence, not so much in themselves as in the way they affect other factors such as health, stress, parenting practices, and the atmosphere in the home (Brooks-Gunn, 2003; Evans, 2004; NICHD Early Child Care Research Network, 2005a; Rouse, Brooks-Gunn, & McLanahan, 2005).

Still, some economically deprived children do better on IQ tests than others. Both genetic and environmental factors are involved. In a study of 1,116 twin pairs born in England and Wales in 1994 and 1995 and assessed at age 5 (Kim-Cohen et al., 2004), children in deprived families tended, as in other studies, to have lower IQs. However, poor children with an outgoing temperament, warm mothering, and stimulating activities in the home (which, again, may be influenced by parental IQ) tended to do better than other economically deprived children.

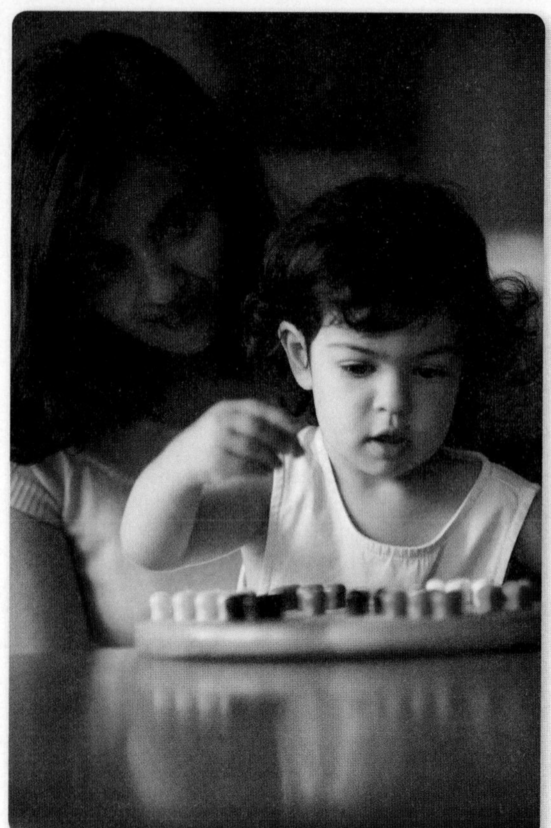

By giving suggestions for solving a puzzle until her daughter can do it on her own, this mother supports the child's cognitive progress.

TESTING AND TEACHING BASED ON VYGOTSKY'S THEORY

According to Vygotsky, children learn by internalizing the results of interactions with adults. This interactive learning is most effective in helping children cross the **zone of proximal development (ZPD),** the imaginary psychological space between what children can do or know by themselves and what they could do or know with help. The ZPD can be assessed by *dynamic tests* that, according to Vygotskyan theory, provide a better measure of children's intellectual potential than do traditional psychometric tests that measure what children have already mastered. Dynamic tests emphasize potential rather than present achievement and strive to measure learning processes directly rather than through the products of past learning. Examiners help the child when necessary by asking questions, giving examples or demonstrations, and offering feedback, making the test itself a learning situation.

The ZPD, in combination with the related concept of **scaffolding,** can help parents and teachers more efficiently guide children's cognitive progress. Scaffolding is the supportive assistance that a more sophisticated interaction partner provides, and ideally it should be aimed at the ZPD. For example, consider what happens when you are trying to learn a new skill, such as playing pool. When you play with someone who is worse than you, you are not likely to improve. Likewise, when you play with someone who is a master, their skills are so above yours that they overwhelm you. However, playing with someone who is just a bit better than you is likely to challenge you, illustrate strategies you might be successful at, and result in the greatest amount of learning.

Ideally, scaffolding is lessened as children gain in skills. The less able a child is to do a task, the more scaffolding, or support, an adult must give. As the child can do more and more, the adult helps less and less. When the child can do the job alone, the adult takes away the scaffold that is no longer needed.

If you were a preschool or kindergarten teacher, would you find it more helpful to know a child's IQ or ZPD?

zone of proximal development (ZPD)
Vygotsky's term for the difference between what a child can do alone and what the child can do with help.

scaffolding
Temporary support to help a child master a task.

By enabling children to become aware of and monitor their own cognitive processes and to recognize when they need help, parents can help children take responsibility for learning. Prekindergarten children who receive scaffolding are better able to regulate their own learning when they get to kindergarten (Neitzel & Stright, 2003). In a longitudinal study of 289 families with infants, the skills children developed during interactions with their mothers at 2 and 3½ enabled them, at 4½, to regulate goal-directed problem solving and to initiate social interactions. Also, 2-year-olds whose mothers helped maintain the child's interest in an activity—for example, by asking questions, making suggestions or comments, or offering choices—tended, at 3½ and 4½, to show independence in cognitive and social skills, such as solving a problem and initiating social interaction (Landry, Smith, Swank, & Miller-Loncar, 2000).

Vygotsky believed play provided children with a great deal of scaffolding, enabling them to work at the higher end of their ZPD. If asked to pretend to be a statue, children are likely to be able to stand still longer than if asked to just remain motionless. The "rules" of being a statue provide support for the emerging regulatory abilities of the children.

study smart

Scaffolding

checkpoint can you . . .

- Describe two individual intelligence tests for preschoolers?
- Discuss the relationship between SES and IQ?
- Explain how a test score based on the ZPD differs from a psychometric test score?

Language Development

Preschoolers are full of questions: "How many sleeps until tomorrow?" "Who filled the river with water?" "What does the fox say?" "Do smells come from inside my nose?" Young children's growing facility with language helps them express their unique view of the world. Between ages 3 and 6, children make rapid advances in vocabulary, grammar, and syntax. The child who, at 3, describes how Daddy "hatches" wood (chops with a hatchet) or asks Mommy to "piece" her food (cut it into little pieces) may, by age 5, tell her mother, "Don't be ridiculous!" or proudly point to her toys and say, "See how I organized everything?"

When exposed to rhymes, 5-year-olds from wealthier families show more localization of language in the left hemisphere (just like adults) than children from poorer families. This may result from children from wealthier homes being exposed to more complex vocabulary and syntax.

Raizada, Richards, Metlzoff, & Kuhl, 2008

VOCABULARY

At age 3 the average child knows and can use 900 to 1,000 words. By age 6, a child typically has an expressive (speaking) vocabulary of 2,600 words and understands more than 20,000. With the help of formal schooling, a child's passive, or receptive, vocabulary (words she can understand) will quadruple to 80,000 words by the time she enters high school (Owens, 1996).

This rapid expansion of vocabulary may occur through **fast mapping,** which allows a child to pick up the approximate meaning of a new word after hearing it only once or twice in conversation. From the context, children seem to form a quick hypothesis about the meaning of the word, which then is refined with further exposure and usage. For example, suppose a child is at the zoo and encounters an emu for the first time. The mother might point to the emu and say, "Look at the emu over there." The child might use what she knows about the rules for forming words, about the context, and about the subject under discussion to form a hypothesis about the meaning of the word *emu.* Names of objects (nouns) seem to be easier to fast map than names of actions (verbs), which are less concrete (Golinkoff, Jacquet, Hirsh-Pasek, & Nandakumar, 1996).

fast mapping
Process by which a child absorbs the meaning of a new word after hearing it once or twice in conversation.

GRAMMAR AND SYNTAX

The ways children combine syllables into words and words into sentences grow increasingly sophisticated during early childhood as their understanding of grammar and syntax becomes more complex. When psychologists speak of grammar, they are not referring to the lessons learned in 7th grade English class; rather, they are referring to the deep underlying structure of a language that enables us to both produce and understand utterances. Syntax is a related concept and involves the rules for putting together sentences in a particular language.

At age 3, children typically begin to use plurals, possessives, and past tense and know the difference between *I, you,* and *we.* They can ask—and answer—what and where questions. However, their sentences are generally short, simple, and declarative ("Kitty wants milk").

Between ages 4 and 5, sentences average four to five words and may be declarative, negative ("I'm not hungry"), interrogative ("Why can't I go outside?"), or imperative ("Catch the ball!"). Four-year-olds use complex, multiclause sentences ("I'm eating because I'm hungry") more frequently if their parents often use such sentences (Huttenlocher, Vasilyeva, Cymerman, & Levine, 2002). They are also affected by their peers. When children interact with peers who have strong language skills, this results in a small but significant positive effect on their own language (Mashburn, Justice, Downer, & Pianta, 2009). Children this age tend to string sentences together in long run-on narratives (". . . And then . . . And then . . ."). In some respects, comprehension may be immature. For example, 4-year-old Noah can carry out a command that includes more than one step ("Pick up your toys and put them in the cupboard"). However, if his mother tells him, "You may watch TV after you pick up your toys," he may process the words in the order in which he hears them and think he can first watch television and then pick up his toys.

By ages 5 to 7, children's speech has become quite adultlike. They speak in longer and more complicated sentences. They use more conjunctions, prepositions, and articles. They use compound and complex sentences and can handle all parts of speech. Still, although children this age speak fluently, comprehensibly, and fairly grammatically, they have yet to master many fine points of language. They rarely use the passive voice ("I was dressed by Grandpa"), conditional sentences ("If I were big, I could drive the bus"), or the auxiliary verb *have* ("I have seen that lady before") (C. S. Chomsky, 1969).

Young children often make errors because they have not yet learned exceptions to rules. Saying "holded" instead of "held" or "eated" instead of "ate" is a normal sign of linguistic progress. When young children discover a rule, such as adding *-ed* to a verb for past tense, they tend to overgeneralize—to use it even with words that do not conform to the rule. Eventually, they notice that *-ed* is not always used to form the past tense of a verb. Training can help children master such syntactical forms (Vasilyeva, Huttenlocher, & Waterfall, 2006).

PRAGMATICS AND SOCIAL SPEECH

pragmatics
The practical knowledge needed to use language for communicative purposes.

Language is a social process. As children learn vocabulary, grammar, and syntax, they also become more competent in **pragmatics.** Pragmatics involves the practical knowledge of how to use language to communicate. For example, a child is more likely to be successful with a request such as "May I please have a cookie?" than with "Give me a cookie now."

Pragmatics is related to theory of mind because to understand how to use language socially, you have to be able to put yourself in other people's shoes. This includes knowing how to ask for things, how to tell a story or joke, how to begin and continue a conversation, and how to adjust comments to the listener's perspective (M. L. Rice, 1982). These are all aspects of **social speech,** speech intended to be understood by a listener. Most 3-year-olds pay attention to the effect of their speech on others. If people cannot understand them, they try to explain themselves more clearly. Four-year-olds, especially girls, simplify their language and use a higher register when speaking to 2-year-olds (Owens, 1996; Shatz & Gelman, 1973).

social speech
Speech intended to be understood by a listener.

Most 5-year-olds can adapt what they say to what the listener knows. They can now use words to resolve disputes, and they use more polite language and fewer direct commands in talking to adults than to other children. Almost half of 5-year-olds can stick to a conversational topic for about a dozen turns—if they are comfortable with their partner and if the topic is one they know and care about.

PRIVATE SPEECH

Anna, age 4, was alone in her room painting. When she finished, she was overheard saying aloud, "Now I have to put the pictures somewhere to dry. I'll put them by the window. They need to get dry now."

private speech
Talking aloud to oneself with no intent to communicate with others.

Private speech—talking aloud to oneself with no intent to communicate with others—is normal and common in childhood. Piaget (1962/1923) saw private speech as a sign of cognitive immaturity. Because young children are egocentric, he suggested, they are unable to recognize others' viewpoints and therefore are unable to communicate meaningfully. Instead, they simply vocalize whatever is on their minds.

Vygotsky (1962/1934) did not look upon private speech as egocentric. He saw it as a special form of communication: conversation with the self. Research generally supports Vygotsky. In a study of 3- to-5-year-olds, 86 percent of the children's remarks were *not* egocentric (Berk, 1986a). The most sociable children and those who engage in the most social speech tend to use the most private speech as well, supporting Vygotsky's view that private speech is stimulated by social experience (Berk, 1992; Kohlberg, Yaeger, & Hjertholm, 1968). There also is evidence for the role of private speech in self-regulation (Berk & Garvin, 1984; Furrow, 1984). Private speech tends to increase when children are trying to solve problems or perform difficult tasks, especially without adult supervision (Berk, 1992).

Vygotsky proposed that private speech increases during the preschool years and then fades away during the early part of middle childhood as children become more able to guide and master their actions. However, the pattern now appears to be more complex. Whereas Vygotsky considered the need for private speech a universal stage of cognitive development, studies have found a wide range of individual differences, with some children using it very little or not at all (Berk, 1992).

DELAYED LANGUAGE DEVELOPMENT

The fact that Albert Einstein did not start to use words until he was between 2 and 3 years old (Isaacson, 2007) may encourage parents of other children whose speech develops later than usual. About 5 to 8 percent of preschool children show speech and language delays (U.S. Preventive Services Task Force, 2006).

Children who speak late do not necessarily lack linguistic input at home. Hearing problems and head and facial abnormalities may be associated with speech and language delays, as are premature birth, family history, socioeconomic factors, and other developmental delays (Dale et al., 1998; U.S. Preventive Services Task Force, 2006). Heredity seems to play a role (Kovas et al., 2005; Spinath, Price, Dale, & Plomin, 2004). Boys are more likely than girls to be late talkers (U.S. Preventive Services Task Force, 2006).

Amalia, one of the children featured in the milestones videos, was diagnosed with a speech delay at 18 months and received speech therapy for approximately 1½ years before she caught up with her peers. You may note that at younger ages her speech is very difficult to understand.

Many children who speak late—especially those whose comprehension is normal—eventually catch up. One of the largest studies to date determined that 80 percent of children with language delays at age 2 catch up with their peers by age 7 (Rice, Taylor, & Zubrick, 2008). However, some children with early language delays, if left untreated, may experience far-reaching cognitive, social, and emotional consequences (U.S. Preventive Services Task Force, 2006).

study smart

Language Challenges

emergent literacy
Preschoolers' development of skills, knowledge, and attitudes that underlie reading and writing.

study smart

Preliteracy

PREPARATION FOR LITERACY

To understand what is on the printed page, children first need to master certain prereading skills. The development of fundamental skills that eventually lead to being able to read is known as **emergent literacy.**

Prereading skills can be divided into two types: (1) oral language skills, such as vocabulary, syntax, narrative structure, and the understanding that language is used to communicate; and (2) specific phonological skills (linking letters with sounds) that help in decoding the printed word. Each of these types of skills seems to have its own independent effect (NICHD Early Child Care Research Network, 2005b; Lonigan, Burgess, & Anthony, 2000). In a 2-year longitudinal study of 90 British schoolchildren, the development of word recognition appeared critically dependent on phonological skills, whereas oral language skills such as vocabulary and grammatical skills were more important predictors of reading comprehension (Muter, Hulme, Snowling, & Stevenson, 2004).

Social interaction is an important factor in literacy development. Children are more likely to become good readers and writers if, during the preschool years, parents provide

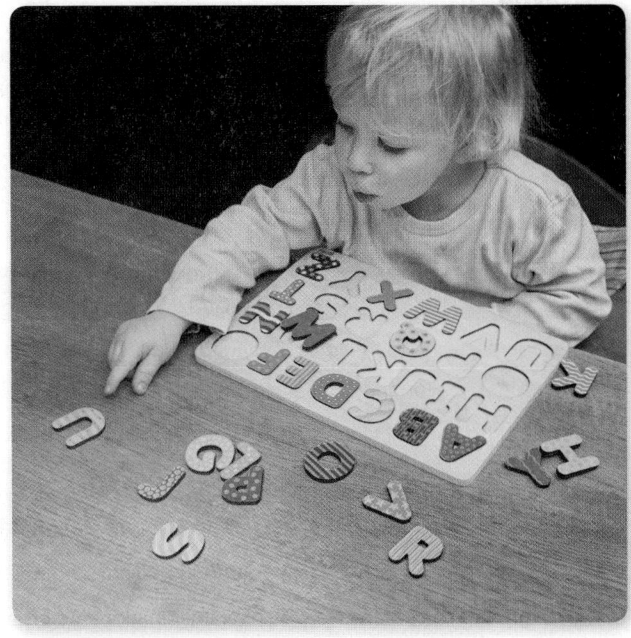

Toys and games that familiarize children with the alphabet and the sounds the letters make can give them a head start in learning to read.

conversational challenges the children are ready for—if they use a rich vocabulary and center dinner-table talk on the day's activities, on mutually remembered past events, or on questions about why people do things and how things work (Reese, 1995; Snow, 1993).

As children learn the skills they will need to translate the written word into speech, they also learn that writing can express ideas, thoughts, and feelings. Preschool children in the United States pretend to write by scribbling, lining up their marks from left to right (Brenneman, Massey, Machado, & Gelman, 1996). Later they begin using letters, numbers, and letterlike shapes to represent words, syllables, or phonemes. Often their spelling is so inventive that they cannot read it themselves (Whitehurst & Lonigan, 1998, 2001)!

Reading to children is one of the most effective paths to literacy. Children who are read to from an early age learn that reading and writing in English move from left to right and from top to bottom and that words are separated by spaces. They also are motivated to learn to read (Siegler, 1998; Whitehurst & Lonigan, 1998, 2001).

checkpoint can you . . .

- Trace normal progress in 3- to 6-year-olds' vocabulary, grammar, syntax, and conversational abilities?
- Give reasons why children use private speech?
- Discuss possible causes, consequences, and treatment of delayed language development?
- Identify factors that promote preparation for literacy?
- Discuss the relationship between media use and cognition?

MEDIA AND COGNITION

Unlike infants and toddlers, preschool-age children comprehend the symbolic nature of television and can readily imitate behaviors they see (Bandura, Ross, & Ross, 1963; Kirkorian, Wartella, & Anderson, 2008). By the age of 3 children are *active media users,* able to pay greater attention to dialogue and narrative (Huston & Wright, 1983). Exposure to television during the first few years of life may be associated with poorer cognitive development, but children over the age of 2 exposed to programs that follow an educational curriculum have demonstrated cognitive enhancement (Kirkorian et al., 2008). In one study, the more time 3- to 5-year-olds spent watching *Sesame Street,* the more their vocabulary improved (M. L. Rice, Huston, Truglio, & Wright, 1990). Program content is an important mediator. Parents who limit screen time, select well-designed, age-appropriate programs, and view the programs with their children can maximize the benefits of media (Table 7).

U.S. booksellers have noted a trend away from picture books and toward chapter books for young children, presumably as a result of parents' concerns about literacy. Do chapter books with fewer pictures and more text help develop children's imagination, or do they push them too quickly?

Bosman, 2010

TABLE 7 Using Media Responsibly

• Limit screen time to the least amount possible.
• Set guidelines for appropriate viewing for all media, including TV, videos/DVDs, movies, and games.
• Protect children from inappropriate media.
• Require that children ask before turning on media.
• Remove TVs, video game systems, and computers from bedrooms.
• Watch programs and movies together and discuss what you are watching.
• Use media in a positive way to spark imagination and creativity.
• Limit the number of products you purchase for your child that are linked to TV programs.

Source: Teachers Resisting Unhealthy Children's Entertainment (TRUCE), 2008.

Early Childhood Education

Going to preschool is an important step, widening a child's physical, cognitive, and social environment. The transition to kindergarten, the beginning of "real school," is another momentous step. Let's look at both of these transitions.

TYPES OF PRESCHOOLS

Preschools vary greatly in their goals and curriculums. Some programs emphasize academic achievement, and others focus on social and emotional development. In some countries, such as China, preschools provide academic preparation for schooling. In contrast, many preschools in the United States have followed progressive, child-centered philosophies stressing social and emotional growth in line with young children's developmental needs. Two of the most influential programs, Montessori and Reggio Emilia, were founded on similar philosophical premises.

The Montessori Method As Italy's first female physician, Maria Montessori dedicated herself to finding new and better methods for educating children with disabilities. Based on her success with these children, she was asked to start a school for underprivileged children living in the slums of Italy. In 1907 Montessori opened Casa dei Bambini and began a movement that has since spread worldwide.

The Montessori method is based on the belief that children's natural intelligence involves rational, spiritual, and empirical aspects (Edwards, 2003). Montessori stresses the importance of children learning independently at their own pace, as they work with developmentally appropriate materials and self-chosen tasks. Children are grouped into multiage classrooms; infancy to age 3 is considered "the unconscious absorbent mind," and age 3 to 6 is considered the "conscious absorbent mind" (Montessori, 1995). Teachers serve as guides, and older children help younger ones. The curriculum is individualized but has a definite scope and prescribed sequencing. Teachers provide an environment of calm productivity, and the classrooms are organized to be orderly, pleasing environments.

Montessori's approach has proven effective. An evaluation of Montessori education in Milwaukee found that 5-year-old Montessori students were better prepared for elementary school in reading and math than children who attended other types of preschools (Lillard & Else-Quest, 2006).

The Reggio Emilia Approach In the late 1940s a group of Italian educators and parents devised a plan to revitalize a crumbling, post–World War II society through a new approach to education for young children. Their goal was to improve the lives of children and families by encouraging nonviolent dialogues and debates, developing problem-solving skills, and forging close, long-term relationships with teachers and classmates. Loris Malaguzzi, the school's founding director, was a social constructivist strongly influenced by Dewey, Piaget, Vygotsky, and Montessori. He envisioned an "education based on relationships" that supported the child's connections to people, society, and the environment (Malaguzzi, 1993).

Reggio Emilia is a less formal model than Montessori. Teachers follow children's interests and support them in exploring and investigating ideas and feelings through words, movement, dramatic play, and music. Learning is purposeful but less defined than with the Montessori curriculum. Teachers ask questions that draw out children's ideas and then create flexible plans to explore these ideas with the children. Classrooms are carefully constructed to offer complexity, beauty, organization, and a sense of well-being (Ceppi & Zini, 1998; Edwards, 2002).

COMPENSATORY PRESCHOOL PROGRAMS

Compensatory preschool programs are designed to aid children who would otherwise enter school poorly prepared to learn. Generally, research has shown that children

The Harlem Children's Zone is an extremely successful current program based in Bronfenbrenner's bioecological model. One reason for its extraordinary success is the systems approach utilized to address children's deficiencies. The focus is as much on the community as it is on the children, with the goal of bringing about a "tipping point" of enriched events and environments that will, it is hoped, at some point become self-perpetuating.

who are enrolled in compensatory preschool programs show academic and cognitive gains (Camilli, Vargas, Ryan, & Barnett, 2010; Ramey & Ramey, 2004). However, teachers and researchers in early childhood education generally work within a model of the whole child, seeking not just to enhance cognitive skills but also to improve physical health and to foster self-confidence and social skills. Because of this whole child focus, compensatory programs offering additional services have been developed. The best known of these programs in the United States is Project Head Start, a federally funded program launched in 1965. Head Start provides medical, dental, and mental health care; social services; and at least one hot meal a day. About 1 out of 3 Head Start children are from non-English-speaking homes (predominantly Hispanic), and a majority live in single-mother homes (Administration for Children and Families [ACF], 2006a).

Has Head Start lived up to its name? Children enrolled in Head Start show academic and social gains in multiple, but not all, target areas immediately following their participation (Garces, Thomas, & Currie, 2000). Head Start children make gains in vocabulary, letter recognition, early writing, early mathematics, and social skills (Figure 5). The gap between their vocabulary and early reading scores and national norms narrows significantly. Furthermore, their skills continue to progress in kindergarten. Gains are closely related to parental involvement (ACF, 2006b).

Some reports suggest that these gains are not maintained over time. These reports have been controversial, in part due to the complexity of comparing outcomes of diverse children in varying programs. About half the number of children who apply for but do not get into Head Start find alternative child care arrangements. Thus the control group—those children who did not participate in Head Start—experience a variety of different child care situations rather than the lack of *any* enriching child care experiences. Some researchers argue that this might help explain why many children who do not participate in Head Start seemed to "catch up" to program participants by first grade. In addition, the pattern of effects may differ for different groups of children. For example, dual language learners and children with special needs who participate in early intervention programs tend to show gains that are both larger and maintained for longer periods of time (National Forum on Early Childhood Policy and Programs, 2010).

FIGURE 5

Academic Outcomes at the Beginning and End of Head Start

These outcomes represent all children who entered Head Start for the first time in the fall of 2009, completed 1 or 2 years of the program, and entered kindergarten in the fall of either 2010 or 2011. Immediate gains are most striking; however, better outcomes do persist over time.

Mean standard score

	Head start entry	Head start exit
Letter-word	95.8	101.3
Spelling	94.8	98.2
Applied problems	89.5	91.8

Source: Aikens, Kopack Klein, Tarullo, & West, 2013.

An analysis of long-term effects of Head Start suggests that the benefits outweigh the costs (Ludwig & Phillips, 2007; Puma et al., 2012). Children from Head Start and other compensatory programs are less likely to be placed in special education or to repeat a grade and are more likely to finish high school than low-income children who did not attend such programs (Deming, 2009; Neisser et al., 1996). "Graduates" of one such program, the Perry Preschool Project, were much less likely to become juvenile delinquents or to become pregnant in their teens (Schweinhart, 2007; Schweinhart, Barnes, & Weikart, 1993). There were differences in long-term outcomes for males and females. At ages 27 and 40, men were less likely to have been involved in criminal activity, and more likely to be employed and have a higher income than controls. For women, there were positive effects on both education and employment at age 19 and 27, and negative effects on criminal activity at age 40 (Heckman et al., 2010). Outcomes are best with earlier and longer-lasting intervention through high-quality, center-based programs (Brooks-Gunn, 2003; Reynolds & Temple, 1998; Zigler & Styfco, 2001).

In 1995, Early Head Start began to offer child and family development services to low-income families with infants and toddlers. At ages 2 and 3, according to randomized studies, participants scored higher on standardized developmental and vocabulary tests and were at less risk of slow development than children not in the program. At age 3, they were less aggressive, more absorbed in play, and more positively engaged with their parents. Early Head Start parents were more emotionally supportive, provided more learning and language stimulation, read to their children more, and spanked less. Programs that offered a mix of center-based services and home visits showed better results than those that concentrated on one setting or the other (Commissioner's Office of Research and Evaluation and Head Start Bureau, 2001; Love et al., 2002, 2005).

Should the primary purpose of preschool be to provide a strong academic foundation or to foster social and emotional development?

A growing consensus among early childhood educators is that the most effective way to ensure that gains achieved in early intervention and compensatory education programs are maintained is through a *PK–3* approach—a systematic program extending from prekindergarten through third grade. Such a program would (1) offer prekindergarten to all 3- and 4-year olds, (2) require full-day kindergarten, and (3) coordinate and align educational experiences and expectations from prekindergarten through Grade 3 through a sequenced curriculum based on children's developmental needs and abilities and taught by skilled professionals (Bogard & Takanishi, 2005).

THE CHILD IN KINDERGARTEN

For many years people thought of kindergarten as a transition time between home or preschool and the structure of grade school and academic instruction. Now kindergarten in the United States has become more like first grade and emphasizes academics. Children spend more time on worksheets and preparing to read and less time on self-chosen activities. It is known that a successful transition from home or preschool to kindergarten lays the foundation for future academic achievement (Schulting, Malone, & Dodge, 2005).

Although some states do not require kindergarten programs or kindergarten attendance, most 5-year-olds attend kindergarten. Since the late 1970s, an increasing number of kindergarteners spend a full day in school, rather than the traditional half day (National Center for Education Statistics [NCES], 2004). A practical impetus for this trend is the growing number of single-parent and dual-earner households. In addition, large numbers of children already have experienced preschool, prekindergarten programs, or full-time child care and are ready for a more rigorous kindergarten curriculum (Walston & West, 2004). Do children learn more in full-day kindergarten? Initially, they do. Full-day kindergarten has been associated with greater growth of reading and math skills from fall until spring, but overall these advantages tend to be small to moderate (Votruba-Drzal, Li-Grining, & Maldonado-Carreno, 2008). By the end of third grade, amount of time spent in kindergarten makes no substantial difference in reading, math, and science achievement (Rathbun, West, & Germino-Hausken, 2004).

Findings highlight the importance of the preparation a child receives *before* kindergarten. The resources with which children come to kindergarten—preliteracy skills and the richness of a home literacy environment—predict reading achievement in first grade, and these individual differences tend to persist or increase throughout the first 4 years of school (Denton, West, & Walston, 2003; Rathbun et al., 2004).

Emotional and social adjustment also affect readiness for kindergarten and strongly predict school success. More important than knowing the alphabet or being able to count to 20, kindergarten teachers say, are the abilities to sit still, follow directions, wait one's turn, and regulate one's own learning (Blair, 2002; Brooks-Gunn, 2003; Raver, 2002). There are individual differences in children's ability to self-regulate, but the environment can either promote or impede regulatory activity, suggesting the importance of classroom management in academic achievement (Rimm-Kaufman, Curby, Grimm, Nathansan, & Brock, 2009). Adjustment to kindergarten can be eased by enabling preschoolers and parents to visit before the start of kindergarten, shortening school days early in the school year, having teachers make home visits, holding parent orientation sessions, and keeping parents informed about what is going on in school (Schulting, Malone, & Dodge, 2005).

checkpoint
can **you** . . .

- Compare goals and effectiveness of varying types of preschool programs?
- Assess the benefits of compensatory preschool education?
- Discuss factors that affect adjustment to kindergarten?

summary and key terms

PHYSICAL DEVELOPMENT

Aspects of Physical Development

- Physical growth continues during the years from 3 to 6, but more slowly than during infancy and toddlerhood. Boys are on average slightly taller, heavier, and more muscular than girls. Internal body systems are maturing.
- Sleep patterns change during early childhood, as throughout life, and are affected by cultural expectations. Occasional sleepwalking, sleep terrors, and nightmares are common, but persistent sleep problems may indicate emotional disturbances.
- Bed-wetting is usually outgrown without special help.
- Brain development continues steadily throughout childhood and affects motor development.
- Children progress rapidly in gross and fine motor skills, developing more complex systems of action.
- Handedness is usually evident by age 3, reflecting dominance by one hemisphere of the brain.
- According to Kellogg's research, stages of art production, which reflect brain development and fine motor coordination, are the scribbling stage, shape stage, design stage, and pictorial stage.

enuresis
gross motor skills
fine motor skills
systems of action
handedness

Health and Safety

- Although major contagious illnesses are rare today in industrialized countries due to widespread immunization, preventable disease continues to be a major problem in the developing world.
- The prevalence of obesity among preschoolers has increased.
- Undernutrition can affect all aspects of development.
- Food allergies are becoming increasingly common.
- Accidents, most frequently in the home, are the leading cause of death in childhood in the United States.
- Environmental factors such as exposure to poverty, homelessness, smoking, air pollution, and pesticides increase the risks of illness or injury. Lead poisoning can have serious physical, cognitive, and behavioral effects.

COGNITIVE DEVELOPMENT

Piagetian Approach: The Preoperational Child

- Children in the preoperational stage show several important advances, as well as some immature aspects of thought.
- The symbolic function enables children to reflect on people, objects, and events that are not physically present. It is shown in deferred imitation, pretend play, and language.
- Symbolic development helps preoperational children make more accurate judgments of spatial relationships. They can link cause and effect with regard to familiar situations, understand the concept of identity, categorize, compare quantities, and understand principles of counting.
- Preoperational children appear to be less egocentric than Piaget thought.
- Centration keeps preoperational children from understanding principles of conservation. Their logic also is limited by irreversibility and a focus on states rather than transformations.
- The theory of mind, which develops markedly between ages 3 and 5, includes awareness of a child's own thought processes, social cognition, understanding that people can hold false beliefs, ability to deceive, ability to distinguish appearance from reality, and ability to distinguish fantasy from reality.
- Maturational and environmental influences affect individual differences in theory-of-mind development.

preoperational stage
symbolic function
pretend play
transduction
animism
centration
decenter
egocentrism
conservation
irreversibility
theory of mind

Information-Processing Approach: Memory Development

- Information-processing models describe three steps in memory: encoding, storage, and retrieval.
- Although sensory memory shows little change with age, the capacity of working memory increases greatly. The central executive controls the flow of information to and from long-term memory.
- At all ages, recognition is better than recall, but both increase during early childhood.
- Early episodic memory is only temporary; it fades or is transferred to generic memory.
- Autobiographical memory typically begins at about age 3 or 4; it may be related to self-recognition and language development.
- According to the social interaction model, children and adults co-construct autobiographical memories by talking about shared experiences.
- Children are more likely to remember unusual activities that they actively participate in. The way adults talk with children about events influences memory formation.

encoding
storage
retrieval
sensory memory
working memory
executive function
long-term memory
central executive
recall
recognition
generic memory
script
episodic memory
autobiographical memory
social interaction model

Intelligence: Psychometric and Vygotskian Approaches

- The two most commonly used psychometric intelligence tests for young children are the Stanford-Binet Intelligence Scales and the Wechsler Preschool and Primary Scale of Intelligence, Revised (WPPSI-IV).
- Intelligence test scores have risen in industrialized countries.
- Intelligence test scores may be influenced by a number of factors, including the home environment and SES.
- Newer tests based on Vygotsky's concept of the zone of proximal development (ZPD) indicate immediate potential for achievement. Such tests, combined with scaffolding, can help parents and teachers guide children's progress.

Stanford-Binet Intelligence Scales
Wechsler Preschool and Primary Scale of Intelligence, Revised (WPPSI-IV)
zone of proximal development (ZPD)
scaffolding

Language Development

- During early childhood, vocabulary increases greatly, and grammar and syntax become fairly sophisticated. Children become more competent in pragmatics.
- Private speech is normal and common; it may aid in the shift to self-regulation.
- Causes of delayed language development are unclear. If untreated, language delays may have serious cognitive, social, and emotional consequences.
- Interaction with adults can promote emergent literacy.
- Well-designed, age-appropriate programming is associated with enhanced cognitive development.

fast mapping
pragmatics
social speech
private speech
emergent literacy

Early Childhood Education

- Goals of preschool education vary across cultures.
- The academic content of early childhood education programs in the United States has increased, but studies support a child-centered approach.
- Compensatory preschool programs have had positive outcomes, and participants' performance is approaching national norms. Compensatory programs that start early may have better results.
- Many children today attend full-day kindergarten. Success in kindergarten depends largely on emotional and social adjustment and prekindergarten preparation.

chapter 8

Psychosocial Development in Early Childhood

outline

The Developing Self

Gender

Play: The Business of Early Childhood

Parenting

Relationships with Other Children

learning objectives

Discuss emotional and personality development in early childhood.

Discuss gender development in early childhood.

Describe play in early childhood.

Explain how parenting practices influence development.

Evaluate young children's relationships with siblings and peers.

did you **know**?

- Young children find it hard to understand that they can have conflicting emotions?
- Gender preferences in toys and playmates appear as early as 12 to 24 months, but boys and girls on average are more alike than different?
- The most effective type of parenting in American culture is warm and accepting but firm in maintaining standards?

In this chapter we discuss preschool children's understanding of themselves and their feelings. We see how their sense of male or female identity arises and how it affects behavior. We describe play, the activity in which children in industrialized countries typically spend most of their time. We consider the influence, for good or ill, of what parents do. Finally, we discuss relationships with siblings and other children.

Play is often talked about as if it were a relief from serious learning. But for children, play is really the work of childhood.

—Fred Rogers

The Developing Self

"Who in the world am I? Ah, *that's* the great puzzle," said Alice in Wonderland, after her size had abruptly changed—again. Solving Alice's "puzzle" is a lifelong process of getting to know one's self.

self-concept
Sense of self; descriptive and evaluative mental picture of one's abilities and traits.

self-definition
Cluster of characteristics used to describe oneself.

THE SELF-CONCEPT AND COGNITIVE DEVELOPMENT

The **self-concept** is our total picture of our abilities and traits. It is "a *cognitive construction* . . . a system of descriptive and evaluative representations about the self" that determines how we feel about ourselves and guides our actions (Harter, 1996, p. 207). The sense of self also has a social aspect: children incorporate into their self-image their growing understanding of how others see them.

The self-concept begins to come into focus in toddlerhood, as children develop self-awareness. It becomes clearer as a person gains in cognitive abilities and deals with the developmental tasks of childhood, of adolescence, and then of adulthood.

Although our self-descriptions do get more accurate with age, even adults wildly overestimate their positive qualities. The only people who are accurate? The clinically depressed.

Changes in Self-Definition: The 5 to 7 Shift Children's **self-definition**—the way they describe themselves—typically changes between about ages 5 and 7, reflecting self-concept development. At age 4, Jason says,

> My name is Jason and I live in a big house with my mother and father and sister, Lisa. I have a kitty that's orange and a television set in my own room. . . . I like pizza and I have a nice teacher. I can count up to 100, want to hear me? I love my dog, Skipper. I can climb to the top of the jungle gym, I'm not scared! Just happy. You can't be happy *and* scared, no way! I have brown hair, and I go to preschool. I'm really strong. I can lift this chair, watch me! (Harter, 1996, p. 208)

The way Jason describes himself is typical of U.S. children his age. They are very concrete in their thinking. Not surprisingly, Jason focuses on what he does, what he looks like, things he owns, and the people and animals in his life. He speaks in specifics, for example, mentioning a particular skill (climbing or counting) rather than general abilities (being athletic or good at math). He is somewhat inaccurate in his description and, like most children, is unrealistically positive about his abilities. Moreover, his understanding of emotions is still forming, and he has difficulty understanding how conflicting emotions can exist simultaneously within one person. At about age 7, Jason will begin to be able to describe himself in terms of generalized traits such as popular, smart, or dumb; recognize that he can have conflicting emotions; and be self-critical while holding a positive overall self-concept.

Jason describes himself in terms of his appearance (brown hair) and his possessions (his dog, Skipper).

What specific changes make up this *age 5 to 7 shift?* A neo-Piagetian analysis (Case, 1992; Fischer, 1980) describes this shift in three steps.

single representations
In neo-Piagetian terminology, first stage in development of self-definition, in which children describe themselves in terms of individual, unconnected characteristics and in all-or-nothing terms.

At 4, Jason is at the first step, **single representations.** His statements about himself are one-dimensional ("I like pizza. . . . I'm really strong"). He cannot imagine having two emotions at once ("You can't be happy *and* scared") because he cannot consider different aspects of himself at the same time. His thinking about himself is all-or-nothing. He cannot acknowledge that his **real self,** the person he actually is, is not the same as his **ideal self,** the person he would like to be.

This is related to why children fail conservation tasks. Just as it is difficult for young children to consider two different aspects of volume (height and width) at the same time, it is difficult for them to consider two different aspects of the self at the same time.

real self
The self one actually is.

ideal self
The self one would like to be.

representational mappings
In neo-Piagetian terminology, second stage in development of self-definition, in which a child makes logical connections between aspects of the self but still sees these characteristics in all-or-nothing terms.

At about age 5 or 6, Jason moves to the second step, **representational mappings.** He begins to make logical connections between one aspect of himself and another: "I can run fast, and I can climb high. I'm also strong. I can throw a ball real far, I'm going to be on a team some day!" (Harter, 1996, p. 215). However, his image of himself is still expressed in completely positive, all-or-nothing terms. He cannot see how he might be good at some things and not at others.

The third step, *representational systems,* takes place in middle childhood when children begin to integrate specific features of the self into a general, multidimensional concept. As all-or-nothing thinking declines, Jason's self-descriptions will become more balanced and realistic: "I'm good at hockey but bad at arithmetic."

SELF-ESTEEM

self-esteem
The judgment a person makes about his or her self-worth.

Self-esteem is the self-evaluative part of the self-concept, the judgment children make about their overall worth. Self-esteem, in part, is based on children's growing cognitive ability to describe and define themselves.

Developmental Changes in Self-Esteem Although children do not generally talk about a concept of self-worth until about age 8, younger children show by their behavior that they have one. In a longitudinal study in Belgium (Verschueren, Buyck, & Marcoen, 2001), researchers measured various aspects of 5-year-olds' self-perceptions, such as physical appearance, scholastic and athletic competence, social acceptance, and behavioral conduct. Children's positive or negative self-perceptions at age 5 tended to predict their self-perceptions and socioemotional functioning at age 8.

Although there are individual differences in self-esteem, most young children wildly overestimate their abilities. Their self-esteem is not based on reality. One reason for this is that self-esteem is, in part, the result of feedback received from other people, and adults tend to give positive and uncritical feedback (Harter, 1998, 2006). For example, a kindergartener's crude lettering is not generally critiqued as being messy; rather, parents and teachers are more likely to praise and encourage the child's efforts.

In addition to being unrealistically high, children's self-esteem tends to be unidimensional. In other words, children believe they are either all good or all bad (Harter, 1998). You may notice that this is similar to what is found in the self-concept, and presumably the same cognitive constraints underlie both processes. In middle childhood, self-esteem will become more realistic as personal evaluations of competence based on internalization of parental and societal standards begin to shape and maintain self-worth (Harter, 1998).

The original research on learned helplessness involved restraining dogs as they were repeatedly shocked. Eventually they stopped struggling to get away and gave up. Research with human participants has to meet rigid ethical criteria, whereas research with animals is less constrained. What do you think of research such as this? Even if it gives us valuable information, is it ethical?

Contingent Self-Esteem: The "Helpless" Pattern When self-esteem is high, a child is generally motivated to achieve. However, if self-esteem is *contingent* on success, children may view failure or criticism as an indictment of their worth and may feel helpless to do better. About one-third to one-half of preschoolers, kindergartners, and first graders show a "learned helplessness" pattern (Dweck & Grant, 2008; Ruble & Dweck, 1995).

Instead of trying a different way to complete a puzzle, "helpless" children feel ashamed and give up. They assume they will fail, and so do not bother to try. Whereas older children

This mother's approval of her 3-year-old son's artwork is an important contributor to his self-esteem. Not until middle childhood do children develop strong internal standards of self-worth.

who fail may conclude that they are "dumb," preschoolers interpret failure as a sign of being "bad." This sense of being a bad person may persist into adulthood.

> *That closet full of participation trophies may not be the best thing for your young child. Research on self-esteem suggests that when children are praised and rewarded for everything they do, regardless of performance, they believe that praise uncritically. When they inevitably fail at a task, they take that as a sign that they are deficient.*
>
> Dweck, 2008

Children whose self-esteem is contingent on success tend to become demoralized when they fail. Often these children attribute poor performance or social rejection to their personality deficiencies, which they believe they are helpless to change. Children with noncontingent self-esteem, in contrast, tend to attribute failure or disappointment to factors outside themselves or to the need to try harder. For example, if such a child is unable to complete a puzzle, she might conclude there are missing pieces, or that perhaps the puzzle is intended for older children. If initially unsuccessful or rejected, they persevere, trying new strategies until they find one that works (Harter, 1998; Pomerantz & Saxon, 2001). Children with high self-esteem tend to have parents and teachers who give specific, focused feedback rather than criticize the child as a person ("Look, the tag on your shirt is showing in front," not "Can't you see your shirt is on backward? When are you going to learn to dress yourself?").

checkpoint can **you** . . .

- Trace early self-concept development?
- Explain the significance of the 5 to 7 shift?
- Tell how young children's self-esteem differs from older children's and explain how the helpless pattern arises?

UNDERSTANDING AND REGULATING EMOTIONS

"I hate you!" Maya, age 5, shouts to her mother. "You're a mean mommy!" Angry because her mother sent her to her room for pinching her baby brother, Maya cannot imagine ever loving her mother again. "Aren't you ashamed of yourself for making the baby cry?" her father asks Maya a little later. Maya nods, but only because she knows what response he wants. In truth, she feels a jumble of emotions.

The ability to understand and regulate, or control, one's feelings is one of the key advances of early childhood (Dennis, 2006). Children who can understand their emotions are better able to control the way they show them and to be sensitive to how others feel (Garner & Estep, 2001; Garner & Power, 1996). Emotional self-regulation

Young children might be able to read your emotions better than you think. New research suggests that children as young as 6 can tell the difference between a real smile and a fake smile. But they're not great at it: they are only accurate about 60 percent of the time.

Gosselin, Perron, & Maassarani, 2009

helps children guide their behavior (Eisenberg, Fabes, & Spinrad, 2006; Laible & Thompson, 1998) and contributes to their ability to get along with others (Denham et al., 2003).

In addition to learning how to regulate their emotions, children come to understand emotions in a more sophisticated manner over time. In preschool, children can talk about their feelings and can read the feelings of others. They know that experiences can elicit emotions and are often based on desires (Saarni, Campos, Camras, & Witherington, 2006; Saarni, Mumme, & Campos, 1998). They understand that people are happy when they get something they want and sad when they do not (Lagattuta, 2005). For example, a child might be able to theorize that a boy who did not get a present on his birthday would be sad, and that another boy who received the toy truck he had been coveting would be happy.

Emotional understanding becomes more complex with age, and there appears to be a fundamental shift in abilities between ages 5 and 7. For example, in one study, 32 children and adults were asked to speculate how a boy would feel if his ball rolled into the street and he either retrieved it or refrained from going into the street to get it. The 4- and 5-year-olds believed the boy would be happy if he got the ball and unhappy if he did not. They ignored that the boy broke a rule about going into the street and did not consider the emotional impact of that. The older children and the adults were more likely to believe that obedience to a rule would make the boy feel good and disobedience would make him feel bad (Lagattuta, 2005).

Children as young as 2 or 3 years of age can experience true clinical depression, although they are unable to verbalize what is going on.

Understanding Conflicting Emotions Many young children do not understand that they can experience contrary emotional reactions at the same time. Individual differences in understanding conflicting emotions are evident by age 3. In one longitudinal study, 3-year-olds who could identify whether a face looked happy or sad and who could tell how a puppet felt when enacting a situation involving happiness, sadness, anger, or fear were better able at the end of kindergarten to explain a story character's conflicting emotions. These children tended to come from families that often discussed why people behave as they do (J. R. Brown & Dunn, 1996). Most children acquire a more sophisticated understanding of conflicting emotions during middle childhood (Harter, 1996).

Temple Grandin, who has autism and speaks widely about her experiences, says people with autism also have difficulty feeling complex emotions. Feeling sad or happy is something she easily understands, but she has difficulty understanding how you can love someone and be angry at them at the same time.

Understanding Emotions Directed toward the Self Emotions directed toward the self, such as guilt, shame, and pride, typically develop by the end of the 3rd year, after children gain self-awareness and accept the standards of behavior their parents have set. However, even children a few years older often lack the cognitive sophistication to *recognize* these emotions and what brings them on (Kestenbaum & Gelman, 1995).

In one study (Harter, 1993), 4- to 8-year-olds were told two stories. In the first story, a child takes a few coins from a jar after being told not to do so; in the second story, a child performs a difficult gymnastic feat—a flip on the bars. Each story was presented in two versions: one in which a parent sees the child doing the act and another in which no one sees the child. The children were asked how they and the parent would feel in each circumstance.

Again, the answers revealed a gradual progression in understanding of feelings about the self, reflecting the 5 to 7 shift (Harter, 1996). At ages 4 to 5, children did not say that either they or their parents would feel pride or shame. Instead they used such terms as "worried" or "scared" (for the money jar incident) and "excited" or "happy" (about the gymnastic accomplishment). At 5 to 6, children said their parents would be ashamed or proud of them but did not acknowledge feeling these emotions themselves. At 6 to 7, children said they would feel proud or ashamed, but only if they were observed. Not until ages 7 to 8 did children say that they would feel ashamed or proud of themselves even if no one saw them.

ERIKSON: INITIATIVE VERSUS GUILT

Megan is starting a new school. On the first day, she is lonely and quiet. When recess arrives, she stands to the side watching other children play, wanting to join them, but afraid of rejection. Biting her lip, she finally walks over to a group of girls playing ball. "Can I play too?" she asks. They consider her briefly, then nod, and Megan smiles in relief and holds her hands out for the ball.

The need to deal with conflicting feelings about the self is at the heart of the third stage of psychosocial development identified by Erik Erikson (1950): **initiative versus guilt.** Preschool children can do—and want to do—more and more. At the same time, they are learning that some of the things they want to do meet social approval, whereas others do not. How do children reconcile their desire to *do* with their desire for approval?

This conflict marks a split between two parts of the personality: the part that remains a child, full of exuberance and a desire to try new things and test new powers, and the part that is becoming an adult, constantly examining the propriety of motives and actions. Children who learn how to regulate these opposing drives develop the virtue of *purpose,* the courage to envision and pursue goals without being unduly inhibited by guilt or fear of punishment (Erikson, 1982).

initiative versus guilt
Erikson's third stage in psychosocial development, in which children balance the urge to pursue goals with reservations about doing so.

checkpoint can you . . .

- Trace two typical developments in understanding of emotions?
- Explain the significance of Erikson's third stage of personality development?

Gender

Gender identity, awareness of one's femaleness or maleness and all it implies in one's society of origin, is an important aspect of the developing self-concept. How different are young boys and girls? What causes those differences? How do children develop gender identity, and how does it affect their attitudes and behavior?

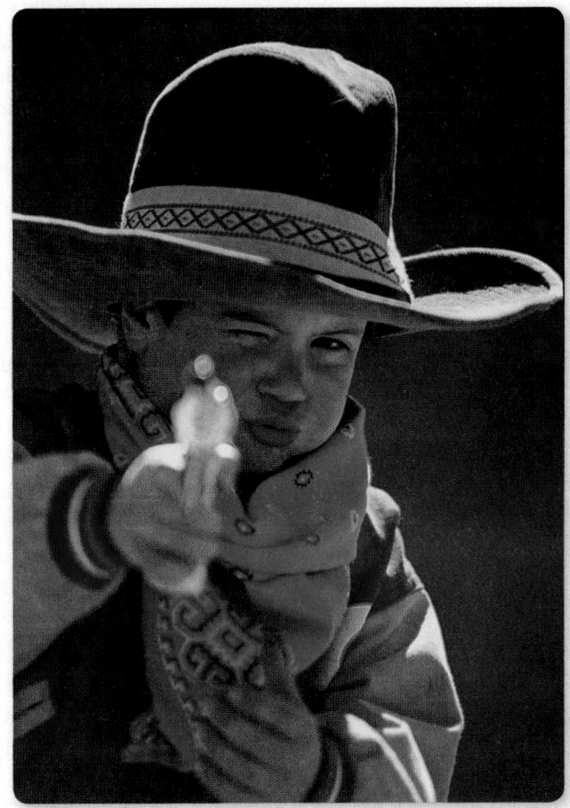

This preschool boy dressed as a cowboy has developed a strong sense of gender roles. One clear behavioral difference between young boys and young girls is boys' greater aggressiveness.

GENDER DIFFERENCES

Gender differences are psychological or behavioral differences between males and females. This is a controversial area of psychology. Measurable differences between baby boys and girls are few. Although some gender differences become more pronounced after age 3, boys and girls on average remain more alike than different. Extensive evidence from many studies supports this *gender similarities hypothesis* (Hyde, 2005), and fully 78 percent of gender differences are small to negligible. Indeed, if gender differences were large and striking, they would not elicit such controversy over their existence and cause.

Physically, among the larger gender differences are boys' higher activity level, superior motor performance, especially after puberty, and their greater propensity for physical aggression (Hyde, 2005) beginning by age 2 (Archer, 2004; Baillargeon et al., 2007; Pellegrini & Archer, 2005). (Aggression is discussed later in this chapter.)

Research involving children age 2½ to 8 has consistently identified striking differences in playtime preferences and styles. Sex-typed preferences increase between toddlerhood and middle childhood, and the degree of sex-typed behavior exhibited early in life is a strong indicator of later gender-based behavior (Golombok et al., 2008).

Cognitive gender differences are few and small (Spelke, 2005). Overall, intelligence test scores show no gender differences (Keenan & Shaw, 1997), perhaps because the most widely used tests are designed to eliminate gender bias. Boys and girls do equally well

Even in the womb, male fetuses are already more active than female fetuses.

gender identity
Awareness, developed in early childhood, that one is male or female.

on tasks involving basic mathematical skills and are equally capable of learning math. However, there are small differences in specific abilities. Girls tend to perform better on tests of verbal fluency, mathematical computation, and memory for locations of objects. Boys tend to perform better in verbal analogies, mathematical word problems, and memory for spatial configurations. In most studies, these differences do not emerge until elementary school or later (Spelke, 2005). Also, boys' mathematical abilities vary more than girls', with more boys at both the highest and lowest ends of the ability range (Halpern et al., 2007). In early childhood and again during preadolescence and adolescence, girls tend to use more responsive language, such as praise, agreement, acknowledgment, and elaboration on what someone else has said (Leaper & Smith, 2004).

checkpoint can you...

▷ Summarize the main behavioral and cognitive differences between boys and girls?

We need to remember, of course, that gender differences are valid for large groups of boys and girls but not necessarily for individuals. By knowing a child's sex, we cannot predict whether that *particular* boy or girl will be faster, stronger, smarter, more obedient, or more assertive than another child.

PERSPECTIVES ON GENDER DEVELOPMENT

What accounts for gender differences, and why do some of them emerge with age? Some explanations center on the differing experiences and social expectations that boys and girls meet almost from birth. These experiences and expectations concern three related aspects of gender identity: *gender roles, gender-typing,* and *gender stereotypes.*

gender roles Behaviors, interests, attitudes, skills, and traits that a culture considers appropriate for each sex; differ for males and females.

Gender roles are the behaviors, interests, attitudes, skills, and personality traits that a culture considers appropriate for males or females. All societies have gender roles. Historically, in most cultures, women have been expected to devote most of their time to caring for the household and children, while men were providers and protectors. Women were expected to be compliant and nurturing; men, to be active, aggressive, and competitive. Today, gender roles, especially in Western cultures, have become more diverse and more flexible.

Even Disney, long criticized for the stereotypical portrayals of women in its movies, has gotten on board with this. Merida from Brave and Anna from Frozen are both attempts to provide viewers with strong female role models.

gender-typing Socialization process whereby children, at an early age, learn appropriate gender roles.

gender stereotypes Preconceived generalizations about male or female role behavior.

Gender-typing, the acquisition of a gender role, takes place early in childhood, but children vary greatly in the degree to which they become gender-typed (Iervolino, Hines, Golombok, Rust, & Plomin, 2005). **Gender stereotypes** are preconceived generalizations about male or female behavior: "All females are passive and dependent; all males are aggressive and independent." Gender stereotypes pervade many cultures. They appear to some degree in children as young as 2 or 3, increase during the preschool years, and reach a peak at age 5 (Campbell, Shirley, & Candy, 2004; Ruble & Martin, 1998).

How do children acquire gender roles, and why do they adopt gender stereotypes? Are these purely social constructs, or do they reflect innate differences between males and females? Let's look at five theoretical perspectives on gender development (summarized in Table 1): *biological, evolutionary, psychoanalytic, cognitive,* and *social learning*. All of these perspectives can contribute to our understanding, and none by itself fully explains why boys and girls differ in some respects and not in others.

Biological Approach The existence of similar gender roles in many cultures suggests that some gender differences may be biologically based. In fact, if gender differences were purely cultural inventions, we would expect to see more variability in male and female roles and characteristics across cultures. Investigators are uncovering evidence of neurological, hormonal, and evolutionary explanations for some gender differences.

By age 5, when the brain reaches approximate adult size, boys' brains are about 10 percent larger than girls' brains, mostly because boys have a greater proportion of gray matter in the cerebral cortex, whereas girls have greater neuronal density (Reiss, Abrams,

TABLE 1 Five Perspectives on Gender Development

Theories	Major Theorists	Key Processes	Basic Beliefs
Biological Approach		Genetic, neurological, and hormonal activity	Many or most behavioral differences between the sexes can be traced to biological differences.
Evolutionary Approach	Charles Darwin	Natural and sexual selection	Child develops gender roles in preparation for adult mating and reproductive behavior.
Psychoanalytic Approach	Sigmund Freud	Resolution of unconscious emotional conflict	Gender identity occurs when the child identifies with the same-sex parent.
Cognitive Approach Cognitive-developmental theory	Lawrence Kohlberg	Self-categorization	Once a child learns she is a girl or he is a boy, the child sorts information about behavior by gender and acts accordingly.
Gender-schema theory	Sandra Bem, Carol Lynn Martin, & Charles F. Halverson	Self-categorization based on processing of cultural information	Child organizes information about what is considered appropriate for a boy or a girl on the basis of what a particular culture dictates and behaves accordingly. Child sorts by gender because the culture dictates that gender is an important schema.
Social Learning Approach Social cognitive theory	Albert Bandura	Observation of models, reinforcement	Child mentally combines observations of gendered behavior and creates own behavioral variations.

Singer, Ross, & Denckla, 1996). However, what may be even more important is what occurs in the womb when the brain is forming. Hormones in the bloodstream before or about the time of birth may affect the developing brain. Although levels of the male hormone testosterone do not appear to be related to aggressiveness in children (Constantino et al., 1993), an analysis of fetal testosterone levels and the development of gender-typical play has shown a link between higher testosterone levels and male-typical play in boys (Auyeng et al., 2009).

Some research focuses on children with unusual prenatal hormonal histories. Girls with a disorder called *congenital adrenal hyperplasia (CAH)* have high prenatal levels of *androgens* (male sex hormones). Although raised as girls, they tend to show preferences for boys' toys, rough play, and male playmates, as well as strong spatial skills. *Estrogens* (female sex hormones), on the other hand, seem to have less influence on boys' gender-typed behavior. However, because these studies are natural experiments, they cannot establish cause and effect. Factors other than hormonal differences also may play a role (Ruble & Martin, 1998).

Perhaps the most dramatic examples of biologically based research have to do with infants born with ambiguous sexual organs that appear to be part male and part female. John Money and his colleagues (Money, Hampson, & Hampson, 1955) recommended that these children be assigned as early as possible to the gender that holds the potential for the most nearly normal functioning.

However, other studies demonstrate the profound difficulty of predicting the outcome of sex assignment at birth. In one study, 14 genetically male children born without normal penises but with testes were legally and surgically assigned to female sex during the 1st month of life and were raised as girls. Between ages 5 and 16, eight declared themselves male (though two were living ambiguously). Five declared unwavering female identity but expressed difficulty fitting in with other girls; and one, after learning that she had been born male, refused to discuss the subject with anyone. Meanwhile, two boys whose parents had refused the initial sexual assignment remained male (Reiner & Gearhart, 2004). Cases such as these strongly suggest that gender identity is rooted in biological factors and is not easily changed (Diamond & Sigmundson, 1997).

For years John Money promoted his most famous study—in which one biologically male twin boy was raised as a girl following a circumcision accident—as a success and hid evidence to the contrary. It later came out that the boy had never successfully adjusted to life as a girl, had been unhappy throughout his childhood, and had several suicide attempts in his youth, finally succeeding in adulthood. Because of Money's research, thousands of gender reassignment surgeries were conducted on infants under the presumption that gender is a malleable social construct. This series of events illustrates one of the primary reasons science needs to be transparent and honest—it can have profound repercussions in the real world.

Evolutionary Approach The evolutionary approach sees gendered behavior as biologically based—with a purpose. From this controversial perspective, children's gender roles underlie the evolved mating and child-rearing strategies of adult males and females.

According to Darwin's (1871) **theory of sexual selection,** the selection of sexual partners is a response to the differing reproductive pressures that early men and women confronted in the struggle for survival of the species (Wood & Eagly, 2002). The more widely a man can "spread his seed," the greater his chances to pass on his genetic inheritance. Thus men tend to prefer more sexual partners than women do. They value physical prowess because it enables them to compete for mates and for control of resources and social status, which women value. Because a woman invests more time and energy in pregnancy and can bear only a limited number of children, each child's survival is of utmost importance to her; so she looks for a mate who will remain with her and support their offspring. The need to raise each child to reproductive maturity also explains why women tend to be more caring and nurturant than men (Bjorklund & Pellegrini, 2000; Wood & Eagly, 2002).

theory of sexual selection
Darwin's theory that gender roles developed in response to men's and women's differing reproductive needs.

According to evolutionary theory, male competitiveness and aggressiveness and female nurturance develop during childhood as preparation for these adult roles (Pellegrini & Archer, 2005). Boys play at fighting; girls play at parenting. In caring for children, women often must put a child's needs and feelings ahead of their own. Thus young girls tend to be better able than young boys to control and inhibit their emotions and to refrain from impulsive behavior (Bjorklund & Pellegrini, 2000).

This approach does not imply that men and women are consciously striving to have lots of kids and pass on their genes. Instead, it is argued that men and women do things—like have sex—that make it more likely they will leave descendants.

Some people misinterpret evolutionary approaches as being deterministic in nature. If evolution plays a role in the development of gender roles, they assume that means gender roles are preordained, and thus should be inflexible and highly resistant to change. For example, as would be predicted, it is indeed the case that in all cultures women tend to be children's primary caregivers (Wood & Eagly, 2002) and men are overwhelmingly responsible for homicides (Daly & Wilson, 1988). But this does not mean that men never care for children, nor does it mean that women are never aggressive. Rather, it means that evolution has given us a slight "push" in one direction or another that can be minimized or maximized by cultural and environmental influences. It is only when large numbers of individuals are examined that gender differences emerge.

Critics of evolutionary theory argue that society and culture are more important than biology in determining gender roles. But evolutionary theorists have never argued that culture is insignificant. Rather, they have argued that men and women have cognitive adaptations designed to be sensitive to environmental input. Research suggests that men's primary ancestral role was to provide for subsistence while women's was to tend to the children, but this does not mean that we are bound to these roles. Indeed, in some nonindustrial societies, women are the main or equal providers, and men and women's mate preferences seem to be less pronounced in egalitarian societies where women have more reproductive freedom and educational opportunities (Wood & Eagly, 2002).

Worried about the boy down the street whose play is always too aggressive? In all likelihood, there's nothing to be concerned about. Research suggests no link between early aggressive play in boys and later criminality.

Parry, 2010

Gender roles are best seen as a dynamic process. Evolutionary psychologists acknowledge that gender roles (such as men's involvement in child rearing) may change in an environment different from that in which these roles initially evolved (Crawford, 1998).

Psychoanalytic Approach "Daddy, where will you live when I grow up and marry Mommy?" asks Mario, age 4. From the psychoanalytic perspective, Mario's question is part of his acquisition of gender identity. That process, according to Freud, is one of **identification,** the adoption of characteristics, beliefs, attitudes, values, and behaviors of the parent of the same sex. Freud considered identification an important personality development of early childhood. Some social learning theorists also have used the term.

identification
In Freudian theory, the process by which a young child adopts characteristics, beliefs, attitudes, values, and behaviors of the parent of the same sex.

According to Freud, identification will occur for Mario when he represses or gives up the wish to possess the parent of the other sex (his mother) and identifies with the parent of the same sex (his father). Although this explanation for gender development has been influential, it has been difficult to test and has little research support (Maccoby, 2000). Most developmental psychologists today favor other explanations.

Cognitive Approach Sarah figures out she is a girl because people call her a girl. As she continues to observe and think about her world, she concludes that she will always be a girl. She comes to understand gender by actively thinking about and constructing her own gender-typing. This is the heart of Lawrence Kohlberg's (1966) cognitive-developmental theory.

Kohlberg's Cognitive-Developmental Theory In Kohlberg's theory, gender knowledge ("I am a boy") precedes gendered behavior ("so I like to do boy things"). Children actively search for cues about gender in their social world. As they realize which gender they belong to, they adopt behaviors they perceive as consistent with being male or female. Thus, 3-year-old Sarah prefers dolls to trucks because she sees girls playing with dolls and therefore views playing with dolls as consistent with her being a girl. And she plays mostly with other girls, whom she assumes will share her interests (Martin & Ruble, 2004).

The acquisition of gender roles, said Kohlberg, hinges on **gender constancy,** also called *sex-category constancy*—a child's realization that his or her gender will always be the same. Once children achieve this realization, they are motivated to adopt behaviors appropriate to their gender. Gender constancy seems to develop in three stages: *gender identity, gender stability,* and *gender consistency* (Martin et al., 2002):

gender constancy
Awareness that one will always be male or female; also called *sex-category constancy.*

Gender

- *Gender identity:* awareness of one's own gender and that of others typically occurs between ages 2 and 3.
- *Gender stability:* awareness that gender does not change. However, children at this stage base judgments about gender on superficial appearances (clothing or hairstyle) and stereotyped behaviors.
- *Gender consistency:* the realization that a girl remains a girl even if she has a short haircut and plays with trucks, and a boy remains a boy even if he has long hair and earrings typically occurs between ages 3 and 7. Once children realize that changes in outward appearance will not affect their gender, they may become less rigid in their adherence to gender norms (Martin et al., 2002).

Much research challenges Kohlberg's view that gender-typing depends on gender constancy. Long before children attain the final stage of gender constancy, they show gender-typed preferences (Bussey & Bandura, 1992; Martin & Ruble, 2004). For example, gender preferences in toys and playmates appear as early as 12 to 24 months. However, these findings do not challenge Kohlberg's basic insight: that gender concepts influence behavior (Martin et al., 2002).

Today, cognitive-developmental theorists no longer claim that gender constancy must precede gender-typing (Martin et al., 2002). Instead, they suggest, gender-typing may be heightened by the more sophisticated understanding that gender constancy brings (Martin & Ruble, 2004). Each stage of gender constancy increases children's attention toward and memory for gender-relevant information. The achievement of gender identity may motivate children to learn more about gender; whereas gender stability and gender consistency may motivate them to be sure they are acting "like a boy" or "like a girl" (Martin et al., 2002).

gender-schema theory
Theory, proposed by Bem, that children socialize themselves in their gender roles by developing a mentally organized network of information about what it means to be male or female in a particular culture.

Gender-Schema Theory Another cognitive approach is **gender-schema theory.** Like cognitive-developmental theory, it views children as actively extracting knowledge about gender from their environment *before* engaging in gender-typed behavior. However, gender-schema theory places more emphasis on the influence of culture. Once children know what sex they are, they develop a concept of what it means to be male or female *in their culture.* Children then match their behavior to their culture's view of what boys and girls are "supposed" to be and do (Bem, 1993; Martin et al., 2002).

According to this theory, gender schemas promote gender stereotypes by influencing judgments about behavior. When a new boy his age moves in next door, 4-year-old Brandon knocks on his door, carrying a toy truck—apparently assuming that the new boy will like the same toys he likes. Bem suggests that children who show such stereotypical behavior may be experiencing pressure for gender conformity that inhibits healthy self-exploration. However, there is little evidence that gender schemas are at the root of stereotyped behavior or that children who are highly gender-typed necessarily feel pressure to conform (Yunger, Carver, & Perry, 2004). Indeed, as many parents will attest, it can be difficult to encourage a child to behave in ways that are not stereotypically masculine or feminine.

Another problem with both gender-schema theory and Kohlberg's theory is that gender-stereotyping does not always become stronger with increased gender knowledge (Bandura & Bussey, 2004; Bussey & Bandura, 1999). In fact, gender-stereotyping rises and then falls in a developmental pattern (Ruble & Martin, 1998; Welch-Ross & Schmidt, 1996). Around ages 4 to 6, when, according to gender-schema theory, children are constructing and then consolidating their gender schemas, they notice and remember only information consistent with these schemas and even exaggerate it. In fact, they tend to *mis*remember information that challenges gender stereotypes, such as photos of a girl sawing wood or a boy cooking, and to insist that the genders in the photos were the other way around. Young children are quick to accept gender labels; when told that an unfamiliar toy is for the other sex, they will drop it like a hot potato, and they expect others to do the same (Martin & Ruble, 2004).

By ages 5 and 6, children develop a repertoire of rigid stereotypes about gender that they apply to themselves and others. A boy will pay more attention to what he considers boys' toys and a girl to girls' toys. Then, around age 7 or 8, schemas become more complex as children begin to take in and integrate contradictory information, such as the fact that many girls have short hair. At this point, children develop more complex beliefs about gender and become more flexible in their views about gender roles (Martin & Ruble, 2004; Trautner et al., 2005).

Coloring book and cereal box characters are not immune from gender stereotypes. Females are more likely to be portrayed as children or humans, males are more likely to be portrayed as animals, adults, and superheroes.

Cognitive approaches to gender development have made an important contribution by exploring how children think about gender and what they know about it at various ages. However, these approaches may not fully explain the link between knowledge and conduct. There is disagreement about precisely what mechanism prompts children to act out gender roles and why some children become more strongly gender-typed than others (Bussey & Bandura, 1992, 1999; Martin & Ruble, 2004; Ruble & Martin, 1998). Some investigators point to socialization.

Social Learning Approach According to Walter Mischel (1966), a traditional social learning theorist, children acquire gender roles by imitating models and being rewarded for gender-appropriate behavior. Typically, one model is a parent, often of the same sex, but children also pattern their behavior after other adults or after peers. Behavioral feedback, together with direct teaching by parents and other adults, reinforces gender-typing. A boy who models his behavior after his father is commended for acting "like a boy." A girl gets compliments on a pretty dress or hairstyle. In this model, *gendered behavior precedes gender knowledge* ("I am rewarded for doing boy things, so I must be a boy").

Since the 1970s, however, studies have cast doubt on the power of same-sex modeling alone to account for gender differences. As cognitive explanations have come to the fore, traditional social learning theory has lost favor (Martin et al., 2002). Albert Bandura's

(1986; Bussey & Bandura, 1999) newer **social cognitive theory,** an expansion of social learning theory, incorporates some cognitive elements.

social cognitive theory Albert Bandura's expansion of social learning theory; holds that children learn gender roles through socialization.

According to social cognitive theory, observation enables children to learn much about gender-typed behaviors before performing them. They can mentally combine observations of multiple models and generate their own behavioral variations. Instead of viewing the environment as a given, social cognitive theory recognizes that children select or even create their environments through their choice of playmates and activities. However, critics say that social cognitive theory does not explain how children differentiate between boys and girls before they have a concept of gender, or what initially motivates children to acquire gender knowledge (Martin et al., 2002).

This explanation of gender development focuses on the learning approaches. Theories help us understand and make sense of the world, and in this case, we use the principles of reinforcement and punishment to explain gender. Note that theories change in response to new data. When research began to indicate that cognition also mattered, the original approach was expanded to accommodate those findings.

For social cognitive theorists, socialization—the way a child interprets and internalizes experiences with parents, teachers, peers, and cultural institutions—plays a central part in gender development. Socialization begins in infancy, long before a conscious understanding of gender begins to form. Gradually, as children begin to regulate their activities, standards of behavior become internalized. A child no longer needs praise, rebukes, or a model's presence to act in socially appropriate ways. Children feel good about themselves when they live up to their internal standards and feel bad when they do not. A substantial part of the shift from socially guided control to self-regulation of gender-related behavior may take place between ages 3 and 4 (Bussey, 2011; Bussey & Bandura, 1992). In the following sections we address three primary sources of social influences on gender development: family, peer, and cultural.

Family Influences When Louisiana governor Kathleen Blanco's 4-year-old grandson David was asked what he wanted to be when he grew up, he wasn't sure. He shrugged off all his mother's suggestions—firefighter, soldier, policeman, airplane pilot. Finally, she asked whether he'd like to be governor. "Mom," he replied, "I'm a boy!" (Associated Press, 2004).

David's response illustrates how strong family influences may be, even fostering counterstereotypical preferences. Usually, though, experience in the family seems to reinforce gender-typical preferences and attitudes. We say "seems" because it is difficult to separate parents' genetic influence from the influence of the environment they create. Also, parents may be responding to rather than encouraging children's gender-typed behavior (Iervolino et al., 2005).

Did you know that pink used to be considered masculine and blue feminine? Blue was considered soothing, and so more appropriate for girls. Pink was a variation of red, a strong and active color, and was seen as more appropriate for boys.

Boys tend to be more strongly gender-socialized concerning play preferences than girls. Parents, especially fathers, generally show more discomfort if a boy plays with a doll than if a girl plays with a truck (Ruble, Martin, & Berenbaum, 2006; Sandnabba & Ahlberg, 1999). Girls have more freedom than boys in their clothes, games, and choice of playmates (Fagot, Rogers, & Leinbach, 2000; Miedzian, 1991).

The division of labor in a household matters too. In an analysis of 43 studies, Tenengaum and Leaper (2002) found that parents who adhered to traditional gender schemas were more likely to have strongly gender-typed children. There are indications that the father's role in gender socialization is especially important, and that viewing fathers engaged in household and child care work is associated with decreased gender-typing (Deutsch, Servis, & Payne, 2001; Turner & Gervai, 1995).

Peer Influences Anna, at age 5, insisted on dressing in a new way. She wanted to wear leggings with a skirt over them, and boots—indoors and out. When her mother asked her why, Anna replied, "Because Katie dresses like this—and Katie's the king of the girls!"

Even in early childhood, the peer group is a major influence on gender-typing. By age 3, preschoolers generally play in sex-segregated groups that reinforce gender-typed behavior, and the influence of the peer group increases with age (Martin et al., 2002; Ruble & Martin, 1998). Children who play in same-sex groups tend to be more gender-typed than children who do not (Maccoby, 2002; Martin & Fabes, 2001). Indeed, play choices at this age may be more strongly influenced by peers than by the models children see at home (Martin & Fabes, 2001; Turner & Gervai, 1995). Generally, however, peer and parental attitudes reinforce each other (Bussey & Bandura, 1999).

Cultural Influences When a young girl in Nepal touched the plow that her brother was using, she was scolded. In this way she learned that as a female she must refrain from acts her brother was expected to perform (D. Skinner, 1989).

In the United States, television is a major format for the transmission of cultural attitudes toward gender. Social learning theory predicts that children who watch a lot of television will become more gender-typed by imitating the stereotyped models they see on the screen. Dramatic supporting evidence emerged from a natural experiment in several Canadian towns with access to television transmission for the first time. Children who had had relatively unstereotyped attitudes showed marked increases in traditional views 2 years later (Kimball, 1986). Movies also have an impact. Research has shown that males in G-rated movies are more likely to be main characters, and females are more likely to be portrayed as young and as possessing traits such as intelligence and beauty (Smith, Pieper, Granados, & Choueiti, 2010).

Children's books, especially illustrated ones, have long been a source of gender stereotypes. An analysis of 200 top-selling and award-winning children's books uncovered nearly twice as many male as female main characters and strong gender-stereotyping. Female main characters nurtured more, were portrayed in indoor settings, and appeared to have no paid occupations (Hamilton, Anderson, Broaddus, & Young, 2006). Fathers were largely absent, and when they appeared, they were shown as withdrawn and ineffectual (Anderson & Hamilton, 2005). Similar results have been found in coloring books, where females are more typically portrayed as children and boys as superheroes, animals, or adults (Fitzpatrick & McPherson, 2010).

checkpoint
can **you** . . .

- Compare five approaches to the study of gender development?
- Assess evidence for biological explanations of gender differences?
- Discuss how various theories explain the acquisition of gender roles, and assess the support for each theory?

Major strengths of the socialization approach include the breadth and multiplicity of processes it examines and the scope for individual differences it reveals. But this very complexity makes it difficult to establish clear causal connections between the way children are raised and the way they think and act. Just what aspects of the home environment and the peer culture promote gender-typing? Do parents and peers treat boys and girls differently because they *are* different or because the culture says they *should be* different? Does differential treatment *produce* or *reflect* gender differences? Or, as social cognitive theory suggests, is there a bidirectional relationship? Further research may help us see how socializing agents mesh with children's biological tendencies and cognitive understandings with regard to gender-related attitudes and behavior.

Play: The Business of Early Childhood

Carmen, age 3, pretends that the pieces of cereal floating in her bowl are "fishies" swimming in the milk, and she "fishes," spoonful by spoonful. After breakfast, she puts on her mother's hat, picks up a briefcase, and is a "mommy" going to work. She rides her tricycle through the puddles, comes in for an imaginary phone call, turns a wooden block into a truck and says, "Vroom, vroom!" Carmen's day is one round of play after another.

Across many animal species, play is practice for skills needed in adulthood. Young prey animals run and jump with each other, predators stalk and attack their littermates. How is children's play helping prepare children for adulthood? What social skills are being practiced?

It would be a mistake to dismiss Carmen's activities as "just fun." Although play does not seem to serve any obvious purpose, it is vitally important to development and has significant current and long-term functions (Bjorklund & Pellegrini, 2002; P. K. Smith, 2005b). Play is important to healthy development of body and brain. It enables children to engage with the world around them, to use their imagination, to discover flexible ways to use objects and solve problems, and to prepare for adult roles. Play is not what children do to burn off energy so they can get to the real business of learning. Play is the context in which much of the most important learning occurs (see Box 1).

Play contributes to all domains of development. Through play, children stimulate the senses, exercise their muscles, coordinate sight with movement, gain mastery over their bodies, make decisions, and acquire new skills. Indeed, play is so important to

research in action

DOES PLAY HAVE AN EVOLUTIONARY BASIS?

Children play for the pure pleasure it brings. Yet, from an evolutionary standpoint, play serves a greater purpose. This activity that (1) takes up considerable time and energy; (2) shows a characteristic age progression, peaking in childhood and declining with sexual maturity; (3) is encouraged by parents; and (4) occurs in all cultures seems to have been naturally selected for its significant benefits for children (Bjorklund & Pellegrini, 2000; P. K. Smith, 2005b).

Many psychologists and educators see play as an adaptive activity characteristic of the long period of immaturity and dependence during which children gain the physical attributes and cognitive and social learning necessary for adult life. Play aids bone and muscle development and gives children a chance to master activities and develop a sense of their capabilities (Bjorklund & Pellegrini, 2000). Through play, children practice, in a risk-free environment, behaviors and skills they will need as adults (Hawes, 1996). Animal studies suggest that the evolution of play may be linked to the evolution of intelligence. The most intelligent animals (birds and mammals) play, whereas less intelligent species (fish, reptiles, and amphibians) do not, as far as we can tell (Hawes, 1996).

Parents, according to evolutionary theory, encourage play because the future benefits of children's skill acquisition outweigh any benefits of current productive activity in which children, at their relatively low skill levels, might engage (P. K. Smith, 2005b). Gender differences in children's play enable boys and girls to practice adult behaviors important for reproduction and survival (Bjorklund & Pellegrini, 2002; Geary, 1999).

Different types of play serve different adaptive functions. Early locomotor play is common among all mammals and may support brain development. Later, exercise play may help develop muscle strength, endurance, physical skills, and efficiency of movement (P. K. Smith, 2005b). Play with objects is found mainly among primates: humans, monkeys, and apes. Object play may have served an evolutionary purpose in the development of tools, by enabling people to learn the properties of objects and what can be done with them (Bjorklund & Pellegrini, 2002). In premodern societies, object play tends to focus on developing useful skills, such as making baskets and pounding grain (P. K. Smith, 2005b). Young mammals, like human children, engage in social play, such as wrestling and chasing each other, which strengthens social bonds, facilitates cooperation, and lessens aggression (Hawes, 1996).

Dramatic play seems to be an almost exclusively human activity. It appears to be universal but is less frequent in societies in which children are expected to participate in adult work (P. K. Smith, 2005a). In traditional hunter-gatherer societies, children imitate adult subsistence activities such as hunting, fishing, and preparing food. These highly repetitive routines seem to serve primarily as practice for adult activities (P. K. Smith, 2005b). As humans began to settle in permanent communities, dramatic play may have evolved so as to practice the changing skills needed for new ways of life. In modern urban industrial societies, themes of dramatic play are highly influenced by the mass media. At least in higher-SES families, dramatic play is encouraged by an abundance of toys, the absence of demands on children to help in subsistence activities, heavy parental involvement in play, and play-based preschool curricula (P. K. Smith, 2005a).

Investigators still have much to learn about the functions and benefits of play, but one thing seems clear: the time children spend playing is time well spent.

From your observations of children's play, what immediate and long-range purposes does it appear to serve?

children's development that the United Nations High Commissioner for Human Rights (1989) has recognized it as a right of every child. Unfortunately, the trend to full-day kindergarten has markedly reduced the time for free play (Ginsburg et al., 2007).

Children need plenty of time for free exploratory play. Today, many parents expose young children to enrichment videos and academically oriented playthings. These activities may—or may not—be valuable in themselves, but not if they interfere with child-directed play (Ginsburg et al., 2007).

Children of differing ages have differing styles of play, play at different things, and spend different amounts of time in various types of play (Bjorklund & Pellegrini, 2002). Physical play, for example, begins in infancy with apparently aimless rhythmic movements. As gross motor skills improve, preschoolers exercise their muscles by running, jumping, skipping, hopping, and throwing. Toward the end of this period and into middle childhood, *rough-and-tumble play* involving wrestling, kicking, and chasing becomes more common, especially among boys.

Researchers categorize children's play in varying ways. One common classification system is by *cognitive complexity*. Another classification is based on the *social dimension* of play.

COGNITIVE LEVELS OF PLAY

functional play
Play involving repetitive large muscular movements.

constructive play
Play involving use of objects or materials to make something.

dramatic play
Play involving imaginary people or situations; also called *pretend play, fantasy play,* or *imaginative play.*

formal games with rules
Organized games with known procedures and penalties.

Courtney, at 3, talked for a doll, using a deeper voice than her own. Miguel, at 4, wore a kitchen towel as a cape and flew around as Batman. These children were engaged in play involving make-believe people or situations—one of four levels of play Smilansky (1968) identified as showing increasing amounts of cognitive complexity. The categories are *functional play, constructive play, dramatic play,* and *games with rules.* Although certain types of play are more common at particular ages, the types of play can occur anytime.

The simplest level, which begins during infancy, is **functional play** (sometimes called *locomotor play*), consisting of repeated practice in large muscular movements, such as rolling a ball (Bjorklund & Pellegrini, 2002).

The second level, **constructive play** (also called *object play*), is the use of objects or materials to make something, such as a house of blocks or a crayon drawing. Children spend an estimated 10 to 15 percent of their time playing with objects (Bjorklund & Pellegrini, 2002).

This young "butterfly" is participating in dramatic play based on the ability to use symbols to stand for people or things.

The third level, **dramatic play** (also called *pretend play, fantasy play,* or *imaginative play*), involves imaginary objects, actions, or roles; it rests on the symbolic function, which emerges during the last part of the second year (Piaget, 1962). Dramatic play involves a combination of cognition, emotion, language, and sensorimotor behavior. More advanced cognitive development affords more sophisticated play, but play also helps strengthen the development of dense connections in the brain and promotes later capacity for abstract thought. Play is not just the response to a developing intellect; it is the driver of it as well. For example, studies have found the quality of dramatic play to be associated with social and linguistic competence (Bergen, 2002). By making "tickets" for an imaginary train trip or "reading eye charts" in a "doctor's office," children build emergent literacy skills (Christie, 1998). Pretend play also may further the development of theory-of-mind skills (Smith, 2005b). Pretending that a banana is a telephone, for example, and understanding that you and I both agree on that pretense, can help children begin to understand others' thoughts.

Dramatic play peaks during the preschool years, increasing in frequency and complexity (Bjorklund & Pellegrini, 2002; Smith, 2005a), and then declines as school-age children become more involved in **formal games with rules**—organized games with known procedures and penalties, such as hopscotch and marbles. However, many children continue to engage in pretending well beyond the elementary school years. An estimated 12 to 15 percent of preschoolers' time is spent in pretend play (Bjorklund & Pellegrini, 2002), but the trend toward academically oriented kindergarten programs may limit the amount of time children can spend in such play (Bergen, 2002; Ginsburg et al., 2007).

THE SOCIAL DIMENSION OF PLAY

study**smart**

Levels of Play

In a classic study done in the 1920s, Mildred B. Parten (1932) identified six types of play ranging from the least to the most social (Table 2). She found that as children get older their play tends to become more social—that is, more interactive and more cooperative. At first children play alone, then alongside other children, and finally together. Although this general progression is common, children of all ages also engage in all of Parten's categories of play (K. H. Rubin, Bukowski, & Parker, 1998).

Parten incorrectly regarded nonsocial play as less mature than social play. She suggested that young children who continue to play alone may develop social, psychological, or educational problems. However, certain types of nonsocial play, particularly parallel play and solitary independent play, may consist of activities that *foster* cognitive, physical, and social development.

Researchers now look not only at *whether* a child plays alone but at *why*. Among 567 kindergartners, teachers, observers, and classmates rated almost 2 out of 3 children who played alone as socially and cognitively competent; they simply preferred to play that way (Harrist, Zain, Bates, Dodge, & Pettit, 1997). On the other hand, solitary play sometimes can be a sign of shyness, anxiety, fearfulness, or social rejection (Coplan, Prakash, O'Neil, & Armer, 2004; Henderson, Marshall, Fox, & Rubin, 2004; Spinrad et al., 2004).

Reticent play, a combination of Parten's unoccupied and onlooker categories, is often a manifestation of shyness (Coplan et al., 2004). However, such reticent behaviors as playing near other children, watching what they do, or wandering aimlessly may sometimes be a prelude to joining in others' play (Spinrad et al., 2004). In a short-term longitudinal study, reticent children were well-liked and showed few problem behaviors (Spinrad et al., 2004). Nonsocial play, then, seems to be far more complex than Parten imagined.

One kind of play that becomes more social during the preschool years is dramatic play (K. H. Rubin et al., 1998). Children typically engage in more dramatic play when

TABLE 2 Parten's Categories of Social and Nonsocial Play

Category	Description
Unoccupied behavior	The child does not seem to be playing but watches anything of momentary interest.
Onlooker behavior	The child spends most of the time watching other children play. The onlooker talks to them, asking questions or making suggestions, but does not enter into the play. The onlooker is definitely observing particular groups of children rather than anything that happens to be exciting.
Solitary independent play	The child plays alone with toys that are different from those used by nearby children and makes no effort to get close to them.
Parallel play	The child plays independently but among the other children, playing with toys like those used by the other children but not necessarily playing with them in the same way. Playing *beside* rather than *with* the others, the parallel player does not try to influence the other children's play.
Associative play	The child plays with other children. They talk about their play, borrow and lend toys, follow one another, and try to control who may play in the group. All the children play similarly if not identically; there is no division of labor and no organization around any goal. Each child acts as she or he wishes and is interested more in being with the other children than in the activity itself.
Cooperative or organized supplementary play	The child plays in a group organized for some goal—to make something, play a formal game, or dramatize a situation. One or two children control who belongs to the group and direct activities. By a division of labor, children take on different roles and supplement each other's efforts.

Source: Adapted from Parten, 1932, pp. 249–251.

playing with someone else than when playing alone (Bjorklund & Pellegrini, 2002). As dramatic play becomes more collaborative, story lines become more complex and innovative, offering rich opportunities to practice interpersonal and language skills and to explore social conventions and roles. In pretending together, children develop joint problem-solving, planning, and goal-seeking skills; gain understanding of other people's perspectives; and construct an image of the social world (Bergen, 2002; Bjorklund & Pellegrini, 2002; P. K. Smith, 2005a).

How do you think the growing use of computers for both games and educational activities might affect preschool children's play?

A common type of dramatic play involves imaginary companions. This normal phenomenon of childhood is seen most often in firstborn and only children, who lack the close company of siblings. Girls are more likely than boys to have imaginary friends, or at least to acknowledge them (Carlson & Taylor, 2005).

Children who have imaginary companions can distinguish fantasy from reality (M. Taylor, Cartwright, & Carlson, 1993). They play more imaginatively than other children and are more cooperative (D. G. Singer & J. L. Singer, 1990); and they do not lack for friends (Gleason, Sebane, & Hartup, 2000). In one study of 152 preschoolers, 4-year-olds who reported having imaginary companions did better on theory-of-mind tasks (such as differentiating appearance and reality and recognizing false beliefs) than children who did not create such companions (M. Taylor & Carlson, 1997), and these children showed greater emotional understanding 3 years later. The positive associations with imaginary companions continue through preschool. Although 5½-year old children with imaginary companions do not have a bigger vocabulary than children without imaginary companions, they tell more elaborate stories about both personal experiences and a storybook (Trionfi & Reese, 2009). These types of results, as a whole, point to the role of play and imagination in the development of essential cognitive and socio-emotional skills.

gender segregation
Tendency to select playmates of one's own gender.

study smart

Emergence of Friendship

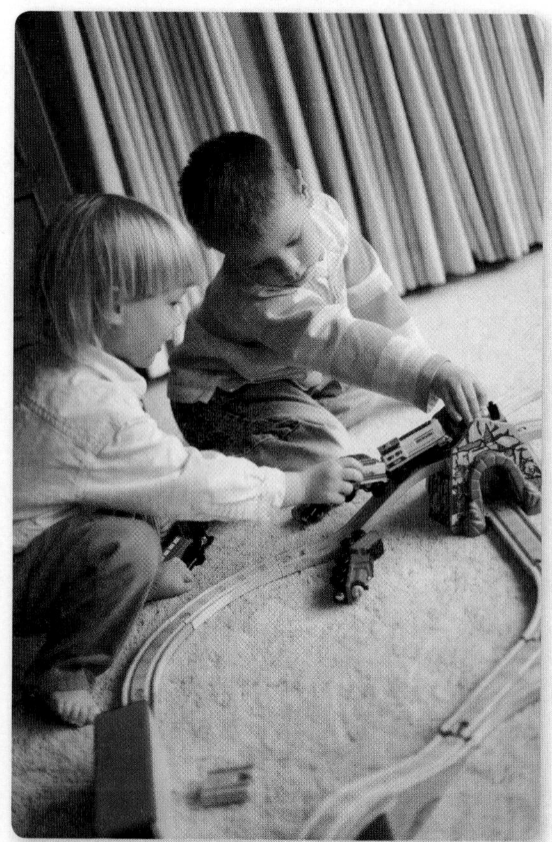

Preschool girls and boys do not typically play together. When they do, they usually play with "masculine" toys such as cars, trains, or blocks.

HOW GENDER INFLUENCES PLAY

As we have mentioned, sex segregation is common among preschoolers and becomes more prevalent in middle childhood. This tendency seems to be universal across cultures (P. K. Smith, 2005a). Although biology (sex hormones), gender identification, and adult reinforcement all seem to influence gender differences in play, the influence of the peer group may be more powerful (P. K. Smith, 2005a). By 3 years of age girls are much more likely to play with dolls and tea sets whereas boys prefer toy guns and trucks (Dunn & Hughes, 2001). Girls tend to select other girls as playmates, and boys prefer other boys (Maccoby & Jacklin, 1987; Martin & Fabes, 2001), a phenomenon known as **gender segregation.** Boys' tendency to be more active and physically aggressive as compared to girls' more nurturing play styles are likely contributors to gender segregation. Boys play spontaneously on sidewalks, streets, or empty lots; girls tend to choose more structured, adult-supervised activities (Bjorklund & Pellegrini, 2002; Fabes, Martin, & Hanish, 2003; P. K. Smith, 2005a). Moreover, this does not seem to be driven by social influences. Regardless of the cultural group they come from, boys tend to engage in more exploratory play, and girls enjoy more symbolic and pretend play (Cote & Bornstein, 2009).

Girls' pretend stories generally focus on social relationships and nurturing, and highlight domestic roles as in playing house (Pellegrini & Archer, 2005; P. K. Smith, 2005a). Boys' pretend play often involves danger or discord and competitive, dominant roles, as in mock battles. Additionally, boys' play is more strongly gender-stereotyped than girls' (Bjorklund & Pellegrini, 2002). Thus, in mixed-sex groups, play tends to revolve around traditionally masculine activities (Fabes et al., 2003).

HOW CULTURE INFLUENCES PLAY

Cultural values affect the play environments adults set up for children, and these environments in turn affect the frequency of specific forms of play across cultures (Bodrova & Leong, 1998, 2005). One observational study compared 48 middle-class Korean American and 48 middle-class Anglo-American children in separate preschools (Farver, Kim, & Lee, 1995). The Anglo-American preschools encouraged independent thinking, active involvement in learning, social interchanges among children, and collaborative activities with teachers. The Korean American preschool emphasized development of academic skills and completion of tasks. Not surprisingly, the Anglo-American children engaged in more social play, whereas the Korean Americans engaged in more unoccupied or parallel play. At the same time, Korean American children played more cooperatively, often offering toys to other children—very likely a reflection of their culture's emphasis on group harmony. Anglo-American children were more aggressive and often responded negatively to other children's suggestions, reflecting the competitiveness of American culture.

checkpoint
can **you**...

- Identify four cognitive levels of play and six categories of social and nonsocial play?
- Explain how cognitive and social dimensions of play may be connected?
- Tell how gender and culture influence the way children play, and give examples?

Parenting

Parenting can be a complex challenge. Parents must deal with small people who have independent minds and wills, but who still have a lot to learn about what kinds of behavior work well in society.

discipline
Methods of molding children's character and of teaching them to exercise self-control and engage in acceptable behavior.

FORMS OF DISCIPLINE

In the field of human development, **discipline** refers to methods of molding character and of teaching self-control and acceptable behavior. In casual speech we tend to think of discipline as involving only punishment, but the psychological definition of the word also includes techniques such as rewarding desired behaviors, and drawing attention to how actions affect others. Discipline can be a powerful tool for socialization with the goal of developing self-discipline. What forms of discipline work best?

A secure attachment with parents or a teacher in early childhood has been related to whether or not children view God as a "loving friend"—someone who is nice, loves you, and makes you happy. If you are religious, do you think your relationship with your parents affects your religious beliefs?

de Roos, 2006

Reinforcement and Punishment "You're such a wonderful helper, Nick! Thank you so much for putting away your toys." Nick's mother smiles warmly at her son as he plops his dump truck into the toy box. Her words and actions provide gentle discipline for her son and teach him that putting away his toys is a positive behavior that should be repeated.

Parents sometimes punish children to stop undesirable behavior, but children usually learn more from being reinforced for good behavior. *External* reinforcements may be tangible (treats, more playtime) or intangible (a smile, a word of praise, or a special privilege). Whatever the reinforcement, the child must see it as rewarding and must receive it fairly consistently after showing the desired behavior. Eventually, the behavior should provide an *internal* reinforcement: a sense of pleasure or accomplishment.

There are occasions, however, when punishment, such as isolation or denial of privileges, is necessary. Children cannot be permitted to run out into traffic or hit another child. In such situations, punishment, if consistent, immediate, and clearly tied to the offense, may be effective. It should be administered calmly, in private, and aimed at eliciting compliance, not guilt. It is most effective when accompanied by a short, simple explanation (AAP Committee on Psychosocial Aspects of Child and Family Health, 1998; Baumrind, 1996a). It is important to remember that, in addition to punishment for undesired behaviors, the desired behaviors should be made clear. Children need to know what should be substituted for misbehavior.

Punishment that is too harsh can be harmful. Children who are punished harshly and frequently may have trouble interpreting other people's actions and words; they may attribute hostile intentions where none exist (Weiss, Dodge, Bates, & Pettit, 1992).

Kids who come from homes in which there is domestic abuse, whether physical or emotional, are more likely to be spanked.

Taylor, Lee, Guterman, & Rice, 2010

Dante Cicchetti from the University of Minnesota has found that children from abusive homes are more likely to respond to a schoolmate's cries with aggression or withdrawal than are children from loving homes, who are more likely to try to comfort their schoolmate or go get a teacher. Why might abused children have developed this tendency? How might their parents' responses to their distress have shaped this?

Young children who have been punished harshly may act aggressively (Nix et al., 1999) or may become passive because they feel helpless. Children may become frightened if parents lose control and may eventually try to avoid a punitive parent, undermining the parent's ability to influence behavior (Grusec & Goodnow, 1994).

Corporal punishment has been defined as "the use of physical force with the intention of causing a child to experience pain, but not injury, for the purpose of correction or control of the child's behavior" (Straus, 1994, p. 4). It can include spanking, hitting, slapping, pinching, shaking (which can be fatal to infants), and other physical acts. Corporal punishment is popularly believed to be more effective than other methods, to instill respect for parental authority, and to be harmless if done in moderation by loving parents (Kazdin & Benjet, 2003; McLoyd & Smith, 2002). However, a growing body of evidence from cross-sectional and longitudinal studies suggests that it is often counterproductive and should be avoided (Straus, 1999; Straus & Stewart, 1999). Research strongly suggests that frequent or severe corporal punishment is harmful to children. Apart from the risk of injury, children who experience corporal punishment may fail to internalize moral messages, develop poor parent-child relationships, and show increased physical aggressiveness or antisocial behavior (Berlin et al., 2009; Gershoff, 2002; MacMillan et al., 1999), even in adulthood (Straus & Stewart, 1999). In addition, spanking has been negatively associated with cognitive development (Berlin et al., 2009), and there is no clear line between mild and harsh spanking—mild spanking often leads to the other (Kazdin & Benjet, 2003).

An ongoing debate about the appropriateness of the use of corporal punishment in schools rages in the United States. Twenty-one states permit the use of corporal punishment in schools. Some educators believe it is an effective deterrent to harmful misbehaviors, like fighting, but others assert that corporal punishment degrades the educational environment (Human Rights Watch, 2008). The American Academy of Pediatrics Committee on Psychosocial Aspects of Child and Family Health (1998) recommends positive reinforcement to encourage desired behaviors and verbal reprimands, time-outs (brief isolation to give the child a chance to cool down), or removal of privileges to discourage undesired behaviors—all within a positive, supportive, loving parent-child relationship.

Inductive Reasoning, Power Assertion, and Withdrawal of Love When Sara took candy from a store, her father did not lecture her on honesty, spank her, or tell her what a bad girl she had been. Instead, he explained how the owner of the store would be harmed by her failure to pay for the candy and how sad he would feel that it was gone. He asked Sara how she would feel in the same situation. Then he took her back to the store to return the candy. Although he did not ask her to do so, Sara told the store owner she was sorry she had made him sad.

Inductive techniques, such as those Sara's father used, are designed to encourage desirable behavior or discourage undesirable behavior by setting limits, demonstrating logical consequences of an action, explaining, discussing, negotiating, and getting ideas from the child about what is fair. They also tend to include appeals to consider how one's actions affect how others feel. Inductive techniques are usually the most effective method of getting children to accept parental standards (M. L. Hoffman, 1970; Kerr, Lopez, Olson, & Sameroff, 2004).

Inductive reasoning tends to arouse empathy for the victim of wrongdoing as well as guilt on the part of the wrongdoer (Kochanska, Gross, Lin, & Nichols, 2002). Kindergartners whose mothers reported using reasoning were more likely to see the moral wrongness of behavior that hurts other people than children whose mothers took away privileges (Jagers et al., 1996).

Two other broad categories of discipline are *power assertion* and *temporary withdrawal of love*. **Power assertion** is intended to stop or discourage undesirable behavior through physical or verbal enforcement of parental control; it includes demands, threats, withdrawal of privileges, spanking, and other types of punishment. **Withdrawal of love** may include ignoring, isolating, or showing dislike for a child. Neither of these is as

corporal punishment
Use of physical force with the intention of causing pain but not injury so as to correct or control behavior.

inductive techniques
Disciplinary techniques designed to induce desirable behavior by appealing to a child's sense of reason and fairness.

power assertion
Disciplinary strategy designed to discourage undesirable behavior through physical or verbal enforcement of parental control.

withdrawal of love
Disciplinary strategy that involves ignoring, isolating, or showing dislike for a child.

effective as inductive reasoning in most circumstances, and both may be harmful (Baumrind, Larzelere, & Owens, 2010; Jagers et al., 1996; McCord, 1996).

The effectiveness of parental discipline may hinge on how well the child understands and accepts the parent's message. For the child to accept the message, the child has to recognize it as appropriate; so parents need to be fair and accurate as well as clear and consistent about their expectations. They need to fit the discipline to the misdeed and to the child's temperament and cognitive and emotional level. A child may be more motivated to accept the message if the parents are normally warm and responsive and if they arouse the child's empathy for someone the child has harmed (Grusec & Goodnow, 1994; Kerr et al., 2004). How well children accept a disciplinary method also may depend on whether the type of discipline used is accepted in the family's culture (Lansford et al., 2005).

One point on which many experts agree is that a child interprets and responds to discipline in the context of an ongoing relationship with a parent. Some researchers therefore look beyond specific parental practices to overall styles, or patterns, of parenting.

checkpoint can **you**...

- Compare five forms of discipline, and discuss their effectiveness?

PARENTING STYLES

Just as children differ in their temperament, parents differ in their approach to parenting. Different styles of parenting may affect children's competence in dealing with their world.

Diana Baumrind and the Effectiveness of Authoritative Parenting In pioneering research, Diana Baumrind (1971, 1996b; Baumrind & Black, 1967) studied 103 preschool children from 95 families. Through interviews, testing, and home studies, she measured how the children were functioning, identified three parenting styles, and described typical behavior patterns of children raised according to each. Baumrind's work and the large body of research it inspired have established associations between each parenting style and some child behaviors (Baumrind, 1989; Darling & Steinberg, 1993; Pettit, Bates, & Dodge, 1997; see Table 3).

Authoritarian parenting emphasizes control and unquestioning obedience. Authoritarian parents try to make children conform to a set standard of conduct and punish them forcefully for violating it. They are less warm than other parents. Their children tend to be more discontented, withdrawn, and distrustful.

Permissive parenting emphasizes self-expression and self-regulation. Permissive parents make few demands. They consult with children about policy decisions and rarely punish. They are warm, noncontrolling, and undemanding. Their preschool children tend to be immature—the least self-controlled and the least exploratory.

Authoritative parenting emphasizes a child's individuality but also stresses social constraints. Authoritative parents are loving and accepting but also demand good behavior and are firm in maintaining standards. They impose limited, judicious punishment when necessary, within the context of a warm, supportive relationship. They favor inductive discipline and encourage verbal give-and-take. Their children feel secure in knowing both that they are loved and what is expected of them. Preschoolers with authoritative parents tend to be the most self-reliant, self-controlled, self-assertive, exploratory, and content.

Eleanor Maccoby and John Martin (1983) added a fourth parenting style—*neglectful,* or *uninvolved*—to describe parents who, sometimes because of stress or depression,

authoritarian parenting
In Baumrind's terminology, parenting style emphasizing control and obedience.

permissive parenting
In Baumrind's terminology, parenting style emphasizing self-expression and self-regulation.

authoritative parenting
In Baumrind's terminology, parenting style blending respect for a child's individuality with an effort to instill social values.

TABLE 3 Parenting Styles

		WARMTH	
		High	**Low**
CONTROL	**High**	Authoritative	Authoritarian
	Low	Permissive	Neglectful

focus on their needs rather than on those of the child. Neglectful parenting has been linked with a variety of behavioral disorders in childhood and adolescence (Steinberg, Eisengard, & Cauffman, 2006).

As a parent, what form of discipline would you favor if your 3-year-old took a cookie from the cookie jar? Refused to nap? Hit his little sister? Tell why.

Why does authoritative parenting seem to enhance children's social competence? It may be because authoritative parents set sensible expectations and realistic standards. By making clear, consistent rules, they let children know what is expected of them. In authoritarian homes, children are so strictly controlled that often they cannot make independent choices about their own behavior. In permissive homes, children receive so little guidance that they may become uncertain and anxious about whether they are doing the right thing. In authoritative homes, children know when they are meeting expectations and can decide whether it is worth risking parental displeasure to pursue a goal. These children are expected to perform well, fulfill commitments, and participate actively in family duties as well as family fun. They know the satisfaction of accepting responsibilities and achieving success.

Support and Criticisms of Baumrind's Model In research based on Baumrind's work, the benefits of authoritative parenting (or similar conceptions of parenting style) have repeatedly been supported. Identifying and promoting positive parenting practices is crucial to preventing early-onset problem behavior (Dishion & Stormshak, 2007). In a longitudinal study of 585 diverse families with children from prekindergarten through Grade 6, four aspects of early supportive parenting—warmth, use of inductive discipline, interest and involvement with children's peers, and proactive teaching of social skills—predicted positive behavioral, social, and academic outcomes (Pettit et al., 1997). Families at high-risk for problem behavior in children who participated in parenting support services were able to improve childhood outcomes by an early focus on positive and proactive parenting practices (Dishion et al., 2008).

Still, Baumrind's model has provoked controversy because it seems to suggest that there is one "right" way to raise children. Also, because Baumrind's findings are correlational, they only establish associations between each parenting style and a particular set of child behaviors. They do not show that different styles of child rearing *cause* children to be more or less competent. It is also impossible to know whether the children Baumrind studied were, in fact, raised in a particular style. It may be that some of the better-adjusted children were raised inconsistently, but by the time of the study their parents had adopted the authoritative pattern (Holden & Miller, 1999). In addition, Baumrind did not consider innate factors, such as temperament, that might have affected children's competence and exerted an influence on the parents.

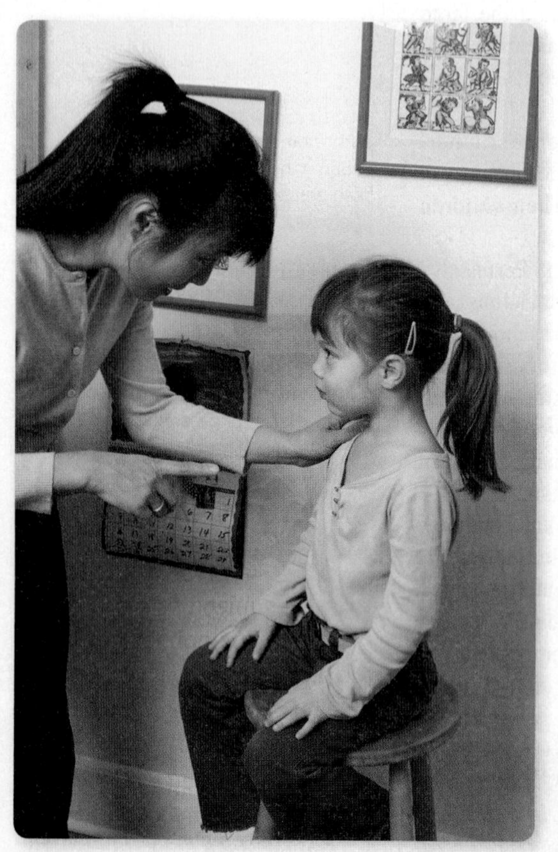

Traditional Asian culture stresses adults' responsibility to maintain the social order by teaching children socially proper behavior.

Cultural Differences in Parenting Styles Another concern is that Baumrind's categories reflect the dominant North American view of child development and may not apply to some cultures or socioeconomic groups. Among Asian Americans, obedience and strictness are not associated with harshness and domination but instead with caring, concern, and involvement and with maintaining family harmony. Traditional Chinese culture, with its emphasis on respect for elders, stresses adults' responsibility to maintain the social order by teaching children socially proper behavior. This obligation is carried out through firm and just control and governance of the child and even by physical punishment if necessary (Zhao, 2002). Although Asian American parenting is frequently described as authoritarian, the warmth and supportiveness that characterize Asian family relationships may more closely resemble Baumrind's authoritative parenting but without the emphasis on the European American values of individuality, choice, and freedom (Chao, 1994) and with stricter parental control (Chao, 2001).

Indeed, a dichotomy between the individualistic values of Western parenting and the collectivist values of Asian parenting may be overly simplistic. In interviews with 64 Japanese mothers of 3- to 6-year-olds (Yamada, 2004), the mothers' descriptions of their parenting practices reflected the search for a balance between granting appropriate autonomy and exercising disciplinary control. The mothers let children make their own decisions within what they saw as the child's personal domain, such as play activities, playmates, and clothing, and this domain enlarged with the child's age. When health, safety, moral issues, or conventional social rules were involved, the mothers set limits or exercised control. When conflicts arose, the mothers used reasoning rather than power-assertive methods or sometimes gave in to the child, apparently on the theory that the issue wasn't worth struggling over—or that the child might be right after all.

checkpoint
can **you** . . .

- Summarize Baumrind's model of parenting styles?
- Explain how parents' way of resolving conflicts with young children can contribute to the success of authoritative child rearing?
- Discuss criticisms of Baumrind's model and cultural variations in parenting styles?

SPECIAL BEHAVIORAL CONCERNS

Three issues of special concern to parents, caregivers, and teachers of preschool children are how to promote altruism, curb aggression, and deal with fears that often arise at this age.

altruism
Behavior intended to help others out of inner concern and without expectation of external reward; may involve self-denial or self-sacrifice.

prosocial behavior
Any voluntary behavior intended to help others.

Prosocial Behavior Alex, at 3½, responded to two preschool classmates' complaints that they did not have enough modeling clay, his favorite plaything, by giving them half of his. Alex was showing **altruism:** motivation to help another person with no expectation of reward. Altruistic acts like Alex's often entail cost, self-sacrifice, or risk. Altruism is at the heart of **prosocial behavior,** voluntary, positive actions to help others.

Remember "harmonizing" with your pals in preschool music circles? Research in Germany suggests that when kids make music together, they are more likely to cooperate with and help each other.

Kirschner & Tomasello, 2010

Even before the second birthday, children often help others, share belongings and food, and offer comfort. Cooperative behavior analysis has revealed three preferences for sharing resources; a preference to share with close relations, reciprocity (a preference to share with people who have shared with you), and indirect reciprocity (a preference to share with people who share with others). In a set of experiments on 3½-year-old children, researchers were able to demonstrate that these preferences are present and functional in young children (Olson & Spelke, 2008).

Babies at about a year of age love give-and-take games, in which a toy is handed back and forth between two people. Researchers have suggested that playing these games might help encourage later sharing behaviors.

Hay, 1994

Is there a prosocial personality or disposition? A longitudinal study that followed 32 4- and 5-year-olds into early adulthood suggests that there is and that it emerges early and remains somewhat consistent throughout life. Preschoolers who were sympathetic and spontaneously shared with classmates tended to show prosocial understanding and empathic behavior as much as 17 years later (Coplan et al., 2004).

Genes and environment each contribute to individual differences in prosocial behavior, an example of gene-environment correlation. This finding comes from a study of 9,319 twin pairs whose prosocial behavior was rated by parents and teachers at ages 3, 4, and 7. Parents who showed affection and followed positive (inductive) disciplinary strategies tended to encourage their children's natural tendency to prosocial behavior (Knafo & Plomin, 2006). Parents of prosocial children typically are prosocial themselves. They point out models of prosocial behavior and steer children toward stories, films, and television programs that depict cooperation, sharing, and empathy and encourage sympathy, generosity, and helpfulness (Singer & Singer, 1998), which have been shown to have prosocial effects by increasing children's altruism, cooperation, and even tolerance for others (Wilson, 2008). Relationships with siblings, peers, and teachers also can model and reinforce prosocial behavior (Eisenberg, 1992).

Children think in concrete terms. When trying to encourage sharing between young children, it is better to encourage them to take turns (a concrete behavior) than to share (an abstract concept).

The kind of aggression involved in fighting over a toy, without intention to hurt or dominate the other child, is instrumental aggression. It surfaces mostly during social play and normally declines as children learn to ask for what they want.

Cultures vary in the degree to which they foster prosocial behavior. Traditional cultures in which people live in extended family groups and share work seem to instill prosocial values more than cultures that stress individual achievement (Eisenberg & Fabes, 1998).

Aggression Noah walks over to Jake, who is playing quietly with a toy car. Noah hits Jake and snatches the car away. He has used aggression as a tool to gain access to a wanted object. This is **instrumental aggression,** or aggression used as an instrument to reach a goal—the most common type of aggression in early childhood. Between ages 2½ and 5, children frequently struggle over toys and control of space. Aggression surfaces mostly during social play; children who fight the most also tend to be the most sociable and competent. In fact, the ability to show some instrumental aggression may be a necessary step in social development.

As children develop more self-control and become better able to express themselves verbally, they typically shift from showing aggression with blows to doing it with words (Coie & Dodge, 1998; Tremblay et al., 2004). However, individual differences remain. In a longitudinal study of 383 preschoolers, 11 percent of the girls and 9 percent of the boys showed high levels of aggression between ages 2 and 5 (Hill, Degnan, Calkins, & Keane, 2006). Children who, as preschoolers, often engage in violent fantasy play may, at age 6, be prone to violent displays of anger (Dunn & Hughes, 2001).

study**smart**

Relational Aggression

Gender Differences in Aggression Aggression is an exception to the generalization that boys and girls are more similar than different (Hyde, 2005). In all cultures studied, as among most mammals, boys are more physically and verbally aggressive than girls. This gender difference is apparent by age 2 (Baillargeon et al., 2007; Pellegrini & Archer, 2005). Research with genetically engineered mice suggests that the Sry gene on the Y chromosome may play a role (Gatewood et al., 2006).

However, when aggression is looked at more closely, it becomes apparent that boys and girls tend to use different kinds of aggression. Boys engage in more **overt (direct) aggression,** and tend to openly direct aggressive acts at a target. Girls, by contrast, tend to engage in a form of indirect social aggression known as **relational aggression** (Putallaz & Bierman, 2004). This more subtle kind of aggression consists of damaging or interfering with relationships, reputation, or psychological well-being, often through teasing, manipulation, ostracism, or bids for control. It may include spreading rumors, name-calling, put-downs, or excluding someone from a group. It can be either overt or covert (indirect)—for example, making mean faces or ignoring someone. Among preschoolers, it tends to be direct and face-to-face ("You can't come to my party if you don't give me that toy") (Archer, 2004; Brendgen et al., 2005).

instrumental aggression
Aggressive behavior used as a means of achieving a goal.

overt (direct) aggression
Aggression that is openly directed at its target.

relational aggression
Aggression aimed at damaging or interfering with another person's relationships, reputation, or psychological well-being.

From an evolutionary perspective, boys' greater overt aggressiveness, like their greater size and strength, may prepare them to compete for a mate (Archer, 2004). Males produce many sperm; females generally produce only one ovum at a time. Males can increase their reproductive output by gaining access to females. Thus males are generally predicted to be more competitive and are more likely to take the risks of physical aggression. Females' reproductive output is limited by their own bodies; thus the need for physical aggression as a means by which to compete is diminished (Pellegrini & Archer, 2005).

Influences on Aggression Why are some children more aggressive than others? Temperament may play a part. Children who are intensely emotional and low in self-control tend to express anger aggressively (Eisenberg, Fabes, Nyman, Bernzweig, & Pinuelas, 1994; Rubin, Burgess, Dwyer, & Hastings, 2003).

Both physical and social aggression have genetic and environmental sources, but their relative influence differs. Among 234 6-year-old twins, physical aggression was

50 to 60 percent heritable; the remainder of the variance was attributable to nonshared environmental influences (unique experiences). Social aggression was much more environmentally influenced; the variance was only 20 percent genetic, 20 percent explained by shared environmental influences, and 60 percent by nonshared experiences (Brendgen et al., 2005).

Parental behaviors strongly influence aggressiveness. In several longitudinal studies, insecure attachment and lack of maternal warmth and affection in infancy predicted aggressiveness in early childhood (Coie & Dodge, 1998; MacKinnon-Lewis, Starnes, Volling, & Johnson, 1997; Rubin, Burgess, & Hastings, 2002). Manipulative behaviors such as withdrawal of love and making a child feel guilty or ashamed may foster social aggression (Brendgen et al., 2005).

Aggressiveness may result from a combination of a stressful and unstimulating home atmosphere, harsh discipline, lack of maternal warmth and social support, family dysfunction, exposure to aggressive adults and neighborhood violence, poverty, and transient peer groups, which prevent stable friendships (Dodge, Pettit, & Bates, 1994; Grusec & Goodnow, 1994; Romano, Tremblay, Boulerice, & Swisher, 2005). In a study of 431 children in an inner-city neighborhood, parents reported that more than half had witnessed gang activity, drug trafficking, police pursuits and arrests, or people carrying weapons. These children showed symptoms of distress at home and aggressive behavior at school (Farver, Xu, Eppe, Fernandez, & Schwartz, 2005).

Culture can influence how much aggressive behavior a child shows. For example, in Japan, anger and aggression contradict the cultural emphasis on harmony. Japanese mothers are more likely than U.S. mothers to use inductive discipline, pointing out how aggressive behavior hurts others. Japanese mothers also show strong disappointment when children fail to meet behavioral standards (Zahn-Waxler et al., 1996).

Why does witnessing violence lead to aggression? In a classic social learning experiment (Bandura, Ross, & Ross, 1961), 3- to 6-year-olds individually watched adult models play with toys. Children in one experimental group saw the adult model play quietly. The model for the other experimental group spent most of the 10-minute session punching, throwing, and kicking a life-size inflated doll. A control group did not see any model. After the sessions, the children who had seen the aggressive model acted much more aggressively than those in the other groups, imitating many of the same things they had seen the model say and do. The children who had seen the quiet model were less aggressive than the control group. This finding suggests that parents may be able to moderate the effects of frustration by modeling nonaggressive behavior.

Fearfulness Passing fears are common in early childhood. Many 2- to 4-year-olds are afraid of animals, especially dogs. By age 6, children are more likely to be afraid of the dark. Other common fears are of thunderstorms, doctors, and imaginary creatures (DuPont, 1983; Stevenson-Hinde & Shouldice, 1996).

Young children's fears stem largely from their intense fantasy life and their tendency to confuse appearance with reality. Sometimes their imaginations get carried away, making them worry about being attacked by a lion or being abandoned. Young children are more likely to be frightened by something that looks scary, such as a cartoon monster, than by something capable of doing great harm, such as a nuclear explosion (Cantor, 1994). For the most part, older children's fears are more realistic (being kidnapped) and self-evaluative (failing a test) (Stevenson-Hinde & Shouldice, 1996).

Fears may come from personal experience or from hearing about other people's experiences (Muris, Merckelbach, & Collaris, 1997). A preschooler whose mother is sick in bed may become upset by a story about a mother's death, even if it is an animal mother. Often fears come from appraisals of danger, such as the likelihood of being bitten by a dog, or are triggered by events, such as a child who was hit by a car becoming afraid to cross the street. Children who have lived through an

A young girl gets up the courage to touch a tarantula as her nervous cousin looks on.

When kids are little, their fears involve darkness, scary monsters, and imaginary threats. As they grow older, their fears become increasingly realistic. Why do you think this happens?

earthquake, kidnapping, war, or some other frightening event may fear that it will happen again (Kolbert, 1994).

It is both normal and appropriate for young children to have fears. It is also normal for these fears to fade as children age. Part of the reason many fears are outgrown is because young children get better at distinguishing the real and the imaginary. Additionally, as children master new skills, they develop an emerging sense of autonomy. When that sense of autonomy is coupled with their increased ability to understand and predict events in their environment, children feel more in control, and thus less frightened (National Scientific Council on the Developing Child, 2010).

Parents can help prevent children's fears by instilling a sense of trust and normal caution without being too protective, and also by overcoming their own unrealistic fears. They can help a fearful child by reassurance and by encouraging open expression of feelings: "I know it is scary, but the thunder can't hurt you." Ridicule ("Don't be such a baby!"), coercion ("Pat the nice doggie—it won't hurt you"), and logical persuasion ("The closest bear is 20 miles away, locked in a zoo!") are not helpful. Not until elementary school can children tell themselves that what they fear is not real (Cantor, 1994).

checkpoint can **you** . . .

- Discuss influences on altruism, aggression, and fearfulness?

Relationships with Other Children

Although the most important people in young children's world are the adults who take care of them, relationships with siblings and playmates become more important in early childhood. Virtually every characteristic activity and personality issue of this age, from gender development to prosocial or aggressive behavior, involves other children. Let's look first at sibling relationships and then at children who have no siblings. Then we will explore relationships with peers and friends.

SIBLING RELATIONSHIPS

"It's mine!"

"No, it's mine!"

"Well, I was playing with it first!"

The earliest, most frequent, and most intense disputes among siblings are over property rights—who owns a toy or who is entitled to play with it. Although exasperated adults may not always see it that way, sibling disputes and their settlement can be viewed as socialization opportunities, in which children learn to stand up for principles and negotiate disagreements (Ross, 1996). Another arena for socialization is joint dramatic play. Siblings who frequently play "let's pretend" develop a history of shared understandings that enable them to more easily resolve issues and build on each other's ideas (Howe, Petrakos, Rinaldi, & LeFebvre, 2005).

Younger siblings are more likely to take risks than older siblings. In one study on baseball statistics, 90 percent of younger brothers in major league baseball stole more bases than their older counterparts.

Sulloway & Zweigenhaft, 2010

Despite the frequency of conflict, sibling rivalry is *not* the main pattern between brothers and sisters early in life. Affection, interest, companionship, and influence are also prevalent in sibling relationships. Observations spanning 3½ years that began when younger siblings were about 1½ and the older siblings ranged from 3 to 4½ found prosocial and play-oriented behaviors to be more common than rivalry, hostility, and competition (Abramovitch, Corter, Pepler, & Stanhope, 1986). Older siblings initiated more behavior, both friendly and unfriendly; younger siblings tended to imitate the older ones. As the younger children reached age 5, the siblings became less physical and more verbal in showing both aggression and care and affection.

At least one finding of this research has been replicated in many studies: same-sex siblings, particularly girls, are closer and play together more peaceably than boy-girl pairs (Kier & Lewis, 1998). Because older siblings tend to dominate younger ones, the quality of the relationship is more affected by the emotional and social adjustment of the older child than the younger one (Pike, Coldwell, & Dunn, 2005).

The quality of sibling relationships tends to carry over to relationships with other children. A child who is aggressive with siblings is likely to be aggressive with friends as well (Abramovitch et al., 1986). Siblings who frequently play amicably together tend to develop prosocial behaviors (Pike et al., 2005).

Likewise, friendships can influence sibling relationships. Older siblings who have experienced a good relationship with a friend before the birth of a sibling are likely to treat their younger siblings better and are less likely to develop antisocial behavior in adolescence (Kramer & Kowal, 2005). For a young child at risk for behavioral problems, a positive relationship with *either* a sibling or a friend can buffer the effects of a negative relationship with the other (McElwain & Volling, 2005).

THE ONLY CHILD

In the United States, approximately 21 percent of children under age 18 are only children (Kreider & Fields, 2005). Are only children selfish, lonely, or spoiled? Generally, this stereotype of only children appears to be false. A meta-analysis of 115 studies found that most "onlies" do well. With respect to academic outcomes and success in work, they perform slightly better than children with siblings. They tend to be more motivated to achieve and to have slightly higher self-esteem; and they do not differ in emotional adjustment, sociability, or popularity.

Only Children

Why do onlies do better on some indices than children with siblings? Evolutionary theory suggests that these children do better because parents, who have limited time and resources to spend, focus more attention on only children, talk to them more, and expect more of them than do parents with more than one child (Falbo, 2006). The more children in a family, the less individual time any one child receives. Most children today spend considerable time in play groups, child care, and preschool, so only children do not lack opportunities for social interaction with peers.

Research in China also has produced largely encouraging findings about only children. In 1979, to control an exploding population, the People's Republic of China established an official policy of limiting families to one child each. Although the policy has since been relaxed, most urban families now have only one child, and most rural families no more than two (Hesketh, Lu, & Xing, 2005). Thus, in many Chinese cities, schoolrooms are almost completely filled with children who have no brothers or sisters. This situation offered researchers a natural experiment: an opportunity to study the adjustment of large numbers of only children.

A review of the literature found no significant differences in behavioral problems (Tao, 1998). Indeed, only children seemed to be at a distinct psychological advantage in a society that favors and rewards such a child. Among 731 urban children and adolescents, those with siblings reported higher levels of fear, anxiety, and depression than only children, regardless of sex or age (Yang, Ollendick, Dong, Xia, & Lin, 1995).

Among 4,000 third and sixth graders, personality differences between only children and those with siblings—as rated by parents, teachers, peers, and the children themselves—were few. Only children's academic achievement and physical growth were about the same as, or better than, children with siblings (Falbo & Poston, 1993). In a randomized study in Beijing first-grade classrooms (Jiao, Ji, & Jing, 1996), only children outperformed classmates with siblings in memory, language, and

Young children learn the importance of being a friend to have a friend.

mathematics skills. This finding may reflect the greater attention, stimulation, hopes, and expectations that parents shower on a baby they know will be their first and last.

PLAYMATES AND FRIENDS

Friendships develop as people develop. Toddlers play alongside or near each other, but not until about age 3 do children begin to have friends. Through friendships and interactions with casual playmates, young children learn how to get along with others. They learn that being a friend is the way to have a friend. They learn how to solve problems in relationships and how to put themselves in another person's place, and they see models of various kinds of behavior. They learn moral values and gender-role norms, and they practice adult roles.

Preschoolers usually like to play with children of the same age and sex. Children who have frequent positive experiences with each other are most likely to become friends (Rubin et al., 1998; Snyder, West, Stockemer, Gibbons, & Almquist-Parks, 1996). About 3 out of 4 preschoolers have such mutual friendships (Hartup & Stevens, 1999).

The traits that young children look for in a playmate are similar to the traits they look for in a friend (C. H. Hart, DeWolf, Wozniak, & Burts, 1992). In one study, 4- to 7-year-olds rated the most important features of friendships as doing things together, liking and caring for each other, sharing and helping one another, and to a lesser degree, living nearby or going to the same school. Younger children rated physical traits, such as appearance and size, higher than older children did and rated affection and support lower (Furman & Bierman, 1983). Preschool children prefer prosocial playmates (C. H. Hart et al., 1992). They reject disruptive, demanding, intrusive, or aggressive children (Ramsey & Lasquade, 1996; Roopnarine & Honig, 1985).

Well-liked preschoolers and kindergartners and those who are rated by parents and teachers as socially competent generally cope well with anger. They avoid insults and threats. Instead, they respond directly, in ways that minimize further conflict and keep relationships going. Less well-liked children tend to hit back or tattle (Fabes & Eisenberg, 1992).

checkpoint can **you** . . .

- Explain how the resolution of sibling disputes contributes to socialization?
- Tell how birth order and gender affect typical patterns of sibling interaction?
- Compare the development of only children with that of children with siblings?
- Discuss how preschoolers choose playmates and friends, how they behave with friends, and how they benefit from friendships?

summary and key terms

The Developing Self

- The self-concept undergoes major change in early childhood. According to a neo-Piagetian model, self-definition shifts from single representations to representational mappings. Young children do not see the difference between the real self and the ideal self.
- Self-esteem in early childhood tends to be global and unrealistic, reflecting adult approval.
- Understanding of emotions directed toward the self and of simultaneous emotions develops gradually.
- According to Erikson, the developmental conflict of early childhood is initiative versus guilt. Successful resolution of this conflict results in the virtue of *purpose*.

self-concept
self-definition
single representations
real self
ideal self
representational mappings
self-esteem
initiative versus guilt

Gender

- Gender identity is an aspect of the developing self-concept.
- The main gender difference in early childhood is boys' greater aggressiveness. Girls tend to be more empathic and prosocial and less prone to problem behavior. Some cognitive differences appear early, others not until preadolescence or later.
- Children learn gender roles at an early age through gender-typing. Gender stereotypes peak during the preschool years.
- Five major perspectives on gender development are biological, evolutionary, psychoanalytic, cognitive, and social learning.

- Evidence suggests that some gender differences may be biologically based.
- Evolutionary theory sees children's gender roles as preparation for adult mating behavior.
- In Freudian theory, a child identifies with the same-sex parent after giving up the wish to possess the other parent.
- Cognitive-developmental theory maintains that gender identity develops from thinking about one's gender. According to Kohlberg, gender constancy leads to acquisition of gender roles. Gender-schema theory holds that children categorize gender-related information by observing what males and females do in their culture.
- According to social cognitive theory, children learn gender roles through socialization. Parents, peers, and culture influence gender-typing.

gender identity
gender roles
gender-typing
gender stereotypes
theory of sexual selection
identification
gender constancy
gender-schema theory
social cognitive theory

Play: The Business of Early Childhood

- Play has physical, cognitive, and psychosocial benefits. Changes in the types of play children engage in reflect cognitive and social development.
- According to Smilansky, children progress cognitively from functional play to constructive play, dramatic play, and then formal games with rules. Dramatic play becomes increasingly common during early childhood and helps children develop social and cognitive skills. Rough-and-tumble play also begins during early childhood.
- According to Parten, play becomes more social during early childhood. However, later research has found that nonsocial play is not necessarily immature.
- Children prefer to play with (and play more socially with) others of their sex.
- Cognitive and social aspects of play are influenced by the culturally approved environments adults create for children.

functional play
constructive play
dramatic play
formal games with rules
gender segregation

Parenting

- Discipline can be a powerful tool for socialization.
- Both positive reinforcement and prudently administered punishment can be appropriate tools of discipline within the context of a positive parent-child relationship.
- Power assertion, inductive techniques, and withdrawal of love are three categories of discipline. Reasoning is generally the most effective and power assertion the least effective in promoting internalization of parental standards. Spanking and other forms of corporal punishment can have negative consequences.
- Baumrind identified three parenting styles: authoritarian, permissive, and authoritative. A fourth style, neglectful or uninvolved, was identified later. Authoritative parents tend to raise more competent children. However, Baumrind's findings may be misleading when applied to some cultures.
- The roots of altruism and prosocial behavior appear early. This may be an inborn disposition, which can be cultivated by parental modeling and encouragement.
- Instrumental aggression—first physical, then verbal—is most common in early childhood.
- Boys tend to practice overt aggression, whereas girls often engage in relational aggression.
- Preschool children show temporary fears of real and imaginary objects and events; older children's fears tend to be more realistic.

discipline
corporal punishment
inductive techniques
power assertion
withdrawal of love
authoritarian parenting
permissive parenting
authoritative parenting
altruism
prosocial behavior
instrumental aggression
overt (direct) aggression
relational aggression

Relationships with Other Children

- Most sibling interactions are positive. Older siblings tend to initiate activities, and younger siblings to imitate. Same-sex siblings, especially girls, get along best.
- Siblings tend to resolve disputes on the basis of moral principles.
- The kind of relationship children have with siblings often carries over into other peer relationships.
- Only children seem to develop at least as well as children with siblings.
- Preschoolers choose playmates and friends who are like them and with whom they have positive experiences.
- Aggressive children are less popular than prosocial children.

part 4

MIDDLE CHILDHOOD

chapter

Physical and Cognitive Development in Middle Childhood

outline

PHYSICAL DEVELOPMENT

Aspects of Physical Development

Health, Fitness, and Safety

COGNITIVE DEVELOPMENT

Piagetian Approach: The Concrete Operational Child

Information-Processing Approach: Planning, Attention, and Memory

Psychometric Approach: Assessment of Intelligence

Language and Literacy

The Child in School

Educating Children with Special Needs

learning objectives

Describe physical changes and health in school-age children.

Describe cognitive development in school-age children.

Explain how language abilities continue developing in school-age children.

Summarize children's adjustment to school and influences on school achievement.

Describe how schools educate children with special needs.

did you know?

- Neuropsychologist Howard Gardner identified eight separate types of intelligence?
- Children who believe they can master schoolwork are more likely to do so?
- Studies support the value of bilingual education?

In this chapter we look at strength, endurance, motor proficiency, and other physical developments. Cognitively, we examine concrete operations, memory, problem solving, intelligence testing, and literacy. We discuss school achievement, methods of teaching reading, and second-language education. Finally, we look at special needs education.

It is easier to build strong children than to repair broken men.

—Frederick Douglass, 1818–1895

PHYSICAL DEVELOPMENT

Aspects of Physical Development

Growth during middle childhood slows considerably. Still, although day-by-day changes may not be obvious, they add up to a startling difference between 6-year-olds, who are still small children, and 11-year-olds, many of whom are now beginning to resemble adults.

HEIGHT AND WEIGHT

Children grow about 2 to 3 inches each year between ages 6 and 11 and approximately double their weight during that period (McDowell, Fryar, Odgen, & Flegal, 2008; Table 1). Girls retain somewhat more fatty tissue than boys, a characteristic that will persist through adulthood. The average 10-year-old weighs about 11 pounds more than 40 years ago—just over 82 pounds for a boy and 83 pounds for a girl (McDowell, Fryar, & Ogden, 2009). African American boys and girls tend to grow faster than white children. By about age 6, African American girls have more muscle and bone mass than European American (white) or Mexican American girls, and Mexican American girls have a higher percentage of body fat than white girls the same size (Ellis, Abrams, & Wong, 1997).

TABLE 1 Physical Growth, Ages 6 to 11 (50th percentile*)

Age	HEIGHT (INCHES)		WEIGHT (POUNDS)	
	Girls	Boys	Girls	Boys
6	46.5	46.8	46.2	48.2
7	48.6	49.6	52.7	56.0
8	51.7	51.7	62.7	61.4
9	53.7	54.1	69.5	70.4
10	56.1	56.3	79.1	79.5
11	59.5	58.0	95.0	87.3

*Fifty percent of children in each category are above this height or weight level and 50 percent are below it.

Source: McDowell, Fryar, & Ogden, 2009.

Almost half of American children 6 to 17 years old have a television in their bedroom.

Sisson, Broyles, Newton, Baker, & Chernausek, 2011

NUTRITION AND SLEEP

To support their steady growth and constant exertion, schoolchildren need, on average, 2,400 calories every day—more for older children and less for younger ones. Nutritionists recommend a varied diet including plenty of whole grains, fruits, and vegetables and complex carbohydrates.

Sleep needs decline from about 11 hours a day at age 5 to a little more than 10 hours at age 9 and about 9 hours at age 13. Sleep problems, such as resistance to going to bed, insomnia, and daytime sleepiness are common in the United States during these years, in part because many children, as they grow older, are allowed to set their own bedtimes (Hoban, 2004) and to have television sets in their bedrooms (National Sleep Foundation, 2004). Unfortunately, this failure to get adequate sleep is associated with a variety of adjustment problems, and this effect is particularly marked when children are African American or come from homes of low socioeconomic status. Sleep, quite plainly, is necessary for optimal outcomes (El-Sheikh, Kelly, Buckhalt, & Hinnant, 2010).

BRAIN DEVELOPMENT

The Developing Brain

A number of cognitive advances occur in middle childhood that can be traced back to changes in the brain's structure and functioning. In general, these changes can be characterized as resulting in faster, more efficient information processing and an increased ability to ignore distracting information (Amso & Casey, 2006). For example, it becomes easier for children to concentrate on the teacher—even if it's a boring lesson—while filtering out the antics of the class clown.

The study of the brain's structure is complex and depends on the interaction between genetic, epigenetic, and environment factors. The use of new technologies has allowed us a window into this process. For example, one technology, *magnetic resonance imaging* (MRI), enables researchers to observe how the brain changes over time and how these changes vary from one child to another (Blakemore & Choudhury, 2006; Kuhn, 2006; Lenroot & Giedd, 2006).

MRI technology shows us that the brain consists of both gray matter and white matter. Gray matter is composed of closely packed neurons in the cerebral cortex. White matter is made of glial cells, which provide support for neurons, and of myelinated axons, which transmit information across neurons. Both types of matter are necessary for effective cognition.

One important maturational change is a *loss in the density of gray matter* (Figure 1). Although "less" gray matter may sound negative, the result is actually the opposite. This loss reflects pruning of unused dendrites. In other words, those connections that are used remain active; the unused connections eventually disappear. The result is that the brain becomes "tuned" to the experiences of the child.

Changes in the volume of gray matter peak at different times in the different lobes. Beneath the cortex, gray matter volume in the caudate—a part of the basal ganglia involved in control of movement and muscle tone and in mediating higher cognitive functions, attention, and emotional states—peaks at age 7 in girls and age 10 in boys. Gray matter volume in the parietal lobes, which deal with spatial understanding, and in the frontal lobes, which handle higher-order functions, peaks at age 11 in girls and age 12 for boys. At age 16 in both boys and girls, gray matter volume peaks in the temporal lobes, which deal with language (Lenroot & Giedd, 2006).

The amount of gray matter in the frontal cortex, which is largely genetic, is likely linked with differences in IQ (Thompson et al., 2001; Toga & Thompson, 2005). Some research suggests, however, that the key may not be how much gray matter a child has but rather the pattern of development of the prefrontal cortex. In children of average intelligence, the prefrontal cortex is relatively thick at age 7, peaks in thickness by age 8, and then gradually thins as unneeded connections are pruned.

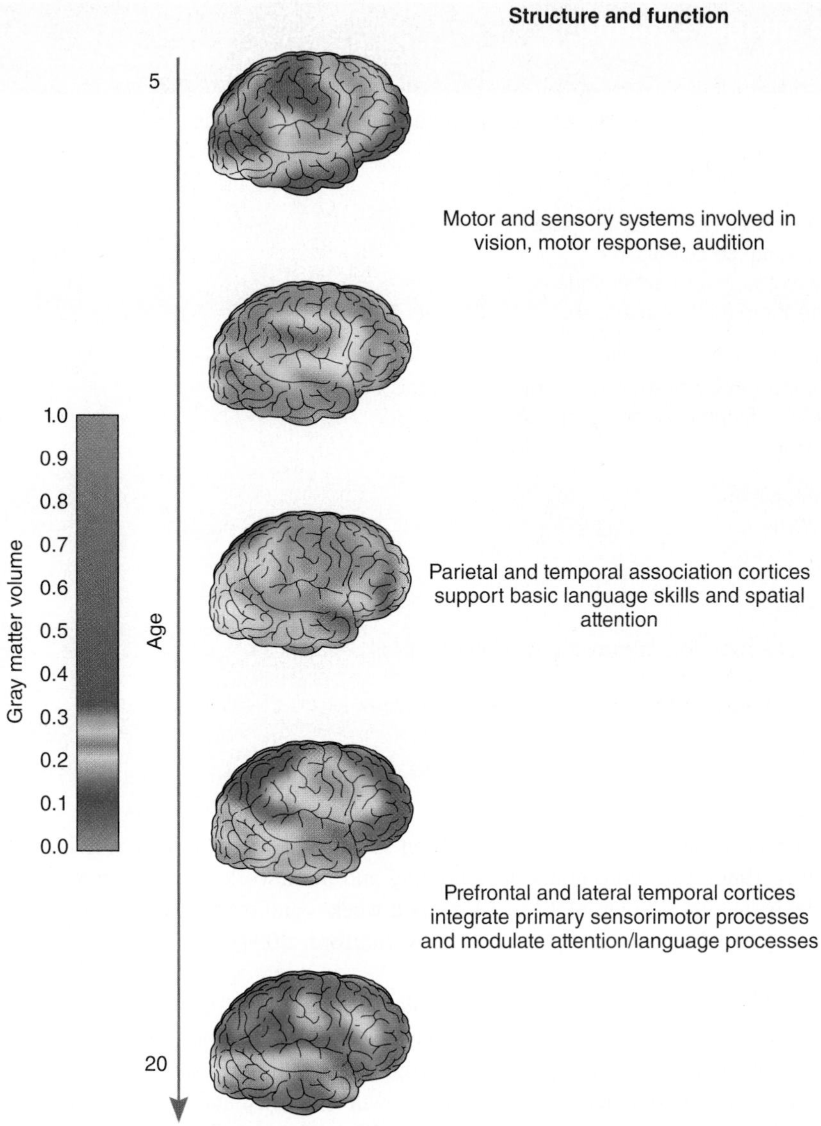

FIGURE 1

Gray-Matter Maturation in the Cerebral Cortex, Ages 5 to 20

Losses in gray matter density reflect maturation of various regions of the cortex, permitting more efficient functioning. Blue areas correspond to specific parts of the cortex undergoing loss of gray matter at a given age. These structures and their functional significance are described.

Structure and function

Age: 5 to 20

Gray matter volume: 1.0, 0.9, 0.8, 0.7, 0.6, 0.5, 0.4, 0.3, 0.2, 0.1, 0.0

Motor and sensory systems involved in vision, motor response, audition

Parietal and temporal association cortices support basic language skills and spatial attention

Prefrontal and lateral temporal cortices integrate primary sensorimotor processes and modulate attention/language processes

Source: Amso & Casey, 2006; adapted from Gogtay et al., 2004.

The loss in density of gray matter with age is balanced by another change—a steady *increase in white matter.* The connections between neurons thicken and myelinate, beginning with the frontal lobes and moving toward the rear of the brain. Between ages 6 and 13, striking growth occurs in connections between the temporal and parietal lobes. In fact, white matter growth may not begin to drop off until well into adulthood (Kuhn, 2006; Lenroot & Giedd, 2006; NIMH, 2001b).

Children's brains also show *changes in the thickness of the cortex.* Researchers have observed cortical thickening between ages 5 and 11 in regions of the temporal and frontal lobes. At the same time, thinning occurs in the rear portion of the frontal and parietal cortex in the brain's left hemisphere. This change correlates with improved performance on the vocabulary portion of an intelligence test (Toga et al., 2006).

checkpoint can **you . . .**

- Summarize typical growth patterns of boys and girls in middle childhood, including ethnic variations?
- Summarize the nutritional and sleep needs of school-age children?
- Discuss changes in the brain at this age and their effects?

MOTOR DEVELOPMENT AND PHYSICAL PLAY

Motor skills continue to improve in middle childhood (Table 2). However, a nationally representative survey based on time-use diaries found that school-age children in the

TABLE 2 Motor Development in Middle Childhood

Age	Selected Behaviors
6	Girls are superior in movement accuracy; boys are superior in forceful, less complex acts. Skipping is possible. Children can throw with proper weight shift and step.
7	One-footed balancing without looking becomes possible. Children can walk 2-inch-wide balance beams. Children can hop and jump accurately into small squares. Children can execute accurate jumping-jack exercise.
8	Children have 12-pound pressure on grip strength. The number of games participated in by both sexes is greatest at this age. Children can engage in alternate rhythmic hopping in a 2-2, 2-3, or 3-3 pattern. Girls can throw a small ball 40 feet.
9	Boys can run 16½ feet per second. Boys can throw a small ball 70 feet.
10	Children can judge and intercept pathways of small balls thrown from a distance. Girls can run 17 feet per second.
11	A standing broad jump of 5 feet is possible for boys and of 4½ feet for girls.

Source: Adapted from Bryant J. Cratty, *Perceptual and Motor Development in Infants and Children,* 3rd ed. Englewood Cliffs, NJ: Prentice Hall, 1986.

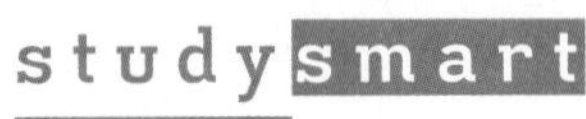

Motor Skills

United States spend less time each week on sports and other outdoor activities than in the early 1980s and more hours on schooling and homework, in addition to time spent on television—an average of 12 to 14 hours a week—and on computer activities, which barely existed 20 years ago (Juster, Ono, & Stafford, 2004).

Recess-Time Play The games children play at recess tend to be informal and spontaneously organized. Boys play more physically active games, whereas girls favor games that include verbal expression or counting aloud, such as hopscotch and jump rope. Such recess-time activities promote growth in agility and social competence and foster adjustment to school (Pellegrini, Kato, Blatchford, & Baines, 2002).

rough-and-tumble play
Vigorous play involving wrestling, hitting, and chasing, often accompanied by laughing and screaming.

About 10 percent of schoolchildren's free play in the early grades consists of **rough-and-tumble play**—wrestling, kicking, tumbling, grappling, and chasing, often accompanied by laughing and screaming (Bjorklund & Pellegrini, 2002). This kind of play may look like fighting but is done playfully among friends (P. K. Smith, 2005a).

Rough-and-tumble play peaks in middle childhood (Bjorklund & Pellegrini, 2002). It seems to be universal, and boys engage in higher levels of it than girls, perhaps because of hormonal differences and socialization (Pellegrini et al., 2002; P. K. Smith, 2005a). These different play styles may help explain sex segregation during play. From an evolutionary standpoint, rough-and-tumble play has important adaptive benefits: it hones skeletal and muscle development, offers safe practice for hunting and fighting skills, and channels aggression and competition. By age 11, it often becomes a way to establish dominance within the peer group (Bjorklund & Pellegrini, 2002; P. K. Smith, 2005b).

Games at recess, such as jump rope, tend to be informal. They promote both agility and social competence.

Sports and Other Physical Activities In a nationally representative survey of U.S. 9- to 13-year-olds and their parents, 38.5 percent reported participation in organized athletics outside of school hours—most of them in baseball, softball, soccer, or basketball. About twice as many children (77.4 percent) participated in unorganized physical activity, such as bicycling and shooting baskets (Duke, Huhman, & Heitzler, 2003).

Besides improving motor skills, regular physical activity has immediate and long-term health benefits: weight control, lower blood pressure, improved cardiorespiratory functioning, and enhanced self-esteem and well-being. Active children tend to become active adults. Thus organized athletic programs should include as many children as possible and should focus on building skills rather than winning games (AAP Committee on Sports Medicine and Fitness, 1992; Council on Sports Medicine and Fitness & Council on School Health, 2006).

checkpoint can **you** . . .

- Contrast boys' and girls' recess-time activities?
- Explain the significance of rough-and-tumble play?
- Tell what types of physical play children engage in as they grow older?

Health, Fitness, and Safety

The development of vaccines for major childhood illnesses has made middle childhood a relatively safe time of life in most of the world. The death rate in these years is the lowest in the life span. Still, too many children are overweight, and some suffer from chronic medical conditions or accidental injuries or from lack of access to health care.

OBESITY AND BODY IMAGE

Obesity in children has become a major health issue worldwide. In the United States, about 17 percent of children between the ages of 2 and 19 are obese and another 16.5 percent are overweight (Fryar, Carroll, & Ogden, 2012; Gundersen, Lohman, Garasky, Stewart, & Eisenmann, 2008). Boys are more likely to be overweight than girls (Ogden et al., 2006). Although overweight has increased in all ethnic groups, it is most prevalent among Mexican American boys (28.9 percent) and non-Hispanic black girls (24.8 percent) (Fryar et al., 2012).

body image
Descriptive and evaluative beliefs about one's appearance.

Unfortunately, children who try to lose weight are not always the ones who need to do so. Concern with **body image**—how one believes one looks—becomes important early in middle childhood, especially for girls, and may develop into eating disorders in adolescence. In one study on the development of body image in 9- to 12-year-old girls, between 49 and 55 percent were dissatisfied with their weight, with heavier girls experiencing overall higher dissatisfaction (Clark & Tiggeman, 2008). Playing with physically unrealistic dolls, such as Barbie, may be an influence in that direction (Box 1).

What's in children's lunchboxes? The typical composition is 1 sandwich, 1 piece of fruit, and 1.5 "extras." The number of extras, which are more likely to be processed and low in nutritional value, peaks on Wednesdays.

Miles, Matthews, Brennan, & Mitchell, 2010

Causes of Obesity Obesity often results from an inherited tendency aggravated by too little exercise and too much or the wrong kinds of food (AAP Committee on Nutrition, 2003; Chen et al., 2004). Children are more likely to be overweight if they have overweight parents or other relatives. Poor nutrition also contributes (Council on Sports Medicine and Fitness & Council on School Health, 2006). Eating out is another culprit; children who eat outside the home consume an estimated 200 more calories a day than when the same foods are eaten at home (French, Story, & Jeffery, 2001). On a typical day, over 30 percent of a nationally representative sample of children and adolescents reported eating fast foods high in fat, carbohydrates, and sugar additives (Bowman, Gortmaker, Ebbeling, Pereira, & Ludwig, 2004).

Inactivity is a major factor in the sharp rise in overweight. Even with the increase in organized sports, school-age children today spend less time than the children of 20 years ago in outdoor play and sports (Juster et al., 2004). Activity levels decrease significantly as children get older, from an average level of approximately 180 minutes of activity per day for 9-year-olds to 40 minutes per day for 15-year-olds (Nader, Bradley, Houts, McRitchie, & O'Brien, 2008).

Childhood Obesity Is a Serious Concern The adverse health effects of obesity for children are similar to those faced by adults. These children are at risk for behavior problems, depression, low self-esteem, and for falling behind in physical and social functioning (AAP Committee on Nutrition, 2003; Datar & Sturm, 2004a; Mustillo et al., 2003; Williams, Wake, Hesketh, Maher, & Waters, 2005). They commonly have medical

research in action

DO BARBIE DOLLS AFFECT GIRLS' BODY IMAGE?

Barbie is the best-selling fashion doll around the world. Although she is sold as "every girl," Barbie is far from average. Her body proportions are "unrealistic, unattainable, and unhealthy" (Dittmar, Halliwell, & Ive, 2006, p. 284). "If she were alive, Barbie would be a woman standing 7 feet tall with a waistline of 18 inches and a bust-line of 38 to 40 inches," writes the psychotherapist Abigail Natenshon (2006). Yet Barbie dolls are role models for young girls, transmitting a cultural ideal of beauty. Girls who do not measure up may experience *body dissatisfaction*—negative thoughts about their bodies, leading to low self-esteem. By age 6, studies show, many girls wish to be thinner than they are.

To test Barbie's effect on young girls' body image, researchers read picture books to 5½- to 8½-year-old girls. One group saw picture stories about Barbie; control groups saw stories about a full-figured fashion doll called Emme or about no doll (Dittmar et al., 2006). Afterward, the girls completed questionnaires in which they were asked to agree or disagree with such statements as "I'm pretty happy about the way I look" and "I really like what I weigh."

The findings were striking. Among the youngest girls (ages 5½ to 6½), a single exposure to the Barbie picture book significantly lowered body esteem and increased the discrepancy between actual and ideal body size. This did not happen with the girls in the two control groups. The effect of Barbie on body image was even stronger in 6½- to 7½-year-olds. However, the findings for the oldest group, ages 7½ to 8½, were completely different: pictures of Barbie had no direct effect on body image at this age.

What accounts for this difference? Girls up to age 7 may be in a sensitive period in which they acquire idealized images of beauty. As girls grow older, they may internalize the ideal of thinness as part of their emerging identity. Once the ideal is internalized, its power no longer depends on direct exposure to the original role model (Dittmar et al., 2006).

Or, it may be that girls simply outgrow Barbie. In another study (Kuther & McDonald, 2004), sixth- through eighth-grade girls were asked about their childhood experiences with Barbie. All the girls had owned at least two Barbie dolls but said they no longer played with them. Looking back, some of the girls saw Barbie as a positive influence: "She is like the perfect person . . . that everyone wants to be like." But most of the girls saw Barbie as an unrealistic role model: "Barbie dolls provide a false stereotype . . . as it is physically impossible to attain the same body size. . . . There wouldn't be enough room for organs and other necessary things. . . . Barbie has this perfect body and now every girl is trying to have her body because they are so unhappy with themselves."

Longitudinal research will help determine whether fashion dolls such as Barbie have a lasting impact on body image.

If you had (or have) a young daughter, would you encourage her to play with Barbie dolls? Why or why not?

Taking in calories through snacks rather than meals is increasingly common in children today. The average child snacks approximately three times a day and takes in 600 calories a day from snacks.

Piernas & Popkin, 2010

hypertension
Chronically high blood pressure.

problems, including high blood pressure (discussed in the next section), high cholesterol, and high insulin levels (NCHS, 2004; Soroff et al., 2004). Childhood diabetes, discussed later in this chapter, is one of the prime results of rising obesity rates (Perrin, Finkle, & Benjamin, 2007). Overweight children often suffer emotionally and may compensate by indulging themselves with treats, making their physical and social problems even worse.

The National Association of State Boards of Education (2000) recommends 150 minutes of physical education each week for elementary students, but the average school offers only 85 to 98 minutes each week (National Center for Education Statistics [NCES], 2006a). An additional 60 minutes of physical education per week in kindergarten and first grade could reduce by half the number of overweight girls at that age (Datar & Sturm, 2004b).

Overweight children tend to become obese adults, at risk for **hypertension** (high blood pressure), heart disease, orthopedic problems, diabetes, and other problems. Indeed, childhood obesity may be a stronger predictor of some diseases than adult obesity (AAP, 2004; Baker, Olsen, & Sorensen, 2007; Li et al., 2004). Children who are obese and who have glucose intolerance and high blood pressure are at risk of premature death (Franks et al., 2010). By midcentury, obesity that starts in childhood may shorten life expectancy by 2 to 5 years (Ludwig, 2007).

Promoting an active lifestyle through both informal and organized sports is an important way to combat the problem of childhood obesity.

Prevention and Treatment Preventing weight gain is easier, less costly, and more effective than treating obesity (Council on Sports Medicine and Fitness & Council on School Health, 2006). Parents should watch children's eating and activity patterns and address excessive weight gain *before* a child becomes severely overweight. The United States Preventive Services Task Force (USPSTF, 2010) recommends screening for children for overweight and obesity starting at the age of 6 years.

To avoid overweight and prevent cardiac problems, children (like adults) should get only 10 percent of their total calories from saturated fat (United States Department of Agriculture, 2010). Studies have found no negative effects on height, weight, body mass, or neurological development from a moderately low-fat diet at this age (Rask-Nissilä et al., 2000; Shea et al., 1993).

Cookie Monster's favorite cookie is chocolate chip, followed by oatmeal. However, since 2006, Cookie Monster admits that cookies are best used as "sometimes snacks."

Effective weight-management programs should include efforts of parents, schools, physicians, communities, and the larger culture (Krishnamoorthy, Hart, & Jelalian, 2006). Treatment should begin early and promote permanent changes in lifestyle, not weight loss alone (Kitzmann & Beech, 2006; Miller-Kovach, 2003). Less time in front of television and computers, changes in food labeling and advertising, healthier school meals, education to help children make better food choices, and more time spent in physical education and informal exercise with family and friends, such as walking and unorganized sports, would help (AAP, 2004). Generally, research supports efforts focused on overall lifestyle changes rather than narrowly defined diets or exercise programs. However, a crucial factor is parental involvement. The most effective interventions are those in which parents are helped to change their own behaviors as well as those of their children (Kitzmann et al., 2010).

checkpoint can **you** . . .

- Discuss the extent of childhood obesity, how it can affect health, and how it can be treated?

OTHER MEDICAL CONDITIONS

Illness in middle childhood tends to be brief. **Acute medical conditions**—occasional, short-term conditions, such as infections and warts—are common. Six or seven bouts a year with colds, flu, or viruses are typical as germs pass among children at school or at play (Behrman, 1992).

acute medical conditions Illnesses that last a short time.

According to a nationally representative survey of more than 200,000 households, an estimated 12.8 percent of U.S. children have or are at risk for **chronic medical conditions:** physical, developmental, behavioral, or emotional conditions that persist for 3 months or more (Kogan, Newacheck, Honberg, & Strickland, 2005). However, despite the rising rates of chronic health conditions in children today, there is hope. In one study following children over a 6-year period, only about 7 percent of children who had a

chronic medical conditions Illnesses or impairments that persist for at least 3 months.

Although generally not an issue in the United States and most industrialized nations, children in tropical countries are at risk for diseases that cause lethargy and problems with attention. The cause? Tropical parasites such as hookworm or schistosomiasis.

Out of sight, out of mind: Hidden cost of neglected tropical diseases, 2010

chronic condition at the beginning of the study still had that same condition when the study concluded, although children who were males, black, Hispanic, or had overweight mothers were at higher risk (Van Cleave, Gortmaker, & Perrin, 2010). Two chronic conditions that have become increasingly common are asthma and diabetes.

asthma
A chronic respiratory disease characterized by sudden attacks of coughing, wheezing, and difficulty in breathing.

Asthma **Asthma** is a chronic, allergy-based respiratory disease characterized by sudden attacks of coughing, wheezing, and difficulty breathing. Its incidence is increasing worldwide (Asher et al., 2006), although it may have leveled off in some parts of the Western world (Eder, Ege, & von Mutius, 2006). Its prevalence in the United States more than doubled between 1980 and 1995 and has since remained at this historically high level (Akinbami, 2006). More than 13 percent of U.S. children and adolescents up to age 17 have been diagnosed with asthma at some time, and 9 percent currently have asthma (Federal Interagency Forum on Child and Family Statistics, 2007). It is 30 percent more likely to be diagnosed in boys than in girls, and 20 percent more likely to be diagnosed in black children than in white children (McDaniel, Paxson, & Waldfogel, 2006).

The causes of the asthma explosion are uncertain, but a genetic predisposition is likely to be involved (Eder et al., 2006). Researchers have identified a gene mutation that increases the risk of developing asthma (Ober et al., 2008). Some researchers point to environmental factors: tightly insulated houses that intensify exposure to indoor air pollutants and allergens such as tobacco smoke, molds, and cockroach droppings. Allergies to household pets also have been suggested as risk factors (Bollinger, 2003; Etzel, 2003). However, findings regarding these proposed causes, except for smoke exposure, are inconclusive. Increasing evidence points to an association between obesity and asthma, perhaps because of an underlying lifestyle factor related to both conditions (Eder et al., 2006).

diabetes
One of the most common diseases of childhood. It is characterized by high levels of glucose in the blood as a result of defective insulin production, ineffective insulin action, or both.

Diabetes **Diabetes** is one of the most common diseases in school-aged children. More than 185,000 children in the United States have diabetes (National Diabetes Information Clearinghouse [NDIC], 2007). Diabetes is characterized by high levels of glucose in the blood as a result of defective insulin production, ineffective insulin action, or both. Type 1 diabetes is the result of an insulin deficiency that occurs when insulin-producing cells in the pancreas are destroyed. Type 1 diabetes accounts for 5 to 10 percent of all diabetes cases and for almost all diabetes in children under 10 years of age. Symptoms include increased thirst and urination, hunger, weight loss, blurred vision, and fatigue. Treatment includes insulin administration, nutrition management, and physical activity (National Diabetes Education Program, 2008).

Type 2 diabetes is characterized by insulin resistance and used to be found mainly in overweight and older adults. With the increase in childhood obesity, more and more children are being diagnosed with this form of diabetes. Each year about 3,700 children are diagnosed with type 2 diabetes, and statistics show increased incidence of the disease among African Americans, American Indians, and Latin Americans. Symptoms are similar to type 1 diabetes (Zylke & DeAngelis, 2007). Nutrition management and increased physical activity can be effective treatments, although glucose-lowering medication or insulin may be needed for resistant cases.

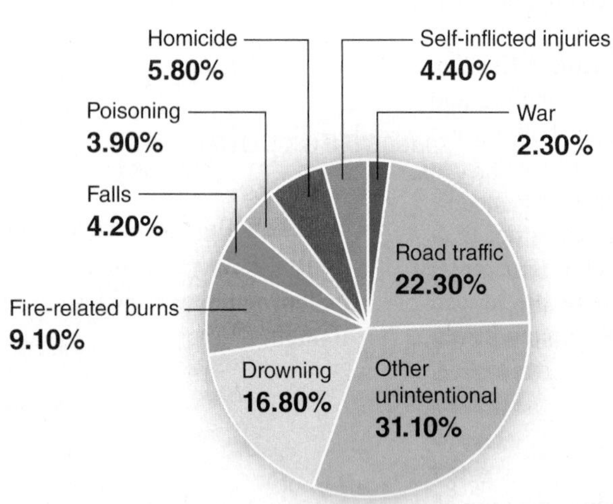

FIGURE 2
Accidental Deaths for Children under Age 18

Traffic accidents, drowning, and burns are the most common causes of accidental deaths among children under 18 years of age.

Source: World Health Organization, 2008.

ACCIDENTAL INJURIES

As in early childhood, accidental injuries are the leading cause of death among school-age U.S. children (Heron et al., 2009). In 2004 nearly 950,000 children under the age of 18 worldwide died of an injury with the majority resulting from traffic accidents, drowning, or burns (WHO, 2008; Figure 2).

An estimated 23,000 children each year suffer serious brain injuries from bicycle accidents, and as many as 88 percent of these injuries could be prevented by using helmets (AAP Committee on

Injury and Poison Prevention, 2001). Protective headgear also is vital for baseball and softball, football, roller skating, in-line skating, skateboarding, scooter riding, horseback riding, hockey, speed sledding, snowmobiling, and tobogganing. For soccer, protective goggles and mouth guards may help reduce head and facial injuries. "Heading" the ball should be minimized because of the danger of brain injury (AAP Committee on Sports Medicine and Fitness, 2001). Also, because of the need for stringent safety precautions and constant supervision for trampoline use, the AAP Committee on Injury and Poison Prevention & Committee on Sports Medicine and Fitness (1999) recommend that parents not buy trampolines and that children not use them on playgrounds or at school.

About half of kids who drown do so within 25 yards of an adult. This happens partly because drowning doesn't look like it does in movies. A drowning child does not yell for help or splash. Signs to look for? Head low in the water, perhaps tilted back with hair covering the eyes, silence, glassy or closed eyes, mouth at or slightly below the water line, and ineffective attempts to roll over to the back or swim.

Vittone, 2010

checkpoint
can **you** . . .

- Distinguish between acute and chronic medical conditions?
- Discuss the incidence and causes of asthma and diabetes?
- Identify factors that increase the risks of accidental injury?

COGNITIVE DEVELOPMENT

Piagetian Approach: The Concrete Operational Child

At about age 7, according to Piaget, children enter the stage of **concrete operations** when they can use mental operations, such as reasoning, to solve concrete (actual) problems. Children can think logically because they can take multiple aspects of a situation into account. However, their thinking is still limited to real situations in the here and now. Now we focus on the cognitive advances typical of this stage of development.

concrete operations
Third stage of Piagetian cognitive development (approximately ages 7 to 12), during which children develop logical but not abstract thinking.

COGNITIVE ADVANCES

In the stage of concrete operations, children have a better understanding than preoperational children of spatial concepts, causality, categorization, inductive and deductive reasoning, conservation, and number (Table 3).

Spatial Relationships and Causality Eight-year-old Ella stares intently at the map. "The star means we are here," she points, "so that must mean the store is there!" Ella turns to her mother with a smile and they both begin walking.

Ella is now in the stage of concrete operations. She is better able to understand spatial relationships. This allows her to interpret a map, find her way to and from school, estimate the time it would take to go from one place to another, and remember routes and landmarks. Experience plays a role in this development because children are more easily able to navigate a physical environment with which they have experience. In addition, these spatial abilities improve as children age (Gauvain, 1993).

Another key development during middle childhood involves the ability to make judgments about cause and effect. These specific abilities also improve as children age. For example, when 5- to 12-year-old children are asked to predict how levers and balance scales work, the older children give more correct answers. In addition, earlier in middle childhood they understand that the number of objects on each side of a scale affects performance, but it is not until later that they understand that the distance of objects from the center of a scale is also important (Amsel, Goodman, Savoie, & Clark, 1996).

TABLE 3 Advances in Selected Cognitive Abilities during Middle Childhood

Ability	Example
Spatial thinking	Danielle can use a map or model to help her search for a hidden object and can give someone else directions for finding the object. She can find her way to and from school, can estimate distances, and can judge how long it will take her to go from one place to another.
Cause and effect	Douglas knows which physical attributes of objects on each side of a balance scale will affect the result (i.e., number of objects matters but color does not). He does not yet know which spatial factors, such as position and placement of the objects, make a difference.
Categorization	Elena can sort objects into categories, such as shape, color, or both. She knows that a subclass (roses) has fewer members than the class of which it is a part (flowers).
Seriation and transitive inference	Catherine can arrange a group of sticks in order, from the shortest to the longest, and can insert an intermediate-size stick into the proper place. She knows that if one stick is longer than a second stick, and the second stick is longer than a third, then the first stick is longer than the third.
Inductive and deductive reasoning	Dominic can solve both inductive and deductive problems and knows that inductive conclusions (based on particular premises) are less certain than deductive conclusions (based on general premises).
Conservation	Felipe, at age 7, knows that if a clay ball is rolled into a sausage, it still contains the same amount of clay (conservation of substance). At age 9, he knows that the ball and the sausage weigh the same. Not until early adolescence will he understand that they displace the same amount of liquid if dropped in a glass of water.
Number and mathematics	Kevin can count in his head, can add by counting up from the smaller number, and can do simple story problems.

Categorization John sits at the kitchen table, working on his class project. He has been asked to make a timeline of six events in his life using photographs. His mother has given him six photographs of himself from infancy to the current time, and John carefully lays them in order from earliest to latest. "There!" he says, "I'm ready to start!"

Part of the reason John is now able to complete tasks such as this class project is because he is becoming better able to categorize objects. This emerging skill involves a series of relatively sophisticated abilities. One such ability is **seriation,** arranging objects in a series according to one or more dimensions. Children become increasingly better at seriation for dimensions such as time (earliest to latest), length (shortest to longest), or color (lightest to darkest) (Piaget, 1952).

seriation
Ability to order items along a dimension.

Another emerging ability is that of **transitive inferences** (if $a < b$ and $b < c$, then $a < c$). This involves the ability to infer a relationship between two objects from the relationship between each of them and a third object. For example, Mateo is shown three sticks: a short yellow stick, a medium-length green stick, and a long blue stick. He is shown that the yellow stick is shorter than the green stick, and is then shown that the green stick is shorter than the blue stick. However, he is not shown all three sticks in order of their length. If Mateo is able to understand transitive inferences, he should be able to quickly and easily infer that the yellow stick is shorter than the blue stick without physically comparing them (Chapman & Lindenberger, 1988; Piaget & Inhelder, 1967).

transitive inferences
Understanding the relationship between two objects by knowing the relationship of each to a third object.

Class inclusion also becomes easier. **Class inclusion** is the ability to see the relationship between a whole and its parts, and to understand the categories within a whole. For example, Piaget (1964) showed preoperational children 10 flowers—7 roses and 3 carnations—and asked them whether there were more roses or more flowers. Children in the preoperational stage of development tended to say there were more roses because they were comparing the roses with the carnations rather than the whole bunch of flowers. However, at about age 7 or 8, when children have reached the concrete operations stage, they are able to understand that roses are a subcategory of the flowers, and that there are therefore more flowers than there are roses (Flavell, Miller, & Miller, 2002).

class inclusion
Understanding of the relationship between a whole and its parts.

Inductive and Deductive Reasoning **Inductive reasoning** involves making observations about particular members of a class of people, animals, objects, or events, and then drawing conclusions about the class as a whole. For example, if one neighbor's dog barks and another neighbor's dog barks, then the conclusion might be that all dogs bark. Inductive reasoning must be tentative, however, because it is always possible to come across new information, such as a dog that does not bark.

inductive reasoning
Type of logical reasoning that moves from particular observations about members of a class to a general conclusion about that class.

Deductive reasoning, by contrast, starts with a general statement—a premise—about a class and applies it to particular members of the class. If a premise is true of the whole class, and the reasoning is sound, then the conclusion must be true. So, for example, if the belief is that all dogs bark, and a new dog comes along, it would be reasonable to conclude that the new dog will also bark.

deductive reasoning
Type of logical reasoning that moves from a general premise about a class to a conclusion about a particular member or members of the class.

Piaget believed that children in the concrete operations stage of cognitive development only used inductive reasoning. Deductive reasoning, according to Piaget, did not develop until adolescence. However, research suggests Piaget underestimated the abilities of children. In one study, researchers gave inductive and deductive reasoning problems to kindergarteners, second graders, fourth graders, and sixth graders. Because they did not want the children to use real world knowledge, they used imaginary terms and words to create both inductive and deductive reasoning problems. For example, one of the inductive problems was "Tombor is a popgop. Tombor wears blue boots. Do all popgops wear blue boots?" The corresponding deductive reasoning problem was "All popgops wear blue boots. Tombor is a popgop. Does Tombor wear blue boots?" Contrary to Piagetian theory, second graders (but not kindergartners) were able to answer both kinds of problems correctly (Galotti, Komatsu, & Voelz, 1997; Pillow, 2002). Given age-appropriate testing methods, evidence of inductive and deductive reasoning is present considerably earlier than Piaget predicted.

How can parents and teachers help children improve their reasoning ability?

Conservation In the preoperational stage of development, children are focused on appearances and have difficulty with abstract concepts. For example, Camilla, who is at the preoperational stage of development, is likely to think that if one of two identical clay balls is rolled into a long thin snake, it will now contain more clay because it is longer. She is deceived by appearances and thus fails this conservation task. However, Michael, who is in the stage of concrete operations, will say that the ball and the snake still contain the same amount of clay. What accounts for his ability to understand that the amount of clay remains unchanged regardless of the form it takes?

In solving various types of conservation problems, children in the stage of concrete operations can work out the answers in their heads. Three primary achievements allow them to do this. First, they understand the principle of *identity.* For instance, Michael understands that the clay is still the same clay even though it has a different shape because nothing was added or taken away from it. He is able to reason that it therefore must still be the same amount of clay for both shapes. Second, children in the concrete operations stage understand the principle of *reversibility.* Michael can picture what would happen if he went backward in time and rolled the snake back into a ball. He can now reason that the snake must still be the same amount of clay. Third, children at this stage can *decenter.* When Camilla looked at the snake, she focused only on its length, ignoring that it was thinner and flatter than the ball of clay. She centered on one dimension (length) while excluding the other (thickness). Michael, however, is able to decenter and look at more than one aspect of the two objects at once. Thus, although the ball is shorter than the snake, it is also thicker.

Children do not gain the ability to pass the various types of conservation tasks at one point in time. Typically, children can solve problems involving conservation of matter, such as the clay task, at about age 7 or 8. However, it is not until age 8 or 9 that children correctly solve conservation of weight tasks in which they are asked, for instance, whether the ball and the snake weigh the same. In tasks involving conservation of volume—in which children must judge whether the snake and ball displace the same amount of liquid when placed in a glass of water—children rarely answer correctly before age 12. Children's thinking at this stage is so concrete, so closely tied to a

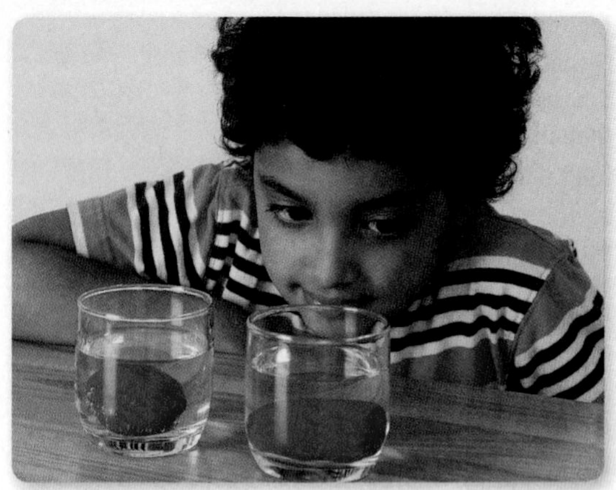

Does one ball of clay displace more water than the other? A child who has achieved conservation of volume knows that the answer does not depend on the ball's shape.

particular situation, that they cannot readily transfer what they have learned about one type of conservation to another type, even though the underlying principles are the same.

Number and Mathematics By age 6 or 7, many children can count in their heads. They also learn to *count on:* to add 5 and 3, they start counting at 5 and then go on to 6, 7, and 8. It may take 2 or 3 more years for them to count down for subtraction, but by age 9 most children can count up and down (Resnick, 1989).

Children also become more adept at solving simple story problems, such as "Pedro went to the store with $5 and spent $2 on candy. How much did he have left?" When the original amount is unknown—"Pedro went to the store, spent $2 and had $3 left. How much did he start out with?"—the problem is harder because the operation needed to solve it (addition) is not as clearly indicated. Few children can solve this kind of problem before age 8 or 9 (Resnick, 1989).

Research with minimally schooled people in developing countries suggests that the ability to add develops nearly universally and often intuitively, through concrete experience in a cultural context (Guberman, 1996; Resnick, 1989). These intuitive procedures are different from those taught in school. In a study of Brazilian street vendors ages 9 to 15, a researcher acting as a customer said, "I'll take two coconuts." Each one cost 40 cruzeiros; she paid with a 500-cruzeiros bill and asked, "What do I get back?" The child counted up from 80: "Eighty, 90, 100. . ." and gave the customer 420 cruzeiros. However, when this same child was given a similar problem in the classroom ("What is 500 minus 80?"), he arrived at the wrong answer by incorrectly using a series of steps learned in school (Carraher, Schliemann, & Carraher, 1988). This finding suggests that there are different routes for cultural learning. In fact, in cultural contexts in which schooling is not as important, children do not generally use abstract counting strategies.

Some intuitive understanding of fractions seems to exist by age 4 (Mix, Levine, & Huttenlocher, 1999), as children show when they deal a deck of cards or distribute portions of pizza or separate a box of chocolates (Frydman & Bryant, 1988; Singer-Freeman & Goswami, 2001; Sophian, Garyantes, & Chang, 1997). However, children tend not to think about the quantity a fraction represents; instead, they focus on the numerals that make it up. Thus they may say that ½ plus ⅓ equals ⅖. It is also difficult for children to grasp that ½ is bigger than ¼—that the smaller fraction (¼) has the larger denominator (Geary, 2006; Siegler, 1998; Sophian & Wood, 1997).

The ability to estimate progresses with age. When asked to place 24 numbers along a line from 0 to 100, kindergartners exaggerate the distances between low numbers and minimize the distances between high numbers. Most second graders produce number lines that are more evenly spaced (Siegler & Booth, 2004). Second, fourth, and sixth graders show a similar progression in producing number lines from 0 to 1,000 (Siegler & Opfer, 2003), most likely reflecting the experience older children gain in dealing with larger numbers. Besides improving in *number line estimation,* school-age children also improve in three other types of estimation: *computational estimation,* such as estimating the sum in an addition problem; *numerosity estimation,* such as estimating the number of candies in a jar; and *measurement estimation,* such as estimating the length of a line (Booth & Siegler, 2006).

INFLUENCES OF NEUROLOGICAL DEVELOPMENT, CULTURE, AND SCHOOLING

Piaget maintained that the shift from the rigid, illogical thinking of younger children to the flexible, logical thinking of older children depends on both neurological development and experience in adapting to the environment. Support for a neurological influence comes from scalp measurements of brain activity during a conservation task. Children who had achieved conservation of volume had different brain wave patterns from those who had not yet achieved it, suggesting that they may have been using different brain regions for the task (Stauder, Molenaar, & Van der Molen, 1993).

Piaget believed his theories described universal aspects of child development, but it may be that abilities such as conservation depend in part on familiarity with the materials being manipulated. Children can think more logically about things they know something about. Thus understanding of conservation may come, not only from new patterns of mental organization but also from culturally defined experience with the physical world.

Today's schoolchildren may not be advancing through Piaget's stages as rapidly as their parents did. When 10,000 British 11- and 12-year-olds were tested on conservation of volume and weight, their performance was 2 to 3 years behind that of their counterparts 30 years earlier (Shayer, Ginsburg, & Coe, 2007). These results suggest that today's teachers may be focusing on the three Rs rather than on hands-on experience with the way materials behave.

MORAL REASONING

Piaget was also interested in how children's ways of thinking might influence their ability to reason about morality. To draw out children's moral thinking, Piaget (1932) would tell them a story about two little boys: "One day Augustus noticed that his father's inkpot was empty and decided to help his father by filling it. While he was opening the bottle, he spilled a lot of ink on the tablecloth. The other boy, Julian, played with his father's inkpot and spilled a little ink on the cloth." Then Piaget would ask, "Which boy was naughtier, and why?" Children younger than 7 usually said Augustus was naughtier because he made the bigger stain. Older children recognized that Augustus meant well and made the large stain by accident, whereas Julian made a small stain while doing something he should not have been doing. Immature moral judgments, Piaget concluded, center only on the *degree* of offense; more mature judgments consider *intent.*

Do you think intent is an important factor in morality? How does the criminal justice system reflect this view?

Piaget (1932; Piaget & Inhelder, 1969) proposed that moral reasoning develops in three stages. He argued that children move gradually from one stage to another, at varying ages.

The first stage (approximately ages 2 to 7, corresponding with the preoperational stage) is based on *rigid obedience to authority.* Young children are egocentric and tend to see things only from their point of view. They cannot imagine that there is more than one way of looking at a moral issue. Moreover, they are rigid in their views. They believe that rules cannot be bent or changed, that behavior is either right or wrong, and that any offense deserves punishment, regardless of intent.

The second stage (ages 7 or 8 to 10 or 11, corresponding with the stage of concrete operations) is characterized by *increasing flexibility.* As children age, they begin to discard the idea that there is a single, absolute standard of right and wrong and develop their own sense of justice based on fairness or equal treatment for all. Because they can consider more than one aspect of a situation, they can make more subtle moral judgments.

Around age 11 or 12, when children may become capable of formal reasoning, the third stage of moral development arrives. The belief that everyone should be treated alike gives way to the ideal of *equity,* of taking specific circumstances into account. According to Piaget, a child of this age might say that a 2-year-old who spilled ink on the tablecloth should be held to a less demanding moral standard than a 10-year-old. With age, there is an increased focus not just on what happened but on the intentions of the actor.

Piaget's classic studies seemed to support the idea that children's moral reasoning progresses broadly in this fashion. However, more recent research suggests that children's moral reasoning is more nuanced at younger ages. For example, negligence—whether or not people who commit a wrongdoing ought to have foreseen the consequences of their actions—influences children's decisions about blame. When negligence is taken into account, younger children are more likely to focus on intentions, and their judgments about punishment look much more like those of adults (Nobes, Panagiotaki, & Pawson, 2009).

checkpoint can **you** . . .

- Identify six cognitive advances during middle childhood?
- Name three principles that help children understand conservation, and discuss influences on its mastery?
- Tell how Piaget's three stages of moral development reflect cognitive maturation?

Information-Processing Approach: Planning, Attention, and Memory

Clara walks by the kitchen and smells the delicious cake she just helped bake cooling on the counter. A few years ago she might have darted into the kitchen and stuck her finger in the cake to steal a few bites. But now, older and wiser, she thinks to herself, "No, that cake is for later. If I take a bite, my mom will get mad at me." Clara's more sophisticated cognitive abilities have allowed her to control her behavior in ways that were previously unavailable to her.

executive function
Conscious control of thoughts, emotions, and actions to accomplish goals or solve problems.

As children move through the school years, they make steady progress in the abilities to regulate and sustain attention, process and retain information, and plan and monitor their behavior. All of these interrelated developments contribute to **executive function,** the conscious control of thoughts, emotions, and actions to accomplish goals or solve problems. As their knowledge expands, children become more aware of what kinds of information are important to pay attention to and remember. School-age children also understand more about how memory works, and this knowledge enables them to plan and use strategies, or deliberate techniques, to help them remember.

HOW DO EXECUTIVE SKILLS DEVELOP?

Attention Span

Executive functions allow children to be more thoughtful in their cognition and behavior, and these skills are vital to successful development. A number of influences help children attain these skills, and as is typical within psychology, we can look at biological and environmental influences as working together to shape the developing child over time.

Executive functioning develops gradually from infancy to adolescence. As might be expected, it is accompanied by brain development, most notably in the prefrontal cortex (Lamm, Zelazo, & Lewis, 2006). As unneeded synapses are pruned away and pathways become myelinated, processing speed improves dramatically (Camarata & Woodcock, 2006). Faster, more efficient processing increases the amount of information children can keep in working memory. As children develop the ability to mentally juggle more concepts at the same time, they are also able to develop more complex thinking and goal-directed planning (Luna et al., 2004).

In addition to the physical development of the brain, environmental influences also matter. For example, the home environment has been documented to contribute to the development of executive skills. In a longitudinal study of 700 children from infancy on, the quality of the family environment—including such factors as available resources, cognitive stimulation, and maternal sensitivity—predicted attentional and memory performance in first grade (NICHD Early Child Care Research Network, 2005c).

As children age, they become increasingly independent and must make decisions for themselves rather than being told what to do. Executive functioning is involved in the capacity to make good decisions and monitor whether goals are being met. These abilities develop gradually, and parenting practices and culture affect the pace at which children are given the opportunity to practice these skills. For example, school-age children develop planning skills by making decisions about their everyday activities. In a 3-year longitudinal study, the responsibility for planning children's informal activities gradually shifted between second and fourth grades from parent to child, and this change was reflected in children's improved ability to plan classroom work (Gauvain & Perez, 2005).

SELECTIVE ATTENTION

School-age children can concentrate longer than younger children and can focus on the information they need and want while screening out irrelevant information. For example, in school, it may be necessary for a child to focus on a teacher's less-than-exciting lesson while simultaneously ignoring the antics of the class clown. This growth in *selective attention*—the ability to deliberately direct one's attention and shut out distractions—may hinge on the executive skill of *inhibitory control,* the voluntary suppression of unwanted responses (Luna et al., 2004).

The increasing capacity for selective attention is believed to be due to neurological maturation and is one of the reasons memory improves during middle childhood (Booth et al., 2003; Harnishfeger & Bjorklund, 1993). Older children may make fewer mistakes in recall than younger children because they are better able to select what they want to remember and what they can forget (Lorsbach & Reimer, 1997).

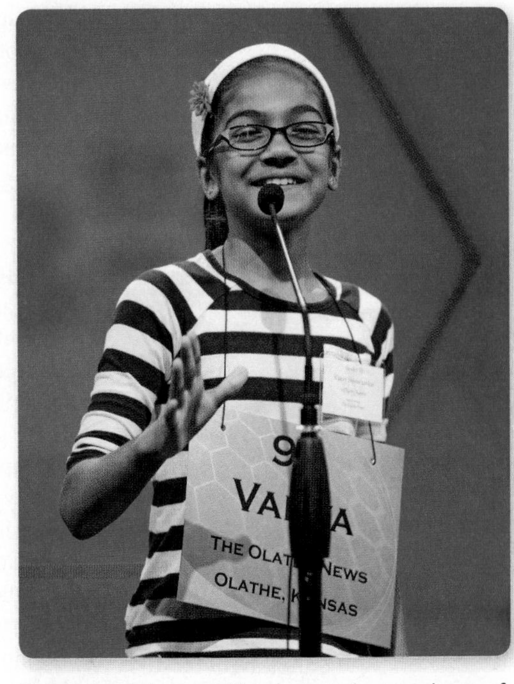

Contestants in a spelling bee make good use of mnemonic strategies—devices to aid memory—such as rehearsal (repetition), organization, and elaboration.

WORKING MEMORY

Working memory involves the short-term storage of information that is being actively processed, like a mental workspace. For example, if you are asked to compute what 42 × 60 is, you would use your working memory to hold part of the answer while you solved the rest of it.

The efficiency of working memory increases greatly in middle childhood, laying the foundation for a wide range of cognitive skills. For example, between the ages of 6 and 10 there are improvements in processing speed (how quickly information is processed) and storage capacity (how many things can be simultaneously held in working memory) (Bayliss, Jarrod, Baddeley, Gunn, & Leigh, 2005). Because working memory is necessary for storing information while other material is being mentally manipulated, the capacity of a child's working memory can directly affect academic success (Alloway, 2006). For example, children with low working memory struggle with structured learning activities. These difficulties are most apparent when there are lengthy instructions because children need to retain multiple items in working memory to be able to follow the instructions (Gathercole & Alloway, 2008). Individual differences in working memory capacity are also linked to a child's ability to acquire knowledge and new skills (Alloway, 2006).

Working Memory Capactiy

Working memory issues are not just a theoretical concern; they are important in education. Research has indicated that as many as 10 percent of school-age children suffer from low working memory (Alloway, Gathercole, Kirkwood, & Elliot, 2009). The adoption of tools that assess working memory in the classroom could greatly influence achievement levels for children identified as possessing low working memory.

METAMEMORY: UNDERSTANDING MEMORY

Between ages 5 and 7, the brain's frontal lobes undergo significant development and reorganization. These changes may make possible improved **metamemory,** knowledge about the processes of memory (Chua, Schacter, Rand-Giovanetti, & Sperling, 2006). Metamemory can be thought of as thinking about memory. In other words, it involves the knowledge of and reflection about memory processes.

metamemory
Understanding of processes of memory.

From kindergarten through fifth grade, children advance steadily in understanding memory (Flavell et al., 2002). Kindergartners and first graders know that people remember better if they study longer, that people forget things with time, and that relearning something is easier than learning it for the first time. By third grade, children know that some people remember better than others and that some things are easier to remember than others.

MNEMONICS: STRATEGIES FOR REMEMBERING

Were you ever taught the saying "please excuse my dear Aunt Sally" as a technique to help you remember the order of operations in solving an equation? This is an example

mnemonic device
Strategy to aid memory.

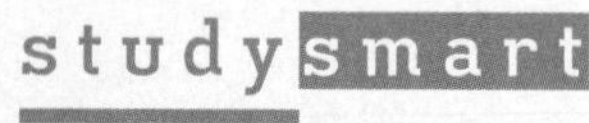

Memory Strategies

external memory aids
Mnemonic strategies using something outside the person.

rehearsal
Mnemonic strategy to keep an item in working memory through conscious repetition.

organization
Mnemonic strategy of categorizing material to be remembered.

elaboration
Mnemonic strategy of making mental associations involving items to be remembered.

of a **mnemonic device,** a strategy to aid memory. The most common mnemonic device among both children and adults is use of *external memory aids.* Other common mnemonic devices are *rehearsal, organization,* and *elaboration.*

Writing down a telephone number, making a list, setting a timer, and putting a library book by the front door are examples of **external memory aids:** prompts by something outside the person. Saying a telephone number over and over after looking it up, so as not to forget it before dialing, is a form of **rehearsal,** or conscious repetition. **Organization** is mentally placing information into categories (such as animals, furniture, vehicles, and clothing) to make it easier to recall. In **elaboration,** children associate items with something else, such as an imagined scene or story. To remember to buy lemons, ketchup, and napkins, for example, a child might visualize a ketchup bottle balanced on a lemon, with a pile of napkins handy to wipe up any spills.

There are developmental changes in children's ability to use these memory strategies. For example, when young children are taught to use a memory strategy, they tend to use it only in the particular context in which they were taught. Older children, however, are more likely to apply it to other situations (Flavell et al., 2002). This process occurs for spontaneous learning as well. As children grow older, they develop better strategies and use them more effectively (Bjorklund, 1997). Older children also often use more than one strategy for a task and choose different kinds of strategies for different problems (Bjorklund, Miller, Coyle, & Slawinski, 1997).

Although it is difficult to teach young children to use mnemonic strategies, teaching older children about them if they are developmentally ready to learn such skills can result in memory gains. Young children have difficulty learning mnemonic strategies because they just aren't ready for them, but once they have the necessary capacities in place, they can benefit from instruction. Indeed, children's memory performance has been linked to aspects of the classroom context. Some teachers ask students to remember more information than other teachers do, and these students tend to use more mnemonic strategies (Coffman, Ornstein, McCall, & Curran, 2008).

checkpoint
can you . . .

- Identify four ways in which information processing improves during middle childhood?
- Explain the importance of executive function, selective attention, working memory, and metamemory?
- Name four common mnemonic aids and discuss developmental differences in their use?
- Give examples of how improved information processing explains cognitive advances Piaget described?

INFORMATION PROCESSING AND PIAGETIAN TASKS

Improvements in information processing may help explain the advances Piaget described. For example, 9-year-olds may be better able than 5-year-olds to find their way to and from school because they can scan a scene, take in its important features, and remember objects in context in the order in which they were encountered (Allen & Ondracek, 1995).

Improvements in memory may contribute to the mastery of conservation tasks. Young children's working memory is so limited that they may not be able to remember all the relevant information (Siegler & Richards, 1982). They may have difficulty holding both the length and width of an item in working memory simultaneously, or have difficulty remembering that two differently shaped pieces of clay were originally identical. Gains in working memory may enable older children to solve such problems.

Psychometric Approach: Assessment of Intelligence

Wechsler Intelligence Scale for Children (WISC-IV)
Individual intelligence test for school-age children, which yields verbal and performance scores as well as a combined score.

Psychometrics is a branch of psychology involved in the quantitative measurement of psychological variables, and psychometric techniques have been used extensively in the development of ways to measure intelligence. The most widely used individual test is the **Wechsler Intelligence Scale for Children (WISC-IV).** This test for ages 6 through 16 measures verbal and performance abilities, yielding separate scores for each as well as a total score. The separate subtest scores pinpoint a child's strengths and help diagnose specific problems. For example, if a child does well on verbal tests (such as general information and basic arithmetic operations) but poorly on performance tests (such as doing a puzzle or drawing the missing part of a picture), the child may be slow in perceptual or motor development. A child who does well on performance tests but poorly on verbal tests may have a language problem. Another commonly used individual test is the Stanford-Binet Intelligence Scales.

A popular group test, the **Otis-Lennon School Ability Test (OLSAT8),** has levels for kindergarten through 12th grade. Children are asked to classify items, show an understanding of verbal and numerical concepts, display general information, and follow directions. Separate scores for verbal comprehension, verbal reasoning, pictorial reasoning, figural reasoning, and quantitative reasoning can identify specific strengths and weaknesses.

Otis-Lennon School Ability Test (OLSAT8)
Group intelligence test for kindergarten through 12th grade.

THE IQ CONTROVERSY

The use of psychometric intelligence tests such as those just described is controversial. On the positive side, because IQ tests have been standardized and widely used, there is extensive information about their norms, validity, and reliability. Scores on IQ tests taken during middle childhood are fairly good predictors of school achievement, especially for highly verbal children, and these scores are more reliable than during the preschool years. IQ at age 11 even has been found to predict length of life, functional independence late in life, and the presence or absence of dementia (Starr, Deary, Lemmon, & Whalley, 2000; Whalley & Deary, 2001; Whalley et al., 2000).

On the other hand, critics claim that the tests underestimate the intelligence of children who are in ill health or, for one reason or another, do not do well on tests (Ceci, 1991; Sternberg, 2004). Because the tests are timed, they equate intelligence with speed and penalize a child who works slowly and deliberately. Their appropriateness for diagnosing learning disabilities also has been questioned (Benson, 2003).

A more fundamental criticism is that IQ tests do not directly measure native ability; instead, they *infer* intelligence from what children already know. As we'll see, it is virtually impossible to design a test that requires no prior knowledge. Further, the tests are validated against measures of achievement, such as school performance, which are affected by such factors as schooling and culture. As we discuss in a later section, there is also controversy over whether intelligence is a single, general ability or whether there are types of intelligence not captured by IQ tests. For these and other reasons, strong disagreement exists over how accurately these tests assess children's intelligence.

checkpoint
can **you . . .**

- Name and describe two traditional intelligence tests for schoolchildren?
- Give arguments for and against IQ tests?

INFLUENCES ON INTELLIGENCE (IQ)

Both heredity and environment influence intelligence. Keeping in mind the controversy over whether IQ tests actually measure intelligence, let's look more closely at these influences.

Brain Development Brain imaging research shows a moderate correlation between brain size or amount of gray matter and general intelligence, especially reasoning and problem-solving abilities (Gray & Thompson, 2004). One study found that the amount of gray matter in the frontal cortex is largely inherited, varies widely among individuals, and is linked with differences in IQ (Thompson et al., 2001). A later study suggests that the key is not the *amount* of gray matter a child has at a certain age, but rather the *pattern of development* of the prefrontal cortex. In children of average IQ, the prefrontal cortex peaks in thickness by age 8, and then gradually thins as unneeded connections are pruned. In the most intelligent 7-year-olds, the cortex does not peak in thickness until age 11 or 12. This pattern may represent an extended critical period for developing high-level thinking circuits (Shaw et al., 2006).

Although reasoning, problem solving, and executive function are linked to the prefrontal cortex, other brain regions under strong genetic influence also contribute to

Asian American children often do well in school. The reasons seem to be cultural, not genetic.

intelligent behavior. So does the speed and reliability of transmission of messages in the brain. Environmental factors, such as the family, schooling, and culture, play a strong role early in life; but heritability of intelligence (an estimate of the degree to which individual differences in intelligence are genetically caused) dramatically increases with age as children select or create environments that fit their genetic tendencies (Davis, Haworth, & Plomin, 2009).

Influence of Schooling on IQ Schooling seems to increase tested intelligence (Neisser et al., 1996). Children whose school entrance was significantly delayed—as happened, for example, in the Netherlands during the Nazi occupation—lost as many as 5 IQ points each year, and some of these losses were never recovered (Ceci & Williams, 1997).

IQ scores also drop during summer vacation (Ceci & Williams, 1997). Among a national sample of 1,500 children, language, spatial, and conceptual scores improved much more between October and April, the bulk of the school year, than between April and October, which includes summer vacation and the beginning and end of the school year (Huttenlocher, Levine, & Vevea, 1998).

Influences of Race/Ethnicity and Socioeconomic Status on IQ Average test scores vary among racial/ethnic groups, inspiring claims that the tests are unfair to minorities. Historically, on average, black children scored about 15 points lower than white children and showed a comparable lag on school achievement tests (Neisser et al., 1996). However, these gaps have narrowed by as much as 4 to 7 points in recent years (Dickens & Flynn, 2006). Average IQ scores of Hispanic American children fall between those of black and white children, and their scores, too, tend to predict school achievement (Ang, Rodgers, & Wanstrom, 2010).

What accounts for racial/ethnic differences in IQ? Some researchers have argued for a substantial genetic factor (Herrnstein & Murray, 1994; Jensen, 1969; Rushton & Jensen, 2005). Although there is strong evidence of a genetic influence on *individual* differences in intelligence, there is *no direct evidence* that IQ differences among ethnic, cultural, or racial *groups* are hereditary (Gray & Thompson, 2004; Neisser et al., 1996; Sternberg et al., 2005). Instead, many studies attribute ethnic differences in IQ to inequalities in environment (Nisbett, 2005)—in income, nutrition, living conditions, health, parenting practices, early child care, intellectual stimulation, schooling, culture, or other circumstances such as the effects of oppression and discrimination that can affect self-esteem, motivation, and academic performance.

The recent narrowing of the gap in test scores parallels an improvement in the life circumstances and educational opportunities of many African American children. In addition, some early intervention programs have had success in raising disadvantaged children's IQs.

The strength of genetic influence itself appears to vary with socioeconomic status. In a longitudinal study of 319 pairs of twins followed from birth, the genetic influence on IQ scores at age 7 among children from impoverished families was close to zero and the influence of environment was strong, whereas among children in affluent families the opposite was true. In other words, high SES strengthens genetic influence, whereas low SES tends to override it (Turkheimer, Haley, Waldron, D'Onofrio, & Gottesman, 2003).

What about Asian Americans, whose scholastic achievements consistently top those of other ethnic groups? Although there is some controversy about their relative performance on intelligence tests, most researchers find that these children do *not* seem to have a significant edge in IQ (Neisser et al., 1996). Instead, Asian American children's strong scholastic achievement seems to be best explained by their culture's emphasis on obedience and respect for elders, the importance Asian American parents place on education as a route to upward mobility, and the devotion of Asian American students to homework and study (Chao, 1996; Fuligni & Stevenson, 1995; Huntsinger & Jose, 1995; H. W. Stevenson, 1995).

Influence of Culture on IQ Various attempts have been made to explain why there are differences in IQ tests for people of different ethnicities. One possibility is that people of different ethnic groups have different cultures. Intelligence and culture are inextricably linked, and behavior seen as intelligent in one culture may be viewed as foolish in another (Sternberg, 2004). For example, when given a sorting task, North Americans would be likely to place a robin under the category of birds, whereas the Kpelle people in North Africa would consider it more intelligent to place the robin in the functional category of flying things (Cole, 1998). Thus a test of intelligence developed in one culture may not be equally valid in another. Furthermore, the schooling offered in a culture may prepare a child to do well in certain tasks and not in others, and the competencies taught and tested in school are not necessarily the same as the practical skills needed to succeed in everyday life (Sternberg, 2004, 2005). Intelligence might thus be better defined as the skills and knowledge needed for success within a particular social and cultural context. The mental processes that underlie intelligence may be the same across cultures, but their products may be different—and so should be the means of assessing performance (Sternberg, 2004). Intelligence tests should be culturally relevant and include activities that are common and necessary in that culture.

These arguments have led to assertions that ethnic differences in IQ are not reflecting intelligence, but rather are an artifact of cultural bias. It may be that some questions use vocabulary or call for information or skills more familiar to some cultural groups than to others (Sternberg, 1985, 1987). Because these intelligence tests are built around the dominant thinking style and language of white people of European ancestry, minority children are at a disadvantage (Heath, 1989; Helms, 1992; Matsumoto & Juang, 2008).

Test developers have tried to design **culture-free tests**—tests with no culture-linked content—by posing tasks that do not require language, such as tracing mazes, putting the right shapes in the right holes, and completing pictures; but they have been unable to eliminate all cultural influences. Test designers also have found it virtually impossible to produce **culture-fair tests** consisting only of experiences common to people in various cultures. Controlled studies have generally failed to show that cultural bias contributes substantially to overall group differences in IQ (Neisser et al., 1996).

culture-free tests
Intelligence tests that, if they were possible to design, would have no culturally linked content.

culture-fair tests
Intelligence tests that deal with experiences common to various cultures, in an attempt to avoid cultural bias.

checkpoint
can you . . .

- Assess the effects of brain development on intellectual functioning?
- Assess the effects of schooling, race/ethnicity, SES, and culture on IQ?

IS THERE MORE THAN ONE INTELLIGENCE?

A serious criticism of IQ tests is that they focus almost entirely on abilities that are useful in school. Doing well in school is important, but doing well in life involves much more than academics. Most IQ tests do not cover other important aspects of intelligent behavior, such as common sense, social skills, creative insight, and self-knowledge. Yet these abilities, in which some children with modest academic skills excel, may become equally or more important in later life and may even be considered separate forms of intelligence. Two of the chief advocates of this position are Howard Gardner and Robert Sternberg.

Gardner's Theory of Multiple Intelligences Is a child who is good at analyzing paragraphs and making analogies more intelligent than one who can play a challenging violin solo or pitch a curve ball at the right time? The answer is no, according to Gardner's (1993, 1998) **theory of multiple intelligences.**

Gardner, a neuropsychologist and educational researcher at Harvard University, identified eight independent kinds of intelligence. According to Gardner, conventional intelligence tests tap only three "intelligences": *linguistic, logical-mathematical,* and, to some extent, *spatial.* The other five, which are not reflected in IQ scores, are *musical,*

theory of multiple intelligences
Gardner's theory that each person has several distinct forms of intelligence.

TABLE 4 Eight Intelligences, According to Gardner

Intelligence	Definition	Fields or Occupations Where Used
Linguistic	Ability to use and understand words and nuances of meaning	Writing, editing, translating
Logical-mathematical	Ability to manipulate numbers and solve logical problems	Science, business, medicine
Spatial	Ability to find one's way around in an environment and judge relationships between objects in space	Architecture, carpentry, city planning
Musical	Ability to perceive and create patterns of pitch and rhythm	Musical composition, conducting
Bodily-kinesthetic	Ability to move with precision	Dancing, athletics, surgery
Interpersonal	Ability to understand and communicate with others	Teaching, acting, politics
Intrapersonal	Ability to understand the self	Counseling, psychiatry, spiritual leadership
Naturalist	Ability to distinguish species and their characteristics	Hunting, fishing, farming, gardening, cooking

Source: Based on Gardner, 1993, 1998.

bodily-kinesthetic, interpersonal, intrapersonal, and *naturalist* (Table 4 gives definitions of each intelligence and examples of fields in which it is most useful).

Gardner argued that these intelligences are distinct from each other and that high intelligence in one area does not necessarily accompany high intelligence in any of the others. A person may be extremely gifted in art (a spatial ability), precision of movement (bodily-kinesthetic), social relations (interpersonal), or self-understanding (intrapersonal), but not have a high IQ. Thus an athlete, an artist, and a musician could be equally intelligent, each in a different area.

Gardner (1995) would assess each intelligence directly by observing its products—how well a child can tell a story, remember a melody, or get around in a strange area—and not with typical standardized tests. The type of intelligence being assessed would determine the type of test required. The purpose would be, not to compare individuals, but to reveal strengths and weaknesses to help people realize their potential.

In which of Gardner's types of intelligence are you strongest? Did your education focus on any of these?

But do Gardner's methods accurately describe and assess intelligence? Critics of Gardner argue that his multiple intelligences are actually more accurately labeled as talents or abilities and assert that *intelligence* is more closely associated with skills that lead to academic achievement. They further question his criteria for defining separate intelligences that largely overlap such as mathematical and spatial intelligence (Willingham, 2004).

triarchic theory of intelligence Sternberg's theory describing three elements of intelligence: componential, experiential, and contextual.

componential element Sternberg's term for the analytic aspect of intelligence.

experiential element Sternberg's term for the insightful or creative aspect of intelligence.

Sternberg's Triarchic Theory of Intelligence Gardner segmented intelligence on the basis of areas of ability, whereas Sternberg's (1985, 2004) **triarchic theory of intelligence** focuses on the processes involved in intelligent behavior. In this approach, intelligence consists of three elements: *componential, experiential,* and *contextual* intelligence.

- The **componential element** is the analytic aspect of intelligence; it determines how efficiently people process information. It helps people solve problems, monitor solutions, and evaluate the results. Some people are more effective information processors than others.
- The **experiential element** is insightful or creative; it determines how people approach novel or familiar tasks. It enables people to compare new information with what they already know and to come up with new ways of putting facts together—in other words, to think originally.

- The **contextual element** is practical; it helps people deal with their environment. It is the ability to size up a situation and decide what to do. What actions are most appropriate for a given situation depend on the context; a person might decide to adapt to a situation, change it, or get out of it.

contextual element
Sternberg's term for the practical aspect of intelligence.

According to Sternberg, everyone has these three abilities to a greater or lesser extent. A person may be strong in one, two, or all three. The *Sternberg Triarchic Abilities Test* (STAT) (Sternberg, 1993) seeks to measure each of the three aspects of intelligence through multiple-choice and essay questions. Because Sternberg focused on processes rather than content, and those processes should predict intelligent behavior across domains of knowledge, three domains of intelligence are assessed: *verbal, quantitative,* and *figural* (or spatial). For example, an item to test practical quantitative intelligence might be to solve an everyday math problem having to do with buying tickets to a ball game or following a recipe for making cookies. A creative verbal item might ask children to solve deductive reasoning problems that start with factually false premises (such as, "Money falls off trees"). An analytical figural item might ask children to identify the missing piece of a figure. Validation studies have found positive correlations between the STAT and several other tests of critical thinking, creativity, and practical problem solving. As predicted, the three kinds of abilities are only weakly correlated with each other (Sternberg, 1997; Sternberg & Clinkenbeard, 1995).

How do Sternberg's tests compare to conventional IQ tests? Conventional tests are relatively good at predicting school performance but are less useful at predicting success in the real world. According to Sternberg, this is to be expected. Conventional IQ tests mainly measure componential ability, and because this ability is the kind most school tasks require, it's not surprising that the tests predict academic success. Their failure to measure experiential (insightful or creative) and contextual (practical) intelligence may explain why they have less utility predicting outcomes in the real world.

In the real world, book knowledge may not always be helpful. For example, children in many cultures have to learn practical skills, known as **tacit knowledge,** in order to succeed. In studies in Usenge, Kenya, and among Yup'ik Eskimo children in southwestern Alaska, children's tacit knowledge of medicinal herbs, hunting, fishing, and preserving plants showed no correlation with conventional measures of intelligence but were necessary for survival (Grigorenko et al., 2004; Sternberg, 2004).

tacit knowledge
Sternberg's term for information that is not formally taught or openly expressed but is necessary to get ahead.

Kaufman Assessment Battery for Children (K-ABC-II)
Nontraditional individual intelligence test designed to provide fair assessments of minority children and children with disabilities.

dynamic tests
Tests based on Vygotsky's theory that emphasize potential rather than past learning.

OTHER DIRECTIONS IN INTELLIGENCE TESTING

Some other diagnostic and predictive tools are based on neurological research and information-processing theory. The second edition of the **Kaufman Assessment Battery for Children (K-ABC-II)** (Kaufman & Kaufman, 1983, 2003), an individual test for ages 3 to 18, is designed to evaluate cognitive abilities in children with diverse needs (such as autism, hearing impairments, and language disorders) and from varying cultural and linguistic backgrounds. It has subtests designed to minimize verbal instructions and responses as well as items with limited cultural content.

Dynamic tests based on Vygotsky's theories emphasize potential rather than present achievement. In contrast with traditional *static tests* that measure a child's current abilities, these tests seek to capture the *dynamic* nature of intelligence by measuring learning processes directly rather than through the products of past learning (Sternberg, 2004). Dynamic tests contain items up to 2 years above a child's current level of competence. Examiners help the child when necessary by asking leading questions, giving examples or demonstrations, and offering feedback; thus the test itself is a learning situation. Because Vygotsky focused on interaction as the context in which development occurred, part of what it means to be intelligent includes the ability to learn via

The Kaufman Assessment Battery for Children (K-ABC-II) is designed to evaluate cognitive abilities in children with diverse needs, such as hearing impairments and language disorders.

checkpoint
can **you** . . .

- Compare Sternberg's and Gardner's theories of intelligence?
- Describe three new types of intelligence testing?

scaffolded interactions. The difference between the items a child can answer alone and the items the child can answer with help is the child's zone of proximal development (ZPD).

By pointing to what a child is ready to learn, dynamic testing may give teachers more useful information than does a psychometric test and can aid in designing interventions to help children progress. However, dynamic testing is quite labor-intensive, and the ZPD may be difficult to measure precisely.

Language and Literacy

Language abilities continue to grow during middle childhood. School-age children are better able to understand and interpret oral and written communication and to make themselves understood. These tasks are especially challenging for children who are not native-language speakers.

VOCABULARY, GRAMMAR, AND SYNTAX

study smart

Forms of Speech

As vocabulary grows during the school years, children use increasingly precise verbs. They learn that a word like *run* can have more than one meaning, and they can tell from the context which meaning is intended. *Simile* and *metaphor,* figures of speech in which a word or phrase that usually designates one thing is compared or applied to another, become increasingly common (Owens, 1996). Although grammar is quite complex by age 6, children during the early school years rarely use the passive voice (as in "The sidewalk is being shoveled").

In 1939, researchers at Iowa University conducted a study in which stuttering was deliberately induced in young children. In this "Monster study," a group of orphans were taunted and harassed over their speech in an attempt to demonstrate that stuttering was the result of psychological pressure. None of the children developed a stuttering problem, but many of them did develop psychological problems as a result of the experiment. Clearly, this study suffered from profound ethical issues, and in 2007 six of the children sued and were awarded settlements of approximately $1 million.

Huge payout in U.S. stuttering case, 2007

Children's understanding of rules of *syntax* (the deep underlying structure of language that organizes words into understandable phrases and sentences) becomes more sophisticated with age (C. S. Chomsky, 1969). For example, most children under age 5 or 6 think the sentences "John promised Bill to go shopping" and "John told Bill to go shopping" both mean that Bill is the one to go to the store. By age 8 most children can interpret the first sentence correctly and by age 9 virtually all children can. They now look at the meaning of a sentence as a whole instead of focusing on word order alone.

Sentence structure continues to become more elaborate. Older children use more subordinate clauses ("The boy *who delivers the newspapers* rang the doorbell."). Still, some constructions, such as clauses beginning with *however* and *although,* do not become common until early adolescence (Owens, 1996).

PRAGMATICS: KNOWLEDGE ABOUT COMMUNICATION

The major area of linguistic growth during the school years is in **pragmatics:** the social context of language. Pragmatics includes both conversational and narrative skills.

pragmatics
The social context of lanuage.

Good conversationalists probe by asking questions before introducing a topic with which the other person may not be familiar. They quickly recognize a breakdown in communication and do something to repair it. There are wide individual differences in such skills; some 7-year-olds are better conversationalists than some adults (Anderson, Clark, & Mullin, 1994). There are also gender differences. In one study, 120 middle-class London fourth graders were paired up to solve a problem. When boys and girls worked together, boys used more controlling statements and negative interruptions, whereas girls phrased their remarks in a more tentative, conciliatory way (Leman, Ahmed, & Ozarow, 2005).

If you want children to tell you the truth, ask them to promise to do so before asking your question. Researchers have found that children are less likely to lie after promising to tell the truth.

Evans & Lee, 2010

Most 6-year-olds can retell the plot of a short book, movie, or television show. They are beginning to describe motives and causal links. By second grade, children's stories become longer and more complex. Fictional tales often have conventional beginnings and endings ("Once upon a time . . ." and "They lived happily ever after"). Word use is more varied than before, but characters do not show growth or change, and plots are not fully developed.

Older children usually set the stage with introductory information about the setting and characters, and they clearly indicate changes of time and place during the story. They construct more complex episodes than younger children do, but with less unnecessary detail. They focus more on the characters' motives and thoughts, and they think through how to resolve problems in the plot.

checkpoint
can **you** . . .

- Summarize improvements in language skills during middle childhood?

SECOND-LANGUAGE LEARNING

In 2007, 21 percent of U.S. children ages 5 to 17 spoke a language other than English at home. The primary language most of these children spoke was Spanish, and more than 5 percent had difficulty speaking English (Federal Interagency Forum on Child and Family Statistics, 2009). About 11 percent of the public school population are defined as *English-language learners* (ELLs) (NCES, 2007b).

Some schools use an **English-immersion approach** (sometimes called ESL, or English as a second language), in which language-minority children are immersed in English from the beginning, in special classes. Other schools have adopted programs of **bilingual education,** in which children are taught in two languages, first learning in their native language with others who speak it and then switching to regular classes in English when they become more proficient in it. These programs can encourage children to become **bilingual** (fluent in two languages) and to feel pride in their cultural identity.

English-immersion approach
Approach to teaching English as a second language in which instruction is presented only in English.

bilingual education
System of teaching non-English-speaking children in their native language while they learn English, and later switching to all-English instruction.

bilingual
Fluent in two languages.

two-way (dual-language) learning
Approach to second-language education in which English speakers and non-English-speakers learn together in their own and each other's languages.

Advocates of early *English immersion* claim that the sooner children are exposed to English and the more time they spend speaking it, the better they learn it. Proponents of *bilingual* programs claim that children progress faster academically in their native language and later make a smoother transition to all-English classrooms (Padilla et al., 1991).

Statistical analyses of multiple studies conclude that children in bilingual programs typically outperform those in all-English programs on tests of English proficiency (Crawford, 2007; Krashen & McField, 2005). Even more successful, according to some research, is another, less common, approach: **two-way (dual-language) learning,** in which English-speaking and foreign-speaking children learn together in their own and each other's languages. This approach avoids any need to place minority children in separate classes. By valuing both languages equally, it reinforces self-esteem and improves school performance. An added advantage is that English speakers learn a foreign language at an early age, when they can acquire it most easily (Collier, 1995; W. P. Thomas & Collier, 1998). However, less than 2 percent of English-language learners nationwide are enrolled in two-way programs (Crawford, 2007).

checkpoint
can **you** . . .

- Describe and evaluate three types of second-language education?

BECOMING LITERATE

Learning to read and write frees children from the constraints of face-to-face communication, giving them access to the ideas and imagination of people in faraway lands and long-ago times. Once children can translate the marks on a page into patterns of sound and meaning, they can develop increasingly sophisticated strategies to understand what they read; and they can use written words to express ideas, thoughts, and feelings.

Reading and Writing Think of what happens in order for a child to learn to read words. First, a child must remember the distinctive features of letters—for example, that, a "c" consists of a curved half-circle and an "o" is a closed circle. Then a child must be able to recognize the different phonemes by breaking down words into their constituent parts. For example, a child must be able to understand that the word *dog* is composed of three different sounds, the "d," the "o," and the "g." Finally, the child must be able to match the visual features of letters and the phonemes and remember

decoding
Process of phonetic analysis by which a printed word is converted to spoken form before retrieval from long-term memory.

phonetic (code-emphasis) approach
Approach to teaching reading that emphasizes decoding of unfamiliar words.

whole-language approach
Approach to teaching reading that emphasizes visual retrieval and use of contextual clues.

visually based retrieval
Process of retrieving the sound of a printed word when seeing the word as a whole.

which ones go together. This process is known as **decoding.** Only when these skills are accomplished can children begin to read. Not surprisingly, learning to read is a complicated and difficult skill.

Because of the difficulties involved in learning how to read, educators have developed a variety of ways to instruct children. Children can learn to identify a printed word in two contrasting ways. In the traditional approach, called the **phonetic (code-emphasis) approach,** the child sounds out the word, translating it from print to speech before retrieving it from long-term memory. To do this, the child must master the phonetic code that matches the printed alphabet to spoken sounds (as described above). Instruction generally involves rigorous, teacher-directed tasks focused on memorizing sound-letter correspondences.

The **whole-language approach** emphasizes visual retrieval and the use of contextual cues. This approach is based on the belief that children can learn to read and write naturally, much as they learn to understand and use speech. By using **visually based retrieval,** the child simply looks at the word and then retrieves it. Whole-language proponents assert that children learn to read with better comprehension and more enjoyment if they experience written language from the outset as a way to gain information and express ideas and feelings, not as a system of isolated sounds and syllables to be learned by memorization and drill. Whole-language programs tend to feature real literature and open-ended, student-initiated activities.

Literacy

Despite the popularity of the whole-language approach, research has found little support for its claims. A long line of research supports the view that phonemic awareness and early phonetics training are keys to reading proficiency for most children (Booth, Perfetti, & MacWhinney, 1999; Hatcher, Hulme, & Ellis, 1994; Jeynes & Littell, 2000; National Reading Panel, 2000).

Many experts recommend a blend of the best features of both approaches (National Reading Panel, 2000). Children can learn phonetic skills along with strategies to help them understand what they read. For example, they might be drilled in sound-letter correspondences, but also be asked to memorize certain common words like *"the"* and *"one"* that are more difficult to decode. Children who can summon both visually based and phonetic strategies become better, more versatile, readers (Siegler, 1998, 2000).

metacognition
Thinking about thinking, or awareness of one's own mental processes.

Metacognitive abilities can help children develop literacy. **Metacognition** involves thinking about thinking. It can help children monitor their understanding of what they read and develop strategies to address challenges. For example, children with good metacognitive skills might use such strategies as reading more slowly, rereading difficult passages, trying to visualize information, or thinking of additional examples when trying to learn information in a challenging written passage. Metacognitive abilities can be encouraged by having students recall, summarize, and ask questions about what they read (National Reading Panel, 2000).

Children who have early reading difficulties are not necessarily condemned to reading failure. One longitudinal study followed the progress of 146 low-income children whose first grade reading scores fell below the 30th percentile. Thirty percent of the children showed steady movement toward average reading skills from second through fourth grade, especially when they had shown emergent literacy skills and better classroom behavior in kindergarten (Spira, Bracken, & Fischel, 2005).

The acquisition of writing skills goes hand in hand with the development of reading. Older preschoolers begin using letters, numbers, and letterlike shapes as symbols to represent words or parts of words (syllables or phonemes). Often their spelling is quite inventive—so much so that they may not be able to read it themselves (Ouellette & Sénéchal, 2008; Whitehurst & Lonigan, 1998).

Writing is difficult for young children. Unlike conversation, which offers constant feedback, writing requires the child to judge independently whether the communicative goal has been met. The child also must keep in mind a variety of other constraints: spelling, punctuation, grammar, and capitalization, as well as the basic physical task of forming letters (Siegler, 1998).

checkpoint
can you . . .

- Compare the phonetic and whole-language methods of teaching reading, and discuss how comprehension improves?
- Identify factors that affect reading improvement in poor beginning readers?
- Explain why writing is hard for young children?

The Child in School

The earliest school experiences are critical in setting the stage for future success or failure. Let's look at the first-grade experience. Then we'll examine influences on school achievement.

ENTERING FIRST GRADE

First grade marks entry into "real school." It is a milestone in academic development. To make the most academic progress, a child needs to be involved in what is going on in class. Interest, attention, and active participation are positively associated with achievement test scores and, even more so, with teachers' marks from first grade through at least fourth grade (K. L. Alexander, Entwisle, & Dauber, 1993).

Did you take psychology because you thought it would be easy? You're not alone. By the age of 7 children believe that psychology is easier than the natural sciences.

Keil, Lockhart, & Schlegel, 2010

In a national longitudinal study, first graders at risk of school failure—either because of low SES or academic, attentional, or behavioral problems—progressed as much as their low-risk peers when teachers offered strong instructional and emotional support. Such support took the form of frequent literacy instruction, evaluative feedback, engaging students in discussions, responding to their emotional needs, encouraging responsibility, and creating a positive classroom atmosphere (Hamre & Pianta, 2005).

checkpoint can you . . .

- Explain the impact of the first-grade experience on a child's school career, and identify factors that affect success in first grade?

INFLUENCES ON SCHOOL ACHIEVEMENT

As Bronfenbrenner's bioecological theory would predict, in addition to children's own characteristics, each level of the context of their lives—from the immediate family to what goes on in the classroom to the messages children receive from peers and from the larger culture—influences how well they do in school. Let's look at this web of influences.

Self-Efficacy Beliefs Think of how you felt the last time you studied for a big exam. Did you feel you could do well as long as you studied, and were you confident in your ability to master the material? Or did you feel that nothing you could do would matter, and that the material was just too hard? Your attitude can be described as involving a construct called *self-efficacy.* Those students high in self-efficacy believe they can master schoolwork and regulate their own learning. They are more likely to succeed than students who do not believe in their abilities (Bandura, Barbaranelli, Caprara, & Pastorelli, 1996; Caprara et al., 2008). Self-regulated learners try hard, persist despite difficulties, and seek help when necessary. Students who do not believe in their ability to succeed tend to become frustrated and depressed—feelings that make success more elusive.

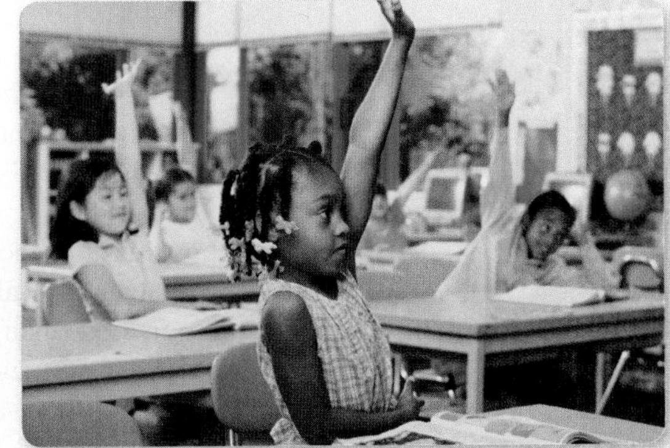

Interest, attention, and active participation all contribute to a child's academic success in school.

Gender Girls tend to do better in school than boys; they receive better grades, on average, in every subject (Halpern et al., 2007), are less likely to repeat grades, have fewer school problems, and outperform boys in national reading and writing assessments (Freeman, 2004). In addition, girls and women tended to do better than boys and men on timed tests (Camarata & Woodcock, 2006). On the other hand, boys do significantly better than girls on science and math tests that are not

In January 2011 a Roslyn, New York, school bought 47 iPads to hand out to students as part of a pilot program. Administrators argue that iPads will replace textbooks, increase homework completion, provide interactive material, and make communication with teachers more likely. What do you think?

Hu, 2011

closely related to material taught in school. However, differences in mathematical abilities in elementary school, when computational facility is stressed, are small and tend to favor girls. Girls' advantage in writing and boys' advantage in science are larger and more reliable (Halpern et al., 2007). Gender differences tend to become more prominent in high school. A combination of several factors—early experience, biological differences (including differences in brain size and structure), and cultural expectations—may help explain these differences (Halpern et al., 2007).

Parenting Practices Parents of high-achieving children create an environment for learning. They provide a place to study and to keep books and supplies; they set times for meals, sleep, and homework; they monitor how much television their children watch and what their children do after school; and they show interest in their children's lives by talking with them about school and being involved in school activities (Hill & Taylor, 2004).

Parenting styles may affect motivation and, thus, school success. In one study, the highest-achieving fifth graders had *authoritative* parents. These children were curious and interested in learning; they liked challenging tasks and enjoyed solving problems by themselves. *Authoritarian* parents, who kept after children to do their homework, supervised closely, and relied on extrinsic motivation, tended to have lower-achieving children. So did children of *permissive* parents, who were uninvolved and did not seem to care how well the children did in school (G. S. Ginsburg & Bronstein, 1993).

This finding is an example of reaction range. Temperamentally difficult infants have a wider reaction range than do easy infants.

The parenting relationship is not a one way street, however. Child temperament interacts with parenting style to influence outcome. For example, some children are more sensitive to the effects of parenting than others. In particular, temperamentally difficult children respond both more positively to sensitive parenting and more negatively to poor parenting. In one study, children who were temperamentally difficult during infancy showed more extreme responses to parenting quality—as measured by first-grade academic competence, social skills, and relationships with others—than those with easy temperaments (Stright et al., 2008).

Socioeconomic Status Socioeconomic status can be a powerful factor in educational achievement—not in and of itself, but through its influence on family atmosphere, choice of neighborhood, parenting practices (Evans, 2004; Rouse et al., 2005), and on parents' expectations for children (Davis-Kean, 2005).

In a nationally representative study of children who entered kindergarten in 1998, achievement gaps between advantaged and disadvantaged students widened during the first 4 years of schooling (Rathbun et al., 2004). Summer vacation contributes to these gaps because of differences in the typical home environment and in the summer learning experiences the children have. Low-income children do not make up for this gap, which can substantially account for differences in high school achievement and completion and college attendance (Alexander, Entwisle, & Olson, 2007).

However, SES is not the only factor in achievement. In a longitudinal study, children whose home environment at age 8 was cognitively stimulating showed higher intrinsic motivation for academic learning at ages 9, 10, and 13 than children who lived in less stimulating homes. This was true over and above effects of SES (Gottfried, Fleming, & Gottfried, 1998).

Why do some young people from disadvantaged homes and neighborhoods do well in school and improve their condition in life? What may make the difference is **social capital:** the networks of community resources children and families can draw on (Coleman, 1988). In a 3-year experimental intervention in which working-poor parents received wage supplements and subsidies for child care and health insurance, their school-age children's academic achievement and behavior improved (Huston et al., 2001). Two years after the families had left the program, the impact on school achievement and motivation held steady, especially for older boys, though the effect on social and problem behavior declined (Huston et al., 2005).

social capital
Family and community resources on which a person can draw.

Peer Acceptance Children who are liked and accepted by peers tend to do better in school. Among 248 fourth graders, those whose teachers reported that they were not liked by peers had poorer academic self-concepts and more symptoms of anxiety or depression in fifth grade and lower reading and math grades in sixth grade. Early teacher identification of children who exhibit social problems could lead to interventions that would improve such children's academic as well as emotional and social outcomes (Flook, Repetti, & Ullman, 2005).

checkpoint
can **you** . . .

- Evaluate how efficacy beliefs, gender, parenting practices, SES, and peer acceptance affect school achievement?

Educational Methods The No Child Left Behind (NCLB) Act of 2001 is a sweeping educational reform emphasizing accountability, expanded parental options, local control, and flexibility. The intent is to funnel federal funding to research-based programs and practices, with special emphasis on reading and mathematics. Students in grades 3 through 8 are tested annually to see if they are meeting statewide progress objectives. Children in schools that fail to meet state standards can transfer to another school.

More than 50 national education, civil rights, children's, and citizens groups have called for substantial changes in NCLB. Critics such as the National Education Association, a national teachers' organization, claim that NCLB emphasizes punishment rather than assistance for failing schools; rigid, largely unfunded, mandates rather than support for proven practices; and standardized testing rather than teacher-led, classroom-focused solutions.

On the other hand, test scores do show improvement. In 2007, for example, math scores for fourth and eighth graders on the National Assessment of Educational Progress (NAEP) rose to their highest levels since the test began in 1990. Black, white, and Hispanic students all improved (NCES, 2007c), but ethnic group gaps remain (Hernandez & Macartney, 2008). Efforts to improve the teaching of reading seem to be paying off more slowly. In the NAEP in 2007, fourth graders' reading scores rose only modestly compared with those in 1990, and eighth graders' scores declined slightly but were better than in 2005 (NCES, 2007d). Meanwhile, in an international literacy test including 38 countries, U.S. fourth graders scored well above average (NCES, 2007e).

Children who have a social network and who are liked and accepted by peers tend to do better in school.

Class Size Most educators consider small class size a key factor in achievement, especially in the early grades, though findings on this point are mixed (Schneider, 2002). A longitudinal study found lasting academic benefits for students randomly assigned to classes of about 15 students in kindergarten through third grade and—especially for low-SES students—a greater likelihood of finishing high school (Finn, Gerber, & Boyd-Zaharias, 2005; Krueger, 2003).

In most places, though, small classes are larger than that. In classroom observations of 890 first graders, classes with 25 students or less tended to be more social and interactive and to enable higher quality instruction and emotional support. Students in these classes tended to score higher on standardized achievement tests and beginning reading skills (NICHD Early Childhood Research Network, 2004b).

Educational Innovations When the Chicago public schools ended *social promotion,* the practice of promoting children to keep them with their age-mates even when they do not meet academic standards, many observers hailed the change. Others warned that, although retention in some cases can be a "wake-up call," more often it is the first step on a remedial track that leads to lowered expectations, poor performance, and dropping out of school (J. M. Fields & Smith, 1998; Lugaila, 2003; Temple, Reynolds, & Miedel, 2000). Indeed, studies found that Chicago's retention policy did *not* improve third graders' test scores, lowered sixth graders' scores, and greatly increased eighth-grade and high school dropout rates for retained students (Nagaoka & Roderick, 2004).

Many educators say the only real solution to a high failure rate is to identify at-risk students early and intervene *before* they fail. One way is to provide alternative schools or programs for at-risk students, offering smaller classes, remedial instruction, counseling, and crisis intervention (NCES, 2003).

Some parents, unhappy with their public schools or seeking a particular style of education, are choosing charter schools or homeschooling. More than 1.3 million U.S. children now attend charter schools, some privately operated and others under charter from public school boards (Center for Education Reform, 2008). Charter schools tend to be smaller than regular public schools and tend to have a unique philosophy, curriculum, structure, or organizational style. Although parents are generally satisfied with their charter schools, studies of their effects on student outcomes have had mixed results (Braun, Jenkins, & Grigg, 2006; Center for Education Reform, 2004; Hoxby, 2004; National Assessment of Educational Progress, 2004; Schemo, 2004).

Homeschooling is legal in all 50 states. In 2007 some 1.5 million U.S. students representing 2.9 percent of the school-age population were homeschooled, 4 out of 5 of them full-time—a 36 percent increase from 2003 (NCES, 2008). In a nationally representative government survey, the main reasons parents gave for choosing to homeschool their children were concern about a poor or unsafe learning environment in the schools and the desire to provide religious or moral instruction (NCES, 2008).

checkpoint
can **you**...

- Discuss changes and innovations in educational philosophy and practice?

Media Use Access to the Internet in public schools has skyrocketed. In 1994 only 3 percent of classrooms had Internet access, compared with 94 percent in 2005 (Wells & Lewis, 2006). However, fewer black, Hispanic, and American Indian children than white and Asian children, and fewer poor children than nonpoor children, use these technologies. Girls and boys spend about the same amount of time on computer and Internet use (Day, Janus, & Davis, 2005; DeBell & Chapman, 2006).

Media influences from home also play a role in children's development. The predominant influence is television. In 2003, 6- to 12-year-old children spent approximately 14 hours per week watching television. Computers also are an influence, although much less time (1 hour and 20 minutes per week) is spent on computers. Of that, the bulk of time is spent on video games, with e-mail, Internet usage, and studying comprising the remainder. This exposure to media has varying influences depending on what type of media is examined as well as the gender of the child. For example, television is associated with the displacement of other more beneficial experiences such as playing or sleeping for all children. Computer usage is associated with increases in achievement and problem-solving abilities for girls. However, for boys, who are more likely to play violent video games, computer usage is associated with increased aggressive behavior problems (Hofferth, 2010).

Computer literacy is an important skill in today's world. However, this tool poses dangers. Foremost is the risk of exposure to harmful or inappropriate material. Also, students need to learn to critically evaluate information they find in cyberspace and to separate facts from opinion and advertising.

checkpoint
can **you**...

- Assess the impact of children's media use?

Educating Children with Special Needs

Public schools have a tremendous job educating children of varying abilities from all sorts of families and cultural backgrounds, including those children with special needs. When we consider special needs, most of us are likely to focus on those children who have learning or behavioral disorders, as those concerns have earned center stage as a major condition affecting the development of school-age children (Pastor & Reuben, 2008). However, special needs also include a focus on children who are gifted, talented, or creative, as they have different educational needs than the typical child.

CHILDREN WITH LEARNING PROBLEMS

Just as educators have become more sensitive to teaching children from varied cultural backgrounds, they also have sought to meet the needs of children with special educational needs.

Intellectual Disability **Intellectual disability** is significantly subnormal cognitive functioning. It is indicated by an IQ of about 70 or less, coupled with a deficiency in age-appropriate adaptive behavior (such as communication, social skills, and self-care), appearing before age 18 (Kanaya, Scullin, & Ceci, 2003). Intellectual disability is sometimes referred to as cognitive disability or mental retardation. Less than 1 percent of U.S. children are intellectually disabled (NCHS, 2004; Woodruff et al., 2004).

intellectual disability
Significantly subnormal cognitive functioning. Also referred to as cognitive disability or mental retardation.

In 30 to 50 percent of cases, the cause of intellectual disability is unknown. Known causes include genetic disorders, traumatic accidents, prenatal exposure to infection or alcohol, and environmental exposure to lead or high levels of mercury (Woodruff et al., 2004). Many cases may be preventable through genetic counseling, prenatal care, amniocentesis, routine screening and health care for newborns, and nutritional services for pregnant women and infants.

Most children with intellectual disabilities can benefit from schooling. Intervention programs have helped many of those mildly or moderately disabled and those considered borderline (with IQs ranging from 70 up to about 85) to hold jobs, live in the community, and function in society. The profoundly disabled need constant care and supervision, usually in institutions. For some, day care centers, hostels for intellectually disabled adults, and homemaking services for caregivers can be less costly and more humane alternatives.

Learning Disorders The two most commonly diagnosed conditions causing behavioral and learning problems in school-age children are learning disability (LD) and attention-deficit/hyperactivity disorder (ADHD). A recent study of more than 23,000 children in the United States revealed that about 5 percent of children have learning disabilities, 5 percent of children have ADHD, and 4 percent of children have both conditions (Pastor & Reuben, 2008).

Learning Disabilities Nelson Rockefeller, former vice president of the United States, was one of many eminent persons with **dyslexia,** a developmental language disorder in which reading achievement is substantially below the level predicted by IQ or age. Other famous people who reportedly have dyslexia include the actor Tom Cruise, the baseball Hall-of-Famer Nolan Ryan, and filmmaker Steven Spielberg.

dyslexia
Developmental disorder in which reading achievement is substantially lower than predicted by IQ or age.

Dyslexia is the most commonly diagnosed of a large number of **learning disabilities (LDs).** These are disorders that interfere with specific aspects of school achievement, such as listening, speaking, reading, writing, or mathematics, resulting in performance substantially lower than would be expected given a child's age, intelligence, and amount of schooling. A growing percentage of U.S. children—9.7 percent in 2003—show LDs at some point in their school career (Altarac & Saroha, 2007); 5 percent are served by federally supported programs (National Center for Learning Disabilities, 2004b).

learning disabilities (LDs)
Disorders that interfere with specific aspects of learning and school achievement.

Children with LDs often have near-average to higher-than-average intelligence and normal vision and hearing, but they seem to have trouble processing sensory information. Although causes are uncertain, one factor is genetic. Research suggests that the genes most responsible for the high heritability of the most common LDs—language impairment, reading disability, and mathematical disability—are also responsible for normal variations in learning abilities (Plomin & Kovas, 2005). Environmental factors may include complications of pregnancy or birth, injuries after birth, nutritional deprivation, and exposure to lead (National Center for Learning Disabilities, 2004b).

People with dyslexia often fail to develop phonological awareness and have difficulty breaking speech sounds into their constituent parts. If you cannot "hear" that the word "dog" is made up of three distinct phonemes, then reading is definitely going to be a challenge.

Shaywitz et al., 2006

About 4 out of 5 children with LDs have been identified as dyslexic. Dyslexia is a chronic, persistent medical condition and tends to run in families (S. E. Shaywitz, 1998, 2003). It hinders the development of oral as well as written language skills and may cause problems with writing, spelling, grammar, and understanding speech as well as with reading (National Center for Learning Disabilities, 2004a). Reading disability is more frequent in boys than in girls (Rutter et al., 2004). Although reading and intelligence are related to each other in children without dyslexia, they are not coupled in this fashion for children with dyslexia. In other words, dyslexia is not an issue of intelligence (Ferrer et al., 2010).

Brain imaging studies have found that dyslexia is due to a neurological defect that disrupts recognition of speech sounds (Shaywitz, Mody, & Shaywitz, 2006). Several identified genes contribute to this disruption (Kere et al., 2005; Meng et al., 2005). Many children—and even adults—with dyslexia can be taught to read through systematic phonological training, but the process does not become automatic, as it does with most readers (Eden et al., 2004; S. E. Shaywitz, 2003).

attention-deficit/hyperactivity disorder (ADHD)
Syndrome characterized by persistent inattention and distractibility, impulsivity, low tolerance for frustration, and inappropriate overactivity.

Attention-Deficit/Hyperactivity Disorder **Attention-deficit/hyperactivity disorder (ADHD)** has been called the most common mental disorder in childhood (Wolraich et al., 2005). It is a chronic condition usually marked by persistent inattention, distractibility, impulsivity, and low tolerance for frustration. Among the well-known people who reportedly have had ADHD are the musician John Lennon, U.S. Senator Robert Kennedy, and the actors Robin Williams and Jim Carrey.

ADHD may affect an estimated 2 to 11 percent of school-age children worldwide (Zametkin & Ernst, 1999). In 2006 about 2.5 million children in the United States were diagnosed with ADHD, a rate of about 4.7 percent. Although the rate of diagnoses of LDs has remained relatively constant, the rate of ADHD increased about 3 percent per year between 1997 and 2006 (Pastor & Reuben, 2008; Figure 3).

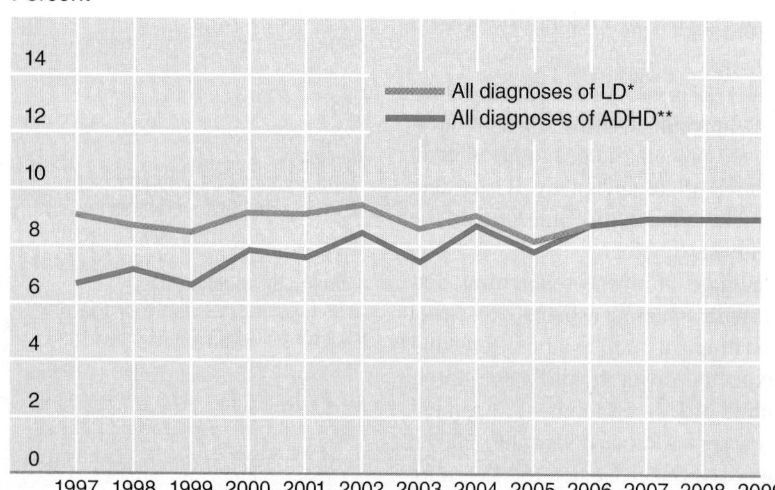

FIGURE 3
U.S. Diagnosis of Attention-Deficit/Hyperactivity Disorder by Year

Diagnosis of learning disabilities has remained constant, but diagnosis of ADHD rose from 1997 to 2009.

Source: CDC/NCHS, National Health Interview Surveys, 1997–2009.

ADHD has two different but sometimes overlapping types of symptoms, making diagnosis imprecise. Some children are inattentive but not hyperactive; others show the reverse pattern (USDHHS, 1999b). Because these characteristics appear to some degree in all children, some practitioners question whether ADHD is actually a distinct neurological or psychological disorder (Bjorklund & Pellegrini, 2002; Furman, 2005). However, most experts agree that there is cause for concern when the symptoms are so severe as to interfere with the child's functioning in school and in daily life (AAP Committee on Children with Disabilities and Committee on Drugs, 1996; Barkley, 1998; USDHHS, 1999b).

Imaging studies reveal that brains of children with ADHD grow in a normal pattern, but the process is delayed by about 3 years in certain regions of the brain, particularly the frontal cortex. These frontal regions enable a person to control movement, suppress inappropriate thoughts and actions, focus attention, remember from moment to moment, and work for rewards—all functions that are often disturbed in children with ADHD. The motor cortex is the only area that matures faster than normal, and this mismatch may account for the restlessness and fidgeting characteristic of the disorder (P. Shaw et al., 2007).

ADHD seems to have a substantial genetic basis with heritability approaching 80 percent (Acosta, Arcos-Burgos, & Muenke, 2004; USDHHS, 1999b). In one of the largest genetic studies of ADHD, over 600,000 genetic markers were examined. Results indicated that many genes are involved in ADHD, each contributing some small effect (Neale et al., 2008). Another group of researchers identified a variation of a gene for dopamine, a brain chemical essential for attention and cognition, low levels of which appear to be associated with ADHD (Shaw et al., 2007; Volkow et al., 2007). Birth complications also may play a part in ADHD. Prematurity, a prospective mother's alcohol or tobacco use, and oxygen deprivation (Barkley, 1998; Thapar et al., 2003; USDHHS, 1999b; Woodruff et al., 2004) have all been linked to ADHD.

Parents and teachers may be able to help children with ADHD by breaking down tasks into small "chunks," providing frequent prompts about rules and time, and giving frequent, immediate rewards for small accomplishments (Barkley, 1998).

ADHD is often managed with drugs, sometimes combined with behavioral therapy, counseling, training in social skills, and special classroom placement. In a 14-month randomized study of 579 children with ADHD, a carefully monitored program of Ritalin treatment, alone or in combination with behavior modification, was more effective than the behavioral therapy alone or standard community care (MTA Cooperative Group, 1999). However, the superior benefits of the program diminished during the following 10 months (MTA Cooperative Group, 2004a). A side effect of the combined treatment was slower growth in height and weight (MTA Cooperative Group, 2004b).

Long-term effects of drug treatment for ADHD are unknown, but leaving the condition untreated also carries risks. If you had a child with ADHD, what would you do?

checkpoint
can **you** . . .

- Discuss the causes, treatments, and prognoses for three conditions that interfere with learning?

Educating Children with Disabilities In 2006–2007, about 9 percent of public school students in the United States were receiving special educational services under the Individuals with Disabilities Education Act, which ensures a free, appropriate public education for all children with disabilities. Most of these children had learning disabilities or speech or language impairments (NCES, 2009c). An individualized program must be designed for each child, with parental involvement. Children must be educated in the "least restrictive environment" appropriate to their needs—which means, whenever possible, the regular classroom.

Programs in which children with special needs are included in the regular classroom are known as inclusion programs. Here, children with disabilities are integrated with nondisabled children for all or part of the day, sometimes with assistance. In 2005, 52 percent of students with disabilities spent at least 80 percent of their time in regular classrooms (NCES, 2007b).

GIFTED CHILDREN

The traditional criterion of giftedness is high general intelligence as shown by an IQ score of 130 or higher. This definition tends to exclude highly creative children (whose unusual answers often lower their test scores), children from minority groups (whose abilities may not be well developed, though the potential is there), and children with specific aptitudes (who may be only average or even show learning problems in other areas).

Most states and school districts have therefore adopted the broader definition in the U.S. Elementary and Secondary Education Act, which encompasses children who show high intellectual, creative, artistic, or leadership capacity or ability in specific academic fields and who need special educational services and activities to fully develop those capabilities. Many school districts now use multiple criteria for admission to programs for the gifted, including achievement test scores, grades,

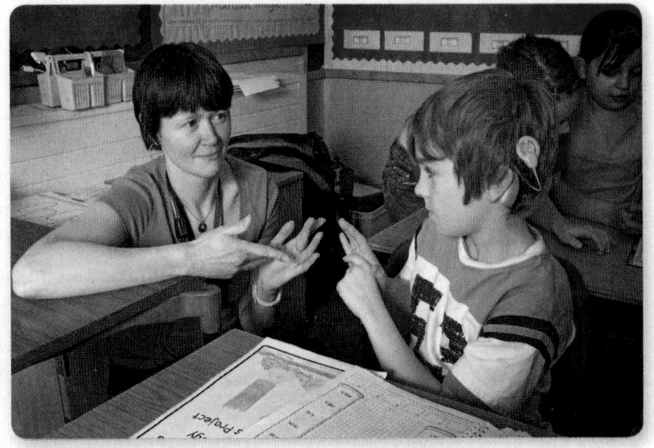
Sign language can be used to integrate deaf children into classrooms with hearing classmates.

classroom performance, creative production, parent and teacher nominations, and student interviews; but IQ remains an important and sometimes the determining factor. An estimated 6 percent of the student population is considered gifted (National Association for Gifted Children [NAGC], n.d.).

What's Special about Gifted Children? Psychologists who study the lives of extraordinary achievers find that high levels of performance require strong intrinsic motivation and years of rigorous training (Bloom, 1985; Csikszentmihalyi, 1996; Gardner, 1993; Gottfried, Cook, Gottfired, & Morris, 2005). However, motivation and training will not produce giftedness unless a child is endowed with unusual ability (Winner, 2000). Conversely, children with innate gifts are unlikely to show exceptional achievement without motivation and hard work (Achter & Lubinski, 2003).

Gifted children tend to grow up in enriched family environments with much intellectual or artistic stimulation. Their parents recognize and often devote themselves to nurturing the children's gifts but also give their children an unusual degree of independence. Parents of gifted children typically have high expectations and are hard workers and high achievers themselves. But, although parenting can enhance the development of gifts, it cannot create them (Winner, 2000).

creativity
Ability to see situations in a new way, to produce innovations, or to discern previously unidentified problems and find novel solutions.

One possible reason creativity and academic achievement don't always relate is that the personality characteristics related to creativity are generally viewed negatively by teachers.

Westby & Dawson, 1995

Defining and Measuring Creativity One definition of **creativity** is the ability to see things in a new light—to produce something never seen before or to discern problems others fail to recognize and find new and unusual solutions. High creativity and high academic intelligence (IQ) do not necessarily go hand in hand (Anastasi & Schaefer, 1971; Getzels, 1984; Getzels & Jackson, 1963).

The reason creativity is not highly correlated with traditional IQ tests is because traditional tests are measuring a different kind of thinking than is characteristic of creativity. J. P. Guilford (1956, 1959, 1960, 1967, 1986) distinguished two kinds of thinking: convergent and divergent. **Convergent thinking**—the kind IQ tests measure—seeks a single correct answer. For example, when solving an arithmetic problem, there is one correct answer upon which everyone is expected to converge. **Divergent thinking,** by contrast, involves coming up with a wide array of fresh possibilities, such as when children are asked to list how many different uses there might be for a paper clip or to write down what a sound brings to mind. There is no one right answer. Tests of creativity call for divergent thinking. This ability can be assessed via the *Torrance Tests of Creative Thinking* (Torrance, 1974; Torrance & Ball, 1984), one of the most widely known tests of creativity. A problem with these tests is that scores depend partly on speed, which is not a hallmark of creativity. Moreover, although the tests yield fairly reliable results, there is dispute over whether they are valid—whether they identify children who are creative in everyday life (Simonton, 1990).

convergent thinking
Thinking aimed at finding the one right answer to a problem.

divergent thinking
Thinking that produces a variety of fresh, diverse possibilities.

enrichment programs
Programs for educating the gifted that broaden and deepen knowledge and skills through extra activities, projects, field trips, or mentoring.

acceleration programs
Programs for educating the gifted that move them through the curriculum at an unusually rapid pace.

Educating Gifted Children Programs for gifted children generally stress either enrichment or acceleration. **Enrichment programs** may deepen students' knowledge and skills through extra classroom activities, research projects, field trips, or expert coaching. **Acceleration programs** speed up their education through early school entrance, grade skipping, placement in fast-paced classes, or advanced courses. Other options include ability grouping within the classroom, which has been found to help children academically and not harm them socially (Winner, 2000), dual enrollment (for example, an eighth grader taking algebra at a nearby high school), magnet schools, and specialized schools for the gifted.

Moderate acceleration does not seem to harm social adjustment, at least in the long run (Winner, 1997). A 30-year study of 3,937 young people who took advanced placement courses in high school found that they were more satisfied with their school experience and ultimately achieved more than equally gifted young people who did not take AP courses (Bleske-Rechek, Lubinski, & Benbow, 2004).

checkpoint
can **you**...

- Tell how gifted children are identified?
- Explain why creativity is hard to measure?
- Compare two approaches to the education of gifted children?

summary and key terms

PHYSICAL DEVELOPMENT

Aspects of Physical Development

- Physical development is less rapid in middle childhood than in earlier years. Wide differences in height and weight exist.
- Proper nutrition and sleep are essential for normal growth and health.
- Changes in brain structure and functioning support cognitive advances.
- Because of improved motor development, boys and girls in middle childhood can engage in a wide range of motor activities.
- Informal recess-time activities help develop physical and social skills. Boys' games tend to be more physical and girls' games more verbal.
- About 10 percent of schoolchildren's play, especially among boys, is rough-and-tumble play.
- Many children, mostly boys, engage in organized, competitive sports. A sound physical education program should aim at skill development and fitness for all children.

rough-and-tumble play

Health, Fitness, and Safety

- Middle childhood is a relatively healthy period; most children are immunized against major illnesses, and the death rate is the lowest in the life span.
- Overweight, which is increasingly common among U.S. children, entails multiple risks. It is influenced by genetic and environmental factors and is more easily prevented than treated. Many children do not get enough physical activity.
- Hypertension is becoming more common along with the rise in overweight.
- Respiratory infections and other acute medical conditions are common at this age. Chronic conditions such as asthma are most prevalent among poor and minority children. Diabetes is one of the most common childhood chronic conditions.
- Accidents are the leading cause of death in middle childhood. Use of helmets and other protective devices and avoidance of trampolines, snowmobiling, and other dangerous sports can greatly reduce injuries.

body image
hypertension
acute medical conditions
chronic medical conditions
asthma
diabetes

COGNITIVE DEVELOPMENT

Piagetian Approach: The Concrete Operational Child

- A child from about age 7 to age 12 is in the stage of concrete operations. Children are less egocentric than before and are more proficient at tasks requiring logical reasoning, such as spatial thinking, understanding of causality, categorization, inductive and deductive reasoning, and conservation. However, their reasoning is largely limited to the here and now.
- Neurological development, culture, and schooling seem to contribute to the rate of development of Piagetian skills.
- According to Piaget, moral development is linked with cognitive maturation and occurs in three stages as children move from rigid to more flexible thinking.

concrete operations
seriation
transitive inference
class inclusion
inductive reasoning
deductive reasoning

Information-Processing Approach: Planning, Attention, and Memory

- Executive skills, reaction time, processing speed, selective attention, metamemory, and use of mnemonic devices improve during the school years.

executive function
metamemory
mnemonic device
external memory aids
rehearsal
organization
elaboration

Psychometric Approach: Assessment of Intelligence

- IQ tests are fairly good predictors of school success but may be unfair to some children.
- Differences in IQ among ethnic groups appear to result to a considerable degree from socioeconomic and other environmental differences.
- Schooling increases measured intelligence.
- Attempts to devise culture-free or culture-fair tests have been unsuccessful. Indeed, intelligence testing seems inextricably linked with culture.
- IQ tests tap only three of the intelligences in Howard Gardner's theory of multiple intelligences.
- According to Robert Sternberg's triarchic theory, IQ tests measure mainly the componential element of intelligence, not the experiential and contextual elements.
- Other directions in intelligence testing include the Sternberg Triarchic Abilities Tests (STAT), Kaufman Assessment Battery for Children (K-ABC-II), and dynamic tests based on Vygotsky's theory.

Wechsler Intelligence Scale for Children (WISC-IV)
Otis-Lennon School Ability Test (OLSAT 8)
culture-free tests
culture-fair tests
theory of multiple intelligences
triarchic theory of intelligence
componential element
experiential element
contextual element
tacit knowledge
Kaufman Assessment Battery for Children (K-ABC-II)
dynamic tests

Language and Literacy

- Use of vocabulary, grammar, and syntax become increasingly sophisticated, but the major area of linguistic growth is in pragmatics.
- Methods of second-language education are controversial. Issues include speed and facility with English, long-term achievement in academic subjects, and pride in cultural identity.
- Despite the popularity of whole-language programs, early phonetics training is a key to reading proficiency.

pragmatics
English-immersion approach
bilingual education
bilingual
two-way (dual-language) learning
decoding
visually based retrieval
phonetic (code-emphasis) approach
whole-language approach
metacognition

The Child in School

- Because schooling is cumulative, the foundation laid in first grade is very important.
- Children's self-efficacy beliefs affect school achievement.
- Girls tend to do better in school than boys.
- Parents influence children's learning by becoming involved in their schooling, motivating them to achieve, and transmitting attitudes about learning. Socioeconomic status can influence parental beliefs and practices that, in turn, influence achievement.
- Peer acceptance and class size affect learning.
- Current educational issues and innovations include social promotion, charter schools, homeschooling, and computer literacy.

social capital

Educating Children with Special Needs

- Three frequent sources of learning problems are intellectual disability, learning disabilities (LDs), and attention-deficit/hyperactivity disorder (ADHD). Dyslexia is the most common learning disability.
- In the United States, all children with disabilities are entitled to a free, appropriate education. Children must be educated in the least restrictive environment possible, often in the regular classroom.
- An IQ of 130 or higher is a common standard for identifying gifted children.
- Creativity and IQ are *not* closely linked. Tests of creativity seek to measure divergent thinking, but their validity has been questioned.
- Special educational programs for gifted children stress enrichment or acceleration.

intellectual disability
dyslexia
learning disabilities (LDs)
attention-deficit/hyperactivity disorder (ADHD)
creativity
convergent thinking
divergent thinking
enrichment programs
acceleration programs

chapter 10

Psychosocial Development in Middle Childhood

outline

The Developing Self

The Child in the Family

The Child in the Peer Group

Mental Health

learning objectives

Discuss emotional and personality development in school-age children.

Describe changes in family relationships in the school-age years.

Identify changes in peer relationships among school-age children.

Describe emotional disorders that can develop in school-age children, along with treatment techniques and children's ability to cope with stress.

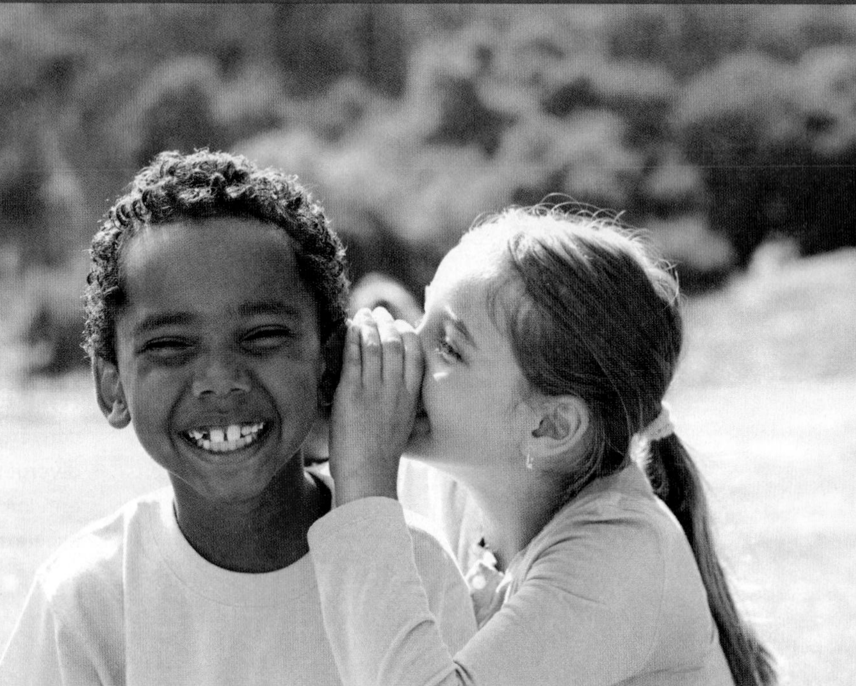

did you **know**?

- Children in single-parent households do better on achievement tests in countries with supportive family policies?
- There are few significant differences in adjustment between adopted and nonadopted children?
- Patterns of bullying and victimization may become established as early as kindergarten?

In this chapter we see how children develop a more realistic self-concept. Through interacting with peers they make discoveries about their own attitudes, values, and skills. Still, the kind of household a child lives in and the relationships in it can profoundly affect psychosocial development. We look at several mental health problems and at resilient children, who can emerge from stress healthy and strong.

Let us put our minds together and see what life we can make for our children.

—Sitting Bull, *Native American Chief of the Lakota Sioux*, 1831–1890

The Developing Self

The cognitive growth that takes place during middle childhood enables children to develop more complex concepts of themselves and to gain in emotional understanding and control.

SELF-CONCEPT DEVELOPMENT: REPRESENTATIONAL SYSTEMS

"At school I'm feeling pretty smart in certain subjects, Language Arts and Social Studies," says 8-year-old Lisa. "I got A's in these subjects on my last report card and was really proud of myself. But I'm feeling really dumb in Arithmetic and Science, particularly when I see how well the other kids are doing. . . . I still like myself as a person, because Arithmetic and Science just aren't that important to me. How I look and how popular I am are more important" (Harter, 1996, p. 208).

Earlier in development young children have difficulty with abstract concepts and with integrating various dimensions of the self. Their self-concepts focus on physical attributes, possessions, and global descriptions. However, at around age 7 or 8, children reach the third stage of self-concept development. At this time judgments about the self become more conscious, realistic, balanced, and comprehensive as children form **representational systems:** broad, inclusive self-concepts that integrate various aspects of the self (Harter, 1993, 1996, 1998).

representational systems
In neo-Piagetian terminology, the third stage in development of self-definition, characterized by breadth, balance, and the integration and assessment of various aspects of the self.

We see these changes in Lisa's self-description. She can now focus on more than one dimension of herself. She has outgrown her earlier all-or-nothing, black-or-white self-definition. Now, she recognizes that she can be "smart" in certain subjects and "dumb" in others. She can verbalize her self-concept better, and she can weigh different aspects of it. She can compare her *real self* (who she is) with her *ideal self* (who she wants to be) and can judge how well she measures up to social standards in comparison with others. All of these changes contribute to the development of self-esteem, her assessment of her *global self-worth* ("I still like myself as a person").

INDUSTRY VERSUS INFERIORITY

According to Erikson (1982), a major determinant of self-esteem is children's view of their capacity for productive work, which develops in his fourth stage of psychosocial development: **industry versus inferiority.** As with all of Erikson's stages, there is an opportunity for growth represented by a sense of industry and a complementary risk represented by inferiority.

industry versus inferiority
Erikson's fourth stage of psychosocial development, in which children must learn the productive skills their culture requires or else face feelings of inferiority.

In the event that children are unable to obtain the praise of adults or peers in their lives, or lack motivation and self-esteem, they may develop a feeling of low self-worth, and thus develop a sense of inferiority. This is problematic because during middle childhood children must learn skills valued in their society. If children feel inadequate compared with their peers, they may retreat to the protective embrace of the family and not venture farther away from home.

Developing a sense of industry, by contrast, involves learning how to work hard to achieve goals. The details may vary across societies: Arapesh boys in New Guinea learn

Hie takes geese to market, developing her sense of competence and building her self-esteem. By taking responsibilities that match her growing capabilities, she also learns how her Vietnamese society works, what her role is in it, and what it means to do a job well.

to make bows and arrows and to lay traps for rats; Arapesh girls learn to plant, weed, and harvest; Inuit children of Alaska learn to hunt and fish; and children in industrialized countries learn to read, write, do math, and use computers. What these different experiences share, however, is an emphasis on developing responsibility and motivation to succeed. If the stage is successfully resolved, children develop a view of themselves as being able to master skills and complete tasks. This can go too far—if children become too industrious, they may neglect social relationships and turn into workaholics.

Parents strongly influence a child's beliefs about competence. In a longitudinal study of 514 middle-class U.S. children, parents' beliefs about their children's competence in math and sports were strongly associated with the children's beliefs (Fredricks & Eccles, 2002).

EMOTIONAL GROWTH AND PROSOCIAL BEHAVIOR

As children grow older, they are more aware of their own and other people's feelings. They can better regulate or control their emotions and can respond to others' emotional distress (Saarni et al., 2006).

studysmart

Emotional Regulation

By age 7 or 8, children typically are aware of feeling shame and pride, and they have a clearer idea of the difference between guilt and shame (Olthof, Schouten, Kuiper, Stegge, & Jennekens-Schinkel, 2000). These emotions affect their opinion of themselves (Harter, 1993, 1996). Children also understand their conflicting emotions. As Lisa says, "Most of the boys at school are pretty yucky. I don't feel that way about my little brother Jason, although he does get on my nerves. I love him but at the same time, he also does things that make me mad. But I control my temper; I'd be ashamed of myself if I didn't" (Harter, 1996, p. 208).

At about the age of 9, white American children start to self-censor their speech so as not to mention the race of others in an attempt to appear unprejudiced.

Apfelbaum et al., 2008

By middle childhood, children are aware of their culture's rules for acceptable emotional expression (Cole et al., 2002). Children learn what makes them angry, fearful, or sad and how other people react to displays of these emotions, and they learn to behave accordingly. When parents respond with disapproval or punishment, emotions such as anger and fear may become more intense and may impair children's social adjustment (Fabes, Leonard, Kupanoff, & Martin, 2001). Or the children may become secretive and anxious about negative feelings. As children approach early adolescence, parental intolerance of negative emotion may heighten parent-child conflict (Eisenberg et al., 1999; Fabes, Leonard, Kupanoff, & Martin, 2001).

Have you ever received a gift you didn't like or had to hold in your anger to avoid getting in trouble? The ability to fake liking a gift or to smile when you are mad involves emotional self-regulation. Emotional self-regulation is effortful (voluntary) control of emotions, attention, and behavior (Eisenberg et al., 2004). There are individual differences in how effective different children are at doing this as well as developmental changes with age.

Self-regulation, specifically self-discipline, is more predictive of academic achievement than IQ.

Duckworth & Seligman, 2005

studysmart

Understanding Emotions

Children low in effortful control tend to become visibly angry or frustrated when interrupted or prevented from doing something they want to do. They cannot easily hide these signals. By contrast, children with high effortful control can stifle the impulse to show negative emotion at inappropriate times. Those children with low effortful control when young are at higher risk for later behavior problems (Eisenberg et al., 2004).

Children tend to become more empathic and more inclined to prosocial behavior in middle childhood. Empathy appears to be "hard wired" into the brains of typical children. As with adults, empathy has been associated with prefrontal activation in children as young as 6 years of age (Light et al., 2009). A recent study of brain activity in 7- to 12-year-olds found parts of their brains were activated when shown pictures of people in pain (Decety, Michalaska, Akitsuki, & Lahey, 2009).

Children with high self-esteem tend to be more willing to volunteer to help those who are less fortunate than they are, and volunteering, in turn, helps build self-esteem (Karafantis & Levy, 2004). Prosocial children tend to act appropriately in social situations, to be relatively free from negative emotion, and to cope with problems constructively (Eisenberg, Fabes, & Murphy, 1996). Parents who acknowledge children's feelings of distress and help them focus on solving the root problem foster empathy, prosocial development, and social skills (Bryant, 1987; Eisenberg et al., 1996).

checkpoint can **you**...

- Discuss how the self-concept develops in middle childhood?
- Describe Erikson's fourth stage of psychosocial development?
- Identify several aspects of emotional growth in middle childhood?

The Child in the Family

School-age children spend more time away from home visiting and socializing with peers than when they were younger. They also spend more time at school and on studies and less time at family meals than children did a generation ago (Juster et al., 2004). Still, home and the people who live there remain an important part of most children's lives. Research suggests that family mealtimes are related both directly and indirectly to children's health and well-being, as discussed in Box 1.

To understand the child in the family, we need to look at the family environment—its atmosphere and structure. These, in turn, are affected by what goes on beyond the walls of the home. As Bronfenbrenner's theory predicts, wider layers of influence—including parents' work and socioeconomic status and societal trends such as urbanization, changes in family size, divorce, and remarriage—help shape the family environment and, thus, children's development.

Culture, too, defines the rhythms of family life and the roles of family members. Many African American families, for example, carry on extended-family traditions that include living near or with kin, a strong sense of family obligation, ethnic pride, and mutual aid (Parke & Buriel, 1998). Latino families tend to stress family commitment, respect for self and others, and moral education (Halgunseth, Ispa, & Rudy, 2006). As we look at the child in the family, then, we need to be aware of outside forces that affect it.

In general, adults are not very good at distinguishing when children lie. Adults are able to identify lies only slightly better than would be predicted by chance.

Stromwall, Granhag, & Landstrom, 2007

FAMILY ATMOSPHERE

Family atmosphere is a key influence on development. One key factor is whether or not conflict is present in the home. Exposure to violence and conflict is harmful to children, both with respect to direct exposure via parental discord (Kaczynski, Lindahl, Malik, & Laurenceau, 2006) and via indirect influences on such variables as low family cohesion and anger regulation strategies (Houltberg, Henry, & Morris, 2012).

Children exposed to family conflict show a variety of responses that can include externalizing or internalizing behaviors. **Internalizing behaviors** include anxiety, fearfulness, and depression—anger turned inward. **Externalizing behaviors** include aggression, fighting, disobedience, and hostility—anger turned outward. Both internalizing behaviors (Fear et al., 2009; Kaczynski et al., 2006) and externalizing behaviors (Houltberg et al., 2012; Kaczynski et al., 2006) are more likely in children who come from families with high levels of discord.

internalizing behaviors
Behaviors by which emotional problems are turned inward; for example, anxiety or depression.

externalizing behaviors
Behaviors by which a child acts out emotional difficulties; for example, aggression or hostility.

Parenting Issues: From Control to Coregulation Babies don't have a lot of say in what happens to them; they are exposed to what their parents choose to expose them to and experience what their parents decide they should experience. However, as children grow and become more autonomous, there is a shift in power. Over the course of childhood, control of behavior gradually shifts from parents to child. Children begin to request certain types of experiences, demand particular foods, negotiate for desired objects, and communicate their shifting needs to parents.

research in action

PASS THE MILK: FAMILY MEALTIMES AND CHILD WELL-BEING

There is no other activity that families share as a group more than daily meals. In one survey 56 percent of families with school-aged children reported eating a meal together 6 to 7 days per week (National Center on Addiction and Substance Abuse, 2006). And that's good news for children's health and well-being. These "densely packed events" that last an average of 20 minutes can have profound effects on a child's health and well-being (Fiese & Schwartz, 2008).

1 A few of the positive outcomes of family mealtimes include:

1. *Promotion of language development.* Frequency of family mealtimes has been linked to vocabulary growth (Beals & Snow, 1994), increased literary skills (Snow & Beals, 2006), and academic achievement (National Center on Addiction and Substance Abuse, 2006).
2. *Reduced risk for eating disorders and childhood obesity.* Families who eat together regularly promote healthy eating habits and report fewer eating disorders (Neumark-Sztainer et al., 2007) and less obesity (Gable, Chung, & Krull, 2007). They eat more fruits and vegetables.
3. *Reduced risk for substance abuse.* Teens who eat regularly with their families are less likely to smoke cigarettes or marijuana and are at reduced risk for alcohol abuse (National Center on Addiction and Substance Abuse, 2007).
4. *Increased awareness of cultural traditions.* Participating in family meals typically offers children opportunities to learn and identify with cultural traditions (Larson, 2008).
5. *Fewer emotional problems.* Mealtimes can offer a venue for positive communication between parents and children. This typically creates an environment where children engage in less risky behavior and have fewer emotional problems (Larson, 2008).

To optimize the likelihood of these positive outcomes, parents need to consider the climate of the mealtime experience. How the family interacts, where the meal is conducted, and the presence of television during the meal strongly influence the mealtime experience. The climate can support or discourage health and well-being. Meals that are well-organized and where parents are responsive to children have been linked to more positive outcomes (Fiese & Schwartz, 2008).

What are some ways busy families can build family mealtimes into their schedules?

coregulation
Transitional stage in the control of behavior in which parents exercise general supervision and children exercise moment-to-moment self-regulation.

In middle childhood, social power becomes more equal between parent and child. Parent and child engage in **coregulation,** a stage that can include strategies in which parents exercise oversight but children enjoy moment-to-moment self-regulation (Maccoby, 1984, 1992). For example, with regard to problems among peers, parents might now rely less on direct intervention and more on discussion with their child (Parke & Buriel, 1998).

Coregulation is affected by the overall relationship between parent and child. Children are more apt to follow their parents' wishes when they believe the parents are fair and concerned about the child's welfare and that they may "know better" because of experience. This is particularly true when parents take pains to acknowledge children's maturing judgment and take strong stands only on important issues (Maccoby, 1984, 1992).

Although school-age children spend less time at home, parents continue to be important in their lives. Parents who enjoy being with their children tend to raise children who feel good about themselves—and about their parents.

The shift to coregulation affects the way parents handle discipline (Kochanska, Aksan, Prisco, & Adams, 2008). Parents of school-age children are more likely to use inductive techniques. For example, 8-year-old Jared's father points out how his actions affect others: "Hitting Jermaine hurts him and makes him feel bad." In other situations, Jared's parents may appeal to his self-esteem ("What happened to the helpful boy who was here yesterday?") or moral values ("A big, strong boy like you shouldn't sit on the train and let an old person stand"). Above all, Jared's parents let him know that he must bear the consequences of his behavior: "No wonder you missed the school bus today—you stayed up too late last night! Now you'll have to walk to school."

Parents also modify their use of physical discipline (such as spanking) as children age. Generally, the use of corporal punishment is associated with negative outcomes for children. Certainly there are parents who never spank; however, parents who do use physical punishment tend to decrease its use as children grow older. When studying parents who do not spank their children past the age of 10 years with those who do, the ones who continue spanking tend to have worse relationships with their children in adolescence, and to have teens with worse behavioral problems (Lansford et al., 2009).

How family conflict is resolved is also important. If family conflict is constructive, it can help children see the need for rules and standards, and learn what issues are worth arguing about and what strategies can be effective (A. R. Eisenberg, 1996). However, as children become preadolescents and their striving for autonomy becomes more insistent, the quality of family problem solving often deteriorates (Vuchinich, Angelelli, & Gatherum, 1996).

Cultural differences are also important. Generally, researchers find that in cultures that stress family interdependence and authoritarian parenting (such as in Turkey, India, and Latin America) this type of parenting is *not* associated with negative maternal feelings or low self-esteem in children (Rudy & Grusec, 2006). Latino parents, for example, tend to exert more control for school-age children than European American parents do (Halgunseth et al., 2006). However, some data suggest that the story may be more complex. For example, children in China, a collectivistic culture, tend to be negatively affected just as are children from the individualistic United States (Pomerantz & Wang, 2009). And, in one study, African American and Latina girls showed more respect for parental authority than did European American girls. However, when minority girls showed low respect, mothers reported more intense arguments than did European American mothers (Dixon, Graber, & Brooks-Gunn, 2008).

checkpoint
can you . . .

- Describe how coregulation works, and how discipline and the handling of family conflict change during middle childhood?

Effects of Parents' Work Most studies of the impact of parents' work on children's well-being have focused on employed mothers. In general, the more satisfied a mother is with her employment status, the more effective she is likely to be as a parent. However, the impact of a mother's work depends on many other factors, including the child's age, sex, temperament, and personality; whether the mother works full-time or part-time; why she is working; whether she has a supportive or unsupportive partner, or none; the family's socioeconomic status; and the type of care the child receives before and/or after school (Parke, 2004a; Parke & Buriel, 1998). Often a single mother must work to stave off economic disaster. How her working affects her children may hinge on how much time and energy she has left to spend with them and what sort of role model she is. How well parents keep track of their children may be more important than whether the mother works for pay (Jacobson & Crockett, 2000). If possible, part-time work may be preferable to full-time. In an analysis of 68 studies, children did slightly better in school if their mothers worked only part time (Goldberg, Prause, Lucas-Thompson, & Himsel, 2008).

In 2009, 66 percent of U.S. mothers worked either full or part time (Parker, 2009b). This necessitates the frequent use of child care arrangements, generally a school- or center-based program. Some children of employed mothers, especially younger children, are supervised by relatives. Many children receive several types of out-of-school care (Carver & Iruka, 2006). Like good child care for preschoolers, good after-school programs have relatively low enrollment, low child-staff ratios, and well-educated staff. Children, especially boys, in organized after-school programs with flexible programming and a positive emotional climate tend to adjust better and do better in school (Mahoney, Lord, & Carryl, 2005; Pierce, Hamm, & Vandell, 1999).

A minority of school-age children and early adolescents are reported to be in *self-care,* regularly caring for themselves at home without adult supervision (NICHD Early Childhood Research Network, 2004a). This arrangement is advisable only for older children who are mature, responsible, and resourceful and know how to get help in an emergency—and, even then, only if a parent can stay in touch by telephone.

If finances permit, should one parent stay home to take care of the children?

Poverty and Parenting About 22 percent of U.S. children up to age 17—including 39 percent of black children and 35 percent of Hispanic children—lived in poverty in 2010. Children living with single mothers were nearly 5 times more likely to be poor than children living with married couples—43 percent as compared with 9 percent (Federal Interagency Forum on Child and Family Statistics, 2012).

Poor children are more likely than other children to have emotional or behavioral problems (Wadsworth, Raviv, Reinhard, Wolff, Santiago, & Einhorn, 2008). In addition, their cognitive potential and school performance suffer even more (Brooks-Gunn, Britto, & Brady, 1998; McLoyd, 1998; Najman, Hayatbakhsh, Heron, Bor, O'Callaghan, & Williams, 2009). Poverty can harm children's development through its impact on parents' emotional state and parenting practices and on the home environment they create.

Vonnie McLoyd (1990, 1998; Mistry, Vandewater, Huston, & McLoyd, 2002) analyzed the effects of poverty. Parents who live in poverty are likely to become anxious, depressed, and irritable and thus may become less affectionate with and less responsive to their children. They may discipline inconsistently, harshly, and arbitrarily. The children tend to become depressed, to have trouble getting along with peers, to lack self-confidence, to develop behavioral and academic problems, and to engage in antisocial acts (Brooks-Gunn et al., 1998; Evans, 2004; J. M. Fields & Smith, 1998; McLoyd, 1998; Mistry et al., 2002).

Fortunately, this pattern is not inevitable. Effective parenting can buffer children from the effects of poverty. Family interventions that reduce family conflict and anger and increase cohesion and warmth are especially beneficial (Repetti, Taylor, & Seeman, 2002). Parents who can turn to relatives or to community resources for emotional support, help with child care, and child-rearing information often can parent their children more effectively. In one study, mothers who, despite economic stress, were emotionally healthy and had relatively high self-esteem tended to have academically and socially competent children who reinforced the mothers' positive parenting. This, in turn, supported the children's continued academic success and socially desirable behavior (Brody, Kim, Murry, & Brown, 2004).

checkpoint
can **you** . . .

- Identify ways in which parents' work can affect children?
- Discuss effects of poverty on parenting?

FAMILY STRUCTURE

Family structure in the United States has changed dramatically. In earlier generations, the vast majority of children grew up in families with two married parents. Today, although about 2 out of 3 children under 18 live with two married biological, adoptive, or stepparents, that proportion represents a dramatic decline—from 77 percent in 1980 to 64 percent in 2012 (Child Trends Data Bank, 2013a; Figure 1). About 10 percent of two-parent families are stepfamilies resulting from divorce and remarriage, and nearly 4 percent are cohabiting families (Kreider & Fields, 2005). Other increasingly common family types are gay and lesbian families and grandparent-headed families.

Other things being equal, children tend to do better in families with two continuously married parents than in cohabiting, divorced, single-parent, or stepfamilies, or when the child

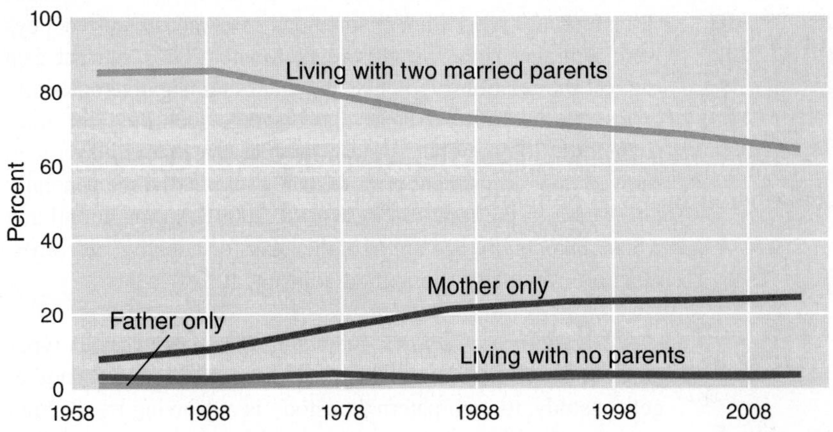

FIGURE 1
Living Arrangements of Children Younger than 18, 1970 to 2012

Most children under 18 in the United States live with two parents, but the prevalence of that household type has been diminishing.

Source: Child Trends Data Bank, 2013.

is born outside of marriage (S. L. Brown, 2004). The distinction is even stronger for children growing up with two *happily* married parents (Amato, 2005). This suggests that the parents' relationship, the quality of their parenting, and their ability to create a favorable family atmosphere may affect children's adjustment more than their marital status does (Amato, 2005; Bray & Hetherington, 1993; Bronstein, Clauson, Stoll, & Abrams, 1993).

Family instability may be more harmful to children than the particular type of family they live in. In a study of a nationally representative sample of 5- to 14-year-olds, children who experienced several family transitions (e.g., moving homes, divorcing parents) were more likely to have behavior problems and to engage in delinquent behavior than children in stable families (Fomby & Cherlin, 2007).

A father's frequent and positive involvement with his child is directly related to the child's well-being and physical, cognitive, and social development (Cabrera et al., 2000; Shannon et al., 2002). Unfortunately, in 2011, more than 30 percent of children lived in homes without a biological father present (National Fatherhood Initiative, 2013). Furthermore, about 18 percent of European American children, 6 percent of black children, and 21 percent of Latino children had never met their father (NCES, 2004).

When Parents Divorce The United States has one of the highest divorce rates in the world. The annual number of divorces has tripled since 1960 (Harvey & Pauwels, 1999), but the divorce *rate* has remained stable at just around 3.5 percent per 1,000 people (Munson & Sutton, 2004; Tejada-Vera & Sutton, 2009). More than 1.5 million children are involved in divorces each year (NIMH, 2002).

Adjusting to Divorce Divorce is stressful for children. First there is the stress of marital conflict and then of parental separation with the departure of one parent, usually the father. Children may not fully understand what is happening. Divorce is, of course, stressful for the parents as well and may negatively affect their parenting. The family's standard of living is likely to drop; and, if a parent moves away, a child's relationship with the noncustodial parent may suffer (Kelly & Emery, 2003). A parent's remarriage or second divorce after remarriage can increase the stress on children, renewing feelings of loss (Ahrons & Tanner, 2003; Amato, 2003).

Children's emotional or behavioral problems also may reflect the level of parental conflict *before* the divorce (Amato, 2005). In a longitudinal study of almost 11,000 Canadian children, those whose parents later divorced showed more anxiety, depression, or antisocial behavior than those whose parents stayed married (Strohschein, 2005). If predivorce parental discord is chronic, overt, or destructive, children may be as well or better off after a divorce (Amato, 2003, 2005; Amato & Booth, 1997).

A child's adjustment to divorce depends in part on the child's age, maturity, gender, temperament, and psychosocial adjustment before the divorce. Children who are younger when their parents divorce tend to suffer from more behavioral problems. By contrast, older children are at higher risk with respect to academic and social outcomes

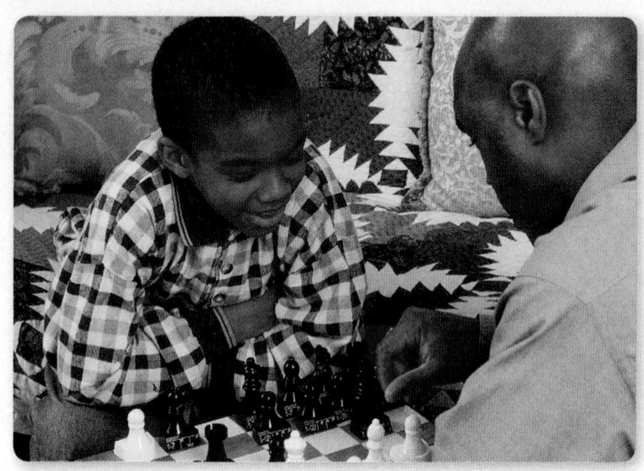

Children of divorce tend to be better adjusted if they have reliable, frequent contact with the noncustodial parent.

(Lansford, 2009). Although previous research suggested boys were at higher risk than girls (e.g., Amato, 2005), current data suggest the relationship between gender and negative outcomes is less clear, with no clear disadvantage identified for boys (Lansford, 2009). What is clear, however, is that children who showed poor adjustment prior to their parent's divorce generally fare worse in the long run (Lansford, 2009). Although children whose parents divorce are at higher risk for negative outcomes, most do eventually show good adjustment.

Custody, Visitation, and Co-parenting There are various types of custody arrangements. In most divorce cases, the mother gets custody, though paternal custody is a growing trend. Joint custody, shared by both parents, is another arrangement. When parents have joint legal custody, they share the right and responsibility to make decisions regarding the child's welfare. When they have joint physical custody (which is less common), the child lives part time with each parent.

When one parent has custody, children do better after divorce if the custodial parent is warm, supportive, and authoritative; monitors the child's activities; and holds age-appropriate expectations. In addition, conflict between the divorced parents needs to be minimal, and the nonresident parent should remain closely involved (Ahrons & Tanner, 2003; Kelly & Emery, 2003). Children living with divorced mothers adjust better when the father pays child support, which may indicate a strong tie between father and child and cooperation between the ex-spouses (Amato & Gilbreth, 1999; Kelly & Emery, 2003). Many children of divorce say that losing contact with a father is one of the most painful results of divorce (Fabricius, 2003). However, frequency of contact with the father is not as important as the quality of the father-child relationship and the level of parental conflict. Children who are close to their nonresident fathers and whose fathers are authoritative parents tend to do better in school and are less likely to have behavior problems (Amato & Gilbreth, 1999; Kelly & Emery, 2003).

Joint custody can be advantageous for the child if the parents can cooperate. An analysis of 33 studies found that children in either legal or physical joint custody were better adjusted and had higher self-esteem and better family relationships than children in sole custody arrangements. In fact, the joint custody children were as well-adjusted as children in nondivorced families (Bauserman, 2002). It is likely, though, that couples who choose joint custody are those that have less conflict.

In a national sample of 354 divorced families, cooperative parenting—active consultation between a mother and a nonresident father on parenting decisions—led to more frequent contact between father and child, and this, in turn, led to better father-child relationships and more responsive fathering (Sobolewski & King, 2005). Unfortunately, cooperative parenting is not the norm (Amato, 2005). Parent education programs that teach separated or divorced couples how to prevent or deal with conflict, keep lines of communication open, develop an effective co-parenting relationship, and help children adjust to divorce have been introduced in many courts with measurable success (Wolchik et al., 2002).

Long-Term Effects Most children of divorce adjust reasonably well. However, the anxiety connected with parental divorce may surface as children enter adulthood and try to form intimate relationships of their own (Amato, 2003; Wallerstein, Lewis, & Blakeslee, 2000). Having experienced their parents' divorce, some young adults are afraid of making commitments that might end in disappointment (Glenn & Marquardt, 2001). According to some research, 25 percent of children of divorce reach adulthood with serious social, emotional, or psychological problems, compared with 10 percent of children whose parents stay together (Hetherington & Kelly, 2002). As adults, the children of divorce tend to have lower SES, poorer psychological well-being, and a greater chance of having a birth outside marriage. Their marriages tend to be less satisfying and are more likely to end in divorce (Amato, 2005). However, much depends on how young people resolve and interpret the experience of parental divorce. Some who saw a high degree of conflict between their parents are able to learn from that negative example and to form highly intimate relationships themselves (Shulman, Scharf, Lumer, & Maurer, 2001).

Living in a One-Parent Family One-parent families result from divorce or separation, unwed parenthood, or death. With rising rates of divorce and of parenthood outside of marriage, the percentage of single-parent families in the United States has more than doubled since 1970 (U.S. Census Bureau, 2008a), reaching a peak in the 1990s. Currently, about 28 percent of children live in a single-parent household (Vespa, Lewis, & Kreider, 2013). More than half of all black children live with a single parent, as compared with 21 percent of non-Hispanic white children and 31 percent of Hispanic children (Vespa, Lewis, & Kreider, 2013). The issue is even more pressing when low-income families are examined, with 66 percent of African American families and 35 percent of both non-Hispanic and Hispanic white children living in single-parent homes (Mather, 2010). Although children are far more likely to live with a single mother than with a single father, the number of father-only families has more than quadrupled since 1970, apparently due largely to the increase in paternal custody after divorce (Fields, 2004).

Children in single-parent families do fairly well overall but tend to lag socially and educationally behind peers in two-parent families (Amato, 2005). Children living with married parents tend to have more daily interaction with their parents, are read to more often, progress more steadily in school, and participate more in extracurricular activities than children living with a single parent (Lugaila, 2003).

However, negative outcomes for children in one-parent families are not inevitable. The child's age and level of development, the family's financial circumstances, whether there are frequent moves, and a nonresident father's involvement make a difference (Amato, 2005; Seltzer, 2000). In a longitudinal study of 1,500 white, black, and Hispanic families with 6- and 7-year-old children, the mother's educational and ability level accounted for most of the negative effects of single parenting on academic performance and behavior (Ricciuti, 1999, 2004). Because single parents often lack the resources needed for good parenting, potential risks to children in these families might be reduced or eliminated through increased access to economic, social, educational, and parenting support. In international math and science tests, the achievement gap between third and fourth graders living in single-parent households and those living with two biological parents was greater for U.S. children than for those in any other country except New Zealand. Children of single parents did better in countries with supportive family policies such as child and family allowances, tax benefits to single parents, maternity leave, and released time from work (Pong, Dronkers, & Hampden-Thompson, 2003).

Living in a Cohabiting Family Cohabiting families are similar in many ways to married families, but the parents tend to be more disadvantaged (Mather, 2010). They traditionally have less income and education, report poorer relationships, and have more mental health problems. Thus it is not surprising that data from a national survey of 35,938 U.S. families showed worse emotional, behavioral, and academic outcomes for 6- to 11-year-old children living with cohabiting biological parents than for those living with married biological parents. The difference in outcomes was due largely to differences in economic resources, parental well-being, and parenting effectiveness (S. L. Brown, 2004).

Furthermore, cohabiting families are more likely to break up than married families. Although about 40 percent of unwed mothers are living with the child's father at the time of birth, 25 percent of cohabiting parents are no longer together 1 year later, and 31 percent break up after 5 years (Amato, 2005). However, some data suggest that the dissolution of a cohabiting couple does not result in the same risk for negative outcomes as does divorce (Wu, Hou, & Schimmele, 2008).

Living in a Stepfamily Most divorced parents eventually remarry, and many unwed mothers marry men who were not the father of their children, forming step-, or blended, families. Sixteen percent of U.S. children live in blended families (Kreider & Ellis, 2011).

Adjusting to a new stepparent may be stressful. A child's loyalties to an absent or dead parent may interfere with forming ties to a stepparent (Amato, 2005). However, some studies have found that boys—who often have more trouble than girls in adjusting to divorce and living with a single mother—benefit from a stepfather. A girl, on the other hand, may find the new man in the house a threat to her independence and to her close relationship with her mother (Bray & Hetherington, 1993; Hetherington, Bridges, & Insalbella, 1998; Hines, 1997). In a longitudinal study of a nationally representative sample of U.S. adults, mothers who remarried or formed new cohabiting relationships tended to use gentler discipline than mothers who remained single, and their children reported better relationships with them. On the other hand, supervision was greater in stable single-mother families (Thomson, Mosley, Hanson, & McLanahan, 2001).

checkpoint
can **you**...

- Assess the impact of parental divorce on children?
- Discuss how living in a single-parent or cohabiting household can affect children?

Living with Gay or Lesbian Parents An estimated 6 million U.S. children and adolescents have at least one gay or lesbian parent (Gates, 2013). Some gays and lesbians are raising children born of previous heterosexual relationships. Others conceive by artificial means, use surrogate mothers, or adopt children (Pawelski et al., 2006; Perrin and AAP Committee on Psychosocial Aspects of Child and Family Health, 2002).

Research has shown that children living with homosexual parents are no more likely than other children to have social or psychological problems or to turn out to be homosexual themselves.

A considerable body of research has examined the development of children of gays and lesbians, including physical and emotional health, intelligence, adjustment, sense of self, moral judgment, and social and sexual functioning, and has found no special concerns (APA, 2004b). There is *no* consistent difference between homosexual and heterosexual parents in emotional health or parenting skills and attitudes; and where there are differences, they tend to favor gay and lesbian parents (Brewaeys, Ponjaert, Van Hall, & Golombok, 1997; Golombok, Mellish, Jennings, Casey, Tasker, & Lamb, 2013; Meezan & Rauch, 2005; Pawelski et al., 2006; Perrin and AAP Committee on Psychosocial Aspects of Child and Family Health, 2002; Wainright, Russell, & Patterson, 2004). Gay or lesbian parents usually have positive relationships with their children, and the children are no more likely than children raised by heterosexual parents to have emotional, social, academic, or psychological problems (APA, 2004b; Chan, Raboy, & Patterson, 1998; Gartrell, Deck, Rodas, Peyser, & Banks, 2005; Golombok et al., 2003; Meezan & Rauch, 2005; Mooney-Somers & Golombok, 2000; Wainright et al., 2004). Furthermore, children of gays and lesbians are no more likely to be homosexual or to be confused about their gender than are children of heterosexuals (Anderssen, Amlie, & Ytteroy, 2002; Golombok et al., 2003; Meezan & Rauch, 2005; Pawelski et al., 2006; Wainright et al., 2004).

The 2010 comedy-drama The Kids Are Alright *encompasses this view within the very title. In this film, a lesbian couple meets the sperm donor they used for their children. Although this introduces challenges into their lives, they, and the kids, ultimately persevere.*

Such findings have social policy implications for legal decisions on custody and visitation disputes, foster care, and adoptions. In the face of controversy over gay and lesbian marriages or civil unions, with its implications for the security of children, several states have considered or adopted legislation sanctioning second-parent adoption by same-sex partners. The American Academy of Pediatrics supports a right to civil marriage for gays and lesbians (Pawelski et al., 2006) and legislative and legal

Those who cite benefits for heterosexual parenting are drawing conclusions that the research does not warrant. Specifically, they often compare two-parent families with single-parent families. The appropriate comparisons are between homosexual and heterosexual two-parent families. And, when this comparison is made, no negative effects are found.

Biblarz & Stacey, 2010

efforts to permit a partner in a same-sex couple to adopt the other partner's child (AAP Committee on Psychosocial Aspects of Child and Family Health, 2002).

Adoptive Families Adoption is found in all cultures throughout history. It is not only for infertile people; single people, older people, gay and lesbian couples, and people who already have biological children have become adoptive parents. In 2004, 1.5 million U.S. children under 18 (about 2.5 percent) lived with at least one adoptive parent (Kreider, 2008) and about 136,000 children are adopted annually (Child Welfare Information Gateway, 2011). An estimated 60 percent of legal adoptions are by stepparents or relatives, usually grandparents (Kreider, 2003).

Adoptions usually take place through public or private agencies. Agency adoptions are intended to be confidential, with no contact between the birth mother and the adoptive parents. However, independent adoptions, made by direct agreement between birth parents and adoptive parents, have become more common (Brodzinsky, 1997; Goodman et al., 1998). Often these are *open adoptions,* in which both parties share information or have direct contact with the child.

Studies suggest that the presumed risks of open adoption, such as fear that a birth mother who knows her child's whereabouts will try to reclaim the child, are overstated (Grotevant, McRoy, Elde, & Fravel, 1994). In a survey of 1,059 California adoptive families, whether an adoption was open bore no relation to the children's adjustment or to the parents' satisfaction with the adoption, both of which were high (Berry, Dylla, Barth, & Needell, 1998). Likewise, in a national study, adoptive parents of adolescents reported no significant difference in their children's adjustment whether the adoption was open or confidential (Von Korff, Grotevant, & McRoy, 2006).

Do you think you would ever try to adopt? If so, would you want the adoption to be open? Why or why not?

Adopting a child carries special challenges: integrating the adopted child into the family, explaining the adoption to the child, helping the child develop a healthy sense of self, and perhaps eventually helping the child find and contact the biological parents. According to a national longitudinal study, two adoptive parents invest just as much energy and resources in their children as two biological parents do, and more than parents in other family types. And adoptive children in two-parent families do as well as biological children in two-parent families (Hamilton, Cheng, & Powell, 2007).

Few significant differences in adjustment between adopted and nonadopted children have been found (Haugaard, 1998; Rueter & Koerner, 2009). Children adopted in infancy are least likely to have adjustment problems (Sharma, McGue, & Benson, 1996b). Any problems that do occur may surface during middle childhood, when children become more aware of differences in the way families are formed (Freeark et al., 2005), or in adolescence (Goodman, Emery, & Haugaard, 1998; Sharma, McGue, & Benson, 1996a), particularly among boys (Freeark et al., 2005).

About 17 percent of adoptions are transracial, most often involving white parents adopting an Asian or Latin American child (Kreider, 2003). Rules governing interracial adoption vary from state to state; some states give priority to same-race adoption, whereas others require that race not be a factor in approval of an adoption.

Adoptions of foreign-born children by U.S. families have nearly quadrupled since 1978, from 5,315 to 20,679, despite a decline in 2006 (Bosch et al., 2003; Crary, 2007). Does foreign adoption entail special problems? Aside from the possibility of malnourishment or medical conditions in children from developing countries (Bosch et al., 2003), a number of studies find no significant problems with the children's psychological adjustment, school adjustment and performance, or observed behavior at home or in the way they cope with being adopted (Levy-Shiff, Zoran, & Shulman, 1997; Sharma et al., 1996a). When foreign adoptees reach adolescence, they may experience feelings of loss of their native culture and growing awareness of racism and discrimination in their adopted culture. Parents who expose their adopted children to experiences that help them identify with their native culture and speak with their children about racism and discrimination may help buffer adopted children from negative effects (Lee, Grotevant, Hellerstedt, Gunnar, & The Minnesota International Adoption Project Team, 2006).

checkpoint
can you . . .

- Identify some special issues and challenges of a stepfamily?
- Summarize findings on outcomes of child raising by gay and lesbian parents?
- Discuss trends in adoption and the adjustment of adopted children?

Culture influences how we interpret parenting choices. In many nonindustrialized cultures, children routinely care for their younger siblings. In countries such as the United States, this might be seen as neglectful, but in many cultures, it is an important culturally defined role for siblings.

SIBLING RELATIONSHIPS

In remote rural areas of Asia, Africa, Oceania, and Central and South America, it is common to see older girls caring for three or four younger siblings. In such a community, older siblings have an important, culturally defined role. Parents train children early to teach younger sisters and brothers how to gather firewood, carry water, tend animals, and grow food. Younger siblings absorb intangible values, such as respecting elders and placing the welfare of the group above that of the individual (Cicirelli, 1994). In industrialized societies such as the United States, parents generally try not to "burden" older children with the regular care of siblings (Weisner, 1993). Older siblings do teach younger siblings, but this usually happens informally and not as an established part of the social system (Cicirelli, 1994).

The number of siblings in a family and their spacing, birth order, and gender often determine roles and relationships. The larger number of siblings in nonindustrialized societies helps the family carry on its work and provide for aging members. In industrialized societies, siblings tend to be fewer and farther apart in age, enabling parents to focus more resources and attention on each child (Cicirelli, 1994).

Sibling relations can be a laboratory for conflict resolution. Siblings are motivated to make up after quarrels, as they know they will see each other every day. They learn that expressing anger does not end a relationship. Children are more apt to squabble with same-sex siblings; two brothers quarrel more than any other combination (Cicirelli, 1976, 1995).

Siblings influence each other, not only *directly,* through their interactions with each other, but also *indirectly,* through their impact on each other's relationship with their parents. Parents' experience with an older sibling influences their expectations and treatment of a younger one (Brody, 2004). Conversely, behavior patterns a child establishes with parents tend to spill over into the child's behavior with siblings. In a study of 101 English families, when the parent-child relationship was warm and affectionate, siblings tended to have positive relationships as well. When the parent-child relationship was conflictual, sibling conflict was more likely (Pike et al., 2005).

study smart

Siblings

checkpoint can you...

- Compare sibling roles in industrialized and nonindustrialized countries?
- Discuss how siblings affect each other's development?

The Child in the Peer Group

In middle childhood the peer group comes into its own. Groups form naturally among children who live near one another or go to school together and often consist of children of the same racial or ethnic origin and similar socioeconomic status. Children who play together are usually close in age and of the same sex (Hartup, 1992; Pellegrini et al., 2002).

How does the peer group influence children? What determines their acceptance by peers and their ability to make friends?

POSITIVE AND NEGATIVE EFFECTS OF PEER RELATIONS

Children benefit from doing things with peers. They develop skills needed for sociability and intimacy, and they gain a sense of belonging. They are motivated to achieve, and they attain a sense of identity. They learn leadership and communication skills, cooperation, roles, and rules.

As children begin to move away from parental influence, the peer group opens new perspectives. In comparing themselves with others their age, children can gauge their abilities more realistically and gain a clearer sense of self-efficacy (Bandura, 1994). The peer group helps children learn how to get along in society—how to adjust their needs and desires to those of others, when to yield, and when to stand firm. The peer group offers emotional security. It is reassuring for children to find out that they are not alone in harboring thoughts that might offend an adult.

Same-sex peer groups may help children learn gender-appropriate behaviors and incorporate gender roles into their self-concept. In a 2-year study of 106 third through seventh graders, a sense of being typical of one's gender and being content with that gender increased self-esteem and well-being, whereas feeling pressure—from parents, peers, or oneself—to conform to gender stereotypes lessened well-being (Yunger et al., 2004).

On the negative side, peer groups may reinforce **prejudice:** unfavorable attitudes toward outsiders, especially members of certain racial or ethnic groups. Children tend to be biased toward children like themselves, but these biases, except for a preference for children of the same sex, diminish with age and cognitive development (Powlishta, Serbin, Doyle, & White, 1994). Prejudice and discrimination can do real damage. In a 5-year longitudinal study of 714 African American 10- to 12-year-olds, those who saw themselves as targets of discrimination tended to show symptoms of depression or conduct problems during the next 5 years (Brody et al., 2006). In a study of 253 English children, prejudice against refugees was reduced by *extended contact:* reading them stories about close friendships between English children and refugee children, followed by group discussions (Cameron, Rutland, Brown, & Douch, 2006).

The peer group also can foster antisocial tendencies. Preadolescent children are especially susceptible to pressure to conform. Of course, some degree of conformity to group standards is healthy. It is unhealthy when it becomes destructive or prompts young people to act against their better judgment. It is usually in the company of peers that some children shoplift and begin to use drugs (Dishion & Tipsord, 2011; Hartup, 1992).

prejudice
Unfavorable attitude toward members of certain groups outside one's own, especially racial or ethnic groups.

By the age of 10, children from both the United States and Korea think it's okay to dislike another child because he or she is aggressive or shy, but it's less acceptable to dislike another child because of his or her race or gender, characteristics that cannot change.

Park & Killen, 2010

POPULARITY

Humans are social creatures, and as such our relationships have a profound effect on our outcomes. Early in life, this need is expressed primarily within the context of attachment relationships with parents. As children age, however, peer relationships become increasingly important. Because children most often interact with each other within the context of school and in groups, researchers have developed means by which to assess their standing in the social group.

Much of research in child development depends on asking children the right questions in the right way. If a researcher asked schoolchildren to tell her the social ranking of all the children in a classroom, she would most likely be met with a blank stare. However, children can easily say who they like to play with, who they like the most, or who they think other kids like the most. This is known as a *positive nomination.*

Children can also easily describe which children they don't like to play with, like the least, or think other kids don't like—this is a *negative nomination.* By asking these types of questions of every child in a classroom, a researcher can use the aggregated responses to get an overall score, or tally, for each child. The tally may be composed of positive nominations, negative nominations, or no nominations. This measure is known as *sociometric popularity.*

Sociometrically *popular* children receive many positive nominations and few negative nominations. They generally have good cognitive abilities, are high achievers, are good at solving social problems, are kind and help other children, and are assertive without being disruptive or aggressive. Their superior social skills make others enjoy being with them (Cillessen & Mayeux, 2004; LaFontana & Cillessen, 2002; Masten & Coatsworth, 1998).

Children can be *unpopular* in one of two ways. Some children are rejected, and they receive a large number of negative nominations. Other children are neglected and receive few nominations of any kind. Some unpopular children are aggressive; others are hyperactive, inattentive, or withdrawn (Dodge, Coie, Pettit, & Price, 1990; LaFontana & Cillessen, 2002; Masten & Coatsworth, 1998). Still others act silly and immature or anxious and uncertain. Unpopular children are often insensitive to other children's feelings and do not adapt well to new situations (Bierman, Smoot, & Aumiller, 1993).

Children who squint are invited to fewer birthday parties.

Mojon-Azzi, Kunz, & Mojon, 2010

Other children can be *average* in their ratings and do not receive an unusual number of either positive or negative nominations. Finally, some children are controversial and receive many positive and negative nominations, indicating that some children like them a great deal and some dislike them a great deal. Less is known about outcomes related to average and controversial sociometric categories.

Popularity is important in middle childhood. Schoolchildren whose peers like them are likely to be well adjusted as adolescents. Those who have trouble getting along with peers are more likely to develop psychological problems, drop out of school, or become delinquent (Dishion & Tipsord, 2011; Hartup, 1992; Kupersmidt & Coie, 1990). Peer rejection has also been linked to lower levels of classroom participation (Ladd, Herald-Brown, & Reiser, 2008).

It is often in the family that children acquire behaviors that affect popularity. Children of authoritarian parents who punish and threaten are likely to threaten or act mean with other children. They are less popular than children whose authoritative parents reason with them and try to help them understand how another person might feel (C. H. Hart, Ladd, & Burleson, 1990). In addition, families can influence popularity by promoting or impeding the development of social competence. In a year-long longitudinal study, 159 fourth-grade children were more socially competent at the end of the study when they were from families in which the parent-child relationships were warm and nurturing, parents provided direct advice about how to manage conflictual social interactions, and parents provided children with appropriate high-quality peer experiences (McDowell & Parke, 2009).

Culture can affect criteria for popularity. One series of studies illustrates how cultural context can vary the meaning of behaviors. Chen, Cen, Li, and He (2005) point to effects of social change resulting from the radical restructuring of China's economic system during the late 1990s. China shifted from a collectivist system in which the people, through their government, owned all means of production and distribution, toward a more competitive, technologically advanced market economy with private ownership and its associated individualist values. Researchers collected data from three cohorts of third and fourth graders in Shanghai schools in 1990, 1998, and 2002. A striking change emerged with regard to shyness and sensitivity. In the 1990 cohort, shy children were accepted by peers and were high in academic achievement, leadership, and teacher-rated competence. By 2002, the results were just the reverse: shy children tended to be rejected by peers, to be depressed, and to be rated by teachers as low in competence. A similar finding was obtained in a more recent comparison of urban and rural children in China. In this study, shyness in urban children was associated with social and school problems, as well as depression, whereas rural children who were shy had positive outcomes (Chen, Wang, & Wang, 2009). In the quasi-capitalist society that China has become, social assertiveness and initiative may be more highly appreciated and encouraged than in the past, and shyness and sensitivity may lead to social and psychological difficulties for children.

checkpoint can you...

- Identify positive and negative effects of the peer group?
- Identify characteristics of popular and unpopular children, and discuss influences on popularity?

FRIENDSHIP

Children may spend much of their free time in groups, but only as individuals do they make friends. Popularity is the peer group's opinion of a child, but friendship is a two-way street.

Children look for friends who are like them in age, sex, and interests. The strongest friendships involve equal commitment and mutual give-and-take. Though children tend to choose friends with similar ethnic backgrounds, cross-racial/ethnic friendships are associated with positive developmental outcomes (Kawabata & Crick, 2008).

With their friends, children learn to communicate and cooperate. They help each other weather stressful situations, such as starting at a new school or adjusting to parents' divorce. The inevitable quarrels help children learn to resolve conflicts (Furman, 1982; Hartup & Stevens, 1999; Newcomb & Bagwell, 1995). Friendship seems to help children feel good about themselves, though it's also likely that children who feel good about themselves have an easier time making friends.

Having friends is important because peer rejection and friendlessness in middle childhood may have long-term negative effects. In one longitudinal study, fifth graders who had no friends were more likely than their classmates to have low self-esteem in young adulthood and to show symptoms of depression (Bagwell, Newcomb, & Bukowski, 1998).

Friends often share secrets—and laughs. Friendships deepen and become more stable in middle childhood, reflecting cognitive and emotional growth. Girls tend to have fewer, more intimate friends than boys.

Children's concepts of friendship and the ways they act with their friends change with age, reflecting cognitive and emotional growth. Preschool friends play together, but friendship among school-age children is deeper and more stable. Children cannot be or have true friends until they achieve the cognitive maturity to consider other people's views and needs as well as their own (Dodge, Coie, & Lynam, 2006; Hartup & Stevens, 1999). On the basis of interviews with people between the ages of 3 and 45, Robert Selman (1980; Selman & Selman, 1979) traced changing conceptions of friendship across development (Table 1). Children from approximately 3 to 7 years of age are at an undifferentiated level of friendship, where they value their friends on selfish, concrete criteria, such as what toys another child has or if that child looks similar to them. In the unilateral stage of friendship at approximately ages 4 to 9, friendship is still based on self-interest and what a friend can do for a child. Between ages 6 and 12, children are starting to engage in reciprocal friendships but are still primarily concerned with their own interests. At ages 9 to 15, in the mutual stage of friendships, true friendships that include commitment and reciprocity begin. And beginning at about age 12, in the

TABLE 1 Selman's Stages of Friendship

Stage	Description	Example
Stage 0: Momentary playmateship (ages 3 to 7)	On this *undifferentiated* level of friendship, children tend to think only about what they want from a relationship. Most very young children define their friends in terms of physical closeness and value them for material or physical attributes.	"She lives on my street" or "He has the Power Rangers."
Stage 1: One-way assistance (ages 4 to 9)	On this *unilateral* level, a "good friend" does what the child wants the friend to do.	"She's not my friend anymore, because she wouldn't go with me when I wanted her to" or "He's my friend because he always says yes when I want to borrow his eraser."
Stage 2: Two-way fair-weather cooperation (ages 6 to 12)	This *reciprocal* level overlaps stage 1. It involves give-and-take but still serves many separate self-interests, rather than the common interests of the two friends.	"We are friends; we do things for each other" or "A friend is someone who plays with you when you don't have anybody else to play with."
Stage 3: Intimate, mutually shared relationships (ages 9 to 15)	On this *mutual* level, children view a friendship as an ongoing, systematic, committed relationship that incorporates more than doing things for each other. Friends become possessive and demand exclusivity.	"It takes a long time to make a close friend, so you really feel bad if you find out that your friend is trying to make other friends too."
Stage 4: Autonomous interdependence (beginning at age 12)	In this *interdependent stage,* children respect friends' needs for both dependency and autonomy.	"A good friendship is a real commitment, a risk you have to take; you have to support and trust and give, but you have to be able to let go too."

Sources: Selman, 1980; Selman & Selman, 1979.

checkpoint can you . . .

- List characteristics children look for in friends?
- Tell how age and gender affect friendships?

interdependent stage of friendship, children depend on others but also respect their need for autonomy.

School-age children distinguish among "best friends," "good friends," and "casual friends" on the basis of intimacy and time spent together (Hartup & Stevens, 1999). Children this age typically have three to five best friends but usually play with only one or two at a time (Hartup, 1992; Hartup & Stevens, 1999). School-age girls seem to care less about having many friends than about having a few close friends they can rely on. Boys have more friendships, but they tend to be less intimate and affectionate (Furman & Buhrmester, 1985; Hartup & Stevens, 1999).

AGGRESSION AND BULLYING

Aggression declines and changes in form during the early school years. After age 6 or 7, most children become less aggressive as they grow less egocentric, more empathic, more cooperative, and better able to communicate. They can now put themselves in someone else's place, can understand another person's motives, and can find positive ways of asserting themselves. *Instrumental aggression,* aggression aimed at achieving an objective—the hallmark of the preschool period—becomes much less common. However, as aggression declines overall, *hostile aggression,* aggression intended to hurt another person, proportionately increases (Dodge, Coie, & Lynam, 2006), often taking verbal rather than physical form (Pellegrini & Archer, 2005). Boys continue to engage in more *direct aggression*, and girls are increasingly more likely to engage in *social* or *indirect aggression*, although some researchers argue the differences have been overstated (Card, Stucky, Sawalani, & Little, 2008).

A small minority of children do not learn to control physical aggression (Coie & Dodge, 1998). These children tend to have social and psychological problems, but it is not clear whether aggression causes these problems or is a response to them, or both (Crick & Grotpeter, 1995). Highly aggressive children often egg each other on to antisocial acts. Thus school-age boys who are physically aggressive may become juvenile delinquents in adolescence (Broidy et al., 2003).

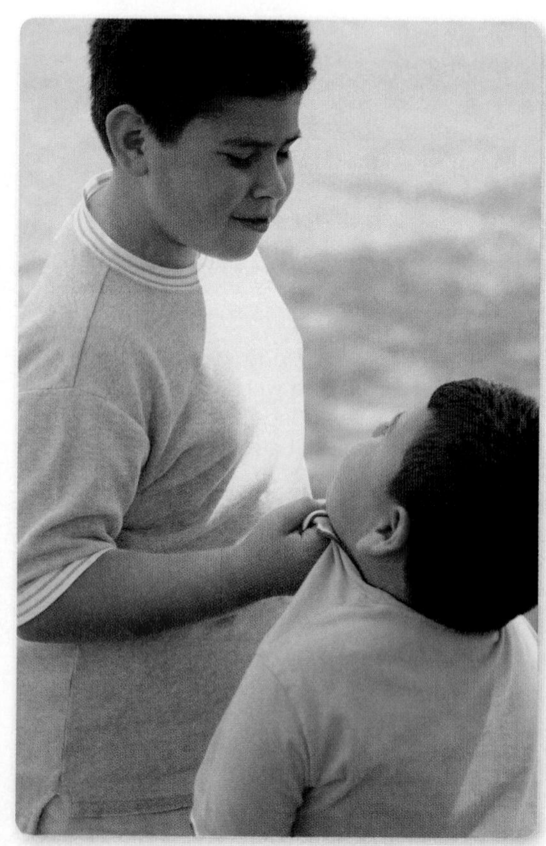

Aggressive boys tend to gain in social status by the end of fifth grade, suggesting that bullying behavior may be seen as cool or glamorous by preadolescents.

Although most aggressors tend to be disliked, physically aggressive boys and some relationally aggressive girls (those who, for example, talk behind another girl's back or exclude her socially) are perceived as among the most popular in the classroom. In a study of fourth graders, aggressive boys tended to increase in social status by the end of fifth grade, suggesting that behavior shunned by younger children may be seen as cool or glamorous by preadolescents (Sandstrom & Coie, 1999). In a longitudinal study of a multiethnic group of 905 urban fifth through ninth graders, physical aggression became less disapproved as children moved into adolescence, and relational aggression was increasingly reinforced by high status among peers (Cillessen & Mayeux, 2004).

Types of Aggression and Social Information Processing What makes children act aggressively? One answer may lie in the way they process social information: what features of the social environment they pay attention to and how they interpret what they perceive.

Instrumental, or *proactive*, aggressors view force and coercion as effective ways to get what they want. They act deliberately, not out of anger. In social learning terms, they are aggressive because they expect to be rewarded for it (Crick & Dodge, 1996). For example, such a child might learn that he can force another child to trade lunch items with him by threatening to hit the other child. If that strategy works, the child has been reinforced for his aggressive acts, and his belief in aggression is confirmed. Other children are more likely to engage in *hostile* or *reactive* aggression. Such a child might, after being accidentally pushed by someone in the lunch line, assume that the bump was on purpose and push back angrily. All children might sometimes assume the worst of others, but children who habitually assume the worst of others in situations such as these are said to have a **hostile attributional bias.** They quickly conclude, in ambiguous situations, that others were acting with ill intent and are likely to strike out in retaliation or self-defense. Generally, other children then respond to this hostility with aggression, thereby confirming the original hostile attributional bias and strengthening it (Crick & Dodge, 1996; de Castro, Veerman, Koops, Bosch, & Monshouwer, 2002; Waldman, 1996).

hostile attribution bias
Tendency to perceive others as trying to hurt one and to strike out in retaliation or self-defense.

Rejected children and those exposed to harsh parenting also tend to have a hostile attribution bias, as do children who seek dominance and control (Coie & Dodge, 1998; de Castro et al., 2002; Erdley et al., 1997; Masten & Coatsworth, 1998; Weiss et al., 1992). Because people often *do* become hostile toward someone who acts aggressively toward them, a hostile bias may become a self-fulfilling prophecy, setting in motion a cycle of aggression (de Castro et al., 2002). Hostile attribution bias becomes more common between ages 6 and 12 (Aber, Brown, & Jones, 2003).

Does Electronic Media Violence Stimulate Aggression? As television, movies, video games, cell phones, and computers take on larger roles in children's daily lives, it is critical to understand the impact mass media has on children's behavior. Children spend more time on entertainment media than on any other activities except school and sleeping. On average, children spend about 4 hours a day in front of a television or computer screen—some much more than that (C. A. Anderson et al., 2003).

Violence is prevalent in U.S. media. About 6 out of 10 television programs portray violence, usually glamorized, glorified, or trivialized (Yokota & Thompson, 2000). Music videos disproportionately feature violence against women and blacks. The motion picture, music, and video game industries aggressively market violent, adult-rated products to children (AAP Committee on Public Education, 2001). In a recent study of U.S. children, 40 movies that were rated R for violence were seen by a median of 12.5 percent of an estimated 22 million children aged 10 to 14 (Worth et al., 2008).

Because of the significant amount of time that children spend interacting with media, the images they see can become primary role models and sources of information about how people behave. Evidence from research conducted over the past 50 years on exposure to violence on TV, movies, and video games supports a causal relationship between media violence and violent behavior on the viewer's part (Huesmann, 2007). Although the strongest single correlate of violent behavior is previous exposure to violence (AAP Committee on Public Education, 2001; Anderson, Berkowitz et al., 2003; Huesmann, Moise-Titus, Podolski, & Eron, 2003), the effect of exposure to violence via mass media is significant (Figure 2).

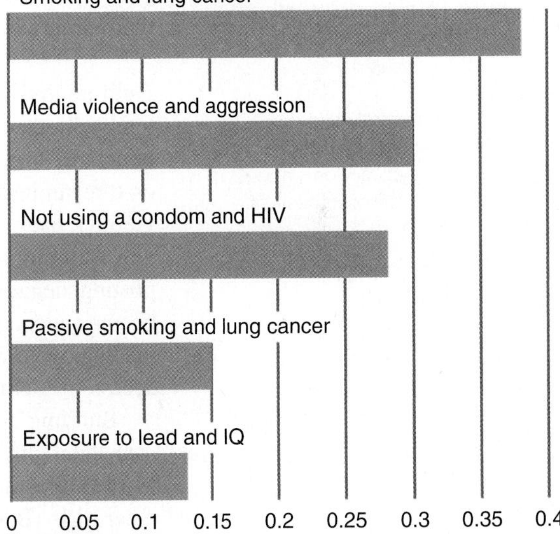

FIGURE 2
Effects of Threats to Public Health

The effect of media violence is the same or greater than the effect of many other recognized threats to public health.

Source: Bushman, B. J., & Rowell Huesmann, L. (2001). Effects of televised violence on aggression. In Dorothy G. Singer and Jerome L. Singer (Eds.), *Handbook of Children and the Media*, p. 235, Figure 11.5. Copyright © 2001 by Sage Publications, Inc. Reproduced with permission of Sage Publications, Inc. in the format Textbook via Copyright Clearance Center.

How does media violence lead to long-term aggressiveness? Longitudinal studies have demonstrated that children's exposure to violent media increases their risk for long-term effects based on observational learning, desensitization, and enactive learning that occur automatically in human children (Huesmann, 2007). Media provides visceral thrills without showing the human cost and leads children to view aggression as acceptable. Children who see characters use violence to achieve their goals are likely to conclude that force is an effective way to resolve conflicts. Repeated exposure can desensitize children. Negative reactions to violent scenes have been shown to decline in intensity with repeated exposure (Huesmann & Kirwil, 2007). The more realistically violence is portrayed, the more likely it is to be accepted (AAP Committee on Public Education, 2001; Anderson, Berkowitz et al., 2003).

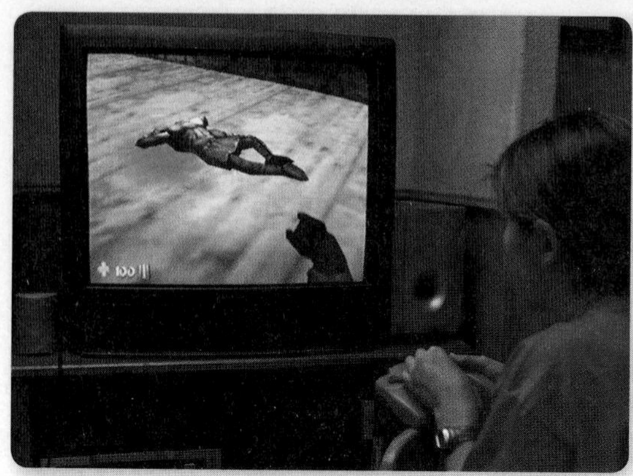

Research shows that children who see televised violence tend to act aggressively. When the violence is child-initiated, as in video games, the effect may be even stronger.

Children are more vulnerable than adults to the influence of televised violence (AAP Committee on Public Education, 2001; Coie & Dodge, 1998). Classic social learning research suggests that children imitate filmed models even more than live ones (Bandura et al., 1963). The influence is stronger if the child believes the violence on the screen is real, identifies with the violent character, finds that character attractive, and watches without parental supervision or intervention (Anderson, Berkowitz et al., 2003; Coie & Dodge, 1998). Highly aggressive children are more strongly affected by media violence than are less aggressive children (Anderson, Berkowitz et al., 2003).

Research on effects of video games and the Internet suggest that long-term increases in violent behavior could be even greater for video games than for TV and movies. Players of violent games are active participants who receive positive reinforcement for violent actions (Huesmann, 2007). In experimental studies, young video game players have shown decreases in prosocial behavior and increases in aggressive thoughts and violent retaliation to provocation (C. Anderson, 2000).

Although the majority of researchers endorse the link between viewing violence and aggression, some believe the link between media violence and aggression may have been overstated (Ferguson, 2013). For example, some researchers argue that methodological flaws such as a failure to consider confounding variables, difficulty generalizing from laboratory studies of aggression to real-world aggressive acts, and inappropriate statistical modeling call into question many of the assertions made in this particular domain (Ferguson & Savage, 2012). In support of this assertion are data indicating that youth violence has declined even though exposure to violent media has remained stable (Ferguson, 2013).

What can and should be done about children's exposure to media violence?

Media-induced aggressiveness can be minimized by cutting down on television use and by parental monitoring and guidance of the shows children watch (Anderson, Berkowitz et al., 2003). The AAP Committee on Public Education (2001) recommends that parents limit children's media exposure to 1 to 2 hours a day.

bullying
Aggression deliberately and persistently directed against a particular target, or victim, typically one who is weak, vulnerable, and defenseless.

Bullies and Victims Aggression becomes **bullying** when it is deliberately, persistently directed against a particular target: a victim. Bullying can be physical (hitting, punching, kicking, or damaging or taking of personal belongings), verbal (name-calling or threatening), or relational or emotional (isolating and gossiping, often behind the victim's back). Bullying can be *proactive*—done to show dominance, bolster power, or win admiration—or *reactive,* responding to a real or imagined attack. *Cyberbullying*—posting negative comments or derogatory photos of the victim on a Web site—has become increasingly common (Berger, 2007). The increase in use of cell phones, text messaging, e-mail, and chat rooms has opened new venues for bullies that provide access to victims without the protection of family and community (Huesmann, 2007).

Bullying may reflect a genetic tendency toward aggressiveness combined with environmental influences, such as coercive parents and antisocial friends (Berger, 2007). Most bullies are boys who tend to victimize other boys; female bullies tend to target other girls (Berger, 2007; Pellegrini & Long, 2002; Veenstra et al., 2005). Male bullies tend to use overt, physical aggression; female bullies may use relational aggression (Boulton, 1995; Nansel et al., 2001). Patterns of bullying and victimization may become established as early as kindergarten; as tentative peer groups form, aggressors soon get to know which children make the easiest targets. Physical bullying declines with age, but other forms of bullying increase, especially at ages 11 to 15. Whereas younger children reject an aggressive child, by early adolescence bullies are often dominant, respected, feared, and even liked (Berger, 2007). Both bullies and victims tend to be deficient in social problem-solving skills, and those who also have academic problems are more likely to be bullies than victims (Cook, Williams, Guerra, Kim, & Sadek, 2010).

Risk factors for victimization seem to be similar across cultures (Schwartz, Chang, & Farver, 2001). Victims do not fit in. They tend to be anxious, depressed, cautious, quiet, and submissive and to cry easily, or to be argumentative and provocative (Hodges, Boivin, Vitaro, & Bukowski, 1999; Olweus, 1995; Veenstra et al., 2005). They have few friends and may live in harsh, punitive family environments (Nansel et al., 2001; Schwartz, Dodge, Pettit, Bates, & Conduct Problems Prevention Research Group, 2000). Victims are apt to have low self-esteem, though it is not clear whether low self-esteem leads to or follows from victimization (Boulton & Smith, 1994; Olweus, 1995). Children who are overweight are most likely to become either victims or bullies (Janssen, Craig, Boyce, & Pickett, 2004).

Some research suggests a transactional pattern between a "typical" victim's internalizing behavior and bullying risk over time. Although most children's risk of bullying does decrease over time as they learn how to discourage bullying (Pellegrini & Long, 2002), a subset of children remains at high risk. These children are different in that they exhibit high levels of internalizing behaviors (such as anxiety and depression) early in their school years. These internalizing behaviors put them at high risk of bullying. When that bullying does occur, they are likely to become even more depressed and anxious, perpetuating a maladaptive style of coping with stressors and making them even more attractive targets for potential bullies (Leadbeater & Hoglund, 2009). Most of these victims are small, passive, weak, and submissive and may blame themselves for being bullied. Other victims are provocative; they goad their attackers, and they may even attack other children themselves (Berger, 2007; Veenstra et al., 2005).

Bullying, especially emotional bullying, is harmful to both bullies and victims—and can even be fatal (Berger, 2007). Bullies are at increased risk of delinquency, crime, or alcohol abuse. In the wave of school shootings since 1994, the perpetrators often had been victims of bullying (Anderson, Kaufman, et al., 2001). Victims of chronic bullying tend to develop behavior problems. They may become more aggressive themselves or may become depressed (Schwartz, McFadyen-Ketchum, Dodge, Pettit, & Bates, 1998; Veenstra et al., 2005). Furthermore, frequent bullying affects the school atmosphere, leading to widespread underachievement, alienation from school, stomachaches and headaches, reluctance to go to school, and frequent absences (Berger, 2007).

The U.S. Department of Health and Human Services has promoted Steps to Respect, a program for grades 3 to 6 that aims to (1) increase staff awareness and responsiveness to bullying, (2) teach students social and emotional skills, and (3) foster socially responsible beliefs. A randomized controlled study of 1,023 third to sixth graders found a reduction in playground bullying and argumentative behavior and an increase in harmonious interactions among children who participated in the program, as well as less bystander incitement to bullying (Frey et al., 2005). However, analysis of research done on a broad variety of these types of intervention programs has indicated that the impact on actual bullying behavior is minimal although the programs may enhance students' social competence and self-esteem (Merrell, Gueldner, Ross, & Isava, 2008).

checkpoint can **you**...

- Tell how aggression changes during middle childhood, and how social information processing and media violence can contribute to it?
- Describe how patterns of bullying and victimization become established and change?

Mental Health

The term *mental health* is a misnomer because it usually refers to emotional health. Although most children are fairly well adjusted, at least 1 in 10 children and adolescents has a diagnosed mental disturbance severe enough to cause some impairment (Leslie, Newman, Chesney, & Perrin, 2005). Diagnosis of mental disorders in children is important because these disorders can lead to psychiatric disorders in adulthood (Kim-Cohen et al., 2003). In fact, half of all mental disorders begin by age 14 (Kessler et al., 2005).

Let's look at several common emotional disturbances and then at types of treatment.

COMMON EMOTIONAL PROBLEMS

Children with emotional, behavioral, and developmental problems tend to be an underserved group. Compared with other children who have special health care needs, they are more likely to have conditions that affect their daily activities and cause them to

Paraplush, a European toy company, has released a line of plush animals illustrating common psychological disorders. Their tagline is "Psychiatry for Abused Toys." The animals include a hallucinating snake, a depressed turtle, a paranoid crocodile, and others. Do you think this approach helps destigmatize mental disorders, or does it promote negative stereotypes and inaccurate perceptions?

miss school. They often have chronic physical conditions. Only about half of all children in the United States who need services for mental health issues currently receive the help they need (Merikangas et al., 2009).

A reported 55.7 percent of children diagnosed with emotional, behavioral, and developmental problems have *disruptive conduct disorders:* aggression, defiance, or antisocial behavior. Almost all the rest, 43.5 percent, have *anxiety* or *mood disorders:* feeling sad, depressed, unloved, nervous, fearful, or lonely (Bethell, Read, & Blumberg, 2005).

Disruptive Conduct Disorders Temper tantrums and defiant, argumentative, hostile, or deliberately annoying behavior—common among 4- and 5-year-olds—typically are outgrown by middle childhood as children get better at controlling these behaviors (Miner & Clarke-Sterwart, 2009). When such a pattern of behavior persists until age 8, children (usually boys) may be diagnosed with **oppositional defiant disorder (ODD),** a pattern of defiance, disobedience, and hostility toward adult authority figures lasting at least 6 months and going beyond the bounds of normal childhood behavior. Children with ODD constantly fight, argue, lose their temper, snatch things, blame others, and are angry and resentful. They have few friends, are in constant trouble in school, and test the limits of adults' patience (National Library of Medicine, 2004).

oppositional defiant disorder (ODD)
Pattern of behavior, persisting into middle childhood, marked by negativity, hostility, and defiance.

conduct disorder (CD)
Repetitive, persistent pattern of aggressive, antisocial behavior violating societal norms or the rights of others.

Some children with ODD may later be diagnosed with **conduct disorder (CD),** a persistent, repetitive pattern, beginning at an early age, of aggressive, antisocial acts, such as truancy, setting fires, habitual lying, fighting, bullying, theft, vandalism, assaults, and drug and alcohol use (National Library of Medicine, 2003). Between 6 and 16 percent of boys and between 2 and 9 percent of girls under age 18 in the United States have been diagnosed with clinical levels of externalizing behavior or conduct problems (Roosa et al., 2005). Some 11- to 13-year-olds progress from conduct disorder to criminal violence—mugging, rape, and break-ins—and by age 17 may be frequent, serious offenders (Coie & Dodge, 1998). Between 25 and 50 percent of these highly antisocial children become antisocial adults (USDHHS, 1999b).

What determines whether a particular child with antisocial tendencies will become severely and chronically antisocial? Neurobiological deficits, such as weak stress-regulating mechanisms, may fail to warn children to restrain themselves from dangerous or risky behavior. Such deficits may be genetically influenced or may be brought on by adverse environments such as hostile parenting or family conflict, or both (van Goozen, Fairchild, Snoek, & Harold, 2007). As an example, in one study the researchers found an interaction between harsh parenting and difficult child temperament. Children who, as infants, were rated as being difficult were at higher risk of developing externalizing behaviors, but only if their mothers also used harsh parenting techniques (Miner & Clarke-Stewart, 2009). Also influential are stressful life events and association with deviant peers (Roosa et al., 2005).

School Phobia and Other Anxiety Disorders Some children have realistic reasons to fear going to school: a sarcastic teacher, overly demanding work, or a bully to avoid. In such cases, the environment may need changing, not the child. However, some children have **school phobia,** an unrealistic fear of going to school. True school phobia may be a type of **separation anxiety disorder,** a condition involving excessive anxiety for at least 4 weeks concerning separation from home or from people to whom the child is attached. Although separation anxiety is normal in infancy, when it persists in older children, it is cause for concern. Separation anxiety disorder affects some 4 percent of children and young adolescents and may persist through the college years. These children often come from close-knit, caring families. They may develop the disorder spontaneously or after a stressful event, such as the death of a pet, an illness, or a move to a new school (American Psychiatric Association, 2000; Harvard Medical School, 2004a).

school phobia
Unrealistic fear of going to school; may be a form of *separation anxiety disorder* or *social phobia*.

separation anxiety disorder
Condition involving excessive, prolonged anxiety concerning separation from home or from people to whom a person is attached.

social phobia
Extreme fear and/or avoidance of social situations.

Sometimes school phobia may be a form of **social phobia,** or *social anxiety:* extreme fear and/or avoidance of social situations such as speaking in class or meeting an acquaintance on the street. Social phobia affects about 5 percent of children; it runs in families, so there may be a genetic component. Often these phobias are triggered by traumatic experiences, such as a child's mind going blank when the child is called on in class (Beidel & Turner, 1998). Social anxiety tends to increase with age, whereas separation anxiety decreases (Costello et al., 2003).

Some children have a **generalized anxiety disorder,** not focused on any specific part of their lives. These children worry about just about everything: school grades, storms, earthquakes, and hurting themselves on the playground. They tend to be self-conscious, self-doubting, and excessively concerned with meeting the expectations of others. They seek approval and need constant reassurance, but their worry seems independent of performance or of how they are regarded by others (Harvard Medical School, 2004a; USDHHS, 1999b). Far less common is **obsessive-compulsive disorder (OCD).** Children with this disorder may be obsessed by repetitive, intrusive thoughts, images, or impulses (often involving irrational fears); or may show compulsive behaviors, such as constant hand-washing; or both (American Psychiatric Association, 2000; Harvard Medical School, 2004a).

generalized anxiety disorder
Anxiety not focused on any single target.

obsessive-compulsive disorder (OCD)
Anxiety aroused by repetitive, intrusive thoughts, images, or impulses, often leading to compulsive ritual behaviors.

Anxiety disorders tend to run in families (Harvard Medical School, 2004a) and are twice as common among girls as among boys. The heightened female vulnerability to anxiety begins as early as age 6. Females also are more susceptible to depression, which is similar to anxiety and often goes hand in hand with it (Lewinsohn, Gotlib, Lewinsohn, Seeley, & Allen, 1998). Both anxiety and depression may be neurologically based or may stem from insecure attachment, exposure to an anxious or depressed parent, or other early experiences that make children feel a lack of control over what happens around them (Chorpita & Barlow, 1998; Harvard Medical School, 2004a).

Childhood Depression **Childhood depression** is a disorder of mood that goes beyond normal, temporary sadness. Depression is estimated to occur in 2 percent of preschool children and up to 2.8 percent of children under the age of 13 years (Costello, Erkanli & Angold, 2006; NCHS, 2004). Symptoms include inability to have fun or concentrate, fatigue, extreme activity or apathy, crying, sleep problems, weight change, physical complaints, feelings of worthlessness, a prolonged sense of friendlessness, or frequent thoughts about death or suicide. Childhood depression may signal the beginning of a recurrent problem that is likely to persist into adulthood (Birmaher, 1998; Cicchetti & Toth, 1998; USDHHS, 1999b; Weissman, Warner, Wickramaratne, & Kandel, 1999).

childhood depression
Mood disorder characterized by such symptoms as a prolonged sense of friendlessness, inability to have fun or concentrate, fatigue, extreme activity or apathy, feelings of worthlessness, weight change, physical complaints, and thoughts of death or suicide.

The exact causes of childhood depression are unknown, but depressed children tend to come from families with high levels of parental depression, anxiety, substance abuse, or antisocial behavior. The atmosphere in such families may increase children's risk of depression (Cicchetti & Toth, 1998; USDHHS, 1999b).

Researchers have found several specific genes related to depression. One gene, *5-HTT,* helps to control the brain chemical serotonin and affects mood. In a longitudinal study of 847 people born in the same year in Dunedin, New Zealand, those who had two short versions of this gene were more likely to become depressed than those who had two long versions (Caspi et al., 2003). A short form of another gene, *SERT-s,* which also controls serotonin, is associated with enlargement of the pulvinar, a brain region involved in negative emotions (Young et al., 2007).

Children as young as 5 or 6 can accurately report depressed moods and feelings that forecast later trouble, from academic problems to major depression and ideas of suicide (Ialongo, Edelsohn, & Kellam, 2001). Depression often emerges during the transition to middle school and may be related to stiffer academic pressures (Cicchetti & Toth, 1998), weak self-efficacy beliefs, and lack of personal investment in academic success (Rudolph, Lambert, Clark, & Kurlakowsky, 2001). Depression becomes more prevalent during adolescence.

TREATMENT TECHNIQUES

Psychological treatment for emotional disturbances can take several forms. In **individual psychotherapy,** a therapist sees a child one-on-one to help the child gain

individual psychotherapy
Psychological treatment in which a therapist sees a troubled person one-on-one.

family therapy
Psychological treatment in which a therapist sees the whole family together to analyze patterns of family functioning.

behavior therapy
Therapeutic approach using principles of learning theory to encourage desired behaviors or eliminate undesired ones; also called *behavior modification.*

art therapy
Therapeutic approach that allows a person to express troubled feelings without words, using a variety of art materials and media.

play therapy
Therapeutic approach that uses play to help a child cope with emotional distress.

drug therapy
Administration of drugs to treat emotional disorders.

insights into his or her personality and relationships and to interpret feelings and behavior. Such treatment may be helpful at a time of stress, such as the death of a parent or parental divorce, even when a child has not shown signs of disturbance. Child psychotherapy is usually more effective when combined with counseling for the parents.

In **family therapy,** the therapist sees the family together, observes how members interact, and points out both growth-producing and growth-inhibiting or destructive patterns of family functioning. Therapy can help parents confront their conflicts and begin to resolve them. This is often the first step toward resolving the child's problems as well.

Behavior therapy, or *behavior modification,* is a form of psychotherapy that uses principles of learning theory to eliminate undesirable behaviors or to develop desirable ones. A statistical analysis of many studies found that psychotherapy is generally effective with children and adolescents, but behavior therapy is more effective than nonbehavioral methods. Results are best when treatment is targeted to specific problems and desired outcomes (Weisz, Weiss, Han, Granger, & Morton, 1995). *Cognitive behavioral therapy,* which seeks to change negative thoughts through gradual exposure, modeling, rewards, or talking to oneself, has proven the most effective treatment for anxiety disorders in children and adolescents (Harvard Medical School, 2004a).

When children have limited verbal and conceptual skills or have suffered emotional trauma, **art therapy** can help them describe what is troubling them without the need to put their feelings into words. The child may express deep emotions through his or her choice of colors and subjects to depict (Kozlowska & Hanney, 1999).

In play therapy, the therapist observes as a child acts out troubled feelings, often using developmentally appropriate materials such as dolls.

Play therapy, in which a child plays freely while a therapist occasionally comments, asks questions, or makes suggestions, has proven effective with a variety of emotional, cognitive, and social problems, especially when consultation with parents or other close family members is part of the process (Athansiou, 2001; Bratton & Ray, 2002; Leblanc & Ritchie, 2001; Ryan & Needham, 2001).

The use of **drug therapy**—antidepressants, stimulants, tranquilizers, or antipsychotic medications—to treat childhood emotional disorders is controversial. During the past decade the rate at which antipsychotic medications are prescribed for children and adolescents has more than quintupled (Olfson, Blanco, Liu, Moreno, & Laje, 2006). For example, from 1999 to 2001 approximately 1 in 650 children were receiving antipsychotic medications; this number rose to 1 in 329 for 2007 (Olfson, Crystal, Huang, & Gerhard, 2010). Sufficient research on the effectiveness and safety of many of these drugs, especially for children, is lacking.

The use of *selective serotonin reuptake inhibitors (SSRIs)* to treat obsessive-compulsive, depressive, and anxiety disorders increased rapidly in the 1990s (Leslie et al., 2005) but has since slipped by about 20 percent (Daly, 2005). Some studies show moderate risks of suicidal thought and behavior for children and adolescents taking antidepressants, whereas others show no significant added risk (Hammad, Laughren, & Racoosin, 2006; Simon, Savarino, Operskalski, & Wang, 2006) or lessened risk (Simon, 2006). An analysis of 27 randomized, placebo-controlled studies found that the benefits of antidepressant use for children and adolescents outweigh the risks (Bridge et al., 2007).

checkpoint
can **you**...

- Discuss causes, symptoms, and treatments of common emotional disorders?

STRESS AND RESILIENCE

Stressful events are part of childhood, and most children learn to cope. Stress that becomes overwhelming, however, can lead to psychological problems. Severe stressors, such as war or child abuse, may have long-term effects on physical and psychological well-being. Yet some individuals show remarkable resilience in surmounting such ordeals.

Stresses of Modern Life The child psychologist David Elkind (1981, 1986, 1997, 1998) has called today's child the "hurried child." He warns that the pressures of modern life are forcing children to grow up too soon and are making their childhood too stressful. Today's children are expected to succeed in school, to compete in sports, and to meet parents' emotional needs. Children are exposed to many adult problems on television and in real life before they have mastered the problems of childhood. They know about sex and violence, and they often must shoulder adult responsibilities. Many children move frequently and have to change schools and leave old friends. The tightly scheduled pace of life can be stressful. Yet children are not small adults. They feel and think like children, and they need the years of childhood for healthy development.

Parents who are burned out at work are more likely to have kids who report they are burned out at school.

Salmela-Aro, Tynkkynen, & Vuori, 2010

Given how much stress children are exposed to, it should not be surprising that anxiety in childhood has increased greatly (Twenge, 2000). Fears of danger and death are the most consistent fears of children at all ages (Gullone, 2000; Silverman, La Greca, & Wasserstein, 1995). This intense anxiety about safety may reflect the high rates of crime and violence in the larger society—including the presence of street gangs and violence in some schools.

Findings about children's fears have been corroborated in a wide range of developed and developing societies. Poor children tend to be more fearful than children of higher socioeconomic status (Gullone, 2000; Ollendick, Yang, King, Dong, & Akande, 1996). Children who grow up constantly surrounded by violence often have trouble concentrating and sleeping. Some become aggressive, and some come to take brutality for granted. Many do not allow themselves to become attached to other people for fear of more hurt and loss (Garbarino, Dubrow, Kostelny, & Pardo, 1992, 1998).

Children are more susceptible than adults to psychological harm from a traumatic event such as war or terrorism, and their reactions vary with age (Wexler, Branski, & Kerem, 2006; Table 2). Younger children, who do not understand why the event occurred, tend to focus on the consequences. Older children are more aware of, and worried about, the underlying forces that caused the event (Hagan et al., 2005).

The impact of a traumatic event is influenced by the type of event, how much exposure children have to it, and how much they and their families and friends are personally affected. Human-caused disasters, such as terrorism and war, are much harder on children psychologically than natural disasters, such as earthquakes and floods. Exposure to graphic news coverage can worsen the effects (Wexler et al., 2006).

TABLE 2 Children's Age-Related Reactions to Trauma

Age	Typical Reactions
5 years or less	Fear of separation from parent; crying, whimpering, screaming, trembling; immobility or aimless motion; frightened facial expressions; excessive clinging; regressive behaviors (thumbsucking, bed-wetting, fear of dark)
6 to 11 years	Extreme withdrawal; disruptive behavior; inability to pay attention; stomachaches or other symptoms with no physical basis; declining school performance, refusal to go to school; depression, anxiety, guilt, irritability, or emotional numbing; regressive behavior (nightmares, sleep problems, irrational fears, outbursts of anger or fighting)
12 to 17 years	Flashbacks, nightmares; emotional numbing, confusion; avoidance of reminders of the traumatic event; revenge fantasies; withdrawal, isolation; substance abuse; problems with peers, antisocial behavior; physical complaints; school avoidance, academic decline; sleep disturbances; depression, suicidal thoughts

Source: NIMH, 2001a.

research in action

TALKING TO CHILDREN ABOUT TERRORISM AND WAR

In today's world, caring adults are faced with the challenge of explaining violence, terrorism, and war to children. Although difficult, these conversations are extremely important. They give parents an opportunity to help their children feel more secure and better understand the world in which they live. Here are some pointers from the American Academy of Child & Adolescent Psychiatry:

2

1. *Listen to children.* Create a time and place for children to ask questions and help them express themselves. Sometimes children are more comfortable drawing pictures or playing with toys rather than talking about their feelings.
2. *Answer their questions.* When you answer tough questions about violence, be honest. Use words the child can understand, and try not to overload him or her with too much information. You may have to repeat yourself. Be consistent and reassuring.
3. *Provide support.* Children are most comfortable with structure and familiarity. Try to establish a predictable routine. Avoid exposure to violent images on TV and video games. Watch for physical signs of stress, such as trouble sleeping or separation anxiety, and seek professional help if symptoms are persistent and/or pronounced.

Many young children feel confused and anxious when faced with the realities of war and terrorism. By creating an open environment where children are free to ask questions and receive honest, consistent, and supportive messages about how to cope with violence, caring adults can reduce the likelihood of emotional difficulties.

Source: Adapted from American Academy of Child & Adolescent Psychiatry (2003).

How might you respond to a 6-year-old who asked you about what happened on September 11, 2001?

Most children who watched news coverage of the September 11, 2001, terrorist attacks on New York and Washington, D.C., experienced profound stress, even if they were not directly affected (Walma van der Molen, 2004).

Children's responses to a traumatic event typically occur in two stages: *first,* fright, disbelief, denial, grief, and relief if their loved ones are unharmed; *second,* several days or weeks later, developmental regression and signs of emotional distress—anxiety, fear, withdrawal, sleep disturbances, pessimism about the future, or play related to themes of the event. If symptoms last for more than a month, the child should receive counseling (Hagan et al., 2005).

For some children, the effects of a traumatic event may remain for years. Children who have been exposed to war or terrorism have high rates of depression, disruptive behaviors, and unexplained, recurring physical symptoms such as stomach distress and headaches. If they and their household have been personally affected, physical pain and loss of home and family may compound the psychological effects (Wexler et al., 2006). Parents' responses to a violent event or disaster and the way they talk with a child about it strongly influence the child's ability to recover (NIMH, 2001a). Providing parents with strategies for addressing terrorism-related news can reduce threat perceptions and lower anxiety related to potential terrorism attacks (Comer, Furr, Beidas, Weiner, & Kendall, 2008; Box 2). Unfortunately, parents tend to underestimate the amount of stress their children are experiencing (APA, 2009) and thus miss opportunities to intervene.

Coping with Stress: The Resilient Child Liz Murray grew up in abject poverty in a small apartment in the Bronx. Both her parents were drug addicts, and her childhood

TABLE 3 Characteristics of Resilient Children and Adolescents

Source	Characteristic
Individual	Good intellectual functioning Appealing, sociable, easygoing disposition Self-efficacy, self-confidence, high self-esteem Talents Faith
Family	Close relationship to caring parent figure Authoritative parenting: warmth, structure, high expectations Socioeconomic advantages Connections to extended supportive family networks
Extrafamilial context	Bonds to prosocial adults outside the family Connections to prosocial organizations Attending effective schools

Source: Masten & Coatsworth, 1998, p. 212.

was marked by poverty, hunger, and chaos. She was teased in school for her dirty clothing, placed in a girls' home for cutting school, and at age 15 ran away from home and spent her nights sleeping on the subways and eating from trash bins. Most children, in this type of situation, would spiral down into a life of further misery. But Liz did not. She was able to realize that education was her ticket to freedom and finished high school while living on the streets. She won a *New York Times* scholarship and was eventually admitted to Harvard. In 2011, she became an author when she published a memoir of her brief but tumultuous life on the streets.

Much of the early history of psychology was marked by investigations into the various risks that can pull a child into a negative developmental trajectory. However, psychologists have increasingly come to realize that there is also value in examining resilience. **Resilient children,** like Liz Murray, are those who weather circumstances that might blight others, who maintain their composure and competence under challenge or threat, or who bounce back from traumatic events. The two most important **protective factors** that help children and adolescents overcome stress and contribute to resilience are *good family relationships* and *cognitive functioning* (Masten & Coatsworth, 1998; see Table 3).

resilient children
Children who weather adverse circumstances, function well despite challenges or threats, or bounce back from traumatic events.

protective factors
Influences that reduce the impact of early stress and tend to predict positive outcomes.

Resilient children also tend to have high IQs and to be good problem solvers, and their cognitive ability may help them cope with adversity, protect themselves, regulate their behavior, and learn from experience. They may attract the interest of teachers, who can act as guides, confidants, or mentors (Masten & Coatsworth, 1998). They may even have protective genes, which may buffer the effects of an unfavorable environment (Caspi et al., 2002; Kim-Cohen et al., 2004).

Other frequently cited protective factors include the following (Ackerman, Kogos, Youngstrom, Schoff, & Izard, 1999; Eisenberg et al., 2004; Masten & Coatsworth, 1998; E. E. Werner, 1993):

- *The child's temperament or personality:* Resilient children are adaptable, friendly, well liked, independent, and sensitive to others. They are competent and have high self-esteem. When under stress, they can regulate their emotions by shifting attention to something else.
- *Compensating experiences:* A supportive school environment or successful experiences in studies, sports, or music or with other children or adults can help make up for a destructive home life.
- *Reduced risk:* Children who have been exposed to only one of a number of factors for psychiatric disorder (such as parental discord, a disturbed

checkpoint can you . . .

- Explain Elkind's concept of the "hurried child"?
- Name the most common sources of fear, stress, and anxiety in children?
- Identify protective factors that contribute to resilience?

mother, a criminal father, and experience in foster care) are often better able to overcome stress than children who have been exposed to more than one risk factor.

This does not mean that bad things that happen in a child's life do not matter. In general, children with unfavorable backgrounds have more adjustment problems than children with more favorable backgrounds, and even some outwardly resilient children may suffer internal distress that may have long-term consequences (Masten & Coatsworth, 1998). Still, what is heartening about these findings is that negative childhood experiences do not necessarily determine the outcome of a person's life and that many children have the strength to rise above the most difficult circumstances.

summary and key terms

The Developing Self

- The self-concept becomes more realistic during middle childhood, when, according to a neo-Piagetian model, children form representational systems.
- According to Erikson, the chief source of self-esteem is children's view of their productive competence. This virtue develops through resolution of the fourth psychosocial conflict, industry versus inferiority.
- School-age children have internalized shame and pride and can better understand and regulate negative emotions.
- Empathy and prosocial behavior increase.
- Emotional growth is affected by parents' reactions to displays of negative emotions.
- Emotional regulation involves effortful control.

representational systems
industry versus inferiority

The Child in the Family

- School-age children spend less time with parents and are less close to them than before, but relationships with parents continue to be important. Culture influences family relationships and roles.
- The family environment has two major components: family structure and family atmosphere.
- The emotional tone of the home, the way parents handle disciplinary issues and conflict, the effects of parents' work, and the adequacy of financial resources all contribute to family atmosphere.
- Development of coregulation may affect the way a family handles conflicts and discipline.
- The impact of mothers' employment depends on many factors concerning the child, the mother's work and her feelings about it, whether she has a supportive partner, the family's socioeconomic status, and the type of care and degree of monitoring the child receives.
- Poverty can harm children's development indirectly through its effects on parents' well-being and parenting practices.
- Many children today grow up in nontraditional family structures. Other things being equal, children tend to do better in traditional two-parent families than in cohabiting, divorced, single-parent, or stepfamilies. The structure of the family, however, is less important than its effects on family atmosphere.
- Children's adjustment to divorce depends on factors concerning the child, the parents' handling of the situation, custody and visitation arrangements, financial circumstances, contact with the noncustodial parent (usually the father), and a parent's remarriage.
- The amount of conflict in a marriage and the likelihood of its continuing after divorce may influence whether children are better off if the parents stay together.
- In most divorces the mother gets custody, though paternal custody is a growing trend. Quality of contact with a noncustodial father is more important than frequency of contact.
- Joint custody can be beneficial to children when the parents can cooperate. Joint legal custody is more common than joint physical custody.
- Although parental divorce increases the risk of long-term problems for children, most adjust reasonably well.
- Children living with only one parent are at heightened risk of behavioral and academic problems, largely related to socioeconomic status.
- Studies have found positive developmental outcomes in children living with gay or lesbian parents.
- Adopted children are generally well adjusted, though they face special challenges.

- The roles and responsibilities of siblings in nonindustrialized societies are more structured than in industrialized societies.
- Siblings learn about conflict resolution from their relationships with each other. Relationships with parents affect sibling relationships.

internalizing behaviors
externalizing behaviors
coregulation

The Child in the Peer Group

- The peer group becomes more important in middle childhood. Peer groups generally consist of children who are similar in age, sex, ethnicity, and socioeconomic status and who live near one another or go to school together.
- The peer group helps children develop social skills, allows them to test and adopt values independent of parents, gives them a sense of belonging, and helps develop their self-concept and gender identity. It also may encourage conformity and prejudice.
- Popularity in middle childhood tends to influence future adjustment. It can be measured sociometrically or by perceived social status, and the results may differ. Popular children tend to have good cognitive abilities and social skills. Behaviors that affect popularity may be derived from family relationships and cultural values.
- Intimacy and stability of friendships increase during middle childhood. Boys tend to have more friends, whereas girls tend to have closer friends.
- During middle childhood, aggression typically declines. Instrumental aggression generally gives way to hostile aggression, often with a hostile bias. Highly aggressive children tend to be unpopular but may gain in status as children move into adolescence.
- Aggressiveness is promoted by exposure to media violence and can extend into adult life.
- Middle childhood is a prime time for bullying, but patterns of bullying and victimization may be established much earlier. Victims tend to be weak and submissive or argumentative and provocative and to have low self-esteem.

prejudice
hostile attribution bias
bullying

Mental Health

- Common emotional and behavioral disorders among school-age children include disruptive behavioral disorders, anxiety disorders, and childhood depression.
- Treatment techniques include individual psychotherapy, family therapy, behavior therapy, art therapy, play therapy, and drug therapy. Often therapies are used in combination.
- As a result of the pressures of modern life, many children experience stress. Children tend to worry about school, health, and personal safety and may be traumatized by exposure to terrorism or war.
- Resilient children are better able than others to withstand stress. Protective factors involve family relationships, cognitive ability, personality, degree of risk, and compensating experiences.

oppositional defiant disorder (ODD)
conduct disorder (CD)
school phobia
separation anxiety disorder
social phobia
generalized anxiety disorder
obsessive-compulsive disorder (OCD)
childhood depression
individual psychotherapy
family therapy
behavior therapy
art therapy
play therapy
drug therapy
resilient children
protective factors

part 5
ADOLESCENCE

chapter 11

Physical and Cognitive Development in Adolescence

outline

learning objectives

Discuss the nature of adolescence.

Describe the changes involved in puberty, as well as the changes in the adolescent brain.

Identify adolescent problems related to health.

Explain cognitive changes in adolescence.

Summarize key aspects of how schools influence adolescent development.

did you know?

- Nearly half of U.S. adolescents have tried illegal drugs by the time they leave high school?
- Depression in young people sometimes looks like irritation or boredom?
- Participation in after-school activities is associated with academic achievement?

In this chapter, we describe the physical transformations of adolescence and how they affect young people's feelings. We look at the not-yet-mature adolescent brain and discuss health issues associated with this time of life. We examine the Piagetian stage of formal operations, information-processing skills, and linguistic and moral development. Finally, we explore educational and vocational issues.

Life would be infinitely happier if we could only be born at the age of eighty and gradually approach eighteen.

—Mark Twain, *American author and humorist,* 1835–1910

Adolescence: A Developmental Transition

This chapter focuses on processes that occur in the long period known as **adolescence**—a developmental transition that involves physical, cognitive, emotional, and social changes and takes varying forms in different social, cultural, and economic settings.

An important physical change is the onset of **puberty,** the process that leads to sexual maturity, or fertility—the ability to reproduce. Traditionally, adolescence and puberty were thought to begin at the same time, around age 13, but physicians in some Western societies now see pubertal changes well before age 10. In this book, we define adolescence roughly as encompassing the years between 11 and 19 or 20.

adolescence
Developmental transition between childhood and adulthood entailing major physical, cognitive, and psychosocial changes.

puberty
Process by which a person attains sexual maturity and the ability to reproduce.

ADOLESCENCE AS A SOCIAL CONSTRUCTION

Adolescence is not a clearly defined physical or biological category—it is a social construction. In other words, the concept of adolescence is in a sense "made up" by culture. In traditional and preindustrial cultures, children generally entered the adult world when they matured physically or when they began a vocational apprenticeship. In the Western world, adolescence was first recognized as a unique period in the life span in the twentieth century. Today adolescence is recognized globally, but it may take different forms in different cultures (Box 1).

The Myth of Adolescence

In most parts of the world, adolescence lasts longer and is less clear-cut than in the past. There are myriad reasons for this social change. First, puberty generally begins earlier, which means that the period of adolescence begins at a younger age than in the past. In addition, as the world becomes more driven by technology and information, the amount of training required to be eligible for higher-paying occupations has increased. Because of this and other factors, the period of adolescence has been extended upward as young adults tend to go to school for more years, delay marriage and childbirth, and settle into permanent careers later and less firmly than in the past.

ADOLESCENCE: A TIME OF OPPORTUNITIES AND RISKS

Any time of transition and change in the life span offers opportunities for both advances and risks. Adolescence is no different. It offers opportunities for growth in cognitive and social competence, autonomy, self-esteem, and intimacy. Young people who have supportive connections with parents, school, and community tend to develop in a positive, healthful way (Youngblade et al., 2007).

However, adolescence is also a time of risk, and adolescents in the United States today face hazards to their well-being, including death from accidents, homicide, and suicide (Eaton et al., 2008). Why is adolescence such a risky stage in the life span? Psychologists believe the tendency to engage in risky behaviors may reflect the immaturity of the adolescent brain. Nonetheless, teens can respond to messages about safety and responsibility.

window on the world

THE GLOBALIZATION OF ADOLESCENCE

1

Young people today live in a global neighborhood. Goods, information, electronic images, songs, entertainment, and fads sweep almost instantaneously around the planet. Western youth dance to Latin rhythms, Arabic girls draw their images of romance from Indian movies, and Maori youth listen to rap music.

Adolescence is no longer solely a Western phenomenon. Globalization and modernization have set in motion changes the world over, including urbanization, longer and healthier lives, reduced birthrates, and smaller families. Earlier puberty and later marriage are increasingly common. More women and fewer children work outside the home. The rapid spread of technologies has made knowledge a prized resource. Young people need more schooling and skills to enter the labor force. Together these changes result in an extended transitional phase between childhood and adulthood.

Puberty in less-developed countries traditionally was marked by initiation rites such as circumcision. Today adolescents in these countries are increasingly identified by their status as students removed from the working world of adults. In this changing world, new pathways are opening up for them. They are less apt to follow in their parents' footsteps and to be guided by their advice.

This does *not* mean that adolescence is the same the world over. In the United States, adolescents are spending less time with their parents and confiding in them less. In India, adolescents may wear Western clothing and use computers, but they maintain strong family ties, and their life decisions often are influenced by traditional Hindu values. In Niger and other African countries, obesity is considered beautiful.

In many non-Western countries, adolescent boys and girls live in two separate worlds. In parts of the Middle East, Latin America, Africa, and Asia, puberty brings more restrictions on girls, whose virginity must be protected to uphold family status and ensure girls' marriageability. Boys, on the other hand, gain more freedom and mobility, and their sexual exploits are tolerated by parents and admired by peers.

Puberty heightens preparation for gender roles, which, for girls in most parts of the world, means preparation for domesticity. In Laos, a girl may spend 2½ hours a day husking, washing, and steaming rice. In Istanbul, a girl must learn the proper way to serve tea when a suitor comes to call. Boys are expected to prepare for adult work and to maintain family honor, but adolescent girls in many less-developed countries, such as rural regions of China, do not go to school because the skills they would learn would be of no use after they married.

This traditional pattern is changing in some parts of the developing world. During the past quarter-century, the advent of public education has enabled more girls to go to school. Better-educated girls tend to marry later and have fewer children, enabling them to seek skilled employment in the new technological society.

Cultural change is complex; it can be both liberating and challenging. Today's adolescents are charting a new course, not always certain where it will lead.

Source: Larson & Wilson, 2004.

Despite the forces of globalization and modernization, preadolescent children in some less-developed societies still follow traditional paths. These 9-year-old schoolgirls in Tehran celebrate the ceremony of Taqlif, which marks their readiness to begin the religious duties of Islam.

Can you think of examples from your experience of how globalization affects adolescents?

Since the 1990s, adolescents are less likely to use alcohol, tobacco, or marijuana; to ride in a car without a seat belt or to ride with a driver who has been drinking; to carry weapons; to have sexual intercourse or to have it without condoms; or to attempt suicide (Centers for Disease Control and Prevention [CDC], 2012; Eaton et al., 2008). These positive trends increase the chance that young people will come through the adolescent years in good health.

Why do you think these encouraging trends are occurring among high school students in recent years?

checkpoint can you . . .

- Point out similarities and differences among adolescents in various parts of the world?
- Identify risky behavior patterns common during adolescence?

PHYSICAL DEVELOPMENT

Puberty

Puberty involves dramatic biological changes. These changes are part of a long, complex process of maturation that begins even before birth, and their psychological ramifications may continue into adulthood.

HOW PUBERTY BEGINS: HORMONAL CHANGES

The advent of puberty is not caused by any single factor. Rather, puberty results from a cascade of hormonal responses (Figure 1). First, the hypothalamus releases elevated

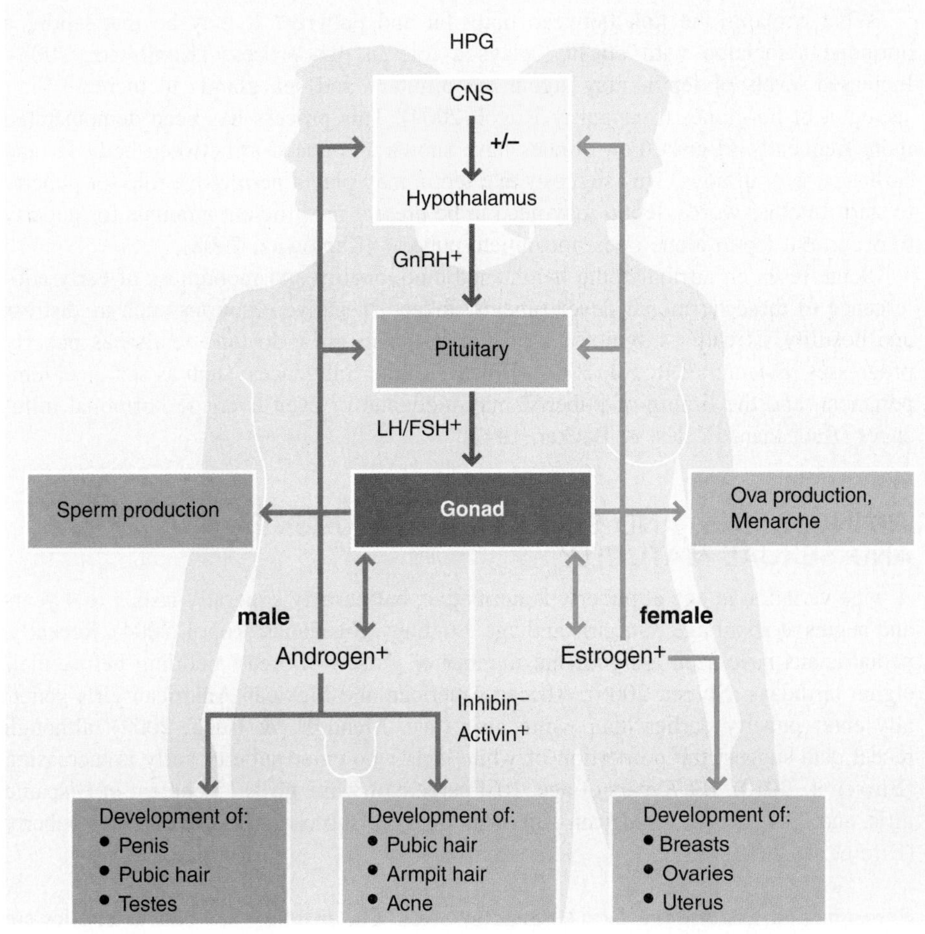

Source: Buck Louis et al., 2008.

FIGURE 1
Regulation of Human Puberty Onset and Progression

HPG (hypothalamuspituitary-gonadal) activation requires a signal from the central nervous system (CNS) to the hypothalamus, which stimulates the production of LH and FSH from the pituitary.

levels of gonadotropin releasing hormone (GnRH). The increased GnRH then triggers a rise in lutenizing hormone (LH) and follicle-stimulating hormone (FSH). These hormones exert their actions differentially on boys and girls. In girls, increased levels of FSH lead to the onset of menstruation. In boys, LH initiates the release of two additional hormones: testosterone and androstendione (Buck Louis et al., 2008).

Puberty can be broken down into two basic stages: adrenarche and gonadarche. Adrenarche occurs between ages 6 and 8. During this stage, the adrenal glands secrete increasing levels of androgens, most notably dehydroepiandrosterone (DHEA) (Susman & Rogol, 2004). Levels increase gradually but consistently, and by the time a child is 10 years of age, the levels of DHEA are 10 times what they were between ages 1 and 4. DHEA influences the growth of pubic, axillary (underarm), and facial hair. It also contributes to faster body growth, oilier skin, and the development of body odor.

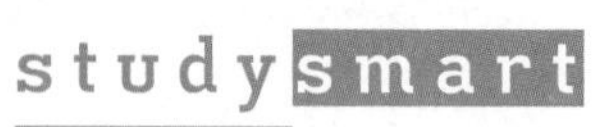

Puberty in Boys

Puberty in Girls

The second stage, gonadarche, is marked by the maturing of the sex organs, which triggers a second burst of DHEA production (McClintock & Herdt, 1996). During this time, a girl's ovaries increase their input of estrogen, which in turn stimulates the growth of female genitals, breasts, and the development of pubic and underarm hair. In boys, the testes increase the production of androgens, especially testosterone. This increase leads to the growth of male genitals, muscle mass, and body hair.

It is important to note that both boys and girls have both types of hormones, and that both types of hormones affect processes in children of both sexes. However, boys have more testosterone and girls have higher levels of estrogens.

What determines the timing of when puberty begins? One factor seems to be reaching a critical amount of body fat necessary for successful reproduction. When this level is hit at a younger age, puberty begins earlier. For example, girls who have a higher percentage of body fat in early childhood tend to show earlier pubertal development (Davison, Susman, & Birch, 2003; Lee et al., 2007).

What explains the link between body fat and puberty? It may be that leptin, a hormone associated with obesity, plays a role in this process (Kaplowitz, 2008). Increased levels of leptin may signal the pituitary and sex glands to increase their secretion of hormones (Susman & Rogol, 2004). This process has been demonstrated more frequently in girls. Few studies have shown a connection between body fat and earlier puberty in boys. This suggests that leptin may play a permissive role for puberty to start. In other words, leptin may need to be present in sufficient amounts for puberty to occur, but leptin alone does not initiate puberty (Kaplowitz, 2008).

Some research attributes the heightened emotionality and moodiness of early adolescence to these hormonal developments. Indeed, negative emotions such as distress and hostility, as well as symptoms of depression in girls, do tend to rise as puberty progresses (Susman & Rogol, 2004). However, other influences, such as sex, age, temperament, and the timing of puberty, may moderate or even override hormonal influences (Buchanan, Eccles, & Becker, 1992).

TIMING, SIGNS, AND SEQUENCE OF PUBERTY AND SEXUAL MATURITY

A wide variation in age at puberty is normative, but puberty generally lasts 3 to 4 years and begins at about age 8 in girls and age 9 in boys (Susman & Rogol, 2004). Recently, pediatricians have seen a significant number of girls with breast budding before their eighth birthdays (Slyper, 2006). African American and Mexican American girls generally enter puberty earlier than white girls (Wu, Mendola, & Buck, 2002), although recent data suggest the proportion of white girls who enter puberty early is increasing (Biro et al., 2010). By 7 years of age, 10.4 percent of white girls, 15 percent of Hispanic girls, and 23.4 percent of African American girls are showing signs of entering puberty (Biro et al., 2010).

primary sex characteristics
Organs directly related to reproduction, which enlarge and mature during adolescence.

Primary and Secondary Sex Characteristics The **primary sex characteristics** are the organs necessary for reproduction. In the female, the sex organs include the ovaries, fallopian tubes, uterus, clitoris, and vagina. In the male, they include the testes, penis, scrotum, seminal vesicles, and prostate gland. During puberty, these organs enlarge and mature.

The **secondary sex characteristics** are physiological signs of sexual maturation that do not directly involve the sex organs, for example, the breasts of females and the broad shoulders of males. Other secondary sex characteristics are changes in the voice and skin texture, muscular development, and the growth of pubic, facial, axillary, and body hair.

secondary sex characteristics Physiological signs of sexual maturation (such as breast development and growth of body hair) that do not involve the sex organs.

These changes unfold in a sequence that is much more consistent than their timing. One girl may develop breasts and body hair at about the same rate; in another girl, body hair may reach adultlike growth a year or so before breasts develop. Similar variations in pubertal status (degree of pubertal development) and timing occur among boys. Let's look more closely at these changes.

Signs of Puberty The first external signs of puberty typically are breast tissue and pubic hair in girls and enlargement of the testes in boys (Susman & Rogol, 2004). A girl's nipples enlarge and protrude, the *areolae* (the pigmented areas surrounding the nipples) enlarge, and the breasts assume first a conical and then a rounded shape. Some adolescent boys experience temporary breast enlargement, much to their distress; this development is normal and generally does not last longer than 18 months.

Pubic hair, at first straight and silky, eventually becomes coarse, dark, and curly. It appears in different patterns in males and females. Adolescent boys are usually happy to see hair on the face and chest; but girls are generally dismayed at the appearance of even a slight amount of hair on the face or around the nipples, though this, too, is normal.

The voice deepens, especially in boys, partly in response to the growth of the larynx and partly in response to the production of male hormones. The skin becomes coarser and oilier, giving rise to pimples and blackheads. Acne is more common in boys and seems related to increased amounts of testosterone.

The Adolescent Growth Spurt The **adolescent growth spurt**—a rapid increase in height, weight, and muscle and bone growth that occurs during puberty—generally begins in girls between ages 9½ and 14½ (usually at about 10) and in boys, between 10½ and 16 (usually at 12 or 13). It typically lasts about 2 years; soon after it ends, the young person reaches sexual maturity. Both growth hormone and the sex hormones (androgens and estrogen) contribute to this normal pubertal growth pattern (Susman & Rogol, 2004).

adolescent growth spurt Sharp increase in height and weight that precedes sexual maturity.

Because girls' growth spurt usually occurs 2 years earlier than that of boys, girls between ages 11 and 13 tend to be taller, heavier, and stronger than boys the same age. After their growth spurt, boys are again larger. Girls typically reach full height at age 15 and boys at age 17 (Gans, 1990).

Boys and girls grow differently, not only in rates of growth, but also in form and shape. A boy becomes larger overall: his shoulders wider, his legs longer relative to his trunk, and his forearms longer relative to his upper arms and his height. A girl's pelvis widens to make childbearing easier, and layers of fat accumulate under her skin, giving her a more rounded appearance. Fat accumulates twice as rapidly in girls as in boys (Susman & Rogol, 2004). Because each of these changes follows its own timetable, parts of the body may be out of proportion for a while.

These striking physical changes have psychological ramifications. Most young teenagers are more concerned about their appearance than about any other aspect of themselves, and some do not like what they see in the mirror. As we discuss in a subsequent section, these attitudes can sometimes lead to eating problems.

Most girls experience a growth spurt 2 years earlier than most boys, so between ages 11 and 13 girls tend to be taller, heavier, and stronger than boys the same age.

Signs of Sexual Maturity: Sperm Production and Menstruation The maturation of the reproductive organs brings the beginning of menstruation in girls and the production of sperm in boys. The principal sign of sexual maturity in boys is the production of sperm. The first ejaculation, or **spermarche,** occurs at an average age of 13. A boy may wake up to find a wet spot or a hardened, dried spot on the sheets—the result of a *nocturnal emission,* an involuntary ejaculation of semen (commonly referred to as a *wet dream*). Most adolescent boys have these emissions, sometimes in connection with an erotic dream.

spermarche
Boy's first ejaculation.

The principal sign of sexual maturity in girls is *menstruation,* a monthly shedding of tissue from the lining of the womb. The first menstruation, called **menarche,** occurs fairly late in the sequence of female development; its normal timing can vary from age 10 to 16½. The average age of menarche in U.S. girls fell from greater than 14 years before 1900 to 12½ years in the 1990s. On average, black girls experience menarche 6 months earlier than white girls (S. E. Anderson, Dallal, & Must, 2003).

menarche
Girl's first menstruation.

Influences on and Effects of Timing of Puberty On the basis of historical sources, developmental scientists have found a **secular trend**—a trend that spans several generations—in the onset of puberty: a drop in the ages when puberty begins and when young people reach adult height and sexual maturity. The trend, which also involves increases in adult height and weight, began about 100 years ago. It has occurred in such places as the United States, Western Europe, and Japan (S. E. Anderson et al., 2003).

secular trend
Trend that can be seen only by observing several generations, such as the trend toward earlier attainment of adult height and sexual maturity, which began a century ago in some countries.

One proposed explanation for the secular trend is a higher standard of living. Children who are healthier, better nourished, and better cared for might be expected to mature earlier and grow bigger (Slyper, 2006). Thus the average age of sexual maturity is earlier in developed countries than in developing countries. Because of the role of body fat in triggering puberty, a contributing factor in the United States during the last part of the twentieth century may have been the increase in obesity among young girls (S. E. Anderson et al., 2003; Lee et al., 2007).

A combination of genetic, physical, emotional, and contextual influences affect individual differences in timing of menarche. Twin studies have documented the heritability of age of menarche (Mendle et al., 2006), and further support for genetic influences is illustrated by the finding that the age of a girl's first menstruation tends to be similar to that of her mother's (Maisonet et al., 2010) if nutrition and standards of living remain stable from one generation to the next (Susman & Rogol, 2004). But genetics are not the only influence. With respect to mothers, studies have shown that earlier menarche is associated with maternal smoking during pregnancy and being the firstborn child (Maisonet et al., 2010) as well as single motherhood (Belsky, Steinberg et al., 2007; Ellis, McFadyen-Ketchum, Dodge, Pettit, & Bates, 1999) and harsh maternal parenting practices (Belsky, Steinberg, Houts, & Halpern-Felsher, 2010). Fathers also play a role. Girls with highly affectionate or involved fathers (Belsky, Steinberg et al., 2007; Mendle et al., 2006) or close supportive relationships with their fathers (Belsky, Steinberg et al., 2007; Ellis et al., 1999) tend to reach menarche later than girls from conflictual homes or who are separated from their fathers (Tither & Ellis, 2008).

Did you mature early, late, or "on time"? How did you feel about the timing of your maturation?

What difference, if any, does timing of puberty make to psychological well-being? It depends on how the adolescent and others interpret the accompanying changes. Effects of early or late maturation are most likely to be negative when adolescents are much more or less developed than their peers; when they do not see the changes as advantageous; and when several stressful events, such as the advent of puberty and the transition to junior high school, occur at about the same time (Petersen, 1993; Simmons, Blyth, & McKinney, 1983). Contextual factors such as ethnicity, school, and neighborhood can make a difference. For example, early-maturing girls are more likely to engage in sexual risk taking (Belsky et al., 2010); and they show more problem behavior in mixed-gender schools than in all-girl schools, and in disadvantaged urban communities than in rural or middle-class urban communities (Caspi, Lynam, Moffitt, & Silva, 1993; Dick, Rose, Kaprio, & Viken, 2000; Ge, Brody, Conger, Simons, & Murry, 2002).

checkpoint
can you . . .

- Tell how puberty begins and how its timing and length vary?
- Describe typical pubertal changes in boys and girls, and identify factors that affect psychological reactions to these changes?

The Adolescent Brain

Pubertal Brain Development

Not long ago, most scientists believed that the brain was fully mature by puberty. However, the adolescent brain is still a work in progress. Dramatic changes in brain structures involved in emotions, judgment, organization of behavior, and self-control take place between puberty and young adulthood (Figure 2). The immaturity of the adolescent brain has raised questions about the extent to which adolescents can reasonably be held legally responsible for their actions (Steinberg & Scott, 2003), prompting the U.S. Supreme Court in 2005 to rule the death penalty unconstitutional for a convicted murderer who was 17 or younger when the crime was committed (Mears, 2005).

Risk-taking appears to result from the interaction of two brain networks: (1) a *socio-emotional network* that is sensitive to social and emotional stimuli, such as peer influence, and (2) a *cognitive-control network* that regulates responses to stimuli. The socio-emotional network becomes more active at puberty, whereas the cognitive-control network matures more gradually into early adulthood. These findings may help explain teenagers' tendency toward emotional outbursts and risky behavior and why risk-taking often occurs in groups (Steinberg, 2007).

A great deal of brain development occurs during adolescence. One important change is a steady increase in white matter (nerve fibers that connect distant portions of the brain). This allows nerve impulses to be transmitted more rapidly and helps neurons synchronize their firing rate (Fields & Stephens-Graham, 2002), thus improving adolescents' information-processing abilities. This increase is most marked in the corpus callosum, a band of axon fibers that connects the two hemispheres of the brain. During adolescence this band thickens, leading to better communication between hemispheres (Geidd, 2008). This increase in white matter also occurs in the frontal, temporal, and parietal lobes (ACT for Youth, 2002; Blakemore & Choudhury, 2006; Kuhn, 2006; National Institute of Mental Health [NIMH], 2001b; Geidd, 2008).

The immaturity of these brain centers, and the consequent propensity to act impulsively and without fully considering consequences, are why some people take issue with the death penalty being applied against teenagers. Do you think this is a valid argument? Why or why not?

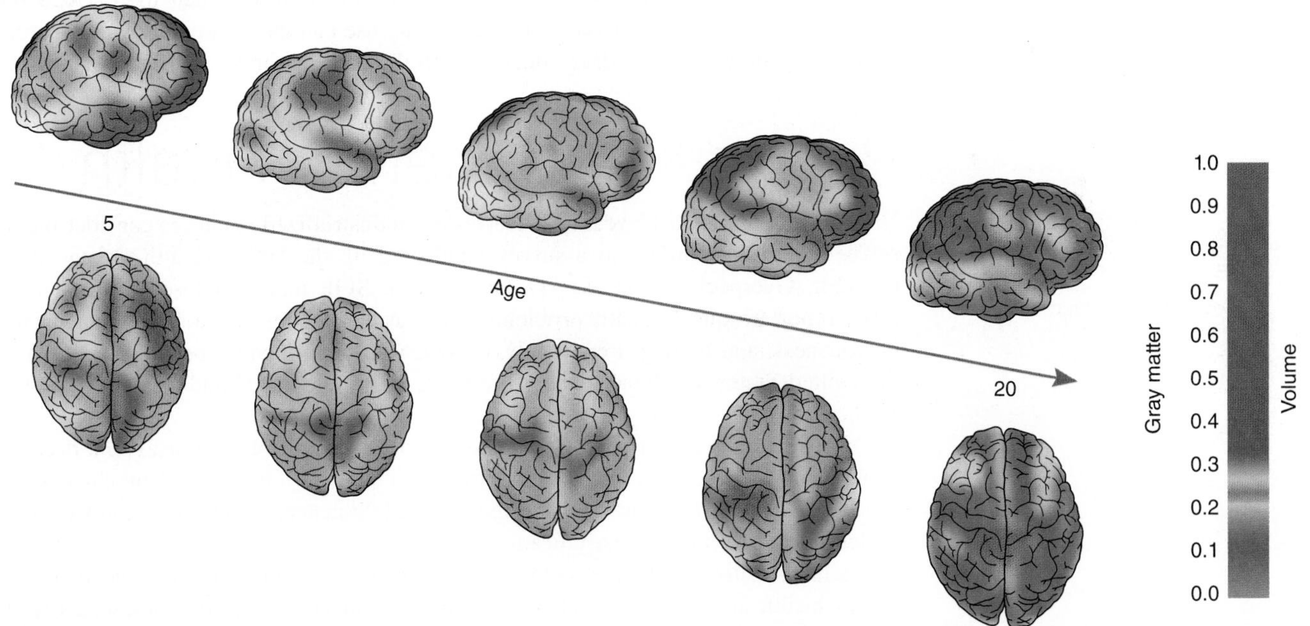

FIGURE 2

Brain Development from 5 to 15 Years of Age

Constructed from MRI scans of healthy children and teens, these images compress 15 years of brain development (ages 5–20). Red indicates more gray matter, blue less gray matter. Gray matter wanes in a back-to-front wave as the brain matures and neural connections are pruned.

Source: Gogtay et al., 2004.

There are also marked changes in gray matter composition. A major spurt in production of gray matter in the frontal lobes begins around puberty. After the growth spurt, the density of gray matter declines greatly, particularly in the prefrontal cortex, as unused synapses (connections between neurons) are pruned and those that remain are strengthened (Blakemore & Choudhury, 2006; Kuhn, 2006). This pruning process begins in the rear portions of the brain and moves forward, generally reaching the frontal lobes during adolescence. By middle to late adolescence young people have fewer but stronger, smoother, and more effective neuronal connections, making cognitive processing more efficient (Kuhn, 2006).

Changes in white and gray matter in the amygdala and prefrontal cortex may help explain why teens sometimes make bad choices based on their emotions rather than more reasoned choices based on logic and foresight. The amygdala, broadly, is involved with strong emotional reactions. It matures before the prefrontal cortex. The prefrontal cortex is involved with planning, reasoning, judgment, emotional regulation, and impulse control. The areas of the brain involved with feeling strong emotions mature prior to the area responsible for making thoughtful decisions (Nelson, Thomas, & deHann, 2006). This might explain some early adolescents' rash choices, such as substance abuse and sexual risk-taking. Immature brain development may permit feelings to override reason and may keep some adolescents from heeding warnings (Yurgelun-Todd, 2002). Underdevelopment of frontal cortical systems associated with motivation, impulsivity, and addiction may help explain why adolescents tend to seek thrills and novelty and why many of them find it hard to focus on long-term goals (Bjork et al., 2004; Chambers, Taylor, & Potenza, 2003).

checkpoint
can **you**...

- Describe two major changes in the adolescent brain?
- Identify immature features of the adolescent brain, and explain how this immaturity can affect behavior?

Because of the vast amount of brain development occurring during adolescence, events experienced at this time affect the shape that development takes. The neuronal connections are retained and strengthened, and this in turn supports further cognitive growth in those areas (Kuhn, 2006). Adolescents who "'exercise' their brains by learning to order their thoughts, understand abstract concepts, and control their impulses are laying the neural foundations that will serve them for the rest of their lives" (ACT for Youth, 2002, p. 1). Alternatively, adolescent drug use can have particularly devastating effects, depending on how drugs interact with the growing brain.

Physical and Mental Health

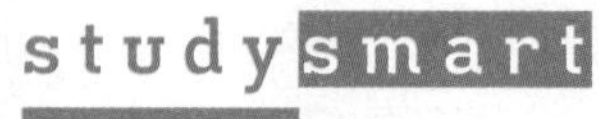

Motor Development

Nine out of ten 11- to 15-year-olds in Western industrialized countries consider themselves healthy, according to a survey conducted by the World Health Organization (Scheidt, Overpeck, Wyatt, & Aszmann, 2000). Still, many adolescents, especially girls, report frequent health problems, such as headache, backache, stomachache, nervousness, and feeling tired, lonely, or low. Such reports are especially common in the United States and Israel, where life tends to be fast paced and stressful (Scheidt et al., 2000).

Many health problems are preventable and stem from lifestyle choices. But because adolescents are generally healthy, they may not feel the effects of their choices for decades. Lifestyle patterns tend to solidify in adolescence, which may result in poor lifelong health habits and early death in adults.

In industrialized countries, adolescents from less affluent families tend to report poorer health and more frequent symptoms (Scheidt et al., 2000). Adolescents from more affluent families tend to have healthier diets and to be more physically active (Mullan & Currie, 2000). Let's look at several specific health concerns: physical fitness, sleep needs, eating disorders, drug abuse, depression, and causes of death in adolescence.

Exercise affects both physical and mental health. The benefits of regular exercise include improved strength and endurance, healthier bones and muscles, weight control, and reduced anxiety and stress, as well as increased self-esteem, school grades, and well-being. Even moderate physical activity has health benefits if done regularly for at least 30 minutes almost every day. A sedentary lifestyle may result in increased risk of obesity, type II diabetes, and an increased likelihood of heart disease and cancer in adulthood (Carnethon, Gulati, & Greenland, 2005; Centers for Disease Control and Prevention [CDC], 2000a; National Center for Health Statistics [NCHS], 2004; Nelson & Gordon-Larsen, 2006).

Unfortunately, only about one-third of U.S. high school students engage in the recommended amounts of physical activity, and the proportion of young people who are inactive increases throughout the high school years (Eaton et al., 2008). Adolescents show a steep drop in physical activity upon entering puberty, shifting from an average of 3 hours per day of physical activity at age 9 to an average of only 49 minutes of activity per day at age 15 (Nader et al., 2008). U.S. adolescents exercise less frequently than in past years and less than adolescents in most other industrialized countries (CDC, 2000a; Hickman et al., 2000).

Adolescents who engage in sports tend to feel better than those who do not.

SLEEP NEEDS AND PROBLEMS

Sleep deprivation among adolescents has been called an epidemic (Hansen, Janssen, Schiff, Zee, & Dubocovich, 2005). A national poll found that 45 percent of adolescents reported getting insufficient sleep, 31 percent were borderline, and only 20 percent slept the recommended amount (Wolfson, Carskadon, Mindell, & Drake, 2006).

Children generally go to sleep later and sleep less on school days the older they get. The average adolescent who slept more than 10 hours at night at age 9 sleeps less than 8 hours at age 16 (Eaton et al., 2008). Actually, adolescents need as much or more sleep than when they were younger (Hoban, 2004; Iglowstein et al., 2003). Sleeping in on weekends does not make up for the loss of sleep on school nights (Hoban, 2004). A pattern of late bedtimes and oversleeping in the mornings can contribute to insomnia, a problem that often begins in late childhood or adolescence (Hoban, 2004).

Although adolescents get less exercise, there is a ray of hope. The most popular extracurricular activity of children ages 12 to 17 years is sports.

Dye & Johnson, 2009

Sleep deprivation can sap motivation and cause irritability, and concentration and school performance can suffer. Sleepiness also can be deadly for adolescent drivers. Studies have found that young people ages 16 to 29 are most likely to be involved in crashes caused by the driver falling asleep (Millman et al., 2005).

Research has repeatedly shown that a short nap can help refresh a tired person. If you can't lie down in bed, the farther you can recline backward, the more restful your nap. And, if you can't lean backward, even putting your head down on an abandoned library table provides clear benefits over no nap at all.

Hayashi & Abe, 2008; Zhao, Zhang, Fu, Tang, & Zhao, 2010

Why do adolescents stay up late? They may need to do homework, want to talk to or text friends or surf the Web. However, sleep experts now recognize that biological changes are also behind adolescents' sleep problems (Sadeh et al., 2000). The timing of secretion of the hormone *melatonin* is a gauge of when the brain is ready for sleep. After puberty, this secretion takes place later at night (Carskadon, Acebo, Richardson, Tate, & Seifer, 1997). But adolescents still need just as much sleep as before; so when they go to bed later than younger children, they need to get up later as well. Yet most secondary schools start *earlier* than elementary schools. Their schedules are out of sync with students' biological rhythms (Hoban, 2004). Teenagers tend to be least alert and most stressed early in the morning and more alert in the afternoon (Hansen et al., 2005). Starting school later, or at least offering difficult courses later in the day, would help improve students' concentration (Crouter & Larson, 1998).

checkpoint can **you**...

- Summarize the status of adolescents' health?
- Explain the importance of physical activity?
- Tell why adolescents often get too little sleep?

NUTRITION AND EATING DISORDERS

Good nutrition is important to support the rapid growth of adolescence and to establish healthy eating habits that will last through adulthood. Unfortunately, U.S. adolescents eat fewer fruits and vegetables and consume more foods that are high in cholesterol, fat, and calories and low in nutrients than adolescents in other industrialized countries (American Heart Association et al., 2006). Deficiencies of calcium, zinc, and iron are common at this age (Bruner, Joffe, Duggan, Casella, & Brandt, 1996; Lloyd et al., 1993).

Worldwide, poor nutrition is most frequent in economically depressed or isolated populations but also may result from concern with body image and weight control (Vereecken & Maes, 2000). Eating disorders, including obesity, are most prevalent in industrialized societies, where food is abundant and attractiveness is equated with slimness; but these disorders appear to be increasing in non-Western countries as well (Makino, Tsuboi, & Dennerstein, 2004).

Obesity U.S. teens are about twice as likely to be overweight as their age-mates in 14 other industrialized countries, according to self-reports of height and weight from more than 29,000 boys and girls ages 13 and 15 (Lissau et al., 2004). About 34 percent of U.S. teens have a body mass index (BMI) at or above the 85th percentile for age and sex. The percentage of U.S. adolescents with BMIs at or above the 95th percentile more than tripled between 1980 and 2008, from 5 percent to nearly 18 percent (Ogden et al., 2010). Among older adolescents, obesity is 50 percent more prevalent in those from poor families (Miech et al., 2006). Mexican American girls and boys and non-Hispanic black girls, who tend to be poorer than their peers, are more likely to be overweight than non-Hispanic white adolescents (Hernandez & Macartney, 2008; NCHS, 2006; Ogden et al., 2010).

Overweight teenagers tend to be in poorer health than their peers and are more likely to have difficulty attending school or engaging in strenuous activity or personal care (Swallen, Reither, Haas, & Meier, 2005). They are at heightened risk of hypertension and diabetes (NCHS, 2005). One in 5 have abnormal lipid levels, including either too much bad cholesterol, too little good cholesterol, or high blood triglycerides (CDC, 2010). They tend to become obese adults, subject to a variety of physical, social, and psychological risks (Gortmaker, Must, Perrin, Sobol, & Dietz, 1993). Given how many adolescents are overweight today, one research team projects that by 2035 more than 100,000 additional cases of cardiovascular disease will be attributable to an increased prevalence of overweight in young and middle-aged men and women (Bibbins-Domingo, Coxson, Pletcher, Lightwood, & Goldman, 2007).

Genetic and other factors, such as faulty regulation of metabolism and, at least in girls, depressive symptoms and having obese parents can increase the likelihood of teenage obesity (Morrison et al., 2005; Stice, Presnell, Shaw, & Rohde, 2005). However some researchers have argued that lack of exercise is the *main* risk factor for overweight in boys and girls (Patrick et al., 2004).

Programs that use behavioral modification techniques to help adolescents make changes in diet and exercise have had some success. Dieting, for adolescents, may be counterproductive, however. In a 3-year study of 8,203 girls and 6,769 boys ages 9 to 14, those who dieted gained more weight than those who did *not* diet (A. E. Field et al., 2003).

body image
Descriptive and evaluative beliefs about one's appearance.

Body Image and Eating Disorders

Body Image and Eating Disorders Sometimes a determination *not* to become overweight can result in graver problems than overweight itself. A concern with **body image** may lead to obsessive efforts at weight control (Davison & Birch, 2001; Vereecken & Maes, 2000). This pattern is more common and less likely to be related to actual weight problems among girls than among boys.

Because of the normal increase in girls' body fat during puberty, many girls, especially if they are advanced in pubertal development, become unhappy about their appearance, reflecting the cultural emphasis on women's physical attributes (Susman & Rogol, 2004). Girls' dissatisfaction with their bodies increases during early to midadolescence, whereas boys, who are becoming more muscular, become more satisfied with their bodies (Feingold & Mazella, 1998; Rosenblum & Lewis, 1999). By age 15, more than half the girls sampled in 16 countries were dieting or thought they should be. The United States was at the top of the list, with 47 percent of 11-year-old girls and 62 percent of 15-year-old girls concerned about their weight (Vereecken & Maes, 2000). African American girls are generally more satisfied with their bodies and less concerned about weight and dieting than are white girls (Kelly, Wall, Eisenberg, Story, & Neumark-Sztainer, 2004; Wardle et al., 2004). According to a large prospective cohort study, parental attitudes and media images play a greater part than peer influences in encouraging weight concerns (A. E. Field et al., 2001).

Excessive concern with weight control and body image may be signs of *anorexia nervosa* or *bulimia nervosa,* both of which involve abnormal patterns of food intake. These chronic disorders occur worldwide, mostly in adolescent girls and young women. The idea that eating disorders are the result of cultural pressure to be thin is too simplistic; biological factors, including genetic factors, play an equally important role (Striegel-Moore & Bulik, 2007). Twin studies have found associations between eating disorders and the brain chemical serotonin; a variant of the protein BDNF, which influences food intake; and estrogen (Klump & Culbert, 2007). Table 1 outlines some of the risk factors and the symptoms for anorexia and bulimia.

TABLE 1 Eating Disorders: Risk Factors and Symptoms

RISK FACTORS	
• Accepting society's attitudes about thinness	
• Being a perfectionist	
• Being female	
• Experiencing childhood anxiety	
• Feeling increased concern or attention to weight and shape	
• Having eating and gastrointestinal problems during early childhood	
• Having a family history of addictions or eating disorders	
• Having parents who are concerned about weight and weight loss	
• Having a negative self-image	
SYMPTOMS	
Anorexia	**Bulimia**
• Using laxatives, enemas, or diuretics inappropriately in an effort to lose weight	• Abuse of laxatives, diuretics, or enemas to prevent weight gain
• Binge eating	• Binge eating
• Going to the bathroom right after meals	• Going to the bathroom right after meals
• Exercising compulsively	• Frequent weighing
• Restricting the amount of food eaten	• Self-induced vomiting
• Cutting food into small pieces	• Overachieving behavior
• Dental cavities due to self-induced vomiting	• Dental cavities due to self-induced vomiting
• Confused or slow thinking	
• Blotchy or yellow skin	
• Depression	
• Dry mouth	
• Extreme sensitivity to cold	
• Fine hair	
• Low blood pressure	
• No menstruation	
• Poor memory or poor judgment	
• Significant weight loss	
• Wasting away of muscle and loss of body fat	

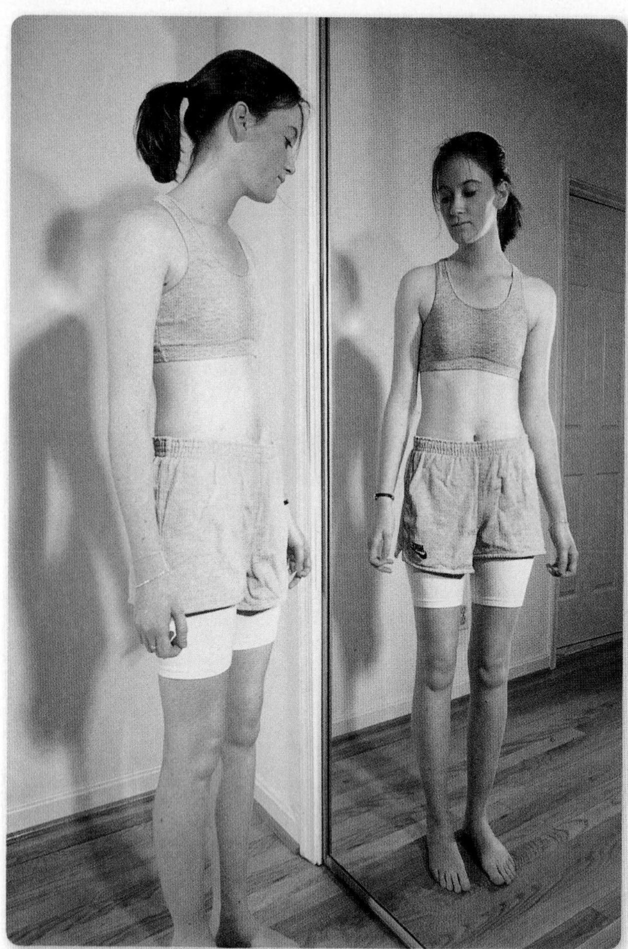

People with anorexia, such as this girl, have a distorted body image. They see themselves as fat even when they are emaciated.

Anorexia Nervosa **Anorexia nervosa,** or *self-starvation,* is potentially life threatening. An estimated 0.3 to 0.5 percent of adolescent girls and young women and a smaller but growing percentage of boys and men in Western countries are known to be affected. People with anorexia have a distorted body image and, though typically severely underweight, think they are too fat. They often are good students but may be withdrawn or depressed and may engage in repetitive, perfectionist behavior. They are extremely afraid of losing control and becoming overweight (AAP Committee on Adolescence, 2003; Wilson, Grilo, & Vitousek, 2007). Early warning signs include determined, secret dieting; dissatisfaction after losing weight; setting new, lower weight goals after reaching an initial desired weight; excessive exercising; and interruption of regular menstruation.

Anorexia is, paradoxically, both deliberate and involuntary: an affected person deliberately refuses food needed for sustenance, yet cannot stop doing so even when rewarded or punished. These behavior patterns have been traced back to medieval times and seem to have existed in all parts of the world. Thus anorexia may be, in part, a reaction to societal pressure to be slender, but this does not seem to be the only factor or even a necessary one (Keel & Klump, 2003; Striegel-Moore & Bulik, 2007).

Bulimia Nervosa **Bulimia nervosa** affects about 1 to 2 percent of international populations (Wilson et al., 2007). A person with bulimia regularly goes on huge, short-lived eating binges (2 hours or less) and then may try to purge the high caloric intake through self-induced vomiting, strict dieting or fasting, excessively vigorous exercise, or laxatives, enemas, or diuretics. These episodes occur at least twice a week for at least 3 months (American Psychiatric Association, 2000). People with bulimia are usually not overweight, but they are obsessed with their weight and shape. They tend to have low self-esteem and may become overwhelmed with shame, self-contempt, and depression (Wilson et al., 2007).

anorexia nervosa
Eating disorder characterized by self-starvation.

bulimia nervosa
Eating disorder in which a person regularly eats huge quantities of food and then purges the body by laxatives, induced vomiting, fasting, or excessive exercise.

A related *binge eating disorder* involves frequent binging but without subsequent fasting, exercise, or vomiting. Not surprisingly, people who binge frequently tend to be overweight and to experience emotional distress and other medical and psychological disorders. An estimated 3 percent of the population are binge eaters (Wilson et al., 2007).

There is some overlap between anorexia and bulimia; some people with anorexia have bulimic episodes, and some people with bulimia lose large amounts of weight ("Eating Disorders—Part I," 1997). Unlike anorexia, there is little evidence of bulimia either historically or in cultures not subject to Western influence (Keel & Klump, 2003).

Treatment and Outcomes of Eating Disorders The immediate goal of treatment for anorexia is to get patients to eat and gain weight—goals that are often difficult to achieve given the strength of patients' beliefs about their bodies. One widely used treatment is a type of family therapy in which parents take control of their child's eating patterns. When the child begins to comply with parental directives, she (or he) may be given more age-appropriate autonomy (Wilson et al., 2007). Cognitive behavioral therapy, which seeks to change a distorted body image and rewards eating with such privileges as being allowed to get out of bed and leave the room, may be part of the treatment (Beumont, Russell, & Touyz, 1993; Wilson et al., 2007). Patients who show signs of severe malnutrition, are resistant to treatment, or do not make progress on an outpatient basis may be admitted to a hospital, where they can be given 24-hour nursing. Once their weight is stabilized, patients may enter less intensive daytime care (McCallum & Bruton, 2003).

Bulimia, too, is best treated with cognitive behavioral therapy (Wilson et al., 2007). Patients keep daily diaries of their eating patterns and are taught ways to avoid the temptation to binge. Individual, group, or family psychotherapy can help both anorexia and bulimia patients, usually after initial behavior therapy has brought symptoms under control. Because these patients are at risk for depression and suicide, antidepressant drugs are often combined with psychotherapy (McCallum & Bruton, 2003), but evidence of their long-term effectiveness on either anorexia or bulimia is lacking (Wilson et al., 2007).

Adolescents, with their need for autonomy, may reject family intervention and may need the structure of an institutional setting. Still, any treatment program for adolescents must involve the family. It also must provide for adolescents' developmental needs, which may be different from the needs of adult patients, and must offer the opportunity to keep up with schooling (McCallum & Bruton, 2003).

Mortality rates among those affected with anorexia nervosa have been estimated at about 10 percent of cases. Among the surviving anorexia patients, less than one-half make a full recovery and only one-third actually improve; 20 percent remain chronically ill (Steinhausen, 2002). It should also be noted that up to one-third of patients drop out of treatment before achieving an appropriate weight (McCallum & Bruton, 2003). Recovery rates from bulimia are a bit better and average 30 to 50 percent after cognitive behavioral therapy (Wilson et al., 2007).

checkpoint
can **you**...

- Identify typical dietary deficiencies of adolescents?
- Discuss risk factors, effects, treatment, and prognoses for obesity, anorexia, and bulimia?

USE AND ABUSE OF DRUGS

Although the great majority of adolescents do not abuse drugs, a significant minority do. **Substance abuse** is harmful use of alcohol or other drugs. Abuse can lead to **substance dependence,** or *addiction,* which may be physiological, psychological, or both and is likely to continue into adulthood. Addictive drugs are especially dangerous because they stimulate parts of the brain that are still developing in adolescence (Chambers et al., 2003). About 12 percent of teens ages 13 to 17 will at some point receive treatment for alcohol use and more than 18 percent for illicit drug use (Substance Abuse and Mental Health Services Administration [SAMHSA], 2013a).

substance abuse
Repeated, harmful use of a substance, usually alcohol or other drugs.

substance dependence
Addiction (physical, or psychological, or both) to a harmful substance.

Substance Abuse

Trends in Drug Use Nearly half (47 percent) of U.S. adolescents have tried illicit drugs by the time they leave high school. An upsurge in drug use during the mid- to late 1990s accompanied a lessening of perceptions of its dangers and a softening of peer disapproval. However, that trend has begun to reverse. Student use of certain drugs, especially central nervous stimulants such as methamphetamine and cocaine, has shown a gradual decline. LSD, ecstacy, and psychoactive drugs such as vicodin have held steady, and use of marijuana and anabolic steroids have shown signs of increased usage.

These findings come from the latest in a series of annual government surveys of a nationally representative sample of 8th, 10th, and 12th graders from more than 400 schools across the United States (Johnston, O'Malley, Bachman, & Schulenberg, 2013; Figure 3). These surveys probably underestimate adolescent drug use because they are based on self-reports and do not reach high school dropouts, who are more likely to use drugs. Continued progress in eliminating drug abuse is slow because new drugs are continually introduced or rediscovered by a new generation, and young people do not necessarily generalize the adverse consequences of one drug to another (Johnston et al., 2013). Table 2 shows risk factors for teenage drug abuse.

A recent trend is the abuse of nonprescription cough and cold medications; 3 percent of 8th graders, 4.7 percent of 10th graders, and 5.6 percent of 12th graders report taking medicines containing dextromethorphan (DXM), a cough suppressant, to get high within the past year (Johnston et al., 2013).

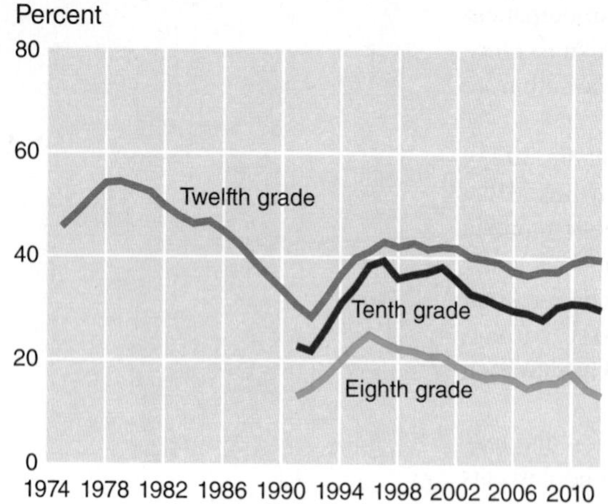

FIGURE 3

Trends in High School Students' Use of Illicit Drugs over the Previous 12 Months

Source: Johnston, O'Malley, Bachman, & Schulenberg, 2013.

binge drinking
Consuming five or more drinks on one occasion.

Alcohol, Marijuana, and Tobacco Alcohol and tobacco use among U.S. teenagers has followed a trend roughly parallel to that of harder drug use, with a dramatic rise during most of the 1990s followed by a smaller, gradual, decline. Marijuana has followed this same pattern for the most part, however its usage has shown an increase in recent years (Johnston et al., 2013). The impact of recent movements to legalize marijuana for recreational use, such as has happened in Colorado and Washington state, remains to be seen.

Alcohol use is a serious problem in many countries (Gabhainn & François, 2000). In 2012, 11 percent of U.S. 8th graders, 27 percent of 10th graders, and 42 percent of 12th graders said they had consumed alcohol at least once during the past 30 days (Johnston et al., 2013). The majority of high school students who drink engage in **binge drinking**—consuming five or more drinks on one occasion. About 25 percent of high school seniors admitted to binge drinking (McQueeny et al., 2009). A recent MRI-based study has revealed that binge drinking in teenagers may affect thinking and memory by damaging sensitive "white matter" in the brain (McQueeny et al., 2009). In a representative national study, binge drinkers were more likely than other students to report poor school performance and to engage in other risky behaviors (Miller, Naimi, Brewer, & Jones, 2007).

Adolescents are more vulnerable than adults to both immediate and long-term negative effects of alcohol on learning and memory (White, 2001). In one study, 15- and 16-year-old alcohol abusers who stopped drinking showed cognitive impairments weeks later in comparison with nonabusing peers (Brown, Tapert, Granholm, & Delis, 2000).

study smart

Attitudes about Drinking

TABLE 2 Risk Factors for Teenage Drug Abuse

What is the likelihood that a particular young person will abuse drugs? Risk factors include the following:
• A "difficult" temperament
• Poor impulse control and a tendency to seek out sensation (which may have a biochemical basis)
• Family influences (such as a genetic predisposition to alcoholism, parental use or acceptance of drugs, poor or inconsistent parenting practices, family conflict, and troubled or distant family relationships)
• Early and persistent behavior problems, particularly aggression
• Academic failure and lack of commitment to education
• Peer rejection
• Associating with drug users
• Alienation and rebelliousness
• Favorable attitudes toward drug use
• Early initiation into drug use
The more risk factors that are present, the greater the chance that an adolescent will abuse drugs.

Sources: Hawkins, Catalano, & Miller, 1992; Johnson, Hoffmann, & Gerstein, 1996; Masse & Tremblay, 1997; Wong et al., 2006.

Despite the decline in *marijuana* use since 1996–1997, it is still by far the most widely used illicit drug in the United States. In 2012, about 11 percent of 8th graders, 28 percent of 10th graders, and 36 percent of 12th graders admitted to having used it in the past year (Johnston et al., 2013).

Marijuana smoke typically contains more than 400 carcinogens, and its potency has doubled in the past 25 years (National Institute on Drug Abuse [NIDA], 2008). Heavy use can damage the brain, heart, lungs, and immune system and can cause respiratory infections, and other physical problems. It may lessen motivation, worsen depression, interfere with daily activities, and cause family problems. Marijuana use also can impede memory, thinking speed, learning, and school performance. Like any drug, if used while driving, it can contribute to traffic accidents (Messinis, Krypianidou, Maletaki, & Papathanasopoulos, 2006; Office of National Drug Control Policy, 2008; SAMHSA, 2006a).

In the United States, approximately 5 percent of 8th graders, 11 percent of 10th graders, and 17 percent of 12th graders are current (past-month) tobacco smokers (Johnston et al., 2013). Although this number is high and cause for concern, there is some good news. Smoking rates have declined one-third to more than one-half among 8th to 12th graders in the United States since the mid-1990s. And adolescent tobacco use is a less widespread problem in the United States than in most other industrialized countries (Gabhainn & Françoise, 2000). Research has indicated that nicotine replacement therapy in concert with behavioral skills training can be effective in helping adolescents stop smoking (Killen et al., 2004).

Marijuana is the most widely used illicit drug in the United States. Aside from its own ill effects, marijuana may lead to other addictions.

Substance use often begins when children enter middle school, where they become more vulnerable to peer pressure. Fourth to sixth graders may start using cigarettes, beer, and inhalants and, as they get older, move on to marijuana or harder drugs (National Parents' Resource Institute for Drug Education, 1999). The earlier young people start using a drug, the more frequently they are likely to use it and the greater their tendency to abuse it (Wong et al., 2006).

Although marijuana clearly has negative effects, there are also documented medical applications. For example, marijuana is an effective treatment for nausea in cancer patients, and it has been used to reduce ocular pressure in glaucoma patients.

The average age for starting to drink is 13 to 14, and some children start earlier. Young people who begin drinking early tend to have behavior problems or to have siblings who are alcohol dependent (Kuperman et al., 2005). Those who start drinking before age 15 are more than 5 times more likely to become alcohol dependent or alcohol abusers than those who do not start drinking until age 21 or later (SAMHSA, 2004a).

A number of states have enacted medical marijuana laws, and Colorado and Washington state have even decriminalized recreational use of marijuana. Should marijuana be legal?

Smoking often begins in the early teenage years as a sign of toughness, rebelliousness, and passage from childhood to adulthood. This desired image enables a young initiate to tolerate the initial distaste for the first few puffs, after which the effects of nicotine begin to take over to sustain the habit. Within a year or two after starting to smoke, these young people inhale the same amount of nicotine as adults and experience the same cravings and withdrawal effects if they try to quit. Young adolescents attracted to smoking often come from homes, schools, and neighborhoods where smoking is common.

Adolescents exposed to alcohol and drugs before the age of 15 demonstrate an increased risk for substance disorders (Hingson, Heeren, & Winter, 2006), risky sexual behavior (Stueve & O'Donnell, 2005), low educational attainment (King, Meehan, Trim, & Chassin, 2006), and crime. Though many adolescents who have been exposed to substances have a history of conduct problems, a recent study has shown that even children with no conduct-problem history were still at an increased risk for negative outcomes based on early exposure to alcohol and drugs (Odgers et al., 2008).

Peer influence on both smoking and drinking has been documented extensively (Center on Addiction and Substance Abuse [CASA] at Columbia University, 1996; Cleveland & Wiebe, 2003). As with hard drugs, the influence of older siblings and their

checkpoint
can **you** . . .

- Summarize recent trends in substance use among adolescents?
- Discuss risk factors and influences connected with use of drugs, specifically alcohol, marijuana, and tobacco?
- Tell why early initiation into substance use is dangerous?

friends increases the likelihood of tobacco and alcohol use (Rende, Slomkowski, Lloyd-Richardson, & Niaura, 2005).

Adolescents who believe that their parents disapprove of smoking are less likely to smoke (Sargent & Dalton, 2001). Rational discussions with parents can counteract harmful influences and discourage or limit drinking (Austin, Pinkleton, & Fujioka, 2000; Turrisi, Wiersman, & Hughes, 2000). However, parents also can be a negative influence. In a longitudinal study that compared 514 children of alcoholics with a matched control group, having an alcoholic parent significantly increased the risk of early alcohol use and later alcohol problems (Wong et al., 2006). The omnipresence of substance use in the media is another important influence. Movies that depict smoking increase early initiation of smoking (Charlesworth & Glantz, 2005).

DEPRESSION

The prevalence of depression increases during adolescence. An annual average of just over 8 percent of young people ages 12 to 17 have experienced at least one episode of major depression, and only about 39 percent of them had been treated (National Survey on Drug Use and Health [NSDUH], 2012). Rates generally increase with increasing age (Figure 4). Depression in young people does not necessarily appear as sadness but as irritability, boredom, or inability to experience pleasure. One reason depression needs to be taken seriously is the danger of suicide (Brent & Birmaher, 2002).

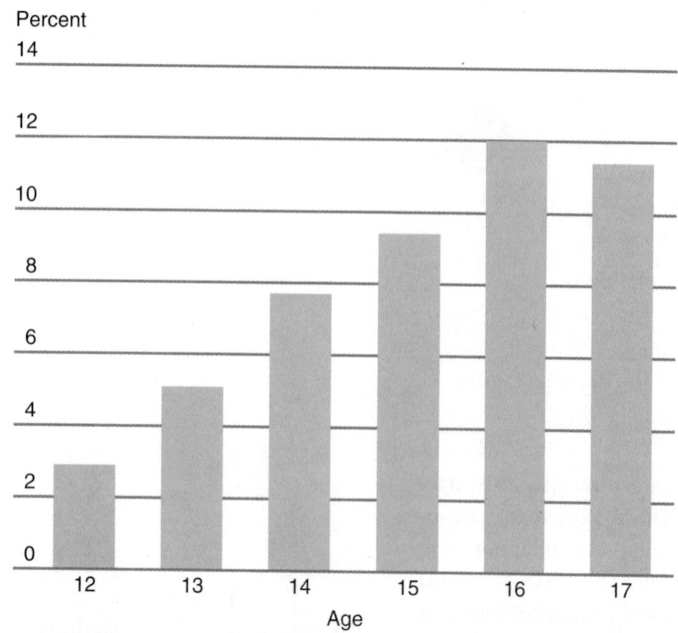

FIGURE 4
Depression Rates for 12- to 17-Year-Olds

Source: NSDUH, 2012.

Adolescent girls, especially early maturing girls, are more likely to be depressed than adolescent boys (Brent & Birmaher, 2002; NSDUH, 2012). This gender difference may be related to biological changes connected with puberty; studies show a correlation between advancing puberty status and depressive symptoms (Susman & Rogol, 2004). Other possible factors are the way girls are socialized (Birmaher et al., 1996) and their greater vulnerability to stress in social relationships (Hankin, Mermelstein, & Roesch, 2007).

In addition to female gender, risk factors for depression include anxiety, fear of social contact, stressful life events, chronic illnesses such as diabetes or epilepsy, parent-child conflict, abuse or neglect, alcohol and drug use, sexual activity, and having a parent with a history of depression. Alcohol and drug use and sexual activity are more likely to lead to depression in girls than in boys (Hallfors, Waller, Bauer, Ford, & Halpern, 2005; NSDUH, 2012; Waller et al., 2006). Body-image problems and eating disturbances can aggravate depressive symptoms (Stice & Bearman, 2001).

Depressed adolescents who do not respond to outpatient treatment or who have substance dependence or psychosis or seem suicidal may need to be hospitalized. At least 1 in 5 persons who experience bouts of depression in childhood or adolescence is at risk for bipolar disorder, in which depressive episodes ("low" periods) alternate with manic episodes ("high" periods) characterized by increased energy, euphoria, grandiosity, and risk-taking (Brent & Birmaher, 2002). Even adolescents with symptoms not severe enough for a diagnosis of depression are at elevated risk of clinical depression and suicidal behavior by age 25 (Fergusson, Horwood, Ridder, & Beautrais, 2005).

One treatment option for depression is psychotherapy; however, studies have found that although it can be effective in the short term, its effects last no more than a year (Weisz, McCarty, & Valeri, 2006). Selective serotonin reuptake inhibitors (SSRIs) are the only antidepressant medications currently approved for adolescents. Although

Playing Tetris can help ameliorate the flashbacks associated with posttraumatic stress disorder.

Holmes, James, Kilford, & Deeprose, 2010

concern about the safety of these medications has been expressed, research suggests that the benefits outweigh the risks (Bridge et al., 2007). In a major federally funded clinical trial, the most effective treatment for depressed adolescents was a combination of fluoxetine and cognitive behavioral therapy (March & the TADS Team, 2007).

This young girl might be sad or worried about grades or a relationship—normal worries for an adolescent. But if sadness persists along with symptoms such as the inability to concentrate, fatigue, apathy, or feelings of worthlessness, it might indicate depression.

DEATH IN ADOLESCENCE

Death this early in life is always tragic and usually accidental but not entirely so. In the United States, 63 percent of all deaths among adolescents result from motor vehicle crashes, other unintentional injuries, homicide, and suicide (National Highway Traffic Safety Administration [NHTSA], 2009; Figure 5). The frequency of violent deaths in this age group reflects a violent culture as well as adolescents' inexperience and immaturity, which often lead to risk-taking and carelessness.

Deaths from Vehicle Accidents and Firearms Motor vehicle collisions are the leading cause of death among U.S. teenagers, accounting for approximately one-third of all deaths in adolescence (Miniño, 2010). The risk of collision is greater among 16- to 19-year-olds than for any other age group and especially so among 16- and 17-year-olds who have recently started to drive (McCartt, 2001; Miniño, Anderson, Fingerhut, Boudreault, & Warner, 2006). Collisions are more likely to be fatal when teenage passengers are in the vehicle, probably because adolescents tend to drive more recklessly in the presence of peers (Chen, Baker, Braver, & Li, 2000). In the United States, 64 percent of all drivers or motorcycle operators ages 15 to 20 who were involved in fatal traffic crashes and had a blood alcohol level of .08 or higher died as a result of the crash, suggesting that alcohol is a major factor in accident-related fatalities. Despite efforts aimed at increasing seat belt use among teens, observed use among teens and young adults was 76 percent in 2006—the lowest of any age group. In fact, in 2006, 58 percent of young people 16 to 20 years old involved in fatal motor vehicle crashes were unbuckled (National Highway Traffic Safety Administration, 2009).

Firearm-related deaths of 15- to 19-year-olds (including homicide, suicide, and accidental deaths) are far more common in the United States than in other industrialized countries. They make up about one-third of all injury deaths and more than 85 percent of homicides in that age group. The chief reason for these grim statistics seems to be the ease of obtaining a gun in the United States (AAP Committee on Injury and Poison Prevention, 2000). However, youth death rates from firearms have declined since 1995 (NCHS, 2006) when police began confiscating guns on the street (T. B. Cole, 1999), and fewer young people have carried them (USDHHS, 1999b).

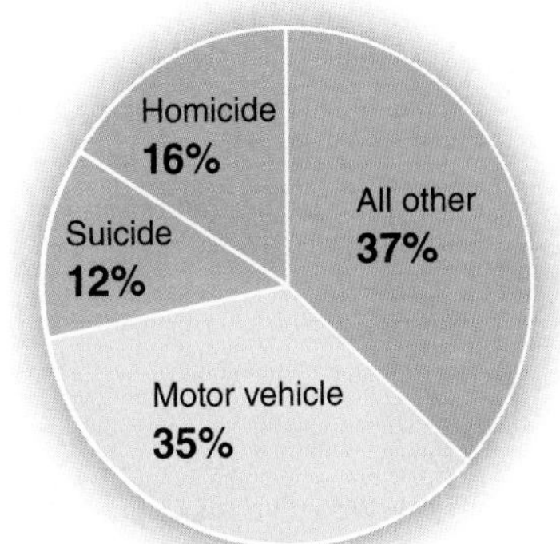

FIGURE 5

Leading Causes of Adolescent Deaths

In the United States, motor vehicle crashes are responsible for the greatest percentage of deaths among adolescents, followed by other unintentional injuries, homicide, and suicide.

Source: National Highway Traffic Safety Administration (NHTSA), 2009.

Suicide Suicide is the fourth leading cause of death among U.S. 15- to 19-year-olds (CDC, 2010; NHTSA, 2009). The teenage suicide rate fell by 34 percent between 1990 and 2006, perhaps in part due to restrictions on children's access to firearms (CDC, 2008c; Lubell, Swahn, Crosby, & Kegler, 2004). In 2004, however, the suicide rate did increase by 8 percent—its highest level in 15 years, with the largest increases among teenage girls. Hanging surpassed handguns as the preferred method among girls, but boys remained more likely to use firearms (Lubell, Kegler, Crosby, & Karch, 2007).

Although suicide occurs in all ethnic groups, Native American boys have the highest rates and African American girls the lowest. Gay, lesbian, and bisexual youths, who have high rates of depression, also have unusually high rates of suicide and attempted suicide (AAP Committee on Adolescence, 2000).

Young people who consider or attempt suicide tend to have histories of emotional illness. They are likely to be either perpetrators or victims of violence and to have school problems, academic or behavioral. Many have suffered from maltreatment in childhood and have severe problems with relationships. They tend to think poorly of themselves, to feel hopeless, and to have poor impulse control and a low tolerance for frustration checkpoint can **you**...

- Discuss factors affecting gender differences in adolescent depression?
- Name the three leading causes of death among adolescents, and identify risk factors for teenage suicide?

and stress. These young people are often alienated from their parents and have no one outside the family to turn to. They also tend to have attempted suicide before or to have friends or family members who did so (Borowsky, Ireland, & Resnick, 2001; Brent & Mann, 2006; Johnson et al., 2002; NIMH, 1999a; "Suicide—Part I," 1996). Alcohol plays a part in half of teenage suicides (AAP Committee on Adolescence, 2000). Perhaps the key factor is a tendency toward impulsive aggression. Imaging and postmortem studies of the brains of persons who have attempted or completed suicide have identified neurocognitive deficits in executive function, risk assessment, and problem solving (Brent & Mann, 2006). Protective factors that reduce the risk of suicide include a sense of connectedness to family and school, emotional well-being, and academic achievement (Borowsky et al., 2001).

COGNITIVE DEVELOPMENT

Aspects of Cognitive Maturation

Adolescents not only look different from younger children, they also think and talk differently. Their speed of information processing continues to increase. Although their thinking may remain immature in some ways, many are capable of abstract reasoning and sophisticated moral judgments and can plan more realistically for the future.

PIAGET'S STAGE OF FORMAL OPERATIONS

formal operations
Piaget's final stage of cognitive development, characterized by the ability to think abstractly.

Piaget's Formal Operations Substage

Adolescents enter what Piaget called the highest level of cognitive development—**formal operations**—when they move away from their reliance on concrete, real-world stimuli and develop the capacity for abstract thought. This development, usually around age 11, gives them a new, more flexible way to manipulate information. They can use symbols to represent other symbols (for example, letting the letter X stand for an unknown numeral) and thus can learn algebra and calculus. They can better appreciate the hidden messages in metaphor and allegory and thus can find richer meanings in literature. They can think in terms of what *might be,* not just what *is*. They can imagine possibilities and can form and test hypotheses.

The ability to think abstractly has emotional implications too. Whereas a young child could love a parent or hate a classmate, "the adolescent can love freedom or hate exploitation. . . . The possible and the ideal captivate both mind and feeling" (H. Ginsburg & Opper, 1979, p. 201).

hypothetical-deductive reasoning
Ability, believed by Piaget, to accompany the stage of formal operations, to develop, consider, and test hypotheses.

Hypothetical-Deductive Reasoning **Hypothetical-deductive reasoning** involves a methodical, scientific approach to problem solving, and it characterizes formal operations thinking. It involves the ability to develop, consider, and test hypotheses, and the young person can be compared to a scientist exploring a problem. To appreciate the difference formal reasoning makes, let's follow the progress of a typical child in dealing with a classic Piagetian problem, the pendulum problem.*

The child, Adam, is shown the pendulum—an object hanging from a string. He is then shown how he can change any of four factors: the length of the string, the weight of the object, the height from which the object is released, and the amount of force he may use to push the object. He is asked to figure out which factor or combination of factors determines how fast the pendulum swings.

*This description of age-related differences in the approach to the pendulum problem is adapted from H. Ginsburg & Opper, 1979.

When Adam first sees the pendulum, he is not yet 7 years old and is in the preoperational stage. Unable to formulate a plan for attacking the problem, he tries one thing after another in a hit-or-miss manner. First, he puts a light weight on a long string and pushes it; then he tries swinging a heavy weight on a short string; then he removes the weight entirely. Not only is his method random, but he also cannot understand or report what has happened.

Adam next encounters the pendulum at age 10, when he is in the stage of concrete operations. This time, he discovers that varying the length of the string and the weight of the object affects the speed of the swing. However, because he varies both factors at the same time, he cannot tell which is critical or whether both are.

Adam is confronted with the pendulum for a third time at age 15, and this time he goes at the problem systematically. He designs an experiment to test all the possible hypotheses, varying one factor at a time—first, the length of the string; next, the weight of the object; then, the height from which it is released; and finally, the amount of force used—each time holding the other three factors constant. In this way, he is able to determine that only one factor—the length of the string—determines how fast the pendulum swings.

Adam's solution of the pendulum problem shows that he has arrived at the stage of formal operations. He is now capable of hypothetical-deductive reasoning. He considers all the relationships he can imagine and tests them systematically, one by one, to eliminate the false and arrive at the true. Hypothetical-deductive reasoning gives him a tool to solve problems, from fixing the family car to constructing a political theory.

How can parents and teachers help adolescents improve their reasoning ability?

What brings about the shift to formal reasoning? Piaget attributed it to a combination of brain maturation and expanding environmental opportunities. Both are essential: even if young people's neurological development has advanced enough to permit formal reasoning, they can attain it only with appropriate stimulation.

As with the development of concrete operations, schooling and culture play a role, as Piaget (1972) ultimately recognized. When adolescents in New Guinea and Rwanda were tested on the pendulum problem, none was able to solve it. On the other hand, Chinese children in Hong Kong, who had been to British schools, did at least as well as U.S. or European children. Schoolchildren in Central Java and New South Wales also showed some formal operational abilities (Gardiner & Kosmitzki, 2005). Apparently, formal reasoning is a learned ability that is not equally necessary or equally valued in all cultures.

Fifty percent of college students, even those enrolled in psychology courses where perception is addressed, believe that vision includes rays coming into our eyes (which is correct) as well as rays bouncing back out of our eyes (which is not). In other words, 50 percent of students think we can see with something akin to X-ray vision.

Gregg, Winer, Cottrell, Hedman, & Fournier, 2001

Evaluating Piaget's Theory Was Piaget right about his beliefs regarding adolescent thought? Psychologists have critiqued Piaget's work on a variety of fronts. The three primary issues are disagreement about the timing; too little attention paid to individual and cultural differences; and a failure to address other, related cognitive advances that influence formal operations reasoning. Here we address each issue in turn.

Although adolescents *do* tend to think more abstractly than younger children, there is debate about the precise age at which this advance occurs (Eccles, Wigfield, & Byrnes, 2003). Piaget's writings provide many examples of children displaying aspects of scientific thinking well before adolescence. At the same time, Piaget seems to have overestimated some older children's abilities. Many late adolescents and adults—perhaps one-third to one-half—seem incapable of abstract thought as Piaget defined it (Gardiner & Kozmitzki, 2005). Thus the timing of formal operations thought processes does not always correspond to when Piaget argued it occurred.

In most of his early writings, Piaget paid little attention to variations in the same child's performance on different kinds of tasks, or to social and cultural influences. In his later years, Piaget himself "came to view his earlier model of the development of children's thinking . . . as flawed because it failed to capture the essential role of the situation in influencing and constraining . . . children's thinking" (Brown, Metz, & Campione, 1996, pp. 152–153). Neo-Piagetian research suggests that children's cognitive processes are closely tied to specific content (what a child is thinking about)

checkpoint
can **you** . . .

- Explain the difference between formal operational and concrete operational thinking, as exemplified by the pendulum problem?
- Identify factors influencing adolescents' development of formal reasoning?
- Evaluate strengths and weaknesses of Piaget's theory of formal operations?

Research has shown that liberals are more creative than conservatives but that conservatives are happier.

Dollinger, 2007; Napier & Jost, 2008

as well as to the context of a problem and the kinds of information and thought a culture considers important (Kuhn, 2006). So, for example, when children or adolescents are asked to reason within the context of familiar situations or objects, they perform at higher levels, suggesting that prior knowledge affects their ability to reason formally.

Finally, Piaget's theory does not adequately consider such cognitive advances as gains in information-processing capacity, accumulation of knowledge and expertise in specific fields, and the role of *metacognition,* the awareness and monitoring of one's own mental processes and strategies (Flavell et al., 2002). This ability to "think about thinking" and, thus, to manage one's mental processes may be the chief advance of adolescent thought (Kuhn, 2006).

CHANGES IN INFORMATION PROCESSING

Changes in the way adolescents process information reflect the maturation of the brain's frontal lobes and may help explain the cognitive advances Piaget described. Which neural connections wither and which become strengthened is highly responsive to experience. Thus progress in cognitive processing varies greatly among individual adolescents (Kuhn, 2006).

Information-processing researchers have identified two broad categories of measurable change in adolescent cognition: *structural change* and *functional change* (Eccles, Wigfield, & Byrnes, 2003).* Let's look at each.

Structural Change *Structural* changes in adolescence include (1) changes in working memory capacity and (2) the increasing amount of knowledge stored in long-term memory.

The capacity of working memory, which enlarges rapidly in middle childhood, continues to increase during adolescence. The expansion of working memory may enable older adolescents to deal with complex problems or decisions involving multiple pieces of information.

Information stored in long-term memory can be *declarative, procedural,* or *conceptual.*

declarative knowledge Acquired factual knowledge stored in long-term memory.

procedural knowledge Acquired skills stored in long-term memory.

conceptual knowledge Acquired interpretive understandings stored in long-term memory.

- **Declarative knowledge** ("knowing that . . .") consists of all the factual knowledge a person has acquired (for example, knowing that 2 + 2 = 4 and that George Washington was the first U.S. president).
- **Procedural knowledge** ("knowing how to . . .") consists of all the skills a person has acquired, such as being able to multiply and divide and to drive a car.
- **Conceptual knowledge** ("knowing why . . .") is an understanding of, for example, why an algebraic equation remains true if the same amount is added or subtracted from both sides.

Confused about the difference between structural and functional brain changes? Structural changes involve changes in the stuff that's in your brain. Functional changes involve changes in how you use that stuff.

Functional Change Processes for obtaining, handling, and retaining information are *functional* aspects of cognition. Among these are learning, remembering, and reasoning, all of which improve during adolescence.

Among the most important functional changes are (1) a continued increase in processing speed (Kuhn, 2006) and (2) further development of executive function, which includes such skills as selective attention, decision making, inhibitory control of impulsive responses, and management of working memory. These skills seem to develop at varying rates (Blakemore & Choudhury, 2006; Kuhn, 2006). In one laboratory study, adolescents reached adult-level performance in response inhibition at age 14, processing speed at 15, and working memory at 19 (Luna et al., 2004). However, improvements observed in laboratory situations may not necessarily reflect real life, in which behavior also depends on motivation and emotion regulation. As we discussed earlier in this chapter, adolescents' rash judgments may be related to immature brain development, which may permit feelings to override reason.

*The discussion in the following two sections is based on Eccles et al., 2003.

LANGUAGE DEVELOPMENT

Children's use of language reflects cognitive development. School-age children are quite proficient in use of language, but adolescence brings further refinements. Vocabulary continues to grow as reading matter becomes more adult. By ages 16 to 18 the average young person knows approximately 80,000 words (Owens, 1996).

With the advent of abstract thought, adolescents can define and discuss such abstractions as *love, justice,* and *freedom.* They more frequently use such terms as *however, otherwise, therefore,* and *probably* to express logical relationships. They become more conscious of words as symbols that can have multiple meanings, and they take pleasure in using irony, puns, and metaphors (Owens, 1996).

Adolescents also become more skilled in social perspective-taking, the ability to tailor their speech to another person's point of view. So, for example, a teen might use simpler words when talking to a child, or swear among friends, and show deference when speaking to an adult. This ability is essential for skilled conversation.

Language is not static; it is fluid and the words and phrases used by people change over time. These changes are striking in the speech of adolescents. In fact, they are so striking that linguist Marcel Danesi (1994) argues that adolescent speech constitutes a dialect of its own: *pubilect,* "the social dialect of puberty" (p. 97). Like any other linguistic code, pubilect serves to strengthen group identity and to shut outsiders (adults) out.

Vocabulary may differ by gender, ethnicity, age, geographical region, neighborhood, and type of school (Labov, 1992) and varies from one clique to another. "Druggies" and "jocks" engage in different kinds of activities, which form the main subjects of their conversation. This talk, in turn, cements bonds within the clique. A study of teenage speech patterns in Naples, Italy, suggests that similar features may emerge "in any culture where teenagerhood constitutes a distinct social category" (Danesi, 1994, p. 123).

Teenage slang is part of the process of developing an independent identity separate from parents and the adult world. In creating such expressions, young people use their newfound ability to play with words "to define their generation's unique take on values, tastes, and preferences" (Elkind, 1998, p. 29).

checkpoint
can **you** . . .

- Name two major types of changes in adolescents' information-processing capabilities, and give examples of each?
- Identify characteristics of adolescents' language development that reflect cognitive advances?
- Explain the uses of pubilect?

MORAL REASONING: KOHLBERG'S THEORY

As children attain higher cognitive levels, they become capable of more complex reasoning about moral issues. Adolescents are better able than younger children to take another person's perspective, to solve social problems, to deal with interpersonal relationships, and to see themselves as social beings. All of these tendencies foster moral development.

Let's look at Lawrence Kohlberg's groundbreaking theory of moral reasoning, at Carol Gilligan's influential work on moral development in women and girls, and at research on prosocial behavior in adolescence.

study**smart**

Moral Reasoning

Heinz's Dilemma A woman is near death from cancer. A druggist has discovered a drug that doctors believe might save her. The druggist is charging $2,000 for a small dose—10 times what the drug costs him to make. The sick woman's husband, Heinz, borrows from everyone he knows but can scrape together only $1,000. He begs the druggist to sell him the drug for $1,000 or let him pay the rest later. The druggist refuses, saying, "I discovered the drug and I'm going to make money from it." Heinz, desperate, breaks into the man's store and steals the drug. Should Heinz have done that? Why or why not? (Kohlberg, 1969).

Heinz's problem is the most famous example of Lawrence Kohlberg's approach to studying moral development. Starting in the 1950s, Kohlberg and his colleagues posed hypothetical dilemmas like this one to 75 boys ages 10, 13, and 16 and continued to question them periodically for more than 30 years. Kohlberg, borrowing Piaget's interview methodology, asked children about how they arrived at their answers. Kohlberg came to believe that moral development was a consequence of moral reasoning, which depended heavily on cognitive development. Moreover, he believed that at the heart of every dilemma was the concept of justice—a universal principle. In other words, Kohlberg believed moral reasoning was fundamentally concerned with sound reasoning about principles of justice.

Kohlberg's Levels and Stages On the basis of thought processes shown by responses to his dilemmas, Kohlberg (1969) described three levels of moral reasoning, each divided into two stages (Table 3):

preconventional morality First level of Kohlberg's theory of moral reasoning in which control is external and rules are obeyed in order to gain rewards or avoid punishment or out of self-interest.

conventional morality (or morality of conventional role conformity) Second level in Kohlberg's theory of moral reasoning in which standards of authority figures are internalized.

postconventional morality (or morality of autonomous moral principles) Third level of Kohlberg's theory of moral reasoning, in which people follow internally held moral principles and can decide among conflicting moral standards.

- *Level I:* **Preconventional morality.** People act under external controls. They obey rules to avoid punishment or reap rewards, or they act out of self-interest. This level is typical of children ages 4 to 10.
- *Level II:* **Conventional morality (or morality of conventional role conformity).** People have internalized the standards of authority figures. They are concerned about being "good," pleasing others, and maintaining the social order. This level is typically reached after age 10; many people never move beyond it, even in adulthood.
- *Level III:* **Postconventional morality (or morality of autonomous moral principles).** People recognize conflicts between moral standards and make their own judgments on the basis of principles of right, fairness, and justice. People generally do not reach this level of moral reasoning until at least early adolescence, or more commonly in young adulthood, if ever.

In Kohlberg's theory, it is the reasoning underlying a person's response to a moral dilemma, not the response itself, that indicates the stage of moral development. As shown in Table 3, two people who give opposite answers may be at the same stage if their reasoning is based on similar factors.

Some adolescents and even some adults remain at Kohlberg's level I. Like young children, they seek merely to avoid punishment or satisfy their needs. Most adolescents and adults seem to be at level II. They conform to social conventions, support the status quo, and "do the right thing" to please others or to obey the law. Stage 4 reasoning (upholding social norms) is less common but increases from early adolescence into adulthood.

Kohlberg added a transitional level between levels II and III, when people no longer feel bound by society's moral standards but have not yet reasoned out their own principles of justice. Instead, they base their moral decisions on personal feelings. Before people can develop a fully principled (level III) morality, he said, they must recognize the relativity of moral standards. Many young people question their earlier moral views when they enter college or the world of work and encounter people whose values, culture, and ethnic background are different from their own. Still, few people reach a level where they can choose among differing moral standards. In fact, at one point Kohlberg questioned the validity of stage 6 because so few people seem to attain it. Later, he proposed a seventh, "cosmic," stage, in which people consider the effect of their actions not only on other people but on the universe as a whole (Kohlberg, 1981; Kohlberg & Ryncarz, 1990).

Evaluating Kohlberg's Theory Kohlberg, building on Piaget, inaugurated a profound shift in the way we look at moral development. Instead of viewing morality solely as the attainment of control over self-gratifying impulses, investigators now study how children and adults base moral judgments on their growing understanding of the social world.

Initial research supported Kohlberg's theory. The American boys that Kohlberg and his colleagues followed through adulthood progressed through Kohlberg's stages in sequence, and none skipped a stage. Their moral judgments correlated positively with age, education, IQ, and socioeconomic status (Colby, Kohlberg, Gibbs, & Lieberman, 1983). More recent research, however, has cast doubt on the delineation of some of Kohlberg's stages (Eisenberg & Morris, 2004). A study of children's judgments about laws and lawbreaking suggests that some children can reason flexibly about such issues as early as age 6 (Helwig & Jasiobedzka, 2001).

TABLE 3 Kohlberg's Six Stages of Moral Reasoning

Levels	Stages of Reasoning	Typical Answers to Heinz's Dilemma
Level I: Preconventional morality (ages 4 to 10)	*Stage 1: Orientation toward punishment and obedience.* "What will happen to me?" Children obey rules to avoid punishment. They ignore the motives of an act and focus on its physical form (such as the size of a lie) or its consequences (for example, the amount of physical damage).	*Pro:* "He should steal the drug. It isn't really bad to take it. It isn't as if he hadn't asked to pay for it first. The drug he'd take is worth only \$200; he's not really taking a \$2,000 drug." *Con:* "He shouldn't steal the drug. It's a big crime. He didn't get permission; he used force and broke and entered. He did a lot of damage and stole a very expensive drug."
	Stage 2: Instrumental purpose and exchange. "You scratch my back, I'll scratch yours." Children conform to rules out of self-interest and consideration for what others can do for them. They look at an act in terms of the human needs it meets and differentiate this value from the act's physical form and consequences.	*Pro:* "It's all right to steal the drug, because his wife needs it and he wants her to live. It isn't that he wants to steal, but that's what he has to do to save her." *Con:* "He shouldn't steal it. The druggist isn't wrong or bad; he just wants to make a profit. That's what you're in business for—to make money."
Level II: Conventional morality (ages 10 to 13 or beyond)	*Stage 3: Maintaining mutual relations, approval of others, the golden rule.* "Am I a good boy or girl?" Children want to please and help others, can judge the intentions of others, and develop their own ideas of what a good person is. They evaluate an act according to the motive behind it or the person performing it, and they take circumstances into account.	*Pro:* "He should steal the drug. He is only doing something that is natural for a good husband to do. You can't blame him for doing something out of love for his wife. You'd blame him if he didn't love his wife enough to save her." *Con:* "He shouldn't steal. If his wife dies, he can't be blamed. It isn't because he's heartless or that he doesn't love her enough to do everything that he legally can. The druggist is the selfish or heartless one."
	Stage 4: Social concern and conscience. "What if everybody did it?" People are concerned with doing their duty, showing respect for higher authority, and maintaining the social order. They consider an act always wrong, regardless of motive or circumstances, if it violates a rule and harms others.	*Pro:* "You should steal it. If you did nothing, you'd be letting your wife die. It's your responsibility if she dies. You have to take it with the idea of paying the druggist." *Con:* "It is a natural thing for Heinz to want to save his wife, but it's still always wrong to steal. He knows he's taking a valuable drug from the man who made it."
Level III: Postconventional morality (early adolescence, or not until young adulthood, or never)	*Stage 5: Morality of contract, of individual rights, and of democratically accepted law.* People think in rational terms, valuing the will of the majority and the welfare of society. They generally see these values as best supported by adherence to the law. While they recognize that there are times when human need and the law conflict, they believe it is better for society in the long run if they obey the law.	*Pro:* "The law wasn't set up for these circumstances. Taking the drug in this situation isn't really right, but it's justified." *Con:* "You can't completely blame someone for stealing, but extreme circumstances don't really justify taking the law into your own hands. You can't have people stealing whenever they are desperate. The end may be good, but the ends don't justify the means."
	Stage 6: Morality of universal ethical principles. People do what they as individuals think is right, regardless of legal restrictions or the opinions of others. They act in accordance with internalized standards, knowing that they would condemn themselves if they did not.	*Pro:* "This is a situation that forces him to choose between stealing and letting his wife die. In a situation where the choice must be made, it is morally right to steal. He has to act in terms of the principle of preserving and respecting life." *Con:* "Heinz is faced with the decision of whether to consider the other people who need the drug just as badly as his wife. Heinz ought to act not according to his feelings for his wife, but considering the value of all the lives involved."

Source: Adapted from Kohlberg, 1969; Lickona, 1976.

One reason the ages attached to Kohlberg's levels are so variable is that people who have achieved a high level of cognitive development do not always reach a comparably high level of moral development. A certain level of cognitive development is *necessary* but not *sufficient* for a comparable level of moral development. In other words, just because a person is capable of moral reasoning does not necessarily mean the person actually engages in moral reasoning. Thus other processes besides cognition must be at work. Some investigators suggest that moral activity is motivated not only by abstract considerations of justice but also by such emotions as empathy, guilt, and distress and the internalization of prosocial norms (Eisenberg & Morris, 2004; Gibbs, 1991, 1995; Gibbs & Schnell, 1985).

Furthermore, there is not always a clear relationship between moral reasoning and moral behavior. For example, most people would characterize the actions of Pol Pot, the despotic Cambodian leader of the Khmer Rouge, as amoral. From 1974 to 1979, the Khmer Rouge killed 1 to 3 million Cambodian people. Most people would consider this mass murder to be profoundly evil. But Pol Pot was driven by his belief in an idyllic Communist agrarian society. He believed that the actions he took were in the service of a higher ideal, and the justifications for the actions he took were cognitively complex and well formed. Although this is an extreme example, it is clear that people at postconventional levels of reasoning do not necessarily act more morally than those at lower levels. Other factors, such as specific situations, conceptions of virtue, and concern for others, contribute to moral behavior (Colby & Damon, 1992; Fischer & Pruyne, 2003). Generally speaking, however, adolescents who are more advanced in moral reasoning do tend to be more moral in their behavior as well as better adjusted and higher in social competence, whereas antisocial adolescents tend to use less mature moral reasoning (Eisenberg & Morris, 2004).

Can you think of a time when you or someone you know acted contrary to personal moral judgment? Why do you think this happened?

Influence of Parents, Peers, and Culture Neither Piaget nor Kohlberg considered parents important to children's moral development, but more recent research emphasizes parents' contribution in both the cognitive and the emotional realms. Adolescents with supportive, authoritative parents who stimulate them to question and expand on their moral reasoning tend to reason at higher levels (Eisenberg & Morris, 2004).

Peers also affect moral reasoning by talking with each other about moral conflicts. Having more close friends, spending quality time with them, and being perceived as a leader are associated with higher moral reasoning (Eisenberg & Morris, 2004).

AN ETHIC OF CARE: GILLIGAN'S THEORY

Do men and women reason in the same fashion? This question was addressed by Carol Gilligan (1982/1993), who asserted that Kohlberg's theory was sexist and oriented toward values more important to men than to women. Gilligan argued that men, Kohlberg included, viewed morality in terms of justice and fairness. Women held a different set of values, however, that placed caring and avoiding harm as higher goals than justice. Kohlberg's typology unfairly categorized women as less morally and cognitive complex because of the exclusive focus on justice (Eisenberg & Morris, 2004).

Research has found little support for Gilligan's claim of a male bias in Kohlberg's stages (Brabeck & Shore, 2003; Jaffee & Hyde, 2000), and she has since modified her position. Generally, gender differences in moral reasoning are small (Jaffee & Hyde, 2000).

PROSOCIAL BEHAVIOR AND VOLUNTEER ACTIVITY

Some researchers have studied prosocial moral reasoning as an alternative to Kohlberg's justice-based system. Prosocial moral reasoning is reasoning about moral dilemmas in which one person's needs conflict with those of others in situations in which social rules or norms are unclear or nonexistent. For example, a child faced with the dilemma of deciding whether or not to intervene when a friend is being teased might run the risk of becoming a target of the bullies too. Such a child might engage in prosocial moral reasoning when deciding on a course of action. Research has shown that, from childhood to early adulthood, prosocial reasoning based on personal reflection about consequences and on internalized values and norms increases with age, whereas reasoning based on stereotypes such as "it's nice to help" decreases with age (Eisenberg & Morris, 2004).

Prosocial behavior, too, typically increases from childhood through adolescence (Eisenberg & Morris, 2004). Girls tend to show more prosocial behavior than boys (Eisenberg & Fabes, 1998), and this difference becomes more pronounced in adolescence (Fabes, Carlo, Kupanoff, & Laible, 1999). Girls tend to see themselves as more empathic and prosocial than boys do, and parents of girls emphasize social responsibility more than parents of boys do (Eisenberg & Morris, 2004). This has been validated cross-culturally in Australia, the United States, Sweden, Hungary, Czech Republic, Bulgaria, and Russia (Flannagan, Bowes, Jonsson, Csapo, & Sheblanova, 1998). Parents who use inductive discipline—including reasoning, explaining consequences, and encouraging teens to consider the effects of their actions on others—are more likely to have prosocial adolescents than parents who use power-assertive discipline.

About half of adolescents engage in some sort of community service or volunteer activity. Girls are more likely to volunteer than boys, and adolescents with high SES volunteer more than those with lower SES (Eisenberg & Morris, 2004). Students who do volunteer work outside of school tend, as adults, to be more engaged in their communities than those who do not. In addition, adolescent volunteers tend to have a higher degree of self-understanding and commitment to others (Eccles, 2004).

checkpoint can **you . . .**

- List Kohlberg's levels and stages, and discuss factors that influence how rapidly children and adolescents progress through them?
- Evaluate Kohlberg's theory with regard to the role of emotion and socialization, parent and peer influences, and cross-cultural validity?
- Explain the difference between Gilligan's and Kohlberg's standards of moral reasoning, and discuss gender effects?
- Discuss individual differences in prosocial behavior, such as volunteering?

Educational and Vocational Issues

School is a central organizing experience in most adolescents' lives. It offers opportunities to learn information, master new skills, and sharpen old skills; to participate in sports, the arts, and other activities; to explore vocational choices; and to be with friends. It widens intellectual and social horizons. Some adolescents, however, experience school not as an opportunity but as one more hindrance on the road to adulthood.

In the United States, as in all other industrialized countries and in some developing countries as well, more students finish high school than ever before, and many enroll in higher education (Eccles et al., 2003; OECD, 2004). In 2009, nearly 76 percent of U.S. 18- to 24-year-olds had received a high school diploma or equivalent credential (Aud, Hussar, Johnson, Kena, & Roth, 2012).

Among the 30 member countries of the Organisation for Economic Cooperation and Development (OECD, 2008), graduation rates vary from 15 percent in Turkey to 62 percent in Iceland. The United States, with an average of 12.7 years of schooling, is on the high end of this international comparison. However, U.S. adolescents, on average, do less well on academic achievement tests than adolescents in many other countries. For example, U.S. students score lower on mathematics and scientific literacy than students in most other countries at a similar level of economic development (Baldi, Jin, Skemer, Green, & Herget, 2007; Lemke et al., 2004). Furthermore, although 4th- and 8th-grade student achievement, as measured by the National Assessment of Educational Progress (NAEP), has improved in some areas, 12th-grade achievement generally has not (NCES, 2009c). An achievement gap still exists between white adolescents and minority teens, but this gap has narrowed in recent years (Rampey, Dion, & Donahue, 2009).

Let's look at influences on school achievement and then at young people who drop out. Finally, we'll consider planning for higher education and vocations.

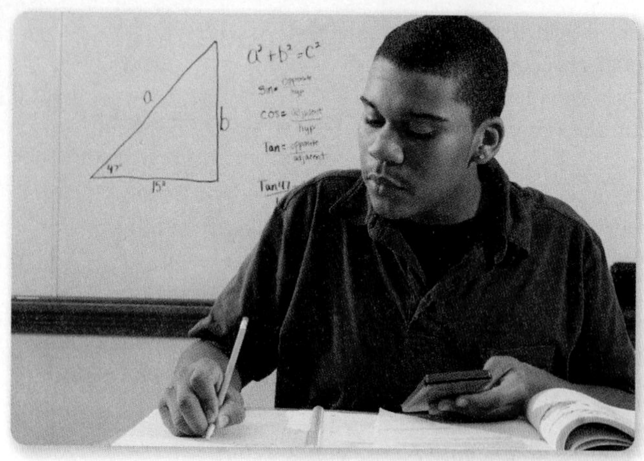

Students who take responsibility for their own learning are likely to do well in school.

INFLUENCES ON SCHOOL ACHIEVEMENT

In adolescence, such factors as parenting practices, socioeconomic status, and the quality of the home environment influence the course of school achievement. Other factors include gender, ethnicity, peer influence, quality of schooling, and students' belief in themselves.

Student Motivation and Self-Efficacy Western educational practices are based on the assumption that students are, or can be, motivated to learn. Educators emphasize the value of intrinsic motivation—the student's desire to learn for the sake of learning (Larson & Wilson, 2004). Unfortunately, many U.S. students are *not* self-motivated, and motivation often declines as they enter high school (Eccles, 2004; Larson & Wilson, 2004). Future-oriented cognitions—hopes and dreams about future jobs—also are related to greater achievement, but this effect seems to be explained by participation in extracurricular activities. It may be that future-oriented cognitions are helpful precisely because they motivate participation in activities that relate to later success (Beal & Crockett, 2010).

In Western cultures, students high in *self-efficacy*—who believe that they can master tasks and regulate their own learning—are likely to do well in school (Zimmerman et al., 1992). So, for example, after failing a test, a student with high self-efficacy might assume that he didn't study enough, and that to do well in future tests he should study more. A student with low self-efficacy, by contrast, might conclude that the material was too hard or the test was unfair. In a study of 140 eighth graders, students' self-discipline was twice as important as IQ in accounting for their grades and achievement test scores and for selection into a competitive high school program (Duckworth & Seligman, 2005).

study smart

Mastery Orientation

In the United States, where opportunities exist for most children, how much children learn is often based on their personal motivation. But in many cultures, education is based on such factors as duty (India), submission to authority (Islamic countries), and participation in the family and community (sub-Saharan Africa). In the countries of east Asia, students are expected to learn to meet family and societal expectations. Learning is expected to require intense effort, and students who fail or fall behind feel obligated to try again. This expectation may help explain why, in international comparisons in science and math, east Asian students substantially surpass U.S. students. In developing countries, issues of motivation pale in the light of social and economic barriers to education: inadequate or absent schools, the need for child labor to support the family, barriers to schooling for girls, and early marriage (Larson & Wilson, 2004). Thus, as we discuss factors in educational success, which are drawn largely from studies in the United States and other Western countries, we need to remember that they do not apply to all cultures.

Gender On a test of adolescents in 43 industrialized countries, girls in all countries were better readers than boys. Boys were ahead in mathematical literacy in about half of the countries, but these gender differences were less pronounced than in reading (OECD, 2004). Overall, beginning in adolescence, girls do better on verbal tasks that involve writing and language usage; boys do better in activities that involve visual and spatial functions helpful in math and science. Despite theories that boys possess some innate ability to do better at math, an evaluation of SAT results and math scores from 7 million students found no gender differences in math performance (Hyde, Lindberg, Linn, Ellis, & Williams, 2008).

What causes the observed gender differences? As with all aspects of development, research points to interacting biological and environmental contributions (Hyde & Mertz, 2009).

Male and female brains do show some differences in structure and organization. Moreover, these differences tend to become more pronounced with age. Girls have more gray matter and the growth of gray matter peaks earlier. Their neurons also have more connections. In addition, their brains are more evenly balanced across the hemispheres, and they have a larger corpus callosum. What are the consequences of these differences? The brain structure of girls appears to permit a wider range of cognitive abilities, and girls are better able to integrate verbal and analytic tasks (which occur in the left brain) with spatial and holistic tasks (which occur in the right brain). This may be related to their more effective language processing. But what about boys? Boys have more connective white matter. In other words, they have more myelin coating the axons of their neurons. Boys also have more cerebrospinal fluid, which cushions the longer paths of nerve impulses. Boys' brains seem to be optimized for activity within each hemisphere—their brains are more specialized and seem to show an advantage for visual and spatial performance (Halpern et al., 2007).

Social and cultural forces that influence gender differences include the following (Halpern et al., 2007):

- *Home influences:* Across cultures, parents' educational level correlates with their children's math achievement. The amount of parental involvement in children's education affects math performance. Parents' gender attitudes and expectations also have an effect.
- *School influences:* Subtle differences in the way teachers treat boys and girls, especially in math and science classes, have been documented.
- *Neighborhood influences:* Boys benefit more from enriched neighborhoods and are hurt more by deprived neighborhoods.
- *Women's and men's roles* in society help shape girls' and boys' choices of courses and occupations.
- *Cultural influences:* Cross-cultural studies show that the size of gender differences in math performance varies among nations and becomes greater by the end of secondary school. These differences correlate with the degree of gender equality in the society.

All in all, science is beginning to find answers to the perplexing question of why boys' and girls' abilities become more different in high school.

Parenting Styles, Ethnicity, and Peer Influence In Western cultures, the benefits of authoritative parenting continue to affect school achievement during adolescence (Baumrind, 1991). *Authoritative parents* urge adolescents to look at both sides of issues, welcome their participation in family decisions, and admit that children sometimes know more than parents. These parents strike a balance between making demands and being responsive. Their children receive praise and privileges for good grades; poor grades bring encouragement to try harder and offers of help.

Authoritarian parents, in contrast, tell adolescents not to argue with or question adults and tell them they will "know better when they are grown up." Good grades bring admonitions to do even better; poor grades may be punished by reduced allowances or grounding. *Permissive parents* seem indifferent to grades, make no rules about watching television, do not attend school functions, and neither help with nor check their children's homework. These parents may not be neglectful or uncaring; they may, in fact, be nurturant. They may simply believe that teenagers should be responsible for their own lives.

What accounts for the academic success of authoritatively raised adolescents? Authoritative parents' greater involvement in schooling may be a factor as well as their encouragement of positive attitudes toward work. A more subtle mechanism, consistent with findings on self-efficacy, may be parents' influence on how children explain success or failure. Examination of 50 studies involving more than 50,000 students revealed that parents who emphasize the value of education, connect academic performance to future goals, and discuss learning strategies have a significant impact on student academic achievement (Hill & Tyson, 2009).

Among some ethnic groups, though, parenting styles may be less important than peer influence on academic motivation and achievement. In one study, Latino and

African American adolescents, even those with authoritative parents, did less well in school than European American students, apparently because of lack of peer support for academic achievement (Steinberg, Dornbusch, & Brown, 1992). On the other hand, Asian American students, whose parents are sometimes described as authoritarian, get high grades and score better than European American students on math achievement tests, apparently because both parents *and* peers prize achievement (C. Chen & Stevenson, 1995). The strong school achievement of many young people from a variety of immigrant backgrounds reflects their families' and friends' strong emphasis on educational success (Fuligni, 1997, 2001).

One of the issues with comparing historical research with current research is that times change, as can the influence of particular variables. Electronic book readers such as the Kindle are becoming increasingly popular. What might this trend mean for the previous finding that number of books in the home is correlated with academic achievement?

Importance of SES and Related Family Characteristics Socioeconomic status is an important predictor of academic success. Parents' educational level and family income indirectly affect educational attainment based on how they influence parenting style, sibling relationships, and adolescent academic engagement (Melby, Conger, Fang, Wickrama, & Conger, 2008). According to a study of 15-year-olds' mathematical literacy in 20 relatively high-income countries, students with at least one postsecondary-educated parent performed better than students whose parents had lower educational levels (Hampden-Thompson & Johnston, 2006). A similar gap occurred between students whose parents had high occupational status and those whose parents were of middle or low occupational status. Having more than 200 books in the home was associated with higher scores, and living in a two-parent family was another key predictor of math competence in all 20 countries.

The School The quality of schooling strongly influences student achievement. A good middle or high school has an orderly, safe environment, adequate material resources, a stable teaching staff, and a positive sense of community. The school culture places a strong emphasis on academics and fosters the belief that all students can learn. It also offers opportunities for extracurricular activities, which keep students engaged and prevent them from getting into trouble after school. Teachers trust, respect, and care about students and have high expectations for them as well as confidence in their own ability to help students succeed (Eccles, 2004).

If adolescents feel support from teachers and other students, and if the curriculum and instruction are meaningful and appropriately challenging and fit their interests and needs, they are more satisfied with school (Samdal & Dür, 2000) and get better grades (Jia et al., 2009). In a survey of students' perceptions of their teachers, high teacher expectations were the most consistent positive predictor of students' goals and interests, and negative feedback was the most consistent negative predictor of academic performance and classroom behavior (Wentzel, 2002).

A decline in academic motivation and achievement often begins with the transition from the intimacy and familiarity of elementary school to the larger, more pressured, and less supportive environment of middle school or junior high school (Eccles, 2004). For this reason, some cities have tried eliminating the middle school transition by extending elementary school to eighth grade or have consolidated some middle schools with small high schools (Gootman, 2007). Some big-city school systems, such as New York's, Philadelphia's, and Chicago's, are experimenting with small schools in which students, teachers, and parents form a learning community united by a common vision of good education and often a special curricular focus, such as music or ethnic studies (Meier, 1995; Rossi, 1996).

Another innovation is Early College High Schools—small, personalized, high-quality schools operated in cooperation with nearby colleges. By combining a nurturing atmosphere with clear, rigorous standards, these schools enable students to complete high school requirements plus the first 2 years of college ("The Early College High School Initiative," n.d.).

checkpoint
can **you** . . .

- Explain how schools in various cultures motivate students to learn?
- Assess the influences of personal qualities, SES, gender, ethnicity, parents, and peers on academic achievement?
- Give examples of educational practices that can help high school students succeed?

Technology The expansion of technology and the major role it plays in children's lives has affected learning. Research indicates that while critical thinking and analysis skills

research in action

MULTITASKING AND GEN M

Multitasking is not a new phenomenon. Humans have always been able to attend to several tasks at once—walking and talking, holding a small child and stirring a pot of soup, chopping vegetables and listening to the radio. What has changed dramatically over the past 15 years is the impact that electronic media has had on the need for and the ability to multitask. A new generation has been added to the Gen Y and Gen X pool—Gen M, short for Generation Media. A recent survey found that teens spend an average of 7.5 hours a day consuming media. However, this is not the whole story. Because multitasking has become increasingly common—most notably with the proliferation of cell phones—teens are exposed to roughly 11 hours of media content a day (Rideout & Foehr, 2010). This trend is likely to continue given the predicted roll-out of wearable media conduits and "smart" machines currently in development.

While the perception is that multitasking saves time, evidence is piling up that suggests the opposite. Trying to accomplish too many tasks at one time increases the likelihood of errors and actually lengthens the time it takes to complete any one single task. Studies on the workings of the brain have shown that task-switching can create a sort of bottleneck effect as the brain struggles to determine which task to perform (Dux, Ivanoff, Asplund, & Marois, 2006). The effects on learning are concerning. Students may have a strong ability to search out and find answers using technology, but their problem-solving and analytical skills are suffering, prompting a number of high-profile schools to block out Internet access during lectures.

Equally disturbing are statistics related to distracted driving. Using cell phones and texting while driving have been linked to hundreds of thousands of injuries and thousands of deaths each year in the United States. In simulated driving studies, researchers found that when drivers used cell phones their reactions were 18 percent slower and that the number of rear end collisions doubled (Strayer & Drews, 2004). These slower reaction rates applied even when there was no manual manipulation of the phone, indicating that hands-free devices are no less likely to slow reaction time or to contribute to accidents (Strayer & Drews, 2007). In a study comparing cell phone use while driving and drunk driving, impairments associated with using a cell phone were determined to be as profound as those associated with driving while drunk (Strayer, Drews, & Crouch, 2006).

Do you consider yourself a member of Gen M? What are some typical tasks you tend to do simultaneously?

have declined as a result of the increased use of computers and video games, visual skills have improved. Students are spending more time multitasking with visual media and less time reading for pleasure (Greenfield, 2009). Reading develops vocabulary, imagination, and induction; skills that are critical to solving more complex problems. Multitasking can prevent a deeper understanding of information. In one study students who were given access to the Internet during class did not process what was presented as well and performed more poorly than students without access (Greenfield, 2009). See Box 2 for more on multitasking.

DROPPING OUT OF HIGH SCHOOL

More U.S. youths are completing high school than ever before. The percentage of those who drop out, known as the status dropout rate, includes all people in the 16- to 24-year-old age group who are not enrolled in school and who have not completed a high school program, regardless of when they left school. In 2009–2010, the status dropout rate for public school students in grades 9–12 was 3.4 percent, representing some 500,000 students. Average dropout rates are lower for white students (2.3 percent) than for both blacks (5.5 percent) and Hispanics (5.0 percent). Asian students at 1.9 percent are the least likely to dropout (Stillwell & Sable, 2013).

The Gates Foundation has provided funding for a new program in which 10th graders who pass proficiency tests will be allowed to graduate early and immediately begin taking community college courses. Proponents argue that a system based on subject mastery rather than accumulated credits will lead to increased motivation for proficient students. Moreover, those students who do not pass the board exams will know which competencies they must work on to engage in college level work. What do you think?

Why are poor and minority adolescents more likely to drop out? One reason may be ineffective schooling: low teacher expectations or differential treatment of these students; less teacher support than at the elementary level; and the perceived irrelevance of the curriculum to culturally underrepresented groups. The transition to high school for African American and Latino students seems to be most risky for those students transitioning from smaller, more supportive junior high schools with significant numbers of minority peers to larger, more impersonal high schools where there are fewer peers from the same racial or ethnic group (Benner & Graham, 2009). In schools that use ability tracking, students in low-ability or noncollege tracks (where minority youth are likely to be assigned) often have inferior educational experiences. Placed with peers who are equally alienated, they may develop feelings of incompetence and negative attitudes toward school and engage in problem behaviors (Eccles, 2004).

There are consequences both for society and for individuals to dropping out. Society suffers when young people do not finish school. Dropouts are more likely to be unemployed or to have low incomes, to end up on welfare, to become involved with drugs, crime, and delinquency. They also tend to be in poorer health (Laird et al., 2006; NCES, 2001, 2003, 2004).

A longitudinal study that followed 3,502 disadvantaged eighth graders into early adulthood points up the difference success in high school can make (Finn, 2006). As young adults, those who successfully completed high school were most likely to obtain postsecondary education, to have jobs, and to be consistently employed. An important factor distinguishing the successful completers was **active engagement:** the "attention, interest, investment, and effort students expend in the work of school" (Marks, 2000, p. 155). On the most basic level, active engagement means coming to class on time, being prepared, listening and responding to the teacher, and obeying school rules. A higher level of engagement consists of getting involved with the coursework—asking questions, taking the initiative to seek help when needed, or doing extra projects. Both levels of active engagement tend to pay off in positive school performance (Finn & Rock, 1997). A number of family characteristics affect school engagement. For example, families where children were praised for academic performance, parents talked to or played with the children 15 minutes a day or more, television was restricted, and where parents and children ate dinner together 5 or more days a week were more likely to have highly engaged children. Participation in extracurricular activities also seemed to make a difference, as did participation in religious activities outside of the school itself (Dye & Johnson, 2009).

active engagement
Personal involvement in schooling, work, family, or other activity.

checkpoint
can **you**...

- Discuss trends in high school completion and causes and effects of dropping out?
- Explain the importance of active engagement in schooling?

Students learn more when they are asked to read materials in a harder-to-read font. The additional processing required to decode the words helps the material stick better.

Diemand-Yauman, Oppenheimer, & Vaughan, 2011

PREPARING FOR HIGHER EDUCATION OR VOCATIONS

How do young people develop career goals? How do they decide whether to go to college and, if not, how to enter the world of work? Many factors enter in, including individual ability and personality, education, socioeconomic and ethnic background, the advice of school counselors, life experiences, and societal values. Let's look at some influences on educational and vocational aspirations. Then we'll examine provisions for young people who do not plan to go to college. We'll also discuss the pros and cons of outside work for high school students.

Influences on Students' Aspirations Self-efficacy beliefs help shape the occupational options students consider and the way they prepare for careers (Bandura, Barbaranelli, Caprara, & Pastorelli, 2001). In addition, parents' values with regard to academic achievement influence adolescents' values and occupational goals (Jodl, Michael, Malanchuk, Eccles, & Sameroff, 2001).

Despite the greater flexibility in career goals today, gender—and gender-stereotyping—still influences vocational choice (Eccles et al., 2003). Girls and boys in the United States are now equally likely to plan careers in math and science. However, boys are much more likely to earn college degrees in engineering, physics, and computer science (NCES, 2001), whereas girls are still more likely to go into nursing, social welfare professions, and teaching (Eccles et al., 2003). Much the same is true in other industrialized countries (OECD, 2004).

The educational system itself may act as a brake on vocational aspirations. Students who can memorize and analyze tend to do well in classrooms where teaching is geared to those abilities. Thus these students are achievers in a system that stresses the abilities in which they happen to excel. Students whose strength is in creative or practical thinking—areas critical to success in certain fields—rarely get a chance to show what they can do (Sternberg, 1997). Recognition of a broader range of intelligences, combined with more flexible teaching and career counseling, could allow more students to meet their educational goals and enter the occupations they desire so they can make the contributions of which they are capable.

Students whose strength is in creative thinking frequently don't get a chance to show what they can do. More flexible teaching and career counseling could allow more students to make the contributions of which they are capable.

Guiding Students *Not* Bound for College Most industrialized countries offer guidance to non-college-bound students. Germany, for example, has an apprenticeship system in which high school students go to school part-time and spend the rest of the week in paid on-the-job training supervised by an employer-mentor.

The United States lacks coordinated policies to help non-college-bound youth make a successful transition from high school to the labor market. Vocational counseling is generally oriented toward college-bound youth. Whatever vocational training programs do exist for high school graduates who do not immediately go on to college tend to be less comprehensive than the German model and less closely tied to the needs of businesses and industries. Most of these young people must get training on the job or in community college courses. Many, ignorant about the job market, do not obtain the skills they need. Others take jobs beneath their abilities. Some do not find work at all (NRC, 1993a).

In some communities, demonstration programs help in the school-to-work transition. The most successful ones offer instruction in basic skills, counseling, peer support, mentoring, apprenticeship, and job placement (NRC, 1993a). In 1994, Congress allocated $1.1 billion to help states and local governments establish school-to-work programs in partnership with employers. Participating students improved their school performance and graduation rates and, when they entered the labor market, were more likely to find jobs and earned higher wages than students who did not participate (Hughes, Bailey, & Mechur, 2001).

Adolescents in the Workplace In the United States, the vast majority of adolescents are employed at some time during high school, mostly in service and retail jobs. Researchers disagree over whether part-time work is beneficial to high school students (by helping them develop real-world skills and a work ethic) or detrimental (by distracting them from long-term educational and occupational goals).

Some research suggests that working students fall into two groups: those who are on an accelerated path to adulthood, and those who make a more leisurely transition, balancing schoolwork, paid jobs, and extracurricular activities. The "accelerators" work more than 20 hours a week during high school and spend little time on school-related leisure activities. Exposure to an adult world may lead them into alcohol and drug use, sexual activity, and delinquent behavior. Many of these adolescents have relatively low SES; they tend to look for full-time work right after high school and not to obtain college degrees. Intensive work experience in high school improves their prospects for work and income after high school, but not for long-term occupational attainment. The "balancers," in contrast, often come from more privileged backgrounds. For them, the effects of part-time work seem entirely benign. It helps them to gain a sense of responsibility, independence, and self-confidence and to appreciate the value of work but does not deter them from their educational path (Staff, Mortimer, & Uggen, 2004).

For high school students who must or choose to work outside of school, then, the effects are more likely to be positive if they try to limit working hours and remain engaged in school activities. Cooperative educational programs that enable students to work part time as part of their school program may be especially protective (Staff et al., 2004).

checkpoint can you...

- Discuss influences on educational and vocational aspirations and planning?

summary and key terms

Adolescence: A Developmental Transition

- Adolescence, in modern industrial societies, is the transition from childhood to adulthood. It lasts from about age 11 until 19 or 20.
- Early adolescence is full of opportunities for physical, cognitive, and psychosocial growth, but also of risks to healthy development. Risky behavior patterns, such as drinking alcohol, drug abuse, sexual and gang activity, and use of firearms, tend to increase throughout the teenage years; but most young people experience no major problems.

adolescence
puberty

PHYSICAL DEVELOPMENT

Puberty

- Puberty is triggered by hormonal changes. Puberty takes about 4 years, typically begins earlier in girls than in boys, and ends when a person can reproduce; but the timing of these events varies considerably.
- Puberty is marked by two stages: (1) the activation of the adrenal glands and (2) the maturing of the sex organs a few years later.
- During puberty, both boys and girls undergo an adolescent growth spurt. The reproductive organs enlarge and mature, and secondary sex characteristics appear.
- A secular trend toward earlier attainment of adult height and sexual maturity began about 100 years ago, probably because of improvements in living standards.
- The principal signs of sexual maturity are production of sperm (for males) and menstruation (for females).

primary sex characteristics
secondary sex characteristics
adolescent growth spurt
spermarche
menarche
secular trend

The Adolescent Brain

- The adolescent brain is not yet fully mature. It undergoes a second wave of overproduction of gray matter, especially in the frontal lobes, followed by pruning of excess nerve cells. Continuing myelination of the frontal lobes facilitates the maturation of cognitive processing.
- Adolescents process information about emotions with the amygdala, whereas adults use the frontal lobe. Thus adolescents tend to make less accurate, less reasoned judgments.
- Underdevelopment of frontal cortical systems connected with motivation, impulsivity, and addiction may help explain adolescents' tendency toward risk-taking.

Physical and Mental Health

- For the most part, the adolescent years are relatively healthy. Health problems often are associated with poverty or lifestyle.
- Many adolescents do not engage in regular vigorous physical activity.
- Many adolescents do not get enough sleep because the high school schedule is out of sync with their natural body rhythms.
- Concern with body image, especially among girls, may lead to eating disorders.

- Three common eating disorders in adolescence are obesity, anorexia nervosa, and bulimia nervosa. All can have serious long-term effects. Anorexia and bulimia affect mostly girls and young women. Outcomes for bulimia tend to be better than for anorexia.
- Adolescent substance use has lessened in recent years; still, drug use often begins as children move into middle school.
- Marijuana, alcohol, and tobacco are the most popular drugs with adolescents. All involve serious risks. Nonmedical use of prescription and over-the-counter drugs is an increasing problem.
- The prevalence of depression increases in adolescence, especially among girls.
- Leading causes of death among adolescents include motor vehicle accidents, firearm use, and suicide.

body image
anorexia nervosa
bulimia nervosa
substance abuse
substance dependence
binge drinking

COGNITIVE DEVELOPMENT

Aspects of Cognitive Maturation

- Adolescents who reach Piaget's stage of formal operations can engage in hypothetical-deductive reasoning. They can think in terms of possibilities, deal flexibly with problems, and test hypotheses.
- Because environmental stimulation plays an important part in attaining this stage, not all people become capable of formal operations; and those who are capable do not always use them.
- Piaget's proposed stage of formal operations does not take into account such developments as accumulation of knowledge and expertise, gains in information processing, and the growth of metacognition. Piaget also paid little attention to individual differences, between-task variations, and the role of the situation.
- Research has found both structural and functional changes in adolescents' information processing. Structural changes include increases in declarative, procedural, and conceptual knowledge and expansion of the capacity of working memory. Functional changes include progress in deductive reasoning. However, emotional immaturity may lead older adolescents to make poorer decisions than younger ones.
- Vocabulary and other aspects of language development, especially those related to abstract thought, such as social perspective-taking, improve in adolescence. Adolescents enjoy wordplay and create their own dialect.
- According to Kohlberg, moral reasoning is based on a developing sense of justice and growing cognitive abilities. Kohlberg proposed that moral development progresses from external control to internalized societal standards to personal, principled moral codes.
- Kohlberg's theory has been criticized on several grounds, including failure to credit the roles of emotion, socialization, and parental guidance. The applicability of Kohlberg's system to women and girls and to people in non-Western cultures has been questioned.

formal operations
hypothetical-deductive reasoning
declarative knowledge
procedural knowledge
conceptual knowledge
preconventional morality
conventional morality (or morality of conventional role conformity)
postconventional morality (or morality of autonomous moral principles)

Educational and Vocational Issues

- Self-efficacy beliefs, parental practices, cultural and peer influences, gender, and quality of schooling affect adolescents' educational achievement.
- Although most Americans graduate from high school, the dropout rate is higher among poor, Hispanic, and African American students. However, this racial/ethnic gap is narrowing. Active engagement in studies is an important factor in keeping adolescents in school.
- Educational and vocational aspirations are influenced by several factors, including self-efficacy and parental values. Gender stereotypes have less influence than in the past.
- High school graduates who do not immediately go on to college can benefit from vocational training.
- Part-time work seems to have both positive and negative effects on educational, social, and occupational development. The long-term effects tend to be best when working hours are limited.

active engagement

chapter 12

Psychosocial Development in Adolescence

outline

The Search for Identity

Sexuality

Relationships with Family, Peers, and Adult Society

Antisocial Behavior and Juvenile Delinquency

learning objectives

Discuss identity formation in adolescence.

Describe adolescent sexuality.

Characterize changes in adolescents' relationships with family and peers.

Describe adjustment problems of adolescents and strategies for intervention and risk reduction.

did you know?

- Sex education programs that encourage *both* abstinence and safe sexual practices are more effective in delaying sexual initiation than abstinence-only programs?
- Most adolescents say they have good relationships with their parents?
- Studies have shown online communication and social networking sites, such as Facebook, strengthen rather than lessen social connectedness?

In this chapter, we turn to psychosocial aspects of the quest for identity. We discuss how adolescents come to terms with their sexuality. We consider how teenagers' burgeoning individuality expresses itself in relationships with parents, siblings, peers, and friends. We examine sources of antisocial behavior and ways of reducing the risks to adolescents to make it a time of positive growth and expanding possibilities.

Life is an experiment. The more experiments you make, the better.

—**Ralph Waldo Emerson**

The Search for Identity

The search for **identity**—which Erikson defined as a coherent conception of the self, made up of goals, values, and beliefs to which the person is solidly committed—comes into focus during the teenage years. Adolescents' cognitive development enables them to construct a "theory of the self" (Elkind, 1998). In other words, adolescence is a time to figure out exactly who you are. As Erikson (1950) emphasized, a teenager's effort to make sense of the self is not "a kind of maturational malaise." It is part of a healthy, vital process that builds on the achievements of earlier stages—on trust, autonomy, initiative, and industry—and lays the groundwork for coping with the challenges of adulthood.

identity
According to Erikson, a coherent conception of the self, made up of goals, values, and beliefs to which a person is solidly committed.

ERIKSON: IDENTITY VERSUS IDENTITY CONFUSION

The chief task of adolescence, said Erikson (1968), is to confront the crisis of **identity versus identity confusion,** or *identity versus role confusion,* so as to become a unique adult with a coherent sense of self and a valued role in society. The concept of the *identity crisis* was based in part on Erikson's life experience. Growing up in Germany as the out-of-wedlock son of a Jewish woman from Denmark, Erikson never knew his biological father. Though adopted at age 9 by his mother's second husband, a German Jewish pediatrician, he felt confusion about who he was. He floundered for some time before settling on his vocation. When he came to the United States, he needed to redefine his identity as an immigrant. Identity, according to Erikson, forms as young people resolve three major issues: the choice of an *occupation,* the adoption of *values* to live by, and the development of a satisfying *sexual identity.*

identity versus identity confusion
Erikson's fifth stage of psychosocial development, in which an adolescent seeks to develop a coherent sense of self, including the role she or he is to play in society. Also called *identity versus role confusion.*

During middle childhood, children acquire skills needed for success in their culture. As adolescents, they need to find ways to use these skills. At least in Western countries such as the United States, adolescence is a relatively long period of time during which young people begin to take on adult responsibilities but are not fully independent. It is also a time during which occupational goals are often developed. Erikson believed this time-out period, which he called *psychosocial moratorium,* was ideal for the development of identity and allowed young people the opportunity to search for commitments to which they could be faithful.

Adolescents who resolve the identity crisis satisfactorily, according to Erikson, develop the virtue of **fidelity:** sustained loyalty, faith, or a sense of belonging to a loved one, friends, or companions. Fidelity also can mean identification with a set of values, an ideology, a religion, a political movement, or an ethnic group (Erikson, 1982). Individuals who do not develop a firm sense of their own identity and do not develop fidelity may have an unstable sense of self, be insecure, and fail to plan for themselves and the future.

fidelity
Sustained loyalty, faith, or sense of belonging that results from the successful resolution of Erikson's *identity versus identity confusion* psychosocial stage of development.

Erikson saw this identity or role confusion as the prime danger of this stage. A failure to form a coherent sense of identity can greatly delay reaching psychological adulthood. (He did not resolve his own identity crisis until his mid-20s.) Some degree of identity confusion is normal. According to Erikson, it accounts for the seemingly chaotic nature of much adolescent behavior and for teenagers' painful

Mastering the challenge of a rope course may help this adolescent girl assess her abilities, interests, and desires. According to Erikson, the process of self-assessment helps adolescents resolve the crisis of identity versus identity confusion.

self-consciousness. Cliquishness and intolerance of differences, both hallmarks of the adolescent social scene, are defenses against identity confusion.

Erikson's theory describes male identity development as the norm. According to Erikson, a man is not capable of real intimacy until he has achieved a stable identity, whereas women define themselves through marriage and motherhood (something that was truer when Erikson developed his theory than it is today). Thus, said Erikson, women (unlike men) develop identity *through* intimacy, not *before* it. As we'll see, this male orientation of Erikson's theory has prompted criticism.

MARCIA: IDENTITY STATUS—CRISIS AND COMMITMENT

Olivia, Isabella, Josh, and Jayden are about to graduate from high school. Olivia has considered her interests and her talents and plans to become an engineer. She has narrowed her college choices to three schools that offer good programs in this field.

Isabella knows exactly what she is going to do with her life. Her mother, a union leader at a plastics factory, has arranged for Isabella to enter an apprenticeship program there. Isabella has never considered doing anything else.

Josh, on the other hand, is agonizing over his future. Should he attend a community college or join the army? He cannot decide what to do now or what he wants to do eventually.

Jayden still has no idea what he wants to do, but he is not worried. He figures he can get some sort of a job and make up his mind about the future when he is ready.

These four young people are involved in identity formation. What accounts for the differences between them? According to research by the psychologist James E. Marcia (1966, 1980), these students are in four different **identity statuses,** or states of ego (self) development.

identity statuses
Marcia's term for states of ego development that depend on the presence or absence of crisis and commitment.

Through 30-minute, semistructured *identity-status interviews* (Table 1), Marcia distinguished four types of identity status: *identity achievement, foreclosure, moratorium,* and *identity diffusion.* The four categories differ according to the presence or absence

TABLE 1 Identity-Status Interview

Sample Questions	Typical Answers for the Four Statuses
About occupational commitment: "How willing do you think you'd be to give up going into ______ if something better came along?"	*Identity achievement.* "Well, I might, but I doubt it. I can't see what 'something better' would be for me."
	Foreclosure. "Not very willing. It's what I've always wanted to do. The folks are happy with it and so am I."
	Moratorium. "I guess if I knew for sure, I could answer that better. It would have to be something in the general area—something related . . ."
	Identity diffusion. "Oh, sure. If something better came along, I'd change just like that."
About ideological commitment: "Have you ever had any doubts about your religious beliefs?"	*Identity achievement.* "Yes, I started wondering whether there is a God. I've pretty much resolved that now. The way it seems to me is . . ."
	Foreclosure. "No, not really; our family is pretty much in agreement on these things."
	Moratorium. "Yes, I guess I'm going through that now. I just don't see how there can be a God and still so much evil in the world. . . ."
	Identity diffusion. "Oh, I don't know. I guess so. Everyone goes through some sort of stage like that. But it really doesn't bother me much. I figure that one religion is about as good as another!"

TABLE 2 Family and Personality Factors Associated with Adolescents in Four Identity Statuses*

Factor	Identity Achievement	Foreclosure	Moratorium	Identity Diffusion
Family	Parents encourage autonomy and connection with teachers; differences are explored within a context of mutuality.	Parents are overly involved with their children; families avoid expressing differences.	Adolescents are often involved in an ambivalent struggle with parental authority.	Parents are laissez-faire in child-rearing attitudes; are rejecting or not available to children.
Personality	High levels of ego development, moral reasoning, self-certainty, self-esteem, performance under stress, and intimacy.	Highest levels of authoritarianism and stereotypical thinking, obedience to authority, dependent relationships, low level of anxiety.	Most anxious and fearful of success; high levels of ego development, moral reasoning, and self-esteem.	Mixed results, with low levels of ego development, moral reasoning, cognitive complexity, and self-certainty; poor cooperative abilities.

*These associations have emerged from a number of separate studies. Because the studies have all been correlational, rather than longitudinal, it is impossible to say that any factor caused placement in any identity status.

Source: Kroger, 1993.

of **crisis** and **commitment,** the two elements Erikson saw as crucial to forming identity. Marcia defined *crisis* as a period of conscious decision making. Crisis, within the context of Erikson's theories, does not refer to a stressful event such as losing your job or not being able to pay your bills. Rather, it refers to the process of grappling with what to believe and who to be.

Identity formation includes attitudes about religion. Research indicates that 84 percent of U.S. teens aged 13 to 17 believe in God, and about half of them say religion is very important to them. This number declines somewhat as teens age; however, by comparison to European countries, U.S. teens show higher religiosity.

Lippman & McIntosh, 2010

Commitment, the other aspect of identity formation, involves a personal investment in an occupation or ideology (system of beliefs). Commitments can be held after they have been deeply considered, after crisis, or can be adopted without much thought put into them. Marcia found relationships between identity status and such characteristics as anxiety, self-esteem, moral reasoning, and patterns of behavior. Building on Marcia's theory, other researchers have identified additional personality and family variables related to identity status (Kroger, 2003; Table 2). Here is a more detailed sketch of young people in each identity status.

crisis
Marcia's term for period of conscious decision making related to identity formation.

commitment
Marcia's term for personal investment in an occupation or system of beliefs.

- **Identity achievement** (*crisis leading to commitment*). Olivia has resolved her identity crisis. During the crisis period, she devoted much thought and some emotional struggle to major issues in her life. She has made choices and expresses strong commitment to them. Her parents have encouraged her to make her own decisions; they have listened to her ideas and given their opinions without pressuring her. Research in a number of cultures has found people in this category to be more mature and socially competent than people in the other three (Kroger, 2003; Marcia, 1993).

identity achievement
Identity status, described by Marcia, that is characterized by commitment to choices made following a crisis, a period spent in exploring alternatives.

- **Foreclosure** (*commitment without crisis*). Isabella has made commitments, not as a result of exploring possible choices, but by accepting someone else's plans for her life. She has not considered whether she believes in her commitments and has uncritically accepted others' opinions. She is happy and self-assured, but she becomes dogmatic when her opinions are questioned. She has close family ties, is obedient, and tends to follow a powerful leader, like her mother, who accepts no disagreement.

foreclosure
Identity status, described by Marcia, in which a person who has not spent time considering alternatives (that is, has not been in crisis) is committed to other people's plans for his or her life.

moratorium
Identity status, described by Marcia, in which a person is currently considering alternatives (in crisis) and seems headed for commitment.

identity diffusion
Identity status, described by Marcia, that is characterized by absence of commitment and lack of serious consideration of alternatives.

- **Moratorium** (*crisis with no commitment yet*). Josh is actively grappling with his identity and trying to decide for himself who he wants to be and the path he wants his life to take. He is lively, talkative, self-confident, and scrupulous but also anxious and fearful. He is close to his mother but resists her authority. He will probably come out of his crisis eventually with the ability to make commitments and achieve identity.
- **Identity diffusion** (*no commitment, no crisis*). Jayden has not seriously considered options and has avoided commitments. He is unsure of himself and tends to be uncooperative. His parents do not discuss his future with him; they say it's up to him. People in this category tend to be unhappy and often lonely.

These categories are not stages; they represent the status of identity development at a particular time, and they may change in any direction as young people continue to develop (Marcia, 1979). Also, because our identity is multidimensional, our identity development is as well. For example, a young person may have decided upon a career path but not yet considered political or religious affiliation. When middle-aged people look back on their lives, they most commonly trace a path from foreclosure to moratorium to identity achievement (Kroger & Haslett, 1991). From late adolescence on, as Marcia proposed, more and more people are in moratorium or achievement: seeking or finding their identity. About half of late adolescents remain in foreclosure or diffusion, but when development does occur, it is typically in the direction Marcia described (Kroger, 2003).

GENDER DIFFERENCES IN IDENTITY FORMATION

Does the identity development of men and women proceed in the same fashion? According to Carol Gilligan (1982/1993, 1987a, 1987b; Brown & Gilligan, 1990), the female sense of self develops not so much through achieving a separate identity as through establishing relationships. Girls and women, says Gilligan, judge themselves on their handling of their responsibilities and on their ability to care for others as well as for themselves.

Some research supports Erikson's view that, for women, identity and intimacy develop together. However, given changes in social structure and the increased role of women in the workplace, it may be that these gender differences are less important than they were previously, and individual differences may play more of a role now (Archer, 1993; Marcia, 1993). In other research on Marcia's identity statuses, few gender differences have appeared (Kroger, 2003).

Although identity formation in men and women may not necessarily conform to Erikson's original conception of it, it does appear that there are differences in the formation of self-esteem. Male self-esteem seems to be linked with striving for individual achievement, whereas female self-esteem depends more on connections with others (Thorne & Michaelieu, 1996). Several large studies have found that self-esteem drops during adolescence, more rapidly for girls than for boys, and then rises gradually into adulthood. These changes may be due in part to body image and other anxieties associated with puberty and with the transitions to junior high or middle school and high school (Robins & Trzesniewski, 2005).

ETHNIC FACTORS IN IDENTITY FORMATION

For a European American young person growing up in a predominantly white culture, the process of ethnic identity formation is not particularly troublesome. However, for many young people in minority groups, race or ethnicity is central to identity formation. Following Marcia's model, some research has identified four ethnic identity statuses (Phinney, 1998):

1. *Diffused:* Juanita hasn't really thought about her identity. She has done little or no exploration of what her heritage means or what she thinks about it.
2. *Foreclosed:* Caleb has strong feelings about his identity, but those feelings are not really based on any serious exploration of his identity. Rather, he has absorbed the attitudes of other important people in his life. These feelings may be positive or negative.

TABLE 3 Representative Quotations from Each Stage of Ethnic Identity Development

Diffusion "Well, yeah, my parents are both Latinos, so I guess I probably am too." (Latina female)
Foreclosure "I am really happy that I am Chinese. My parents have always made me go to Chinese classes and participate in Chinese cultural events so that's just how I've always been." (Chinese male)
Moratorium "I've heard people say that racism doesn't exist anymore, but I disagree. I've had some experiences that have really made me stop and think. I haven't figured it out yet, but I know that being black is different than being white" (black female)
Achieved "My parents are first-generation immigrants, and I was born here. When I think about myself, I think I am a mix of their culture, and of American culture too. I think it helps me be flexible in social situations – I know that people are different in many ways, but also the same in many ways." (Latino male)

Source: Adapted from Phinney, 1998, p. 277, Table 2.

3. *Moratorium:* Cho-san has begun to think about what her ethnicity means to her but is still confused about it. She asks questions of others, talks about it with her parents, and thinks a great deal about it.
4. *Achieved:* Diego has spent a good deal of time thinking about who he is and what his ethnicity means within that context. He now understands and accepts his ethnicity.

Table 3 includes representative statements by minority young people in each status. A study of 940 African Americans found evidence of all four identity statuses across age groups. Only 27 percent of the adolescents were in the achieved group, as compared with 47 percent of the college students and 56 percent of the adults. Instead, adolescents were more likely to be in moratorium (42 percent). Twenty-five percent of the adolescents were in foreclosure. All three of these groups (achieved, in moratorium, and foreclosed) reported more positive regard for being African American than the 6 percent of adolescents who were diffused. Those of any age who were in the achieved status were most likely to view race as central to their identity (Yip, Seaton, & Sellers, 2006). And, reaching this stage of racial identity formation has practical applications. Although the effect is stronger for males than for females, increases in racial identity over 1 year have been related to a decreased risk of depressive symptoms (Mandara, Gaylord-Harden, Richards, & Ragsdale, 2009).

Another model focuses on three aspects of racial/ethnic identity: *connectedness* to one's own racial/ethnic group, *awareness of racism,* and *embedded achievement,* the belief that academic achievement is a part of group identity. A longitudinal study of low-income minority youth found that all three aspects of identity appear to stabilize and even to increase slightly by midadolescence. Thus a positive racial/ethnic identity may buffer tendencies toward a drop in grades and connection to school during the transition from middle school to high school (Altschul, Oyserman, & Bybee, 2006). On the other hand, perceived discrimination during the transition to adolescence can interfere with positive identity formation and lead to conduct problems or depression. As an example, perceptions of discrimination in Chinese American adolescents are associated with depressive symptoms, alienation, and a drop in academic performance (Benner & Kim, 2009). Protective factors are nurturant, involved parenting; prosocial friends; and strong academic performance (Brody et al., 2006).

One study of African American, Latino American, and European American adolescents investigated *group esteem* (feeling good about one's ethnicity) and *exploration of the meaning of ethnicity* in one's life. Group esteem rose during both early and middle adolescence, especially for African Americans and Latinos, for whom it

cultural socialization
Parental practices that teach children about their racial/ethnic heritage and promote cultural practices and cultural pride.

checkpoint
can **you**...

- List the three major issues involved in identity formation, according to Erikson?
- Describe four types of identity status found by Marcia?
- Discuss how gender and ethnicity affect identity formation?

was lower to begin with. Exploration increased only in middle adolescence, perhaps reflecting the transition to more ethnically diverse high schools. Interactions with members of other ethnic groups may stimulate young people's curiosity about their own ethnic identity (French, Seidman, Allen, & Aber, 2006). Girls may undergo the process of identity formation earlier than boys (Portes, Dunham, & Del Castillo, 2000). For example, one study showed that over a 4-year period Latina girls went through exploration, resolution, and affirmation of positive feelings about their ethnic identities, whereas boys showed increases only in affirmation. This finding is important because the increase in exploration—which the boys did not demonstrate—was the only factor tied to increase in self-esteem (Umana-Taylor, Gonzales-Backen, & Guimond, 2009).

The term **cultural socialization** refers to practices that teach children about their racial or ethnic heritage, promote cultural customs and traditions, and foster racial/ethnic and cultural pride. For example, think about the holidays you celebrate. Participating in those traditions and rituals was part of your cultural socialization. Adolescents who have experienced cultural socialization tend to have stronger and more positive ethnic identities than those who have not (Hughes et al., 2006).

Sexuality

Seeing oneself as a sexual being, recognizing one's sexual orientation, and forming romantic or sexual attachments all are parts of achieving *sexual identity.* Awareness of sexuality is an important aspect of identity formation. Although this process is biologically driven, its expression is in part culturally defined.

During the twentieth century a major change in sexual attitudes and behavior in the United States and other industrialized countries brought more widespread acceptance of premarital sex, homosexuality, and other previously disapproved forms of sexual activity. With widespread access to the Internet, casual sex with fleeting acquaintances met in online chat rooms or singles' meeting sites has become more common. Cell

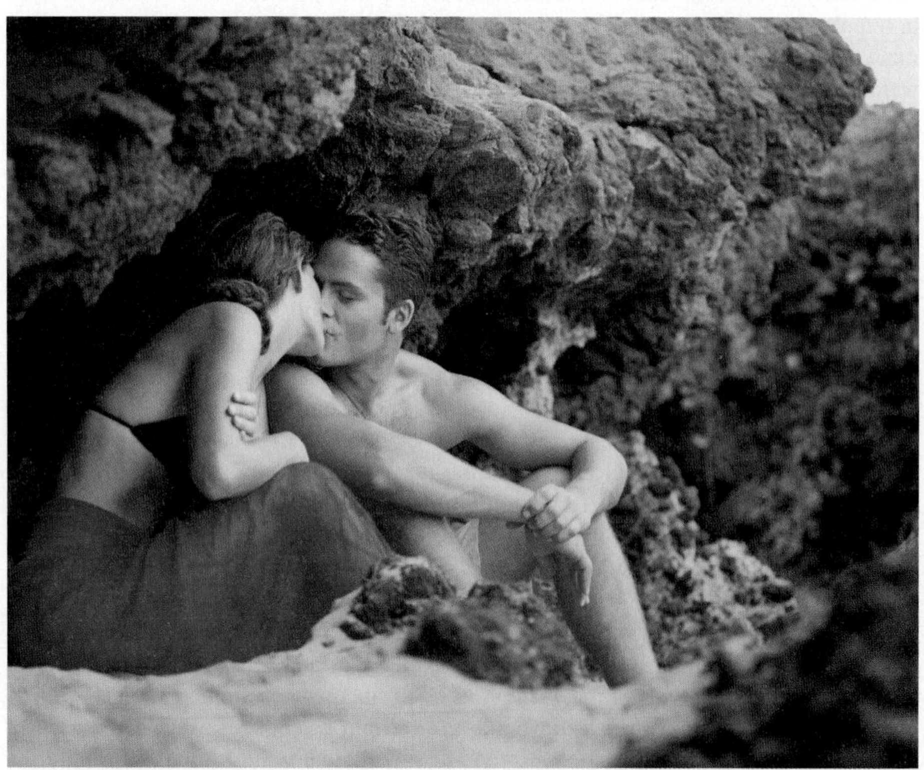

Attitudes toward sexuality have liberalized in the United States in the past 50 years. This trend includes more open acceptance of sexual activity and a decline in the double standard by which males are freer sexually than females.

phones, e-mail, and instant messaging make it easy for adolescents to arrange hookups with disembodied strangers. All of these changes have brought increased concerns about sexual risk-taking. On the other hand, the AIDS epidemic has led many young people to abstain from sexual activity outside of committed relationships or to engage in safer sexual practices.

sexual orientation
Focus of consistent sexual, romantic, and affectionate interest, either heterosexual, homosexual, or bisexual.

SEXUAL ORIENTATION AND IDENTITY

It is in adolescence that a person's **sexual orientation** generally becomes more clear: whether that person will consistently be sexually attracted to persons of the other sex (*heterosexual*), of the same sex (*homosexual*), or of both sexes (*bisexual*). And, as with other important areas of development, teens may hold varying identity statuses as they form their sexual identity. The prevalence of homosexual orientation varies widely. Depending on whether it is measured by sexual or romantic *attraction or arousal* or by sexual *behavior* or sexual *identity,* the rate of homosexuality in the U.S. population ranges from 1 to 21 percent (Savin-Williams, 2006).

Many young people have one or more homosexual experiences, but isolated experiences or even occasional attractions or fantasies do not determine sexual orientation. In a national survey, 4.5 percent of 15- to 19-year-old boys and 10.6 percent of girls in that age group reported ever having had same-sex sexual contact, but only 2.4 percent of the boys and 7.7 percent of the girls reported having done so in the past year (Mosher, Chandra, & Jones, 2005). Social stigma may bias such self-reports, underestimating the prevalence of homosexuality and bisexuality.

Most people experience their first crush at about 10 years of age, a process that appears to be related to the maturation of the adrenal glands. For those who will later identify as homosexual, this first crush is often on a member of the same sex.

Herdt & McClintock, 2000

Origins of Sexual Orientation Much research on sexual orientation has focused on efforts to explain homosexuality. Although it once was considered a mental illness, several decades of research have found no association between homosexual orientation and emotional or social problems—apart from those apparently caused by societal treatment of homosexuals (APA, n.d.; Meyer, 2003; C. J. Patterson, 1992, 1995a, 1995b). These findings led the psychiatric profession in 1973 to stop classifying homosexuality as a mental disorder.

Homosexual teens are at risk for depression and suicide largely due to contextual variables such as bullying and a lack of acceptance. In 2010, columnist and author Dan Savage created a YouTube video that went viral and has now resulted in the "It Gets Better" campaign. In this video, teens are assured that happiness and hope are a distinct possibility for the future—that, indeed, it does get better.

Sexual orientation seems to be at least partly genetic (Diamond & Savin-Williams, 2003). The first full genome-wide scan for male sexual orientation has identified three stretches of DNA on chromosomes 7, 8, and 10 that appear to be involved (Mustanski et al., 2005). However, because identical twins are not perfectly concordant for sexual orientation, nongenetic factors also play a part (Diamond & Savin-Williams, 2003). Among more than 3,800 Swedish same-sex twin pairs, genes explained about 34 percent of the variation in men and 18 percent in women. Shared family influences accounted for about 16 percent of the variation in women but had no effect in men (Långström, Rahman, Carlström, & Lichtenstein, 2008).

The more older biological brothers a man has, the more likely he is to be gay. Each older biological brother increases the chances of homosexuality in a younger brother by 33 percent. This phenomenon may be a cumulative immune-like response to the presence of successive male fetuses in the womb (Bogaert, 2006).

Imaging studies have found striking similarities of brain structure and function between homosexuals and heterosexuals of the other sex. Brains of gay men and straight women are symmetrical, whereas in lesbians and straight men the right hemisphere is slightly larger. Also, in gays and lesbians, connections in the amygdala, which is involved in emotion, are typical of the other sex (Savic & Lindström, 2008). One researcher reported a difference in the size of the hypothalamus, a brain structure that governs sexual activity, in heterosexual and gay men (LeVay, 1991). In brain imaging studies on pheromones, odors that attract mates, the odor of male sweat activated the hypothalamus in gay men much as it did in heterosexual women. Similarly, lesbian women and straight men reacted more positively to female pheromones than to male ones (Savic, Berglund, & Lindström, 2005, 2006). However, these differences may be an effect of homosexuality, not a cause.

checkpoint can **you**...

- Summarize research findings regarding origins of sexual orientation?
- Discuss homosexual identity and relationship formation?

Homosexual and Bisexual Identity Development Despite the increased acceptance of homosexuality in the United States, many adolescents who openly identify as gay, lesbian, or bisexual feel isolated. They may be subject to discrimination or violence. Others may be reluctant to disclose their sexual orientation, even to their parents, for fear of strong disapproval or a rupture in the family (Hillier, 2002). They may find it difficult to meet and identify potential same-sex partners (Diamond & Savin-Williams, 2003). Notice that, as in ethnic identity formation, not being from the majority group makes the process of identity formation more complex.

There is no single route to the development of sexual identity and behavior. Because of the lack of socially sanctioned ways to explore their sexuality, many gay and lesbian adolescents experience identity confusion (Sieving, Oliphant, & Blum, 2002). Gay, lesbian, and bisexual youth who are unable to establish peer groups that share their sexual orientation may struggle with the recognition of same-sex attractions (Bouchey & Furman, 2003).

SEXUAL BEHAVIOR

According to national surveys, 42.5 percent of never-married 15- to 19-year-olds have had sex (Abma, Martinez, & Copen, 2010) and 77 percent of young people in the United States have had sex by age 20 (Finer, 2007). This proportion has been roughly the same since the mid-1960s and the advent of the pill (Finer, 2007). The average girl has her first sexual intercourse at 17, the average boy at 16, and approximately one-fourth of boys and girls report having had intercourse by age 15 (Klein & AAP Committee on Adolescence, 2005). African Americans and Latinos tend to begin sexual activity earlier than white youth (Kaiser Family Foundation, Hoff, Greene, & Davis, 2003). Though teenage boys historically have been more likely to be sexually experienced than teenage girls, trends are shifting. In 2011, 44 percent of 12th grade boys and 51 percent of girls in that age group reported being sexually active (USDHHS, 2012; Figure 1).

Sexual Risk-Taking Two major concerns about adolescent sexual activity are the risks of contracting sexually transmitted infections (STIs) and, for heterosexual activity, of pregnancy. Most at risk are young people who start sexual activity early, have multiple partners, do not use contraceptives regularly, and have inadequate information—or

FIGURE 1
Percentage of Students in Grades 9 through 12 Who Report They Are Sexually Active

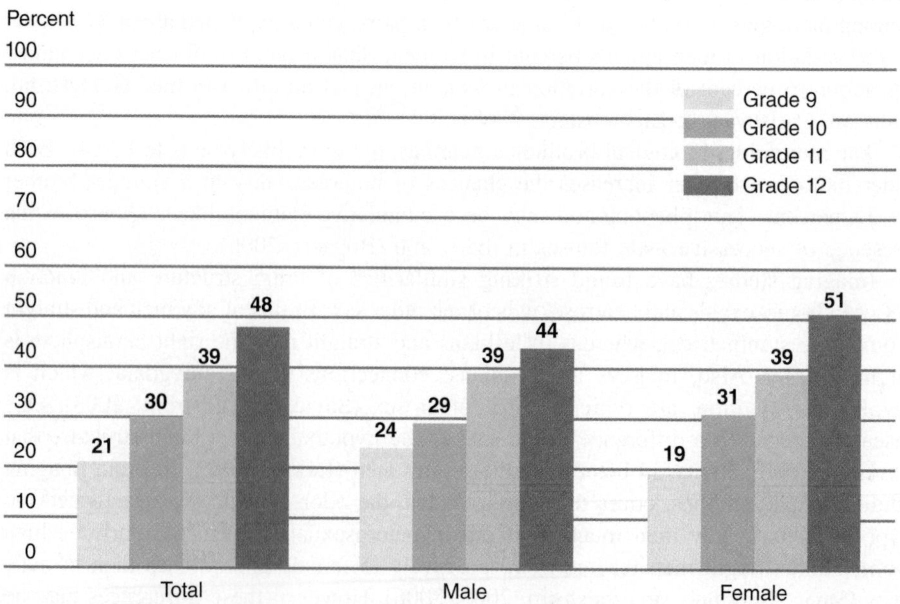

Source: Child Trends Databank, 2012.

misinformation—about sex (Abma et al., 1997). Other risk factors are living in a socio-economically disadvantaged community, substance use, antisocial behavior, and association with deviant peers. Parental monitoring can help reduce these risks (Baumer & South, 2001; Capaldi, Stoolmiller, Clark, & Owen, 2002).

Why do some adolescents become sexually active at an early age? Early puberty, poverty, poor school performance, lack of goals, a history of sexual abuse or parental neglect, and cultural or family patterns of early sexual experience may play a part (Klein & AAP Committee on Adolescence, 2005). The absence of a father, especially early in life, is a strong factor (Ellis et al., 2003). For those teens in two-parent families, having fathers who know more about their friends and activities is associated with delays in sexual activity (Coley, Votruba-Drzal, & Schindler, 2009). Teenagers who have close, warm relationships with their mothers are also likely to delay sexual activity, especially if they perceive that their mothers would disapprove (Jaccard & Dittus, 2000; Sieving, McNeely, & Blum, 2000). Generally, an involved and engaged relationship with teens is associated with decreases in risk of early sexual activity. For example, participating in regular family activities predicts declines in teenaged sexual activity (Coley et al., 2009). Other reasons teenagers give for not yet having had sex are that it is against their religion or morals and that they do not want to get (or get a girl) pregnant (Abma et al., 2010).

One of the most powerful influences is perception of peer group norms. Young people often feel under pressure to engage in sexual activities. In a nationally representative survey, nearly one-third of 15- to 17-year-olds, especially boys, said they had experienced pressure to have sex (Kaiser Family Foundation et al., 2003).

As U.S. adolescents have become more aware of the risks of sexual activity, the percentage who have ever had intercourse has declined, especially among boys (Abma et al., 2004). However, noncoital forms of genital sexual activity, such as oral and anal sex and mutual masturbation, are common. Many heterosexual teens do not regard these activities as "sex" but as substitutes for, or precursors of, sex, or even as abstinence (Remez, 2000). In one national survey, just over half of teenage boys and girls reported having given or received oral sex, more than had had vaginal intercourse (Mosher et al., 2005).

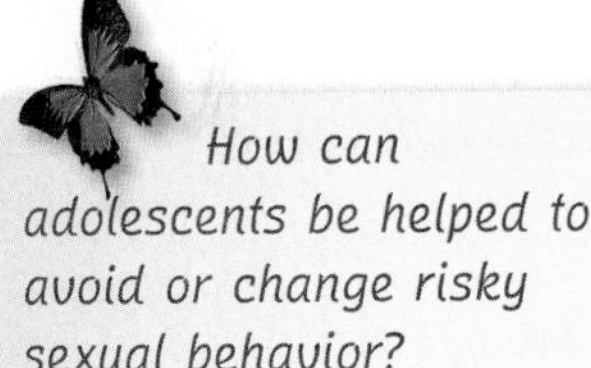
How can adolescents be helped to avoid or change risky sexual behavior?

Use of Contraceptives The use of contraceptives among teenagers has increased since the 1990s (Abma et al., 2004). Teens who, in their first relationship, delay intercourse, discuss contraception before having sex, or use more than one method of contraception are more likely to use contraceptives consistently throughout that relationship (Manlove, Ryan, & Franzetta, 2003).

The best safeguard for sexually active teens is regular use of condoms, which give some protection against STIs as well as against pregnancy. The first time they have sex teens use contraception, most often condoms, almost 80 percent of the time (Martinez, Copen, & Abma, 2011). The use of many types of contraceptives has increased among sexually active teenage girls in recent years, including the pill and new hormonal and injectable methods or combinations of methods (CDC, 2012b). In 2011, 52 percent of sexually active high school girls and 75 percent of sexually active high school boys reported having used condoms the last time they had intercourse (Martinez, Copen, & Abma, 2011). Adolescents who start using prescription contraceptives often stop using condoms, in some cases not realizing that they leave themselves unprotected against STIs (Klein & AAP Committee on Adolescence, 2005).

Condoms have been in use for at least 400 years.

Where Do Teenagers Get Information about Sex? Adolescents get their information about sex primarily from friends, parents, sex education in school, and the media (Kaiser Family Foundation et al., 2003). Adolescents who can talk about sex with older siblings as well as with parents are more likely to have positive attitudes toward safer sexual practices (Kowal & Pike, 2004).

Since 1998, federal- and state-funded sex education programs stressing abstinence until marriage as the best option have become common. Programs that encourage abstinence but also discuss STI prevention and safer sexual practices have been found to delay sexual initiation and increase contraceptive use (AAP Committee on Psychosocial Aspects of Child and Family Health and Committee on Adolescence, 2001).

However, some school programs promote abstinence as the *only* option, even though abstinence-only courses do not delay sexual activity (AAP Committee on Psychosocial Aspects of Child and Family Health and Committee on Adolescence, 2001; Satcher, 2001; Trenholm et al., 2007). Likewise, pledges to maintain virginity have shown little impact on sexual behavior other than a *decrease* in the likelihood to take precautions during sex (Rosenbaum, 2009).

Unfortunately, many teenagers get much of their "sex education" from the media, which present a distorted view of sexual activity, associating it with fun, excitement, competition, or violence and rarely showing the risks of unprotected sex. Teens exposed to highly sexual television content were twice as likely to experience a pregnancy compared with lower level or no exposure (Chandra et al., 2008).

checkpoint
can **you**...

- Cite trends in sexual activity among adolescents?
- Identify factors that increase or decrease the risks of sexual activity?

SEXUALLY TRANSMITTED INFECTIONS (STIs)

sexually transmitted infections (STIs) Infections and diseases spread by sexual contact.

Sexually transmitted infections (STIs) are diseases spread by sexual contact. An estimated 19 million new STIs are diagnosed each year, and 65 million Americans have an uncurable STI (Wildsmith, Schelar, Peterson, & Manlove, 2010). An estimated 3.2 million adolescent girls in the United States—about 1 in 4 of those ages 14 to 19—has had at least one STI (Forhan et al., 2008). The chief reasons for the prevalence of STIs among teenagers include early sexual activity; multiple partners; failure to use condoms or to use them regularly and correctly; and, for women, a tendency to have sex with older partners (CDC, 2000b; Forhan et al., 2008). Despite the fact that teens are at higher risk for contracting STIs, they perceive their own personal risk as low (Wildsmith et al., 2010).

STIs in adolescent girls are most likely to develop undetected. In a *single* unprotected sexual encounter with an infected partner, a girl runs a 1 percent risk of acquiring HIV, a 30 percent risk of acquiring genital herpes, and a 50 percent risk of acquiring gonorrhea (Alan Guttmacher Institute [AGI], 1999). Although teenagers tend to view oral sex as less risky than intercourse, a number of STIs, especially pharyngeal gonorrhea, can be transmitted in that way (Remez, 2000).

According to Piaget, teens perceiving low personal risk is an example of adolescent egocentrism. Piaget called this the personal fable. Teens often seem to behave as if they believe that bad things won't happen to them because their "personal story" is different and unique.

The most common STI, accounting for about half of all STI infections diagnosed in 15- to 24-year-olds each year, is human papilloma virus (HPV), or genital warts, the leading cause of cervical cancer in women (Weinstock et al., 2004). Among girls with three or more partners, the risk jumps to 50 percent (Forhan et al., 2008). There are approximately 40 types of HPV virus, a number of which have been identified as the leading cause of cervical cancer in women. A vaccine is available that prevents the types of HPV that cause most cases of cervical cancer and genital warts. The Centers for Disease Control (2013a) recommends routine vaccination for all female adolescents and young adults starting at age 11 or 12.

The most common *curable* STIs are chlamydia and gonorrhea. These diseases, if undetected and untreated, can lead to severe health problems, including, in women, pelvic inflammatory disease (PID), a serious abdominal infection. In the United States, close to 1 in 10 teenage girls and 1 in 5 boys are affected by either chlamydia or gonorrhea, or both (Forhan et al., 2008). Although the occurrence rates of gonorrhea and syphilis have remained stable, chlamydia has increased sharply (Figure 2).

Genital herpes simplex is a chronic, recurring, often painful, and highly contagious disease. It can be fatal to a person with a deficiency of the immune system or to the newborn infant of a mother who has an outbreak at the time of delivery. Its incidence has increased dramatically during the past three decades. Hepatitis B remains a prominent STI despite the availability, for more than 20 years, of a preventive vaccine. Also common among young people is trichomoniasis, a parasitic infection that may be passed along by moist towels and swimsuits (Weinstock, Berman, & Cates, 2004).

The human immunodeficiency virus (HIV), which causes AIDS, is transmitted through bodily fluids, usually by sharing intravenous drug needles or by sexual contact with an infected partner. The virus attacks the body's immune system, leaving a person vulnerable to a variety of fatal diseases. Symptoms of AIDS include extreme fatigue, fever, swollen lymph nodes, weight loss, diarrhea, and night sweats.

There were 2.3 million new HIV infections worldwide last year, representing a 33 percent decline from 2001 (UNAIDS, 2013). As of now, AIDS is incurable, but increasingly the related infections that kill people are being stopped with antiviral therapy (UNAIDS, 2013; Weinstock et al., 2004).

Comprehensive sex and STI/HIV education is critical to promoting responsible decision making and controlling the spread of STIs. Evidence for the positive impact of such programs is strong: more than 60 percent of programs that emphasized abstinence and condom use delayed and/or reduced sexually activity and increased the use of condoms or contraceptives. Further, the programs did not increase sexual activity. In contrast, programs that emphasize abstinence-only have shown little evidence of affecting sexual behavior (Kirby & Laris, 2009).

Rate per 100,000
2200
2000
1800
1600
1400
1200
1000
800
600
400
200
0
1996 1997 1998 1999 2000 2001 2002 2003 2004 2005 2006 2007 2008 2009 2010 2011
Year
Chlamydia
Gonorrhea
Syphilis

FIGURE 2

Chlamydia, Gonorrhea, and Syphilis Rates for Adolescents Aged 15 to 19

Source: Child Trends Databank, 2013.

checkpoint
can **you** . . .

- Identify and describe the most common sexually transmitted infections?
- List risk factors for developing an STI during adolescence, and identify effective prevention methods?

TEENAGE PREGNANCY AND CHILDBEARING

More than 7 in 10 adolescent girls in the United States have been pregnant at least once before age 20 (Kost, Henshaw, & Carlin, 2013). More than half (51 percent) of pregnant teenagers in the United States have their babies (Klein & AAP Committee on Adolescence, 2005). Sixty-seven percent of teens who carry the pregnancies to term are between the ages of 18 and 19 years, and 31 percent are 15 to 17 years of age, with 2 percent of live births accounted for by teens under the age of 15 (National Center for Health Statistics, 2009a). Overall, 35 percent of adolescents choose to abort (Figure 3), and 14 percent of teen pregnancies end in miscarriage or stillbirth (Klein & AAP Committee on Adolescence, 2005).

A substantial decline in teenage pregnancy has accompanied steady decreases in early intercourse and in sex with multiple partners and an increase in contraceptive use. In 2011, birthrates for teens dropped to their lowest level yet, 31.3 per 1,000 women ages 15 to 19 years (CDC, 2012a; Martin et al., 2012).

Programs that focus on teen outreach also have had some success. Such programs generally combine comprehensive sex education and access to family planning services. With the use of such a program, California—the only state that refused abstinence-only federal dollars—went from having the highest teen pregnancy rate to showing the steepest decline, effectively halving their rates (Boonstra, 2010). Similar results have been found with teen outreach programs that also focus on raising self-esteem, handling emotions, and dealing effectively with peers and adults (Allen & Philliber, 2001).

Although declines in teenage pregnancy and childbearing have occurred among all population groups, birthrates have fallen most sharply among black teenagers. Still, black and Hispanic girls are more

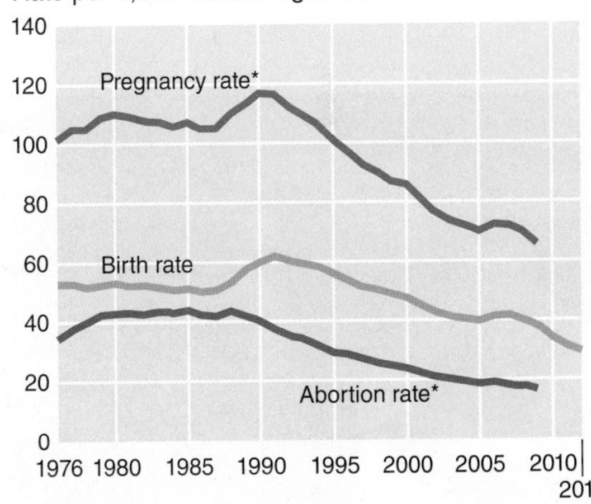

FIGURE 3

Pregnancy, Birth, and Abortion Rates for U.S. Teenagers Ages 15 to 19

Source: CDC, 2013b.

likely to have babies than white, American Indian, or Asian American girls (Martin et al., 2012).

More than 90 percent of pregnant teenagers describe their pregnancies as unintended, and 50 percent of teen pregnancies occur within 6 months of sexual initiation (Klein & AAP Committee on Adolescence, 2005). Many of these girls grew up fatherless (Ellis et al., 2003). Research suggests contributing factors include having been physically, emotionally, or sexually abused and/or exposed to parental divorce or separation, domestic violence, substance abuse, or a household member who was mentally ill or engaged in criminal behavior (Hillis et al., 2004). Teenage fathers, too, tend to have limited financial resources, poor academic performance, and high dropout rates. Many teenage parents are themselves products of adolescent pregnancy (Campa & Eckenrode, 2006; Klein & AAP Committee on Adolescence, 2005).

Outcomes of Teenage Pregnancy Teenage pregnancies often have poor outcomes. Many of the mothers are impoverished and poorly educated, and some are drug users. Many do not eat properly, do not gain enough weight, and get inadequate prenatal care, or none at all. Their babies are likely to be premature or dangerously small and are at heightened risk of other birth complications (Wen, Wen, Fleming, Demissie, Rhoads, & Walker, 2007). They are also at heightened risk for health and academic problems; abuse and neglect; and developmental disabilities that may continue into adolescence (AAP Committee on Adolescence and Committee on Early Childhood, Adoption, and Dependent Care, 2001; Children's Defense Fund, 2004; Klein & AAP Committee on Adolescence, 2005; Menacker, Martin, MacDorman, & Ventura, 2004).

Teenage unwed mothers and their families are likely to suffer financially. Teenage mothers are likely to drop out of school and to have repeated pregnancies. They and their partners may lack the maturity, skills, and social support to be good parents. Their children, in turn, tend to have developmental and academic problems, to be depressed, to engage in substance abuse and early sexual activity, to engage in gang activity, to be unemployed, and to become adolescent parents themselves (Klein & AAP Committee on Adolescence, 2005; Pogarsky, Thornberry, & Lizotte, 2006).

Poor outcomes of teenage parenting are far from inevitable, however. Several long-term studies find that, two decades after giving birth, most former adolescent mothers are not on welfare; many have finished high school and secured steady jobs; and they do not have large families. Comprehensive adolescent pregnancy and home visitation programs seem to contribute to good outcomes (Klein & AAP Committee on Adolescence, 2005), as do contact with the father (Howard, Lefever, Borkowski, & Whitman, 2006), and involvement in a religious community (Carothers, Borkowski, Lefever, & Whitman, 2005).

MTV's Teen Mom franchise, originally criticized for glamorizing teen pregnancy, may instead be partially responsible for the recent declines in teenage motherhood (Kearney & Levine, 2014).

Preventing Teenage Pregnancy Teenage pregnancy and birthrates in the United States are many times higher than in other industrialized countries, despite similar levels of sexual activity (Guttmacher Institute, 2013). Teenage birthrates are nearly 5 times as high in the United States as in Denmark, Finland, France, Germany, Italy, the Netherlands, Spain, Sweden, and Switzerland and 12 times as high as in Japan (Ventura, Mathews, & Hamilton, 2001).

Why are U.S. rates so high? Some observers point to such factors as the reduced stigma on unwed motherhood, media glorification of sex, the lack of a clear message that sex and parenthood are for adults, the influence of childhood sexual abuse, and failure of parents to communicate with children. Comparisons with the European experience suggest the importance of other factors: U.S. girls are more likely to have multiple sex partners and are less likely to use contraceptives (Darroch et al., 2001).

Europe's industrialized countries have provided universal, comprehensive sex education for a much longer time than the United States. Comprehensive programs encourage young teenagers to delay intercourse but also aim to improve contraceptive use among sexually active adolescents. Such programs include education about sexuality and acquisition of skills for making responsible sexual decisions and communicating with partners. They provide information about risks and consequences of teenage pregnancy, about birth control methods, and about where to get medical and contraceptive help (AAP Committee on Psychosocial Aspects of Child and Family Health and Committee on Adolescence, 2001).

In the United States the provision and content of sex education programs are political issues. Some critics claim that community- and school-based sex education leads to more or earlier sexual activity, even though evidence shows otherwise (Kirby & Laris, 2009).

An important component of pregnancy prevention in European countries is access to reproductive services. Contraceptives are provided free to adolescents in many countries. Sweden showed a fivefold reduction in the teenage birthrate following introduction of birth control education, free access to contraceptives, and free abortion on demand (Bracher & Santow, 1999).

Do you favor or oppose programs that provide contraceptives to teenagers?

The problem of teenage pregnancy requires a multifaceted solution. It must include programs and policies to encourage postponing or refraining from sexual activity, but it also must recognize that many young people do become sexually active and need education and information to prevent pregnancy and STIs. It requires attention to underlying factors that put teenagers and families at risk—reducing poverty, school failure, behavioral and family problems, and expanding employment, skills training, and family life education (CDC, 2013c)—and it should target those young people at highest risk (Klein & AAP Committee on Adolescence, 2005). Comprehensive early intervention programs for preschoolers and elementary school students have reduced teenage pregnancy (Lonczak, Abbott, Hawkins, Kosterman, & Catalano, 2002; Schweinhart et al., 1993).

Because adolescents with high aspirations are less likely to become pregnant, programs that motivate young people to achieve and raise their self-esteem have had some success. Teen Outreach Program (TOP), which began in 1978, helps teenagers make decisions, handle emotions, and deal with peers and adults. Among 1,600 students in TOP and 1,600 in a control group, TOP participants had about half the risk of pregnancy as nonparticipants (Allen & Philliber, 2001).

checkpoint
can you . . .

- Summarize trends in teenage pregnancy and birthrates?
- Discuss risk factors, problems, and outcomes connected with teenage pregnancy?
- Describe educational programs that can prevent teenage pregnancy?

Relationships with Family, Peers, and Adult Society

Age becomes a powerful bonding agent in adolescence. Adolescents spend more time with peers and less with family. Even as adolescents increasingly turn toward peers to fulfill many of their social needs, they still look to parents for a secure base from which they can try their wings, and their fundamental values stay more similar than most people realize (Offer & Church, 1991). You may recall that toddlers who use their parents as a secure base feel safer exploring the world—they know they have someone to count on if things go wrong.

Similarly, those adolescents who have the most secure attachment relationships tend to have strong, supportive relationships with parents who permit and encourage their strivings for independence while providing a safe haven in times of emotional stress (Allen et al., 2003).

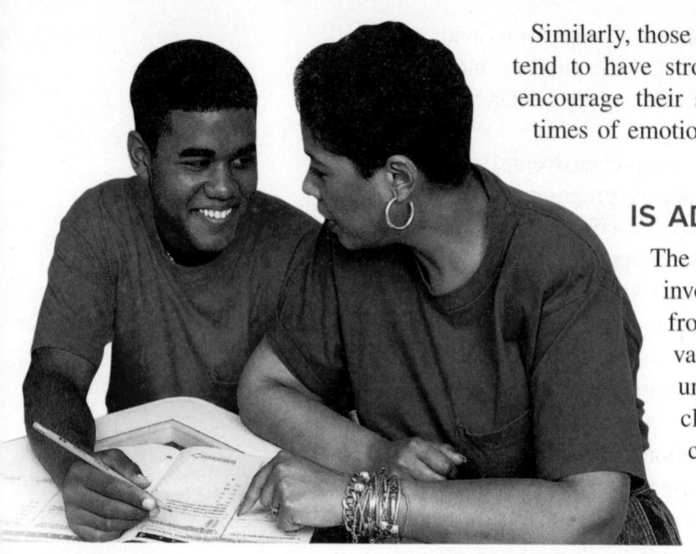

Contrary to popular belief, most adolescents are not ticking time bombs. Those raised in homes with a positive family atmosphere tend to come through adolescence with no serious problems.

IS ADOLESCENT REBELLION A MYTH?

The teenage years have been called a time of **adolescent rebellion,** involving emotional turmoil, conflict within the family, alienation from adult society, reckless behavior, and rejection of adult values. Yet full-fledged rebellion now appears to be relatively uncommon even in Western societies, at least among middle-class adolescents who are in school. Most young people feel close to and positive about their parents, share similar opinions on major issues, and value their parents' approval (Blum & Rinehart, 2000; Offer & Church, 1991).

adolescent rebellion
Pattern of emotional turmoil, characteristic of a minority of adolescents, that may involve conflict with family, alienation from adult society, reckless behavior, and rejection of adult values.

In a 34-year longitudinal study of 67 suburban boys 14 years old when the study began, the vast majority adapted well to their life experiences (Offer, Offer, & Ostrov, 2004). The relatively few deeply troubled adolescents tended to come from disrupted families and, as adults, continued to have unstable family lives and to reject cultural norms. Those raised in homes with a positive family atmosphere tended to come through adolescence with no serious problems and, as adults, to have solid marriages and lead well-adjusted lives (Offer, Kaiz, Ostrov, & Albert, 2002).

Still, adolescence can be a tough time for young people and their parents. Family conflict, depression, and risky behavior are more common than during other parts of the life span (Arnett, 1999; Petersen et al., 1993). And family conflict, while relatively infrequent, has a significant impact on emotional distress. This finding is particularly true for girls and for those teens whose parents are foreign-born (Chung, Flook, & Fuligni, 2009). Negative emotions and mood swings are most intense during early adolescence, perhaps due to the stress connected with puberty. By late adolescence, emotionality tends to become more stable (Larson, Moneta, Richards, & Wilson, 2002).

study smart

Adolescence as a Social Construction

Recognizing that adolescence may be a difficult time can help parents and teachers put trying behavior in perspective. But adults who assume that adolescent turmoil is normal and necessary may fail to heed the signals of the relatively few young persons who need special help.

checkpoint
can you . . .

- Assess the extent of storm and stress during the teenage years?

CHANGING TIME USE AND CHANGING RELATIONSHIPS

One way to measure changes in adolescents' relationships with the important people in their lives is to see how they spend their discretionary time. The amount of time U.S. adolescents spend with their families declines dramatically during the teenage years. However, this disengagement is not a rejection of the family but a response to developmental needs. Early adolescents often retreat to their rooms; they seem to need time alone to step back from the demands of social relationships, regain emotional stability, and reflect on identity issues (Larson, 1997).

Cultural variations in time use reflect varying cultural needs, values, and practices (Verma & Larson, 2003). Young people in tribal or peasant societies spend most of their time producing bare necessities of life and have much less time for socializing than adolescents in technologically advanced societies (Larson & Verma, 1999). In some postindustrial societies such as Korea and Japan, where the pressures of schoolwork and family obligations are strong, adolescents have relatively little free time. To relieve stress, they spend their time in passive pursuits, such as watching television and "doing nothing" (Verma & Larson, 2003). In India's family-centered culture, on the other hand, middle-class urban eighth graders spend 39 percent of their waking hours with family (as compared with 23 percent for U.S. eighth graders) and report being happier when with their families than the U.S. eighth graders do. For these young people, the task of adolescence is not to separate from the family but to become more integrated with it. Similar findings have been reported in Indonesia, Bangladesh, Morocco, and Argentina (Larson & Wilson, 2004). In comparison, U.S. adolescents have a good deal of discretionary time, most of which they spend with peers, increasingly of the other sex (Juster et al., 2004; Larson & Seepersad, 2003; Verma & Larson, 2003). They spend a growing proportion of this down time engaged in consuming various forms of media, including watching television, listening to music, surfing the Web, playing video games, and watching movies. For example, from 2004 to 2009, teens increased their media usage from 6:21 to 7:38 minutes a day, every day, and often used several forms of media at the same time. These trends have been most pronounced in younger teens aged 11 to 14 years and in African American and Latino adolescents (Rideout, Fochet, & Roberts, 2010).

Ethnicity may affect family connectedness. In some research, African American teenagers, who may look on their families as havens in a hostile world, tended to maintain more intimate family relationships and less intense peer relations than white teenagers (Giordano, Cernkovich, & DeMaris, 1993). Among 489 ninth graders, however, those with European backgrounds reported as much or more family identification and closeness as did minority students. On the other hand, those from Mexican and Chinese families, particularly immigrant families, reported a stronger sense of family obligation and assistance and spent more time on activities that carried out those obligations (Hardway & Fuligni, 2006). It may be that while the overall amount of assistance provided to their families varies across ethnic and cultural groups, providing assistance to their family is associated with feelings of connectedness, and is thus beneficial. For example, research has shown that Asian, Latino, and European American teens all tend to show higher levels of happiness when they participate in activities that help the family (Telzer & Fulingi, 2009).

With such cultural variations in mind, let's look more closely at relationships with parents, and then with siblings and peers.

checkpoint
can **you** . . .

- Identify and discuss age and cultural differences in how young people spend their time?

ADOLESCENTS AND PARENTS

Relationships with parents during adolescence are grounded largely in the emotional closeness developed in childhood. And adolescent relationships with parents, in turn, set the stage for the quality of the relationship with a partner in adulthood (Overbeek, Stattin, Vermulst, Ha, & Engels, 2007).

Most adolescents report good relations with their parents (Gutman & Eccles, 2007). Still, adolescence brings special challenges. Just as adolescents feel tension between dependency on their parents and the need to break away, parents want their children to be independent yet find it hard to let go. Tensions can lead to family conflict, and parenting styles can influence its shape and outcome. Effective monitoring depends on how much adolescents let parents know about their daily lives, and such disclosures may depend on the atmosphere parents have established. Also, as with younger children, adolescents' relationships with parents are affected by the parents' life situation—their work and marital and socioeconomic status. Personality is also an important factor. Agreeableness in adolescents and extraversion in parents both predict relationship warmth (Denissen, van Aken, & Dubas, 2009).

Individuation and Family Conflict If you were like most teens, you probably listened to different music from your parents, dressed in a different style of clothing, and felt it was reasonable to keep certain things private from them. This process, called **individuation** by psychologists, begins in infancy and continues throughout adolescence. It involves the struggle for autonomy and differentiation, or personal identity. An important aspect of individuation is carving out boundaries of control

individuation
Adolescents' struggle for autonomy and personal identity.

study smart

Conflict with Parents

between self and parents (Nucci, Hasebe, & Lins-Dyer, 2005), and this process may entail family conflict.

In a longitudinal study, 1,357 European American and African American youth were interviewed between high school entry and 11th grade. Results showed that young people who saw themselves as having a great deal of autonomy over their everyday activities tended to spend more time in unsupervised socializing with peers and were at risk for problem behavior by 11th grade. Those who perceived their parents as highly intrusive in their personal lives were influenced by negative peer interactions and joined their friends in risky behaviors. Thus parents of young adolescents must strike a delicate balance between too much freedom and too much intrusiveness (Goldstein, Davis-Kean, & Eccles, 2005).

Arguments most often concern control over everyday personal matters—chores, schoolwork, dress, money, curfews, dating, and friends—rather than issues of health and safety or right and wrong (Adams & Laursen, 2001; Steinberg, 2005). Teens generally feel they should have autonomy over personal matters. The emotional intensity of these conflicts may reflect the underlying individuation process. In a longitudinal study of 99 families, both individuation and family connectedness during adolescence predicted well-being in middle age (Bell & Bell, 2005).

The process of individuation can be rocky, and as teens work out the details of their new power dynamic, conflict may result. Both family conflict and positive identification with parents are highest at age 13 and then diminish until age 17, when they stabilize or increase somewhat. This shift reflects increased opportunities for independent adolescent decision making (Gutman & Eccles, 2007), enlarging the boundaries of what is considered the adolescent's own business (Steinberg, 2005). There are also cultural differences. Younger American teens define themselves in terms of their relationship with their parents, but the tendency to do this diminishes with age. By contrast, Chinese teens continue to view themselves as interconnected across younger and later adolescence (Pomerantz, Qin, Wang, & Chen, 2009).

Especially for girls, family relations can affect mental health. Adolescents who are given more decision-making opportunities report higher self-esteem than those who are given fewer such opportunities. In addition, negative family interactions are related to adolescent depression, whereas positive family identification is related to less depression (Gutman & Eccles, 2007). Moreover, family conflict tends to go down over time in warm, supportive families, but increases in hostile, coercive, or critical families (Rueter & Conger, 1995). In addition, autonomy support on the part of parents is associated with more adaptive self-regulation of negative emotions and academic engagement (Roth et al., 2009).

What issues caused the most conflict in your family when you were a teenager, and how were they resolved?

Parenting Styles and Parental Authority Authoritative parenting continues to foster healthy psychosocial development (Baumrind, 2005). Overly strict, authoritarian parenting may lead an adolescent to reject parental influence and to seek peer support and approval at all costs (Fuligni & Eccles, 1993), and expressions of disappointment are more effective in motivating responsible behavior than is harsh punishment (Krevans & Gibbs, 1996).

Authoritative parents insist on important rules, norms, and values but are willing to listen, explain, and negotiate. They exercise appropriate control over a child's conduct (*behavioral control*) but not over the child's feelings, beliefs, and sense of self (*psychological control*) (Steinberg & Darling, 1994). So, for example, they might ground their teenage son for breaking a rule, but they would not insist that the teen agree with them about the wisdom of the broken rule. Generally, behavioral control is preferable. Psychological control, exerted through such emotionally manipulative techniques as withdrawal of love, can harm adolescents' psychosocial development and mental health (Steinberg, 2005). For example, withdrawal of love as a control strategy is associated with an increase in resentment toward parents and a decrease in teens' ability to self-regulate negative emotions (Roth et al., 2009). Parents who are psychologically controlling tend to be unresponsive to their children's growing need for *psychological autonomy,* the right to their own thoughts and feelings (Steinberg, 2005). By contrast, parents who are open to new experiences themselves are more likely to allow their teens greater freedom (Denissen et al., 2009).

Authoritative parenting bolsters adolescents' self-image. Generally, teens whose parents firmly enforce behavioral rules have more self-discipline and fewer behavior problems than those with more permissive parents. In addition, when parents grant teens psychological autonomy, they tend to become more self-confident and competent. Together such research indicates that parents who provide both structure and autonomy help teens develop rules of conduct, psychosocial skills, and good mental health (Gray & Steinberg, 1999).

Problems arise when parents overstep what adolescents perceive as appropriate bounds of legitimate parental authority. The existence of a mutually agreed personal domain in which authority belongs to the adolescent has been found in various cultures and social classes from Japan to Brazil. This domain expands as parents and adolescents continually renegotiate its boundaries (Nucci et al., 2005). When teens feel their parents are trying to dominate their behavior, and particularly their psychological experience, their emotional health suffers.

Parental Monitoring and Adolescents' Self-disclosure A large body of research shows that parental monitoring is one of the most consistently identified protective factors for teens (Barnes, Hoffman, & Welte, 2006; Racz & McMahon, 2011). Parental monitoring broadly involves keeping track of the young person's activities, for example, by signing the teen up for after-school activities, checking in with parents of their teen's friends, and keeping track of a teen's whereabouts (Barnes et al., 2006).

Part of monitoring involves knowing what a teen is up to. Young people's growing autonomy and the shrinking areas of perceived parental authority redefine the types of behavior adolescents are expected to disclose to parents (Smetana, Crean, & Campione-Barr, 2005; Table 4). In a study of 276 ethnically diverse suburban 9th and 12th graders, both adolescents and parents saw *prudential* issues, behavior related to health and safety (such as smoking, drinking, and drug use), as most subject to disclosure; followed by *moral* issues (such as lying); *conventional* issues (such as bad manners or swearing); and *multifaceted,* or borderline, issues (such as seeing an R-rated movie), which lie at the boundary between personal matters and one of the other categories. Both adolescents and parents saw *personal* issues (such

TABLE 4 Items Used to Assess Perceived Areas of Parental versus Adolescent Authority

Moral Items	Conventional Items	Prudential Items	Multifaceted Items	Multifaceted Friendship	Personal Items
Stealing money from parents	Not doing assigned chores	Smoking cigarettes	Not cleaning bedroom	When to start dating	Sleeping late on weekends
Hitting siblings	Talking back to parents	Drinking beer or wine	Getting ears pierced with multiple holes	Staying over at a friend's house	Choosing how to spend allowance money
Lying to parents	Using bad manners	Doing drugs	Staying out late	Seeing friends whom parents don't like	Choosing own clothes or hairstyles
Breaking a promise to parents	Cursing	Having sex	Watching cable TV	Seeing friends rather than going out with family	Choice of music

Source: Adapted from Smetana, Crean, & Campione-Barr, 2005.

as how teens spend their time and money) as least subject to disclosure. However, for each type of behavior parents wanted more disclosure than adolescents were willing to provide. This discrepancy diminished with age as parents modified their expectations to fit adolescents' growing maturity (Smetana, Metzger, Gettman, & Campione-Barr, 2006).

In a study of 690 Belgian adolescents, teens disclosed more information when parents maintained a warm, responsive family climate and provided clear expectations without being overly controlling (Soenens, Vansteenkiste, Luyckx, & Goossens, 2006)—in other words, when parenting was authoritative. This link between warmth and disclosure also has been found in various ethnic groups in the United States, including Chinese, Mexican American, and European American youth (Yau, Tasopoulos-Chan, & Smetana, 2009). Adolescents, especially girls, tend to have closer, more supportive relationships with their mothers than with their fathers (Smetana et al., 2006), and girls confide more in their mothers (Yau et al., 2009). Moreover, relationship quality seems to matter more in girls' willingness to confide in their parents. In other words, boys' secret keeping depends less on relationship warmth than does that of girls' (Keijsers et al., 2010).

Family Structure and Family Atmosphere Conflict in the home can affect the process of individuation. In a longitudinal study of 451 adolescents and their parents, changes in marital distress or conflict predicted corresponding changes in adolescents' adjustment (Cui, Conger, & Lorenz, 2005). Divorce can affect this process as well. Adolescents whose parents later divorced showed more academic, psychological, and behavioral problems before the breakup than peers whose parents did not later divorce (Sun, 2001). Moreover, research has shown that teens whose parents are still married report a close relationship with their father 48 percent of the time, whereas those whose parents are divorced report being close to their father only 25 percent of the time (Scott, Booth, King, & Johnson, 2007).

Adolescents living with their continuously married parents tend to have significantly fewer behavioral problems than those in other family structures (single-parent, cohabiting, or stepfamilies). An important factor is father involvement. High-quality involvement by a nonresident father helps a great deal, but not as much as the involvement of a father living in the home (Carlson, 2006).

Adolescents in cohabiting families, like younger children, tend to have greater behavioral and emotional problems than adolescents in married families; and, when one of the cohabiting parents is not a biological parent, school engagement suffers as well. For adolescents, unlike younger children, these effects are independent of economic resources, parental well-being, or effectiveness of parenting, suggesting that parental cohabitation itself may be more troublesome for adolescents than for younger children (S. L. Brown, 2004).

On the other hand, a multiethnic study of single mothers found no negative effects of single parenting on school performance or on problem behavior. What mattered most were the mother's educational level and ability, family income, and the quality of the home environment (Ricciuti, 2004). This finding suggests that negative effects of living in a single-parent home can be offset by positive factors.

Mothers' Employment and Economic Stress The impact of a mother's work outside the home may depend on how many parents are present in the household. Often a single mother must work to stave off economic disaster; how her working affects her teenage children may hinge on how much time and energy she has left over to spend with them, and how much parental monitoring she is able to provide. The type of after-school care and supervision is particularly important. Those who are on their own, away from home, tend to become involved in alcohol and drug use and in misconduct in school, especially if they have an early history of problem behavior. However, this is less likely to happen when parents monitor their children's activities and neighbors are actively involved (Coley, Morris, & Hernandez, 2004).

As we discussed earlier, a major problem in many single-parent families is lack of money. In a national longitudinal study, adolescent children of low-income single mothers were more likely to drop out of school and show declines in self-esteem and mastery if their mothers had unstable employment or were out of work for 2 years (Kalil & Ziol-Guest, 2005). Furthermore, family economic hardship during adolescence can affect adult well-being, especially if parents see their situation as stressful and if that stress interferes with family relationships and affects children's educational and occupational attainments (Sobolewski & Amato, 2005).

On the other hand, many adolescents in economically distressed families benefit from accumulated social capital—the support of kin and community. In 51 poor, urban African American families in which teenagers were living with their mothers, grandmothers, or aunts, women who had strong kinship networks exercised firmer control and closer monitoring while granting appropriate autonomy, and their teenage charges were more self-reliant and had fewer behavior problems (R. D. Taylor & Roberts, 1995).

checkpoint
can you . . .

- Identify factors that affect conflict with parents and adolescents' self-disclosure?
- Discuss the impact on adolescents of parenting styles and of marital status, mothers' employment, and economic stress?

ADOLESCENTS AND SIBLINGS

If you have one or more brothers or sisters, did your relationships with them change during adolescence?

There are several trends in sibling relationships across adolescence. In general, siblings spend less time together, their relationships become more equal, and they become more similar in their levels of competence.

Changes in sibling relationships in many ways precede and mirror the changes we see in the relationships of adolescents and their parents. As young people develop, they become more independent, and they begin to exert their autonomy and spend less time with their parents and more time with their peers. Sibling processes are similar. As adolescents spend more time with peers, they spend less time with siblings. Generally, and perhaps as a result of this, adolescents tend to be less close to siblings than to friends and are less influenced by them. This distance grows across adolescence (Laursen, 1996). Moreover, as children approach high school, their relationships with their siblings become progressively more equal. As relative age differences shrink, so do differences in competence and independence (Buhrmester & Furman, 1990).

Research has shown that sisters generally report more intimacy than brothers or mixed pairs. Mixed-sex siblings become less intimate between middle childhood and early adolescence, but more so in middle adolescence, a time when most young people become more interested in the other sex. Sibling conflict declines across middle adolescence (Kim, McHale, Osgood, & Courter, 2006).

Sibling relationships also reflect both parent-child relations and the parents' marital relationship. For example, in one study siblings were more intimate if their mother was warm and accepting. Parent-child conflict was associated with sibling conflict. However, when fathers became less happy in their marriage, siblings became closer and quarreled less (Kim et al., 2006).

Siblings can exert positive or negative effects. In single-mother homes, a warm and nurturing relationship with an older sister tended to prevent a younger sister from engaging in substance use and risky sexual behavior. On the other hand, having a domineering older sister tended to increase a younger sibling's high-risk sexual behavior (East & Khoo, 2005). Older siblings may influence a younger one to smoke, drink, or use drugs (Pomery et al., 2005; Rende et al., 2005).

Sibling relationships become more equal as younger siblings approach or reach adolescence and the relative age difference diminishes. Even so, younger siblings still look up to their older siblings and may try to emulate them.

checkpoint
can **you**...

- Identify typical changes in sibling relationships during adolescence and factors that affect these relationships?

Younger siblings hanging out with an antisocial older brother are at serious risk for adolescent antisocial behavior, drug use, sexual behavior, and violence, regardless of parental discipline (Snyder, Bank, & Burraston, 2005). A meta-analysis supports the strong connection between warm relationships with little conflict and healthier psychological adjustment in siblings (Buist, Dekovic, & Prinzie, 2013).

ADOLESCENTS AND PEERS

As an adolescent, were you part of a clique or crowd? If so, how did it affect your social relationships and attitudes?

An important influence in adolescence is the peer group. The peer group is a source of affection, sympathy, understanding, and moral guidance; a place for experimentation; and a setting for achieving autonomy and independence from parents. It is a place to form intimate relationships that serve as rehearsals for adult intimacy.

In childhood, most peer interactions are *dyadic,* or one-to-one, though larger groupings begin to form in middle childhood. As children move into adolescence, the peer social system becomes more diverse. *Cliques*—structured groups of friends who do things together—become more important. A larger type of grouping, the *crowd,* which does not normally exist before adolescence, is based not on personal interactions but on reputation, image, or identity. Crowd membership is a social construction: for example, the jocks, the nerds, or the stoners. All three levels of peer groupings may exist simultaneously, and some may overlap in membership, which may change over time. Both clique and crowd affiliations tend to become looser as adolescence progresses (B. B. Brown & Klute, 2003).

The influence of peers normally peaks at ages 12 to 13 and declines during middle and late adolescence. At age 13 or 14, popular adolescents may engage in mildly antisocial behaviors, such as trying drugs or sneaking into a movie without paying, to demonstrate to their peers their independence from parental rules (Allen, Porter, McFarland, Marsh, & McElhaney, 2005).

Risk-taking, especially in early adolescence, is higher in the company of peers than when alone (Gardner & Steinberg, 2005). However, attachment to peers in early adolescence is not likely to forecast real trouble unless the attachment is so strong that the young person is willing to give up obeying household rules, doing schoolwork, and developing his or her own talents in order to win peer approval and popularity (Fuligni, Eccles, Barber, & Clements, 2001).

study**smart**

Cliques and Crowds

Friendships The intensity of friendships and the amount of time spent with friends may be greater in adolescence than at any other time. Friendships become more reciprocal, equal, and stable. Those that are less satisfying become less important or are abandoned.

The increased intimacy of adolescent friendship reflects cognitive as well as emotional development. Closer intimacy means a greater ability and desire to share emotions and feelings.

Greater intimacy, loyalty, and sharing with friends mark a transition toward adultlike friendships. Adolescents begin to rely more on friends than on parents for intimacy and support, and they share confidences more than younger friends do (Hartup & Stevens, 1999; Nickerson & Nagle, 2005). Girls' friendships tend to be more intimate than boys', with frequent sharing of confidences (B. B. Brown & Klute, 2003). Intimacy with same-sex friends increases during early to midadolescence, after which it typically declines as intimacy with the other sex grows (Laursen, 1996).

The increased intimacy of adolescent friendship reflects cognitive as well as emotional development. Adolescents are now better able to express their private thoughts and feelings. They can more readily consider another person's point of view, so it is easier for them to understand a friend's thoughts and feelings. Confiding in a friend helps young people explore their own feelings, define their identity, and validate their self-worth (Buhrmester, 1996).

Humans are social animals, and as such the quality of our relationships matters greatly to outcomes. Friends are important. Thus it is not surprising that the capacity for intimacy is related to psychological adjustment and social competence. Adolescents who have close, stable, supportive friendships generally have a high opinion of themselves, do well in school, are sociable, and are unlikely to be hostile, anxious, or depressed (Berndt & Perry, 1990; Buhrmester, 1990; Hartup & Stevens, 1999). They also tend to have established strong bonds with parents (B. B. Brown & Klute, 2003). A bidirectional process seems to be at work: good relationships foster adjustment, which in turn fosters good friendships. Online communication has had both positive and negative effects on adolescents' social relationships (Box 1).

There are indications that administering oxytocin, a hormone involved in social affiliation, results in better social cognitive abilities, but only for those people who are deficient in this hormone to start with.

Bartz, 2010

It is true that those around you influence your propensity to take risks, but it is also true that some people, by virtue of their genetic makeup, are more likely to take risks. Researchers have recently found that mutations linked to the production of dopamine are involved in sensation-seeking.

Derringer et al., 2011

Romantic Relationships Romantic relationships are a central part of most adolescents' social worlds. With the onset of puberty, most heterosexual boys and girls begin to think about and interact more with members of the other sex. Typically, they move from mixed groups or group dates to one-on-one romantic relationships that, unlike other-sex friendships, they describe as involving passion and a sense of commitment (Bouchey & Furman, 2003; Furman & Wehner, 1997).

There are social consequences to online communities . . . and there are academic ones as well. Students who are on Facebook while they study earn 20 percent lower grades than their peers who turn the computer off.

Kirschner & Karpinski, 2010

study smart

Social Networking

Romantic relationships tend to become more intense and more intimate across adolescence. Early adolescents think primarily about how a romantic relationship may affect their status in the peer group (Bouchey & Furman, 2003). In midadolescence, most young people have at least one exclusive partner lasting for several months to about a year, and the effect of the choice of partner on peer status tends to become less important (Furman & Wehner, 1997). By age 16, adolescents interact with and think about romantic partners more than parents, friends, or siblings (Bouchey & Furman, 2003). Not until late adolescence or early adulthood, though, do romantic relationships begin to serve the full gamut of emotional needs that such relationships can serve and then only in relatively long-term relationships (Furman & Wehner, 1997).

Relationships with parents and peers may affect the quality of romantic relationships. The parent's own marriage or romantic relationship may serve as a model for their adolescent child. The peer group forms the context for most romantic relationships and may affect an adolescent's choice of a partner and the way the relationship develops (Bouchey & Furman, 2003).

study smart

Dating

Dating Violence Dating violence is a significant problem in the United States. The three common forms of dating violence are:

Physical—when a partner is hit, pinched, shoved, or kicked

Emotional—when a partner is threatened or verbally abused

Sexual—when a partner is forced to engage in a nonconsensual sex act

Statistics indicate that about 10 percent of students have been victims of physical dating violence, but the rate is almost certainly underreported. The rates for emotional

research in action

CONSEQUENCES OF THE SOCIAL NETWORK

The explosion of online communication technologies such as instant messaging, e-mail, and text messaging, as well as social networking sites like Snapchat and Instagram, has changed the way many adolescents communicate. As a group, adolescents are the primary users of social interaction technologies. They spend more time online than adults, and spend a majority of their online time using the Internet to communicate. Early research suggested that online communication would reduce adolescents' social connectedness with friends and family members. Studies on the effects of Internet use in the 1990s and early 2000 showed that adolescents who spent a lot of time on the Internet spent less time with friends (Nie, 2001), had fewer friends (Mesch, 2001), and showed reduced social connectedness and well-being (Kraut et al., 1998).

As access to the Internet has increased and as more sophisticated technologies like instant messaging (IM) and Facebook have replaced public chat rooms, the effect of increased Internet use has shifted from negative to positive. European and U.S. studies have shown that 88 percent of adolescents use IM to communicate with existing friends (Valkenburg & Peter, 2007). Recent studies have shown that online communication stimulates rather than reduces social connectedness (Kraut et al., 2002). One study determined that the number of months a person is active on Twitter and the more hours per week he or she spends tweeting is positively related to camaraderie and connection to an online community (Chen, 2010).

The ability of online communication to enhance online self-disclosure has been identified as a primary reason for improved social connectedness and well-being. Individuals often become unusually intimate in an online environment with reduced visual and auditory contextual cues. They are less concerned about how others perceive them and more free to express themselves (Tidewell & Walther, 2002; Valkenburg & Peter, 2009). Because adolescents connect self-disclosure with quality friendships, the elevated level of self-disclosure in online environments can also be linked to friendship quality and formation (McKenna & Bargh, 2000; Valkenburg & Peter, 2007), which in turn elevates social connectedness and well-being.

The aspects of online communication that enhance connectedness—the level of anonymity—has made it appealing for electronic bullies. Bullying is a form of aggression intended to harm. Verbal and physical bullying are the more prevalent types of bullying, but cyber bullying and victimization rates have been reported by about 25 percent of middle school students (Willard, 2006). Also, although self-disclosure is more common online, so is lying. People are more likely to lie over e-mail than over old-fashioned pen and paper (Naquin, Kurtzberg, & Belkin, 2010).

What do you think are the pros and cons of using social network sites?

checkpoint
can **you** . . .

- List several functions of the peer group in adolescence, and discuss the role of peer influence?
- Identify important features of adolescent friendships?
- Trace developmental changes in romantic relationships?

abuse are even higher: as many as 3 in 10 adolescents report being verbally or psychologically abused (Halpern, Young, Waller, Martin, & Kupper, 2003). Altogether, 1 in 4 adolescents reports verbal, physical, emotional, or sexual abuse from a dating partner each year (CDC, 2008a).

In addition to the physical harm caused by this type of abuse, teens who are victims of dating violence are more likely to do poorly in school and to engage in risky behaviors like drug and alcohol use. These students are also subject to eating disorders, depression, and suicide. Boys report slightly higher levels of victimization, but girls are disproportionately victims in cases of severe violence (Mulford & Giordano, 2008).

Risk factors that may predict violence include substance abuse, conflict and/or abuse in the home, antisocial peers, and living in neighborhoods with high crime and drug use rates (Child Trends, 2010a, 2010b). Unhealthy relationships can last a lifetime as victims carry patterns of violence into future relationships.

Antisocial Behavior and Juvenile Delinquency

What influences young people to enage in—or refrain from—violence (Box 2) or other antisocial acts? By what processes do antisocial tendencies develop? What determines whether a juvenile delinquent will grow up to be a hardened criminal? Human behavior is complex, and no one factor is responsible for antisocial behavior. Rather, the development of antisocial behavior involves a complex and reciprocal interaction between environment and biological risk factors (van Goozen et al., 2007).

BECOMING A DELINQUENT: GENETIC AND NEUROLOGICAL FACTORS

Antisocial behavior tends to run in families. Analyses of many studies have concluded that genes influence 40 to 50 percent of the variation in antisocial behavior within a population, and 60 to 65 percent of the variation in aggressive antisociality (Rhee & Waldman, 2002; Tackett, Krueger, Iacono, & McGue, 2005). Genes alone, however, are not predictive of antisocial behavior. Recent research findings suggest that although genetics influences delinquency, environmental influences including family, friends, and school affect gene expression (Guo, Roettger, & Cai, 2008).

Neurobiological deficits, particularly in the portions of the brain that regulate reactions to stress, may help explain why some children become antisocial. As a result of these neurological deficits, which may result from the interaction of genetic factors or difficult temperament with adverse early environments, children may not receive or heed normal warning signals to restrain impulsive or reckless behavior (van Goozen et al., 2007).

Teens who drop out of high school cost society approximately $240,000 in lost tax revenue, increased use of social services, and greater likelihood of being on welfare or incarcerated. In October 2008, approximately 30 million 16- to 24-year-olds were not in school and had not earned a high school diploma. This represents approximately 8 percent of eligible teens.

Chapman et al., 2010

BECOMING A DELINQUENT: HOW FAMILY, PEER, AND COMMUNITY INFLUENCES INTERACT

Researchers have identified two types of antisocial behavior: an *early-onset* type, beginning by age 11, which tends to lead to chronic juvenile delinquency in adolescence; and a milder, *late-onset* type, beginning after puberty, which tends to arise temporarily in response to the changes of adolescence: the mismatch between biological and social maturity, increased desire for autonomy, and decreased adult supervision. Late-onset adolescents tend to commit relatively minor offenses (Schulenberg & Zarrett, 2006).

The early-onset type of antisocial behavior is influenced, as Bronfenbrenner's theory would suggest, by interacting factors ranging from microsystem influences, such as parent-child hostility, poor parenting practices, and peer deviance, to macrosystem influences, such as community structure and neighborhood social support (Buehler, 2006; Tolan, Gorman-Smith, & Henry, 2003). Evidence suggests that early-onset offenders are likely different from very early on, explaining both the early onset of their behaviors as well as their persistence into adulthood. For example, such adolescents show poor impulse control, are aggressive, and tend not to think about their future (Monahan, Cauffman, & Steinberg, 2009).

Parents of children who become chronically antisocial may have failed to reinforce good behavior in early childhood and may have been harsh or inconsistent, or both, in punishing misbehavior (Coie & Dodge, 1998; Snyder, Cramer, Afrank, & Patterson, 2005). Through the years these parents may not have been closely and positively involved in their children's lives (G. R. Patterson, DeBaryshe, & Ramsey, 1989). The children may get payoffs for antisocial behavior: when they act up, they may gain attention or get their own way. These early negative patterns pave the way for negative peer influences that promote and reinforce antisocial behavior (B. B. Brown, Mounts, Lamborn, & Steinberg, 1993; Collins et al., 2000).

research in action

THE YOUTH VIOLENCE EPIDEMIC

In April 1999, two Columbine High School students in Littleton, Colorado, killed 12 classmates and 1 teacher before shooting themselves. In April 2007, a 23-year-old Virginia Tech student killed 32 people before shooting himself. And in December 2012, a 20-year-old man first shot his mother, and then 20 children and 6 adults at Sandy Hook Elementary School in Newtown, Connecticut, before taking his own life.

2

Although the publicity surrounding such acts of violence makes them highly salient to most people, in actuality they are rare, representing only 1 percent of homicides among school-age youth. Most homicides involve only a single killer and victim. Indeed, despite the wave of school killings since 1999, rates of school-associated homicides have declined (Modzeleski et al., 2008).

Sadly, though, victims of these highly publicized cases are only a small fraction of those affected by youth violence. In 2005, more than 721,000 young people ages 10 to 24 were treated in emergency departments for injuries sustained from violence (CDC, 2007b). Persons under age 25 comprised 44.5 percent of persons arrested for violent crime (FBI, 2007).

What causes such destructive behavior? Many influences may push young people to violent acts:

- The immature adolescent brain, particularly the prefrontal cortex, which is critical to judgment and impulse suppression.
- Ready access to guns in a culture that "romanticizes gunplay" (Weinberger, 2001, p. 2).
- The presence of gangs at school (NCES, 2003; "Youth Violence," 2001).
- A rejecting, coercive, or chaotic childhood home environment, which tends to produce aggressive behavior in children that is then exacerbated in their interactions with others (Staub, 1996).
- Living in unstable, inner-city neighborhoods with low community involvement and support (Tolan et al., 2003).
- Having witnessed or having been victims of neighborhood violence, or having been exposed to media violence (Brookmeyer, Henrich, & Schwab-Stone, 2005).

Psychologists point to potential warning signs. Adolescents likely to commit violence often refuse to listen to parents and teachers, ignore the feelings and rights of others, mistreat people, rely on violence or threats to solve problems, and believe that life has treated them unfairly. They tend to do poorly in school; to cut classes; to be held back or suspended or to drop out; to be victims of bullying; to use alcohol and drugs; to engage in early sexual activity; to join gangs; and to fight, steal, or destroy property (Smith-Khuri et al., 2004; "Youth Violence," 2001).

One of the worst myths is that nothing can be done to prevent or treat violent behavior. This is not true. School-based programs for *all* children, not just those at risk, have reduced violence and aggressiveness at all grade levels. These programs are designed to prevent violent behavior by promoting social skills and emotional awareness and control (R. Hahn et al., 2007).

What do you think is the most important factor in preventing youth violence?

By early adolescence, open hostility may exist between parent and child. When constant criticism, angry coercion, or rude, uncooperative behavior characterizes parent-child interactions, the child tends to show aggressive behavior problems, which worsen the parent-child relationship (Buehler, 2006). Ineffective parenting can leave younger siblings to the powerful influence of a deviant older brother, especially if the siblings are close in age (Snyder, Bank, & Burraston, 2005).

The choice of antisocial peers is affected mainly by environmental factors (Iervolino et al., 2002). Young people gravitate to others brought up like themselves who are similar in school achievement, adjustment, and prosocial or antisocial tendencies (Collins et al., 2000). As in childhood, antisocial adolescents tend to have antisocial friends, and their antisocial behavior increases when they associate with each other

(Dishion, McCord, & Poulin, 1999; Hartup & Stevens, 1999). The way antisocial teenagers talk, laugh, or smirk about rule breaking and nod knowingly among themselves seems to constitute a sort of "deviancy training" (Dishion, McCord, & Poulin, 1999). These problem children continue to elicit ineffective parenting, which predicts delinquent behavior and association with deviant peer groups or gangs (Simons, Chao, Conger, & Elder, 2001; Tolan et al., 2003).

Authoritative parenting, which involves high levels of warmth as well as control and rules, can help young people internalize standards that may insulate them against negative peer influences and open them to positive influences (Collins et al., 2000; Mounts & Steinberg, 1995). Improved parenting during adolescence can reduce delinquency by discouraging association with deviant peers (Simons et al., 2001). Adolescents whose parents know where they are and what they are doing are less likely to engage in delinquent acts (Laird, Pettit, Bates, & Dodge, 2003) or to associate with deviant peers (Lloyd & Anthony, 2003). In sum, parents who are warm, who monitor their teens, and who have clearly defined and well-enforced rules are the least likely to have delinquent adolescents.

What are the chances this gang member will become a hardened criminal? Teenagers who don't have positive alternatives are more likely to adopt antisocial lifestyles.

Family economic circumstances may influence the development of antisocial behavior. Persistent economic deprivation can undermine sound parenting by depriving the family of social capital. Poor children are more likely than other children to commit antisocial acts, and those whose families are continuously poor tend to become more antisocial with time. Conversely, when families rise from poverty while a child is still young, the child is no more likely to develop behavior problems than a child whose family was never poor (Macmillan, McMorris, & Kruttschnitt, 2004).

Weak neighborhood social organization in a disadvantaged community can influence delinquency through its effects on parenting behavior and peer deviance (Chung & Steinberg, 2006). *Collective efficacy* is a neighborhood-level influence involving the willingness of individuals in a neighborhood to work together to achieve a common goal, intervene if a problem is apparent, and help each other out in times of need (Sampson, 1997). A combination of nurturant, involved parenting and collective efficacy can discourage adolescents from association with deviant peers (Brody et al., 2001).

LONG-TERM PROSPECTS

The vast majority of young people who engage in juvenile delinquency do not become adult criminals (Kosterman, Graham, Hawkins, Catalano, & Herrenkohl, 2001). Delinquency peaks at about age 15 and then declines as most adolescents and their families come to terms with young people's need to assert independence. However, teenagers who do not see positive alternatives or who come from dysfunctional families are more likely to adopt a permanently antisocial lifestyle (Schulenberg & Zarrett, 2006). Those most likely to persist in violence are boys who had early antisocial influences. Least likely to persist are boys and girls who were early school achievers and girls who showed early prosocial development (Kosterman et al., 2001). Because adolescent character is still in flux, it may be premature to transfer juvenile offenders from the juvenile court system, which is aimed at rehabilitation, to criminal courts where they can be tried and sentenced as adults (Steinberg & Scott, 2003).

PREVENTING AND TREATING DELINQUENCY

Because juvenile delinquency has roots early in childhood, so should preventive efforts that attack the multiple factors that can lead to delinquency. Adolescents who have taken part in certain early childhood intervention programs are less likely to get in trouble than their equally underprivileged peers (Yoshikawa, 1994). Effective programs target high-risk urban children and last at least 2 years during the child's first 5 years. They influence children directly, through high-quality day care or education, and at the same time indirectly, by offering families assistance and support geared to their needs (Schweinhart et al., 1993; Seitz, 1990; Yoshikawa, 1994; Zigler et al., 1992).

These programs operate on Bronfenbrenner's mesosystem by affecting interactions between the home and the school or child care center. The programs also go one step further, to the exosystem, by creating supportive parent networks and linking parents with such community services as prenatal and postnatal care and educational and vocational counseling (Yoshikawa, 1994; Zigler et al., 1992). Through their multipronged approach, these interventions have an impact on several early risk factors for delinquency.

One such program is the Chicago Child-Parent Centers, a preschool program for disadvantaged children in the Chicago Public Schools that offers follow-up services through age 9. Participants studied at age 20 had better educational and social outcomes and fewer juvenile arrests than a comparison group who had received less extensive early interventions (Reynold, Temple, Robertson, & Mann, 2001).

Once children reach adolescence, especially in poor, crime-ridden neighborhoods, interventions need to focus on spotting troubled adolescents and preventing gang recruitment (Tolan et al., 2003). Successful programs boost parenting skills through better monitoring, behavioral management, and neighborhood social support. For example, recent research has shown that in early adolescence, maintaining appropriate levels of control and nurturing a close and positive relationship has protective effects against teenage antisocial behaviors later in adolescence, especially for mothers (Vieno, Nation, Pastore, & Santinello, 2009). Research such as this has clear practical applications for the development of interventions targeting adolescent misbehavior.

Programs such as teen hangouts and summer camps for behaviorally disturbed youth can be counterproductive because they bring together groups of deviant youth who tend to reinforce each other's deviancy. More effective programs—Scouts, sports, and church activities—integrate deviant youth into the nondeviant mainstream. Structured, adult-monitored or school-based activities after school, on weekend evenings, and in summer, when adolescents are most likely to be idle and to get in trouble, can reduce their exposure to settings that encourage antisocial behavior (Dodge, Dishion, & Lansford, 2006). Getting teenagers involved in constructive activities or job skills programs during their free time can pay long-range dividends. Participation in extracurricular school activities tends to cut down on dropout and criminal arrest rates among high-risk boys and girls (Mahoney, 2000).

Fortunately, the great majority of adolescents do not get into serious trouble. Those who show disturbed behavior can—and should—be helped. With love, guidance, and support, adolescents can avoid risks, build on their strengths, and explore their possibilities as they approach adult life.

The normal developmental changes in the early years of life are obvious and dramatic signs of growth. The infant lying in the crib becomes an active, exploring toddler. The young child enters and embraces the worlds of school and society. The adolescent, with a new body and new awareness, prepares to step into adulthood.

checkpoint can you...

- Explain how parental, peer, and neighborhood influences may interact to promote antisocial behavior and delinquency?
- Identify characteristics of programs that have been successful in preventing or stopping delinquency and other risky behavior?

summary and key terms

The Search for Identity

- A central concern during adolescence is the search for identity, which has occupational, sexual, and values components. Erik Erikson described the psychosocial conflict of adolescence as *identity versus identity confusion*. The virtue that should arise from this conflict is *fidelity*.
- James Marcia, in research based on Erikson's theory, described four identity statuses: identity achievement, foreclosure, moratorium, and identity diffusion.
- Researchers differ on whether girls and boys take different paths to identity formation. Although some research suggests that girls' self-esteem tends to fall in adolescence, later research does not support that finding.
- Ethnicity is an important part of identity. Minority adolescents seem to go through stages of ethnic identity development much like Marcia's identity statuses.

identity

identity versus identity confusion

fidelity
identity statuses
crisis
commitment
identity achievement
foreclosure
moratorium
identity diffusion
cultural socialization

Sexuality

- Sexual orientation appears to be influenced by an interaction of biological and environmental factors and to be at least partly genetic.
- Because of lack of social acceptance, the course of homosexual identity and relationship development may vary.
- Teenage sexual activity involves risks of pregnancy and sexually transmitted infections. Adolescents at greatest risk are those who begin sexual activity early, have multiple partners, do not use contraceptives, and are ill-informed about sex.
- Regular condom use is the best safeguard for sexually active teens.
- Comprehensive sex education programs delay sexual initiation and encourage contraceptive use. Abstinence-only programs have not been as effective.
- STIs are most likely to develop undetected in girls.
- Teenage pregnancy and birthrates in the United States have declined.
- Teenage childbearing often has negative outcomes. Teenage mothers and their families tend to suffer ill health and financial hardship, and the children often suffer from ineffective parenting.

sexual orientation
sexually transmitted infections (STIs)

Relationships with Family, Peers, and Adult Society

- Although relationships between adolescents and their parents are not always easy, full-scale adolescent rebellion is unusual. For the majority of teens, adolescence is a fairly smooth transition. For the minority who seem more deeply troubled, it can predict a difficult adulthood.
- Adolescents spend an increasing amount of time with peers, but relationships with parents continue to be influential.
- Conflict with parents tends to be greatest during early adolescence. Authoritative parenting is associated with the most positive outcomes.
- Effects of family structure and maternal employment on adolescents' development may depend on such factors as economic resources, the quality of the home environment, and how closely parents monitor adolescents' whereabouts.
- Relationships with siblings tend to become more distant during adolescence, and the balance of power between older and younger siblings becomes more equal.
- The influence of the peer group is strongest in early adolescence. The structure of the peer group becomes more elaborate, involving cliques and crowds as well as friendships.
- Friendships, especially among girls, become more intimate, stable, and supportive in adolescence.
- Romantic relationships meet a variety of needs and develop with age and experience.

adolescent rebellion
individuation

Antisocial Behavior and Juvenile Delinquency

- Chronic delinquency generally stems from early-onset antisociality. It is associated with multiple, interacting risk factors, including ineffective parenting, school failure, peer and neighborhood influence, and low socioeconomic status. Programs that attack risk factors from an early age have had success.

part 6
EMERGING AND YOUNG ADULTHOOD

chapter 13

Physical and Cognitive Development in Emerging and Young Adulthood

outline

learning objectives

Describe the transition from adolescence to adulthood.

Summarize physical development in young adults.

Discuss sexuality in young adults.

Characterize cognitive changes in early adulthood.

Identify examples of the roles of experience, culture, and gender in adult moral development.

Explain how emerging adults make the transitions to higher education and work.

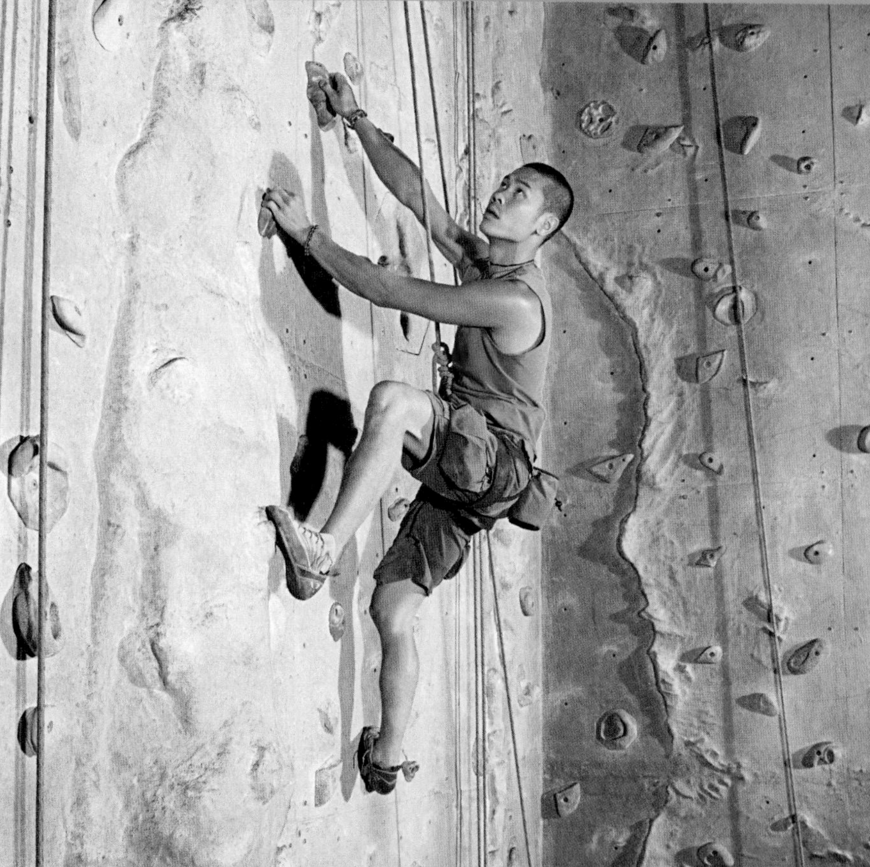

did you know?

- U.S. adults ages 20 to 40 are the most likely to be poor and the least likely to have health insurance?
- The tendency to engage in reflective thinking seems to emerge between ages 20 and 25?
- For both immediate and long-term cognitive benefits, going to college—any college—is more important than which college a person attends?

In this chapter, we look at emerging and young adults' physical functioning and factors that can affect health, fitness, sexuality, and reproduction. We discuss features of their cognition and how education can stimulate its growth. We examine moral development. Finally, we discuss entering the world of work.

I t takes courage to grow up and become who you really are.

—e. e. cummings

Emerging Adulthood

When does a person become an adult? Contemporary U.S. society has a variety of markers. *Sexual maturity* arrives during adolescence; *cognitive* maturity generally takes longer. The definition of *legal* adulthood varies: at 18, young people can vote, and, in most states, they can marry without their parents' permission; at 18 to 21 (depending on the state), they can enter into binding contracts. Using *sociological* definitions, people may be considered adults when they are self-supporting or have chosen a career, have married or formed a significant romantic partnership, or have started a family.

Psychological maturity may depend on such achievements as discovering one's identity, becoming independent of parents, developing a system of values, and forming relationships. Some psychologists suggest that the onset of adulthood is marked, not by external criteria, but by such internal indicators as a sense of autonomy, self-control, and personal responsibility—that it is more a state of mind than a discrete event (Shanahan, Porfeli, & Mortimer, 2005). From this point of view, some people never become adults, no matter what their chronological age.

For most laypeople, though, three criteria define adulthood: (1) accepting responsibility for oneself, (2) making independent decisions, and (3) becoming financially independent (Arnett, 2006). In industrialized countries, the achievement of these goals takes longer and follows far more varied routes than in the past. Before the mid-twentieth century, a young man just out of high school typically would seek a stable job, marry, and start a family. For a young woman, the usual route to adulthood was marriage, which occurred as soon as she found a suitable mate.

Since the 1950s, the technological revolution has made higher education or specialized training increasingly essential. The typical ages of first marriage and first childbirth have shifted sharply upward as both women and men pursue higher education or vocational opportunities (Furstenberg, Rumbaut, & Setterstein, 2005; Fussell & Furstenberg, 2005) prior to forming long-term relationships. Today the road to adulthood may be marked by multiple milestones—entering college (full- or part-time), working (full- or part-time), moving away from home, getting married, and having children—and the order and timing of these transitions vary (Schulenberg, O'Malley, Bachman, & Johnston, 2005).

Thus some developmental scientists suggest that, for the many young people in industrialized societies, the late teens through the mid- to late 20s has become a distinct period of the life. This period of the life span is known as **emerging adulthood,** and it represents a period of time during which young adults can figure out who they are and what they want to be. In essence, it is a time during which young people are no longer adolescents but have not yet settled into adult roles (Arnett, 2000, 2004, 2006; Furstenberg et al., 2005). Although the uncertainty and turmoil that can mark this process can be distressing, overall most young people have a positive view of their future and look forward to their adult lives (Arnett, 2007a).

As we look more closely at the varied paths of emerging adults, it is important to note that this exploratory process is not shared by all young adults in the world. It is largely tied to development in Western countries, especially among relatively affluent young people.

What criteria for adulthood do you consider most relevant? Do you think those criteria are influenced by the culture in which you live or grew up?

emerging adulthood
Proposed transitional period between adolescence and adulthood commonly found in industrialized countries.

checkpoint
can you . . .

- **Explain how entrance to adulthood has changed in industrialized societies?**

PHYSICAL DEVELOPMENT

Health and Fitness

Young adults in the United States generally enjoy the benefits of good health, but they increasingly suffer from a range of health-related risks tied to modern lifestyles. In the following section, we review some of the more important influences.

HEALTH STATUS AND HEALTH ISSUES

During this period, the foundation for lifelong physical functioning continues to be laid. Health may be influenced by the genes, but behavioral factors—what young adults eat, whether they get enough sleep, how physically active they are, and whether they smoke, drink, or use drugs—contribute greatly to health and well-being. Moreover, these environmental factors can result in epigenetic changes in the expression of particular genes that can have lifelong consequences (Dolinoy & Jirtle, 2008).

Most emerging and young adults in the United States report that they are in good to excellent health. The most common causes of activity limitations are arthritis and other muscular and skeletal disorders (NCHS, 2006). Accidents are the leading cause of death for young Americans aged 20 to 44 (Xu et al., 2010). Still, mortality rates for this group as a whole have been nearly cut in half in the past 50 years (Kochanek, Murphy, Anderson, & Scott, 2004). The health issues of these years mirror those of adolescence; however, rates of injury, homicide, and substance use peak at this time. Whites and Asians are the most likely to be in good health, although whites' health tends to decline as they age into adulthood. The worst health prognosis is generally found for Native Americans, followed by African Americans. Latinos generally occupied a middle position (Harris, Gordon-Larson, Chantala, & Udry, 2006).

In the past, young people generally aged out of many social service programs such as Medicaid, State Children's Health Insurance programs, or support systems in place within the school system. At the same time, many moved away from home and began living independently. Emerging and young adults have the highest poverty rate and the lowest level of health insurance of any age group, and often have no regular access to health care (Callahan & Cooper, 2005; Park, Mulye, Adams, Brindis, & Irwin, 2006). The implementation of the Affordable Care Act in 2014 may improve this situation.

GENETIC INFLUENCES ON HEALTH

Mapping the human genome has enabled us to examine more clearly the genetic roots of many disorders. The expression of any disorder, from obesity to certain cancers to mental health conditions (such as alcoholism and depression) is the product of an interaction between genes and environment. For example, people with more copies of a gene that helps fight HIV are less likely to become infected with the virus or to develop AIDS than people with fewer copies (Gonzalez et al., 2005). In this case, the genetic profile of the individual affects the likelihood of not being infected via behaviors (i.e., exposure to the virus).

A similar process occurs with cholesterol-related heart disease. Some cholesterol is necessary for optimal functioning, but elevated cholesterol levels increase the risk for coronary heart disease. A genetic propensity for elevated cholesterol can put a person at risk, but *only* in the presence of an unhealthy diet (Verschuren et al., 1995). In this case, the genetic propensity is apparent only when the environmental conditions allow it to exert its effects. Similarly, a person's likelihood of developing symptoms of depression is affected by a genetic variant. However, this particular variant is highly affected by environmental influences. In the presence of a supportive family environment, depression risk is not elevated. In the absence of

Wakeboarding takes strength, energy, endurance, and muscular coordination. Most young adults, like this young man, are in prime physical condition.

such an environment, however, the gene influences risk (S. E. Taylor, Lehman, Kiefe, & Seeman, 2006).

BEHAVIORAL INFLUENCES ON HEALTH AND FITNESS

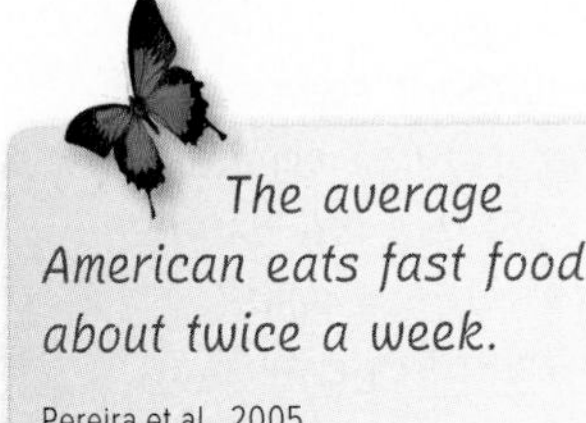

The average American eats fast food about twice a week.

Pereira et al., 2005

The link between behavior and health illustrates the interrelationship among physical, cognitive, and emotional aspects of development. What people know about health affects what they do, and what they do affects how they feel. Yet *knowing* about good (and bad) health habits is not enough. Personality, emotions, and social surroundings often outweigh what people know they should do and lead them into unhealthful behavior. In the next section, we look at both direct and indirect influences on health.

What specific things could you do to have a healthier lifestyle?

Diet and Nutrition The saying "You are what you eat" sums up the importance of nutrition for physical and mental health. What people eat affects how they look, how they feel, and how likely they are to get sick and even die. An estimated 365,000 U.S. adults die each year from causes related to poor diet and lack of physical activity (Mokdad, Marks, Stroup, & Gerberding, 2005). In a 15-year longitudinal study of 18- to 30-year-olds, those who ate plenty of fruits, vegetables, and other plant foods were less likely to develop high blood pressure than those who ate a diet heavy in meat (Steffen et al., 2005).

The World Health Organization recommends a "Mediterranean" style diet rich in fruits, vegetables, whole grains, and unsaturated fats. Although such a diet is associated with reduced risk for a wide variety of different cancers (Cuoto, Boffetta, Lagiou, Ferrari, Buckland et al., 2011), that reduced risk may well be the result of other factors: for example, people who eat such a diet tend to live overall healthier lives (Boffeta et al., 2010).

Obesity/Overweight Worldwide trends indicate obesity is on the rise. Between 1980 and 2008, the global obesity rate doubled, from 4.8 to 9.8 percent in men, and from 7.9 to 13.8 percent in women. Much of this increase can be attributed to unintended consequences of globalization, including increases in the availability of nutrient poor, high calorie processed foods and urbanization of the environment (Malik, Willet, & Hu, 2012; Figure 1).

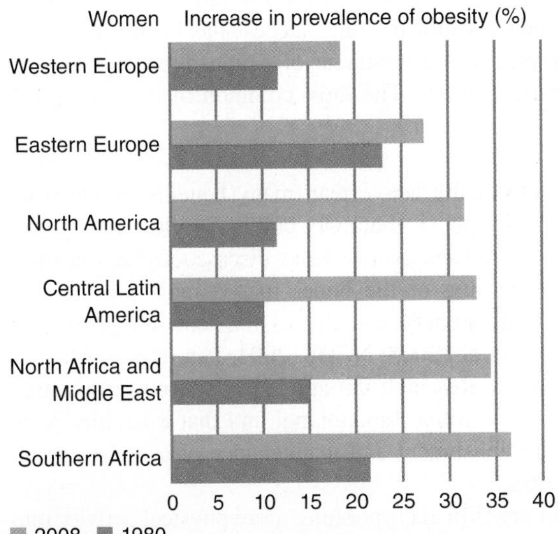

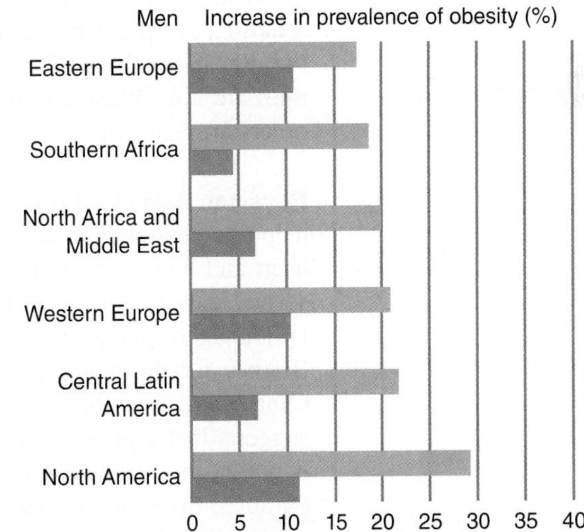

FIGURE 1

Global Trends in Obesity for Women and Men, 1980 and 2008

The greatest increases in obesity occurred in central Latin America, North America, North Africa, and the Middle East.

Source: Malik, Willett, & Hu, 2012.

Here are five easy things you can do to decrease your calorie intake without even noticing: (1) use smaller plates; (2) use tall, skinny glasses; (3) use small rather than large serving utensils; (4) buy food in smaller packages, or put snacks in plastic baggies rather than eating from the bag; and (5) keep snacks in the cupboard rather than out on plates or easily accessible.

Wansink, 2010

In the United States, the average man or woman is more than 24 pounds heavier than in the early 1960s but is only about 1 inch taller. About 34 percent of men and women 20 years and older were obese in 2007–2008. If overweight and obesity are considered together (BMI greater than 25), some 68 percent of the United States population meets the criteria. The obesity rates of women have not changed in the last 10 years, but men's weight continues to creep up (Flegal, Carrol, Ogden, & Curtin, 2010).

What explains the obesity epidemic? Experts point to an increase in snacking (Zizza, Siega-Riz, & Popkin, 2001), availability of inexpensive fast foods, supersized portions, high-fat diets, labor-saving technologies including highly processed foods, and sedentary recreational pursuits, such as television and computers (Harvard Medical School, 2004c; Pereira et al., 2005). As in childhood and adolescence development, an inherited tendency toward obesity may interact with such environmental and behavioral factors.

Obesity can lead to depression, and vice versa (Markowitz, Friedman, & Arent, 2008). It also carries risks of high blood pressure, heart disease, stroke, diabetes, gallstones, arthritis and other muscular and skeletal disorders, and some cancers, and it diminishes quality and length of life (Gregg et al., 2005; Harvard Medical School, 2004c; Hu et al., 2004; NCHS, 2004; Ogden, Carroll, McDowell, & Flegal, 2007; Peeters et al., 2003; Pereira et al., 2005). Lifestyle changes (dietary change plus exercise) or drug treatments have sustained weight-loss targets for 2 or more years (Powell, Calvin, & Calvin, 2007), but such losses are difficult for many people to sustain for longer periods of time. However, research with animal models suggests that calorie restriction, and the attendant weight maintenance of a thinner frame, is associated with increased health and longevity over the life span (Bodkin, Alexander, Ortmeyer, Johnson, & Hansen, 2003; Omodei & Fontana, 2011). Some researchers, however, have questioned whether humans would respond in the same way (Dolinsky & Dyck, 2011).

checkpoint can you . . .

- Summarize the typical health status of young adults in the United States and identify the leading cause of death in young adulthood?
- Tell how some dietary factors can affect the likelihood of cancer and heart disease?
- Give reasons for the obesity epidemic?

Eating Disorders While eating too much and gaining excessive weight is the more common nutritional issue, eating disorders that focus on attempts to keep weight low also are a problem in many countries, especially developed ones such as the United States (Makino, Tsuboi, & Dennerstein, 2004). Overall, lifetime prevalence rates of eating disorders are low, somewhere between 0.3 and 0.6 percent (Favaro, Ferrara, & Santonastaso, 2004), but this still represents a substantial amount of pain and suffering, especially since many of those suffering from eating disorders fail to get treatment (Hudson, Hiripa, Pope, & Kessler, 2007). Although some success has been found with the use of cognitive behavioral therapies in the treatment of eating disorders, success rates are low (Wilson, Grilo, & Vitousek, 2007). The most common of the eating disorders are anorexia nervosa and bulimia nervosa.

Physical Activity People who are physically active reap many benefits. Aside from helping to maintain desirable body weight, physical activity builds muscles; strengthens heart and lungs; lowers blood pressure; protects against heart disease, stroke, diabetes, several cancers, and osteoporosis (a thinning of the bones that is most prevalent in middle-aged and older women); relieves anxiety and depression; and lengthens life (Barnes & Schoenborn, 2003; Bernstein et al., 2005; NCHS, 2004; Pan, Ugnat, Mao, & Canadian Cancer Registries Epidemiology Research Group, 2005). Moreover, research suggests that exercise is also related to cognitive functioning, and that a healthy body is one of the variables related to the establishment and maintenance of a healthy mind (Kramer, Erickson, & Colcombe, 2006).

Even moderate exercise has health benefits. Incorporating more physical activity into daily life—for example, by walking instead of driving short distances—can be as effective as structured exercise. However, maintaining a healthy weight generally requires both physical activity and diet changes. In a randomized trial of 201 sedentary women, a combination of diet and exercise (primarily walking) for 12 months produced significant weight loss and improved cardiorespiratory fitness (Jakicic, Marcus, Gallagher, Napolitano, & Lang, 2003).

Unfortunately, although people are aware of the need to monitor their weight and establish healthy habits, this is easier said than done. Despite public health recommendations from both the Centers for Disease Control and the American College of Sports Medicine regarding guidelines for appropriate levels of exercise and strength training, Americans have not made substantial progress toward implementing these recommendations (CDC, 2000a). Generally, adults aged 18 to 64 should engage in 75 to 150 minutes of aerobic exercise (depending on intensity levels) and muscle-strengthening activities on at least 2 days a week (CDC, 2011). Despite the fact that this represents less than half an hour a day of exercise, many Americans do not meet these guidelines. Furthermore, most diets are unsuccessful in the long term. Moreover, many people engage in unhealthy "yo-yo" dieting, which ultimately results in a lowered metabolism, and hence even more difficulty with weight management. Current trends suggest that obesity and overweight will continue to be major health risk factors in the coming years.

Incorporating more activity into daily life, say, by biking to work instead of driving, can be as effective as structured exercise.

Stress Despite the generally positive experiences of most emerging adults, the dynamics of this stage in life can lead to increases in perceived stress (Arnett, 2005; Brougham, Zail, Mendoza, & Miller, 2009). A growing body of research suggests that our psychological health affects our physical health, and that high levels of chronic stress are related to a host of physical and immunological impairments (Ho, Neo, Chua, Cheak, & Mak, 2010).

> *Stressed out? Having a good laugh over a bad day might be helpful. Although the research is still equivocal, there are indications that humor can be an effective strategy for managing stress. So laugh a little bit!*
>
> Moran & Hughes, 2006

There are individual differences in how young adults handle stress. In some cases, stress may lead young adults to engage in risky behaviors such as drinking or smoking to manage that stress (White et al., 2006; Rice & Van Arsdale, 2010), behaviors that have consequences for their health. Also, stressed out college students are more likely to eat junk food, are less likely to exercise (Hudd et al., 2000), and tend to have poor quality or insufficient sleep (Lund, Reider, Whiting, & Prichard, 2010).

There are gender differences in how young adults typically manage stress. Generally, coping has been split into two broad categories. Emotion-focused coping consists of attempts to manage the emotions associated with experiencing a particular event by such tactics as refusing to think about an issue or reframing the event in a positive light. Problem-focused coping involves addressing an issue head-on and developing action-oriented ways of managing and changing a bad situation (Lazarus & Folkman, 1984). College-aged women are also more likely to use emotion-focused strategies than are college-aged men. Moreover, at the same time, college-aged women experience overall higher levels of stress (Brougham et al., 2009). Relationships may help people cope with stress. In one study, individuals who were secure in their relationships with others experienced less interpersonal stress and used more adaptive coping styles (Sieffge-Krenke, 2006).

Sleep The 20s and 30s are busy times, so it is not surprising that many emerging and young adults often go without adequate sleep. Among college students, family life stress, together with academic stress, is associated with high levels of insomnia (Bernert, Merrill, Braithwaite, Van Orden, & Joiner, 2007; Lund et al., 2010).

> *Younger people are more likely than older adults to dream in color, a phenomenon that may be tied to exposure to color versus black and white television and film.*
>
> Murzyn, 2008

Sleep deprivation affects not only physical health but cognitive, emotional, and social functioning as well. In a poll by the National Sleep Foundation (2001), respondents said they were more likely to make mistakes, become impatient or aggravated when waiting, or get upset with their children or others when they had not had enough sleep the night before. Sleep deprivation can be dangerous on the road. Indeed, performance impairments related to even partial sleep deprivation have been shown to be similar to those found after drinking alcohol (Elmenhorst et al., 2009). Lack of sleep tends to impair verbal learning (Horne, 2000), some aspects of memory (Harrison & Horne, 2000b), high-level decision making (Harrison & Horne, 2000a), and speech articulation (Harrison & Horne, 1997), and increases distractibility (Blagrove, Alexander, & Horne, 1995). Chronic sleep deprivation (less than 6 hours' sleep each night for three or more nights) can seriously worsen cognitive performance (Van Dongen, Maislin, Mullington, & Dinges, 2003). Finally, chronic sleep deprivation has been linked to depression (Taylor, Lichstein, Durrence, Reidel, & Bush, 2005), and insomnia and sleep disturbances also are related to the risk of postpartum depression (Wisner, Parry, & Piontek, 2002).

Poor cognitive performance due to sleep deprivation is why pulling an all-nighter for an exam is a bad idea.

Adequate sleep improves learning of complex motor skills (Walker, Brakefield, Morgan, Hobson, & Stickgold, 2002) and consolidates previous learning. Even a short nap can prevent burnout—oversaturation of the brain's perceptual processing systems (Mednick et al., 2002).

Because smoking is addictive, it is hard to quit despite awareness of health risks. Smoking is especially harmful to African Americans, whose blood metabolizes nicotine rapidly, heightening their risk of lung cancer.

Smoking Smoking is the leading preventable cause of death among U.S. adults, linked not only to lung cancer but also to increased risks of heart disease, stroke, and chronic lung disease (NCHS, 2004). Exposure to passive, or secondhand, smoke has been shown to cause circulatory problems and increase the risk of cardiovascular disease (Otsuka et al., 2001) and may increase the risk of cervical cancer (Trimble et al., 2005). In 2000, smoking killed almost 5 million people worldwide, about half in developing countries and half in industrialized countries (Ezzati & Lopez, 2004). Despite recent attempts by cities such as New York and Portland to limit or ban smoking in public locations, smoking continues to be a significant and common risk factor.

More than 26.3 percent of men and 21.7 percent of women over age 12 in the United States are current smokers (SAMHSA, 2009a). Emerging adults are more likely to smoke than any other age group. More than 40 percent of 21- to 25-year-olds report using cigarettes (SAMHSA, 2007a). Given the known risks, why do so many people smoke? For one thing, smoking is addictive. A tendency to addiction may be genetic (Lerman et al., 1999; Pianezza, Sellers, & Tyndale, 1998; Sabol et al., 1999). And the link between genetic susceptibility and likelihood of addiction is strongest for those who begin to smoke at a young age (Weiss et al., 2008). Smoking is strongly associated with socioeconomic level as well; those adults with less than a high school education are 3 times more likely to be smokers than those with a bachelor's degree or higher (NCHS, 2008).

Giving up smoking reduces the risks of heart disease, cancer, and stroke (USDHHS, 2010). Nicotine chewing gum, nicotine patches, and nicotine nasal sprays and inhalers, especially when combined with counseling, can help addicted persons taper off gradually and safely (Cepeda-Benito, Reynoso, & Erath, 2004). New e-cigarettes show promise as well (Siegal, Tanwar, & Wood, 2011; Cahn & Siegal, 2011). The use of drugs that help manage cravings without the provision of nicotine also can be helpful (Gonzalez et al., 2006). Quitting smoking is difficult, and many smoking cessation programs have low success rates. However, most smokers attempt to quit on their own, and tend not to use either behavioral therapies or medical support (Shiffman, Brockwell, Pillitteri, & Gitchell, 2008). Only about 4 to 7 percent of smokers manage to quit for good on any one attempt, although medication can increase the 6-month success rate to approximately 25 to 33 percent (American Cancer Society, 2011). Many smokers require multiple attempts to quit the habit.

Alcohol Use The United States is a drinking society. Advertising associates liquor, beer, and wine with the good life and with being grown-up. Alcohol use peaks in emerging adulthood. Among adults from the ages of 18 to 25, approximately 57 percent of women and 65 percent of men drink alcohol (SAMHSA, 2008).

College is a prime time and place for drinking, and college students tend to drink more frequently and more heavily than their non-collegiate peers (SAMHSA, 2004b). In 2007, nearly 64 percent of full-time college students ages 18 to 20 had used alcohol in the past month; 17.2 percent heavily; and about 43.6 percent had engaged in binge drinking (SAMHSA, 2008; Figure 2). Although light to moderate alcohol consumption seems to reduce the risk of fatal heart disease and stroke, and also of dementia later in life (Ruitenberg et al., 2002), heavy drinking over the years may lead to cirrhosis of the liver, other gastrointestinal disorders (including ulcers), pancreatic disease, certain cancers, heart failure, stroke, damage to the nervous system, psychoses, and other medical problems (AHA, 1995; Fuchs et al., 1995).

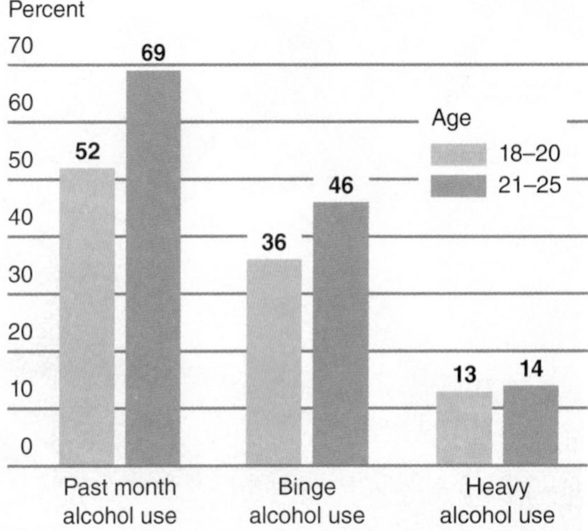

FIGURE 2
Current (Past Month) Alcohol Use, Binge Drinking, and Heavy Alcohol Use among Full-Time College Students Ages 18 to 25

Source: SAMHSA, 2008.

Alcohol use is associated with other risks characteristic of emerging adulthood, such as traffic accidents, crime, HIV infection (Leigh, 1999), illicit drug and tobacco use (Hingson, Heeren, Winter, & Wechsler, 2005), and the likelihood of committing sexual assault (Brecklin & Ullman, 2010). From 2004 to 2006, an estimated 15 percent of U.S. drivers age 18 or older said that in the past year they drove under the influence of alcohol, and nearly 5 percent said they drove under the influence of drugs (SAMHSA, 2008). Alcoholism, or long-term addiction, is discussed later in this chapter under "Mental Health Problems."

Risky drinking is defined as consuming more than 14 drinks a week or 4 drinks on any single day for men, and more than 7 drinks a week or 3 drinks on any single day for women. Approximately 3 out of 10 people are risky drinkers, at risk for alcoholism and liver disease, as well as physical, mental, and social problems as a result of their drinking (National Institute on Alcohol Abuse and Alcoholism, n.d.).

risky drinking
Consuming more than 14 drinks a week or 4 drinks on any single day for men, and more than 7 drinks a week or 3 drinks on any single day for women.

Individual variables affect the likelihood of alcohol consumption. For example, race and ethnicity can affect drinking patterns. The group reporting the highest consumption of alcohol is Native Americans, followed by whites, and the lowest levels of use are reported by Central Americans, African Americans, and Asian Americans (Wallace et al., 2005). Gender affects consumption patterns as well, with females generally consuming less alcohol overall as well as having lower levels of binge drinking. However, this gender gap in alcohol consumption appears to be shrinking (Keyes, Grant, & Hasin, 2007).

checkpoint
can you . . .

- Cite the benefits of exercise?
- Explain why sleep deprivation is harmful?
- Discuss trends and risks involved in smoking and alcohol use?

INDIRECT INFLUENCES ON HEALTH

Apart from the things people do, or refrain from doing, that affect their health directly, there are indirect influences on health. Among these are income, education, and race/ethnicity. Relationships also seem to make a difference, as do the paths young people take into adulthood.

Socioeconomic Status and Race/Ethnicity The connection between socioeconomic status (SES) and health has been widely documented. Higher-income people rate their health as better and live longer than lower-income people (NCHS, 2006). Education is important too. The less schooling people have had, the greater the chance that they will develop and die from communicable diseases, injuries, or chronic ailments, or that they will become victims of homicide or suicide (NCHS, 2004; Pamuk, Makuc, Heck, Reuben, & Lochner, 1998). Socioeconomic circumstances in both childhood and

Living in poverty, as do this mother and her daughter who share a room in a shelter, can affect health through poor nutrition, substandard housing, and inadequate health care.

adulthood are important determinants of risk for cardiovascular disease, and, even more so, of stroke (Galobardes, Smith, & Lynch, 2006).

This does not mean that income and education *cause* good health; instead, they are related to environmental and lifestyle factors that tend to be causative. In other words, their influences are indirect. Better-educated and more affluent people tend to have healthier diets and better preventive health care and medical treatment. They exercise more, are less likely to be overweight, smoke less, are less likely to use illicit drugs, and are more likely to use alcohol in moderation (NCHS, 2004; SAMHSA, 2004b). Moreover, the less affluent are more likely to live close to a polluting facility (Mohai, Lantz, Morenoff, House, & Mero, 2009) and show elevated levels of lead and other toxins in their blood (Bellinger, 2008).

Because many minorities in the United States also tend to have a lower SES, their health issues stem from that rather than from minority status per se (Kiefe et al., 2000). Thirty-nine percent of African American men and 43 percent of African American women aged 20 years and older suffer from high blood pressure (CDC, 2011a). African Americans also are more likely to be diagnosed with diabetes, and more likely to eventually die from the disease as well (Kirk et al., 2006). African Americans are about twice as likely as white people to die in young adulthood, in part because young African American men are far more likely to be victims of homicide (NCHS, 2006).

Factors associated with SES do not tell the whole story, however. For example, although African Americans smoke less than white Americans, they metabolize more nicotine in the blood, face higher risks of lung cancer, and have more trouble breaking the habit. Possible reasons may be genetic, biological, or behavioral (Caraballo et al., 1998; Pérez-Stable, Herrera, Jacob, & Benowitz, 1998; Sellers, 1998). It is unfortunate that despite the potentially elevated health consequences for minority people, cigarette companies have nonetheless chosen to specifically target ethnic minority groups in a variety of marketing campaigns (American Heart Association, 2011). A review of more than 100 studies found that racial/ethnic minorities tend to receive lower-quality health care than white people do, even when insurance status, income, age, and severity of conditions are similar (Smedley, Stith, & Nelson, 2002).

Relationships and Health Social relationships seem to be vital to health and well-being. Research has identified at least two interrelated aspects of the social environment that can promote health: *social integration* and *social support* (Cohen, 2004).

Social integration is active engagement in a broad range of social relationships, activities, and roles (spouse, parent, neighbor, friend, colleague, and the like). Social networks can influence emotional well-being as well as participation in healthful behaviors, such as exercising, eating nutritiously, and refraining from substance use (Cohen, 2004). Social integration has repeatedly been associated with lower mortality rates (Berkman & Glass, 2000; Rutledge et al., 2004). People with wide social networks and multiple social roles are more likely to survive heart attacks and less likely to be anxious or depressed than people with more limited social networks and roles (Cohen, Gottlieb, & Underwood, 2000) and even are less susceptible to colds (Cohen, Doyle, Skoner, Rabin, & Gwaltney, 1997). In addition, it appears that online social networking sites, such as Facebook, can provide some of those benefits via online interaction and support (Ellison, Steinfield, & Lampe, 2007). Some of these processes may be mediated

This happily married couple is the picture of good health. Although there is a clear association between relationships and health, it's not clear which is the cause and which the effect.

by stress hormones such as cortisol. In other words, the beneficial effects of social integration may in part be due to the decreases in stress levels that strong social ties can engender (Grant, Hamer, & Steptoe, 2009).

Social support refers to material, informational, and psychological resources derived from the social network, on which a person can rely for help in coping with stress. In highly stressful situations, people who are in touch with others may be more likely to eat and sleep sensibly, get enough exercise, and avoid substance abuse, and are less likely to be distressed, anxious, or depressed or even to die (Cohen, 2004). In sum, people with good, healthy social relationships enjoy better health.

Because marriage offers a readily available system for both social integration and social support, it is not surprising that marriage tends to benefit health, especially for men (Wu & Hart, 2002). An interview survey of 127,545 U.S. adults found that married people, particularly in young adulthood, tend to be healthier physically and psychologically than those who are never-married, cohabiting, widowed, separated, or divorced (Schoenborn, 2004). Dissolving a marriage, or a cohabitation, tends to have negative effects on physical or mental health or both—but so, apparently, does remaining in a bad relationship (Wu & Hart, 2002). People in an unhappy marriage have poorer health than single adults, and even a supportive network of friends and family does not buffer this effect (Holt-Lundstad, Birmingham, & Jones, 2008).

However, the effects of marriage and health can be both direct and indirect. Most notably, two-income families are more likely to have access to health insurance. And access to high-quality health care is related to general well-being, as well as people's ability to seek appropriate care in the event of a health issue. Therefore, some of the links between marriage and health are the result of correlates of marriage rather than a direct effect of marriage itself. This can help explain the higher risk for negative health consequences for some people in same-sex relationships, as they are less likely to have health insurance and are more likely to delay or fail to receive preventative health care (Buchmueller & Carpenter, 2010). In addition, passage of same-sex marriage laws seems to result in broad health benefits to gay couples, perhaps as a result of decreasing discrimination and prejudice (Hatzenbeuhler, O'Cleirigh, & Bradbord, 2012).

checkpoint can **you**...

- Point out differences in health and mortality that reflect income, education, and race/ethnicity?
- Discuss how relationships may affect physical and mental health?

MENTAL HEALTH PROBLEMS

For most emerging adults, mental health and well-being improve and problem behaviors diminish. Yet, at the same time, the incidence of psychological disorders increases for conditions such as major depression, schizophrenia, and bipolar disorders. What explains this apparent paradox? The emerging adult transition brings an end to the relatively structured years of high school. The freedom to make life decisions and choose diverse paths is often liberating, but the responsibility to rely on oneself and to become financially self-supporting can be overwhelming (Schulenberg & Zarrett, 2006). Let's look at some specific disorders that can occur in young adulthood: alcoholism, drug abuse, and depression.

Alcoholism Alcohol abuse and dependence are the most prevalent substance disorders, reported by 8.5 percent of the U.S. adult population. Alcohol dependence, or **alcoholism,** is a long-term physical condition characterized by compulsive drinking that a person is unable to control. The heritability of a tendency to alcoholism is 50 to 60 percent (Bouchard, 2004). Alcoholism, like other addictions, such as getting hooked on smoking, seems to result from long-lasting changes in patterns of neural signal transmission in the brain. Exposure to the addictive substance (in this case, alcohol) creates a euphoric mental state accompanied by neurological changes that produce feelings of discomfort and craving when it is no longer present. From 6 to 48 hours after the last drink, alcoholics experience strong physical withdrawal symptoms (anxiety, agitation, tremors, elevated blood pressure, and sometimes seizures). Alcoholics, like drug addicts, develop a tolerance for the substance and need more and more to get the desired high (NIAAA, 1996).

alcoholism
Chronic disease involving dependence on use of alcohol, causing interference with normal functioning and fulfillment of obligations.

Treatment for alcoholism may include detoxification (removing all alcohol from the body), hospitalization, medication, individual and group psychotherapy, and referral to a support organization, such as Alcoholics Anonymous. Although not a cure, treatment can give alcoholics new tools to cope with their addiction and lead productive lives.

Drug Use and Abuse Use of illicit drugs peaks at ages 18 to 25; almost 20 percent of this age group report using illicit drugs during the past month. As young adults settle down, get married, and take responsibility for their future, they tend to cut down on drug use. Usage rates drop sharply during the 20s, and then continues to decline, albeit more slowly as people enter later adulthood and old age (SAMHSA, 2013c; Figure 3).

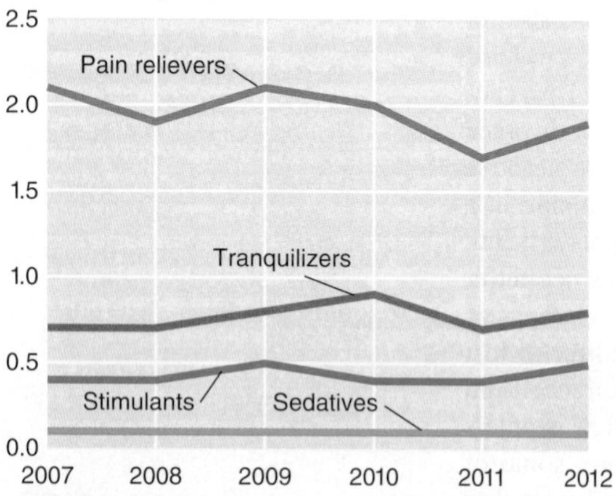

FIGURE 3
Past Month Nonmedical Use of Types of Psychotherapeutic Drugs among Persons Aged 12 or Older

Source: SAMHSA, 2013.

As in adolescence, marijuana is by far the most popular illicit drug among young adults. In 2006, 18.7 percent of 18- to 25-year-olds had used marijuana within the previous month (SAMHSA, 2013c). In general, although a substantial proportion of young adults will experiment with alcohol, cigarettes, or marijuana, a much smaller proportion will try other drugs such as ecstasy, methamphetamines, or heroin; and an even smaller number will become chronic and heavy users of illegal drugs (Johnston, O'Malley, Bachman, & Schulenberg, 2009). However, despite the relatively moderate prevalence numbers for heavy abuse, drug abuse still results in significant costs to the user personally and to society at large. The Office of National Drug Control Policy (2004) estimates that illegal drugs cost society approximately $181 billion yearly.

About 20 percent of persons with substance use disorders also have mood (depression) or anxiety disorders (Grant et al., 2004). Moreover, there is a relationship between the occurrence of personality disorders and the abuse of both illegal drugs and alcohol (Grant et al., 2007). The causal relationship here is unclear. It may be that the use of illegal drugs puts young people at risk for the development of a variety of psychopathologies. Alternatively, it could be the case that those people who suffer from psychological distress self-medicate and thus are more prone to addiction and other risky behaviors.

Depression Adolescence and emerging adulthood appear to be sensitive periods for the onset of depressive disorders. Between ages 15 and 22, the incidence of depression increases gradually (Schulenberg & Zarrett, 2006). Depression can be characterized in a number of different ways. Depressive mood is an extended period of sadness. Depressive syndrome is an extended period of sadness along with a variety of other symptoms such as crying and feelings of worthlessness or hopelessness. A major depressive disorder, by contrast, is a clinical diagnosis with a specific set of symptoms, is considered to be the most serious, and generally requires medical intervention. People who are diagnosed with major depressive disorder often have depressed or irritable moods for most of the day, every day, show reduced interest in and enjoyment of previously pleasurable activities, often either gain or lose significant amounts of weight, have difficulties sleeping too little or too much, and often show a variety of cognitive biases and maladaptive recurrent thoughts (American Psychiatric Association, n.d.).

Childhood-or-adolescent-onset depression and adult-onset depression seem to have different origins and developmental paths. Adolescents who are depressed, and whose depression carries over into adulthood, tend to have had significant childhood risk factors, such as neurological or developmental disorders, dysfunctional or unstable families, and childhood behavioral disorders. They may have difficulty negotiating the transition to emerging adulthood. For some of them, on the other hand, emerging adulthood represents a new start, a chance to find new social roles and settings more conducive to mental health. The adult-onset group tend to have had low levels of childhood risk factors and to possess more resources to deal with the challenges of emerging adulthood; but the sudden decline in structure and support that accompanies adult life may throw them off course (Schulenberg & Zarrett, 2006).

Generally, young women are more likely to suffer from a major depressive episode, and this difference in prevalence becomes particularly acute after the onset of puberty (Wasserman, 2006). Women are also more likely than men to show atypical symptoms, to have an additional psychopathology along with their depressive disorders, and to attempt (but not succeed in) suicide (Gorman, 2006). In addition, women and men may respond to antidepressants differently, with women showing a greater likelihood of adverse drug reactions (Franconi, Brunelleschi, Steardo, & Cuomo, 2007).

checkpoint can **you**...

- Discuss mental health problems common in emerging and young adulthood?

Sexual and Reproductive Issues

Sexual and reproductive activities are often a prime preoccupation of emerging and young adulthood. These natural and important functions may involve physical concerns. Three such concerns are disorders related to menstruation, sexually transmitted infections (STIs), and infertility.

Kissing occurs in over 90 percent of cultures. When kissing, men tend to prefer wetter kisses using more tongue. Men might want to think about this—research has shown that 66 percent of women can be put off by a bad kisser.

Hughes, Harrison, & Gallup, 2007

SEXUAL BEHAVIOR AND ATTITUDES

What are the recent trends in sexual behaviors in young adults? Today almost all U.S. adults have had sexual relations before marriage (Lefkowitz & Gillen, 2006). According to a nationally representative in-person survey, 75 percent of adults have had premarital sex by age 20; 95 percent have done so by age 44. The percentages rise sharply in more recent age cohorts; among girls who turned 15 between 1964 and 1993, at least 91 percent had had premarital sex by age 30 (Finer, 2007).

Variety in sexual activity is common. Among 25- to 44-year-olds, 97 percent of men and 98 percent of women have had vaginal intercourse; 90 percent of men and 88 percent of women have had oral sex with a partner of the other sex; and 40 percent of men and 35 percent of women have had anal sex with an other-sex partner. About 6.5 percent of men and 11 percent of women have had sex with a same-sex partner (Mosher et al., 2005).

Emerging adults tend to have more sexual partners than in older age groups, but they have sex less frequently. People who become sexually active during emerging adulthood tend to engage in fewer risky behaviors—those that may lead to STIs or unplanned pregnancies—than those who began in adolescence. Condoms are the most commonly used contraceptive, though their use is inconsistent (Lefkowitz & Gillen, 2006).

Casual sex (hooking up) is fairly common, especially on college campuses. Sexual assaults on women are also a problem in this age group. Both are often associated with other, nonsexual risky behaviors such as drinking and drug use (Santelli, Carter, Orr, & Dittus, 2007). College students, in particular, are becoming less judgmental and more open-minded about sexual activity. However, a double standard still exists: men are expected to have more sexual freedom than women.

By emerging adulthood, most lesbian, gay, bisexual, and transgender persons are clear about their sexual identity. Many first come out to others during this period (Lefkowitz & Gillen, 2006). In general, more recent generations in the United States are coming out at an earlier age, and men are more likely to come out at an earlier age (by approximately 2 years) than women. Ethnic minority youth are equally likely to be open about their sexual orientation to their friends, but they are more likely to keep this information secret from their parents (Grov, Bimbi, Nanin, & Parsons, 2006).

SEXUALLY TRANSMITTED INFECTIONS (STIs)

Sexually transmitted infections, also known as sexually transmitted diseases (STDs), are illnesses that are transmitted by having sex. Because people can carry infections for years without displaying signs of active disease, *STIs* is becoming the preferred term. By far the highest rates of STIs in the United States are among emerging adults ages 18 to 25, especially among those who use alcohol and/or illicit drugs (SAMHSA, 2007b). An estimated 1 in 4 persons who have been sexually active, but nearly half of new STI cases, are in that age group, and many do not get medical diagnosis and care (Lefkowitz & Gillen, 2006). There are also indications that risk is higher among certain ethnic groups. For example, there are elevated rates of STIs for African American (Hallfors, Iritani, Miller, & Bauer, 2006; Kaplan, Crespo, Huguet, & Marks, 2009), and Latino/a young adults (Kaplan et al., 2009).

The number of people living with HIV has risen in every region of the world since 2002, with the steepest increases in East and Central Asia and Eastern Europe. Still, sub-Saharan Africa remains by far the worst affected. Infection can theoretically occur with any transmission of body fluids, although some activities are clearly riskier than others. A growing proportion of new infections occur in women, especially in places where heterosexual transmission is predominant, such as sub-Saharan Africa and the Caribbean. In the United States, most infections occur through drug abusers sharing contaminated hypodermic needles, unprotected sex among gay or bisexual men (who may then pass on the infection to female partners), or commercial sex with prostitutes (UNAIDS/WHO, 2004).

With highly active antiviral therapy, death rates of persons diagnosed with HIV have dropped dramatically, and their average life span has increased to more than 35 years (Bhaskaran et al., 2008; Lohse et al., 2007). In the United States in 1995, AIDS was the leading cause of death for 25- to 44-year-olds; by 2003, it had fallen to ninth (Hoyert, Kochanek, & Murphy, 1999; NCHS, 2006). Use of condoms is the most effective means of preventing STIs. A three-session intervention among U.S. Marine security guards resulted in increased perception of social support for condom use and stronger intentions to practice safer sex (Booth-Kewley, Minagawa, Shaffer, & Brodine, 2002). Unfortunately, interventions focused on STI transmission within the context of intravenous drug use are not as effective and have not been shown to significantly reduce either needle sharing or risky sexual behaviors in drug addicts (Crepaz et al., 2009; Herbst et al., 2006).

MENSTRUAL DISORDERS

Premenstrual syndrome (PMS) is a disorder that produces physical discomfort and emotional tension for up to 2 weeks before a menstrual period. Symptoms may include fatigue, headaches, swelling and tenderness of the breasts, swollen hands or feet, abdominal bloating, nausea, cramps, constipation, food cravings, weight gain, anxiety, depression, irritability, mood swings, tearfulness, and difficulty concentrating or remembering (American College of Obstetricians & Gynecologists [ACOG], 2013). Up to 85 percent of menstruating women may have some symptoms, but only 5 to 10 percent warrant a diagnosis of PMS (ACOG, 2000).

premenstrual syndrome (PMS)
Disorder producing symptoms of physical discomfort and emotional tension for up to 2 weeks before a menstrual period.

The cause of PMS is not fully understood, but it appears to be a response to normal monthly surges of the female hormones estrogen and progesterone (Schmidt, Nieman, Danaceau, Adams, & Rubinow, 1998) as well as to levels of the male hormone testosterone and of serotonin, a brain chemical (ACOG, 2000). Smoking may put women at increased risk for the development of PMS (Bertone-Johnson, Hankinson, Johnson, & Manson, 2008).

The symptoms of PMS can sometimes be alleviated or minimized through aerobic exercise, eating frequent small meals, a diet high in complex carbohydrates and low in salt and caffeine, and regular sleep routines. Calcium, magnesium, and vitamin E supplements may help. Medications may relieve specific symptoms—for example, a diuretic for bloating and weight gain (ACOG, 2013; Moline & Zendell, 2000).

PMS may include the presence of cramps, but it is not the same thing. PMS can be confused with *dysmenorrhea* (painful menstruation, or "cramps"). Cramps tend to affect younger women, whereas PMS is more typical in women in their 30s or older. Dysmenorrhea is caused by contractions of the uterus, which are set in motion by prostaglandin, a hormone-like substance; it can be treated with prostaglandin inhibitors, such as ibuprofen (Wang et al., 2004). Dysmenorrhea is estimated to affect up to 90 percent of women, and approximately 15 percent experience severe symptoms that can affect educational and occupational responsibilities (Mannix, 2008).

infertility
Inability to conceive a child after 12 months of sexual intercourse without the use of birth control.

INFERTILITY

An estimated 7 percent of U.S. couples experience **infertility:** the inability to conceive a baby after 12 months of intercourse in the absence of birth control methods (CDC, 2005; Wright, Chang, Jeng, & Macaluso, 2006). Women's fertility begins to decline in their late 20s, with substantial decreases during their 30s. By their 40s, many women are not able to become pregnant without the use of artificial reproduction technologies (ART). Men's fertility is less affected by age but declines significantly by their late 30s (Dunson, Colombo, & Baird, 2002). Infertility can burden a relationship emotionally, but only when infertility leads to permanent, involuntary childlessness is it associated with long-term psychological distress (McQuillan, Greil, White, & Jacob, 2003).

The most common cause of infertility in men is production of too few sperm. In some

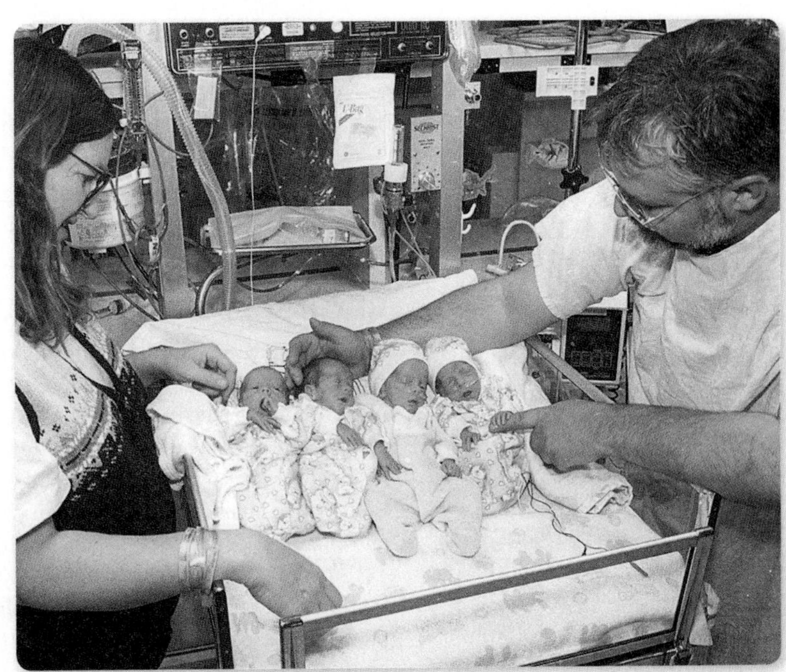

Delayed childbearing, use of fertility drugs, and assisted reproductive techniques such as in vitro fertilization increase the likelihood of multiple, usually premature, births.

instances an ejaculatory duct may be blocked, preventing the exit of sperm, or sperm may be unable to swim well enough to reach the cervix. Some cases of male infertility seem to have a genetic basis (O'Flynn O'Brien, Varghese, & Agarwal, 2010).

In women, the common causes of infertility include the failure to produce ova or to produce normal ova; mucus in the cervix, which might prevent sperm from penetrating it; or a disease of the uterine lining, which might prevent implantation of the fertilized ovum. A major cause of declining fertility in women after age 30 is deterioration in the quality of ova (van Noord-Zaadstra et al., 1991). However, the most common cause is blockage of the fallopian tubes, preventing ova from reaching the uterus. In about half of these cases, the tubes are blocked by scar tissue from sexually transmitted infections (King, 1996). In addition, some women suffer from physical disorders affecting fertility, such as polycystic ovarian syndrome (Franks, 2009) or primary ovarian insufficiency (Welt, 2008).

In both men and women, modifiable environmental factors are related to infertility. For example, overweight men (Sallmen, Sandler, Hoppin, Blair, & Day, 2006) and women (Maheshwari, 2010) are more likely to have issues with fertility. Smoking also appears to have a strong negative effect on fertility. Other factors, such as psychological stress, high levels of caffeine and alcohol consumption, and exposure to environmental pollutants have been implicated, but the evidence for their negative effects is less strong (Hofman, Davies, & Norman, 2007).

Sometimes hormone treatment, drug therapy, or surgery may correct the problem. However, fertility drugs increase the likelihood of multiple, high-risk births. Men undergoing fertility treatment are at increased risk of producing sperm with chromosomal abnormalities (Levron et al., 1998).

Unless there is a known cause for failure to conceive, the chances of success after 18 months to 2 years are high (Dunson, 2002). For couples struggling with infertility, science today offers several alternative ways to parenthood; these are discussed in Box 1.

checkpoint can **you**...

- Summarize trends in sexual behavior and attitudes among emerging and young adults?
- Discuss the spread of STIs and ways to control them?
- Discuss the symptoms and likely causes of PMS and ways to manage it?
- Identify common causes of male and female infertility?

COGNITIVE DEVELOPMENT

Perspectives on Adult Cognition

Developmentalists have studied cognition from a variety of perspectives. Here, we address three important perspectives on cognition in young adulthood.

reflective thinking
Type of logical thinking that becomes more prominent in adulthood, involving continuous, active evaluation of information and beliefs in the light of evidence and implications.

BEYOND PIAGET: NEW WAYS OF THINKING IN ADULTHOOD

Piaget believed that the pinnacle of cognitive development was formal operations thought. In this stage, adults were presumed to be capable of fully abstract thought and formal hypothesis testing. However, some developmental scientists maintain that changes in cognition extend beyond that stage. One line of neo-Piagetian theory and research concerns higher levels of *reflective thinking,* or abstract reasoning. Another line of investigation deals with *postformal thought,* which combines logic with emotion and practical experience in the resolution of ambiguous problems.

Why is it so much more irritating to listen to a cell phone conversation than a conversation between two physically present people? Well, as we only hear half the conversation, it takes more work to interpret and understand this "halfalogue"—which is why it's more distracting and so much more irritating.

Emberson, Lupyan, Goldstein, & Spivey, 2010

Reflective Thinking **Reflective thinking** was first defined by the American philosopher and educator John Dewey (1910/1991) as "active, persistent, and careful consideration" of information or beliefs in the light of the evidence that supports them and the conclusions to which they lead. Reflective thinkers continually question supposed facts, draw inferences, and make connections. In other words, they frequently and spontaneously engage in critical thinking. Building on Piaget's stage of formal operations,

research in action

ASSISTED REPRODUCTIVE TECHNOLOGY

More than 3 million children worldwide have been conceived through *assisted reproductive technology (ART)* (Reaney, 2006; ICMART, 2006). In 2005, U.S. women delivered more than 52,000 babies with technological help, representing 1 percent of all babies born in the United States in that year (Wright, Chang, Jeng, & Macaluso, 2008).

In vitro fertilization (IVF) accounts for 99 percent of all ARTs and is the most common assisted reproductive technique (CDC, 2009a). With IVF, women receive fertility drugs to increase production of ova. Then ova are surgically removed, fertilized in a laboratory dish, and implanted in the woman's uterus. Because several embryos are typically transferred to the uterus to increase the chances of pregnancy, this procedure increases the likelihood of multiple, usually premature, births (Wright et al., 2006). The odds of a successful pregnancy resulting in a live birth decline with age (CDC, 2009a).

A newer technique, *in vitro maturation (IVM),* is performed when egg follicles are developing. Harvesting a large number of follicles before ovulation and then allowing them to mature in the laboratory can make hormone injections unnecessary and diminish the likelihood of multiple births (Duenwald, 2003).

IVF also addresses severe male infertility. A single sperm can be injected into the ovum—a technique called *intracytoplasmic sperm injection (ICSI).* This procedure is now used in 63 percent of IVF cycles (CDC, 2009a).

Artificial insemination—injection of sperm into a woman's vagina, cervix, or uterus—can be used to facilitate conception if a man has a low sperm count. If the man is infertile, a couple may choose *artificial insemination by a donor (AID).*

Although success rates have improved (Duenwald, 2003), only 35 percent of women who attempted assisted reproduction in 2005 had live births (Wright et al., 2008). The likelihood of success with IVF using a mother's own ova drops precipitously with maternal age as the quality of her ova declines (Van Voorhis, 2007).

A woman who is producing poor-quality ova or who has had her ovaries removed may try *ovum transfer.* In this procedure, an ovum, or *donor egg,* provided by a fertile younger woman is fertilized in the laboratory or via artificial insemination in the donor and implanted in the prospective mother's uterus. IVF using donor eggs tends to be highly successful (Van Voorhis, 2007). Success rates for fresh embryos (approximately 55 percent) tend to be higher than for frozen embryos (approximately 30 percent) (CDC, 2009a).

Two other techniques with relatively higher success rates are *gamete intrafallopian transfer (GIFT)* and *zygote intrafallopian transfer (ZIFT),* in which either the egg and sperm or the fertilized egg are inserted in the fallopian tube (CDC, 2002; Society for Assisted Reproductive Technology, 2002).

In *surrogate motherhood,* a fertile woman is impregnated by the prospective father, usually by artificial insemination. She agrees to carry the baby to term and give it to the father and his partner. The American Academy of Pediatrics (AAP) Committee on Bioethics (1992) recommends that surrogacy be considered a tentative, preconception adoption agreement. The committee also recommends a prebirth agreement on the period of time in which the surrogate may assert parental rights.

Assisted reproduction can result in a tangled web of legal, ethical, and psychological dilemmas (Schwartz, 2003). The issues multiply when a surrogate is involved (Schwartz, 2003). Who is the real parent—the surrogate or the woman whose baby she bears? What if a surrogate wants to keep the baby? Another controversial aspect of surrogacy is the payment of money. The creation of a "breeder class" of poor and disadvantaged women who carry the babies of the well-to-do strikes many people as wrong. Some countries, such as France and Italy, have banned commercial surrogacy. In the United States, it is illegal in some states and legal in others, and regulations differ from state to state (Warner, 2008).

One thing seems certain: as long as there are people who want children but are unable to conceive or bear them, human ingenuity and technology will come up with ways to satisfy their desire. Unfortunately, our means of handling these issues in a socially responsible, legal, and ethical manner have not caught up to that desire.

If you or your partner were infertile, would you seriously consider or undertake one of the methods of assisted reproduction described here? Why or why not?

1

Ever see seminars or classes offered that claim to be able to help you think with your right brain and therefore release your creative juices more effectively? Although it sounds nice, unfortunately, there doesn't seem to be any scientific basis for these types of claims. A review of 72 neuro-imaging studies showed no relationship between creativity and right brain activation.

Dietrich & Kanso, 2010

reflective thinkers can also create complex intellectual systems that reconcile apparently conflicting ideas or considerations—for example, by putting together various theories of human development into a single overarching theory that explains many different kinds of behavior (Fischer & Pruyne, 2003).

At approximately 20 to 25 years of age, the brain forms new neurons, synapses, and dendritic connections, and the cortical regions that handle higher-level thinking become fully myelinated. A rich and stimulating environment can stimulate the development of thicker, denser, cortical connections. These physical changes in the brain allow more complex thinking to occur. Although almost all adults develop the *capacity* for becoming reflective thinkers, few attain optimal proficiency in this skill, and even fewer can apply it consistently to various kinds of problems. For many adults, college education stimulates progress toward reflective thinking (Fischer & Pruyne, 2003).

Postformal Thought Research and theoretical work since the 1970s suggest that mature thinking is more complex than Piaget described, and that it encompasses more than just the capacity for abstract thought. This higher stage of adult cognition, which tends to emerge in early adulthood, is sometimes called **postformal thought.** As with reflective thinking, exposure to higher education is often a catalyst for the development of this ability (Labouvie-Vief, 2006).

postformal thought
Mature type of thinking that relies on subjective experience and intuition as well as logic and allows room for ambiguity, uncertainty, inconsistency, contradiction, imperfection, and compromise.

Postformal thought is characterized by the ability to deal with inconsistency, contradiction, and compromise. Life is messy and complex, and some people are better able to deal with its inherent uncertainty. Thus postformal thinking is in some way as much a personality style as it is a mode of thinking.

Another characteristic of postformal thought is its flexibility. Postformal thought draws on different aspects of cognition when needed. At times, formal logical thought is the appropriate tool to solve a problem. The problems that Piaget examined tended to be like this—they involved physical phenomena and required dispassionate, objective observation and analysis. But other times, especially in ambiguous circumstances, the fruits of experience can help us understand a situation more effectively. Postformal thought draws on intuition and emotion as well as logic to help people cope with situations such as social dilemmas, which are often less clearly structured and are fraught with emotion (Berg & Klaczynski, 1996; Sinnot, 2003).

Postformal thought is also relativistic. Immature thinking tends to be black and white—there is one right answer and one wrong one. Relativistic thought, by contrast, acknowledges that there may be more than one valid way of viewing an issue and that the world is made up of shades of gray. This allows adults to transcend a single logical system (such as an established political system and ideology) and reconcile or choose among conflicting ideas (such as those of the Israelis and Palestinians) when each of these ideas may have a valid claim as the truth (Sinnott, 2003). Relativistic thinking often develops in response to events or interactions that open up unaccustomed ways of looking at things and challenge a simple, polarized view of the world.

Research has found a progression toward postformal thought throughout young and middle adulthood. In one study, participants were asked to judge what caused the outcomes of a series of ambiguous hypothetical situations, such as a marital conflict. Adolescents and young adults tended to blame individuals, whereas middle-aged people were more likely to attribute behavior to the interplay among persons and environment (Blanchard-Fields & Norris, 1994).

SCHAIE: A LIFE-SPAN MODEL OF COGNITIVE DEVELOPMENT

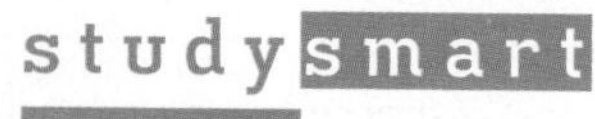

Perspectives on Thinking and Memory

K. Warner Schaie's life-span model of cognitive development (1977-1978; Schaie & Willis, 2000) looks at the developing uses of intellect and cognition within a social context. His seven stages revolve around what motivates cognition at various stages of life. These goals shift from acquisition of information and skills (*what I need to know*) to practical integration of knowledge and skills (*how to use what I know*) to a search for meaning and purpose (*why I should know*). The seven stages are as follows:

1. *Acquisitive stage* (childhood and adolescence). Children and adolescents acquire information and skills mainly for their own sake or as preparation for participation in society. For example, a child might read about dinosaurs out of pure interest in the topic.
2. *Achieving stage* (late teens or early 20s to early 30s). Young adults no longer acquire knowledge merely for its own sake; they use what they know to pursue goals, such as career and family. For example, a young adult might take a college class as preparation for a career in a particular area.
3. *Responsible stage* (late 30s to early 60s). Middle-aged people use their minds to solve practical problems associated with responsibilities to others, such as family members or employees. For example, an adult might figure out a more efficient way to complete a task at work.
4. *Executive stage* (30s or 40s through middle age). People in the executive stage are responsible for societal systems (such as governmental or business organizations) or social movements. They deal with complex relationships on multiple levels. For example, an adult might mediate a disagreement between two coworkers so the office runs more smoothly.
5. *Reorganizational stage* (end of middle age, beginning of late adulthood). People who enter retirement reorganize their lives and intellectual energies around meaningful pursuits that take the place of paid work. A retired adult, for example, might decide to volunteer at a local botanical garden.
6. *Reintegrative stage* (late adulthood). Older adults may be experiencing biological and cognitive changes and tend to be more selective about what tasks they expend effort on. They focus on the purpose of what they do and concentrate on tasks that have the most meaning for them. For example, a person feeling the effects of age on her joints might decide to take a daily walk rather than a run for health.
7. *Legacy-creating stage* (advanced old age). Near the end of life, once reintegration has been completed (or along with it), older people may create instructions for the disposition of prized possessions, make funeral arrangements, provide oral histories, or write their life stories as a legacy for their loved ones. An older adult might, for instance, complete an advance directive and distribute that to his children.

This approach suggests that intelligence looks different depending on the stage of life of the person. So traditional psychometric tests, which use the same kinds of tasks to measure intelligence at all periods of life, may be inappropriate. For example, tests developed to measure knowledge and skills in children may not be suitable for measuring cognitive competence in adults, who use knowledge and skills to solve practical problems and achieve self-chosen goals. Also, not everyone goes through the stages within the suggested time frame.

checkpoint
can you . . .

- Differentiate between reflective and postformal thinking?
- Tell why postformal thought may be especially suited to solving social problems?
- Identify Schaie's seven stages of cognitive development?

STERNBERG: INSIGHT AND KNOW-HOW

Alix, Barbara, and Courtney applied to graduate programs at Yale University. Alix had earned almost straight A's in college and had scored high on the Graduate Record Examination (GRE). Barbara's grades were fair, and her GRE scores were low by Yale's standards, but her letters of recommendation enthusiastically praised her exceptional research and creative ideas. Courtney's grades, GRE scores, and recommendations were good but not among the best.

Alix and Courtney were admitted to the graduate program. Barbara was not admitted but was hired as a research associate and took graduate classes on the side. Alix did very well for the first year or so, but less well after that when asked to develop independent research ideas. Barbara confounded the admissions committee by doing outstanding work. Courtney's performance in graduate school was only fair, but she had the easiest time getting a good job afterward (Trotter, 1986).

study smart

Sternberg's Theory of Intelligence

This vignette illustrates that doing well in life involves more than just exam grades. The triarchic theory of intelligence is comprised of three elements: *componential, experiential,* and *contextual knowledge* (Sternberg, 1985, 1987). Alix's analytical abilities illustrated componential knowledge, which helped her sail through examinations and do well in situations in which academic rigor was important. She scored very well on traditional psychometric tests, which are highly predictive of academic success. However, componential knowledge such as this is not always sufficient to do well in life. Also important are experiential elements (how insightful or creative a person is) and contextual knowledge (the practical aspect of intelligence).

In graduate school, where original thinking is expected, Barbara's superior experiential intelligence—her fresh insights and original ideas—began to shine. So did Courtney's practical, contextual intelligence. Courtney knew her way around. She chose hot research topics, submitted papers to the right journals, and knew when and how to apply for jobs.

tacit knowledge
Sternberg's term for information that is not formally taught but is necessary to get ahead.

An important aspect of practical intelligence is **tacit knowledge:** "inside information," "know-how," or "savvy" that is not formally taught or openly expressed. Tacit knowledge is commonsense knowledge of how to get ahead—how to win a promotion or cut through red tape. It is not well correlated with measures of general cognitive ability, but it may be a better predictor of managerial success (Sternberg, Grigorenko, & Oh, 2001).

Tacit knowledge may include *self-management* (knowing how to motivate oneself and organize time and energy), *management of tasks* (knowing how to write a term paper or grant proposal), and *management of others* (knowing when and how to reward or criticize subordinates) (E. A. Smith, 2001). Sternberg's method of testing tacit knowledge in adults is to compare a test-taker's chosen course of action in hypothetical, work-related situations (such as how best to angle for a promotion) with the choices of experts in the field and with accepted rules of thumb. Tacit knowledge, measured in this way, seems to be unrelated to IQ and predicts job performance better than do psychometric tests (Herbig, Büssing, & Ewert, 2001; Sternberg, Wagner, Williams, & Horvath, 1995).

We remember more events from our young adult years than at any other point in the life span, a phenomenon known as the reminiscence bump.

Janssen, Murre, & Meeter, 2007

Of course, tacit knowledge is not all that is needed to succeed; other aspects of intelligence count too. In studies of business managers, tests of tacit knowledge *together with* IQ and personality tests predicted virtually all of the variance in performance, measured by such criteria as salary, years of management experience, and the company's success (Sternberg et al., 1995). In one study, tacit knowledge was related to the salaries managers earned at a given age and to how high their positions were, independent of family background and education. The most knowledgeable managers were not those who had spent many years with a company or many years as managers, but those who had worked for the most companies, perhaps gaining a greater breadth of experience (Sternberg et al., 2000).

checkpoint
can **you** . . .

- Tell why Sternberg's three kinds of intelligence may be especially applicable to adults?

EMOTIONAL INTELLIGENCE

emotional intelligence (EI)
Salovey and Mayer's term for the ability to understand and regulate emotions; an important component of effective, intelligent behavior.

Peter Salovey and John Mayer (1990) coined the term **emotional intelligence (EI).** It refers to four related skills: the abilities to *perceive, use, understand,* and *manage,* or regulate, emotions—our own and those of others—so as to achieve goals. Emotional intelligence enables a person to harness emotions to deal more effectively with the social environment. It requires awareness of the type of behavior that is appropriate in a given social situation.

To measure emotional intelligence, psychologists use the Mayer-Salovey-Caruso Emotional Intelligence Test (MSCEIT) (Mayer, Salovey, & Caruso, 2002), a 40-minute battery of questions that generates a score for each of the four abilities, as well as a total score. The test includes such questions as, "Tom felt anxious and became a bit stressed when he thought about all the work he needed to do. When his supervisor brought him an additional project, he felt (a) overwhelmed, (b) depressed, (c) ashamed, (d) self-conscious, or (e) jittery."

Emotional intelligence affects the quality of personal relationships. Studies have found that college students who score high on the MSCEIT are more likely to report positive relationships with parents and friends (Lopes, Salovey, & Straus, 2003), that college-age men who score low on the MSCEIT report engaging in more drug use and consuming more alcohol (Brackett, Mayer, & Warner, 2004), and that close friends of college students who score well on the MSCEIT rate them as more likely to provide emotional support in time of need (Lopes et al., 2004). College-age couples in which both partners scored high on the MSCEIT reported the happiest relationships, whereas couples who scored low were unhappiest (Brackett, Cox, Gaines, & Salovey, 2005).

Emotional intelligence also affects effectiveness at work. Among a sample of employees of a Fortune 500 insurance company, those with higher MSCEIT scores were rated higher by colleagues and supervisors on sociability, interpersonal sensitivity, leadership potential, and ability to handle stress and conflict. High scores also were related to higher salaries and more promotions (Lopes, Grewal, Kadis, Gall, & Salovey, 2006).

Ultimately, acting on emotions often comes down to a value judgment. Is it smarter to obey or disobey authority? To inspire others or exploit them? "Emotional skills, like intellectual ones, are morally neutral. . . . Without a moral compass to guide people in how to employ their gifts, emotional intelligence can be used for good or evil" (Gibbs, 1995, p. 68). Let's look next at the development of that "moral compass" in adulthood.

In what kinds of situations would emotional intelligence be most useful? Give specific examples. Do the same for reflective thought, postformal thought, and tacit knowledge.

Generally, we think of the capacity to empathize with others as a good thing. But what if you work in a job where you frequently see people in pain? Research has shown that doctors suppress this empathic response, allowing them to focus on treatment more effectively.

Decety, Yang, & Chen, 2010

checkpoint can you . . .

- Explain the concept of emotional intelligence and how it is tested?

Moral Reasoning

In Kohlberg's theory, moral development of children and adolescents is closely tied to cognitive maturation. Young people advance in moral judgment as they shed egocentrism and become capable of abstract thought. In adulthood, however, moral judgments become more complex.

Recall that Kohlberg broke moral development into three stages. In the final stage, postconventional morality, Kohlberg believed that people became capable of fully principled moral reasoning, and that they made moral decisions on the basis of universal principles of justice. Kohlberg argued that most people did not reach this level until their 20s, if at all (Kohlberg, 1973). He believed that the acquisition of this style of thinking was primarily a function of experience. In particular, when young people encounter values that conflict with their own (as might happen in college or foreign travel) and when they are responsible for the welfare of others (as in parenthood), their development of moral reasoning abilities increases.

There is some support for the view that experience may lead adults to reevaluate their criteria for what is right and wrong. For example, when asked about moral dilemmas, some adults spontaneously offer their own personal experiences as explanations for why they answered as they did. For instance, people who have had cancer or whose relatives or friends have had cancer are more likely to condone a man's stealing an expensive drug to save his dying wife (Bielby & Papalia, 1975). Experiences themselves can also shape moral reasoning more broadly. Students who attend church are less likely to cheat on a task than those who attend church less regularly (Bloodgood, Turnley, & Mudrack, 2008). On the other hand, people exposed to war (Haskuka, Sunar, & Alp, 2008) or who suffer from posttraumatic stress disorder as a result of combat experience (Taylor, 2007) show a reduced tendency to reach Kohlberg's higher levels of moral reasoning. In short, personal experiences can affect the likelihood of engaging in certain types of moral reasoning.

Shortly before his death, Kohlberg proposed an additional seventh state of moral reasoning. He believed it was possible for people to achieve "a sense of unity with the cosmos, nature or God," which enabled them to see moral issues from "the standpoint of the universe as a whole" (Kohlberg & Ryncarz, 1990, pp. 191, 207). Rather than seeing morality as tied to justice, adults at this stage might instead reflect on the question, "Why be moral?"

CULTURE AND MORAL REASONING

Culture affects the understanding of morality. Heinz's dilemma was revised for use in Taiwan. In the revision, a shopkeeper will not give a man *food* for his sick wife. This version would seem unbelievable to Chinese villagers, who are more accustomed to hearing a shopkeeper in such a situation say, "You have to let people have things whether they have money or not" (Wolf, 1968, p. 21).

Cultures like the United States tend to focus on individual autonomy, whereas cultures like China are more concerned with group dynamics and harmony. This may help explain some of the cultural differences in moral reasoning. Whereas Kohlberg's system is based on justice, the Chinese ethos leans toward conciliation and harmony. In Kohlberg's format, respondents make an either-or decision based on their own value system. In Chinese society, people faced with moral dilemmas are expected to discuss them openly, be guided by community standards, and try to find a way of resolving the problem to please as many parties as possible. In the West, even good people may be harshly punished if, under the force of circumstances, they break a law. The Chinese are unaccustomed to universally applied laws; they are taught to abide by the decisions of a wise judge (Dien, 1982).

Have you ever observed or had an experience with a person from another culture that revealed cultural differences in moral principles?

This example illustrates a wider critique leveled at Kohlberg's approach. Kohlberg believed that certain cultures were more likely to provide opportunities for people to attain the highest levels of moral reasoning (Jenson, 1997). This underlying belief in the superiority of a particular worldview has been criticized as being too narrow, and as being biased toward Western cultural norms of individuality and a nonreligious mindset. For example, many cultures provide moral dictates focused on divine authority and tradition, and there is no reason for these beliefs to be viewed as morally inferior or as reflecting a less sophisticated form of reasoning (Shweder et al., 2006). Similarly, who is to say that caring for justice is morally superior to caring for others?

GENDER AND MORAL REASONING

Carol Gilligan was bothered by what she perceived as a male bias in Kohlberg's approach. She believed that women's central dilemma was the conflict between their needs and the needs of others rather than the principles of abstract justice and fairness delineated by Kohlberg. Women's moral reasoning was not less complex than men's, she argued, it merely had a different focus.

In her research, Gilligan (1982/1993) interviewed 29 pregnant women about their decision to continue or end their pregnancies. As with Kohlberg, the key feature was not the particular decision each woman made, but rather the reasoning behind that decision. What Gilligan found was that the women in her research saw morality in terms of selfishness versus responsibility, which was generally understood as an obligation to exercise care and avoid hurting others. Gilligan concluded that women were more concerned with their responsibilities to others than about independently derived abstract ideals. Table 1 lists Gilligan's proposed levels of moral development in women.

Which, if either, do you consider to be higher moral priorities: justice and rights, or compassion and responsibility?

Other research has not found consistent gender differences in moral reasoning (Brabeck & Shore, 2003). A recent analysis of 113 studies found that although women were more likely to think in terms of care, and men in terms of justice, these differences were small. It is interesting, however, that in brain imaging studies (Harenski, Antonenko, Shane, & Keihl, 2008) women showed more activity in areas of the brain associated with care-based reasoning (the posterior, anterior cingulated, and anterior insula) and men showed more activity in areas of the brain associated with justice-based

TABLE 1 Gilligan's Levels of Moral Development in Women

Stage	Description
Level 1: Orientation of individual survival	The woman concentrates on herself—on what is practical and what is best for her.
Transition 1: From selfishness to responsibility	The woman realizes her connection to others and thinks about what the responsible choice would be in terms of other people (including her unborn baby), as well as herself.
Level 2: Goodness as self-sacrifice	This conventional feminine wisdom dictates sacrificing the woman's own wishes to what other people want—and will think of her. She considers herself responsible for the actions of others, while holding others responsible for her own choices. She is in a dependent position, one in which her indirect efforts to exert control often turn into manipulation, sometimes through the use of guilt.
Transition 2: From goodness to truth	The woman assesses her decisions not on the basis of how others will react to them but on her intentions and the consequences of her actions. She develops a new judgment that takes into account her own needs, along with those of others. She wants to be "good" by being responsible to others, but also wants to be "honest" by being responsible to herself. Survival returns as a major concern.
Level 3: Morality of nonviolence	By elevating the injunction against hurting anyone (including herself) to a principle that governs all moral judgment and action, the woman establishes a "moral equality" between herself and others and is then able to assume the responsibility for choice in moral dilemmas.

Source: Reprinted and adapted by permission of the publisher from *In a Different Voice: Psychological Theory and Women's Development* by Carol Gilligan, Cambridge, Mass: Harvard University Press, Copyright © 1982, 1993 by Carol Gilligan.

processing (superior temporal sulcus). Still, the weight of evidence does not appear to back up either of Gilligan's original contentions: a male bias in Kohlberg's theory or a distinct female perspective on morality (L. Walker, 1995).

In her later research, Gilligan described moral development in *both* men and women as evolving beyond abstract reasoning. In studies using real-life moral dilemmas (such as whether a woman's lover should confess their affair to her husband), rather than hypothetical dilemmas like the ones Kohlberg used, Gilligan and her colleagues found that many people in their 20s become dissatisfied with a narrow moral logic and become more able to live with moral contradictions (Gilligan, Murphy, & Tappan, 1990). It seems, then, that if Gilligan's earlier research reflected an alternative value system, it was not gender-based. At the same time, with the inclusion of his seventh stage, Kohlberg's thinking evolved to a point of greater agreement with Gilligan's. Both theories now place responsibility to others at the highest level of moral thought.

checkpoint
can **you** . . .

- Give examples of the roles of experience and culture in adult moral development?
- State Gilligan's original position on gender differences in moral development, and summarize research findings on the subject?

Education and Work

Unlike young people in past generations, who typically could expect to move directly from school to work and financial independence, many emerging adults today do not have a clear career path. Some alternate between education and work; others pursue both at the same time. Most of those who do not enroll in postsecondary education, or do not finish, enter the job market, but many return later for more schooling (Furstenberg et al., 2005; Hamilton & Hamilton, 2006; NCES, 2005b). Some, especially in the United Kingdom, take a year off from formal education or the workplace—a *gap year*—to gain new skills, do volunteer work, travel, or study abroad (Jones, 2004). And some combine college with marriage and child rearing (Fitzpatrick & Turner, 2007). Many emerging adults who are in school or living in their parents' homes are financially dependent (Schoeni & Ross, 2005).

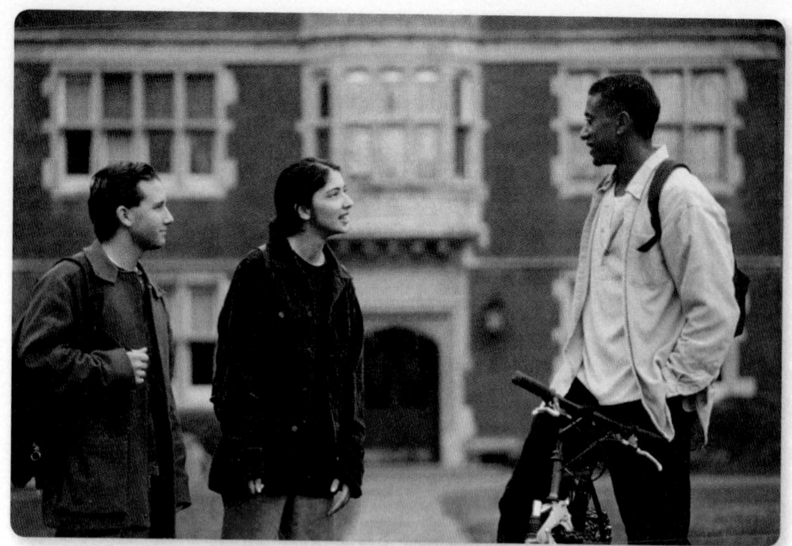

College enrollments in the United States are at an all-time high. More than 2 out of 3 high school graduates go right to college.

Educational and vocational choices after high school may present opportunities for cognitive growth. Exposure to a new educational or work environment offers the opportunity to hone abilities, question long-held assumptions, and try out new ways of looking at the world. For the increasing number of students of nontraditional age (age 25 and up), college or workplace education is rekindling intellectual curiosity, improving employment opportunities, and enhancing work skills.

THE COLLEGE TRANSITION

College is an increasingly important path to adulthood, though it is only one such path and, until recently, not the most common one (Montgomery & Côté, 2003). Between 1975 and 2011, the proportion of U.S. high school graduates who went straight into a 2- or 4-year college grew from about half (51 percent) to more than two-thirds (68 percent; NCES, 2013).

Fewer than one-third of young adults have basic knowledge of interest rates, inflation, and risk diversification. Going to college helps: higher education is associated with increases in financial literacy.

Lusardi, Mitchell, & Curto, 2009

College courses and even complete degree or certificate programs are now widely available by *distance learning,* in which courses are delivered via mail, e-mail, the Internet, or other technological means. About 4.6 million students took at least one online course during the fall of 2008, and more than 1 in 4 students will take an online course at some point in their college career. In fact, online enrollment is now growing faster than traditional higher education enrollment numbers (Allen & Seeman, 2010). Colleges also are increasingly experimenting with hybrid courses, which utilize a mixture of both online and in person techniques. In general, research seems to suggest that learning outcomes are similar for online, hybrid, and traditional students, although a wide variety of variables can affect outcomes (Tallent-Runnels et al., 2006).

Some colleges, including Stanford University and MIT, have offered massive, open, online courses (MOOCs) that allow any person with an Internet connection to take the course for free. Although such courses show promise, especially with respect to opening avenues of affordable knowledge in far-flung locales, they also suffer from high rates of attrition and are subject to cheating (Daniel, 2012). Their effect remains to be determined.

Gender, Socioeconomic Status, and Race/Ethnicity U.S. college enrollment has continued to reach new highs each year, an increase primarily driven by larger numbers of female students (NCES, 2012b). In a reversal of the traditional gender gap, women now make up a larger percentage of the student population. In 2006, women made up 66 percent of U.S. undergraduate students (NCES, 2007a), and in 2010, slightly over 57 percent of those earning bachelor's degrees (NCES, 2012a). By comparison, in 1970, women made up only 42 percent of those earning bachelor's degrees (NCES, 2009b). This development is due in part to a decline in gender discrimination and in part to women's growing awareness of the need to support themselves (Buchmann & DiPrete, 2006). Similarly, women have higher postsecondary enrollment rates than men in most European countries, as well as in Australia, Canada, New Zealand, Japan, and the Russian Federation (Buchmann & DiPrete, 2006; Sen, Partelow, & Miller, 2005). U.S. women are more likely than men to enroll in graduate school and earn master's degrees (59 percent) and almost as likely to complete doctoral degrees (NCES, 2007b).

Despite increases in tuition and fees, data by the College Board suggests that long-term benefits of going to college still exist, and are in fact growing.

Baum, Ma, & Payea, 2010

Still, gender differences are evident at these highest educational levels (Halpern et al., 2007). In the United States, women remain more likely than men to major in traditionally women's fields, such as education, nursing, English literature, and psychology, and not in math and science (NCES, 2007a). Although women generally do better than men in high school math and science courses, they tend to score lower on standardized college and graduate school entrance tests—a fact that may relate to men's advantage at the upper end of the mathematical, visual, and spatial ability range, or perhaps to differences in the way men and women solve novel problems (Halpern et al., 2007). Even so, women have made gains in almost every field (NCES, 2006b). More women than in the past now earn engineering degrees, though at least 80 percent of bachelor's degrees in that field still go to men (Halpern et al., 2007; NCES, 2007b). The percentage of professional degrees (law, medicine, dentistry, and so forth) awarded to women has risen dramatically since 1970 (NCES, 2005c). In 1960 women earned only 10 percent of postgraduate degrees, averaged across all fields, but women now earn approximately 57 percent of postgraduate degrees (NCES, 2009b).

Socioeconomic status and race/ethnicity affect access to postsecondary education. In 2011, 82 percent of high school graduates from high-income families, as compared with only 52 percent from low-income families, enrolled in college immediately after high school (NCES, 2012a). From the 2000–2001 academic year to the 2010–2011 academic year, prices for tuition, room, and board rose 42 percent at public institutions and 31 percent at private, not-for-profit institutions (NCES, 2012a), making the attainment of higher education increasingly difficult for low- and middle-income families. Thus many students from more modest circumstances are likely to work while attending college, which often serves to slow their progress (Dey & Hurtado, 1999). In addition, students from wealthier families are less likely to drop out of college before graduating (Hamilton & Hamilton, 2006).

Currently, approximately 72 percent of bachelor's degrees are earned by white students (NCES, 2009b). Minority participation, however, has risen at all levels. More than 50 percent of Hispanics and blacks who finished high school in 2005 went directly to college. And the percentage of college students who are minorities is rising, primarily due to increased numbers of Latinos, Pacific Islanders, and Asian Americans (NCES, 2009b). It is likely, given the current demographic composition of the United States, that this trend will continue.

Adjusting to College Many freshmen feel overwhelmed by the demands of college. Family support seems to be a key factor in adjustment, both for students commuting from home and for those living on campus. Students who are adaptable, have high aptitude and good problem-solving skills, become actively engaged in their studies and in the academic environment, and enjoy close but autonomous relationships with their parents tend to adjust best and get the most out of college. Also important is being able to build a strong social and academic network among peers and instructors (Montgomery & Côté, 2003). In fact, relatively cost-effective peer support interventions can significantly ease the transition to college (Mattanah et al., 2010).

Studies show that Web sites such as Facebook help students build connections between budding college communities and are associated with students' psychological well-being.

Ellison et al., 2007

Cognitive Growth in College College can be a time of intellectual discovery and personal growth, especially in verbal and quantitative skills, critical thinking, and moral reasoning (Montgomery & Côté, 2003). Students change in response to (1) the curriculum, which offers new insights and new ways of thinking; (2) other students who challenge long-held views and values; (3) the student culture, which is different from the culture of society at large; and (4) faculty members, who provide new role models. In terms of both immediate and long-term benefits, going to college—any college—is more important than which college a person attends (Montgomery & Côté, 2003).

The college experience can be an exciting time of intellectual growth and discovery. Indeed, researchers have found that going to college can result in a fundamental change in the way young people think (Fischer & Pruyne, 2003). In a groundbreaking study, William Perry (1970) interviewed 67 Harvard and Radcliffe students throughout their undergraduate years and found patterns in the way they approached learning and knowledge. Overall, their thinking progressed from rigidity to flexibility, and ultimately to choosing their own beliefs on the basis of reflection.

Many students come to college with rigid ideas about how the world works. They tend to believe that there is a "right" answer that can be found and defended. As they begin to encounter a wider range of ideas and viewpoints, they are forced to examine

The future looks bright for this young woman. Today, more women than men enter college and earn degrees, and many colleges offer support and facilities for students with disabilities. A college education is often the key to a successful career and a healthy, satisfying life.

their assumptions about the "truth." However, they consider this stage as temporary, and are generally certain they will learn the "one right answer" eventually.

As students gain more experience and think more deeply and from a greater wealth of accumulated knowledge, they begin to realize that much of knowledge and many values are somewhat relative. They realize that different individuals or cultures may hold different values than they do, and thus see the world in different ways. Although they believe their unique view has value, they have difficulty finding meaning in the maze of systems and beliefs to which they have been exposed. How do they decide what to believe?

Ultimately, students achieve what has been called *commitment within relativism.* At this point, students make their own judgments; they decide for themselves, finally, what they want to believe. They give credence to the inherent uncertainty of belief but feel confident in their choices and values and trust in their own opinions.

A diverse student body also contributes to cognitive growth. Discussions that include mixed-race participants produce greater novelty and complexity of ideas than all-white discussions (Antonio et al., 2004). In general, research also supports the social benefits of diversity. For example, research has shown that those campuses with more diverse student bodies result in greater amounts of interracial friendships rather than in continued or increased segregation (Fischer, 2008) and that a diverse campus is related to intellectual and academic gains (Gurin, Dey, Gurin, & Hurtado, 2003). Interestingly, in one study students who shared a dorm room with someone of a different race showed decreases in their racial stereotypes and less anxiety about interracial group experiences over the course of the study (Shook & Fazio, 2008).

Completing College Although college entrance has become more common in the United States, *finishing* college has not. Only 1 out of 4 young people who start college (1 out of 2 at 4-year institutions) have received a degree after 5 years (Horn & Berger, 2004; NCES, 2004). This does not mean that the rest drop out. A growing number of students, especially men, remain in college more than 5 years or switch from 2-year to 4-year institutions (Horn & Berger, 2004; Peter & Horn, 2005).

Whether a person completes college may depend not only on motivation, academic aptitude and preparation, and ability to work independently, but also on social integration and social support: employment opportunities, financial support, suitability of living arrangements, quality of social and academic interactions, and the fit between what the college offers and what the student wants and needs. Intervention programs for at-risk students have improved college attendance rates by creating meaningful bonds between students and teachers, finding opportunities for students to work while in college, providing academic assistance, and helping students see how college can move them toward a better future (Montgomery & Côté, 2003).

checkpoint
can **you** . . .

- Discuss factors affecting who goes to college and who finishes?
- Tell how college can affect cognitive development?

ENTERING THE WORLD OF WORK

By their mid-20s, most emerging adults are either working or pursuing advanced education or both (Hamilton & Hamilton, 2006). Those who enter the workforce face a rapidly changing picture. The nature of work is changing, and work arrangements are becoming more varied and less stable. Where previous generations of employees often could expect to remain at a company from their start date until retirement, that pattern of employment is becoming increasingly rare. More and more adults are self-employed, working at home, telecommuting, on flexible work schedules, or acting as independent contractors. These changes, together with a more competitive job market and the demand for a highly skilled workforce, make education and training more vital than ever before (Corcoran & Matsudaira, 2005).

Higher education expands employment opportunities and earning power (Figure 4) and enhances long-term quality of life for adults worldwide (Centre for Educational Research and Innovation, 2004; Montgomery & Côté, 2003). In the United States, adults with advanced degrees earn 4 times more than those with less than a high school diploma (U.S. Census Bureau, 2007a). For adults without higher education, unemployment rates are high (U.S. Census Bureau, 2006), and it may be difficult to earn enough to establish an independent household. A cross-national survey in Belgium, Canada, Germany, and Italy found a decline in economic self-sufficiency among 18- to 34-year-old men and among women in their early 20s between the mid-1980s and 1995–2000 (Bell, Burtless, Gornick, & Smeeding, 2007). And workers in their 20s, especially their early 20s, tend to be concentrated in low-wage, low-skilled positions and frequently change jobs (Hamilton & Hamilton, 2006).

Although income differentials between male and female workers exist at all levels of educational attainment, these gaps have narrowed considerably. In 1980, the average young man with a bachelor's degree earned 36 percent more than the average young woman; in 2002 the difference was 23 percent (NCES, 2007b). However, a report by the American Association of University Women (2007) found that the earnings gap increases during the 10 years after graduation, so that women at that point earn only 69 percent of what their male counterparts do. Furthermore, one-fourth of the pay gap is unexplained by such factors as hours, occupations, and parenthood, suggesting that it stems from gender discrimination. Data from the last U.S. Census survey reveals that as of 2009 women still earned only 78 cents for every dollar a man earns (Getz, 2010).

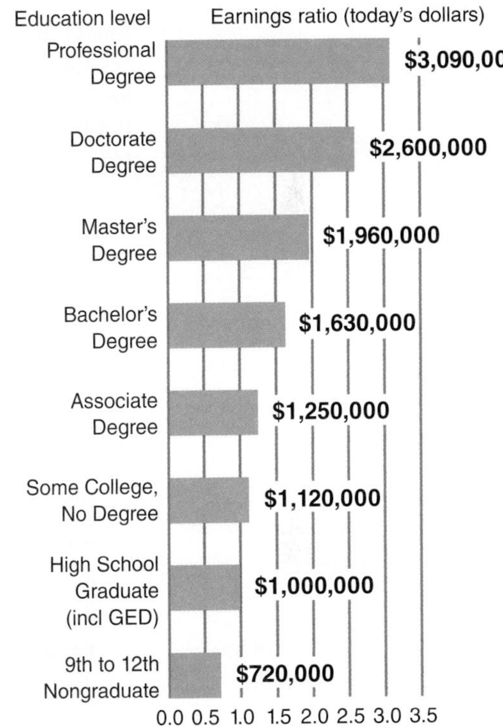

FIGURE 4

Expected Lifetime Earnings (Present Value) by Educational Level: United States, 2008

Even considering the cost of an education, higher educational levels mean more lifetime earnings.

Note: Income multiples are calculated on median earnings by educational attainment level for the population age 25 to 64 as of March 2007.

Source: U.S. Census Bureau, CPS 2008 Annual Social and Economic Supplement, PINC-03.

Combining Work and Schooling How does juggling work and study affect cognitive development and career preparation? One longitudinal study followed a random sample of incoming freshmen through their first 3 years of college. During the first 2 years, on- or off-campus work had little or no effect on reading comprehension, mathematical reasoning, or critical thinking skills. By the 3rd year, part-time work had a positive effect, perhaps because employment forces students to organize their time efficiently and learn better work habits. However, working more than 15 to 20 hours a week tended to have a negative impact (Pascarella, Edison, Nora, Hagedorn, & Terenzini, 1998) and is associated with a failure to graduate.

Working during college may also affect the likelihood of attending graduate programs. Although grants and loans are available to some students, many students must work to help support their educational aspirations. Such work cuts into the time they have available to engage in other activities, such as participation in research groups, internships, and volunteer work. These activities are optional but allow students a more competitive application into graduate school. Therefore, although work itself may not be detrimental to an undergraduate education, it may be related to difficulties meeting criteria for graduate programs.

Cognitive Growth at Work Do people change as a result of the kind of work they do? Some research says yes: people seem to grow in challenging jobs, the kind that are becoming increasingly prevalent today.

substantive complexity
Degree to which a person's work requires thought and independent judgment.

This research has revealed a reciprocal relationship between the **substantive complexity** of work—the degree of thought and independent judgment it requires—and a person's flexibility in coping with cognitive demands (Kohn, 1980).

Brain research casts light on how people deal with complex work. A great deal of development in the frontal lobes occurs in young adulthood (Luciana, 2010). Full development of this area of the brain during young adulthood may better equip people to handle several tasks at the same time. Magnetic resonance imaging shows that the most frontward part of the frontal lobes has a special function and plays a major role in problem solving and planning. This portion of the brain springs into action when a person needs to put an unfinished task on hold and shift attention to another task. It permits a worker to keep the first task in working memory while attending to the second—for example, to resume reading a report after being interrupted by the telephone (Koechlin, Basso, Pietrini, Panzer, & Grafman, 1999). Other aspects of brain development also influence why, as young people enter adulthood, they become less likely to take risks and are better able to control their behaviors (Luciana, 2010).

spillover hypothesis
Hypothesis that there is a carryover of cognitive gains from work to leisure that explains the positive relationship between activities in the quality of intellectual functioning.

Cognitive growth need not stop at the end of the workday. According to the **spillover hypothesis,** cognitive gains from work carry over to nonworking hours. Studies support this hypothesis: substantive complexity of work strongly influences the intellectual level of leisure activities (Kohn, 1980; K. Miller & Kohn, 1983).

Smoothing the Transition to the Workplace What does it take to achieve a successful transition from school to work? A review of the literature points to four key factors: (1) competence (in general and at work); (2) personal characteristics such as initiative, flexibility, purposefulness, and a sense of urgency; (3) positive personal relationships; and (4) links between schooling and employment (Blustein, Juntunen, & Worthington, 2000).

Some developmental scientists (Furstenberg et al., 2005; Settersten, 2005) suggest measures to strengthen the links between work and educational institutions, especially community colleges:

- Improve dialogue between educators and employers.
- Modify school and work schedules to adapt to the needs of working students.
- Let employers help design work-study programs.
- Increase availability of temporary and part-time work.
- Relate better what students learn at work and in school.
- Improve training of vocational guidance counselors.
- Make better use of study and support groups and tutoring and mentoring programs.
- Provide scholarships, financial aid, and health insurance to part-time as well as full-time students and employees.

Work affects day-to-day life, not only on the job but at home, and it brings both satisfaction and stress.

checkpoint
can you . . .

- Summarize recent changes in the workplace?
- Discuss the impact of combining work and schooling?
- Explain the relationship between substantive complexity of work and cognitive development?
- List proposals for easing the transition to the workplace?

summary and key terms

Emerging Adulthood

- For many young people in advanced technological societies, entrance into adulthood is not clearly marked; it takes longer and follows more varied routes than in the past. Some developmental scientists suggest that the late teens through the mid-20s has become a transitional period called emerging adulthood.
- Emerging adulthood consists of multiple milestones or transitions, and their order and timing varies. Passage of these milestones may determine when a young person becomes an adult.

emerging adulthood

PHYSICAL DEVELOPMENT

Health and Fitness

- Physical and sensory abilities are typically at their peak in emerging and young adulthood.
- Accidents are the leading cause of death in this age group.
- The mapping of the human genome is enabling the discovery of genetic bases for certain disorders.
- Lifestyle factors such as diet, obesity, exercise, sleep, smoking, and substance use or abuse can affect health, survival, and may have epigenetic consequences for the regulation of when genes turn on and off.
- Good health is related to higher income and education. African Americans and some other minorities tend to be less healthy than other Americans. Although much of this is due to SES, there also are indications that people of different ethnicities might respond differently to some environmental influences on health.
- Social relationships, especially marriage, tend to be associated with physical and mental health.
- Mental health is generally good in early adulthood, but certain conditions, such as depression, become more prevalent. Alcohol abuse and alcoholism are the most common substance disorders.

risky drinking

alcoholism

Sexual and Reproductive Issues

- Almost all U.S. young adults have sexual relations before marriage.
- Sexually transmitted infections, menstrual disorders, and infertility can be concerns during young adulthood.
- The highest rates of STIs in the United States are among emerging adults, particularly among young women.
- The most common cause of infertility in men is a low sperm count; the most common cause in women is blockage of the fallopian tubes.
- Infertile couples now have many options for assisted reproduction. These techniques involve ethical and practical issues.

premenstrual syndrome (PMS)

infertility

COGNITIVE DEVELOPMENT

Perspectives on Adult Cognition

- Some investigators propose distinctively adult forms of cognition beyond formal operations. Reflective thinking emphasizes complex logic; postformal thought involves intuition and emotion as well.
- Schaie proposed seven stages of age-related cognitive development: acquisitive (childhood and adolescence), achieving (young adulthood), responsible and executive (middle adulthood), and reorganizational, reintegrative, and legacy-creating (late adulthood).
- According to Sternberg's triarchic theory of intelligence, the experiential and contextual elements become particularly important during adulthood. Tests that measure tacit knowledge can be useful complements to traditional intelligence tests.
- Emotional intelligence plays an important part in life success.

reflective thinking

postformal thought

tacit knowledge

emotional intelligence (EI)

Moral Reasoning

- According to Kohlberg, moral development in adulthood depends primarily on experience, though it cannot exceed the limits set by cognitive development. Experience may be interpreted differently in various cultural contexts, and not all cultures support Kohlberg's more advanced stages of moral development.
- Gilligan initially proposed that women have an ethic of care, whereas Kohlberg's theory emphasizes justice. However, later research, including her own, has not supported a distinction between men's and women's moral outlook.

Education and Work

- A majority of emerging adults now go to college, either to 2-year or 4-year institutions. More women than men now go to college, and an increasing percentage pursue advanced degrees even in traditionally male-dominated fields. Minority participation is growing, but more slowly. Many students enter college, but fewer graduate with a degree.
- According to Perry, college students' thinking tends to progress from rigidity to flexibility to freely chosen commitments.
- Research has found a relationship between substantive complexity of work and cognitive growth, as well as between complex work and intellectually demanding leisure activities.
- Changes in the workplace call for higher education or training. Higher education greatly expands workplace opportunities and earnings.
- The transition to the workplace could be eased through measures to strengthen vocational education and its links with work.
- **substantive complexity**
- **spillover hypothesis**

chapter 14

Psychosocial Development in Emerging and Young Adulthood

outline

learning objectives

Describe identity development and the relationship with parents in emerging adulthood.

Summarize theoretical perspectives on adult personality development.

Identify key aspects of intimate relationships and love.

Characterize marital and nonmarital lifestyles.

Discuss parenthood and the pressures on dual-income families.

Identify trends in divorce and remarriage.

did you know?

- Historically and across cultures, marriages arranged by either parents or professional matchmakers are the most common means of finding a mate?
- In 1970, only 4 percent of women 35–44 years of age made more money than their husband; by 2007 this number had increased to 22 percent?
- Half of young parents say they have too little time with their children, according to national surveys?

Personal choices made in emerging and young adulthood establish a framework for the rest of life. In this chapter, we examine the choices that frame personal and social life: adopting a sexual lifestyle; marrying, cohabiting, or remaining single; having children or not; and establishing and maintaining friendships.

The great challenge of adulthood is holding on to your idealism after you lose your innocence.

—Bruce Springsteen

Emerging Adulthood: Patterns and Tasks

VARIED PATHS TO ADULTHOOD

Paths to adulthood are far more varied than in the past. Before the 1960s, young people in the United States typically finished school, left home, got a job, got married, and had children, in that order. By the 1990s, only 1 in 4 young adults followed that sequence (Mouw, 2005).

For many young people today, emerging adulthood is a time of experimentation before assuming adult roles and responsibilities. A young man or woman may get a job and an apartment and revel in the single life. A young married couple may move in with parents while they finish school or get on their feet or after a job loss. Such traditional developmental tasks as finding stable work and developing long-term romantic relationships may be postponed until the 30s or even later (Roisman, Masten, Coatsworth, & Tellegen, 2004). What influences affect these varied paths to adulthood?

Influences on Paths to Adulthood Individual paths to adulthood are influenced by such factors as gender, academic ability, early attitudes toward education, race and ethnicity, expectations in late adolescence, and social class. Increasingly, emerging adults of both sexes extend education and delay parenthood (Osgood, Ruth, Eccles, Jacobs, & Barber, 2005), and these decisions are usually keys to future success on the job (Sandefur, Eggerling-Boeck, & Park, 2005) as well as to current well-being. In a longitudinal study that followed a nationally representative sample of high school seniors each year since 1975, emerging adults with the highest well-being were those who were not yet married, had no children, attended college, and lived away from their childhood home (Schulenberg et al., 2005). In another study, youth who were downwardly mobile tended to leave home earlier, get less support from parents, forgo higher education, and have children earlier. Early parenthood particularly limited future prospects (Boden, Fergusson, & Horwood, 2008; Mollenkopf, Waters, Holdaway, & Kasinitz, 2005).

What path have you taken, or are you taking, toward adulthood? Do you have friends who took other paths?

Some emerging adults have more resources—financial and developmental—than others. Much depends on *ego development:* a combination of ability to understand oneself and one's world, to integrate and synthesize what one perceives and knows, and to take charge of planning one's life course. Family influences are important. Young people whose ego development tended to be "stuck" at a less mature level at age 25 were more likely to have had parents who, at age 14, inhibited their autonomy, devalued them, and were more hostile in conversations (Billings, Hauser, & Allen, 2008). As a result of these and other influences, some emerging adults have more highly developed egos than others and are therefore more ready to learn to stand alone (Tanner, 2006).

checkpoint
can you . . .

- Give examples of various paths to adulthood?
- Discuss influences on paths young people take to adulthood?

IDENTITY DEVELOPMENT IN EMERGING ADULTHOOD

Adolescence is a time of great change, from the developing body to the changing brain to developing the new social roles thrust upon young people as they move

research in action

THE MILLENNIALS

Do you . . .

1. Watch more than an hour of television a day?
2. Have a tattoo or piercing in a place other than your earlobe?
3. Send more than 10 text messages a day?
4. Have a profile on a social networking site?

If you answered "yes" to the above questions, you have a lot in common with today's young adults. Every cohort of young adults is affected by a different constellation of influences, and today's—known as the millennials—are no exception. They are making their way into adulthood at a tumultuous period in U.S. history, particularly when viewed against the backdrop of changing economic circumstances and the pervasive media and networking influences on daily life. These millennials are more racially and ethnically diverse than previous generations, and, although they are likely to pray as much as previous generations, only 1 in 4 characterizes him- or herself as belonging to any particular religious group. They are rapidly becoming the most highly educated cohort in U.S. history, however, the economic recession of the late 2000s has also resulted in the highest levels of unemployment for 18- to 29-year-olds in roughly 30 years. Approximately 40 percent of these young adults were raised by divorced or single parents, and perhaps as a result millennials seem more reluctant to marry than previous generations, and the percentage of unwed mothers is (at roughly 30 percent) the highest in U.S. history. Despite (or perhaps because of) the involvement of the United States in two wars in the 2000s, young adults are less likely to have served in the military or to be veterans. They are more likely to be liberal, and 60 percent of them supported Barack Obama's bid for the presidency.

They are also more likely to vote, however, current data suggests they appear to be losing some confidence in the government and that these voting gains may not persist. Last, they are profoundly plugged in to social media, emerging technologies, and the Internet. Eighty percent sleep with their cell phone within reach, and 75 percent have created an online profile for themselves. They are also more likely to text frequently and utilize wireless technology (Pew Research Center, 2010a).

Pew Research Center, 2011

How do you think the characteristics of the millennials in young adulthood might affect their development at midlife? In what ways do you think they will be different from—or similar to—the current generation of middle-age adults?

toward independence. Erikson saw the search for identity as a lifelong task focused largely on this stage of the life span. Emerging adulthood offers a moratorium, or time out, from developmental pressures and allows young people the freedom to experiment with various roles and lifestyles (Box 1). However, it also represents a turning point during which adult role commitments gradually crystallize. In postindustrialized countries today, the active search for identity is more and more likely to extend into emerging adulthood (Côté, 2006).

recentering
Process that underlies the shift to an adult identity.

Recentering **Recentering** is a name for the process that underlies the shift to an adult identity. It is the primary task of emerging adulthood. Recentering is a three-stage process in which power, responsibility, and decision making gradually shift from the family of origin to the independent young adult (Tanner, 2006):

- At *stage 1,* the beginning of emerging adulthood, the individual is still embedded in the family of origin, but expectations for self-reliance and self-directedness begin to increase. So, for example, a young adult might still live at home and attend high school but would be expected to schedule and monitor his own activities during nonschool hours.

- In *stage 2,* during emerging adulthood, the individual remains connected to but no longer embedded within the family of origin. So, for example, an undergraduate student might live in a college dorm but still be supported financially by her parents as she attends school. Temporary, exploratory involvements in a variety of college courses, jobs, and intimate partners mark this stage. Toward its end, the individual is moving toward serious commitments and gaining the resources to support them.
- In *stage 3,* usually by age 30, the individual moves into young adulthood. This stage is marked by independence from the family of origin (while retaining close ties to it) and commitment to a career, a partner, and possibly children. Here, a young adult might be settling into a career or marriage and live independently but still remain close to his or her parents and family of origin.

The Contemporary Moratorium A fragmented, postindustrial society offers many emerging adults little guidance and less pressure to grow up (Heinz, 2002). Not everyone is equally up to the task (Côté, 2006). In general, there is a shift in goals related to the process of recentering over time. Many young people shift away from goals related to education, travel, and friends and toward goals that are health, family, and work related (Salmela-Aro, Aunola, & Nurmi, 2007).

Identity status research has found that only about a third of Western youth seem to go through what Marcia named the *moratorium* status, a self-conscious crisis that ideally leads to a resolution and identity achievement status. However, approximately 15 percent seem to regress during emerging adulthood, and about half show no significant changes at all (Kroger, Martinussen, & Marcia, 2009). Rather than actively and thoughtfully exploring their identity, many young adults seem to do little active, conscious deliberation, instead taking a passive (diffused) approach or taking the lead from their parents (foreclosure). Nevertheless, about 3 out of 4 eventually settle on some sort of occupational identity by the end of their 20s. Identity confusion persists for 10 to 20 percent, who lack what Erikson called *fidelity:* faith in something larger than themselves (Côté, 2006).

Racial/Ethnic Identity Exploration Identity exploration is different for racial/ethnic minorities than for the majority white population. Ethnic identity can be defined as one's identity as a member of a particular ethnic group (Phinney, 2003) and is part of the wider social identity of an individual (Tajfel, 1981). Many minority youth, often out of economic concerns, must take on adult responsibilities earlier than their peers. At the same time, they tend to value close and interdependent family relations and may feel obligated to assist their families financially. They may be under pressure to marry and have children at an early age, or to enter the workforce immediately rather than spending years in higher education. Thus, for them, some of the processes of emerging adulthood may be curtailed. On the other hand, they must deal with more complex identity issues regarding their ethnicity, and this process may extend well beyond the 20s (Phinney, 2006).

To achieve a secure ethnic identity, they must come to understand themselves both as part of an ethnic group and as part of the wider, diverse society, and to have a positive view of both the minority and majority cultures in which they live. Multiracial young people have the added challenge of figuring out where they fit in. Still, many reach a resolution that leads to identity achievement, as in the following:

> When I was younger I felt I didn't belong anywhere. But now I've just come to the conclusion that . . . that's just the way I am, . . . and my home is inside myself. . . . I no longer feel the compulsion to fit in 'cause if you're just trying to fit in you never do. (Alipuria, 2002, p. 143)

checkpoint
can **you** . . .

- Define *recentering* and summarize its three stages?
- Discuss identity status research on emerging adults in postindustrial societies?
- Explain why identity development of racial/ethnic minorities is complex?

As might be expected, the formation of a secure ethnic identity has wide repercussions. For example, secure ethnic identity is related to higher self-esteem (Umana-Taylor & Updegraff, 2006). And because a secure ethnic identity involves positive feelings about both one's own personal identity and the wider culture (Phinney, 1989), it is not surprising to find that secure ethnic identity is related to greater acceptance of other groups (Phinney, Ferguson, & Tate, 1997). Presumably, then, such feelings might result in more positive interactions between different groups and reductions in discrimination (Phinney, Jacoby, & Silva, 2007).

What are some examples in your community of ethnic identity influencing interactions between groups?

DEVELOPING ADULT RELATIONSHIPS WITH PARENTS

As young people leave home, they must complete the negotiation of autonomy begun in adolescence and redefine their relationship with their parents as one between adults. Parents who are unable to acknowledge this change may slow their children's development (Aquilino, 2006).

Influences on Relationships with Parents Even though they are no longer children, emerging adults still need parental acceptance, empathy, and support, and attachment to the parents remains a key ingredient of well-being. Financial support from parents, especially for education, enhances emerging adults' chances of success in adult roles (Aquilino, 2006).

Positive parent-child relationships during early adolescence predict warmer and less conflicted relationships with both parents when the children reach age 26 (Belsky, Jaffee, Hsieh, & Silva, 2001). These relationships are better when the young adult is married but childless, engaging in productive activity (either school, employment, or homemaking), and not living in the childhood home. Generally, parents and young adult children get along best when the young adult is following a normative life course but has deferred the responsibility of parenthood until other adult roles are well established (Belsky, Jaffee, Caspi, Moffitt, & Silva, 2003).

The quality of the parent–adult child relationship may be affected by the relationship between the mother and father (Aquilino, 2006). When the young adult becomes "caught in the middle" between two conflictual parents, relaying messages from one parent to the other, and attempting to minimize conflicts between them (Amato & Afifi, 2006), there can be negative consequences. For example, one study of 426 adolescents showed that such situations resulted in higher levels of internalizing symptoms and depressive thoughts 3 years later (Buehler & Welsh, 2009).

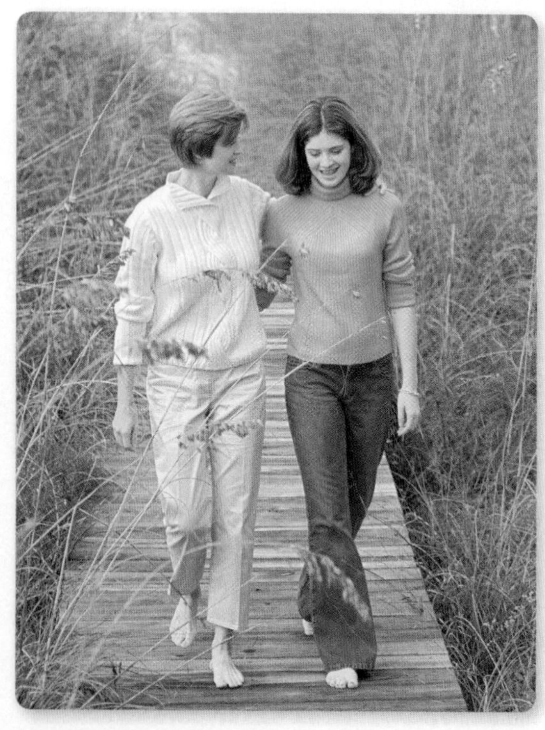

Although emerging adults may no longer rely on parents for basic sustenance, they still benefit from parental companionship and social support.

Failure to Launch In the movie *Failure to Launch,* Matthew McConaughey plays a 30-year-old man who still lives with his parents, much to their dismay. This scenario has become increasingly common in the United States, especially in high-income families (Hill & Holzer, 2007). The stereotypical view—that these young adults who do not move out of their parents' homes are selfish slackers who refuse to grow up and accept responsibility—is largely inaccurate (Arnett, 2007b). Rather, they are forced to remain somewhat dependent largely out of economic concerns and the need to obtain training or schooling to a greater degree than previous generations. However, adult children who continue to live with parents may have trouble renegotiating their relationship. The process may be a gradual one that takes many years, especially when the adult child still needs parental financial support (Aquilino, 2006).

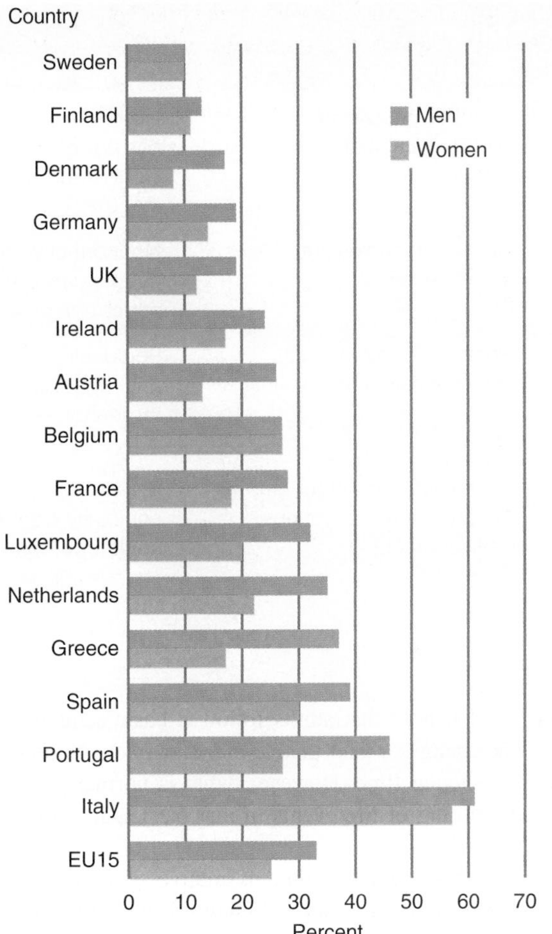

FIGURE 1

Percent of European Young Adults Ages 18 to 34 Who Do Not Have Their Own Partners or Children and Are Living with Parents

Many young adults fail to launch from the nest at the expected time or return to it in times of trouble.

Source: Newman & Aptekar, 2007, figure 1.

The trend for emerging adults to live in the parents' home also exists in some European countries where government benefits to unemployed youth are lacking; in Italy, more than half of young men live with their parents until age 30. Although living with parents has been associated with lower life satisfaction, this is becoming less true as the practice becomes widespread. In over half of European families, young adult children living at home is viewed in a positive light (Guerrero, 2001). Indeed, Europeans may be witnessing a new developmental stage, *in-house adulthood,* in which live-in adult children and their parents treat each other as equals (Newman & Aptekar, 2007; Figure 1).

checkpoint
can **you**...

- Explain how relationships with parents affect adjustment to adulthood and how emerging adults renegotiate their relationships with their parents?
- Discuss the trend of young adults living in the parental home?

Personality Development: Four Views

What is personality? The answer depends in part on how we study and measure it. Four approaches to adult psychosocial development are represented by *normative-stage models,* the *timing-of-events model, trait models,* and *typological models.* These four approaches ask different questions about adult personality, look at different aspects of its development, and often use different methods (Table 1).

NORMATIVE-STAGE MODELS

At what age should people marry? Have children? Decide on a career? Every culture has norms about the "right" time for major life events to occur. **Normative-stage models** are

normative-stage models
Theoretical models that describe psychosocial development in terms of a definite sequence of age-related changes.

TABLE 1 Four Views of Personality Development

Models	Questions Asked	Methods Used	Change or Stability
Normative-stage models	Does personality change in typical ways at certain periods throughout the life course?	In-depth interviews, biographical materials	Normative personality changes having to do with personal goals, work, and relationships occur in stages.
Timing-of-events model	When do important life events typically occur? What if they occur earlier or later than usual?	Statistical studies, interviews, questionnaires	Nonnormative timing of life events can cause stress and affect personality development.
Trait models	Do personality traits fall into groups, or clusters? Do these clusters of traits change with age?	Personality inventories, questionnaires, factor analysis	Personality changes substantially until age 30, more slowly thereafter.
Typological models	Can basic personality types be identified, and how well do they predict the life course?	Interviews, clinical judgments, Q-sorts, behavior ratings, self-reports	Personality types tend to show continuity from childhood through adulthood, but certain events can change the life course.

theoretical approaches that hold that adults follow a basic sequence of age-related psychosocial changes. The changes are normative in that they are common for most members of a population at a particular time. However, what is normative is dependent upon the expectations about the timing of life events in that particular cultural group.

Erikson: Intimacy versus Isolation One normative-stage model is Erikson's psychosocial approach. Erikson argued that at each stage in the life span people address particular crises. The normative crisis of young adulthood is **intimacy versus isolation.**

intimacy versus isolation
Erikson's sixth stage of psychosocial development, in which young adults either form strong, long-lasting bonds with friends and romantic partners or face a possible sense of isolation and self-absorption.

Recall that Erikson argued that successful resolution of a psychosocial crisis puts people in a good position to successfully address the next one. The psychosocial crisis in adolescence, according to Erikson, is identity formation. He believed that young people who develop a strong sense of self during adolescence are in a better position, in early adulthood, to fuse their identity with that of another. In other words, knowing who you are and what you want makes it more likely you will end up with a compatible partner who fulfills your needs.

Why is intimacy a trait to strive for? According to Erikson, if adults cannot make deep personal commitments to others, they risk becoming overly isolated and self-absorbed. The process of forming a sense of intimacy is important as well. Intimate relationships demand sacrifice and compromise. As young adults work to resolve conflicting demands for intimacy and competitiveness, they develop an ethical sense, which Erikson considered a marker of adulthood.

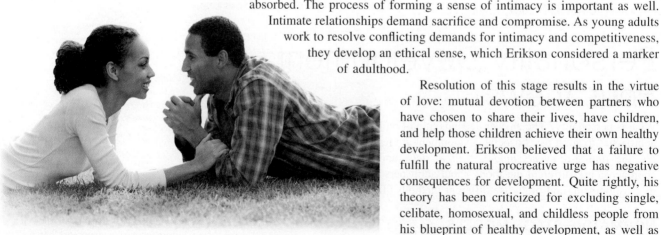

Young adults who have a strong sense of self are likely to be ready for the demands of an intimate relationship, according to Erikson.

Resolution of this stage results in the virtue of love: mutual devotion between partners who have chosen to share their lives, have children, and help those children achieve their own healthy development. Erikson believed that a failure to fulfill the natural procreative urge has negative consequences for development. Quite rightly, his theory has been criticized for excluding single, celibate, homosexual, and childless people from his blueprint of healthy development, as well as for describing the male pattern of developing intimacy after identity as the norm.

Despite these critiques, however, normative-stage research has had a continuing impact on the field. Psychologists, drawing on the work of Erikson, have identified developmental tasks that need to be accomplished for successful adaptation to each stage of life (Roisman et al., 2004). Among the typical developmental tasks of young adulthood are leaving the childhood home for advanced schooling, work, or military service; developing new and more intimate friendships and romantic relationships; and developing self-reliance and independence (Arnett, 2004; Scharf, Mayseless, & Kivenson-Baron, 2004). Perhaps the most important message of normative-stage models is that development is not just about the attainment of adulthood. Normative-stage research supports the idea that development is continuous throughout the life span. In other words, people continue to change and develop throughout their entire lives, not just during childhood.

Both the Grant Study and Levinson's early work were based on small groups of men and women born in the 1920s, 1930s, and 1940s. Thus their development was affected by societal events unique to their cohorts, as well as by their socioeconomic status, ethnicity, and gender. Today, young adults follow much more diverse developmental paths and, as a result, may develop differently than did the people in these studies. In addition, the findings of normative-stage research may not apply to other cultures, some of which have very different patterns of life-course development.

Nevertheless, normative-stage research has had a continuing impact on the field. Psychologists, drawing especially on the work of Erikson, have identified developmental tasks that need to be accomplished for successful adaptation to each stage of life (Roisman et al., 2004). Among the developmental tasks of young adulthood are leaving the childhood home for advanced schooling, work, or military service; developing new and more intimate friendships and romantic relationships; and developing a sense of the self as independent and self-reliant (Arnett, 2004; Scharf, Mayseless, & Kivenson-Baron, 2004). Other developmental tasks of this period include completing education, entering the world of work, and becoming financially independent.

Perhaps the most important message of normative-stage models is that development is not merely about the attainment of adulthood. Whether or not people follow the specific patterns suggested by these models, normative-stage research supports the idea that human beings do continue to change and develop throughout their lives.

TIMING-OF-EVENTS MODEL

Instead of looking at adult personality development purely as a function of age, the **timing-of-events model,** supported by Bernice Neugarten and others (Neugarten, Moore, & Lowe, 1965; Neugarten & Neugarten, 1987), holds that the course of development depends on when certain events occur in people's lives. **Normative life events** (also called *normative age-graded events*) are those that typically happen at certain times of life—such events as marriage, parenthood, grandparenthood, and retirement. According to this model, people usually are keenly aware of both their timing and the **social clock**—their society's norms or expectations for the appropriate timing of life events.

If events occur on time, development proceeds smoothly. If not, stress can result. Stress may come from an unexpected event (such as losing a job), an event that happens off time (being widowed at age 35 or being forced to retire at 50), or the failure of an expected and wanted event to occur at all (never being married, or being unable to have a child). Personality differences influence the way people respond to life events and may even influence their timing. For example, a resilient person is likely to experience an easier transition to adulthood and the tasks and events that lie ahead than an overly anxious person, who may put off relationship or career decisions.

The typical timing of events varies from culture to culture and from generation to generation. Indeed, more recent cohorts of young adults are completing the developmental

timing-of-events model
Theoretical model of personality development that describes adult psychosocial development as a response to the expected or unexpected occurrence and timing of important life events.

normative life events
In the timing-of-events model, commonly expected life experiences that occur at customary times.

social clock
Set of cultural norms or expectations for the times of life when certain important events, such as marriage, parenthood, entry into work, and retirement, should occur.

tasks of this period at later ages than were previously normative, indicating that the timing of the social clock in U.S. culture has shifted somewhat in recent years (Arnett, 2010).

The rise in the average age when adults first marry in the United States (U.S. Census Bureau, 2010a) and the trend toward delayed first childbirth (Martin, Hamilton, et al., 2010) are two examples of events for which timing has shifted. A timetable that seems right to people in one cohort or cultural group may not seem so to the next.

Since the mid-twentieth century, the social clocks in many Western societies have become more widely age-graded. Today people are more accepting of 40-year-old first-time parents and 40-year-old grandparents, 50-year-old retirees and 75-year-old workers, 60-year-olds in jeans and 30-year-old college presidents. This widened range of age norms undermines the predictability on which the timing-of-events model is based.

The timing-of-events model has made an important contribution to our understanding of adult personality by emphasizing the individual life course and challenging the idea of universal, age-related change. However, its usefulness may well be limited to cultures and historical periods in which norms of behavior are stable and widespread.

TRAIT MODELS: COSTA AND MCCRAE'S FIVE FACTORS

When most people are asked to describe themselves, they often provide a list of adjectives. They might describe themselves as shy or outgoing, as friendly or neurotic, or as honest and hardworking. All of these descriptions focus on what psychologists call *traits*. Traits can be thought of as mental, emotional, temperamental, or behavioral attributes that vary between people. **Trait models** are psychological models that focus on the measurement and examination of these different traits. One of the best known of these models is Paul T. Costa and Robert R. McCrae's **five-factor model** (Figure 2) consisting of factors, or dimensions, that seem to underlie five groups of associated traits, known as the "Big Five." They are (1) *neuroticism (N),* (2) *extraversion (E),* (3) *openness to experience (O),* (4) *conscientiousness (C),* and (5) *agreeableness (A).*

trait models
Theoretical models of personality development that focus on mental, emotional, temperamental, and behavioral traits, or attributes.

five-factor model
Theoretical model of personality, developed and tested by Costa and McCrae, based on the "Big Five" factors underlying clusters of related personality traits: neuroticism, extraversion, openness to experience, conscientiousness, and agreeableness.

Each personality trait, called a cluster, has a number of traits, or facets, associated with it. *Neuroticism* includes six factors: anxiety, hostility, depression, self-consciousness, impulsiveness, and vulnerability. *Extraversion* also has six facets: warmth, gregariousness, assertiveness, activity, excitement-seeking, and positive emotions. People who are *open to experience* are willing to try new things and embrace new ideas. *Conscientious* people are achievers: they are competent, orderly, dutiful, deliberate, and disciplined. *Agreeable* people are trusting, straightforward, altruistic, compliant, modest, and easily swayed.

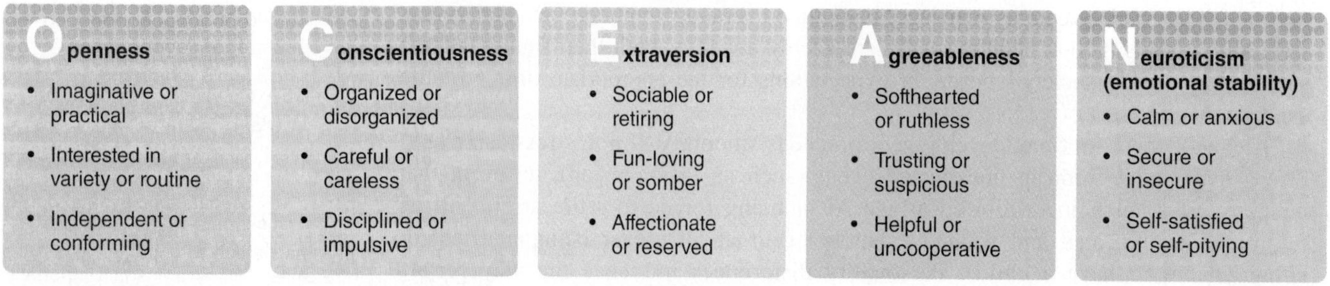

Openness
- Imaginative or practical
- Interested in variety or routine
- Independent or conforming

Conscientiousness
- Organized or disorganized
- Careful or careless
- Disciplined or impulsive

Extraversion
- Sociable or retiring
- Fun-loving or somber
- Affectionate or reserved

Agreeableness
- Softhearted or ruthless
- Trusting or suspicious
- Helpful or uncooperative

Neuroticism (emotional stability)
- Calm or anxious
- Secure or insecure
- Self-satisfied or self-pitying

FIGURE 2
Costa and McCrae's Five Factors of Personality

Each factor, or dimension, of personality represents a cluster of related traits. Use the acronym OCEAN to remember the main five: openness, conscientiousness, extraversion, agreeableness, and neuroticism.

Continuity and Change in the Five-Factor Model Do people change or stay the same? In analyses of longitudinal and cross-sectional samples of U.S. men and women, Costa and McCrae (1980, 1988, 1994a, 1994b, 2006; Costa et al., 1986; McCrae, 2002; McCrae & Costa, 1984; McCrae, Costa, & Busch, 1986) found considerable continuity within people as well as normative developmental change in all five dimensions between adolescence and age 30, with much slower change thereafter. However, the *direction* of change varied for different personality factors. Agreeableness and conscientiousness generally increased, whereas neuroticism, extraversion, and openness to experience declined (McCrae et al., 2000). These patterns of age-related change appeared to be universal across cultures and, thus, according to these authors, maturational (McCrae, 2002).

Other research found important change in almost all personality traits throughout adulthood (Roberts & Mroczek, 2008; Roberts, Walton, & Viechtbauer, 2006a, 2006b). Similar to Costa and McCrae, these lines of research also found that traits changed more markedly in young adulthood than in any other period. In addition, the changes they observed were uniformly in a positive direction, with especially large increases in social dominance (assertiveness, a facet of extraversion), conscientiousness, and emotional stability. Personality showed clear, generally positive change after age 30, even in old age; and changes that occurred tended to be retained. Furthermore, there was little evidence for maturational or genetic causes for the early adult changes: "We believe that life experiences . . . centered in young adulthood are the most likely reason for the patterns of development we see" (Roberts et al., 2006a, p. 18).

Of course, some people change more, others less; and not all change is positive. People with successful, satisfying careers in young adulthood tend to show disproportionate increases in emotional stability and conscientiousness, whereas people who shirk or act aggressively at work tend to show decreases in those traits (Roberts & Mroczek, 2008).

The Big Five appear to be linked to various aspects of health and well-being. In a study of representative samples of adults ages 25 to 65 in the United States and Germany, the Big Five (especially neuroticism) were associated with subjective feelings of health and well-being (Staudinger, Fleeson, & Baltes, 1999). Conscientiousness has been linked with health-related behaviors that contribute to long life (Bogg & Roberts, 2004). Big Five traits also have been associated with marital satisfaction (Gattis, Berns, Simpson, & Christensen, 2004), parent-infant relationships (Kochanska, Friesenborg et al., 2004), work-family conflict (Wayne, Musisca, & Fleeson, 2004), and personality disorders. People high in neuroticism tend to be subject to anxiety and depression; people low in extraversion are prone to agoraphobia (fear of open spaces) and social phobias (Bienvenu et al., 2001).

Do you have a blog? If so, the words you use may reflect how you would score on the Big Five measures. People who are high on neuroticism are likely to use words associated with negative emotions and have a fondness for the word "irony." Extraverted people use positive words, and are more likely to use the word "drinks" and less likely to use the word "computer." Open people use lots of prepositions and long words as well as, oddly, the word "ink." Conscientious people like the word "completed," and agreeable people favor "wonderful" and aren't particularly fond of "porn."

Yarkoni, 2010

Evaluating the Five-Factor Model One of the great strengths of the scientific approach is that theories are modified and updated when new data is unearthed. Costa and McCrae's body of work originally made a powerful case for continuity of personality, especially after age 30. More recent research has eroded that conclusion, and Costa and McCrae have now modified their perspective and acknowledge that change occurs throughout the life span.

However, the question of causation needs further study: Do maturational changes impel people to seek out social roles that fit their maturing personalities, or do adults change to meet the demands of their new roles? Or is change bidirectional? In a longitudinal study of 980 people in New Zealand, personality traits at age 18 affected work experiences in emerging adulthood, and these work experiences, in turn, affected changes in personality as measured at age 26. For example, adolescents who were sociable and affable tended to rise faster in their early careers; and, in turn, those who were in higher-status, more satisfying jobs tended to become more sociable and affable

Facebook profiles are more likely to reflect actual individual differences in the Big Five factors of personality than an idealized version of who you are. This is most true for extraversion and openness, and least true for neuroticism. So be careful what you write!

Back et al., 2010

(Roberts, Caspi, & Moffitt, 2003). So it seems that personality in adulthood may be more malleable and more complex than previous trait research suggests.

Other criticisms of the five-factor model are methodological. Jack Block (1995a, 1995b) argues that, because the five-factor model is based largely on subjective ratings, it may lack validity unless supplemented by other measures. Moreover, the selection of factors and their associated facets is both an art and a science and perhaps not all-inclusive. Other researchers have chosen different factors and have divided up the associated traits differently. For example, one might wonder if warmth is a facet of extraversion, as in the Big Five model, or might it be better classified as an aspect of agreeableness? Finally, personality is more than a collection of traits. A model that looks only at individual differences in trait groupings offers no theoretical framework for understanding how personality works within the person.

TYPOLOGICAL MODELS

typological approach
Theoretical approach that identifies broad personality types, or styles.

ego-resiliency
Dynamic capacity to modify one's level of ego-control in response to environmental and contextual influences.

ego-control
Self-control and the self-regulation of impulses.

Jack Block (1971; Block & Block, 2006) was a pioneer in the **typological approach.** Typological research seeks to complement and expand trait research by looking at personality as a functioning whole.

Researchers have identified three personality types: *ego-resilient, overcontrolled,* and *undercontrolled.* These three types differ in **ego-resiliency,** or adaptability under stress, and **ego-control,** or self-control. *Ego-resilient* people are well-adjusted: self-confident, independent, articulate, attentive, helpful, cooperative, and task-focused. *Overcontrolled* people are shy, quiet, anxious, and dependable; they tend to keep their thoughts to themselves and to withdraw from conflict, and they are the most subject to depression. *Undercontrolled* people are active, energetic, impulsive, stubborn, and easily distracted. Ego resiliency interacts with ego control to determine whether or not behavior is adaptive or maladaptive. For example, underrcontrol can lead to creativity and resourcefulness or, if it is excessive, to externalizing and antisocial behaviors. By the same token, overcontrol can help make a person highly focused and planful, or it can lead to an inflexible and inhibited style of behavior. More extreme forms of either overcontrol or undercontrol are generally associated with low levels of ego resilience (Kremen & Block, 1998). These or similar personality types seem to exist in both sexes, across cultures and ethnic groups, and in children, adolescents, and adults (Caspi, 1998; Hart, Hofmann, Edelstein, & Keller, 1997; Pulkkinen, 1996; Robins, John, Caspi, Moffitt, & Stouthamer-Loeber, 1996; van Lieshout, Haselager, Riksen-Walraven, & van Aken, 1995).

A longitudinal study in Munich demonstrated the lasting influence of childhood personality. Teachers and parents assessed 103 children annually between ages 3 and 12, and then again at ages 17 and 23. Children who had been overcontrolled between ages 4 and 6 tended to be shy in late adolescence and emerging adulthood, whereas those who had been undercontrolled in early childhood were more aggressive; and these traits became more accentuated between ages 17 and 23. In addition, both overcontrolled and undercontrolled types had more difficulty than more resilient types in assuming adult social roles: leaving the parental home, establishing romantic relationships, and getting part-time jobs (Denissen, Asendorpf, & van Aken, 2008).

Which of the models presented here seems to you to most accurately describe psychosocial development in adulthood?

Of course, the finding of a tendency toward continuity of attitudes and behavior does not mean that personalities never change, or that certain people are condemned to a life of maladjustment. Undercontrolled children may get along better in early adulthood if they find niches in which their energy and spontaneity are considered a plus. Overcontrolled youngsters may come out of their shell if they find that their quiet dependability is valued. And, although personality types established in childhood may predict long-term patterns of behavior, certain events may change the life course (Caspi, 1998). For young people with adjustment problems, for example, marriage to a supportive person can lead to more positive outcomes.

checkpoint
can you . . .

- **Compare four theoretical approaches to adult psychosocial development?**

Foundations of Intimate Relationships

Erikson saw the development of intimate relationships as the crucial task of young adulthood. The need to form strong, stable, close, caring relationships is a powerful motivator of human behavior. People become intimate—and remain intimate—through shared disclosures, responsiveness to one another's needs, and mutual acceptance and respect.

Intimate relationships require self-awareness; empathy; the ability to communicate emotions, resolve conflicts, and sustain commitments; and, if the relationship is potentially a sexual one, sexual decision making. Such skills are pivotal as young adults decide whether to marry or form intimate partnerships and to have or not to have children (Lambeth & Hallett, 2002). Moreover, the formation of new relationships (such as with romantic partners), and the renegotiation of existing relationships (such as with parents), has implications for personality. For example, people high in neuroticism tend to end up in relationships in which they feel less secure, and these chronic feelings of insecurity serve to make them more neurotic over time (Neyer & Lehnart, 2007). In short, personality and relationships can be viewed as co-influencing each other.

Let's look at two expressions of intimacy in young adulthood: friendship and love.

People with larger amygdalae—a part of the brain involved in emotions—tend to have larger social circles.

Bickart, Wright, Duatoff, Dickerson, & Feldman, 2010

FRIENDSHIP

Friendships during young adulthood are often less stable than in either adolescence or later adulthood, primarily because people in emerging adulthood relocate more frequently than at other points in the life span (Collins & Van Dulmen, 2006). Nonetheless, many young adults manage to maintain high-quality, committed, long-distance friendships (Johnson, Becker, Craig, Gilchrist, & Haigh, 2009), sometimes using social networking sites to keep in touch across geographical distance (Subrahmanyam, Reich, Waecheter, & Espinoza, 2008). Indeed, some friendships are more stable than ties to a lover or a spouse. But regardless of whether the friendships are virtual or not, they tend to center on work and parenting activities, sharing confidences, and advice. Some friendships are intimate and supportive, whereas others are marked by frequent conflict (Hartup & Stevens, 1999).

fictive kin
Friends who are considered and behave like family members.

Friendships in emerging adulthood show developmental change. Young single adults tend to rely on friendships to fulfill their social needs more than young married adults or young parents do. Over the course of young adulthood, the number of friends and the amount of time spent with them gradually decreases, presumably as leisure time decreases and responsibility to others increases. Still, despite spending less time on them, friendships remain important to young adults. People with friends tend to have a sense of well-being—although it is unclear if friendship causes well-being, or if people who feel good about themselves have an easier time making friends (Myers, 2000).

Women typically have more intimate friendships than men do. Women are more likely to share confidences with friends (Rosenbluth & Steil, 1995), to talk with their friends about marital problems, and to receive advice and support (Helms, Crouter, & McHale, 2003). Men, by contrast, are more likely to share information and activities (Rosenbluth & Steil, 1995).

Close supportive friendships are sometimes incorporated into family networks. These types of friends are known as "**fictive kin**"—they are treated as family members despite a lack of blood relationship. For example, fictive kinship relationships often develop for gay and lesbian people who have straight friends of the opposite sex, particularly if those friends are unmarried or have an unconventional lifestyle (Muraco, 2006).

Intimate relationships involve self-awareness, empathy, and the ability to communicate. Such skills are pivotal as young adults decide whether to marry or form partnerships.

Like tearjerkers? Well, such movies may have an unintended effect. Women's tears have been shown to lead to lower levels of sexual arousal in men. Researchers believe that close contact sends an olfactory chemical message to the man's brain, and the message the tears are sending is "back off."

Gelstein et al., 2011

triangular theory of love
Sternberg's theory that patterns of love hinge on the balance among three elements: intimacy, passion, and commitment.

Sternberg's Triangular Theory of Love

In recent years, young adults' use of social networking sites has increased dramatically (Facebook, 2011). In fact, the number of people using such sites doubled between 2008 and 2010 (Hampton, Goulet, Rainie, & Purcell, 2011). Some people have argued that such sites can be harmful, and that online relationships can interfere with the formation of high-quality friendships in real life (McPherson, Smith-Lovin, & Brashears, 2006). However, social networking sites can have advantages. For example, recent research indicates that social networking sites are often used to maintain and strengthen ties to others (Hampton et al., 2011; Subrahmanyam et al., 2008), and they are related to increased participation in political discussion and activities (Hampton et al., 2011; Zhang, Johnson, Seltzer, & Bichard, 2010).

LOVE

Most people like love stories, including their own. According to Robert J. Sternberg's **triangular theory of love** (1995, 1998b, 2006), the way love develops *is* a story. The lovers are its authors, and the story they create reflects their personalities and their conceptions of love.

Thinking of love as a story may help us see how people select and mix the elements of the plot. According to Sternberg (1986, 1998a, 2006), the three elements, or components, of love are intimacy, passion, and commitment. *Intimacy,* the emotional element, involves self-disclosure, which leads to connection, warmth, and trust. For example, new lovers might share stories of their childhood or their hopes for the future. *Passion,* the motivational element, is based on inner drives that translate physiological arousal into sexual desire. Passion might include feelings of sexual attraction, intrusive thoughts of the romantic partner, or sexual activity itself. *Commitment,* the cognitive element, is the decision to love and to stay with the beloved. So, for example, commitment might include a decision to make the relationship exclusive or to marry. The degree to which each of the three elements is present determines what type of love people feel (Table 2).

TABLE 2 Patterns of Loving

Type	Description
Nonlove	All three components of love—intimacy, passion, and commitment—are absent. This describes most interpersonal relationships, which are simply casual interactions.
Liking	Intimacy is the only component present. There is closeness, understanding, emotional support, affection, bondedness, and warmth. Neither passion nor commitment is present.
Infatuation	Passion is the only component present. This is "love at first sight," a strong physical attraction and sexual arousal, without intimacy or commitment. Infatuation can flare up suddenly and die just as fast—or, given certain circumstances, can sometimes last for a long time.
Empty love	Commitment is the only component present. Empty love is often found in long-term relationships that have lost both intimacy and passion, or in arranged marriages.
Romantic love	Intimacy and passion are both present. Romantic lovers are drawn to each other physically and bonded emotionally. They are not, however, committed to each other.
Companionate love	Intimacy and commitment are both present. This is a long-term, committed friendship, often occurring in marriages in which physical attraction has died down but in which the partners feel close to each other and have made the decision to stay together.
Fatuous love	Passion and commitment are present without intimacy. This is the kind of love that leads to a whirlwind courtship, in which a couple make a commitment on the basis of passion without allowing themselves the time to develop intimacy. This kind of love usually does not last, despite the initial intent to commit.
Consummate love	All three components are present in this "complete" love, which many people strive for, especially in romantic relationships. It is easier to achieve it than to hold on to it. Either partner may change what he or she wants from the relationship. If the other partner changes, too, the relationship may endure in a different form. If the other partner does not change, the relationship may dissolve.

Source: Based on Sternberg, 1986.

Communication is an essential part of intimacy. In a cross-cultural study, 263 young adult couples in Brazil, Italy, Taiwan, and the United States reported on communication and satisfaction in their romantic relationships. In all four places, couples who communicated constructively tended to be more satisfied with their relationships than those who did not (Christensen, Eldridge, Catta-Preta, Lim, & Santagata, 2006).

The formation of a sense of identity achievement also seems to affect the quality of romantic relationships. In one study of 710 emerging adults, identity achievement status was associated with stronger feelings of companionship, worth, affection and emotional support within romantic relationships (Barry, Madsen, Nelson, Carroll, & Badger, 2009). This supports Erikson's (1973) assertions that the formation of a secure sense of identity is necessary for the establishment of high-quality intimate relationships.

study smart

Falling in Love

checkpoint can **you** . . .

- List skills that promote and maintain intimacy?
- Identify characteristic features of friendship in young adulthood?
- Identify the three components of love, according to Sternberg?

Marital and Nonmarital Lifestyles

In many Western countries, today's rules for socially acceptable lifestyles are more flexible than they were during the first half of the twentieth century. People marry later, if at all; more people have children outside of marriage, if at all; and more people end their marriages. Some people remain single, some remarry, and others live with a partner of either sex. Some married couples with separate careers have *commuter marriages* (Adams, 2004). All in all, there is no such thing as a "typical" marriage or family.

In this section, we look more closely at marital and nonmarital lifestyles. In the next section we examine parenthood.

More and more, people are using online sites to meet potential dates and romantic partners. But can we trust what people say? For the most part it seems we can, but people do tend to lie about (in order) weight, age, and height. So, when relationship shopping, be sure to ask for a current photo!

Toma, Hancock, & Ellison, 2008

SINGLE LIFE

The proportion of young adults ages 25 to 34 in the United States who have not yet married tripled between 1970 and 2005 (U.S. Census Bureau, 2007b) and reached an all-time high of 54 percent in 2010 (Mather & Lavery, 2012). This decline in marriage has occurred across all age groups but is most prominent in young adults (Cohn, Passel, Wang, & Livingston, 2011). The trend is particularly pronounced among African American women, 35 percent of whom are still single in their late 30s (Teachman et al., 2000). Between 1970 and 2007, there has been a significant decline in the marriage rate in almost all countries (Figure 3).

There are indications that religious beliefs might affect the marriage rate. Urban mothers who had a baby out of wedlock were more likely to eventually marry if they attended church on a regular basis. It may be that participation in a social group in which marriage and family concerns are modeled and supported on a regular basis socializes these women to expect and desire marriage to a greater degree (Wilcox & Wolfinger, 2007).

Some young adults stay single because they have not found the right mate; others are single by choice. More women today are self-supporting, and there is less social pressure to marry. At the same time, many single adults are postponing marriage and children due to economic instability (Wang & Morin, 2009) or out of a desire for self-fulfillment. Some enjoy sexual freedom. Some find the lifestyle exciting. Some just like being alone. And some postpone or avoid marriage because of fear that it will end in divorce.

Venus Williams is just one of many African American women who remain single through young adulthood.

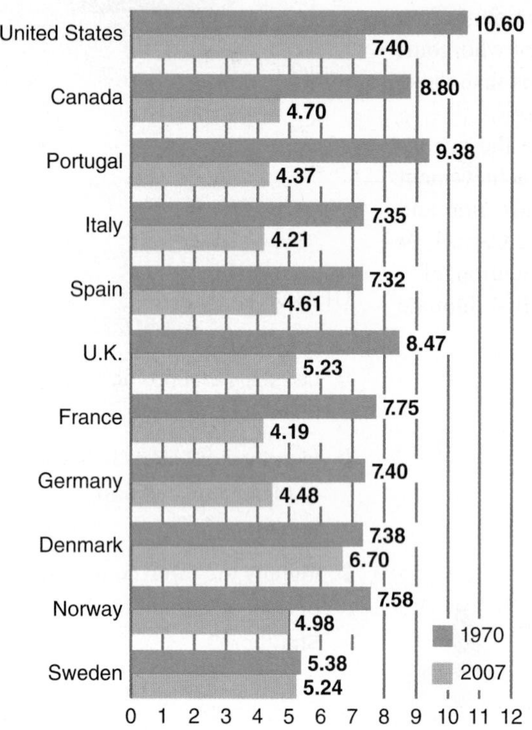

FIGURE 3

Marriage Rates by Country, 1970 and 2007

Source: National Healthy Marriage Resource Center, n.d.

GAY AND LESBIAN RELATIONSHIPS

In the past 40 years or so, gay and lesbian adults have increasingly come out of the closet and are living openly. Surveys suggest that 40 to 60 percent of gay men and 45 to 80 percent of lesbians in the United States are in romantic relationships, and 8 to 28 percent of these couples have lived together for at least 10 years (Kurdek, 2004). This increasing openness has led to greater societal acceptance of homosexuality. Currently, approximately 4 in 10 Americans has a close friend or family member who is gay and about half of Americans support gay marriage (Morin, 2013). It may be that the increasing openness with which gay and lesbian people are living their lives is affecting public opinion; those who are close to a gay or lesbian person are more likely to be supportive of gay marriage and the antidiscrimination laws focused on gay and lesbian people (Neidorf & Morin, 2011). This is relevant to the strength of these relationships, as research has shown that support from family and friends is related to how well and how long the relationship lasts (Kurdek, 2008).

In most ways, gay and lesbian relationships mirror heterosexual relationships. Gay and lesbian couples tend to be at least as satisfied with their relationships as heterosexual couples. The factors that predict the quality of both homosexual and heterosexual relationships—personality traits, perceptions of the relationship by the partners, ways of communicating and resolving conflicts, and social support—are similar (Kurdek, 2005, 2006). Indeed, committed same-sex relationships are hardly distinguishable in quality from committed heterosexual relationships (Roisman, Clausell, Holland, Fortuna, & Elieff, 2008).

Differences between gay and lesbian couples and heterosexual couples also have emerged from research (Kurdek, 2006). First, gay and lesbian couples are more likely than heterosexual couples to negotiate household chores to achieve a balance that works for them and accommodates the interests, skills, and schedules of both partners. Second, they tend to resolve conflicts in a more positive atmosphere than heterosexual couples do. Third, gay and lesbian relationships tend to be less stable than heterosexual relationships, mainly due to the lack of institutional supports. However, although gay and lesbian couples may receive less support from friends and family, they may compensate for this with friends, social groups, and organizations friendly to the lesbian-gay-bisexual community (Pope, Murray, & Mobley, 2010). On the basis of such research and in view of the similarities between same-sex and heterosexual relationships, the American Psychological Association (2004a) has declared it unfair and discriminatory to deny same-sex couples legal access to civil (i.e., nonreligious) marriage.

Should gays and lesbians be allowed to marry? Adopt children? Be covered by a partner's health care plan?

Gay marriage is now legal in more than a dozen European countries (Pew Research Center, 2014). In addition, civil unions, in which couples have some of the economic and other benefits, rights, and responsibilities of marriage, are recognized in several countries in Europe and in Israel and New Zealand.

In the United States, gays and lesbians are struggling to obtain legal recognition of their unions and the right to adopt children or raise their own. They argue that same-sex marriage offers benefits that civil unions do not (Herek, 2006; King & Bartlett, 2006). Emerging research suggests that this is indeed the case. For example, one study comparing four groups of gay and lesbian people—single, dating, in a committed relationship, and in a legally recognized relationship—found that those couples who were able to legally marry showed lower levels of depression, stress, and internalized homophobia and felt they had more meaning in their lives (Riggle, Rotosky, & Riggle, 2010).

As of January 2014, same-sex marriage was legal in 17 states and the District of Columbia: California, Connecticut, Delaware, Hawaii, Illinois, Iowa, Maine, Maryland, Massachusetts, Minnesota, New Hampshire, New Jersey, New York, New Mexico, Rhode

Island, Vermont, and Washington. Currently 29 states have amended their constitutions to define marriage as being between a man and a woman. In 2013 the United States Supreme Court ruled that the federal government was obligated to recognize gay marriages that were conducted in states where it is legal (Pew Research Center, 2013). Much of the opposition to gay marriage correlates with political orientation: approximately 69 percent of Democrats support same-sex marriage, whereas only 32 percent of Republicans support it (Pew Research Center, 2012). Religion also plays a role. Of those people who characterize themselves as unaffiliated with any religion, 60 percent support gay marriage. By contrast, 85 percent of people who attend services at least once a week are opposed. In addition, age has been implicated in the debate, with younger generations becoming increasingly accepting of same-sex marriage (Pew Research Center, 2012).

COHABITATION

Cohabitation is an increasingly common lifestyle in which an unmarried couple involved in a sexual relationship live together. Its rise in recent decades reflects the exploratory nature of emerging adulthood and the trend toward postponing marriage.

Types of Cohabitation: International Comparisons Surveys in 14 European countries, Canada, New Zealand, and the United States found wide variations in the cohabitation rates, ranging from more than 14 percent in France down to less than 2 percent in Italy (Figure 4). In all countries, the overwhelming majority of cohabiting women have never been married. Cohabitors who do not marry tend to stay together longer in countries in which cohabitation is an *alternative to* or *tantamount to* marriage than in countries where it usually leads to marriage (Heuveline & Timberlake, 2004).

Consensual or *informal unions,* almost indistinguishable from marriage, have long been as accepted as marriage in many Latin American countries, especially for low-SES couples (Phillips & Sweeney, 2005). In such countries, cohabiting couples have practically the same legal rights as married couples (Seltzer, 2000). In Canada, too, cohabitors have gained legal benefits and obligations close to those of married couples (Cherlin, 2004; Le Bourdais & Lapierre-Adamcyk, 2004). In most Western countries, unmarried couples who cohabit typically intend to, and do, marry; and these cohabitations tend to be relatively short (Heuveline & Timberlake, 2004). Premarital cohabitation in Great Britain and in the United States has accompanied a trend toward delayed marriage (Ford, 2002).

Cohabitation in the United States In 2010 there were an estimated 7.5 million unmarried couples living together in the United States, an increase of 13 percent over 2009 (Kreider, 2010). The increase in cohabitation in the United States has occurred among all racial/ethnic groups and at all educational levels, but people with less education are more likely to cohabit than those with higher education (Fields, 2004; Seltzer, 2004). Cohabiters also are likely to be less religious, less traditional, have less confidence in their relationships, be more accepting of divorce, be more negative and aggressive in their interactions with their romantic partners, and communicate less effectively (Jose, O'Leary, & Moyer, 2010).

Although U.S. family law currently gives cohabitors few of the legal rights and benefits of marriage, this situation is changing, particularly with regard to protection for children of cohabiting couples (Cherlin, 2004; Seltzer, 2004).

Cohabiting relationships tend to be less satisfying and less stable than marriages (Binstock & Thornton, 2003; Heuveline & Timberlake, 2004;

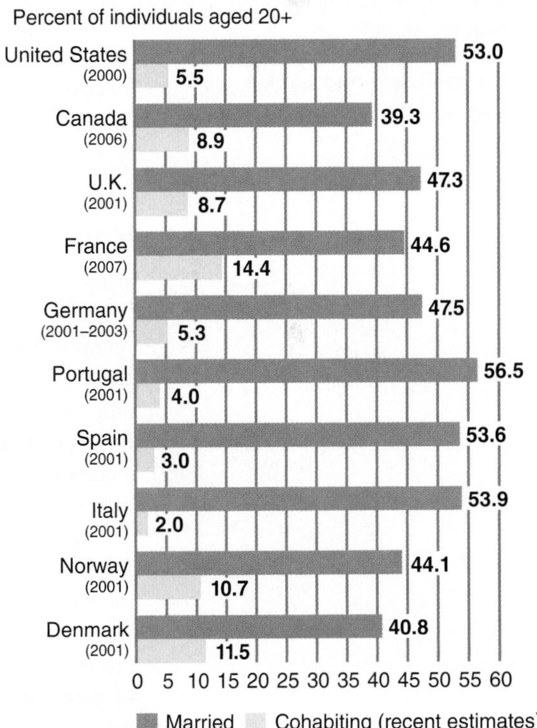

FIGURE 4

Marriage and Cohabitation Rates of Individuals Aged 20+ by Country

Source: National Healthy Marriage Resource Center, n.d.

Seltzer, 2004). In particular, cohabiting couples who have divergent expectations about the division of household labor are highly likely to break up (Hohmann-Marriott, 2006). Many cohabitors who want to marry put off marriage until they feel their economic circumstances permit it (Smock, Manning, & Porter, 2005). These young adults are not generally using cohabitation to replace marriage, but rather view it as one step along the way to marriage (Manning, Longmore, & Giordano, 2007).

From your experience or observation, is it a good idea to cohabit before marriage? Why or why not? Does it make a difference if children are involved?

Some research suggests that cohabiting couples who marry tend to have unhappier marriages and greater likelihood of divorce than those who wait to live together until marriage (Bramlett & Mosher, 2002; Dush, Cohan, & Amato, 2003). However, in a nationally representative cross-sectional survey of 6,577 women ages 15 to 45, women who cohabited or had premarital sex *only with their future husbands* had no special risk of marital dissolution (Teachman, 2003). Moreover, it appears there may be fundamental differences in types of cohabiting couples, with those couples who eventually marry having more stable and happier relationships than those who do not, perhaps as a result of a stronger initial commitment to the relationship (Jose et al., 2010).

Beliefs about cohabitation, cohabitation patterns, and the stability of cohabitation vary among racial/ethnic groups and are very complex in nature. Couples who cohabitate, on average, are younger, black, and less religious (Pew Research Center, 2007a). Perhaps for economic reasons, black and Hispanic couples are less likely than non-Hispanic white couples to regard cohabitation as a trial marriage and more likely to regard it as a substitute for marriage (Phillips & Sweeney, 2005). And white couples who cohabit are more likely than other groups to end the relationship; their children have almost 10 times the risk of going through a parental separation (Osborne, Manning, & Smock, 2007). Older and younger adults show a distinct difference in their views of the morality of cohabitation, with younger adults much more likely to think living together without being married is not wrong (Pew Research Center, 2012).

checkpoint
can **you**...

- State reasons why people remain single?
- Compare gay and lesbian relationships with heterosexual relationships?

Cohabitation after divorce is more common than premarital cohabitation and may function as a form of remarriage mate selection. However, postdivorce cohabitation, especially with serial partners, greatly delays remarriage and contributes to instability in a new marriage (Xu, Hudspeth, & Bartkowski, 2006).

MARRIAGE

In most societies, the institution of marriage is considered the best way to ensure the protection and raising of children. It allows for a division of labor and a sharing of material goods. Ideally, it offers intimacy, commitment, friendship, affection, sexual fulfillment, companionship, and an opportunity for emotional growth, as well as new sources of identity and self-esteem (Gardiner & Kosmitzki, 2005; Myers, 2000). Despite these positive associations with marriage, the United States and other postindustrial societies have seen a weakening of the social norms that once made marriage almost universal.

Marriage in the United States has been affected by wider demographic and economic changes in the population. For example, more recent cohorts of young women are likely to have attained a higher educational level than previous generations of women and are generally more economically successful. For many couples, this has altered the dynamics of marriage. Specifically, in 1970, only 4 percent of women 35 to 44 years of age made more money than their husbands, but by 2007 this number had increased to 22 percent. One consequence is that marriage is now associated with increases in economic security for both men and women (Cohn & Fry, 2010).

What Marriage Means to Emerging and Young Adults Today In the United States, despite the vast demographic changes of the last half-century, some 90 percent of adults will still opt to marry at some point in their lives (Whitehead & Poponoe, 2003). Although the proportion of emerging and young adults who choose to marry is not much different from what it was at the beginning of the twentieth century

(Fussell & Furstenberg, 2005), they do seem to think about it differently. For example, in one research study, young adults viewed traditional marriage with its rigid gender roles as no longer viable in today's world. Instead, they expected greater space for individual interests and pursuits, both within and outside of the marriage. They put more emphasis on friendship and compatibility and less on romantic love (Kefalas, Furstenberg, & Napolitano, 2005). Indeed, the vast majority of adults in the United States today view the primary purpose of marriage as "the mutual happiness and fulfillment of adults" rather than as being based on parenting and children (Pew Research Center, 2007a).

Instead of seeing marriage as an inevitable step toward adulthood, as in the past, today's young adults tend to believe that, to be married, one should already *be* an adult. Most plan to marry, but only when they feel ready; and they see getting on their feet financially and establishing themselves in stable jobs or careers as formidable obstacles (Kefalas et al., 2005).

This mass wedding in India, organized by social workers for members of impoverished families, is an example of the variety of marriage customs around the world.

Entering Matrimony For the reasons just mentioned—as well as because of the increasing enrollment in higher education—the typical marrying age has risen in industrialized countries. Thirty to 50 years ago, most people married in or before their early 20s. In the United States in 2009 the median age of first-time bridegrooms was 28.3 and of first-time brides, 25.8 (Copen, Daniels, Vespa, & Mosher, 2012). And slightly more women are living without a spouse than with one. In England, France, Germany, and Italy, the average marrying age is even higher: 29 or 30 for men and 27 for women (van Dyk, 2005).

Historically and across cultures the most common way of selecting a mate has been through arrangement, either by the parents or by professional matchmakers. Generally, one of the primary beliefs about the role of marriage is focused on the union of two families, rather than on love between two individuals. Given this orientation, it is perhaps not surprising to find that couples in arranged marriages have very different expectations of their spouses. There are decreased expectations of intimacy and love, and responsibility and commitment are emphasized. Only in modern times has free choice of mates on the basis of love become the norm in the Western world (Broude, 1994; Ingoldsby, 1995). However, despite these variations in beliefs about what marriage should look like, couples in arranged marriages appear to be equally happy in their relationships (Myers, Madithil, & Tingle, 2005). In many cultures, the Western ideal of a relationship based on love and personal attraction seems to have changed the nature of arranged marriage, with "semi-arranged" marriages becoming more and more common (Naito & Gielen, 2005). In these situations, parents are heavily involved in the process of finding a marriage partner, but the young adult holds veto power over potential spouses.

The transition to married life brings major changes in sexual functioning, living arrangements, rights and responsibilities, attachments, and loyalties. Among other tasks, marriage partners need to redefine the connection with their original families, balance intimacy with autonomy, and establish a fulfilling sexual relationship.

Sexual Activity after Marriage Americans apparently have sex less often than media images suggest, and married people have sex more often than singles, though not as often as cohabitors. However, married couples report more emotional satisfaction from sex than single or cohabiting couples (Waite & Joyner, 2000).

It is hard to know just how common extramarital sex is, because there is no way to tell how truthful people are about their sexual practices, but surveys suggest that it is much less common than is generally assumed. About 18 percent of married people report having had extramarital relations at some time during their married lives. Current extramarital activity is most prevalent among younger adults and about twice as common among husbands as among wives (T. W. Smith, 2003). Generally, extramarital activity occurs earlier in the relationship; marriages that last for long periods of time show decreasing risk (DeMaris, 2009).

Only about a third of married couples have sex at least twice a week.

Laumann & Michael, 2000

Young adults of both sexes have become less permissive in their attitudes toward extramarital sex (T. W. Smith, 2005). In fact, disapproval of extramarital sex is even greater in U.S. society today (94 percent) than disapproval of homosexuality. The pattern of strong disapproval of homosexuality, even stronger disapproval of extramarital sex, and far weaker disapproval of premarital sex also holds true in such European countries as Britain, Ireland, Germany, Sweden, and Poland, though degrees of disapproval differ from one country to another. The United States has more restrictive attitudes than any of these countries except Ireland, where the influence of the Catholic Church is strong (Scott, 1998).

Marital Satisfaction Married people tend to be happier than unmarried people, though those in unhappy marriages are less happy than those who are unmarried or divorced (Myers, 2000). People who marry and stay married, especially women, tend to become better off financially than those who do not marry or who divorce (Hirschl, Altobelli, & Rank, 2003; Wilmoth & Koso, 2002). However, we do not know that marriage causes wealth; it may be that people who seek wealth and who have characteristics favorable to obtaining it are more likely to marry and to stay married (Hirschl et al., 2003). Nor is it certain that marriage causes happiness; it may be that the greater happiness of married people reflects a greater tendency of happy people to marry (Lucas, Clark, Georgellis, & Diener, 2003; Stutzer & Frey, 2006).

Marriages, by and large, seem to be just about as happy as they were a quarter-century ago, but husbands and wives spend less time doing things together. Those conclusions come from two national surveys of married persons. Marital happiness was positively affected by increased economic resources, equal decision making, nontraditional gender attitudes, and support for the norm of lifelong marriage; marital happiness was negatively affected by premarital cohabitation, extramarital affairs, wives' job demands, and wives' longer working hours. Increases in husbands' share of housework appeared to lower marital satisfaction among husbands but improved it among wives (Amato, Johnson, Booth, & Rogers, 2003). In fact "sharing household chores" is viewed as very important to marital success by approximately 62 percent of American respondents (Pew Research Center, 2007b). A large difference in wage earning potential between spouses was associated with decreases in happiness (Stuzer & Frey, 2006). In a study of 197 Israeli couples, a tendency toward emotional instability and negativity in either spouse was a strong predictor of marital unhappiness (Lavee & Ben-Ari, 2004).

One factor underlying marital satisfaction may be a difference in what the man and woman expect from marriage. Women tend to place more importance on emotional expressiveness—their own and their husbands'—than men do (Lavee & Ben-Ari, 2004). Men's efforts to express positive emotion to their wives, to pay attention to the dynamics of the relationship, and to set aside time for activities focused on building the relationship are important to women's perceptions of marital quality (Wilcox & Nock, 2006).

Factors in Marital Success Can the outcome of a marriage be predicted before the couple ties the knot? In one study, researchers followed 100 mostly European American couples for 13 years, starting before they married. Such factors as premarital income and education levels, whether a couple cohabited before marriage or had premarital sex, and how long they had known each other or dated before marriage had no effect on marital success. What did matter were the partners' happiness with the relationship, their sensitivity to each other, their validation of each other's feelings, and their communication and conflict management skills (Clements, Stanley, & Markman, 2004). In a similar vein, longitudinal research conducted with newlywed couples showed that empathy, validation, and caring were related to feelings of intimacy and better relationship quality (Sullivan, Pasch, Johnson, & Bradbury, 2010). Couples who engaged in premarital counseling tend to be more satisfied with and committed to their marriages than couples who did not have such counseling, and their marriages are less likely to end in divorce (Stanley, Amato, Johnson, & Markman, 2006).

The way people describe their marriage can tell much about its likelihood of success. In a nationally representative longitudinal study, 2,034 married people age 55 or younger were asked what held their marriages together. Those who perceived the cohesiveness of their marriage as based on *rewards,* such as love, respect, trust, communication, compatibility, and commitment to the partner, were more likely to be happy in marriage and to remain married after 14 years than people who referred to *barriers* to leaving the marriage, such as children, religious beliefs, financial interdependence, and commitment to the institution of marriage (Previti & Amato, 2003).

checkpoint
can **you...**

- Identify several benefits of marriage?
- Discuss differences between traditional views of marriage and the way emerging and young adults view it today?
- Note cultural differences in methods of mate selection and historical changes in marrying age?
- Cite findings on sexual relations in and outside of marriage?
- Identify factors in marital satisfaction and success?

Parenthood

People in industrial societies typically have fewer children today than in earlier generations, and they start having them later in life, in many cases because they spend their emerging adult years getting an education and establishing a career. In 2011 the average age of first births in the United States had risen to 25.4 years (Martin, Hamilton, Ventura, et al., 2013; Figure 5), and the percentage of women who give birth for the first time in their late 30s and even in their 40s and 50s has increased dramatically, often with the help of fertility treatments (Martin et al., 2013).

Both mothers and fathers prefer to hold babies on the left side of their bodies.

Scola & Vauclair, 2010

A woman's age at first birth varies with ethnic and cultural background. In 2008, Asian American and Pacific Islander women had their first babies at an average age of 28.7, whereas American Indian and Alaska Native women gave birth for the first time, on average, at just under age 22 (Martin et al., 2010).

The number of children born to unwed mothers has been rising for the last half century; however, the proportion of unwed mothers has risen particularly sharply since 2002 (Cohn, 2009). In 2012, 40.7 percent of U.S. births were to unmarried women, a decline for the third straight year from the historic high of 41 percent in 2009 (Martin et al., 2013). The U.S. fertility rate is higher than that in several other developed countries, such as Japan and the United Kingdom, where the average age at first birth is about 29 (Martin et al., 2002; van Dyk, 2005).

At the same time, an increasing proportion of U.S. couples remain childless. The percentage of households with children fell from 45 percent in 1970 (Fields, 2004) to approximately 30 percent in 2010 (Jacobsen, Mark, & Dupuis, 2012). The aging of the population as well as delays in marriage and childbearing may help explain these data, but some couples undoubtedly remain childless by choice. Some see marriage primarily as a way to enhance their intimacy, not as an institution dedicated to the bearing and raising of children (Popenoe & Whitehead, 2003). Others may be discouraged by the financial burdens of parenthood and the difficulty of combining parenthood with employment. Better child care and other support services might help couples make truly voluntary decisions.

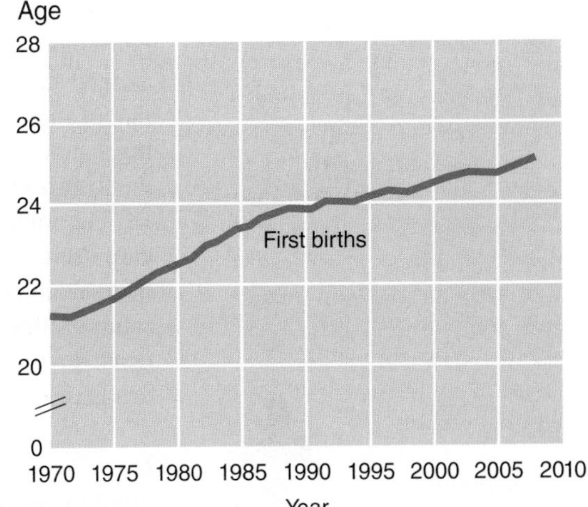

FIGURE 5
Mean Age of Mother at First Birth: United States

Many women today start families at a later age than in their parents' generation, raising the average age at first birth.

Source: Martin, Hamilton, et al., 2010.

PARENTHOOD AS A DEVELOPMENTAL EXPERIENCE

Any major life transition—starting college, embarking on a career, or retiring—is a time of developmental change that can result in positive

Celebrating a child's birthday is one of the many joys of parenthood.

or negative outcomes. Among key experiences in life is the birth of a child. Along with feeling excitement, wonder, and awe, most new parents experience some anxiety about the responsibility of caring for a child, the commitment of time and energy it entails, and the feeling of permanence that parenthood imposes on a marriage. Pregnancy and the recovery from childbirth can affect a couple's relationship, sometimes increasing intimacy and sometimes creating barriers. In addition, many couples find their relationship becoming more "traditional" following the birth of a child, with the woman often engaging in the bulk of caregiving and housekeeping (Cox & Paley, 2003).

Men's and Women's Involvement in Parenthood Even though most mothers now work outside the home, women spend more time on child care than their counterparts did in the 1960s, when 60 percent of children lived with a breadwinner father and a stay-at-home mother. Today, only about 30 percent of children live in such families. Yet married mothers spent 12.9 hours a week on child care in 2000 compared with 10.6 hours in 1965, and single mothers spent 11.8 hours a week on child care as compared with 7.5 hours in 1965 (Bianchi, Robinson, & Milkie, 2006). Despite this increase in overall hours spent parenting, many mothers say they have too little time with their children (Milkie, Mattingly, Nomaguchi, Bianchi, & Robinson, 2004).

How and why do they do it? For one thing, many mothers delay parenting until a time when they want to spend time with their children. Also, social norms have changed; today's mothers feel more pressure to invest time and energy in child rearing. And they feel a need to keep a closer eye on their children because of concerns about crime, school violence, and other negative influences (Bianchi et al., 2006).

What about fathers? Generally, most fathers are not as involved as mothers are (Yeung, Sandberg, Davis-Kean, & Hofferth, 2001). However, the amount of time fathers spend with their children has gone up. For example, married fathers spent more than twice as much time with child care (6.5 hours) and housework (9.7 hours) in 2000 than they did in 1965 (Bianchi et al., 2006). And on weekends, and as their children get older, the time fathers spend with their children is more equal to that of mothers (Yeung et al., 2001). Work affects this as well. Fathers with long working hours report wanting more time to spend with their children but being unable to do so (Milkie et al., 2004).

The impacts of having children are also indirect. In addition to time spent in child care itself, fathers living with dependent children are less likely to be involved in their own independent social activities. However, they are more likely to be engaged in school-related activities, church groups, and community service organizations. The result of this is generally positive—the most involved fathers also report the highest levels of satisfaction (Eggebeen & Knoester, 2001).

Having children doesn't just change fathers' lives, it changes their physiology. Fathers who are involved in a pregnancy show decreased levels of testosterone over the course of the pregnancy.

Berg & Wynne-Edwards, 2001

How Parenthood Affects Marital Satisfaction How does parenthood affect the relationship between marriage partners? Results are mixed. Some studies show that marital satisfaction typically declines during the child-raising years—and the more children, the greater the decline. Moreover, mothers of young infants tend to feel the effects most strongly. For example, only 38 percent of new mothers report high marital satisfaction compared with 62 percent of childless wives (Twenge, Campbell, & Foster, 2003).

Why do these declines occur? New parents are likely to experience stressors that can affect their health and state of mind. Taking care of newborn babies is difficult and often comes with sleep deprivation, uncertainty, and isolation. Nighttime crying, for example, is associated with a decrease in marital satisfaction in the 1st year of the child's life (Meijer & van den Wittenboer, 2007). If the woman was working outside the home and is now staying home, the burden of housework and child care may fall mostly on her. Indeed, the division of household tasks is a common issue among new parents (Schulz, Cowan, & Cowan, 2006).

However, the picture is not all bad. Other studies tell a different story, and it may be that additional variables are needed to truly understand the effect of a new baby. For example, whether or not the couple was happy prior to the pregnancy, and whether or not the pregnancy was planned, affects marital satisfaction after the birth of a child (Lawrence, Rothman, Cobb, Rothman, & Bradbury, 2008). Other studies have found no differences in marital satisfaction a year into the marriage (McHale & Huston, 1985) or even increases in satisfaction peaking at 1 month postpartum (Wallace & Gotlib, 1990).

A recent attempt to make sense of these contrasting findings suggests that when studies are examined in concert, a small but significant decrease in marital satisfaction is common 1 to 2 years after the birth of a child. However, this decline is also found in married couples without a child. Thus it may be a general relational process rather than one specific to the parenting transition (Mitnick, Heyman, & Slep, 2009).

There are indications, too, that declines in satisfaction are not inevitable. Parents who participate in professionally led couples discussion groups about parenting issues and relationships, beginning in the last trimester of pregnancy, report significantly smaller declines in satisfaction (Schultz et al., 2006). It may be that the adjustment is easier when parents have more accurate perceptions of the impact a new child is likely to have on the marriage (Kalmus, Davidson, & Cushman, 1992).

checkpoint can **you**...

- Describe trends in family size and age of parenthood?
- Compare men's and women's attitudes toward and exercise of parental responsibilities?
- Discuss how parenthood affects marital satisfaction?

HOW DUAL-INCOME FAMILIES COPE

In married family life of the past, men were traditionally viewed as the main providers, and women, if they worked, as secondary providers. These traditional gender roles are changing. In the United States today, most families are composed of two working parents (Gauthier & Furstenberg, 2005), and women are providing an increasingly large percentage of family income. For example, in 1973 women's income accounted for only about 26 percent of family income, whereas in 2003 women brought in 35 percent of family income. Moreover, 25 percent of working wives earned *more* than their husbands (Bureau of Labor Statistics, 2005).

How does having two working parents affect families? Generally, combining work and family roles is good for both men's and women's mental and physical health and has positive effects on the strength of their relationship (Barnett & Hyde, 2001). However, juggling multiple roles—partner, parent, and employee—is often difficult. Working couples face extra demands on time and energy, conflict between work and family, possible rivalry between spouses, and anxiety and guilt about meeting children's needs. The family role is most demanding, especially for women, when children are young (Milkie & Peltola, 1999; Warren & Johnson, 1995), and the career role is most demanding when a worker is getting established or being promoted. Therefore, the benefits of these multiple roles depend on how many roles each partner carries, the demands of each role, the success or satisfaction the partners derive from their roles, and the extent to which the couples hold traditional or nontraditional attitudes about gender roles (Barnett & Hyde, 2001; Voydanoff, 2004).

For those parents who are not able to establish a satisfactory work-family balance, negative effects may snowball. Negative effects can either spill over from work to family, or from family to work, although work stress seems to affect family life to a greater degree (Ford, Heinen, & Langkamer, 2007; Schulz, Cowan, Cowan, & Brennan, 2004). To cope with this, new parents may cut back on working hours, refuse overtime, or turn down jobs that require excessive travel to increase family time and reduce stress (Barnett & Hyde, 2001; Becker & Moen, 1999; Crouter & Manke, 1994). Or a couple may make a trade-off, trading a career for a job, or trading off whose work takes precedence depending on shifts in career opportunities and family responsibilities. Women are more likely to do the scaling back, which usually occurs during the early years of child rearing (Becker & Moen, 1999; Gauthier & Furstenberg, 2005).

To lessen the pressures on dual-income families, most countries have adopted workplace protection for such families (Heymann, Siebert, & Wei, 2007). Fathers in

65 countries—but not in the United States—get *paid* paternity leave. (The U.S. Family and Medical Leave Act of 1993 grants 12 weeks of *unpaid* leave.) At least 34 countries—but not the United States—set a maximum length for the work week. In the United States, approximately 48 percent of workers in the private sector do not have paid leave to care for themselves, and even more lack paid care for other family members such as children. Moreover, even of those who are legally entitled to take family leave, 78 percent do not because they cannot afford to do so (Quamie, 2010). The United States is the only industrialized nation without paid maternity leave although a few states have adopted paid family plans. President Obama's 2012 budget included $50 million for start-up funds for grants to help states provide paid family leave to workers (Office of Management and Budget, 2011).

checkpoint
can **you** . . .

- Identify benefits and drawbacks of a dual-earner household?

When Marriage Ends

In the United States, the average marriage that ends in divorce does so after 7 or 8 years (Kreider, 2005). Divorce, more often than not, leads to remarriage with a new partner and the formation of a stepfamily, which includes children born to or adopted by one or both partners before the current marriage.

DIVORCE

The U.S. divorce rate hit its lowest point since 1970 in 2008 at 3.5 divorces per 1,000 married women (Tejada-Vera & Sutton, 2009). This rate is about twice what it was in 1960 but has fallen gradually since its peak in 1981. About 1 in 5 U.S. adults has been divorced (Kreider, 2005).

The sharpest drop in divorce has occurred among younger cohorts—those born since the mid-1950s (U.S. Census Bureau, 2007b). College-educated women, who previously had the most permissive views about divorce, have become less so, whereas women with lower educational levels have become more permissive and thus more likely to divorce (Martin & Parashar, 2006). Age at marriage is another predictor of whether a union will last. The decline in divorce may reflect higher educational levels as well as the later age of first marriages, both of which are associated with marital stability (Popenoe & Whitehead, 2004). It also may reflect the rise in cohabitation, which, if it ends, does not end in divorce (A. Cherlin in Lopatto, 2007). Teenagers, high school dropouts, and nonreligious persons have higher divorce rates (Bramlett & Mosher, 2002; Popenoe & Whitehead, 2004). The rates of marital disruption for black women remain higher than for white or Latino women (Bulanda & Brown, 2007; Sweeney & Phillips, 2004). In addition, interracial couples, particularly those involving white females with Asian or black males, are more likely to divorce than same-race couples (Bratter & King, 2008).

The highest divorce rates in the United States are in Nevada, so reconsider that Vegas wedding!

National Center for Health Statistics, 2009b

Why Do Marriages Fail? Looking back on their marriages, 130 divorced U.S. women who had been married an average of 8 years showed remarkable agreement on the reasons for the failure of their marriages. The most frequently cited reasons were incompatibility and lack of emotional support; for more recently divorced, presumably younger, women, this included lack of career support. Spousal abuse was third, suggesting that intimate partner violence may be more frequent than is generally realized (Dolan & Hoffman, 1998; Box 2).

According to a randomized telephone survey of 1,704 married people, the greatest likelihood of *either* spouse's bringing up divorce exists when the couple's economic resources are about equal and their financial obligations to each other are relatively small (Rogers, 2004). Instead of staying together "for the sake of the children," many embattled spouses conclude that exposing children to continued parental conflict does greater damage. And, for the increasing number of childless couples, it's easier to return to a single state (Eisenberg, 1995).

When considering affairs, men are less likely to break up with a woman who had a homosexual rather than a heterosexual affair. For women, on the other hand, a homosexual affair on the part of their male partner is more likely to end the relationship.

Confer & Cloud, 2011

research in action

INTIMATE PARTNER VIOLENCE

Intimate partner violence (IPV), or domestic violence, is the physical, sexual, or psychological maltreatment of a spouse, a former spouse, or an intimate partner. Each year U.S. women are the victims of about 4.8 million intimate partner–related physical assaults, and U.S. men are the victims of about 2.9 million such assaults (CDC, 2009c). In 2005, intimate partner violence resulted in 1,510 deaths, 22 percent of them males and 78 percent females (CDC, 2009c). The true extent of domestic violence is difficult to ascertain because the victims are often too ashamed or afraid to report what has happened, especially if the victim is male.

Most studies in the United States find that men are far more likely than women to perpetrate intimate partner violence (Tjaden & Thoennes, 2000). Women's violence against men in domestic relationships does happen, but it is typically less injurious, and less likely to be motivated by a desire to dominate or control their partner (Kimmel, 2002). Both women and men who have been victimized or threatened by IPV tend to report more chronic health conditions and health risk behaviors than those who have not experienced IPV. However, it is not clear whether these conditions and behaviors are a cause or a result of the violence (Black & Breiding, 2008).

Research on intimate partner violence has identified three types of violence: situational couple violence, emotional abuse, and intimate terrorism (DeMaris, Benson, Fox, Hill, & Van Wyk, 2003; Frye & Karney, 2006; Leone, Johnson, Cohan, & Lloyd, 2004). Situational couple violence refers to physical confrontations that develop in the heat of an argument. This type of violence, in the context of marriage, may reflect poor marital adjustment or acute stress (Frye & Karney, 2006). It may be initiated by either partner and is unlikely to escalate in severity (DeMaris et al., 2003). It is often related to the use of drugs or alcohol (CDC, 2011b).

Emotional abuse, such as insults and intimidation, may occur either with or without physical violence (Kaukinen, 2004; WHO, 2005). In a survey of 25,876 Canadian men and women, emotional abuse of women tended to occur when a woman's education, occupational status, and income were higher than her partner's. Such behavior may be a man's way of asserting dominance (Kaukinen, 2004).

The most serious type of partner violence is intimate terrorism—systematic use of emotional abuse, coercion, and, sometimes, threats and violence to gain or enforce power or control over a partner. This type of abuse tends to become more frequent and more severe as time goes on. Its most important distinguishing characteristic is its underlying control-seeking motivation (DeMaris et al., 2003; Leone et al., 2004). Victims of intimate terrorism are most likely to be female and to experience physical injuries, time lost from work, poor health, and psychological distress (Leone et al., 2004).

2

Why do victims stay with partners who abuse or terrorize them? Some blame themselves. Constant ridicule, criticism, threats, punishment, and psychological manipulation destroy their self-confidence and overwhelm them with self-doubt. Some are more concerned about preserving the family than about protecting themselves. Often victims feel trapped in an abusive relationship. Their partners isolate them from family and friends. They may be financially dependent and lack outside social support. Some are afraid to leave—a realistic fear, as some abusive husbands track down, harass, and beat or even kill their estranged wives (Fawcett, Heise, Isita-Espejel, & Pick, 1999; Harvard Medical School, 2004b; Walker, 1999).

The U.S. Violence Against Women Act, adopted in 1994, provides for tougher law enforcement, funding for shelters, a national domestic violence hotline, and educating judges and court personnel, as well as young people, about domestic violence. To be effective, shelters need to offer expanded employment and educational opportunities for abused women who are economically dependent on their partners. Health providers need to question women about suspicious injuries and tell them about the physical and mental health risks of staying with abusive partners (Kaukinen, 2004). Community standards can make a difference. In communities where neighborhood cohesion and informal social control are strong, rates of intimate partner violence and homicide tend to be low, and women are more likely to disclose their problems and seek social support (Browning, 2002).

What more do you think can or should be done to prevent or stop intimate partner violence?

Divorce breeds more divorce. Adults with divorced parents are more likely to expect that their marriages will not last (Glenn & Marquardt, 2001) and to become divorced themselves than those whose parents remained together (Shulman et al., 2001). However, this process may be affected by a subsequent parental marriage. Young adults who had remarried parents currently modeling a high-quality relationship in their second marriage were not more likely to get a divorce themselves, suggesting that current influences play a strong role in relationships (Yu & Adler-Baeder, 2007).

Divorce can be catching. People who have others in their social network who are divorcing are more likely to get divorced themselves.

McDermott, Fowler, & Christakis, 2009

Adjusting to Divorce Ending even an unhappy marriage can be painful for both partners, especially when there are young children in the home. Issues concerning custody and visitation often force divorced parents to maintain contact with each other, and these contacts may be stressful (Williams & Dunne-Bryant, 2006).

Divorce tends to reduce long-term well-being, especially for the partner who did not initiate the divorce or does not remarry (Amato, 2000). Especially for men, divorce can have negative effects on physical or mental health or both (Wu & Hart, 2002). Women are more likely than men to experience a sharp reduction in economic resources and living standards after separation or divorce (Kreider & Fields, 2002; Williams & Dunne-Bryant, 2006); however, women in unhappy marriages benefit more from the dissolution of the relationship than men in unhappy marriages (Waite, Luo, & Lewin, 2009). People who were—or thought they were—happily married tend to react more negatively and adapt more slowly to divorce (Lucas et al., 2003). On the other hand, when a marriage was highly conflicted, its ending may improve well-being in the long run (Amato, 2000).

An important factor in adjustment is emotional detachment from the former spouse. People who argue with their ex-mates or who have not found a new partner or spouse experience more distress. An active social life, both at the time of divorce and afterward, helps (Amato, 2000; Thabes, 1997).

REMARRIAGE AND STEPPARENTHOOD

Remarriage, said the essayist Samuel Johnson, "is the triumph of hope over experience." Evidence for the truth of that statement is that remarriages are more likely than first marriages to end in divorce (Adams, 2004).

In the United States and abroad, rates of remarriage are high and rising (Adams, 2004). More than 1 out of 3 U.S. marriages are remarriages for both bride and groom (Kreider, 2005). Half of those who remarry after divorce from a first marriage do so within 3 to 4 years (Kreider, 2005). Men and women living with children from a previous relationship are most likely to form a new union with someone who also has resident children, thus forming a his-and-hers stepfamily (Goldscheider & Sassler, 2006). And families in which both parents bring children into the marriage are marked by higher levels of conflict (Heatherington, 2006).

The more recent the current marriage and the older the stepchildren, the harder stepparenting seems to be. Women, especially, seem to have more difficulties in raising stepchildren than in raising biological children, perhaps because women generally spend more time with the children than men do (MacDonald & DeMaris, 1996).

Still, the stepfamily has the potential to provide a warm, nurturing atmosphere, as does any family that cares about all its members. One researcher (Papernow, 1993) identified several stages of adjustment: At first, adults expect a smooth, rapid adjustment, while children fantasize that the stepparent will go away and the original parent will return. As conflicts develop, each parent may side with his or her biological children. Eventually, the adults form a strong alliance to meet the needs of all the children. The stepparent gains the role of a significant adult figure, and the family becomes an integrated unit with its own identity.

checkpoint can **you**...

- Give reasons for the decrease in divorce since 1981?
- Discuss factors in adjustment to divorce?
- Discuss factors in adjustment to remarriage and stepparenthood?

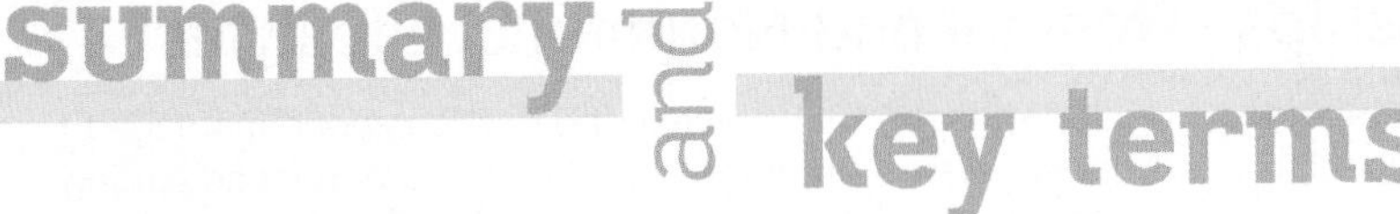

Emerging Adulthood: Patterns and Tasks

- Emerging adulthood is often a time of experimentation before assuming adult roles and responsibilities. Such traditional developmental tasks as finding stable work and developing long-term romantic relationships may be postponed until the 30s or even later.
- Paths to adulthood may be influenced by such factors as gender, academic ability, early attitudes toward education, expectations in late adolescence, social class, and ego development.
- Identity development in emerging adulthood may take the form of recentering, the gradual development of a stable adult identity. For racial/ethnic minorities, the task of identity formation may be accelerated.
- Emerging adulthood offers a moratorium, a period in which young people are free from pressure to make lasting commitments.
- A measure of how successfully emerging adults handle the developmental task of leaving the childhood home is their ability to maintain close but autonomous relationships with their parents.
- Remaining in the parental home is increasingly common among emerging and young adults, who do so often for financial reasons. This can complicate the negotiation of an adult relationship with parents.

recentering

Personality Development: Four Views

- Four theoretical perspectives on adult personality development are normative-stage models, the timing-of-events model, trait models, and typological models.
- Normative-stage models hold that age-related social and emotional change emerges in successive periods sometimes marked by crises. In Erikson's theory, the major issue of young adulthood is intimacy versus isolation.
- The timing-of-events model, advocated by Neugarten, proposes that adult psychosocial development is influenced by the occurrence and timing of normative life events. As society becomes less age-conscious, however, the social clock has less meaning.
- The five-factor model of Costa and McCrae is organized around five groupings of related traits: neuroticism, extraversion, openness to experience, conscientiousness, and agreeableness. Current studies find that each of these traits changes during young adulthood and to some extent throughout life.
- Typological research, pioneered by Jack Block, has identified personality types that differ in ego-resiliency and ego-control. These types seem to persist from childhood through adulthood.

normative-stage models
intimacy versus isolation
timing-of-events model
normative life events
social clock
trait models
five-factor model
typological approach
ego-resiliency
ego-control

Foundations of Intimate Relationships

- Young adults seek intimacy in relationships with peers and romantic partners. Self-disclosure is an important aspect of intimacy.
- Most young adults have friends but have increasingly limited time to spend with them. Women's friendships tend to be more intimate than men's.
- Many young adults have friends who are considered fictive kin or psychological family.
- According to Sternberg's triangular theory of love, love has three aspects: intimacy, passion, and commitment.

fictive kin

triangular theory of love

Marital and Nonmarital Lifestyles

- Today, more adults than in the past postpone marriage or never marry. The trend is particularly pronounced among African American women and people from lower socioeconomic classes.
- Reasons for staying single include career opportunities, travel, sexual and lifestyle freedom, a desire for self-fulfillment, women's greater self-sufficiency, reduced social pressure to marry, financial constraints, fear of divorce, difficulty in finding a suitable mate, and lack of dating opportunities or of available mates.
- The ingredients of long-term satisfaction are similar in homosexual and heterosexual relationships.
- Gays and lesbians in the United States are fighting for rights other people enjoy, such as the right to marry.
- With the new stage of emerging adulthood and the delay in age of marriage, cohabitation has increased and has become the norm in some countries.
- Cohabitation can be a trial marriage, an alternative to marriage, or, in some places, almost indistinguishable from marriage. Cohabiting relationships in the United States tend to be less stable than marriages.
- Marriage (in a variety of forms) is universal and meets basic economic, emotional, sexual, social, and child-raising needs.
- Mate selection and marrying age vary across cultures. People in industrialized nations now marry later than in past generations.
- Success in marriage may depend on partners' sensitivity to each other, their validation of each other's feelings, and their communication and conflict management skills. Men's and women's differing expectations may be important factors in marital satisfaction.

Parenthood

- Today women in industrialized societies are having fewer children and having them later in life, and an increasing number choose to remain childless.
- Fathers are usually less involved in child raising than mothers, but more so than in previous generations.
- Marital satisfaction typically declines during the childbearing years.
- In most cases, the burdens of a dual-earner lifestyle fall most heavily on the woman.
- Family-friendly workplace policies may help alleviate marital stress.

When Marriage Ends

- Divorce rates in the United States have fallen from their high in 1981. Among the likely reasons are increasing educational levels, the delay in age of marriage, and the rise in cohabitation.
- Adjusting to divorce can be painful. Emotional distance from the ex-spouse is a key to adjustment.
- Many divorced people remarry within a few years, but remarriages tend to be less stable than first marriages.
- Stepfamilies may go through several stages of adjustment.

part 7

MIDDLE ADULTHOOD

chapter 15

Physical and Cognitive Development in Middle Adulthood

outline

Middle Age: A Social Construct

PHYSICAL DEVELOPMENT

Physical Changes

Physical and Mental Health

COGNITIVE DEVELOPMENT

Measuring Cognitive Abilities in Middle Age

The Distinctiveness of Adult Cognition

Creativity

Work and Education

learning objectives

Explain how midlife is changing and define *middle adulthood.*

Discuss physical changes in middle adulthood.

Characterize health and well-being in middle age.

Identify cognitive changes in middle adulthood.

Describe creative achievement and the relationship between creativity and age.

Discuss trends in work, retirement, and education in middle adulthood.

did you know?

- One-third of Americans in their 70s think of themselves as middle-aged?
- Positive personality traits are related to good health and long life?
- Middle-aged people who engage in complex work tend to show stronger cognitive performance than their peers?

In this chapter, we examine physical changes during midlife as well as physical, sexual, and mental health issues. We look at factors that affect intelligence, thought processes, and creativity. Finally, we look at work, retirement, and educational pursuits.

To be a healthy person, you have to be sympathetic to the child you once were and maintain the continuity between you as a child and you as an adult.

—Maurice Sendak

Middle Age: A Social Construct

We described adolescence as a stage of life that ultimately is a social construct. The same is true of midlife. The term *midlife* first came into the dictionary in 1895 (Lachman, 2004) as life expectancy began to lengthen. Today, in industrial societies, middle adulthood is considered to be a distinct stage of life with its own societal norms, roles, opportunities, and challenges. However, some traditional societies, such as upper-caste Hindus in rural India (Menon, 2001) and the Gusii in Kenya, do not recognize a middle stage of adulthood at all.

When would you say middle age begins? Think of several people you know who are middle-aged. Do they seem to be in good health? How involved are they in work or other activities?

We define *middle adulthood* in chronological terms as the years between ages 40 and 65, but this definition is arbitrary. There is no consensus on when middle age begins and ends or on specific biological or social events that mark its boundaries. With improvements in health and length of life, the subjective upper limits of middle age are rising (Lachman, 2004).

As the United States entered the twenty-first century, more than 80 million baby boomers, born between 1946 and 1964, were between ages 35 and 54 and constituted about 30 percent of the total population (U.S. Census Bureau, 2000). On the whole, this is the best educated and most affluent cohort ever to reach middle age anywhere, and it is changing our perspective on that time of life (Eggebeen & Sturgeon, 2006; Willis & Reid, 1999).

The Midlife in the United States (MIDUS) study, a comprehensive survey of a national sample of 7,189 noninstitutionalized adults ages 25 to 75, has enabled researchers to study factors that influence health, well-being, and productivity in midlife and how adults navigate the transition to old age (Brim, Ryff, & Kessler, 2004). According to the MIDUS data, most middle-aged people are in good physical, cognitive, and emotional shape and feel good about the quality of their lives (Fleeson, 2004; Figure 1). However, the experience of middle age varies with health,

Many middle-aged people are at the peak of their careers, enjoying a sense of freedom, responsibility, and control over their lives and making important contributions to social betterment. Bono, lead singer for the rock band U2, is a philanthropist who has done exactly that. As cofounder and spokesperson for ONE Campaign, he has helped with many causes, especially those related to AIDS and poverty in African countries.

FIGURE 1
How U.S. Adults of Various Ages Rate Aspects of Their Quality of Life and Overall Quality of Life

Source: Fleeson, 2004; data from MacArthur Foundation Research Network on Successful Midlife Development (the MIDUS National Survey).

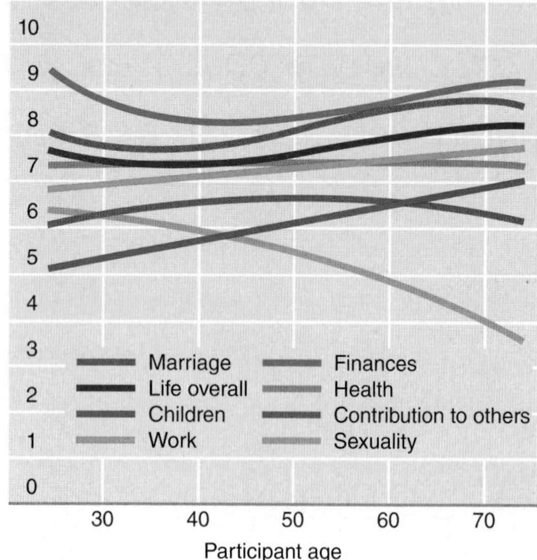

gender, race/ethnicity, socioeconomic status, cohort, and culture, as well as with personality, marital and parental status, and employment (Lachman, 2004). For example, older adults who maintain their physical health tend to have more stable personality traits (Stephan, Sutin, & Terracciano, 2013). Furthermore, the experiences, roles, and issues of early middle age differ from those of late middle age (Keegan, Gross, Fisher, & Remez, 2004).

According to the MIDUS research, "aging, at least up until the midseventies, appears to be a positive phenomenon" (Fleeson, 2004, p. 269). At the same time, the middle years are marked by growing individual differences and a multiplicity of life paths (Lachman, 2004). Some middle-aged people can run marathons; others get winded climbing a steep stairway. Some have a sharper memory than ever; others feel their memory beginning to slip. Many adults in the middle years feel a stable sense of control over their lives (Skaff, 2006) as they handle weighty responsibilities and multiple, demanding roles: running households, departments, or enterprises; launching children; and perhaps caring for aging parents or starting new careers. Others, having made their mark and raised their children, have an increased feeling of freedom and independence (Lachman, 2001). What people do and how they live has much to do with how they age. Middle age can be a time not just of decline and loss but of mastery, competence, and growth.

checkpoint can you . . .

- Cite individual differences in the experience of middle age?

PHYSICAL DEVELOPMENT

Physical Changes

"Use it or lose it!" Research bears out the wisdom of that popular creed. Although some physiological changes are direct results of biological aging and genetic makeup, behavioral and lifestyle factors dating from youth can affect the likelihood, timing, and extent of physical change. By the same token, health and lifestyle habits in the middle years influence what happens in the years beyond (Lachman, 2004; Whitbourne, 2001). The life-span developmental approach presumes that middle adulthood is characterized not just as a time of losses but also as a time for gains.

The more people do, the more they *can* do. People who become active early in life reap the benefits of more stamina and more resilience after age 60 (Spirduso & MacRae, 1990). People who are sedentary lose muscle tone and energy and become less inclined to exert themselves physically. Still, it is never too late to adopt a healthier lifestyle.

People perceive their hands to be shorter and fatter than they actually are.

Longo & Haggard, 2010

SENSORY AND PSYCHOMOTOR FUNCTIONING

From young adulthood through the middle years, sensory and motor changes are almost imperceptible—until one day a 45-year-old man realizes that he cannot read the telephone directory without eyeglasses, or a 60-year-old woman has to admit that she is not as quick on her feet as she was. With increasing age, it is common for adults to experience a variety of perceptual declines, including hearing and visual difficulties (Pleis & Lucas, 2009).

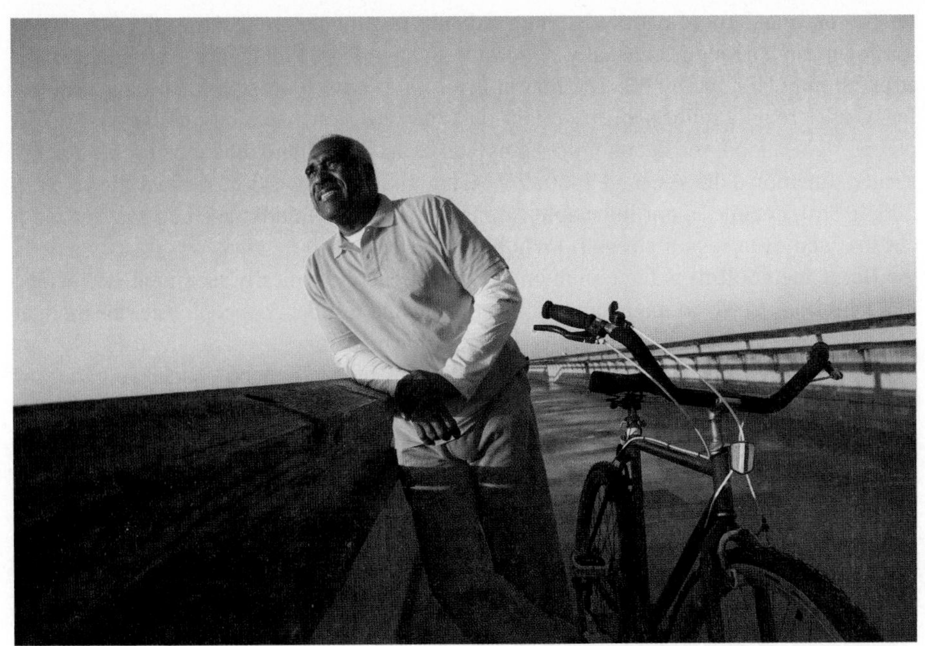

Though strength and coordination may decline, many middle-aged people who remain active show benefits in both psychological and physical health.

Age-related visual problems occur mainly in five areas: near vision, dynamic vision (reading moving signs), sensitivity to light, visual search (locating a car in a parking lot), and speed of processing visual information (Kline & Scialfa, 1996). Some adults also show a slight loss in visual acuity, or sharpness of vision. You may have seen older people using reading glasses, or holding books or newspapers as far out as possible with one arm when trying to focus. As people age, they have difficulty focusing on near objects, a condition known as **presbyopia.** The incidence of **myopia** (nearsightedness) also increases throughout middle age (Merrill & Verbrugge, 1999). Overall, approximately 12 percent of adults age 45 to 64 experience declines in their vision (Pleis & Lucas, 2009). This change usually becomes noticeable in early middle age and is generally complete by age 60 (Kline & Scialfa, 1996).

presbyopia
Age-related, progressive loss of the eyes' ability to focus on nearby objects due to loss of elasticity in the lens.

myopia
Nearsightedness.

How do people adjust to these changes? Middle-aged people often need brighter lighting to see well. Because of changes in the eye, they need about one-third more brightness to compensate for the loss of light reaching the retina (Troll, 1985). Reading glasses, bifocals, and trifocals are also used to aid the eye in focusing on objects.

Age-related, gradual hearing loss is known as **presbycusis.** It is rarely noticed earlier in life, but it generally speeds up and becomes noticeable in the 50s (Merrill & Verbrugge, 1999). Presbycusis normally is limited to higher-pitched sounds than those used in speech (Kline & Scialfa, 1996) and thus is less disruptive than it otherwise might be. Hearing loss proceeds twice as quickly in men as in women (Pearson et al., 1995). Today, a preventable increase in hearing loss is occurring among 45- to 64-year-olds due to continuous or sudden exposure to noise at work, at loud concerts, through earphones, and the like (Wallhagen, Strawbridge, Cohen, & Kaplan, 1997). Almost 18 percent of these adults experience hearing problems (Pleis & Lucas, 2009). Hearing losses due to environmental noise can be avoided by wearing hearing protectors, such as earplugs or special earmuffs.

presbycusis
Age-related, gradual loss of hearing, which accelerates after age 55, especially with regard to sounds at higher frequencies.

Sensitivity to taste and smell generally begins to decline in midlife (Stevens, Cain, Demarque, & Ruthruff, 1991). As the taste buds become less sensitive and the number of olfactory cells diminishes, foods may seem more bland (Merrill & Verbrugge, 1999). Women tend to retain these senses longer than men. There are individual differences, however. One person may become less sensitive to salty foods, another to sweet, bitter, or sour foods. And the same person may remain more sensitive to some of these tastes than to others (Stevens, Cruz, Hoffman, & Patterson, 1995; Whitbourne, 1999).

Strength and coordination decline gradually from their peak during the 20s. Some loss of muscle strength is usually noticeable by age 45; 10 to 15 percent of maximum strength may be gone by 60. The reason is a loss of muscle fiber, which is replaced by fat. Grip strength reflects birth weight and muscle growth earlier in life as well as parents' childhood socioeconomic status and is an important predictor of future disability, functional losses, and mortality (Guralnik, Butterworth, Wadsworth, & Kuh, 2006). Still, decline is not inevitable; strength training in middle age can prevent muscle loss and even regain strength (Whitbourne, 2001).

basal metabolism
Use of energy to maintain vital functions.

Basal metabolism is the minimum amount of energy, typically measured in calories, that your body needs to maintain vital functions while resting. As people age, the amount of energy needed to maintain the body goes down, particularly after age 40. So, for example, older people often put on weight later in life despite no change in eating or exercise habits. This affects endurance, as loss of endurance is partly due to declines in basal metabolism (Merrill & Verbrugge, 1999). Once again, however, "use it or lose it" holds. Often-used skills are more resistant to the effects of aging than those used less, and athletes often show a smaller-than-average loss in endurance (Stones & Kozma, 1996).

Manual dexterity generally becomes less efficient after the midthirties (Vercruyssen, 1997), though some pianists, such as Vladimir Horowitz, have continued to perform brilliantly in their 80s. Simple reaction time (as in pressing a button when a light flashes) slows very little until about age 50, but choice reaction time (as in pressing one of four numbered buttons when the same number appears on a screen) slows gradually throughout adulthood (Der & Deary, 2006). When a vocal rather than a manual response is called for, age differences in simple reaction time are substantially less (S. J. Johnson & Rybash, 1993).

One set of researchers noted this distractibility during their brain scans of younger and older adults. They realized the performance of the older adults was being disrupted by the banging and clanging of the MRI machine.

Stevens et al., 2008

THE BRAIN AT MIDLIFE

In general, the aging brain can be described in two ways: as working more slowly and as having difficulty juggling multiple tasks. This general process affects multiple tasks across many different areas—from understanding complex language to driving a car skillfully to learning new skills. What these disparate tasks have in common is the necessity to quickly process complex information and pay attention to relevant stimuli while simultaneously ignoring irrelevant stimuli. In particular, the ability to ignore distractions gradually declines with age, which makes multitasking increasingly challenging (Madden & Langley, 2003; Stevens, Hasher, Chiew, & Grady, 2008). So, for example, driving while listening to the radio or focusing on one conversation while ignoring the buzz of the crowded room become much more difficult.

Why do these changes occur? Physical changes in the aging brain contribute to the decline in functioning. Myelin, the fatty sheath that lines nerve axons and helps impulses move more quickly through the brain, begins to break down with age (Bartzokis et al., 2008). This helps explain why processing speed slows. Also, when people show atrophy in the left insula, an area of the brain associated with speech production, they more frequently experience the tip-of-the-tongue (TOT) phenomenon (Shafto et al., 2007). In the TOT phenomenon a person knows he knows a word, and can often even specify how many syllables it contains, but cannot access the word.

Another way to keep your brain sharp? Google it. Older adults asked to surf the Web showed significant activation in areas of the brain related to reasoning and decision making. This effect was strongest for experienced surfers, but the researchers argued that even technologically unsophisticated adults should benefit.

Small, Moody, Siddarth, & Bookheimer, 2009

Although some declines are likely, declines are neither inevitable nor necessarily permanent. Older brains are still flexible and can respond positively. For example, when a group of "aging couch potatoes" enrolled in a physical education program, they showed corresponding changes in both gray and white brain matter volume, especially if they engaged in aerobic fitness activities (Colcombe et al., 2006). Overall, keeping the body healthy is associated with retention of cognitive abilities (Doaga & Lee, 2008).

Moreover, even if declines do occur, knowledge based on experience can compensate for the physical changes. For example, middle-aged adults are better drivers than younger ones (McFarland, Tune, & Welford, 1964), and 60-year-old typists are as efficient as 20-year-olds (Spirduso & MacRae, 1990). Similarly, skilled industrial workers in their 40s and 50s are often more productive than younger workers, and they are less likely to suffer disabling injuries on the job. This is partly because they tend to be more conscientious and careful (Salthouse & Maurer, 1996), which is likely a consequence of experience and good judgment.

vital capacity
Amount of air that can be drawn in with a deep breath and expelled.

STRUCTURAL AND SYSTEMIC CHANGES

Changes in appearance may become noticeable during the middle years. By the fifth or sixth decade, the skin may become less taut and smooth as the layer of fat below the surface becomes thinner, collagen molecules more rigid, and elastin fibers more brittle. Hair may become thinner due to a slowed replacement rate, and grayer as production of melanin, the pigmenting agent, declines. Middle-aged people tend to gain weight as a result of accumulation of body fat and lose height due to shrinkage of the intervertebral disks (Merrill & Verbrugge, 1999; Whitbourne, 2001).

Bone density normally peaks in the 20s or 30s. From then on, people typically experience some bone loss as more calcium is absorbed than replaced, causing bones to become thinner and more brittle. Bone loss accelerates in the 50s and 60s; it occurs twice as rapidly in women as in men, sometimes leading to osteoporosis (Merrill & Verbrugge, 1999; Whitbourne, 2001). Smoking, alcohol use, and a poor diet earlier in adulthood tend to speed bone loss; it can be slowed by aerobic exercise, resistance training with weights, increased calcium intake, and vitamin C. Joints may become stiffer as a result of accumulated stress. Exercises that expand range of motion and strengthen the muscles supporting a joint can improve functioning (Whitbourne, 2001).

Large proportions of middle-aged and even older adults show little or no decline in organ functioning (Gallagher, 1993). In some, however, the heart begins to pump more slowly and irregularly in the midfifties; by 65, it may lose up to 40 percent of its aerobic power. Arterial walls may become thicker and more rigid. Heart disease becomes more common beginning in the late 40s or early 50s. **Vital capacity**—the maximum volume of air the lungs can draw in and expel—may begin to diminish at about age 40 and may drop by as much as 40 percent by age 70. Temperature regulation and immune response may begin to weaken, and sleep may become less deep (Merrill & Verbrugge, 1999; Whitbourne, 2001).

Research suggests it's the quantity and depth of your wrinkles, not their location, that makes you appear older.

Aznar-Casanova, Torro-Alves, & Fukusima, 2010

checkpoint
can **you** . . .

- Summarize changes in sensory and motor functioning and body structure and systems that may begin during middle age?
- Identify factors that contribute to individual differences in physical condition?

SEXUALITY AND REPRODUCTIVE FUNCTIONING

Sexuality is not only a hallmark of youth. Although both sexes experience losses in reproductive capacity sometime during middle adulthood—women become unable to bear children and men's fertility begins to decline—sexual enjoyment continues throughout adult life. (Changes in the male and female reproductive systems are summarized in Table 1.)

TABLE 1 Changes in Human Reproductive Systems during Middle Age

	Female	Male
Hormonal change	Drop in estrogen and progesterone	Drop in testosterone
Symptoms	Hot flashes, vaginal dryness, urinary dysfunction	Undetermined
Sexual changes	Less intense arousal, frequent and quicker orgasms	Loss of psychological arousal, less frequent erections, slower orgasms, longer recovery between ejaculations, increased risk of erectile dysfunction
Reproductive capacity	Ends	Continues; some decrease in fertility occurs

TABLE 2 Symptoms of Menopause and Aging

Symptom
Hot flashes, night sweats
Vaginal dryness, painful intercourse
Sleep disturbances
Mood disturbances (depression, anxiety, irritability)
Urinary incontinence
Cognitive disturbances (i.e., forgetfulness)
Somatic symptoms (back pain, tiredness, stiff or painful joints)
Sexual dysfunction

Source: NCCAM, 2008.

Menopause and Its Meanings **Menopause** takes place when a woman permanently stops ovulating and menstruating and can no longer conceive a child; it is generally considered to have occurred one year after the last menstrual period. This happens, on average, at about age 50 to 52, with most women experiencing it between 45 and 55 (Avis & Crawford, 2006).

Menopause is not a single event; it is a process called the *menopausal transition.* It begins with **perimenopause,** also known as the *climacteric.* During this time, a woman's production of mature ova begins to decline, and the ovaries produce less estrogen. Menstruation becomes less regular, with less flow than before, and there is a longer time between menstrual periods. Eventually, menstruation ceases altogether. The menopausal transition generally begins in the midthirties to midforties, and can take approximately 3 to 5 years.

Attitudes toward Menopause During the early nineteenth century in Western cultures, menopause was seen as a disease, a failure of the ovaries to perform their natural function. In the United States today, most women who have gone through menopause view it positively, as a natural process (Avis & Crawford, 2006; Rossi, 2004). Menopause can be seen as a sign of a transition into the second half of adult life—a time of role changes, greater independence, and personal growth.

menopause
Cessation of menstruation and of ability to bear children.

perimenopause
Period of several years during which a woman experiences physiological changes of menopause; includes first year after end of menstruation; also called *climacteric*.

Symptoms Most women experience some symptoms during the menopausal transition. Some have no symptoms at all, and racial/ethnic variations exist. Table 2 summarizes the current evidence concerning reported symptoms.

Most commonly reported are hot flashes and night sweats, sudden sensations of heat that flash through the body due to erratic changes in hormone secretion that affect the temperature control centers in the brain. There is strong evidence that the menopausal transition is responsible for these symptoms. Interestingly, some women never have them, and others have them almost every day (Avis & Crawford, 2006; Rossi, 2004).

Some women find intercourse painful because of thinning vaginal tissues and inadequate lubrication (NIH, 2005). Water-soluble lubricants may help relieve this problem. In addition, some women of menopausal age may experience mood disturbances, such as irritability, nervousness, tension, and depression. Additional research needs to be conducted to understand the relationship between menopause and mood changes (Avis, 1999; Lachman, 2004; NIH, 2005; Rossi, 2004; Whitbourne, 2001).

All in all, the research suggests that some of the symptoms of menopause may be related to other natural changes of aging (National Center for Complementary and Alternative Medicine [NCCAM], 2008). They also may reflect societal views of women and of aging (Box 1). In cultures in which women view menopause positively or in which older women acquire social, religious, or political power after menopause, few problems are associated with this natural event (Aldwin & Levenson, 2001; Avis, 1999).

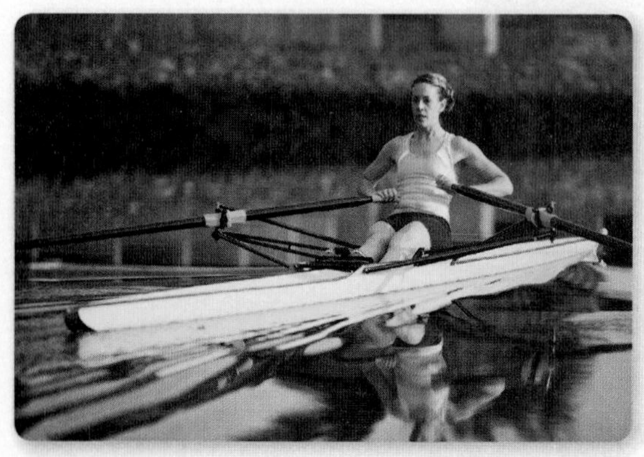

Women of menopausal age report many different symptoms. Physical exercise may alleviate some of them.

Treatment of Menopausal Symptoms Short-term, low-dose administration of artificial estrogen is one way to alleviate hot flashes, but it carries serious risks (Avis & Crawford, 2006; NIH, 2005). Various nonhormonal therapies have been tried. Studies have found some evidence of effectiveness for certain antidepressant drugs as well as for the antihypertensive clonidine and the anticonvulsive drug gabapentin in treating hot flashes in women with severe symptoms, but adverse effects and high costs may limit their usefulness for most women (Nelson et al., 2006). Some women have turned to alternative therapies, such as phytomedicines, St. John's wort, vitamin E, black cohosh, and other natural or herbal preparations, as well as mind-body therapies, energy therapies, and non-Western medicine, but none have been found effective (Avis & Crawford, 2006; Nedrow et al., 2006; Newton et al., 2006;

window on the world

CULTURAL DIFFERENCES IN WOMEN'S EXPERIENCE OF MENOPAUSE

Many women accept hot flashes and night sweats as normal, though unwelcome, accompaniments of menopause. Yet women in some cultures rarely or never experience these symptoms.

In research conducted by Margaret Lock, fewer than 10 percent of Japanese women whose menstruation was becoming irregular reported having had hot flashes during the previous 2 weeks, compared with about 40 percent of a Canadian sample and 35 percent of a U.S. sample. In fact, fewer than 20 percent of Japanese women had ever experienced hot flashes, compared with 65 percent of Canadian women, and most of the Japanese women who had experienced hot flashes reported little or no physical or psychological discomfort. Furthermore, only about 3 percent of the Japanese women said they experienced night sweats, and they were far less likely than Western women to suffer from insomnia, depression, irritability, or lack of energy (Lock, 1994).

In Japan, menopause is not regarded as a medical condition, and the end of menstruation has far less significance than it does for Western women. The closest term for it, *kônenki,* refers not specifically to what Westerners call menopause but to a considerably longer period comparable to perimenopause (Lock, 1994, 1998). There also is no specific Japanese term for "hot flash," even though the Japanese language makes many subtle distinctions among body states. Aging itself is less feared in Japan than in the West; it brings newfound freedom—as does menopause (Lock, 1998). It has been suggested that because women's diet in Japan is high in plant foods containing phytoestrogens, estrogen-like compounds, Japanese women may not experience symptoms of dramatic declines in estrogen levels.

Attitudes toward menopause vary greatly across cultures. In some cultures, such as that of the southwestern Papago Indians, menopause seems to be virtually ignored. In other cultures, such as those of India and South Asia, it is a welcome event; women's status and freedom of movement increase once they are free of taboos connected with menstruation and fertility (Avis, 1999; Lock, 1994).

In the United States, a national study of women's health came up with some paradoxical findings. African American women tended to have more positive feelings about menopause than did Caucasian women, perhaps because in comparison with racism, which many African American women have experienced, menopause is perceived as a minor stressor (Avis & Crawford, 2006; Sommer et al., 1999). Yet, in other studies, African American women have reported more frequent hot flashes than did white women (Avis & Crawford, 2006). In the national women's study, white women agreed that menopause signaled freedom and independence (Sommer et al., 1999). Yet, in a large, community-based study, white women were more likely to experience psychological distress during menopause than women of other racial/ethnic groups (Bromberger et al., 2001). In the national women's study, Japanese American and Chinese American women reported the most negative feelings about menopause, contrary to the findings about Japanese women in Japan (Avis & Crawford, 2006; Sommer et al., 1999).

Clearly, more research is needed. However, these findings show that even such a universal biological event as menopause has major cultural variations, once again affirming the importance of cross-cultural research.

What do you think might explain cultural differences in women's experience of menopause?

NIH, 2005). However, most of the studies have been small or poorly designed. Also, there is a placebo effect; women in control groups, who are not given the therapy being tested, improve more than 30 percent (NIH, 2005).

Changes in Male Sexual Functioning Men remain fertile throughout the life span and do not go through menopause in the same dramatic fashion as do women. Men do have a biological clock, however, and they also experience age-associated changes. Starting at about age 30, testosterone levels begin to decline at a rate of about 1 percent a year, although there are wide individual variations (Asthana et al., 2004; Lewis, Legato, & Fisch, 2006). Although men can still father children, sperm count declines with age, making conception less likely. Moreover, the genetic quality of their sperm declines as well, and advanced paternal age has been implicated as a source of birth defects (Lewis et al., 2006).

Men's changing hormone levels affect more than just their sexual organs. The decline in testosterone has been associated with reductions in bone density and muscle mass (Asthana et al., 2004) as well as decreased energy, lower sex drive, overweight, emotional irritability, and depressed mood. Low testosterone has also been linked to diabetes and cardiovascular disease and has been theorized to increase mortality (Lewis et al., 2006).

Many men suffer no ill effects from declines in testosterone production, but some middle-aged and older men experience erectile dysfunction (ED; commonly called *impotence*). **Erectile dysfunction** is defined as a persistent inability to achieve or maintain an erect enough penis for satisfactory sexual performance. An estimated 39 percent of 40-year-old men and 67 percent of 70-year-old men experience ED at least sometimes (Feldman, Goldstein, Hatzichristou, Krane, & McKinlay, 1994; Goldstein et al., 1998). There are multiple potential causes for ED. Diabetes, hypertension, high cholesterol, kidney failure, depression, neurological disorders, and many chronic diseases have been implicated. In addition, alcohol and drug use, as well as smoking, may contribute. Poor sexual techniques, lack of knowledge, unsatisfying relationships, anxiety, and stress may be contributing factors as well (Lewis et al., 2006; Utiger, 1998).

erectile dysfunction
Inability of a man to achieve or maintain an erect penis sufficient for satisfactory sexual performance.

Sildenafil (Viagra) and other similar testosterone therapies have been found safe and effective (Goldstein et al., 1998; Nurnberg et al., 2003; Utiger, 1998), and their use has mushroomed. However, they should not be prescribed indiscriminately—only for men with known testosterone deficiency (Lewis et al., 2006; Whitbourne, 2001). If there is no apparent physical problem, psychotherapy or sex therapy (with the support and involvement of the partner) may help (NIH, 1992).

checkpoint
can you . . .

- Contrast men's and women's reproductive changes at midlife?
- Identify factors that can affect women's experience of menopause?
- Tell which reported symptoms have been found to be related to menopause, and which have not?
- Identify changes in male sexual functioning in middle age?
- Discuss changes in sexual activity during middle age?

Sexual Activity Myths about sexuality in midlife—for example, the idea that satisfying sex ends at menopause—have sometimes become self-fulfilling prophecies. Now advances in health care and more liberal attitudes toward sex are making people more aware that sex can be a vital part of life during these and even later years.

Frequency of sexual activity and satisfaction with sex life do tend to diminish gradually during the 40s and 50s. In the MIDUS study, 61 percent of married or cohabiting premenopausal women but only 41 percent of postmenopausal women reported having sex once a week or more. This decline was related, not to menopause but to age and physical condition (Rossi, 2004). Possible physical causes include chronic disease, surgery, medications, and too much food or alcohol. Often, however, a decline in frequency has nonphysiological causes: monotony in a relationship, preoccupation with business or financial worries, mental or physical fatigue, depression, failure to make sex a high priority, fear of failure to attain an erection, or lack of a partner (King, 1996; Masters & Johnson, 1966; Weg, 1989). Treating these causes may bring renewed vitality to a couple's sex life.

Physical and Mental Health

Most middle-aged Americans, like middle-aged people in other industrialized countries, are quite healthy. All but 12 percent of 45- to 54-year-olds and 18 percent of 55- to 64-year-olds consider themselves in good to excellent health. Only 12.5 percent of 45- to 54-year-olds and 20 percent of 55- to 64-year-olds are limited in activities because of chronic conditions (chiefly arthritis and circulatory conditions), which increase with age (National Center for Health Statistics [NCHS], 2006; Schiller & Bernadel, 2004).

However, baby boomers may be less healthy than previous generations. In a comparison of three birth cohorts—aged 60–69, 70–79, and 80 and older—the younger cohorts showed sharper increases in health problems including basic activities associated with daily living, performing everyday chores such as making dinner or using a bathroom, and mobility issues. In this group, disability increased between 40 percent and 70 percent in each area. By contrast, these changes were not seen in the older cohorts. This research suggests that people now entering their 60s could face significant disabilities—more so than their counterparts in previous generations—and exert a substantial cost on the already overburdened health care system (Seeman, Merkin, Crimmins, & Karlamangla, 2009). Not surprisingly, research also has shown increases in the use of medical services. The percentage of medical appointments in which five or more drugs were prescribed has doubled—to 25 percent—in the last 10 years. Moreover, hospitalization rates for coronary stent insertion and hip and knee replacements rose sharply, as did many types of less extensive surgical procedures (Freid & Bernstein, 2010).

HEALTH TRENDS AT MIDLIFE

Despite their generally good health, many people in midlife, especially those with low SES, experience increasing health problems (Lachman, 2004) or are concerned about signs of potential decline. They may have less energy than in their youth and are likely to experience occasional or chronic pains and fatigue. The prevalence of physical limitations increases with age, from about 16 percent at ages 50–59, to almost 23 percent at the end of the 60s; and this effect is most marked for African Americans and women (Holmes, Powell-Griner, Lerthbridge-Cejku, & Heyman, 2009). Many adults can no longer stay awake late with ease. They are more likely to contract certain diseases, such as hypertension and diabetes, and they take longer to recover from illness or extreme exertion (Merrill & Verbrugge, 1999; Siegler, 1997).

A relatively simple question, "How are you?" can help alert physicians to quality of life issues that might affect health and health outcomes. Researchers have suggested that such questions be incorporated in all medical appointments for older adults.

Hahn et al., 2007

Hypertension (chronically high blood pressure) is an increasingly important concern from midlife on as a risk factor for cardiovascular disease and kidney disease. Almost 41 percent of adults aged 55–64 suffer from hypertension (Schoenborn & Heyman, 2009). People who consume more vegetable protein tend to have lower blood pressure (Elliott et al., 2006). Impatience and hostility increase the long-term risk of developing hypertension (Yan et al., 2003). Hypertension can be controlled through blood pressure screening, a low-salt diet, and medication.

hypertension
Chronically high blood pressure.

Hypertension is 60 percent more prevalent in Europe than in the United States and Canada (Wolf-Maier et al., 2003). The proportion of the world's population with high blood pressure is expected to increase from one-quarter to one-third by 2025, leading to a predicted epidemic of cardiovascular disease, which already is responsible for 30 percent of all deaths worldwide (Kearney et al., 2005).

In the United States, cancer has replaced heart disease as the leading cause of death between ages 45 and 64 (Miniño, Xu, & Kochanek, 2010). Overall, death rates have declined sharply since the 1970s for people in this age bracket, in large part because of improvements in treatment of heart attack patients (Hoyert, Arias, Smith, Murphy, & Kochanek, 2001; Rosamond et al., 1998). Chest pain is the most common symptom of a heart attack in both men and women, but women may experience other symptoms, such as back and jaw pain, nausea and vomiting, indigestion, difficult breathing, or palpitations (Patel, Rosengren, & Ekman, 2004).

The prevalence of **diabetes** doubled in the 1990s (Weinstein et al., 2004). The most common type, mature-onset (type 2) diabetes, typically develops after age 30 and becomes more prevalent with age. Unlike juvenile-onset (type 1), or insulin-dependent, diabetes, in which the level of blood sugar rises because the body does not produce enough insulin, in mature-onset diabetes glucose levels rise because the cells lose their ability to use the insulin the body produces. As a result, the body may try to compensate by producing too much insulin. People with mature-onset diabetes often do not realize they have it until they develop such serious complications as heart disease, stroke, blindness, kidney disease, or loss of limbs (American Diabetes Association, 1992).

diabetes
Disease in which the body does not produce or properly use *insulin*, a hormone that converts sugar, starches, and other foods into energy needed for daily life.

BEHAVIORAL INFLUENCES ON HEALTH

The behavioral patterns that young adults set will affect them in middle age and beyond. This includes such lifestyle factors as nutrition, smoking, alcohol and drug use, and physical activity. Many of these patterns are established during what is for most people a relatively healthy portion of the life span, and people may not feel the effects of an unhealthy lifestyle until years later.

What are the factors that can lead to problems in middle age and beyond? On average, Americans who smoke, are overweight, and have high blood pressure and high blood sugar have a life expectancy 4 years less than those who do not (Danaei et al., 2010). By the same token, people who do not smoke, who exercise regularly, drink alcohol in moderation, and eat plenty of fruits and vegetables have 4 times less risk of dying in midlife and old age (Khaw et al., 2008). Perhaps more important from a quality of life perspective, people who guard their health not only live longer but also have shorter periods of disability at the end of life (Vita, Terry, Hubert, & Fries, 1998).

Weight in particular seems to affect health. Even small changes in weight can make a big difference (Byers, 2006). Excess weight in middle age increases the risk of impaired health and death (Jee et al., 2006), even in healthy people (Yan et al., 2006) and for those who have never smoked (Adams et al., 2006). Weight also interacts with ethnicity, making some ethnic groups more likely to become overweight or obese. For example, when considering overweight, Hispanics have the highest prevalence rate at 84.2 percent, in comparison to non-Hispanic whites at 70.8 percent and non-Hispanic blacks at 76 percent. By contrast, when considering obesity, non-Hispanic blacks (52.9 percent) demonstrate the highest prevalence rate, with non-Hispanic whites (34.9 percent) and Hispanics (42 percent) at lower risk (Flegal et al., 2010).

Physical activity in midlife is an important protective factor, particularly given that declines in cardiovascular fitness are steep after age 45 (Jackson, Sui, Hébert, Church, & Blair, 2009). Physical activity can increase the chances of remaining mobile in old age (Patel et al., 2006), of avoiding weight gain (Lee, Djoussé, & Sesso, 2010), and of staying healthier longer (Jackson et al., 2009). Adults who engage in regular, moderate, or vigorous exercise are about 35 percent less likely to die in the next 8 years than those with a sedentary lifestyle. And those with cardiovascular risk factors, including smoking, diabetes, high blood pressure, and a history of coronary heart disease, benefit the most from being physically active (Richardson, Kriska, Lantz, & Hayward, 2004).

Unfortunately, only about a third of U.S. adults show good compliance with health recommendations, most notably with respect to suggested dietary guidelines (Wright, Hirsch, & Wang, 2009). Although adhering to a healthy lifestyle throughout life is ideal, changes later in life can reverse some of the damage. Middle-aged men and women who stop smoking reduce their risk of heart disease and stroke (AHA, 1995; Wannamethee, Shaper, Whincup, & Walker, 1995). And previously sedentary women can significantly increase fitness with as little as 72 minutes a week of exercise (Church, Earnest, Skinner, & Blair, 2007).

There are also indirect influences on health, such as socioeconomic status, race/ethnicity, and gender. Social relationships matter, too (Ryff, Singer, & Palmersheim, 2004). Loneliness in middle adulthood predicts declines in physical activity (Hawkley, Thisted, & Cacioppo, 2009). Another important influence is stress; the cumulative effects of stress on both physical and mental health often begin to appear in middle age (Aldwin & Levenson, 2001).

SOCIOECONOMIC STATUS AND HEALTH

Social inequalities continue to affect health in middle age (Marmot & Fuhrer, 2004). People with low socioeconomic status tend to have poorer health, shorter life expectancy, more activity limitations due to chronic disease, lower well-being, and more restricted access to health care than people with higher SES (Spiro, 2001). In the MIDUS study, low SES was linked with self-reported health status, overweight, and psychological well-being (Marmot & Fuhrer, 2004). In a follow-up study of 2,606 stroke patients, SES affected the likelihood of death independent of the severity of the stroke (Arrich, Lalouschek, & Müllner, 2005).

In part, the reasons for the connection between SES and health may be psychosocial. People with low SES tend to have more negative emotions and thoughts and live in more stressful environments (Gallo & Matthews, 2003). In addition, even when younger, they tend to engage in unhealthy behaviors at higher rates than do those with high SES (Stringhini et al., 2010). People with higher SES, by contrast, tend to have a greater sense of control over what happens to them as they age, They tend to choose healthier lifestyles and to seek medical attention and social support when they need it (Lachman & Firth, 2004; Marmot & Fuhrer, 2004; Whitbourne, 2001), and they tend to show higher compliance with lifestyle modifications recommended to improve health indices (Wright, Hirsch, & Yang, 2009). However, there are wide individual differences in health among low-SES adults. Protective influences include the quality of social relationships and the level of religious engagement from childhood on (Ryff, Singer, & Palmersheim, 2004). In past years, poverty has been highly associated with lack of health insurance and health care access, but passage of the Affordable Care Act may ameliorate this issue.

Research suggests that regular church attendance is related to decreases in the risk of death and increases in health. Some of these influences appear to be indirect—for example, those who attend church frequently are less likely to abuse alcohol and smoke—but others may be direct—those who attend church regularly show higher subjective well-being. In other words, they just plain feel better.

Koenig & Vaillant, 2009

RACE/ETHNICITY AND HEALTH

Even though racial and ethnic disparities have decreased in the United States since 1990, substantial differences persist (Bach et al., 2002; Keppel, Pearcy, & Wagener, 2002). In trying to determine the cause of these disparities, researchers have looked to the human genome. Research in this area has found distinctive variations in the DNA code among people of European, African, and Chinese ancestry (Hinds et al., 2005). These variations are linked to predispositions to various diseases, from cancer to obesity, and such data may ultimately open the way to targeted treatments of preventive measures.

Although genetics may offer some clues to differences in health as a function of race or ethnicity, by far the most research has focused on correlates of ethnicity, and how those might be related to differences in health. Poverty is most likely the largest single underlying factor in this link. People who live in poverty generally have poorer access to health care, more stressful lives, and are exposed to more potential toxins in their everyday environment. For African Americans, for example, poverty has been related to poor nutrition, substandard housing, and poor access to health care (Smedley & Smedley, 2005). Still, poverty cannot be the sole explanation because the death rate of middle-aged Hispanic Americans, who are also disproportionately poor, is lower than that of white Americans (Kochanek et al., 2004).

There are other differences between people of different ethnicities. From young adulthood throughout middle age, African Americans have higher overall death rates (Kochanek, Aksan, Knaach, & Rhines, 2004), higher incidence of hypertension (NCHS, 2009) and obesity, and poorer cardiovascular fitness (Office of Minority Health Centers for Disease Control, 2005). Perhaps these factors occur as a consequence of African Americans' lower likelihood of participating in regular, moderate physical activity (Lavie, Kuruyanka, Milani, Prasad, & Ventura, 2004; Office of Minority Health, Centers for Disease Control, 2005). Hispanic Americans, like African Americans, have a disproportionate incidence of stroke, liver disease, diabetes, HIV infection, homicide, and cancers of the cervix and stomach (Office of Minority Health, Centers for Disease Control, 2005). They are also much less likely, particularly if they are limited English proficient, to have health insurance and a regular source of health care (Martorell & Martorell, 2006). Not surprising, they are also less likely to be screened for cholesterol and for breast, cervical, and colorectal cancers, or to receive influence and pneumonia vaccines (Balluz, Okoro, & Strine, 2004).

checkpoint
can **you** . . .

- Describe the typical health status in middle age, and identify health concerns that become more prevalent at this time?
- Discuss behavioral, socioeconomic, and racial/ethnic factors in health and mortality at middle age?

Women's greater longevity has been attributed to genetic protection given by the second X chromosome (which men do not have) and, before menopause, to beneficial effects of the female hormone estrogen, particularly on cardiovascular health.

GENDER AND HEALTH

Which are healthier: women or men? We know that women have a higher life expectancy than men and lower death rates throughout life (Miniño, Heron, Murphy, & Kochanek, 2007). Women's greater longevity has been attributed to genetic protection given by the second X chromosome (which men do not have) and, before menopause, to beneficial effects of the female hormone estrogen, particularly on cardiovascular health (Rodin & Ickovics, 1990; USDHHS, 1992). However, psychosocial and cultural factors, such as men's greater propensity for risk-taking, also may play a part (Liebman, 1995; Schardt, 1995).

Despite their longer life, women are more likely than men to report being in fair or poor health, and they go to doctors or seek outpatient or emergency room care more often. Men are less likely to seek professional help for health problems, they have longer hospital stays, and their health problems are more likely to be chronic and life-threatening (Addis & Mahalik, 2003; Kroenke & Spitzer, 1998; NCHS, 2004; Rodin & Ickovics, 1990). According to the MIDUS survey, middle-aged women tend to report more specific symptoms and chronic conditions, and men are more likely to report alcohol or drug problems (Cleary, Zaborski, & Ayanian, 2004).

Women's greater tendency to seek medical care does not necessarily mean that they are in worse health than men, nor that they are imagining ailments or are preoccupied with illness. They may simply be more health-conscious. Women devote more effort to maintaining their health (Cleary, Zaborski, & Ayanian, 2004). Men may feel that admitting illness is not masculine, and seeking help means a loss of control (Addis & Mahalik, 2003). It may well be that the better care women take of themselves helps them live longer than men.

Even just an hour a day spent in moderate exercise such as walking, doing housework, or going on an easy bike ride can prevent unhealthy weight gain in women.

Public awareness of men's health issues has increased. The availability of impotence treatment and of screening tests for prostate cancer is bringing more men into doctor's offices. In a 40-year prospective cohort study of 5,820 middle-aged Japanese American men in Honolulu, 42 percent survived to age 85. Good grip strength together with avoidance of overweight, smoking, hypertension, and high blood sugar (which can lead to diabetes) increased the chances of long and healthy lives.

Meanwhile, as women's lifestyles have become more like men's, so—in some ways—have their health patterns. The gender gap in deaths from heart disease has narrowed primarily because heart attack rates in women have risen. Explanations for this increase rely in part on rising rates of obesity and diabetes in women, and in part on the tendency of doctors to assume heart disease is less likely in women, leading to a better focus on controlling risk factors in men (Towfighi, Zheng, & Ovbiagele, 2009; Vaccarino et al., 2009). This trend may help explain why the difference between women's and men's life expectancy shrank from 7.6 years in 1970 to 5.2 years in 2005 (Kung, Hoyert, Xu, & Murphy, 2007; NCHS, 2004).

Women are at increased risk after menopause, particularly for osteoporosis, breast cancer, and heart disease. With longer life spans, women in many developed countries now can expect to live half their adult lives after menopause. As a result, increasing attention is being paid to women's health issues at this time of life (Barrett-Connor et al., 2002).

Bone Loss and Osteoporosis In women, bone loss rapidly accelerates in the first 5 to 10 years after menopause as levels of estrogen, which helps in calcium absorption, fall. Extreme bone loss may lead to **osteoporosis** ("porous bones"), a condition in which the bones become thin and brittle as a result of calcium depletion. Common signs of osteoporosis are marked loss in height and a hunchbacked posture that results from compression and collapse of a weakened spinal column. In a

osteoporosis
Condition in which the bones become thin and brittle as a result of rapid calcium depletion.

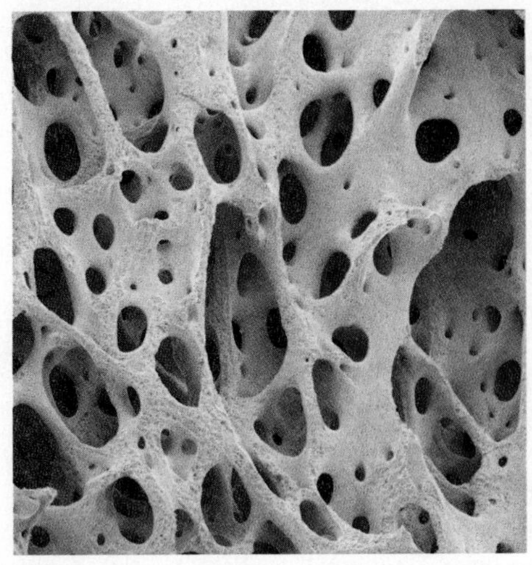
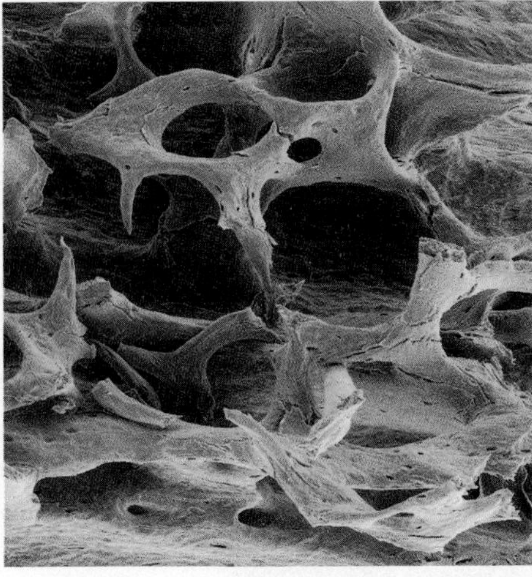

Images of normal (left) and osteoporotic (right) bones.

national observational study of more than 200,000 postmenopausal women, almost half had previously undetected low bone mineral density, and 7 percent of these women had osteoporosis (Siris et al., 2001). Osteoporosis is a major cause of broken bones in old age and can greatly affect quality of life and even survival (NIH, 2003; NIH Consensus Development Panel on Osteoporosis Prevention, Diagnosis, and Therapy, 2001).

Almost 3 out of 4 cases of osteoporosis occur in white women, most often in those with fair skin, small frame, low weight and BMI, and a family history of the condition, and those whose ovaries were surgically removed before menopause (NIH Consensus Development Panel, 2001; Siris et al., 2001). Other risk factors, besides age, include smoking and lack of exercise (Siris et al., 2001). A predisposition to osteoporosis seems to have a genetic basis, so measurement of bone density is an especially wise precaution for women with affected family members (Prockop, 1998; Uitterlinden et al., 1998). However, good lifestyle habits make a significant difference, especially if started early in life (NIH Consensus Development Panel, 2001).

Even if bone loss has started, it can be slowed or even reversed with proper nutrition, weight-bearing exercise, and avoidance of smoking (Barrett-Connor et al., 2002). High-intensity strength training and resistance training have proven particularly effective (Layne & Nelson, 1999). Women over age 40 should get 1,000 to 1,500 milligrams of dietary calcium a day, along with recommended daily amounts of vitamin D, which helps the body absorb calcium (NIA, 1993). Studies have found that calcium and vitamin D supplements improve bone density (Jackson et al., 2006).

Alendronate (Fosamax) and risedronate (Actonel) have been found to reduce hip fractures (Black et al., 2007). Raloxifene, one of a group of designer estrogens, seems to favorably affect bone density and possibly cholesterol levels and reduce the risk of genetic breast cancer (Barrett-Connor et al., 2002). A once-a-year intravenous infusion of zoledronic acid can reduce the risk of vertebral, hip, and other fractures (Black et al., 2007; Compston, 2007). Other FDA-approved medications for osteoporosis include teriparatide (Forteo) and calcitonin (Miacalcin or Calcimar). However, most of these drugs have side effects, and their long-term effects are unknown.

Breast Cancer and Mammography One in 8 American women and 1 in 9 British women develop breast cancer at some point in their lives (American Cancer Society, 2001; Pearson, 2002). As with other cancers, the chances of developing breast cancer increase with age (Barrett-Connor et al., 2002).

About 5 to 10 percent of breast cancer cases are thought to be hereditary, resulting from inherited mutations. The most common of these are mutations of the *BRCA1* and *BRCA2* genes. Women who have a *BRCA1* or *BRCA2* mutation have as much as an

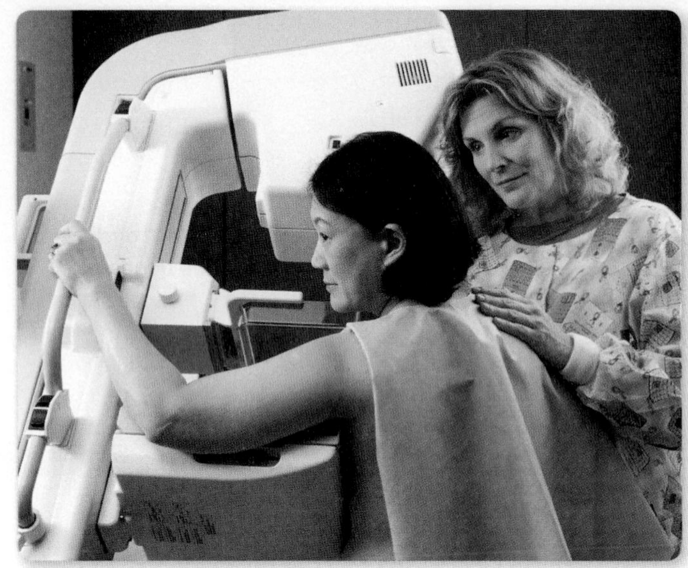

Routine mammography to screen for breast cancer is generally recommended for older women. If cancer is detected before it spreads, women have about a 98 percent chance of surviving at least 5 years after diagnosis.

80 percent chance of developing breast cancer (American Cancer Society, 2007).

However, the vast majority of breast cancer cases are environmentally influenced. Once found mostly in affluent countries, breast cancer is becoming a worldwide problem as Western lifestyles move into the developing world (Porter, 2008). Overweight women, those who drink alcohol, those who experienced early menarche and late menopause, those with a family history of breast cancer, and those who have no children or who bore children later in life have a greater risk of breast cancer, whereas those who are moderately physically active and eat low-fat, high-fiber diets are at less risk (ACS, 2007; McTiernan et al., 2003; U.S. Preventive Services Task Force, 2002). Weight gain, especially after menopause, increases a woman's risk of breast cancer, and weight loss decreases the risk (Eliassen, Colditz, Rosner, Willett, & Hankinson, 2006).

Advances in diagnosis and treatment have dramatically improved prospects for some breast cancer patients. Fully 98 percent of U.S. women with breast cancer now survive at least 5 years if the cancer is caught before it spreads (Ries et al., 2007). The benefits of **mammography,** diagnostic X-ray examination of the breasts, appear to be greatest for women over 50. In 2009, the United States Preventive Services Task Force issued a new set of guidelines recommending that women begin routine screening for breast cancer at 50, rather than at 40 years of age as had been previously suggested. Currently, however, government insurance programs are still covering mammograms for women ages 40 and older.

mammography
Diagnostic X-ray examination of the breasts.

Hormone Therapy The most troublesome physical effects of menopause are linked to reduced levels of estrogen, and **hormone therapy (HT)** has been used to address these effects. HT is treatment with artificial estrogen, sometimes in combination with progesterone, to help relieve symptoms of menopause. Estrogen taken alone increases the risk of uterine cancer, so women whose uterus has not been surgically removed are usually given estrogen in combination with progestin, a form of the female hormone progesterone. Now, however, medical evidence challenges some of HT's presumed benefits and bears out some suspected risks.

hormone therapy (HT)
Treatment with artificial estrogen, sometimes in combination with the hormone progesterone, to relieve or prevent symptoms caused by decline in estrogen levels after menopause.

On the positive side, HT, when started at menopause and continued for at least 5 years, can prevent or stop bone loss after menopause (Barrett-Connor et al., 2002; Lindsay, Gallagher, Kleerekoper, & Pickar, 2002) and can prevent hip and other bone fractures (Writing Group for the Women's Health Initiative Investigators, 2002). However, bone loss resumes within 3 years if and when HT stops (Heiss et al., 2008) and, as discussed, can be treated in safer ways.

Contrary to early correlational research, which suggested that HT cut the risk of heart disease (Davidson, 1995; Ettinger, Friedman, Bush, & Quesenberry, 1996; Grodstein, 1996), a large-scale randomized, controlled study found that hormone treatment either provides *no* cardiovascular benefit to high-risk women—those who already have heart disease or related conditions—or actually *increases* the risks (Grady et al., 2002; Hulley et al., 2002; Petitti, 2002). Then, the Women's Health Initiative (WHI), a large-scale randomized, controlled trial of estrogen plus progestin in healthy women was stopped after 5 years because of evidence that the risks of breast cancer, heart attack, stroke, and blood clots exceeded the benefits (NIH, 2005; Wassertheil-Smoller et al., 2003). The cardiovascular risks dropped back to normal within 3 years after the end of the trial (Heiss et al., 2008). However, age may make a difference. The results of the WHI study were driven mainly by effects on older women (Mendelsohn & Karas, 2007). Estrogen therapy does reduce clogging of the coronary arteries in women in their 50s who have recently gone through menopause (Manson et al., 2007).

Still, the American Heart Association now advises *against* HT, though the decision should, of course, be made in consultation with a physician (Mosca et al., 2001). Lifestyle changes such as losing weight and stopping smoking, together with any necessary drugs to lower cholesterol and blood pressure, appear to be wiser courses for heart disease prevention in most women (Manson & Martin, 2001).

Risks of breast cancer and other cancers *rose* slightly after the WHI treatment ended. In fact, the combined risk of all cancers increased throughout and after the trial (Heiss et al., 2008). Heightened risk of breast cancer seems to occur mainly among current or recent estrogen users, and the risk increases with length of use (Chen, Weiss, Newcomb, Barlow, & White, 2002; Willett, Colditz, & Stampfer, 2000). Long-term estrogen use also has been associated with heightened risk of ovarian cancer (Lacey et al., 2002; Rodriguez, Patel, Calle, Jacob, & Thun, 2001) and gallbladder disease (Cirillo et al., 2005).

Finally, studies have found, contrary to earlier research (Zandi et al., 2002), that estrogen—either alone or with progestin—does not improve cognition or prevent cognitive impairment after age 65. Instead, it *increases* the risk of dementia or cognitive decline (Espeland et al., 2004; Rapp et al., 2003; Shumaker et al., 2004). However, in a randomized 1-year study of 5,692 postmenopausal women in Australia, New Zealand, and the United Kingdom, HT improved health-related quality of life (Welton et al., 2008).

checkpoint
can you . . .

- Discuss changes in women's health risks after menopause, and weigh the risks and benefits of hormone replacement therapy?

STRESS IN MIDDLE AGE

Stress is the damage that occurs when perceived environmental demands, or **stressors,** exceed a person's capacity to cope with them. The body's capacity to adapt to stress involves the brain, which perceives danger (either real or imagined); the adrenal glands, which mobilize the body to fight it; and the immune system, which provides the defenses.

stress
Response to physical or psychological demands.

stressors
Perceived environmental demands that may produce stress.

People early in middle age tend to experience higher levels of stress and more frequent stress than other age groups. For example, in a nationally representative study (American Psychological Association, 2007), 39 percent of U.S. 35- to 55-year-olds reported extreme stress approximately 25 percent of the time. Younger adults (ages 18 to 34) and late middle-aged and older adults (age 55 and up) reported lower stress levels, with 29 percent and 25 percent, respectively, reporting high stress. Similar results were found in the MIDUS study, with middle-aged adults reporting more frequent, multiple, and severe stressors than older adults, as well as a greater degree of overload and disruption in their daily lives (Almeida, Serido, & McDonald, 2006).

People who chew gum on a regular basis report being less stressed.
Smith, 2009

The different age groups also vary on the sources of stress. Younger adults are more stressed by unhealthy behaviors, such as smoking, losing sleep, and skipping meals. Older adults tend to report stress as a response to issues related to health and aging. However, middle-aged adults report being most stressed by family relationships, work, money, and housing (American Psychological Association, 2007). Specifically, stress in middle age is more likely to come from role changes, career transitions, grown children leaving home, and the renegotiation of family relationships. Although the frequency of interpersonal tensions, such as arguments with spouses, decreases with age, stressors involving, for example, a sick friend or relative increase. Stressors posing financial risk or involving children exist at high levels in the middle-aged (Almeida et al., 2006).

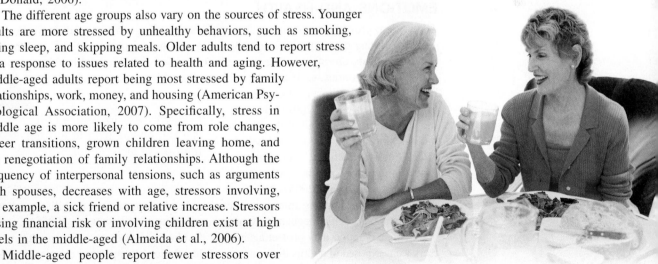

Women are likely to tend and befriend as a way of dealing with stress.

Middle-aged people report fewer stressors over which they have little or no control (Almeida & Horn, 2004), which may be due in part to middle-aged people being better equipped to cope with stress than those in

A positive outlook may guard against disease and buffer the impact of stress. People with a positive outlook tend to take care of their health.

other age groups (Lachman, 2004). They have a better sense of what they can do to change stressful circumstances and may be better able to accept what cannot be changed. They also have learned more effective strategies for avoiding or minimizing stress. For example, instead of having to worry about running out of gas on a long trip, they are likely to check to make sure the gas tank is full before starting out (Aldwin & Levenson, 2001).

What are the main sources of stress in your life? How do you handle stress? What methods have you found most successful?

Women tend to report more extreme stress than men (35 percent compared to 28 percent) and to be more concerned about stress (American Psychological Association, 2007). The classic stress response—*fight or flight*—may be more characteristic of men, activated in part by testosterone. Women's response pattern is typically *tend and befriend*—nurturant activities that promote safety, and reliance on social networks to exchange resources and responsibilities. These patterns, activated by oxytocin and other female reproductive hormones, may have evolved through natural selection and may draw on women's involvement in attachment and caregiving (Taylor, 2006).

EMOTIONS AND HEALTH

The ancient proverb of Solomon, "A merry heart doeth good like medicine" (Proverbs 17:22), is being borne out by contemporary research. Negative emotions, such as anxiety and despair, are often associated with poor physical and mental health, and positive emotions, such as hope, with good health and longer life (Ray, 2004; Salovey, Rothman, Detweiler, & Steward, 2000; Spiro, 2001). Because the brain interacts with all of the body's biological systems, feelings and beliefs affect bodily functions, including the functioning of the immune system (Ray, 2004; Richman et al., 2005). Negative moods seem to suppress immune functioning and increase susceptibility to illness; positive moods seem to enhance immune functioning (Salovey et al., 2000).

People who smile widely and more in photos tend to live longer than those who do not.

Abel & Kruger, 2010

Positive emotion may protect against the development of disease. When adult volunteers were exposed to a virus that can cause colds, those with a positive emotional outlook were less likely to get sick (Cohen, Doyle, Turner, Alper, & Skoner, 2003). In a study of patients in a large medical practice, two positive emotions—hope and curiosity—were found to lessen the likelihood of having or developing hypertension, diabetes, or respiratory tract infections (Richman et al., 2005).

However, we can't be sure that outcomes such as this are *caused* by the emotions shown. People with a positive emotional outlook are likely to engage in more healthful practices, such as regular sleep and exercise, and to pay more attention to health-related information. Positive emotions also may affect health indirectly by softening the impact of stressful life events (Cohen & Pressman, 2006; Richman et al., 2005).

Not only specific emotions but also personality traits seem to be related to health. In prospective studies, neuroticism and hostility are consistently associated with serious illness and reduced longevity, whereas optimism and conscientiousness are associated with better health and longer life (Kern & Friedman, 2008; Lahey, 2009; T. W. Smith, 2006). Optimism has been related to decreases in risk for coronary heart disease and mortality for postmenopausal women, whereas hostility has been related to the opposite pattern (Tindle et al., 2009). However, the underlying mechanisms have yet to be identified and tested (T. W. Smith, 2006).

checkpoint
can **you**...

- Explain how emotions and personality may affect health?
- Identify risk factors for psychological distress and depressive symptoms?

MENTAL HEALTH

Perhaps not surprising given the findings on higher levels of stress in middle-aged adults (American Psychological Association, 2007), middle-aged adults are also more likely to suffer from serious psychological distress (Pratt, Dey, & Cohen, 2007). For example, in a large national study of middle-aged women, 1 in 4 showed depressive symptoms, and their depression was associated with poor health, high stress, and lack of social support (Bromberger, Harlow, Avis, Kravitz, & Cordal, 2004). Indeed, adults with serious psychological distress are more likely than their peers to be diagnosed with heart disease, diabetes, arthritis, or stroke, and to report needing help with activities of daily living such as bathing and dressing (Pratt et al., 2007). In the following section, we address research on the link between stress and health.

TABLE 3 Stress from Life Changes, United States, 1967 and 2007

	LIFE CHANGE UNITS (LCUS)	
	1967	2007
Death of spouse	100	80
Death of family member	63	70
Divorce/separation	73/65	66
Job layoff or firing	47	62
Birth of child/pregnancy	40	60
Death of a friend	37	58
Marriage	50	50
Retirement	45	49
Marital reconciliation	45	48
Change job field	36	47
Child leaves home	29	43

Note: A comparison of First 30 Days findings and the Social Readjustment Rating Scale, Thomas H. Holmes and Richard H. Rahe, *Journal of Psychosomatic Research.* Stress levels from many life changes have increased. Because the study methods differ, findings should be interpreted as relative and directional.

Source: "First 30 Days," 2008.

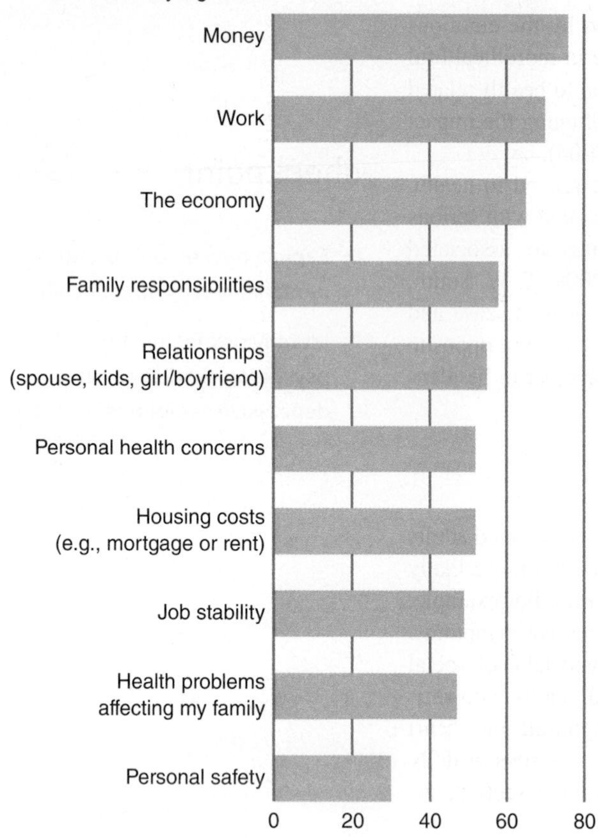

FIGURE 2

Significant Sources of Stress, United States, 2010

Work and money are greater stressors than relationships or health, a national survey found.

Source: American Psychological Association, 2011.

How Stress Affects Health How does stress produce illness? And why do some people handle stress better than others? The stress response system and the immune system are closely linked and work together to keep the body healthy. However, at times, especially during highly stressful events, the body may not be able to cope. For example, chronic stress can lead to persistent inflammation and disease (Miller & Blackwell, 2006). A propensity to respond in a negative fashion to stress may interact with genetic predispositions. So, even if similar stressors are experienced, some people respond more negatively than others. For example, a particular version of a serotonin transponder gene is associated with a higher likelihood of depression in the face of stress; a different version is associated with a more robust outcome (Caspi et al., 2003).

Research has shown a number of life events to be highly stressful, including divorce, the death of a spouse or other family member, or the loss of a job. It is clear that change in life—even positive change—can be stressful. The more stressful the changes that take place in a person's life, the greater likelihood of serious illness within the next year or 2 (Holmes & Rahe, 1976). Moreover, research shows that the stress of adjusting to such life events was 45 percent higher in 1997 than in 1967 (Miller and Rahe, 1997), and that it continues to increase ("First 30 Days," 2008; Table 3).

Generally, acute, or short-term, stress, such as the challenge of taking a test or speaking before an audience, strengthens the immune system (Segerstrom & Miller, 2004). We are adapted to dealing with such events, and our bodies quickly and efficiently respond and then recover from the event (Sapolsky, 1992). For example, the most common response to a highly traumatic event, such as the 9/11 attacks, is resilience (Bonanno, Galea, Bucciarelli, & Vlahov, 2006), particularly if people are buffered from stress by the presence of supportive social relationships (Bonanno, 2005). However, intense or prolonged stress, such as might result from poverty or disability, can weaken or break down the body, increasing the susceptibility to disease (Sapolsky, 1992; Segerstrom, & Miller, 2004). In support of this assertion, research has found suppressed immune function in breast cancer patients (Compas & Luecken, 2002), abused women, hurricane survivors, and men with a history of post-traumatic stress disorders (PTSD) (Harvard Medical School, 2002). Unsafe neighborhoods with poor-quality housing and few resources also may produce or worsen depression (Cutrona, Wallace, & Wesner, 2006).

We are affected not just by major life events but also by the daily hassles of life. Daily stressors such as irritations, frustrations, and overloads may be less severe in their impact than life changes, but their buildup can affect health and emotional adjustment (Almeida et al., 2006; American Psychological Association, 2011; Figure 2). This is of concern because stress has been increasingly implicated as a factor in such age-related diseases as hypertension, heart disease, stroke, diabetes, osteoporosis, peptic ulcers, depression, HIV/AIDS, and cancer (Baum, Cacioppo, Melamed, Gallant, & Travis, 1995; Cohen, Janicki-Deverts, & Miller, 2007; Levenstein, Ackerman, Kiecolt-Glaser, & Dubois, 1999; Light et al., 1999, Sapolsky, 1992; Wittstein et al., 2005).

In addition to its direct effects on our bodies, stress may harm us through other lifestyle factors. People under stress tend to sleep less, smoke and drink more, eat poorly, and pay too little attention to their health (American Psychological Association, 2007), even though regular exercise, good nutrition, at least 7 hours of sleep a night, and frequent socializing are associated with lower stress (Baum et al., 1995). People who believe they have control over their lives also tend to engage in healthier behaviors and have fewer illnesses and better physical functioning (Lachman & Firth, 2004).

checkpoint
can you . . .

- Discuss causes and effects of stress and sources of stress in middle age?
- Explain how stress affects health?

COGNITIVE DEVELOPMENT

What happens to cognitive abilities in middle age? Do they improve or decline, or both? Do people develop distinctive ways of thinking at this time of life? How does age affect the ability to solve problems, to learn, to create, and to perform on the job?

Measuring Cognitive Abilities in Middle Age

The status of cognitive abilities in middle age has been a subject of much debate. Studies using different methodologies and measuring different characteristics have had somewhat different findings. Here, we look at two important lines of research, K. Warner Schaie's Seattle Longitudinal Study and Horn and Cattell's studies of fluid and crystallized intelligence.

Good spellers seem to remain good at spelling as they age. Poor spellers, however, get worse.

Margolin & Abrams, 2007

SCHAIE: THE SEATTLE LONGITUDINAL STUDY

Cognitively speaking, in many respects middle-aged people are in their prime. The Seattle Longitudinal Study of Adult Intelligence, conducted by K. Warner Schaie and his colleagues (Schaie, 1990, 1994, 1996a, 1996b, 2005; Willis & Schaie, 1999, 2006), demonstrates this fact.

The study began in 1956 with 500 randomly chosen men and women across a variety of different age brackets ranging from 22 to 67 years of age. The participants were then followed longitudinally, and assessed every 7 years on timed tests of six primary mental abilities (Table 4 gives definitions and sample tasks for each ability).

Perspectives on Thinking and Memory

Recall that longitudinal studies follow one cohort of people over time, and thus it can be difficult to tell whether that particular cohort had different experiences than

TABLE 4 Tests of Primary Mental Abilities Given in Seattle Longitudinal Study of Adult Intelligence

Test	Ability Measured	Task	Type of Intelligence*
Verbal meaning	Recognition and understanding of words	Find synonym by matching stimulus word with another word from multiple-choice list	Crystallized
Word fluency	Retrieving words from long-term memory	Think of as many words as possible beginning with a given letter, in a set time period	Part crystallized, part fluid
Number	Performing computations	Do simple addition problems	Crystallized
Spatial orientation	Manipulating objects mentally in two-dimensional space	Select rotated examples of figure to match stimulus figure	Fluid
Inductive reasoning	Identifying patterns and inferring principles and rules for solving logical problems	Complete a letter series	Fluid
Perceptual speed	Making quick, accurate discriminations between visual stimuli	Identify matching and nonmatching images flashed on a computer screen	Fluid

*Fluid and crystallized intelligence are defined in the next section.

Sources: Schaie, 1989; Willis & Schaie, 1999.

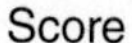

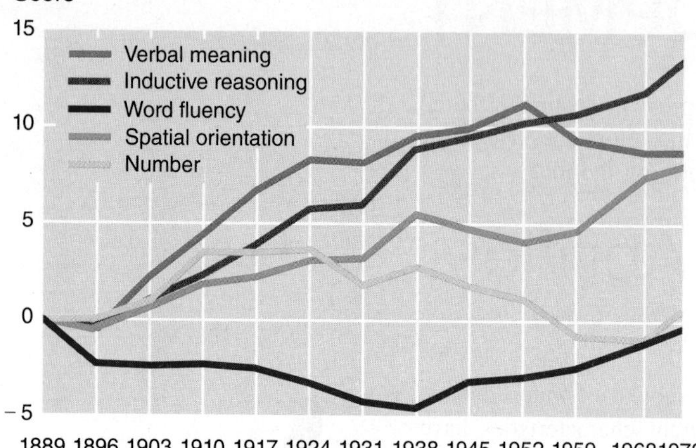

FIGURE 3

Cohort Differences in Scores on Tests of Primary Mental Abilities

More recent cohorts scored higher on inductive reasoning, word fluency, and spatial orientation.

Source: From K. W. Schaie, *Developmental Influences on Adult Intelligence: The Seattle Longitudinal Study* (2005), Fig. 6.1, p. 137. By permission of Oxford University Press, Inc.

other cohorts. If those experiences affected their development, then any changes seen might apply *only* to that cohort. By contrast, cross-sectional studies, which examine people of various ages at one point in time, have an analogous problem. Here it can be difficult to determine whether the variations seen across different ages are really due to developmental change. By using multiple cohorts—people of different ages, all followed over time—Schaie and his colleagues were able to tease apart the different influences and conduct more sophisticated analyses.

Most participants showed remarkable stability over time, and no significant reductions in most abilities until after age 60, and then not in most areas. Virtually no one declined on all fronts, and most people improved in some areas. However, there were wide individual differences. One participant might decline early, whereas another might show great plasticity.

Similarly, there were no uniform patterns of age-related change across cognitive abilities. For example, several abilities peaked during middle age, and verbal meaning even showed improvements into old age. By contrast, about 13 to 17 percent of adults declined in number, memory recall, or verbal fluency between ages 39 and 53 (Schaie, 1994, 2005; Willis & Schaie, 2006).

Schaie and his colleagues also found that successive cohorts scored progressively higher at the same ages on most abilities, possibly because of improvements in education, healthy lifestyles, and other positive environmental influences. However, numerical ability showed overall declines after the 1924 cohort, and verbal meaning declined after the 1952 cohort (Willis & Schaie, 2006; Figure 3).

Individuals who scored highest tended to have high educational levels, to have flexible personalities, to be in intact families, to pursue cognitively complex occupations and other activities, to be married to someone more cognitively advanced, to be satisfied with their accomplishments (Schaie, 1994, 2005; Willis & Schaie, 2006), and to be high in the personality dimension of openness to experience (Sharp, Reynolds, Pedersen, & Gatz, 2010). Given the strong cognitive performance of most middle-agers, evidence of substantial cognitive decline in persons younger than 60 may indicate a neurological problem (Schaie, 2005; Willis & Shaie, 1999). In particular, midlife decline in memory recall and verbal fluency, a measure of executive functioning, can predict cognitive impairment in old age (Willis & Schaie, 2006).

In another longitudinal study of 384 Baltimore adults age 50 and above, those with larger social networks better maintained their cognitive functioning 12 years later. It is not clear, however, whether more social contacts produce or merely reflect better cognitive functioning. If the former, the benefit may result from the wider variety of informational and interactional opportunities that a wide circle of friends and families provides (Holtzman et al., 2004).

Our growing knowledge about the brain's genetic aging may shed light on patterns of cognitive decline. Researchers who examined postmortem brain tissue from 30 people ages 26 to 106 identified two groups of genes that tend to become damaged with age. Among these were genes involved in learning and memory. Middle-aged brains showed the greatest variability, some exhibiting gene patterns much like those of young adults and others showing gene patterns more like older adults (Lu et al., 2004). This finding may help account for the wide range of individual differences in cognitive functioning in midlife.

HORN AND CATTELL: FLUID AND CRYSTALLIZED INTELLIGENCE

Imagine a glass of water. If you tilt it, the water sloshes around in random swirls and waves. By contrast, a block of ice has a rigid crystalline structure, with every molecule in its place. This is the metaphor used by another set of cognitive researchers (Cattell, 1965; Horn, 1967, 1968, 1970, 1982a, 1982b; Horn & Hofer, 1992) to describe the different types of intelligence. They distinguish between two aspects of intelligence: *fluid* and *crystallized*. **Fluid intelligence** is the ability to solve novel problems on the fly. Such problems require little or no previous knowledge, such as realizing that a hanger can be used to fix a leaky toilet, or discovering the pattern in a sequence of figures. It involves perceiving relations, forming concepts, and drawing inferences. These abilities are largely determined by neurological status. **Crystallized intelligence,** by contrast, is the ability to remember and use information acquired over a lifetime, such as finding a synonym for a word or solving a math problem. It is fixed, as is the structure of ice. Crystallized intelligence is measured by tests of vocabulary, general information, and responses to social situations and dilemmas—abilities that depend largely on education and cultural experience.

These two types of intelligence follow different paths. Typically, fluid intelligence has been found to peak in young adulthood. This is particularly true for perceptual speed, which peaks quite early, beginning in the 20s. Working memory capacity also declines with age. However, these changes are gradual and do not generally cause functional impairment (Lachman, 2004; Willis & Schaie, 1999), and regular exercise can slow this process (Singh-Manoux, Hillsdon, Brunner, & Marmot, 2005). Morever, the losses in fluid intelligence may be offset by improvements in crystallized intelligence, which increase through middle age and often until near the end of life (Horn, 1982a, 1982b; Horn & Donaldson, 1980).

fluid intelligence
Type of intelligence, proposed by Horn and Cattell, that is applied to novel problems and is relatively independent of educational and cultural influences.

crystallized intelligence
Type of intelligence, proposed by Horn and Cattell, involving the ability to remember and use learned information; it is largely dependent on education and culture.

checkpoint
can you . . .

- Summarize results of the Seattle Longitudinal Study?
- Distinguish between fluid and crystallized intelligence, and tell how they are affected by age?
- Compare the findings of the Seattle study with those of Horn and Cattell?

The Distinctiveness of Adult Cognition

Instead of measuring the same cognitive abilities at different ages, some developmental scientists look for distinctive qualities in the thinking of mature adults. Some, working within the psychometric tradition, claim that accumulated knowledge changes the way fluid intelligence operates. Others maintain that mature thought represents a new stage of cognitive development—a "special form of intelligence" (Sinnott, 1996, p. 361) that may underlie mature interpersonal skills and contribute to practical problem solving.

THE ROLE OF EXPERTISE

Two young resident physicians in a hospital radiology laboratory examine a chest X-ray. They study an unusual white blotch on the left side. "Looks like a large tumor," one of them says finally. The other nods. Just then, a longtime staff radiologist walks by and looks over their shoulders at the X-ray. "That patient has a collapsed lung and needs immediate surgery," he declares (Lesgold et al., 1988).

Why do mature adults show increasing competence in solving problems in their chosen fields? One answer seems to lie in *specialized knowledge,* or *expertise*—a form of crystallized intelligence that is related to the process of encapsulation.

The type of knowledge children accumulate—such as how to read, complete math problems, or understand metaphor—is fairly uniform. Most children learn similar things at roughly the same time. In adulthood, however, paths of learning diverge and adults become more or less learned in whatever domain of knowledge they pursue. Some may be experts in sports strategy, some in physics, others in legal issues. These advances in expertise continue at least through middle adulthood and, for the most part, are not

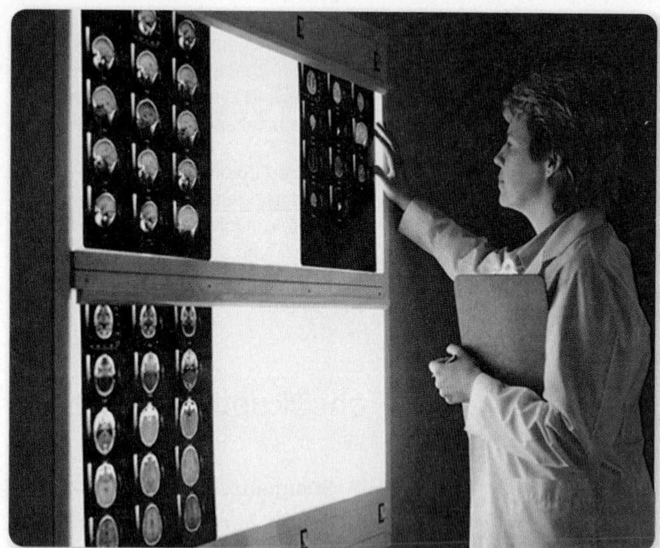

Expertise in interpreting X-rays, as in many other fields, depends on accumulated, specialized knowledge, which continues to increase with age. Experts often appear to be guided by intuition and cannot explain how they arrive at conclusions.

related to general intelligence. Moreover, they usually do not depend on the brain's information-processing machinery because some adults' fluid intelligence abilities become *encapsulated*—that is, dedicated to handling specific kinds of knowledge. In other words, it is as if they have bundles of linked information that work together when the area of expertise is needed. This process of **encapsulation** makes that knowledge easier to access, to add to, and to use. It may take middle-aged people longer than younger people to process *new* information. But when it comes to solving problems *within* their field of expertise, their encapsulated knowledge compensates and allows them to rapidly and effectively solve a problem (Hoyer & Rybash, 1994; Rybash, Hoyer, & Roodin, 1986).

In one classic study (Ceci & Liker, 1986), researchers identified 30 middle-aged and older men who were avid horse-racing fans. On the basis of skill in picking winners, the investigators divided the men into two groups: "expert" and "nonexpert." The experts used a more sophisticated method of reasoning, incorporating interpretations of much interrelated information, whereas nonexperts used simpler, less successful methods. Superior reasoning was not related to IQ; there was no significant difference in average measured intelligence between the two groups, and experts with lower IQs used more complex reasoning than nonexperts with higher IQs.

encapsulation
In Hoyer's terminology, the process that allows expertise to compensate for declines in information-processing ability by bundling relevant knowledge together.

Experts notice different aspects of a situation than novices do, and they process information and solve problems differently. Their thinking is often more flexible and adaptable. They assimilate and interpret new knowledge more efficiently by referring to a rich, highly organized storehouse of mental representations of what they already know. They sort information on the basis of underlying principles, rather than surface similarities and differences. And they are more aware of what they do *not* know (Charness & Schultetus, 1999; Goldman, Petrosino, & Cognition and Technology Group at Vanderbilt, 1999).

Studies of people in such diverse occupations as chess players, street vendors, abacus counters, physics experts, hospitality workers, airline counter workers, and airplane pilots illustrate how specific knowledge contributes to superior performance in a particular domain (Billet, 2001) and can help buffer age-related declines in cognitive resources when solving problems in that domain (Morrow, Menard, Stine-Morrow, Teller, & Bryant, 2001).

Cognitive performance is not the only ingredient of expertise. Problem solving occurs in a social context. Ability to make expert judgments depends on familiarity with the way things are done—with the expectations and demands of the job and the culture of the community or enterprise. Even concert pianists, who spend hours practicing in isolation, must adapt to various concert halls with different acoustics, to the musical conventions of the time and place, and to the musical tastes of their audiences (Billet, 2001).

If you needed surgery, would you rather go to a middle-aged doctor or one who is considerably older or younger? Why?

Expert thinking often seems automatic and intuitive. Experts generally are not fully aware of the thought processes that lie behind their decisions (Charness & Schultetus, 1999; Dreyfus, 1993-1994; Rybash et al., 1986). They cannot readily explain how they arrive at a conclusion or where a nonexpert has gone wrong. (The experienced radiologist could not see why the residents would even consider diagnosing a collapsed lung as a tumor.) Such intuitive, experience-based thinking is also characteristic of what has been called postformal thought.

INTEGRATIVE THOUGHT

Although not limited to any particular period of adulthood, postformal thought seems well suited to the complex tasks, multiple roles, and perplexing choices and challenges of midlife, such as the need to synthesize and balance work and family demands

(Sinnott, 2003). An important feature of postformal thought is its *integrative* nature. Mature adults integrate logic with intuition and emotion; they put together conflicting facts and ideas; and they compare new information with what they already know. They interpret what they read, see, or hear in terms of its meaning for them. Instead of accepting something at face value, they filter it through their life experience and previous learning.

In one study (C. Adams, 1991), early and late adolescents and middle-aged and older adults were asked to summarize a Sufi teaching tale. In the story, a stream was unable to cross a desert until a voice told it to let the wind carry it; the stream was dubious but finally agreed and was blown across. Adolescents recalled more details of the story than adults did, but their summaries were largely limited to repeating the story line. Adults, especially women, gave summaries that were rich in interpretation, integrating what was in the text with its psychological and metaphorical meaning for them, as in this response of a 39-year-old:

> I believe what this story was trying to say was that there are times when everyone needs help and must sometimes make changes to reach their goals. Some people may resist change for a long time until they realize that certain things are beyond their control and they need assistance. When this is finally achieved and they can accept help and trust from someone, they can master things even as large as a desert. (p. 333)

Society benefits from this integrative feature of adult thought. Generally, it is mature adults who translate their knowledge about the human condition into inspirational stories to which younger generations can turn for guidance.

checkpoint
can you . . .

- Discuss the relationship between expertise, knowledge, and intelligence?
- Give an example of integrative thinking?

Creativity

At about age 40, Frank Lloyd Wright designed Robie House in Chicago, Agnes deMille choreographed the Broadway musical *Carousel,* and Louis Pasteur developed the germ theory of disease. Charles Darwin was 50 when he presented his theory of evolution. Toni Morrison won the Pulitzer Prize for *Beloved,* a novel she wrote at about 55. Many creative people have reached their greatest achievements in middle age.

CHARACTERISTICS OF CREATIVE ACHIEVERS

Where does creativity come from? What are the characteristics of those who achieve highly creative work? Although a certain baseline general intelligence, or IQ, is needed (Guilford, 1956), creative performance is not strongly related to general intelligence (Simonton, 2000). Moreover, even though intelligence shows high heritability estimates (Plomin & Thompson, 1993), strong genetic contributions have not been found for creativity (Reuter, Roth, Holve, & Hennig, 2006). Whereas children often show strong creative potential, in adults what matters is creative performance—what, and how much, a creative mind produces (Sternberg & Lubart, 1995). So, if not intelligence, genetics, or childhood, how does creativity emerge?

Helen Mirren, long a highly respected, classically trained actress, reached the apex of her career at the age of 61, when she won the Academy Award for Best Actress for her portrayal of a proud, aging Queen Elizabeth II in the film The Queen.

Creativity seems to be the product of particular social contexts as well as individual proclivities. With respect to environment, creativity seems to develop from diverse experiences that weaken conventional constraints and challenging experiences that strengthen the ability to persevere and overcome obstacles (Sternberg & Lubart, 1995). The environment, in fact, need not be nurturing.

Individual differences also can make creativity more likely. For example, highly creative people are self-starters and risk-takers. They tend to be independent, nonconformist, unconventional, and flexible, and they are open to new ideas and experiences. Their thinking processes are often unconscious, leading to sudden moments of illumination (Simonton, 2000; Torrance, 1988). They look at problems more deeply and come up with solutions that do not occur to others (Sternberg & Horvath, 1998).

However, this is not enough. Creative people are not generally creative in all areas. Extraordinary creative achievement requires deep, highly organized knowledge of a subject, and a strong emotional attachment to the work, which spurs the creator to persevere in the face of obstacles. A person must first be thoroughly grounded in a field before she or he can see its limitations, envision radical departures, and develop a new and unique point of view (Keegan, 1996).

Think of an adult you know who is a creative achiever. To what combination of personal qualities and environmental forces would you attribute her or his creative performance?

CREATIVITY AND AGE

Is there a relationship between creative performance and age? On psychometric tests of divergent thinking, age differences consistently appear. Whether data are cross-sectional or longitudinal, scores peak, on average, around the late 30s. A similar age curve emerges when creativity is measured by variations in output (number of publications, paintings, or compositions). A person in the last decade of a creative career typically produces only about half as much as during the late 30s or early 40s, though somewhat more than in the 20s (Simonton, 1990).

However, the age curve varies depending on the field. Poets, mathematicians, and theoretical physicists tend to be most prolific in their late 20s or early 30s. Research psychologists reach a peak around age 40, followed by a moderate decline. Novelists, historians, and philosophers become increasingly productive through their late 40s or 50s and then level off. These patterns hold true across cultures and historical periods (Dixon & Hultsch, 1999; Simonton, 1990). Losses in productivity may be offset by gains in quality. A study of the swan songs of 172 composers found that their last works—usually fairly short and melodically simple—were among their richest, most important, and most successful (Simonton, 1989).

Research suggests that this decline in productivity may no longer be characteristic for newer cohorts of researchers.

Stroebe, 2010

checkpoint can **you** . . .

- Discuss prerequisites for creative achievement?
- Summarize the relationship between creative performance and age?

Work and Education

In industrialized societies, occupational roles typically are based on age. Young people are students; young and middle-aged adults are workers; older adults organize their lives around retirement and leisure. In postindustrial societies, people make multiple transitions throughout their adult lives (Czaja, 2006). College students take work-study programs or stop for a while before resuming their education. Emerging adults explore various avenues before settling into careers, and even then, their decisions may be open-ended. A person may have several careers in succession, each requiring additional education or training. Mature adults take evening classes or take time off work to pursue a special interest. People retire earlier or later than in the past, or not at all. Retirees devote time to study or to a new line of work, paid or unpaid.

We become more ambidextrous—using either hand rather than a dominant hand to perform functions—as we get older. Researchers suggest this may be tied to retirement. Generally, we intensify this dominance in everyday activities. Once retirement occurs and those activities change, so may our dominance.

Kalisch, Wilimzig, Kleibel, Tegenthoff, & Dinse, 2006

WORK VERSUS EARLY RETIREMENT

Before 1985, people retired earlier and earlier. The average age of retirement moved steadily downward. Since then, the trend has reversed. Before bringing their working lives to a complete stop, people may reduce work hours or days, gradually moving into retirement over a number of years. This practice is called *phased retirement.* Or they may switch to another company or a new line of work, a practice called *bridge employment* (Czaja, 2006). About half of workers ages 55 to 65 take a bridge job before moving to full retirement (Purcell, 2002).

What has brought about this change? People may continue working to maintain their physical and emotional health and their personal and social roles, or simply because they enjoy the stimulation of work, and their reasons may change at different times (Czaja, 2006; Sterns & Huyck, 2001). Others work primarily for financial reasons. The recession, as well as long-term labor trends in the United States, also seem to affect retirement age with a higher proportion of adults aged 55 to 64 now reporting they plan to delay retirement until age 66, and a full 16 percent saying they never plan to retire (Morin, 2009). Many of today's middle-aged and older workers have inadequate savings or pensions or need continued health insurance. The rise in the Social Security retirement age to 67 for full benefits offers an inducement to keep working. The Age Discrimination in Employment Act, which eliminated mandatory retirement ages for most occupations, and the Americans with Disabilities Act, which requires employers to make reasonable accommodations for workers with disabilities, have helped mature workers to keep their jobs. Furthermore, baby boomers, now nearing retirement age, are better educated than in previous generations, and their options therefore are wider (Czaja, 2006).

WORK AND COGNITIVE DEVELOPMENT

"Use it or lose it" applies to the mind as well as the body. Work can influence cognitive functioning.

Adults can affect their cognitive development by the occupational choices they make. For example, flexible thinkers tend to seek out and obtain substantively complex work—work that requires thought and independent judgment. In turn, complex work stimulates more flexible thinking, and flexible thinking then increases the ability to do such work (Kohn, 1980). Work need not necessarily be construed in the traditional way, and the same is true of men and women engaged in complex household work, such as planning a budget or a household move or making complicated repairs like putting in new plumbing (Caplan & Schooler, 2006). Regardless of the specifics, people who are deeply engaged in complex work tend to show stronger cognitive performance than their peers as they age (Avolio & Sosik, 1999; Kohn & Schooler, 1983; Schaie, 1984; Schooler, 1990).

Openness to experience—a personality variable—also affects cognitive performance over time (Sharp et al., 2010). People who are high on openness to experience are more likely to retain their faculties and show high work performance. Similarly, those people who consistently seek more stimulating opportunities are likely to remain mentally sharp (Avolio & Sosik, 1999).

This suggests that if work, both on the job and at home, could be made meaningful and challenging, more adults might retain or improve their cognitive abilities. This seems to be happening to some extent. The gains in cognitive abilities seen in older cohorts may well reflect workplace changes that emphasize self-managed, multifunctional teams and put a premium on adaptability, initiative, and decentralized decision making. Unfortunately, older workers are less likely than younger workers to be offered, or to volunteer for, training, education, and challenging job assignments, sometimes out of the mistaken belief that older people cannot handle such opportunities (Avolio & Sosik, 1999).

checkpoint can **you . . .**

- Discuss trends in work and retirement in middle age?
- Explain how work can affect cognitive functioning?

THE MATURE LEARNER

In 2005, 44 percent of U.S. adults, including 48 percent of 45- to 54-year-olds and 40 percent of 55- to 64-year-olds, reported having participated in adult education, 27 percent in work-related courses (National Center for Education Statistics, 2007; O'Donnell, 2006).

Why do middle-aged people engage in formal education? Education enables adults to develop their cognitive potential, improve their self-esteem, help their children with homework, or keep up with the changing world of work. Some seek specialized training to update their knowledge and skills. Some train for new occupations. Some want to move up the career ladder or to go into business for themselves. Some women who have devoted their young adult years to homemaking and parenting are taking their first steps toward reentering the job market. People close to retirement often want to expand their minds and skills to make more productive and interesting use of leisure. Some people simply enjoy learning and want to keep doing it throughout life.

From what you have seen, do students of nontraditional age seem to do better or worse in college than younger students? How would you explain your observation?

literacy
In an adult, ability to use printed and written information to function in society, achieve goals, and develop knowledge and potential.

Adult Education and Work Skills Changes in the workplace often entail a need for more training or education. Expanding technology and shifting job markets require a life-span approach to learning. Technological skills are increasingly necessary for success in the modern world and are a major component of work-related adult education. With experience, middle-aged people can perform computer-based tasks as well as young adults (Czaja, 2006).

Employers see benefits of workplace education in improved morale, increased quality of work, better teamwork and problem solving, and greater ability to cope with new technology and other changes in the workplace (Conference Board, 1999).

Literacy Training **Literacy** is a fundamental requisite for participation not only in the workplace but in all facets of a modern, information-driven society. Literate adults can use printed and written information to function in society, achieve their goals, and develop their knowledge and potential. At the turn of the century, a person with a fourth-grade education was considered literate; today, a high school diploma is barely adequate.

In 2003, the most recent year for which data are available, 14 percent of U.S. adults could not locate clearly identifiable information in brief English prose, 22 percent could not perform simple numerical operations such as addition, and 12 percent could not read documents well enough to succeed in today's economy—all components of basic literacy (NCES, 2006c). Also in 2003, U.S. adults performed worse on an international literacy test than adults in Bermuda, Canada, Norway, and Switzerland but better than those in Italy (Lemke et al., 2005; NCES, 2005b).

Middle-aged and older adults tend to have lower literacy levels than young adults, but the average literacy level of adults ages 50 to 59 has increased since 1992. Adults below basic literacy are less likely to be employed than adults at higher literacy levels (Kutner et al., 2007; NCES, 2006c).

Globally, 774 million adults—about 1 in 5—are illiterate, mostly in sub-Saharan Africa and East and South Asia (UNESCO, 2004, 2007). Illiteracy is especially common among women in developing nations, where education typically is considered unimportant for them. In 1990, the United Nations launched literacy programs in such developing countries as Bangladesh, Nepal, and Somalia (Linder, 1990). More recently, the UN named 2003 to 2012 the Literacy Decade and sponsored conferences and programs to promote literacy development. In the United States, the National Literacy Act requires the states to establish literacy training centers with federal funding assistance.

checkpoint can **you . . .**

- Give reasons why mature adults return to the classroom?
- Discuss the importance of literacy and literacy training in the United States and internationally?

summary and key terms

Middle Age: A Social Construct

- The concept of middle age is a social construct. It came into use in industrial societies as an increasing life span led to new roles at midlife.
- The span of middle adulthood is often subjective.
- Middle adulthood is a time of both gains and losses.
- Most middle-aged people are in good physical, cognitive, and emotional condition. They have heavy responsibilities and multiple roles and feel competent to handle them.
- Middle age is a time for taking stock and making decisions about the remaining years.

PHYSICAL DEVELOPMENT

Physical Changes

- Although some physiological changes result from aging and genetic makeup, behavior and lifestyle can affect their timing and extent.
- Most middle-aged adults compensate well for gradual, minor declines in sensory and psychomotor abilities. Losses in bone density and vital capacity are common.
- Symptoms of menopause and attitudes toward it may depend on cultural factors and natural changes of aging.
- Although men can continue to father children until late in life, many middle-aged men experience a decline in fertility and in frequency of orgasm.

- A large proportion of middle-aged men experience erectile dysfunction. Erectile dysfunction can have physical causes but also may be related to health, lifestyle, and emotional well-being.
- Sexual activity generally diminishes gradually in middle age.

presbyopia
myopia
presbycusis
basal metabolism
vital capacity
menopause
perimenopause
erectile dysfunction

Physical and Mental Health

- Most middle-aged people are healthy and have no functional limitations; however, baby boomers may be less healthy than previous generations at middle age.
- Hypertension is a major health problem beginning in midlife. Cancer has passed heart disease as the number one cause of death in midlife. The prevalence of diabetes has doubled, and it is now the fourth leading cause of death in this age group.
- Diet, exercise, alcohol use, and smoking affect present and future health. Preventive care is important.
- Low income is associated with poorer health, in part because of lack of insurance.
- Racial and ethnic disparities in health and health care have decreased but still persist.
- Postmenopausal women become more susceptible to heart disease as well as to bone loss leading to osteoporosis. Chances of developing breast cancer also increase with age, and routine mammography is recommended for women beginning at age 40.
- Mounting evidence suggests that the risks of hormone therapy outweigh its benefits.
- Stress occurs when the body's ability to cope is not equal to the demands on it. Stress is often greatest in middle age and can be related to a variety of practical problems. Severe stress can affect immune functioning.
- Role and career changes and other experiences typical of middle age can be stressful, but resilience is common.
- Personality and negative emotionality can affect health. Positive emotions tend to be associated with good health.
- Psychological distress becomes more prevalent in middle age.

hypertension
diabetes
osteoporosis
mammography
hormone therapy (HT)
stress
stressors

COGNITIVE DEVELOPMENT

Measuring Cognitive Abilities in Middle Age

- The Seattle Longitudinal Study found that several of the primary mental abilities remain strong during middle age, but there is great individual variability.
- Fluid intelligence declines earlier than crystallized intelligence.

fluid intelligence
crystallized intelligence

The Distinctiveness of Adult Cognition

- Some theorists propose that cognition takes distinctive forms at midlife. Advances in expertise, or specialized knowledge, have been attributed to encapsulation of fluid abilities within a person's chosen field.
- Postformal thought seems especially useful in situations calling for integrative thinking.

encapsulation

Creativity

- Creative performance depends on personal attributes and environmental forces.
- Creativity is not strongly related to intelligence.
- An age-related decline appears in both psychometric tests of divergent thinking and actual creative output, but peak ages for output vary by occupation. Losses in productivity with age may be offset by gains in quality.

Work and Education

- A shift away from early retirement and toward more flexible options is occurring.
- Complex work may improve cognitive flexibility.
- Many adults participate in educational activities, often to improve work-related skills and knowledge.
- Literacy training is an urgent need in the United States and globally.

literacy

chapter 16

Psychosocial Development in Middle Adulthood

outline

learning objectives

Discuss stability and change in development in middle adulthood.

Summarize personality development and psychological adjustment in middle age.

Identify some important aspects of close relationships in middle adulthood.

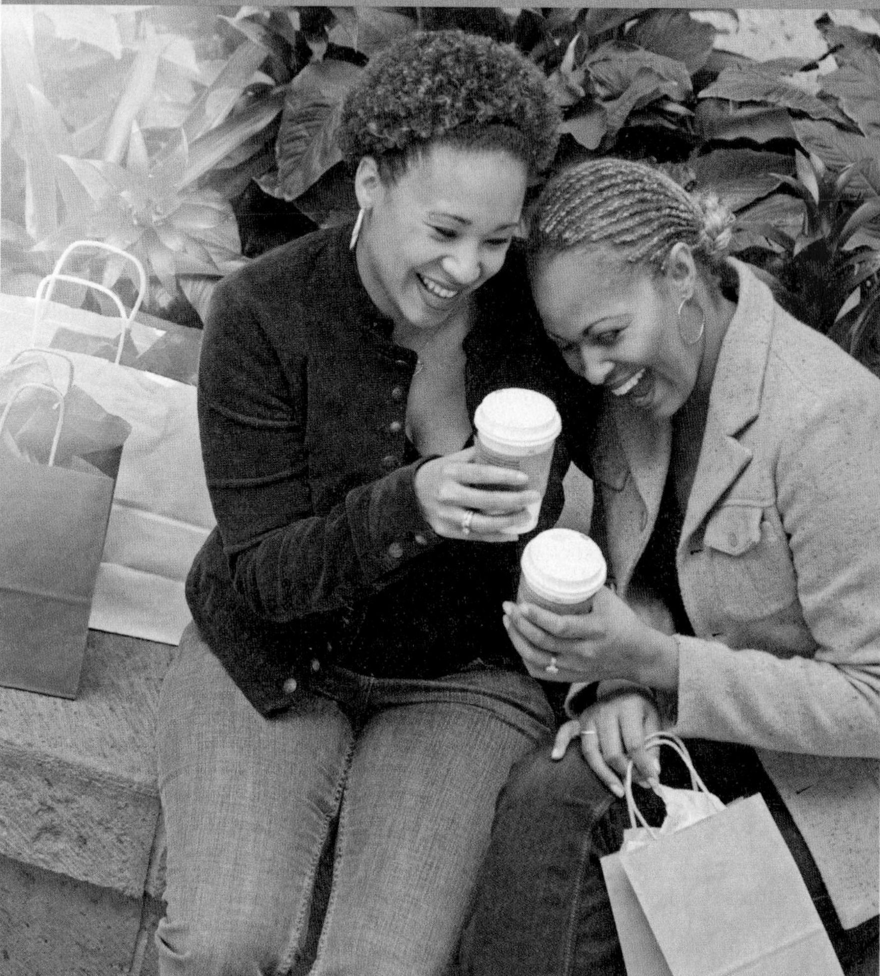

did you know?

- The idea of a midlife crisis has been largely discredited, and it is fairly unusual to have one?
- Marital satisfaction generally bottoms in early middle age and peaks when children are grown?
- With adequate support, caring for an infirm parent can be an opportunity for personal growth?

In this chapter we look at theoretical perspectives and research on psychosocial issues and themes at midlife. We then focus on intimate relationships: marriage, cohabitation, and divorce; gay and lesbian relationships; friendships; and relationships with maturing children, aging parents, siblings, and grandchildren. All these may be woven into the rich texture of the middle years.

One of the many things nobody ever tells you about middle age is that it's such a nice change from being young.

—William Feather

Looking at the Life Course in Middle Age

Developmental scientists view the course of midlife psychosocial development in several ways. *Objectively,* they look at trajectories or pathways, such as a once-traditional wife and mother's pursuit of a midlife career. *Subjectively,* they look at how people construct their identity and the structure of their lives (Moen & Wethington, 1999).

Development in the middle years must be seen in the perspective of the entire life span, but early patterns are not necessarily blueprints for later patterns (Lachman & James, 1997). And there are differences between early and late middle age. Just compare the typical concerns of a 40-year-old with those of a 60-year-old. Today, of course, it is hard to say what life course, if any, is typical. At 40, some people become parents for the first time, and others become grandparents. At 50, some people are starting new careers, and others are taking early retirement. Furthermore, lives do not progress in isolation. Individual pathways intersect with those of family members, friends, acquaintances, and strangers. Work and personal roles are interdependent, and those roles are affected by trends in the larger society.

Cohort, gender, ethnicity, culture, and socioeconomic status can profoundly affect the life course. (See Box 1 for a discussion about a society with no concept of middle age.) The path of a woman with a midlife career may be very different from that of her mother, who made her family her total life's work. This woman's course also may be different from that of an educated young woman today who embarks on a career before marriage and motherhood. Her path most likely would have been different, too, had she been a man, or had she been too poor or poorly educated to aspire to a career, or had she grown up in a highly traditional society. All these factors, and more, enter into the study of psychosocial development in middle adulthood.

checkpoint
can you . . .

- Distinguish between objective and subjective views of the life course?
- Identify factors that affect the life course in middle age?

Change at Midlife: Theoretical Approaches

In psychosocial terms, middle adulthood once was considered a relatively settled period. Freud (1906/1942), for example, believed personality is permanently formed well before that age.

In contrast, humanistic theorists such as Abraham Maslow and Carl Rogers saw middle age as an opportunity for positive change. According to Maslow (1968), the full realization of human potential, which he called *self-actualization,* can come only with maturity. Rogers (1961) held that full human functioning requires a constant, lifelong process of bringing the self in harmony with experience.

Longitudinal studies show that psychosocial development involves both stability and change (Franz, 1997; Helson, 1997). But what *types* of changes occur and what brings them about? Several theorists have sought to answer that question.

window on the world

1

A SOCIETY WITHOUT MIDDLE AGE

The Gusii are a rural society of more than 1 million people in southwestern Kenya (Levine, 1980; LeVine & LeVine, 1998). They have a *life plan,* a hierarchy of stages based largely on the achievement of reproductive capacity and its extension through the next generation.

The Gusii have no words for "adolescent," "young adult," or "middle-aged." A boy or girl is circumcised sometime between ages 9 and 11 and becomes an elder when his or her first child marries. Between these two events, a man is in the stage of omomura, or "warrior." The omomura stage may last anywhere from 25 to 40 years, or even longer. Because of the importance of marriage in a woman's life, women have an additional stage: omosubaati, or "young married woman."

Childbearing is not confined to early adulthood. As in other preindustrial societies, where many hands are needed to raise crops, and death in infancy or early childhood is common, fertility is highly valued. People continue to reproduce as long as they are physiologically able. The average woman bears 10 children. When a woman reaches menopause, her husband may take a younger wife and create another family.

In Gusii society, then, transitions depend on life events. Status is linked to circumcision, marriage (for women), having children, and, finally, becoming a parent of a married child and thus a prospective grandparent and respected elder. The Gusii have a *social clock,* a set of expectations for the ages at which these events should normally occur. People who marry late or do not marry at all, men who become impotent or sterile, and women who fail to conceive, have their first child late, bear no sons, or have few children are ridiculed and ostracized and may undergo rituals to correct the situation.

Although the Gusii have no recognized midlife transition, some of them do reassess their lives around the time they are old enough to be grandparents. Awareness of mortality and of waning physical powers, especially among women, may lead to a career as a ritual healer. The quest for spiritual powers has a generative purpose too: elders are responsible for ritually protecting their children and grandchildren from death or illness. Many older women who become ritual practitioners or witches seek power either to help people or to harm them, perhaps to compensate for their lack of personal and economic power in a male-dominated society.

Gusii society has undergone change, particularly since the 1970s, as a result of British colonial rule and its aftermath. With infant mortality curtailed, rapid population growth is straining the supply of food and other resources; and a life plan organized around maximizing reproduction is no longer adaptive. Growing acceptance of birth limitation among younger Gusii suggests that "conceptions of adult maturity less centered on fertility will eventually become dominant in the Gusii culture" (LeVine & LeVine, 1998, p. 207).

Given the current dramatic changes in Gusii society, would you expect shifts in the way the Gusii define life's stages? If so, in what direction?

TRAIT MODELS

Recall that the best known trait model of personality described the individual differences between people as consisting of five different factors: neuroticism, extraversion, openness to experience, conscientiousness, and agreeableness (Costa & McCrae, 1980). The research in this area originally claimed that these traits, known as the Big Five, were relatively continuous and were not believed to change in any appreciable way after the age of 30. More recent data suggests that slow change during the middle and older years is common (Costa & McCrae, 2006), and that significant positive changes during those years are possible (Roberts & Mroczek, 2008).

What specific changes have been noted? Conscientiousness—being deliberate, organized, and disciplined—tends to be highest in middle age (Donnellan & Lucas, 2008), perhaps as a consequence of work experience or because of increases in social maturity and emotional stability (Roberts & Mroczek, 2008). Individual life trajectories can affect this process as well. For example, compared to people who continue to work, retirees tend to increase in agreeableness—being straightforward, altruistic, and modest—and decrease in activity (Lockenhoff, Terracciano, & Costa, 2009). And middle-aged men who remarry in middle age tend to become less neurotic (Roberts & Mroczek, 2008).

Research across 55 nations has shown that sex differences in personality traits are larger in more prosperous nations where women have more equality. In such nations, women tend to report higher levels of neuroticism, extraversion, agreeableness, and conscientiousness than men.

Schmitt, Realo, Voracek, & Allik, 2008

The Big Five traits are related to actual, physical differences in brain structures of adults. For example, extraversion is correlated to the size of the medial orbitofrontal cortex—an area of the brain involved in processing rewards—and neuroticism is related to the volume of brain areas associated with threat and punishment. This supports a biologically based model of the Big Five.

DeYoung et al., 2010

NORMATIVE-STAGE MODELS

Two early normative-stage theorists whose work continues to provide a frame of reference for much developmental theory and research on middle adulthood are Carl G. Jung and Erik Erikson.

Carl G. Jung: Individuation and Transcendence The Swiss psychologist Carl Jung (1933, 1953, 1969, 1971) held that healthy midlife development calls for **individuation,** the emergence of the true self through balancing or integrating conflicting parts of the personality, including those parts that previously have been neglected. Until about age 40, said Jung, adults concentrate on obligations to family and society and develop aspects of personality that will help them reach external goals. Women emphasize expressiveness and nurturance; men are primarily oriented toward achievement. At midlife, people shift their preoccupation to their inner, spiritual selves. Both men and women seek a *union of opposites* by expressing their previously disowned aspects. In short, individuation involves combining the various conscious and unconscious aspects of the psyche into an integrated whole.

individuation
Jung's term for emergence of the true self through balancing or integration of conflicting parts of the personality.

Two necessary but difficult tasks of midlife are giving up the image of youth and acknowledging mortality. According to Jung (1966), the need to acknowledge mortality requires a search for meaning within the self. This inward turn may be unsettling. Yet people who avoid this transition and do not reorient their lives appropriately miss the chance for psychological growth.

Erik Erikson: Generativity versus Stagnation In contrast to Jung, who saw midlife as a time of turning inward, Erikson believed middle age was more characterized by an outward turn. As with all stages of the life span, there was a challenge to be faced, with both risks and positive outcomes possible. Erikson believed that the years around age 40 were a time when people entered their seventh normative stage: **generativity versus stagnation. Generativity,** as Erikson defined it, involved finding meaning through contributing to society and leaving a legacy for future generations. The virtue of this period is *care:* "a widening commitment to *take care* of the persons, the products and the ideas one has learned *to care for*" (Erikson, 1985, p. 67). People who do not find an outlet for generativity run the risk of becoming self-absorbed, self-indulgent, and stagnant. Adults who slide into stagnation may find themselves disconnected from their communities because of their failure to find a way to contribute.

study smart

Erikson's Stages of Psychosocial Development

generativity versus stagnation
Erikson's seventh stage of psychosocial development, in which the middle-aged adult develops a concern with establishing, guiding, and influencing the next generation or else experiences stagnation (a sense of inactivity or lifelessness).

generativity
Erikson's term for concern of mature adults for finding meaning through contributing to society and leaving a legacy for future generations.

Forms of Generativity What form does generativity take? What does it look like? For many adults, generativity is expressed through parenting and grandparenting. However, this is not the only path; generativity can derive from involvement in multiple roles (Staudinger & Bluck, 2001). It can be expressed through teaching or mentorship, productivity or creativity, and self-generation or self-development. It can extend to the world or work, to politics, to religion, to hobbies, to art, to music, and to other spheres; or as Erikson called it, "maintenance of the world." Regardless of its form, generativity tends

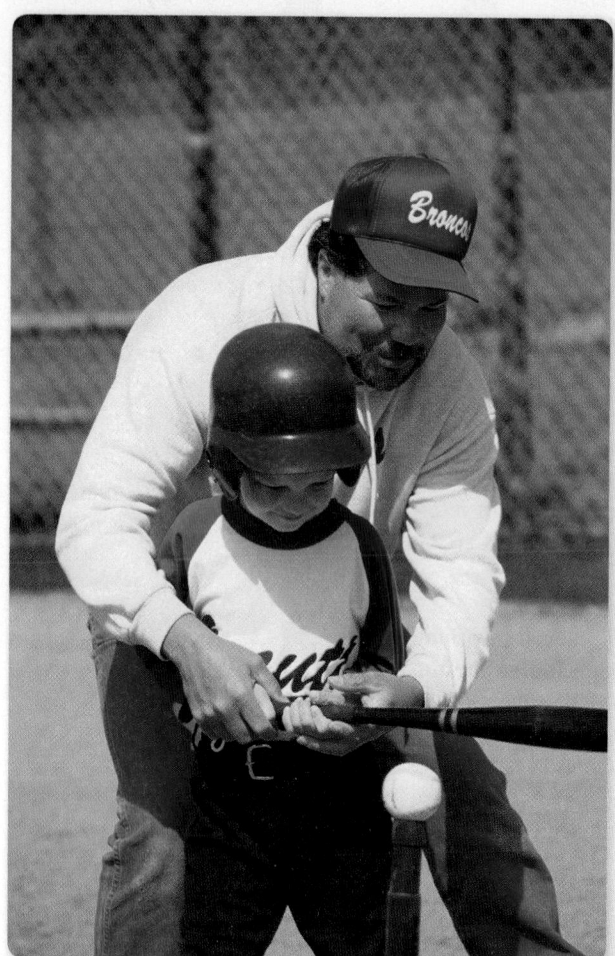

Generativity, a concern for guiding the younger generation, can be expressed through coaching or mentoring. Generativity may be a key to well-being in midlife.

to be associated with prosocial behavior (McAdams, 2006). So, for example, volunteering for community service or for a political cause is an expression of generativity (Hart, Southerland, & Atkins, 2003).

High levels of generativity are linked to positive outcomes. For example, highly generative people tend to report greater well-being and satisfaction in midlife (McAdams, 2001) and in later adulthood (Sheldon & Kasser, 2001), perhaps through the sense of having contributed meaningfully to society. The direction of effects, however, is unclear. Because such research is correlational, we cannot be sure that generativity causes well-being. It could be the case that those people who are happy with their lives are more likely to be generative (McAdams, 2001).

Generativity, Age, and Gender Why is generativity important during midlife? Erikson believed that generativity was especially salient during midlife because of the demands placed on adults through work and family. Research, using techniques such as behavior checklists and self-reports (Table 1), supports that middle-aged people do indeed score higher on generativity than younger and older ones. The age at which individuals achieve generativity varies, as does its strength at any particular time, and some people are more generative than others (Keyes & Ryff, 1998; McAdams, 2006; Steward & Vandewater, 1998). These variations in generativity affect the way people interact with others. For example, highly generative parents tend to be more involved in their children's schooling than those who are less generative, and they tend to have authoritative parenting styles (McAdams, 2006).

How does gender affect generativity? Early in adulthood, women report higher levels of generativity. However, this difference fades in late adulthood (Keyes & Ryff, 1998). Apparently, even those adults who enter midlife with low levels of generativity can catch up to their peers later (Whitbourne, Sneed, & Sayer, 2009). It may be that relief from primary family and work responsibilities frees middle-aged and older adults to express generativity on a broader scale (Keyes & Ryff, 1998). This finding underscores Erikson's assertion that positive change is possible at any point in the life span. Because of the centrality of generativity in middle age, we return to generativity later in this chapter.

interiority
Neugarten's term for a concern with inner life (introversion or introspection), which usually appears in middle age.

Jung's and Erikson's Legacy: Vaillant and Levinson Jung's and Erikson's ideas and observations inspired George Vaillant's (1977, 1989) and Daniel Levinson's (1978) longitudinal studies of men. Both described major midlife shifts—from occupational striving in the 30s to reevaluation and often drastic restructuring of lives in the 40s to mellowing and relative stability in the 50s.*

Vaillant, like Jung, reported a lessening of gender differentiation at midlife and a tendency for men to become more nurturant and expressive. Likewise, Levinson's men at midlife became less obsessed with personal achievement and more concerned with relationships; and they showed generativity by becoming mentors to younger people.

Vaillant echoed Jung's concept of turning inward. In the 40s, many of the men in his Grant Study of Harvard graduates abandoned the "compulsive, unreflective busy-work of their occupational apprenticeships and once more [became] explorers of the world within" (1977, p. 220). Bernice Neugarten (1977) noted a similar introspective tendency at midlife, which she called **interiority.** For Levinson's men, the transition to middle adulthood was stressful enough to be considered a crisis.

On the basis of your observations, do you believe that adults' personalities change significantly during middle age? If so, do such changes seem related to maturation, or do they accompany important events, such as divorce, occupational change, or grandparenthood?

*Levinson's description of the 50s was only projected.

TABLE 1 A Self-Report Test for Generativity

• I try to pass along the knowledge I have gained through my experiences.
• I do not feel that other people need me.
• I think I would like the work of a teacher.
• I feel as though I have made a difference to many people.
• I do not volunteer to work for a charity.
• I have made and created things that have had an impact on other people.
• I try to be creative in most things that I do.
• I think that I will be remembered for a long time after I die.
• I believe that society cannot be responsible for providing food and shelter for all homeless people.
• Others would say that I have made unique contributions to society.
• If I were unable to have children of my own, I would like to adopt children.
• I have important skills that I try to teach others.
• I feel that I have done nothing that will survive after I die.
• In general, my actions do not have a positive effect on others.
• I feel as though I have done nothing of worth to contribute to others.
• I have made many commitments to many different kinds of people, groups, and activities in my life.
• Other people say that I am a very productive person.
• I have a responsibility to improve the neighborhood in which I live.
• People come to me for advice.
• I feel as though my contributions will exist after I die.

Source: Copyright © 1992 by the American Psychological Association. Reproduced with permission. McAdams, D. P., & de St. Aubin, E. (1992). A theory of generativity and its assessment through self-report, behavioral acts, and narrative themes in autobiography. *Journal of Personality and Social Psychology,* 62(6), 1003–1015 (from the Appendix, p. 1015). No further reproduction or distribution is permitted without written permission from the American Psychological Association.

Vaillant (1993) also studied the relationship between generativity, age, and mental health. As his Harvard alumni approached and moved through middle age, an increasing proportion were rated as having achieved generativity. In their 50s, the best-adjusted men were the most generative (Soldz & Vaillant, 1998).

TIMING OF EVENTS: THE SOCIAL CLOCK

Every culture has a social clock describing the ages at which people are expected to reach certain milestones. In Western cultures, middle age often brings a restructuring of social roles. A parent may launch children from the family home or become a grandparent, change careers or jobs, or retire. Timing of events models suggest that development is more affected by when these events occur in a person's life than by a person's chronological age. In other words, what matters is not that a person turns 65 but that the person retires.

In previous generations, the occurrence and timing of major events in the social clock were fairly predictable. When occupational patterns were more stable and retirement at age 65 was almost universal, the meaning of work was more similar for all working adults nearing retirement age. Today lifestyles have become increasingly diverse, and the boundaries of middle adulthood have become blurred (Josselson, 2003). In a time of frequent job changes, downsizing, and either early or delayed retirement, the meaning of work is more variable. Similarly, when women's lives revolved around bearing and rearing children, the end of the reproductive years meant something different from what it means now when so many middle-aged women are part of the workforce. When people died at younger ages, those who survived into middle age were more likely to feel that they were reaching the end of their life. Today middle-aged people may be raising children, being parents to adolescents and young adults, or serving as caregivers to aging parents. They are likely to be busier and more involved in life than ever. Fortunately, despite the multiple challenges and variable events of midlife, most middle-aged adults seem well able to handle this life stage (Lachman, 2004).

Research suggests that people who are required to wear a uniform at work have lower morbidity than those who can wear what they choose. The researchers suggest that clothing is often an environmental cue to aging, and uniforms, because everyone must wear the same thing, removes that cue and thereby primes improved health.

Hsu, Chung, & Langer, 2010

checkpoint can **you**...

- Summarize important changes that occur at midlife, according to trait and normative-stage theory and research?
- Tell how historical and cultural changes have affected the social clock for middle age?

The Self at Midlife: Issues and Themes

"I'm a completely different person now from the one I was twenty years ago," said a 47-year-old architect as six friends, all in their 40s and 50s, nodded vigorously in agreement. Many people feel and observe personality change occurring at midlife. Whether we look at middle-aged people objectively, in terms of their outward behavior, or subjectively, in terms of how they describe themselves, certain issues and themes emerge. Is there such a thing as a midlife crisis? How does identity develop in middle age? Do men and women change in different ways? What contributes to psychological well-being? All of these questions revolve around the self.

IS THERE A MIDLIFE CRISIS?

The middle-aged man who impulsively buys an expensive sports car or the woman who suddenly leaves her job and home to travel to find herself are familiar stereotypes. Often, changes in personality and lifestyle such as these during the early to middle 40s are attributed to what has been called a **midlife crisis.** What brings it on is awareness of mortality (Jaques, 1967). At about this age, many people realize that they will not be able to fulfill the dreams of their youth, or that fulfillment of their dreams has not brought the satisfaction they expected, and they become more aware of their own mortality. The midlife crisis is a supposedly stressful period triggered by this review and reevaluation of one's life.

midlife crisis
In some normative-crisis models, stressful life period precipitated by the review and reevaluation of one's past, typically occurring in the early to middle 40s.

This midlife turmoil is an inevitable part of the struggle to restructure life at middle age (Levinson, 1996). However, the term *midlife crisis* is now considered an inaccurate representation of what most people experience in midlife. In fact, its occurrence seems to be fairly unusual (Aldwin & Levenson, 2001; Heckhausen, 2001; Lachman, 2004). Some middle-aged people may experience crisis or turmoil, but others feel at the peak of their powers. Still others may fall somewhere in between—with neither a peak nor a crisis—or may experience both crisis and competence at different times or in different domains of life (Lachman, 2004).

The onset of middle age may be stressful, but no more so than some events of young adulthood (Chiriboga, 1997; Wethington et al., 2004). Indeed, some researchers have proposed the occurrence of a *quarterlife crisis* in the mid-20s to early 30s, as emerging adults seek to settle into satisfying work and relationships (Lachman, 2004; Robbins & Wilner, 2001).

Apparently, midlife is just one of life's **turning points**—psychological transitions that involve significant change or transformation in the perceived meaning, purpose, or direction of a person's life. Turning points may be triggered by major life events, normative changes, or a new understanding of past experience, either positive or negative, and they may be stressful. However, in the MIDUS survey and a follow-up study of psychological turning points (PTP), many respondents reported positive growth from successful resolution of stressful situations (Wethington et al., 2004; Figure 1).

turning point
Psychological transitions that involve significant change or transformation in the perceived meaning, purpose, or direction of a person's life.

midlife review
Introspective examination that often occurs in middle age, leading to reappraisal and revision of values and priorities.

ego-resiliency
The ability to adapt flexibly and resourcefully to potential sources of stress.

identity process theory (IPT)
Whitbourne's theory of identity development based on processes of assimilation and accommodation.

identity schemas
Accumulated perceptions of the self shaped by incoming information from intimate relationships, work-related situations, and community and other experiences.

Turning points often involve an introspective review and reappraisal of values and priorities (Helson, 1997; Reid & Willis, 1999; Robinson, Rosenberg, & Farrell, 1999). The **midlife review** involves recognizing the finiteness of life and can be a time of stocktaking, discovering new insights about the self, and spurring midcourse corrections in the design and trajectory of one's life. However, it can also involve regret over failure to achieve a dream or a keener awareness of *developmental deadlines*—time constraints on, say, the ability to have a child or to make up with an estranged friend or family member (Heckhausen, 2001; Heckhausen, Wrosch, & Fleeson, 2001).

As far as you know, did one or both of your parents go through what appeared to be a midlife crisis? If you are middle-aged or older, did you go through such a crisis? If so, what issues made it a crisis? Did it seem more serious than transitions at other times of life?

Whether a turning point becomes a crisis may depend less on age than on individual circumstances and personal resources. People high in neuroticism are more likely to experience midlife crises (Lachman, 2004). People with **ego-resiliency**—the ability to adapt flexibly and resourcefully to potential sources of stress—and those who have a sense of mastery and control are more likely to navigate the midlife crossing successfully (Heckhausen, 2001; Klohnen, 1996; Lachman, 2004; Lachman & Firth, 2004). For people with resilient personalities, even negative events, such as an unwanted divorce, can become springboards for positive growth (Klohnen, 1996; Moen & Wethington, 1999). Table 2 outlines qualities considered most and least characteristic of ego-resilient adults.

IDENTITY DEVELOPMENT

Although Erikson defined identity formation as the main concern of adolescence, he noted that identity continues to develop. Indeed, some developmental scientists view the process of identity formation as the central issue of adulthood (McAdams & de St. Aubin, 1992). Let's look at theories and research on identity development, particularly in middle age.

Susan Krauss Whitbourne: Identity Processes According to the **identity process theory (IPT)** of Susan Krauss Whitbourne (1987, 1996; Jones, Whitbourne, & Skultety, 2006; Whitbourne & Connolly, 1999), identity is made up of accumulated perceptions of the self. Perceived physical characteristics, cognitive abilities, and personality traits ("I am sensitive" or "I am stubborn") are incorporated into **identity schemas.** These self-perceptions are continually confirmed or revised in response to incoming information, which can come from intimate relationships, work-related situations, community activities, and other experiences.

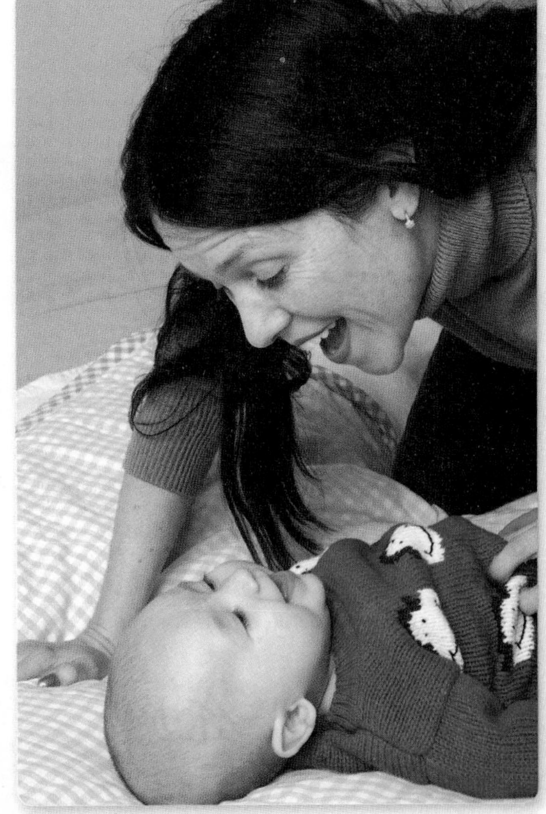

A midlife review might inspire a woman who senses her biological clock ticking to move forward on her wish to have a child.

Piaget described two processes involved in cognitive development that have been applied toward understanding identity development. *Assimilation,* according to Piaget, is the interpretation of new information

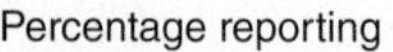

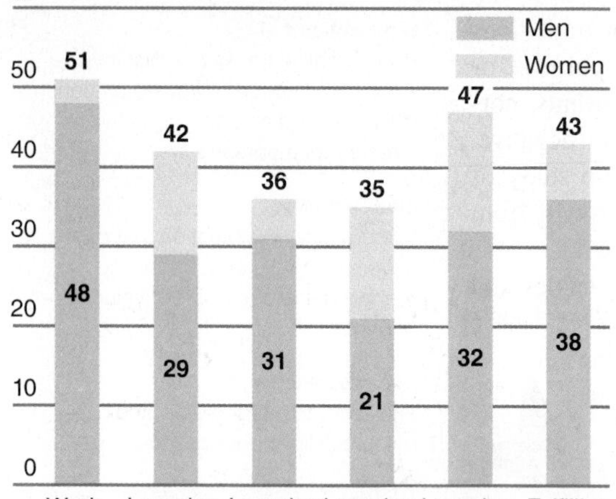

FIGURE 1

Turning Points Reported by 25- to 74-Year-Olds as Having Occurred in the Past 5 Years

Source: Wethington, E., Kessler, R. C., & Pixley, J. E. (2004). Turning points in adulthood. In O. G. Brim, C. D. Ryff, & R. C. Kessler, (Eds.), *How Healthy Are We? A National Study of Well-Being at Midlife*, Figure 3, p. 600. © 2004 by The University of Chicago. Reprinted by permission of The University of Chicago Press.

encountered in the environment via existing cognitive structures. It involves "fitting in" new information with what is already known. Sometimes, however, discrepancies are found between what is known and what is encountered; and this eventually leads to accommodation. *Accommodation* involves changing cognitive structures to more closely align with what is encountered. Piaget argued that these two complementary processes drive the development of new cognitive schemas, and analogous arguments can be made for identity schemas. **Identity assimilation** involves holding onto a consistent sense of self in the face of new experiences that do not fit the current understanding of the self. Contradictory or confusing information is absorbed without changing one's identity schema. **Identity accommodation,** in contrast, involves adjusting the identity schema to fit new experiences. Here discontinuity of the self is the result because identity accommodation involves changing the understanding of the self.

Ideally, people are able to achieve **identity balance** and maintain a stable sense of self while adjusting their self-schemas to incorporate new information, such as the effects of aging. People who achieve identity balance recognize changes and respond flexibly; they seek to control what can be controlled and accept what cannot. A strong stable identity helps people resist negative self-stereotyping, seek help when needed, and face the future without panic or undue anxiety (Jones et al., 2006).

Overuse of either assimilation or accommodation is unhealthy, according to Whitbourne and her colleagues. People who constantly assimilate are inflexible and do not learn from experience. They may seek, perhaps unrealistically, to maintain a youthful self-image and ignore what is going on in their body. This process of denial may make it harder for them to confront the reality of aging when it can no longer be ignored. By contrast, people who constantly accommodate are weak and highly vulnerable to criticism. Their identity is easily undermined.

TABLE 2 Characteristics of Ego-Resilient Adults

Most Characteristic	Most Uncharacteristic
Has insight into own motives and behavior	Has brittle ego-defense; maladaptive under stress
Has warmth; capacity for close relationships	Is self-defeating
Has social poise and presence	Is uncomfortable with uncertainty and complexities
Is productive; gets things done	Overreacts to minor frustrations; is irritable
Is calm, relaxed in manner	Denies unpleasant thoughts and experiences
Is skilled in social techniques of imaginary play	Does not vary roles; relates to all in same way
Is socially perceptive of interpersonal cues	Is basically anxious
Can see to the heart of important problems	Gives up and withdraws from frustration or adversity
Is genuinely dependable and responsible	Is emotionally bland
Responds to humor	Is vulnerable to real or fancied threat; fearful
Values own independence and autonomy	Tends to ruminate and have preoccupying thoughts
Tends to arouse liking and acceptance	Feels cheated and victimized by life
Initiates humor	Feels a lack of personal meaning in life

Note: These items are used as criteria for rating ego-resiliency, using the California Adult Q-Set.

Source: Adapted from Block, 1991, as reprinted in Klohnen, 1996.

They may overreact to early signs of aging, such as the first gray hair, and their pessimism may hasten physical and cognitive declines.

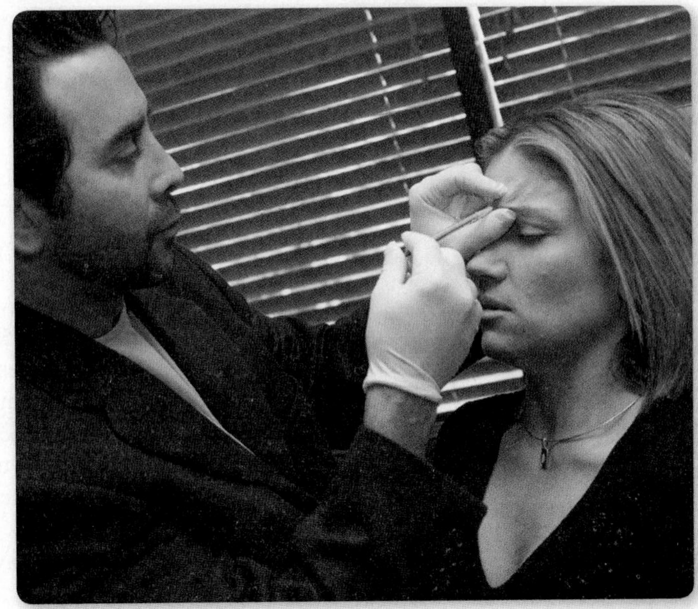

The popularity of regular Botox injections to temporarily smooth lines and wrinkles may express what Whitbourne calls an assimilative identity style.

Generativity and Identity Erikson saw generativity as an aspect of identity formation. Research supports this connection.

Among 40 middle-class, female bank employees in their early 40s who were mothers of school-age children, the women who had achieved identity were the most psychologically healthy. They also expressed the greatest degree of generativity, bearing out Erikson's view that successful achievement of identity paves the way for other tasks (DeHaan & MacDermid, 1994). In a cross-sectional study of 333 female, mostly white, University of Michigan graduates in their 60s, high levels of generativity went hand in hand with increased certainty about their identity and a sense of confidence in their powers (Zucker, Ostrove, & Stewart, 2002). In the Radcliffe class of 1984, women who had attained generativity at age 43, as measured by a Q-sort instrument, reported greater investment 10 years later in their cross-generational roles as daughter and mother and felt less burdened by the care of aging parents (Peterson, 2002). And, once established, generativity appears to pave the way for positive life outcomes. For example, in one study of middle-aged women, generativity predicted positive feelings about marriage and motherhood, and was related to successful aging (Peterson & Duncan, 2007).

identity assimilation
Whitbourne's term for effort to fit new experience into an existing self-concept.

identity accommodation
Whitbourne's term for adjusting the self-concept to fit new experience.

identity balance
Whitbourne's term for a tendency to balance assimilation and accommodation.

Narrative Psychology: Identity as a Life Story We all carry with us the story of who we are: how we came to be the person we are today, what shaped us over time and how, and who we wish to be in the future. The field of *narrative psychology* views the development of the self as a continuous process of constructing one's life story—a dramatic narrative, or personal myth, to help make sense of one's life and connect the past and present with the future (McAdams, 2006). This evolving story provides a person with a "narrative identity" (Singer, 2004). Indeed, some narrative psychologists view identity itself as this internalized *script* or story. People follow the script they have created as they act out their identity (McAdams, Diamond, de St. Aubin, & Mansfield, 1997). Midlife often is a time for revision of the life story (McAdams, 1993; Rosenberg, Rosenberg, & Farrell, 1999).

Studies in narrative psychology are based on a standardized 2-hour life-story interview. The participant is asked to think of his or her life as a book, to divide the book into chapters, and to recall eight key scenes, each of which includes a turning point. Research using this technique has found that people's scripts tend to reflect their personalities (McAdams, 2006).

Highly generative adults tend to construct *generativity scripts.* These scripts often feature a theme of *redemption,* or deliverance from suffering, and are associated with psychological well-being. In one such story, a nurse devotes herself to the care of a good friend during a fatal illness. Although devastated by her friend's death, she comes out of the experience with a renewed sense of confidence and determination to help others (McAdams, 2006).

Often the main characters in these redemptive stories enjoyed advantaged childhoods—a special talent, or a privileged home environment—but were deeply troubled by the suffering of others. This moral contrast inspired them to want to give back to society. As children and adolescents, they internalized a stable sense of moral values. As adults, they dedicate their lives to social improvement and do not swerve from that mission despite frustrating obstacles, which eventually have positive resolutions. They anticipate the future with optimism (McAdams, 2006).

checkpoint
can you . . .

- Compare the concepts of the midlife crisis and of turning points and discuss their relative prevalence?
- State typical concerns of the midlife transition and factors that affect how successfully people come through it?
- Summarize Whitbourne's identity process theory and tell how identity assimilation, identity accommodation, and identity balance differ, especially in response to signs of aging?

From what you have observed, do men seem to become less masculine and women less feminine at midlife?

gender crossover
Gutmann's term for reversal of gender roles after the end of active parenting.

checkpoint can you . . .

- Explain the connection between generativity and identity and discuss research on generativity and age?
- Explain the concept of identity as a life story, and how it relates to generativity?
- Compare Jung's and Gutmann's concepts of changes in gender identity at midlife, and assess their research support?

study smart

Multiple Dimensions of Well-Being

We get more nostalgic as we age. One of the consequences of this is it makes us more susceptible to advertisements that appeal to nostalgia and makes us more likely to purchase an item.

Kusumi, Matsuda, & Sugimori, 2010

Gender Identity and Gender Roles As Erikson observed, identity is closely tied to social roles and commitments ("I am a parent," "I am a teacher," "I am a citizen"). Changing roles and relationships at midlife may affect gender identity (Josselson, 2003).

In many studies during the 1960s, 1970s, and 1980s, middle-aged men were more open about feelings, more interested in intimate relationships, and more nurturing—characteristics traditionally labeled as feminine—than at earlier ages, whereas middle-aged women became more assertive, self-confident, and achievement-oriented, characteristics traditionally labeled as masculine (Cooper & Gutmann, 1987; Cytrynbaum et al., 1980; Helson & Moane, 1987; Huyck, 1990, 1999; Neugarten, 1968). Jung saw these changes as part of the process of individuation, or balancing the personality. The psychologist David Gutmann (1975, 1977, 1985, 1987) offers an explanation that goes further than Jung's.

Traditional gender roles, according to Gutmann, evolved to ensure the well-being of growing children: the mother must be the caregiver, the father the provider. Once active parenting is over, there is not just a balancing but a reversal of roles—a **gender crossover.** Men, now free to explore their previously repressed feminine side, become more passive; women, free to explore their masculine side, become more dominant and independent.

These changes may have been normative in the preliterate, agricultural societies Gutmann studied, which had distinct gender roles, but they are not necessarily universal (Franz, 1997). In U.S. society today, men's and women's roles are becoming less distinct. In an era in which most young women combine employment with child rearing, when many men take an active part in parenting, and when childbearing may not even begin until midlife, gender crossover in middle age seems less likely (Antonucci & Akiyama, 1997; Barnett, 1997; James & Lewkowicz, 1997). In fact, an analysis of longitudinal studies of men's and women's personality change during the life course found little support for the gender crossover hypothesis, or even for the idea that men and women change in different ways, or in ways related to their changing gender roles (Roberts et al., 2006a, 2006b).

PSYCHOLOGICAL WELL-BEING AND POSITIVE MENTAL HEALTH

Mental health is not just the absence of mental illness. *Positive* mental health involves a sense of psychological well-being, which goes hand in hand with a healthy sense of self (Keyes & Shapiro, 2004). This subjective sense of well-being, or happiness, is a person's evaluation of his or her life (Diener, 2000). How do developmental scientists measure well-being, and what factors affect well-being at midlife?

Emotionality, Personality, and Age Many studies, including the MIDUS survey, have found a gradual average decline in negative emotions through midlife and beyond, though women in the MIDUS study reported slightly more negative emotionality (such as anger, fear, and anxiety) at all ages than men (Mroczek, 2004). According to the MIDUS findings, positive emotionality (such as cheerfulness) increases, on average, among men but falls among women in middle age and then rises sharply for both sexes, but especially men, in late adulthood. The general trends in positive and negative emotionality seem to suggest that as people age they tend to have learned to accept what comes (Carstensen, Pasupathi, Mayr, & Nesselroade, 2000) and to regulate their emotions effectively (Lachman, 2004).

Middle-aged and younger adults in the MIDUS study showed greater individual variation in emotionality than older adults; however, the factors that affected emotionality differed. Only physical health had a consistent impact on emotionality in adults of all ages, but two other factors—marital status and education—had significant impacts in middle age. Married people at midlife tended to report more positive emotion and less negative emotion than unmarried people. People with higher education also reported more positive emotion and less negative emotion—but only when stress was controlled (Mroczek, 2004).

Subjective well-being (how happy a person feels) also is known to be related to dimensions of personality identified by the five-factor model. In particular, people who are emotionally stable (low in neuroticism), physically and socially active (high in extraversion), and highly conscientious tend to feel happiest (Weiss, Bates, & Luciano, 2008).

The Red Hat Society, whose members go to tea in red hats and purple dresses, began with a few women friends' decision to greet middle age with verve, humor, and élan.

Life Satisfaction and Age In numerous surveys worldwide using various techniques for assessing subjective well-being, most adults of all ages, both sexes, and all races report being satisfied with their lives (Myers, 2000; Myers & Diener, 1995, 1996; Walker, Skowronski, & Thompson, 2003). One reason for this general finding of life satisfaction is that the positive emotions associated with pleasant memories tend to persist, whereas the negative feelings associated with unpleasant memories fade. Most people have good coping skills (Walker et al., 2003). After either especially happy or distressing events, such as marriage or divorce, they generally adapt, and subjective well-being returns to, or close to, its previous level (Lucas et al., 2003; Diener, 2000).

Social support—friends and spouses—and religiosity are important contributors to life satisfaction (Csikszentmihalyi, 1999; Diener, 2000; Myers, 2000). So are certain personality dimensions—extraversion and conscientiousness (Mroczek & Spiro, 2005; Siegler & Brummett, 2000)—and the quality of work and leisure (Csikszentmihalyi, 1999; Diener, 2000; Myers, 2000).

Does life satisfaction change with age? Although a majority of older adults report rising levels of life satisfaction as they age, this is certainly not the case for every adult. Adults who report poor social relationships and a lack of a sense of control tend to report declines in life satisfaction (Rocke & Lachman, 2008). There are also developmental changes that can best be described as fitting a U-shaped curve. For example, in a 22-year longitudinal study of 1,927 men, life satisfaction gradually rose, peaked at age 65, and then slowly declined (Mroczek & Spiro, 2005). In another study done with Mills College alumnae, life satisfaction tended to peak in the latter part of middle age. Most of the Mills alumnae found their early 40s a time of turmoil but by the early 50s rated their quality of life as high (Helson & Wink, 1992).

Among a subsample of middle-aged MIDUS respondents, life satisfaction was strongly affected by physical health, a capacity for enjoying life, and positive feelings about the self (Markus, Ryaff, Curhan, & Palmershein, 2004). It is likely that how you feel about yourself affects how satisfied you are with your life. In one 16-year longitudinal study of more than 3,500 adults, self-esteem showed a path similar to that of life satisfaction, suggesting a link between the two. Self-esteem seems to increase until middle adulthood, peak at 60 years of age, and then decline. Although there were no cohort differences, African Americans showed greater declines in old age (Orth, Trzesniewski, & Robins, 2010).

Enhanced life satisfaction may be the outcome of a midlife review or revision—a search for balance through the pursuit of previously submerged desires and aspirations (Josselson, 2003). In the Radcliffe study previously mentioned, about two-thirds of the women made major life changes between ages 37 and 43. Women who had midlife regrets—many about educational or work options they had put aside to assume traditional family roles—and changed their lives accordingly, had greater well-being and better psychological adjustment in the late 40s than those who had regrets but did not make the desired changes (Stewart & Ostrove, 1998; Stewart & Vandewater, 1999).

Carol Ryff: Multiple Dimensions of Well-Being Within the discipline of psychology, a subjective sense of happiness is characterized as well-being. Although people generally have an overall sense of how happy they are, happiness is multidimensional,

study smart

Perspectives on Emotion

and people can be more or less pleased with various aspects of their life. How do we parse these various dimensions of well-being? Carol Ryff and colleagues developed a model that includes six dimensions of well-being referred to as the Ryff Well-Being Inventory (Keyes & Ryff, 1999; Ryff, 1995; Ryff & Keyes, 1995; Ryff & Singer, 1998). The first dimension of the model is *self-acceptance,* which involves a positive attitude toward the self that acknowledges both good and bad *qualities*. The second dimension is *positive relations with others*, warm, trusting relationships with others and an understanding of the dynamics of human relationships. The third dimension, *autonomy*, is about being independent and assured in interactions and beliefs. The fourth dimension is *environmental mastery*, the ability to manage the environment to achieve goals, perhaps by choosing or creating contexts to maximize opportunities. The fifth domain is *purpose in life*, having goals and a sense of directedness. Last is *personal growth,* a feeling of continued development and openness to new experiences. As described in Table 3, those who score higher on these dimensions may have a stronger sense of well-being than those who score lower.

TABLE 3 Definitions of Theory-Guided Dimensions of Well-Being

SELF-ACCEPTANCE
High scorer: maintains positive feelings about the self, integrating both positive and negative aspects of the multidimensional self; is satisfied with past life choices. *Low scorer:* is dissatisfied with the self and dislikes personal characteristics; would prefer to be different and is troubled and disappointed with past life choices.
POSITIVE RELATIONS WITH OTHERS
High scorer: has high quality, loving and trusting relationships with others; expresses empathy for others and concern with their welfare; appreciates the dynamic and interactive give and take that relationships require. *Low scorer:* is distant and mistrustful; shows little empathy or warmth toward others; tends to remain isolated and unhappy in relationships; unwilling to make compromises.
AUTONOMY
High scorer: is self-sufficient and independent; acts in accordance with personal standards and is not easily swayed by societal pressures; has internal regulation of behavior. *Low scorer:* worries about the opinions of others; looks to others for standards of behavior and guidance on important decisions; tends to conform.
ENVIRONMENTAL MASTERY
High scorer: feels confident in abilities and is capable of managing the environment; is able to effectively utilize emerging opportunities; uses personal needs as a guide in the creation or selection of contexts suitable for those needs. *Low scorer:* is ineffective at managing everyday responsibilities; feels helpless in the face of difficulty; fails to recognize available opportunities or potential changes that might improve situations; lacks a sense of personal control over events.
PURPOSE IN LIFE
High scorer: has articulated personal goals and has a sense of purpose in life; has beliefs, aims, and objectives that guide life choices; feels a sense of meaning that incorporates both past and present life. *Low scorer:* drifts through life without a clear sense of direction; lacks personal goals and sees little purpose to past life; feels as if life has little meaning.
PERSONAL GROWTH
High scorer: feels that the self is continually developing and expanding over time and has a sense of realizing his or her potential; is open to new experiences; believes that personal improvement of the self and behavior is ongoing; works to improve and expand self-knowledge. *Low scorer:* feels stuck in the present self and feels a sense of stagnation in the present life; fails to develop new attitudes or patterns of behavior; is apathetic and bored with life.

Source: Adapted from Keyes & Ryff, 1999, p. 163, Table 1.

A series of cross-sectional studies using Ryff's scale have shown midlife to be a period of generally positive mental health (Ryff & Singer, 1998). Middle-aged people expressed greater well-being than older and younger adults in some areas, though not in others. They were more autonomous than younger adults but somewhat less purposeful and less focused on personal growth—future-oriented dimensions that declined even more sharply in late adulthood. Environmental mastery, on the other hand, increased between middle and late adulthood. Self-acceptance was relatively stable for all age groups. Of course, because this research was cross-sectional, we do not know whether the differences were due to maturation, aging, or cohort factors. Overall, men's and women's well-being were quite similar, but women had more positive social relationships (Ryff & Singer, 1998).

When Ryff's scale was used to measure the psychological well-being of minority group members, the collective portrait replicated these age-related patterns. Still, black and Hispanic women scored lower than black and Hispanic men in several areas, revealing "a wider expanse of compromised well-being among ethnic/minority women of differing ages" (Ryff, Keyes, & Hughes, 2004, p. 417). However, when employment and marital status were controlled, minority status predicted positive well-being in several areas, even when education and perceived discrimination were accounted for. It may be that such factors as self-regard, mastery, and personal growth are strengthened by meeting the challenges of minority life (Ryff et al., 2004).

Research suggests that immigrants to the United States may be more physically and mentally healthy than those who have been here for two or more generations. One study, which assessed 312 first-generation Mexican American and Puerto Rican immigrants and 242 second-generation Puerto Ricans, found that resistance to assimilation promotes well-being in the immigrant generation, especially in the domains of autonomy, quality of relationships, and purpose in life. The researchers propose the term *ethnic conservatism* for this tendency to resist assimilation and cling to familiar values and practices that give meaning to life. Ethnic conservatism was less effective in promoting well-being among the second generation, who may find it harder or more psychologically conflicting to resist the pull of assimilation (Horton & Schweder, 2004).

checkpoint
can **you**...

- Explain the concept of positive mental health?
- Discuss age trends in emotionality, personality, life satisfaction, and psychological well-being?
- Explain the importance of a multifaceted measure of well-being, and name and describe the six dimensions in Ryff's model?

Relationships at Midlife

It is hard to generalize about the meaning of relationships in middle age today. Not only does that period cover a quarter-century of development; it also embraces a greater multiplicity of life paths than ever before (S. L. Brown, Bulanda, & Lee, 2005). For most middle-aged people, however, relationships with others are very important—perhaps in a different way than earlier in life.

THEORIES OF SOCIAL CONTACT

How do we describe the nature of our social relationships across time? According to **social convoy theory**, people move through life surrounded by *social convoys:* circles of close friends and family members of varying degrees of closeness, on whom they can rely for assistance, well-being, and social support, and to whom they in turn also offer care, concern, and support (Antonucci & Akiyama, 1997; Kahn & Antonucci, 1980). Characteristics of the person (gender, race, religion, age, education, and marital status) together with characteristics of that person's situation (role expectations, life events, financial stress, daily hassles, demands, and resources) influence the size and composition of the convoy, or support network; the amount and kinds of social support a person receives; and the satisfaction derived from this

social convoy theory
Theory, proposed by Kahn and Antonucci, that people move through life surrounded by concentric circles of intimate relationships on which they rely for assistance, well-being, and social support.

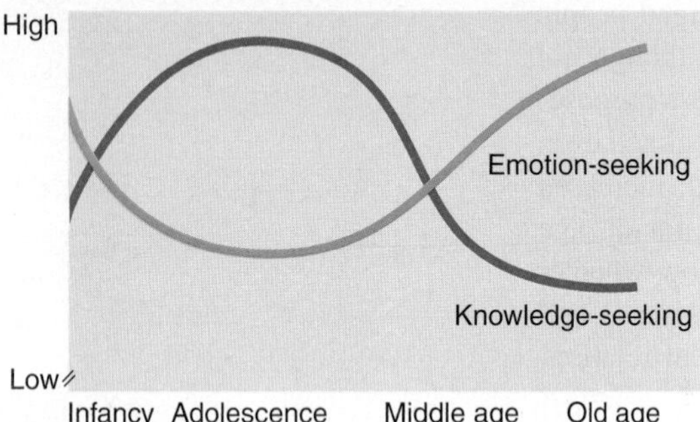

FIGURE 2

How Motives for Social Contact Change across the Life Span

According to socioemotional selectivity theory, infants seek social contact primarily for emotional comfort. In adolescence and young adulthood, people tend to be most interested in seeking information from others. From middle age on, emotional needs increasingly predominate.

Source: Adapted from Carstensen, Gross, & Fung, 1997.

support. All of these factors contribute to health and well-being (Antonucci, Akiyama, & Merline, 2001).

Although convoys usually show long-term stability, their composition can change. At one time, bonds with siblings may be more significant; at another time, ties with friends (Paul, 1997). Middle-aged people in industrialized countries tend to have the largest convoys because they are likely to be married, to have children, to have living parents, and to be in the workforce unless they have retired early (Antonucci et al., 2001). Women's convoys, particularly the inner circle, tend to be larger than men's (Antonucci & Akiyama, 1997).

Laura Carstensen's (1991, 1995, 1996; Carstensen, Isaacowitz, & Charles, 1999) **socioemotional selectivity theory** offers a life-span perspective on how people choose with whom to spend their time. In this approach, it is assumed that we select our friends based on their ability to meet our goals. According to Carstensen, social interaction has three main goals: (1) it is a source of information; (2) it helps people develop and maintain a sense of self; and (3) it is a source of pleasure and comfort, or emotional well-being. In infancy, the third goal, the need for emotional support, is paramount. From childhood through young adulthood, information-seeking comes to the fore. As young people strive to learn about their society and their place in it, strangers may well be the best sources of knowledge. By middle age, although information-seeking remains important (Fung, Carstensen, & Lang, 2001), the original, emotion-regulating function of social contacts begins to reassert itself. In other words, middle-aged people increasingly seek out others who make them feel good (Figure 2).

socioemotional selectivity theory Theory, proposed by Carstensen, that people select social contacts on the basis of the changing relative importance of social interaction as a source of information, as an aid in developing and maintaining a self-concept, and as a source of emotional well-being.

RELATIONSHIPS, GENDER, AND QUALITY OF LIFE

For most middle-aged adults, relationships are the most important key to well-being (Markus et al., 2004). They can be a major source of health and satisfaction (Lachman, 2004). Indeed, having a partner and being in good health are the biggest factors in well-being for women in their 50s, according to two national surveys. Having or not having children made little difference. Least happy, loneliest, and most depressed were mothers who were single, divorced, or widowed (Koropeckyj-Cox, Pienta, & Brown, 2007).

However, relationships also can present stressful demands (Lachman, 2004), which tend to fall most heavily on women. A sense of responsibility and concern for others may impair a woman's well-being when problems or misfortunes beset her mate, children, parents, friends, or coworkers. This vicarious stress may help explain why middle-aged women are especially susceptible to depression and other mental health problems and why, as we will see, they tend to be unhappier with their marriages than are men (Antonucci & Akiyama, 1997; S. P. Thomas, 1997).

In studying midlife social relationships, then, we need to keep in mind that their effects can be both positive and negative. In the remaining sections of this chapter, we examine how intimate relationships develop during the middle years. We look first at relationships with spouses, cohabiting partners, homosexual partners, and friends; next at bonds with maturing children; and then at ties with aging parents, siblings, and grandchildren.

checkpoint can **you**...

- Summarize two theoretical models of the selection of social contacts?
- Discuss how relationships can affect quality of life in middle adulthood?

Consensual Relationships

Marriages, cohabitations, homosexual unions, and friendships typically involve two people of the same generation who mutually choose each other. How do these relationships fare in middle age?

MARRIAGE

Midlife marriage is very different from what it used to be. When life expectancies were shorter, couples who remained together for 25, 30, or 40 years were rare. The most common pattern was for marriages to be broken by death and for survivors to remarry. People had many children and expected them to live at home until they married. It was unusual for a middle-aged husband and wife to be alone together. Today, more marriages end in divorce, but couples who stay together can often look forward to 20 or more years of married life after the last child leaves home.

What happens to the quality of a longtime marriage? An analysis of two surveys of 8,929 men and women in first marriages found a U-shaped curve. During the first 20 to 24 years of marriage, the longer a couple had been married, the less satisfied they tended to be. Then the association between marital satisfaction and length of marriage begins to turn positive. At 35 to 44 years of marriage, a couple tends to be even more satisfied than during the first 4 years (Orbuch, House, Mero, & Webster, 1996).

Marital satisfaction generally hits bottom early in middle age, when many couples have teenage children and are heavily involved in careers. Satisfaction usually reaches a height when children are grown; many people are retired or entering retirement, and a lifetime accumulation of assets helps ease financial worries (Orbuch et al., 1996). On the other hand, these changes may produce new pressures and challenges (Antonucci et al., 2001).

Sexual satisfaction affects marital satisfaction and stability, according to a longitudinal study of 283 married couples. Those who were satisfied with their sex lives tended to be satisfied with their marriages, and better marital quality led to longer marriages for both men and women (Yeh, Lorenz, Wickrama, Conger, & Elder, 2006).

Some research suggests that people married for 25 years or more begin to look like each other. Certainly diet and lifestyle may play a role, but researchers think it has more to do with empathy. Long-term couples mirror each other's facial expressions, and over time, their wrinkles set into similar grooves.

Zajonc et al., 1987

How many longtime happily married couples do you know? Can you tell whether their marriages followed patterns similar to those mentioned in this section?

COHABITATION

Although cohabitation has increased greatly in the United States, it is only half as common in midlife as in young adulthood (Blieszner & Roberto, 2006). With the aging of the baby boom generation, however, it is becoming more common (S. L. Brown et al., 2005).

Do cohabitants reap the same rewards as married people? Although there is little research on cohabitation among middle-aged and older people, one study suggests that the answer, at least for men, is no. Among 18,598 Americans over age 50, cohabiting men (but not cohabiting women) were more likely to be depressed than their married counterparts, even when such variables as physical health, social support, and economic resources were controlled. Indeed, cohabiting men were about as likely to be depressed as men without partners. It may be that men and women view their relationships differently. Women, like men, may want an intimate companion but may be able to enjoy that companionship without the commitment of formal marriage—a commitment that, in middle age, may come to mean the possibility of having to care for an infirm husband. Aging men, by the same token, may need or anticipate needing the kind of care that wives traditionally provide and may worry about not getting it (S. L. Brown et al., 2005).

Former Vice-President Gore and his wife Tipper divorced in 2010 after 40 years of marriage. Although many people were shocked by this, it's not that unusual. The lifetime risk for couples in their age range hovers just under 50 percent.

DIVORCE

Although divorce in midlife is more common than in the past (Aldwin & Levenson, 2001; Blieszner & Roberto, 2006), the break-up can still be traumatic. In an American Association of Retired Persons (AARP) survey of men and women who had been divorced at least once in their 40s, 50s, or 60s, most respondents described the experience as more emotionally devastating than losing a job and about as devastating as a major illness, though less devastating than a spouse's death. Midlife divorce seems especially hard for women, who are more negatively affected by divorce at any age than men are (Marks & Lambert, 1998; Montenegro, 2004). Marital loss is associated with an elevated chance of chronic health conditions in both sexes, perhaps driven by the disruption and stress such a loss entails (Hughes & Waite, 2009). Luckily, most middle-aged divorced people bounce back eventually. On average, the AARP respondents rated their outlook on life as highly as does the general over-45 population and higher than that of singles in their age group. Three out of 4 said that ending their marriage was the right decision. About 1 out of 3 (32 percent) had remarried—6 percent to their former spouses—and their outlook was better than that of those who had not remarried (Montenegro, 2004).

marital capital
Financial and emotional benefits built up during a long-standing marriage, which tend to hold a couple together.

Long-standing marriages may be less likely to break up than more recent ones. Why might this be the case? One possible explanation lies with the concept of **marital capital.** The longer a couple is married, the more likely they are to have built up joint financial assets, to share the same friends, to go through important experiences together, and to get used to the emotional benefits that marriage can provide. This accumulated "capital" can be difficult to give up, and thus might explain the decreased likelihood of a breakup (Becker, 1991; Jones, Tepperman, & Wilson, 1995).

All else being equal, couples with daughters are more likely to divorce than those with sons.

Dahl & Moretti, 2004

Another important factor that keeps many couples from divorcing is finances. According to the AARP survey, loss of financial security is a major concern of people in their 40s who divorce (Montenegro, 2004). After the first decade of marriage, educated couples who have accumulated marital assets have much to lose financially from divorce and are less likely to divorce or separate (Hiedemann, Suhomilinova, & O'Rand, 1998). Middle-aged divorcees, especially women who do not remarry, tend to be less financially secure than those who remain married (Wilmoth & Koso, 2002) and may have to work outside of the home, perhaps for the first time (Huyck, 1999).

When they do divorce, why do middle-aged people do so? The number one reason given by the AARP respondents was partner abuse—verbal, physical, or emotional. Other frequent reasons were differing values or lifestyles, infidelity, alcohol or drug abuse, and simply falling out of love.

Still, stress often remains. Divorce does not eliminate stress, although it may change the source of it. Nearly half (49 percent) of the AARP respondents, especially women, said they suffered greatly from stress and 28 percent from depression. These proportions are similar to the rates among singles the same age (Montenegro, 2004). On the positive side, the stress of divorce may lead to personal growth (Aldwin & Levenson, 2001; Helson & Roberts, 1994).

The sense of violated expectations may be diminishing as midlife divorce becomes more common (Marks & Lambert, 1998; Norton & Moorman, 1987). This change appears to be due largely to women's growing economic independence (Hiedemann et al., 1998). Even in long marriages, the increasing number of years that people can expect to live in good health after child rearing ends may make the dissolution of a marginal marriage and the prospect of possible remarriage a more practical and attractive option (Hiedemann et al., 1998).

Indeed, divorce today may be *less* a threat to well-being in middle age than in young adulthood. That conclusion comes from a 5-year longitudinal study that compared the reactions of 6,948 young and middle-aged adults taken from a nationally representative sample. The researchers used Ryff's six-dimensional measure of psychological well-being, as well as other criteria. In almost all respects, middle-aged people showed more adaptability than younger people in the face of separation or divorce (Marks & Lambert, 1998).

MARITAL STATUS, WELL-BEING, AND HEALTH

As in young adulthood, marriage offers major benefits. For example, marriage can provide social support and is associated with the encouragement of health-promoting behaviors. Moreover, married couples generally have greater socioeconomic resources (Gallo, Troxel, Matthews, & Kuller, 2003). In cross-sectional studies, married people appear to be healthier, both physically and mentally, in middle age and tend to live longer than single, separated, or divorced people (S. L. Brown et al., 2005; Kaplan &

Kronick, 2006; Zhang, 2006). Marital quality appears to be a key factor in well-being. In one longitudinal study, women in highly satisfying marital or cohabitating relationships had lower risk factors for cardiovascular disease than single women or women in unsatisfying relationships (Gallo et al., 2003).

A good marital relationship can buffer people against life stressors, whereas a poor marital relationship can make people vulnerable to them. For example, marital strains increased both men's and women's aging-related declines in health, and this effect was stronger the older a couple was (Umberson, Williams, Powers, Liu, & Needham, 2006). In addition, women who are in unsatisfying married or cohabiting relationships are at higher risk for cardiovascular disease and other health problems, especially if marital conflict is involved (Gallo et al., 2003; Kiecolt-Glaser & Newton, 2001).

In comparison to their unmarried peers, married couples also show an advantage. In the MIDUS sample, single people, especially men, were more likely to be anxious, sad, or restless, and to be less generative than their younger counterparts. Formerly married, noncohabitating women and men reported more negative emotionality than those still in a first marriage (Marks, Bumpass, & Jun, 2004). And those who never marry may be at the highest risk for cardiovascular and other disease (Kaplan & Kronick, 2006).

The relationship between health and marriage may be mediated by immune function. Being in a good marriage can provide a person with buffers against life's stressors in the form of a friend and confidante. This appears to bolster the immune system, and marriage, in these cases, is related to good health. However, being in a bad marriage and experiencing elevated levels of stress and conflict is a stressor that can result in dampened immune system functioning. Therefore, it is not surprising that marriage can be related to poor health (Graham, Christian, & Kiecolt-Glaser, 2006).

Individual differences still matter with respect to the link between marriage and health. When personal resources such as mastery, agency, and self-sufficiency are included in analyses, those adults low on such measures show ill effects relative to their married counterparts, whereas those adults who score high show greater well-being than married couples (Bookwala & Fekete, 2009). Similarly, midlife women who are divorced, remarried, or cohabitating experience more well-being than their younger counterparts, perhaps because life experience is an asset for women in such situations (Marks, Bumpass, & Jun, 2004).

checkpoint can **you**...

- Describe the typical age-related pattern of marital satisfaction, and cite factors that may help explain it?
- Compare the benefits of marriage and cohabitation in middle age?
- Give reasons for the tendency for divorce to occur early in a marriage, and cite factors that may increase the risk of divorce in midlife?
- Discuss the effects of marriage, cohabitation, and divorce on well-being and physical and mental health?

GAY AND LESBIAN RELATIONSHIPS

Gays and lesbians now in middle age grew up at a time when homosexuality was considered a mental illness, and homosexuals tended to be isolated not only from the larger community but from each other.

One factor that seems to affect relationship quality in gays and lesbians is whether or not they have internalized society's negative views on homosexuality. Those gays and lesbians who have internalized the homophobic attitudes held by others are more likely to show symptoms of depression, presumably because these attitudes affect their overall self-concept. And when depressive symptoms increase, so do relationship issues (Frost & Meyer, 2009).

The timing of coming out can affect aspects of development. Some middle-aged gays and lesbians may be associating openly for the first time and establishing relationships. Many are still working out conflicts with parents and other family members (sometimes including spouses) or hiding their homosexuality from them. Some move to cities with large gay populations where they can more easily seek out and form relationships.

Gay men who do not come out until midlife often go through a prolonged search for identity, marked by guilt, secrecy, heterosexual marriage, and conflicted relationships with both sexes. In contrast, those who recognize and accept their sexual orientation early in life often cross racial, socioeconomic, and age barriers within the gay community.

Some gay men and women do not come out until well into adulthood and so may develop intimate relationships later in life than their heterosexual counterparts.

checkpoint can you . . .

▷ Discuss issues regarding gay and lesbian relationships at midlife?

Midlife friendships often have a special importance for homosexuals. Lesbians are more likely to get emotional support from lesbian friends, lovers, and even ex-lovers than from relatives. Gay men, too, rely on friendship networks, or *fictive kin*, which they actively create and maintain. Friendship networks for gays and lesbians provide solidarity and contact with younger people, which middle-aged heterosexuals normally get through family rather than friendship networks.

FRIENDSHIPS

As Carstensen's theory predicts, social networks tend to become smaller and more intimate at midlife. Still, friendships persist and are a strong source of emotional support and well-being, especially for women (Adams & Allan, 1998; Antonucci et al., 2001). Midlife baby boomers have as many as seven good friends on average (Blieszner & Roberto, 2006). Friendships often revolve around work and parenting; others are based on neighborhood contacts or on association in volunteer organizations (Antonucci et al., 2001; Hartup & Stevens, 1999).

The quality of midlife friendships often makes up for what they lack in quantity of time spent. Especially during a crisis, such as a divorce or a problem with an aging parent, adults turn to friends for emotional support, practical guidance, comfort, companionship, and talk (Antonucci & Akiyama, 1997; Hartup & Stevens, 1999; Suitor & Pillemer, 1993). The quality of such friendships can affect health, as can lack of friendships. Loneliness, for example, is predictive of increases in blood pressure, even when such variables as age, gender, race, and cardiovascular risk factors are taken into account (Hawkley, Thisted, Masi, & Cacioppo, 2010). However, sometimes friendships themselves can be stressful. Conflicts with friends often center on differences in values, beliefs, and lifestyles; yet friends usually can talk out these conflicts while maintaining mutual dignity and respect (Hartup & Stevens, 1999).

Loneliness is contagious. Recent research conducted on social networks suggests lonely people act in less affirming ways to others. Their behavior is often interpreted as implying rejection or indifference, which then makes those people feel more lonely too.

Cacioppo, Fowler, & Christakis, 2010

checkpoint can you . . .

▷ Summarize the quantity, quality, and importance of friends in middle age?

Relationships with Maturing Children

Parenthood is a process of letting go, and this process usually approaches or reaches its climax during the parents' middle age (Marks et al., 2004). It is true that, with contemporary trends toward delayed marriage and parenthood, some middle-aged people now face such issues as finding a good day care or preschool program and screening the content of Saturday morning cartoons. However, most parents in the early part of middle age must cope with a different set of issues, which arise from living with children who will soon be leaving home. Once children become adults and have their own children, the intergenerational family multiplies in number and in connections. It is middle-aged parents, usually women, who tend to be the family *kinkeepers,* maintaining ties among the various branches of the extended family (Putney & Bengtson, 2001). So, for example, a mother might insist that all her children and their partners and families come home for holidays, and she may be the catalyst for setting such events in motion.

Families today are diverse and complex. Increasingly, middle-aged parents have to deal with an adult child's continuing to live in the family home or leaving it only to return. One thing, though, has not changed: parents' well-being tends to hinge on how well their children turn out (Allen, Blieszner, & Roberto, 2000). Fortunately, the parent-child relationship often improves with age (Blieszner & Roberto, 2006).

ADOLESCENT CHILDREN: ISSUES FOR PARENTS

Ironically, the people at the two times of life popularly linked with emotional crises—adolescence and midlife—often live in the same household. It is usually middle-aged adults who are the parents of adolescent children. While dealing with their own special concerns, parents have to cope daily with young people who are undergoing great physical, emotional, and social changes.

Although research contradicts the stereotype of adolescence as a time of inevitable turmoil and rebellion, some rejection of parental authority is necessary. An important task for parents is to accept maturing children as they are, not as what the parents had hoped they would be.

Theorists from a variety of perspectives have described this period as one of questioning, reappraisal, or diminished well-being for parents, but this is not inevitable. In the MIDUS study, being a parent was associated with more psychological distress than being child-free, but it also brought greater psychological wellness and generativity, especially to men (Marks et al., 2004).

A questionnaire survey of 129 two-parent families with a firstborn son or daughter between the ages of 10 and 15 illustrates this complexity. For some parents, especially white-collar and professional men with sons, a child's adolescence brought increased satisfaction, well-being, and even pride. For most parents, however, the normative changes of adolescence elicited a mixture of positive and negative emotions. This was particularly true of mothers with early adolescent daughters, whose relationships tend to be both close and conflict-filled (Silverberg, 1996).

WHEN CHILDREN LEAVE: THE EMPTY NEST

Research is challenging popular ideas about the **empty nest**—a supposedly difficult transition, especially for women, that occurs when the youngest child leaves home. Although some women, heavily invested in mothering, do have problems in adjusting to the empty nest, they are far outnumbered by those who find the departure liberating (Antonucci et al., 2001; Antonucci & Akiyama, 1997; Barnett, 1985; Chiriboga, 1997; Helson, 1997; Mitchell & Helson, 1990). For some women, the empty nest may bring relief from what Gutmann called the "chronic emergency of parenthood" (Cooper & Gutmann, 1987, p. 347). They can pursue their own interests as they bask in their grown children's accomplishments.

empty nest
Transitional phase of parenting following the last child's leaving the parents' home.

When children are not accomplished, however, this process may be more difficult. Typically, when adult children have greater needs, parents provide more material and financial support to them (Fingerman, Miller, Birditt, & Zarit, 2009). Given this tendency, it is not surprising to also find that such parents are likely to feel torn between wanting their adult children to assert their independence and a desire to step in and help. Men, in particular, seem to be more affected by their children's successes and failures (Birditt, Fingerman, & Zarit, 2010). Some ambivalence during these situations is standard, but far more stress results when there is already tension in the relationship (Birditt, Miller, Fingerman, & Lefkowitz, 2009) or when grown children return home (Thomas, 1997).

Feeling lonely? Try heating your house. Research suggests that how warm the temperature of a room is affects how socially connected we feel. Warmer rooms are associated with feelings of closeness to others.

Ijzerman & Semin, 2009

The effects of the empty nest on a marriage depend on its quality and length. In a good marriage, the departure of grown children may usher in a second honeymoon. The departure of children from the family home generally increases marital satisfaction, perhaps because of the additional time partners now have to spend with each other (Gorhoff, John, & Helson, 2008). The empty nest may be harder on couples whose identity is dependent on the parental role, or who now must face marital problems they had previously pushed aside under the press of parental responsibilities (Antonucci et al., 2001).

The empty nest does not signal the end of parenthood. It is a transition to a new stage: the relationship between parents and adult children.

PARENTING GROWN CHILDREN

Even after the years of active parenting are over and children have left home for good, parents are still parents. The midlife role of parent to young adults raises new issues and calls for new attitudes and behaviors on the part of both generations (Marks et al., 2004).

Parents are more likely to show favoritism for adult children than young children, in particular when those children are daughters, live nearby, share their values, have avoided deviant behaviors, and have previously helped them out.

Suitor, Seechrist, Plikuhn, & Pillemer, 2008

Middle-aged parents generally give their children more help and support than they get from them as the young adults establish careers and families (Antonucci et al., 2001). Parents give the most help to children who need it most, typically those who are single or are single parents (Blieszner & Roberto, 2006). At the same time, adult children's problems reduce their parents' well-being (Greenfield & Marks, 2006). Some parents have difficulty treating their offspring as adults, and many young adults have difficulty accepting their parents' continuing concern about them. In a warm, supportive family environment, such conflicts can be managed by an open airing of feelings (Putney & Bengtson, 2001).

Most young adults and their middle-aged parents enjoy each other's company and get along well. However, intergenerational families do not all fit one mold. An estimated 25 percent of intergenerational families are *tight-knit,* both geographically and emotionally; they have frequent contact with mutual help and support. Another 25 percent are *sociable,* but with less emotional affinity or commitment. About 16 percent have *obligatory* relationships, with much interaction but little emotional attachment; and 17 percent are *detached,* both emotionally and geographically. An in-between category consists of those who are *intimate but distant* (16 percent), spending little time together but retaining warm feelings that might lead to a renewal of contact and exchange. Adult children tend to be closer to their mothers than to their fathers (Bengtson, 2001; Silverstein & Bengtson, 1997).

Do you think it is a good idea for adult children to live with their parents?

PROLONGED PARENTING: THE "CLUTTERED NEST"

revolving door syndrome
Tendency for young adults who have left home to return to their parents' household in times of financial, marital, or other trouble.

What happens if the nest does not empty when it normally should, or unexpectedly refills? Since the 1980s, in most Western nations, more and more adult children have delayed leaving home until the late 20s or beyond (Mouw, 2005). Furthermore, the **revolving door syndrome,** sometimes called the *boomerang phenomenon,* has become more common. Increasing numbers of young adults, especially men, return to their parents' home, sometimes more than once, and sometimes with their own families (Aquilino, 1996; Blieszner & Roberto, 2006; Putney & Bengtson, 2001).

Prolonged parenting may lead to intergenerational tension when it contradicts parents' normative expectations. As children move from adolescence to young adulthood, parents typically expect them to become independent, and children expect to do so. An adult child's autonomy is a sign of parental success. As the timing-of-events model would predict, then, a grown child's delayed departure from the nest or return to it may produce family stress (Antonucci et al., 2001; Aquilino, 1996). Parents and adult children tend to get along best when the young adults are employed and living on their own (Belsky et al., 2003). When adult children live with parents, relations tend to be smoother when the parents see the adult child moving toward autonomy—for example, by enrolling in college (Antonucci et al., 2001).

However, the nonnormative experience of parent-child coresidence is becoming less so, especially for parents with more than one child. Rather than an abrupt leave-taking, the empty nest transition is coming to be seen as a more prolonged process of separation, often lasting several years (Aquilino, 1996; Putney & Bengtson, 2001). Coresidence with adult children may be seen as an expression of family solidarity, an extension of the normative expectation of assistance from parents to young adult children.

checkpoint
can **you** . . .

- Discuss the changes parents of adolescent children go through?
- Compare how women and men respond to the empty nest?
- Describe typical features of relationships between parents and grown children?
- Give reasons for the prolonged parenting phenomenon, and discuss its effects?

Other Kinship Ties

Except in times of need, ties with the family of origin—parents and siblings—tend to recede in importance during young adulthood, when work, spouses or partners, and children take precedence. At midlife, these earliest kinship ties may reassert themselves in a new way, as the responsibility for care and support of aging parents may begin to shift to their middle-aged children. In addition, a new relationship often begins at this time of life: grandparenthood.

RELATIONSHIPS WITH AGING PARENTS

The middle years may bring dramatic, though gradual, changes in parent-child relationships. Many middle-aged people look at their parents more objectively than before, seeing them as individuals with both strengths and weaknesses. Something else may happen during these years: one day a middle-aged adult may look at a mother or father and see an old person, who may need a daughter's or son's care.

Most middle-aged adults and their aging parents have warm, affectionate relationships.

Contact and Mutual Help Even when they do not live close to each other, most middle-aged adults and their parents have warm, affectionate relationships based on frequent contact, mutual help, feelings of attachment, and shared values. Daughters and older mothers tend to be especially close (Bengtson, 2001; Fingerman & Dolbin-MacNab, 2006; Willson, Shuey, & Elder, 2003). Positive relationships with parents contribute to a strong sense of self and to emotional well-being at midlife (Blieszner & Roberto, 2006).

Mostly, help and assistance continue to flow from parents to child. The majority of help consists of assistance with everyday needs and, less commonly, emergencies and crises. This pattern is true of most families; however, the dynamics change in situations in which parents are disabled or experience some sort of crisis themselves. Not surprisingly, in these cases, adult children often provide resources to their middle-aged parents (Fingerman, Pitzer, Birditt, Franks, & Zarit, 2010).

With the changing demographics of the United States, particularly the lengthening of the life span, some developmental scientists have proposed a new stage of life. In this stage, termed **filial maturity,** middle-aged children must "learn to accept and to meet their parents' dependency needs" (Marcoen, 1995, p. 125). For example, a son might realize that his mother is no longer able to drive and might decide to stop by the grocery store once a week for her, or a daughter might realize her father is no longer able to remember to pay bills unassisted and set up payments for him. This normative development is seen as the healthy outcome of a **filial crisis,** in which adults learn to balance love and duty to their parents with autonomy in a two-way relationship. Although striking this balance can be challenging, most middle-aged people willingly accept their obligations to their parents (Antonucci et al., 2001).

filial maturity
Stage of life, proposed by Marcoen and others, in which middle-aged children, as the outcome of a filial crisis, learn to accept and meet their parents' need to depend on them.

filial crisis
In Marcoen's terminology, normative development of middle age, in which adults learn to balance love and duty to their parents with autonomy within a two-way relationship.

However, family relations in middle and late adulthood can be complex. With increasing longevity, middle-aged couples with limited emotional and financial resources may need to allocate them among two sets of aging parents as well as provide for their own (and possibly their own adult children's) needs. In one study, researchers interviewed 738 middle-aged sons and daughters from 420 close-knit, mostly two-parent, households. More than 25 percent of the relationships between adult children and their aging parents or in-laws were characterized by ambivalence—nearly 8 percent highly so (Willson et al., 2003).

Ambivalence may surface in trying to juggle competing needs. In a national longitudinal survey of 3,622 married couples with at least one surviving parent, the allocation of assistance to aging parents involved tradeoffs and often depended on family lineage. Most couples contributed time or money, but not both, and few assisted both sets of parents. Couples tended to respond more readily to the needs of the wife's parents, presumably because of her greater closeness to them. African American and Hispanic couples were more likely than white couples to provide consistent assistance of all types to parents on each side of the family (Shuey & Hardy, 2003).

Becoming a Caregiver for Aging Parents The generations typically get along best while parents are healthy and vigorous. When older people become infirm, the burden of caring for them may strain the relationship (Antonucci et al., 2001; Marcoen, 1995). Given the high cost of nursing homes and most older people's reluctance to stay in them, many dependent elders receive long-term care in their own home or that of a caregiver.

The world over, caregiving is typically a female function (Kinsella & Velkoff, 2001). When an ailing mother is widowed or a divorced woman can no longer manage alone, it is most likely that a daughter will take on the caregiving role (Pinquart & Sörensen, 2006; Schulz & Martire, 2004). Sons do contribute to caregiving, but they are less likely to provide primary, personal care (Blieszner & Roberto, 2006; Marks, 1996).

Strains of Caregiving Caregiving can be stressful. Many caregivers find the task a physical, emotional, and financial burden, especially if they work full-time, have limited financial resources, or lack support and assistance (Lund, 1993a; Schulz & Martire, 2004). It is hard for women who work outside the home to assume an added caregiving role, and reducing work hours or quitting a job to meet caregiving obligations can increase financial stress. Flexible work schedules and family and medical leave could help alleviate this problem.

Emotional strain may come not only from caregiving itself but from the need to balance it with the many other responsibilities of midlife (Antonucci et al., 2001; Climo & Stewart, 2003). Elderly parents may become dependent at a time when middle-aged adults need to launch their children or, if parenthood was delayed, to raise them. Caregiving can also lead to marriage problems. Adult caregivers report less marital happiness, great marital inequality, more hostility, and, for women, a greater degree of depressive symptomatology and depression over time (Bookwala, 2009). Members of this generation in the middle, sometimes called the **sandwich generation,** may be caught in a squeeze between these competing needs and their limited resources of time, money, and energy. Also, a middle-aged child, who may be preparing to retire, can ill afford the additional costs of caring for a frail older person or may have health problems of his or her own (Kinsella & Velkoff, 2001).

sandwich generation
Middle-aged adults squeezed by competing needs to raise or launch children and to care for elderly parents.

Caring for a person with physical impairments is hard. It can be even more difficult to care for someone with dementia, who, in addition to being unable to carry on basic functions of daily living, may be incontinent, suspicious, agitated or depressed, subject to hallucinations, likely to wander about at night, dangerous to self and others, and in need of constant supervision (Schultz & Martire, 2004). Sometimes the caregiver becomes physically or mentally ill under the strain (Pinquart & Sörensen, 2007; Schultz & Martire, 2004; Vitaliano, Zhang, & Scanlan, 2003). Because women are more likely than men to give personal care, their mental health and well-being may be more likely to suffer (Amirkhanyan & Wolf, 2006; Climo & Stewart, 2003; Pinquart & Sörensen, 2006). Sometimes the stress created by the incessant, heavy demands of caregiving is so great as to lead to abuse, neglect, or even abandonment of the dependent elderly person.

A result of these and other strains may be **caregiver burnout,** a physical, mental, and emotional exhaustion that can affect adults who care for aged relatives (Barnhart, 1992). Even the most patient, loving caregiver may become frustrated, anxious, or resentful under the constant strain of meeting an older person's seemingly endless needs. Often families and friends fail to recognize that caregivers have a right to feel discouraged, frustrated, and put upon. Caregivers need a life of their own, beyond the

caregiver burnout
Condition of physical, mental, and emotional exhaustion affecting adults who provide continuous care for sick or aged persons.

loved one's disability or disease. Sometimes other arrangements, such as institutionalization, assisted living, or a division of responsibilities among siblings, must be made (Shuey & Hardy, 2003).

Community support programs can reduce the strains and burdens of caregiving, prevent burnout, and postpone the need for institutionalization of the dependent person. Support services may include meals and housekeeping; transportation and escort services; and adult day care centers, which provide supervised activities and care while caregivers work or attend to personal needs. *Respite care* (substitute supervised care by visiting nurses or home health aides) gives regular caregivers some time off, whether for a few hours, a day, a weekend, or a week. Temporary admission of the patient to a nursing home is another alternative. Through counseling, support, and self-help groups, caregivers can share problems, gain information about community resources, and improve skills.

Community support may improve caregivers' morale and reduce stress (Gallagher-Thompson, 1995). More broadly based interventions target both the caregiver and the patient, offering individual or family counseling, case management, skills training, environmental modification, and behavior management strategies. Such a combination of diverse services and supports can reduce caregivers' burdens and improve their skills, satisfaction, and well-being—and even, sometimes, improve the patient's symptoms (Schulz & Martire, 2004).

Some family caregivers, looking back, regard the experience as uniquely rewarding. If a caregiver deeply loves an infirm parent, cares about family continuity, looks at caregiving as a challenge, and has adequate personal, family, and community resources to meet that challenge, caregiving can be an opportunity for personal growth in competence, compassion, self-knowledge, and self-transcendence (Bengtson, 2001; Bengtson, Rosenthal, & Burton, 1996; Biegel, 1995; Climo & Stewart, 2003; Lund, 1993a).

What would you do if one or both of your parents required long-term care? To what extent should children or other relatives be responsible for such care? To what extent, and in what ways, should society help?

RELATIONSHIPS WITH SIBLINGS

Sibling ties are the longest-lasting relationships in most people's lives. In some cross-sectional research, sibling relationships over the life span look like an hourglass, with the most contact at the two ends—childhood and middle to late adulthood—and the least contact during the child-raising years. After establishing careers and families, siblings may renew their ties (Bedford, 1995; Cicirelli, 1995; Putney & Bengtson, 2001). Other studies indicate a decline in contact throughout adulthood. Sibling conflict tends to diminish with age—perhaps because siblings who do not get along see each other less (Putney & Bengtson, 2001).

Relationships with siblings who remain in contact can be central to psychological well-being in midlife (Antonucci et al., 2001; Spitze & Trent, 2006). As in young adulthood, sisters tend to be closer than brothers (Blieszner & Roberto, 2006; Spitze & Trent, 2006).

Dealing with the care of aging parents can bring siblings closer together but also can cause resentment and conflict (Blieszner & Roberto, 2006; Ingersoll-Dayton, Neal, Ha, & Hammer, 2003). Disagreements may arise over the division of care or over an inheritance, especially if the sibling relationship has not been good.

checkpoint can you . . .

- Describe the change in the balance of filial relationships that often occurs between middle-aged children and elderly parents?
- Cite sources of potential strain in caregiving for elderly parents?
- Discuss the nature of sibling relationships in middle age?

GRANDPARENTHOOD

Often grandparenthood begins before the end of active parenting. Adults in the United States become grandparents, on average, around age 45 (Blieszner & Roberto, 2006). With today's lengthening life spans, many adults spend several decades as grandparents and live to see grandchildren become adults. Eighty percent of people over the age of 65 have grandchildren, and about a third of them list grandparenting as the most valued aspect of getting older (Livingston & Parker, 2010).

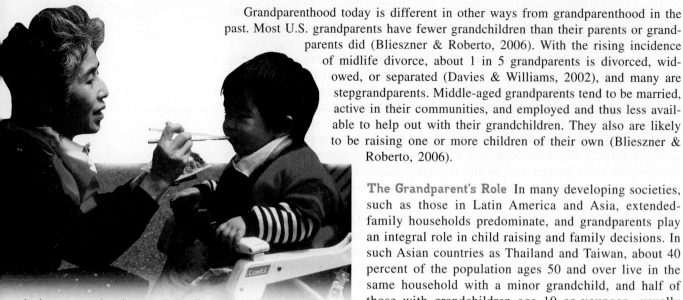

In Japan, grandmothers traditionally wear red as a sign of their noble status. Grandparenthood is an important milestone in Western societies as well.

Grandparenthood today is different in other ways from grandparenthood in the past. Most U.S. grandparents have fewer grandchildren than their parents or grandparents did (Blieszner & Roberto, 2006). With the rising incidence of midlife divorce, about 1 in 5 grandparents is divorced, widowed, or separated (Davies & Williams, 2002), and many are stepgrandparents. Middle-aged grandparents tend to be married, active in their communities, and employed and thus less available to help out with their grandchildren. They also are likely to be raising one or more children of their own (Blieszner & Roberto, 2006).

The Grandparent's Role In many developing societies, such as those in Latin America and Asia, extended-family households predominate, and grandparents play an integral role in child raising and family decisions. In such Asian countries as Thailand and Taiwan, about 40 percent of the population ages 50 and over live in the same household with a minor grandchild, and half of those with grandchildren age 10 or younger—usually grandmothers—provide care for the child (Kinsella & Velkoff, 2001).

In the United States, the extended family household is common in some minority communities, but the dominant household pattern is the nuclear family. When children grow up, they typically leave home and establish new, autonomous nuclear families wherever their inclinations, aspirations, and job hunts take them. Although 68 percent of the grandparents in an AARP survey see at least one grandchild every 1 or 2 weeks, 45 percent live too far away to see their grandchildren regularly (Davies & Williams, 2002). However, distance does not necessarily affect the quality of relationships with grandchildren (Kivett, 1991, 1993, 1996).

In general, grandmothers have closer, warmer, more affectionate relationships with their grandchildren (especially granddaughters) than grandfathers do, and see them more (Putney & Bengtson, 2001). Grandparents who have frequent contact with their grandchildren, feel good about grandparenthood, attribute importance to the role, and have high self-esteem tend to be more satisfied with being grandparents (Reitzes & Mutran, 2004).

Have you had a close relationship with a grandmother or grandfather? If so, in what specific ways did that relationship influence your development?

About 15 percent of U.S. grandparents provide child care for working parents (Davies & Williams, 2002). Indeed, grandparents are almost as likely to be child care providers as organized child care centers or preschools; 30 percent of children under age 5 with employed mothers are under a grandparent's care while the mothers are at work (U.S. Census Bureau, 2008b).

Grandparenting after Divorce and Remarriage One result of the rise in divorce and remarriage is a growing number of grandparents and grandchildren whose relationships are endangered or severed. After a divorce, because the mother usually has custody, her parents tend to have more contact and stronger relationships with their grandchildren, and the paternal grandparents tend to have less (Cherlin & Furstenberg, 1986; Myers & Perrin, 1993). A divorced mother's remarriage typically reduces her need for support from her parents, but not their contact with their grandchildren. For paternal grandparents, however, the new marriage increases the likelihood that they will be displaced or that the family will move away, making contact more difficult (Cherlin & Furstenberg, 1986).

Because ties with grandparents are important to children's development, every state has given grandparents (and in some states, great-grandparents, siblings, and others) the right to visitation after a divorce or the death of a parent if a judge finds it in the best interest of the child. However, a few state courts have struck down such laws for being too broad and potentially infringing on parental rights (Greenhouse, 2000), and some legislatures have restricted grandparents' visitation rights. For example, in June of 2000, the Supreme Court invalidated the state of Washington's "grandparents' rights" statute, arguing that the criteria for awarding visitation be changed from "the best interest of the child" to whether or not upholding the parent's interests might cause "harm" to the child. Currently, the laws vary state by state, and the burden of proof is generally on the grandparents.

Raising Grandchildren Many grandparents are their grandchildren's sole or primary caregivers. One reason, in developing countries, is the migration of rural parents to urban areas to find work. These *skip-generation* families exist in all regions of the world, particularly in Afro-Caribbean countries. In sub-Saharan Africa, the AIDS epidemic has left many orphans whose grandparents step into the parents' place (Kinsella & Velkoff, 2001).

In the United States, about 1 in 10 grandparents is raising a grandchild, and this number is rising (Livingston & Parker, 2010). Many are serving as *parents by default* for children whose parents are unable to care for them—often as a result of teenage pregnancy, substance abuse, illness, divorce, or death (Allen et al., 2000; Blieszner & Roberto, 2006). Surrogate parenting by grandparents is a well-established pattern in African American families (Blieszner & Roberto, 2006).

Unexpected surrogate parenthood can be a physical, emotional, and financial drain on middle-aged or older adults (Blieszner & Roberto, 2006). They may have to quit their jobs, shelve their retirement plans, drastically reduce their leisure pursuits and social life, and endanger their health.

Most grandparents who take on the responsibility to raise their grandchildren do it because they do not want their grandchildren placed in a stranger's foster home. However, the age difference can become a barrier, and both generations may feel cheated out of their traditional roles. At the same time, grandparents often have to deal with a sense of guilt because the adult children they raised have failed their own children, and also with the rancor they may feel toward these adult children. For some caregiver couples, the strains produce tension in their relationship. And, if one or both parents resume their normal roles, it may be emotionally wrenching to return the child (Crowley, 1993; Larsen, 1990–1991).

kinship care
Care of children living without parents in the home of grandparents or other relatives, with or without a change of legal custody.

Grandparents providing **kinship care** who do not become foster parents or gain custody have no legal status and no more rights than unpaid babysitters. They may face many practical problems, from enrolling the child in school and gaining access to academic records to obtaining medical insurance for the child. Grandchildren are usually not eligible for coverage under employer-provided health insurance even if the grandparent has custody. Like working parents, working grandparents need good, affordable child care and family-friendly workplace policies, such as time off to care for a sick child. The federal Family and Medical Leave Act of 1993 does cover grandparents who are raising grandchildren, but many do not realize it.

Grandparents can be sources of guidance, companions in play, links to the past, and symbols of family continuity. They express generativity, a longing to transcend mortality by investing themselves in the lives of future generations. Men and women who do not become grandparents may fulfill generative needs by becoming foster grandparents or volunteering in schools or hospitals. By finding ways to develop what Erikson called the virtue of *care,* adults prepare themselves to enter the culminating period of adult development.

checkpoint can **you . . .**

- Tell how parents' divorce and remarriage can affect grandparents' relationships with grandchildren?
- Discuss the challenges involved in raising grandchildren?
- Tell how grandparenthood has changed in recent generations?
- Describe the roles grandparents play in family life?

summary and key terms

Looking at the Life Course in Middle Age

- Developmental scientists view midlife psychosocial development both objectively, in terms of trajectories or pathways, and subjectively, in terms of people's sense of self and the way they actively construct their lives.
- Change and continuity must be seen in context and in terms of the whole life span.

Change at Midlife: Theoretical Approaches

- Although some theorists held that personality is essentially formed by midlife, there is a growing consensus that midlife development shows change as well as stability.
- Humanistic theorists such as Maslow and Rogers saw middle age as an opportunity for positive change.
- Costa and McCrae's five-factor model shows slowed change after age 30. Other trait research has found more significant positive change with individual differences.
- Jung held that men and women at midlife express previously suppressed aspects of personality. Two necessary tasks are giving up the image of youth and acknowledging mortality.
- Erikson's seventh psychosocial stage is generativity versus stagnation. Generativity can be expressed through parenting and grandparenting, teaching or mentorship, productivity or creativity, self-development, and "maintenance of the world." The virtue of this period is *care*. Current research on generativity finds it most prevalent at middle age but not universally so.
- Vaillant and Levinson found major midlife shifts in lifestyle and personality.
- The greater fluidity of the life cycle today has partly undermined the assumption of a "social clock."

individuation
generativity versus stagnation
generativity
interiority

The Self at Midlife: Issues and Themes

- Key psychosocial issues and themes during middle adulthood concern the existence of a midlife crisis, identity development (including gender identity), and psychological well-being.
- Research does not support a normative midlife crisis. It is more accurate to refer to a transition that may be a psychological turning point.
- According to Whitbourne's identity process theory, people continually confirm or revise their perceptions about themselves on the basis of experience and feedback from others. Identity processes typical of an individual can predict adaptation to aging.
- Generativity is an aspect of identity development.
- Narrative psychology describes identity development as a continuous process of constructing a life story. Highly generative people tend to focus on a theme of redemption.
- Some research has found increasing "masculinization" of women and "feminization" of men at midlife, but this may be largely a cohort effect. Research does *not* support Gutmann's proposed gender crossover.
- Emotionality and personality are related to psychological well-being.
- Research based on Ryff's six-dimensional scale has found that midlife is generally a period of positive mental health and well-being, though socioeconomic status is a factor.

midlife crisis
turning points
midlife review
ego-resiliency
identity process theory (IPT)
identity schemas
identity assimilation
identity accommodation
identity balance
gender crossover

Relationships at Midlife

- Two theories of the changing importance of relationships are Kahn and Antonucci's social convoy theory and Carstensen's socioemotional selectivity theory. According to both theories, socioemotional support is an important element in social interaction at midlife and beyond.
- Relationships at midlife are important to physical and mental health but also can present stressful demands.

social convoy theory
socioemotional selectivity theory

Consensual Relationships

- Research on the quality of marriage suggests a dip in marital satisfaction during the years of child rearing, followed by an improved relationship after the children leave home.
- Cohabitation in midlife may negatively affect men's well-being.
- Divorce at midlife can be stressful and life-changing. Marital capital tends to dissuade midlife divorce.
- Divorce today may be less threatening to well-being in middle age than in young adulthood.
- Married people tend to be happier at middle age than people with any other marital status.
- Because some gays and lesbians delayed coming out, at midlife they may be just establishing intimate relationships.
- Middle-aged people tend to invest less time in friendships than younger adults do but depend on friends for emotional support and practical guidance.

marital capital

Relationships with Maturing Children

- Parents of adolescents have to come to terms with a loss of control over their children's lives.
- The emptying of the nest is liberating for many women but may be stressful for couples whose identity is dependent on the parental role or those who now must face previously submerged marital problems.
- Middle-aged parents tend to remain involved with their adult children, and most are generally happy with the way their children turned out. Conflict may arise over grown children's need to be treated as adults and parents' continuing concern about them.
- Today, more young adults are delaying departure from their childhood home or are returning to it, sometimes with their own families. Adjustment tends to be smoother if the parents see the adult child as moving toward autonomy.

empty nest
revolving door syndrome

Other Kinship Ties

- Relationships between middle-aged adults and their parents are usually characterized by a strong bond of affection. The two generations generally maintain frequent contact and offer and receive assistance. Aid flows mostly from parents to children.
- As life lengthens, more and more aging parents become dependent for care on their middle-aged children. Acceptance of these dependency needs is the mark of filial maturity and may be the outcome of a filial crisis.
- The chances of becoming a caregiver to an aging parent increase in middle age, especially for women.
- Caregiving can be a source of considerable stress but also of satisfaction. Community support programs can help prevent caregiver burnout.
- Although siblings tend to have less contact at midlife than before and after, most middle-aged siblings remain in touch, and their relationships are important to well-being.
- Most U.S. adults become grandparents in middle age and have fewer grandchildren than in previous generations.
- Geographic separation does not necessarily affect the quality of grandparenting relationships.
- Divorce and remarriage of an adult child can affect grandparent-grandchild relationships.
- A growing number of grandparents are raising grandchildren whose parents are unable to care for them. Raising grandchildren can create physical, emotional, and financial strains.

filial maturity
filial crisis
sandwich generation
caregiver burnout
kinship care

part 8

LATE ADULTHOOD

chapter 17

Physical and Cognitive Development in Late Adulthood

outline

learning objectives

Discuss the causes and impact of the aging population.

Characterize longevity and discuss biological theories of aging.

Describe physical changes in late adulthood.

Identify factors that influence health and well-being in late adulthood.

Describe the cognitive functioning of older adults.

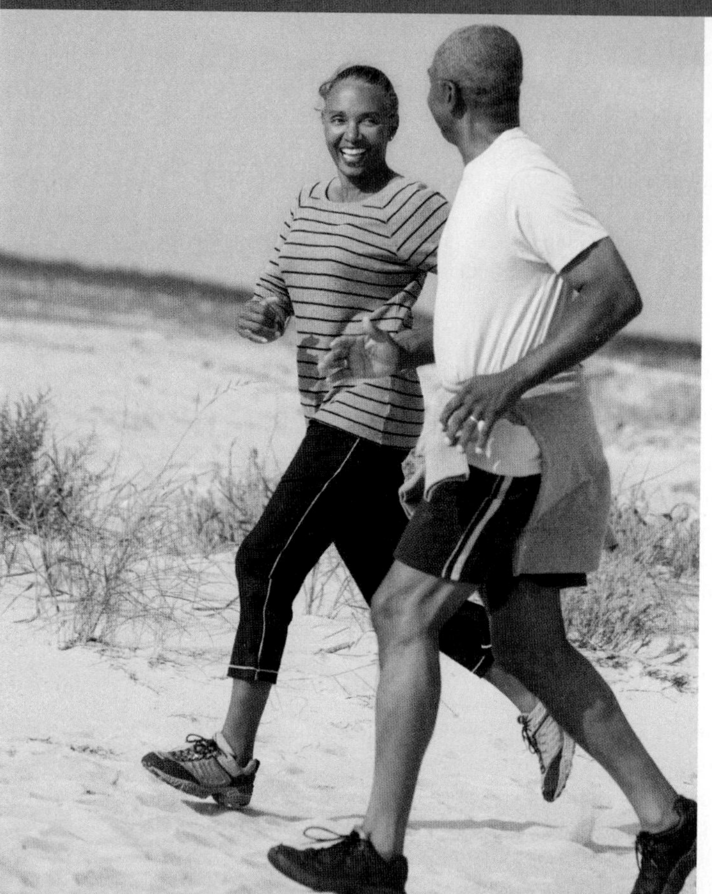

did you know?

- By 2040 the population of people 65 and over is projected to be 1.3 billion worldwide?
- In many parts of the world, the fastest-growing age group consists of people in their 80s and older?
- Older brains can grow new nerve cells—something once thought impossible?

In this chapter, we begin by sketching demographic trends among today's older population. We look at the increasing length and quality of life in late adulthood and at causes of biological aging. We examine physical changes and health. We then turn to cognitive development: changes in intelligence and memory, the emergence of wisdom, and the influence of continuing education in late life.

Old age is just a record of one's whole life.

—Muhammad Ali

Old Age Today

In Japan, old age is a status symbol; travelers checking into hotels there are often asked their age to ensure that they will receive proper deference. In the United States, by contrast, aging is generally seen as undesirable. In research, the most consistent stereotypes that have emerged regarding the elderly are that while older people are generally seen as warm and loving, they are incompetent and of low status (Cuddy, Norton, & Fiske, 2005). These stereotypes about aging, internalized in youth and reinforced for decades by societal attitudes, may become self-stereotypes, unconsciously affecting older people's expectations about their behavior and often acting as self-fulfilling prophecies (Levy, 2003).

What stereotypes about aging have you heard in the media and in everyday life?

ageism
Prejudice or discrimination against a person (most commonly an older person) based on age.

Today, efforts to combat **ageism**—prejudice or discrimination based on age—are making headway, thanks to the growing visibility of active, healthy older adults. Reports about aging achievers appear frequently in the media. On television, older people are less often portrayed as doddering and helpless and more often as level-headed, respected, and wise, a shift that may be important in the reduction of negative stereotypes about the elderly (Bodner, 2009).

We need to look beyond distorted images of age to its true, multifaceted reality. What does today's older population look like?

The growing visibility of such active, healthy older adults as actress Betty White is changing the perception of old age. At age 88, she became the oldest host on Saturday Night Live, *where she kept up with the younger actors. She is also a well-known animal health advocate and author.*

THE GRAYING OF THE POPULATION

The global population is aging. In 2010, nearly 524 million people worldwide were age 65 or older, and by 2050 the total population in that age group is projected to reach 1.5 billion. Estimates are that by about 2016 people age 65 and older will for the first time outnumber children age 5 and younger. The most rapid increases will be in developing countries, where the number of older people is projected to increase more than 250 percent by 2050 (National Institute on Aging, 2011; Figure 1). Aging populations result from declines in fertility accompanied by economic growth, better nutrition, healthier lifestyles, improved control of infectious disease, safer water and sanitation facilities, and advances in science, technology, and medicine (Dobriansky, Suzman, & Hodes, 2007).

The aged population itself is aging. In many parts of the world, the fastest-growing age group consists of people in their 80s and older. The population of people 85 and older is projected to increase 351 percent between 2010 and 2050 (Kinsella & He, 2009). By contrast, the percentage rate increase predicted for adults 65 and older is 188 percent, and the overall increase expected for people under age 65 is just 22 percent (National Institute on Aging, 2011). In the United States, the graying of the population is due to high birthrates and high immigration rates during the early to mid-twentieth century and a trend toward

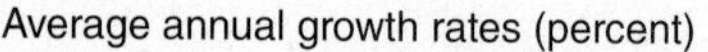

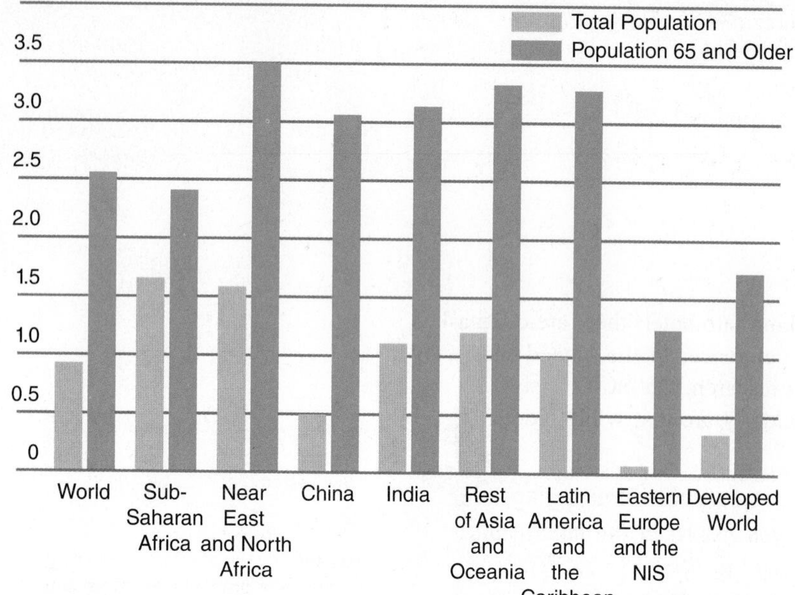

FIGURE 1

Change in the World's Older Population and Total Population by Region, 2002–2025

The growth of the population age 65 and up is projected to be faster than that of any other segment of the population in all world regions. Growth will be greatest in much of the developing world.

Source: U.S. Census Bureau, 2004; data from U.S. Census Bureau International Programs Center, International Data Base and unpublished tables.

smaller families, which has reduced the relative size of younger age groups. Since 1900, the proportion of Americans age 65 and up has more than tripled, from 4.1 to 12.8 percent. With the baby boomers turning 65, nearly 19 percent of Americans—72.1 million—are likely to be 65 and older in 2030, about twice as many as in 2000 (Administration on Aging, 2010; Federal Interagency Forum on Aging-Related Statistics, 2010).

Ethnic diversity among older adults is increasing. In 2005, 18.5 percent of older Americans were members of minority groups; by 2040, 24 percent will be. The older Hispanic population is projected to grow most rapidly, from 6 percent of the over-65 population in 2004 to almost 20 percent in 2050 (Administration on Aging, 2010; Federal Interagency Forum on Aging-Related Statistics, 2010).

YOUNG OLD TO OLDEST OLD

The economic impact of a graying population depends on the proportion of the population that is healthy and able-bodied. In this regard, the trend is encouraging. Many problems that we used to think were the result of age have been determined to be due to lifestyle factors or disease.

primary aging
Gradual, inevitable process of bodily deterioration throughout the life span.

secondary aging
Aging processes that result from disease and bodily abuse and disuse and are often preventable.

Primary aging is a gradual, inevitable process of bodily deterioration that begins early in life and continues through the years irrespective of what people do to stave it off. In this view, aging is an unavoidable consequence of getting older. **Secondary aging** results from disease, abuse, and disuse—factors that are often within a person's control (J. C. Horn & Meer, 1987). These two philosophies of aging can be likened to the familiar nature-nurture debate. Primary aging is a nature process governed by biology. Secondary aging is the result of nurture, the environmental insults that accrue over the course of a lifetime. As always, the truth lies somewhere in between and both factors matter.

activities of daily living (ADLs)
Essential activities that support survival, such as eating, dressing, bathing, and getting around the house.

functional age
Measure of a person's ability to function effectively in his or her physical and social environment in comparison with others of the same chronological age.

gerontology
Study of the aged and the process of aging.

Today, social scientists who specialize in the study of aging refer to three groups of older adults: the "young old," "old old," and "oldest old." These terms represent social constructions similar to the concept of adolescence. Chronologically, *young old* generally refers to people ages 65 to 74, who are usually active, vital, and vigorous. The *old old,* ages 75 to 84, and the *oldest old,* age 85 and above, are more likely to be frail and infirm and to have difficulty managing **activities of daily living (ADLs).** As a result, the oldest old consume a disproportionate number of resources such as pensions or health care costs given their population size (Kinsella & He, 2009).

A more meaningful classification is **functional age:** how well a person functions in a physical and social environment in comparison with others of the same chronological age. For example, a person of 90 who is still in good health and can live independently may be functionally younger than a 75-year-old suffering the effects of dementia.

The use of these terms and age distinctions has arisen out of research and service needs. **Gerontology** is the study of the aged and aging processes. Gerontologists are interested in differences between elderly people because these differences can influence outcomes. Likewise, researchers and service providers in **geriatrics,** the branch of medicine concerned with aging, are concerned with differences among the elderly. Understanding differences among the elderly has underlined the need for support services that people in age groups such as the *oldest old* may need. For example, some in this age group have outlived their savings and cannot pay for their own care.

checkpoint
can **you** . . .

- Discuss the causes and impact of the aging population?
- State two criteria for differentiating among the young old, old old, and oldest old?
- Differentiate between primary and secondary aging?

PHYSICAL DEVELOPMENT

Longevity and Aging

How long will you live? Why do you have to grow old? Human beings have been wondering about these questions for thousands of years.

Life expectancy is the age to which a person born at a certain time and place is statistically likely to live, given his or her current age and health status. Life expectancy is based on the average **longevity,** or actual length of life, of members of a population. Gains in life expectancy reflect declines in *mortality rates,* or death rates (the proportions of a total population or of certain age groups who die in a given year). The human **life span** is the longest period that members of our species can live. The longest documented life span thus far is that of Jeanne Clement, a French woman who died at 122 years of age.

Keep in mind life expectancy doesn't reflect the average age at which someone dies. It includes deaths across the life span. Therefore, a short life expectancy can often signify a high infant mortality rate, which pulls down the number.

geriatrics
Branch of medicine concerned with processes of aging and medical conditions associated with old age.

life expectancy
Age to which a person in a particular cohort is statistically likely to live (given his or her current age and health status), on the basis of average longevity of a population.

longevity
Length of an individual's life.

life span
The longest period that members of a species can live.

TRENDS AND FACTORS IN LIFE EXPECTANCY

The average American is getting older, a phenomenon that has been called "the graying of the population." This reflects a rapid rise in life expectancy. A baby born in the United States in 2010 can expect to live to 78.7 years, about 29 years longer than a baby born in 1900 and more than 4 times longer than a baby born at the dawn of human history (National Center for Health Statistics, 2012; Wilmoth, 2000; Figure 2). However, in the absence of major lifestyle changes, some gerontologists predict that life expectancy in the United States may halt its upward trend and even decline in coming decades as a rise in obesity-related and infectious diseases offsets gains from medical advances (Olshansky et al., 2005; Preston, 2005).

Gender Differences Nearly all over the world, women typically live longer and have lower mortality rates at all ages than men. The gender gap is widest in high-income industrialized nations, where female mortality dropped sharply with improvements in prenatal and obstetric care. Women's longer lives also have been attributed to their greater tendency to take care of themselves and to seek medical care, the higher level of social support they enjoy, the rise in women's socioeconomic status in recent decades, and men's higher death rates throughout life. Further, men are more likely to smoke, drink, and be exposed to dangerous toxins (Kinsella & He, 2009).

In the United States, women's life expectancy in 1900 was only 2 years longer than men's. The gender gap widened to 7.8 years in the late 1970s, mainly because more men were dying from smoking-related illnesses (heart disease and lung cancer) and fewer women were dying in childbirth. Since then the gap has narrowed to about 5 years (Heron, Hoyert,

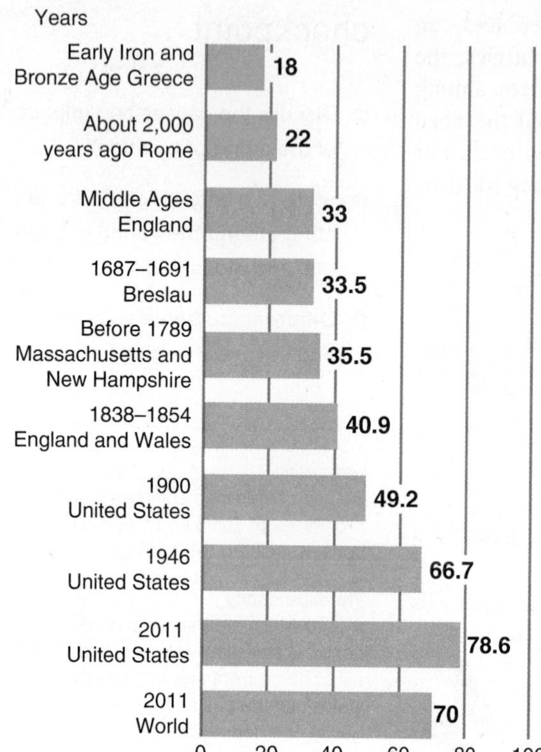

FIGURE 2

Changes in Life Expectancy from Ancient to Modern Times

Source: Adapted from Katchadourian, 1987; 2011 U.S. and World data from World Bank, n.d., and WHO, n.d., respectively.

Xu, Scott, & Tejada-Vera, 2008), largely because more women are smoking (Gorman & Read, 2007). With the exception of Eastern Europe and the former Soviet Union, similar trends have been noted in other developed countries (Kinsella & He, 2009). Because of the difference in life expectancy, older women in the United States outnumber older men by nearly 3 to 2 (Administration on Aging, 2006), and this disparity increases with advancing age.

Regional and Racial/Ethnic Differences The gap in life expectancies between developed and developing countries is vast. In the African nation of Sierra Leone, a man born in 2009 could expect to live 48 years, as compared to 82 years for a man in San Marino, a tiny republic surrounded by Italy (WHO, 2011). On average, a child born in a developed country can expect to live for 14 years more than a child born in a developing country (Kinsella & He, 2009).

The most dramatic improvements in developing regions have occurred in East Asia, where life expectancy grew from less than 45 years in 1950 to more than 74 years today. Almost all nations have shown improvement, with the exception of Africa, due to the AIDS epidemic (National Institute on Aging, 2011).

Wide racial/ethnic, socioeconomic, and geographic disparities in life expectancy exist in the United States. In contrast to the upward national trend, life expectancy has stagnated or even declined since 1983 in many of the nation's poorest counties, mainly in the Deep South, along the Mississippi River, in Appalachia, and in Texas and the southern Plains region (Ezzati, Friedman, Kulkarni, & Murray, 2008). On average, white Americans live about 4 years longer than African Americans (National Center for Health Statistics, 2012), though this difference has narrowed somewhat with greater reductions in African American death rates from homicide, HIV, accidents, cancer, diabetes, influenza, pneumonia, and, among women, heart disease (Harper, Lynch, Burris, & Smith, 2007; Heron et al., 2008; NCHS, 2007). African Americans, especially men, are more vulnerable than white Americans to illness and death from infancy through middle adulthood. However, the gap begins to close in older adulthood, and by age 85 African Americans can expect slightly more remaining years than white Americans (NCHS, 2007). Somewhat surprisingly, Hispanic Americans have the highest life expectancy (81.2 years), an advantage of approximately 2.5 years over white Americans and 6.5 years over African Americans (National Center for Health Statistics, 2012; Table 1). The reasons for this are somewhat unclear but may include cultural lifestyle issues or migration effects (e.g., those who migrate to the United States tend to be healthier) (Arias, 2010).

TABLE 1 Life Expectancy in Years for . . .

	At Birth	At Age 65
Hispanic men	77.9	84.0
Hispanic women	83.1	86.7
White men	75.6	82.1
White women	80.4	84.7
African American men	69.2	80.0
African American women	76.2	83.4

Source: Arias, 2010.

A new way to look at life expectancy is in terms of the number of years a person can expect to live in good health, free of disabilities. In this regard United States ranks 33rd worldwide, with an average healthy life expectancy of 77.9 years. Reasons for this relatively poor showing as compared with other industrialized nations include ill health among the urban poor and some ethnic groups, a relatively large proportion of HIV-related death and disability in young and middle adulthood, high rates of lung disease and coronary heart disease, and fairly high levels of violence (WHO, 2000, 2007b).

checkpoint can **you** . . .

- Distinguish life expectancy, longevity, and life span?
- Summarize trends in life expectancy, including gender, regional, and ethnic differences?

WHY PEOPLE AGE

As we get older, we move slower, we become wrinkled, and we may feel the effects of various chronic conditions or diseases. This process is known as **senescence,** the decline in body functioning associated with aging. Why does senescence occur? Why do we grow old? Most theories about biological aging fall into one of two categories (summarized in Table 2): *genetic-programming theories* and *variable-rate theories.*

senescence
Period of the life span marked by declines in physical functioning usually associated with aging; begins at different ages for different people.

Genetic-Programming Theories Is aging an inevitable biological process? Are we programmed to age? **Genetic-programming theories** hold that this is indeed the case. These theories propose that people's bodies age according to instructions built into the genes, and that aging is a normal part of development.

genetic-programming theories
Theories that explain biological aging as resulting from a genetically determined developmental timetable.

If genes control the aging process, then studying twins should give us some indication of the strength of this process. Twin studies have shown that genetic differences account for about one-fourth of the variance in the adult human life span. And the genetic influences on aging appear to become stronger over time, especially after age 60 (Molofsky et al., 2006; Willcox et al., 2008). It is likely that aging involves many gene variants, each with small effects.

Aging also may be influenced by specific genes "switching off," after which age-related losses (such as declines in vision, hearing, and motor control) occur. This process, broadly described as *epigenesis,* involves genes being turned on and off by molecular "tags," or instructions. Epigenetic changes do not involve changes in the underlying genetic code; rather, they involve changes in how genes are expressed. Some researchers suggest that the accumulation of epigenetic changes is partly responsible for aging (Skulachev et al., 2009). Consider this, however. Because epigenetic changes are dynamic and modifiable by environmental influences, positive interventions may be able to combat the effects of aging (Gravina & Vijg, 2010).

TABLE 2 Theories of Biological Aging

Genetic-Programming Theories	Variable-Rate Theories
Programmed senescence theory. Aging is the result of the sequential switching on and off of certain genes. Senescence is the time when the resulting age-associated deficits become evident.	*Wear-and-tear theory.* Cells and tissues have vital parts that wear out.
Endocrine theory. Biological clocks act through hormones to control the pace of aging.	*Free-radical theory.* Accumulated damage from oxygen radicals causes cells and eventually organs to stop functioning.
Immunological theory. A programmed decline in immune system functions leads to increased vulnerability to infectious disease and thus to aging and death.	*Rate-of-living theory.* The greater an organism's rate of metabolism, the shorter its life span.
Evolutionary theory. Aging is an evolved trait thus genes that promote reproduction are selected at higher rates than genes that extend life.	*Autoimmune theory.* Immune system becomes confused and attacks its own body cells.

Source: Adapted from NIH/NIA, 1993, p. 2.

This Japanese woman's active lifestyle has contributed to her long healthy life and to her country's lengthy healthy life expectancy.

Another factor that affects aging are processes within cells themselves. For example, *mitochondria*—tiny organisms that generate energy for cell processes—play an important role in helping cells survive under stress. In a study of worms, it was found that the fragmentation of mitochondria prompted cells to self-destruct (Jagasia, Grote, Westermann, & Conradt, 2005). These defects may be a major cause of aging (Holliday, 2004) and may apply to humans as well.

Another cellular process involves *telomeres,* the protective fragments of DNA on the tips of chromosomes. Every time a cell divides, replicating its genetic code, the telomeres become shorter. Some theorists argue that cells can only divide a fixed number of times—eventually they run out of telomeres. When cells can no longer divide, the body loses its ability to repair damaged tissue, and thus begins to age. Research has found that shorter telomeres are related to early death, particularly from heart and infectious disease, in people over the age of 60 (Cawthon, Smith, O'Brien, Sivatchenko, & Kerber, 2003), although other data have failed to support this finding (Bischoff et al., 2006). There are some indications that telomere length may not predict life expectancy but might predict how many years of life are healthy (Njajou et al., 2009), in conjunction with environmental factors. For example, telomere change is affected by stress (Epel et al., 2004), and stress is predictive of cardiovascular disease and cancer (M. Simon et al., 2006), both of which can shorten one's life.

The above processes are likely to be intimately related, and result in a series of interacting changes. Mitochondrial dysfunction may lead to damage in DNA, which in turn leads to a more rapid shortening of telomere length and accelerated aging (Sahin & DePinho, 2010).

According to *endocrine theory,* the biological clock acts through genes that control hormonal changes. Loss of muscle strength, accumulation of fat, and atrophy of organs may be related to declines in hormonal activity (Lamberts, van den Beld, & van der Lely, 1997). There are suggestions that the longevity effect seen as a result of calorie restriction might be mediated by endocrine activity. In other words, what may be causing the increase in life span is not the direct consequence of the decrease in calories, but rather the result of the alterations in endocrine activity calorie restriction brings about (Redman & Ravussin, 2009). *Immunological theory* proposes that certain genes may cause problems in the immune system (Holliday, 2004; Kiecolt-Glaser & Glaser, 2001) that then leads to an increased susceptibility to diseases, infections, and cancer (DiCarlo, Fuldner, Kaminski, & Hodes, 2009).

Still another variant of genetic-programming theory is the *evolutionary theory of aging.* According to evolutionary theory, reproductive fitness is the primary aim of natural selection. Therefore, natural selection acts most strongly on the young, who have many years of potential reproduction ahead of them. If a trait favoring reproductive output in the young is present, it will be spread throughout the population, even if the effects are damaging to the individual later in life (Baltes, 1997). Moreover, natural selection results in energy resources being allocated to protect and maintain the body until reproduction, but not necessarily after. After reproduction has ceased, the molecular integrity of the body cells and systems deteriorate beyond the body's ability to repair them, resulting in increased vulnerability to disease and death (Hayflick, 2004). This deterioration occurs because there is no selective pressure to prevent it once genes have been passed on to the next generation.

Variable-Rate Theories Why might one older adult suffer from arthritis, poor health, and declining perceptual abilities and another remain active and engaged? Why do some people age more quickly or slowly than others? According to **variable-rate theories,** aging is the result of random processes that vary from person to person. They are also called *error theories* because these processes often involve damage due to chance errors in, or environmental assaults on, biological systems.

variable-rate theories
Theories that explain biological aging as a result of processes that involve damage to biological systems and that vary from person to person.

One such theory, *wear-and-tear theory,* holds that the body ages as a result of accumulated damage to the system at the molecular level (Hayflick, 2004; Holliday, 2004). The body's cells constantly multiply through cell divisions. As cells age, some become damaged or useless and must be replaced in order for organs and body systems to function effectively. If a person's body is unable to do this, it eventually runs down. Internal and external stressors (including the accumulation of harmful materials, such as chemical by-products of metabolic processes) may aggravate the wearing-down process.

Another theory of aging, known as the *free-radical theory,* proposes that aging results from the formation of **free radicals,** a by-product of metabolic processes. Free radicals are molecules with unpaired electrons. This makes them very reactive because they seek to pair their electrons and will "steal" electrons from neighboring atoms. This process can ultimately damage cell membranes, cell proteins, fats, carbohydrates, and even DNA. Moreover, free-radical damage accumulates with age and has been associated with arthritis, muscular dystrophy, cataracts, cancer, late-onset diabetes, and neurological disorders such as Parkinson's disease (Stadtman, 1992; Wallace, 1992). Support for free-radical theory comes from research in which fruit flies, given extra copies of genes that eliminate free radicals, lived as much as one-third longer than usual (Orr & Sohal, 1994). Conversely, a strain of mice bred without a gene called *MsrA,* which normally protects against free radicals, had shorter-than-normal life spans (Moskovitz et al., 2001).

free radicals
Unstable, highly reactive atoms or molecules, formed during metabolism, that can cause internal bodily damage.

Is there any way to protect ourselves from the action of free radicals? Antioxidants are molecules that stabilize the action of free radicals and theoretically might be used to prevent their negative effects. Unfortunately, antioxidant supplementation has not been shown to be helpful in prolonging the human life span, and it may even have negative effects (Bjelakovic, Nikolova, Gluud, Simonetti, & Gluud, 2008).

The *rate-of-living theory* postulates that there is a balance between metabolism, or energy use, and life span. The faster a body's metabolism, the shorter its life span, and vice versa. So, for example, a hummingbird would be predicted to have a far shorter life than a sloth. In support of this assertion, fish whose metabolism is lowered by putting them in cooler water live longer than they would in warmer water (Schneider, 1992). Additional evidence suggests that reduced calorie diets, which result in slowed metabolism, increase longevity across a variety of species (Bordone & Guarente, 2005).

Autoimmune theory suggests that an aging immune system can become "confused" and release antibodies that attack the body's own cells. This malfunction, called **autoimmunity,** is thought to be responsible for some aging-related diseases and disorders (Holliday, 2004).

autoimmunity
Tendency of an aging body to mistake its own tissues for foreign invaders and to attack and destroy them.

Genetic-programming and variable-rate theories have practical implications. If human beings are programmed to age at a certain rate, they can do little to retard the process. If, on the other hand, aging is variable, then lifestyle practices may influence it. However, there is no evidence to support the profusion of commercial "anti-aging" remedies now on the market (International Longevity Center, 2002; Olshansky, Hayflick, & Perls, 2004). Instead of looking for anti-aging remedies, many gerontologists urge that more resources be devoted to research on "longevity medicine"—ways to combat specific diseases and thus prolong life (International Longevity Center, 2002; Olshansky et al., 2002a). Moreover, some researchers have suggested that rather than focusing on how to extend the human life span, it makes more sense to consider how we can improve human health *while* aging (Partridge, 2010).

It seems likely that many of these theoretical perspectives offer parts of the truth. Controllable environmental and lifestyle factors may interact with genetic factors to determine how long a person lives and in what condition. And epigenetic processes are also likely to be at play here (Migliore & Coppede, 2008).

HOW FAR CAN THE LIFE SPAN BE EXTENDED?

The idea that people can control the length and quality of their lives goes back to Luigi Cornaro, a nobleman of the sixteenth-century Italian Renaissance (Haber, 2004).

research in action

CENTENARIANS

1

A century ago, most people did not live to their 50th birthdays. Today people over 100—known as centenarians—are a fast-growing segment of the world population. Researchers estimate that by 2040 there will be 2.3 million centenarians worldwide, a change of 746 percent since 2005 (Kinsella & He, 2009).

Leading gerontologists worry that a longer life span means an increasing number of people with chronic disease, but that prediction may not necessarily come true. Remarkably, among 424 centenarians in the United States and Canada, about one-half of both men and women were free of heart disease, stroke, and cancer (other than skin cancer), the three most common causes of mortality in old age. The researchers found three alternative patterns in the centenarians' health histories. Nearly 1 in 5 (32 percent of the men and 15 percent of the women) were *escapers*—they were disease-free. *Survivors* (24 percent of the men and 43 percent of the women) had been diagnosed with an age-associated illness such as stroke, heart disease, cancer, hypertension, diabetes, or chronic obstructive pulmonary disease before age 80 but had survived it. The largest category, *delayers* (44 percent of the men and 42 percent of the women), had managed to delay the onset of age-related disease until age 80 or later. Altogether, 87 percent of the men and 83 percent of the women had escaped or delayed these diseases (Evert, Lawler, Bogan, & Perls, 2003).

What might explain this pattern? One possibility is exceptional genes. Centenarians tend to be relatively free of genes linked to age-related fatal diseases such as cancer and Alzheimer's. A region on chromosome 4, shared by many of the centenarians studied, has been linked to exceptionally long life (Perls, Kunkel, & Puca, 2002a, 2002b; Puca et al., 2001) and also to healthy aging (Reed, Dick, Uniacke, Foroud, & Nichols, 2004). In other research, a gene variant studied in people of Ashkenazi (Eastern European) Jewish descent age 95 and older seemed to protect memory and the ability to think and learn (Barzilai, Atzmon, Derby, Bauman, & Lipton, 2006).

Centenarians studied in eight New England towns vary widely in educational level, socioeconomic status, religion, ethnicity, and diet patterns. Some are vegetarians, and others eat a lot of saturated fats. Some were athletes, and some did no strenuous activity. However, few are obese, and heavy smoking is rare among them. A disproportionate number are never-married women; and, among those who are mothers, a disproportionate number had children after age 40. The only shared personality trait is the ability to manage stress (Perls, Alpert, & Fretts, 1997; Perls, Hutter-Silver, & Lauerman, 1999; Silver, Bubrick, Jilinskaia, & Perls, 1998). Perhaps this quality was best exemplified by Anna Morgan of Rehoboth, Massachusetts. Before her death at 101, she made her own funeral arrangements. "I don't want my children to be burdened with all this," she explained to the researchers. "They're old, you know" (Hilts, 1999).

Have you ever known someone who lived past 100? If so, to what did that person attribute his or her longevity? Did he or she have family members who also were long-lived?

Cornaro practiced moderation in all things, and he lived to be 98—close to what scientists once considered the upper limit of the human life span. Today that limit has been greatly exceeded by the growing number of centenarians—people who live past 100 (Box 1). Is it possible for human beings to live even longer?

survival curve
A curve on a graph showing the percentage of people or animals alive at various ages.

Most people understand that more people survive to the age of 40 than to 60, and that more people survive to the age of 60 than to 80. When translated into statistical terms, this concept is known as a **survival curve.** A survival curve represents the percentage of people or animals alive at various ages. Survival curves support the idea of a biological limit to the life span because more members of a species die as they approach the upper limit. With respect to humans, the curve currently ends roughly at age 100. Why is the human life span about 100 years? One reason may be that there are limits on how many times our cells can divide.

Leonard Hayflick (1974) found that human cells will divide in the laboratory no more than 50 times. This is called the **Hayflick limit,** and it has been shown to be genetically controlled. If, as Hayflick (1981) suggested, cells go through the same process in the body as in a laboratory culture, there might be a biological limit to the life span of human cells, and therefore of human life—a limit Hayflick estimated at 110 years.

Misao Okawa of Japan is the oldest living person with documentation of her age. She was born March 5, 1898. Two of her children are still alive, and they are in their 90s.

However, the pattern appears to change at very old ages. In Sweden, for example, the maximum life span increased from about 101 years in the 1860s to 108 years in the 1990s, mainly due to reductions in death rates after age 70 (Wilmoth, Deegan, Lundstrom, & Horiuchi, 2000). Furthermore, death rates actually *decrease* after 100 (Coles, 2004). People at 110 are no more likely to die in a given year than people in their 80s (Vaupel et al., 1998). In other words, people hardy enough to reach a certain age are likely to go on living a while longer. This is why life expectancy at 65, for example, is longer than life expectancy at birth (Administration on Aging, 2006). From this and other demographic evidence, at least one researcher suggests that there is no fixed limit on the human life span (Wilmoth, 2000). However, newer mathematical models, bolstered by data on long-lived Swedish women, suggest that the maximum life span for humans may be somewhere in the range of 126 years (Weon & Je, 2009).

Hayflick limit
Genetically controlled limit, proposed by Hayflick, on the number of times cells can divide in members of a species.

Because genetics plays at least a partial role in human longevity (Coles, 2004), some believe the idea of an exponential increase in the human life span is unrealistic. Gains in life expectancy since the 1970s have come from reductions in age-related diseases, such as heart disease, cancer, and stroke, and further gains will be far more difficult to achieve unless scientists find ways to modify the basic processes of aging—a feat some gerontologists consider impossible (Hayflick, 2004; Holliday, 2004).

If you could live as long as you wanted to, how long would you choose to live? What factors would affect your answer?

Animal research, however, challenges the idea of an unalterable biological limit for each species. Scientists have extended the healthy life spans of worms, fruit flies, and mice through slight genetic mutations (Ishii et al., 1998; Kolata, 1999; Lin, Seroude, & Benzer, 1998; Parkes et al., 1998; Pennisi, 1998). Such research suggests the possibility of delayed senescence and a significant increase in the average and maximum life spans (Arking, Novoseltsev, & Novoseltseva, 2004). In human beings, of course, genetic control of a biological process may be far more complex. Because no single gene or process seems responsible for senescence and the end of life, we are less likely to find genetic quick fixes for human aging (Holliday, 2004). Moreover, techniques that show promise in shorter-lived species may not apply to humans. However, a more general and holistic approach to aging, with medications used *before* the advent of aging-related disease, might show more promise for extending life in humans (Partridge, 2010).

People who, when they were young, held negative stereotypes of the elderly, were more likely to experience heart problems later in life.

Levy, Zonderman, Slade, & Ferrucci, 2009

One promising line of research—inspired by rate-of-living theories that view the speed of metabolism, or energy use, as the crucial determinant of aging—is on dietary restriction. Drastic caloric reduction (but still including all necessary nutrients) has been found to greatly extend life in worms, fish, and monkeys—in fact, in nearly all animal species on which it has been tried (Bodkin et al., 2003; Heilbronn & Ravussin, 2003). A review of 15 years of research suggests that calorie restriction can have beneficial effects on human aging and life expectancy (Fontana & Klein, 2007).

The Calorie Restriction Society practices voluntary caloric restriction, avoiding processed foods rich in refined carbohydrates and partially hydrogenated oils. In comparison with control groups eating a typical Western diet, society members show many of the same improvements in metabolic and organ function previously reported in calorie-restricted rhesus monkeys, among them, a low percentage of body fat, and a decreased incidence of diabetes, cancer, and age-related disease. Calorie restricted

checkpoint
can **you**...

- Compare two types of theories of biological aging and discuss their implications and supporting evidence?
- Discuss findings of life-extension research and its limitations in human beings?

monkeys also show less of the brain atrophy that sometimes accompanies aging (Colman et al., 2009). However, the optimal amount of caloric restriction in humans is not known, nor it is known if there are any adverse effects of such extreme restriction. In addition, it is unclear if exercise-induced leanness has the same positive benefits as leanness resulting from mere calorie restriction. For these reasons, and because a very-low-calorie diet takes great discipline to maintain, there is increasing interest in developing drugs that mimic the effects of caloric restriction (Fontana, Klein, & Holloszy, 2010).

If human beings someday realize the dream of a fountain of youth, some gerontologists fear a rise in age-related diseases and disabling infirmities (Stock & Callahan, 2004). Life-extension studies in animals and research on human centenarians, though, suggest that such fears may be unwarranted and that fatal diseases would come very near the end of a longer life (International Longevity Center, 2002).

Physical Changes

Some physical changes typically associated with aging are obvious to a casual observer. Older skin tends to become paler and less elastic; and, as fat and muscle shrink, the skin may wrinkle. Varicose veins may appear on the legs. The hair on the head thins and turns gray and then white, and body hair becomes sparser.

Older adults become shorter as the disks between their spinal vertebrae atrophy. Especially in women with osteoporosis, thinning of the bones may cause *kyphosis,* commonly called a "dowager's hump," an exaggerated curvature of the spine that generally occurs between ages 50 and 59 (Ball, 2009). In addition, the chemical composition of the bones changes, creating a greater risk of fractures. Less visible but equally important changes affect internal organs and body systems; the brain; and sensory, motor, and sexual functioning.

Kyphosis is not inevitable—spine extension exercises can help prevent or delay it.

Ball, 2009

ORGANIC AND SYSTEMIC CHANGES

Changes in organic and systemic functioning are highly variable. Some body systems decline rapidly, others hardly at all (Figure 3). Aging, together with chronic stress, can depress immune function, making older people more susceptible to respiratory infections (Kiecolt-Glaser & Glaser, 2001) and less likely to ward them off (Koivula, Sten, & Makela, 1999). Chronic stress in older adults is also related to chronic low-grade inflammation (Bauer, Jeckel, & Luz, 2009). The digestive system, on the other hand, remains relatively efficient (Harris, Davies, Ward, & Haboubi, 2008). The rhythm of the heart tends to become slower and more irregular. Deposits of fat accumulate around the heart and may interfere with functioning, and blood pressure often rises.

reserve capacity
Ability of body organs and systems to put forth 4 to 10 times as much effort as usual under acute stress; also called *organ reserve.*

Car batteries supply electrical energy to a car, and the number of minutes a battery can function without recharging is the reserve capacity. When conditions are good, such as in warm weather, you may not see the effects of an old battery. When conditions are poor, however, such as during cold weather, an old battery may not start your car. We can use this analogy to describe the functioning of human body systems. In this case, **reserve capacity** is the backup capacity that helps body systems function to their utmost limits in times of stress. With age, reserve levels tend to drop, and many older people cannot respond to extra physical demands as they once did. For example, a person who used to be able to shovel snow and then ski afterward may become exhausted just from the shoveling, or may have to stop shoveling altogether.

Still, many older adults barely notice changes in systemic functioning. By pacing themselves, most older adults can do almost anything they need and want to do.

checkpoint
can **you**...

- Summarize common changes and variations in systemic functioning during late life?

THE AGING BRAIN

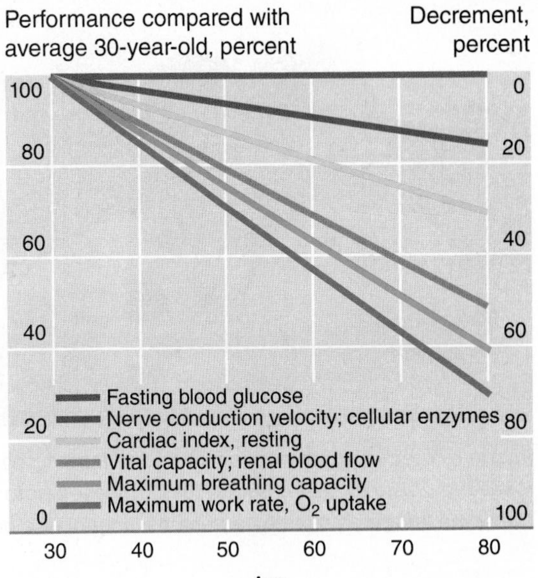

FIGURE 3

Declines in Organ Functioning

Differences in functional efficiency of various internal body systems are typically slight in young adulthood but widen by old age.

Source: Katchadourian, 1987.

In normal, healthy people, changes in the aging brain are generally subtle and make little difference in functioning. The brain's plasticity can "reorganize neural circuitry to respond to the challenge of neurobiological aging" (Park & Gutchess, 2006, p. 107). In fact, some researchers have suggested that the brain's continued flexibility and plasticity is responsible for the fact that although processing speed, memory, and inhibition all decline with advanced age, there are *increases* in prefrontal activity (Park & Reuter-Lorenz, 2009). Similarly, MRI studies have shown that when engaged in cognitive tasks the brains of older adults show more diffuse activation than the brains of younger adults (Brayne, 2007). These processes may be compensatory. Given declines in certain areas, the brain works around those issues by utilizing alternative cognitive pathways, and thus the declines seen in the aging brain are not as severe as they otherwise might have been.

In late adulthood, the brain gradually diminishes in volume and weight, particularly in the frontal cortex, which controls executive functions (Park & Gutchess, 2006; von Hippel, 2007). This gradual shrinkage was formerly attributed to a loss of neurons (nerve cells). However, most researchers now agree that—except in certain specific brain areas, such as the cerebellum, which coordinates sensory and motor activity—neuronal loss is not substantial and does not affect cognition (Burke & Barnes, 2006; Finch & Zelinski, 2005). However, when the pace of these brain changes increases, cognitive declines are increasingly likely (Carlson et al., 2008).

Another typical change is a decrease in the number, or density, of dopamine neurotransmitters due to losses of synapses (neuronal connections). Dopamine receptors are important as they help in regulating attention (Park & Reuter-Lorenz, 2009). Not surprisingly, this decline generally results in slowed response time.

Beginning in the mid-fifties, the myelin sheathing that enables neuronal impulses to travel rapidly between brain regions begins to thin out (Hinman & Abraham, 2007). This deterioration of the brain's myelin, or white matter, is associated with cognitive and motor declines (Andrews-Hanna et al., 2007; Finch & Zelinski, 2005).

Postmortem examinations of brain tissue have found significant DNA damage in certain genes that affect learning and memory in most very old people and some middle-aged people (Lu et al., 2004). Although adults over the age of 90 years are more than 25 times more likely to develop dementia than adults aged 65 to 69 years (Brayne, 2007), such deterioration is *not* inevitable. A postmortem examination of the brain of a Dutch woman who died at 115 found no evidence of dementia. Two to three years before her death, her neurological and cognitive performance tested better than that of the average 60- to 75-year-old (den Dunnen et al., 2008).

Not all changes in the brain are destructive. Researchers have discovered that older brains can grow new nerve cells from stem cells—something once thought impossible. Evidence of cell division has been found in the hippocampus, a portion of the brain involved in learning and memory (Van Praag et al., 2002). It appears likely that in humans, physical activity paired with cognitive challenges may be most effective in promoting the growth of new cells in the hippocampus (Fabel & Kempermann, 2008).

Changes in the brain can have social as well as cognitive consequences. Loss of executive function in the frontal cortex can lessen the ability to inhibit irrelevant or unwanted thoughts; thus older adults may talk too much about matters apparently unconnected to the topic of conversation. On the positive side, the amygdala, the seat of emotions, shows lessened response to negative, but not positive, events; thus older adults tend to be more constructive in resolving conflicts than are younger adults (von Hippel, 2007).

checkpoint
can **you** . . .

- **Identify several age-related changes in the brain and their effects on cognitive and social functioning?**

In age-related macular degeneration, the leading cause of visual impairment in older adults, the center of the retina gradually loses the ability to distinguish details. In these photos, the left is an image as seen by a person with normal vision and the right is the same image as seen by a person with macular degeneration.

SENSORY AND PSYCHOMOTOR FUNCTIONING

Individual differences in sensory and motor functioning increase with age (Steinhagen-Thiessen & Borchelt, 1993). Some older people experience sharp declines; others find their abilities virtually unchanged. Visual and hearing problems may deprive them of social relationships and independence (Desai, Pratt, Lentzner, & Robinson, 2001; O'Neill, Summer, & Shirey, 1999), and motor impairments may limit everyday activities.

Vision and Hearing Older eyes need more light to see, are more sensitive to glare, and may have trouble locating and reading signs. Thus driving may become hazardous, especially at night. Older adults may have difficulty with depth or color perception or with such daily activities as reading, sewing, shopping, and cooking (Desai et al., 2001). Losses in visual contrast sensitivity can cause difficulty reading very small or very light print (Kline & Scialfa, 1996). Vision problems also can cause accidents and falls (Kulmala et al., 2009). Many community-dwelling older adults report difficulty with bathing, dressing, and walking around the house, in part because they are visually impaired (Desai et al., 2001).

People with moderate visual losses often can be helped by corrective lenses or changes in the environment. Still, 17 percent of U.S. older adults and 30 percent of those 85 and older have trouble seeing, even when wearing glasses or contact lenses (Schoenborn, Vickerie, & Powell-Griner, 2006), and women are generally more impaired than are men, at least until age 85 (Schoenborn & Heyman, 2009).

cataracts
Cloudy or opaque areas in the lens of the eye, which cause blurred vision.

Cataracts, cloudy or opaque areas in the lens of the eye, are common in older adults and eventually cause blurred vision (Schaumberg et al., 2004). Surgery to remove cataracts is one of the most frequent operations among older Americans.

age-related macular degeneration
Condition in which the center of the retina gradually loses its ability to discern fine details; leading cause of irreversible visual impairment in older adults.

The leading cause of visual impairment in older adults is **age-related macular degeneration.** In our eye, the macula is a small spot in the center of the retina that helps us keep objects directly in our line of sight in sharp focus. In the most common form of macular degeneration, the retinal cells in this area degenerate over time, and the center of the retina gradually loses the ability to sharply distinguish fine details. Activities such as reading and driving become extremely problematic, as the exact area in which a person focuses becomes blurry. In some cases, treatments such as laser surgery, photodynamic therapy, and antioxidant and zinc supplements can prevent further vision loss (Foundation Fighting Blindness, 2005).

glaucoma
Irreversible damage to the optic nerve caused by increased pressure in the eye.

Glaucoma is irreversible damage to the optic nerve caused by increased pressure in the eye. If left untreated, it can cause blindness. Early treatment can lower elevated pressure in the eye and delay the onset of the condition (Heijl et al., 2002). Worldwide, glaucoma is the second leading cause of blindness (Quigley & Broman, 2006). However, even with treatment, 10 percent of people who get glaucoma will eventually go blind (Glaucoma Research Foundation, 2010).

Hearing impairments increase with age, affecting 31.6 percent of Americans ages 65 to 74 and 62.1 percent of those 85 and over. Men are more likely to experience hearing loss than women, and white people more than black people (Schoenborn & Heyman, 2009). Hearing loss may contribute to a false perception of older people as distractible, absentminded, and irritable and tends to have a negative impact on the well-being not only of the impaired person but of his or her spouse or partner (Wallhagen, Strawbridge, Shema, & Kaplan, 2004). Hearing aids can help but are expensive and may magnify background noises as well as the sounds a person wants to hear.

Changes in environmental design, such as brighter reading lights, a closed captioning option on television sets, and built-in telephone amplifiers can help many older adults with sensory limitations.

Strength, Endurance, Balance, and Reaction Time Adults generally lose about 10 to 20 percent of their strength up to age 70 and more after that. Endurance declines more consistently with age, especially among women, than some other aspects of fitness, such as flexibility (Van Heuvelen, Kempen, Ormel, & Rispens, 1998). Declines in muscle strength and power may result from a combination of natural aging, decreased activity, and disease (Barry & Carson, 2004).

These losses seem to be partly reversible. In controlled studies with people in their 60s to 90s, weight training, power training, or resistance training programs lasting 8 weeks to 2 years increased muscle strength, size, and mobility; speed, endurance, and leg muscle power; and spontaneous physical activity (Ades, Ballor, Ashikaga, Utton, & Nair, 1996; Fiatarone et al., 1994; Foldvari et al., 2000; McCartney, Hicks, Martin, & Webber, 1996). Although these gains may result to some extent from improvements in muscle mass, the primary factor in older adults is likely to be a training-induced adaptation in the brain's ability to activate and coordinate muscular activity (Barry & Carson, 2004). This evidence of plasticity in older adults is especially important because people whose muscles have atrophied are more likely to suffer falls and fractures and to need help with tasks of day-to-day living (Agency for Healthcare Research and Quality and CDC, 2002). Indeed, weight training has been used to restore physical functioning in elderly subjects recovering from hip replacement surgery and has been shown to be much more effective than the standard physical therapy generally used in rehabilitation (Suetta et al., 2008).

Falls, and the injuries that often occur as a result, are the leading cause of hospitalization in the elderly (Centers for Disease Control, and Merck Company Foundation, 2007). Many falls and fractures are preventable by boosting muscle strength, balance, and gait speed and by eliminating hazards commonly found in the home (Agency for Healthcare Research and Quality and CDC, 2002; Table 3). The Korean martial art of *tae kwon do* is effective in improving balance and walking ability (Cromwell, Meyers, Meyers, & Newton, 2007). In one study, explosive heavy resistance training, which involves the rapid lifting of heavy weights, was well tolerated by women aged 60 to 89 years of age and resulted in increases in muscle power and strength, and consequently in a decreased risk of falling (Casserotti, Aarguard, Larsen, & Puggaard, 2008).

SLEEP

Older people tend to sleep less and dream less than before. Their hours of deep sleep are more restricted, and they may awaken more easily because of physical problems, exposure to light (Czeisler et al., 1999), or perhaps as a result of age-related changes in the body's ability to regulate circadian cycles of sleep and wakefulness (Cajochen, Münch, Knoblauch, Blatter, & Wirz-Justice, 2006). However, the assumption that sleep problems are normal in old age can be dangerous. Chronic *insomnia,* or sleeplessness, can be a symptom of, or if untreated, a forerunner of depression. Either too much sleep or too little sleep is associated with an increased risk of mortality (Gangswisch et al., 2008).

TABLE 3 Safety Checklist for Preventing Falls in the Home

Stairways, hallways, and pathways	Free of clutter Good lighting, especially at top of stairs Light switches at top and bottom of stairs Tightly fastened handrails on both sides and full length of stairs Carpets firmly attached and not frayed; rough-textured or abrasive strips to secure footing
Bathrooms	Grab bars conveniently located inside and outside of tubs and showers and near toilets Nonskid mats, abrasive strips, or carpet on all surfaces that may get wet Night lights
Bedrooms	Telephones and night lights or light switches within easy reach of beds
All living areas	Electrical cords and telephone wires out of walking paths Rugs and carpets well secured to floor No exposed nails or loose threshold trim Furniture and other objects in familiar places and not in the way; rounded or padded table edges Couches and chairs proper height to get into and out of easily

Source: Adapted from NIA, 1993.

Drugs such as benzodiazepines are commonly used to treat sleep problems (Salzman, 2008). Additionally, cognitive behavioral therapy (staying in bed only when asleep, getting up at the same time each morning, and learning about false beliefs pertaining to sleep needs) has produced long-term improvement, with or without drug treatment (Morin, Colecchi, Stone, Sood, & Brink, 1999; Reynolds, Buysse, & Kupfer, 1999).

In a recent study, about a third of men ages 75 to 95 reported having had sex in the previous year.

Hyde et al., 2010

SEXUAL FUNCTIONING

The most important factor in maintaining sexual functioning is consistent sexual activity over the years. In a national survey, 53 percent of U.S. adults ages 65 to 74 and 26 percent of those ages 75 to 85 reported being sexually active. Men are much more likely than women to remain sexually active in old age, largely because, being less numerous, they are more likely to have a spouse or partner (Lindau et al., 2007).

Sex is different in late adulthood from what it was earlier. Men typically take longer to develop an erection and to ejaculate, may need more manual stimulation, and may experience longer intervals between erections. Women's breast engorgement and other signs of sexual arousal are less intense than before, and they may experience issues with lubrication. In the survey just mentioned, about half of both men and women who were sexually active reported sexual problems (Lindau et al., 2007). Health problems are more likely to affect the sex life of women than men, but poor mental health and relationship dissatisfaction are associated with sexual dysfunction in both men and women (Laumann, Das, & Waite, 2008).

Sexual activity in older people is normal and healthy. Housing arrangements and care providers should consider the sexual needs of elderly people. Satisfaction with life, cognitive functioning, and psychological well-being are all strongly related to interest in and having sex (Trudel, Villeneuve, Anderson, & Pilon, 2008). Physicians should avoid prescribing drugs that interfere with sexual functioning if alternatives are available and, when such a drug must be taken, should alert the patient to its effects.

checkpoint
can **you** . . .

- **Describe typical changes in sensory and motor functioning and in sleep needs, and tell how they can affect everyday living?**
- **Summarize changes in sexual functioning and possibilities for sexual activity in late life?**

Physical and Mental Health

Increasing life expectancy is raising pressing questions about the relationship between longevity and health, both physical and mental. How healthy are older adults today, and how can they stave off declines in health?

HEALTH STATUS

Poor health is *not* an inevitable consequence of aging (Moore, Moir, & Patrick, 2004). About 76 percent of U.S. adults age 65 and older consider themselves in good to excellent health. As earlier in life, poverty is strongly related to poor health and to limited access to, and use of, health care (Federal Interagency Forum on Aging-Related Statistics, 2006; Schoenborn et al., 2006). For instance, poverty is related to a higher incidence of arthritis, diabetes, high blood pressure, heart disease, depression, and stroke in the elderly (Menec, Shooshtari, Nowicki, & Fournier, 2010). Adults who live in poverty are less likely to engage in such healthy behaviors as leisure-time physical activity, avoidance of smoking, and maintenance of appropriate body weight (Schoenborn et al., 2006).

Exposure to words that evoke stereotypes of the elderly lead to slower walking in young people. How might these stereotypes affect someone who is old?

Bargh, Chen, & Burrows, 1996

CHRONIC CONDITIONS AND DISABILITIES

At least 80 percent of older Americans have at least one chronic condition, and 50 percent have at least two (Moore et al., 2004). A much smaller proportion—but about half of those over 85—are frail: weak and vulnerable to stress, disease, disability, and death (Ostir, Ottenbacher, & Markides, 2004).

Common Chronic Conditions Six of the seven leading causes of death in old age in the United States are chronic conditions: heart disease, cancer, stroke, chronic lower respiratory disease, diabetes, and influenza/pneumonia (which government health authorities count as a single condition). In fact, heart disease, cancer, and stroke account for about 60 percent of deaths among older Americans (Federal Interagency Forum on Aging-Related Statistics, 2006; NCHS, 2007). However, cancer deaths have declined since the early 1990s due to reductions in smoking, early screening, and more effective treatment (Howe et al., 2006). Worldwide, the leading causes of death at age 60 and above are heart disease, stroke, chronic pulmonary disease, lower respiratory infections, and lung cancer (WHO, 2003). As we will discuss, many of these deaths could be prevented through healthier lifestyles. If Americans were to quit smoking, eat a healthier diet, and engage in higher levels of physical activity, estimates are that approximately 35 percent of deaths could be prevented in the elderly (Centers for Disease Control & Merck Company Foundation, 2007). Almost 95 percent of health care costs for older Americans are for chronic diseases (Moore et al., 2004), and the overall need for health care services for this population is expected to increase markedly over the next two decades (Centers for Disease Control & Merck Company Foundation, 2007).

Hypertension and diabetes are increasing in prevalence, affecting about 56 percent and 19 percent of the older population, respectively (Federal Interagency Forum on Aging-Related Statistics, 2010). Hypertension, which can affect blood flow to the brain, is related to declines in attention, learning, memory, executive functions, psychomotor abilities, and visual, perceptual, and spatial skills and is a risk factor for stroke. Table 4 lists warning signs of stroke.

TABLE 4 Warning Signs of Stroke
The first letters of four warning signs of stroke spell the word **FAST.**
Face Drooping—Does one side of the face droop or is it numb? Ask the person to smile to see if the person's smile is uneven.
Arm Weakness—Is one arm weak or numb? Ask the person to raise both arms. Does one arm drift downward?
Speech Difficulty—Is speech slurred? Ask the person to repeat a simple sentence.
Time to call 911—If someone shows any of these symptoms, call 911 and get the person to the hospital immediately.

Source: American Heart Association, 2013.

Aside from hypertension and diabetes, the most common chronic conditions are arthritis (50 percent), heart disease (31 percent), and cancer (21 percent). Women are more likely to report hypertension, stroke, asthma, chronic bronchitis, emphysema, and arthritis, whereas men are more likely to have heart disease, cancer, and diabetes (Federal Interagency Forum on Aging-Related Statistics, 2010).

Chronic conditions vary by race/ethnicity. In 2007–2008, 71 percent of older blacks had hypertension, compared with slightly more than 50 percent of older whites and Hispanics. Older blacks and Hispanics were significantly more likely than older whites to have diabetes—30 percent and 27 percent, respectively, as compared with 16 percent for older whites. On the other hand, 25 percent of older whites had cancer, compared with approximately 13 percent of older blacks and Hispanics (Federal Interagency Forum on Aging-Related Statistics, 2010).

Disabilities and Activity Limitations The proportion of older adults in the United States with chronic physical disabilities or activity limitations has declined since the mid-1980s (Federal Interagency Forum on Aging-Related Statistics, 2010), perhaps due in part to the increasing number of older people who are educated and knowledgeable about preventive measures. However, the proportion of people who have difficulty with functional activities such as walking, climbing stairs, and lifting objects rises sharply with age (NCHS, 2010).

When a condition is not severe, it can often be managed so that it does not interfere with daily life. A person who is arthritic or short of breath may take fewer steps or move items to lower shelves within easy reach. However, in the presence of chronic conditions and loss of reserve capacity, even a minor illness or injury can have serious repercussions. In one study looking at older adults hospitalized after a fall, those adults were more likely to die or be placed in a nursing home than adults admitted to the hospital for reasons unrelated to a fall (Aitken, Burmeister, Lang, Chaboyer, & Richmond, 2010). Even older people who say they have no difficulty walking may have trouble rapidly walking a quarter of a mile. In one study, 70- to 79-year-olds who could not complete this test were at greater risk of cardiovascular disease, mobility limitations or disabilities, and death after age 80, and each extra minute necessary to complete the test heightened these risks (Newman et al., 2006).

checkpoint
can **you**...

- Summarize the health status of older adults, and identify common chronic conditions common in late life?

LIFESTYLE INFLUENCES ON HEALTH AND LONGEVITY

The chances of remaining healthy and fit in late life often depend on lifestyle choices, especially related to smoking, heavy drinking, and exercise (Vu, Liu, Garside, & Daviglus, 2009).

Physical Activity When Yuichiro Miura first scaled the summit of Mount Everest, he was 70 years old. Not satisfied, he continued to train with weights and a treadmill, hoping to capture that distinction again. Miura is one of Japan's "old men of the mountain," a small group of aging climbers who seek the title of oldest person to have conquered the world's tallest peak (Watanabe, 2007).

Not every older adult can aspire to climb a mountain, but a lifelong program of exercise may prevent many physical changes once associated with normal aging. Regular exercise can strengthen the heart and lungs and decrease stress. It can protect against hypertension, hardening of the arteries, heart disease, osteoporosis, and diabetes. It helps maintain speed, stamina, strength, and endurance, and such basic functions as circulation and breathing. It reduces the chance of injuries by making joints and muscles stronger and more flexible, and it helps prevent or relieve lower-back pain and symptoms of arthritis. It can enable people with such conditions as lung disease and arthritis to remain independent and can help prevent the development of limitations on mobility. In addition, it may improve mental alertness and cognitive performance, help relieve anxiety and mild depression, and enhance feelings of mastery and well-being (Agency for Healthcare Research and Quality and CDC, 2002; Butler, Davis, Lewis, Nelson, &

The benefits these cross-country skiers gain from this lifelong activity are numerous. Exercise helps them live longer, healthier lives, and the social aspect of their sport helps keep them mentally healthy.

Strauss, 1998a, 1998b; Kramer et al., 1999; Kritchevsky et al., 2005; Mazzeo et al., 1998; Netz, Wu, Becker, & Tenenbaum, 2005; NIH Consensus Development Panel, 2001).

*In*activity contributes to heart disease, diabetes, colon cancer, and high blood pressure. It may lead to obesity, which affects the circulatory system, the kidneys, and sugar metabolism; contributes to degenerative disorders; and tends to shorten life. In a longitudinal study of 7,553 white older women, those who increased their activity levels over a 6-year period had lower death rates during the following 6½ years (Gregg et al., 2003). In a 12-month randomized, controlled study of 201 adults age 70 and older, a combination of exercise, training in self-management of chronic disease, and peer support improved the ability of those with mild to moderate disabilities to carry out activities of daily living (Phelan, Williams, Penninx, LoGerfo, & Leveille, 2004). An analysis of many studies found that aerobic activity of moderate intensity was most beneficial to well-being (Netz et al., 2005).

Do you engage regularly in physical exercise? How many of the older people you know do so? What types of physical activity do you expect to maintain as you get older?

Nutrition Five out of six Americans age 60 and older have diets that are poor or need improvement. Older women tend to have healthier diets than older men (Ervin, 2008).

Nutrition plays a large part in susceptibility to such chronic illnesses as atherosclerosis, heart disease, and diabetes as well as functional and activity limitations. Excessive body fat, which can come from a diet heavy in red and processed meats and alcohol, has been linked to several types of cancer (World Cancer Research Fund, 2007). However, while weight gain is not healthy for older adults, neither is excessive weight loss. Excessive weight loss can lead to muscle weakness and general frailty, and can be as debilitating to older adults as weight gain (Schlenker, 2010).

A healthy diet can reduce risks of obesity as well as of high blood pressure and cholesterol (Federal Interagency Forum on Aging-Related Statistics, 2006). A diet high in olive oil, whole grains, vegetables, and nuts has been found to reduce cardiovascular risk (Esposito et al., 2004) and—in combination with physical activity, moderate alcohol use, and refraining from smoking—cut 10-year mortality from all causes in healthy 70- to 90-year-old Europeans by nearly two-thirds (Rosamund et al., 2008). Eating fruits and vegetables—especially those rich in vitamin C, citrus fruits and juices, green leafy vegetables, broccoli, cabbage, cauliflower, and brussels sprouts—lowers the risk of cancer and heart disease (Takachi et al., 2007).

checkpoint can you . . .

▷ Give evidence of the influences of exercise and nutrition on health and longevity?

Periodontal disease is a chronic inflammation of the gums caused by the bacteria in plaque. It can result in tender or bleeding gums and eventual tooth loss. Although more aging Americans are keeping their natural teeth than ever before, more than 1 in 4 have lost all their teeth (Schoenborn et al., 2006). And those older adults with fewer than 20 teeth may suffer from malnutrition (Budtz-Jorgensen & Rapin, 2001) as a result of the increased difficulty in adequately chewing food. Periodontal disease has also been related to cognitive declines (Kaye et al., 2010) and cardiovascular disease (Blaizot, Vergnes, Nuwwareh, Amar, & Sixou, 2009). In fact, some suggest it may impair the regulation of blood sugar (Zadik, Bechor, Galor, & Levin, 2010).

MENTAL AND BEHAVIORAL PROBLEMS

Pet therapy results in decreased depressive symptoms and improvements in cognitive functioning for the elderly.

Moretti et al., 2010

Only 6 percent of older Americans report frequent mental distress (Moore et al., 2004). However, mental and behavioral disturbances that do occur can result in functional impairment in major life activities as well as cognitive decline (van Hooren et al., 2005).

Many older people with mental and behavioral problems tend not to seek help for their issues. Among these issues are drug intoxication, delirium, metabolic or infectious disorders, malnutrition, anemia, low thyroid functioning, minor head injuries, alcoholism, and depression (NIA, 1993; Wykle & Musil, 1993). The primary reason older people do not seek help is difficulty accessing needed support services (Mackenzie, Scott, Mather, & Sareen, 2008). Indeed, there is a shortage of trained mental health professionals for the elderly, and this shortage is likely to increase in line with projected increases in the elderly population (American Psychological Association, 2011).

Depression In 2006, 10 percent of older men and 18 percent of older women in the United States reported symptoms of clinical depression (Federal Interagency Forum on Aging-Related Statistics, 2010). Heredity may account for 40 to 50 percent of the risk for major depression (Bouchard, 2004; Harvard Medical School, 2004c). Vulnerability seems to result from the influence of multiple genes interacting with environmental factors. Special risk factors in late adulthood include chronic illness or disability, cognitive decline, and divorce, separation, or widowhood (Harvard Medical School, 2003; Mueller et al., 2004).

Depression is often coupled with other medical conditions. Some physicians, when treating multiple illnesses, may give depression lower priority than a physical ailment, such as diabetes or arthritis. Yet in a study of 1,801 older adults with clinically severe depression—each of whom had, on average, four chronic medical illnesses—depression played a more pervasive role in mental functional status, disability, and quality of life than did any of the other conditions (Noël et al., 2004).

Depression can be treated by antidepressant drugs, psychotherapy, or both, and antidepressant drugs appear to work equally as well as they do at younger ages (Blazer, 2009). Regular aerobic exercise can reduce symptoms of mild to moderate depression (Dunn, Trivedi, Kampert, Clark, & Chambliss, 2005).

dementia
Deterioration in cognitive and behavioral functioning due to physiological causes.

Dementia Sixty-nine-year-old Rose has become increasingly forgetful. Although her memory for long-ago events is sharp and detailed, she often repeats herself or finds herself standing in her kitchen, unsure of why she walked in. Always responsible in the past, she now has multiple unpaid bills and got lost driving home from the store in the past week. It is likely that Rose is experiencing the effects of dementia. **Dementia** is the general term for physiologically caused cognitive and behavioral decline sufficient to interfere with daily activities. Cognitive decline becomes increasingly common with advanced age, affecting 5 percent of U.S. adults in their 70s, 24 percent in their 80s, and 37.4 percent of those 90 and older (Plassman et al., 2007). Still, cognitive impairment severe enough to be diagnosed as dementia is not inevitable.

Most forms of dementia are irreversible, but about 10 percent of cases can be reversed with early diagnosis and treatment (NIA, 1993; Wykle & Musil, 1993).

Although there are about 50 causes of dementia of known origin, the vast majority of cases (about two-thirds) are caused by **Alzheimer's disease,** a progressive, degenerative brain disorder (Gatz, 2007). **Parkinson's disease,** the second most common disorder involving progressive neurological degeneration, is characterized by tremor, stiffness, slowed movement, and unstable posture (Nussbaum, 1998). These two diseases, together with *multi-infarct dementia (MD),* which is caused by a series of small strokes, account for at least 8 out of 10 cases of dementia, all irreversible.

Because our pet population is living longer too, dementia also occurs in dogs and is known as canine cognitive dysfunction syndrome. Common signs include accidents in the house, wandering in circles or staring, and changes in appetite and circadian rhythms.

Alzheimer's disease
Progressive, irreversible, degenerative brain disorder characterized by cognitive deterioration and loss of control of bodily functions, leading to death.

Parkinson's disease
Progressive, irreversible degenerative neurological disorder, characterized by tremor, stiffness, slowed movement, and unstable posture.

A variety of factors protect people from developing dementia. Certain personality traits seem to confer protection. In particular, high extraversion and low neuroticism (Wang et al., 2009) and high conscientiousness (Wilson, Schneider, Arnold, Bienias, & Bennett, 2007) offer advantages. Cognitive characteristics can also buffer a person. Education is protective (Mortimer, Snowdon, & Markesbery, 2002; Tyas et al., 2007), as is a challenging job (Seidler et al., 2004), lifelong bilingualism (Bialystok, Craik, & Freeman, 2007), and high linguistic ability early in life (Snowden et al., 1996). Drinking small amounts of alcohol has been associated with a decrease in risk (Peters, Peters, Warner, Beckett, & Bulpitt, 2008). Staying engaged with others is also beneficial. Older adults who have large social networks or frequent contact with others are less likely to show cognitive declines (Holtzman et al., 2004).

Cognitive impairment is more likely in people with poor health, especially those who experience strokes or diabetes (Tilvis et al., 2004). A lack of regular physical activity puts people at risk for later dementia (Abbott et al., 2004; van Gelder et al., 2004; Weuve et al., 2004), and instituting an exercise program even late in life may help reverse some of the early signs of cognitive impairment in otherwise healthy adults (Lautenschlager et al., 2008).

checkpoint
can you . . .

- Tell why late-life depression may be more common than is generally realized?
- Name the three main causes of dementia in older adults?

Alzheimer's Disease Alzheimer's disease (AD) is one of the most common and most feared terminal illnesses among aging persons. It gradually robs patients of intelligence, awareness, and even the ability to control their bodily functions—and finally kills them. The disease affects more than 26 million people throughout the world, and its incidence is expected to quadruple by 2050 (Brookmeyer, Johnson, Ziegler-Graham, & Arrighi, 2007).

In the United States, AD was the sixth leading cause of death in 2007 (Xu et al., 2010). An estimated 5.3 million people in the United States are living with AD, and by 2050 the incidence could reach between 11 and 16 million. Furthermore, as many as half a million people under 65 may have an early-onset form of the disease (Alzheimer's Association, 2010). The risk rises dramatically with age; thus increases in longevity mean that more people will survive to an age when the risk of AD is greatest (Hebert, Scherr, Bienias, Bennett, & Evans, 2003).

Symptoms The classic symptoms of Alzheimer's disease are memory impairment, deterioration of language, and deficits in visual and spatial processing. The most prominent early symptom is inability to recall recent events or take in new information. A person may repeat questions that were just answered or leave an everyday task unfinished. These early signs may be overlooked because they look like ordinary forgetfulness or may be interpreted as signs of normal aging.

Personality changes—for instance, rigidity, apathy, egocentricity, and impaired emotional control—tend to occur early in the disease's development (Balsis, Carpenter, & Storandt, 2005). There are indications that these personality changes may be useful in predicting which healthy adults might be at risk of developing dementia (Duchek, Balota, Storandt, & Larsen, 2007). More symptoms follow: irritability, anxiety, depression, and,

TABLE 5 Alzheimer's Disease versus Normal Behavior

Symptoms of Disease	Normal Behavior
Permanently forgetting recent events; asking the same questions repeatedly	Temporarily forgetting things
Inability to do routine tasks with many steps such as making and serving a meal	Inability to do some challenging tasks
Forgetting simple words	Forgetting unusual or complex words
Getting lost on one's own block	Getting lost in a strange city
Forgetting that a child is in one's care and leaving the house	Becoming momentarily distracted and failing to watch a child
Forgetting what the numbers in a checkbook mean and what to do with them	Making mistakes in balancing a checkbook
Putting things in inappropriate places where one cannot usefully retrieve them (e.g., a wristwatch in a fishbowl)	Misplacing everyday items
Rapid, dramatic mood swings and personality changes; loss of initiative	Occasional mood changes

later, delusions, delirium, and wandering. Long-term memory, judgment, concentration, orientation, and speech all become impaired, and patients have trouble handling basic activities of daily life. By the end, the patient cannot understand or use language, does not recognize family members, cannot eat without help, cannot control the bowels and bladder, and loses the ability to walk, sit up, and swallow solid food. Death usually comes within 8 to 10 years after symptoms appear (Cummings, 2004). Table 5 compares early warning signs of Alzheimer's disease with normal mental lapses.

Causes and Risk Factors Accumulation of an abnormal protein called *beta amyloid peptide* appears to be the main culprit contributing to the development of Alzheimer's disease (Gatz et al., 2006). The brain of a person with AD contains excessive amounts of **neurofibrillary tangles** (twisted masses of dead neurons) and large waxy clumps of **amyloid plaque** (nonfunctioning tissue formed by beta amyloid in the spaces between neurons). Because these plaques are insoluble, the brain cannot clear them away. They may become dense, spread, and destroy surrounding neurons. The breakdown of myelin may promote the buildup of plaques (Bartzokis et al., 2007).

neurofibrillary tangles
Twisted masses of protein fibers found in brains of persons with Alzheimer's disease.

amyloid plaque
Waxy chunks of insoluble tissue found in brains of persons with Alzheimer's disease.

Alzheimer's disease, or at least its age of onset, is strongly heritable (Gatz et al., 2006). A variant of the *APOE* gene has been found to contribute to susceptibility to late-onset AD, the most common form, which typically develops after age 65 (Gatz, 2007). A variant of another gene called *SORL1* was found to stimulate the formation of amyloid plaque (Meng et al., 2007; Rogaeva et al., 2006). Another gene variant involved in the manufacture of amyloid precursors, Cathepsine D, moderately increases the risk as well (Schuur et al., 2009). However, identified genes are thought to explain no more than half of all AD cases. Epigenetic modifications that determine whether a particular gene is activated may play a part (Gatz, 2007).

Although a number of lifestyle factors have been studied regarding their potential impact on AD, results are mixed and conclusions difficult to make. For example, lifestyle factors, such as diet and physical activity, have been implicated especially for persons who are not at genetic risk (Gatz, 2007). Foods rich in vitamin E, Omega-3 fatty acids, and unhydrogenated unsaturated fats—such as oil-based salad dressings, nuts, seeds, fish, mayonnaise, and eggs—may be protective against AD, whereas foods high in saturated and transunsaturated fats, such as red meats, butter, and ice cream, may be harmful (Morris, 2004). Smokers have increased risk of AD (Launer et al., 1999).

Esther Lipman Rosenthal's battle with Alzheimer's disease is evident in her artwork. She created the picture on the left, showing her husband golfing, at age 55 and the picture on the right, showing him on cross-country skis, at age 75, during the early and middle stages of her disease. Photos courtesy of Linda Goldman.

Use of nonsteroidal anti-inflammatory drugs such as aspirin and ibuprofen may cut the risk of AD (Vlad, Miller, Kowall, & Felson, 2008).

Education and cognitively stimulating activities have been associated with reduced risk of the disorder (Billings, Green, McGaugh, & LaFerla, 2007; Wilson, Scherr, Schneider, Tang, & Bennett, 2007) even when the presence of risky APOE genes is accounted for (Sando et al., 2008). The protective effect appears to be due not to education itself, but to the fact that educated people tend to be cognitively active (Wilson & Bennett, 2003). How might cognitive activity protect against AD? One hypothesis is that ongoing cognitive activity may build **cognitive reserve** and thus delay the onset of dementia (Stern, 2009). Cognitive reserve, like organ reserve, may enable a deteriorating brain to continue to function under stress, up to a point, without showing signs of impairment. An analysis of 26 studies worldwide concluded that a mere 5 percent increase in cognitive reserve could prevent one-third of Alzheimer's cases (de la Fuente-Fernandez, 2006). However, a recent NIH Consensus Development statement regarding preventing AD and cognitive decline (Daviglus et al., 2010) finds that "firm conclusions cannot be drawn about the association of any modifiable risk factor with cognitive decline or Alzheimer's Disease" (p. 2).

cognitive reserve
Hypothesized fund of energy that may enable a deteriorating brain to continue to function normally.

Diagnosis and Prediction Although it appears that definitive tests for AD are on the horizon (Kolata, 2010), until recently AD could be diagnosed definitively only by postmortem examination of brain tissue. Neuroimaging has been particularly useful in excluding alternative causes of dementia (Cummings, 2004) and in allowing researchers to see brain lesions indicative of AD in a living patient (Shoghi-Jadid et al., 2002). Noninvasive PET (positron emission tomography) scanning has been used to detect the plaques and tangles characteristic of Alzheimer's, and the results were as good as those obtained by autopsy (Mosconi et al., 2008; Small et al., 2006). Whatever the technique used, the identification of AD prior to symptom onset would have a variety of important applications, from assessing those individuals at risk of developing dementia to monitoring interventions and drug treatments of affected people.

If these tests are successful, it would allow researchers and health care professional to, for the first time, diagnose early signs of Alzheimer's in patients who have not yet started showing symptoms of the disease.

Kolata, 2010

Other researchers have focused on identifying not Alzheimer's per se but rather mild cognitive impairments that, if left untreated, might eventually result in the

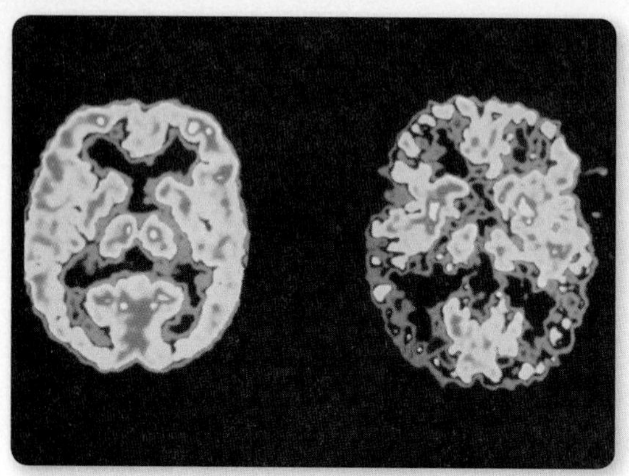

These PET (position emission tomography) scans show dramatic deterioration in the brain of an Alzheimer's patient (right) as compared with a normal brain (left). The red and yellow areas represent high brain activity; the blue and black areas, low activity. The scan on the right shows reduction of both function and blood flow in both sides of the brain.

disease. In other words, they are searching for risk factors that might indicate early signs of the disease in an attempt to diagnose it before extensive damage has occurred. A longitudinal study found that reduced metabolic activity in the hippocampus of healthy adults can accurately predict who will get Alzheimer's or a related memory impairment within the next 9 years (Mosconi et al., 2005). In what could lead to a definitive test for early AD, researchers have used technology to detect amyloid beta-derived diffusible ligands (ADDLs) in cerebral and spinal fluid (Georganopoulou et al., 2005). In addition, certain blood tests and electroencephalogram (EEG) results may predict AD in the early stages (Gandhi, Green, Kounios, Clark, & Polikar, 2006; Ray et al., 2007).

Degenerative changes in brain structure also can forecast AD. For example, in one study, brain scans of older adults who were considered cognitively normal found less gray matter in memory processing areas of the brain in those who were diagnosed with AD 4 years later (C. D. Smith et al., 2007). Cognitive tests alone may distinguish between patients experiencing cognitive changes related to normal aging and those in early stages of dementia. In the Seattle Longitudinal Study of Adult Intelligence, results of psychometric tests predicted dementia as much as 14 years prior to diagnosis (Schaie, 2005). In the Nun Study, a research team examined autobiographies the nuns had written in their early 20s. The women whose autobiographies were densely packed with ideas were least likely to become cognitively impaired or to develop Alzheimer's disease later in life (Riley, Snowdon, Desrosiers, & Markesbery, 2005). However, cognitive tests used together with brain imaging studies might provide a more precise way of assessing which adults are at risk of dementia. For example, in a study of adults with mild cognitive impairments, changes in the medial temporal lobe and fusiform gyrus occurred 3 years before the diagnosis of the disease (Whitwell et al., 2007).

Despite the identification of several genes associated with AD, genetic testing so far has a limited role in prediction and diagnosis. Still, it may be useful in combination with cognitive tests, brain scans, and clinical evidence of symptoms. There is evidence that people alter their health behaviors if told they have genes making them vulnerable to dementia (Chao et al., 2008), so such information may someday become part of the way in which the medical profession addresses risk in individuals.

Treatment Although no cure has yet been found, early diagnosis and treatment can slow the progress of Alzheimer's disease and improve quality of life. Currently, the U.S. Food and Drug Administration has approved five drugs that have been shown to slow, though not stop, the progression of Alzheimer's disease for up to a year (Alzheimer's Association, 2010). One medication is memantine (commercially known as Namenda). Daily doses of memantine taken for as long as a year reduced deterioration in patients with moderate to severe AD without significant adverse effects (Reisberg et al., 2006).

A promising experimental approach is immunotherapy, and researchers think a vaccine for Alzheimer's based on the immunotherapy approach is possible (Solomon & Frankel, 2010).

In the absence of a cure, management of the disease is critical. In the early stages, cognitive training interventions have been demonstrated to result in gains in both cognitive and behavioral areas (Sitzer, Twamley, & Jeste, 2006). Behavioral therapies can slow deterioration, improve communication, and reduce disruptive behavior (Barinaga, 1998). Drugs can relieve agitation, lighten depression, and help patients sleep. Proper nourishment and fluid intake together with exercise, physical therapy, and control of other medical conditions are important, and cooperation between the physician and the caregiver is essential (Cummings, 2004).

checkpoint
can **you**...

- Summarize what is known about the prevalence, symptoms, causes, risk factors, diagnosis, and treatment of Alzheimer's disease?

COGNITIVE DEVELOPMENT

Aspects of Cognitive Development

Old age "adds as it takes away," wrote the poet William Carlos Williams in one of three books of verse he produced between his first stroke at the age of 68 and his death at 79. This comment seems to characterize a number of trends in cognitive functioning in late adulthood. As Baltes's life-span developmental approach suggests, age brings gains as well as losses. Let's look first at intelligence and general processing abilities, then at memory, and then at wisdom, which is popularly associated with the later years.

INTELLIGENCE AND PROCESSING ABILITIES

Does intelligence diminish in late adulthood? The answer depends on what abilities are being measured, and how. Some abilities, such as speed of mental processes and abstract reasoning, may decline in later years, but other abilities tend to improve throughout most of adult life. Although changes in processing abilities may reflect neurological deterioration, there is much individual variation, suggesting that declines in functioning are not inevitable and may be preventable.

The effects of aging aren't all bad. As we get older, we are more likely to attend to and process positive, happy faces than negative ones, a tendency that may have implications for how we handle real-life problems.

Mather & Carstenson, 2003

The impact of cognitive changes is influenced by earlier cognitive ability, SES, and educational status. Childhood intelligence test scores reliably predict cognitive ability at age 80; and SES and educational level predict cognitive status after age 70 better than do health ratings or the presence or severity of medical conditions (Finch & Zelinski, 2005). Moreover, having higher childhood intelligence may predict not just the overall level of functioning but also whether or not declines are likely. One study looking at children assessed at 11, and then again at approximately 66 to 80 years of age, showed that those children who started off lower on the intelligence scale were more likely to experience cognitive declines in late adulthood (Bourne, Fox, Deary, & Whalley, 2007).

Measuring Older Adults' Intelligence To measure the intelligence of older adults, researchers often use the **Wechsler Adult Intelligence Scale (WAIS).** The WAIS is a standardized measure that allows assessment of a person's intellectual functioning at different ages. Scores on the WAIS subtests yield a verbal IQ, a performance IQ, and a total IQ. Older adults tend not to perform as well as younger adults on the WAIS, but the difference is primarily in processing speed and nonverbal performance. On the five subtests in the performance scale (such as identifying the missing part of a picture or mastering a maze), scores drop with age; but on the six tests making up the verbal scale—particularly tests of vocabulary, information, and comprehension—scores fall only slightly (Figure 4). This is called the *classic aging pattern* (Botwinick, 1984). This age disparity in performance, particularly for processing speed, is smaller in more recent cohorts (Miller, Myers, Prinzi, & Mittenberg, 2009).

Wechsler Adult Intelligence Scale (WAIS)
Intelligence test for adults that yields verbal and performance scores as well as a combined score.

What might account for this pattern? The pattern is likely a consequence of muscular and neurological slowing. For tasks that do not require speed, declines are less likely. For example, verbal items that hold up with age are based on knowledge and

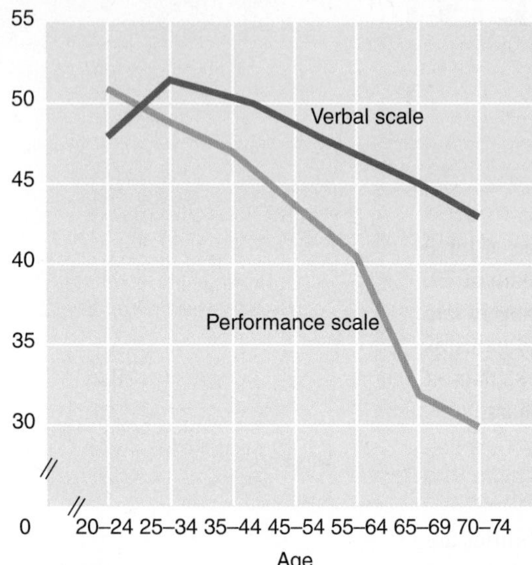

FIGURE 4

Classic Aging Pattern on the Revised Version of the Wechsler Adult Intelligence Scale (WAIS-R)

Scores on the performance subtests decline far more rapidly with age than scores on the verbal subtests.

Source: Botwinick, 1984.

do not require the test-taker to figure out or do anything new. The performance tasks involve the processing of new information and require perceptual speed and motor skills. The variance in retention of different types of cognitive skills in old age has generated several lines of theory and research.

The Seattle Longitudinal Study: Use It or Lose It If we do not consistently challenge our muscles, eventually they atrophy and our bodies become weaker. In some ways, the mind can be thought of as a muscle. It too responds to use, and it too declines if not engaged in the world around us. This "use it or lose it" dynamic is illustrated with research from the Seattle Longitudinal Study of Adult Intelligence. Researchers measured six primary mental abilities: verbal meaning, word fluency, number (computational ability), spatial orientation, inductive reasoning, and perceptual speed. Consistent with other studies, perceptual speed tended to decline earliest and most rapidly. Cognitive decline in other respects was slower and more variable. Very few people weakened in all abilities, and many improved in some areas. Most fairly healthy older adults showed only small losses until the late 60s or 70s. Not until the 80s did they fall below the average performance of younger adults, and even then declines in verbal abilities and reasoning were modest (Schaie, 2005).

The most striking feature of the Seattle findings was the tremendous variation among individuals. Some participants showed declines during their 40s, but a few maintained full functioning very late in life. Those most likely to show declines were men who had low educational levels, were dissatisfied with their success in life, and exhibited a significant decrease in flexibility of personality. Some health-related variables also were important, most notably, hypertension and diabetes. Participants who engaged in cognitively complex work and who were in good health tended to retain their abilities longer. Engaging in activities that challenge cognitive skills promotes the retention or growth of those skills and, as we mentioned earlier, appears to protect against dementia (Willis & Schaie, 2005).

What are some ways to sustain a high level of intellectual activity in late life? Do you think you need to develop new or broader interests that you will want to pursue as you age?

Longitudinal findings suggest that cognitive training may enable older adults not only to recover lost competence but even to surpass their previous attainments (Schaie & Willis, 1996). In the Seattle study, participants who underwent an intervention focused on training them in reasoning skills showed decreased likelihood of dementia 7 years after the training occurred (Blaskewicz, Boron, Willis, & Schaie, 2007).

Cognitive deterioration, then, often may be related to disuse. Much as many aging athletes can call on physical reserves, older people who get training, practice, and social support seem to be able to draw on mental reserves. Adults may be able to maintain or expand this reserve capacity by engaging in a lifelong program of mental exercise (Vance et al., 2008).

Everyday Problem Solving The purpose of intelligence, of course, is not to take tests but to deal with the challenges of daily life. In many studies, the quality of practical decisions (such as what car to buy or how to compare insurance policies) bore only a modest relationship, if any, to performance on tasks like those on intelligence tests (Blanchard-Fields, 2007) and, often, no relationship to age (Meyer et al., 1995). Similarly, much research on everyday problem solving (such as what to do about a flooded basement) has not found as early a decline as is often seen in measures of fluid intelligence, and some research has found marked improvement (Blancher-Fields, Stein, & Watson, 2004), particularly when the contexts being assessed are those that older people are familiar with (Aristico, Orom, Cervone, Krauss, & Houston, 2010).

Age differences are reduced in studies that focus on *interpersonal* problems—such as how to deal with a new mother who insists on showing her older mother-in-law how to hold the baby—rather than on *instrumental* problems—such as how to return defective merchandise (Thornton & Dumke, 2005). Older adults have more extensive repertoires of strategies to apply to interpersonal situations than younger adults do, and they are more likely to chose a highly effective strategy than are younger adults (Blanchard-Fields, Mienaltowski, & Seay, 2007).

checkpoint can **you . . .**

- Compare the classic aging pattern on the WAIS with those of the Seattle Longitudinal Study with regard to cognitive changes in old age?
- Cite evidence of the plasticity of cognitive abilities in late adulthood?
- Discuss the relationship between practical (everyday) problem solving and age?

Changes in Processing Abilities What explains the varied course of cognitive abilities in late adulthood? In many older adults, a general slowdown in central nervous system functioning is a major contributor to losses of efficiency of information processing and changes in cognitive abilities. Speed of processing, one of the first abilities to decline, is related to health status, balance, and gait and to performance of activities of daily living, such as looking up phone numbers and counting out change (Ball, Edwards, & Ross, 2007).

One ability that tends to slow with age is ease in switching attention from one task or function to another (Bucur & Madden, 2010). This finding may help explain why many older adults have difficulty driving, which requires rapid attentional shifts (Bialystok, Craik, Klein, & Viswanathan, 2004). Training can increase older adults' processing speed—their ability to process more information in shorter periods of time. Training typically involves practice, feedback, and learning task-specific strategies. In studies of several training programs, participants who started with the worst performance made the most gains. A method aimed at improving driving ability was the most successful, perhaps because it had a concrete, practical goal. This research underlines the brain's plasticity even with regard to a basic fluid ability, speed of processing (Ball et al., 2007). Additionally, folic acid (given adequate levels of B-12) and vitamin D may have a facilitative effect on cognitive processes (Buell et al., 2009; Morris, Jacques, Rosenberg, & Selhub, 2007) such as memory, processing speed, and sensorimotor speed (Durga et al., 2007). Similarly, vitamin D has been shown to have a facilitative effect (Buell et al., 2009).

Although age-related declines in processing abilities occur, it is not inevitable that older adults will show declines in everyday life. Many older adults naturally compensate. For example, strong negative emotions are likely to make processing more challenging. However, older adults tend to show fewer negative moods and more positive moods overall, diminishing this effect. Additionally, they use their vast reservoirs of knowledge to compensate for declines that do occur (Peters, Hess, Västfjäall, & Auman, 2007). Generally, older adults tend to do better on tasks that depend on ingrained habits and knowledge (Bialystok et al., 2004). It is likely that older adults are using alternative, although complementary, neural circuits for more difficult tasks, and it may be that cognitive interventions are exerting their influence here by restructuring the pathways used to complete such tasks (Park & Reuter-Lorenz, 2009).

Cognitive Abilities and Mortality Psychometric intelligence may be an important predictor of how long and in what condition adults will live. In one longitudinal study, boys who scored an average of 15 points higher on an IQ test were 79 percent more likely to live to age 76 (Gottfredson & Deary, 2004), and 27 percent less likely to die of cancer (Deary, Whalley, & Starr, 2003).

However, in another study, reaction time at age 56 more strongly predicted mortality by age 70 than did IQ, suggesting that efficiency of information processing may explain the link between intelligence and timing of death (Deary & Der, 2005). Another possible explanation is that intelligent people learn information and problem-solving skills that help them prevent chronic disease and accidental injury and cooperate in their treatment when they do get sick or hurt (Deary & Der, 2005). Yet another interpretation is that, given that most studies are retrospective, results may be misleading. As many diseases, such as diabetes and hypertension, may lead both to cognitive declines earlier in life and an earlier death, data showing a link between the two may reflect the action of the disease instead of an association between IQ and mortality (Batty, Deary, & Gottfredson, 2007).

checkpoint can **you . . .**

- Discuss findings on the slowdown in neural processing and its relationship to cognitive decline?
- Discuss the relationship of intelligence to health and mortality?

study smart

Three Types of Memory

MEMORY: HOW DOES IT CHANGE?

Failing memory is often considered a sign of aging. Loss of memory is the chief worry reported by older Americans (National Council on the Aging, 2002). An estimated 1 in 5 adults over age 70 has some degree of memory impairment short of dementia (Plassman et al., 2008). Yet in memory, as in other cognitive abilities, older people's functioning declines slowly and varies greatly.

To understand age-related memory decline, we need to review the various memory systems that enable the brain to process information for use at a later time (Budson & Price, 2005). These systems are traditionally classified as "short-term" and "long-term."

Short-Term Memory Researchers assess short-term memory by asking a person to repeat a sequence of numbers, either in the order in which they were presented (*digit span forward*) or in reverse order (*digit span backward*). Digit span forward ability holds up well with advancing age (Craik & Jennings, 1992; Wingfield & Stine, 1989) but digit span backward performance does not (Craik & Jennings, 1992; Lovelace, 1990). Why? One reason may involve the differentiation of sensory and working memory. **Sensory memory** involves the brief storage of sensory information. For example, when you see the trail left behind by a fourth of July sparkler, you are seeing the trace left by your sensory memory. **Working memory** involves the short-term storage of information being actively processed, such as when you calculate the tip on a restaurant bill in your head. Some theorists argue that forward repetition requires only sensory memory, which retains efficiency throughout life. Therefore, declines in this area are more rare. However, backward repetition requires the manipulation of information in working memory, which gradually shrinks in capacity with age (Gazzaley, Sheridan, Cooney, & D'Esposito, 2007), making it harder to handle more than one task at a time (E. E. Smith et al., 2001).

sensory memory
Initial, brief, temporary storage of sensory information.

working memory
Short-term storage of information being actively processed.

A key factor in memory performance is the complexity of the task (Park & Reuter-Lorenz, 2009). Tasks that require only *rehearsal,* or repetition, show very little decline. Tasks that require *reorganization* or *elaboration* show greater falloff (Emery, Heaven, Paxton, & Braver, 2008). If you are asked to verbally rearrange a series of items (such as "Band-Aid, elephant, newspaper") in order of increasing size ("Band-Aid, newspaper, elephant"), you must call to mind your previous knowledge of Band-Aids, newspapers, and elephants (Cherry & Park, 1993). More mental effort is needed to keep this additional information in mind, using more of the limited capacity of working memory.

Long-Term Memory Information-processing researchers divide long-term memory into three major systems: *episodic memory, semantic memory,* and *procedural memory.*

Do you remember what you had for breakfast this morning? Such information is stored in **episodic memory,** the long-term memory system most likely to deteriorate with age (Park & Gutchess, 2005). Episodic memory is linked to specific events; you retrieve an item by reconstructing the original experience in your mind. Older adults are less able than younger people to do so, perhaps because they focus less on context (where something happened, who was there), and rely more on gist than details (Dodson & Schacter, 2002). Because of this, they have fewer connections to jog their memory (Lovelace, 1990). Also, older people have had many similar experiences that tend to run together. When older people perceive an event as distinctive, they can remember it nearly as well as younger people (Geraci, McDaniel, Manzano, & Roediger, 2009).

episodic memory
Long-term memory of specific experiences or events, linked to time and place.

Some types of long-term memories remain vigorous as people age. **Semantic memory** consists of meanings, facts, and concepts accumulated over a lifetime of learning. It is like a mental encyclopedia; it is not about when and where something was learned but rather consists of our general knowledge of the world. Semantic memory shows little decline with age, although infrequently used or highly specific information

semantic memory
Long-term memory of general factual knowledge, social customs, and language.

may sometimes be difficult to retrieve (Luo & Craik, 2008). Indeed, some aspects of semantic memory, such as vocabulary and knowledge of rules of language, may even increase with age (Camp, 1989).

Another long-term memory system that remains relatively unaffected is procedural memory. **Procedural memory** includes motor skills (like riding a bike) and habits (like taking a particular street home) that, once learned, take little conscious effort. If you have ever intended to stop by the grocery store on your way home, and ended up pulling into your driveway instead without thinking about it, you have experienced the automaticity that is characteristic of procedural memory. It is relatively unaffected by age (Fleischman, Wilson, Gabriele, Bienias, & Bennett, 2004). Moreover, new procedural memories that are formed in old age may be retained for at least 2 years (Smith et al., 2005) even though they may take a bit more time to learn initially (Iaria, Palermo, Committeri, & Barton, 2009).

Riding a bicycle requires procedural memory. Once learned, procedural skills can be activated without conscious effort, even after a long period of disuse.

procedural memory
Long-term memory of motor skills, habits, and ways of doing things, which can be recalled without conscious effort; sometimes called *implicit memory*.

Speech and Memory: Effects of Aging As people become older, they often begin to have minor difficulties with language. However, these experiences are not generally due to issues related to language per se but rather are the result of problems accessing and retrieving information from memory. Thus they are considered memory problems rather than language problems. For example, have you ever been unable to come up with a word that you knew perfectly well? This is known as the tip-of-the-tongue (TOT) phenomenon; it occurs in people of all ages but becomes more common in late adulthood (Burke & Shafto, 2004). Presumably, the TOT phenomenon results from a failure in working memory (Schwartz, 2008). Other problems in verbal retrieval include errors in naming pictures of objects aloud, more ambiguous references and slips of the tongue in everyday speech, more use of nonfluencies (such as "um" and "er") in speech, and a tendency to misspell words (such as *indict*) that are spelled differently than they sound (Burke & Shafto, 2004). Older adults also may show declines in the complexity of grammar used in speech (Kemper, Thompson, & Marquix, 2001).

Why Do Some Memory Systems Decline? What explains older adults' memory losses? Investigators have offered several hypotheses. One approach focuses on the biological structures that make memory work. Another approach looks at problems with the three steps required to process information in memory: *encoding, storage,* and *retrieval*.

Neurological Change The decline in processing speed described earlier in this chapter seems to be a fundamental contributor to age-related memory loss. In one study, controlling for processing speed eliminated most of the age-related drop in memory performance (Hedden, Lautenschlager, & Park, 2005).

Different memory systems depend on different brain structures. Thus a disorder that damages a particular brain structure may impair the type of memory associated with it. For example, Alzheimer's disease disrupts working memory (located in the prefrontal cortex at the front of the frontal lobes) as well as semantic and episodic memory (located in the frontal and temporal lobes); Parkinson's disease affects procedural memory, located in the cerebellum, basal ganglia, and other areas (Budson & Price, 2005).

The main structures involved in normal memory processing and storage include the *frontal lobes* and the *hippocampus*. The *frontal lobes* are active in both encoding and retrieval of episodic memories. Dysfunction of the frontal lobes may cause false memories—"remembering" events that never occurred. Early decline in the prefrontal cortex may underlie such common problems as inability to concentrate or pay attention and difficulty in performing a task with several steps. The *hippocampus,* a small, centrally located structure deep in the temporal lobe, seems critical to the ability to store new information in episodic memory. Lesions in the hippocampus or other brain structures involved in episodic memory may result in loss of recent memories (Budson & Price, 2005).

The brain often compensates for age-related declines in specialized regions by tapping other regions to help. In one study, when asked to remember sets of letters on a computer screen, college students used only the left hemisphere; when asked to remember the locations of points on the screen, they used only the right hemisphere. Older adults, who did just as well as the students, used *both* the right and left frontal lobes for both tasks (Reuter-Lorenz, Stanczak, & Miller, 1999; Reuter-Lorenz et al., 2000). This suggests that older adults' brains were compensating: because the task was harder for them, they utilized more brain areas than the younger adults (Park & Reuter-Lorenz, 2009). In another study, educated younger adults performing memory tasks relied more on the medial temporal lobes, whereas educated older adults doing the same tasks relied more on the frontal lobes (Springer, McIntosh, Winocur, & Grady, 2005). The brain's ability to shift functions may help explain why symptoms of Alzheimer's disease often do not appear until the disease is well advanced, and previously unaffected regions of the brain, which have taken over for impaired regions, lose their own working capacity ("Alzheimer's Disease, Part I," 1998; Finch & Zelinski, 2005).

Memory can be improved with a simple technique—saying words out loud, even if you just mouth the words.

McLeod, Gopie, Hourihan, Neary, & Ozubko, 2010

Problems in Encoding, Storage, and Retrieval Episodic memory is particularly vulnerable to the effects of aging; an effect that is aggravated as memory tasks become more complex or demanding, or require the free recall of information as opposed to recognition of previously seen material (Cansino, 2009). Older adults seem to have greater difficult *encoding* new episodic memories, presumably because of difficulties in forming and later recalling a coherent and cohesive episode (Naveh-Benjamin, Brav, & Levy, 2007). They tend to be less efficient and precise than younger adults in the use of strategies to make it easier to remember—for example, by arranging material alphabetically or creating mental associations (Craik & Byrd, 1982). Most studies have found that older and younger adults are about equally knowledgeable as to effective encoding strategies (Salthouse, 1991). Yet in laboratory experiments, older adults are less likely to *use* such strategies unless trained—or at least prompted or reminded—to do so (Craik & Jennings, 1992; Salthouse, 1991). However, when they do use associative strategies such as these, the age-related declines in encoding can be greatly reduced (Naveh-Benjamin et al., 2007).

As an example of one frequent consequence in the real world, medically fragile adults are more likely to have problems with memory, and thus are less likely to take their medications.

Insel, Morrow, Brewer, & Figueredo, 2006

Another hypothesis is that material in *storage* may deteriorate to the point where retrieval becomes difficult or impossible. Some research suggests that a small increase in "storage failure" may occur with age (Lustig & Flegal, 2008). However, traces of decayed memories are likely to remain, and it may be possible to reconstruct them, or at least to relearn the material speedily (Camp & McKitrick, 1989; Chafetz, 1992). In particular, it appears as if memories that contain an emotional component are more resistant to the effects of decay (Kensinger, 2009). For example, studies have found that older adults are motivated to preserve memories that have positive emotional meaning to them (Carstensen & Mikels, 2005). Thus emotional factors need to be considered in studying memory changes in old age.

We should keep in mind that most of the research on encoding, storage, and retrieval has been done in the laboratory. But memory may operate differently in the real world. In one naturalistic study, when 333 older adults were asked to keep daily diaries, they were more likely to report memory failures on days when they experienced stress, especially from other people (Neupert, Almeida, Mroczek, & Spiro, 2006).

checkpoint
can you . . .

- Identify two aspects of memory that tend to decline with age, and give reasons for this decline?
- Discuss neurological changes related to memory?
- Explain how problems in encoding, storage, and retrieval may affect memory in late adulthood, and discuss how emotional factors may affect memory?

WISDOM

Wisdom has been defined as "exceptional breadth and depth of knowledge about the conditions of life and human affairs and reflective judgment about the application of this knowledge. It may involve insight and awareness of the uncertain, paradoxical nature of reality and may lead to *transcendence,* detachment from preoccupation with the self" (Kramer, 2003, p. 132). Some theorists define wisdom as an extension of postformal thought, a synthesis of reason and emotion (Labouvie-Vief, 1990a, 1990b). Quite simply, wisdom is the ability to navigate the messiness of life. It involves understanding how people work and how to accomplish goals. People who are wise, according to psychologists, are also comfortable with uncertainty and understand that different people have different viewpoints and that sometimes there is no one right answer.

The most extensive research on wisdom as a cognitive ability has been done by the late Paul Baltes and his colleagues. In a series of studies, Baltes and his associates at the Max Planck Institute in Berlin asked adults of various ages and occupations to think aloud about hypothetical dilemmas. Responses were rated according to whether they showed rich factual and procedural knowledge about the human condition and about dealing with life's problems. Other criteria were awareness that contextual circumstances can influence problems, that problems tend to lend themselves to multiple interpretations and solutions, and that choices of solutions depend on individual values, goals, and priorities (Baltes & Staudinger, 2000; Pasupathi, Staudinger, & Baltes, 2001).

In one of these studies, 60 well-educated German professionals ages 25 to 81 were given four dilemmas involving such issues as weighing career against family needs and deciding whether to accept early retirement. Of 240 solutions, only 5 percent were rated wise, and these responses were distributed nearly evenly among young, middle-aged, and older adults. Participants showed more wisdom about decisions applicable to their own stage of life. For example, the oldest group gave its best answers to the problem of a 60-year-old widow who, having just started her own business, learns that her son has been left with two young children and wants her to help care for them (J. Smith & Baltes, 1990).

Think of the wisest person you know. Which, if any, of the criteria for wisdom mentioned in this chapter seem to describe this person? If none do, how would you define and measure wisdom?

Apparently, then, wisdom is not necessarily a property of old age—or of any age. Instead, it appears to be a rather rare and complex phenomenon that shows relative stability or slight growth in certain individuals (Staudinger & Baltes, 1996; Staudinger, Smith, & Baltes, 1992). A variety of factors, including personality and life experience—either direct or vicarious—may contribute to it (Shedlock & Cornelius, 2003), and guidance from mentors may help prepare the way (Baltes & Staudinger, 2000; Pasupathi et al., 2001).

Research on physical functioning, cognition, and aging is more encouraging than some might expect. Older adults tend to make the most of their abilities, often exploiting gains in one area to offset declines in another. Research highlights the widely varying paths of physical and cognitive development among individuals. It also points to the importance of emotional well-being in late adulthood.

checkpoint can **you** . . .

- Compare various approaches to the study of wisdom?
- Discuss findings from Baltes's studies of wisdom?

summary and key terms

Old Age Today

- Efforts to combat ageism are making headway, thanks to the visibility of a growing number of active, healthy older adults.
- The proportion of older people in the United States and world populations is greater than ever before and is expected to continue to grow. People over 80 are the fastest-growing age group.
- Although effects of primary aging may be beyond people's control, they often can avoid effects of secondary aging.
- Specialists in the study of aging sometimes refer to people between ages 65 and 74 as the *young old*, those over 75 as the *old old*, and those over 85 as the *oldest old*. However, these terms may be more useful when used to refer to functional age.

ageism
primary aging
secondary aging
activities of daily living (ADLs)
functional age
gerontology
geriatrics

PHYSICAL DEVELOPMENT

Longevity and Aging

- Life expectancy has increased dramatically. The longer people live, the longer they are likely to live.
- In general, life expectancy is greater in developed countries than in developing countries, among Hispanics and white Americans than among African Americans, and among women as compared to men.
- Recent gains in life expectancy come largely from progress toward reducing death rates from diseases affecting older people. Further large improvements in life expectancy may depend on whether scientists can learn to modify basic processes of aging.
- Theories of biological aging fall into two categories: genetic-programming theories and variable-rate, or error, theories.
- Research on extension of the life span through genetic manipulation or caloric restriction has challenged the idea of a biological limit to the life span.

life expectancy
longevity
life span
senescence
genetic-programming theories
variable-rate theories
free radicals
autoimmunity
survival curves
Hayflick limit

Physical Changes

- Changes in body systems and organs are highly variable. Most body systems continue to function fairly well, but the heart becomes more susceptible to disease. Reserve capacity declines.
- Although the brain changes with age, the changes are usually modest. They include loss of volume and weight and a slowing of responses. However, the brain can grow new neurons and build new connections late in life.
- Vision and hearing problems may interfere with daily life but often can be corrected. Irreversible damage may result from age-related macular degeneration or glaucoma. Losses in taste and smell may lead to poor nutrition. Training can improve muscular strength, balance, and reaction time. Older adults tend to be susceptible to accidents and falls.
- Older people tend to sleep less and dream less than before, but chronic insomnia can be an indication of depression.
- Many older adults remain sexually active.

reserve capacity
cataracts
age-related macular degeneration
glaucoma

Physical and Mental Health

- Most older people are reasonably healthy, especially if they follow a healthy lifestyle. Many do have chronic conditions, but these usually do not greatly limit activities or interfere with daily life.
- Exercise and diet are important influences on health. Loss of teeth can seriously affect nutrition.
- Most older people are in good mental health. Depression, alcoholism, and many other conditions can be reversed with treatment; a few, such as Alzheimer's disease, are irreversible.
- Alzheimer's disease becomes more prevalent with age. It is highly heritable, but diet, exercise, and other lifestyle factors may play a part. Cognitive activity may be protective by building up a cognitive reserve that enables the brain to function under stress. Behavioral and drug therapies can slow deterioration. Mild cognitive impairment can be an early sign of the disease, and researchers are developing tools for early diagnosis.

dementia
Alzheimer's disease
Parkinson's disease
neurofibrillary tangles
amyloid plaque
cognitive reserve

COGNITIVE DEVELOPMENT

Aspects of Cognitive Development

- Older adults do better on the verbal portion of the Wechsler Adult Intelligence Scale than on the performance portion.
- The Seattle Longitudinal Study found that cognitive functioning in late adulthood is highly variable. Few people decline in all or most areas, and many people improve in some. The engagement hypothesis seeks to explain these differences.
- Older adults are more effective in solving practical problems that have emotional relevance for them.
- A general slowdown in central nervous system functioning may affect the speed of information processing.
- Intelligence may be a predictor of longevity.
- Sensory memory, semantic memory, and procedural memory appear nearly as efficient in older adults as in younger adults. The capacity of working memory and episodic memory are often less efficient.
- Older adults have more problems with oral word retrieval and spelling than younger adults. Grammatical complexity and content of speech decline.
- Neurological changes and problems in encoding, storage, and retrieval may account for much of the decline in memory functioning in older adults. However, the brain can compensate for some age-related declines.
- Older people show considerable plasticity in cognitive performance and can benefit from training.
- According to Baltes's studies, wisdom is not age-related, but people of all ages give wiser responses to problems affecting their own age group.

Wechsler Adult Intelligence Scale (WAIS)
sensory memory
working memory
episodic memory
semantic memory
procedural memory

chapter 18

Psychosocial Development in Late Adulthood

outline

learning objectives

Discuss theories and research on personality changes in late adulthood.

Identify strategies and resources that contribute to older adults' well-being and mental health.

Discuss aging and adaptation to work and retirement.

Characterize the social relationships of aging adults.

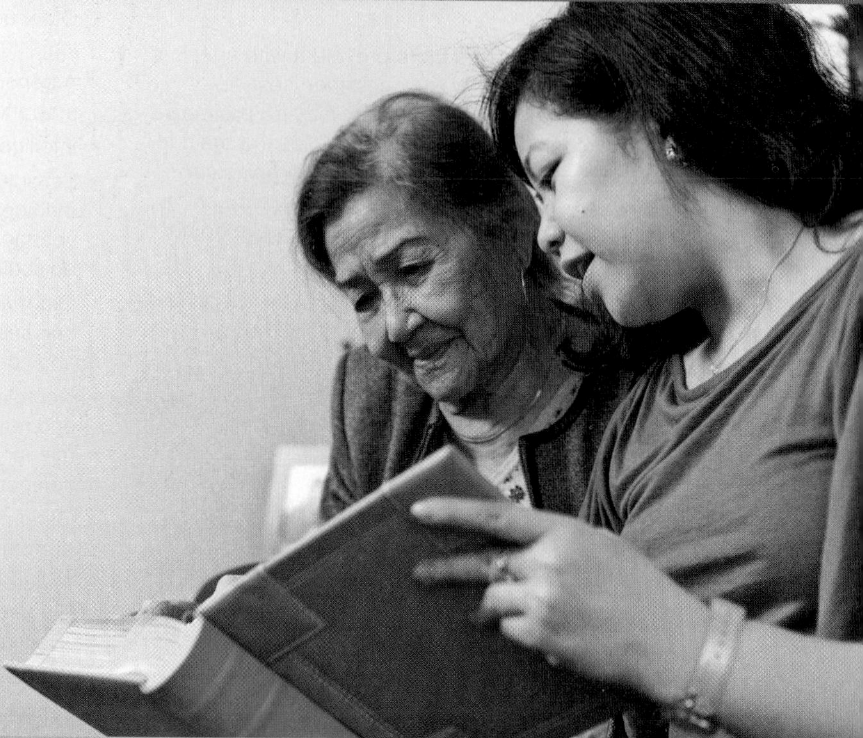

did you know?

- Productive activity seems to play an important part in successful aging?
- In most developed countries, older women are more likely to live alone than older men?
- People who can confide their feelings and thoughts to friends tend to deal better with the changes and challenges of aging?

In this chapter, we look at theory and research on psychosocial development in late adulthood and discuss such late-life options as work, retirement, and living arrangements and their impact on society's ability to support and care for an aging population. Finally, we look at relationships with families and friends, which greatly affect the quality of these last years.

I am still every age that I have been.

—Madeleine L'Engle

Theory and Research on Personality Development

In the early 1980s, when the writer Betty Friedan was asked to organize a seminar at Harvard University on "Growth in Aging," the distinguished behaviorist B. F. Skinner declined to participate. Age and growth, he said, were "a contradiction in terms" (Friedan, 1993, p. 23). Skinner was far from alone in that belief. Yet three decades later, late adulthood is increasingly recognized as a time of potential growth.

Most theorists view late adulthood as a developmental stage with its own special issues and tasks. It is a time when people can reexamine their lives, complete unfinished business, and decide how best to channel their energies and spend their remaining days, months, or years. Some wish to leave a legacy to their grandchildren or to the world, pass on the fruits of their experience, or validate the meaning of their lives. Others simply want to enjoy favorite pastimes or to do things they never had enough time for when they were younger. "Growth in aging" *is* possible; and many older adults experience this last stage of life as a positive one.

> When does "old age" begin? That depends on who you ask. People who are under the age of 30 are pretty sure it begins sometime before you turn 60 years old. However, the older you get, the later you think old age begins—at 75 years of age, only 35 percent of people consider themselves old.
>
> Pew Research Center, 2009a

Let's see what theory and research can tell us about personality in this final phase of the life span and about the psychosocial challenges and opportunities of aging. In the next section, we discuss how older adults cope with stress and loss and what constitutes successful aging.

ERIK ERIKSON: NORMATIVE ISSUES AND TASKS

What factors contribute to personal growth? According to normative-stage theorists, growth depends on carrying out the psychological tasks of each stage of life in an emotionally healthy way.

For Erikson, the crowning achievement of late adulthood is a sense of *ego integrity,* or integrity of the self, an achievement based on reflection about one's life. In the eighth and final stage of the life span, **ego integrity versus despair,** older adults need to evaluate and accept their lives so as to accept death. Building on the outcomes of the seven previous stages, they struggle to achieve a sense of coherence and wholeness, rather than give way to despair over their inability to relive the past differently (Erikson, Erikson, & Kivnick, 1986). People who succeed in this final, integrative task gain a sense of the meaning of their lives within the larger social order. The virtue that may develop during this stage is *wisdom,* an "informed and detached concern with life itself in the face of death itself" (Erikson, 1985, p. 61).

Wisdom, said Erikson, means accepting the life one has lived, without major regrets: without dwelling on "should-have-dones" or "might-have-beens." It means accepting imperfection in the self, in parents, in children, and in life. (This definition of *wisdom*

ego integrity versus despair
According to Erikson, the eighth and final stage of psychosocial development, in which people in late adulthood either achieve a sense of integrity of the self by accepting the lives they have lived, and thus accept death, or yield to despair that their lives cannot be relived.

Jimmy Carter, one of the most active ex-presidents in American history, won the Nobel Prize at age 78 for his continuing work in human rights, education, preventive health research, and conflict resolution, much of it in developing countries. He was born in 1924.

as an important psychological resource differs from the largely cognitive definitions explored in the discussion about physical and cognitive development in late adulthood.)

Although integrity must outweigh despair if this stage is to be resolved successfully, Erikson maintained that some despair is inevitable. People need to mourn—not only for their own misfortunes and lost chances but for the vulnerability and transience of the human condition.

Yet, Erikson believed, even as the body's functions weaken, people must maintain a "vital involvement" in society. On the basis of studies of life histories of people in their 80s, he concluded that ego integrity comes not just from reflecting on the past but from continued stimulation and challenge—whether through political activity, fitness programs, creative work, or relationships with grandchildren (Erikson et al., 1986).

According to Erikson, ego integrity in late adulthood requires continuing stimulation and challenge, which, for this sculptor, come from creative work.

THE FIVE-FACTOR MODEL: PERSONALITY TRAITS IN OLD AGE

Does personality change in late life? The answer may depend in part on the way stability and change are measured.

Measuring Stability and Change in Late Adulthood The long-term stability reported by Costa and McCrae is in *average levels* of various traits within a population. According to the five-factor model and its supporting research, hostile people, on average, are unlikely to mellow much with age, and optimistic people are likely to remain their hopeful selves. However, other longitudinal and cross-sectional studies using a modified version of this model found continued change in late adulthood: decreases in neuroticism over time (Allemand, 2007); increases in self-confidence, warmth, and emotional stability (Roberts & Mroczek, 2008); and increases in conscientiousness (Donnellan & Lucas, 2008) accompanied by declines in social vitality (gregariousness) and openness to experience (Roberts & Mroczek, 2008).

One way to measure stability or change is in *rank-order comparisons* of different people on a given trait. When personality change is measured in this fashion, relative differences among individuals seem to become increasingly stable for a period of time and then plateau. Some researchers believe this to happen relatively early in life—at approximately 30 years of age (Terraciao, McCrae, & Costa, 2009)—others believe this occurs sometime between ages 50 and 70 (Roberts & DelVecchio, 2000). A recent study of over 800 adults suggests that this stability in rank-ordering is strongly influenced by genetics (Johnson, McGue, & Krueger, 2005). The best way to conceptualize personality stability in later adulthood is as relatively consistent, shaped by both genetics and active niche picking, but as still being subject to the continuing influences of a changing biological and social world.

Early cross-sectional research suggested that personality becomes more rigid in old age. However, personality tests of 3,442 participants in the Seattle Longitudinal Study found no age-related trends in inflexibility (Schaie, 2005). And people in more recent cohorts seem to be more flexible (that is, less rigid) than previous cohorts. These findings fly in the face of the widespread stereotype that older people become rigid and set in their ways.

Personality as a Predictor of Emotionality, Health, and Well-Being Personality is a strong predictor of emotionality and subjective well-being—stronger in most respects than social relationships and health (Isaacowitz & Smith, 2003). In a longitudinal study that followed four generations for 23 years, self-reported *negative* emotions such as restlessness, boredom, loneliness, unhappiness, and depression decreased with age. At the same time, *positive* emotionality—excitement, interest, pride, and a sense of accomplishment—tended to remain stable until late life and then declined only slightly and gradually (Charles, Reynolds, & Gatz, 2001).

A possible explanation for this generally positive picture comes from socioemotional selectivity theory: as people get older, they tend to seek out activities and people that give them emotional gratification. In addition, older adults' greater ability to regulate their emotions may help explain why they tend to be happier and more cheerful than younger adults and to experience negative emotions less often and more fleetingly (Blanchard-Fields, Stein, & Watson, 2004; Carstensen, 1999). Moreover, emotions are part and parcel of personality. For example, neuroticism is in many respects a characteristically negative way of viewing the world. Therefore, it is not surprising that personality variables might be related to general well-being and satisfaction with life (Lucas & Diener, 2009).

Two of the Big Five personality traits—extraversion and neuroticism—demonstrate this relationship. As Costa and McCrae (1980) predicted, people with *extraverted* personalities (outgoing and socially oriented) tend to report especially high levels of positive emotion initially and are more likely than others to retain their positivity throughout life (Charles et al., 2001; Isaacowitz & Smith, 2003).

People with *neurotic* personalities (moody, touchy, anxious, and restless) tend to report negative and not positive emotions, and they tend to become even less positive as they age (Charles et al., 2001; Isaacowitz & Smith, 2003). Neuroticism is a far more powerful predictor of moods and mood disorders than variables such as age, health status, education, or gender (Siedlecki, Tucker-Drop, Oishi, & Salthouse, 2008). Highly neurotic people who become more neurotic as they age have low survival rates, possibly because they are likely to smoke or use alcohol or drugs to help calm their negative emotions and because they are ineffective in managing stress (Mroczek & Spiro, 2007). In contrast, *conscientiousness,* or dependability, has been found to predict health and mortality, most likely because conscientious people tend to avoid risky behaviors and to engage in activities that promote their health (Martin, Friedman, & Schwartz, 2007).

In January of 2011, the oldest baby boomers started turning 65, and apparently they "can't get no satisfaction." Researchers report they are more pessimistic than previous generations and upcoming younger generations.

Cohn & Taylor, 2010

checkpoint
can you . . .

- Discuss Erikson's stage of ego integrity versus despair, and tell what Erikson meant by *wisdom*?
- Summarize research about stability of personality and its effects on emotionality and well-being in old age?

Well-Being in Late Adulthood

In general, older adults have fewer mental disorders and are happier and more satisfied with life than younger adults (Mroczek & Kolarz, 1998; Yang, 2008). In fact, a recent study of 340,000 adults showed that happiness is high at approximately 18 years of age, declines until people reach 50 years of age, and then tends to rise again until 85 years of age—at that point reaching levels even higher than in the teenage years (Stone, Schwartz, Broderick, & Deacon, 2010). What accounts for this remarkable ability to cope, and what contributes to successful aging?

The rise in happiness later in life may in part reflect the value of a mature outlook, but it also may reflect the selective survival of happier people. Still, some cohort variations and social disparities exist. For example, baby boomers report lower levels of happiness than do earlier and later cohorts, perhaps due to the immense size of their generation and the resulting competitive strains for schooling, jobs, and economic security, as well as the turbulent societal events of their formative years. Gender, racial/ethnic, and educational disparities in happiness have narrowed or, in the case of gender, disappeared, especially since the mid-1990s. Furthermore, social disparities may have less impact in old age as biological changes, life events, the ability to cope with stress, and access to social welfare and support services play a more important role (Yang, 2008).

COPING AND MENTAL HEALTH

Coping is adaptive thinking or behavior aimed at reducing or relieving stress that arises from harmful, threatening, or challenging conditions. It is an important aspect of mental health. Let's look at two theoretical approaches to the study of coping: adaptive defenses and the cognitive-appraisal model. Then we'll examine a support system to which many older adults turn: religion.

coping
Adaptive thinking or behavior aimed at reducing or relieving stress that arises from harmful, threatening, or challenging conditions.

"Elderspeak"—the use of words or phrases such as "How are we feeling?" or "good girl"—is often used in an attempt to be helpful or kindly, but it is more likely to be viewed as demeaning or condescending.

Balsis & Carpenter, 2006

George Vaillant: Adaptive Defenses What makes for positive mental health in old age? According to three prospective studies covering more than 60 years, an important predictive factor is the use of mature *adaptive defenses* in coping with problems earlier in life.

Vaillant (2000) looked at the survivors of his earlier studies as well as at a subsample of women from Terman's study of gifted California schoolchildren born about 1910. Those who, in old age, showed the best psychosocial adjustment were those who, earlier in adulthood, had used such mature adaptive defenses as altruism, humor, suppression (keeping a stiff upper lip), anticipation (planning for the future), and sublimation (redirecting negative emotions into productive pursuits).

How do adaptive defenses work? According to Vaillant (2000), they can change people's perceptions of realities they are powerless to change. For example, in the studies just mentioned, the use of adaptive defenses predicted *subjective* physical functioning even though it did not predict *objective* physical health as measured by physicians.

Adaptive defenses may be unconscious or intuitive. In contrast, the cognitive-appraisal model, to which we turn now, emphasizes consciously chosen coping strategies.

studysmart

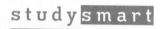

Perspectives on Emotion

Cognitive-Appraisal Model People respond to stressful situations differently. For example, think of how you felt when facing your last large exam. Were you anxious? Confident? Did you think the test would be fair? Did you feel you were capable of getting a good grade? What did you do to handle the stress?

In the **cognitive-appraisal model** (Lazarus & Folkman, 1984), people respond to stressful or challenging situations on the basis of two types of analyses. In *primary appraisal,* people analyze a situation and decide, at some level, whether or not the situation is a threat to their well-being. In *secondary appraisal,* people evaluate what can be done to prevent harm and choose a coping strategy to handle the situation. Coping includes anything an individual thinks or does in trying to adapt to stress, regardless of how well it works. Choosing the most appropriate strategy, and adapting to the various stressors of life, requires a continuous reappraisal of the relationship between person and environment.

cognitive-appraisal model
Model of coping, proposed by Lazarus and Folkman, that holds that, on the basis of continuous appraisal of their relationship with the environment, people choose appropriate coping strategies to deal with situations that tax their normal resources.

problem-focused coping
In the cognitive-appraisal model, coping strategy directed toward eliminating, managing, or improving a stressful situation.

Coping Strategies: Problem-Focused versus Emotion-Focused Coping strategies may be either problem-focused or emotion-focused. **Problem-focused coping** involves the use of *instrumental,* or action-oriented, strategies to eliminate, manage, or improve a stressful condition. This type of coping is more common when a person sees a realistic chance to change the situation. For example, some students may feel they are capable of learning the relevant material and will do well on an upcoming exam. To achieve this, they may use such problem-focused coping strategies as going to the professor for extra help or spending more time studying. By addressing the source of stress, people using problem-focused coping seek to lessen any harm to the self.

emotion-focused coping
In the cognitive-appraisal model, coping strategy directed toward managing the emotional response to a stressful situation so as to lessen its physical or psychological impact.

Emotion-focused coping, by contrast, involves attempting to manage the emotional response to a stressful situation to relieve its physical or psychological impact. People are more likely to use this coping strategy when they conclude that little or nothing can be done about the situation itself. Thus they direct their energy toward "feeling better" rather than toward any actions meant to change the situation. For example, when faced with a difficult test, students who feel they are unable to learn the material well enough to earn a good grade may select coping strategies that focus on emotions rather than actions. They might ignore the upcoming test and go out with friends instead of studying, decide the class is not important after all, or become angry with the professor for being unfair. There are two types of emotion-focused coping: *proactive* (confronting or expressing one's emotions or seeking social support) and *passive* (avoidance, denial, suppression of emotions, or acceptance of the situation as it is).

Age Differences in Choice of Coping Styles Older adults tend to do more emotion-focused coping than younger people (Blanchard-Fields, 2007); this is particularly true when looking at the oldest old (Martin et al., 2008). Generally, emotion-focused coping is less adaptive than problem-focused coping, but this is only true when something can realistically be done about the problem. When a solution is not available, it may be more adaptive to control negative or unpleasant emotions. When both emotion- and problem-focused coping are used together, a wider and more flexible range of responses to stressful events is possible.

In studies in which young, middle-aged, and older adults were asked how they would deal with various kinds of problems, participants, regardless of age, most often picked problem-focused strategies (either direct action or analyzing the problem so as to understand it better). The largest age differences appeared in problems with highly emotional or stressful implications, such as that of a divorced man who is allowed to see his child only on weekends but wants to see the child more often. Adults of all ages were more likely to use emotion-focused coping in such situations, but older adults chose emotion-focused strategies (such as doing nothing, waiting until the child is older, or trying not to worry about it) more often than younger adults did (Blanchard-Fields et al., 2004).

Apparently, with age, people develop this more flexible repertoire of coping strategies. Older adults *can* employ problem-focused strategies but may be more able than younger adults to use emotion regulation when a situation seems to call for it—when problem-focused action might be futile or counterproductive (Blanchard-Fields et al., 2004).

ambiguous loss
A loss that is not clearly defined or does not bring closure.

Emotion-focused coping can be especially useful in coping with what the family therapist Pauline Boss (2007) calls **ambiguous loss.** Boss applies that term to losses that are not clearly defined or do not bring closure, such as the loss of a still-living loved one to Alzheimer's disease or the loss of a homeland, which elderly immigrants may feel as long as they live. In such situations, experience may teach people to accept what they cannot change—a lesson often reinforced by religion.

Which type of coping do you tend to use more: problem-focused or emotion-focused? Which type do your parents use more? Your grandparents? In what kinds of situations does each type of coping seem most effective?

Coping styles are related not only to emotional and psychological well-being but also to physical well-being. In general, happier people are healthier people, and how a person copes with the trials and tribulations of life is related to a number of important health outcomes. Why does this link exist? Research suggests that adaptive coping is related to health via stress hormone pathways (Carver, 2007). In one study of more than 500 older adults, those adults who used problem-focused coping strategies and sought social support in the face of stressful events showed lower levels of cortisol, a stress hormone, over the course of the day (O'Donnell, Badrick, Kumari, & Steptoe, 2008).

Does Religion or Spirituality Affect Health and Well-Being? Religion becomes increasingly important to many people as they age. In a nationally representative survey, about 50 percent of U.S. adults in their 70s and 80s said they attend services every week (Cornwell, Laumann, & Schumm, 2008). Religion seems to play a supportive role for many older people. Some possible explanations include social support, encouragement of healthy lifestyles, the perception of a measure of control over life through prayer, fostering of positive emotional states, reduction of stress, and faith in God as a way of interpreting misfortunes (Seybold & Hill, 2001). But does religion actually improve health and well-being?

Religious activity seems to help many people cope with stress and loss in later life, and some research suggests that its effect on health and well-being may be real.

Many studies suggest a positive link between religion or spirituality and health (Lawler-Rowe & Elliot, 2009). In fact, a review of studies with relatively sound methodology found a 25 percent reduction in risk of mortality among healthy adults who attended religious services weekly (Powell, Shahabi, & Thoresen, 2003). Another research review found positive associations between religiosity or spirituality and measures of health, well-being, marital satisfaction, and psychological functioning and negative associations with suicide, delinquency, criminality, and drug and alcohol use (Seybold & Hill, 2001). It seems that part of the reason for the links between health and spirituality is because people who belong to a church are more likely to engage in healthy behaviors and have higher levels of social support. Interestingly, church membership per se—rather than frequency of attendance—is the crucial variable (Lawler-Row & Elliot, 2009). Although the cited study focused on church membership only, it is likely that participation in other religious traditions and communities acts similarly.

Relatively little of the research on religion and spirituality has been done with racial/ethnic minorities. In one such study, among 3,050 older Mexican Americans, those who attended church once a week had a 32 percent lower mortality risk than those who never attended (Hill, Angel, Ellison, & Angel, 2005). For elderly black people, religion is closely related to life satisfaction and well-being (Coke & Twaite, 1995; Krause, 2004a). A special factor is the belief held by many black people that the church helps sustain them in confronting racial injustice (Ellison, Musick, & Henderson, 2008).

checkpoint can you . . .

- Name five mature adaptive mechanisms identified by Vaillant, and discuss how they work?
- Describe the cognitive-appraisal model of coping, and explain the relationship between age and choice of coping strategies?
- Discuss how religiosity and spirituality relate to mortality risk, health, and well-being in late life?

MODELS OF "SUCCESSFUL," OR "OPTIMAL," AGING

With a growing number of active, healthy older adults, the concept of aging has shifted. *Successful,* or *optimal, aging* has largely replaced the idea that aging results from inevitable, intrinsic processes of loss and decline. Given that modifiable factors play a role in at least some aspects of aging, it follows that some people may age more successfully than others (Rowe & Kahn, 1997).

A considerable body of work has identified three main components of successful aging: (1) avoidance of disease or disease-related disability, (2) maintenance of high physical and cognitive functioning, and (3) sustained, active engagement in social and productive activities (activities, paid or unpaid, that create social value). Successful agers tend to have social support, both emotional and material, which aids mental health; and as long as they remain active and productive, they do not think of themselves as old (Rowe & Kahn, 1997). Another approach emphasizes subjective well-being and satisfaction with life (Jopp & Smith, 2006). Agreement on what constitutes successful aging is surprisingly absent (Depp & Jeste, 2009). However, a meta-analysis of studies that included quantitative data as well as a definition of "successful aging" found that approximately one-third of adults over the age of 60 engage in successful aging (Depp & Jeste, 2009).

Many people argue that the definitions of *successful,* or *optimal, aging* are value-laden. These terms, critics say, may burden, rather than liberate, older people by putting pressure on them to meet standards they cannot or do not wish to meet. The concept of successful aging, according to these critics, does not pay enough attention to the constraints that may limit lifestyle choices. Not all adults have the good genes, education, and favorable circumstances to "construct the kind of life they choose." An unintended result of labeling older adults as "successful" or "unsuccessful" may be to blame the victims and drive them to self-defeating, antiaging, strategies. It also tends to demean old age itself and to deny the importance of accepting, or adapting to, what cannot be changed (Holstein & Minkler, 2003).

Keeping these concerns in mind, let's look at some classic and current theories and research about aging well.

checkpoint can you . . .

- Tell what is meant by *successful,* or *optimal, aging* and why the concept is controversial.

disengagement theory
Theory of aging that holds that successful aging is characterized by mutual withdrawal of the older person and society.

Disengagement Theory versus Activity Theory Who is making a healthier adjustment to old age: a person who peacefully watches the world go by from a rocking chair or one who keeps busy from morning till night? According to **disengagement theory,** a normal part of aging involves a gradual reduction in social involvement and greater preoccupation with the self. According to **activity theory,** the more active older people remain, the better they age.

activity theory
Theory of aging that holds that to age successfully a person must remain as active as possible.

Disengagement theory was one of the first theories in gerontology. Its proponents (Cumming & Henry, 1961) regarded disengagement as a normative, or typical, part of aging. They argued that awareness of the approach of death and declines in physical functioning resulted in a gradual, inevitable withdrawal from social roles. Moreover, because society stops providing useful roles for the older adult, the disengagement is mutual—others do not try to stop it. Introspection and a quieting of the emotions also accompany disengagement.

For a time this approach was influential, but more than five decades of research has provided little support for disengagement theory, and its influence has largely waned (Achenbaum & Bengtson, 1994). This approach may have reflected beliefs about aging at the time it was developed (Moody, 2009) rather than described a normative and healthy developmental process.

The second approach, *activity theory,* takes the opposing viewpoint. In this theory, we are what we do (Moody, 2009). Rather than retreating from life, adults who age successfully tend to remain engaged with social roles and connections. The more active they remain in those roles, the more satisfied with life they are likely to be. When they lose a role, such as when they retire, they find a substitute role, such as volunteering (Neugarten, Havighurst, & Tobin, 1968). Research generally supports this approach, showing that people who retain their major role identities tend to report greater well-being and better mental health (Greenfield & Marks, 2004).

continuity theory
Theory of aging, described by Atchley, that holds that in order to age successfully people must maintain a balance of continuity and change in both the internal and external structures of their lives.

How has this theory held up over time? As originally framed, activity theory is now regarded as overly simplistic. Early research did indeed suggest that activity was associated with life satisfaction (Neugarten et al., 1968); however, the interpretation of this finding may have been flawed. Rather than activity driving satisfaction, it may have been relationships that were responsible for the effect. People who remain active are more likely to maintain high-quality social relationships, and the presence of these relationships is likely to positively affect life satisfaction (Litwing & Shiovitz-Ezra, 2006). In addition, a good proportion of disengaged people are nonetheless happy with their lives, and recent research suggests that disengagement and activity theory may both speak to successful aging. Specifically, adults who believed themselves to be aging successfully struck a balance between self-acceptance and being happy with themselves as they were and remaining simultaneously engaged and involved with life (Reichstadt, Sengupta, Depp, Palinkas, & Jeste, 2010). Findings such as these suggest that activity may work best for most people but disengagement may be appropriate for others, and that it may be unwise to make generalizations about a particular pattern of successful aging (Moen, Dempster-McClain, & Williams, 1992; Musick, Herzog, & House, 1999).

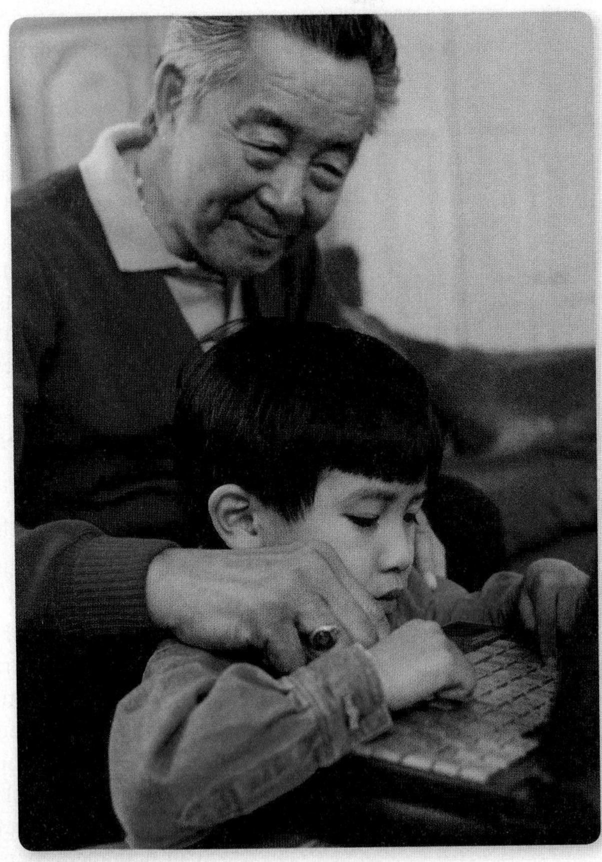

Older people who feel useful to others, as this grandparent does to his grandson, are more likely to age successfully.

Continuity Theory Are you happiest being out and about, visiting friends, and staying busy? Or do you prefer a quiet night spent watching a movie by yourself? What you prefer prior to the later stages of life may influence what you prefer when you reach them. In other words, if you are happy being active now, you are likely to be happy being active later. However, if you are happy being less active now, you may prefer a quieter lifestyle later in life too (Pushkar et al., 2009). This is the primary premise of **continuity theory** (Atchley, 1989). In this approach, people's need to maintain a connection between past and present is emphasized, and activity is viewed as important, not for its own sake but because it represents continuation of a previous lifestyle. For example, many retired people are happiest pursuing work or leisure activities similar to those they enjoyed in the past (Pushkar et al., 2010). Women who have been involved in multiple roles (such as wife, mother, employee, or volunteer) tend to continue those involvements as they age—and remain happier for having done so (Moen et al., 1992). And people who, in middle age, enjoyed leisure activities such as reading books, pursuing a hobby, or gardening tended to engage in these activities in old age as well (Agahi, Ahacic, & Parker, 2006). Continuity in activities is not always possible because some older adults must cut back on participation in favorite events due to visual, motor, or cognitive impairments. Older adults are likely to be happier, however, if they can maintain their favorite activities to some extent.

The Role of Productivity Some researchers focus on productive activity, either paid or unpaid, as a key to aging well. In one study of more than 1,200 older adults, both the number of productive activities and the amount of time spent on those activities were related to subjective well-being and feelings of happiness (Baker, Cahalil, Gerst, & Burr, 2005). Similarly, a 6-year longitudinal study of 3,218 older adults in Manitoba, Canada, found that *social* and *productive activities* (such as visiting family or housework and gardening) were related to self-rated happiness, better physical functioning, and less chance of having died 6 years later. Although *solitary activities,* such as reading and handiwork, did not have physical benefits, they were nonetheless related to happiness, perhaps by promoting a sense of engagement with life (Menec, 2003).

checkpoint can **you**...

- Compare disengagement theory, activity theory, and continuity theory?
- Discuss the importance of productivity in late adulthood?

Some research suggests that frequent participation in *leisure activities* can be as beneficial to health and well-being as frequent participation in productive activities, although this effect may be stronger for women (Agahi & Parker, 2008). It may be that *any* regular activity that expresses and enhances some aspect of the self can contribute to successful aging (Herzog, Franks, Markus, & Holmberg, 1998).

Selective Optimization with Compensation According to Paul Baltes and his colleagues (Baltes, 1997), successful aging involves strategies that enable people to adapt to the changing balance of growth and decline throughout life. In childhood, resources are primarily used for growth, and in early adulthood resources are used to maximize reproductive fitness. In old age, resources are increasingly directed toward the maintenance of health and the management of loss (Baltes & Smith, 2004; Jopp & Smith, 2006). Older adults allocate these resources via a process called **selective optimization with compensation (SOC).** SOC involves developing abilities that allow for maximum gain, as well as developing abilities that compensate for decline and could lead to loss. According to SOC, older adults conserve their resources by:

selective optimization with compensation (SOC)
Enhancing overall cognitive functioning by using stronger abilities to compensate for those that have weakened.

- *Selecting* fewer and more meaningful activities or goals.
- *Optimizing,* or making the most of, the resources they have to achieve their goals.
- *Compensating* for losses by using resources in alternative ways to achieve their goals.

Are you satisfied with any of the definitions of successful, or optimal, aging presented in this section? Why or why not?

For example, the celebrated concert pianist Arthur Rubenstein gave his farewell concert at age 89. He was able to compensate for his age-related memory loss by selecting a smaller repertoire of material to play and by practicing longer each day to optimize his performance. He also compensated for declines in motor abilities by slowing down his playing immediately before fast movements, thus heightening the contrast and making the music sound faster (Baltes & Baltes, 1990).

The same life-management strategies apply to psychosocial development. According to Carstensen's (1991, 1995, 1996) socioemotional selectivity theory, older adults become more selective about social contacts, keeping up with friends and relatives who can best meet their current needs for emotional satisfaction. In this way, even though older adults may have fewer friends, the friends that they do have are closer and provide more rewarding social contact.

Research has found that use of SOC is associated with positive developmental outcomes, including greater well-being (Baltes & Smith, 2004). Eventually, though, older people may reach the limit of their available resources, and compensatory efforts may no longer seem to work. In a 4-year longitudinal study of 762 adults, compensatory efforts increased up to age 70 but then declined. Adjusting one's personal standards to changes in what is possible to achieve may be essential to maintaining a positive outlook on life (Rothermund & Brandtstädter, 2003). The argument about what constitutes successful or optimal aging and what contributes to well-being in old age is far from settled, and may never be. One thing is clear: people differ greatly in the ways they can and do live—and want to live—in the later years of life.

checkpoint
can **you** . . .

- Explain how selective optimization with compensation helps older adults deal with losses?

Practical and Social Issues Related to Aging

Whether and when to retire are among the most crucial lifestyle decisions people make as they approach late adulthood. These decisions affect their financial situation and emotional state, as well as the ways they spend their waking hours and the ways they relate to family and friends. The need to provide financial support for large numbers of retired older people also has serious implications for society, especially as the baby boom generation starts to retire. Another social issue is the need for appropriate living arrangements and care for older people who can no longer manage on their own. (Box 1 reports on issues related to support of the aging in Asia.)

Despite the fact that more women develop Alzheimer's disease, men tend to have earlier and more problems with forgetting, a tendency that may have more immediate practical consequences for those entering the later states of life.

Petersen et al., 2010

WORK AND RETIREMENT

Retirement took hold in many industrialized countries during the late nineteenth and early twentieth centuries as life expectancy increased. In the United States, the creation of the Social Security system in the 1930s, together with company-sponsored pension plans negotiated by labor unions, made it possible for many older workers to retire with financial security. Eventually, mandatory retirement at age 65 became almost universal. However, in 1983, an amendment was passed in which the age for full eligibility for retirement benefits was raised to 67 years for people born in 1960 or later, and more stringent penalties were instituted for early retirement at age 62. Despite these changes, the number of people receiving benefits has continued to rise in concert with the changing demographics of the United States (Duggan, Singleton, & Song, 2007).

Today, compulsory retirement has been virtually outlawed in the United States as a form of age discrimination (except for certain occupations, such as airline pilots), and the line between work and retirement is not as clear as it used to be. There are no longer norms concerning the timing of retirement, how to plan for it, and what to do afterward. Adults have many choices. The biggest factors in the decision usually are health and financial considerations. For many older adults, retirement is a "phased phenomenon, involving multiple transitions out of and into paid and unpaid 'work'" (Kim & Moen, 2001, p. 489). Only 40 percent of those older adults who stop working in their 50s and 60s stop for good; the remainder go back to work either part or full time before permanently exiting the workforce (Maestas, 2010).

Although you may have more time to enjoy a glass of wine after you retire, unfortunately, you'll pay more for it the next day. Older people metabolize wine more slowly and have less liquid in their bodies. Therefore, blood alcohol level rises more quickly and is likely to result in a more severe hangover.

National Institute on Alcohol Abuse and Alcoholism, 2010

Trends in Late-Life Work and Retirement In the United States, most adults who *can* retire *do* retire; and, with increasing longevity, they spend more time in retirement than in the past (Dobriansky et al., 2007). However, the proportion of workers older than 65 years of age has increased sharply between 1997 and 2007, reaching a high of 56 percent in 2007. This graying of the working population is expected to continue to increase (U.S. Bureau of Labor Statistics, 2008b).

At what age, if ever, do you expect to retire? Why? How would you like to spend your time if and when you retire?

window on the world

AGING IN ASIA

Challenges of an aging population are common to Eastern and Western societies, but differing cultural traditions and economic systems affect the way societies deal with these challenges. In East Asia, in particular, the shifting balance of young and old, together with rapid economic development, has caused societal dislocations and cultural strains, upsetting ancient traditions.

1 One dramatic result of an aging population is fewer young people to care for the old. By 2030 Japan, for example, is projected to have twice as many older adults, nearly 40 percent of them at least 80 years old, as children. Pension reserves will likely be exhausted, and retirement and health care costs for the elderly may consume nearly three-fourths of the national income (Dobriansky et al., 2007; Kinsella & Phillips, 2005).

In China, the over-60 population is growing faster than in any other major country. By midcentury, about 430 million Chinese—one-third of the population—will be retirees (United Nations, 2007). In its rapid transition to a market economy, China has not established a fully functioning system of old-age insurance. A steady rise in the number of retirees together with a decline in the ratio of workers to pensioners threaten the stability of the system. One possible solution—raising the currently low retirement age—would make jobs for the 30 percent of recent university graduates who are unemployed even more scarce (Dobriansky et al., 2007; French, 2007).

Throughout Asia, a large proportion of older people still live with their children in the Confucian tradition of spiritual obligation to aid and care for parents. However, this tradition is eroding. In Hong Kong, China, Korea, and Japan, significant numbers of older adults now live alone (Dobriansky et al., 2007; Kinsella & Phillips, 2005; Silverstein, Cong, & Li, 2006).

All of these changes make the tradition of home care of the elderly less feasible. Institutionalization—virtually nonexistent in 1960—is seen as a violation of traditional obligations, but the exploding older Japanese population is outgrowing family-based care. To halt this trend, the government has made it a legal obligation to care for elderly relatives and has provided tax relief to those who give them financial help (Lin et al., 2003).

In urban areas of China, where housing is scarce, older parents continue to live with adult children, usually married sons, following the traditional patriarchal custom (Pimentel & Liu, 2004; Silverstein et al., 2006; Zhang, 2004). In rural areas, however, where many working-age adults have migrated to cities in search of jobs, a decline in multigenerational households undermines Confucian ideals. Still, in the absence of universal public pensions and long-term care programs, older parents remain largely dependent on their children. In one rural province, more than half (51 percent) of older parents live with adult children, grandchildren, or both, and almost all receive material assistance from their children—but for many parents such assistance is less important than maintaining the tradition of a multigenerational household (Silverstein et al., 2006).

Because of China's one-child policy, in force since 1979, singleton adult children, usually daughters-in-law who may be in the workforce, are expected to care for two parents and four grandparents, a task that will become increasingly unworkable. The aging population has increased the prevalence of chronic diseases and disabilities and expanded the need for long-term care. The government has begun to develop disease-prevention programs and long-term care systems, but it is doubtful that enough funding will be available to cover rising health care costs (Kaneda, 2006).

In what ways is aging in Asia becoming similar to aging in the United States? In what ways is it different?

How Does Age Affect Attitudes toward Work and Job Performance? Prior to the economic downturn, which began in 2007, people who continued to work after age 65 typically liked their work and did not find it unduly stressful. They tended to be better educated and in better health than those who retired earlier (Kiefer, Summer, & Shirey, 2001; Kim & Moen, 2001). However, the changing economic climate has meant that many older workers are now forced to work not because they want to but because they are forced to by their financial situation and escalating medical costs (Sterns, 2010).

Contrary to ageist stereotypes, older workers can be as productive as younger workers. Although they may work more slowly than younger people, they are more accurate (Czaja & Sharit, 1998; Salthouse & Maurer, 1996). A key factor may be experience rather than age: when older people perform better, it may be because they have been on a job, or have done similar work, longer (Cleveland & Lim, 2007). The greatest declines in productivity for older workers are seen when problem solving, learning, or speed are important. When experience or verbal abilities matter more, productivity of older workers matches or even exceeds that of younger workers (Skirbekk, 2008).

In the United States, the Age Discrimination in Employment Act (ADEA), which applies to firms with 20 or more employees, protects workers ages 40 and older from being denied a job, fired, paid less, or forced to retire because of age. Still, many employers exert subtle pressures on older employees (Landy, 1994), and age discrimination cases can be difficult to prove. Approximately 14,500 age discrimination claims—primarily focused on termination rather than hiring decisions—are filed each year, suggesting that age discrimination is still a factor in employment for older adults (Neumark, 2008).

About 500,000 older Americans volunteer through the Senior Corps program. These volunteers are building a home for a low-income family through Habitat for Humanity.

Life after Retirement Retirement is not a single event but a dynamic adjustment process that is best conceptualized as a form of decision making. Personal resources (health, SES, and personality), economic resources, and social-relational resources, such as support from a partner and friends, can affect how well retirees weather this transition (Wang & Shultz, 2009). So can a person's attachment to work (van Solinge & Henkens, 2005).

In a 2-year longitudinal study of 458 relatively healthy married men and women ages 50 to 72, men whose morale at work had been low tended to enjoy a boost during the "honeymoon period" immediately following retirement, but *continuous* retirement was associated with an increase in depressive symptoms. Women's well-being was less influenced by retirement—their own or their husbands'; their morale was more affected by marital quality. A sense of personal control was a key predictor of morale in both men and women (Kim & Moen, 2002).

Volunteer work is closely tied to well-being during retirement (Hao, 2008). In a sample of adults ages 65 to 74 from the MIDUS study, volunteering predicted positive emotionality. It also tended to protect against declines in well-being associated with major role-identity losses (Greenfield & Marks, 2004) and declines in mental health (Hao, 2008). In Japan, older adults who are healthy and active are encouraged to be volunteers. In a longitudinal study of older Japanese adults, those who rated themselves as useful to others and to society were more likely to survive 6 years later, even after adjustment for self-rated health (Okamoto & Tanaka, 2004). It is important to note that those older adults who volunteer are more likely to be higher in resources than those who do not (Li & Ferraro, 2005). However, despite this selection bias, it does appear that volunteering has a positive effect on older adults.

The many paths to a meaningful, enjoyable retirement have two things in common: doing satisfying things and having satisfying relationships. For most older people, both "are an extension of histories that have developed throughout the life course" (J. R. Kelly, 1994, p. 501).

HOW DO OLDER ADULTS FARE FINANCIALLY?

Since the 1960s, Social Security has provided the largest share of older Americans' income—39 percent in 2013 (Social Security Administration, 2013). Other sources of income include income from assets (13 percent), private pensions (19 percent), and earnings (30 percent) (Federal Interagency Forum on Aging Related Statistics, 2010). Dependence on Social Security and asset income rises dramatically with age and decreases with income level (Federal Interagency Forum on Aging-Related Statistics, 2006).

checkpoint can you . . .

- Describe current trends in late-life work and retirement?
- Cite findings on the relationship between aging and work attitudes and skills?
- Discuss how retirement can affect well-being?
- Discuss the economic status of older adults and issues concerning Social Security?

Social Security and other government programs, such as Medicare, which covers basic health insurance for U.S. residents who are 65 or older or are disabled, have enabled today's older Americans, as a group, to live fairly comfortably. Since 1959 the proportion of older adults living in poverty fell from 35 percent to less than 10 percent in 2008 (Administration on Aging, 2009), and the poverty rate for older adults now is lower than that of the total population (U.S. Census Bureau, 2010b). However, with a graying population and proportionately fewer workers to contribute to the Social Security system, it seems likely that, unless changes are made, benefits will eventually decline, though the timing and severity of the problem are in dispute (Sawicki, 2005).

Women—especially if they are single, widowed, separated, or divorced or if they were previously poor or worked only part-time in middle age—are more likely (12 percent) than men (7 percent) to live in poverty in old age. There are also ethnic differences. Older African Americans and Hispanic Americans, at rates of 23 and 17 percent, respectively, are more likely to live in poverty than older white Americans at 7.4 percent. The highest poverty rates are among older Hispanic women (20 percent) and older African American women (27 percent) who live alone (Federal Interagency Forum on Aging Related Statistics, 2010).

LIVING ARRANGEMENTS

In developing countries, older adults typically live with adult children and grandchildren in multigenerational households, though this custom is declining. In developed countries, most older people live alone or with a partner or spouse (Kinsella & Phillips, 2005).

In the United States, in 2009, about 7 percent of adults aged 65 and older live in senior housing of various types, generally taking advantage of supportive services (Federal Interagency Forum on Aging-Related Statistics, 2012). Because of women's greater life expectancy, about 72 percent of noninstitutionalized men but only about 42 percent of noninstitutionalized women lived with a spouse. Nineteen percent of the men and 37 percent of the women lived alone, although the proportion living alone increases with advancing age. For example, by the age of 75 years, nearly half of all women live alone. Approximately 9 percent of the men and 20 percent of the women lived with other relatives or nonrelatives, including partners and children. Minority elders, especially Asian and Hispanic Americans, in keeping with their traditions, were more likely than white elders to live in extended-family households (Administration on Aging, 2009; Federal Interagency Forum on Aging-Related Statistics, 2010; Figure 1).

Living arrangements alone do not tell us much about older adults' well-being. For example, living alone does not necessarily imply lack of family cohesion and support; instead, it may reflect an older person's good health, economic self-sufficiency, and

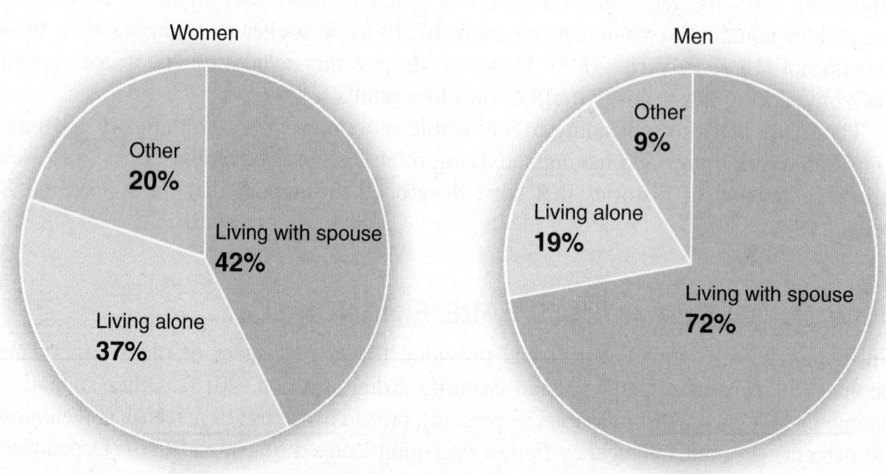

Source: Federal Interagency Forum on Aging-Related Statistics, 2012.

FIGURE 1
Living Arrangements of Noninstitutionalized Men and Women Age 65 and Over, United States, 2010

In part because of women's longer life expectancy, they are more likely to live alone (especially as they get older), whereas men are more likely to live with a spouse. The "Other" category includes those living with adult children, other relatives, or nonrelatives.

desire for independence. By the same token, living with adult children tells us nothing about the quality of relationships in the household (Kinsella & Velkoff, 2001).

Aging in Place Most older adults in industrialized countries prefer, if possible, to stay in their own homes and communities (Kinsella & Phillips, 2005). This option, called **aging in place,** makes sense for those who can manage on their own or with minimal help, have an adequate income or a paid-up mortgage, can handle the upkeep, are happy in the neighborhood, and want to be independent, to have privacy, and to be near friends, adult children, or grandchildren. Most informal caregivers, such as family, who provide aging in place care do so willingly, but it can be a significant source of stress and worry for them (Sanders, Stone, Meador, & Parker, 2010). Partially in response to this, naturally occurring retirement communities (NORCs) are neighborhoods in which a large proportion of residents happen to be older adults. In general, NORCs are not the result of deliberate planning; rather, they are the result of the simultaneous aging of community residents or migration of large numbers of older adults to a particular location. A national initiative of the U.S. Administration on Aging seeks to enhance supportive services for people living in NORCs (Bernstein, 2008), a process that is likely to be of growing importance with the graying of the population.

aging in place
Remaining in one's own home, with or without assistance, in later life.

For older people with impairments that make it hard to get along entirely on their own, minor support—such as meals, transportation, and home health aides—often can help them stay put. So can ramps, grab bars, and other modifications within the home (Newman, 2003). Most older people do not need much help; and those who do can often remain in the community if they have at least one person to depend on. In fact, the single most important factor keeping people out of institutions is being married. As long as a couple are in relatively good health, they can usually live fairly independently and care for each other. The issue of living arrangements becomes more pressing and institutionalization more likely when one or both become frail, infirm, or disabled, or when one spouse dies (Nihtilä & Martikainen, 2008).

Let's look more closely at the two most common living arrangements for older adults without spouses—living alone and living with adult children—and then at living in institutions and alternative forms of group housing.

Living Alone Because women live longer than men and are more likely to be widowed, older women in the United States are more than twice as likely as older men to live alone, and the likelihood increases with age. Older people living alone are more likely than older people with spouses to be poor (Administration on Aging, 2009) and to end up in institutions (Kaspar, Pezzin, & Rice, 2010).

The picture is similar in most developed countries: older women are more likely to live alone than older men. The growth of elderly single-person households has been spurred by greater longevity, increased benefits and pensions, increased home ownership, more elder-friendly housing, more availability of community support, and reduced public assistance with nursing home costs (Kinsella & Phillips, 2005).

The older you are, the more you are likely to say that a television is a necessity versus a luxury. Younger people show the opposite pattern.

Taylor & Wang, 2010

It might seem that older people who live alone, particularly the oldest old, would be lonely. However, such factors as personality, cognitive abilities, physical health, and a depleted social network may play a greater role in loneliness (Martin, Kliegel, Rott, Poon, & Johnson, 2007). Social activities, such as going to a senior center or doing volunteer work, can help an older person living alone stay connected to the community (Hendricks & Cutler, 2004; Kim & Moen, 2001). Loneliness is more closely tied to disability and withdrawal from the social world than it is to age itself (Jyhla, 2004).

Living with Adult Children Historically, older people in many African, Asian, and Latin American societies could expect to live and be cared for in their children's or grandchildren's homes, but this pattern is changing rapidly. Most older people in developed countries, even when in difficult circumstances, prefer not to live with their children (Kinsella & Phillips, 2005). They are reluctant to burden their families and to give up their freedom. It can be inconvenient to absorb an extra person into a household, and everyone's privacy—and relationships—may suffer. The parent may feel useless, bored, and isolated from friends. If the adult child is married and the spouse and parent do not get along well, or caregiving duties become too burdensome, the marriage may be threatened (Shapiro & Cooney, 2007).

The success of such an arrangement depends largely on the quality of the relationship that has existed in the past and on the ability of both generations to communicate fully and frankly. The decision to move a parent into an adult child's home should be mutual and needs to be thought through carefully and thoroughly. Parents and children need to respect each other's dignity and autonomy and accept their differences (Shapiro, 1994).

Living in Institutions The use of nonfamily institutions for care of the frail elderly varies greatly around the world. Institutionalization has been rare in developing regions but is becoming less so in Southeast Asia, where declines in fertility have resulted in a rapidly aging population and a shortage of family caregivers (Kinsella & Velkoff, 2001). Comprehensive geriatric home visitation programs in some countries, such as the United Kingdom, Denmark, and Australia, have been effective in holding down nursing home admissions (Stuck, Egger, Hammer, Minder, & Beck, 2002).

A recent movement toward "consistent assignment" in nursing homes involves having the same caregivers care for an elderly person on a regular basis, rather than the more common rotation of caregivers. This consistency allows for better monitoring of care and condition, as well as affording the elderly person an opportunity to establish relationships with caregivers.

Span, 2010

In all countries, the likelihood of living in a nursing home increases with age—in the United States, from about 1 percent at ages 65 to 74 to 15.4 percent at age 85 and over (Administration on Aging, 2009). Most older nursing home residents worldwide and almost 3 out of 4 in the United States are women (Federal Interagency Forum on Aging-Related Statistics, 2004; Kinsella & Velkoff, 2001). In addition to gender, being poor and living alone significantly increase the risk of entering long-term care (Martainkainen et al., 2009).

The number of U.S. nursing home residents has increased considerably since the late 1970s due to growth of the older population. In addition, liberalization of Medicare long-term care coverage and the emergence of widespread private long-term care insurance have spurred a shift from institutionalization to less expensive alternative living options (discussed in the next section) and home health care (Ness, Ahmed, & Aronow, 2004). However, as the baby boom generation ages and if current nursing home usage rates continue, the number of residents is projected to rise sharply (Seblega et al., 2010). Such growth would greatly burden Medicaid, the national health insurance program for low-income persons and the major source of payments for nursing home usage (Ness et al., 2004).

Federal law sets strict requirements for nursing homes and gives residents the right to choose their own doctors, to be fully informed about their care and treatment, and to be free from physical or mental abuse, corporal punishment, involuntary seclusion, and

Older adults in a retirement village with supportive living facilities keep their minds active. These women are taking a computer class in cooperation with a nearby community college.

physical or chemical restraints. Some states train volunteer ombudsmen to act as advocates for nursing home residents, to explain their rights, and to resolve their complaints about such matters as privacy, treatment, food, and financial issues.

An essential element of good care is the opportunity for residents to make decisions and exert some control over their lives. Among 126 elderly nursing home residents, those who lived in nursing homes that supported their autonomy showed increases in perceptions of the choices and freedom available to them. Those perceptual changes, in turn, led to increases in motivation in attempting various daily activities, and were related to psychological adjustment and well-being (Phillippe & Vallerand, 2008).

Alternative Housing Options Some older adults who cannot or do not want to maintain a house, do not need special care, do not have family nearby, prefer a different locale or climate, or want to travel move into maintenance-free or low-maintenance townhouses, condominiums, cooperative or rental apartments, or mobile homes. A relatively new but growing segment of the housing market is in age-qualified active adult communities. In these communities, for people age 55 and older, residents can walk out their front door and find a variety of leisure opportunities, such as fitness centers, tennis courts, and golf courses, close by.

For those who cannot or prefer not to live completely independently, a wide array of group housing options, many of them described in Table 1, have emerged.

TABLE 1 Group Living Arrangements for Older Adults

Facility	Description
Retirement hotel	Hotel or apartment building remodeled to meet the needs of independent older adults. Typical hotel services (switchboard, maid service, message center) are provided.
Retirement community	Large, self-contained development with owned or rental units or both. Support services and recreational facilities are often available as in active adult communities.
Shared housing	Housing can be shared informally by adult parents and children or by friends. Other times social agencies match people who need a place to live with people who have houses or apartments with extra rooms. The older person usually has a private room but shares living, eating, and cooking areas and may exchange services such as light housekeeping for rent.
Accessory apartment or ECHO (elder cottage housing opportunity) housing	An independent unit created so that an older person can live in a remodeled single-family home or in a portable unit on the grounds of a single-family home—often, but not necessarily, that of an adult child. Units offer privacy, proximity to caregivers, and security.
Congregate housing	Private or government-subsidized rental apartment complexes or mobile home parks designed for older adults provide meals, housekeeping, transportation, social and recreational activities, and sometimes health care. One type of congregate housing is a *group home:* a social agency that owns or rents a house brings together a small number of elderly residents and hires helpers to shop, cook, do heavy cleaning, drive, and give counseling. Residents take care of their personal needs and take some responsibility for day-to-day tasks.
Assisted-living facility	Semi-independent living in one's own room or apartment. Similar to congregate housing, but residents receive personal care (bathing, dressing, and grooming) and protective supervision according to their needs and desires. *Board-and-care homes* are similar but smaller and offer more personal care and supervision.
Foster-care home	Owners of a single-family residence take in an unrelated older adult and provide meals, housekeeping, and personal care.
Continuing care retirement community	Long-term housing planned to provide a full range of accommodations and services for affluent elderly people as their needs change. A resident may start out in an independent apartment; then move into congregate housing with such services as cleaning, laundry, and meals; then into an assisted-living facility; and finally into a nursing home. *Life-care communities* are similar but guarantee housing and medical or nursing care for a specified period or for life; they require a substantial entry fee in addition to monthly payments.

Source: Laquatra & Chi, 1998; Porcino, 1993.

As you become older and possibly at least partly incapacitated, what type of living arrangement would you prefer?

checkpoint can you . . .

- Compare various kinds of living arrangements for older adults, their relative prevalence, and their advantages and disadvantages?

Some of these newer arrangements enable older people with health problems or disabilities to receive needed services or care without sacrificing autonomy, privacy, and dignity.

One popular option is *assisted living,* housing specifically for older adults (Hawes, Phillips, Rose, Holan, & Sherman, 2003). Assisted-living facilities enable tenants to live in their own homelike space while giving them easy 24-hour access to needed personal and health care services. In most of these facilities a person can move, when and if necessary, from relative independence (with housekeeping and meals provided) to help with bathing, dressing, managing medications, and using a wheelchair to get around. However, assisted-living facilities vary widely in accommodations, operation, philosophy, and rates, and those offering adequate privacy and services are generally not affordable for moderate- and low-income persons unless they dispose of or spend down their assets to supplement their income (Hawes et al., 2003). Indeed, facilities are disproportionately found in areas with more educated residents and higher incomes (Stevenson & Grabowski, 2010).

Personal Relationships in Late Life

Our stereotypes of the elderly often lead us to believe that old age is a time of loneliness and isolation. Work is often a convenient source of social contact; longtime retirees have fewer social contacts than more recent retirees or those who continue to work. For some older adults, infirmities make it harder to get out and see people. All in all, older adults report only half as many people in their social networks as younger adults do (Lang, 2001), and men's social networks tend to be somewhat smaller than those of women (McLaughlin, Vagenas, Pachana, Begum, & Dobson, 2010). However, research suggests that even though age may result in a shrinking of the size of social networks, older adults retain a close circle of confidants (Cornwell et al., 2008). Furthermore, the relationships older adults *do* maintain are more important to their well-being than ever (Charles & Carstensen, 2007) and help keep their minds and memories sharp (Crooks, Lubben, Petitti, Little, & Chiu, 2008; Ertel, Glymour, & Berkman, 2008). In a National Council on Aging (2002) survey, only about 1 out of 5 U.S. older adults reported loneliness as a serious problem, and nearly 9 out of 10 placed the highest importance on family and friends for a meaningful, vital life.

People tend to gain emotional intelligence with age. They respond more empathically to sad events or stimuli and are better at reframing that information in a positive way.

Seider, Shiota, Whalen, & Levenson, 2010

THEORIES OF SOCIAL CONTACT AND SOCIAL SUPPORT

According to *social convoy theory,* aging adults maintain their level of social support by identifying members of their social network who can help them and avoiding those who are not supportive. As former coworkers and casual friends drop away, most older adults retain a stable inner circle of social convoys: close friends and family members on whom they can rely and who strongly affect their well-being (Antonucci & Akiyama, 1995).

A somewhat different explanation of changes in social contact comes from *socioemotional selectivity theory* (Carstensen, 1991, 1995, 1996). As remaining time becomes short, older adults choose to spend time with people and in activities that meet immediate emotional needs. A college student may put up with a disliked teacher for the sake of gaining needed knowledge; an older adult may be less willing to spend precious time with a friend who gets on her nerves. Young adults with a free half-hour may spend it with someone they would like to get to know better; older adults tend to spend free time with someone they know well.

Thus, even though older adults may have smaller social networks than younger adults do, they tend to have as many very close relationships (Cornwell et al., 2008) and tend to be quite satisfied with those they have (Fiori, Smith, & Antonucci, 2007).

Their positive feelings toward old friends are as strong as those of young adults, and their positive feelings toward family members are stronger (Charles & Piazza, 2007).

Among a nationally representative sample, older adults tended to see friends less often but family about as frequently as before. This finding, consistent with socioemotional selectivity theory, suggests that as people age, they invest the time and energy they still have in maintaining more intimate relationships. In line with social convoy theory, the researchers also found a shifting balance of tangible, informational, and emotional support; as they age, adults, especially men, give less support to others but receive more. As older adults give up some of the support they formerly received from friends, they gain more emotional support from a smaller network of family ties (Shaw, Krause, Liang, & Bennett, 2007).

THE IMPORTANCE OF SOCIAL RELATIONSHIPS

Humans are a profoundly social species. Most of us want and need the support and love of others around us, and we are happier when part of a social community. Even if the size of that community might shrink with age, we need interaction. Because of this need, social isolation—or loneliness—is an important outcome variable that affects both psychological and physical health. Indeed, strong social relationships are as important for health and mortality as smoking, being obese, and abusing alcohol (Holt-Lunstad, Smith, & Layton, 2010).

People who are socially isolated tend to show more rapid physical and cognitive declines than those who are not isolated (Hawkley & Cacioppo, 2007; Holtzman et al., 2004). Moreover, the feeling of being useless to others is a strong factor for disabilities and mortality (Gruenewal, Karlamangla, Greendale, Singer, & Seeman, 2007). To be beneficial, however, relationships must be of good quality. If they are marked by criticism, rejection, competition, violation of privacy, or lack of reciprocity, they can serve as chronic stressors (Krause & Rook, 2003).

Strong, positive social ties can literally be a lifesaver. One longitudinal study showed that socially isolated men were 53 percent more likely than the most socially connected men to die of cardiovascular disease and more than twice as likely to die from accidents or suicide (Eng, Rimm, Fitzmaurice, & Kawachi, 2002). Similar data with women showed that older women who received the most social support—including a sense of being needed and valued, a sense of belonging, and emotional intimacy—were 2 times less likely to die during a 10-year period than those who received the least such support (Lyyra & Heikkinen, 2006). Emotional support helps older people maintain life satisfaction in the face of stress and trauma (Krause, 2004b), and positive ties tend to improve health and well-being.

THE MULTIGENERATIONAL FAMILY

The late-life family has special characteristics. Historically, families rarely spanned more than three generations. Today, many families in developed countries can include four or more generations, making it possible for a person to be both a grandparent and a grandchild at the same time (Costanzo & Hoy, 2007).

Have you ever lived in a multigenerational household? Do you think you ever might? What aspects of this lifestyle do or do not appeal to you, and why?

The presence of so many family members can be enriching (McIlvane, Ajrouch, & Antonucci, 2007) but also can create special pressures. Increasing numbers of families are likely to have at least one member who has lived long enough to have several chronic illnesses and whose care may be physically and emotionally draining (C. L. Johnson, 1995). Now that the fastest-growing group in the population is age 85 and over, many people in their late 60s or beyond, whose own health and energy may be faltering, find themselves serving as caregivers. Generally, the burden of this intergenerational care falls to women (Grundy & Henretta, 2006), due in part to gender role norms of women as caregivers (Brody, 2004).

A new term has emerged to describe these caregivers: the sandwich generation.

checkpoint can **you...**

- Tell how social contact changes in late life, and discuss theoretical explanations of this change?
- Explain the importance of positive social contact and social support, and cite evidence for a relationship between social interaction and health?
- Discuss issues concerning the new multigenerational family?

The ways families deal with these issues often have cultural roots. For example, people from cultures that strongly focus on familial bonds are, not surprisingly, more receptive to the needs of their aging parents and more likely to offer support than are people from more individualistic cultures (Kalmijn & Saraceno, 2008; Tomassini, Glaser, & Stuchbury, 2007). These varied cultural patterns affect family relationships and responsibilities toward the older generation. For example, the nuclear family and the desire of older adults to live apart from their children reflect dominant U.S. values of individualism, autonomy, and self-reliance. Hispanic and Asian American cultures traditionally emphasize *lineal,* or intergenerational, obligations with power and authority lodged in the older generation, a belief system that differs sharply from dominant U.S. cultural values (C. L. Johnson, 1995) and that has implications for the type of care people are willing to provide their aging parents. There are suggestions that the accelerating pace of globalization will result in a movement away from the more traditionally oriented family bonds found in many countries and toward the individualistic style more characteristic of more economically stable nations (Costanzo & Hoy, 2007).

In the remainder of this chapter we look more closely at older people's relationships with family and friends. We also examine the lives of older adults who are divorced, remarried, or widowed, those who have never married, and those who are childless. Finally, we consider the importance of a new role: that of great-grandparent.

Marital Relationships

Unlike other family relationships, marriage—at least in contemporary Western cultures—is generally formed by mutual consent. Thus its effect on well-being has characteristics of both friendship and kinship ties (Antonucci & Akiyama, 1995). It can provide both the highest emotional highs and the lowest lows a person experiences. What happens to marital quality in late life?

LONG-TERM MARRIAGE

Because women usually marry older men and outlive them and because men are more likely to remarry after divorce or widowhood, a higher proportion of men than women throughout the world are married in late life (Federal Interagency Forum on Aging-Related Statistics, 2012; Figure 2).

Married couples who are still together in late adulthood are more likely than middle-aged couples to report higher satisfaction and fewer adjustment problems in their marriages (Orathinkal & Vansteenwegen, 2007). Because divorce has been easier to obtain for some years, spouses who remain together are likely to have worked out their differences and to have arrived at mutually satisfying accommodations (Huyck, 1995). Children tend to become a source of shared pleasure and pride rather than conflict (Carstensen, Graff, Levenson, & Gottman, 1996). According to the MacArthur Successful Aging Study, men receive social support primarily from their wives, whereas women rely more heavily on friends, relatives, and children (Gurung, Taylor, & Seeman, 2003).

The way couples resolve conflicts is key to marital satisfaction throughout adulthood. Married people with much discord in their marriages tend to be anxious and depressed, whereas those with less discordant marriages tend to have higher self-esteem (Whisman, Uebelacker, Tolejko, Chatav, & McKelvie, 2006) and report higher levels of marital satisfaction (Schmitt, Kliegel, & Shapiro, 2007). Patterns of conflict resolution tend to remain fairly constant throughout a marriage, but older couples' greater ability to regulate their emotions may make their conflicts less severe (Carstensen et al., 1996).

Married people are healthier (Schoenborn, 2004) and live longer than unmarried people (Kaplan & Kronick, 2006), but the relationship between marriage and health may be different for husbands than for wives. Whereas *being* married seems to have health benefits for older men, older women's health seems to be linked more to the *quality* of the marriage (Carstensen et al., 1996).

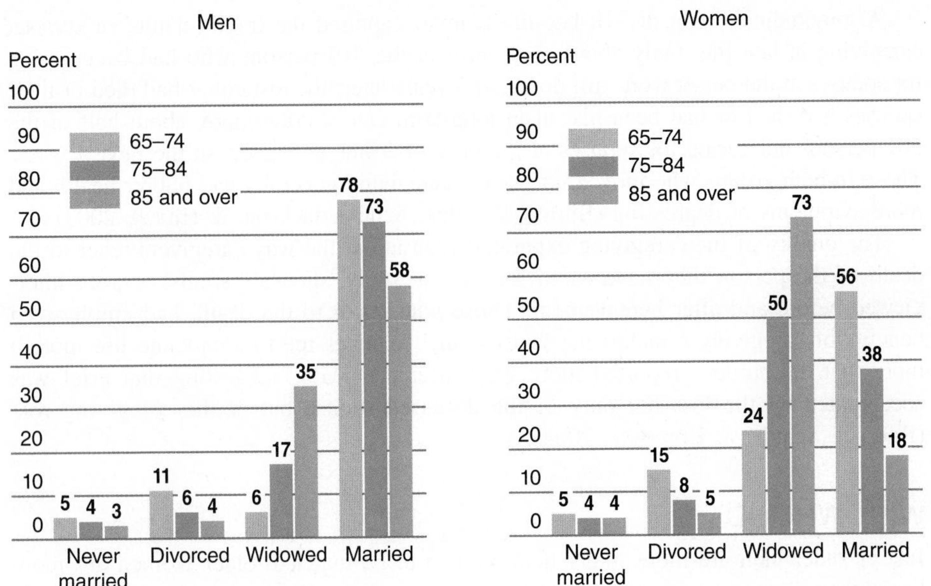

Note: Married includes married, spouse present; married, spouse absent; and separated. These data refer to the civilian noninstitutionalized population.

Source: Federal Interagency Forum on Aging-Related Statistics, 2012.

FIGURE 2

Marital Status of the U.S. Population Age 65 and Over by Age Group and Sex, 2010

Because of women's greater longevity, they are more likely than men to be widowed in late life, whereas men are more likely to be married or remarried in late life.

Late-life marriage can be severely tested by advancing age and physical ills, though a close marital relationship can moderate the negative psychological effects of functional disabilities by reducing anxiety and depression and increasing self-esteem (Mancini & Bonanno, 2006). Spouses who must care for disabled partners may feel isolated, angry, and frustrated, especially if they are in poor health themselves. Such couples may be caught in a vicious cycle: the illness puts strains on the marriage, and these strains may aggravate the illness, stretching coping capacity to the breaking point (Karney & Bradbury, 1995) and putting the caregiver's health and well-being at risk (Graham et al., 2006). Indeed, a study of more than 500,000 couples on Medicare found that when one spouse was hospitalized, the other's risk of death increased (Christakis & Allison, 2006).

Many couples who are still together late in life say they are happier in marriage than they were in their younger years. Important benefits of marriage include intimacy, sharing, and a sense of belonging to one another.

A longitudinal study of 818 late-life couples captured the fragile nature of spousal caregiving in late life. Only about one-fourth of the 317 persons who had been caring for spouses at the outset were still doing so 5 years later; the rest either had died or their spouses had died or had been placed in long-term care. Furthermore, about half of the 501 persons not caring for spouses at the outset became caregivers in the next 5 years. Those in both groups who moved into heavy caregiving generally had poorer health and more symptoms of depression (Burton, Zdaniuk, Schulz, Jackson, & Hirsch, 2003).

The quality of the caregiving experience can affect the way caregivers react to the death of the person they have cared for. In one study, spousal caregivers were interviewed before and after bereavement. Those who, prior to the death, had emphasized benefits of caregiving ("makes me feel useful," "enables me to appreciate life more") more than its burdens reported more grief after the death, suggesting that grief was accentuated by the loss not only of the deceased spouse but of the caregiving role (Boerner, Schulz, & Horowitz, 2004).

WIDOWHOOD

Just as older men are more likely than women to be married, older women are more likely than men to be widowed, and for similar reasons. Women tend to outlive their husbands and are less likely than men to marry again. As Figure 2 shows, U.S. women age 65 and over are far more likely than men of the same age to be widowed (Federal Interagency Forum on Aging-Related Statistics, 2012). However, as the gender gap in life expectancy narrows, as it has done in the United States since 1990, an increasing proportion of older men will outlive their wives (Hetzel & Smith, 2001). By the age of 65, women are 4 times as likely as men to be widowers (Federal interagency Forum on Aging-Related Statistics, 2012). And older widowed men are far more likely to be institutionalized than older widowed women following the death of a spouse (Nihtila & Martikainen, 2008). In most countries, more than half of older women are widows (Kinsella & Velkoff, 2001).

DIVORCE AND REMARRIAGE

Divorce in late life is rare; only about 11 percent of U.S. adults age 65 and over were divorced and not remarried in 2005. However, these numbers have nearly doubled since 1980 and probably will continue to increase as younger cohorts with larger proportions of divorced people reach late adulthood (Administration on Aging, 2006).

Remarriage in late life may have a special character. Among 125 well-educated, fairly affluent men and women, those in late-life remarriages seemed more trusting and accepting and less in need of deep sharing of personal feelings than in earlier marriages. Men, but not women, tended to be more satisfied in late-life remarriages than in midlife remarriages (Bograd & Spilka, 1996).

Remarriage has societal benefits. Older married people are less likely than those living alone to need help from the community. Remarriage could be encouraged by letting people keep pension and Social Security benefits derived from a previous marriage and by greater availability of group housing and other shared living quarters.

checkpoint can you...

- Discuss factors affecting marital satisfaction in late adulthood?
- Explain gender differences in the prevalence of widowhood?
- Tell why divorce in late life is rare, and identify the special character of remarriage in late adulthood?

Nonmarital Lifestyles and Relationships

SINGLE LIFE

In most countries, 5 percent or less of older men and 10 percent or less of older women have never married. In Europe, this gender difference may reflect the toll on marriageable men taken by World War II, when today's older cohort were of marrying age. In some

Latin American and Caribbean countries, proportions of never-marrieds are higher, probably due to the prevalence of consensual unions (Kinsella & Phillips, 2005). In the United States, only about 5 percent of men and women 65 years and older have never married (Federal Interagency Forum on Aging-Related Statistics, 2012; see Figure 2). This percentage is likely to increase as today's middle-aged adults grow old because larger proportions of that cohort, especially African Americans, have remained single (U.S. Bureau of the Census, 1991a, 1991b, 1992, 1993).

Older never-married people in the United States are more likely than older divorced or widowed people to prefer single life and less likely to be lonely (Dykstra, 1995), even though they are most likely to live alone and receive the least social support. They are least likely to experience "single strain"—chronic practical and emotional stressors attributed to the lack of an intimate partner. The reasons may be that never-marrieds have never gone through the stress of transitioning out of marriage and have developed earlier in adult life skills and resources such as autonomy and self-reliance that help them cope with singlehood. They also have greater tangible resources: they are in better health and have higher education and income than those who have been married (Pudrovska, Schieman, & Carr, 2006).

White never-married women report more single strain than their male counterparts. Women in older cohorts were socialized to view the roles of wife and mother as normative and may face negative cultural attitudes if they do not marry. Black women show less single strain than white women; with a shortage of marriageable black men, being single is normative and statistically more prevalent among black women (Prudrovska et al., 2006).

Previously married older men are much more likely to date than previously married older women, probably because of the greater availability of women in this age group. Most elderly daters are sexually active but do not expect to marry. Among both whites and blacks, men are more interested in romantic involvement than women, who may fear getting locked into traditional gender roles (R. A. Bulcroft & Bulcroft, 1991; Tucker, Taylor, & Mitchell-Kernan, 1993).

COHABITATION

Older adults are increasingly likely to cohabit, as are younger adults, but for them cohabitation typically comes after a prior marriage, not before marriage. More than 1 million U.S. older adults, 4 percent of the unmarried population, currently cohabit, and 9 out of 10 of them were previously married (S. L. Brown, Lee, & Bulanda, 2006).

Older cohabitors have certain disadvantages as compared with older people who are remarried. Older cohabitors, particularly women, tend to have lower incomes and are less likely to own their homes. In comparison with older adults without partners, on the other hand, they tend to have higher household incomes and are more likely to have full-time jobs. In comparison with *both* the remarried and the unpartnered, they are less likely to be religious or to have friends or relatives living nearby (S. L. Brown et al., 2006).

Women, especially, seem to be disadvantaged by cohabiting. For example, they are three times more likely to have no health insurance than either remarried or unpartnered women. For men there is no such difference. In fact, marital status makes more difference overall for women than for men (S. L. Brown et al., 2006).

GAY AND LESBIAN RELATIONSHIPS

There is little research on homosexual relationships in old age, largely because the current cohort of older adults grew up at a time when living openly as a homosexual was rare (Fredriksen-Goldsen & Muraco, 2010). For aging gays and lesbians who recognized their homosexuality before the rise of the gay liberation movement in the late 1960s, their self-concept tended to be shaped by the then-prevailing stigma against homosexuality. Those who came of age after the liberation movement (and the shift

Intimacy is important to older gay men, as it is to older heterosexual adults. Contrary to stereotype, homosexual relationships in late life are strong and supportive.

in public discourse it brought about) was in full swing are more likely to view their homosexuality simply as a *status:* a characteristic of the self like any other (Rosenfeld, 1999).

Gay and lesbian relationships in late life tend to be strong, supportive, and diverse. Many homosexuals have children from earlier marriages; others have adopted children. Friendship networks or support groups may substitute for the traditional family (Reid, 1995). Those who have maintained close relationships and strong involvement in the homosexual community tend to adapt to aging with relative ease (Friend, 1991; Reid, 1995).

The main problems of many older gays and lesbians grow out of societal attitudes: strained relationships with the family of origin, discrimination in nursing homes and elsewhere, lack of medical or social services and social support, insensitive policies of social agencies, and, when a partner falls ill or dies, dealing with health care providers, bereavement and inheritance issues, and lack of access to a partner's Social Security benefits (Kimmel, 1990; Knochel, Quam, & Chroghan, 2011; Reid, 1995).

FRIENDSHIPS

Maintaining friendships is important for well-being. Most older people have close friends, and, as in early and middle adulthood, those with an active circle of friends tend to be healthier and happier (Antonucci & Akiyama, 1995; Golden, Conroy, & Lawlor, 2009). People who can confide their feelings and thoughts and can talk about their worries and pain with friends tend to deal better with the changes and crises of aging (Genevay, 1986) and to live longer (Steinbach, 1992). The element of choice in friendship may be especially important to older people (Golden et al., 2009), who may feel their control over their lives slipping away (R. G. Adams, 1986). Intimacy is another important benefit of friendship for older adults, who need to know that they are still valued and wanted despite physical and other losses (Essex & Nam, 1987).

Older people enjoy time spent with their friends more than time spent with their families. As earlier in life, friendships revolve around pleasure and leisure, whereas family relationships tend to involve everyday needs and tasks (Antonucci & Akiyama, 1995). Friends are a powerful source of *immediate* enjoyment; the family provides greater emotional security and support. Thus friendships have the greatest positive effect on older people's well-being; but when family relationships are poor or absent, the negative effects can be profound (Antonucci & Akiyama, 1995). In line with socioemotional selectivity theory, older adults tend to have stronger positive feelings about old friends than about new friends (Charles & Piazza, 2007).

People usually rely on neighbors in emergencies and on relatives for long-term commitments, such as caregiving; but friends may, on occasion, fulfill both these functions. Although friends cannot replace a spouse or partner, they can help compensate for the lack of one (Hartup & Stevens, 1999) by playing the role of fictive kin, a psychological family. Among 131 older adults in the Netherlands who were never married or were divorced or widowed, those who received high levels of emotional and practical support from friends were less likely to be lonely (Dykstra, 1995).

In line with social convoy and socioemotional selectivity theories, longtime friendships often persist into very old age (Hartup & Stevens, 1999). Sometimes, however, relocation, illness, or disability make it hard to keep up with old friends. Although many older people do make new friends, even after age 85 (C. L. Johnson & Troll, 1994), older adults are more likely than younger adults to attribute the benefits of friendship (such as affection and loyalty) to specific individuals, who cannot easily be replaced if they die, go into a nursing home, or move away (de Vries, 1996).

checkpoint
can you . . .

- Discuss differences between never-married and previously married singles in late life?
- Tell why older women who are cohabiting may be at a disadvantage?
- Discuss strengths and problems of gay and lesbian relationships in late life?
- Identify special characteristics of friendship in old age?

Nonmarital Kinship Ties

Some of the most lasting and important relationships in late life come not from mutual choice (as marriages, cohabitations, homosexual partnerships, and friendships do) but from kinship bonds. Let's look at these.

RELATIONSHIPS WITH ADULT CHILDREN

Parent-child bonds remain strong in old age. Children provide a link with other family members, especially grandchildren. Parents who have good relationships with their adult children are less likely to be lonely or depressed than those whose parent-child relationships are not so good (Koropeckyj-Cox, 2002).

Most older people have living children, but, because of global trends toward smaller families, have fewer of them than in previous generations (Dobriansky et al., 2007; Kinsella & Phillips, 2005). In European countries, about one-third of adults in their 60s live with an adult child, and almost half live within 15 miles of an adult child. These proportions remain fairly stable or increase with age. Coresidence is most common in the more traditional Mediterranean countries (Greece, Italy, and Spain) and least common in the Scandinavian countries (Denmark and Sweden) with their strong welfare services and cultural emphasis on autonomy. About half of older parents below age 80 report contact with a child, most often a daughter, at least once a week (Hank, 2007). In the United States, immigrants who arrived as older adults are most likely to live with adult children and to be dependent on them (Glick & Van Hook, 2002).

A study of 60- to 90-year-old participants asked to evaluate a man who either bragged about himself or about his son showed that bragging about the achievements of those close to us—a process known as burnishing—can lead to perceptions of a person as less capable.

Tal-Or, 2010

The mother-daughter relationship tends to be especially close. In one study, researchers recorded conversations between 48 mostly European American, well-educated, mother-daughter pairs. The mothers were over age 70 and in good health. Each pair was asked to construct a story about a picture of an older and a younger woman. These conversations were characterized by warmth and mutual affection, encouragement, and support, with little criticism or hostility. Both mothers and daughters held their relationship in high regard, reporting that they had many positive feelings and few negative ones toward each other (Lefkowitz & Fingerman, 2003).

The balance of mutual aid between parents and their adult children tends to shift as parents age, with children providing a greater share of support (Bengtson et al., 1990, 1996). Mothers'—but not fathers'—willingness to ask adult children for help reflects their earlier parenting styles. Warm, responsive mothers are more likely to ask for financial help or personal advice than mothers who were more dominant or restrictive during their children's adolescence and young adulthood (Schooler, Revell, & Caplan, 2007). In the United States and other developed countries, institutional supports such as Social Security and Medicare have lifted some responsibilities for older adults from family members; but many adult children do provide significant assistance and direct care. The trend toward smaller families means fewer potential family caregivers for ailing, aging parents (Kinsella & Phillips, 2005), increasing the strains on those who do serve as caregivers—strains that may lead to mistreatment of a "difficult" frail patient (Box 2).

Older parents who can do so often continue to provide financial support to children. In less developed countries, older parents contribute through housekeeping, child care, and socialization of grandchildren (Kinsella & Phillips, 2005). Older parents continue to show strong concern about their children (Bengtson et al., 1996). They tend to be distressed if their children have serious problems and may consider such problems a sign of their failure as parents (G. R. Lee, Netzer, & Coward, 1995; Pillemer & Suitor, 1991; Suitor, Pillemer, Keeton, & Robison, 1995; Troll & Fingerman, 1996). Many older people whose adult children are mentally ill, retarded, physically disabled, or stricken with serious illnesses serve as primary caregivers for as long as both parent and child live (Brabant, 1994; Greenberg & Becker, 1988; Ryff & Seltzer, 1995).

research in action

MISTREATMENT OF THE ELDERLY

A middle-aged woman drives up to a hospital emergency room in a middle-sized U.S. city. She lifts a frail, elderly woman (who appears somewhat confused) out of the car and into a wheelchair, wheels her into the emergency room, and quietly walks out and drives away, leaving no identification (Barnhart, 1992).

"Granny dumping" is an example of *elder abuse:* maltreatment or neglect of dependent older persons or violation of their personal rights. Mistreatment of the elderly may fall into any of six categories: (1) *physical abuse*—physical force that may cause bodily injury, physical pain, or impairment; (2) *sexual abuse*—nonconsensual sexual contact with an elderly person; (3) *emotional or psychological abuse*—infliction of anguish, pain, or distress (such as the threat of abandonment or institutionalization); (4) *financial or material exploitation*—illegal or improper use of an elder's funds, property, or assets; (5) *neglect*—refusal or failure to fulfill any part of one's obligations or duties to an elder; and (6) *self-neglect*—behaviors of a depressed, frail, or mentally incompetent elderly person that threaten his or her health or safety, such as failure to eat or drink adequately or to take prescribed medications (National Center on Elder Abuse & Westat, Inc., 1998). The American Medical Association (1992) has added a seventh category: *violating personal rights*—for example, the older person's right to privacy and to make her or his personal and health decisions.

In almost 9 out of 10 maltreatment cases with a known perpetrator, that person is a family member; and 2 out of 3 of these perpetrators are spouses or adult children (National Center for Elder Abuse, 2014). Neglect by family caregivers is usually unintentional. Many do not know how to give proper care or are in poor health themselves. The states of mind of caregivers and the older persons under their care may reinforce each other. When older women receiving informal long-term care feel respected and valued by their caregivers, they are less likely to be depressed (Wolff & Agree, 2004).

Other types of elder abuse should be recognized as forms of domestic violence. Abusers need counseling or treatment to recognize what they are doing and assistance to reduce the stress of caregiving (AARP, 1993). Self-help groups may help victims acknowledge what is happening, recognize that they do not have to put up with mistreatment, and find out how to stop it or get away from it.

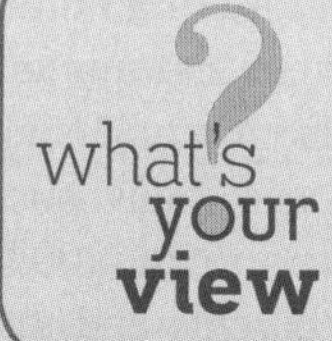

In your opinion, what steps could be taken to reduce mistreatment of the elderly?

Furthermore, a growing number of older adults, particularly African Americans, raise or help raise grandchildren or great-grandchildren. These nonnormative caregivers, pressed into active parenting at a time when such a role is unexpected, frequently feel strain. Often ill-prepared physically, emotionally, and financially for the task, they may not know where to turn for help and support (Abramson, 1995).

What about the increasing number of older adults *without* living children? According to questionnaires and interviews with a nationally representative sample of late middle-aged and older adults, the impact of childlessness on well-being is influenced by gender and by a person's feelings about being childless. Childless women who said it would be better to have a child were more likely to be lonely and depressed than women who did not agree with that statement. That was not true of men, probably because of the greater importance of motherhood to women's identity. However, mothers *and* fathers who had poor relationships with their children were more likely to be lonely or depressed. Thus parenthood does not guarantee well-being in old age, nor does childlessness necessarily harm it. Attitudes and the quality of relationships are what count (Koropeckyj-Cox, 2002).

RELATIONSHIPS WITH SIBLINGS

Brother and sisters play an important role in older people's support networks. Siblings, more than other family members, tend to provide companionship as older adults. They also, more than friends, tend to provide emotional support (Bedford, 1995). Although siblings often engage in conflict when young, overt rivalry generally decreases with age, especially for sisters (Cicirelli, 1995).

Sibling commitment, meaning the degree to which siblings keep in contact with and help each other out, is relatively stable across the life span (Rittenour, Myers, & Braun, 2007). Most older siblings say they stand ready to provide tangible help, and would turn to a sibling for such help as needed, although relatively few actually do so unless facing an emergency (Cicirelli, 1995). For those that do, however, both giving support (Gierveld & Dykstra, 2008) and receiving support (Thomas, 2010) are associated with positive outcomes such as reductions in loneliness. Surviving siblings with a poor relationship are at higher risk of depression (Cicirelli, 2009).

Bessie and Sadie Delany were best friends all their lives. Elderly siblings are an important part of each other's support network, and sisters are especially vital in maintaining family relationships.

The nearer older people live to their siblings and the more siblings they have, the more they are likely to confide in them (Connidis & Davies, 1992). Reminiscing about shared early experiences becomes more frequent in old age and may help in reviewing a life and putting the significance of family relationships into perspective (Cicirelli, 1995).

Sisters are especially vital in maintaining family relationships and well-being, perhaps because of women's emotional expressiveness and traditional role as nurturers (Bedford, 1995; Cicirelli, 1995). Older people who are close to their sisters feel better about life and worry less about aging than those without sisters or without close ties to them (Cicirelli, 1989).

Although the death of a sibling in old age may be understood as a normative part of that stage of life, survivors may grieve intensely and become lonely or depressed (Cicirelli, 2009). The loss of a sibling represents not only a loss of someone to lean on and a shift in the family constellation, but perhaps even a partial loss of identity. To mourn for a sibling is to mourn for the lost completeness of the original family within which one came to know oneself and can bring home one's own nearness to death (Cicirelli, 1995).

BECOMING GREAT-GRANDPARENTS

As grandchildren grow up, grandparents generally see them less often. Then, when grandchildren become parents, grandparents move into a new role: great-grandparenthood.

Because of age, declining health, and the scattering of families, great-grandparents tend to be less involved than grandparents in a child's life; and, because four- or five-generation families are relatively new, there are few generally accepted guidelines for what great-grandparents are supposed to do (Cherlin & Furstenberg, 1986). Still, most great-grandparents find the role fulfilling (Pruchno & Johnson, 1996). Great-grandparenthood offers a sense of personal and family renewal, a source of diversion, and a mark of longevity. When 40 great-grandfathers and great-grandmothers, ages 71 to 90, were interviewed, 93 percent made such comments as "Life is starting again in my family," "Seeing them grow keeps me young," and "I never thought I'd live to see it" (Doka & Mertz, 1988, pp. 193–194). More than one-third of the sample (mostly women) were close to their great-grandchildren. The ones with the most intimate connections were likely to live nearby and to be close to the children's parents and grandparents as well, often helping out with loans, gifts, and babysitting.

Grandparents and great-grandparents are important to their families. They are sources of wisdom, companions in play, links to the past, and symbols of the continuity of family life. They are engaged in the ultimate generative function: expressing the human longing to transcend mortality by investing themselves in the lives of future generations.

checkpoint can **you**...

- Tell how contact and mutual aid between parents and grown children changes during late adulthood, and how childlessness can affect older people?
- Discuss the importance of sibling relationships in late life?
- Identify several values great-grandparents find in their role?

summary and key terms

Theory and Research on Personality Development

- Erik Erikson's final stage, ego integrity versus despair, culminates in the virtue of *wisdom,* or acceptance of one's life and impending death.
- Erikson believed that people must maintain a vital involvement in society.
- Personality traits tend to remain fairly stable in late adulthood, depending on how they are measured.
- Older adults in recent cohorts seem to be less rigid in personality than in previous cohorts.
- Emotionality tends to become more positive and less negative in old age, but personality traits can modify this pattern.

ego integrity versus despair

Well-Being in Late Adulthood

- George Vaillant found that the use of mature adaptive defenses earlier in adulthood predicts psychosocial adjustment in late life.
- In research based on the cognitive-appraisal model, adults of all ages generally prefer problem-focused coping, but older adults do more emotion-focused coping than younger adults when the situation calls for it.
- Religion is an important source of emotion-focused coping for many older adults. Links have been found between religion or spirituality and health, longevity, and well-being.
- The concept of successful, or optimal, aging reflects the growing number of healthy, vital older adults, but there is dispute over how to define and measure it and over the validity of the concept.
- Two contrasting early models of *successful,* or *optimal,* aging are disengagement theory and activity theory. Disengagement theory has little support, and findings on activity theory are mixed. Newer refinements of activity theory include continuity theory and an emphasis on productive activity.
- Baltes and his colleagues suggest that successful aging, in the psychosocial as well as the cognitive realm, may depend on selective optimization with compensation.

coping
cognitive-appraisal model
problem-focused coping
emotion-focused coping
ambiguous loss
disengagement theory
activity theory
continuity theory
selective optimization with compensation (SOC)

Practical and Social Issues Related to Aging

- Some older adults continue to work for pay, but most are retired. However, many retired people start new careers or do part-time paid or volunteer work. Often retirement is a phased process.
- Older adults tend to be more satisfied with their work and often more productive than younger ones. Age has both positive and negative effects on job performance, and individual differences are more significant than age differences.
- Retirement is an ongoing process. Personal, economic, and social resources may affect morale.
- The financial situation of older Americans has improved, and fewer live in poverty. Women, Hispanic Americans, and African Americans are most likely to be poor in old age.
- In developing countries, the elderly often live with children or grandchildren. In developed countries, most older people live with a spouse or live alone. Minority elders are more likely than white elders to live with extended family members.
- Most older adults in industrialized nations prefer to age in place. Most can remain in the community if they can depend on a spouse or someone else for help.
- Older women are more likely than older men to live alone.
- Older adults in developed countries typically do not expect to live with adult children and do not wish to do so.
- Institutionalization is rare in developing countries. Its extent varies in developed countries. Most likely to be institutionalized are older women, older adults who live alone or do not take part in social activities, those who have poor health or disabilities, and those whose informal caregivers are overburdened.
- Fast-growing alternatives to institutionalization include assisted-living facilities and other types of group housing.

aging in place

Personal Relationships in Late Life

- Relationships are important to older people, even though frequency of social contact declines in old age.
- According to social convoy theory, reductions or changes in social contact in late life do not impair well-being because a stable inner circle of social support is maintained. According to socioemotional selectivity theory, older people choose to spend time with people who enhance their emotional well-being.
- Social interaction is associated with good health and life satisfaction, and isolation is a risk factor for mortality.
- The way multigenerational late-life families function often has cultural roots.

Marital Relationships

- As life expectancy increases, so does the potential longevity of marriage. More men than women are married in late life. Marriages that last into late adulthood tend to be relatively satisfying.
- Although a growing proportion of men are widowed, women tend to outlive their husbands and are less likely to marry again.
- Divorce is uncommon among older people, and most older adults who have been divorced are remarried. Remarriages may be more relaxed in late life.

Nonmarital Lifestyles and Relationships

- A small but increasing percentage of adults reach old age without marrying. Never-married adults are less likely to be lonely than divorced or widowed ones.
- Older adults are more likely to cohabit after a prior marriage than before marriage.
- Many gays and lesbians adapt to aging with relative ease, particularly if they maintain relationships as well as involvement in the gay community. Adjustment may be influenced by coming-out status.
- Most older adults have close friends, and those who do are healthier and happier.
- Older people enjoy time spent with friends more than with family, but the family is the main source of emotional and practical support.

Nonmarital Kinship Ties

- Older parents and their adult children frequently see or contact each other, are concerned about each other, and offer each other assistance. Many older parents are caregivers for adult children, grandchildren, or great-grandchildren.
- In some respects, childlessness does not seem to be an important disadvantage in old age.
- Often siblings offer each other emotional support, and sometimes more tangible support as well. Sisters, in particular, maintain sibling ties.
- Great-grandparents are usually less involved in children's lives than grandparents are, but most find the role fulfilling.

part 9

THE END OF LIFE

chapter 19

Dealing with Death and Bereavement

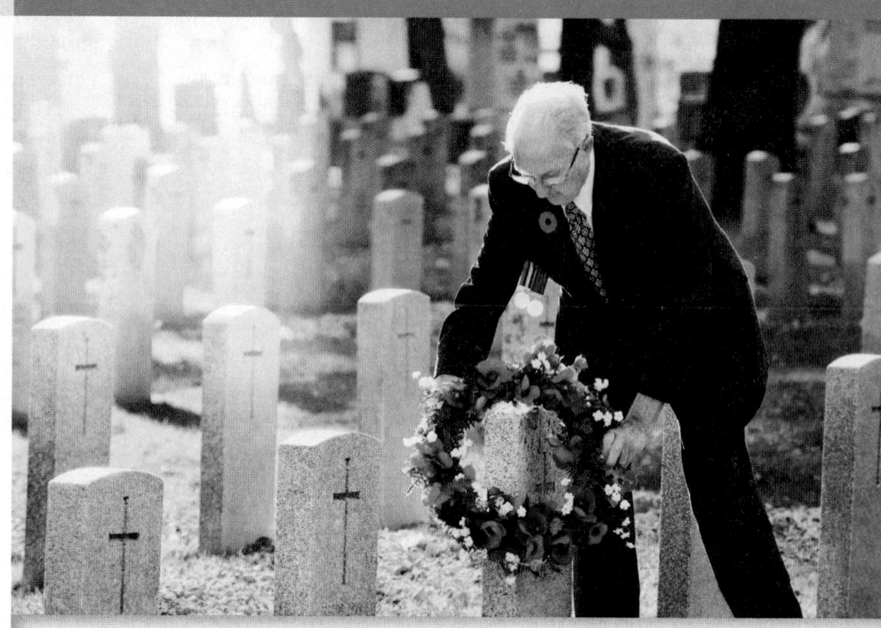

outline

learning objectives

Describe the cultural and historical contexts of death and dying.

Discuss death and bereavement as well as attitudes about death and dying across the life span.

Identify the challenges of coping with the death of another person.

Evaluate issues involved in decisions about death.

did you know?

- A marked cognitive decline, in the absence of known physical illness, can predict death nearly 15 years later?
- Research has challenged earlier notions of a single, "normal" pattern of grieving?
- Children as young as 4 may have some understanding of what happens after death but may not fully understand it until well into the school years?

In this chapter we discuss how people of different cultures and ages think and feel about death and dying. We examine patterns of grief and how people cope with significant loss. We look at questions raised about life support and examine whether people have the right to die. Finally, we consider how confronting death can give life greater purpose.

Death is not the opposite of life, but a part of it.

—Haruki Murakami

The Many, Changing Meanings of Death and Dying

Death is a *biological* fact; but it also has *social, cultural, historical, religious, legal, psychological, developmental, medical,* and *ethical* aspects, and often these are closely intertwined.

Although death and loss are universal experiences, they have a cultural and historical context. Cultural and religious attitudes toward death and dying affect how people regard their own. Death may mean one thing to an elderly Japanese person, imbued with Buddhist teachings of accepting the inevitable, and another to a third-generation Japanese American youth who has grown up with a belief in directing one's own destiny. Death used to come early and frequently in the life of a family and community and was a constant household companion. Today people in most countries live longer, and death is a less frequent and less visible occurrence.

Let's look more closely at death and mourning in their cultural and historical context.

THE CULTURAL CONTEXT

Customs concerning disposal and remembrance of the dead, transfer of possessions, and even expression of grief vary greatly from culture to culture and often are governed by religious or legal prescriptions that reflect a society's view of what death is and what happens afterward. Cultural aspects of death include care of and behavior toward the dying and the dead, the setting where death usually takes place, and mourning customs and rituals—from the all-night Irish wake, at which friends and family toast the memory of the dead person, to the weeklong Jewish *shiva,* at which mourners vent their feelings and share memories of the deceased. Some cultural conventions, such as flying a flag at half-mast after the death of a public figure, are codified in law.

In ancient Greece, bodies of heroes were publicly burned as a sign of honor. Cremation still is widely practiced by Hindus in India and Nepal. In contrast, cremation is prohibited under Orthodox Jewish law in the belief that the dead will rise again for a Last Judgment and the chance for eternal life (Ausubel, 1964).

In Japan, religious rituals encourage survivors to maintain contact with the deceased. Families keep an altar in the home dedicated to their ancestors; they talk to their dead loved ones and offer them food or cigars. In Gambia the dead are considered part of the community; among Native Americans, the Hopi fear the spirits of the dead and try to forget a deceased person as quickly as possible. Muslims in Egypt show grief through expressions of deep sorrow; Muslims in Bali are encouraged to suppress sadness, to laugh, and to be joyful (Stroebe, Gergen, Gergen, & Stroebe, 1992). All these varied customs and practices help people deal with death and bereavement through well-understood cultural meanings that provide a stable anchor amid the turbulence of loss.

Even when brain dead, it is possible for spinal reflexes to cause movement. In one particularly creepy variation, called the Lazarus sign, the dead person raises her or his arms and crosses them over the chest.

Urasaki, Tokimura, Kumai, & Yokota, 1992

Most gladiators died as a result of traumatic brain injury.

Kanz & Grossschmidt, 2006

checkpoint can you . . .

▷ Give examples of cross-cultural differences in customs and attitudes related to death?

Some modern social customs have evolved from ancient ones. Embalming goes back to the ancient practice of mummification common in ancient Egypt and China: preserving a body so the soul can return to it. A traditional Jewish custom is never to leave a dying person alone. Anthropologists suggest that the original reason for this may have been a belief that evil spirits hover around, trying to enter the dying body (Ausubel, 1964). Such rituals give people facing a loss something predictable and important to do at a time when they otherwise might feel confused and helpless.

THE MORTALITY REVOLUTION

Until the twentieth century, in all societies throughout history, death was a frequent, expected event, sometimes welcomed as a peaceful end to suffering. Caring for a dying loved one at home was a common experience, as it still is in some rural communities.

Great historical changes regarding death and dying have taken place since the late nineteenth century, especially in developed countries. Advances in medicine and sanitation, new treatments for many once-fatal illnesses, and a better-educated, more health-conscious population have brought about a *mortality revolution.* Women today are less likely to die in childbirth, infants are more likely to survive their 1st year, children are more likely to grow to adulthood, young adults are more likely to reach old age, and older people often can overcome illnesses they grew up regarding as fatal. The top causes of death in the United States in the 1900s were diseases that most often affected children and young people: pneumonia and influenza, tuberculosis, diarrhea, and enteritis. Today, despite recent increases in apparently drug-related deaths of people in their 20s and in early middle age as well as a spike in midlife suicide, nearly three-quarters of deaths in the United States still occur among people age 65 and over; and close to one-half of deaths are from heart disease, cancer, and stroke—the three leading causes of death in late adulthood (Xu et al., 2010).

thanatology
Study of death and dying.

hospice care
Personal, patient- and family-centered care for a person with a terminal illness.

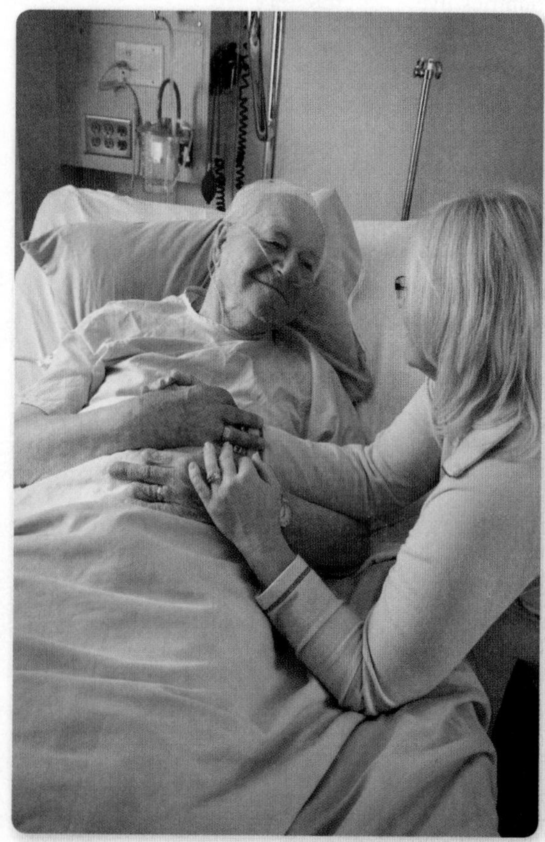

Hospice care seeks to ease patients' pain and treat their symptoms to keep them as comfortable and alert as possible. It also helps families deal with illness and death.

Amid all this progress in improving health and lengthening life, something important may have been lost. Looking death in the eye, bit by bit, day by day, people growing up in traditional societies absorbed an important truth: dying is part of living. As death increasingly became a phenomenon of late adulthood, it became "invisible and abstract" (Fulton & Owen, 1987–1988, p. 380). Care of the dying and the dead became largely a task for professionals. Such social conventions as placing the dying person in a hospital or nursing home and refusing to openly discuss his or her condition reflected and perpetuated attitudes of avoidance and denial of death. Death—even of the very old—came to be regarded as a failure of medical treatment rather than as a natural end to life (McCue, 1995).

Today, this picture again is changing. **Thanatology,** the study of death and dying, is arousing interest, and educational programs have been established to help people deal with death. Because of the prohibitive cost of extended hospital care that cannot save the terminally ill, many more deaths are now occurring at home, as they once did the world over.

CARE OF THE DYING

Edith, 82 years old, died of organ failure in a hospital following a 5-day stay. She died alone, afraid, hooked up to machines to help sustain her life for as long as possible, and confused about what was going on. Is this how you would choose to die?

Along with a growing tendency to face death more honestly, movements have arisen to make dying more humane. Primary among these movements is the establishment of **hospice care** for dying persons. Hospice care is personal, patient- and family-centered, compassionate care for the terminally ill. Hospice facilities generally provide **palliative care,** which includes relief of pain and suffering, control of symptoms, alleviation of stress, and attempts to maintain a satisfactory quality of life. However, palliative care is not intended to cure or reverse the course of disease.

Hospice facilities offer a specialized type of palliative care for people whose life expectancy is 6 months or less. The goal is to allow the person to die in peace and dignity, while minimizing any pain and suffering, and it often includes self-help support groups for both dying people and their families.

Hospice care may take place at home; but such care can be given in a hospital or another institution, at a hospice center, or through a combination of home and institutional care. Family members often take an active part. Palliative care also can be introduced earlier in an illness that is not yet terminal, and may lead to increases in quality of life. For example, in one study tracking newly diagnosed advanced metastatic lung cancer patients, those that began to receive palliative care immediately at the time of diagnosis had a higher quality of life, better emotional state, and even longer median survival time than patients who received standard oncological care only (Temel et al., 2010).

What does it mean to preserve the dignity of a patient who is dying? One research team decided to ask patients themselves. From interviews with 50 Canadian patients with advanced terminal cancer, researchers concluded that dignity-conserving care depends not only on how patients are treated but on how they are regarded: "When dying patients are seen, and know that they are seen, as being worthy of honor and esteem by those who care for them, dignity is more likely to be maintained" (Chochinov, Hack, McClement, Harlos, & Kristjanson, 2002, p. 2259).

A study of objects placed by the bedside of people in hospice care showed that almost all clients had objects to remind them of home—a source of comfort in their last days.

Kellehear, Pugh, & Atter, 2009

palliative care
Care aimed at relieving pain and suffering and allowing the terminally ill to die in peace, comfort, and dignity.

checkpoint
can you . . .

- Discuss the mortality revolution in developed countries?
- Identity the chief goals of hospice care?

Facing Death and Loss

Death is an important chapter in human development. People change in response to death and dying, whether their own or that of a loved one. What changes do people undergo shortly before death? How do they come to terms with its imminence? How do people handle grief? How do attitudes toward death change across the life span?

PHYSICAL AND COGNITIVE CHANGES PRECEDING DEATH

Even without any identifiable illness, people around the age of 100—close to the present limit of the human life span—tend to experience functional declines, lose interest in eating and drinking, and die a natural death (Johansson et al., 2004; Singer, Verhaeghen, Ghisletta, Lindenberger, & Baltes, 2003; B. J. Small, Fratiglioni, von Strauss, & Bäckman, 2003). Such changes also have been noted in younger people whose death is near. In a 22-year longitudinal study of 1,927 men, life satisfaction showed steep declines within 1 year before death, regardless of self-rated health (Mroczek & Spiro, 2005).

Terminal drop, or *terminal decline,* refers specifically to a widely observed decline in cognitive abilities shortly before death, even when factors such as demographics and health are controlled for (Weatherbee & Allaire, 2008). This effect has been found in longitudinal studies in various countries—not only of the very old (Johansson et al., 2004; T. Singer et al., 2003; B. J. Small et al., 2003), but also of adults of a wide range of ages (Rabbitt et al., 2002; B. J. Small et al., 2003) with no signs of dementia. Losses of perceptual speed have been found to predict death nearly 15 years later (Thorvaldsson et al., 2008). Declines in verbal ability, spatial reasoning, and everyday cognition are other important markers of terminal drop (Rabbitt et al., 2002; Thorvaldsson et al., 2008).

terminal drop
A frequently observed decline in cognitive abilities near the end of life. Also called *terminal decline.*

Some people who have come close to dying have told of *near-death experiences (NDE),* often involving a sense of being out of the body or sucked into a tunnel and visions of bright lights or mystical encounters. These reports are highly subjective, and skeptics generally interpret them as resulting from physiological changes that accompany

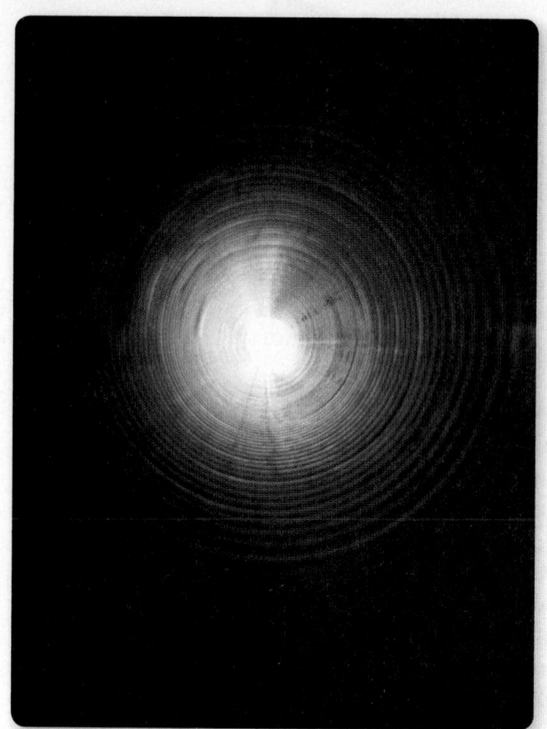

When a brain is deprived of oxygen, certain images arise due to alterations in the visual cortex and can result in the perception of a tunnel, like the images reported by people who have had near-death experiences.

the process of dying. According to one Dutch anesthesiologist, near-death experiences are probably biological events in the brain, and the similarities in individuals' reports about their experiences reflect the common bodily structures affected by the process of dying, in particular, the oxygen deprivation that occurs in 9 out of 10 dying persons (Woerlee, 2005). However, not everyone who experiences oxygen deprivation experiences a NDE. In one study of cardiac patients who were "brought back" after clinical death, only about 21 percent reported a NDE (Klemenc-Ketis, Kersnik, & Grmec, 2010). Therefore, anoxia cannot be the sole cause of NDEs.

Some people may be biologically predisposed to near-death experiences. One study found altered functioning of the temporal lobes in people who experience near-death imagery (Britton & Bootzin, 2004). In another study, patients who experienced a NDE during resuscitation were more likely to have experienced multiple sessions of CPR during their hospital stay, and were more likely to die within 30 days of their NDE than similar patients who did not experience a NDE (van Lommel, van Wees, Meyers, & Elfferich, 2001).

CONFRONTING ONE'S OWN DEATH

The psychiatrist Elisabeth Kübler-Ross, in her pioneering work with dying people, found that most of them welcomed an opportunity to speak openly about their condition and were aware of being close to death, even when they had not been told. After speaking with some 500 terminally ill patients, Kübler-Ross (1969, 1970) outlined five stages in coming to terms with death: (1) *denial* ("This can't be happening to me!"); (2) *anger* ("Why me?"); (3) *bargaining for extra time* ("If I can only live to see my daughter married, I won't ask for anything more"); (4) *depression;* and ultimately (5) *acceptance.* She also proposed a similar progression in the feelings of people facing imminent bereavement (Kübler-Ross, 1975).

How do people on death row confront their death? In a survey of their last statements, death row inmates are most likely to talk about forgiveness, claims of innocence, silence, love, activism, and a belief in the afterlife.

Heflick, 2005

Kübler-Ross's model has been criticized and modified by other professionals who work with dying patients. Although the emotions she described are common, not everyone goes through all five stages and not necessarily in the same sequence. A person may go back and forth between anger and depression, for example, or may feel both at once. Unfortunately, some health professionals assume that these stages are inevitable and universal, and others feel that they have failed if they cannot bring a patient to the final stage of acceptance.

Dying, like living, is an individual experience. For some people, denial or anger may be a healthier way to face death than calm acceptance. Kübler-Ross's findings, valuable as they are in helping us understand the feelings of those who are facing the end of life, should not be considered the sole model or criterion for a "good death."

studysmart

Perspectives on Death and Dying

PATTERNS OF GRIEVING

The death of a loved one is a difficult thing. First, there is **grief,** the emotional response that generally follows closely on the heels of death. This is followed by **bereavement.** Bereavement is a response to the loss of someone to whom a person feels close. But bereavement is not just an event, and it is not just grief—it is also a process of adjustment.

grief
Emotional response experienced in the early phases of bereavement.

bereavement
Loss, due to death, of someone to whom one feels close and the process of adjustment to the loss.

Bereavement often brings about a change in role or status. For example, a person may have to adjust to becoming a widow after previously being a wife, or as an orphan after previously being a son or daughter. There may be social or economic consequences as well—a loss of friends and sometimes of income. In short, bereavement can affect practically all aspects of a person's life.

Bereavement, like dying, is a highly personal experience. Today research has challenged earlier notions of a single, "normal" pattern of grieving and a "normal" timetable for recovery. A widow talking to her late husband might once have been considered emotionally disturbed; now this is recognized as a common and helpful behavior (Lund, 1993b). Some people recover fairly quickly after bereavement; others never do.

Should bereavement be medicated? One study showed that approximately half of doctors believe medicating grief is warranted despite the risk of long-term use or addiction.

Cook, Biyanova, & Marshall, 2007

The Classic Grief Work Model How do people grieve? A classic pattern of grief is three stages in which the bereaved person accepts the painful reality of the loss, gradually lets go of the bond with the dead person, and readjusts to life by developing new interests and relationships. This process of **grief work,** the working out of psychological issues connected with grief, often takes the following path—though, as with Kübler-Ross's stages, it may vary (J. T. Brown & Stoudemire, 1983; R. Schulz, 1978).

grief work
Working out of psychological issues connected with grief.

1. *Shock and disbelief.* Immediately following a death, survivors often feel lost and confused. As awareness of the loss sinks in, the initial numbness gives way to overwhelming feelings of sadness and frequent crying. This first stage may last several weeks, especially after a sudden or unexpected death.
2. *Preoccupation with the memory of the dead person.* In the second stage, which may last 6 months to 2 years or so, the survivor tries to come to terms with the death but cannot yet accept it. A widow may relive her husband's death and their entire relationship. From time to time, she may be seized by a feeling that her dead husband is present. These experiences diminish with time, though they may recur—perhaps for years—on such occasions as the anniversary of the marriage or of the death.
3. *Resolution.* The final stage has arrived when the bereaved person renews interest in everyday activities. Memories of the dead person bring fond feelings mingled with sadness rather than sharp pain and longing.

studysmart

Classic Grief Work Model

What advice would you give a friend about what to say—and what not to say—to a person in mourning?

Grieving: Multiple Variations Although the pattern of grief work just described is common, grieving does not necessarily follow a straight line from shock to resolution. One team of psychologists (Wortman & Silver, 1989) found three main patterns of grieving. In the *commonly expected* pattern, the mourner goes from high to low distress. In the *absent grief* pattern, the mourner does not experience intense distress, either immediately or later. In the *chronic grief* pattern, the mourner remains distressed for a long time (Wortman & Silver, 1989). Chronic grief may be especially painful and acceptance most difficult when a loss is *ambiguous,* as when a loved one is missing and presumed dead (Box 1).

In another study, researchers interviewed 1,532 married older adults and then did follow-up interviews with 185 (161 women and 24 men) whose spouses had died. The interviews took place 6 months after and again up to 4 years after the loss (Boerner, Wortman, & Bonanno, 2005; Bonanno, Wortman, & Nesse, 2004). The typical pattern of grieving (shown by 46 percent of the sample) was *resilience:* a low and gradually diminishing level of distress. The resilient mourners expressed acceptance of death as a natural process. After their loss, they spent relatively little time thinking and talking about it or searching for meaning in it, though the majority did report some yearning and emotional pangs during the first 6 months. These findings challenge the assumption that something is wrong if a bereaved person shows only mild distress. They demonstrate that "'doing well' after a loss is not necessarily a cause for concern but rather a normal response for many older adults" (Boerner et al., 2005, p. P72).

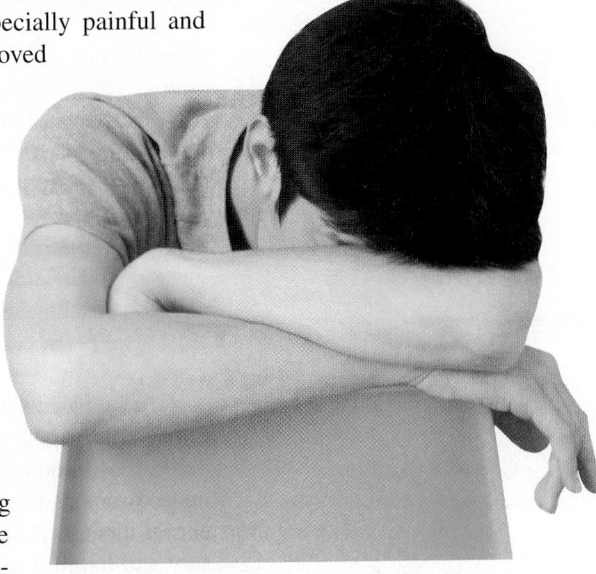

Some people recover quickly from the loss of a loved one, others never do.

research in action

AMBIGUOUS LOSS

A woman whose husband was in the World Trade Center on September 11, 2001, did not truly believe he was dead until months later, when cleanup workers turned up a shard of one of his bones. Victims of the tsunami in Southeast Asia in 2005 continue to grieve for partners, children, and parents swept away without a trace by the massive waves. Middle-aged women and men fly to Vietnam and Cambodia to search for the remains of husbands and fathers whose
1 planes were shot down decades ago.

Dealing with the death of a loved one is difficult enough under normal circumstances. But when there is no body—no clear evidence of death—it can be harder to face the finality of loss. "People yearn for a body," says the family therapist Pauline Boss (2002, p. 15), "because, paradoxically, *having* the body enables them to let go of it." Viewing the body overcomes confusion, "provides cognitive certainty of death," and thus enables the bereaved to begin mourning. Without a body, survivors feel cheated out of the chance to say good-bye and to honor the loved one properly.

Ambiguous loss occurs when there is no tangible confirmation of a death, as when a body cannot be found. People are denied ritual and emotional closure, and their grief may remain frozen. The path forward is not clear. People may find themselves unable to go on with the necessary tasks of reorganizing family roles and relationships, and their feelings are often confusing and difficult to resolve. When such a loss continues on without resolution, it can create physical and emotional exhaustion, and the support of friends and family may drop away with time. Ambiguous loss is not a psychological disorder; rather, it is a relational disorder.

The concept of ambiguous loss can also be applied to situations in which the loved one is physically present but psychologically absent, such as in Alzheimer's disease, drug addiction, or chronic mental illness (Boss, 2000). In these situations, the person is alive; however, there is grief for the person he or she used to be, and there is no clear way to ameliorate such feelings. These processes also can be present in the families of deployed military personnel (Huebner, Mancini, Wilcox, Grass, & Grass, 2007), and these feelings may be exacerbated by the fear that loved ones will be injured or killed.

People who can best tolerate ambiguous loss tend to have certain characteristics: (1) They are deeply spiritual and do not expect to understand what happens in the world—they have faith and trust in the unknown. (2) They are optimistic by nature. (3) They can hold two opposite ideas at one time ("I need to reorganize my life but keep hope alive") and thus can live with uncertainty. (4) Often they grew up in a family or culture where mastery, control, and finding answers to questions was less important than learning to live with what is.

Therapy can help people to "understand, cope, and move on after the loss, even if it remains unclear" (Boss, 1999, p. 7). Telling and hearing stories about the missing person may begin the healing process. Reconstructing family rituals can affirm that family life goes on.

Therapists working with people suffering from ambiguous loss need to be able to tolerate ambiguity themselves. They must recognize that the classic stages of grief work (described in this chapter) do not apply. Pressing for closure will bring resistance. Families can learn to manage the stress of ambiguous loss at their own pace and in their own way.

Sources: Boss, 1999, 2000, 2002, 2004, 2006, 2007; Boss, Beaulieu, Wieling, Turner, & LaCruz , 2003.

Have you ever experienced an ambiguous loss, or do you know someone who has? If so, what coping strategies seemed most effective?

The knowledge that grief takes varied forms and patterns has important implications for helping people deal with loss (Boerner et al., 2004, 2005; Bonanno et al., 2002); Table 1 lists some suggestions for helping those who have lost a loved one. It may be unnecessary and even harmful to urge or lead mourners to work through a loss or to expect them to follow a set pattern of emotional reactions—just as it may be unnecessary and harmful to expect all dying patients to experience Kübler-Ross's stages. And while bereavement therapy may help some people, the evidence suggests that grief work is not necessary for recovery (Stroebe, Schut, & Stroebe, 2005) and that many people

TABLE 1 Helping Someone Who Has Lost a Loved One

These suggestions from mental health professionals may enable you to help someone you know through the grieving process:

- ***Share the sorrow.*** Allow—or encourage—the bereaved person to talk about feelings of loss and share memories of the deceased person.
- ***Don't offer false comfort.*** Saying such things as "It's all for the best" or "You'll get over it in time" is not helpful. Instead, simply express sorrow—and take time to listen.
- ***Offer practical help.*** Babysitting, cooking, and running errands are ways to help someone who is grieving.
- ***Be patient.*** It can take a long time to recover from a significant loss. Be available to talk and listen.
- ***Suggest professional help when necessary.*** Don't hesitate to recommend professional help when it appears that someone is experiencing too much pain to cope alone.

Source: National Mental Health Association, n.d.

will recover on their own if given time (Neimeyer & Currier, 2009). Respect for different ways of showing grief can help the bereaved deal with loss without making them feel that their reactions are abnormal.

checkpoint
can **you** . . .

- Summarize changes that may occur in a person close to death?
- Cite possible explanations for near-death experiences?
- Name Kübler-Ross's five stages of confronting death, and tell why her work is controversial?
- Identify the three stages commonly described as *grief work,* and discuss newer findings of variations in the grieving process?

ATTITUDES ABOUT DEATH AND DYING ACROSS THE LIFE SPAN

There is no single way of viewing death at any age; people's attitudes toward it reflect their personality and experience, as well as how close they believe they are to dying. Still, broad developmental differences apply. As the timing-of-events model suggests, death probably does not mean the same thing to an 85-year-old man with excruciatingly painful arthritis, a 56-year-old woman at the height of a brilliant legal career who discovers she has breast cancer, and a 15-year-old who dies of an overdose of drugs. Typical changes in attitudes toward death across the life span depend both on cognitive development and on the normative or nonnormative timing of the event.

Childhood and Adolescence According to early neo-Piagetian research (Speece & Brent, 1984), sometime between ages 5 and 7 most children come to understand that death is *irreversible*—that a dead person, animal, or flower cannot come to life again. At about the same age, children realize two other important concepts about death: first, that it is *universal* (all living things die) and therefore *inevitable;* and second, that a dead person is *nonfunctional* (all life functions end at death). Before then, children may believe that certain groups of people (say, teachers, parents, and children) do not die, that a person who is smart enough or lucky enough can avoid death, and that they themselves will be able to live forever. They also may believe that a dead person still can think and feel. The concepts of irreversibility, universality, and cessation of functions, these studies suggest, usually develop during the shift from preoperational to concrete operational thinking, when concepts of causation become more mature.

More recent research suggests that children may acquire a partial understanding of what happens after death as early as age 4, but that understanding may not be complete until well into the school years. In a series of studies at two university-affiliated schools, most preschoolers and kindergartners expressed knowledge that a dead mouse will never be alive again or grow up to be an old mouse, but 54 percent said the mouse might still need to eat. By age 7, 91 percent of the children were consistent in their knowledge that such biological processes as eating and drinking cease at death. Yet, when similar questions were put in psychological terms ("Is he still hungry?"), children this age and younger were less consistent. Only 21 percent of kindergartners and 55 percent of early elementary students knew, for example, that a dead mouse would no longer feel sick, compared with 75 percent of late elementary students ages 11 to 12. The understanding that cognitive states cease at death lagged even further; only 30 percent of the late elementary group consistently answered questions about whether thoughts, feelings, and desires persist after death (Bering & Bjorklund, 2004).

Children can better understand death if they are introduced to the concept at an early age and are encouraged to talk about it. The death of a pet may provide a natural opportunity. If another child dies, teachers and parents need to try to allay the surviving children's anxieties. For children with terminal illnesses, the need to understand death may be more pressing and more concrete. Yet parents may avoid bringing up the subject, whether because of their own difficulty in accepting the prospect of loss or because they are trying to protect their child. In so doing, they may miss an opportunity for the child and family to prepare emotionally for what is to come (Wolfe, 2004).

Like their understanding of death, the way children show grief depends on cognitive and emotional development (Table 2). Children sometimes express grief through anger, acting out, or refusal to acknowledge a death, as if the pretense that a person is still alive will make it so. They may be confused by adults' euphemisms: that someone "passed on" or that the family "lost" someone or that someone is "asleep" and will never awaken.

Children's confusion is related to their cognitive development. In the Piagetian framework discussed in other chapters, we learned that children have difficulty with abstract thought, so euphemisms used to describe death can be confusing to them.

Adjusting to loss is more difficult if a child had a troubled relationship with the person who died; if a surviving parent depends too much on the child; if the death was unexpected, especially if it was a murder or suicide; if the child has had previous behavioral or emotional problems; or if family and community support are lacking (AAP Committee on Psychosocial Aspects of Child and Family Health, 1992).

Parents and other adult caregivers can help children deal with bereavement by explaining that death is final and inevitable and that they did not cause the death by their misbehavior or thoughts. Children need reassurance that they will continue to receive care from loving adults. It is usually advisable to make as few changes as possible in a child's environment, relationships, and daily activities; to answer questions simply and honestly; and to encourage the child to talk about his or her feelings and about the person who died (AAP Committee on Psychosocial Aspects of Child and Family Health, 2000).

TABLE 2 Manifestations of Grief in Children

Under 3 Years	3 to 5 Years	School-Age Children	Adolescents
Regression Sadness Fearfulness Loss of appetite Failure to thrive Sleep disturbance Social withdrawal Developmental delay Irritability Excessive crying Increased dependency Loss of speech	Increased activity Constipation Soiling Bed-wetting Anger and temper tantrums Out-of-control behavior Nightmares Crying spells	Deterioration of school performance caused by loss of concentration, lack of interest, lack of motivation, failure to complete assignments, and daydreaming in class Resistance to attending school Crying spells Lying Stealing Nervousness Abdominal pain Headaches Listlessness Fatigue	Depression Somatic complaints Delinquent behavior Promiscuity Suicide attempts Dropping out of school

Source: Adapted from AAP Committee on Psychosocial Aspects of Child and Family Health, 1992.

For adolescents, death is not something they normally think much about unless they are directly faced with it. Many of them take unnecessary risks. They hitchhike, drive recklessly, or experiment with drugs and sex—often with tragic results. In their urge to discover and express their identity, they tend to focus more on *how* they live than on how *long* they are likely to live.

The unnecessary risks adolescents sometimes take can have tragic results.

Adulthood Young adults who have finished their education and have embarked on careers, marriage, or parenthood are generally eager to live the lives they have been preparing for. If they are suddenly struck by a potentially fatal illness or injury, they are likely to be extremely frustrated and angry. People who develop terminal illnesses in their 20s or 30s must face issues of death and dying at an age when they normally would be dealing with such issues of young adulthood as establishing an intimate relationship. Rather than having a long lifetime of losses as gradual preparation for the final loss of life, they find their entire world collapsing at once.

In middle age, most adults understand that they are indeed going to die. Their bodies send them signals that they are not as young, agile, and hearty as they once were. More and more they think about how many years they may have left and how to make the most of those years (Neugarten, 1967). Often—especially after the death of both parents—there is a new awareness of being the older generation or the next in line to die (Scharlach & Fredriksen, 1993). Middle-aged and older adults may prepare for death emotionally as well as in practical ways by making a will, planning their funerals, and discussing their wishes with family and friends.

Older adults may have mixed feelings about the prospect of dying. Physical losses and other problems and losses of old age may diminish their pleasure in living and their will to live (McCue, 1995). Some older adults give up on achieving unfulfilled goals. Others push harder to do what they can with life in the time they have left. Many try to extend their remaining time by adopting healthier lifestyles or struggle to live even when they are profoundly ill (Cicirelli, 2002). When they think or talk of their impending death, some older adults express fear. Others, especially the devoutly religious, compare death to falling asleep, an easy and painless transition to an afterlife (Cicirelli, 2002).

Try to imagine that you are terminally ill. What do you imagine your feelings would be? Would they be similar to or different from those described with reference to your age group?

According to Erikson, older adults who resolve the final critical alternative of *integrity versus despair* achieve acceptance both of what they have done with their lives and of their impending death. One way to accomplish this resolution is through a *life review,* discussed later in this chapter. People who feel that their lives have been meaningful and who have adjusted to their losses may be better able to face death.

checkpoint can you . . .

- Discuss how people of different ages understand and cope with death and bereavement?

Significant Losses

Especially difficult losses that may occur during adulthood are the deaths of a spouse, a parent, or a child. The loss of a potential offspring through miscarriage or stillbirth also can be painful but usually draws less social support.

SURVIVING A SPOUSE

Because women tend to live longer than men and to be younger than their husbands, they are more likely to be widowed. They also tend to be widowed at an earlier age.

Some 25 percent of U.S. women, but only 7 percent of U.S. men, lose their spouse by age 65 (Federal Interagency Forum on Aging-Related Statistics, 2010).

The stress of widowhood often affects physical and mental health. Bereavement can impair the immune system, resulting in headaches, dizziness, indigestion, or chest pain. It also entails higher risks of disability, drug use, hospitalization, and even death (Stroebe, Schut, & Stroebe, 2007). In a large-scale Finnish study, men who lost their wives within the 5-year period of the study were 21 percent more likely to die within the same period than men who remained married, and widowed women were 10 percent more likely to die than nonwidowed women (Martikainen & Valkonen, 1996). The risk of either natural death or suicide is greatest in the early months after a loss and is higher for younger adults. Bereavement also can lead to memory problems, loss of appetite, and difficulty with concentration, and it heightens the risks of anxiety, depression, insomnia, and social dysfunction. These reactions may range from fairly short and mild to extreme and long lasting, sometimes even for years (Stroebe et al., 2007).

Social relationships are related to good health. Thus the loss of companionship may help explain why a widowed person, especially a widower, may soon follow the spouse to the grave (Ray, 2004). However, a more practical explanation also may apply; after the death of a spouse, there may be no one to remind an older widow to take her pills or to make sure a widowed man adheres to a special diet. Those who receive such reminders (say, from children or health workers) tend to improve in health habits and reported health (Williams, 2004).

The quality of the marital relationship that has been lost may affect the degree to which widowhood affects mental health. In one study, widowed persons who had been especially close to, or highly dependent on, their spouses tended to become more anxious and yearned more for their partners 6 months after the death than did widowed persons who had not been so close or dependent (Carr et al., 2000). The loss of a husband may be especially hard for a woman who has structured her life and her identity around pleasing or caring for him (Marks & Lambert, 1998). Such a woman has lost not only a companion but an important, perhaps central, role (Lucas et al., 2003).

Widowhood can create practical problems too. Widows whose husbands were chief breadwinners may experience economic hardship or fall into poverty (Hungerford, 2001). Widowed husbands may have to buy household services a homemaker wife provided. When both spouses were employed, the loss of one income can be hard. For women, the main consequences of widowhood are more likely to be economic strain, whereas for men the chief consequences are more likely to be social isolation and loss of emotional intimacy (Pudrovska et al., 2006). Older widows are more likely than older widowers to stay in touch with friends from whom they receive social support (Kinsella & Velkoff, 2001).

Ultimately, the distress of loss can be a catalyst for introspection and growth—for discovering submerged aspects of oneself and learning to stand on one's own feet (Lieberman, 1996). In one study, widows continued to talk and think about their deceased husbands decades after the loss, but these thoughts rarely upset them. Instead, these women said they had become stronger and more self-confident as a result of their loss (Carnelley, Wortman, Bolger, & Burke, 2006).

Older widows are more likely than older widowers to stay in touch with friends and benefit from the support of a social network.

LOSING A PARENT IN ADULTHOOD

The loss of a parent at any time is difficult, even in adulthood. In-depth interviews with 83 volunteers ages 35 to 60 found a majority of bereaved adult children still experiencing emotional distress—ranging from sadness and crying to depression and thoughts of suicide—after 1 to 5 years, especially following loss of a mother (Scharlach & Fredriksen, 1993). Still, the death of a parent can be a maturing experience. It can push adults into resolving important developmental issues: achieving a stronger sense of self and a more pressing, realistic awareness of their own mortality, along with a greater sense of responsibility, commitment, and attachment to others (M. S. Moss & Moss, 1989; Scharlach & Fredriksen, 1993, Table 3).

TABLE 3 Self-Reported Psychological Impacts of a Parent's Death on Adult Children

Impacts	Death of Mother (percent)	Death of Father (percent)
Self-concept		
More "adult"	29	43
More self-confident	19	20
More responsible	11	4
Less mature	14	3
Other	8	17
No impact	19	12
Feelings about mortality		
Increased awareness of own mortality	30	29
More accepting of own death	19	10
Made concrete plans regarding own death	10	4
Increased fear of own death	10	18
Other	14	16
No impact	17	23
Religiosity		
More religious	26	29
Less religious	11	2
Other	3	10
No impact	60	59
Personal priorities		
Personal relationships more important	35	28
Simple pleasures more important	16	13
Personal happiness more important	10	7
Material possessions less important	5	8
Other	20	8
No impact	14	36
Work or career plans		
Left job	29	16
Adjusted goals	15	10
Changed plans due to family needs	5	6
Moved	4	10
Other	13	19
No impact	34	39

Source: From Scharlach, A. E., & Fredriksen, K. I. (1993). Reactions to the death of a parent during midlife. *Omega: Journal of Death and Dying,* 27, p. 311, Table 1. Copyright 1993 by Baywood Publishing Company, Inc. Reproduced with permission of Baywood Publishing Company, Inc. in the format Textbook via Copyright Clearance Center.

The death of a parent often brings changes in other relationships. A bereaved adult child may assume more responsibility for the surviving parent and for keeping the family together (Aldwin & Levenson, 2001). The intense emotions of bereavement may draw siblings closer, or they may become alienated over differences that arose during the parent's final illness. A parent's death may free an adult child to spend more time and energy on relationships that were temporarily neglected to meet demands of caregiving. Or the death may free an adult child to shed a relationship that was being maintained to meet the parent's expectations (M. S. Moss & Moss, 1989; Scharlach & Fredriksen, 1993).

The death of a second parent can have especially great impact. The adult child may feel a sharpened sense of mortality now that the buffer of the older generation is gone

(Aldwin & Levenson, 2001). This awareness can be an opportunity for growth, leading to a more mature outlook on life and a greater appreciation of the value of personal relationships (Scharlach & Fredriksen, 1993). Recognition of the finality of death and of the impossibility of saying anything more to the deceased parent motivates some people to resolve disturbances in their ties to the living while there is still time. Some people are moved to reconcile with their adult children. Sometimes estranged siblings, realizing that the parent who provided a link between them is no longer there, try to mend the rift.

LOSING A CHILD

A parent is rarely prepared emotionally for the death of a child. Such a death, no matter at what age, comes as a cruel, unnatural shock, an untimely event that, in the normal course of things, should never happen. The parents may feel they have failed, no matter how much they loved and cared for the child, and they may find it hard to let go. If a marriage is strong, the couple may draw closer together, supporting each other in their shared loss. In other cases, the loss weakens and eventually destroys the marriage (Brandt, 1989). Parents, especially mothers, who have lost a child are at heightened risk of being hospitalized for mental illness (Li, Laursen, Precht, Olsen, & Mortensen, 2005). The stress of a child's loss may even hasten a parent's death (Li, Precht, Mortensen, & Olsen, 2003).

Many parents hesitate to discuss a terminally ill child's impending death with the child, but those who do so tend to achieve a sense of closure that helps them cope after the loss. In 2001, a Swedish research team surveyed 449 Swedish parents who had lost a child to cancer 4 to 9 years earlier. About one-third of the parents said they had talked with their children about their impending death, and none of these parents regretted having done so, whereas 27 percent of those who had not brought up the subject regretted it.

The impact of parental bereavement may vary depending on such factors as the age of the child, the cause of death, and the number of remaining children a couple has. In a longitudinal study, 219 Dutch couples who had lost a child were followed for 20 months after the death. Grief was greater the older the child (up to age 17). Parents whose child had died a traumatic death grieved more than those whose child had died of an illness or disorder or those who experienced a stillbirth or neonatal death. Parents who had expected the death and those who had other children expressed the least grief. Mothers tended to grieve more than fathers. As time went by, grief tended to diminish, especially among couples who became pregnant again (Wijngaards-de Meij et al., 2005).

Have you lost a parent, a sibling, a spouse, a child, or a friend? If not, which of these losses do you imagine would be hardest to bear, and why? If you have experienced more than one of these types of loss, how did your reactions differ?

Although each bereaved parent must cope with grief in his or her own way, some have found that plunging into work, interests, and other relationships or joining a support group eases the pain. Some well-meaning friends tell parents not to dwell on their loss, but remembering the child in a meaningful way may be exactly what they need to do. When asked what most helped them cope with the end of their child's life, 73 percent of parents whose children died in intensive-care units gave religious or spiritual responses. They mentioned prayer, faith, discussions with clergy, or a belief that the parent-child relationship endures beyond death. Parents also said they were guided by insight and wisdom, inner values, and spiritual virtues such as hope, trust, and love (Robinson, Thiel, Backus, & Meyer, 2006).

MOURNING A MISCARRIAGE

At a Buddhist temple in Tokyo, small statues of infants accompanied by toys and gifts are left as offerings to Jizo, an enlightened being who is believed to watch over miscarried and aborted fetuses and eventually, through reincarnation, to guide them into a new life. The ritual of *mizuko kuyo,* a rite of apology and remembrance, is observed as a means of making amends to the aborted life (Orenstein, 2002).

The Japanese word *mizuko* means "water child." Japanese Buddhists believe that life flows into an organism gradually, like water, and a mizuko is somewhere on the continuum between life and death (Orenstein, 2002). In English, in contrast, there is no special word for a miscarried or aborted fetus and, in American life, no customary ritual for mourning the loss. Families, friends, and health professionals tend to avoid talking about such losses, which often are considered insignificant compared with the loss of a living child (Van, 2001). Grief can be more wrenching without social support.

How do prospective parents cope with the loss of a child they never knew? Each person's or couple's experience of loss is unique, although grief, especially in women, is the most common response (Brier, 2008). In one small study, 11 men whose child had died in utero reported being overcome with frustration and helplessness during and after the delivery, but several found relief in supporting their partners (Samuelsson, Radestad, & Segesten, 2001). In another study, grieving parents perceived their spouses and extended families as most helpful and their doctors as least helpful. Some bereaved parents benefited from a support group, and some not (DiMarco, Menke, & McNamara, 2001). Whether married or living together, couples who experience a miscarriage prior to 20 weeks gestation are 22 percent more likely to break up than couples who have a successful pregnancy. When the miscarriage occurs after 20 weeks gestation, that risk is elevated by as much as 40 percent (Gold, Sen, & Hayward, 2010).

In response to the wishes of many parents who have experienced stillbirth, as of July 2011, laws had been enacted in 28 states providing birth certificates for stillborn babies to recognize and validate the births.

checkpoint
can you . . .

- Identify specific challenges involved in losing a spouse?
- Discuss ways in which an adult's loss of a spouse or parent can be a maturing experience?
- Explain why parents are rarely prepared emotionally for the death of a child?
- Suggest ways to help expectant parents cope with the loss of a pregnancy?

Medical, Legal, and Ethical Issues: The "Right to Die"

Do people have a right to die? If so, under what circumstances? Should a terminally ill person who wants to commit suicide be allowed or helped to do so? Should a doctor prescribe medicine that will relieve pain but may shorten the patient's life? What about giving a lethal injection to end a patient's suffering? Who decides that a life is not worth prolonging? These are some of the thorny moral, ethical, and legal questions that face individuals, families, physicians, and society—questions involving the quality of life and the nature and circumstances of death.

SUICIDE

Although suicide is no longer a crime in modern societies, there is still a stigma against it, based in part on religious prohibitions and in part on society's interest in preserving life. A person who expresses suicidal thoughts may be considered mentally ill. On the other hand, a growing number of people consider a mature adult's deliberate choice of a time to end his or her life a rational decision and a right to be defended.

Suicide rates in the United States began declining in the late 1990s after a 25 percent rise from 1981 to 1997; however, a significant increase of 3.7 percent occurred between 2006 and 2007 (Xu et al., 2010), with more than 34,500 people taking their own lives in 2007. Still, the suicide rate in the United States—11.5 deaths per 100,000 population (Xu et al., 2010)—is lower than in many other industrialized countries (Kinsella & Velkoff, 2001).

Statistics probably understate the number of suicides; many go unreported and some (such as traffic "accidents" and "accidental" medicinal overdoses) are not recognized as such. Also, the figures on suicides often do not include suicide *attempts;* an estimated 20 to 60 percent of people in the United States who commit suicide have tried before,

Most people believe suicide terrorists are motivated by religious extremism. However, a small and controversial group of researchers argues that their motivation is, more simply, driven by the same desire to commit suicide and the same risk factors that have been found in other clinical populations.

Lankford, 2010

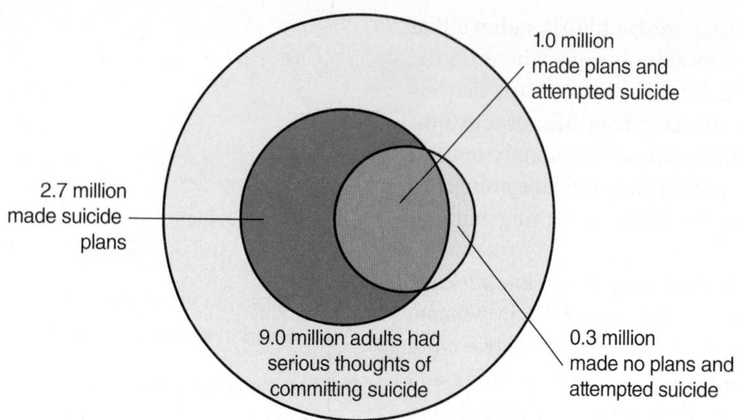

FIGURE 1

About 1.3 million people attempted suicide in 2012.

Source: SMHSA, 2013.

and about 10 percent of people who attempt suicide will kill themselves within 10 years (Harvard Medical School, 2003).

In most nations, suicide rates rise with age and are higher among men than among women (Kinsella & Velkoff, 2001; Nock et al., 2008), though more women consider or attempt suicide (Figure 1). Young, unmarried women with little education and those who are unusually impulsive, anxious, or depressed are most at risk for suicidal thoughts and behavior (Nock et al., 2008). Historically males were far more likely to succeed in taking their own life, but this gap has greatly diminished in recent years and males are only marginally more likely to attempt suicide (National Survey on Drug Use and Health, 2009). Men's suicide rates are higher mainly because they are far more likely to use reliable methods, such as firearms, whereas women are more likely to choose other means, such as poisoning or hanging. More than half of completed suicides are by gunshot (CDC, 2007a; Kung et al., 2008; Miniño et al., 2007).

The highest rate of suicide is among white men age 75 and over; the risk rises among men 85 and older. Older people are more likely than younger people to be depressed and socially isolated.

Among racial/ethnic groups, white and Native American men have the highest suicide rates. Older blacks are only about one-third as likely to commit suicide as older whites (NCHS, 2006), perhaps because of religious commitment and because they may be accustomed to hard knocks (NIMH, 1999a). However, suicide rates among black people, especially those who are younger and less educated, have increased significantly since the mid-1980s (Joe, Baser, Breeden, Neighbors, & Jackson, 2006).

Due to a recent unexplained jump in midlife suicide (Table 4), U.S. suicide rates now reach a high for adults in their 40s and early 50s and then subside and rise again after age 75 (Xu et al., 2010).

A family history of suicide or suicide attempts greatly raises the risk of completing suicide. An apparent hereditary vulnerability may be related to low activity of the mood- and impulse-regulating brain chemical serotonin in the prefrontal cortex, the seat of judgment, planning, and inhibition (Harvard Medical School, 2003).

Although some people intent on suicide carefully conceal their plans, most give warning signs. These may include talking about death or suicide; giving away prized possessions; abusing drugs or alcohol; and personality changes, such as unusual anger, sadness, boredom, or apathy. People who are about to kill themselves may neglect their appearance and sleep or eat much more or less than usual. They often show signs of depression, such as unusual difficulty concentrating, loss of self-esteem, and feelings of helplessness, hopelessness, or panic (American College of Emergency Physicians, 2008; Harvard Medical School, 2003).

Survivors of people who take their own lives have been called "suicide's other victims." Many blame themselves for failing to recognize the signs. They "obsessively replay the events leading up to the death, imagining how they could have prevented it and berating themselves for their failure to do so" (Goldman & Rothschild, n.d.). Because of the stigma attached to suicide, these survivors often struggle with their

The world's most popular suicide spot is the Golden Gate Bridge in San Francisco, California. Because of this, city officials are considering installing a safety net.

Fleming, 2010; Pogash, 2014

TABLE 4 Changes in Suicide Rates by Age, United States, 1999–2003

Suicide rates rose the most among middle-aged people while decreasing for the elderly, whose risk nevertheless remains the highest.

SUICIDE RATE, PER 100,000 PEOPLE		
Age Group	Rate in 2000	Rate in 2010
15 to 24	10.2	10.5
25 to 34	12.0	14.0
35 to 44	14.5	16.0
45 to 54	**14.4**	**19.6**
55 to 64	**12.1**	**17.5**
65 to 74	12.5	13.7
75 to 84	17.6	15.7
85 and over	19.6	17.6

Source: CDC, 2012.

emotions alone rather than share them with others who might understand. (Table 5 lists warning signs of suicide and steps to take if someone threatens suicide.)

HASTENING DEATH

How do we decide if someone is truly dead? Is it ever right to hasten the process? Two recent events illustrate the importance of such questions. In November 2013 a pregnant woman, Marlize Nicole Muñoz, experienced a suspected pulmonary embolism, and upon reaching the hospital was declared to be brain dead. Despite evidence she would not have wanted to be kept on life support, as well as the wishes of her family, she was placed on life support machines. In Texas, her home state, any advance directives are considered null and void if a woman is pregnant. Her family fought to be allowed to remove her from life support, and in January 2014 they were allowed to lay her to rest.

In December of that same year, 13-year-old Jahi McMath underwent surgery in California to relieve sleep apnea. Despite waking up alert, she suffered a cardiac arrest and massive blood loss shortly thereafter. She was also declared brain dead. However, in this situation, the hospital wanted to remove her from life support but her family held out hope of some recovery and resisted the process. After a protracted legal battle, her family was allowed to claim her body and move her to an undisclosed facility. Both of these tragic events illustrate how medical technology has outpaced our legal system and ethics and are reminders that not everyone views life and death in the same way.

Until recent decades, the idea of helping a suffering loved one hasten death was virtually unheard of. Changing attitudes toward hastening death can be attributed largely to revulsion against technologies that keep patients alive against their will despite intense suffering, and sometimes even after the brain has stopped functioning.

Is euthanasia a moral way to end life? *Euthanasia* means "good death" and is intended to end suffering or to allow a terminally ill person to die with dignity. People differ in their beliefs about this process, and some draw distinctions between the types of euthanasia used. **Passive euthanasia** involves withholding or discontinuing treatment that might extend the life of a terminally ill patient, such as medication, life support systems, or feeding tubes. Many people would characterize turning off the life support systems for Marlize Muñoz as passive euthanasia, although the case is complicated by

passive euthanasia
Withholding or discontinuation of life-prolonging treatment of a terminally ill person in order to end suffering or allow death with dignity.

TABLE 5 Preventing Suicide

WARNING SIGNS OF SUICIDE:
• Feeling depressed, down, or excessively sad.
• Feelings of hopelessness, worthlessness, or having no purpose in life, along with a loss of interest or pleasure in doing things.
• Preoccupation with death, dying, or violence, or talking about wanting to die.
• Seeking access to medications, weapons, or other means of committing suicide.
• Wide mood swings—feeling extremely up one day and terribly down the next.
• Feelings of great agitation, rage, or uncontrolled anger, or wanting to get revenge.
• Changes in eating and sleeping habits, appearance, behavior, or personality.
• Risky or self-destructive behavior, such as driving recklessly or taking illegal drugs.
• Sudden calmness (a sign that a person has made the decision to attempt suicide).
• Life crises, trauma, or setbacks, including school, work, or relationship problems, job loss, divorce, death of a loved one, financial difficulties, diagnosis of a terminal illness.
• Putting one's affairs in order, including giving away belongings, visiting family members and friends, drawing up a will, or writing a suicide note.
IF SOMEONE THREATENS SUICIDE:
• Stay calm.
• Take the threat seriously.
• Don't leave the person alone. Prevent access to firearms, knives, medications, or any other item the person may use to commit suicide.
• Don't try to handle the situation alone. Call 911 or the local emergency response number. Phone the person's doctor, the police, a local crisis intervention team, or others who are trained to help.
• While waiting for help, listen closely to the person. Let the person know you're listening by maintaining eye contact, moving closer, or holding his or her hand, if appropriate.
• Ask questions to determine what method of suicide the person is considering and whether he or she has an organized plan.
• Remind the person that help is available.
• If the person does attempt suicide, immediately call for emergency medical assistance and administer first aid, if necessary.

Source: Adapted from American College of Emergency Physicians, 2008.

active euthanasia
Deliberate action taken to shorten the life of a terminally ill person in order to end suffering or to allow death with dignity; also called *mercy killing.*

the fact that brain dead people are considered legally dead even if their heart continues to beat. Passive euthanasia is generally legal. **Active euthanasia** (sometimes called *mercy killing*) involves action taken directly or deliberately to shorten a life, and it is generally illegal. An important question regarding either form of euthanasia is whether it is done at the direct request, or to carry out the express wishes, of the person whose death results.

Advance Directives Many of the issues surrounding how much medical technology should be used to keep a person alive near the end of life can be addressed if people's wishes are made clear before they are incapacitated. The U.S. Supreme Court held, in the case of Nancy Cruzan, that a person whose wishes are clearly known has a constitutional right to refuse or discontinue life-sustaining treatment (*Cruzan v. Director, Missouri Department of Health,* 1990). A mentally competent person's wishes can be spelled out in advance in a document called an **advance directive (living will),** which contains instructions for when and how to discontinue futile medical care. All 50 states have since legalized some form of advance directive or adopted other provisions governing the making of end-of-life decisions.

> *At the time of death, more than a quarter of elderly patients are incapable of making medical care decisions. This illustrates why, difficult as they may be, discussions about the end of life are important.*
>
> Silveira, Kim, & Langa, 2010

A *living will* may contain specific provisions with regard to circumstances in which treatment should be discontinued, what extraordinary measures—if any—should be taken to prolong life, and what kind of pain management is desired. A person also may specify, through a donor card or a signature on the back of his or her driver's license, that his or her organs be donated to someone in need of an organ transplant. Such advance care planning is beneficial not just to the dying person, but also to the family. Deciding on a plan of action in the event that death is imminent leads to improved end-of-life care and results in higher levels of family satisfaction, and reductions in stress, anxiety, and depression in family members of the terminally ill patient (Detering, Hancock, Reade, & Silvester, 2010).

advance directive (living will)
Document specifying the type of care wanted by the maker in the event of an incapacitating or terminal illness.

> *As of May 2011, more than 110,500 people were waiting for an organ donation in the United States, and the need is particularly acute for minority candidates. Would you donate an organ to a friend or family member who needed it? To a stranger? Why or why not?*
>
> *The need is real*, n.d.

Some living will legislation applies only to terminally ill patients, not to those who are incapacitated by illness or injury but may live many years in severe pain. Nor do advance directives help many patients in comas or in persistent vegetative states. Such situations can be covered by a **durable power of attorney,** which appoints another person to make decisions if the maker of the document becomes incompetent to do so. A number of states have adopted a simple form known as a *medical durable power of attorney* expressly for decisions about health care. However, even with advance directives, many patients have undergone protracted, fruitless treatment against their expressed wishes (SUPPORT Principal Investigators, 1995).

durable power of attorney
Legal instrument that appoints an individual to make decisions in the event of another person's incapacitation.

Such situations led the American Medical Association to form a Task Force on Quality Care at the End of Life. Many hospitals now have ethics committees that create guidelines, review cases, and help doctors, patients, and their families with decisions about end-of-life care (Simpson, 1996); and some hospitals employ full-time ethics consultants.

Assisted Suicide: Pros and Cons **Assisted suicide**—in which a physician or someone else helps a person bring about a self-inflicted death by, for example, prescribing or obtaining drugs or enabling a patient to inhale a deadly gas—commonly refers to situations in which people with incurable, terminal illnesses request help in ending their lives. Assisted suicide is still illegal in most places but in recent years has come to the forefront of public debate. It may be similar in principle to voluntary active euthanasia, in which, for example, a patient asks for, and receives, a lethal injection; but in assisted suicide the person who wants to die performs the actual deed.

assisted suicide
Suicide in which a physician or someone else helps a person take his or her own life.

In the United States, assisted suicide is illegal in almost all states but often goes on covertly, without regulation. The American Medical Association opposes physician aid in dying as contrary to a practitioner's oath to "do no harm." Doctors are permitted to give drugs that may shorten a life if the purpose is to relieve pain (Gostin, 1997; Quill, Lo, & Brock, 1997), but some physicians refuse for reasons of personal or medical ethics (APA Online, 2001).

The *ethical arguments for* assisted suicide are based on the principles of autonomy and self-determination: that mentally competent persons should have the right to control the quality of their own lives and the timing and nature of their death. Proponents of assisted suicide place a high value on preserving the dignity and personhood of the dying human being. *Medical arguments* hold that a doctor is obligated to take all measures necessary to relieve suffering. Besides, in assisted suicide the patient is the one who takes the actual step to end life. A *legal argument* is that legalizing assisted suicide would permit the regulation of practices that now occur anyway out of compassion for suffering patients. It is argued that adequate safeguards against abuse can be put in place through a combination of legislation and professional regulation (APA Online, 2001).

Some ethical and legal scholars go further: They favor legalizing all forms of *voluntary euthanasia* with safeguards against involuntary euthanasia. The key issue, according to these scholars, is not how death occurs but who makes the decision. They see no difference in principle between pulling the plug on a respirator, pulling out feeding tubes, giving a lethal injection, or prescribing an overdose of pills at the patient's request. They maintain that aid in dying, if openly available, would reduce fear and helplessness by enabling patients to control their own fate (APA Online, 2001; Orentlicher, 1996).

Ethical arguments against assisted suicide center on two principles: (1) the belief that taking a life, even with consent, is wrong; and (2) concern for protection of the disadvantaged. Opponents of aid-in-dying point out that autonomy is often limited by poverty or disability or membership in a stigmatized social group, and they fear that persons in these categories may be subtly pressured into choosing suicide with cost containment as an underlying factor. *Medical arguments* against assisted suicide include the possibility of misdiagnosis, the potential future availability of new treatments, the likelihood of incorrect prognosis, and the belief that helping someone die is incompatible with a physician's role as healer and that adequate safeguards are not possible. *Legal arguments* against assisted suicide include concerns about enforceability of safeguards and about lawsuits when family members disagree about the propriety of terminating a life (APA Online, 2001).

Because self-administered pills do not always succeed, some opponents contend that physician-assisted suicide would lead to voluntary active euthanasia (Groenewoud et al., 2000). The next step on the slippery slope, some warn, would be involuntary euthanasia—not only for the terminally ill but for others, such as people with disabilities, whose quality of life is perceived as diminished. The opponents claim that people who want to die are often temporarily depressed and might change their minds with treatment or palliative care (APA Working Group on Assisted Suicide and End-of-Life Decisions, 2005; Butler, 1996; Quill et al., 1997).

Legalizing Physician Aid in Dying Since 1997, when a unanimous U.S. Supreme Court left regulation of physician aid-in-dying up to the states, measures to legalize assisted suicide for the terminally ill have been introduced in several states. Oregon was the first state to pass such a law, the Death with Dignity Act (DWDA). In 1994, Oregonians voted to let mentally competent patients, who have been told by two doctors that they have less than 6 months to live, to request a lethal prescription with strong safeguards to make sure the request is serious and voluntary and that all other alternatives have been considered. In January 2006 the Supreme Court upheld the Oregon law (Gostin, 2006; Greenhouse, 2005).

In September 1996, a 66-year-old Australian man with advanced prostate cancer was the first person to die legally by assisted suicide.

What has been the experience under the Oregon law? The legalization of assisted suicide has resulted in improvements of palliative care and an increased number of deaths occurring at home rather than in the hospital (Steinbrook, 2008). Since DWDA was enacted, 752 terminally ill patients were reported to state health officials to have taken their lives, 122 of them in 2013. The concerns most frequently mentioned by patients who requested and used lethal prescriptions were loss of autonomy (93 percent), loss of ability to participate in activities that make life enjoyable (88.7 percent), and loss of dignity (73.2 percent) (Oregon Health Authority, n.d.).

Active euthanasia remains illegal in the United States but not in the Netherlands, where in 2002 a law permitting voluntary euthanasia for patients in a state of continuous, unbearable, and incurable suffering went into effect. In such cases, doctors can now inject a lethal dose of medication. In 2005, a reported 1.8 percent of deaths in the Netherlands resulted from euthanasia or assisted suicide (Van der Heide et al., 2007).

Before 2002, both assisted suicide and active euthanasia were technically illegal in the Netherlands, but physicians who engaged in these practices could avoid prosecution under strict conditions of reporting and government oversight (Simons, 1993). A similar situation still exists in Switzerland and Belgium (Steinbrook, 2008). In France, a law effective in February 2006 authorizes doctors to withhold unnecessary medical treatment or to intensify pain relief, even if these decisions unintentionally hasten death. In many cases, assisted suicide occurs regardless of laws against it, but it is an underground practice (Steinbrook, 2008).

Do you think assisted suicide should be legalized? If so, what safeguards should be provided? Would your answers be the same or different for voluntary active euthanasia? Do you see an ethical distinction between euthanasia and oversedation of the terminally ill?

End-of-Life Decisions and Cultural Attitudes It is hard to compare the experience of the Netherlands, which has a homogeneous population and universal national health coverage, with that of such a large, diverse country as the United States. Nevertheless, with increasing numbers of Americans favoring euthanasia for a patient who is incurably ill and wants to die, some U.S. doctors have agreed to help patients requesting assistance in hastening death. A nationwide survey of 1,902 physicians whose specialties involve care of dying patients found that, of those who had received requests for help with suicide (18 percent) or lethal injections (11 percent), about 7 percent had complied at least once (Meier et al., 1998).

The first representative study of end-of-life decisions in six European countries (Belgium, Denmark, Italy, the Netherlands, Sweden, and Switzerland) found important cultural differences. In all six countries, physicians reported withholding or withdrawing life-prolonging treatment—most typically medication, followed by hydration or nutrition—but the frequency varied greatly, from 41 percent of deaths in Switzerland to 6 percent in Italy (Bosshard et al., 2005). Active forms of physician-assisted death were most prevalent in the Netherlands and Belgium (van der Heide et al., 2003). In a later survey of physicians in the same six countries, direct physician-assisted deaths were rare; but in one-quarter to one-half of all deaths (23 percent in Italy, 51 percent in Switzerland), physicians made death-hastening decisions, such as deep sedation, sometimes accompanied by withdrawal of artificial nutrition and hydration (Bilsen, Cohen, & Deliens, 2007). Most Americans—roughly 84 percent—support a terminally ill person's right to decide whether or not to be kept alive with medical treatment, and approximately 70 percent agree that there are some circumstances in which a person should be allowed to die. Only 22 percent of Americans believe everything possible should always be done to save the life of a patient (Parker, 2009a).

Author Aldous Huxley, best known for his dystopic novel Brave New World, *died while high on an intramuscular injection of LSD, administered to him by his wife, at his request.*

End-of-Life Options and Diversity Concerns One beneficial result of the aid-in-dying controversy has been to call attention to the need for better palliative care and closer attention to patients' motivation and state of mind. When doctors talk openly with patients about their physical and mental symptoms, their expectations, their fears and goals, their options for end-of-life care, their family concerns, and their need for meaning and quality of life, ways may be found to diminish these concerns without the taking of life (Bascom & Tolle, 2002).

In the United States, with its ethnically diverse population, issues of social and cultural diversity need to be addressed in end-of-life decision making. Planning for death is inconsistent with traditional Navajo values, which avoid negative thinking and talk. Chinese families may seek to protect a dying person from unfavorable information, including knowledge of his or her impending death. Recent Mexican or Korean immigrants may believe less in individual autonomy than is customary in the dominant U.S. culture. Among some ethnic minorities, the value of longevity may take priority over health. Both African Americans and Hispanic Americans, for example, are more likely than European Americans to prefer life-sustaining treatment regardless of the state of the disease and of their educational level (APA Working Group on Assisted Suicide, 2005).

Issues of hastening death will become more pressing as the population ages. In years to come, both the courts and the public will be forced to come to terms with these issues as increasing numbers of people claim a right to die with dignity and with help.

checkpoint
can you . . .

- Explain why intent to commit suicide is sometimes not recognized, and list warning signs?
- Discuss the ethical, practical, and legal issues involved in advance directives, euthanasia, and assisted suicide?

Finding Meaning and Purpose in Life and Death

The struggle to find meaning in life and in death—often dramatized in books and movies—has been borne out by research. Studies examining religion and death have found that such beliefs are generally beneficial for the dying (Edmondson, Park, Chaudoir, & Wortmann, 2008). In one study of 39 women whose average age was 76, those who saw the most purpose in life had the least fear of death (Durlak, 1973). Conversely, according to Kübler-Ross (1975), facing the reality of death is a key to living a meaningful life:

> It is the denial of death that is partially responsible for [people] living empty, purposeless lives; for when you live as if you'll live forever, it becomes too easy to postpone the things you know that you must do. In contrast, when you fully understand that each day you awaken could be the last you have, you take the time that day to grow, to become more of who you really are, to reach out to other human beings. (p. 164)

Some theorists have suggested that one of the primary functions of religion is to provide comfort in the face of our certain death.

Edmondson et al., 2008

REVIEWING A LIFE

In Charles Dickens's *A Christmas Carol,* Scrooge changes his greedy, heartless ways after seeing ghostly visions of his past, his present, and his future death. In the movie *It's a Wonderful Life,* when an angel helps George Bailey (played by Jimmy Stewart) to see the world without himself in it, he realizes how meaningful his life is. These fictional characters make their remaining time more purposeful through **life review,** a process of reminiscence that enables a person to see the significance of his or her life.

life review
Reminiscence about one's life in order to see its significance.

Life review can, of course, occur at any time. However, it may have special meaning in old age, when it can foster ego integrity—according to Erikson, the final critical task of the life span. As the end of their journey approaches, people may look back over their accomplishments and failures and ask themselves what their lives have meant. Awareness of mortality may be an impetus for reexamining values and seeing one's experiences and actions in a new light. Some people find the will to complete unfinished tasks, such as reconciling with estranged family members or friends, and thus to achieve a satisfying sense of closure.

Not all memories are equally conducive to mental health and growth. Older people who use reminiscence for self-understanding show the strongest ego integrity, whereas those who entertain only pleasurable memories show less. Most poorly adjusted are those who keep recalling negative events and are obsessed with regret, hopelessness, and fear of death; their ego integrity has given way to despair (Sherman, 1993).

Life review therapy can help focus the natural process of life review and make it more conscious, purposeful, and efficient (Butler, 1961; M. I. Lewis & Butler, 1974). Methods often used for uncovering memories in life review therapy (which also may be used by individuals on their own) include recording an autobiography; constructing a family tree; spending time with scrapbooks, photo albums, old letters, and other memorabilia; making a trip back to scenes of childhood and young adulthood; reuniting with former classmates or colleagues or distant family members; describing ethnic traditions; and summing up one's life's work.

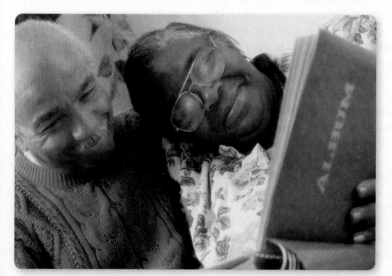

Sharing memories evoked by a photo album is one way to review a life. Life review can help people recall important events and can motivate them to rebuild damaged relationships or complete unfinished tasks.

DEVELOPMENT: A LIFELONG PROCESS

In his late 70s, the artist Pierre-Auguste Renoir had crippling arthritis and chronic bronchitis and had lost his wife. He spent his days in a wheelchair, and his pain was so great that he could not sleep through the night. He was unable to hold a palette or grip a brush: his brush had to be tied to his right hand. Yet he continued to produce brilliant paintings, full of color and vibrant life. Finally, stricken by pneumonia, he lay in bed, gazing at some anemones his attendant had picked. He gathered enough strength to sketch the form of these beautiful flowers, and then—just before he died—lay back and whispered, "I think I am beginning to understand something about it" (L. Hanson, 1968).

Even dying can be a developmental experience. As one health practitioner put it, "there are things to be gained, accomplished in dying. Time with and for those whom we are close to, achieving a final and enduring sense of self-worth, and a readiness to let go are priceless elements of a good death" (Weinberger, 1999).

Within a limited life span, no person can realize all capabilities, gratify all desires, explore all interests, or experience all the richness that life has to offer. The tension between possibilities for growth and a finite time in which to do the growing defines human life. By choosing which possibilities to pursue and by continuing to follow them as far as possible, even up to the very end, each person contributes to the unfinished story of human development.

checkpoint can **you** . . .

- Explain why life review can be especially helpful in old age and how it can help overcome fear of death?
- Tell what types of memories are most conducive to a life review?
- List several activities used in life review therapy?
- Explain how dying can be a developmental experience?

summary and key terms

The Many, Changing Meanings of Death and Dying

- Death has biological, social, cultural, historical, religious, legal, psychological, developmental, medical, and ethical aspects.
- Customs surrounding death and mourning vary greatly from one culture to another, depending on the society's view of the nature and consequences of death. Some modern customs have evolved from ancient beliefs and practices.
- Death rates dropped drastically during the twentieth century, especially in developed countries.
- Nearly three-quarters of deaths in the United States occur among the elderly, and the top causes of death are diseases that primarily affect older adults.
- As death became primarily a phenomenon of late adulthood, it became largely "invisible," and care of the dying took place in isolation, by professionals.
- There is now an upsurge of interest in understanding and dealing realistically and compassionately with death. Examples of this tendency are a growing interest in thanatology and increasing emphasis on hospice care and palliative, or comfort, care.

thanatology
hospice care
palliative care

Facing Death and Loss

- People often undergo cognitive and functional declines shortly before death.
- Some people who come close to dying have "near-death" experiences that may result from physiological changes.
- Elisabeth Kübler-Ross proposed five stages in coming to terms with dying: denial, anger, bargaining, depression, and acceptance. These stages, and their sequence, are not universal.
- There is no universal pattern of grief. The most widely studied pattern moves from shock and disbelief to preoccupation with the memory of the dead person and finally to resolution. However, research has found wide variations and a prevalence of resilience.
- Children's understanding of death develops gradually. Young children can better understand death if it is part of their own experience. Children show grief in age-related ways based on cognitive and emotional development.
- Although adolescents generally do not think much about death, violence and the threat of death are part of some adolescents' daily life. Adolescents tend to take needless risks.
- Realization and acceptance of the inevitability of death increases throughout adulthood.

terminal drop
grief
bereavement
grief work

Significant Losses

- Women are more likely to be widowed, and widowed younger, than men, and may experience widowhood somewhat differently. Physical and mental health tend to decline after widowhood, but for some people widowhood can ultimately become a positive developmental experience.
- Death of a parent can precipitate changes in the self and in relationships with others.
- The loss of a child can be especially difficult because it is no longer normative.
- Because miscarriage and stillbirth are not generally considered significant losses in U.S. society, those who experience such losses are often left to deal with them with little social support.

Medical, Legal, and Ethical Issues: The "Right to Die"

- Although suicide is no longer illegal in modern societies, there is still a stigma attached to it. Some people maintain a "right to die," especially for people with long-term degenerative illness.
- The number of suicides is probably underestimated. It is often related to depression, isolation, family conflict, financial troubles, and debilitating ailments. There are many more suicide attempts than actual deaths.
- Euthanasia and assisted suicide involve controversial ethical, medical, and legal issues.
- To avoid unnecessary suffering through artificial prolongation of life, passive euthanasia is generally permitted with the patient's consent or with advance directives. However, such directives are not consistently followed. Most hospitals now have ethics committees to deal with decisions about end-of-life care.
- Active euthanasia and assisted suicide are generally illegal, but public support for physician aid-in-dying has increased. The state of Oregon has a law permitting physician-assisted suicide for the terminally ill. The Netherlands and Belgium have legalized both euthanasia and assisted suicide.
- Forgoing or withdrawing treatment of newborns who cannot survive or who can do so only with extremely poor quality of life is becoming a more widely accepted practice than in the past, especially in some European countries.
- The aid-in-dying controversy has focused more attention on the need for better palliative care and understanding of patients' state of mind. Issues of social and cultural diversity need to be considered.

passive euthanasia
active euthanasia
advance directive (living will)
durable power of attorney
assisted suicide

Finding Meaning and Purpose in Life and Death

- The more meaning and purpose people find in their lives, the less they tend to fear death.
- Life review can help people prepare for death and give them a last chance to complete unfinished tasks.
- Even dying can be a developmental experience.

life review

glossary

acceleration programs Programs for educating the gifted that move them through the curriculum at an unusually rapid pace.

accommodation Piaget's term for changes in a cognitive structure to include new information.

acquired immune deficiency syndrome (AIDS) Viral disease that undermines effective functioning of the immune system.

active engagement Personal involvement in schooling, work, family, or other activity.

active euthanasia Deliberate action taken to shorten the life of a terminally ill person in order to end suffering or to allow death with dignity; also called *mercy killing*.

activities of daily living (ADLs) Essential activities that support survival, such as eating, dressing, bathing, and getting around the house.

activity theory Theory of aging that holds that to age successfully a person must remain as active as possible.

acute medical conditions Illnesses that last a short time.

adaptation Piaget's term for adjustment to new information about the environment, achieved through processes of assimilation and accommodation.

adolescence Developmental transition between childhood and adulthood entailing major physical, cognitive, and psychosocial changes.

adolescent growth spurt Sharp increase in height and weight that precedes sexual maturity.

adolescent rebellion Pattern of emotional turmoil, characteristic of a minority of adolescents, that may involve conflict with family, alienation from adult society, reckless behavior, and rejection of adult values.

advance directive (living will) Document specifying the type of care wanted by the maker in the event of an incapacitating or terminal illness.

ageism Prejudice or discrimination against a person (most commonly an older person) based on age.

age-related macular degeneration Condition in which the center of the retina gradually loses its ability to discern fine details; leading cause of irreversible visual impairment in older adults.

aging in place Remaining in one's own home, with or without assistance, in later life.

alcoholism Chronic disease involving dependence on use of alcohol, causing interference with normal functioning and fulfillment of obligations.

alleles Two or more alternative forms of a gene that occupy the same position on paired chromosomes and affect the same trait.

altruism Behavior intended to help others out of inner concern and without expectation of external reward; may involve self-denial or self-sacrifice.

altruistic behavior Activity intended to help another person with no expectation of reward.

Alzheimer's disease Progressive, irreversible, degenerative brain disorder characterized by cognitive deterioration and loss of control of bodily functions, leading to death.

ambiguous loss A loss that is not clearly defined or does not bring closure.

ambivalent (resistant) attachment Pattern in which an infant becomes anxious before the primary caregiver leaves, is extremely upset during his or her absence, and both seeks and resists contact on his or her return.

amyloid plaque Waxy chunks of insoluble tissue found in brains of persons with Alzheimer's disease.

animism Tendency to attribute life to objects that are not alive.

anorexia nervosa Eating disorder characterized by self-starvation.

anoxia Lack of oxygen, which may cause brain damage.

anticipatory smiling Infant smiles at an object and then gazes at an adult while still smiling.

Apgar scale Standard measurement of a newborn's condition; it assesses appearance, pulse, grimace, activity, and respiration.

art therapy Therapeutic approach that allows a person to express troubled feelings without words, using a variety of art materials and media.

assimilation Piaget's term for incorporation of new information into an existing cognitive structure.

assisted suicide Suicide in which a physician or someone else helps a person take his or her own life.

asthma A chronic respiratory disease characterized by sudden attacks of coughing, wheezing, and difficulty in breathing.

attachment Reciprocal, enduring tie between two people—especially between infant and caregiver—each of whom contributes to the quality of the relationship.

attention-deficit/hyperactivity disorder (ADHD) Syndrome characterized by persistent inattention and distractibility, impulsivity, low tolerance for frustration, and inappropriate overactivity.

authoritarian parenting In Baumrind's terminology, parenting style emphasizing control and obedience.

authoritative parenting In Baumrind's terminology, parenting style blending respect for a child's individuality with an effort to instill social values.

autobiographical memory Memory of specific events in one's life.

autoimmunity Tendency of an aging body to mistake its own tissues for foreign invaders and to attack and destroy them.

autonomy versus shame and doubt Erikson's second stage in psychosocial development, in which children achieve a balance between self-determination and control by others.

autosomes In humans, the 22 pairs of chromosomes not related to sexual expression.

avoidant attachment Pattern in which an infant rarely cries when separated from the primary caregiver and avoids contact on his or her return.

basal metabolism Use of energy to maintain vital functions.

basic sense of trust versus mistrust Erikson's first stage in psychosocial development, in which infants develop a sense of the reliability of people and objects.

Bayley Scales of Infant and Toddler Development Standardized test of infants' and toddlers' mental and motor development.

behavioral genetics Quantitative study of relative hereditary and environmental influences on behavior.

behaviorism Learning theory that emphasizes the predictable role of environment in causing observable behavior.

behaviorist approach Approach to the study of cognitive development that is concerned with basic mechanics of learning.

behavior therapy Therapeutic approach using principles of learning theory to encourage desired behaviors or eliminate undesired ones; also called *behavior modification.*

bereavement Loss, due to death, of someone to whom one feels close and the process of adjustment to the loss.

bilingual Fluent in two languages.

bilingual education System of teaching non-English-speaking children in their native language while they learn English, and later switching to all-English instruction.

binge drinking Consuming five or more drinks on one occasion.

bioecological theory Bronfenbrenner's approach to understanding processes and contexts of human development that identifies five levels of environmental influence.

body image Descriptive and evaluative beliefs about one's appearance.

Brazelton Neonatal Behavioral Assessment Scale (NBAS) Neurological and behavioral test to measure neonate's responses to the environment.

bulimia nervosa Eating disorder in which a person regularly eats huge quantities of food and then purges the body by laxatives, induced vomiting, fasting, or excessive exercise.

bullying Aggression deliberately and persistently directed against a particular target, or victim, typically one who is weak, vulnerable, and defenseless.

canalization Limitation on variance of expression of certain inherited characteristics.

caregiver burnout Condition of physical, mental, and emotional exhaustion affecting adults who provide continuous care for sick or aged persons.

case study Study of a single subject, such as an individual or family.

cataracts Cloudy or opaque areas in the lens of the eye, which cause blurred vision.

cell death In brain development, normal elimination of excess brain cells to achieve more efficient functioning.

central executive In Baddeley's model, element of working memory that controls the processing of information.

central nervous system Brain and spinal cord.

centration In Piaget's theory, the tendency of preoperational children to focus on one aspect of a situation and neglect others.

cephalocaudal principle Principle that development proceeds in a head-to-tail direction, that is, that upper parts of the body develop before lower parts of the trunk.

cesarean delivery Delivery of a baby by surgical removal from the uterus.

child-directed speech (CDS) Form of speech often used in talking to babies or toddlers; includes slow, simplified speech, a high-pitched tone, exaggerated vowel sounds, short words and sentences, and much repetition; also called *parentese* or *motherese.*

childhood depression Mood disorder characterized by such symptoms as a prolonged sense of friendlessness, inability to have fun or concentrate, fatigue, extreme activity or apathy, feelings of worthlessness, weight change, physical complaints, and thoughts of death or suicide.

chromosomes Coils of DNA that consist of genes.

chronic medical conditions Illnesses or impairments that persist for at least 3 months.

circular reactions Piaget's term for processes by which an infant learns to reproduce desired occurrences originally discovered by chance.

classical conditioning Learning based on associating a stimulus that does not ordinarily elicit a response with another stimulus that does elicit the response.

class inclusion Understanding of the relationship between a whole and its parts.

code mixing Use of elements of two languages, sometimes in the same utterance, by young children in households where both languages are spoken.

code switching Changing one's speech to match the situation, as in people who are bilingual.

cognitive-appraisal model Model of coping, proposed by Lazarus and Folkman, that holds that, on the basis of continuous appraisal of their relationship with the environment, people choose appropriate coping strategies to deal with situations that tax their normal resources.

cognitive development Pattern of change in mental abilities, such as learning, attention, memory, language, thinking, reasoning, and creativity.

cognitive neuroscience Study of links between neural processes and cognitive abilities.

cognitive neuroscience approach Approach to the study of cognitive development that links brain processes with cognitive ones.

cognitive perspective View that thought processes are central to development.

cognitive reserve Hypothesized fund of energy that may enable a deteriorating brain to continue to function normally.

cognitive-stage theory Piaget's theory that children's cognitive development advances in a series of four stages involving qualitatively distinct types of mental operations.

cohort A group of people born at about the same time.

commitment Marcia's term for personal investment in an occupation or system of beliefs.

committed compliance Kochanska's term for wholehearted obedience of a parent's orders without reminders or lapses.

componential element Sternberg's term for the analytic aspect of intelligence.

conceptual knowledge Acquired interpretive understandings stored in long-term memory.

concordant Term describing tendency of twins to share the same trait or disorder.

concrete operations Third stage of Piagetian cognitive development (approximately ages 7 to 12), during which children develop logical but not abstract thinking.

conduct disorder (CD) Repetitive, persistent pattern of aggressive, antisocial behavior violating societal norms or the rights of others.

conscience Internal standards of behavior, which usually control one's conduct and produce emotional discomfort when violated.

conservation Piaget's term for awareness that two objects that are equal according to a certain measure remain equal in the face of perceptual alteration so long as nothing has been added to or taken away from either object.

constructive play Play involving use of objects or materials to make something.

contextual element Sternberg's term for the practical aspect of intelligence.

contextual perspective View of human development that sees the individual as inseparable from the social context.

continuity theory Theory of aging, described by Atchley, that holds that in order to age successfully people must maintain a balance of continuity and change in both the internal and external structures of their lives.

control group In an experiment, a group of people, similar to those in the experimental group, who do not receive the treatment under study.

conventional morality (or morality of conventional role conformity) Second level in Kohlberg's theory of moral reasoning in which standards of authority figures are internalized.

convergent thinking Thinking aimed at finding the one right answer to a problem.

coping Adaptive thinking or behavior aimed at reducing or relieving stress that arises from harmful, threatening, or challenging conditions.

coregulation Transitional stage in the control of behavior in which parents exercise general supervision and children exercise moment-to-moment self-regulation.

corporal punishment Use of physical force with the intention of causing pain but not injury so as to correct or control behavior.

correlational study Research design intended to discover whether a statistical relationship between variables exists.

creativity Ability to see situations in a new way, to produce innovations, or to discern previously unidentified problems and find novel solutions.

crisis Marcia's term for period of conscious decision making related to identity formation.

critical period Specific time when a given event or its absence has a specific impact on development.

cross-modal transfer Ability to use information gained by one sense to guide another.

cross-sectional study Study designed to assess age-related differences, in which people of different ages are assessed on one occasion.

crystallized intelligence Type of intelligence, proposed by Horn and Cattell, involving the ability to remember and use learned information; it is largely dependent on education and culture.

cultural socialization Parental practices that teach children about their racial/ethnic heritage and promote cultural practices and cultural pride.

culture A society's or group's total way of life, including customs, traditions, beliefs, values, language, and physical products—all learned behavior, passed on from parents to children.

culture-fair tests Intelligence tests that deal with experiences common to various cultures, in an attempt to avoid cultural bias.

culture-free tests Intelligence tests that, if they were possible to design, would have no culturally linked content.

decenter In Piaget's terminology, to think simultaneously about several aspects of a situation.

declarative knowledge Acquired factual knowledge stored in long-term memory.

decoding Process of phonetic analysis by which a printed word is converted to spoken form before retrieval from long-term memory.

deductive reasoning Type of logical reasoning that moves from a general premise about a class to a conclusion about a particular member or members of the class.

deferred imitation Piaget's term for reproduction of an observed behavior after the passage of time by calling up a stored symbol of it.

dementia Deterioration in cognitive and behavioral functioning due to physiological causes.

Denver Developmental Screening Test Screening test given to children 1 month to 6 years old to determine whether they are developing normally.

deoxyribonucleic acid (DNA) Chemical that carries inherited instructions for the development of all cellular forms of life.

dependent variable In an experiment, the condition that may or may not change as a result of changes in the independent variable.

depth perception Ability to perceive objects and surfaces three-dimensionally.

diabetes (1) One of the most common diseases of childhood. It is characterized by high levels of glucose in the blood as a result of defective insulin production, ineffective insulin action, or both. (2) Disease in which the body does not produce or properly use *insulin,* a hormone that converts sugar, starches, and other foods into energy needed for daily life.

differentiation Process by which cells acquire specialized structures and functions.

"difficult" children Children with irritable temperament, irregular biological rhythms, and intense emotional responses.

discipline Methods of molding children's character and of teaching them to exercise self-control and engage in acceptable behavior.

disengagement theory Theory of aging that holds that successful aging is characterized by mutual withdrawal of the older person and society.

dishabituation Increase in responsiveness after presentation of a new stimulus.

disorganized-disoriented attachment Pattern in which an infant, after separation from the primary caregiver, shows contradictory, repetitious, or misdirected behaviors on his or her return.

divergent thinking Thinking that produces a variety of fresh, diverse possibilities.

dizygotic twins Twins conceived by the union of two different ova (or a single ovum that has split) with two different sperm cells; also called *fraternal twins*; they are no more alike genetically than any other siblings.

dominant inheritance Pattern of inheritance in which, when a child receives different alleles, only the dominant one is expressed.

doula An experienced mentor who furnishes emotional support and information for a woman during labor.

Down syndrome Chromosomal disorder characterized by moderate-to-severe mental retardation and by such physical signs as a downward-sloping skin fold at the inner corners of the eyes. Also called *trisomy-21.*

dramatic play Play involving imaginary people or situations; also called *pretend play, fantasy play,* or *imaginative play.*

drug therapy Administration of drugs to treat emotional disorders.

dual representation hypothesis Proposal that children under age 3 have difficulty grasping spatial relationships because of the need to keep more than one mental representation in mind at the same time.

durable power of attorney Legal instrument that appoints an individual to make decisions in the event of another person's incapacitation.

dynamic systems theory (DST) Esther Thelen's theory, which holds that motor development is a dynamic process of active coordination of multiple systems within the infant in relation to the environment.

dynamic tests Tests based on Vygotsky's theory that emphasize potential rather than past learning.

dyslexia Developmental disorder in which reading achievement is substantially lower than predicted by IQ or age.

early intervention Systematic process of providing services to help families meet young children's developmental needs.

"easy" children Children with a generally happy temperament, regular biological rhythms, and a readiness to accept new experiences.

ecological theory of perception Theory developed by Eleanor and James Gibson, which describes developing motor and perceptual abilities as interdependent parts of a functional system that guides behavior in varying contexts.

egocentrism Piaget's term for inability to consider another person's point of view; a characteristic of young children's thought.

ego-control Self-control and the self-regulation of impulses.

ego integrity versus despair According to Erikson, the eighth and final stage of psychosocial development, in which people in late adulthood either achieve a sense of integrity of the self by accepting the lives they have lived, and thus accept death, or yield to despair that their lives cannot be relived.

ego-resiliency (1) Dynamic capacity to modify one's level of ego-control in response to environmental and contextual influences. (2) The ability to adapt flexibly and resourcefully to potential sources of stress.

elaboration Mnemonic strategy of making mental associations involving items to be remembered.

electronic fetal monitoring Mechanical monitoring of fetal heartbeat during labor and delivery.

elicited imitation Research method in which infants or toddlers are induced to imitate a specific series of actions they have seen but not necessarily done before.

embryonic stage Second stage of gestation (2 to 8 weeks), characterized by rapid growth and development of major body systems and organs.

emergent literacy Preschoolers' development of skills, knowledge, and attitudes that underlie reading and writing.

emerging adulthood Proposed transitional period between adolescence and adulthood commonly found in industrialized countries.

emotional intelligence (EI) Salovey and Mayer's term for the ability to understand and regulate emotions; an important component of effective, intelligent behavior.

emotional maltreatment Rejection, terrorization, isolation, exploitation, degradation, ridicule, or failure to provide emotional support, love, and affection; or other action or inaction that may cause behavioral, cognitive, emotional, or mental disorders.

emotion-focused coping In the cognitive-appraisal model, coping strategy directed toward managing the emotional response to a stressful situation so as to lessen its physical or psychological impact.

emotions Subjective reactions to experience that are associated with physiological and behavioral changes.

empathy Ability to put oneself in another person's place and feel what the other person feels.

empty nest Transitional phase of parenting following the last child's leaving the parents' home.

encapsulation In Hoyer's terminology, the process that allows expertise to compensate for declines in information-processing ability by bundling relevant knowledge together.

encoding Process by which information is prepared for long-term storage and later retrieval.

English-immersion approach Approach to teaching English as a second language in which instruction is presented only in English.

enrichment programs Programs for educating the gifted that broaden and deepen knowledge and skills through extra activities, projects, field trips, or mentoring.

enuresis Repeated urination in clothing or in bed.

environment Totality of nonhereditary, or experiential, influences on development.

epigenesis Mechanism that turns genes on or off and determines functions of body cells.

episodic memory Long-term memory of specific experiences or events, linked to time and place.

equilibration Piaget's term for the tendency to seek a stable balance among cognitive elements; achieved through a balance between assimilation and accommodation.

erectile dysfunction Inability of a man to achieve or maintain an erect penis sufficient for satisfactory sexual performance.

ethnic gloss Overgeneralization about an ethnic or cultural group that obscures differences within the group.

ethnic group A group united by ancestry, race, religion, language, or national origins, which contribute to a sense of shared identity.

ethnographic study In-depth study of a culture, which uses a combination of methods including participant observation.

ethology Study of distinctive adaptive behaviors of species of animals that have evolved to increase survival of the species.

evolutionary psychology Application of Darwinian principles of natural selection and survival of the fittest to individual behavior.

evolutionary/sociobiological perspective View of human development that focuses on evolutionary and biological bases of behavior.

executive function Conscious control of thoughts, emotions, and actions to accomplish goals or solve problems.

experiential element Sternberg's term for the insightful or creative aspect of intelligence.

experiment Rigorously controlled, replicable procedure in which the researcher manipulates variables to assess the effect of one on the other.

experimental group In an experiment, the group receiving the treatment under study.

explicit memory Intentional and conscious memory, generally of facts, names, and events.

extended family Multigenerational kinship network of parents, children, and other relatives, sometimes living together in an extended-family household.

externalizing behaviors Behaviors by which a child acts out emotional difficulties; for example, aggression or hostility.

external memory aids Mnemonic strategies using something outside the person.

family therapy Psychological treatment in which a therapist sees the whole family together to analyze patterns of family functioning.

fast mapping Process by which a child absorbs the meaning of a new word after hearing it once or twice in conversation.

fertilization Union of sperm and ovum to produce a zygote; also called *conception*.

fetal alcohol syndrome (FAS) Combination of mental, motor, and developmental abnormalities affecting the offspring of some women who drink heavily during pregnancy.

fetal stage Final stage of gestation (from 8 weeks to birth), characterized by increased differentiation of body parts and greatly enlarged body size.

fictive kin Friends who are considered and behave like family members.

fidelity Sustained loyalty, faith, or sense of belonging that results from the successful resolution of Erikson's *identity versus identity confusion* psychosocial stage of development.

filial crisis In Marcoen's terminology, normative development of middle age, in which adults learn to balance love and duty to their parents with autonomy within a two-way relationship.

filial maturity Stage of life, proposed by Marcoen and others, in which middle-aged children, as the outcome of a filial crisis, learn to accept and meet their parents' need to depend on them.

fine motor skills Physical skills that involve the small muscles and eye–hand coordination.

five-factor model Theoretical model of personality, developed and tested by Costa and McCrae, based on the "Big Five" factors underlying clusters of related personality traits: neuroticism, extraversion, openness to experience, conscientiousness, and agreeableness.

fluid intelligence Type of intelligence, proposed by Horn and Cattell, that is applied to novel problems and is relatively independent of educational and cultural influences.

foreclosure Identity status, described by Marcia, in which a person who has not spent time considering alternatives (that is, has not been in crisis) is committed to other people's plans for his or her life.

formal games with rules Organized games with known procedures and penalties.

formal operations Piaget's final stage of cognitive development, characterized by the ability to think abstractly.

free radicals Unstable, highly reactive atoms or molecules, formed during metabolism, that can cause internal bodily damage.

functional age Measure of a person's ability to function effectively in his or her physical and social environment in comparison with others of the same chronological age.

functional play Play involving repetitive large muscular movements.

gender Significance of being male or female.

gender constancy Awareness that one will always be male or female; also called *sex-category constancy.*

gender crossover Gutmann's term for reversal of gender roles after the end of active parenting.

gender identity Awareness, developed in early childhood, that one is male or female.

gender roles Behaviors, interests, attitudes, skills, and traits that a culture considers appropriate for each sex; differ for males and females.

gender-schema theory Theory, proposed by Bem, that children socialize themselves in their gender roles by developing a mentally organized network of information about what it means to be male or female in a particular culture.

gender segregation Tendency to select playmates of one's own gender.

gender stereotypes Preconceived generalizations about male or female role behavior.

gender-typing Socialization process by which children, at an early age, learn appropriate gender roles.

generalized anxiety disorder Anxiety not focused on any single target.

generativity Erikson's term for concern of mature adults for finding meaning through contributing to society and leaving a legacy for future generations.

generativity versus stagnation Erikson's seventh stage of psychosocial development, in which the middle-aged adult develops a concern with establishing, guiding, and influencing the next generation or else experiences stagnation (a sense of inactivity or lifelessness).

generic memory Memory that produces scripts of familiar routines to guide behavior.

genes Small segments of DNA located in definite positions on particular chromosomes; functional units of heredity.

genetic code Sequence of bases within the DNA molecule; governs the formation of proteins that determine the structure and functions of living cells.

genetic counseling Clinical service that advises prospective parents of their probable risk of having children with hereditary defects.

genetic-programming theories Theories that explain biological aging as resulting from a genetically determined developmental timetable.

genotype Genetic makeup of a person, containing both expressed and unexpressed characteristics.

genotype-environment correlation Tendency of certain genetic and environmental influences to reinforce each other; may be passive, reactive (evocative), or active. Also called *genotype-environment covariance.*

genotype-environment interaction The portion of phenotypic variation that results from the reactions of genetically different individuals to similar environmental conditions.

geriatrics Branch of medicine concerned with processes of aging and medical conditions associated with old age.

germinal stage First 2 weeks of prenatal development, characterized by rapid cell division, blastocyst formation, and implantation in the wall of the uterus.

gerontology Study of the aged and the process of aging.

gestation Period of development between conception and birth.

gestational age Age of an unborn baby, usually dated from the first day of an expectant mother's last menstrual cycle.

glaucoma Irreversible damage to the optic nerve caused by increased pressure in the eye.

goodness of fit Appropriateness of environmental demands and constraints to a child's temperament.

grief Emotional response experienced in the early phases of bereavement.

grief work Working out of psychological issues connected with grief.

gross motor skills Physical skills that involve the large muscles.

guided participation Adult's participation in a child's activity that helps to structure it and bring the child's understanding of it closer to the adult's.

habituation Type of learning in which familiarity with a stimulus reduces, slows, or stops a response.

handedness Preference for using a particular hand.

haptic perception Ability to acquire information about properties of objects, such as size, weight, and texture, by handling them.

Hayflick limit Genetically controlled limit, proposed by Hayflick, on the number of times cells can divide in members of a species.

heredity Inborn traits or characteristics inherited from the biological parents.

heritability Statistical estimate of contribution of heredity to individual differences in a specific trait within a given population.

heterozygous Possessing differing alleles for a trait.

historical generation A group of people strongly influenced by a major historical event during their formative period.

holophrase Single word that conveys a complete thought.

Home Observation for Measurement of the Environment (HOME) Instrument to measure the influence of the home environment on children's cognitive growth.

homozygous Possessing two identical alleles for a trait.

hormone therapy (HT) Treatment with artificial estrogen, sometimes in combination with the hormone progesterone, to relieve or prevent symptoms caused by decline in estrogen levels after menopause.

hospice care Personal, patient- and family-centered care for a person with a terminal illness.

hostile attribution bias Tendency to perceive others as trying to hurt one and to strike out in retaliation or self-defense.

human development Scientific study of processes of change and stability throughout the human life span.

human genome Complete sequence of genes in the human body.

hypertension Chronically high blood pressure.

hypotheses Possible explanations for phenomena, used to predict the outcome of research.

hypothetical-deductive reasoning Ability, believed by Piaget, to accompany the stage of formal operations, to develop, consider, and test hypotheses.

ideal self The self one would like to be.

identification In Freudian theory, the process by which a young child adopts characteristics, beliefs, attitudes, values, and behaviors of the parent of the same sex.

identity According to Erikson, a coherent conception of the self, made up of goals, values, and beliefs to which a person is solidly committed.

identity accommodation Whitbourne's term for adjusting the self-concept to fit new experience.

identity achievement Identity status, described by Marcia, that is characterized by commitment to choices made following a crisis, a period spent in exploring alternatives.

identity assimilation Whitbourne's term for effort to fit new experience into an existing self-concept.

identity balance Whitbourne's term for a tendency to balance assimilation and accommodation.

identity diffusion Identity status, described by Marcia, that is characterized by absence of commitment and lack of serious consideration of alternatives.

identity process theory (IPT) Whitbourne's theory of identity development based on processes of assimilation and accommodation.

identity schemas Accumulated perceptions of the self shaped by incoming information from intimate relationships, work-related situations, and community and other experiences.

identity statuses Marcia's term for states of ego development that depend on the presence or absence of crisis and commitment.

identity versus identity confusion Erikson's fifth stage of psychosocial development, in which an adolescent seeks to develop a coherent sense of self, including the role she or he is to play in society. Also called *identity versus role confusion.*

implantation The attachment of the blastocyst to the uterine wall, occurring at about day 6.

implicit memory Unconscious recall, generally of habits and skills; sometimes called *procedural memory.*

imprinting Instinctive form of learning in which, during a critical period in early development, a young animal forms an attachment to the first moving object it sees, usually the mother.

incomplete dominance Pattern of inheritance in which a child receives two different alleles, resulting in partial expression of a trait.

independent variable In an experiment, the condition over which the experimenter has direct control.

individual differences Differences in characteristics, influences, or developmental outcomes.

individual psychotherapy Psychological treatment in which a therapist sees a troubled person one-on-one.

individuation (1) Adolescents' struggle for autonomy and personal identity. (2) Jung's term for emergence of the true self through balancing or integration of conflicting parts of the personality.

inductive reasoning Type of logical reasoning that moves from particular observations about members of a class to a general conclusion about that class.

inductive techniques Disciplinary techniques designed to induce desirable behavior by appealing to a child's sense of reason and fairness.

industry versus inferiority Erikson's fourth stage of psychosocial development, in which children must learn the productive skills their culture requires or else face feelings of inferiority.

infant mortality rate Proportion of babies born alive who die within the 1st year.

infertility Inability to conceive a child after 12 months of sexual intercourse without the use of birth control.

information-processing approach (1) Approach to the study of cognitive development by observing and analyzing the mental processes involved in perceiving and handling information. (2) Approach to the study of cognitive development that analyzes processes involved in perceiving and handling information.

initiative versus guilt Erikson's third stage in psychosocial development, in which children balance the urge to pursue goals with reservations about doing so.

instrumental aggression Aggressive behavior used as a means of achieving a goal.

integration Process by which neurons coordinate the activities of muscle groups.

intellectual disability Significantly subnormal cognitive functioning. Also referred to as cognitive disability or mental retardation.

intelligent behavior Behavior that is goal oriented and adaptive to circumstances and conditions of life.

interiority Neugarten's term for a concern with inner life (introversion or introspection), which usually appears in middle age.

internalization During socialization, process by which children accept societal standards of conduct as their own.

internalizing behaviors Behaviors by which emotional problems are turned inward; for example, anxiety or depression.

intimacy versus isolation Erikson's sixth stage of psychosocial development, in which young adults either form strong, long-lasting bonds with friends and romantic partners or face a possible sense of isolation and self-absorption.

invisible imitation Imitation with parts of one's body that one cannot see.

IQ (intelligence quotient) tests Psychometric tests that seek to measure intelligence by comparing a test-taker's performance with standardized norms.

irreversibility Piaget's term for a preoperational child's failure to understand that an operation can go in two or more directions.

kangaroo care Method of skin-to-skin contact in which a newborn is laid face down between the mother's breasts for an hour or so at a time after birth.

Kaufman Assessment Battery for Children (K-ABC-II) Nontraditional individual intelligence test designed to provide fair assessments of minority children and children with disabilities.

kinship care Care of children living without parents in the home of grandparents or other relatives, with or without a change of legal custody.

laboratory observation Research method in which all participants are observed under the same controlled conditions.

language Communication system based on words and grammar.

language acquisition device (LAD) In Chomsky's terminology, an inborn mechanism that enables children to infer linguistic rules from the language they hear.

lateralization Tendency of each of the brain's hemispheres to have specialized functions.

learning disabilities (LDs) Disorders that interfere with specific aspects of learning and school achievement.

learning perspective View of human development that holds that changes in behavior result from experience or from adaptation to the environment.

life expectancy Age to which a person in a particular cohort is statistically likely to live (given his or her current age and health status), on the basis of average longevity of a population.

life review Reminiscence about one's life in order to see its significance.

life span The longest period that members of a species can live.

life-span development Concept of human development as a lifelong process, which can be studied scientifically.

linguistic speech Verbal expression designed to convey meaning.

literacy (1) Ability to read and write. (2) In an adult, ability to use printed and written information to function in society, achieve goals, and develop knowledge and potential.

longevity Length of an individual's life.

longitudinal study Study designed to assess age changes in a sample over time.

long-term memory Storage of virtually unlimited capacity that holds information for long periods.

low-birth-weight babies Weight of less than 5½ pounds (2500 grams) at birth because of prematurity or being small-for-date.

mammography Diagnostic X-ray examination of the breasts.

marital capital Financial and emotional benefits built up during a long-standing marriage, which tend to hold a couple together.

maturation Unfolding of a natural sequence of physical and behavioral changes.

mechanistic model Model that views human development as a series of predictable responses to stimuli.

menarche Girl's first menstruation.

menopause Cessation of menstruation and of ability to bear children.

metacognition Thinking about thinking, or awareness of one's own mental processes.

metamemory Understanding of processes of memory.

midlife crisis In some normative-crisis models, stressful life period precipitated by the review and reevaluation of one's past, typically occurring in the early to middle 40s.

midlife review Introspective examination that often occurs in middle age, leading to reappraisal and revision of values and priorities.

mirror neurons Neurons that fire when a person does something or observes someone else doing the same thing.

mnemonic device Strategy to aid memory.

monozygotic twins Twins resulting from the division of a single zygote after fertilization; also called *identical twins*; they are genetically similar.

moratorium Identity status, described by Marcia, in which a person is currently considering alternatives (in crisis) and seems headed for commitment.

multifactorial transmission Combination of genetic and environmental factors to produce certain complex traits.

mutations Permanent alterations in genes or chromosomes that may produce harmful characteristics.

mutual regulation Process by which infant and caregiver communicate emotional states to each other and respond appropriately.

myelination Process of coating neural pathways with a fatty substance called myelin, which enables faster communication between cells.

myopia Nearsightedness.

nativism Theory that human beings have an inborn capacity for language acquisition.

natural childbirth Method of childbirth that seeks to prevent pain by eliminating the mother's fear through education about the physiology of reproduction and training in breathing and relaxation during delivery.

naturalistic observation Research method in which behavior is studied in natural settings without intervention or manipulation.

neglect Failure to meet a dependent's basic needs.

neonatal jaundice Condition, in many newborn babies, caused by immaturity of liver and evidenced by yellowish appearance; can cause brain damage if not treated promptly.

neonatal period First 4 weeks of life, a time of transition from intrauterine dependency to independent existence.

neonate Newborn baby, up to 4 weeks old.

neurofibrillary tangles Twisted masses of protein fibers found in brains of persons with Alzheimer's disease.

neurons Nerve cells.

niche-picking Tendency of a person, especially after early childhood, to seek out environments compatible with his or her genotype.

nonnormative Characteristic of an unusual event that happens to a particular person or a typical event that happens at an unusual time of life.

nonorganic failure to thrive Slowed or arrested physical growth with no known medical cause, accompanied by poor developmental and emotional functioning.

nonshared environmental effects The unique environment in which each child grows up, consisting of distinctive influences or influences that affect one child differently than another.

normative Characteristic of an event that occurs in a similar way for most people in a group.

normative life events In the timing-of-events model, commonly expected life experiences that occur at customary times.

normative-stage models Theoretical models that describe psychosocial development in terms of a definite sequence of age-related changes.

nuclear family Two-generational kinship, economic, and household unit consisting of one or two parents and their biological children, adopted children, or stepchildren.

obesity Extreme overweight in relation to age, sex, height, and body type as defined by having a body mass index at or above the 95th percentile.

object permanence Piaget's term for the understanding that a person or object still exists when out of sight.

observational learning Learning through watching the behavior of others.

obsessive-compulsive disorder (OCD) Anxiety aroused by repetitive, intrusive thoughts, images, or impulses, often leading to compulsive ritual behaviors.

operant conditioning (1) Learning based on association of behavior with its consequences. (2) Learning based on reinforcement or punishment.

operational definition Definition stated solely in terms of the operations or procedures used to produce or measure a phenomenon.

oppositional defiant disorder (ODD) Pattern of behavior, persisting into middle childhood, marked by negativity, hostility, and defiance.

organismic model Model that views human development as internally initiated by an active organism and as occurring in a sequence of qualitatively different stages.

organization (1) Piaget's term for the creation of categories or systems of knowledge. (2) Mnemonic strategy of categorizing material to be remembered.

osteoporosis Condition in which the bones become thin and brittle as a result of rapid calcium depletion.

Otis-Lennon School Ability Test (OLSAT 8) Group intelligence test for kindergarten through 12th grade.

overt (direct) aggression Aggression that is openly directed at its target.

palliative care Care aimed at relieving pain and suffering and allowing the terminally ill to die in peace, comfort, and dignity.

Parkinson's disease Progressive, irreversible degenerative neurological disorder, characterized by tremor, stiffness, slowed movement, and unstable posture.

participant observation Research method in which the observer lives with the people or participates in the activity being observed.

parturition The act or process of giving birth.

passive euthanasia Withholding or discontinuation of life-prolonging treatment of a terminally ill person in order to end suffering or allow death with dignity.

perimenopause Period of several years during which a woman experiences physiological changes of menopause; includes first year after end of menstruation; also called *climacteric.*

permissive parenting In Baumrind's terminology, parenting style emphasizing self-expression and self-regulation.

personality The relatively consistent blend of emotions, temperament, thought, and behavior that makes a person unique.

phenotype Observable characteristics of a person.

phonetic (code-emphasis) approach Approach to teaching reading that emphasizes decoding of unfamiliar words.

physical abuse Action taken deliberately to endanger another person, involving potential bodily injury.

physical development Growth of body and brain, including patterns of change in sensory capacities, motor skills, and health.

Piagetian approach Approach to the study of cognitive development that describes qualitative stages in cognitive functioning.

plasticity (1) Range of modifiability of performance. (2) Modifiability, or "molding," of the brain through experience.

play therapy Therapeutic approach that uses play to help a child cope with emotional distress.

polygenic inheritance Pattern of inheritance in which multiple genes at different sites on chromosomes affect a complex trait.

postconventional morality (or morality of autonomous moral principles) Third level of Kohlberg's theory of moral reasoning, in which people follow internally held moral principles and can decide among conflicting moral standards.

postformal thought Mature type of thinking that relies on subjective experience and intuition as well as logic and allows room for ambiguity, uncertainty, inconsistency, contradiction, imperfection, and compromise.

postmature A fetus not yet born as of 2 weeks after the due date or 42 weeks after the mother's last menstrual period.

power assertion Disciplinary strategy designed to discourage undesirable behavior through physical or verbal enforcement of parental control.

pragmatics (1) The practical knowledge needed to use language for communicative purposes. (2) The social context of language.

preconventional morality First level of Kohlberg's theory of moral reasoning in which control is external and rules are obeyed in order to gain rewards or avoid punishment or out of self-interest.

prejudice Unfavorable attitude toward members of certain groups outside one's own, especially racial or ethnic groups.

prelinguistic speech Forerunner of linguistic speech; utterance of sounds that are not words. Includes crying, cooing, babbling, and accidental and deliberate imitation of sounds without understanding their meaning.

premenstrual syndrome (PMS) Disorder producing symptoms of physical discomfort and emotional tension for up to 2 weeks before a menstrual period.

preoperational stage In Piaget's theory, the second major stage of cognitive development, in which symbolic thought expands but children cannot yet use logic.

prepared childbirth Method of childbirth that uses instruction, breathing exercises, and social support to induce controlled physical responses to uterine contractions and reduce fear and pain.

presbycusis Age-related, gradual loss of hearing, which accelerates after age 55, especially with regard to sounds at higher frequencies.

presbyopia Age-related, progressive loss of the eyes' ability to focus on nearby objects due to loss of elasticity in the lens.

pretend play Play involving imaginary people and situations; also called *fantasy play, dramatic play,* or *imaginative play.*

preterm (premature) infants Infants born before completing the 37th week of gestation.

primary aging Gradual, inevitable process of bodily deterioration throughout the life span.

primary sex characteristics Organs directly related to reproduction, which enlarge and mature during adolescence.

private speech Talking aloud to oneself with no intent to communicate with others.

problem-focused coping In the cognitive-appraisal model, coping strategy directed toward eliminating, managing, or improving a stressful situation.

procedural knowledge Acquired skills stored in long-term memory.

procedural memory Long-term memory of motor skills, habits, and ways of doing things, which can be recalled without conscious effort; sometimes called *implicit memory.*

prosocial behavior Any voluntary behavior intended to help others.

protective factors (1) Influences that reduce the impact of potentially negative influences and tend to predict positive outcomes. (2) Influences that reduce the impact of early stress and tend to predict positive outcomes.

proximodistal principle Principle that development proceeds from within to without, that is, that parts of the body near the center develop before the extremities.

psychoanalytic perspective View of human development as shaped by unconscious forces that motivate human behavior.

psychometric approach Approach to the study of cognitive development that seeks to measure intelligence quantitatively.

psychosexual development In Freudian theory, an unvarying sequence of stages of childhood personality development in which gratification shifts from the mouth to the anus and then to the genitals.

psychosocial development (1) Pattern of change in emotions, personality, and social relationships. (2) In Erikson's eight-stage theory, the socially and culturally influenced process of development of the ego, or self.

puberty Process by which a person attains sexual maturity and the ability to reproduce.

punishment The process by which a behavior is weakened, decreasing the likelihood of repetition.

qualitative change Discontinuous changes in kind, structure, or organization.

qualitative research Research that focuses on nonnumerical data, such as subjective experiences, feelings, or beliefs.

quantitative change Changes in number or amount, such as in height, weight, size of vocabulary, or frequency of communication.

quantitative research Research that deals with objectively measurable data.

random assignment Assignment of participants in an experiment to groups in such a way that each person has an equal chance of being placed in any group.

random selection Selection of a sample in such a way that each person in a population has an equal and independent chance of being chosen.

reaction range Potential variability, depending on environmental conditions, in the expression of a hereditary trait.

real self The self one actually is.

recall Ability to reproduce material from memory.

recentering Process that underlies the shift to an adult identity.

receptive cooperation Kochanska's term for eager willingness to cooperate harmoniously with a parent in daily interactions, including routines, chores, hygiene, and play.

recessive inheritance Pattern of inheritance in which a child receives identical recessive alleles, resulting in expression of a nondominant trait.

reciprocal determinism Bandura's term for bidirectional forces that affect development.

recognition Ability to identify a previously encountered stimulus.

reflective thinking Type of logical thinking that becomes more prominent in adulthood, involving continuous, active evaluation of information and beliefs in the light of evidence and implications.

reflex behaviors Automatic, involuntary, innate responses to stimulation.

rehearsal Mnemonic strategy to keep an item in working memory through conscious repetition.

reinforcement The process by which a behavior is strengthened, increasing the likelihood that the behavior will be repeated.

relational (social or indirect) aggression Aggression aimed at damaging or interfering with another person's relationships, reputation, or psychological well-being.

representational ability Piaget's term for capacity to store mental images or symbols of objects and events.

representational mappings In neo-Piagetian terminology, second stage in development of self-definition, in which a child makes logical connections between aspects of the self but still sees these characteristics in all-or-nothing terms.

representational systems In neo-Piagetian terminology, the third stage in development of self-definition, characterized by breadth, balance, and the integration and assessment of various aspects of the self.

reserve capacity Ability of body organs and systems to put forth 4 to 10 times as much effort as usual under acute stress; also called *organ reserve.*

resilient children Children who weather adverse circumstances, function well despite challenges or threats, or bounce back from traumatic events.

retrieval Process by which information is accessed or recalled from memory storage.

revolving door syndrome Tendency for young adults who have left home to return to their parents' household in times of financial, marital, or other trouble.

risk factors Conditions that increase the likelihood of a negative developmental outcome.

risky drinking Consuming more than 14 drinks a week or 4 drinks on any single day for men, and more than 7 drinks a week or 3 drinks on any single day for women.

rough-and-tumble play Vigorous play involving wrestling, hitting, and chasing, often accompanied by laughing and screaming.

sample Group of participants chosen to represent the entire population under study.

sandwich generation Middle-aged adults squeezed by competing needs to raise or launch children and to care for elderly parents.

scaffolding Temporary support to help a child master a task.

schemes Piaget's term for organized patterns of thought and behavior used in particular situations.

schizophrenia Mental disorder marked by loss of contact with reality; symptoms include hallucinations and delusions.

school phobia Unrealistic fear of going to school; may be a form of *separation anxiety disorder* or *social phobia.*

scientific method System of established principles and processes of scientific inquiry, which includes identifying a problem to be studied, formulating a hypothesis to be tested by research, collecting data, analyzing the data, forming tentative conclusions, and disseminating findings.

script General remembered outline of a familiar, repeated event, used to guide behavior.

secondary aging Aging processes that result from disease and bodily abuse and disuse and are often preventable.

secondary sex characteristics Physiological signs of sexual maturation (such as breast development and growth of body hair) that do not involve the sex organs.

secular trend Trend that can be seen only by observing several generations, such as the trend toward earlier attainment of adult height and sexual maturity, which began a century ago in some countries.

secure attachment Pattern in which an infant cries or protests when the primary caregiver leaves and actively seeks out the caregiver on his or her return.

selective optimization with compensation (SOC) Enhancing overall cognitive functioning by using stronger abilities to compensate for those that have weakened.

self-awareness Realization that one's existence and functioning are separate from those of other people and things.

self-concept Sense of self; descriptive and evaluative mental picture of one's abilities and traits.

self-conscious emotions Emotions, such as embarrassment, empathy, and envy, that depend on self-awareness.

self-definition Cluster of characteristics used to describe oneself.

self-efficacy Sense of one's capability to master challenges and achieve goals.

self-esteem The judgment a person makes about his or her self-worth.

self-evaluative emotions Emotions, such as pride, shame, and guilt, that depend on both self-awareness and knowledge of socially accepted standards of behavior.

self-regulation A child's independent control of behavior to conform to understood social expectations.

semantic memory Long-term memory of general factual knowledge, social customs, and language.

senescence Period of the life span marked by declines in physical functioning usually associated with aging; begins at different ages for different people.

sensitive periods Times in development when a person is particularly open to certain kinds of experiences.

sensorimotor stage Piaget's first stage in cognitive development, in which infants learn through senses and motor activity.

sensory memory Initial, brief, temporary storage of sensory information.

separation anxiety Distress shown by someone, typically an infant, when a familiar caregiver leaves.

separation anxiety disorder Condition involving excessive, prolonged anxiety concerning separation from home or from people to whom a person is attached.

sequential study Study design that combines cross-sectional and longitudinal techniques.

seriation Ability to order items along a dimension.

sex chromosomes Pair of chromosomes that determines sex: XX in the normal human female, XY in the normal human male.

sex-linked inheritance Pattern of inheritance in which certain characteristics carried on the X chromosome inherited from the mother are transmitted differently to her male and female offspring.

sexual abuse Physically or psychologically harmful sexual activity or any sexual activity involving a child and an older person.

sexually transmitted infections (STIs) Infections and diseases spread by sexual contact.

sexual orientation Focus of consistent sexual, romantic, and affectionate interest, either heterosexual, homosexual, or bisexual.

shaken baby syndrome Form of maltreatment in which shaking an infant or toddler can cause brain damage, paralysis, or death.

single representations In neo-Piagetian terminology, first stage in development of self-definition, in which children describe themselves in terms of individual, unconnected characteristics and in all-or-nothing terms.

situational compliance Kochanska's term for obedience of a parent's orders only in the presence of signs of ongoing parental control.

"slow-to-warm-up" children Children whose temperament is generally mild but who are hesitant about accepting new experiences.

small-for-date (small-for-gestational-age) infants Infants whose birth weight is less than that of 90 percent of babies of the same gestational age, as a result of slow fetal growth.

social capital Family and community resources on which a person can draw.

social clock Set of cultural norms or expectations for the times of life when certain important events, such as marriage, parenthood, entry into work, and retirement, should occur.

social cognition The ability to understand that others have mental states and to gauge their feelings and actions.

social cognitive theory Albert Bandura's expansion of social learning theory; holds that children learn gender roles through socialization.

social construction A concept or practice that may appear natural and obvious to those who accept it, but that in reality is an invention of a particular culture or society.

social-contextual approach Approach to the study of cognitive development that focuses on environmental influences, particularly parents and other caregivers.

social convoy theory Theory, proposed by Kahn and Antonucci, that people move through life surrounded by concentric circles of intimate relationships on which they rely for assistance, well-being, and social support.

social interaction model Model, based on Vygotsky's sociocultural theory, that proposes children construct autobiographical memories through conversation with adults about shared events.

socialization Development of habits, skills, values, and motives shared by responsible, productive members of a society.

social learning theory Theory that behaviors are learned by observing and imitating models. Also called *social cognitive theory.*

social phobia Extreme fear and/or avoidance of social situations.

social referencing Understanding an ambiguous situation by seeking another person's perception of it.

social smiling Beginning in the 2nd month, newborn infants gaze at their parents and smile at them, signaling positive participation in the relationship.

social speech Speech intended to be understood by a listener.

sociocultural theory Vygotsky's theory of how contextual factors affect children's development.

socioeconomic status (SES) Combination of economic and social factors describing an individual or family, including income, education, and occupation.

socioemotional selectivity theory Theory, proposed by Carstensen, that people select social contacts on the basis of the changing relative importance of social interaction as a source of information, as an aid in developing and maintaining a self-concept, and as a source of emotional well-being.

spermarche Boy's first ejaculation.

spillover hypothesis Hypothesis that there is a carryover of cognitive gains from work to leisure that explains the positive relationship between activities in the quality of intellectual functioning.

spontaneous abortion Natural expulsion from the uterus of an embryo that cannot survive outside the womb; also called *miscarriage.*

Stanford-Binet Intelligence Scales Individual intelligence tests for ages 2 and up used to measure fluid reasoning, knowledge, quantitative reasoning, visual-spatial processing, and working memory.

state of arousal An infant's physiological and behavioral status at a given moment in the periodic daily cycle of wakefulness, sleep, and activity.

stillbirth Death of a fetus at or after the 20th week of gestation.

storage Retention of information in memory for future use.

stranger anxiety Wariness of strange people and places, shown by some infants during the second half of the 1st year.

Strange Situation Laboratory technique used to study infant attachment.

stress (1) Physical or psychological demands on a person or organism. (2) Response to physical or psychological demands.

stressors Perceived environmental demands that may produce stress.

substance abuse Repeated, harmful use of a substance, usually alcohol or other drugs.

substance dependence Addiction (physical, or psychological, or both) to a harmful substance.

substantive complexity Degree to which a person's work requires thought and independent judgment.

sudden infant death syndrome (SIDS) Sudden and unexplained death of an apparently healthy infant.

survival curve A curve on a graph showing the percentage of people or animals alive at various ages.

symbolic function Piaget's term for ability to use mental representations (words, numbers, or images) to which a child has attached meaning.

syntax Rules for forming sentences in a particular language.

systems of action Increasingly complex combinations of motor skills, which permit a wider or more precise range of movement and more control of the environment.

tacit knowledge Sternberg's term for information that is not formally taught but is necessary to get ahead.

telegraphic speech Early form of sentence use consisting of only a few essential words.

temperament Characteristic disposition, or style of approaching and reacting to situations.

teratogen Environmental agent, such as a virus, a drug, or radiation, that can interfere with normal prenatal development and cause developmental abnormalities.

terminal drop A frequently observed decline in cognitive abilities near the end of life. Also called *terminal decline.*

thanatology Study of death and dying.

theory Coherent set of logically related concepts that seeks to organize, explain, and predict data.

theory of mind Awareness and understanding of mental processes.

theory of multiple intelligences Gardner's theory that each person has several distinct forms of intelligence.

theory of sexual selection Darwin's theory that gender roles developed in response to men's and women's differing reproductive needs.

timing-of-events model Theoretical model of personality development that describes adult psychosocial development as a response to the expected or unexpected occurrence and timing of important life events.

trait models Theoretical models of personality development that focus on mental, emotional, temperamental, and behavioral traits, or attributes.

transduction Piaget's term for a preoperational child's tendency to mentally link particular phenomena, whether or not there is logically a causal relationship.

transitive inference Understanding the relationship between two objects by knowing the relationship of each to a third object.

triangular theory of love Sternberg's theory that patterns of love hinge on the balance among three elements: intimacy, passion, and commitment.

triarchic theory of intelligence Sternberg's theory describing three elements of intelligence: componential, experiential, and contextual.

turning points Psychological transitions that involve significant change or transformation in the perceived meaning, purpose, or direction of a person's life.

two-way (dual-language) learning Approach to second-language education in which English speakers and non-English-speakers learn together in their own and each other's languages.

typological approach Theoretical approach that identifies broad personality types, or styles.

ultrasound Prenatal medical procedure using high-frequency sound waves to detect the outline of a fetus and its movements, so as to determine whether a pregnancy is progressing normally.

variable-rate theories Theories that explain biological aging as a result of processes that involve damage to biological systems and that vary from person to person.

violation-of-expectations Research method in which dishabituation to a stimulus that conflicts with experience is taken as evidence that an infant recognizes the new stimulus as surprising.

visible imitation Imitation with parts of one's body that one can see.

visual cliff Apparatus designed to give an illusion of depth and used to assess depth perception in infants.

visual guidance Use of the eyes to guide movements of the hands or other parts of the body.

visually based retrieval Process of retrieving the sound of a printed word when seeing the word as a whole.

visual preference Tendency of infants to spend more time looking at one sight than another.

visual recognition memory Ability to distinguish a familiar visual stimulus from an unfamiliar one when shown both at the same time.

vital capacity Amount of air that can be drawn in with a deep breath and expelled.

Wechsler Adult Intelligence Scale (WAIS) Intelligence test for adults that yields verbal and performance scores as well as a combined score.

Wechsler Intelligence Scale for Children (WISC-IV) Individual intelligence test for school-age children, which yields verbal and performance scores as well as a combined score.

Wechsler Preschool and Primary Scale of Intelligence, Revised (WPPSI-IV) Individual intelligence test for children ages 2½ to 7 that yields verbal and performance scores as well as a combined score.

whole-language approach Approach to teaching reading that emphasizes visual retrieval and use of contextual clues.

withdrawal of love Disciplinary strategy that involves ignoring, isolating, or showing dislike for a child.

working memory Short-term storage of information being actively processed.

zone of proximal development (ZPD) Vygotsky's term for the difference between what a child can do alone and what the child can do with help.

zygote One-celled organism resulting from fertilization.

bibliography

Abbott, R. D., White, L. R., Ross, G. W., Masaki, K. H., Curb, J. D., & Petrovitch, H. (2004). Walking and dementia in physically capable elderly men. *Journal of the American Medical Association, 292,* 1447–1453.

Abel, E., & Kruger, M. (2010). Smile intensity in photographs predicts longevity. *Psychological Science, 21,* 542–544. doi: 10.1177/0956797610363775

Aber, J. L., Brown, J. L., & Jones, S. M. (2003). Developmental trajectories toward violence in middle childhood: Course, demographic differences, and response to school-based intervention. *Developmental Psychology, 39,* 324–348.

Abma, J. C., Chandra, A., Mosher, W. D., Peterson, L., & Piccinino, L. (1997). Fertility, family planning, and women's health: New data from the 1995 National Survey of Family Growth. *Vital Health Statistics, 23*(19). Washington, DC: National Center for Health Statistics.

Abma, J. C., Martinez, G. M., & Copen, C. E. (2010). Teenagers in the United States: Sexual activity, contraceptive use, and childbearing, National Survey of Family Growth 2006–2008. *Vital Health Statistics, 23*(30). Washington, DC: National Center for Health Statistics.

Abma, J. C., Martinez, G. M., Mosher, W. D., & Dawson, B. S. (2004). Teenagers in the United States: Sexual activity, contraceptive use, and childbearing, 2002. *Vital Health Statistics, 23*(24). Washington, DC: National Center for Health Statistics.

Abramovitch, R., Corter, C., Pepler, D., & Stanhope, L. (1986). Sibling and peer interactions: A final follow-up and comparison. *Child Development, 57,* 217–229.

Abramson, T. A. (1995, Fall). From nonnormative to normative caregiving. *Dimensions: Newsletter of American Society on Aging,* pp. 1–2.

Achenbaum, W. A., & Bengtson, V. L. (1994). Re-engaging the disengagement theory of aging: On the history and assessment of theory development in gerontology. *Gerontologist, 34,* 756–763.

Achter, J. A., & Lubinski, D. (2003). Fostering exceptional development in intellectually talented populations. In W. B. Walsh (Ed.), *Counseling psychology and optimal human functioning* (pp. 279–296). Mahwah, NJ: Erlbaum.

Ackerman, B. P., Kogos, J., Youngstrom, E., Schoff, K., & Izard, C. (1999). Family instability and the problem behaviors of children from economically disadvantaged families. *Developmental Psychology, 35*(1), 258–268.

Ackerman, M. J., Siu, B. L., Sturner, W. Q., Tester, D. J., Valdivia, C. R., Makielski, J. C., & Towbin, J. A. (2001). Postmortem molecular analysis of SCN5A defects in sudden infant death syndrome. *Journal of the American Medical Association, 286,* 2264–2269.

Acosta, M. T., Arcos-Burgos, M., & Muenke, M. (2004). Attention deficit/hyperactivity disorder (ADHD): Complex phenotype, simple genotype? *Genetics in Medicine, 6,* 1–15.

ACT for Youth Upstate Center of Excellence. (2002). *Adolescent brain development. Research facts and findings* [A collaboration of Cornell University, University of Rochester, and the NYS Center for School Safety]. Retrieved from www.human.cornell.edu/actforyouth

Adam, E. K., Gunnar, M. R., & Tanaka, A. (2004). Adult attachment, parent emotion, and observed parenting behavior: Mediator and moderator models. *Child Development, 75,* 110–122.

Adams, B. N. (2004). Families and family study in international perspective. *Journal of Marriage and Family, 66,* 1076–1088.

Adams, C. (1991). Qualitative age differences in memory for text: A life-span developmental perspective. *Psychology and Aging, 6,* 323–336.

Adams, K. F., Schatzkin, A., Harris, T. B., Kipnis, V., Mouw, T., Ballard-Barbash, R., . . . Leitzmann, M. F. (2006). Overweight, obesity, and mortality in a large prospective cohort of persons 50 to 71 years old. *New England Journal of Medicine, 355,* 763–778.

Adams, L. A., & Rickert, V. I. (1989). Reducing bedtime tantrums: Comparison between positive routines and graduated extinction. *Pediatrics, 84,* 756–761.

Adams, R., & Laursen, B. (2001). The organization and dynamics of adolescent conflict with parents and friends. *Journal of Marriage and the Family, 63,* 97–110.

Adams, R. G. (1986). Friendship and aging. *Generations, 10*(4), 40–43.

Adams, R. G., & Allan, G. (1998). *Placing friendship in context.* Cambridge, MA: Cambridge University Press.

Addis, M. E., & Mahalik, J. R. (2003). Men, masculinity, and the contexts of help seeking. *American Psychologist, 58,* 5–14.

Ades, P. A., Ballor, D. L., Ashikaga, T., Utton, J. L., & Nair, K. S. (1996). Weight training improves walking endurance in healthy elderly persons. *Annals of Internal Medicine, 124,* 568–572.

Administration for Children and Families. (2006a). *FACES 2003 research brief and program quality in Head Start.* Washington, DC: Author.

Administration for Children and Families. (2006b). *FACES findings: New research on Head Start outcomes and program quality.* Washington, DC: Author.

Adminstration on Aging. (2006). *A profile of older Americans: 2006.* Washington, DC: U.S. Department of Health and Human Services.

Administration on Aging. (2009). *A profile of older Americans: 2009.* Retrieved from http://www.aoa.gov/AoARoot/Aging_Statistics/Profile/2009/2.aspx

Administration on Aging. (2010). *Aging statistics.* Retrieved from http://www.aoa.gov/AoARoot/Aging_Statistics/index.aspx

Adolph, K. E. (2000). Specificity of learning: Why infants fall over a veritable cliff. *Psychological Science, 11,* 290–295.

Adolph, K. E. (2008). Learning to move. *Current Directions in Psychological Science, 17,* 213–218.

Adolph, K. E., & Eppler, M. A. (2002). Flexibility and specificity in infant motor skill acquisition. In J. Fagen & H. Hayne (Eds.), *Progress in infancy research* (Vol. 2, pp. 121–167). Mahwah, NJ: Erlbaum.

Adolph, K. E., Vereijken, B., & Shrout, P. E. (2003). What changes in infant walking and why. *Child Development, 74,* 475–497.

Agahi, N., Ahacic, K., & Parker, M. G. (2006). Continuity of leisure participation from middle age to old age. *Journal of Gerontology: Social Sciences, 61B,* S340–S346.

Agahi, N., & Parker, M. G. (2008). Leisure activities and mortality: Does gender matter? *Journal of Aging and Health, 20*(7), 855–871.

Agency for Healthcare Research and Quality and the Centers for Disease Control. (2002). *Physical activity and older Americans: Benefits and strategies.* Retrieved from www.ahrq.gov/ppip/activity.htm

Ahnert, L., Gunnar, M. R., Lamb, M. E., & Barthel, M. (2004). Transition to child care: Associations with infant-mother attachment, infant negative emotion and corticol elevation. *Child Development, 75,* 639–650.

Ahnert, L., & Lamb, M. E. (2003). Shared care: Establishing a balance between home and child care settings. *Child Development, 74,* 1044–1049.

Ahrons, C. R., & Tanner, J. L. (2003). Adult children and their fathers: Relationship changes 20 years after parental divorce. *Family Relations, 52,* 340–351.

Aikens, N., Kopack Klein, A., Tarullo, L., & West, J. (2013). Getting ready for kindergarten: Children's progress during Head Start. *FACES 2009 Report.* OPRE Report 2013-21a. Washington, DC: Office of Planning, Research and Evaluation, Administration for Children and Families, U.S. Department of Health and Human Services.

Ainsworth, M. D. S. (1967). *Infancy in Uganda: Infant care and the growth of love.* Baltimore: Johns Hopkins University Press.

Ainsworth, M. D. S., Blehar, M. C., Waters, E., & Wall, S. (1978). *Patterns of attachment: A psychological study of the strange situation.* Hillsdale, NJ: Erlbaum.

Aitken, L., Burmeister, E., Lang, J., Chaboyer, W., & Richmond, T. S. (2010). Characteristics and outcomes of injured older adults after hospitalization. *Journal of the American Geriatrics Society, 58*(3), 442–449.

Akinbami, L. (2006). The state of childhood asthma, United States, 1980–2005. *Advance Data from Vital and Health Statistics, 381.* Hyattsville, MD: National Center for Health Statistics.

Alaimo, K., Olson, C. M., & Frongillo, E. A. (2001). Food insufficiency and American school-aged children's cognitive, academic, and psychosocial development. *Pediatrics, 108,* 44–53.

Alan Guttmacher Institute (AGI). (1999). *Facts in brief: Teen sex and pregnancy.* Retrieved from www.agi_usa.org/pubs/fb_teen_sex.html#sfd

Alati, R., Al Mamun, A., Williams, G. M., O'Callaghan, M., Najman, J. M., & Bor, W. (2006). In utero alcohol exposure and prediction of alcohol disorders in early adulthood: A birth cohort study. *Archives of General Psychiatry, 63*(9), 1009–1016.

Aldwin, C. M., & Levenson, M. R. (2001). Stress, coping, and health at midlife: A developmental perspective. In M. E. Lachman (Ed.), *Handbook of midlife development* (pp. 188–214). New York: Wiley.

Alexander, K. L., Entwisle, D. R., & Dauber, S. L. (1993). First-grade classroom behavior: Its short- and long-term consequences for school performance. *Child Development, 64,* 801–814.

Alexander, K. L., Entwisle, D. R., & Olson, L. S. (2007). Lasting consequences of the summer learning gap. *American Sociological Review, 72,* 167–180.

Alfred, Lord Tennyson. (1850). "In Memoriam A. H. H., Canto 54."

Alibeik, H., & Angaji, S. A. (2010). Developmental aspects of left handedness. *Australian Journal of Basic and Applied Sciences, 4*(5), 881–977.

Alipuria, L. (2002). Ethnic, racial, and cultural identity/self: An integrated theory of identity/self in relation to large-scale social cleavages. *Dissertation Abstracts International, 63B,* 583. (UMI No. 3039092).

Allemand, M. (2007). Cross-sectional age differences and longitudinal age changes of personality in middle adulthood and old age. *Journal of Personality, 75*(2), 323–358.

Allen, G. L., & Ondracek, P. J. (1995). Age-sensitive cognitive abilities related to children's acquisition of spatial knowledge. *Developmental Psychology, 31,* 934–945.

Allen, I. E., & Seeman, J. (2010). *Learning on demand: Online education in the United States, 2009.* Retrieved from http://sloanconsortium.org/publications/survey/pdf/learningondemand.pdf

Allen, J. P., McElhaney, K. B., Land, D. J., Kuperminc, G. P., Moore, C. W., O'Beirner-Kelly, H., & Kilmer, S. L. (2003). A secure base in adolescence: Markers of attachment security in the mother-adolescent relationship. *Child Development, 74,* 292–307.

Allen, J. P., & Philliber, S. (2001). Who benefits most from a broadly targeted prevention program? Differential efficacy across populations in the Teen Outreach Program. *Journal of Community Psychology, 29,* 637–655.

Allen, J. P., Porter, M. R., McFarland, F. C., Marsh, P., & McElhaney, K. B. (2005). The two faces of adolescents' success with peers: Adolescent popularity, social adaptation, and deviant behavior. *Child Development, 76*(3), 747–760.

Allen, K. R., Blieszner, R., & Roberto, K. A. (2000). Families in the middle and later years: A review and critique of research in the 1990s. *Journal of Marriage and Family, 62,* 911–926.

Alloway, T. P. (2006). How does working memory work in the classroom? *Education Research and Reviews, 1,* 134–139.

Alloway, T. P., Gathercole, S. E., Kirkwood, H., & Elliot, J. (2009). The cognitive and behavioral characteristics of children with low working memory. *Child Development, 80*(2), 606–621.

Almeida, D. M., & Horn, M. C. (2004). Is daily life more stressful during adulthood? In O. G. Brim, C. D. Riff, & R. C. Kessler (Eds.), *How healthy are we? A national study of well-being at midlife* (pp. 425–451). Chicago: University of Chicago Press.

Almeida, D. M., Serido, J., & McDonald, D. (2006). Daily life stressors of early and late baby boomers. In S. K. Whitbourne & S. L. Willis (Eds.), *The baby boomers grow up: Contemporary perspectives on midlife* (pp. 165–183). Mahwah, NJ: Erlbaum.

Almli, C. R., Ball, R. H., & Wheeler, M. E. (2001). Human fetal and neonatal movement patterns: Gender differences and fetal-to-natal continuity. *Developmental Psychobiology, 38*(4), 252–273.

Als, H., Duffy, F. H., McAnulty, G. B., Rivkin, M. J., Vajapeyam, S., Mulkern, R. V., . . . Eichenwald, E. C. (2004). Early experience alters brain function and structure. *Pediatrics, 113,* 846–857.

Altarac, M., & Saroha, E. (2007). Lifetime prevalence of learning disabilities among U.S. children. *Pediatrics, 119*(Suppl. 1), S77–S83.

Altschul, I., Oyserman, D., & Bybee, D. (2006). Racial-ethnic identity in mid-adolescence: Content and change as predictors of academic achievement. *Child Development, 77,* 1155–1169.

Aluti, A., Cattaneo, F., Galimberti, S., Benninghoff, U., Cassani, B., Callegaro, L., . . . Roncarolo, M. G. (2009). Gene therapy for immunodeficiency due to adenosine deaminase deficiency. *New England Journal of Medicine, 360,* 447–458.

Alzheimer's Association. (2010). *Alzheimer's disease: Facts and figures.* Retrieved from http://www.alz.org/documents_custom/report_alzfactsfigures2010.pdf

Alzheimer's Disease: The search for causes and treatments—Part I. (1998, August). *Harvard Mental Health Letter, 15*(2).

Amato, P. R. (2000). The consequences of divorce for adults and children. *Journal of Marriage and Family, 62,* 1269–1287.

Amato, P. R. (2003). Reconciling divergent perspectives: Judith Wallerstein, quantitative family research, and children of divorce. *Family Relations, 52,* 332–339.

Amato, P. R. (2005). The impact of family formation change on the cognitive, social, and emotional well-being of the next generation. *Future of Children, 15,* 75–96.

Amato, P. R., & Afifi, T. D. (2006). Feeling caught between parents: Adult children's relations with parents and subjective well-being. *Journal of Marriage and Family, 68,* 222–235.

Amato, P. R., & Booth, A. (1997). *A generation at risk: Growing up in an era of family upheaval.* Cambridge, MA: Harvard University Press.

Amato, P. R., & Gilbreth, J. G. (1999). Nonresident fathers and children's well-being: A meta-analysis. *Journal of Marriage and Family, 61,* 557–573.

Amato, P. R., Johnson, D. R., Booth, A., & Rogers, S. J. (2003). Continuity and change in marital quality between 1980 and 2000. *Journal of Marriage and Family, 65,* 1–22.

America's youngest outcasts 2010. (2011). National Center on Family Homelessness, Needham, MA. Retrieved from www.HomelessChildrenAmerica.org

American Academy of Child & Adolescent Psychiatry (AACAP). (1997). *Children's sleep problems* [Fact Sheet No. 34]. Retrieved from www.aacap.org/publications/

American Academy of Child & Adolescent Psychiatry. (2003). *Talking to children about terrorism and war* [Facts for Families #87]. Retrieved from www.aacap.org/publications/factsfam/87.htm

American Academy of Pediatrics (AAP). (1986). *Positive approaches to day care dilemmas: How to make it work.* Elk Grove Village, IL: Author.

American Academy of Pediatrics (AAP). (1992, Spring). Bedtime doesn't have to be a struggle. *Healthy Kids,* pp. 4–10.

American Academy of Pediatrics (AAP). (2000). *Shaken baby syndrome.* Retrieved from www.medemcom/search/article_display.cfm?path=\\TANQUERAY\M_ContentItem&mstr=/M_ContentItem/ZZZM8JMMH4C.html&soc=AAP&srch_typ=NAV_SERCH

American Academy of Pediatrics (AAP). (2004, September 30). *American Academy of Pediatrics (AAP) supports Institute of Medicine's (IOM) childhood obesity recommendation* [Press release].

American Academy of Pediatrics (AAP) and Canadian Paediatric Society. (2000). Prevention and management of pain and stress in the neonate. *Pediatrics, 105*(2), 454–461.

American Academy of Pediatrics (AAP) Committee on Adolescence. (2000). Suicide and suicide attempts in adolescents. *Pediatrics, 105*(4), 871–874.

American Academy of Pediatrics (AAP) Committee on Adolescence. (2003). Policy statement: Identifying and treating eating disorders. *Pediatrics, 111*, 204–211.

American Academy of Pediatrics (AAP) Committee on Adolescence and Committee on Early Childhood, Adoption, and Dependent Care. (2001). Care of adolescent parents and their children. *Pediatrics, 107*, 429–434.

American Academy of Pediatrics (AAP) Committee on Bioethics. (1992, July). Ethical issues in surrogate motherhood. *AAP News*, pp. 14–15.

American Academy of Pediatrics (AAP) Committee on Children with Disabilities and Committee on Drugs. (1996). Medication for children with attentional disorders. *Pediatrics, 98*, 301–304.

American Academy of Pediatrics (AAP) Committee on Drugs. (2000). Use of psychoactive medication during pregnancy and possible effects on the fetus and newborn. *Pediatrics, 105*, 880–887.

American Academy of Pediatrics (AAP) Committee on Drugs. (2001). The transfer of drugs and other chemicals into human milk. *Pediatrics, 108*(3), 776–789.

American Academy of Pediatrics (AAP) Committee on Environmental Health. (2005). Lead exposure in children: Prevention, detection, and management. *Pediatrics, 116*, 1036–1046.

American Academy of Pediatrics (AAP) Committee on Fetus and Newborn & American College of Obstetricians and Gynecologists (ACOG) Committee on Obstetric Practice. (1996). Use and abuse of the Apgar score. *Pediatrics, 98*, 141–142.

American Academy of Pediatrics (AAP) Committee on Genetics. (1996). Newborn screening fact sheet. *Pediatrics, 98*, 1–29.

American Academy of Pediatrics (AAP) Committee on Injury and Poison Prevention. (2000). Firearm-related injuries affecting the pediatric population. *Pediatrics, 105*(4), 888–895.

American Academy of Pediatrics (AAP) Committee on Injury and Poison Prevention. (2001). Bicycle helmets. *Pediatrics, 108*(4), 1030–1032.

American Academy of Pediatrics (AAP) Committee on Injury and Poison Prevention and Committee on Sports Medicine and Fitness. (1999). Policy statement: Trampolines at home, school, and recreational centers. *Pediatrics, 103*, 1053–1056.

American Academy of Pediatrics (AAP) Committee on Nutrition. (2003). Prevention of pediatric overweight and obesity. *Pediatrics, 112*, 424–430.

American Academy of Pediatrics (AAP) Committee on Nutrition. (2006). Dietary recommendations for children and adolescents: A guide for practitioners. *Pediatrics, 117*(2), 544–559.

American Academy of Pediatrics (AAP) Committee on Practice and Ambulatory Medicine and Section on Ophthalmology. (1996). Eye examination and vision screening in infants, children, and young adults. *Pediatrics, 98*, 153–157.

American Academy of Pediatrics (AAP) Committee on Practice and Ambulatory Medicine and Section on Ophthalmology. (2002). Use of photoscreening for children's vision screening. *Pediatrics, 109*, 524–525.

American Academy of Pediatrics (AAP) Committee on Psychosocial Aspects of Child and Family Health. (1992). The pediatrician and childhood bereavement. *Pediatrics, 89*(3), 516–518.

American Academy of Pediatrics (AAP) Committee on Psychosocial Aspects of Child and Family Health. (1998). Guidance for effective discipline. *Pediatrics, 101*, 723–728.

American Academy of Pediatrics (AAP) Committee on Psychosocial Aspects of Child and Family Health. (2000). The pediatrician and childhood bereavement. *Pediatrics, 105*, 445–447.

American Academy of Pediatrics (AAP) Committee on Psychosocial Aspects of Child and Family Health. (2002). Coparent or second-parent adoption by same-sex parents. *Pediatrics, 109*(2), 339–340.

American Academy of Pediatrics (AAP) Committee on Psychosocial Aspects of Child and Family Health and Committee on Adolescence. (2001). Sexuality education for children and adolescence. *Pediatrics, 108*(2), 498–502.

American Academy of Pediatrics (AAP) Committee on Public Education (2001). Policy statement: Children, adolescents, and television. *Pediatrics, 107*, 423–426.

American Academy of Pediatrics (AAP) Committee on Sports Medicine and Fitness. (1992). Fitness, activity, and sports participation in the preschool child. *Pediatrics, 90*, 1002–1004.

American Academy of Pediatrics (AAP) Committee on Sports Medicine and Fitness. (2001). Risk of injury from baseball and softball in children. *Pediatrics, 107*(4), 782–784.

American Academy of Pediatrics (AAP) Committee on Sports Medicine and Fitness and Committee on School Health. (2001). Organized sports for children and preadolescents. *Pediatrics, 107*(6), 1459–1462.

American Academy of Pediatrics (AAP) Committee on Substance Abuse. (2001). Tobacco's toll: Implications for the pediatrician. *Pediatrics, 107*, 794–798.

American Academy of Pediatrics (AAP) Section on Breastfeeding. (2005). Breastfeeding and the use of human milk. *Pediatrics, 115*, 496–506.

American Academy of Pediatrics (AAP), Stirling, J., Jr., and the Committee on Child Abuse and Neglect and Section on Adoption and Foster Care; American Academy of Child and Adolescent Psychiatry, Amaya-Jackson, L.; & National Center for Child Traumatic Stress, Amaya-Jackson, L. (2008). Understanding the behavioral and emotional consequences of child abuse. *Pediatrics, 122*(3), 667–673.

American Academy of Pediatrics (AAP) Task Force on Infant Sleep Position and Sudden Infant Death Syndrome. (2000). Changing concepts of sudden infant death syndrome: Implications for infant sleeping environment and sleep position. *Pediatrics, 105*, 650–656.

American Academy of Pediatrics (AAP) Task Force on Sudden Infant Death Syndrome. (2005). The changing concept of sudden infant death syndrome: Diagnostic coding shifts, controversies regarding sleeping environment, and new variables to consider in reducing risk. *Pediatrics, 116*, 1245–1255.

American Association of Retired Persons (AARP). (1993). *Abused elders or battered women?* Washington, DC: Author.

American Association of University Women. (2007). *Behind the pay gap*. Washington, DC: AAUW Educational Foundation.

American Cancer Society. (2001). *Cancer facts and figures*. Atlanta: Author.

American Cancer Society. (2007). What are the risk factors for breast cancer? *Cancer Reference Information*. Oklahoma City, OK: Author.

American Cancer Society. (2011). *Guide to quitting smoking*. Retrieved from http://www.cancer.org/docroot/PED/content/PED_10_13X_Guide_for_Quitting_Smoking.asp?from=fast

American College of Emergency Physicians. (2008, March 10). *Know suicide's warning sign* [Press release]. Irving, TX: Author.

American College of Nurse-Midwives. (2005). *Position statement: Home births*. Silver Spring, MD: Author.

American College of Obstetricians and Gynecologists (ACOG). (2000). Premenstrual syndrome. *ACOG Practice Bulletin, No. 15*. Washington, DC: Author.

American College of Obstetricians and Gynecologists (ACOG). (2002). *Early pregnancy loss: Miscarriage and molar pregnancy*. Washington, DC: Author.

American College of Obstetricians and Gynecologists (ACOG). (2008, February 6). *ACOG news release: ACOG statement on home births*. Retrieved from www.acog.org/fromhome/publications/pressreleases/nr02-06-08-2.cfm

American College of Obstetricians and Gynecologists (ACOG). (2013). *Premenstrual syndrome*. Retrieved from http://www.acog.org/~/media/For%20Patients/faq057.pdf

American Congress of Obstetricians and Gynecologists. (2002). Exercise during pregnancy and the post partum period. ACOG Committee Opinion No. 267. *Obstetrics and Gynecology, 99*, 171–173.

American Congress of Obstetricians and Gynecologists. (2010). *New VBAC guidelines*. Retrieved from http://www.acog.org/~/media/ACOG%20Today/acogToday0810.pdf?dmc=1&ts=20140209T2027089834

American Diabetes Association. (1992). *Diabetes facts*. Alexandria, VA: Author.

American Heart Association (AHA). (1995). *Silent epidemic: The truth about women and heart disease*. Dallas: Author.

American Heart Association (AHA). (2011). *Tobacco industry's targeting of youth, minorities, and women.* Retrieved from http://www.americanheart.org/presenter.jhtml?identifier=11226

American Heart Association (AHA). (2013). *Stroke warning signs and symptoms.* Retrieved from http://www.strokeassociation.org/STROKEORG/WarningSigns/Stroke-Warning-Signs-and-Symptoms_UCM_308528_SubHomePage.jsp

American Heart Association, Gidding, S. S., Dennison, B. A., Birch, L. L., Daniels, S. R., Gilman, M. W., Lichtenstein, A. H., . . . & Van Horn, L. (2006). Dietary recommendations for children and adolescents: a guide for practitioners. *Pediatrics, 117*(2), 544–559.

American Medical Association (AMA). (1992). *Diagnosis and treatment guidelines on elder abuse and neglect.* Chicago: Author.

American Medical Association House of Delegates. (2008, June). *Resolution 205: Home deliveries.* Proceedings of the American Medical Association House of Delegates, Fifteenth Annual Meeting, Chicago, IL. Retrieved from www.ama-assn.org/ama1/pub/upload/mm/471/205.doc

American Psychiatric Association. (2000). *Diagnostic and statistical manual of mental disorders* (4th ed., Text Revision). Washington, DC: Author.

American Psychological Association (APA). (2002). Ethical principles of psychologists and code of conduct. *American Psychologist, 57,* 1060–1073.

American Psychological Association (APA). (2004a). *Resolution on sexual orientation and marriage.* Retrieved from www.apa.org/pi/lgbc/policy/marriage.pdf

American Psychological Association (APA). (2004b, July). *Resolution on sexual orientation, parents, and children.* Retrieved from www.apa.org/pi/lgbc/policy/parents.html

American Psychological Association (APA). (2007). *Stress in America.* Washington, DC: Author.

American Psychological Association (APA). (2009). *Stress in America.* Retrieved from http://www.apa.org/news/press/releases/stress-exec-summary.pdf

American Psychological Association (APA). (2011). *Mental and behavioral health and older Americans.* Retrieved from http://www.apa.org/about/gr/issues/aging/mental-health.aspx

American Psychological Association (APA). (n.d.). *Answers to your questions about sexual orientation and homosexuality* [Brochure]. Washington, DC: Author.

American Psychological Association (APA). (n.d.). *Depression.* Retrieved from http://www.apa.org/topics/depress/index.aspx

American Psychological Association (APA) Online. (2001). *End-of-life issues and care.* Retrieved from www.apa.org/pi/eol/arguments.html

American Psychological Association (APA) Working Group on Assisted Suicide and End-of-Life Decisions. (2005). *Orientation to end-of-life decision-making.* Retrieved from www.apa.org/pi/aseol/section1.html

American Public Health Association. (2004). *Disparities in infant mortality* [Fact sheet]. Retrieved from www.medscape.com/viewarticle/472721

Ames, E. W. (1997). *The development of Romanian orphanage children adopted to Canada: Final report* (National Welfare Grants Program, Human Resources Development, Canada). Burnaby, BC, Canada: Fraser University, Psychology Department.

Amirkhanyan, A. A., & Wolf, D. A. (2006). Parent care and the stress process: Findings from panel data. *Journal of Gerontology: Social Sciences, 61B,* S248–S255.

Amsel, E., Goodman, G., Savoie, D., & Clark, M. (1996). The development of reasoning about causal and noncausal influences on levers. *Child Development, 67,* 1624–1646.

Amso, D., & Casey, B. J. (2006). Beyond what develops when: Neuroimaging may inform how cognition changes with development. *Current Directions in Psychological Science, 15,* 24–29.

Anastasi, A. (1988). *Psychological testing* (6th ed.). New York: Macmillan.

Anastasi, A., & Schaefer, C. E. (1971). Note on concepts of creativity and intelligence. *Journal of Creative Behavior, 3,* 113–116.

Anderson, A. H., Clark, A., & Mullin, J. (1994). Interactive communication between children: Learning how to make language work in dialog. *Journal of Child Language, 21,* 439–463.

Anderson, C. (2000). *The impact of interactive violence on children.* Statement before the Senate Committee on Commerce, Science, and Transportation, 106th Congress, 1st session.

Anderson, C. A., Berkowitz, L., Donnerstein, E., Huesmann, L. R., Johnson, J. D., Linz, D., Malamuth, N. M., & Wartella, E. (2003). The influence of media violence on youth. *Psychological Science in the Public Interest, 4,* 81–110.

Anderson, D. A., & Hamilton, M. (2005). Gender role stereotyping of parents in children's picture books: The invisible father. *Sex Roles, 52,* 145–151.

Anderson, D. R., & Pempek, T. A. (2005). Television and very young children. *American Behavioral Scientist, 48*(5), 505–522.

Anderson, M., Kaufman, J., Simon, T. R., Barrios, L., Paulozzi, L., Ryan, G., . . . the School-Associated Violent Deaths Study Group. (2001). School-associated violent deaths in the United States, 1994–1999. *Journal of the American Medical Association, 286*(21), 2695–2702.

Anderson, P., Doyle, L. W., & the Victorian Infant Collaborative Study Group. (2003). *Journal of the American Medical Association, 289,* 3264–3272.

Anderson, R. N., & Smith, B. L. (2005). Deaths: Leading causes for 2002. *National Vital Statistics Reports, 53*(17). Hyattsville, MD: National Center for Health Statistics.

Anderson, S. E., Dallal, G. E., & Must, A. (2003). Relative weight and race influence average age at menarche: Results from two nationally representative surveys of U.S. girls studied 25 years apart. *Pediatrics, 111,* 844–850.

Anderson, S. E., & Whitaker, R. C. (2010). Household routines and obesity in US preschool-aged children. *Pediatrics, 125*(3), 420–428. doi: 10.1542/peds.2009-0417

Anderssen, N., Amlie, C., & Ytteroy, E. A. (2002). Outcomes for children with lesbian or gay parents: A review of studies from 1978 to 2000. *Scandinavian Journal of Psychology, 43*(4), 335–351.

Andrews-Hanna, J. R., Snyder, A. Z., Vincent, J. L., Lustig, C., Head, D., Raichie, M. E., & Buckner, R. L. (2007). Disruption of large-scale brain systems in advanced aging. *Neuron, 56,* 924–935.

Ang, S., Rodgers, J. L., & Wanstrom, L. (2010). The Flynn Effect within subgroups in the U.S.: Gender, race, income, education, and urbanization differences in the NLSY-Children data. *Intelligence, 38*(4), 367–384.

Antonio, A. L., Chang, M. J., Hakuta, K., Kenny, D. A., Levin, S., & Milem, J. F. (2004). Effects of racial diversity on complex thinking in college students. *Psychological Science, 15,* 507–510.

Antonucci, T., & Akiyama, H. (1997). Concern with others at midlife: Care, comfort, or compromise? In M. E. Lachman & J. B. James (Eds.), *Multiple paths of midlife development* (pp. 145–169). Chicago: University of Chicago Press.

Antonucci, T. C., & Akiyama, H. (1995). Convoys of social relations: Family and friendships within a life-span context. In R. Blieszner & V. Hilkevitch (Eds.), *Handbook of aging and the family* (pp. 355–371). Westport, CT: Greenwood Press.

Antonucci, T. C., Akiyama, H., & Merline, A. (2001). Dynamics of social relationships in midlife. In M. E. Lachman (Ed.), *Handbook of midlife development* (pp. 571–598). New York: Wiley.

Apfelbaum, E. P., Pauker, K., Ambady, N., Sommers, S. R., & Norton, M. I. (2008). Learning (not) to talk about race: When older children underperform in social categorization. *Developmental Psychology, 44*(5), 1513–1518. doi:10.1037/a0012835

Apgar, V. (1953). A proposal for a new method of evaluation of the newborn infant. *Current Research in Anesthesia and Analgesia, 32,* 260–267.

Aquilino, W. S. (1996). The returning adult child and parental experience at midlife. In C. Ryff & M. M. Seltzer (Eds.), *The parental experience in midlife* (pp. 423–458). Chicago: University of Chicago Press.

Aquilino, W. S. (2006). Family relationships and support systems in emerging adulthood. In J. J. Arnett & J. L. Tanner (Eds.), *Emerging adults in America: Coming of age in the 21st century* (pp. 193–217). Washington, DC: American Psychological Association.

Archer, J. (2004). Sex differences in aggression in real-world settings: A meta-analytic review. *Review of General Psychology, 8,* 291–322.

Archer, S. L. (1993). Identity in relational contexts: A methodological proposal. In J. Kroger (Ed.), *Discussions on ego identity* (pp. 75–99). Hillsdale, NJ: Erlbaum.

Arcus, D., & Kagan, J. (1995). Temperament and craniofacial variation in the first two years. *Child Development, 66,* 1529–1540.

Arend, R., Gove, F., & Sroufe, L. A. (1979). Continuity of individual adaptation from infancy to kindergarten: A predictive study of ego-resiliency and curiosity in preschoolers. *Child Development, 50*(4), 950–959.

Arias, E. (2010). United States life tables by Hispanic origin. *Vital Health Statistics, 2*(152), 1–33. Hyattsville, MD: National Center for Health Statistics.

Arias, E., MacDorman, M. F., Strobino, D. M., & Guyer, B. (2003). Annual summary of vital statistics—2002. *Pediatrics, 112,* 1215–1230.

Artistico, D., Orom, H., Cervone, D., Krauss, S., & Houston, E. (2010). Everyday challenges in context: The influence of contextual factors on everyday problem solving among young, middle-aged and older adults. *Experimental Aging Research, 36*(2), 230–247.

Arking, R., Novoseltsev, V., & Novoseltseva, J. (2004). The human life span is not that limited: The effect of multiple longevity phenotypes. *Journal of Gerontology: Biological Sciences, 59A,* 697–704.

Arner, P. (2000). Obesity—a genetic disease of adipose tissue? *British Journal of Nutrition, 83*(1), 9–16.

Arnestad, M., Crotti, L., Rognum, T. O., Insolia, R., Pedrazzini, M., Ferrandi, C., . . . Schwartz, P. J. (2007). Prevalence of long-qt syndrome gene variants in sudden infant death syndrome. *Circulation, 115,* 361–367.

Arnett, J. J. (1999). Adolescent storm and stress, reconsidered. *American Psychologist, 54,* 317–326.

Arnett, J. J. (2000). Emerging adulthood: A theory of development from the late teens through the twenties. *American Psychologist, 55,* 469–480.

Arnett, J. J. (2004). *Emerging adulthood.* New York: Oxford University Press.

Arnett J. J. (2005). The developmental context of substance use in emerging adulthood. *Journal of Drug Issues, 35,* 235–254.

Arnett, J. J. (2006). Emerging adulthood: Understanding the new way of coming of age. In J. J. Arnett & J. L. Tanner (Eds.), *Emerging adults in America: Coming of age in the 21st century* (pp. 3–19). Washington, DC: American Psychological Association.

Arnett, J. J. (2007a). Emerging adulthood: What is it, and what is it good for? *Child Development Perspectives, 1,* 68–73.

Arnett, J. J. (2007b), Suffering, selfish slackers? Myths and reality about emerging adults. *Journal of Youth and Adolescence, 36,* 23–39.

Arnett, J. J. (2010). Oh, grow up! Generational grumbling and the new life stage of emerging adulthood. *Perspectives on Psychological Science, 5,* 89–92.

Arrich, J., Lalouschek, W., & Müllner, M. (2005). Influence of socioeconomic status on mortality after stroke: Retrospective cohort study. *Stroke, 36,* 310–314.

Asher, M. I., Montefort, S., Björkstén, B., Lai, C. K., Strachan, D. P., Weiland, S. K., . . . the ISAAC Phase Three Study Group. (2006). Worldwide time trends in the prevalence of symptoms of asthma, allergic rhinoconjunctivitis, and eczema in childhood: ISAAC phases one and three repeat multicountry cross-sectional surveys. *Lancet, 368*(9537), 733–743.

Ashman, S. B., & Dawson, G. (2002). Maternal depression, infant psychobiological development, and risk for depression. In S. H. Goodman & I. H. Gotlib (Eds.), *Children of depressed parents: Mechanisms of risk and implications for treatment* (pp. 37–58). Washington, DC: American Psychological Association.

Associated Press. (2004, April 29). *Mom in C-section case received probation: Woman originally charged with murder for delaying operation.* Retrieved from www.msnbc.msn.com/id/4863415/

Asthana, S., Bhasin, S., Butler, R. N., Fillit, H., Finkelstein, J., Harman, S. M., . . . Urban, R. (2004). Masculine vitality: Pros and cons of testosterone in treating the andropause. *Journal of Gerontology: Medical Sciences, 59A,* 461–466.

Astington, J. W. (1993). *The child's discovery of the mind.* Cambridge, MA: Harvard University Press.

Atchley, R. C. (1989). A continuity theory of normal aging. *Gerontologist, 29,* 183–190.

Athansiou, M. S. (2001). Using consultation with a grandmother as an adjunct to play therapy. *Family Journal—Consulting and Therapy for Couples and Families, 9,* 445–449.

Aud, S., Hussar, W., Johnson, F., Kena, G., & Roth, E. (2012). *The condition of education 2012.* (NCES 2012045). Hyattsville, MD: National Center on Education Statistics.

Austin, E. W., Pinkleton, B. E., & Fujioka, Y. (2000). The role of interpretation processes and parental discussion in the media's effects on adolescents' use of alcohol. *Pediatrics, 105*(2), 343–349.

Ausubel, N. (1964). *The book of Jewish knowledge.* New York: Crown.

Auyeng, B., Baron-Cohen, S., Ashwin, E., Kinckmeyer, R., Taylor, K., Hackett, G., & Hines, M. (2009). Fetal testosterone predicts sexually differentiated childhood behavior in girls and in boys. *Psychological Science, 20,* 144–148.

Avis, N. E. (1999). Women's health at midlife. In S. L. Willis & J. D. Reid (Eds.), *Life in the middle: Psychological and social development in middle age* (pp. 105–146). San Diego: Academic Press.

Avis, N. E., & Crawford, S. (2006). Menopause: Recent research findings. In S. K. Whitbourne & S. L. Willis (Eds.), *The baby boomers grow up: Contemporary perspectives on midlife* (pp. 75–109). Mahwah, NJ: Erlbaum.

Avolio, B. J., & Sosik, J. J. (1999). A life-span framework for assessing the impact of work on white-collar workers. In S. L. Willis & J. D. Reid (Eds.), *Life in the middle: Psychological and social development in middle age.* San Diego: Academic Press.

Aznar-Casanova, J., Torro-Alves, N., & Fukusima, S. (2010). How much older do you get when a wrinkle appears on your face? Modifying age estimates by number of wrinkles. *Aging, Neuropsychology, and Cognition, 17*(4), 406–421. doi: 10.1080/13825580903420153

Babu, A., & Hirschhorn, K. (1992). *A guide to human chromosome defects* (Birth Defects: Original Article Series, 28[2]). White Plains, NY: March of Dimes Birth Defects Foundation.

Bach, P. B., Schrag, D., Brawley, O. W., Galaznik, A., Yakren, S., & Begg, C. B. (2002). Survival of blacks and whites after a cancer diagnosis. *Journal of the American Medical Association, 287,* 2106–2113.

Back, M. D., Stopfer, J. M., Vazire, S., Gaddis, S., Schmukle, S. C., Egloff, B., & Gosling, S. D. (2010). Facebook profiles reflect actual personality, not self-idealization. *Psychological Science, 21*(3), 372–374.

Bada, H. S., Das, A., Bauer, C. R., Shankaran, S., Lester, B., LaGasse, L., . . . Higgins, R. (2007). Impact of prenatal cocaine exposure on child behavior problems through school age. *Pediatrics, 119,* 348–359.

Baddeley, A. (1998). Recent developments in working memory. *Current Opinion in Neurobiology, 8,* 234–238.

Baddeley, A. D. (2001). Is working memory still working? *American Psychologist, 56,* 851–864.

Baer, J. S., Sampson, P. D., Barr, H. M., Connor, P. D., & Streissguth, A. P. (2003). A 21-year longitudinal analysis of the effects of prenatal alcohol exposure on young adult drinking. *Archives of General Psychiatry, 60,* 377–385.

Bagwell, C. L., Newcomb, A. F., & Bukowski, W. M. (1998). Preadolescent friendship and peer rejection as predictors of adult adjustment. *Child Development, 69,* 140–153.

Baillargeon, R. (1994). How do infants learn about the physical world? *Current Directions in Psychological Science, 3,* 133–140.

Baillargeon, R. (1999). Young infants' expectations about hidden objects. *Developmental Science, 2,* 115–132.

Baillargeon, R., & DeVos, J. (1991). Object permanence in young infants: Further evidence. *Child Development, 62,* 1227–1246.

Baillargeon, R. H., Zoccolillo, M., Keenan, K., Côté, S., Pérusse, D., Wu, H.-X., . . . Tremblay, R. E. (2007). Gender differences in physical aggression: A prospective population-based survey of children before and after 2 years of age. *Developmental Psychology, 43,* 13–26.

Bainbridge, J. W. B., Smith, A. J., Barker, S. S., Robbie, S., Henderson, R., Balaggan, K., . . . Ali, R. R. (2008). Effect of gene therapy on visual function in Leber's congenital amaurosis. *New England Journal of Medicine, 358,* 2231–2239.

Baird, A. A., Gruber, S. A., Fein, D. A., Maas, L. C., Steingard, R. J., Renshaw, P. F., . . . Yurgelon-Todd, D. A. (1999). Functional magnetic resonance imaging of facial affect recognition in children and adolescents. *Journal of the American Academy of Child and Adolescent Psychiatry, 38*, 195–199.

Baird, G., Pickles, A., Simonoff, E., Charman, T., Sullivan, P., Chandler, S., . . . Brown, D. (2008). Measles vaccination and antibody response in autism spectrum disorders. *Archives of Disease in Childhood.* Advance online publication. doi: 10.1136/adc.2007.122937

Baker, J. L., Olsen, L. W., & Sorensen, T. I. A. (2007). Childhood body-mass index and the risk of coronary heart disease in adulthood. *New England Journal of Medicine, 357*, 2329–2336.

Baker, L., Cahalin, L. P., Gerst, K., & Burr, J. A. (2005). Productive activities and subjective well-being among older adults: The influence of number of activities and time commitment. *Social Indicators Research, 73*, 431–458.

Baldi, S., Jin, Y., Skemer, M., Green, P. J., & Herget, D. (2007). *Highlights from PISA 2006: Performance of U.S. 15-year-old students in science and mathematics literacy in an international context* (NCES 2008-016). Washington, DC: U.S. Department of Education, National Center for Education Statistics.

Ball, J. M. (2009). Spinal extension exercises prevent natural progression of kyphosis. *Osteoporosis International, 20*(3), 481–489.

Ball, K., Edwards, J. D., & Ross, L. A. (2007). The impact of speed of processing training on cognitive and everyday functions [Special issue I]. *Journal of Gerontology: Psychological Sciences, 62B*, 19–31.

Balluz, L. S., Okoro, C. A., & Strine, T. W. (2004). Access to health-care preventive services among Hispanics and non-Hispanics—United States, 2001–2002. *Morbidity and Mortality Weekly Report, 53*, 937–941.

Balsis, S., & Carpenter, B. (2006). Evaluations of elderspeak in a caregiving context. *Clinical Gerontologist, 29*(1), 79–96. doi: 10.1300/J018v29n01_07

Balsis, S., Carpenter, B. D., & Storandt, M. (2005). Personality change precedes clinical diagnosis of dementia of the Alzheimer type. *Journal of Gerontology: Psychological Sciences, 60B*, P98–P101.

Baltes, P. B. (1987). Theoretical propositions of life-span development psychology: On the dynamics between growth and decline. *Developmental Psychology 23*(5), 611–626.

Baltes, P. B. (1997). On the incomplete architecture of human ontogeny: Selection, optimization, and compensation as foundation of developmental theory. *American Psychologist, 52*, 366–380.

Baltes, P. B., & Baltes, M. M. (1990). Psychological perspectives on successful aging: The model of selective optimization with compensation. In P. B. Baltes & M. M. Baltes (Eds.), *Successful aging: Perspectives from the behavioral sciences* (pp. 1–34). New York: Cambridge University Press.

Baltes, P. B., Lindenberger, U., & Staudinger, U. M. (1998). Life-span theory in developmental psychology. In R. M. Lerner (Ed.), *Handbook of child psychology: Vol. 1. Theoretical models of human development* (pp. 1029–1143). New York: Wiley.

Baltes, P. B., & Smith, J. (2004). Lifespan psychology: From developmental contextualism to developmental biocultural co-constructivism. *Research in Human Development, 1*, 123–144.

Baltes, P. B., & Staudinger, U. M. (2000). Wisdom: A metaheuristic (pragmatic) to orchestrate mind and virtue toward excellence. *American Psychologist, 55*, 122–136.

Bandura, A. (1977). *Social learning theory.* Englewood Cliffs, NJ: Prentice Hall.

Bandura, A. (1986). *Social foundations of thought and action: A social cognitive theory.* Englewood Cliffs, NJ: Prentice Hall.

Bandura, A. (1989). Social cognitive theory. In R. Vasta (Ed.), *Annals of child development* (Vol. 6, pp. 1–60). Greenwich, CT: JAI.

Bandura, A. (1994). Self-efficacy. In V. S. Ramachaudran (Ed.), *Encyclopedia of human behavior* (Vol. 4, pp. 71–81). New York: Academic Press.

Bandura, A., Barbaranelli, C., Caprara, G. V., & Pastorelli, C. (1996). Multifaceted impact of self-efficacy beliefs on academic functioning. *Child Development, 67*, 1206–1222.

Bandura, A., Barbaranelli, C., Caprara, G. V., & Pastorelli, C. (2001). Self-efficacy beliefs as shapers of children's aspirations and career trajectories. *Child Development 72*(1), 187–206.

Bandura, A., & Bussey, K. (2004). On broadening the cognitive, motivational, and sociostructural scope of theorizing about gender development and functioning: Comment on Martin, Ruble, and Szkrybalo (2002). *Psychological Bulletin, 130*(5), 691–701.

Bandura, A., Ross, D., & Ross, S. A. (1961). Transmission of aggression through imitation of aggressive models. *Journal of Abnormal and Social Psychology, 63*, 575–582.

Bandura, A., Ross, D., & Ross, S. A. (1963). Imitation of film-mediated aggressive models. *Journal of Abnormal and Social Psychology, 66*, 3–11.

Bandura, A., & Walters, R. H. (1963). *Social learning and personality development.* New York: Holt, Rinehart & Winston.

Banks, E. (1989). Temperament and individuality: A study of Malay children. *American Journal of Orthopsychiatry, 59*, 390–397.

Banta, D., & Thacker, S. B. (2001). Historical controversy in health technology assessment: The case of electronic fetal monitoring. *Obstetrical and Gynecological Survey, 56*(11), 707–719.

Bargh, J. A., Chen, M., & Burrows, L. (1996). Automaticity of social behavior: Direct effects of trait construct and stereotype activation on action. *Journal of Personality and Social Psychology, 71*, 230–244.

Barinaga, M. (1998). Alzheimer's treatments that work now. *Science, 282*, 1030–1032.

Barkley, R. A. (1998, September). Attention-deficit hyperactivity disorder. *Scientific American*, pp. 66–71.

Barnes, G. M., Hoffman, J. H., & Welte, J. W. (2006). Effects of parental monitoring and peer deviance in substance abuse and delinquency. *Journal of Marriage and Family, 68*, 1084–1104.

Barnes, P. M., & Schoenborn, C. A. (2003). Physical activity among adults: United States, 2000. *Advance Data from Vital and Health Statistics,* No. 133. Hyattsville, MD: National Center for Health Statistics.

Barnett, R. (1985, March). *We've come a long way—But where are we and what are the rewards?* Paper presented at the conference on Women in Transition, New York University School of Continuing Education, Center for Career and Life Planning, New York.

Barnett, R. C. (1997). Gender, employment, and psychological well-being: Historical and life-course perspectives. In M. E. Lachman & J. B. James (Eds.), *Multiple paths of midlife development* (pp. 325–343). Chicago: University of Chicago Press.

Barnett, R. C., & Hyde, J. S. (2001). Women, men, work, and family. *American Psychologist, 56*, 781–796.

Barnhart, M. A. (1992, Fall). Coping with the Methuselah syndrome. *Free Inquiry,* pp. 19–22.

Baron-Cohen, S. (2005). The essential difference: The male and female brain. *Phi Kappa Phi Forum, 85*(1), 23–26.

Baron-Cohen, S., Leslie, A. M., & Frith, U. (1985). Does the autistic child have a "theory of mind"? *Cognition, 21*(1), 37–46.

Barnett, W. S., Jung, K., Yarosc, D. J., Thomas, J., Hornbeck, A., Stechuk, R. A., & Burns, M. S. (2008). Educational effects of the tools of the mind curriculum: A randomized trial. *Early Childhood Research Quarterly, 23*(3), 299–313.

Barrett-Connor, E., Hendrix, S., Ettinger, B., Wenger, N. K., Paoletti, R., Lenfant, C. J. M., & Pinn, V. W. (2002). *Best clinical practices: Chapter 13. International position paper on women's health and menopause: A comprehensive approach.* Washington, DC: National Heart, Lung, and Blood Institute.

Barry, B. K., & Carson, R. G. (2004). The consequences of resistance training for movement control in older adults. *Journal of Gerontology: Medical Sciences, 59A*, 730–754.

Barry, C. M., Madsen, S. D., Nelson, L. J., Carroll, J. S., & Badger, S. (2009). Friendship and romantic relationship qualities in emerging adulthood: Differential associations with identity development and achieved adulthood criteria. *Journal of Adult Development, 16*(4), 209–222.

Bartick, M., & Reinhold, A. (2010). The burden of suboptimal breastfeeding in the United States: A pediatric cost analysis. *Pediatrics 125*, e1048–e1056.

Bartoshuk, L. M., & Beauchamp, G. K. (1994). Chemical senses. *Annual Review of Psychology, 45*, 419–449.

Bartz, J. A. (2010). Oxytocin electively improves empathic accuracy. *Psychological Science, 21*(10), 1426–1428. doi: 10.1177/0956797610383439

Bartzokis, G., Lu, P. H., Tingus, K., Mendez, M. F., Richard, A., Peters, D. G., . . . Mintz, J. (2008). Lifespan trajectory of myelin integrity and maximum motor speed. *Neurobiology and Imaging, 31*(9), 1554–1562.

Bartzokis, G., Lu, P. H., Tishler, T. A., Fong, S. M., Oluwadara, B., Finn, J. P., . . . Perlman, S. (2007). Myelin breakdown and iron changes in Huntington's disease: Pathogenesis and treatment implications. *Neurochemical Research, 32*(10), 1655–1664.

Barzilai, N., Atzmon, G., Derby, C. A., Bauman, J. M., & Lipton, R. B. (2006). A genotype of exceptional longevity is associated with preservation of cognitive function. *Neurology, 67*, 2170–2175.

Bascom, P. B., & Tolle, S. W. (2002). Responding to requests for physician-assisted suicide: "These are uncharted waters for both of us. . . ." *Journal of the American Medical Association, 288*, 91–98.

Bates, E., O'Connell, B., & Shore, C. (1987). Language and communication in infancy. In J. D. Osofsky (Ed.), *Handbook of infant development* (2nd ed.). New York: Wiley.

Batty, G. D., Deary, I. J., & Gottfredson, L. S. (2007). Premorbid (early life) IQ and later mortality risk: Systematic review. *Annals of Epidemiology, 17*(4), 278–288.

Bauer, M. E., Jeckel, C. M. M., & Luz, C. (2009). The role of stress factors during aging of the immune system. *Annals of the New York Academy of Sciences, 1153*, 39–152. doi: 10.1111/j.1749-6632.2008.03966.x

Bauer, P. J. (2002). Long-term recall memory: Behavioral and neurodevelopmental changes in the first 2 years of life. *Current Directions in Psychological Science, 11*, 137–141.

Bauer, P. J., Wenner, J. A., Dropik, P. L., & Wewerka, S. S. (2000). Parameters of remembering and forgetting in the transition from infancy to early childhood. *Monographs of the Society for Research in Child Development, 65*(4, Serial No. 263). Malden, MA: Blackwell.

Bauer, P. J., Wiebe, S. A., Carver, L. J., Waters, J. M., & Nelson, C. A. (2003). Developments in long-term explicit memory late in the first year of life: Behavioral and electrophysiological indices. *Psychological Science, 14*, 629–635.

Baum, A., Cacioppo, J. T., Melamed, B. G., Gallant, S. J., & Travis, C. (1995). *Doing the right thing: A research plan for healthy living.* Washington, DC: American Psychological Association Science Directorate.

Baum, S., Ma, J., & Payea, K. (2010). *Education pays.* Retrieved from http://trends.collegeboard.org/education_pays

Baumer, E. P., & South, S. J. (2001). Community effects on youth sexual activity. *Journal of Marriage and Family, 63*, 540–554.

Baumrind, D. (1971). Harmonious parents and their preschool children. *Developmental Psychology, 41*, 92–102.

Baumrind, D. (1989). Rearing competent children. In W. Damon (Ed.), *Child development today and tomorrow* (pp. 349–378). San Francisco: Jossey-Bass.

Baumrind, D. (1991). Parenting styles and adolescent development. In J. Brooks-Gunn, R. Lerner, & A. C. Peterson (Eds.), *The encyclopedia of adolescence* (pp. 746–758). New York: Garland.

Baumrind, D. (1996a). A blanket injunction against disciplinary use of spanking is not warranted by the data. *Pediatrics, 88*, 828–831.

Baumrind, D. (1996b). The discipline controversy revisited. *Family Relations, 45*, 405–414.

Baumrind, D. (2005). Patterns of parental authority and adolescent autonomy. In J. Smetana (Ed.), *Changing boundaries of parental authority during adolescence* (New Directions for Child and Adolescent Development, No. 108, pp. 61–70). San Francisco: Jossey-Bass.

Baumrind, D., & Black, A. E. (1967). Socialization practices associated with dimensions of competence in preschool boys and girls. *Child Development, 38*, 291–327.

Baumrind, D., Larzelere, R. E., & Owens, E. B. (2010). Effects of preschool parents' power assertive patterns and practices on adolescent development. *Parenting: Science and Practice, 10*(3), 157–201.

Bauserman, R. (2002). Child adjustment in joint-custody versus sole-custody arrangements: A meta-analytic review. *Journal of Family Psychology, 16*, 91–102.

Bayley, N. (1969). *Bayley Scales of Infant Development.* New York: Psychological Corporation.

Bayley, N. (1993). *Bayley Scales of Infant Development: II.* New York: Psychological Corporation.

Bayley, N. (2005). *Bayley Scales of Infant Development, Third Ed. (Bayley-III).* New York: Harcourt Brace.

Bayliss, D. M., Jarrold, C., Baddeley, A. D., Gunn, D. M., & Leigh, E. (2005). Mapping the developmental constraints on working memory span performance. *Developmental Psychology, 41*(4), 579–597.

Beal, S. J., & Crockett, L. J. (2010). Adolescents' occupational and educational aspirations and expectations: Links to high school activities and adult educational achievement. *Developmental Psychology, 46*(1), 258–265.

Beals, D. E., & Snow, C. E. (1994). Thunder is when the angels are upstairs bowling: Narratives and explanations at the dinner table. *Journal of Narrative and Life History, 4*, 331–352.

Beauchamp, G. K., & Mennella, J. A. (2009). Early flavor learning and its impact on later feeding behavior. *Journal of Pediatric Gastroenterology and Nutrition, 48*, 25–30.

Becker, G. S. (1991). *A treatise on the family* (Enlarged ed.). Cambridge, MA: Harvard University Press.

Becker, P. E., & Moen, P. (1999). Scaling back: Dual-earner couples' work–family strategies. *Journal of Marriage and Family, 61*, 995–1007.

Beckett, C., Maughan, B., Rutter, M., Castle, J., Colvert, E., Groothues, C., . . . Sonuga-Barke, E. J. S. (2006). Do the effects of severe early deprivation on cognition persist into early adolescence? Findings from the English and Romanian adoptees study. *Child Development, 77*, 696–711.

Bedford, V. H. (1995). Sibling relationships in middle and old age. In R. Blieszner & V. Hilkevitch (Eds.), *Handbook of aging and the family* (pp. 201–222). Westport, CT: Greenwood Press.

Behrman, R. E. (1992). *Nelson textbook of pediatrics* (13th ed.). Philadelphia: Saunders.

Behne, R., Carpenter, M., Call, J., & Tomasello, M. (2005). Unwilling versus unable: Infants' understanding of intentional action. *Developmental Psychology, 41*, 328–337.

Beidel, D. C., & Turner, S. M. (1998). *Shy children, phobic adults: Nature and treatment of social phobia.* Washington, DC: American Psychological Association.

Belizzi, M. (2002, May). *Obesity in children—What kind of future are we creating?* Presentation at the 55th World Health Assembly Technical Briefing, Geneva.

Bell, L., Burtless, G., Gornick, J., & Smeedling, T. M. (2007). A cross-national survey of trends in the transition to economic independence. In S. Danzinger & C. Rouse (Eds.), *The price of independence: The economics of early adulthood* (pp. 27–55). New York: Russell Sage Foundation.

Bell, L. G., & Bell, D. C. (2005). Family dynamics in adolescence affect midlife well-being. *Journal of Family Psychology, 19*, 198–207.

Bell, M. A., & Fox, N. A. (1992). The relations between frontal brain electrical activity and cognitive development during infancy. *Child Development, 63*, 1142–1163.

Bell, J. F., Zimmerman, F. J., & Diehr, P. K. (2008). Maternal work and birth outcome disparities. *Maternal & Child Health Journal, 12*, 415–426.

Bellinger, D. C. (2008). Lead neurotoxicity and socioeconomic status: Conceptual and analytic issues. *NeuroToxicology, 29*(5), 828–832.

Belsky, J. (1984). Two waves of day care research: Developmental effects and conditions of quality. In R. Ainslie (Ed.), *The child and the day care setting.* New York: Praeger.

Belsky, J. (1997). Variation in susceptibility to environmental influence: An evolutionary argument. *Psychological Inquiry, 8*, 230–235.

Belsky, J. (2005). Differential susceptibility to rearing influence: An evolutionary hypothesis and some evidence. In B. J. Ellis & D. F. Bjorklund (Eds.), *Origins of the social mind: Evolutionary psychology and child development* (pp. 139–163). New York: Guilford Press.

Belsky, J., Fish, M., & Isabella, R. (1991). Continuity and discontinuity in infant negative and positive emotionality: Family antecedents and attachment consequences. *Developmental Psychology, 27*, 421–431.

Belsky, J., Jaffee, S., Hsieh, K., & Silva, P. A. (2001). Childrearing antecedents of intergenerational relations in young adulthood: A prospective study. *Developmental Psychology, 37*, 801–814.

Belsky, J., Jaffee, S. R., Caspi, A., Moffitt, T., & Silva, P. A. (2003). Intergenerational relationships in young adulthood and their life course, mental health, and personality correlates. *Journal of Family Psychology, 17*, 460–471.

Belsky, J., & Pluess, M. (2009). Beyond diathesis stress: Differential susceptibility to environmental influences. *Psychological Bulletin, 135*(6), 885–908. doi: 10.1037/a0017376

Belsky, J., Steinberg, L., Houts, R. M., & Halpern-Felsher, B. L. (2010). The development of reproductive strategy in females: Early maternal harshness—earlier menarch—increased sexual risk taking. *Developmental Psychology, 46*(1), 120–128.

Belsky, J., Steinberg, L. D., Houts, R. M., Friedman, S. L., DeHart, G., Cauffman, E., . . . NICHD Early Child Care Research Network. (2007). Family rearing antecedents of pubertal timing. *Child Development, 78*(4), 1302–1321.

Bem, S. L. (1993). *The lenses of gender: Transforming the debate on sexual inequality.* New Haven, CT: Yale University Press.

Benes, F. M., Turtle, M., Khan, Y., & Farol, P. (1994). Myelination of a key relay zone in the hippocampal formation occurs in the human brain during childhood, adolescence, and adulthood. *Archives of General Psychiatry, 51*, 447–484.

Bengtson, V. L. (2001). Beyond the nuclear family: The increasing importance of multigenerational bonds. *Journal of Marriage and Family, 63*, 1–16.

Bengtson, V. L., Rosenthal, C., & Burton, L. (1996). Paradoxes of families and aging. In R. H. Binstock & L. K. George (Eds.), *Handbook of aging and the social sciences* (4th ed., pp. 253–282). San Diego: Academic Press.

Bengtson, V. L., Rosenthal, C. J., & Burton, L. M. (1990). Families and aging: Diversity and heterogeneity. In R. Binstock & L. George (Eds.), *Handbook of aging and the social sciences* (3rd ed., pp. 263–287). San Diego: Academic Press.

Benner, A. D., & Graham, S. (2009). The transition to high schools as a developmental process among multiethnic urban youth. *Child Development, 80*(2), 356–376.

Benner, A. D., & Kim, S. Y. (2009). Experiences of discrimination among Chinese American adolescents and the consequences for socioemotional and academic development. *Developmental Psychology, 45*(6), 1682–1694.

Benson, E. (2003). Intelligent intelligence testing. *Monitor on Psychology, 43*(2), 48–51.

Berg, C. A., & Klaczynski, P. A. (1996). Practical intelligence and problem solving: Search for perspectives. In F. Blanchard-Fields & T. M. Hess (Eds.), *Perspectives on cognitive change in adulthood and aging* (pp. 323–357). New York: McGraw-Hill.

Berg, S. J., & Wynne-Edwards, K. E. (2001). Changes in testosterone, cortisol, and estradiol levels in men becoming fathers. *Mayo Clinic Proceedings, 76*(6), 582–592.

Bergeman, C. S., & Plomin, R. (1989). Genotype-environment interaction. In M. Bornstein & J. Bruner (Eds.), *Interaction in human development* (pp. 157–171). Hillsdale, NJ: Erlbaum.

Bergen, D. (2002). The role of pretend play in children's cognitive development. *Early Childhood Research & Practice,* 4(1). Retrieved from http://ecrp.uiuc.edu/v4n1/bergen.html

Berger, K. S. (2007). Update on bullying at school: Science forgotten? *Developmental Review, 27*, 91–92.

Berger, R. M., & Kelly, J. J. (1986). Working with homosexuals of the older population. *Social Casework, 67*, 203–210.

Bering, J. M., & Bjorklund, D. F. (2004). The natural emergence of reasoning ability about the afterlife as a developmental regularity. *Developmental Psychology, 40*, 217–233.

Berk, L. E. (1986a). Development of private speech among preschool children. *Early Child Development and Care, 24*, 113–136.

Berk, L. E. (1992). Children's private speech: An overview of theory and the status of research. In R. M. Diaz & L. E. Berk (Eds.), *Private speech: From social interaction to self-regulation* (pp. 17–53). Hillsdale, NJ: Erlbaum.

Berk, L. E., & Garvin, R. A. (1984). Development of private speech among low income Appalachian children. *Developmental Psychology, 20*, 271–286.

Berkman, L. F., & Glass, T. (2000). Social integration, social networks, social support, and health. In L. F. Berkman & I. Kawachi (Eds.), *Social epidemiology* (pp. 137–173). New York: Oxford University Press.

Berkowitz, G. S., Skovron, M. L., Lapinski, R. H., & Berkowitz, R. L. (1990). Delayed childbearing and the outcome of pregnancy. *New England Journal of Medicine, 322*, 659–664.

Berkowitz, R. I., Stallings, V. A., Maislin, G., & Stunkard, A. J. (2005). Growth of children at high risk of obesity during the first 6 years of life: Implications for prevention. *American Journal of Clinical Nutrition, 81*, 140–146.

Berlin, L. J., Ispa, J. M., Fine, M. A., Malone, P. S., Brooks-Gunn, J., Brady-Smith, C., . . . Bai, Y. (2009). Correlates and consequences of spanking and verbal punishment for low income White, African American and Mexican American toddlers. *Child Development, 80*(5), 1403–1420.

Berndt, T. J., & Perry, T. B. (1990). Distinctive features and effects of early adolescent friendships. In R. Montemayor, G. R. Adams, & T. P. Gullotta (Eds.), *From childhood to adolescence: A transitional period?* (Vol. 2, pp. 269–287). Newbury Park, CA: Sage.

Bernert, R. A., Merrill, K. A., Braithwaite, S. R., Van Orden, K. A., & Joiner, T. E. (2007). Family life stress and insomnia symptoms in a prospective evaluation of young adults. *Journal of Family Psychology, 21*, 58–66.

Bernier, A., Carlson, S. M., & Whipple, N. (2010). From external regulation to self-regulation: Early parenting precursors of young children's executive functioning. *Child Development, 81*, 326–339. doi: 10.1111/j.1467-8624.2009.01397.x

Bernier, A., & Meins, E. (2008). A threshold approach to understanding the origins of attachment disorganization. *Developmental Psychology, 44*, 969–982.

Bernstein, L., Patel A. V., Sullivan-Halley, J., Press, M. F., Deapen, D., Berlin, J. A., . . . Spirtas, R. (2005). Lifetime recreational exercise activity and breast cancer risk among black women and white women. *Journal of the National Cancer Institute, 97*, 1671–1679.

Bernstein, N. (2008). *"Aging in place" communities offer seniors independence and support.* Retrieved from www.caring.com/articles/aging-in-place

Bernstein, P. S. (2003, December 12). Achieving equity in women's and perinatal health. *Medscape Ob/Gyn & Women's Health, 8.*

Berrick, J. D. (1998). When children cannot remain home: Foster family care and kinship care. *Future of Children, 8*, 72–87.

Berry, M., Dylla, D. J., Barth, R. P., & Needell, B. (1998). The role of open adoption in the adjustment of adopted children and their families. *Children and Youth Services Review, 20*, 151–171.

Berry, R. J., Li, Z., Erickson, J. D., Li, S., Moore, C. A., Wang, H., . . . Correa, A. for the China-U.S. Collaborative Project for Neural Tube Defect Prevention. (1999). Prevention of neural-tube defects with folic acid in China. *New England Journal of Medicine, 341*, 1485–1490.

Bertenthal, B. I., & Campos, J. J. (1987). New directions in the study of early experience. *Child Development, 58*, 560–567.

Bertenthal, B. I., Campos, J. J., & Barrett, K. C. (1984). Self-produced locomotion: An organizer of emotional, cognitive, and social development in infancy. In R. N. Emde & R. J. Harmon (Eds.), *Continuities and discontinuities in development.* New York: Plenum Press.

Bertenthal, B. I., Campos, J. J., & Kermoian, R. (1994). An epigenetic perspective on the development of self-produced locomotion and its consequences. *Current Directions in Psychological Science, 3*(5), 140–145.

Bertenthal, B. I., & Clifton, R. K. (1998). Perception and action. In W. Damon (Series Ed.), D. Kuhn, & R. S. Siegler (Vol. Eds.), *Handbook of child psychology: Vol. 2. Cognition, perception, and language* (pp. 51–102). New York: Wiley.

Bertone-Johnson, E. R., Hankinson, S. E., Johnson, S. R., & Manson, J. E. (2008). Cigarette smoking and the development of premenstrual syndrome. *American Journal of Epidemiology, 168*(8), 938–945.

Bethell, C. D., Read, D., & Blumberg, S. J. (2005). Mental health in the United States: Health care and well-being of children with chronic emotional, behavioral, or developmental problem—United States, 2001. *Morbidity and Mortality Weekly Report, 54*, 985–989.

Beumont, P. J. V., Russell, J. D., & Touyz, S. W. (1993). Treatment of anorexia nervosa. *Lancet, 341*, 1635–1640.

Beversdorf, D. Q., Manning, S. E., Anderson, S. L., Nordgren, R. E., Walters, S. E., Cooley, W. C., . . . Bauman, M. L. (2001, November 10–15). *Timing of prenatal stressors and autism*. Presentation at the 31st annual meeting of the Society for Neuroscience, San Diego.

Bhaskaran, K., Hamouda, O., Sannesa, M., Boufassa, F., Johnson, A. M., Lambert, P. C., & Porter, K., for the CASCADE Collaboration. (2008). Changes in the risk of death after HIV seroconversion compared with mortality in the general population. *Journal of the American Medical Association, 300,* 51–59.

Bialystok, E., & Senman, L. (2004). Executive processes in appearance-reality tasks: The role of inhibition of attention and symbolic representation. *Child Development, 75,* 562–579.

Bialystok, E., Craik, F. I. M., & Freeman, M. (2007). Bilingualism as a protection against the onset of symptoms of dementia. *Neuropsychologia, 45*(2), 459–464.

Bialystok, E., Craik, F. I. M., Klein, R., & Viswanathan, M. (2004). Bilingualism, aging, and cognitive control: Evidence from the Simon task. *Psychology and Aging, 19,* 290–303.

Bianchi, S., Robinson, J., & Milkie, M. (2006). *The changing rhythms of American family life.* New York: Russell Sage Foundation.

Biason-Lauber, A., Konrad, D., Navratil, F., & Schoenle, E. J. (2004). A WNT4 mutation associated with Mullerian-duct regression and virilization in a 46,XX woman. *New England Journal of Medicine, 351,* 792–798.

Bibbins-Domingo, K., Coxson, P., Pletcher, M. J., Lightwood, J., & Goldman, L. (2007). Adolescent overweight and future adult coronary heart disease. *New England Journal of Medicine, 357,* 2371–2379.

Biblarz, T. J., & Stacey, J. (2010). How does gender of the parent matter? *Journal of Marriage and Family, 72,* 3–22.

Bickart, K. C., Wright, C. I., Duatoff, R. J., Dickerson, B. C., & Feldman, B. L. (2010). Amygdala volume and social network size in humans. *Nature Neuroscience, 14,* 163–164. doi:10.1038/nn.2724

Biegel, D. E. (1995). Caregiver burden. In G. E. Maddox (Ed.), *The encyclopedia of aging* (2nd ed., pp. 138–141). New York: Springer.

Bielby, D., & Papalia, D. (1975). Moral development and perceptual role-taking egocentrism: Their development and interrelationship across the lifespan. *International Journal of Aging and Human Development, 6*(4), 293–308.

Bienvenu, O. J., Nestadt, G., Samuels, J. F., Costa, P. T., Howard, W. T., & Eaton, W. W. (2001). Phobic, panic, and major depressive disorders and the five-factor model of personality. *Journal of Mental Diseases, 189,* 154–161.

Bierman, K. L., Smoot, D. L., & Aumiller, K. (1993). Characteristics of aggressive rejected, aggressive (nonrejected), and rejected (non-aggressive) boys. *Child Development, 64,* 139–151.

Billet, S. (2001). Knowing in practice: Reconceptualising vocational expertise. *Learning and Instruction, 11,* 431–452.

Billings, L. M., Green, K. N., McGaugh, J. L., & LaFerla, F. M. (2007). Learning decreases A beta*56 and tau pathology and ameliorates behavioral decline in 3xTg-AD mice. *Journal of Neuroscience, 27*(4), 751–761.

Billings, R. L., Hauser, S. T., & Allen, J. P. (2008). Continuity and change from adolescence to emerging adulthood: Adolescence-limited vs. life-course-persistent profound ego development arrests. *Journal of Youth and Adolescence, 37*(10), 1178–1192.

Bilsen, J., Cohen, J., & Deliens, L. (2007). End of life in Europe: An overview of medical practices. *Populations and Societies* (No. 430). Paris: INED.

Binstock, G., & Thornton, A. (2003). Separations, reconciliations, and living apart in cohabiting and marital units. *Journal of Marriage and Family, 65,* 432–443.

Birditt, K. S., Fingerman, K. L., & Zarit, S. H. (2010). Adult children's problems and successes: Implications for intergenerational ambivalence. *Journal of Gerontology, 65*(2), 145–153.

Birditt, K. S., Miller, L. M., Fingerman, K. L., & Lefkowitz, E. S. (2009). Tensions in the parent and adult child relationship: Links to solidarity and ambivalence. *Psychology and Aging, 24*(2), 287–295.

Birmaher, B. (1998). Should we use antidepressant medications for children and adolescents with depressive disorders? *Psychopharmacology Bulletin, 34,* 35–39.

Birmaher, B., Ryan, N. D., Williamson, D. E., Brent, D. A., Kaufman, J., Dahl, R. E., Perel, J., & Nelson, B. (1996). Childhood and adolescent depression: A review of the past 10 years. *Journal of the American Academy of Child and Adolescent Psychiatry, 35,* 1427–1440.

Biro, F. M., Galvez, M. P., Greenspan, L. C., Succop, P. A., Vangeepuram, N., Pinney, S. N., . . . Wolff, M. S. (2010). Pubertal assessment method and baseline characteristics in a mixed longitudinal study of girls. *Pediatrics, 126*(3), e583–590.

Bischoff, C., Petersen, H. C., Graakjaer, J., Andersen-Ranberg, K., Vaupel, J. W., Bohr, V. A., . . . Christensen, K. (2006). No association between telomere length and survival among the elderly and the oldest old. *Epidemiology, 17,* 190–194.

Bittles, A. H., Bower, C., Hussain, R., & Glasson, E. J. (2006). The four ages of Down syndrome. *European Journal of Public Health, 17*(2), 221–225.

Bjelakovic, G., Nikolova, D., Gluud, L. L., Simonetti, R. G., & Gluud, C. (2008). Antioxidant supplements for prevention of mortality in healthy participants and patients with various diseases. *Cochrane Database of Systematic Reviews, 2008*(2), CD007176.

Bjork, J. M., Knutson, B., Fong, G. W., Caggiano, D. M., Bennett, S. M., & Hommer, D. W. (2004). Incentive-elicited brain activities in adolescents: Similarities and differences from young adults. *Journal of Neuroscience, 24,* 1793–1802.

Bjorklund, D. F. (1997). The role of immaturity in human development. *Psychological Bulletin, 122,* 153–169.

Bjorklund, D. F., Miller, P. H., Coyle, T. R., & Slawinski, J. L. (1997). Instructing children to use memory strategies: Evidence of utilization deficiencies in memory training studies. *Developmental Review, 17*(4), 411–441.

Bjorklund, D. F., & Pellegrini, A. D. (2000). Child development and evolutionary psychology. *Child Development, 71,* 1687–1708.

Bjorklund, D. F., & Pellegrini, A. D. (2002). *The origins of human nature: Evolutionary developmental psychology.* Washington, DC: American Psychological Association.

Black, D. M., Delmas, P. D., Eastell, R., Reid, I. R., Boonen, S., Cauley, J. A., . . . the HORIZON Pivotal Fracture Trial. (2007). Once-yearly Zoledronic acid for treatment of postmenopausal osteoporosis. *New England Journal of Medicine, 356,* 1809–1822.

Black, J. E. (1998). How a child builds its brain: Some lessons from animal studies of neural plasticity. *Preventive Medicine, 27,* 168–171.

Black, M. C., & Breiding, M. J. (2008). Adverse health conditions and health risk behaviors associated with intimate partner violence—United States, 2005. *Morbidity and Mortality Weekly Report, 57,* 113–117.

Black, M. M., & Krishnakumar, A. (1998). Children in low-income, urban settings: Interventions to promote mental health and well-being. *American Psychologist, 53,* 636–646.

Black, R. E., Morris, S. S., & Bryce, J. (2003). Where and why are 10 million children dying each year? *Lancet, 361,* 2226–2234.

Blagrove, M., Alexander, C., & Horne, J. A. (1995). The effects of chronic sleep reduction on the performance of cognitive tasks sensitive to sleep deprivation. *Applied Cognitive Psychology, 9,* 21–40.

Blair, C. (2002). School readiness: Integrating cognition and emotion in a neurobiological conceptualization of children's functioning at school entry. *American Psychologist, 57,* 111–127.

Blaizot, A., Vergnes, J. N., Nuwwareh, S., Amar, J., & Sixou, M. (2009). Periodontal diseases and cardiovascular events: Meta-analysis of observational studies. *International Dental Journal, 59*(4), 197–209.

Blakemore, S., & Choudhury, S. (2006). Development of the adolescent brain: Implications for executive function and social cognition. *Journal of Child Psychology and Psychiatry, 47*(3), 296–312.

Blakeslee, S. (1997, April 17). Studies show talking with infants shapes basis of ability to think. *New York Times,* p. D21.

Blanchard-Fields, F. (2007). Everyday problem solving and emotion: An adult developmental perspective. *Current Directions in Psychological Science, 16*(1), 26–31.

Blanchard-Fields, F., Mienaltowski, A., & Seay, R. B. (2007). Age differences in everyday problem-solving effectiveness: Older adults select more effective strategies for interpersonal problems. *Journal of Gerontology: Psychological Sciences, 62B*, P61–P64.

Blanchard-Fields, F., & Norris, L. (1994). Causal attributions from adolescence through adulthood: Age differences, ego level, and generalized response style. *Aging and Cognition, 1*, 67–86.

Blanchard-Fields, F., Stein, R., & Watson, T. L. (2004). Age differences in emotion-regulation strategies in handling everyday problems. *Journal of Gerontology: Psychological Sciences, 59B*, P261–P269.

Blaskewicz, B. J., Willis, S. L., & Schaie, K. W. (2007). Cognitive training gains as a predictor of mental status. *Journal of Gerontology, 62B*, 45–52.

Blazer, D. G. (2009). Depression in late life: Review and commentary. *Focus, 7*(1), 118–136.

Bleske-Rechek, A., Lubinski, D., & Benbow, C. P. (2004). Meeting the educational needs of special populations. Advanced placement's role in developing exceptional human capital. *Psychological Sciences, 15*, 217–224.

Blieszner, R., & Roberto, K. (2006). Perspectives on close relationships among the baby boomers. In S. K. Whitbourne & S. L. Willis (Eds.), *The baby boomers grow up: Contemporary perspectives on midlife* (pp. 261–279). Mahwah, NJ: Erlbaum.

Block, J. (1971). *Lives through time.* Berkeley, CA: Bancroft.

Block, J. (1991). *Prototypes for the California Adult Q-set.* Berkeley: University of California, Department of Psychology.

Block, J. (1995a). A contrarian view of the five-factor approach to personality description. *Psychological Bulletin, 117*, 187–215.

Block, J. (1995b). Going beyond the five factors given: Rejoinder to Costa and McCrae (1995) and Goldberg and Saucier (1995). *Psychological Bulletin, 117*, 226–229.

Block, J., & Block, J. H. (2006). Venturing a 30-year longitudinal study. *American Psychologist, 61*, 315–327.

Block, R. W., Krebs, N. F., Committee on Child Abuse and Neglect, & Committee on Nutrition. (2005). Failure to thrive as a manifestation of child neglect. *Pediatrics, 116*(5), 1234–1237.

Bloodgood, J. M., Turnley, W. H., & Mudrack, P. (2008). The influence of ethics instruction, religiosity and ethics on cheating behavior. *Journal of Business Ethics, 82*(3), 0167–4544.

Bloom, B. (1985). *Developing talent in young people.* New York: Ballantine.

Blum, R., & Reinhart, P. (2000). *Reducing the risk: Connections that make a difference in the lives of youth.* Minneapolis: University of Minnesota, Division of General Pediatrics and Adolescent Health.

Blustein, D. L., Juntunen, C. L., & Worthington, R. L. (2000). The school-to-work transition: Adjustment challenge for the forgotten half. In S. D. Brown & R. W. Lent (Eds.), *Handbook of counseling psychology* (pp. 435–470). New York: Wiley.

Boatman, D., Freeman, J., Vining, E., Pulsifer, M., Miglioretti, D., Minahan, R., . . . McKhann, G. (1999). Language recovery after left hemispherectomy in children with late onset seizures. *Annals of Neurology, 46*(4), 579–586.

Bochukova, E. G., Huang, N., Keogh, J., Henning, E., Plurmann, C., Blaszczyk, K., . . . Faroqui, I. S. (2009). Large, rare chromosomal deletions associated with severe early-onset obesity. *Nature, 463*, 666–670.

Bocskay, K. A., Tang, D., Orjuela, M. A., Liu, X., Warburton, D. P., & Perera, F. P. (2005). Chromosomal aberrations in cord blood are associated with prenatal exposure to carcinogenic polycyclic aromatic hydrocarbons. *Cancer Epidemiology Biomarkers and Prevention, 14*, 506–511.

Boden, J. M., Fergusson, D. M., & Horwood, L. J. (2008). Early motherhood and subsequent life outcomes. *Journal of Child Psychology and Psychiatry, 49*(2), 151–160.

Bodkin, N. L., Alexander, T. M., Ortmeyer, H. K., Johnson, E., & Hansen, B. C. (2003). Mortality and morbidity in laboratory-maintained rhesus monkeys and effects of long-term dietary restriction. *Journal of Gerontology: Biological Sciences, 58A*, 212–219.

Bodner, E. (2009). On the origins of ageism in older and younger workers. *International Psychogeriatrics, 21*, 1003–1014.

Bodrova, E., & Leong, D. J. (1998). Adult influences on play: The Vygotskian approach. In D. P. Fromberg & D. Bergen (Eds.), *Play from birth to twelve and beyond: Contexts, perspectives, and meanings* (pp. 277–282). New York: Garland.

Bodrova, E., & Leong, D. J. (2005). High quality preschool programs: What would Vygotsky say? *Early Education & Development, 16*(4), 437–446.

Boerner, K., Schulz, R., & Horowitz, A. (2004). Positive aspects of caregiving and adaptation to bereavement. *Psychology and Aging, 19*, 668–675.

Boerner, K., Wortman, C. B., & Bonanno, G. A. (2005). Resilient or at risk? A 4-year study of older adults who initially showed high or low distress following conjugal loss. *Journal of Gerontology: Psychological Sciences, 60B*, P67–P73.

Boffetta, P., Couto, E., Wichman, J., Ferrari, P., Trichopoulos, D., Bas Bueno-de-Mesquita, H., . . . Trichopoulou, A. (2010). Fruit and vegetable intake and overall cancer risk in the European Prospective Investigation into Cancer and Nutrition (EPIC). *Journal of the National Cancer Institute, 102*(8), 529–537.

Bogaert, A. F. (2006). Biological versus nonbiological older brothers and men's sexual orientation. *Proceedings of the National Academy of Sciences, 103*, 10771–10774.

Bogard, K., & Takanishi, R. (2005). Pre-K through 3: An aligned and coordinated approach to education for children 3–8 years old. *Social Policy Report, 19*(3).

Bogg, T., & Roberts, B. W. (2004). Conscientiousness and health-related behaviors: A meta-analysis of the leading behavioral contributors to mortality. *Psychological Bulletin, 130*, 887–919.

Bograd, R., & Spilka, B. (1996). Self-disclosure and marital satisfaction in mid-life and late-life remarriages. *International Journal of Aging and Human Development, 42*(3), 161–172.

Bojczyk, K. E., & Corbetta, D. (2004). Object retrieval in the 1st year of life: Learning effects of task exposure and box transparency. *Developmental Psychology, 40*, 54–66.

Bollinger, M. B. (2003). Involuntary smoking and asthma severity in children: Data from the Third National Health and Nutrition Examination Survey (NHANES III). *Pediatrics, 112*, 471.

Bonanno, G. A. (2005). Resilience in the face of potential trauma. *Current Directions in Psychological Science, 14*, 135–138.

Bonanno, G. A., Galea, S., Bucciarelli, A., & Vlahov, D. (2006). Psychological resilience after disaster. *Current Directions in Psychological Science, 17*, 181–186.

Bonanno, G. A., Wortman, C. B., Lehman, D. R., Tweed, R. G., Haring, M., Sonnega, J., . . . Nesse, R. M. (2002). Resilience to loss and chronic grief: A prospective study from preloss to 18-month postloss. *Journal of Personality and Social Psychology*, 1150–1164.

Bonanno, G. A., Wortman, C. B., & Nesse, R. M. (2004). Prospective patterns of resilience and maladjustment during widowhood. *Psychology and Aging, 19*, 260–271.

Bookwala, J. (2009). The impact of adult care on marital quality and well-being in adult daughters and sons. *Journal of Gerontology, 64B*(3), 339–347.

Bookwala, J., & Fekete, E. (2009). The role of psychological resources in the affective well-being of never married adults. *Journal of Social and Personal Relationships, 26*(4), 411–428.

Boonstra, H. D. (2010). Winning campaign: California's concerted effort to reduce its teen pregnancy rate. *Gottmacher Policy Review, 13*(2), 18–24.

Booth, J. R., Burman, D. D., Meyer, J. R., Lei, Z., Trommer, B. L., Davenport, D., . . . Mesulam, M. M. (2003). Neural development of selective attention and response inhibition. *Neuroimage, 20*, 737–751.

Booth, J. L., & Siegler, R. S. (2006). Developmental and individual differences in pure numerical estimation. *Developmental Psychology, 41*, 189–201.

Booth, J. R., Perfetti, C. A., & MacWhinney, B. (1999). Quick, automatic, and general activation of orthographic and phonological representations in young readers. *Developmental Psychology, 35*(1), 3–19.

Booth-Kewley, S., Minagawa, R. Y., Shaffer, R. A., & Brodine, S. K. (2002). A behavioral intervention to prevent sexually transmitted diseases/human immunodeficiency virus in a Marine Corps sample. *Military Medicine, 167*, 145–150.

Bordone, L., & Guarente, L. (2005). Calorie restriction, SIRT1 and metabolism: Understanding longevity. *Nature Reviews Molecular Cell Biology, 6*(4), 298–305.

Bornstein, M. H., & Cote, L. R., with Maital, S., Painter, K., Park, S. Y., Pascual, L., . . .

Vyt, A. (2004). Cross-linguistic analysis of vocabulary in young children: Spanish, Dutch, French, Hebrew, Italian, Korean, and American English. *Child Development, 75*, 1115–1139.

Bornstein, M. H., Haynes, O. M., O'Reilly, A. W., & Painter, K. (1996). Solitary and collaborative pretense play in early childhood: Sources of individual variation in the development of representational competence. *Child Development, 67*, 2910–2929.

Bornstein, M. H., & Tamis-LeMonda, C. S. (1994). Antecedents of information processing skills in infants: Habituation, novelty responsiveness, and cross-modal transfer. *Infant Behavior and Development, 17*, 371–380.

Borse, N. N., Gilchrist, J., Dellinger, A. M., Rudd, R. A., Ballesteros, M. F., & Sleet, D. A. (2008). *CDC childhood injury reports: Patterns of unintentional injuries among 0–19 year olds in the United States, 2000–2006.* Atlanta, GA: Centers for Disease Control and Prevention, National Center for Injury Prevention and Control.

Borowsky, I. A., Ireland, M., & Resnick, M. D. (2001). Adolescent suicide attempts: Risks and protectors. *Pediatrics, 107*(3), 485–493.

Bosch, J., Sullivan, S., Van Dyke, D. C., Su, H., Klockau, L., Nissen, K., . . . Eberly, S. S. (2003). Promoting a healthy tomorrow here for children adopted from abroad. *Contemporary Pediatrics, 20*(2), 69–86.

Bosman, J. (2010, October). Picture books no longer a staple for children. *The New York Times.* Retrieved from http://www.nytimes.com/2010/10/08/us/08picture.html?emc=eta1

Boss, P. (1999). *Ambiguous loss.* Cambridge, MA: Harvard University Press.

Boss, P. (2000). *Ambiguous loss: Learning to live with unresolved grief.* Cambridge, MA: Harvard University Press.

Boss, P. (2002). Ambiguous loss: Working with the families of the missing. *Family Process, 41*, 14–17.

Boss, P. (2004). Ambiguous loss research, theory, and practice: Reflections after 9/11. *Journal of Marriage and Family, 66*(3), 551–566.

Boss, P. (2006). *Loss, trauma, and resilience: Therapeutic work with ambiguous loss.* New York: Norton.

Boss, P. (2007). Ambiguous loss theory: Challenges for scholars and practitioners. *Family Relations, 56*(2), 105–111.

Boss, P., Beaulieu, L., Wieling, E., Turner, W., & LaCruz, S. (2003). Healing loss, ambiguity, and trauma: A community-based intervention with families of union workers missing after the 9/11 attack in New York City. *Journal of Marital and Family Therapy, 29*(4), 455–467.

Bosshard, G., Nilstun, T., Bilsen, J., Norup, M., Miccinesi, G., vanDelden, J. J. M., . . . van der Heide, A., for the European End-of-Life (EURELD) Consortium. (2005). Forgoing treatment at the end of life in 6 European countries. *Archives of Internal Medicine, 165*, 401–407.

Botwinick, J. (1984). *Aging and behavior* (3rd ed.). New York: Springer.

Bouchard, T. J. (1994). Genes, environment, and personality. *Science, 264*, 1700–1701.

Bouchard, T. J. (2004). Genetic influence on human psychological traits: A survey. *Current Directions in Psychological Science, 13*, 148–154.

Bouchard, T. J., & McGue, M. (2003). Genetic and environmental influences on human psychological differences. *Developmental Neurobiology, 54*(1), 4–45.

Bouchey, H. A., & Furman, W. (2003). Dating and romantic experiences in adolescence. In G. R. Adams & M. D. Berzonsky (Eds.), *Blackwell handbook of adolescence* (pp. 313–329). Oxford, UK: Blackwell.

Boulton, M. J. (1995). Playground behaviour and peer interaction patterns of primary school boys classified as bullies, victims and not involved. *British Journal of Educational Psychology, 65*, 165–177.

Boulton, M. J., & Smith, P. K. (1994). Bully/victim problems in middle school children: Stability, self-perceived competence, peer perception, and peer acceptance. *British Journal of Developmental Psychology, 12*, 315–329.

Bourne, V. J., Fox, H. C., Deary, I. J., & Whalley, L. J. (2007). Does childhood intelligence predict variation in cognitive change in later life? *Personality and Individual Differences, 42*(8), 1551–1559.

Bowlby, J. (1951). Maternal care and mental health. *Bulletin of the World Health Organization, 3*, 355–534.

Bowlby, J. (1969). *Attachment and loss: Vol. I. Attachment.* London: Hogarth Press & the Institute of Psychoanalysis.

Bowman, S. A., Gortmaker, S. L., Ebbeling, C. B., Pereira, M. A., & Ludwig, D. S. (2004). Effects of fast food consumption on energy intake and diet quality among children in a national household survey. *Pediatrics, 113*, 112–118.

Boyce J. A., Assa'ad, A., Burks A. W., et al. (2010). Guidelines for the diagnosis and management of food allergy in the United States: Report of the NIAID-sponsored expert panel. *Journal of Allergy and Clinical Immunology, 126* (suppl 6), S1–S58.

Boyles, S. (2002, January 27). Toxic landfills may boost birth defects. *WebMD Medical News.* Retrieved from www.webmd.com/content/article/25/3606_1181.htm

Brabant, S. (1994). An overlooked AIDS affected population: The elderly parent as caregiver. *Journal of Gerontological Social Work, 22*, 131–145.

Brabeck, M. M., & Shore, E. L. (2003). Gender differences in intellectual and moral development? The evidence refutes the claims. In J. Demick & C. Andreoletti (Eds.), *Handbook of adult development* (pp. 351–368). New York: Plenum Press.

Bracher, G., & Santow, M. (1999). Explaining trends in teenage childbearing in Sweden. *Studies in Family Planning, 30*, 169–182.

Brackett, M. A., Cox, A., Gaines, S. O., & Salovey, P. (2005). *Emotional intelligence and relationship quality among heterosexual couples.* Unpublished data, Yale University.

Brackett, M. A., Mayer, J. D., & Warner, R. M. (2004). Emotional intelligence and the prediction of behavior. *Personality and Individual Differences, 36*, 1387–1402.

Bradley, R. H. (1989). Home measurement of maternal responsiveness. In M. H. Bornstein (Ed.), *Maternal responsiveness: Characteristics and consequences* (New Directions for Child Development, No. 43). San Francisco: Jossey-Bass.

Bradley, R., & Caldwell, B. (1982). The consistency of the home environment and its relation to child development. *International Journal of Behavioral Development, 5*, 445–465.

Bradley, R., Caldwell, B., & Rock, S. (1988). Home environment and school performance: A ten-year follow-up and examination of three models of environmental action. *Child Development, 59*, 852–867.

Bradley, R. H., Caldwell, B. M., Rock, S. L., Ramey, C. T., Barnard, K. E., Gray, C., . . . Johnson, D. L. (1989). Home environment and cognitive development in the first 3 years of life: A collaborative study involving six sites and three ethnic groups in North America. *Developmental Psychology, 25*, 217–235.

Bradley, R. H., Corwyn, R. F., Burchinal, M., McAdoo, H. P., & Coll, C. G. (2001). The home environment of children in the United States: Part II: Relations with behavioral development through age thirteen. *Child Development, 72*(6), 1868–1886.

Bradley, R. H., Corwyn, R. F., McAdoo, H. P., & Coll, C. G. (2001). The home environment of children in the United States: Part I: Variation by age, ethnicity, and poverty status. *Child Development, 72*(6), 1844–1867.

Braine, M. (1976). Children's first word combinations. *Monographs of the Society for Research in Child Development, 41*(1, Serial No. 164).

Bramlett, M. D., & Mosher, W. D. (2001). First marriage dissolution, divorce, and remarriage: United States. *Advance Data from Vital and Health Statistics, No. 323.* Hyattsville, MD: National Center for Health Statistics.

Bramlett, M. D., & Mosher, W. D. (2002). Cohabitation, marriage, divorce, and remarriage in the United States. *Vital Health Statistics, 23*(22). Hyattsville, MD: National Center for Health Statistics.

Brandt, B. (1989). A place for her death. *Humanistic Judaism, 17*(3), 83–85.

Brannon, E. M. (2002). The development of ordinal numerical knowledge in infancy. *Cognition, 83*, 223–240.

Branum, A., & Lukacs, S. L. (2008). *Food allergy among U.S. children: Trends in prevalence and hospitalizations* (Data Brief No. 10). Hyattsville, MD: National Center for Health Statistics.

Branum, A. M., & Lukacs, S. L. (2009). Food allergy among children in the United States. *Pediatrics, 124*(6) 1549–1555. doi:10.1542/peds.2009-1210

Brass, L. M., Isaacsohn, J. L., Merikangas, K. R., & Robinette, C. D. (1992). A study of twins and stroke. *Stroke, 23*(2), 221–223.

Braswell, G. S. (2006). Sociocultural contexts for the early development of semiotic production. *Psychological Bulletin, 132*, 877–894.

Bratter, J. L., & King, R. B. (2008). "But will it last?": Marital instability among interracial and same-race couples. *Family Relations, 57*(2), 160–171.

Bratton, S. C., & Ray, D. (2002). Humanistic play therapy. In D. J. Cain (Ed.), *Humanistic psychotherapies: Handbook of research and practice* (pp. 369–402). Washington, DC: American Psychological Association.

Braun, H., Jenkins, F., & Grigg, W. (2006). *A closer look at charter schools using hierarchical linear modeling* (NCES 2006-460). Washington, DC: U.S. Government Printing Office.

Braungart, J. M., Plomin, R., DeFries, J. C., & Fulker, D. W. (1992). Genetic influence on tester-rated infant temperament as assessed by Bayley's Infant Behavior Record: Nonadoptive and adoptive siblings and twins. *Developmental Psychology, 28*, 40–47.

Braungart-Rieker, J. M., Garwood, M. M., Powers, B. P., & Wang, X. (2001). Parental sensitivity, infant affect, and affect regulation: Predictors of later attachment. *Child Development, 72*(1), 252–270.

Bray, J. H., & Hetherington, E. M. (1993). Families in transition: Introduction and overview. *Journal of Family Psychology, 7*, 3–8.

Brayne, C. (2007). The elephant in the room—Healthy brains in later life, epidemiology and public health. *Neuroscience, 8*(3), 233–239.

Brayne, C., Ince, P. G., Keage, H. A. D., McKeith, I. G., Matthews, F. E., Polvikoski, T., & Sulkava, R. (2010). Education, the brain and dementia: Neuroprotection or compensation? *Brain: A Journal of Neurology, 133*(8), 2210–2216.

Brazelton, T. B. (1973). *Neonatal Behavioral Assessment Scale.* Philadelphia: Lippincott.

Brazelton, T. B. (1984). *Neonatal Behavioral Assessment Scale* (2nd ed.). Philadelphia: Lippincott.

Brazelton, T. B., & Nugent, J. K. (1995). *Neonatal Behavioral Assessment Scale* (3rd ed.). Cambridge: Cambridge University Press.

Brazelton, T. B., & Nugent, J. K. (2011). *Neonatal Behavioral Assessment Scale* (4th ed.). Hoboken, NJ: Wiley.

Breastfeeding and HIV International Transmission Study Group. (2004). Late postnatal transmission of HIV-1 in breast-fed children: An individual patient data meta-analysis. *Journal of Infectious Diseases, 189*, 2154–2166.

Brecklin, L. R., & Ullman, S. E. (2010). The roles of victim and offender substance use in sexual assault outcomes. *Journal of Interpersonal Violence, 25*(8), 1503–1522. doi: 0886260509354584

Brendgen, M., Dionne, G., Girard, A., Boivin, M., Vitaro, F., & Perusse, D. (2005). Examining genetic and environmental effects on social aggression: A study of 6-year-old twins. *Child Development, 76*, 930–946.

Brenneman, K., Massey, C., Machado, S. F., & Gelman, R. (1996). Young children's plans differ for writing and drawing. *Cognitive Development, 11*, 397–419.

Brent, M. R., & Siskind, J. M. (2001). The role of exposure to isolated words in early vocabulary development. *Cognition, 81*, 33–34.

Brent, D. A., & Birmaher, B. (2002). Adolescent depression. *New England Journal of Medicine, 347*, 667–671.

Brent, D. A., & Mann, J. J. (2006). Familial pathways to suicidal behavior—Understanding and preventing suicide among adolescents. *New England Journal of Medicine, 355*, 2719–2721.

Bretherton, I. (1990). Communication patterns, internal working models, and the intergenerational transmission of attachment relationships. *Infant Mental Health Journal, 11*(3), 237–252.

Brewaeys, A., Ponjaert, I., Van Hall, V. E., & Golombok, S. (1997). Donor insemination: Child development and family functioning in lesbian mother families. *Human Reproduction, 12*, 1349–1359.

Brier, N. (2008). Grief following miscarriage: A comprehensive review of the literature. *Journal of Women's Health, 17*(3), 451–464.

Bridge, J. A., Iyengar, S., Salary, C. B., Barbe, R. P., Birmaher, B., Pincus, H. A., . . . Brent, D. A. (2007). Clinical response and risk for reported suicidal ideation and suicide attempts in pediatric antidepressant treatment: A meta-analysis of randomized controlled trials. *Journal of the American Medical Association, 297*, 1683–1696.

Briggs, J. L. (1970). *Never in anger.* Cambridge, MA: Harvard University Press.

Briggs, G. G., Freeman, R. K., & Yaffe, S. J. (2012). *Drugs in pregnancy and lactation: A reference guide to fetal and neonatal risk.* Baltimore, MD: Lippincott Williams & Wilkins.

Brim, O. G., Ryff, C. D., & Kessler, R. C. (2004). The MIDUS National Survey: An overview. In O. G. Brim, C. D. Ryff, & R. C. Kessler (Eds.), *How healthy are we? A national study of well-being at midlife.* Chicago: University of Chicago Press.

Britton, W. B., & Bootzin, R. R. (2004). Near-death experiences and the temporal lobe. *Psychological Science, 15*, 254–258.

Brody, E. M. (2004). *Women in the middle: Their parent care years* (2nd ed.). New York: Springer.

Brody, G. H. (1998). Sibling relationship quality: Its causes and consequences. *Annual Review of Psychology, 49*, 1–24.

Brody, G. H. (2004). Siblings' direct and indirect contributions to child development. *Current Directions in Psychological Science, 13*, 124–126.

Brody, G. H., Chen, Y.-F., Murry, V. M., Ge, X., Simons, R. L., Gibbons, F. X., . . . Cutrona, C. E. (2006). Perceived discrimination and the adjustment of African American youths: A five-year longitudinal analysis with contextual moderation effects. *Child Development, 77*(5), 1170–1189.

Brody, G. H., Ge., X., Conger, R., Gibbons, F. X., Murry, V. M., Gerrard, M., & Simons, R. L. (2001). The influence of neighborhood disadvantage, collective socialization, and parenting on African American children's affiliation with deviant peers. *Child Development, 72*(4), 1231–1246.

Brody, G. H., Kim, S., Murry, V. M., & Brown, A. C. (2004). Protective longitudinal paths linking child competence to behavioral problems among African American siblings. *Child Development, 75*, 455–467.

Brody, J. E. (1995, June 28). Preventing birth defects even before pregnancy. *The New York Times*, p. C10.

Brody, L. R., Zelazo, P. R., & Chaika, H. (1984). Habituation-dishabituation to speech in the neonate. *Developmental Psychology, 20*, 114–119.

Brodzinsky, D. (1997). Infertility and adoption adjustment: Considerations and clinical issues. In S. R. Leiblum (Ed.), *Infertility: Psychological issues and counseling strategies* (pp. 246–262). New York: Wiley.

Broidy, L. M., Tremblay, R. E., Brame, B., Fergusson, D., Horwood, J. L., Laird, R., . . . Vitaro, F. (2003). Developmental trajectories of childhood disruptive behaviors and adolescent delinquency: A six-site cross-national study. *Developmental Psychology, 39*, 222–245.

Bromberger, J. T., Harlow, S., Avis, N., Kravitz, H. M., & Cordal, A. (2004). Racial/ethnic differences in the prevalence of depressive symptoms among middle-aged women: The study of women's health across the nation (SWAN). *American Journal of Public Health, 94*, 1378–1385.

Bromberger, J. T., Meyer, P. M., Kravitz, H. M., Sommer, B., Cordal, A., Powell, L., . . . Sutton-Tyrell, K. (2001). Psychologic distress and natural menopause: A multiethnic community study. *American Journal of Public Health, 91*, 1435–1442.

Bronfenbrenner, U. (1979). *The ecology of human development.* Cambridge, MA: Harvard University Press.

Bronfenbrenner, U. (1986). Ecology of the family as a context for human development: Research perspectives. *Developmental Psychology, 22*, 723–742.

Bronfenbrenner, U. (1994). Ecological models of human development. In T. Husen & T. N. Postlethwaite (Eds.), *International encyclopedia of education* (Vol. 3, 2nd ed., pp. 1643–1647). Oxford: Pergamon Press/Elsevier Science.

Bronfenbrenner, U., & Morris, P. A. (1998). The ecology of developmental processes. In W. Damon (Series Ed.) & R. Lerner (Vol. Ed.), *Handbook of child psychology: Vol. 1. Theoretical models of human development* (5th ed., pp. 993–1028). New York: Wiley.

Bronstein, P. (1988). Father-child interaction: Implications for gender role socialization. In P. Bronstein & C. P. Cowan (Eds.), *Fatherhood today: Men's changing role in the family.* New York: Wiley.

Bronstein, P., Clauson, J., Stoll, M. F., & Abrams, C. L. (1993). Parenting behavior and children's social, psychological, and academic adjustment in diverse family structures. *Family Relations, 42*, 268–276.

Brookmeyer, K. A., Henrich, C. C., & Schwab-Stone, M. (2005). Adolescents who witness community violence: Can parent support and prosocial cognitions protect them from committing violence? *Child Development, 76*, 917–929.

Brookmeyer, R., Johnson, E., Ziegler-Graham, K., & Arrighi, H. M. (2007). Forecasting the global burden of Alzheimer's disease. *Alzheimer's and Dementia, 3*(3), 186–191. Paper also presented in June 2007 at the meeting of the second Alzheimer's Association International Conference on Prevention of Dementia, Washington, DC.

Brooks, R., & Meltzoff, A. N. (2002). The importance of eyes: How infants interpret adult looking behavior. *Developmental Psychology, 38*, 958–966.

Brooks, R., & Meltzoff, A. N. (2005). The development of gaze following and its relation to language. *Developmental Science, 8*, 535–543.

Brooks-Gunn, J. (2003). Do you believe in magic? What can we expect from early childhood intervention programs? *SRCD Social Policy Report, 17*(1).

Brooks-Gunn, J., Britto, P. R., & Brady, C. (1998). Struggling to make ends meet: Poverty and child development. In M. E. Lamb (Ed.), *Parenting and child development in "nontraditional" families* (pp. 279–304). Mahwah, NJ: Erlbaum.

Brooks-Gunn, J., Han, W.-J., & Waldfogel, J. (2002). Maternal employment and child cognitive outcomes in the first three years of life: The NICHD study of early child care. *Child Development, 73*, 1052–1072.

Broude, G. J. (1994). *Marriage, family, and relationships: A cross-cultural encyclopedia.* Santa Barbara, CA: ABC-CLIO.

Broude, G. J. (1995). *Growing up: A crosscultural encyclopedia.* Santa Barbara, CA: ABC-CLIO.

Brougham, R. R., Zail, C. M., Mendoza, C. M., & Miller, J. R. (2009). Stress, sex differences, and coping strategies among college students. *Current Psychology, 28*(2), 85–97.

Brousseau, E. (2006, May). *The effect of maternal body mass index on efficacy of dinoprostone vaginal insert for cervical ripening.* Paper presented at the annual meeting of the American College of Obstetricians and Gynecologists, Washington, DC.

Brown, A. L., Metz, K. E., & Campione, J. C. (1996). Social interaction and individual understanding in a community of learners: The influence of Piaget and Vygotsky. In A. Tryphon & J. Voneche (Eds.), *Piaget-Vygotsky: The social genesis of thought* (pp. 145–170). Hove, UK: Psychology Press.

Brown, A. S., Begg, M. D., Gravenstein, S., Schaefer, C. A., Wyatt, R. J., Bresnahan, M., . . . Susser, E. S. (2004). Serologic evidence of prenatal influence in the etiology of schizophrenia. *Archives of General Psychiatry, 61*, 774–780.

Brown, A. S., Tapert, S. F., Granholm, E., & Delis, D. C. (2000). Neurocognitive functioning of adolescents: Effects of protracted alcohol use. *Alcoholism: Clinical and Experimental Research, 24*, 64–171.

Brown, B. B., & Klute, C. (2003). Friendships, cliques, and crowds. In G. R. Adams & M. D. Berzonsky (Eds.), *Blackwell handbook of adolescence* (pp. 330–348). Malden, MA: Blackwell.

Brown, B. B., Mounts, N., Lamborn, S. D., & Steinberg, L. (1993). Parenting practices and peer group affiliation in adolescence (pp. 245–270). Cambridge, UK: Cambridge University Press.

Brown, J. L. (1987). Hunger in the U.S. *Scientific American, 256*(2), 37–41.

Brown, J. R., & Dunn, J. (1996). Continuities in emotion understanding from three to six years. *Child Development, 67*, 789–802.

Brown, J. T., & Stoudemire, A. (1983). Normal and pathological grief. *Journal of the American Medical Association, 250*, 378–382.

Brown, L. M., & Gilligan, C. (1990, April). *The psychology of women and the development of girls.* Paper presented at the Laurel-Harvard Conference on the Psychology of Women and the Education of Girls, Cleveland, OH.

Brown, P. (1993, April 17). Motherhood past midnight. *New Scientist*, pp. 4–8.

Brown, S. L. (2004). Family structure and child well-being: The significance of parental cohabitation. *Journal of Marriage and Family, 66*, 351–367.

Brown, S. L., Bulanda, J. R., & Lee, G. R. (2005). The significance of nonmarital cohabitation: Marital status and mental health benefits among middle-aged and older adults. *Journal of Gerontology: Social Sciences, 60B*, S21–S29.

Brown, S. L., Lee, G. R., & Bulanda, J. R. (2006). Cohabitation among older adults: A national portrait. *Journal of Gerontology: Social Sciences, 61B*, S71–S79.

Browne, A., & Finkelhor, D. (1986). Impact of child sexual abuse: A review of research. *Psychological Bulletin, 99*(1), 66–77.

Brownell, C. A., Ramani, G. B., & Zerwas, S. (2006). Becoming a social partner with peers: Cooperation and social understanding in one- and two-year-olds. *Child Development, 77*, 803–821.

Browning, C. R. (2002). The span of collective efficacy: Extending social disorganization theory to partner violence. *Journal of Marriage and Family, 64*, 833–850.

Bruer, J. T. (2001). A critical and sensitive period primer. In D. B. Bailey, J. T. Bruer, F. J. Symons, & J. W. Lichtman (Eds.), *Critical thinking about critical periods: A series from the National Center for Early Development and Learning* (pp. 289–292). Baltimore, MD: Paul Brooks Publishing.

Bruner, A. B., Joffe, A., Duggan, A. K., Casella, J. F., & Brandt, J. (1996). Randomised study of cognitive effects of iron supplementation in non-anaemic iron-deficient adolescent girls. *Lancet, 348*, 992–996.

Brunson, K. L., Kramar, E., Lin, B., Chen, Y., Colgin, L. L., Yanagihara, T. K., Lynch, G., & Baram, T. Z. (2005). Mechanisms of late-onset cognitive decline after early-life stress. *Journal of Neurosicence, 25*(41), 9328–9338.

Bryant, B. K. (1987). Mental health, temperament, family, and friends: Perspectives on children's empathy and social perspective taking. In N. Eisenberg & J. Strayer (Eds.), *Empathy and its development of competence in adolescence* (pp. 245–270). Cambridge, UK: Cambridge University Press.

Bryce, J., Boschi-Pinto, C., Shibuya, K., Black, R. E., & the WHO Child Health Epidemiology Reference Group. (2005). WHO estimates of the causes of death in children. *Lancet, 365*, 1147–1152.

Buchanan, C. M., Eccles, J. S., & Becker, J. B. (1992). Are adolescents the victims of raging hormones? Evidence for activational effects of hormones on moods and behavior at adolescence. *Psychological Bulletin, 111*(1), 62–107.

Buck Louis, G., Gray, L., Marcus, M., Ojeda, S., Pescovitz, O., Witchel, S., . . . Euling, S. Y. (2008). Environmental factors and puberty timing: Expert panel research needs. *Pediatrics, 121*, S192–S207.

Buchmann, C., & DiPrete, T. A. (2006). The growing female advantage in college completion: The role of family background and academic achievement. *American Sociological Review, 71*, 515–541.

Buck-Morss, S. (1975). Social-economic bias in Piaget's theories and its implication for cross-cultural study. *Human Development, 18*(1–2), 35–49.

Buchmueller, T., & Carpenter, C. (2010). Disparities in health insurance coverage, access and outcomes for individuals in same-sex versus different-sex relationships, 2000–2007. *American Journal of Public Health, 100*(3), 489–495.

Bucur, B., & Madden, D. J. (2010). Effects of adult age and blood pressure on executive function and speech of processing. *Experimental Aging Research, 36*(2), 153–168.

Budson, A. E., & Price, B. H. (2005). Memory dysfunction. *New England Journal of Medicine, 352*, 692–699.

Budtz-Jørgensen, E., Chung, J. P., & Rapin, C. H. (2001). Nutrition and oral health. *Best Practice & Research Clinical Gastroenterology, 15*(6), 885–896.

Buehler, C. (2006). Parents and peers in relation to early adolescent problem behavior. *Journal of Marriage and Family, 68*, 109–124.

Buehler, C., & Welsh, D. P. (2009). A process model of adolescents' triangulation into parents' marital conflict: The role of emotional reactivity. *Journal of Family Psychology, 23*(2), 167–180.

Buell, J. S., Scott, T. M., Dawson-Hughes, B., Dallal, G. E., Rosenberg, I. H., Folstein, M. F., & Tucker, K. L. (2009). Vitamin D is associated with cognitive function in elders receiving home health services. *Journals of Gerontology, 64A*(8), 888–895.

Buhrmester, D. (1990). Intimacy of friendship, interpersonal competence, and adjustment during preadolescence and adolescence. *Child Development, 61*, 1101–1111.

Buhrmester, D., & Furman, W. (1990). Perceptions of sibling relationships during middle childhood and adolescence. *Child Development, 61*, 138–139.

Buist, K. L., Dekovic, M., & Prinzie, P. (2013). Sibling relationship quality and psychopathology of children and adolescents: A meta-analysis. *Clinical Psychology Review, 33*(1), 97–106.

Bulanda, J. R., & Brown, S. L. (2007). Race-ethnic differences in marital quality and divorce. *Social Science Research, 36*(3), 945–967.

Bulcroft, R. A., & Bulcroft, K. A. (1991). The nature and function of dating in later life. *Research on Aging, 13*, 244–260.

Bunikowski, R., Grimmer, I., Heiser, A., Metze, B., Schafer, A., & Obladen, M. (1998). Neurodevelopmental outcome after prenatal exposure to opiates. *European Journal of Pediatrics, 157*, 724–730.

Burchinal, M. R., Roberts, J. E., Nabors, L. A., & Bryant, D. M. (1996). Quality of center child care and infant cognitive and language development. *Child Development, 67*, 606–620.

Bureau of Labor Statistics. (2005). *Data on unemployment rate.* Retrieved from www.bls.gov/cps/home.htm

Burke, D. M., & Shafto, M. A. (2004). Aging and language production. *Current Directions in Psychological Science, 13*, 81–84.

Burke, S. N., & Barnes, C. A. (2006). Neural plasticity in the ageing brain. *Nature Review Neuroscience, 7*, 30–40.

Burns, B. J., Phillips, S. D., Wagner, H. R., Barth, R. P., Kolko, D. J., Campbell, Y., & Landsverk, J. (2004). Mental health need and access to mental health services by youths involved with child welfare: A national survey. *Journal of the American Academy of Child & Adolescent Psychiatry, 43*, 960–970.

Burton, L. C., Zdaniuk, B., Schulz, R., Jackson, S., & Hirsch, C. (2003). Transitions in spousal caregiving. *Gerontologist, 43*, 230–241.

Bushman, B. J.; Huesmann, Rowell. (2001). *Effects of televised violence on aggression.* In Dorothy G. Singer and Jerome L. Singer (Eds.), *Handbook of Children and the Media,* p. 235, Figure 11.5. Sage Publications, Inc.

Bushnell, E. W., & Boudreau, J. P. (1993). Motor development and the mind: The potential role of motor abilities as a determinant of aspects of perceptual development. *Child Development, 64*, 1005–1021.

Bussey, K., & Bandura, A. (1992). Self-regulatory mechanisms governing gender development. *Child Development, 63*, 1236–1250.

Bussey, K., & Bandura, A. (1999). Social cognitive theory of gender development and differentiation. *Psychological Review, 106*, 676–713.

Bussey, K. (2011). Gender identity development. In S. J. Schwarts, K. Luyckx, & V. L. Vignoles (Eds.), *Handbook of identity theory and research: Vol. 1. Structures and processes* (pp. 603–628). New York: Springer.

Butler, R. (1961). Reawakening interests. *Nursing Homes: Journal of the American Nursing Home Association, 10*, 8–19.

Butler, R. (1996). The dangers of physician-assisted suicide. *Geriatrics, 51*, 7.

Butler, R. N., Davis, R., Lewis, C. B., Nelson, M. E., & Strauss, E. (1998a). Physical fitness: Benefits of exercise for the older patient. *Geriatrics 53*, 46, 49–52, 61–62.

Butler, R. N., Davis, R., Lewis, C. B., Nelson, M. E., & Strauss, E. (1998b). Physical fitness: How to help older patients live stronger and longer. *Geriatrics, 53*, 26–28, 31–32, 39–40.

Byers, T. (2006). Overweight and mortality among baby boomers—Now we're getting personal. *New England Journal of Medicine, 355*, 758–760.

Byers-Heinlein, K., Burns, T. C., & Werker, J. F. (2010). The roots of bilingualism in newborns. *Psychological Science, 21*(3), 343–348. doi:10.1177/0956797609360758

Byrne, M., Agerbo, E., Ewald, H., Eaton, W. W., & Mortensen, P. B. (2003). Parental age and risk of schizophrenia. *Archives of General Psychiatry, 60*, 673–678.

Byrnes, J. P., & Fox, N. A. (1998). The educational relevance of research in cognitive neuroscience. *Educational Psychology Review, 10*, 297–342.

Bystron, I., Rakic, P., Molnar, Z., & Blakemore, C. (2006). The first neurons of the human cerebral cortex. *Nature Neuroscience, 9*(7), 880–886.

Caballero, B. (2006). Obesity as a consequence of undernutrition. *Journal of Pediatrics, 149*(5, Suppl. 1), 97–99.

Cabrera, N. J., Tamis-LeMonda, C. S., Bradley, R. H., Hofferth, S., & Lamb, M. E. (2000). Fatherhood in the twenty-first century. *Child Development, 71*, 127–136.

Cacciatore, J., DeFrain, J., & Jones, K. L. C. (2008). When a baby dies: Ambiguity and stillbirth. *Marriage & Family Review, 44*(4), 439–454.

Cahn, Z., & Siegel, M. (2011). Electronic cigarettes as a harm reduction strategy for tobacco control: A step forward or a repeat of past mistakes? *Journal of Public Health Policy, 32*, 16–31. doi: 10.1057/jphp2010.41

Cajochen, C., Münch, M., Knoblauch, V., Blatter, K., & Wirz-Justice, A. (2006). Age-related changes in the circadian and homeostatic regulation of human sleep. *Chronobiology International, 23*(1–2), 461–474.

Caldwell, B. M., & Bradley, R. H. (1984). *Home observation for measurement of the environment.* Unpublished manuscript, University of Arkansas at Little Rock.

Calkins, S. D., & Fox, N. A. (1992). The relations among infant temperament, security of attachment, and behavioral inhibition at twenty-four months. *Child Development, 63*, 1456–1472.

Callahan, S. T., & Cooper, W. O. (2005). Uninsurance and health care access among young adults in the United States. *Pediatrics, 116*, 88–95.

Camarata, S., & Woodcock, R. (2006). Sex differences in processing speed: Developmental effects in males and females. *Intelligence, 34*(3), 231–252.

Cameron, L., Rutland, A., Brown, R., & Douch, R. (2006). Changing children's intergroup attitudes towards refugees: Testing different models of extended contact. *Child Development, 77*, 1208–1219.

Camilli, G., Vargas, S., Ryan, S., & Barnett, W. S. (2010). Meta-analysis of the effects of early education interventions on cognitive and social development. *Teachers College Record, 112*(3), 579–620.

Camp, C. J. (1989). World-knowledge systems. In L. W. Poon, D. C. Rubin, & B. A. Wilson (Eds.), *Everyday cognition in adulthood and late life.* Cambridge, UK: Cambridge University Press.

Camp, C. J., & McKitrick, L. A. (1989). The dialectics of remembering and forgetting across the adult lifespan. In D. Kramer & M. Bopp (Eds.), *Dialectics and contextualism in clinical and developmental psychology: Change, transformation, and the social context* (pp. 169–187). New York: Springer.

Campa, M. J., & Eckenrode, J. J. (2006). Pathways to intergenerational adolescent childbearing in a high-risk sample. *Journal of Marriage and Family, 68*, 558–572.

Campbell, F. A., Ramey, C., Pungello, E., Sparling, J., & Miller-Johnson, S. (2002). Early childhood education: Young adult outcomes from the Abecedarian Project. *Applied Developmental Science, 6*(1), 42–57.

Campbell, A., Shirley, L., & Candy, J. (2004). A longitudinal study of gender-related cognition and behaviour. *Developmental Science, 7*, 1–9.

Campbell, A., Shirley, L., Heywood, C., & Crook, C. (2000). Infants' visual preference for sex-congruent babies, children, toys, and activities: A longitudinal study. *British Journal of Developmental Psychology, 18*, 479–498.

Campos, J., Bertenthal, B., & Benson, N. (1980, April). *Self-produced locomotion and the extraction of form invariance.* Paper presented at the meeting of the International Conference on Infant Studies, New Haven, CT.

Cansino, S. (2009). Episodic memory decay along the adult lifespan: A review of behavioral and neurophysiological evidence. *International Journal of Psychophysiology, 71*(1), 64–69.

Cantor, J. (1994). Confronting children's fright responses to mass media. In D. Zillman, J. Bryant, & A. C. Huston (Eds.), *Media, children, and the family: Social scientific, psychoanalytic, and clinical perspectives* (pp. 139–150). Hillsdale, NJ: Erlbaum.

Cao, A., Rosatelli, M. C., Monni, G., & Galanello, R. (2002). Screening for thalassemia: A model of success. *Obstetrics and Gynecology Clinics of North America, 29*(2), 305–328.

Capaldi, D. M., Stoolmiller, M., Clark, S., & Owen, L. D. (2002). Heterosexual risk behaviors in at-risk young men from early adolescence to young adulthood: Prevalence, prediction, and STD contraction. *Developmental Psychology, 38*, 394–406.

Caplan, L. J., & Schooler, C. (2006). Household work complexity, intellectual functioning, and self-esteem in men and women. *Journal of Marriage and Family, 68*, 883–900.

Caprara, G. V., Fida, R., Vecchione, M., Del Bove, G., Vecchio, G. M., Barbaranelli, C., &

Bandura, A. (2008). Longitudinal analysis of the role of perceived self-efficacy for self-regulated learning in academic continuance and achievement. *Journal of Educational Psychology, 100*(3), 525–534.

Capute, A. J., Shapiro, B. K., & Palmer, F. B. (1987). Marking the milestones of language development. *Contemporary Pediatrics, 4*(4), 24.

Caraballo, R. S., Giovino, G. A., Pechacek, T. F., Mowery, P. D., Richter, P. A., Strauss, W. J., . . . Maurer, K. R. (1998). Racial and ethnic differences in serum cotinine levels of cigarette smokers. *Journal of the American Medical Association, 280*, 135–139.

Card, N., Stucky, B., Sawalani, G., & Little, T. (2008). Direct and indirect aggression during childhood and adolescence: A meta-analytic review of gender differences, intercorrelations, and relations to maladjustment. *Child Development, 79*(5), 1185–1229.

Carlson, E. A. (1998). A prospective longitudinal study of attachment disorganization/disorientation. *Child Development, 69*(4), 1107–1128.

Carlson, M. J. (2006). Family structure, father involvement, and adolescent behavioral outcomes. *Journal of Marriage and Family, 68*, 137–154.

Carlson, N. E., Moore, M. M., Dame, A., Howieson, D., Silbert, L. C., Quinn, J. F., & Kaye, J. A. (2008). Trajectories of brain loss in aging and the development of cognitive impairment. *Neurology, 79*(11), 828–833.

Carlson, S. M., Moses, L. J., & Hix, H. R. (1998). The role of inhibitory processes in young children's difficulties with deception and false belief. *Child Development, 69*(3), 672–691.

Carlson, S. M., & Taylor, M. (2005). Imaginary companions and impersonated characters: Sex differences in children's fantasy play. *Merrill-Palmer Quarterly, 51*(1), 93–118.

Carmichael, M. (2004, January 26). In parts of Asia, sexism is ingrained and gender selection often means murder. No girls, please. *Newsweek*, p. 50.

Carnelley, K. B., Wortman, C. B., Bolger, N., & Burke, C. T. (2006). The time course of grief reactions to spousal loss: Evidence from a national probability sample. *Journal of Personality and Social Psychology, 91*, 476–492.

Carnethon, M. R., Gulati, M., & Greenland, P. (2005). Prevalence and cardiovascular disease correlates of low cardiorespiratory fitness in adolescents and adults. *Journal of the American Medical Association, 294*, 2981–2988.

Carothers, S. S., Borkowski, J. G., Lefever, J. B., & Whitman, T. L. (2005). Religiosity and the socioemotional adjustment of adolescent mothers and their children. *Journal of Family Psychology, 19*, 263–275.

Carr, D., House, J. S., Kessler, R. C., Nesse, R. M., Sonnega, J., & Wortman, C. (2000). Marital quality and psychological adjustment to widowhood among older adults: A longitudinal analysis. *Journal of Gerontology: Social Sciences, 55B*, S197–S207.

Carraher, T. N., Schliemann, A. D., & Carraher, D. W. (1988). Mathematical concepts in everyday life. In G. B. Saxe & M. Gearhart (Eds.), *Children's mathematics* (New Directions in Child Development, No. 41, pp. 71–87). San Francisco: Jossey-Bass.

Carrel, L., & Willard, B. F. (2005). X-inactivation profile reveals extensive variability in X-linked gene expression in females. *Nature, 434*, 400–404.

Carskadon, M. A., Acebo, C., Richardson, G. S., Tate, B. A., & Seifer, R. (1997). Long nights protocol: Access to circadian parameters in adolescents. *Journal of Biological Rhythms, 12*, 278–289.

Carstensen, L. L. (1991). Selectivity theory: Social activity in life-span context. In *Annual Review of Gerontology and Geriatrics* (Vol. 11, pp. 195–217). New York: Springer.

Carstensen, L. L. (1995). Evidence for a life-span theory of socioemotional selectivity. *Current Directions in Psychological Science, 4*, 150–156.

Carstensen, L. L. (1996). Socioemotional selectivity: A life-span developmental account of social behavior. In M. R. Merrens & G. G. Brannigan (Eds.), *The developmental psychologists: Research adventures across the life span* (pp. 251–272). New York: McGraw-Hill.

Carstensen, L. L. (1999). *Elderly show their emotional know-how.* Paper presented at the meeting of the American Psychological Society, Denver, CO.

Carstensen, L. L., Graff, J., Levenson, R. W., & Gottman, J. M. (1996). Affect in intimate relationships: The development course of marriage. In C. Magai & S. H. McFadden (Eds.), *Handbook of emotion, adult development, and aging* (pp. 227–247). San Diego: Academic Press.

Carstensen, L. L., Gross, J., & Fung, H. (1997). The social context of emotion. *Annual Review of Geriatrics and Gerontology, 17*, 331.

Carstensen, L. L., Isaacowitz, D. M., & Charles, S. T. (1999). Taking time seriously: A theory of socioemotional selectivity. *American Psychologist, 54*, 165–181.

Carstensen, L. L., & Mikels, J. A. (2005). At the intersection of emotion and cognition: Aging and the positivity effect. *Current Directions in Psychological Science, 14*, 117–122.

Carstensen, L. L., Pasupathi, M., Mayr, U., & Nesselroade, J. (2000). Emotional experience in everyday life across the adult life span. *Journal of Personality and Social Psychology, 79*, 644–655.

Carter, R. C., Jacobson, S. W., Molteno, C. D., Chiodo, L. M., Viljoen, D., & Jacobson, J. L. (2005). Effects of prenatal alcohol exposure on infant visual acuity. *Journal of Pediatrics, 147*(4), 473–479.

Carver, C. S. (2007). Stress, coping, and health. In H. S. Friedman, & R. C. Silver (Eds.), *Foundations of health psychology* (pp. 117–144). New York: Oxford University Press.

Carver, P. R., & Iruka, I. U. (2006). *After-school programs and activities: 2005* (NCES 2006-076). Washington, DC: National Center for Education Statistics.

Casaer, P. (1993). Old and new facts about perinatal brain development. *Journal of Child Psychology and Psychiatry, 34*(1), 101–109.

Case, R. (1992). Neo-Piagetian theories of child development. In R. Sternberg & C. Berg (Eds.), *Intellectual development* (pp. 161–196). New York: Cambridge University Press.

Casper, L. M. (1997). My daddy takes care of me: Fathers as care providers. *Current Population Reports* (P70–59). Washington, DC: U.S. Bureau of the Census.

Caspi, A. (1998). Personality development across the life course. In W. Damon (Series Ed.) & N. Eisenberg (Vol. Ed.), *Handbook of child psychology: Vol. 3. Social, emotional, and personality development* (5th ed., pp. 311–388). New York: Wiley.

Caspi, A. (2000). The child is father of the man: Personality continuity from childhood to adulthood. *Journal of Personality and Social Psychology, 78*, 158–172.

Caspi, A., Lynam, D., Moffitt, T. E., & Silva, P. A. (1993). Unraveling girls' delinquency: Biological, dispositional, and contextual contributions to adolescent misbehavior. *Developmental Psychology, 29*(1), 19–30.

Caspi, A., McClay, J., Moffitt, T. E., Mill, J., Martin, J., Craig, I. W., . . . Poulton, R. (2002). Role of genotype in the cycle of violence in maltreated children. *Science, 297*, 851–854.

Caspi, A., Sugden, K., Moffitt, T. E., Taylor, A., Craig, I. W., Harrington, H., . . . Poulton, R. (2003). Influence of life stress on depression: Moderation by a polymorphism in the 5-HTT gene. *Science, 301*, 386–389.

Casserotti, P., Aarguard, P., Larsen, J. B., & Puggaard, L. (2008). Explosive heavy-resistance training in old and very old adults: Changes in rapid muscle force, strength and power. *Scandanavian Journal of Medicine and Science in Sport, 18*(6), 773–782.

Cassidy, K. W., Werner, R. S., Rourke, M., Zubernis, L. S., & Balaraman, G. (2003). The relationship between psychological understanding and positive social behaviors. *Social Development, 12*, 198–221.

Cattell, R. B. (1965). *The scientific analysis of personality.* Baltimore: Penguin Books.

Caughey, A. B., Hopkins, L. M., & Norton, M. E. (2006). Chorionic villus sampling compared with amniocentesis and the difference in the rate of pregnancy loss. *Obstetrics and Gynecology, 108*, 612–616.

Cawthon, R. M., Smith, K. R., O'Brien, E., Sivatchenko, A., & Kerber, R. A. (2003). Association between telomere length in blood and mortality in people aged 60 years or older. *Lancet, 361*, 393–394.

Ceci, S., & Liker, J. (1986). A day at the races: A study of IQ, expertise, and cognitive complexity. *Journal of Experimental Psychology: General, 114*, 255–266.

Ceci, S. J. (1991). How much does schooling influence general intelligence and its cognitive components? A reassessment of the evidence. *Developmental Psychology, 27*, 703–722.

Ceci, S. J., & Williams, W. M. (1997). Schooling, intelligence, and income. *American Psychologist, 52*(10), 1051–1058.

Celis, W. (1990). More states are laying school paddle to rest. *The New York Times,* pp. A1, B12.

Center for Education Reform. (2004, August 17). *Comprehensive data discounts* New York Times *account; reveals charter schools performing at or above traditional schools* [Press release]. Retrieved from http://edreform.com/indexcfm?fuseAction=document&documentID=1806

Center for Education Reform. (2008, October 23). *Charter school numbers 2008: Count 'em up* [Press release]. Retrieved from http://www.edreform.com/Press_Box/Press_releases/?Charter_School_Numbers_2008_Count_Em_Up& year=2008

Center on Addiction and Substance Abuse at Columbia University (CASA). (1996, June). *Substance abuse and the American woman.* New York: Author.

Centers for Disease Control and Prevention (CDC). (2000a). *CDC's guidelines for school and community programs: Promoting lifelong physical activity.* Retrieved from www.cdc.gov/nccdphp/dash/phactaag.htm

Centers for Disease Control and Prevention (CDC). (2000b). *Tracking the hidden epidemic: Trends in STDs in the U.S., 2000.* Washington, DC: Author.

Centers for Disease Control and Prevention (CDC). (2002). Youth risk behavior surveillance—United States, 2001. *Morbidity and Mortality Weekly Report, 51*(4). Atlanta, GA: Author.

Centers for Disease Control and Prevention (CDC). (2004). National, state, and urban area vaccination coverage among children aged 19–36 months—United States, 2003. *Morbidity and Mortality Weekly Report, 53,* 658–661.

Centers for Disease Control and Prevention (CDC). (2005). *Assisted reproductive technology: Home.* Retrieved from www.cdc.gov/ART/

Centers for Disease Control and Prevention (CDC). (2006a). Achievements in public health: Reduction in perinatal transmission of HIV infection—United States, 1985–2005. *Morbidity and Mortality Weekly Report, 55*(21), 592–597.

Centers for Disease Control and Prevention (CDC). (2006b). Improved national prevalence estimates for 18 selected major birth defects—United States, 1999–2001. *Morbidity and Mortality Weekly Report, 54*(51–52), 1301–1305.

Centers for Disease Control and Prevention (CDC). (2006c). National, state, and urban area vaccination coverage among children aged 19–35 months—United States, 2005. *Morbidity and Mortality Weekly Report, 55*(36), 988–993.

Centers for Disease Control and Prevention (CDC). (2007a, Summer). *Suicide: Facts at a Glance.* Retrieved from www.cdc.gov/ncipc/dvp/Suicide/SuicideDataSheet.pdf

Centers for Disease Control and Prevention (CDC). (2007b). *Web-Based Injury Statistics Query and Reporting System.* Retrieved from www.cdc.gov/ncipc/wisqars/default.htm

Centers for Disease Control and Prevention (CDC). (2008a). *Understanding teen dating violence* [Fact sheet]. Atlanta, GA: Author.

Centers for Disease Control and Prevention (CDC). (2008c). *Surveillance summaries.* Atlanta, GA: Author.

Centers for Disease Control and Prevention (2009a). *2007 assisted reproductive technology success rates: National summary and fertility clinic reports.* Retrieved from http://www.cdc.gov/art/ART2007/PDF/COMPLETE_2007_ART.pdf

Centers for Disease Control and Prevention (2009b). Prevalence of autism spectrum disorders—Autism and developmental disabilities monitoring network, United States, 2006. *Morbidity and Mortality Weekly Report, 58*(SS10), 1–20.

Centers for Disease Control and Prevention (2009c). *Understanding intimate partner violence* [Fact sheet]. Retrieved from http://www.cdc.gov/violenceprevention/pdf/IPV_factsheet-a.pdf

Centers for Disease Control and Prevention (CDC). (2010). *Mortality among teenagers aged 12–19 years: United States, 1999–2006.* NCHS Data Brief. Retrieved from http://www.cdc.gov/nchs/data/databriefs/db37.htm

Centers for Disease Control and Prevention (CDC). (2011). *How much physical activity do adults need?* Retrieved from http://www.cdc.gov/physicalactivity/everyone/guidelines/adults.html

Centers for Disease Control and Prevention. (2011a). *Fast stats. Health of Black or African American population.* Retrieved from http://www.cdc.gov/nchs/fastats/black_health.htm

Centers for Disease Control and Prevention. (2011b). *Understanding intimate partner violence.* Retrieved from http://www.cdc.gov/violenceprevention/pdf/IPV_factsheet-a.pdf

Centers for Disease Control and Prevention (CDC). (2012). *Death rates for suicide, by sex, race, Hispanic origin, and age: United States, selected years 1950–2010.* Retrieved from www.cdc.gov/nchs/data/hus/2012/035.pdf

Centers for Disease Control and Prevention (CDC). (2012a). *Birth rates for U.S. teenagers reach historic lows for all age and ethnic groups.* Retrieved from http://www.cdc.gov/nchs/data/daabriefs/db89.htm

Centers for Disease Control and Prevention (CDC). (2012b). Sexual experience and contraceptive use among female teens—United States, 1995, 2002, and 2006–2010. *Morbidity and Mortality Weekly Report, 61*(17), 297–301.

Centers for Disease Control and Prevention (CDC). (2012c). *Youth risk behavior survellience–2011.* Retrieved from http://www.cdc.gov/mmwr/pdf/ss/ss6104.pdf

Centers for Disease Control and Prevention (CDC). (2013a). *HPV (Human Papillomavirus) Gardasil VIS.* Retrieved from http://www.cdc.gov/vaccines/hcp/vis/vis-statements/hpv-gardasil.html#who

Centers for Disease Control and Prevention (CDC). (2013b). *Pregnancy rates for U.S. women continue to drop.* Retrieved from http://www.cdc.gov/nchs/data/databriefs/db136.pdf, fig. 3

Centers for Disease Control and Prevention (CDC). (2013c). *Reducing teen pregnancy: Engaging communities.* Retrieved from http://www.cdc.gov/Features/TeenPregnancy/

Centers for Disease Control and Prevention and The Merck Company Foundation. (2007). *The state of aging and health care in America.* Whitehouse Station, NJ: The Merck Company Foundation. Retrieved from http://www.cdc.gov/Aging/pdf/saha_2007.pdf

Centers for Medicare and Medicaid Services. (2009). *Low cost health insurance for families and children.* Retrieved from www.cms.hhs.gov/lowcosthealthinsfamchild/

Centre for Educational Research and Innovation. (2004). Education at a Glance: OECD indicators—2004. *Education and Skills, 2004*(14), 1–456.

Cepeda-Benito, A., Reynoso, J. T., & Erath, S. (2004). Meta-analysis of the efficacy of nicotine replacement therapy for smoking cessation: Differences between men and women. *Journal of Consulting and Clinical Psychology, 72,* 712–722.

Ceppi, G., & Zini, M. (1998). *Children, spaces, relations: Metaproject for an environment for young children.* Eggio Emilia, Italy: Municipality of Reggio Emilia Inanzia ricerca.

Chafetz, M. D. (1992). *Smart for life.* New York: Penguin Books.

Chambers, R. A., Taylor, J. R., & Potenza, M. N. (2003). Developmental neurocircuitry of motivation in adolescence: A critical period of addiction vulnerability. *American Journal of Psychiatry, 160,* 1041–1052.

Champagne, F. A., & Mashoodh, R. (2009). Genes in context: Gene-environment interactions and the origins of individual differences in behavior. *Current Directions in Psychological Science, 18*(3), 127–131.

Chan, R. W., Raboy, B., & Patterson, C. J. (1998). Psychosocial adjustment among children conceived via donor insemination by lesbian and heterosexual mothers. *Child Development, 69,* 443–457.

Chandra, A., Martin, S., Collins, R., Elliott, M., Berry, S., Kanouse, D., & Miu, A. (2008). Does watching sex on television predict teen pregnancy? Findings from a National Longitudinal Survey of Youth. *Pediatrics, 122*(5), 1047–1054.

Chao, R. (1996). Chinese and European American mothers' beliefs about the role of parenting in children's school success. *Journal of Cross-Cultural Psychology, 27,* 403–423.

Chao, R. K. (1994). Beyond parental control and authoritarian parenting style: Understanding Chinese parenting through the cultural notion of training. *Child Development, 65,* 1111–1119.

Chao, R. K. (2001). Extending research on the consequences of parenting style for Chinese Americans and European Americans. *Child Development, 72,* 1832–1843.

Chao, S., Roberts, J. S., Marteau, T. M., Silliman, R., Cupples, L. A., & Green, R. C. (2008). Health behavior changes after genetic risk assessment for Alzheimer disease: The REVEAL study. *Alzheimer Disease Association, 22*(1), 94–97.

Chapman, C., Laird, J., & Kewal-Ramani, A. (2010). *Trends in high school dropout and completion rates in the United States: 1972–2008* (NCES 2011-012). Retrieved from National Center for Education Statistics website: http://nces.ed.gov/pubsearch

Chapman, M., & Lindenberger, U. (1988). Functions, operations, and décalage in the development of transitivity. *Developmental Psychology, 24*, 542–551.

Charles, S. T., & Carstensen, L. L. (2007). Emotion regulation and aging. In J. J. Gross (Ed.), *Handbook of emotion regulation* (pp. 307–330). New York: Guilford Press.

Charles, S. T., & Piazza, J. R. (2007). Memories of social interactions: Age differences in emotional intensity. *Psychology and Aging, 22*, 300–309.

Charles, S. T., Reynolds, C. A., & Gatz, M. (2001). Age-related differences and change in positive and negative affect over 23 years. *Journal of Personality and Social Psychology, 80*, 136–151.

Charlesworth, A., & Glantz, S. A. (2005). Smoking in the movies increases adolescent smoking: A review. *Pediatrics, 116*, 1516–1528.

Charness, N., & Schultetus, R. S. (1999). Knowledge and expertise. In F. T. Durso (Ed.), *Handbook of applied cognition* (pp. 57–81). Chichester, England: Wiley.

Chen, H., Chauhan, S. P., Ananth, C. V., Vintzileos, A. M., & Abuhamad, A. Z. (2013). Electronic fetal heart rate monitoring and its relationship to neonatal and infant mortality in the United States. *American Journal of Obstetrics and Gynecology, 204*(6), 491–501.

Chen, A., & Rogan, W. J. (2004). Breast-feeding and the risk of postneonatal death in the United States. *Pediatrics, 113*, e435–e439.

Chen, C., & Stevenson, H. W. (1995). Motivation and mathematics achievement: A comparative study of Asian-American, Caucasian-American, and East Asian high school students. *Child Development, 66*, 1215–1234.

Chen, C. L., Weiss, N. S., Newcomb, P., Barlow, W., & White, E. (2002). Hormone replacement therapy in relation to breast cancer. *Journal of the American Medical Association, 287*, 734–741.

Chen, E., Matthews, K. A., & Boyce, W. T. (2002). Socioeconomic differences in children's health: How and why do these relationships change with age? *Psychological Bulletin, 128*, 295–329.

Chen, G. M. (2010). Tweet this: A uses and gratifications perspective on how active Twitter use gratifies a need to connect with others. *Computers in Human Behavior*, 27(2), 755–762. doi: 10.1016/j.chb.2010.10.023

Chen, L., Baker, S. B., Braver, E. R., & Li, G. (2000). Carrying passengers as a risk factor for crashes fatal to 16- and 17-year-old drivers. *Journal of the American Medical Association, 283*(12), 1578–1582.

Chen, P-L., Avramopoulos, D., Lasseter, V. K., McGrath, J. A., Fallin, M. D., Liang, K-Y., . . . Valle, D. (2009). Fine mapping on chromosome 10q22-q23 implicates *Neuregulin 3* in schizophrenia. *American Journal of Human Genetics, 84*, 21–34.

Chen, W., Li, S., Cook, N. R., Rosner, B. A., Srinivasan, S. R., Boerwinkle, E., & Berenson, G. S. (2004). An autosomal genome scan for loci influencing longitudinal burden of body mass index from childhood to young adulthood in white sibships. The Bogalusa Heart Study. *International Journal of Obesity, 28*, 462–469.

Chen, X., Cen, G., Li, D., & He, Y. (2005). Social functioning and adjustment in Chinese children: The imprint of historical time. *Child Development, 76*, 182–195.

Chen, P. C., & Wang, J. D. (2006). Parental exposure to lead and small for gestational age births. *American Journal of Industrial Medicine, 49*(6), 417–422.

Chen, X., Wang, L., & Wang, Z. (2009). Shyness-sensitivity and social, school and psychological adjustment in rural migrant and urban children in China. *Child Development, 80*(5), 1499–1513.

Cherlin, A. (2004). The deinstitutionalization of American marriage. *Journal of Marriage and Family, 66*, 848–861.

Cherlin, A., & Furstenberg, F. F. (1986). *The new American grandparent.* New York: Basic Books.

Cherry, K. E., & Park, D. C. (1993). Individual differences and contextual variables influence spatial memory in younger and older adults. *Psychology and Aging, 8*, 517–526.

Cheruku, S. R., Montgomery-Downs, H. E., Farkas, S. L., Thoman, E. B., & Lammi-Keefe, C. J. (2002). Higher maternal plasma docosahexaenoic acid during pregnancy is associated with more mature neonatal sleep-state patterning. *American Journal of Clinical Nutrition, 76*, 608–613.

Child Trends. (2010a). *Children in poverty.* Retrieved from www.childtrendsdatabank.org/?q=node/221

Child Trends. (2010b). *Physical Fighting by Youth.* Retrieved from www.childtrendsdatabank.org/?q=node/136

Child Trends Databank. (2012). *Sexually active teens: Indicators on children and youth.* Retrieved from http://www.childtrendsdatabank.org/sites/default/files/23_Sexually_Active_Teens.pdf

Child Trends Databank. (2013a). *Family structure: Indicators on children and youth.* Retrieved from http://www.childtrendsdatabank.org/sites/default/files/59_Family_Structure.pdf

Child Trends Databank. (2013b). *Sexually transmitted infections (STIs): Indicators on children and youth.* Retrieved from http://www.childtrends.org/?indicators=sexually-transmitted-infections-stis

Child Welfare Information Gateway. (2008). *Child abuse and neglect fatalities: Statistics and interventions.* Retrieved from www.childwelfare.gov/pubs/factsheets/fatality.cfm

Child Welfare Information Gateway. (2011). *How many children were adopted in 2007 and 2008?* Washington, DC: U.S. Department of Health and Human Services, Children's Bureau.

Child Welfare Information Gateway. (2013). *Child abuse and neglect fatalities 2011: Statistics and interventions.* Washington, DC: Author. Retrieved from https://www.childwelfare.gov/pubs/factsheets/fatality.pdf

Children in North America Project. (2008). *Growing up in North America: The economic well-being of children in Canada, the United States, and Mexico.* Baltimore, MD: Annie E. Casey Foundation.

Children's Defense Fund (CDF). (2004). *The state of America's children, 2004.* Washington, DC: Author.

Children's Defense Fund. (2008). *The state of America's children 2008.* Washington, DC: Author.

Children's Defense Fund. (2012). *The state of America's children handbook 2012.* Retrieved from http://www.childrensdefense.org/child-research-data-publications/data/soac-2012-handbook.pdf

Chiriboga, C. A., Brust, J. C. M., Bateman, D., & Hauser, W. A. (1999). Dose-response effect of fetal cocaine exposure on newborn neurologic function. *Pediatrics, 103*, 79–85.

Chiriboga, D. A. (1997). Crisis, challenge, and stability in the middle years. In M. E. Lachman & J. B. James (Eds.), *Multiple paths of midlife development* (pp. 293–322). Chicago: University of Chicago Press.

Chochinov, H. M., Hack, T., McClement, S., Harlos, M., & Kristjanson, L. (2002). Dignity in the terminally ill: A developing empirical model. *Social Science Medicine,* 54, 433–443.

Chodirker, B. N., Cadrin, C., Davies, G. A. L., Summers, A. M., Wilson, R. D., Winsor, E. J. T., & Young, D. (2001, July). Canadian guidelines for prenatal diagnosis: Techniques for prenatal diagnosis. *JOGC Clinical Practice Guidelines,* No. 105.

Chomitz, V. R., Cheung, L. W. Y., & Lieberman, E. (1995). The role of lifestyle in preventing low birth weight. *Future of Children, 5*(1), 121–138.

Chomsky, C. S. (1969). *The acquisition of syntax in children from five to ten.* Cambridge, MA: MIT Press.

Chomsky, N. (1957). *Syntactic structures.* The Hague: Mouton.

Chomsky, N. (1972). *Language and mind* (2nd ed.). New York: Harcourt Brace Jovanovich.

Chomsky, N. (1995). *The minimalist program.* Cambridge, MA: MIT Press.

Chorpita, B. P., & Barlow, D. H. (1998). The development of anxiety: The role of control in the early environment. *Psychological Bulletin, 124*, 3–21.

Christakis, D. A., Zimmerman, F. J., DiGiuseppe, D. L., & McCarty, C. A. (2004). Early television exposure and subsequent attentional problems in children. *Pediatrics, 113*, 708–713.

Christakis, N. A., & Allison, P. D. (2006). Mortality after the hospitalization of a spouse. *New England Journal of Medicine, 354*, 719–730.

Christensen, A., Eldridge, K., Catta-Preta, A. B., Lim, V. R., & Santagata, R. (2006). Cross-cultural consistency of the demand/withdraw interaction pattern in couples. *Journal of Marriage and Family, 68*, 1029–1044.

Christian, M. S., & Brent, R. L. (2001). Teratogen update: Evaluation of the reproductive and developmental risks of caffeine. *Teratology, 64*(1), 51–78.

Christie, J. F. (1998). Play as a medium for literacy development. In D. P. Fromberg & D. Bergen (Eds.), *Play from birth to 12 and beyond: Contexts, perspectives, and meanings* (pp. 50–55). New York: Garland.

Chua, E. F., Schacter, D. L., Rand-Giovanetti, E., & Sperling, R. A. (2006). Understanding metamemory: Neural correlates of the cognitive process and subjective level of confidence in recognition memory. *Neuroimage, 29*(4), 1150–1160.

Chu, S. Y., Bachman, D. J., Callaghan, W. M., Whitlock, E. P., Dietz, P. M., Berg, C. J., . . . Hornbrook, M. C. (2008). Association between obesity during pregnancy and increased use of health care. *New England Journal of Medicine, 358*, 1444–1453.

Chung, G. H., Flook, L., & Fuligni, A. J. (2009). Daily family conflict and emotional distress among adolescents from Latin American, Asian and European backgrounds. *Developmental Psychology, 45*(5), 1406–1415.

Chung, H. L., & Steinberg, L. (2006). Relations between neighborhood factors, parenting behaviors, peer deviance, and delinquency among serious juvenile offenders. *Developmental Psychology, 42*, 319–331.

Church, T. S., Earnest, C. P. Skinner, J. S., & Blair, S. N. (2007). Effects of different doses of physical activity on cardiorespiratory fitness among sedentary, overweight or obese postmenopausal women with elevated blood pressure. *Journal of the American Medical Association, 297*, 2081–2091.

Cicchetti, D., & Toth, S. L. (1998). The development of depression in children and adolescents. *American Psychologist, 53*, 221–241.

Cicchino, J. B., & Rakison, D. H. (2008). Producing and processing self-propelled motion in infancy. *Developmental Psychology, 44*, 1232–1241.

Cicero, S., Curcio, P., Papageorghiou, A., Sonek, J., & Nicolaides, K. (2001). Absence of nasal bone in fetuses with trisomy 21 at 11–14 weeks of gestation: An observational study. *Lancet, 358*, 1665–1667.

Cicirelli, V. G. (1976). Family structure and interaction: Sibling effects on socialization. In M. F. McMillan & S. Henao (Eds.), *Child psychiatry: Treatment and research.* New York: Brunner/Mazel.

Cicirelli, V. G. (1989). Feelings of attachment to siblings and well-being in later life. *Psychology and Aging, 4*(2), 211–216.

Cicirelli, V. G. (1994). Sibling relationships in cross-cultural perspective. *Journal of Marriage and Family, 56*, 7–20.

Cicirelli, V. G. (1995). *Sibling relationships across the life span.* New York: Plenum Press.

Cicirelli, V. G. (Ed.). (2002). *Older adults' views on death.* New York: Springer.

Cicirelli, V. G. (2009). Sibling death and death fear in relation to depressive symptomatology in older adults. *Journals of Gerontology Series B: Psychological Sciences and Social Sciences, 64*(1), 24–32.

Cillessen, A. H. N., & Mayeux, L. (2004). From censure to reinforcement: Developmental changes in the association between aggression and social status. *Child Development, 75*, 147–163.

Cirillo, D. J., Wallace, R. B., Rodabough, R. J., Greenland, P., LaCroix, A. Z., Limacher, M. C., & Larson, J. C. (2005). Effect of estrogen therapy on gallbladder disease. *Journal of the American Medical Association, 293*, 330–339.

Clark, S. L. (2012). Strategies for reducing maternal mortality. *Seminars in Perinatology, 36*(1), 42–47.

Clark, L., & Tiggeman, M. (2008). Sociocultural and individual psychology predictors of body image in young girls: A prospective study. *Developmental Psychology, 44*, 1124–1134.

Clarke-Stewart, K. A. (1987). Predicting child development from day care forms and features: The Chicago study. In D. A. Phillips (Ed.), *Quality in child care: What does the research tell us?* (Research Monographs of the National Association for the Education of Young Children). Washington, DC: National Association for the Education of Young Children.

Clavel-Chapelon, G., & the E3N-EPIC Group. (2002). Differential effects of reproductive factors on the risk of pre- and post-menopausal breast cancer: Results from a large cohort of French women. *British Journal of Cancer, 86*, 723–727. doi: 10.1038/sj/bjc/6600124

Clayton, E. W. (2003). Ethical, legal, and social implications of genomic medicine. *New England Journal of Medicine, 349*, 562–569.

Cleary, P. D., Zaborski, L. B., & Ayanian, J. Z. (2004). Sex differences in health over the course of midlife. In O. G. Brim, C. E. Ryff, & R. C. Kessler (Eds.), *How healthy are we? A national study of well-being at midlife.* Chicago: University of Chicago Press.

Clements, M. L., Stanley, S. M., & Markman, H. J. (2004). Before they said "I do": Discriminating among marital outcomes over 13 years. *Journal of Marriage and Family, 66*, 613–626.

Cleveland, J. N., & Lim, A. S. (2007). Employee age and evaluation in organizations. In K. S. Shultz & G. A. Adams (Eds.), *Aging and work in the 21st century* (pp. 109–137). Mahwah, NJ: Lawrence Erlbaum.

Cleveland, E. S., & Reese, E. (2005). Maternal structure and autonomy support in conversations about the past: Contributions to children's autobiographical memory. *Developmental Psychology, 41*(2), 376.

Cleveland, H. H., & Wiebe, R. P. (2003). The moderation of adolescent-to-peer similarity in tobacco and alcohol use by school level of substance use. *Child Development, 74*, 279–291.

Clifton, R. K., Muir, D. W., Ashmead, D. H., & Clarkson, M. G. (1993). Is visually guided reaching in early infancy a myth? *Child Development, 64*, 1099–1110.

Climo, A. H., & Stewart, A. J. (2003). Eldercare and personality development in middle age. In J. Demick & C. Andreoletti (Eds.), *Handbook of adult development.* New York: Plenum Press.

Cloak, C. C., Ernest, T., Fujii, L., Hedemark, B., & Chang, L. (2009). Lower diffusion in white matter of children with prenatal methamphetamine exposure. *Neurology, 72*(24), 2068–2975. doi: 10.1212/01.wnl.0000346516.49126.20 Ch. 3

Coffman, J. L., Ornstein, P. A., McCall, L. W., & Curran, P. J. (2008). Linking teachers' memory-relevant language and the development of children's memory skills. *Developmental Psychology, 44*,1640–1654.

Cohen, L. B., & Amsel, L. B. (1998). Precursors to infants' perception of the causality of a simple event. *Infant Behavior and Development, 21*, 713–732.

Cohen, L. B., Chaput, H. H., & Cashon, C. H. (2002). A constructivist model of infant cognition. *Cognitive Development, 17*, 1323–1343.

Cohen, S. (2004). Social relationships and health. *American Psychologist, 59*, 676–684.

Cohen, S., Doyle, W. J., Skoner, D. P., Rabin, B. S., & Gwaltney, J. M., Jr. (1997). Social ties and susceptibility to the common cold. *Journal of the American Medical Association, 277*, 1940–1944.

Cohen, S., Doyle, W. J., Turner, R. B., Alper, C. M., & Skoner, D. P. (2003). Emotional style and susceptibility to the common cold. *Psychosomatic Medicine, 65*, 652–657.

Cohen, S., Gottlieb, B., & Underwood, L. (2000). Social relationships and health. In S. Cohen, L. Underwood, & B. Gottlieb (Eds.), *Measuring and intervening in social support* (pp. 3–25). New York: Oxford University Press.

Cohen, L. B., & Marks, K. S. (2002). How infants process addition and subtraction events. *Developmental Science, 5*, 186–201.

Cohen, S., Janicki-Deverts, D., & Miller, G. E. (2007). Psychological stress and disease. *Journal of the American Medical Association, 298*, 1685–1687.

Cohen, S., & Pressman, S. D. (2006). Positive affect and health. *Current Directions in Psychological Science, 15*, 122–125.

Cohn, D. (2009). *Public has split verdict on increased level of unmarried motherhood.* Retrieved from http://pewsocialtrends.org/2009/03/19/public-has-split-verdict-on-increased-level-of-unmarried-motherhood/

Cohn, D., & Fry, R. (2010). *Women, men and the new economics of marriage.* Retrieved from http://pewsocialtrends.org/2010/01/19/women-men-and-the-new-economics-of-marriage/

Cohn, D., & Taylor, P. (2010, December 20). *Baby boomers approach 65—glumly.* Retrieved from http://pewsocialtrends.org/2010/12/20/baby-boomers-approach-65-glumly/

Cohn, D., Passel, J. S., Wang, W., & Livingston, G. (2011). *Barely half of U.S adults are married—a record low.* Pew Research Center. Retrieved from http://www.pewsocialtrends.org/2011/12/14/barely-half-of-u-s-adults-are-married-a-record-low/

Coie, J. D., & Dodge, K. A. (1998). Aggression and antisocial behavior. In W. Damon (Series Ed.) & N. Eisenberg (Vol. Ed.), *Handbook of child psychology: Vol. 3. Social, emotional, and personality development* (5th ed., pp. 780–862). New York: Wiley.

Coke, M. M., & Twaite, J. A. (1995). *The black elderly: Satisfaction and quality of later life.* New York: Haworth.

Colby, A., & Damon, W. (1992). *Some do care: Contemporary lives of moral commitment.* New York: Free Press.

Colby, A., Kohlberg, L., Gibbs, J., & Lieberman, M. (1983). A longitudinal study of moral development. *Monographs of the Society for Research in Child Development, 48*(1–2, Serial No. 200).

Colcombe, S. J., Erickson, K. I., Scalf, P. E., Kim, J. S., Prakash, R., McAuley, E., . . . Kramer, A. F. (2006). Aerobic exercise training increases brain volume in aging humans. *Journals of Gerontology. Series A, 61*(11), 1166–1170.

Cole, M. (1998). *Cultural psychology: A once and future discipline.* Cambridge, MA: Belknap.

Cole, P. M., Barrett, K. C., & Zahn-Waxler, C. (1992). Emotion displays in two-year-olds during mishaps. *Child Development, 63*, 314–324.

Cole, P. M., Bruschi, C. J., & Tamang, B. L. (2002). Cultural differences in children's emotional reactions to difficult situations. *Child Development, 73*(3), 983–996.

Cole, S. W. (2009). Social regulation of human gene expression. *Current Directions in Psychological Science, 18*(3), 132–137.

Cole, T. B. (1999). Ebbing epidemic: Youth homicide rate at a 14-year low. *Journal of the American Medical Association, 281*, 25–26.

Coleman, J. S. (1988). Social capital in the creation of human capital. *American Journal of Sociology, 94*(Suppl. 95), S95–S120.

Colman, R. J., Anderson, R. M., Johnson, S. C., Kastman, E. K., Kosmatka, K. J., Beasley, T. M., . . . Weindruch, R. (2009). Caloric restriction delays disease onset and mortality in Rhesus monkeys. *Science, 325*(5937), 201–204.

Coleman-Phox, K., Odouli, R., & De-Kun, L. (2008). Use of a fan during sleep and the risk of sudden infant death syndrome. *Archives of Pediatric & Adolescent Medicine, 162*(10), 963–968.

Coles, L. S. (2004). Demography of human supercentenarians. *Journal of Gerontology: Biological Sciences, 59A*, 579–586.

Coley, R. L., Morris, J. E., & Hernandez, D. (2004). Out-of-school care and problem behavior trajectories among low-income adolescents: Individual, family, and neighborhood characteristics as added risks. *Child Development, 75*, 948–965.

Coley, R. L., Votruba-Drzal, E., & Schindler, H. S. (2009). Fathers' and mothers' parenting predicting and responding to adolescent sexual risk behaviors. *Child Development, 80*(3), 808–827.

Collier, V. P. (1995). Acquiring a second language for school. *Directions in Language and Education, 1*(4), 1–11.

Collins, W. A., Maccoby, E. E., Steinberg, L., Hetherington, E. M., & Bornstein, M. H. (2000). Contemporary research in parenting: The case for nature and nurture. *American Psychologist, 55*, 218–232.

Collins, W. A., & van Dulmen, M. (2006). Friendships and romance in emerging adulthood: Assessing the distinctiveness in close relationships. In J. J. Arnett & J. L. Tanner (Eds.), *Emerging adults in America: Coming of age in the 21st century* (pp. 219–234). Washington DC: American Psychological Association.

Colombo, J. (2002). Infant attention grows up: The emergence of a developmental cognitive neuroscience perspective. *Current Directions in Psychological Science, 11*, 196–200.

Colombo, J., Kannass, K. N., Shaddy, J., Kundurthi, S., Maikranz, J. M., Anderson, C. J., . . . Carlson, S. E. (2004). Maternal DHA and the development of attention in infancy and toddlerhood. *Child Development, 75*, 1254–1267.

Comer, J., Furr, J., Beidas, R., Weiner, C., & Kendall, P. (2008). Children and terrorism related news: Training parents in coping and media literacy. *Journal of Consulting and Clinical Psychology, 76*(4), 568–578.

Commissioner's Office of Research and Evaluation and Head Start Bureau, Department of Health and Human Services. (2001). *Building their futures: How Early Head Start programs are enhancing the lives of infants and toddlers in low-income families* [Summary report]. Washington, DC: Author.

Committee on Obstetric Practice. (2002). ACOG committee opinion: Exercise during pregnancy and the postpartum period. *International Journal of Gynecology & Obstetrics, 77*(1), 79–81.

Community Paediatrics Committee, Canadian Paediatrics Society. (2005). Management of primary nocturnal enuresis. *Paediatrics and Child Health, 10*, 611–614.

Compas, B. E., & Luecken, L. (2002). Psychological adjustment to breast cancer. *Current Directions in Psychological Science, 11*, 111–114.

Compston, J. (2007). Treatments for osteoporosis—Looking beyond the HORIZON. *New England Journal of Medicine, 356*, 1878–1880.

Conde-Agudelo, A., Rosas-Bermúdez, A., & Kafury-Goeta, A. C. (2006). Birth spacing and risk of adverse perinatal outcomes: A meta-analysis. *Journal of the American Medical Association, 295*, 1809–1823.

Confer, J., & Cloud, M. (2011). Sex differences in response to imagining a partner's heterosexual or homosexual affair. *Personality and Individual Differences, 50*(2), 129–134. doi: 10.1016/j.paid.2010.09.007

Conference Board. (1999, June 25). *Workplace education programs are benefiting U.S. corporations and workers* [Press release]. Retrieved from www.newswise.com/articles/1999/6/WEP.TCB.html

Connidis, I. A., & Davies, L. (1992). Confidants and companions: Choices in later life. *Journal of Gerontology: Social Sciences, 47*(30), S115–S122.

Constantino, J. N. (2003). Autistic traits in the general population: A twin study. *Archives of General Psychiatry, 60*, 524–530.

Constantino, J. N., Grosz, D., Saenger, P., Chandler, D. W., Nandi, R., & Earls, F. J. (1993). Testosterone and aggression in children. *Journal of the Academy of Child and Adolescent Psychiatry, 32*, 1217–1222.

Cook, C. R., Williams, K. R., Guerra, N. G., Kim, T. E., & Sadek, S. (2010). Predictors of bullying and victimization in childhood and adolescence: A meta-analytic investigation. *Social Psychology Quarterly, 25*(2), 65–83.

Cook, J. M., Biyanova, T., & Marshall, R. (2007). Medicating grief with benzodiazepines: Physician and patient perspectives. *Archives of Internal Medicine, 167*(18), 2006–2007.

Cooper, K. L., & Gutmann, D. L. (1987). Gender identity and ego mastery style in middle-aged, pre- and post-empty nest women. *Gerontologist, 27*(3), 347–352.

Cooper, R. P., & Aslin, R. N. (1990). Preference for infant-directed speech in the first month after birth. *Child Development, 61*, 1584–1595.

Cooper, W. O., Hernandez-Diaz, S., Arbogast, P. G., Dudley, J. A., Dyer, S., Gideon, P. S., Hall, K., & Ray, W. A. (2006). Major congenital formations after first-trimester exposure to ACE inhibitors. *New England Journal of Medicine, 354*, 2443–2451.

Copen, C. E., Daniels, K., Vespa, J., & Mosher, W. D. (2012). First marriages in the United States: Data from the 2006–2010 National Survey of Family Growth. *National Health Statistics Reports, 49.* Hyattsville, MD: National Center for Health Statistics.

Coplan, R. J., Prakash, K., O'Neil, K., & Armer, M. (2004). Do you "want" to play? Distinguishing between conflicted-shyness and social disinterest in early childhood. *Developmental Psychology, 40*, 244–258.

Corbet, A., Long, W., Schumacher, R., Gerdes, J., Cotton, R., & the American Exosurf Neonatal Study Group 1. (1995). Double-blind developmental evaluation at 1-year corrected age of 597 premature infants with birth weight from 500 to 1,350 grams enrolled in three placebo-controlled trials of prophylactic synthetic surfactant. *Journal of Pediatrics, 126*, S5–S12.

Corcoran, M., & Matsudaira, J. (2005). Is it getting harder to get ahead? Economic attainment in early adulthood for two cohorts. In R. A. Settersten Jr., F. F. Furstenberg Jr., & R. G. Rumbaut (Eds.), *On the frontier of adulthood: Theory, research, and public policy* (pp. 356–395). Chicago: University of Chicago Press.

Cornwell, B., Laumann, E. O., & Schumm, L. P. (2008). The social connectedness of older adults: A national profile. *American Sociological Review, 73*, 185–203.

Correa, A., Botto, L., Liu, V., Mulinare, J., & Erickson, J. D. (2003). Do multivitamin supplements attenuate the risk for diabetes-associated birth defects? *Pediatrics, 111*, 1146–1151.

Correa, A., Gilboa, S. M., Besser, L. M., Botto, L. D., Moore, C. A., Hobbs, C. A., . . . Reece, E. A. (2008). Diabetes mellitus and birth defects. *American Journal of Obstetrics & Gynecology, 199*(237), e1–e9.

Corriveau, K. H., Harris, P. L., Meins, E., Fernyhough, C., Arnott, B., Elliott, L., . . . deRosnay, M. (2009). Young children's trust in their mother's claims: Longitudinal links with attachment security in infancy. *Child Development, 80*(3), 750–761.

Costa, P. T., Jr., & McCrae, R. R. (1980). Still stable after all these years: Personality as a key to some issues in adulthood and old age. In P. B. Baltes Jr. & O. G. Brim (Eds.), *Lifespan development and behavior* (Vol. 3, pp. 65–102). New York: Academic Press.

Costa, P. T., Jr., & McCrae, R. R. (1988). Personality in adulthood: A six-year longitudinal study of self-reports and spouse ratings on the NEO Personality Inventory. *Journal of Personality and Social Psychology, 54,* 853–863.

Costa, P. T., Jr., & McCrae, R. R. (1994a). Set like plaster? Evidence for the stability of adult personality. In T. F. Heatherton & J. L. Weinberger (Eds.), *Can personality change?* (pp. 21–41). Washington, DC: American Psychological Association.

Costa, P. T., Jr., & McCrae, R. R. (1994b). Stability and change in personality from adolescence through adulthood. In C. F. Halverson, G. A. Kohnstamm, & R. P. Martin (Eds.), *The developing structure of temperament and personality from infancy to adulthood.* Hillsdale, NJ: Erlbaum.

Costa, P. T., Jr., & McCrae, R. R. (2006). Age changes in personality and their origins: Comments on Roberts, Walton, and Viechtbauer (2006). *Psychological Bulletin, 1,* 26–28.

Costa, P. T., Jr., McCrae, R. R., Zonderman, A. B., Barbano, H. E., Lebowitz, B., & Larson, D. M. (1986). Cross-sectional studies of personality in a national sample: 2. Stability in neuroticism, extraversion, and openness. *Psychology and Aging, 1*, 144–149.

Costanzo, P. R., & Hoy, M. B. (2007). Intergenerational relations: Themes, prospects, and possibilities. *Journal of Social Issues, 63*(4), 885–902.

Costello, E. J., Compton, S. N., Keeler, G., & Angold, A. (2003). Relationship between poverty and psychopathology: A natural experiment. *Journal of the American Medical Association, 290*, 2023–2029.

Costello, E. J., Erklani, A., & Angold, A. (2006). Is there an epidemic of child or adolescent depression? *Journal of Child Psychology and Psychiatry, 47*, 1263–1271.

Côté, J. E. (2006). Emerging adulthood as an institutionalized moratorium: Risks and benefits to identity formation. In J. J. Arnett & J. L. Tanner (Eds.), *Emerging adults in America: Coming of age in the 21st century* (pp. 85–116). Washington, DC: American Psychological Association.

Cote, L. R., & Bornstein, M. H. (2009). Child and mother play in three U.S. cultural groups: Comparisons and associations. *Journal of Family Psychology, 23*(3), 355–363.

Council on Sports Medicine and Fitness & Council on School Health. (2006). Active healthy living: Prevention of childhood obesity through increased physical activity. *Pediatrics, 117*, 1834–1842.

Courage, M. L., & Howe, M. L. (2002). From infant to child: The dynamics of cognitive change in the second year of life. *Psychological Bulletin, 128*, 250–277.

Couto, E., Boffetta, P., Lagiou, P., Ferrari, P., Buckland, G., et al. (2011). Mediterranean dietary pattern and cancer risk in the EPIC cohort. *British Journal Cancer, 104*(9), 1493–1499.

Cox, M. J., & Paley, B. (2003). Understanding families as systems. *Current Directions in Psychological Science, 12*(5), 193–196.

Cowan, W. M. (1979). The development of the brain. *Scientific American, 241*(3), 113–133.

Cowan, N., Nugent, L. D., Elliott, E. M., Ponomarev, I., & Saults, J. S. (1999). The role of attention in the development of short-term memory: Age differences in the verbal span of apprehension. *Child Development*, *70*(5), 1082–1097.

Craik, F. I. M., & Byrd, M. (1982). Aging and cognitive deficits: The role of attentional resources. In F. I. M. Craik & S. Trehub (Eds.), *Aging and cognitive processes* (pp. 191–221). New York: Plenum Press.

Craik, F. I. M., & Jennings, J. M. (1992). Human memory. In F. I. M. Craik & T. A. Salthouse (Eds.), *Handbook of aging and cognition* (pp. 51–110). Hillsdale, NJ: Erlbaum.

Crary, D. (2007, January 6). After years of growth, foreign adoptions by Americans decline sharply. *Associated Press.* Retrieved from www.chron.com/disp/story.mpl/nation/4452317.html

Cratty, Bryant J. (1986). *Perceptual and Motor Development in Infants and Children,* 3rd ed. Englewood Cliff, NJ: Prentice Hall

Crawford, C. (1998). Environments and adaptations: Then and now. In C. Crawford & D. L. Krebs (Eds.), *Handbook of evolutionary psychology: Ideas, issues, and applications* (pp. 275–302). Mahwah, NJ: Erlbaum.

Crawford, J. (2007). The decline of bilingual education: How to reverse a troubling trend? *International Multilingual Research Journal, 1*(1), 33–38.

Crepaz, N., Lyles, C. M., Passin, R. J., Rama, S. M., Herbst, J. H., Malow, R. W., & Stal, R. (2009). Do prevention interventions reduce HIV risk behaviours among people living with HIV? A meta-analytic review of controlled trials. *AIDS, 20*(2), 143–157.

Crick, N. R., & Dodge, K. A. (1996). Social information-processing mechanisms in reactive and proactive aggression. *Child Development, 67*, 993–1002.

Crick, N. R., & Grotpeter, J. K. (1995). Relational aggression, gender, and social psychological adjustment. *Child Development, 66*, 710–722.

Crider, K. S., Cleves, M. A., Reefhuis, J., Berry, R. J., Hobbs, C. A., & Hu, D. (2009). Antibacterial medication use during pregnancy and risk of birth defects. *Archives of Pediatrics & Adolescent Medicine, 163*(11), 978–985.

Crockenberg, S. C. (2003). Rescuing the baby from the bathwater: How gender and temperament influence how child care affects child development. *Child Development, 74*, 1034–1038.

Cromwell, R. L., Meyers, P. M., Meyers, P. E., & Newton, R. A. (2007). Tae kwon do: An effective exercise for improving balance and walking ability in older adults. *Journal of Gerontology: Biological and Medical Sciences, 62*, 641–646.

Cronk, L. B., Ye, B., Tester, D. J., Vatta, M., Makielski, J. C., & Ackerman, M. J. (2006, May). *Identification of CAV3-encoded caveolin-3 mutations in sudden infant death syndrome.* Presentation at Heart Rhythm 2006, the 27th annual Scientific Sessions of the Heart Rhythm Society, Boston.

Crooks, V. C., Lubben, J., Petitti, D. B., Little, D., & Chiu, V. (2008). Social network, cognitive function, and dementia incidence among elderly women. *American Journal of Public Health, 98,* 1221–1227.

Crouter, A., & Larson, R. (Eds.). (1998). *Temporal rhythms in adolescence: Clocks, calendars, and the coordination of daily life* (New Directions in Child and Adolescent Development, No. 82). San Francisco: Jossey-Bass.

Crouter, A. C., & Manke, B. (1994). The changing American workplace: Implications for individuals and families. *Family Relations, 43*, 117–124.

Crowley, S. L. (1993, October). Grandparents to the rescue. *AARP Bulletin,* pp. 1, 16–17.

Cruzan v. Director, Missouri Department of Health, 110 S. Ct. 2841 (1990).

Csikszentmihalyi, M. (1996). *Creativity: Flow and the psychology of discovery and invention.* New York: HarperCollins.

Csikszentmihalyi, M. (1999). If we are so rich, why aren't we happy? *American Psychologist, 54*, 821–827.

Cuddy, A. J. C., Norton, M. I., & Fiske, S. T. (2005). This old stereotype: The pervasiveness and persistence of the elderly stereotype. *Journal of Social Issues, 61*(2), 267–285.

Cui, M., Conger, R. D., & Lorenz, F. O. (2005). Predicting change in adolescent adjustment from change in marital problems. *Developmental Psychology, 41*, 812–823.

Cumming, E., & Henry, W. (1961). *Growing old.* New York: Basic Books.

Cummings, J. L. (2004). Alzheimer's disease. *New England Journal of Medicine, 351*, 56–67.

Cunniff, C., & Committee on Genetics. (2004). Prenatal screening and diagnosis for pediatricians. *Pediatrics, 114,* 889–894.

Cunningham, F. G., & Leveno, K. J. (1995). Childbearing among older women: The message is cautiously optimistic. *New England Journal of Medicine, 333*, 1002–1004.

Curtiss, S. (1977). *Genie.* New York: Academic Press.

Cutrona, C. E., Wallace, G., & Wesner, K. A. (2006). Neighborhood characteristics and depressions: An examination of stress processes. *Current Directions in Psychological Science, 15,* 188–192.

Cytrynbaum, S., Bluum, L., Patrick, R., Stein, J., Wadner, D., & Wilk, C. (1980). Midlife development: A personality and social systems perspective. In L. Poon (Ed.), *Aging in the 1980s.* Washington, DC: American Psychological Association.

Czaja, A. J., & Sharit, J. (1998). Ability-performance relationships as a function of age and task experience for a data entry task. *Journal of Experimental Psychology—Applied, 4,* 332–351.

Czaja, S. J. (2006). Employment and the baby boomers: What can we expect in the future? In S. K. Whitbourne & S. L. Willis (Eds.), *The baby boomers grow up: Contemporary perspectives on midlife* (pp. 283–298). Mahwah, NJ: Erlbaum.

Czeisler, C. A., Duffy, J. F., Shanahan, T. L., Brown, E. N., Mitchell, J. F., Rimmer, D. W., . . . Kronauer, R. E. (1999). Stability, precision, and near 24-hour period of the human circadian pacemaker. *Science, 284,* 2177–2181.

Dahl G. B., & Moretti, E. (2004). *The demand for sons: Evidence from divorce, fertility, and shotgun marriage* (Working Paper No. 10281). Cambridge, MA: National Bureau of Economic Research (NBER).

Dale, P. S., Simonoff, E., Bishop, D. V. M., Eley, T. C., Oliver, B., Price, T. S., . . . Plomin, R. (1998). Genetic influence on language delay in two-year-old children. *Nature Neuroscience, 1,* 324–328.

Daly, R. (2005). Drop in youth antidepressant use prompts call for FDA monitoring. *Psychiatric News, 40*(19), 18.

Daly, M., & Wilson, M. (1988). *Homicide.* Hawthorne, NY: Aldine de Gruyter.

Danaei, G., Rimm, E. B., Oza, S., Kulkarni, S. C., Murray, C. J. L., & Ezzati, M. (2010). The promise of prevention: The effects of four preventable risk factors on national life expectancy and life expectancy disparities by race and county in the United States. *PLoS Medicine, 7*(3) e1000248. doi:10.1371/journal.pmed.1000248

Danesi, M. (1994). *Cool: The signs and meanings of adolescence.* Toronto: University of Toronto Press.

Daniel, J. (2012). Making sense of MOOCs: Musing in a maze of myth, paradox and possibility. *Journal of Interactive Media in Education, 18*(3), 1–20.

Darling, N., Kolasa, M., & Wooten, K. G. (2008). National, state, and local area vaccination coverage among children aged 19–35 months—United States, 2007. *Morbidity & Mortality Weekly Report, 57*(35), 961–966.

Darling, N., & Steinberg, L. (1993). Parenting style as context: An integrative model. *Psychological Bulletin, 113,* 487–496.

Darroch, J. E., Singh, S., Frost, J. J., & the Study Team. (2001). Differences in teenage pregnancy rates among five developed countries: The roles of sexual activity and contraceptive use. *Family Planning Perspectives, 33,* 244–250, 281.

Darwin, C. (1871/2004). *The descent of man.* London, UK: Penguin.

Datar, A., & Sturm, R. (2004a). Childhood overweight and parent- and teacher-reported behavior problems. *Archives of Pediatric and Adolescent Medicine, 158,* 804–810.

Datar, A., & Sturm, R. (2004b). Duke physical education in elementary school and body mass index: Evidence from the Early Childhood Longitudinal Study. *American Journal of Public Health, 94,* 1501–1507.

David and Lucile Packard Foundation. (2004). Children, families, and foster care: Executive summary. *Future of Children, 14*(1). Retrieved from www.futureofchildren.org

Davidson, N. E. (1995). Hormone-replacement therapy—Breast versus heart versus bone. *New England Journal of Medicine, 332,* 1638–1639.

Davies, C., & Williams, D. (2002). *The grandparent study 2002 report.* Washington, DC: American Association of Retired Persons.

Daviglus, M. L., Bell, C. C., Berrettini, W., Bowen, P. E., Connolly, E. S., Cox, N. J., . . . Trevisan, M. (2010). Preventing Alzheimer's disease and cognitive decline. *NIH Consensus State-of-the-Science Statements, 27*(4), 1–30.

Davis, A. S. (2008). Children with Down syndrome: Implications for assessment and intervention in the school. *School Psychology Quarterly, 23,* 271–281.

Davis, B. E., Moon, R. Y., Sachs, H. C., & Ottolini, M. C. (1998). Effects of sleep position on infant motor development. *Pediatrics, 102*(5), 1135–1140.

Davis, M., & Emory, E. (1995). Sex differences in neonatal stress reactivity. *Child Development, 66,* 14–27.

Davis, O. S. P., Haworth, C. M. A., & Plomin, R. (2009). Dramatic increases in heritability of cognitive development from early to middle childhood: An 8-year longitudinal study of 8,700 pairs of twins. *Psychological Science, 20*(10), 1301–1308.

Davis-Kean, P. E. (2005). The influence of parent education and family income on child achievement: The indirect role of parental expectation and the home environment. *Journal of Family Psychology, 19,* 294–304.

Davison, K. K., & Birch, L. L. (2001). Weight status, parent reaction, and self-concept in 5-year-old girls. *Pediatrics, 107,* 46–53.

Davison, K. K., Susman, E. J., & Birch, L. L. (2003). Percent body fat at age 5 predicts earlier pubertal development among girls at age 9. *Pediatrics, 111,* 815–821.

Dawson, G. (2007). Despite major challenges, autism research continues to offer hope. *Archives of Pediatric and Adolescent Medicine, 161,* 411–412.

Dawson, G., Frey, K., Panagiotides, H., Yamada, E., Hessl, D., & Osterling, J. (1999). Infants of depressed mothers exhibit atypical frontal electrical brain activity during interactions with mother and with a familiar nondepressed adult. *Child Development, 70,* 1058–1066.

Dawson, G., Klinger, L. G., Panagiotides, H., Hill, D., & Spieker, S. (1992). Frontal lobe activity and affective behavior of infants of mothers with depressive symptoms. *Child Development, 63,* 725–737.

Day, J. C., Janus, A., & Davis, J. (2005). Computer and Internet use in the United States: 2003. *Current Population Reports* (P23–P208). Washington, DC: U.S. Census Bureau.

Day, S. (1993, May). Why genes have a gender. *New Scientist, 138*(1874), 34–38.

de Castro, B. O., Veerman, J. W., Koops, W., Bosch, J. D., & Monshouwer, H. J. (2002). Hostile attribution of intent and aggressive behavior: A meta-analysis. *Child Development, 73,* 916–934.

de la Fuente-Fernandez, R. (2006). Impact of neuroprotection on incidence of Alzheimer's disease. *PloS ONE, 1*(1), e52. doi: 10.1371/journal.pone.0000052. Retrieved from www.pubmedcentral.nih.gov/articlerender.fcgi?artid=1762379

de Kieviet, J. F., Piek, J. P., Aarnoudse-Moens, C. S., & Oosterlaan, J. (2009). Motor development in very preterm and very-low-birth-weight children from birth to adolescence. *Journal of the American Medical Association, 302*(20), 2235–2242. doi: 10.1001/jama.2009.1708

de Roos, S. (2006). Young children's God concepts: Influences of attachment and religious socialization in a family and school context. *Religious Education, 101*(1), 84–103.

de Vries, B. (1996). The understanding of friendship: An adult life course perspective. In C. Magai & S. H. McFadden (Eds.), *Handbook of emotion, adult development, and aging* (pp. 249–269). San Diego: Academic Press.

Deary, I. J., & Der, G. (2005). Reaction time explains IQ's association with death. *Psychological Science, 16,* 64–69.

Deary, I. J., Whalley, L. J., & Starr, J. M. (2003). IQ at age 11 and longevity: Results from a follow-up of the Scottish Mental Survey 1932. In C. D. Finch, J.-M. Robine, & Y. Christen (Eds.), *Brain and longevity: Perspectives in longevity* (pp. 153–164). Berlin: Springer.

DeBell, M., & Chapman, C. (2006). *Computer and Internet use by students in 2003: Statistical analysis report* (NCES 2006-065). Washington, DC: National Center for Education Statistics.

DeCasper, A. J., Lecanuet, J. P., Busnel, M. C., Granier-Deferre, C., & Maugeais, R. (1994). Fetal reactions to recurrent maternal speech. *Infant Behavior and Development, 17,* 159–164.

DeCasper, A. J., & Spence, M. J. (1986). Prenatal maternal speech influences newborns' perceptions of speech sounds. *Infant Behavior and Development, 9,* 133–150.

Decety, J., Michalaska, K., Akitsuki, Y., & Lahey, B. (2009). Atypical empathetic responses in adolescents with aggressive conduct disorder: A functional MRI investigation. *Biological Psychology, 80,* 203–211.

Decety J., Yang, C. Y., & Cheng, Y. (2010). Physicians down-regulate their pain empathy response: An event-related brain potential study. *NeuroImage, 50*(4), 1676–1682.

Dee, D. L., Li, R., Lee, L., & Grummer-Strawn, L. M. (2007). Association between breastfeeding practices and young children's language and motor development. *Pediatrics, 119*(Suppl. 1), 592–598.

DeHaan, L. G., & MacDermid, S. M. (1994). Is women's identity achievement associated with the expression of generativity? Examining identity and generativity in multiple roles. *Journal of Adult Development, 1*, 235–247.

DeLoache, J. S. (2006). Mindful of symbols. *Scientific American Mind, 17*, 70–75.

DeLoache, J. S., Chiong, C., Sherman, K., Islam, N., Vanderborgt, M., Troseth, G. L., . . . O'Dougherty, K. (2010). Do babies learn from baby media? *Psychological Science, 21*(11), 1570–1574.

DeLoache, J., & Gottlieb, A. (2000). If Dr. Spock were born in Bali: Raising a world of babies. In J. DeLoache & A. Gottlieb (Eds.), *A world of babies: Imagined childcare guides for seven societies* (pp. 1–27). New York: Cambridge University Press.

DeLoache, J. S., Miller, K. F., & Pierroutsakos, S. L. (1998). Reasoning and problem solving. In D. Kuhn & R. S. Siegler (Eds.), *Handbook of child psychology: Vol. 2. Cognition, perception, and language* (5th ed., pp. 801–850). New York: Wiley.

DeLoache, J. S., Pierroutsakos, S. L., & Uttal, D. H. (2003). The origins of pictorial competence. *Current Directions in Psychological Science, 12*, 114–118.

DeLoache, J. S., Uttal, D. H., & Rosengren, K. S. (2004). Scale errors offer evidence for a perception-action dissociation early in life. *Science, 304*, 1027–1029.

DeMaris, A. (2009). Distal and proximal influences on the risk of extramarital sex: A prospective study of longer duration marriages. *Journal of Sex Research*, *46*(6), 597–607.

DeMaris, A., Benson, M. L., Fox, G. L., Hill, T., & Van Wyk, J. (2003). Distal and proximal factors in domestic violence: A test of an integrated model. *Journal of Marriage and Family, 65*, 652–667.

Deming, D. (2009). Early childhood intervention and life-cycle skill development: Evidence from Head Start. *American Economic Journal: Applied Economics, 1*(3), 111–134.

den Dunnen, W. F. A., Bouwer, W. H., Bijlard, E., Kamphuis, J., van Linschoten, K., Eggens-Meijer, E., & Holstege, G. (2008). No disease in the brain of a 115-year-old woman. *Neurobiology of Aging, 29*, 1127–1132.

DeNavas-Walt, C., Proctor, B. D., & Smith, J. C. (2012). *U.S. Census Bureau, current population reports, income, poverty, and health insurance coverage in the United States: 2011* (pp. 60–243). Washington, DC: U.S. Government Printing Office.

Denham, S. A., Blair, K. A., DeMulder, E., Levitas, J., Sawyer, K., Auerbach-Major, S., & Queenan, P. (2003). Preschool emotional competence: Pathway to social competence? *Child Development, 74*, 238–256.

Denissen, J. J. A., Asendorpf, J. B., & van Aken, M. A. G. (2008). Childhood personality predicts long-term trajectories of shyness and aggressiveness in the context of demographic transitions in emerging adulthood. *Journal of Personality, 76*, 67–99.

Denissen, J. J. A., van Aken, M. A. G., & Dubas, J. S. (2009). It takes two to tango: How parents' and adolescents' personalities link to the quality of their mutual relationship. *Developmental Psychology, 45*(4), 928–941.

Dennis, T. (2006). Emotional self-regulation in preschoolers: The interplay of child approach reactivity, parenting, and control capacities. *Developmental Psychology, 42*, 84–97.

Denton, K., West, J., & Walston, J. (2003). Reading—Young children's achievement and classroom experiences: Findings from *The Condition of Education 2003*. Washington, DC: National Center for Education Statistics.

Deutsch, F. M., Servis, L. J., & Payne, J. D. (2001). Paternal participation in child care and its effects on children's self-esteem and attitudes toward gender roles. *Journal of Family Issues, 22*(8), 1000–1024.

Department of Immunization, Vaccines, and Biologicals, World Health Organization; United Nations Children's Fund; Global Immunization Division, National Center for Immunization and Respiratory Diseases (proposed); & McMorrow, M. (2006). Vaccine preventable deaths and the global immunization vision and strategy, 2006–2015. *Morbidity and Mortality Weekly Report, 55*, 511–515.

Depp, C. A., & Jeste, D. V. (2009). Definitions and predictors of successful aging: A comprehensive review of larger quantitative studies. *Focus, 7*, 137–150.

Der, G., & Deary, I. J. (2006). Age and sex differences in reaction time in adulthood: Results from the United Kingdom Health and Lifestyle Study. *Psychology and Aging, 21*, 62–73.

Derringer, J., Krueger, R. F., Dick, D. M., Saccone, S., Grucza, R. A., Agrawal, A., . . . Gene Environment Association Studies (GENEVA) Consortium. (2011). Predicting sensation seeking from dopamine genes: A candidate-system approach. *Psychological Science, 2*, 413–415. doi:10.1177/0956797610380699

Desai, M., Pratt, L. A., Lentzner, H., & Robinson, K. N. (2001). Trends in vision and hearing among older Americans. *Aging Trends,* No. 2. Hyattsville, MD: National Center for Health Statistics.

Detering, K. M., Hancock, A. D., Reade, M. C., & Silvester, W. (2010). The impact of advance care planning on end of life care in elderly patients: Randomised controlled trial. *British Medical Journal, 340*, 1345. doi:10.1136/bmj.c1345

Devoe, J. E., Ray, M., Krois, L., & Carlson, M. J. (2010). Uncertain health insurance coverage and unmet children's health care needs. *Family Medicine, 42*(2), 121–132.

Dewey, J. (1910/1991). *How we think*. Amherst, NY: Prometheus Books.

Dey, E. L., & Hurtado, S. (1999). Students, colleges and society: Considering the interconnections. In P. G. Altbach, R. O. Berndahl, & P. J. Gumport (Eds.), *American higher education in the twenty-first century: Social, political and economic challenges* (pp. 298–322). Baltimore, MD: Johns Hopkins University Press.

DeYoung, C. G., Hirsh, J. B., Shane, M. S., Papademetris, X., Rajeevan, N., & Gray, J. R. (2010). Testing predictions from personality neuroscience: Brain structure and the Big Five. *Psychological Science, 21*(6), 820–828.

Diamond, A. (1991). Neuropsychological insights into the meaning of object concept development. In S. Carey & R. Gelman (Eds.), *Epigensis of mind* (pp. 67–110). Hillsdale, NJ: Erlbaum.

Diamond, A. (2002). Normal development of prefrontal cortex from birth to young adulthood: Cognitive functions, anatomy, and biochemistry. In D. T. Strauss & R. T. Knight (Eds.), *Principles of frontal lobe function* (pp. 466–503). New York: Oxford University Press.

Diamond, L. M., & Savin-Williams, R. C. (2003). The intimate relationships of sexual-minority youths. In G. R. Adams & M. D. Berzonsky (Eds.), *Blackwell handbook of adolescence* (pp. 393–412). Malden, MA: Blackwell.

Diamond, M., & Sigmundson, H. K. (1997). Sex reassignment at birth: Longterm review and clinical implications. *Archives of Pediatric and Adolescent Medicine,* 151, 298–304.

DiCarlo, A. L., Fuldner, R., Kaminski, J., & Hodes, R. (2009). Aging in the context of immunological architecture, function and disease outcomes. *Trends in Immunology, 30*(7), 293–294.

Dick, D. M., Rose, R. J., Kaprio, J., & Viken, R. (2000). Pubertal timing and substance use: Associations between and within families across late adolescence. *Developmental Psychology, 36*, 180–189.

Dickens, W. T., & Flynn, J. R. (2006). Black Americans reduce the racial IQ gap: Evidence from standardization samples. *Psychological Science, 17*(10), 913–920.

Diemand-Yauman, C., Oppenheimer, D., & Vaughan, E. (2011). Fortune favors the bold (and the italicized): Effects of disfluency on educational outcomes. *Cognition, 118*(1), 111–115. doi: 10.1016/j.cognition.2010.09.012

Dien, D. S. F. (1982). A Chinese perspective on Kohlberg's theory of moral development. *Developmental Review, 2*, 331–341.

Diener, E. (2000). Subjective well-being: The science of happiness and a proposal for a national index. *American Psychologist, 55*, 34–43.

Dietert, R. R. (2005). Developmental immunotoxicology (DIT): Is DIT testing necessary to ensure safety? *Proceedings of the 14th Immunotoxicology Summer School, Lyon, France, October 2005*, 246–257.

Dietrich, A., & Kanso, R. (2010). A review of EEG, ERP, and neuroimaging studies of creativity and insight. *Psychological Bulletin, 136*(5), 822–848.

DiFranza, J. R., Aligne, C. A., & Weitzman, M. (2004). Prenatal and postnatal environmental tobacco smoke exposure and children's health. *Pediatrics, 113*, 1007–1015.

Dilworth-Bart, J. E., & Moore, C. F. (2006). Mercy mercy me: Social injustice and the prevention of environmental pollutant exposures among ethnic minority and poor children. *Child Development, 77*(2), 247–265.

DiMarco, M. A., Menke, E. M., & McNamara, T. (2001). Evaluating a support group for perinatal loss. *MCN American Journal of Maternal and Child Nursing, 26*, 135–140.

DiPietro, J. A. (2004). The role of prenatal maternal stress in child development. *Current Directions in Psychological Science, 13*(2), 71–74.

DiPietro, J. A., Bornstein, M. H., Costigan, K. A., Pressman, E. K., Hahn, C. S., Painter, K., Smith, B. A., & Yi, L. J. (2002). What does fetal movement predict about behavior during the first two years of life? *Developmental Psychobiology, 40*(4), 358–371.

DiPietro, J. A., Hodgson, D. M., Costigan, K. A., Hilton, S. C., & Johnson, T. R. B. (1996). Development of fetal movement—Fetal heart rate coupling from 20 weeks through term. *Early Human Development, 44*, 139–151.

DiPietro, J. A., Kivlighan, K. T., Costigan, K. A., Rubin, S. E., Shiffler, D. E., Henderson, J. L., & Pillion, J. P. (2010). Prenatal antecedents of newborn neurological maturation. *Child Development, 81*(1), 115–130. doi: 10.1111/j.1467-8624.2009.01384.x

DiPietro, J. A., Novak, M. F. S. X., Costigan, K. A., Atella, L. D., & Reusing, S. P. (2006). Maternal psychological distress during pregnancy in relation to child development at age 2. *Child Development, 77*(3), 573–587.

Dirix, C. E. H., Nijhuis, J. G., Jongsma, H. W., & Hornstra, G. (2009). Aspects of fetal learning and memory. *Child Development, 80*(4), 1251–1258.

Dishion, T. J., McCord, J., & Poulin, F. (1999). When intervention harms. *American Psychologist, 54*, 755–764.

Dishion, T. J., Shaw, D., Connell, A., Garnder, F., Weaver, C., & Wilson, M. (2008). The family check-up with high-risk indigent families: Preventing problem behavior by increasing parents' positive behavior support in early childhood. *Child Development, 79*, 1395–1414.

Dishion, T. J., & Stormshak, E. (2007). *Intervening in children's lives: An ecological, family-centered approach to mental healthcare.* Washington, DC: APA Books.

Dishion, T. J., & Tipsord, J. M. (2011). Peer contagion in child and adolescent social and emotional development. *Annual Review of Psychology, 62*, 189–214.

Dittmar, H., Halliwell, E., & Ive, S. (2006). Does Barbie make girls want to be thin? The effect of experimental exposure to images of dolls on the body image of 5- to 8-year-old girls. *Developmental Psychology, 42*, 283–292.

Dixon, R. A., & Hultsch, D. F. (1999). Intelligence and cognitive potential in late life. In J. C. Cavanaugh & S. K. Whitbourne (Eds.), *Gerontology: An interdisciplinary perspective.* New York: Oxford University Press.

Dixon, S. V., Graber, J. A., & Brooks-Gunn, J. (2008). The roles of respect for authority and parenting practices in parent-child conflict among African American, Latino, and European American families. *Journal of Family Psychology, 22*, 1–10.

Doaga, D., & Lee, T. (2008). What could be behind your elderly patient's subjective memory complaints? *Journal of Family Practice, 57*(3), 333–334.

Dobriansky, P. J., Suzman, R. M., & Hodes, R. J. (2007). *Why population aging matters: A global perspective.* Washington, DC: U.S. Department of State and Department of Health and Human Services, National Institute on Aging, & National Institutes of Health.

Dodge, K. A., Coie, J. D., & Lynam, D. (2006). Aggression and antisocial behavior in youth. In N. Eisenberg, W. Damon, & R. Lerner (Eds.), *Handbook of Child Psychology: Vol. 3, Social, emotional and personality development* (6th ed., pp. 719–788). Hoboken, NJ: Wiley.

Dodge, K. A., Coie, J. D., Pettit, G. S., & Price, J. M. (1990). Peer status and aggression in boys' groups: Developmental and contextual analysis. *Child Development, 61*, 1289–1309.

Dodge, K. A., Dishion, T. J., & Lansford, J. E. (2006). Deviant peer influences in intervention and public policy for youth. *Social Policy Report, 20*, 3–19.

Dodge, K. A., Pettit, G. S., & Bates, J. E. (1994). Socialization mediators of the relation between socioeconomic status and child conduct problems. *Child Development, 65*, 649–665.

Dodson, C. S., & Schacter, D. L. (2002). Aging and strategic retrieval processes: Reducing false memories with a distinctiveness heuristic. *Psychology and Aging, 17*(3), 405–415.

Doherty, W. J., Kouneski, E. F., & Erickson, M. F. (1998). Responsible fathering: An overview and conceptual framework. *Journal of Marriage and Family, 60*, 277–292.

Doka, K. J., & Mertz, M. E. (1988). The meaning and significance of great-grandparenthood. *Gerontologist, 28*(2), 192–197.

Dolan, M. A., & Hoffman, C. D. (1998). Determinants of divorce among women: A reexamination of critical influences. *Journal of Divorce and Remarriage, 28*, 97–106.

Dolinoy, D. C., & Jirtle, R. L. (2008). Environmental epigenomics in human health and disease. *Environmental and Molecular Mutagenesis, 49*, 4–8.

Dolinsky, V. W., & Dyck, J. R. B. (2011). Calorie restriction and resveratrol in cardiovascular health and disease. *Biochimica et Biophysica Acta (BBA), Molecular Basis of Disease, 1812*(11), 1477–1489.

Dollinger, S. J. (2007). Creativity and conservatism. *Personality and Individual Differences, 43*, 1025–1035.

Donnellan, M. B., & Lucas, R. E. (2008). Age differences in the big five across the life span: Evidence from two national samples. *Psychology and Aging, 23*(3), 558–566.

Donovan, W. L., Leavitt, L. A., & Walsh, R. O. (1998). Conflict and depression predict maternal sensitivity to infant cries. *Infant Behavior and Development, 21*, 505–517.

Dougherty, T. M., & Haith, M. M. (1997). Infant expectations and reaction time as predictors of childhood speed of processing and IQ. *Developmental Psychology, 33*, 146–155.

Dowshen, S., Crowley, J., & Palusci, V. J. (2004). *Shaken baby/shaken impact syndrome.* Retrieved from www.kidshealth.org/parent/medical/brain/shaken.html

Dozier, M., Stovall, K. C., Albus, K. E., & Bates, B. (2001). Attachment for infants in foster care: The role of caregiver state of mind. *Child Development, 72*, 1467–1477.

Dreyfus, H. L. (1993-1994, Winter). What computers still can't do. *Key Reporter,* pp. 4–9.

Drewnowski, A., & Eichelsdoerfer, P. (2009). The Mediterranean diet: Does it have to cost more? *Public Health Nutrition, 12*(9A), 1621–1628.

Dube, S. R., Anda, R. F., Felitti, V. J., Chapman, D. P., Williamson, D. F., & Giles, W. H. (2001). Childhood abuse, household dysfunction, and the risk of attempted suicide throughout the life span: Findings from the Adverse Childhood Experiences Study. *Journal of the American Medical Association, 286*(24), 3089–3096.

Dube, S. R., Felitti, V. J., Dong, M., Chapman, D. P., Giles, W. H., & Anda, R. F. (2003, March). Childhood abuse, neglect, and household dysfunction and the risk of illicit drug use: The Adverse Childhood Experiences Study. *Pediatrics, 111*(3), 564–572.

Dubowitz, H. (1999). The families of neglected children. In M. E. Lamb (Ed.), *Parenting and child development in "nontraditional" families* (pp. 327–345). Mahwah, NJ: Erlbaum.

Duchek, J. M., Balota, D. A., Storandt, M., & Larsen, R. (2007). The power of personality in discriminating between healthy aging and early-stage Alzheimer's disease. *Journals of Gerontology, 62*(6, Series A), 353–361.

Duckworth, A., & Seligman, M. E. P. (2005). Self-discipline outdoes IQ in predicting academic performance of adolescents. *Psychological Science, 26*, 939–944.

Duenwald, M. (2003, July 15). After 25 years, new ideas in the prenatal test tube. *The New York Times.* Retrieved from www.nytimes.com/2003/07/15/health/15IVF.html?ex

Duggan, M., Singleton, P., & Song, J. (2007). Aching to retire? The rise in the full retirement age and its impact on the Social Security disability rolls. *Journal of Public Economics, 91*(7–8), 1327–1350.

Duke, J., Huhman, M., & Heitzler, C. (2003). Physical activity levels among children aged 9–13 years—United States, 2002. *Morbidity and Mortality Weekly Report, 52*, 785–788.

Duncan, J. R., Paterson, D. S., Hoffman, J. M., Mokler, D. J., Borenstein, N. S., Belliveau, R. A., . . . Kinney, H. C. (2010). Brainstem serotonergic deficiency in sudden infant death syndrome. *Journal of the American Medical Association, 303*(5), 430–437. doi: 10.1001/jama.2010.45

Dunham, P., Dunham, F., & O'Keefe, C. (2000). Two-year-olds' sensitivity to a parent's knowledge state: Mind reading or contextual cues? *British Journal of Developmental Psychology, 18*(4), 519–532.

Dunn, A. L., Trivedi, M. H., Kampert, J. B., Clark, C. G., & Chambliss, H. O. (2005). Exercise treatment for depression: Efficacy and dose response. *American Journal of Preventive Medicine, 28*, 1–8.

Dunn, J. (1991). Young children's understanding of other people: Evidence from observations within the family. In D. Frye & C. Moore (Eds.), *Children's theories of mind: Mental states and social understanding.* Hillsdale, NJ: Erlbaum.

Dunn, J. (2006). Moral development in early childhood and social interaction in the family. In M. Killen & J. Smetana (Eds.), *Handbook of moral development* (pp. 331–350). Mahwah, NJ: Earlbaum.

Dunn, J., Brown, J., Slomkowski, C., Tesla, C., & Youngblade, L. (1991). Young children's understanding of other people's feelings and beliefs: Individual differences and antecedents. *Child Development, 62*, 1352–1366.

Dunn, J., & Hughes, C. (2001). "I got some swords and you're dead!": Violent fantasy, antisocial behavior, friendship, and moral sensibility in young children. *Child Development, 72*, 491–505.

Dunn, J., & Munn, P. (1985). Becoming a family member: Family conflict and the development of social understanding in the second year. *Child Development, 56*, 480–492.

Dunson, D. (2002). *Late breaking research session. Increasing infertility with increasing age: Good news and bad news for older couples.* Paper presented at the 18th annual meeting of the European Society of Human Reproduction and Embryology, Vienna.

Dunson, D. B., Colombo, B., & Baird, D. D. (2002). Changes with age in the level and duration of fertility in the menstrual cycle. *Human Reproduction, 17*, 1399–1403.

DuPont, R. L. (1983). Phobias in children. *Journal of Pediatrics, 102*, 999–1002.

Durga, J., van Boxtel, M. P. J., Schouten, E. G., Kok, F. J., Jolles, J., Katan, M. B., & Verhoef, P. (2007). Effect of 3-year folic acid supplementation on cognitive function in older adults in the FACIT trial: A randomized, double blind controlled study. *Lancet, 369*, 208–216.

Durlak, J. A. (1973). Relationship between attitudes toward life and death among elderly women. *Developmental Psychology, 8*(1), 146.

Dush, C. M. K., Cohan, C. L., & Amato, P. R. (2003). The relationship between cohabitation and marital quality and stability: Change across cohorts? *Journal of Marriage and Family, 65*, 539–549.

Dux, P. E., Ivanoff, J. G., Asplund, C. L., & Marois, R. (2006). Isolation of a central bottleneck of information processing with time-resolved fMRI. *Neuron, 52*(6), 1109–1120.

Dweck, C. S. (2008). Mindsets: How praise is harming youth and what can be done about it. *School Library Medical Activities Monthly, 24*(5), 55–58.

Dweck, C. S., & Grant, H. (2008). Self theories, goals, and meaning. In J. Y. Shaw and W. L. Gardner (Eds.), *Handbook of motivation science* (pp. 405–416). New York: Guilford Press.

Dwyer, T., Ponsonby, A. L., Blizzard, L., Newman, N. M., & Cochrane, J. A. (1995). The contribution of changes in the prevalence of prone sleeping position to the decline in sudden infant death syndrome in Tasmania. *Journal of the American Medical Association, 273*, 783–789.

Dye, J. L., & Johnson, T. D. (2009). A child's day: 2006 (selected indicators of child well-being). *Current Population Reports* (P70–118). Washington, DC: U.S. Census Bureau.

Dye, J. L. (2010). *Fertility of American women: 2008.* Retrieved from http://www.census.gov/prod/2010pubs/p20-563.pdf

Dye, M. (2010, July 13). Why Johnny can't name his colors. *The Scientific American.* Retrieved from http://www.scientificamerican.com/article.cfm?id=why-johnny-name-colors

Dykstra, P. A. (1995). Loneliness among the never and formerly married: The importance of supportive friendships and a desire for independence. *Journal of Gerontology: Social Sciences, 50B*, S321–S329.

Early college high school initiative. (n.d.). Retrieved from www.earlycolleges.org

East, P. L., & Khoo, S. T. (2005). Longitudinal pathways linking family factors and sibling relationship qualities to adolescent substance use and sexual risk behaviors. *Journal of Family Psychology, 19*, 571–580.

Eating disorders—Part I. (1997, October). *Harvard Mental Health Letter,* pp. 1–5.

Eaton, D. K., Kann, L., Kinchen, S., Shanklin, S., Ross, J., Hawkins, J., . . . Wechsler, H. (2008). Youth risk behavior surveillance—United States, 2007. *Morbidity and Mortality Weekly Report, 57*(SS-4), 1–131.

Eccles, R. (1978). The central rhythm of the nasal cycle. *Acta Oto-laryngologica, 86*(5–6), 464–468.

Eccles, A. (1982). *Obstetrics and gynaecology in Tudor and Stuart England.* Kent, OH: Kent State University Press.

Eccles, J. S. (2004). Schools, academic motivation, and stage-environment fit. In R. M. Lerner & L. Steinberg (Eds.), *Handbook of adolescent development* (2nd ed., pp. 125–153). Hoboken, NJ: Wiley.

Eccles, J. S., Wigfield, A., & Byrnes, J. (2003). Cognitive development in adolescence. In I. B. Weiner (Series Ed.), R. M. Lerner, M. A. Easterbrooks, & J. Mistry (Vol. Eds.), *Handbook of psychology: Vol. 6. Developmental psychology.* New York: Wiley.

Ecker, J. L., & Frigoletto, F. D., Jr. (2007). Cesarean delivery and the risk-benefit calculus. *New England Journal of Medicine, 356*, 885–888.

Eckerman, C. O., Davis, C. C., & Didow, S. M. (1989). Toddlers' emerging ways of achieving social coordination with a peer. *Child Development, 60*, 440–453.

Eckerman, C. O., & Didow, S. M. (1996). Nonverbal imitation and toddlers' mastery of verbal means of achieving coordinated action. *Developmental Psychology, 32*, 141–152.

Eddleman, K. A., Malone, F. D., Sullivan, L., Dukes, K., Berkowitz, R. L., Kharbutli, Y., . . . D'Alton, M. E. (2006). Pregnancy loss rates after midtrimester amniocentesis. *Obstetrics and Gynecology, 108*(5), 1067–1072.

Eden, G. F., Jones, K. M., Cappell, K., Gareau, L., Wood, F. B., Zeffiro, T. A., . . . Flowers, D. L. (2004). Neural changes following remediation in adult developmental dyslexia. *Neuron, 44*, 411–422.

Eder, W., Ege, M. J., & von Mutius, E. (2006). The asthma epidemic. *New England Journal of Medicine, 355*, 2226–2235.

Edmondson, D., Park, C. L., Chaudoir, S. R., & Wortman, J. H. (2008). Death without God: Religious struggle, death concerns, and depression in the terminally ill. *Psychological Science, 19*(8), 754–758.

Edwards, C. P. (1994, April). *Cultural relativity meets best practice, or, anthropology and early education, a promising friendship.* Paper presented at the meeting of the American Educational Research Association, New Orleans.

Edwards, C. P. (2002). Three approaches from Europe: Waldorf, Montessori, and Reggio Emilia. *Early Childhood Research and Practice, 4*(1), 14–38.

Edwards, C. P. (2003). "Fine designs" from Italy: Montessori education and the Reggio Emilia approach. *Montessori Life: Journal of the American Montessori Society, 15*(1), 33–38.

Eggebeen, D. J., & Knoester, C. (2001). Does fatherhood matter for men? *Journal of Marriage and Family, 63*, 381–393.

Eggebeen, D. J., & Sturgeon, S. (2006). Demography of the baby boomers. In S. K. Whitbourne & S. L. Willis (Eds.), *The baby boomers grow up: Contemporary perspectives on midlife* (pp. 3–21). Mahwah, NJ: Erlbaum.

Ehrenreich, B., & English, D. (2005). *For her own good: Two centuries of the experts' advice to women.* New York: Anchor.

Eichler, E. E., & Zimmerman, A. W. (2008). A hot spot of genetic instability in autism. *New England Journal of Medicine, 358*, 737–739.

Eimas, P., Siqueland, E., Jusczyk, P., & Vigorito, J. (1971). Speech perception in infants. *Science, 171*, 303–306.

Einarson, A., & Boskovic, R. (2009). Use and safety of antipsychotic drugs during pregnancy. *Journal of Psychiatric Practice, 15*(3), 183–192.

Eisenberg, A. R. (1996). The conflict talk of mothers and children: Patterns related to culture, SES, and gender of child. *Merrill-Palmer Quarterly, 42*, 438–452.

Eisenberg, L. (1995, Spring). Is the family obsolete? *Key Reporter*, pp. 1–5.

Eisenberg, N. (1992). *The caring child.* Cambridge, MA: Harvard University Press.

Eisenberg, N. (2000). Emotion, regulation, and moral development. *Annual Review of Psychology, 51*, 665–697.

Eisenberg, N., & Fabes, R. A. (1998). Prosocial development. In W. Damon (Series Ed.) & N. Eisenberg (Vol. Ed.), *Handbook of child psychology: Vol. 3. Social, emotional, and personality development* (5th ed., pp. 701–778). New York: Wiley.

Eisenberg, N., Fabes, R. A., & Murphy, B. C. (1996). Parents' reactions to children's negative emotions: Relations to children's social competence and comforting behavior. *Child Development, 67*, 2227–2247.

Eisenberg, N., Fabes, R. A., Nyman, M., Bernzweig, J., & Pinuelas, A. (1994). The relations of emotionality and regulation to children's anger-related reactions. *Child Development, 65*, 109–128.

Eisenberg, N., Fabes, R. A., Shepard, S. A., Guthrie, I. K., Murphy, B. C., & Reiser, M. (1999). Parental reactions to children's negative emotions: Longitudinal relations to quality of children's social functioning. *Child Development, 70*(2), 513–534.

Eisenberg, N., Fabes, R. A., & Spinrad, T. L. (2006). Prosocial development. In W. Damon & R. M. Lerner (Series Eds.) & N. Eisenberg (Vol. Ed.), *Handbook of child psychology: Vol 3. Social, emotional and personality development* (6th ed., pp. 646–718). Hoboken: NJ: Wiley.

Eisenberg, N., & Morris, A. D. (2004). Moral cognitions and prosocial responding in adolescence. In R. M. Lerner & L. Steinberg (Eds.), *Handbook of adolescent psychology* (2nd ed., pp. 155–188). Hoboken, NJ: Wiley.

Eisenberg, N., Spinrad, T. L., Fabes, R. A., Reiser, M., Cumberland, A., Shepard, S. A., . . . Thompson, M. (2004). The relations of effortful control and impulsivity to children's resiliency and adjustment. *Child Development, 75*, 25–46.

Eliassen, H., Colditz, G. A., Rosner, B., Willett, W. C., & Hankinson, S. E. (2006). Adult weight change and risk of postmenopausal breast cancer. *Journal of the American Medical Association, 296*, 193–201.

Elicker, J., Englund, M., & Sroufe, L. A. (1992). Predicting peer competence and peer relationships in childhood from early parent-child relationships. In R. Parke & G. Ladd (Eds.), *Family peer relationships: Modes of linkage* (pp. 77–106). Hillsdale, NJ: Erlbaum.

Elkind, D. (1981). *The hurried child.* Reading, MA: Addison-Wesley.

Elkind, D. (1986). *The miseducation of children: Superkids at risk.* New York: Knopf.

Elkind, D. (1997). *Reinventing childhood: Raising and educating children in a changing world.* Rosemont, NJ: Modern Learning Press.

Elkind, D. (1998). *Teenagers in crisis: All grown up and no place to go.* Reading, MA: Perseus Books.

Elliott, P., Stamler, J., Dyer, A. R., Appel, L., Dennis, B., Kesteloot, H., . . . Zhou, B. for the INTERMAP Cooperative Research Group. (2006). Association between protein intake and blood pressure. *Annals of Internal Medicine, 166*, 79–87.

Ellis, A., & Oakes, L. M. (2006). Infants flexibly use different dimensions to categorize objects. *Developmental Psychology, 42*, 1000–1011.

Ellis, B. J., Bates, J. E., Dodge, K. A., Fergusson, D. M., Horwood, L. J., Pettit, G. S., & Woodward, L. (2003). Does father-absence place daughters at special risk for early sexual activity and teenage pregnancy? *Child Development, 74*, 801–821.

Ellis, B. J., McFadyen-Ketchum, S., Dodge, K. A., Pettit, G. S., & Bates, J. E. (1999). Quality of early family relationships and individual differences in the timing of pubertal maturation in girls: A longitudinal test of an evolutionary model. *Journal of Personality and Social Psychology, 77*, 387–401.

Ellis, K. J., Abrams, S. A., & Wong, W. W. (1997). Body composition of a young, multiethnic female population. *American Journal of Clinical Nutrition, 65*, 724–731.

Ellison, C. G., Musick, M. A., & Henderson, A. K. (2008). Balm in Gilead: Racism, religious involvement, and psychological distress among African American adults. *Journal for the Scientific Study of Religion, 47*, 291–309.

Ellison, N. B., Steinfield, C., & Lampe, C. (2007). The benefits of Facebook "friends": Social capital and college students' use of online social network sites. *Journal of Computer-Mediated Communication, 12*(4), 1143–1168.

Elmenhorst, D., Elmenhorst, E., Luks, N., Maass, H., Mueller, E., Vejvoda, M., . . . Samuel, A. (2009). Performance impairment after four days partial sleep deprivation compared with acute effects of alcohol and hypoxia. *Sleep Medicine, 10*, 189–197.

El-Sheikh, M., Kelly, R. J., Buckhalt, J. A., & Hinnant, J. B. (2010). Children's sleep and adjustment over time: The role of socioeconomic context. *Child Development, 81*, 870–883. doi: 10.1111/j.1467-8624.2010.01439.x

Eltzschig, H. K., Lieberman, E. S., & Camann, W. R. (2003). Regional anesthesia and analgesia for labor and delivery. *New England Journal of Medicine, 348*, 319–332.

Emberson, L. L., Lupyan, G., Goldstein, M. H., & Spivey, M. J. (2010). Overheard cell phone conversations: When speech is more distracting. *Psychological Science, 21*(10), 1383–1388.

Emde, R. N., Plomin, R., Robinson, J., Corley, R., DeFries, J., Fulker, D. W., . . . Zahn-Waxler, C. (1992). Temperament, emotion, and cognition at 14 months: The MacArthur Longitudinal Twin Study. *Child Development, 63*, 1437–1455.

Emery, L., Heaven, T. J., Paxton, J. L., & Braver, T. S. (2008). Age-related changes in neural activity during performance matched working memory manipulation. *NeuroImage, 42*(4), 1577–1586.

Eng, P. M., Rimm, E. B., Fitzmaurice, G., & Kawachi, I. (2002). Social ties and change in social ties in relation to subsequent total and cause-specific mortality and coronary heart disease incidence in men. *American Journal of Epidemiology, 155*, 700–709.

Engle, P. L., & Breaux, C. (1998). Fathers' involvement with children: Perspectives from developing countries. *Social Policy Report, 12*(1), 1–21.

Epel, E. S., Blackburn, E. H., Lin, J., Dhabhar, F. S., Adler, N. E., Morrow, J. D., & Cawthon, R. M. (2004). Accelerated telomere shortening in response to life stress. *Proceedings of the National Academy of Sciences, 101*, 17312–17315.

Engle, P. L., Black, M. M., Behrman, J. R., de Mello, M. C., Gertler, P. J., Kapiriri, L., Martorell, R., & Young, M. E. (2007). Strategies to avoid the loss of developmental potential in more than 200 million children in the developing world. *The Lancet, 369*(9557), 20–26.

Erikson, E. H. (1950). *The life cycle completed.* New York: Norton.

Erikson, E. H. (1968). *Identity: Youth and crisis.* New York: Norton.

Erikson, E. H. (1973). The wider identity. In K. Erikson (Ed.), *In search of common ground: Conversations with Erik H. Erikson and Huey P. Newton.* New York: Norton.

Erikson, E. H. (1982). *The life cycle completed.* New York: Norton.

Erikson, E. H. (1985). *The life cycle completed* (Paperback reprint ed.). New York: Norton.

Erikson, E. H., Erikson, J. M., & Kivnick, H. Q. (1986). *Vital involvement in old age: The experience of old age in our time.* New York: Norton.

Ertel, K. A., Glymour, M. M., & Berkman, L. F. (2008). Effects of social integration on preserving memory function in a nationally representative elderly population. *American Journal of Public Health, 98*, 1215–1220.

Ervin, R. B. (2008). Healthy Index Eating scores among adults, 60 years of age and over, by sociodemographic and health characteristics: United States, 1999–2002. *Advance Data from Vital and Health Statistics*, No. 395. Hyattsville, MD: National Center for Health Statistics.

Espeland, M. A., Rapp, S. R., Shumaker, S. A., Brunner, R., Manson, J. E., Sherwin, B. B., . . . Hays, J., for the Women's Health Initiative Memory Study Investigators. (2004). Conjugated equine estrogens and global cognitive function in postmenopausal women: Women's Health Initiative Memory Study. *Journal of the American Medical Association, 21*, 2959–2968.

Esposito, K., Marfella, R., Ciotola, M., DiPalo, C., Giugliano, F., Giugliano, G., . . . Giugliano, D. (2004). Effects of a Mediterranean-style diet on endothelial dysfunction and markers of vascular inflammation in the metabolic syndrome: A randomized trial. *Journal of the American Medical Association, 292*, 1440–1446.

Essex, M. J., & Nam, S. (1987). Marital status and loneliness among older women: The differential importance of close family and friends. *Journal of Marriage and Family, 49*, 93–106.

Ettinger, B., Friedman, G. D., Bush, T., & Quesenberry, C. P. (1996). Reduced mortality associated with long-term postmenopausal estrogen therapy. *Obstetrics & Gynecology, 87*, 6–12.

Etzel, R. A. (2003). How environmental exposures influence the development and exacerbation of asthma. *Pediatrics, 112*(1), 233–239.

Evans, A. D., & Lee, K. (2010). Promising to tell the truth makes 8- to 16-year-olds more honest. *Behavioral Sciences and the Law, 28*(6), 801–811.

Evans, G. W. (2004). The environment of childhood poverty. *American Psychologist, 59,* 77–92.

Evert, J., Lawler, E., Bogan, H., & Perls, T. (2003). Morbidity profiles of centenarians: Survivors, delayers, and escapers. *Journal of Gerontology: Medical Sciences, 58A,* 232–237.

Ezzati, M., Friedman, A. B., Kulkarni, S. C., & Murray, C. J. L. (2008). The reversal of fortunes: Trends in country mortality and cross-country mortality disparities in the United States. *PloS Medicine, 5*(4), e66. doi: 10:1371/journal.pmed.0050066

Ezzati, M., & Lopez, A. D. (2004). Regional, disease specific patterns of smoking-attributable mortality in 2000. *Tobacco Control, 13,* 388–395.

Fabel, K., & Kempermann, G. (2008). Physical activity and the regulation of neurogenesis in the adult and aging brain. *Neuromolecular Medicine, 10*(2), 59–66.

Fabes, R. A., Carlo, G., Kupanoff, K., & Laible, D. (1999). Early adolescence and prosocial/moral behavior: I. The role of individual processes. *Journal of Early Adolescence, 19,* 5–16.

Fabes, R. A., & Eisenberg, N. (1992). Young children's coping with interpersonal anger. *Child Development, 63,* 116–128.

Fabes, R. A., Leonard, S. A., Kupanoff, K., & Martin, C. L. (2001). Parental coping with children's negative emotions: Relations with children's emotional and social responding. *Child Development, 72,* 907–920.

Fabes, R. A., Leonard, S. A., Kupanoff, K., & Martin, C. L. (2001). Parental coping with children's negative emotions: Relations with children's emotional and social responding. *Child Development, 72*(3), 907–920.

Fabes, R. A., Martin, C. L., & Hanish, L. D. (2003). Young children's play qualities in same-, other-, and mixed-gender peer groups. *Child Development, 74*(3), 921–932.

Fabricius, W. V. (2003). Listening to children of divorce: New findings that diverge from Wallerstein, Lewis, and Blakeslee. *Family Relations, 52,* 385–394.

Facebook. (2011). *Statistics.* Retrieved from http://www.facebook.com/press/info.php?statistics

Fagan, J. F., Holland, C. R., & Wheeler, K. (2007). The prediction, from infancy, of adult IQ. *Intelligence, 35,* 225–231.

Fagot, B. I. (1997). Attachment, parenting, and peer interactions of toddler children. *Developmental Psychology, 33,* 489–499.

Fagot, B. I., Rogers, C. S., & Leinbach, M. D. (2000). Theories of gender socialization. In T. Eckes & H. M. Trautner (Eds.), *The developmental social psychology of gender.* Mahwah, NJ: Earlbaum.

Falbo, T. (2006). *Your one and only: Educational psychologist dispels myths surrounding only children.* Retrieved from www.utexas.edu/features/archive/2004/single.htm

Falbo, T., & Poston, D. L. (1993). The academic, personality, and physical outcomes of only children in China. *Child Development, 64,* 18–35.

Fantz, R. L. (1963). Pattern vision in newborn infants. *Science, 140,* 296–297.

Fantz, R. L. (1964). Visual experience in infants: Decreased attention to familiar patterns relative to novel ones. *Science, 146,* 668–670.

Fantz, R. L. (1965). Visual perception from birth as shown by pattern selectivity. In H. E. Whipple (Ed.), *New issues in infant development. Annals of the New York Academy of Science, 118,* 793–814.

Fantz, R. L., Fagen, J., & Miranda, S. B. (1975). Early visual selectivity. In L. Cohen & P. Salapatek (Eds.), *Infant perception: From sensation to cognition: Vol. 1. Basic visual processes* (pp. 249–341). New York: Academic Press.

Fantz, R. L., & Nevis, S. (1967). Pattern preferences and perceptual-cognitive development in early infancy. *Merrill-Palmer Quarterly, 13,* 77–108.

Farver, J. A. M., Kim, Y. K., & Lee, Y. (1995). Cultural differences in Korean and Anglo-American preschoolers' social interaction and play behavior. *Child Development, 66,* 1088–1099.

Farver, J. A. M., Xu, Y., Eppe, S., Fernandez, A., & Schwartz, D. (2005). Community violence, family conflict, and preschoolers' socioemotional functioning. *Developmental Psychology, 41,* 160–170.

Fasig, L. (2000). Toddlers' understanding of ownership: Implications for self-concept development. *Social Development, 9,* 370–382.

Favaro, A., Ferrara, S., & Santonastaso, P. (2004). The spectrum of eating disorders in young women: A prevalence study in a general population sample. *Psychosomatic Medicine, 65,* 701–708.

Fawcett, G. M., Heise, L. L., Isita-Espejel, L., & Pick, S. (1999). Change community responses to wife abuse: A research and demonstration project in Iztacalco, Mexico. *American Psychologist, 54,* 41–49.

Fear, J. M., Champion, J. E., Reeslund, K. L., Forehand, R., Colletti, C., Roberts, L., & Compas, B. E. (2009). Parental depression and interparental conflict: Children and adolescents' self-blame and coping responses. *Journal of Family Psychology, 23*(5), 762–766. doi:10.1037/a0016381

Fearon, P., O'Connell, P., Frangou, S., Aquino, P., Nosarti, C., Allin, M., . . . Murray, R. (2004). Brain volume in adult survivors of very low birth weight: A sibling-controlled study. *Pediatrics, 114,* 367–371.

Fearon, R. P., Bakermans-Kranenburg, M. J., Van IJzendoorn, M. H., Lapsley, A.-M., & Roisman, G. I. (2010). The significance of insecure attachment and disorganization in the development of children's externalizing behavior: A meta-analytic study. *Child Development, 81,* 435–456. doi: 10.1111/j.1467-8624.2009.01405.x

Federal Bureau of Investigation (FBI). (2007). *Crime in the United States, 2005.* Retrieved from www.fbi.gov/ucr/05cius

Federal Interagency Forum on Aging-Related Statistics. (2004). *Older Americans 2004: Key indicators of well-being.* Washington, DC: U.S. Government Printing Office.

Federal Interagency Forum on Aging-Related Statistics. (2006). *Older Americans update 2006: Key indicators of well-being.* Washington, DC: U.S. Government Printing Office.

Federal Interagency Forum on Aging-Related Statistics. (2010). *Older Americans 2010: Key indicators of well-being.* Washington, DC: U.S. Government Printing Office.

Federal Interagency Forum on Aging-Related Statistics. (2012). *Older Americans 2012: Key indicators of well-being.* Washington, DC: U.S. Government Printing Office.

Federal Interagency Forum on Child and Family Statistics. (2005). *America's children: Key national indicators of well-being, 2005.* Washington, DC: U.S. Government Printing Office.

Federal Interagency Forum on Child and Family Statistics. (2007). *America's children: Key indicators of well-being, 2007.* Washington, DC: U.S. Government Printing Office.

Federal Interagency Forum on Child and Family Statistics. (2008). *Table PHY1a: Outdoor air quality: Percentage of children ages 0–17 living in counties in which levels of one or more air pollutants were above allowable levels, 1999–2007.* Washington, DC: U.S. Government Prining Office. Retrieved from http://www.childstats.gov/americaschildren/tables/phy1a.asp

Federal Interagency Forum on Child and Family Statistics. (2009). *America's children: Key national indicators of well-being, 2009.* Retrieved from www.childstats.gov/americas-children/eco3.asp

Federal Interagency Forum on Child and Family Statistics. (2012). *America's children: Key indicators of well-being.* Retrieved from http://www.childstats.gov/americaschildren/eco.asp

Feingold, A., & Mazzella, R. (1998). Gender differences in body image are increasing. *Psychological Science, 9*(3), 190–195.

Feldman, H. A., Goldstein, I., Hatzichristou, D. G., Krane, R. J., & McKinlay, J. B. (1994). Impotence and its medical and psychosocial correlates: Results of the Massachusetts Male Aging Study. *Journal of Urology, 151,* 54–61.

Feldman, R. (2007). Parent-infant synchrony: Biological foundations and developmental outcomes. *Current Directions in Psychological Science, 16*(6), 340–345.

Ferber, R. (1985). *Solve your child's sleep problems.* New York: Simon & Schuster.

Ferber, S. G., & Makhoul, I. R. (2004). The effect of skin-to-skin contact (Kangaroo Care) shortly after birth on the neuro-behavioral responses of the term newborn: A randomized, controlled trial. *Pediatrics, 113,* 858–865.

Ferguson, C. J. (2013). Violent video games and the Supreme Court: Lessons for the scientific community in the wake of Brown vs. Entertainment Merchant's Association. *American Psychologist, 68*(2), 57–74.

Fergusson, D. M., Horwood, L. J., Ridder, E. M., & Beautrais, A. L. (2005). Sub-threshold depression in adolescence and mental health outcomes in adulthood. *Archives of General Psychiatry, 62*(1), 66–72.

Ferguson, C. J., & Savage, J. (2012). Have recent studies addressed methodological issues raised by five decades of televised violence research? A critical review. *Aggression and Violent Behavior, 17,* 129–139.

Fernald, A., Perfors, A., & Marchman, V. A. (2006). Picking up speed in understanding: Speech processing efficiency and vocabulary growth across the second year. *Developmental Psychology, 42,* 98–116.

Fernald, A., Swingley, D., & Pinto, J. P. (2001). When half a word is enough: Infants can recognize spoken words using partial phonetic information. *Child Development, 72,* 1003–1015.

Fernauld, A. (1985). Four-month-old infants prefer to listen to motherease. *Infant Behavior and Development, 8,* 181–195.

Ferrer, E., Shaywitz, B. A., Holahan, J. M., Marchione, K., & Shaywitz, S. E. (2010). Uncoupling of reading and IQ over time: Empirical evidence for a definition of dyslexia. *Psychological Science, 21*(1), 93–101.

Fiatarone, M. A., O'Neill, E. F., Ryan, N. D., Clements, K. M., Solares, G. R., Nelson, M. E., . . . Evans, W. J. (1994). Exercise training and nutritional supplementation for physical frailty in very elderly people. *New England Journal of Medicine, 330,* 1769–1775.

Field, A. E., Austin, S. B., Taylor, C. B., Malspeis, S., Rosner, B., Rockett, H. R., . . . Colditz, G. A. (2003). Relation between dieting and weight change among preadolescents and adolescents. *Pediatrics, 112*(4), 900–906.

Field, A. E., Camargo, C. A., Taylor, B., Berkey, C. S., Roberts, S. B., & Colditz, G. A. (2001). Peer, parent, and media influence on the development of weight concerns and frequent dieting among preadolescent and adolescent girls and boys. *Pediatrics, 107*(1), 54–60.

Field, T. (1995). Infants of depressed mothers. *Infant Behavior and Development, 18,* 1–13.

Field, T. (1998a). Emotional care of the at-risk infant: Early interventions for infants of depressed mothers. *Pediatrics, 102,* 1305–1310.

Field, T. (1998b). Massage therapy effects. *American Psychologist, 53,* 1270–1281.

Field, T. (1998c). Maternal depression effects on infants and early intervention. *Preventive Medicine, 27,* 200–203.

Field, T., Diego, M., & Hernandez-Reif, M. (2007). Massage therapy research. *Developmental Review, 27,* 75–89.

Field, T., Diego, M., Hernandez-Reif, M., Schanberg, S., & Kuhn, C. (2003). Depressed mothers who are "good interaction" partners versus those who are withdrawn or intrusive. *Infant Behavior & Development, 26,* 238–252.

Field, T., Fox, N. A., Pickens, J., Nawrocki, T., & Soutollo, D. (1995). Right frontal EEG activation in 3- to 6-month-old infants of depressed mothers. *Developmental Psychology, 31,* 358–363.

Field, T., Grizzle, N., Scafidi, F., Abrams, S., Richardson, S., Kuhn, C., & Schanberg, S. (1996). Massage therapy for infants of depressed mothers. *Infant Behavior and Development, 19,* 107–112.

Field, T. M. (1978). Interaction behaviors of primary versus secondary caretaker fathers. *Developmental Psychology, 14,* 183–184.

Field, T. M., & Roopnarine, J. L. (1982). Infant-peer interaction. In T. M. Field, A. Huston, H. C. Quay, L. Troll, & G. Finley (Eds.), *Review of human development.* New York: Wiley.

Field, T. M., Sandberg, D., Garcia, R., Vega-Lahr, N., Goldstein, S., & Guy, L. (1985). Pregnancy problems, postpartum depression, and early infant-mother interactions. *Developmental Psychology, 21,* 1152–1156.

Fields, R. D., & Stevens-Graham, B. (2002). New insights into neuron–glia communication. *Science, 298,* 556–562.

Fields, J. (2004). America's families and living arrangements: 2003. *Current Population Reports* (P20-553). Washington, DC: U.S. Census Bureau.

Fields, J. M., & Smith, K. E. (1998, April). *Poverty, family structure, and child well-being: Indicators from the SIPP* (Population Division Working Paper No. 23, U.S. Bureau of the Census). Paper presented at the annual meeting of the Population Association of America, Chicago.

Fiese, B., & Schwartz, M. (2008). Reclaiming the family table: Mealtimes and child health and wellbeing. *Society for Research in Child Development Social Policy Report, 23*(4).

Fifer, W. P., & Moon, C. M. (1995). The effects of fetal experience with sound. In J. P. Lecanuet, W. P. Fifer, N. A. Krasnegor, & W. P. Smotherman (Eds.), *Fetal development. A psychobiological perspective* (pp. 351–366). Hillsdale, NJ: Erlbaum.

Finch, C. E., & Zelinski, E. M. (2005). Normal aging of brain structure and cognition: Evolutionary perspectives. *Research in Human Development, 2,* 69–82.

Finer, L. B. (2007). Trends in premarital sex in the United States, 1954–2003. *Public Health Reports, 122,* 73–78.

Fingerman, K., & Dolbin-MacNab, M. (2006). The baby boomers and their parents: Cohort influences and intergenerational ties. In S. K. Whitbourne & S. L. Willis (Eds.), *The baby boomers grow up: Contemporary perspectives on midlife* (pp. 237–259). Mahwah, NJ: Erlbaum.

Fingerman, K., Miller, L., Birditt, K., & Zarit, S. (2009). Giving to the good and to the needy: Parental support of grown children. *Journal of Marriage and Family, 71,* 1220–1233.

Fingerman, K. L., Pitzer, L. M., Chan, W., Birditt, K., Franks, M. M., & Zarit, S. (2010). Who gets what and why? Help middle-aged adults provide to parents and grown children. *Journal of Gerontology, 10,* 1–12.

Finn, J. D. (2006). *The adult lives of at-risk students: The roles of attainment and engagement in high school* (NCES 2006-328). Washington, DC: U.S. Department of Education, National Center for Education Statistics.

Finn, J. D., Gerber, S. B., & Boyd-Zaharias, J. (2005). Small classes in the early grades, academic achievement, and graduating from high school. *Journal of Educational Psychology, 97,* 214–223.

Finn, J. D., & Rock, D. A. (1997). Academic success among students at risk for dropout. *Journal of Applied Psychology, 82,* 221–234.

Fiori, K. L., Smith, J., & Antonucci, T. C. (2007). Social network types among older adults: A multidimensional approach. *Journals of Gerontology, 62*(6, Series A), 322–330.

First 30 days. (2008). *The change report* (Research conducted by Southeastern Institute of Research). Retrieved from www.first30days.com/pages/the_change_report.html

Fiscella, K., Kitzman, H. J., Cole, R. E., Sidora, K. J., & Olds, D. (1998). Does child abuse predict adolescent pregnancy? *Pediatrics, 101,* 620–624.

Fischer, K. (1980). A theory of cognitive development: The control and construction of hierarchies of skills. *Psychological Review, 87,* 477–531.

Fischer, K. W. (2008). Dynamic cycles of cognitive and brain development: Measuring growth in mind, brain, and education. In A. M. Battro, K. W. Fischer, & P. Léna (Eds.), *The educated brain* (pp. 127–150). Cambridge UK: Cambridge University Press.

Fischer, K. W., & Pruyne, E. (2003). Reflective thinking in adulthood. In J. Demick & C. Andreoletti (Eds.), *Handbook of adult development.* New York: Plenum Press.

Fischer, K. W., & Rose, S. P. (1994). Dynamic development of coordination of components in brain and behavior: A framework for theory and research. In G. Dawson & K. W. Fischer (Eds.), *Human behavior and the developing brain* (pp. 3–66). New York: Guilford Press.

Fischer, K. W., & Rose, S. P. (1995, Fall). Concurrent cycles in the dynamic development of brain and behavior. *SRCD Newsletter,* pp. 3–4, 15–16.

Fisher, C. B., Hoagwood, K., Boyce, C., Duster, T., Frank, D. A., Grisso, T., . . . Luis, H. (2002). Research ethics for mental health science involving ethnic minority children and youth. *American Psychologist, 57,* 1024–1040.

Fischer, M. J. (2008). Does campus diversity promote friendship diversity? A look at interracial friendships in college. *Social Science Quarterly, 89*(3), 631–655.

Fitzpatrick, M. D., & Turner, S. E. (2007). Blurring the boundary: Changes in the transition from college participation to adulthood. In S. Danziger & C. Rouse (Eds.), *The price of independence: The economics of early adulthood* (pp. 107–137). New York: Russell Sage Foundation.

Fitzpatric, M. J., & McPhearson, B. J. (2010). Coloring within the lines: Gender stereotypes in contemporary coloring books. *Sex Roles, 62,* 127–137. doi: 10.1008/s11199-009-9703-8

Fivush, R., & Haden, C. A. (2006). Elaborating on elaborations: Role of maternal reminiscing style in cognitive and socioemotional development. *Child Development, 77,* 1568–1588.

Fivush, R., & Nelson, K. (2004). Culture and language in the emergence of autobiographical memory. *Psychological Science, 15,* 573–577.

Flannagan, C. A., Bowes, J. M., Jonsson, B., Csapo, B., & Sheblanova, E. (1998). Ties that bind: Correlates of adolescents' civic commitment in seven countries. *Journal of Social Issues, 54*, 457–475.

Flavell, J. H. (1993). Young children's understanding of thinking and consciousness. *Current Directions in Psychological Science, 2*, 40–43.

Flavell, J. H. (2000). Development of children's knowledge about the mental world. *International Journal of Behavioral Development, 24*(1), 15–23.

Flavell, J. H., Green, F. L., & Flavell, E. R. (1986). Development of knowledge about the appearance-reality distinction. *Monographs of the Society for Research in Child Development, 51*(1, Serial No. 212).

Flavell, J. H., Green, F. L., & Flavell, E. R. (1995). Young children's knowledge about thinking. *Monographs of the Society for Research in Child Development, 60*(1, Serial No. 243).

Flavell, J. H., Green, F. L., Flavell, E. R., & Grossman, J. B. (1997). The development of children's knowledge about inner speech. *Child Development, 68*, 39–47.

Flavell, J. H., Miller, P. H., & Miller, S. A. (2002). *Cognitive development.* Englewood Cliffs, NJ: Prentice Hall.

Flaxman, S. M., & Sherman, P. W. (2000). Morning sickness: A mechanism for protecting mother and embryo. *Quarterly Review of Biology*, 113–148.

Fleeson, W. (2004). The quality of American life at the end of the century. In O. G. Brim, C. D. Ryff, & R. C. Kessler (Eds.), *How healthy are we? A national study of well-being at midlife* (pp. 252–272). Chicago: University of Chicago Press.

Flegal, K. M., Carroll, M. D., Ogden, C. L., & Curtin, L. R. (2010). Prevalence and trends in obesity among U.S. adults, 1999–2008. *Journal of the American Medical Association, 303*, 235–241.

Fleischman, D. A., Wilson, R. S., Gabrieli, J. D. E., Bienias, J. L., & Bennett, D. A. (2004). A longitudinal study of implicit and explicit memory in old persons. *Psychology and Aging, 19*(4), 617–625. doi: 10.1037/0882-7974.19.4.617

Fleming, B. M. (2010). Suicide from the Golden Gate Bridge. *American Journal of Psychiatry, 166*(10), 1111–1116.

Flook, L., Repetti, R. L., & Ullman, J. B. (2005). Classroom social experiences as predictors of academic performance. *Developmental Psychology, 41*, 319–327.

Flores, G., Fuentes-Afflick, E., Barbot, O., Carter-Pokras, O., Claudio, L., Lara, M., . . . Weitzman, M. (2002). The health of Latino children: Urgent priorities, unanswered questions, and a research agenda. *Journal of the American Medical Association, 288*, 82–90.

Flores, G., Olson, L., & Tomany-Korman, S. C. (2005). Racial and ethnic disparities in early childhood health and health care. *Pediatrics, 115*, e183–e193.

Flynn, J. R. (1984). The mean IQ of Americans: Massive gains 1932 to 1978. *Psychological Bulletin, 95*, 29–51.

Flynn, J. R. (1987). Massive IQ gains in 14 nations: What IQ tests really measure. *Psychological Bulletin, 101*, 171–191.

Foldvari, M., Clark, M., Laviolette, L. C., Bernstein, M. A., Kaliton, D., Castaneda, C., . . . Singh, M. A. (2000). Association of muscle power with functional status in community-dwelling elderly women. *Journal of Gerontology: Biological and Medical Sciences, 55*, M192–M199.

Fomby, P., & Cherlin, A. J. (2007). Family instability and child well-being. *American Sociological Review, 72*(2), 181–204.

Fontana, L., & Klein, S. (2007). Aging, adiposity, and calorie restriction. *Journal of the American Medical Association, 297*, 986–994.

Fontana, L., Klein, S., & Holloszy, J. (2010). Effects of long-term calorie restriction and endurance exercise on glucose tolerance, insulin action, and adipokine production. *Age, 32*(1), 97–108. doi: 10.1007/s11357-009-9118-z

Fontanel, B., & d'Harcourt, C. (1997). *Babies, history, art and folklore.* New York: Abrams.

Ford, M. T., Heinen, B. A., & Langkamer, K. L. (2007). Work and family satisfaction and conflict: A meta-analysis of cross-domain relations. *Journal of Applied Psychology, 92*(1), 57–80.

Ford, P. (April 10, 2002). In Europe, marriage is back. *Christian Science Monitor,* p. l.

Ford, R. P., Schluter, P. J., Mitchell, E. A., Taylor, B. J., Scragg, R., & Stewart, A. W. (1998). Heavy caffeine intake in pregnancy and sudden infant death syndrome (New Zealand Cot Death Study Group). *Archives of Disease in Childhood, 78*(1), 9–13.

Forget-Dubois, N., Dionne, G., Lemelin, J.-P., Pérusse, D., Tremblay, R. E., & Boivin, M. (2009). Early child language mediates the relation between home environment and school readiness. *Child Development, 80*, 736–749. doi: 10.1111/j.1467-8624.2009.01294.x

Forhan, S. E., Gottlieb, S. L., Sternberg, M. R., Xu, F., Datta, D., Berman, S., & Markowitz, L. E. (2008, March 13). *Prevalence of sexually transmitted infections and bacterial vaginosis among female adolescents in the United States: Data from the National Health and Nutritional Examination Survey (NHANES) 2003–2004.* Oral presentation at the meeting of the 2008 National STD Prevention Conference, Chicago.

Foster, E. M., & Watkins, S. (2010). The value of reanalysis: TV viewing and attention problems. *Child Development, 81*(1), 368–375. doi: 10.1111/j.1467-8624.2009.01400.x

Foundation for Child Development. (2010). *Child and youth well-being index.* Retrieved from http://www.fcd-us.org/sites/default/files/FINAL%202010%20CWI%20Annual%20Release.pdf

Foundation Fighting Blindness. (2005). *Macular degeneration—Treatments.* Retrieved from www.blindness.org/disease/treatmentdetail.asp?typed=2&id=6

Fox, M. K., Pac, S., Devaney, B., & Jankowski, L. (2004). Feeding Infants and Toddlers Study: What foods are infants and toddlers eating? *Journal of the American Dietetic Association, 104*, 22–30.

Fox, N. A., Hane, A. A., & Pine, D. S. (2007). Plasticity for affective neurocircuitry: How the environment affects gene expression. *Current Directions in Psychological Science, 16*(1), 1–5.

Fraga, M., F., Ballestar, E., Paz, M. F., Ropero, S., Setien, F., Ballestar, M. L., . . . Esteller, M. (2005). Epigenetic differences arise during the lifetime of monozygotic twins. *Proceedings of the National Academy of Sciences, USA, 102*, 10604–10609.

Franconi, F., Brunelleschi, S., Steardo, L., & Cuomo, V. (2007). Gender differences in drug responses. *Pharmacological Research, 55*, 81–95.

Frank, D. A., Augustyn, M., Knight, W. G., Pell, T., & Zuckerman, B. (2001). Growth, development, and behavior in early childhood following prenatal cocaine exposure. *Journal of the American Medical Association, 285*, 1613–1625.

Frankenburg, W. K., Dodds, J., Archer, P., Bresnick, B., Maschka, P., Edelman, N., & Shapiro, H. (1992). *Denver II training manual.* Denver: Denver Developmental Materials.

Frankenburg, W. K., Dodds, J. B., Fandal, A. W., Kazuk, E., & Cohrs, M. (1975). *The Denver Developmental Screening Test: Reference manual.* Denver: University of Colorado Medical Center.

Franks, P. W., Hanson, R. L., Knowler, W. C., Sievers, M. L., Bennett, P. H., & Looker, H. C. (2010). Childhood obesity, other cardiovascular risk factors and premature death. *New England Journal of Medicine, 362*(6), 485–493.

Franks, S. (2009). Polycystic ovary syndrome. *Medicine, 37*(9), 441–444.

Frans, E. M., Sandin, S., Reichenberg, A., Lichtenstein, P., Långström, N., & Hultman, C. M. (2008). Advancing paternal age and bipolar disorder. *Archives of General Psychiatry, 65*, 1034–1040.

Franz, C. E. (1997). Stability and change in the transition to midlife: A longitudinal study of midlife adults. In M. E. Lachman & J. B. James (Eds.), *Multiple paths of mid-life development* (pp. 45–66). Chicago: University of Chicago Press.

Fraser, A. M., Brockert, J. F., & Ward, R. H. (1995). Association of young maternal age with adverse reproductive outcomes. *New England Journal of Medicine, 332*(17), 1113–1117.

Fredricks, J. A., & Eccles, J. S. (2002). Children's competence and value beliefs from childhood through adolescence: Growth trajectories in two male-sex-typed domains. *Developmental Psychology, 38*, 519–533.

Fredriksen-Goldsen, K. I., & Muraco, A. (2010). Aging and sexual orientation: A 25-year review of the literature. *Research on Aging, 32*(3), 372–413.

Freeark, K., Rosenberg, E. B., Bornstein, J., Jozefowicz-Simbeni, D., Linkevich, M., & Lohnes, K. (2005). Gender differences and dynamics shaping the adoption life cycle: Review of the literature and recommendations. *American Journal of Orthopsychiatry, 75*, 86–101.

Freeman, C. (2004). *Trends in educational equity of girls & women: 2004* (NCES 2005-016). Washington, DC: National Center for Education Statistics.

Freid, V. M., & Bernstein, A. B. (2010). Health care utilization among adults aged 55–64 years: How has it changed over the past 10 years? *NCHS Data Brief, 32*. Hyattsville, MD: National Center for Health Statistics.

French, H. W. (2007, March 22). China scrambles for stability as its workers age. *The New York Times*, p. A1.

French, R. M., Mareschal, D., Mermillod, M., & Quinn, P. C. (2004). The role of bottom-up processing in perceptual categorization by 3- to 4-month old infants: Simulations and data. *Journal of Experimental Psychology: General, 133*(3), 382–397.

French, S. A., Story, M., & Jeffery, R. W. (2001). Environmental influences on eating and physical activity. *Annual Review of Public Health, 22*, 309–335.

French, S. E., Seidman, E., Allen, L., & Aber, J. L. (2006). The development of ethnic identity during adolescence. *Developmental Psychology, 42*, 1–10.

Freud, S. (1942). On psychotherapy. In E. Jones (Ed.), *Collected papers*. London: Hogarth. (Original work published 1906)

Freud, S. (1953). *A general introduction to psychoanalysis* (J. Rivière, Trans.). New York: Permabooks. (Original work published 1935)

Freud, S. (1964a). New introductory lectures on psychoanalysis. In J. Strachey (Ed. & Trans.), *The standard edition of the complete psychological works of Sigmund Freud* (Vol. 22). London: Hogarth. (Original work published 1933)

Freud, S. (1964b). An outline of psychoanalysis. In J. Strachey (Ed. & Trans.), *The standard edition of the complete psychological works of Sigmund Freud* (Vol. 23). London: Hogarth. (Original work published 1940)

Frey, K. S., Hirschstein, M. K., Snell, J. L., Edstrom, L. V. S., MacKenzie, E. P., & Broderick, C. J. (2005). Reducing playground bullying and supporting beliefs: An experimental trial of the Steps to Respect program. *Developmental Psychology, 41*, 479–491.

Fried, P. A., & Smith, A. M. (2001). A literature review of the consequences of prenatal marijuana exposure: An emerging theme of a deficiency in aspects of executive function. *Neurotoxicology and Teratology, 23*, 1–11.

Friedan, B. (1993). *The fountain of age*. New York: Simon & Schuster.

Friend, R. A. (1991). Older lesbian and gay people: A theory of successful aging. In J. A. Lee (Ed.), *Gay midlife and maturity* (pp. 99–118). New York: Haworth.

Fries, A. B. W., Ziegler, T. E., Kurian, J. R., Jacoris, S., & Pollak, S. D. (2005). Early experiences in humans is associated with changes in neuropeptides critical for regulating social behavior. *Proceedings of the National Academy of Sciences, USA, 102*, 17237–17240.

Froehlich, T. E., Lanphear, B. P., Auinger, P., Hornung, R., Epstein, J. N., Braun, J., & Kahn, R. S. (2009). Association of tobacco and lead exposures with attention-deficit/hyperactivity disorder. *Pediatrics, 124*(6), e1054–e1063. doi: 10.1542/peds.2009-0738

Fromkin, V., Krashen, S., Curtiss, S., Rigler, D., & Rigler, M. (1974). The development of language in Genie: Acquisition beyond the "critical period." *Brain and Language, 15*(9), 28–34.

Frost, D. M., & Meyer, I. H. (2009). Internalized homophobia and relationship quality among lesbians, gay men and bisexuals. *Journal of Counseling Psychology, 56*(1), 97–109.

Fryar, C. D., Carroll, M. D., & Ogden, C. L. (2012). Prevalence of obesity among children and adolescents: United States, trends 1963–1965 through 2009–2010. National Center for Health Statistics. *Health E-Stats*, 1–6.

Frydman, O., & Bryant, P. (1988). Sharing and the understanding of number equivalence by young children. *Cognitive Development, 3*, 323–339.

Frye, N. E., & Karney, B. R. (2006). The context of aggressive behavior in marriage: A longitudinal study of newlyweds. *Journal of Family Psychology, 20*, 12–20.

Fuchs, C. S., Stampfer, M. J., Colditz, G. A., Giovannucci, E. L., Manson, J. E., Kawachi, I., . . . Willett, W. C. (1995). Alcohol consumption and mortality among women. *New England Journal of Medicine, 332*, 1245–1250.

Fuligni, A. J. (1997). The academic achievement of adolescents from immigrant families: The roles of family background, attitudes, and behavior. *Child Development, 68*, 351–363.

Fuligni, A. J. (2001). Family obligation and the academic motivation of adolescents from Asian, Latin American, and European backgrounds. *New Directions for Child and Adolescent Development, 94*, 61–76.

Fuligni, A. J., & Eccles, J. S. (1993). Perceived parent-child relationships and early adolescents' orientation toward peers. *Developmental Psychology, 29*, 622–632.

Fuligni, A. J., Eccles, J. S., Barber, B. L., & Clements, P. (2001). Early adolescent peer orientation and adjustment during high school. *Developmental Psychology, 37*(1), 28–36.

Fuligni, A. J., & Stevenson, H. W. (1995). Time use and mathematics achievement among American, Chinese, and Japanese high school students. *Child Development, 66*, 830–842.

Fulton, R., & Owen, G. (1987-1988). Death and society in twentieth-century America. *Omega: Journal of Death and Dying, 18*(4), 379–395.

Fung, H. H., Carstensen, L. L., & Lang, F. R. (2001). Age-related patterns in social networks among European-Americans and African-Americans: Implications for socioemotional selectivity across the life span. *International Journal of Aging and Human Development, 52*, 185–206.

Furman, L. (2005). What is attention-deficit hyperactivity disorder (ADHD)? *Journal of Child Neurology, 20*, 994–1003.

Furman, W. (1982). Children's friendships. In T. M. Field, A. Huston, H. C. Quay, L. Troll, & G. E. Finley (Eds.), *Review of human development*. New York: Wiley.

Furman, W., & Bierman, K. L. (1983). Developmental changes in young children's conception of friendship. *Child Development, 54*, 549–556.

Furman, W., & Buhrmester, D. (1985). Children's perceptions of the personal relationships in their social networks. *Developmental Psychology, 21*, 1016–1024.

Furman, W., & Wehner, E. A. (1997). Adolescent romantic relationships: A developmental perspective. In S. Shulman & A. Collins (Eds.), *Romantic relationships in adolescence: Developmental perspectives* (New Directions for Child and Adolescent Development, No. 78, pp. 21–36). San Francisco: Jossey-Bass.

Furrow, D. (1984). Social and private speech at two years. *Child Development, 55*, 355–362.

Furstenberg, F. F., Jr., Rumbaut, R. G., & Setterstein, R. A., Jr. (2005). On the frontier of adulthood: Emerging themes and new directions. In R. A. Settersten Jr., F. F. Furstenberg Jr., & R. G. Rumbaut (Eds.), *On the frontier of adulthood: Theory, research, and public policy* (pp. 3–25). Chicago: University of Chicago Press.

Fussell, E., & Furstenberg, F. (2005). The transition to adulthood during the twentieth century: Race, nativity, and gender. In R. A. Settersten Jr., F. F. Furstenberg Jr., & R. G. Rumbaut (Eds.), *On the frontier of adulthood: Theory, research, and public policy* (pp. 29–75). Chicago: University of Chicago Press.

Gabbard, C. P. (1996). *Lifelong motor development* (2nd ed.). Madison, WI: Brown & Benchmark.

Gabhainn, S., & François, Y. (2000). Substance use. In C. Currie, K. Hurrelmann, W. Settertobulte, R. Smith, & J. Todd (Eds.), Health behaviour in school-aged children: A WHO cross-national study (HBSC) international report (pp. 97–114). *WHO Policy Series: Healthy Policy for Children and Adolescents, Series No. 1*. Copenhagen, Denmark: World Health Organization Regional Office for Europe.

Gable, S., Chang, Y., & Krull, J. L. (2007). Television watching and frequency of family meals are predictive of overweight onset and persistence in a national sample of school-age children. *Journal of the American Dietetic Association, 107*, 53–61.

Gaffney, M., Gamble, M., Costa, P., Holstrum, J., & Boyle, C. (2003). Infants tested for hearing loss—United States, 1999–2001. *Morbidity and Mortality Weekly Report, 51*, 981–984.

Gagne, J. R., & Saudino, K. J. (2010). Wait for it! A twin study of inhibitory control in early childhood. *Behavioral Genetics, 40*(3), 327–337.

Gallagher, W. (1993, May). Midlife myths. *Atlantic Monthly*, pp. 51–68.

Gallagher-Thompson, D. (1995). Caregivers of chronically ill elders. In G. E. Maddox (Ed.), *The encyclopedia of aging* (pp. 141–144). New York: Springer.

Gallo, L. C., & Matthews, K. A. (2003). Understanding the association between socioeconomic status and physical health: Do negative emotions play a role? *Psychological Bulletin, 129*, 10–51.

Gallo, L. C., Troxel, W. M., Matthews, K. A., & Kuller, L. H. (2003). Marital status and quality in middle-aged women: Associations with levels and trajectories of cardiovascular risk factors. *Health Psychology, 22*, 453–463.

Galobardes, B., Smith, G. D., & Lynch, J. W. (2006). Systematic review of the influence of childhood socioeconomic circumstances on risk for cardiovascular disease in adulthood. *Annals of Epidemiology, 16*, 91–104.

Galotti, K. M., Komatsu, L. K., & Voelz, S. (1997). Children's differential performance on deductive and inductive syllogisms. *Developmental Psychology, 33*, 70–78.

Gandhi, H., Green, D., Kounios, J., Clark., C. M., & Polikar, R. (2006, September). *Stacked generalization for early diagnosis of Alzheimer's disease*. Paper presented at the meeting of the 28th International Conference of the IEEE Engineering in Medicine and Biology Society, New York.

Ganger, J., & Brent, M. R. (2004). Reexamining the vocabulary spurt. *Developmental Psychology, 40*, 621–632.

Gangwisch, J. E., Heymsfield, S. B., Boden-Albala, B., Buijs, R. M., Kreier, F., Opler, M. G., . . . Pickering, T. G. (2008). Sleep duration associated with mortality in elderly, but not middle-aged, adults in a large U.S. sample. *Sleep, 31*(8), 1087–1096.

Gannon, P. J., Holloway, R. L., Broadfield, D. C., & Braun, A. R. (1998). Asymmetry of chimpanzee planum temporale: Human-like pattern of Wernicke's brain language homolog. *Science, 279*, 22–222.

Gans, J. E. (1990). *America's adolescents: How healthy are they*? Chicago: American Medical Association.

Garbarino, J., Dubrow, N., Kostelny, K., & Pardo, C. (1992). *Children in danger: Coping with the consequences of community violence*. San Francisco: Jossey-Bass.

Garbarino, J., Dubrow, N., Kostelny, K., & Pardo, C. (1998). *Children in danger: Coping with the consequences of community violence*. San Francisco: Jossey-Bass.

Garbarino, J., & Kostelny, K. (1993). Neighborhood and community influences on parenting. In T. Luster & L. Okagaki (Eds.), *Parenting: An ecological perspective* (pp. 203–226). Hillsdale, NJ: Erlbaum.

Garces, E., Thomas, D., & Currie, J. (2000). *Longer term effects of Head Start* (No. w8054). Washington, DC: National Bureau of Economic Research.

Gardiner, H. W., & Kosmitzki, C. (2005). *Lives across cultures: Cross-cultural human development*. Boston: Allyn & Bacon.

Gardner, H. (1993). *Frames of mind: The theory of multiple intelligences*. New York: Basic Books. (Original work published 1983)

Gardner, H. (1995). Reflections on multiple intelligences: Myths and messages. *Phi Delta Kappan*, pp. 200–209.

Gardner, H. (1998). Are there additional intelligences? In J. Kane (Ed.), *Education, information, and transformation: Essays on learning and thinking*. Englewood Cliffs, NJ: Prentice Hall.

Gardner, M., & Steinberg, L. (2005). Peer influence on risk taking, risk preference, and risky decision making in adolescence and adulthood: An experimental study. *Developmental Psychology, 41*, 625–635.

Garlick, D. (2003). Integrating brain science research with intelligence research. *Current Directions in Psychological Science, 12*, 185–192.

Garner, P. W., & Power, T. G. (1996). Preschoolers' emotional control in the disappointment paradigm and its relation to temperament, emotional knowledge, and family expressiveness. *Child Development, 67*, 1406–1419.

Garner, P. W., & Estep, K. M. (2001). Emotional competence, emotional socialization, and young children's peer-related social competence. *Early Education & Development, 12*(1), 29–48.

Gartrell, N., Deck, A., Rodas, C., Peyser, H., & Banks, A. (2005). The National Lesbian Family Study: Interviews with the 10-year-old children. *American Journal of Orthopsychiatry, 75*, 518–524.

Gates, G. J. (2013). *LBGT parenting in the United States*. Retrieved from http://williamsinstitute.law.ucla.edu/wp-content/uploads/LGBT-Parenting.pdf

Gatewood, J. D., Wills, A., Shetty, S., Xu, J., Arnold, A. P., Burgoyne, P. S., & Rissman, E. F. (2006). Sex chromosome complement and gonadal sex influence aggressive and parental behaviors in mice. *Journal of Neuroscience, 26*, 2335–2342.

Gathercole, S. E., & Alloway, T. P. (2008). *Working memory and learning: A practical guide*. Thousand Oaks, CA: Sage.

Gattis, K. S., Berns, S., Simpson, L. E., & Christensen, A. (2004). Birds of a feather or strange birds? Ties among personality dimensions, similarity, and marital quality. *Journal of Family Psychology, 18*, 564–574.

Gatz, M. (2007). Genetics, dementia, and the elderly. *Current Directions in Psychological Science, 16*, 123–127.

Gatz, M., Reynolds, C. A., Fratiglioni, L., Johansson, B., Mortimer, J. A., Berg, S., . . . Pederson, N. L. (2006). Role of genes and environments for explaining Alzheimer disease. *Archives of General Psychiatry, 63*, 168–174.

Gauthier, A. H., & Furstenberg, F. F., Jr. (2005). Historical trends in patterns of time use among young adults in developed countries. In R. A. Settersten Jr., F. F. Furstenberg Jr., & R. G. Rumbaut (Eds.), *On the frontier of adulthood: Theory, research, and public policy* (pp. 150–176). Chicago: University of Chicago Press.

Gauvain, M. (1993). The development of spatial thinking in everyday activity. *Developmental Review, 13*, 92–121.

Gauvain, M., & Perez, S. M. (2005). Parent-child participation in planning children's activities outside of school in European American and Latino families. *Child Development, 76*, 371–383.

Gazzaley, A., Sheridan, M. A., Cooney, J. W., & D'Esposito, M. (2007). Age-related deficits in component processes of working memory. *Neuropsychology, 21*(5), 532–539. doi: 10.1037/0894-4105.21.5.532

Ge, X., Brody, G. H., Conger, R. D., Simons, R. L., & Murry, V. (2002). Contextual amplification of pubertal transitional effect on African American children's problem behaviors. *Developmental Psychology, 38*, 42–54.

Geary, D. C. (1999). Evolution and developmental sex differences. *Current Directions in Psychological Science, 8*(4), 115–120.

Geary, D. C. (2006). Development of mathematical understanding. In W. Damon (Ed.), & D. Kuhl & R. S. Siegler (Vol. Eds.), *Handbook of child psychology: Cognition, perception, and language, Vol 2*. (6th ed., pp. 777–810). Hoboken, NJ: Wiley.

Gedo, J. (2001). *The enduring scientific contributions of Sigmund Freud*. Retrieved from http://www.pep-web.org/document.php?id=AOP.029.0105A

Geen, R. (2004). The evolution of kinship care: Policy and practice. *Future of Children, 14*(1). (David and Lucile Packard Foundation.) Retrieved from www.futureofchildren.org

Geidd, J. N. (2008). The teen brain: Insights from neuroimaging. *Journal of Adolescent Health, 42*, 321–323.

Gelfand, D. M., & Teti, D. M. (1995, November). How does maternal depression affect children? *Harvard Mental Health Letter*, p. 8.

Gélis, J. (1991). *History of childbirth: Fertility, pregnancy, and birth in early modern Europe*. Boston: Northeastern University Press.

Gelman, R. (2006). Young natural-number mathematicians. *Current Directions in Psychological Science, 15*, 193–197.

Gelman, R., Spelke, E. S., & Meck, E. (1983). What preschoolers know about animate and inanimate objects. In D. R. Rogers & J. S. Sloboda (Eds.), *The acquisition of symbolic skills* (pp. 297–326). New York: Plenum Press.

Gelstein, S., Yeshurun, Y., Rosenkrantz, S., Shushan, S., Frumin, I., Roth, Y., & Sobel, N. (2011). Human tears contain a chemosignal. *Science, 331*(6014), 226–230. doi: 10.1126/science.1198331

Genesee, F., Nicoladis, E., & Paradis, J. (1995). Language differentiation in early bilingual development. *Journal of Child Language, 22*, 611–631.

Genevay, B. (1986). Intimacy as we age. *Generations, 10*(4), 12–15.

Georganopoulou, D. G., Chang, L., Nam, J.-M., Thaxton, C. S., Mufson, E. J., Klein, W. L., & Mirkin, C. A. (2005). Nanoparticle-based detection in cerebral spinal fluid of a soluble pathogenic biomarker for Alzheimer's disease. *Proceedings of the National Academy of Sciences, 102*, 2273–2276.

George, C., Kaplan, N., & Main, M. (1985). *The Berkeley Adult Attachment Interview.* [Unpublished protocol]. Department of Psychology, University of California, Berkeley.

Geraci, L., McDaniel, M. A., Manzano, I., & Roediger, H. L. (2009). The influence of age on memory for distinctive events. *Memory & Cognition, 37*(2), 175–180.

Gershoff, E. T. (2002). Corporal punishment by parents and associated child behaviors and experiences: A meta-analytic and theoretical review. *Psychological Bulletin, 128,* 539–579.

Gervai, J., Nemoda, Z., Lakatos, K., Ronai, Z., Toth, I., Ney, K., & Sasvari-Szekely, M. (2005). Transmission disequilibrium tests confirm the link between DRD4 gene polymorphism and infant attachment. *American Journal of Medical Genetics, Part B (Neuropsychiatric Genetics), 132B,* 126–130.

Getz, D. (2010). *American community survey briefs: Men's and women's earnings for states and metropolitan statistical areas: 2009* (ACSBR/09-3). Washington DC: U.S. Census Bureau. Retrieved from http://www.census.gov/prod/2010pubs /acsbr09-3.pdf

Getzels, J. W. (1984, March). *Problem finding in creativity in higher education.* The Fifth Rev. Charles F. Donovan, S. J., Lecture, Boston College, School of Education, Boston, MA.

Getzels, J. W., & Jackson, P. W. (1963). The highly intelligent and the highly creative adolescent: A summary of some research findings. In C. W. Taylor & F. Baron (Eds.), *Scientific creativity: Its recognition and development* (pp. 161–172). New York: Wiley.

Gibbons, L., Belizan, J. M., Lauer, J. A., Betran, A. P., Merialdi, M., & Althabe, F. (2010). The global numbers and costs of additionally needed and unnecessary caesarean sections performed per year: Overuse as a barrier to universal coverage. *World Health Report, 30.*

Gibbs, J. C. (1991). Toward an integration of Kohlberg's and Hoffman's theories of moral development. In W. M. Kurtines & J. L. Gewirtz (Eds.), *Handbook of moral behavior and development: Advances in theory, research, and application* (Vol. 1). Hillsdale, NJ: Erlbaum.

Gibbs, J. C. (1995). The cognitive developmental perspective. In W. M. Kurtines & J. L. Gewirtz (Eds.), *Moral development: An introduction.* Boston: Allyn & Bacon.

Gibbs, J. C., & Schnell, S. V. (1985). Moral development "versus" socialization. *American Psychologist, 40*(10), 1071–1080.

Gibson, E. J. (1969). *Principles of perceptual learning and development.* New York: Appleton-Century-Crofts.

Gibson, E. J., & Pick, A. D. (2000). *An ecological approach to perceptual learning and development.* New York: Oxford University Press.

Gibson, E. J., & Walker, A. S. (1984). Development of knowledge of visual tactual affordances of substance. *Child Development, 55,* 453–460.

Gibson, J. J. (1979). *The ecological approach to visual perception.* Boston: Houghton-Mifflin.

Gierveld, J. D. J., & Dykstra, P. A. (2008). Virtue is its own reward? Support-giving in the family and loneliness in middle and old age. *Ageing and Society, 28*(2), 271–287.

Gilboa, S., Correa, A., Botto, L., Rasmussen, S., Waller, D., Hobbs, C., . . . Riehle-Colarusso, T. J. (2009). Association between prepregnancy body mass index and congenital heart defects. *American Journal of Obstetrics and Gynecology, 202*(1), 51–61.

Gilligan, C. (1982/1993). *In a different voice: Psychological theory and women's development.* Cambridge, MA: Harvard University Press.

Gilligan, C. (1987a). Adolescent development reconsidered. In E. E. Irwin (Ed.), *Adolescent social behavior and health.* San Francisco: Jossey-Bass.

Gilligan, C. (1987b). Moral orientation and moral development. In E. F. Kittay & D. T. Meyers (Eds.), *Women and moral theory* (pp. 19–33). Totowa, NJ: Rowman & Littlefield.

Gilligan, C., Murphy, J. M., & Tappan, M. B. (1990). Moral development beyond adolescence. In C. N. Alexander & E. J. Langer (Eds.), *Higher stages of human development* (pp. 208–228). New York: Oxford University Press.

Gilmore, J., Lin, W., Prastawa, M. W., Looney, C. B., Vetsa, Y. S. K., Knickmeyer, R. C., . . . Gerig, G. (2007). Regional gray matter growth, sexual dimorphism, and cerebral asymmetry in the neonatal brain. *Journal of Neuroscience, 27*(6), 1255–1260.

Ginsburg, G. S., & Bronstein, P. (1993). Family factors related to children's intrinsic/extrinsic motivational orientation and academic performance. *Child Development, 64,* 1461–1474.

Ginsburg, H., & Opper, S. (1979). *Piaget's theory of intellectual development* (2nd ed.). Englewood Cliffs, NJ: Prentice Hall.

Ginsburg, K., & Committee on Communications and Committee on Psychosocial Aspects of Child and Family Health, American Academy of Pediatrics (AAP). (2007). The importance of play in promoting healthy child development and maintaining strong parent-child bonds. *Pediatrics, 119,* 182–191.

Giordano, P. C., Cernkovich, S. A., & DeMaris, A. (1993). The family and peer relations of black adolescents. *Journal of Marriage and Family, 55,* 277–287.

Giscombé, C. L., & Lobel, M. (2005). Explaining disproportionately high rates of adverse birth outcomes among African Americans: The impact of stress, racism, and related factors in pregnancy. *Psychological Bulletin, 131,* 662–683.

Gjerdingen, D. (2003). The effectiveness of various postpartum depression treatments and the impact of antidepressant drugs on nursing infants. *Journal of American Board of Family Practice, 16,* 372–382.

Glaser, D. (2000). Child abuse and neglect and the brain: A review. *Journal of Child Psychiatry, 41,* 97–116.

Glasson, E. J., Bower, C., Petterson, B., de Klerk, N., Chaney, G., & Hallmayer, J. F. (2004). Perinatal factors and the development of autism: A population study. *Archives of General Psychiatry, 61,* 618–627.

Glaucoma Research Foundation. (2010). *Four key facts about glaucoma.* Retrieved from http://www.glaucoma.org/learn/glaucoma_facts.php

Gleason, T. R., Sebanc, A. M., & Hartup, W. W. (2000). Imaginary companions of preschool children. *Developmental Psychology, 36,* 419–428.

Glenn, N., & Marquardt, E. (2001). *Hooking up, hanging out, and hoping for Mr. Right: College women on dating and mating today.* New York: Institute for American Values.

Glick, J. E., & Van Hook, J. (2002). Parents' coresidence with adult children: Can immigration explain racial and ethnic variation? *Journal of Marriage and Family, 64,* 240–253.

Gluckman, P. D., Wyatt, J. S., Azzopardi, D., Ballard, R., Edwards, A. D., Ferriero, D. M., . . . Gunn, A. J. (2005). Selective head cooling with mild systemic hypothermia after neonatal encephalopathy: Multicentre randomized trial. *Lancet, 365,* 663–670.

Goetz, P. J. (2003). The effects of bilingualism on theory of mind development. *Bilingualism: Language and Cognition, 6,* 1–15.

Gogtay, N., Giedd, J. N., Lusk, L., Hayashi, K. M., Greenstein, D., Vaituzis, A. C., . . . Thompson, P. M. (2004). Dynamic mapping of human cortical development during childhood through early adulthood. *Proceedings of the National Academy of Sciences, USA, 101,* 8174–8179.

Gold, K. J., Sen, A., & Hayward, R. A. (2010). Marriage and cohabitation outcomes after pregnancy loss. *Pediatrics, 125*(5), e1202–e1207.

Golden, J., Conroy, R. M., & Lawlor, B. A. (2009). Social support network structure in older people: Underlying dimensions and association with psychological and physical health. *Psychology, Health & Medicine, 14*(3), 280–290.

Goldberg, W. A., Prause, J. A., Lucas-Thompson, R., & Himsel, A. (2008). Maternal employment and children's achievement in context: A meta-analysis of four decades of research. *Psychological Bulletin, 134,* 77–108.

Goldenberg, R. L., Kirby, R., & Culhane, J. F. (2004). Stillbirth: A review. *Journal of Maternal-Fetal & Neonatal Medicine, 16*(2), 79–94.

Goldenberg, R. L., & Rouse, D. J. (1998). Prevention of premature labor. *New England Journal of Medicine, 339,* 313–320.

Goldin-Meadow, S. (2007). Pointing sets the stage for learning language—And creating language. *Child Development, 78*(3), 741–745.

Goldman, L., Falk, H., Landrigan, P. J., Balk, S. J., Reigart, J. R., & Etzel, R. A. (2004). Environmental pediatrics and its impact on government health policy. *Pediatrics, 113,* 1146–1157.

Goldman, L. L., & Rothschild, J. (n.d.). *Healing the wounded with art therapy.* Unpublished manuscript.

Goldman, S. R., Petrosino, A. J., & Cognition and Technology Group at Vanderbilt. (1999).

Design principles for instruction in content domains: Lessons from research on expertise and learning. In F. T. Durso (Ed.), *Handbook of applied cognition* (pp. 595–627). Chichester, England: Wiley.

Goldscheider, F., & Sassler, S. (2006). Creating stepfamilies: Integrating children into the study of union formation. *Journal of Marriage and Family, 68*, 275–291.

Goldstein, I., Padma-Nathan, H., Rosen, R. C., Steers, W. D., & Wicker, P. A., for the Sildenafil Study Group. (1998). Oral sildenafil in the treatment of erectile dysfunction. *New England Journal of Medicine, 338*, 1397–1404.

Goldstein, M., King, A., & West, M. (2003). Social interaction shapes babbling: Testing parallels between birdsong and speech. *Proceedings of the National Academy of Sciences, USA, 100*, 8030–8035.

Goldstein, M. H., Schwade, J. A., & Bornstein, M. H. (2009). The value of vocalizing: Five-month-old infants associate their own noncry vocalizations with responses from caregivers. *Child Development, 80*(3), 636–644.

Goldstein, S. E., Davis-Kean, P. E., & Eccles, J. E. (2005). Parents, peers, and problem behavior: A longitudinal investigation of the impact of relationship perceptions and characteristics on the development of adolescent problem behavior. *Developmental Psychology, 2*, 401–413.

Goler, N. C., Armstrong, M. A., Taillac, C. J., & Osejo, V. M. (2008). Substance abuse treatment linked with prenatal visits improves perinatal outcomes: A new standard. *Journal of Perinatology, 28*, 597–603.

Golinkoff, R. M., & Hirsch-Pasek, K. (2006). Baby wordsmith. *Current Directions in Psychological Science, 15*, 30–33.

Golinkoff, R. M., Jacquet, R. C., Hirsh-Pasek, K., & Nandakumar, R. (1996). Lexical principles may underlie the learning of verbs. *Child Development, 67*, 3101–3119.

Golombok, S., Mellish, L., Jennings, S., Casey, P., Tasker, F., & Lamb, M. E. (2013). Adoptive gay father families: Parent–child relationships and children's psychological adjustment. *Child Development.* doi: 10.1111/cdev.12155

Golombok, S., Perry B., Burston, A., Murray, C., Mooney-Summers, J., Stevens, M., & Golding, J. (2003). Children with lesbian parents: A community study. *Developmental Psychology, 39*, 20–33.

Golombok, S., Rust, J., Zervoulis, K., Croudace, T., Golding, J., & Hines, M. (2008). Developmental trajectories of sex-typed behaviors in boys and girls: A longitudinal general population study of children aged 2.5–8 years. *Child Development, 79*, 1583–1593.

Göncü, A., Mistry, J., & Mosier, C. (2000). Cultural variations in the play of toddlers. *International Journal of Behavioral Development, 24*(3), 321–329.

Gonzalez, D., Rennard, S. I., Nides, M., Oncken, C., Azouley, S., Billing, C., . . . Reeves, K. R. (2006). Verenicline, an $\alpha_4\beta_2$ nicotinic acetylcholine receptor partial agonist, vs. sustained-release bupropion and placebo for smoking cessation. *Journal of the American Medical Association, 296*, 47–55.

Gonzalez, E., Kulkarni, H., Bolivar, H., Mangano, A., Sanchez, R., Catano, G., . . . Ahuja, S. K. (2005). The influence of CCL3L1 gene-containing segmental duplications on HIV-1/AIDS susceptibility. *Science, 307*(5714), 1434–1440. doi: 10.1126/science.1101160

Gonzales, N. A., Cauce, A. M., & Mason, C. A. (1996). Interobserver agreement in the assessment of parental behavior and parent-adolescent conflict: African American mothers, daughters, and independent observers. *Child Development, 67*, 1483–1498.

Goodman, G. S., Emery, R. E., & Haugaard, J. J. (1998). Developmental psychology and law: Divorce, child maltreatment, foster care, and adoption. In W. Damon (Series Ed.), I. E. Sigel & K. A. Renninger (Vol. Eds.), *Handbook of child psychology* (Vol. 4, pp. 775–874). New York: Wiley.

Gootman, E. (2007, January 22). Taking middle schoolers out of the middle. *The New York Times,* p. A1.

Gorchoff, S. M., John, O. P., & Helson, R. (2008). Contextualizing change in marital satisfaction during middle age. *Psychological Science, 19*(11), 1194–1200.

Gorman, B. K., & Read, J. G. (2007). Why men die younger than women. *Geriatrics and Aging, 10*, 182–191.

Gorman, J. (2006). Gender differences in depression and response to psychotropic medication. *Gender Medicine, 3*(2), 93–109.

Gortmaker, S. L., Must, A., Perrin, J. M., Sobol, A. M., & Dietz, W. H. (1993). Social and economic consequences of overweight in adolescence and young adulthood. *New England Journal of Medicine, 329*, 1008–1012.

Gosselin, P., Perron, M., & Maassarani, R. (2009). Children's ability to distinguish between enjoyment and non-enjoyment smiles. *Infant and Child Development, 19*(3), 297–312. doi: 10.1002/icd.648

Gostin, L. O. (1997). Deciding life and death in the courtroom: From Quinlan to Cruzan, Glucksberg, and Vacco—A brief history and analysis of constitutional protection of the "right to die." *Journal of the American Medical Association, 278*, 1523–1528.

Gostin, L. O. (2006). Physician-assisted suicide. *Journal of the American Medical Association, 295*, 1941–1943.

Gottfredson, L. S., & Deary, I. J. (2004). Intelligence predicts health and longevity, but why? *Current Directions in Psychological Science, 13*, 1–4.

Gottfried, A. E., Fleming, J. S., & Gottfried, A. W. (1998). Role of cognitively stimulating home environment in children's academic intrinsic motivation: A longitudinal study. *Child Development, 69*, 1448–1460.

Gottfried, A. W., Cook, C. R., Gottfried, A. E., & Morris, P. E. (2005). Educational characteristics of adolescents with gifted academic intrinsic motivation: A longitudinal investigation from school entry through early adulthood. *Gifted Child Quarterly, 49*(2), 172–186.

Gottlieb, G. (1991). Experiential canalization of behavioral development theory. *Developmental Psychology, 27*(1), 4–13.

Gottlieb, G. (1997). *Synthesizing nature-nurture: Prenatal roots of instinctive behavior.* Mahwah, NJ: Erlbaum.

Gottlieb, G. (2007). Probabilistic epigenesis. *Developmental Science, 10*, 1–11.

Goubet, N., & Clifton, R. K. (1998). Object and event representation in 6½-month-old infants. *Developmental Psychology, 34*, 63–76.

Gould, E., Reeves, A. J., Graziano, M. S. A., & Gross, C. G. (1999). Neurogenesis in the neocortex of adult primates. *Science, 286*, 548–552.

Grady, D. (2010, July 21). New guidelines seek to reduce repeat caesareans. *The New York Times*. Retrieved from http://www.nytimes.com/2010/07/22/health/22birth.html?_r=1&emc=eta1

Grady, D., Herrington, D., Bittner, V., Blumenthal, R., Davidson, M., Hlatky, M., . . . Wenger, N. (2002). Cardiovascular disease outcomes during 6.8 years of hormone therapy: Heart and Estrogen/Progestin Replacement Study follow-up (HERS II). *Journal of the American Medical Association, 288*, 49–57.

Graham, J. E., Christian, L. M., & Kiecolt-Glaser, J. K. (2006). Marriage, health and immune function: A review of key findings and the role of depression. In S. Beach & M. Wimboldt (Eds.), *Relational processes in mental health* (Vol. 11, pp. 61–76). Arlington, VA: American Psychiatric Publishing.

Grant, B. F., Stinson, F. S., Chou, D. A., Raun, P., June, W., & Pickering, R. P. (2007). Co-occurrence of 12-month alcohol and drug use disorders and personality disorders in the United States: Results from the National Epidemiologic Survey on alcohol and related conditions. *Alcohol Research and Health, 29*(2), 121–130.

Grant, B. F., Stinson, F. S., Dawson, D. A., Chou, S. P., Dufour, M. C., Compton, W., Pickering, R. P., & Kaplan, K. (2004). Prevalence and co-occurrence of substance use disorders and independent mood and anxiety disorders: Results from the National Epidemiologic Survey on Alcohol and Related Conditions. *Archives of General Psychiatry, 61*, 807–816.

Grant, N., Hamer, M., & Steptoe, A. (2009). Social isolation and stress-related cardiovascular, lipid, and cortisol responses. *Annals of Behavioral Medicine, 37*(1), 29–37.

Grantham-McGregor, S., Powell, C., Walker, S., Chang, S., & Fletcher, P. (1994). The long-term follow-up of severely malnourished children who participated in an intervention program. *Child Development, 65*, 428–439.

Gravina, S., & Vijg, J. (2010). Epigenetic factors in aging and longevity. *Pflugers Archives, European Journal of Physiology, 459*(2), 241–258. doi: 10.1007/s00424-009-0730-7 Ch. 17

Gray, J. R., & Thompson, P. M. (2004). Neurobiology of intelligence: Science and ethics. *Neuroscience, 5*, 471–492.

Gray, M. R., & Steinberg, L. (1999). Unpacking authoritative parenting: Reassessing a multidimensional construct. *Journal of Marriage and Family, 61*, 574–587.

Graziano, A. M., & Mooney, K. C. (1982). Behavioral treatment of "nightfears" in children: Maintenance and improvement at 2½- to 3-year follow-up. *Journal of Counseling and Clinical Psychology, 50,* 598–599.

Green, R. E., Krause, J., Briggs, A. W., Maricic, T., Stenzel, U., Kircher, M., . . . Paabo, S. (2010). A draft sequence of the Neandertal genome. *Science, 7*(328), 710–722. doi: 10.1126/science.1188021

Greenberg, J., & Becker, M. (1988). Aging parents as family resources. *Gerontologist, 28*(6), 786–790.

Greenfield, E. A., & Marks, N. F. (2004). Formal volunteering as a protective factor for older adults' psychological well-being. *Journal of Gerontology: Social Sciences, 59B*, S258–S264.

Greenfield, E. A., & Marks, N. F. (2006). Linked lives: Adult children's problems and their parents' psychological and relational well-being. *Journal of Marriage and Family, 68*, 442–454.

Greenfield, P. M. (2009). Technology and informal education: What is taught, what is learned. *Science, 323*(5910), 69–71. doi: 10.1126/science.1167190

Greenfield, P. M., & Childs, C. P. (1978). Understanding sibling concepts: A developmental study of kin terms in Zinacanten. In P. R. Dasen (Ed.), *Piagetian psychology* (pp. 335–358). New York: Gardner.

Greenhouse, L. (2000, June 6). Justices reject visiting rights in divided case: Ruling favors mother over grandparents. *The New York Times* (National ed.), pp. A1, A15.

Greenhouse, L. (2005, February 23). Justices accept Oregon case weighing assisted suicide. *The New York Times,* p. A1.

Gregg, E. W., Cauley, J. A., Stone, K., Tompson, T. J., Bauer, D. C., Cummings, S. R., & Ensrud, K. E., for the Study of Osteoporotic Fractures Research Group. (2003). Relationship of changes in physical activity and mortality among older women. *Journal of the American Medical Association, 289*, 2379–2386.

Gregg, E. W., Cheng, Y. J., Cadwell, B. L., Imperatore, G., Williams, D. E., Flegal, K. M., . . . Williamson, D. F. (2005). Secular trends in cardiovascular disease risk factors according to body mass index in U.S. adults. *Journal of the American Medical Association, 293*, 1868–1874.

Gregg, V. R., Winer, G. A., Cottrell, J. E., Hedman, K. E., & Fournier, J. S. (2001). The persistence of a misconception about vision after educational interventions. *Psychonomic Bulletin and Review, 8,* 622–626.

Grigorenko, E. L., Meier, E., Lipka, J., Mohatt, G., Yanez, E., & Sternberg, R. J. (2004). Academic and practical intelligence: A case study of the Yup'ik in Alaska. *Learning and Individual Differences, 14*(4), 183–207.

Grodstein, F. (1996). Postmenopausal estrogen and progestin use and the risk of cardiovascular disease. *New England Journal of Medicine, 335,* 453.

Groenewoud, J. H., van der Heide, A., Onwuteaka-Philipsen, B. D., Willems, D. L., van der Maas, P. J., & van der Wal, G. (2000). Clinical problems with the performance of euthanasia and physician-assisted suicide in the Netherlands. *New England Journal of Medicine, 342*, 551–556.

Grotevant, H. D., McRoy, R. G., Eide, C. L., & Fravel, D. L. (1994). Adoptive family system dynamics: Variations by level of openness in the adoption. *Family Process, 33*(2), 125–146.

Grov, C., Bimbi, D. S., Nanin, J. E., & Parsons, J. T. (2006). Race, ethnicity, gender and generational factors associated with the coming-out process among gay, lesbian and bisexual individuals. *Journal of Sex Research, 43*(2), 115–121.

Gruenewald, T. L., Karlamangla, A. S., Greendale, G. A., Singer, B. H., & Seeman, T. E. (2007). Feelings of usefulness to others, disability, and mortality in older adults: The MacArthur Study of Successful Aging. *Journal of Gerontology: Psychological Sciences, 62B*, P28–P37.

Grundy, E., & Henretta, J. C. (2006). Between elderly parents and adult children: A new look at intergenerational care provided by the "sandwich generation." *Ageing and Society, 26*(5), 707–722.

Grusec, J. E., & Goodnow, J. J. (1994). Impact of parental discipline methods on the child's internalization of values: A reconceptualization of current points of view. *Developmental Psychology, 30*, 4–19.

Guberman, S. R. (1996). The development of everyday mathematics in Brazilian children with limited formal education. *Child Development, 67*, 1609–1623.

Guegen, N. (2007). Courtship compliance: The effect of touch on women's behaviour. *Social Influence, 2*, 81–97.

Guendelman, S., Kosa, J. L., Pearl, M., Graham, S., Goodman, J., & Kharrazi, M. (2009). Juggling work and breastfeeding: Effects of maternity leave and occupational characteristics. *Pediatrics, 123,* e38–e46.

Guerrero, T. J. (2001). *Youth in transition: Housing, employment, social policies and families in France and Spain.* Aldershot, Hants, England: Ashgate.

Guilford, J. P. (1956). Structure of intellect. *Psychological Bulletin, 53*, 267–293.

Guilford, J. P. (1959). Three faces of intellect. *American Psychologist, 14*, 469–479.

Guilford, J. P. (1960). Basic conceptual problems of the psychology of thinking. *Proceedings of the New York Academy of Sciences, 91*, 6–21.

Guilford, J. P. (1967). *The nature of human intelligence.* New York: McGraw-Hill.

Guilford, J. P. (1986). *Creative talents: Their nature, uses and development.* Buffalo, NY: Bearly.

Guilleminault, C., Palombini, L., Pelayo, R., & Chervin, R. D. (2003). Sleeping and sleep terrors in prepubertal children: What triggers them? *Pediatrics, 111*, e17–e25.

Gullone, E. (2000). The development of normal fear: A century of research. *Clinical Psychology Review, 20*, 429–451.

Gundersen, C., Lohman, B. J., Garasky, S., Stewart, S., & Eisenmann, J. (2008). Food security, maternal stressors, and overweight among low-income U.S. children: Results from the National Health and Nutrition Examination Survey (1999–2002). *Pediatrics, 122,* e529–e540.

Gunnar, M. R., Larson, M. C., Hertsgaard, L., Harris, M. L., & Brodersen, L. (1992). The stressfulness of separation among 9-month-old infants: Effects of social context variables and infant temperament. *Child Development, 63*, 290–303.

Gunnar, M. R., Kryzer, E., Van Ryzin, M. J., & Phillips, D. A. (2010). The rise in cortisol in family day care: Associations with aspects of care quality, child behavior, and child sex. *Child Development, 81*, 851–869. doi: 10.1111/j.1467-8624.2010.01438.x

Gunturkun, O. (2003). Human behaviour: Adult persistence of head-turning asymmetry. *Nature, 421*, 711. doi:10.1038/421711a

Guo, G., Roettger, M., & Cai, T. (2008). The integration of genetic propensities into social-control models of delinquency and violence among male youths. *American Sociological Review, 73,* 543–568.

Guralnik, J. M., Butterworth, S., Wadsworth, M. E. J., & Kuh, D. (2006). Childhood socioeconomic status predicts physical functioning a half century later. *Journal of Gerontology: Medical Sciences, 61A*, 694–701.

Gurin, P. Y., Dey, E. L., Gurin, G., & Hurtado, S. (2003). How does racial/ethnic diversity promote education? *Western Journal of Black Studies, 27*(1), 20.

Gurung, R. A. R., Taylor, S. E., & Seeman, T. E. (2003). Accounting for changes in social support among married older adults: Insights from the MacArthur studies of successful aging. *Psychology and Aging, 18*, 487–496.

Gutman, L. M., & Eccles, J. S. (2007). Stage-environment fit during adolescence: Trajectories of family relations and adolescent outcomes. *Developmental Psychology, 43*, 522–537.

Gutmann, D. (1975). Parenting: A key to the comparative study of the life cycle. In N. Datan & L. H. Ginsberg (Eds.), *Life-span developmental psychology: Normative life crises.* New York: Academic Press.

Gutmann, D. (1977). The cross-cultural perspective: Notes toward a comparative psychology of aging. In J. E. Birren & K. W. Schaie (Eds.), *Handbook of the psychology of aging* (pp. 302–326). New York: Van Nostrand Reinhold.

Gutmann, D. (1985). The parental imperative revisited. In J. Meacham (Ed.), *Family and individual development.* Basel, Switzerland: Karger.

Gutmann, D. L. (1987). *Reclaimed powers; Toward a new psychology of men and women in later life.* New York: Basic Books.

Guttmacher Institute. (2013). *Facts on American teens' sexual and reproductive health.* Retrieved from http://www.guttmacher.org/pubs/FB-ATSRH.html#6

Haber, C. (2004). Life extension and history: The continual search for the Fountain of Youth. *Journal of Gerontology: Biological Sciences, 59A*, 515–522.

Hack, M., Youngstrom, E. A., Cartar, L., Schluchter, M., Taylor, H. G., Flannery, D., . . . Borawski, E. (2004). Behavioral outcomes and evidence of psychopathology among very low birth weight infants at age 20 years. *Pediatrics, 114*, 932–940.

Hagan, J. F., Committee on Psychosocial Aspects of Child and Family Health, & Task Force on Terrorism. (2005). Psycho-social implications of disaster or terrorism on children: A guide for pediatricians. *Pediatrics, 116*, 787–796.

Hahn, E. A., Cella, D., Chassany, O., Faiclough, D. L., Wong, G. Y., Hays, R. D., & Clinical Significance Consensus Meeting Group. (2007). Precision of health-related quality-of-life data compared with other clinical measures. *Mayo Clinic Proceedings, 82*(10), 1244–1254.

Hahn, R., Fuqua-Whitley, D., Wethington, H., Lowy, J., Liberman, A., Crosby, A., . . . Dahlberg, L. (2007). The effectiveness of universal school-based programs for the prevention of violent and aggressive behavior: A report on recommendations of the Task Force on Community Preventive Services. *Morbidity and Mortality Weekly Report, 56*(RR07), 1–12.

Haith, M. M. (1986). Sensory and perceptual processes in early infancy. *Journal of Pediatrics, 109*(1), 158–171.

Haith, M. M. (1998). Who put the cog in infant cognition? Is rich interpretation too costly? *Infant Behavior and Development, 21*(2), 167–179.

Haith, M. M., & Benson, J. B. (1998). Infant cognition. In D. Kuhn & R. S. Siegler (Eds.), *Handbook of child psychology: Vol. 2. Cognition, perception, and language* (5th ed., pp. 199–254). New York: Wiley.

Halgunseth, L. C., Ispa, J. M., & Rudy, D. (2006). Parental control in Latino families: An integrated review of the literature. *Child Development, 77*, 1282–1297.

Hallfors, D. D., Iritani, B. J., Miller, W. C., & Bauer, D. J. (2006). Sexual and drug behavior patterns and HIV and STD racial disparities: The need for new directions. *American Journal of Public Health, 97*(1), 125–132.

Hallfors, D. D., Waller, M. W., Bauer, D., Ford, C. A., & Halpern, C. T. (2005). Which comes first in adolescence—Sex and drugs or depression? *American Journal of Preventive Medicine, 29*, 1163–1170.

Halpern, C., Young, M., Waller, M., Martin, S., & Kupper, L. (2003). Prevalence of partner violence in same-sex romantic and sexual relationships in a national sample of adolescents. *Journal of Adolescent Health, 35*(2), 124–131.

Halpern, D. F., Benbow, C. P., Geary, D. C., Gur, R. C., Hyde, J. S., & Gernsbacher, M. A. (2007). The science of sex differences in science and mathematics. *Psychological Science in the Public Interest, 8*, 1–51.

Hamilton, L., Cheng, S., & Powell, B. (2007). Adoptive parents, adaptive parents: Evaluating the importance of biological ties for parental involvement. *American Sociological Review, 72*, 95–116.

Hamilton, M. C., Anderson, D., Broaddus, M., & Young, K. (2006). Gender stereotyping and underrepresentation of female characters in 200 popular children's picture books: A 21st century update. *Sex Roles: A Journal of Research, 55*, 757–765.

Hamilton, S. F., & Hamilton, M. A. (2006). School, work, and emerging adulthood. In J. J. Arnett & J. L. Tanner (Eds.), *Emerging adults in America: Coming of age in the 21st century* (pp. 257–277). Washington, DC: American Psychological Association.

Hamlin, J. K., Wynn, K., & Bloom, P. (2007). Social evaluation by preverbal infants. *Nature, 450*, 557–559.

Hammad, T. A., Laughren, T., & Racoosin, J. (2006). Suicidality in pediatric patients treated with antidepressant drugs. *Archives of General Psychiatry, 63*, 332–339.

Hampden-Thompson, G., & Johnston, J. S. (2006). *Variation in the relationship between nonschool factors and student achievement on international assessments* (NCES 2006-014). Washington, DC: U.S. Department of Education, National Center for Education Statistics.

Hampton, K. N., Goulet, L. S., Rainie, L., & Purcell, K. (2011). *Social networking sites and our lives.* Pew Research Center's Internet and American Life Project. Retrieved from http://www.namingandtreating.com/wp-content/uploads/2011/07/PIP-Social-networking-sites-and-our-lives.pdf

Hamre, B. K., & Pianta, R. C. (2005). Can instructional and emotional support in the first-grade classroom make a difference for children at risk of school failure? *Child Development, 76*, 949–967.

Handmaker, N. S., Rayburn, W. F., Meng, C., Bell, J. B., Rayburn, B. B., & Rappaport, V. J. (2006). Impact of alcohol exposure after pregnancy recognition on ultrasonographic fetal growth measures. *Alcoholism: Clinical and Experimental Research, 30*, 892–898.

Hank, K. (2007). Proximity and contacts between older parents and their children: A European comparison. *Journal of Marriage and Family, 69*, 157–173.

Hankin, B. L., Mermelstein, R., & Roesch, L. (2007). Sex differences in adolescent depression: Exposure and reactivity models. *Child Development, 78*, 279–295.

Hannigan, J. H., & Armant, D. R. (2000). Alcohol in pregnancy and neonatal outcome. *Seminars in Neonatology, 5*, 243–254.

Hansen, M., Janssen, I., Schiff, A., Zee, P. C., & Dubocovich, M. L. (2005). The impact of school daily schedule on adolescent sleep. *Pediatrics, 115*, 1555–1561.

Hanson, L. (1968). *Renoir: The man, the painter, and his world.* New York: Dodd, Mead.

Hao, Y. (2008). Productive activities and psychological well-being among older adults. *Journals of Gerontology, 63*(2, Series A), S64–S72.

Hardway, C., & Fuligni, A. J. (2006). Dimensions of family connectedness among adolescents with Mexican, Chinese, and European backgrounds. *Developmental Psychology, 42*, 1246–1258.

Hardy, R., Kuh, D., Langenberg, C., & Wadsworth, M. E. (2003). Birth weight, childhood social class, and change in adult blood pressure in the 1946 British birth cohort. *Lancet, 362*, 1178–1183.

Hardy-Brown, K., & Plomin, R. (1985). Infant communicative development: Evidence from adoptive and biological families for genetic and environmental influences on rate differences. *Developmental Psychology, 21*, 378–385.

Hardy-Brown, K., Plomin, R., & DeFries, J. C. (1981). Genetic and environmental influences on rate of communicative development in the first year of life. *Developmental Psychology, 17*, 704–717.

Harenski, C. L., Antonenko, O., Shane, M. S., & Keihl, K. A. (2008). Gender differences in neural mechanisms underlying moral sensitivity. *Social Cognitive and Affective Neuroscience, 3*, 313–321.

Harlow, H. F., & Harlow, M. K. (1962). The effect of rearing conditions on behavior. *Bulletin of the Menninger Clinic, 26*, 213–224.

Harlow, H. F., & Zimmerman, R. R. (1959). Affectional responses in the infant monkey. *Science, 130*, 421–432.

Harnishfeger, K. K., & Bjorklund, D. F. (1993). The ontogeny of inhibition mechanisms: A renewed approach to cognitive development. In M. L. Howe & R. P. Pasnak (Eds.), *Emerging themes in cognitive development* (Vol. 1, pp. 28–49). New York: Springer-Verlag.

Harper, S., Lynch, J., Burris, S., & Smith, G. D. (2007). Trends in the black-white life expectancy gap in the United States, 1983–2003. *Journal of the American Medical Association, 297*, 1224–1232.

Harris, D. G., Davies, C., Ward, H., & Haboubi, N. Y. (2008). An observational study of screening for malnutrition in elderly people living in sheltered accommodation. *Journal of Human Nutrition and Dietetics, 21*(1), 3–9.

Harris, G. (1997). Development of taste perception and appetite regulation. In G. Bremner, A. Slater, & G. Butterworth (Eds.), *Infant development: Recent advances* (pp. 9–30). East Sussex, UK: Psychology Press.

Harris, K. M., Gordon-Larsen, P., Chantala, K., & Udry, J. R. (2006). Longitudinal trends in race/ethnic disparities in leading health indicators from adolescence to young adulthood. *Archives of Pediatric and Adolescent Medicine, 160*, 74–81.

Harrison, Y., & Horne, J. A. (1997). Sleep deprivation affects speech. *Sleep, 20*, 871–877.

Harrison, Y., & Horne, J. A. (2000a). Impact of sleep deprivation on decision making: A review. *Journal of Experimental Psychology, 6*, 236–249.

Harrison, Y., & Horne, J. A. (2000b). Sleep loss and temporal memory. *Quarterly Journal of Experimental Psychology: Human Experimental Psychology, 53A*, 271–279.

Harrist, A. W., Zain, A. F., Bates, J. E., Dodge, K. A., & Pettit, G. S. (1997). Subtypes of social withdrawal in early childhood: Sociometric status and social-cognitive differences across four years. *Child Development, 68*, 278–294.

Hart, C. H., DeWolf, M., Wozniak, P., & Burts, D. C. (1992). Maternal and paternal disciplinary styles: Relations with preschoolers' playground behavioral orientation and peer status. *Child Development, 63*, 879–892.

Hart, C. H., Ladd, G. W., & Burleson, B. R. (1990). Children's expectations of the outcome of social strategies: Relations with sociometric status and maternal disciplinary style. *Child Development, 61*, 127–137.

Hart, D., Hofmann, V., Edelstein, W., & Keller, M. (1997). The relation of childhood personality types to adolescent behavior and development: A longitudinal study of Icelandic children. *Developmental Psychology, 33*, 195–205.

Hart, D., Southerland, N., & Atkins, R. (2003). Community service and adult development. In J. Demick & C. Andreoletti (Eds.), *Handbook of adult development* (pp. 585–597). New York: Plenum Press.

Harter, S. (1993). Developmental changes in self-understanding across the 5 to 7 shift. In A. Sameroff & M. Haith (Eds.), *Reason and responsibility: The passage through childhood* (pp. 207–236). Chicago: University of Chicago Press.

Harter, S. (1996). Developmental changes in self-understanding across the 5 to 7 shift. In A. J. Sameroff & M. M. Haith (Eds.), *The five to seven year shift: The age of reason and responsibility* (pp. 207–235). Chicago: University of Chicago Press.

Harter, S. (1998). The development of self-representations. In W. Damon (Series Ed.) & N. Eisenberg (Vol. Ed.), *Handbook of child psychology: Vol. 3. Social, emotional, and personality development* (5th ed., pp. 553–617). New York: Wiley.

Harter, S. (2006). The self. In W. Damon & R. M. Lerner (Series Eds.) & N. Eisenberg (Vol. Ed.), *Handbook of child psychology: Vol 3. Social, emotional and personality development* (pp. 505–570). Hoboken: NJ: Wiley.

Hartshorn, K., Rovee-Collier, C., Gerhardstein, P., Bhatt, R. S., Wondoloski, R. L., Klein, P., . . . Campos-de-Carvalho, M. (1998). The ontogeny of long-term memory over the first year-and-a-half of life. *Developmental Psychobiology, 32*, 69–89.

Hartup, W. W. (1992). Peer relations in early and middle childhood. In V. B. Van Hasselt & M. Hersen (Eds.), *Handbook of social development: A lifespan perspective* (pp. 257–281). New York: Plenum Press.

Hartup, W. W. (1996a). The company they keep: Friendships and their developmental significance. *Child Development, 67*, 1–13.

Hartup, W. W. (1996b). Cooperation, close relationships, and cognitive development. In W. M. Bukowski, A. F. Newcomb, & W. W. Hartup (Eds.), *The company they keep: Friendship in childhood and adolescence* (pp. 213–237). New York: Cambridge University Press.

Hartup, W. W., & Stevens, N. (1999). Friendships and adaptation across the life span. *Current Directions in Psychological Science, 8*, 76–79.

Harvard Medical School. (2002). The mind and the immune system—Part I. *Harvard Mental Health Letter, 18*(10), 1–3.

Harvard Medical School. (2003, May). Confronting suicide—Part I. *Harvard Mental Health Letter, 19*(11), 1–4.

Harvard Medical School. (2004a, December). Children's fears and anxieties. *Harvard Mental Health Letter, 21*(6), 1–3.

Harvard Medical School. (2004b, April). Countering domestic violence. *Harvard Mental Health Letter, 20*(10), pp. 1–5.

Harvard Medical School. (2004c, May). Women and depression: How biology and society may make women more vulnerable to mood disorders. *Harvard Mental Health Letter, 20*(11), 1–4.

Harvey, J. H., & Pauwels, B. G. (1999). Recent developments in close relationships theory. *Current Directions in Psychological Science, 8*(3), 93–95.

Haskuka, M., Sunar, D., & Alp, I. E. (2008). War exposure, attachment and moral reasoning. *Journal of Cross Cultural Psychology, 39*(4), 381–401.

Haswell, K., Hock, E., & Wenar, C. (1981). Oppositional behavior of preschool children: Theory and prevention. *Family Relations, 30*, 440–446.

Hatcher, P. J., Hulme, C., & Ellis, A. W. (1994). Ameliorating early reading failure by integrating the teaching of reading and phonological skills: The phonolgical linkage hypotheses. *Child Development, 65*, 41–57.

Hatzenbuehler, M. L., O'Cleirigh, C., & Bradford, J. (2012). Effect of same-sex marriage laws on health care use and expenditures on sexual minority men: A quasi-natural experiment. *American Journal of Public Health, 102*(2), 285–291.

Hauck, F. R., Herman, S. M., Donovan, M., Iyasu, S., Moore, C. M., Donoghue, E., . . . Willinger, M. (2003). Sleep environment and the risk of sudden infant death syndrome in an urban population: The Chicago Infant Mortality Study. *Pediatrics, 111*, 1207–1214.

Hauck, F. R., Omojokun, O. O., & Siadaty, M. S. (2005). Do pacifiers reduce the risk of sudden infant death syndrome? A meta-analysis. *Pediatrics, 116*, e716–e723.

Haugaard, J. J. (1998). Is adoption a risk factor for the development of adjustment problems? *Clinical Psychology Review, 18*, 47–69.

Hawes, A. (1996). Jungle gyms: The evolution of animal play. *ZooGoer, 25*(1). Retrieved from http://nationalzoo.si.edu/Publications/ZooGoer.1996/1/junglegyms.cfm

Hawes, C., Phillips, C. D., Rose, M., Holan, S., & Sherman, M. (2003). A national survey of assisted living facilities. *Gerontologist, 43*, 875–882.

Hawkins, J. D., Catalano, R. F., & Miller, J. Y. (1992). Risk and protective factors for alcohol and other drug problems in adolescence and early adulthood: Implications for substance abuse programs. *Psychological Bulletin, 112*(1), 64–105.

Hawkley, L. C., & Cacioppo, J. T. (2007). Aging and loneliness: Downhill quickly? *Current Directions in Psychological Science, 16*, 187–191.

Hawkley, L. C., Thisted, R. A., & Cacioppo, J. T. (2009). Loneliness predicts reduced physical activity: Cross-sectional and longitudinal analyses. *Health Psychology, 28*(3), 354–363.

Hay, D. (1994). Prosocial development. *Journal of Child Psychology and Psychiatry, 35*, 29–71.

Hay, D. (2003). Pathways to violence in the children of mothers who were depressed postpartum. *Developmental Psychology, 39*, 1083–1094.

Hay, D. F., Pawlby, S., Waters, C. S., Perra, O., & Sharp, D. (2010). Mothers' antenatal depression and their children's antisocial outcomes. *Child Development, 81*(1), 149–165.

Hay, D. F., Pedersen, J., & Nash, A. (1982). Dyadic interaction in the first year of life. In K. H. Rubin & H. S. Ross (Eds.), *Peer relationships and social skills in children.* New York: Springer.

Hayashi, M., & Abe, A. (2008). Short daytime naps in a car seat to counteract daytime sleepiness: The effect of backrest angle. *Sleep and Biological Rhythms, 6*, 34–44. doi: 10.1111/j.1479-8425.2008.00333.x

Hayes, A., & Batshaw, M. L. (1993). Down syndrome. *Pediatric Clinics of North America, 40*, 523–535.

Hayflick, L. (1974). The strategy of senescence. *Gerontologist, 14*(1), 37–45.

Hayflick, L. (1981). Intracellular determinants of aging. *Mechanisms of Aging and Development, 28*, 177.

Hayflick, L. (2004). "Anti-aging" is an oxymoron. *Journal of Gerontology: Biological Sciences, 59A*, 573–578.

Healy, A. J., Malone, F. D., Sullivan, L. M., Porter, T. F., Luthy, D. A., Comstock, C. H., . . . D'Alton, M. E. (2006). Early access to prenatal care: Implications for racial disparity in perinatal mortality. *Obstetrics and Gynecology, 107*, 625–631.

Heath, S. B. (1989). Oral and literate tradition among black Americans living in poverty. *American Psychologist, 44*, 367–373.

Heatherington, E. M. (2006). The influence of conflict, marital problem solving and parenting on children's adjustment in nondivorced, divorced and remarried families. In A. Clarke-Stewart & J. Dunn (Eds.), *Families count: Effects on child and adolescent development* (pp. 203–237). New York: Cambridge University Press.

Hebert, L. E., Scherr, P. A., Bienias, J. L., Bennett, D. A., & Evans, D. A. (2003). Alzheimer disease in the U.S. population:

Prevalence estimates using the 2000 census. *Archives of Neurology, 60*, 1119–1122.
Heckhausen, J. (2001). Adaptation and resilience in midlife. In M. E. Lachman (Ed.), *Handbook of midlife development* (pp. 345–394). New York: Wiley.
Heckhausen, J., Wrosch, C., & Fleeson, W. (2001). Developmental regulation before and after a developmental deadline: The sample case of biological clock for childbearing. *Psychology and Aging, 16*, 400–413.
Heckman, J. J., Moon, S. H., Pinto, R., Savelyev, P. A., & Yavitz, A. (2010). The rate of return to the High/Scope Perry Preschool Program. *Journal of Public Economics, 94*(1), 114–128.
Hedden, T., Lautenschlager, G., & Park, D. C. (2005). Contributions of processing ability and knowledge to verbal memory tasks across the adult life-span. *Quarterly Journal of Experimental Psychology. A Human Experimental Psychology, 58*(1), 169–190.
Heffner, L. J. (2004). Advanced maternal age—How old is too old? *New England Journal of Medicine, 351*, 1927–1929.
Helflick, N. A. (2005). Sentenced to die: Last statements and dying on death row. *Journal of Death and Dying, 51*(4), 323–336.
Heijl, A., Leske, M. C., Bengtsson, B., Hyman, L., Bengtsson, B., & Hussein, M., for the Early Manifest Glaucoma Trial Group. (2002). Reduction of intraocular pressure and glaucoma progression: Results from the Early Manifest Glaucoma Trial. *Archives of Ophthalmology, 120*, 1268–1279.
Heilbronn, L. K., & Ravussin, E. (2003). Calorie restriction and aging: Review of the literature and implications for studies in humans. *American Journal of Clinical Nutrition, 78*, 361–369.
Heinz, W. (2002). Self-socialization and post-traditional society. *Advances in Life Course Research, 7*, 41–64.
Heiss, G., Wallace, R., Anderson, G. L., Aragaki, A., Beresford, S. A. A., Brzyski, R., . . . Stefanick, M. L., for the WHI Investigators. (2008). Health risks and benefits 3 years after stopping randomized treatment with estrogen and progestin. *Journal of the American Medical Association, 299*, 1036–1045.
Helms, H. M., Crouter, A. C., & McHale, S. M. (2003). Marital quality and spouses' marriage work with close friends and each other. *Journal of Marriage and Family, 65*, 963–977.
Helms, J. E. (1992). Why is there no study of cultural equivalence in standardized cognitive ability testing? *American Psychologist, 47*, 1083–1101.
Helms, J. E., Jernigan, M., & Mascher, J. (2005). The meaning of race in psychology and how to change it: A methodological perspective. *American Psychologist, 60*, 27–36.
Helson, R. (1997). The self in middle age. In M. E. Lachman & J. B. James (Eds.), *Multiple paths of midlife development* (pp. 21–43). Chicago: University of Chicago Press.
Helson, R., & Moane, G. (1987). Personality change in women from college to midlife. *Journal of Personality and Social Psychology, 53*, 176–186.
Helson, R., & Roberts, B. W. (1994). Ego development and personality change in adulthood. *Journal of Personality and Social Psychology, 66*, 911–920.
Helson, R., & Wink, P. (1992). Personality change in women from the early 40s to the early 50s. *Psychology and Aging, 7*(1), 46–55.
Helwig, C. C., & Jasiobedzka, U. (2001). The relation between law and morality: Children's reasoning about socially beneficial and unjust laws. *Child Development, 72*, 1382–1393.
Henderson, H. A., Marshall, P. J., Fox, N. A., & Rubin, K. H. (2004). Psychophysiological and behavioral evidence for varying forms and functions of nonsocial behavior in preschoolers. *Child Development, 75*, 251–263.
Hendricks, J., & Cutler, S. J. (2004). Volunteerism and socioemotional selectivity in later life. *Journal of Gerontology: Social Sciences, 59B*, S251–S257.
Herbig, B., Büssing, A., & Ewert, T. (2001). The role of tacit knowledge in the work context of nursing. *Journal of Advanced Nursing, 34*, 687–695.
Herbst, J. H., Kay, L. S., Passin, W. F., Lyles, C. M., Crepaz, N., & Marin, B. V. (2006). A systematic review and meta-analysis of behavioral interventions to reduce HIV risk behaviors of Hispanics in the United States and Puerto Rico. *AIDS and Behavior, 11*(1), 25–47.
Herdt, G., & McClintock, M. (2000). The magical age of ten. *Archives of Sexual Behavior, 29*(6), 587–606. doi: 10.1023/A:1002006521067
Herek, G. M. (2006). Legal recognition of same-sex unions in the United States: A social science perspective. *American Psychologist, 61*, 607–621.
Hernandez, D. J. (2004, Summer). Demographic change and the life circumstances of immigrant families. In R. E. Behrman (Ed.), *Children of immigrant families* (pp. 17–48). *Future of Children, 14*(2). Retrieved from www.futureofchildren.org
Hernandez, D. J., Denton, N. A., & Macartney, S. E. (2007). *Children in immigrant families—The U.S. and 50 states: National origins, language, and early education.* (Child Trends and the Center for Social and Demographic Analysis, 2007 Research Brief Series.) Albany: SUNY.
Hernandez, D. J., & Macartney, S. E. (2008, January). *Racial-ethnic inequality in child well-being from 1985–2004: Gaps narrowing, but persist* (No. 9). New York: Foundation for Child Development.
Heron, M. P., Hoyert, D. L., Murphy, S. L., Xu, J. Q., Kochanek, K. D., & Tejada-Vera, B. (2009). Deaths: Final data for 2006. *National Vital Statistics Reports, 57*(14). Hyattsville, MD: National Center for Health Statistics.
Heron, M. P., Hoyert, D. L., Xu, J., Scott, C., & Tejada-Vera, B. (2008). Deaths: Preliminary data for 2006. *National Vital Statistics Reports, 56*(16). Hyattsville, MD: National Center for Health Statistics.
Herrnstein, R. J., & Murray, C. (1994). *The bell curve: Intelligence and class structure in American life.* New York: Free Press.
Hertenstein, M. J., & Campos, J. J. (2004). The retention effects of an adult's emotional displays on infant behavior. *Child Development, 75*, 595–613.
Hertz-Pannier, L., Chiron, C., Jambaque, I., Renaux-Kieffer, V., Van de Moortele, P., Delalande, O., . . . Le Bihan, D. (2002). Late plasticity for language in a child's non-dominant hemisphere. A pre- and post-surgery fMRI study. *Brain, 125*(2), 361–372.
Herzog, A. R., Franks, M. M., Markus, H. R., & Holmberg, D. (1998). Activities and well-being in older age: Effects of self-concept and educational attainment. *Psychology and Aging, 13*(2), 179–185.
Hesketh, T., Lu, L., & Xing, Z. W. (2005). The effect of China's one-child policy after 25 years. *New England Journal of Medicine, 353*, 1171–1176.
Hespos, S. J., & Baillargeon, R. (2008). Young infants' actions reveal their developing knowledge of support variables: Converging evidence for violation-of-expectation findings. *Cognition, 107*(1), 304–316.
Hesso, N. A., & Fuentes, E. (2005). Ethnic differences in neonatal and postneonatal mortality. *Pediatrics, 115*, e44–e51.
Hess, S. Y., & King, J. C. (2009). Effects of maternal zinc supplementation on pregnancy and lactation outcomes. *Food and Nutrition Bulletin, 30*(1), 60–78.
Hetherington, E. M., Bridges, M., & Insabella, G. M. (1998). What matters? What does not? Five perspectives on the association between marital transitions and children's adjustment. *American Psychologist, 53*, 167–184.
Hetherington, E. M., & Kelly, J. (2002). *For better or worse: Divorce reconsidered.* New York: Norton.
Hetzel, L., & Smith, A. (2001). *The 65 years and over population: 2000* (Census 2000 Brief C2KBR/01-10). Washington, DC: U.S. Census Bureau.
Heuveline, P., & Timberlake, J. M. (2004). The role of cohabitation in family formation: The United States in comparative perspective. *Journal of Marriage and Family, 66*, 1214–1230.
Hewlett, B. S. (1987). Intimate fathers: Patterns of paternal holding among Aka pygmies. In M. E. Lamb (Ed.), *The father's role: Cross-cultural perspectives* (pp. 295–330). Hillsdale, NJ: Erlbaum.
Hewlett, B. S. (1992). Husband-wife reciprocity and the father-infant relationship among Aka pygmies. In B. S. Hewlett (Ed.), *Father-child relations: Cultural and biosocial contexts* (pp. 153–176). New York: de Gruyter.
Hewlett, B. S., Lamb, M. E., Shannon, D., Leyendecker, B., & Schölmerich, A. (1998). Culture and early infancy among central African foragers and farmers. *Developmental Psychology, 34*(4), 653–661.
Heymann, J., Siebert, W. S., & Wei, X. (2007). The implicit wage costs of family friendly work

practices. *Oxford Economic Papers, 59*(2), 275–300.

Hickling, A. K., & Wellman, H. M. (2001). The emergence of children's causal explanations and theories: Evidence from everyday conversations. *Developmental Psychology, 37*(5), 668–683.

Hickman, M., Roberts, C., & de Matos, M. G. (2000). Exercise and leisure time activities. In C. Currie, K. Hurrelmann, W. Settertobulte, R. Smith, & J. Todd (Eds.), Health and health behaviour among young people: A WHO cross-national study (HBSC) international report (pp. 73–82.). *WHO Policy Series: Health Policy for Children and Adolescents, Series No. 1.* Copenhagen, Denmark: World Health Organization Regional Office for Europe.

Hiedemann, B., Suhomilinova, O., & O'Rand, A. M. (1998). Economic independence, economic status, and empty nest in midlife marital disruption. *Journal of Marriage and Family, 60*, 219–231.

Hill, A. L., Degnan, K. A., Calkins, S. D., & Keane, S. P. (2006). Profiles of externalizing behavior problems for boys and girls across preschool: The roles of emotional regulation and inattention. *Developmental Psychology, 42*, 913–928.

Hill, C., & Holzer, H. (2007). Labor market experiences and the transition to adulthood. In S. Danziger & C. Rouse (Eds.), *The price of independence: The economics of early adulthood* (pp. 141–169). New York: Russell Sage Foundation.

Hill, D. A., Gridley, G., Cnattingius, S., Mellemkjaer, L., Linet, M., Adami, H.-O., . . . Fraumeni, J. F. (2003). Mortality and cancer incidence among individuals with Down syndrome. *Archives of Internal Medicine, 163*, 705–711.

Hill, J. L., Waldfogel, J., Brooks-Gunn, J., & Han, W.-J. (2005). Maternal employment and child development: A fresh look using newer methods. *Developmental Psychology, 41*, 833–850.

Hill, N., & Tyson, D. (2009). Parental involvement in middle school: A metaanalytical assessment of the strategies that promote achievement. *Developmental Psychology, 45*(3), 740–763.

Hill, N. E., & Taylor, L. C. (2004). Parental school involvement and children's academic achievement: Pragmatics and issues. *Current Directions in Psychological Science, 13*, 161–168.

Hill, T. D., Angel, J. L., Ellison, C. G., & Angel, R. J. (2005). Religious attendance and mortality: An 8-year follow-up of older Mexican Americans. *Journal of Gerontology: Social Sciences, 60B*, S102–S109.

Hillier, L. (2002). "It's a catch-22": Same-sex-attracted young people on coming out to parents. In S. S. Feldman & D. A. Rosenthal (Eds.), *Talking sexuality* (New Directions for Child and Adolescent Development, No. 97, pp. 75–91). San Francisco: Jossey-Bass.

Hillis, S. D., Anda, R. F., Dubé, S. R., Felitti, V. J., Marchbanks, P. A., & Marks, J. S. (2004). The association between adverse childhood experiences and adolescent pregnancy, long-term psychosocial consequences, and fetal death. *Pediatrics, 113*, 320–327.

Hilts, P. J. (1999, June 1). Life at age 100 is surprisingly healthy. *The New York Times*, p. D7.

Hinckley, A. F., Bachand, A. M., & Reif, J. S. (2005). Late pregnancy exposures to disinfection by-products and growth-related birth outcomes. *Environmental Health Perspectives, 113*, 1808–1813.

Hinds, D. A., Stuve, L. L., Nilsen, G. B., Halperin, E., Eskin, E., Ballinger, D. G., . . . Cox, D. R. (2005). Whole-genome patterns of common DNA variation in three human populations. *Science, 307*, 1072–1079.

Hines, A. M. (1997). Divorce-related transitions, adolescent development, and the role of the parent-child relationship: A review of the literature. *Journal of Marriage and Family, 59*, 375–388.

Hingson, R. W., Heeren, T., & Winter, M. R. (2006). Age at drinking onset and alcohol dependence: Age at onset, duration, and severity. *Archivers of Pediatrics & Adolescent Medicine, 160*, 739–746.

Hingson, R., Heeren, T., Winter, M., & Wechsler, H. (2005). Magnitude of alcohol-related mortality and morbidity among U.S. college students ages 18–24: Changes from 1998–2001. *Annual Reviews, 26*, 259–279.

Hinman, J. D., & Abraham, C. R. (2007). What's behind the decline? The role of white matter in brain aging. *Neurochemical Research, 32*(12), 2023–2031.

Hirschl, T. A., Altobelli, J., & Rank, M. R. (2003). Does marriage increase the odds of affluence? Exploring the life course probabilities. *Journal of Marriage and Family, 65*, 927–938.

Hitchins, M. P., & Moore, G. E. (2002, May 9). Genomic imprinting in fetal growth and development. *Expert Reviews in Molecular Medicine.* Retrieved from www.expertreviews.org/0200457Xh.htm

Hitlin, S., Brown, J. S., & Elder, G. H. (2006). Racial self-categorization in adolescence: Multiracial development and social pathways. *Child Development, 77*, 1298–1308.

Hjelmborg, J., Iachine, I., Skytthe, A., Vaupel, J., McGue, M., et al. (2006). Genetic influence on human lifespan and longevity. *Human Genetics 199*(3), 312–321.

Ho, R. C. M., Neo, L. F., Chua, A. N. C., Cheak, A. A. C., & Mak, A. (2010). Research on psychoneuroimmunology: Does stress influence immunity and coronary artery disease? *Annals Academy of Medicine Singapore, 39*, 191–196.

Hoban, T. F. (2004). Sleep and its disorders in children. *Seminars in Neurology, 24*, 327–340.

Hobson, J. A., & Silvestri, L. (1999, February). Parasomnias. *Harvard Mental Health Letter*, 3–5.

Hodges, E. V. E., Boivin, M., Vitaro, F., & Bukowski, W. M. (1999). The power of friendship: Protection against an escalating cycle of peer victimization. *Developmental Psychology, 35*, 94–101.

Hodnett, E. D., Gates, S., Hofmeyr, G. J., & Sakala, C. (2005). Continuous support for women during childbirth (Cochrane Review). *The Cochrane Library*, Issue 1, Oxford.

Hoff, E. (2003). The specificity of environmental influence: Socioeconomic status affects early vocabulary development via maternal speech. *Child Development, 74*, 1368–1378.

Hoff, E. (2006). How social contexts support and shape language development. *Developmental Review, 26*, 55–88.

Hofferth, S. L. (2010). Home media and children's achievement and behavior, *Child Development, 81*, 1598–1619. doi: 10.1111/j.1467-8624.2010.01494.x

Hoffman, G. F., Davies, M., & Norman, R. (2007). The impact of lifestyle factors on reproductive perfomance in the general population and those undergoing infertility treatment: A review. *Human Reproduction Update, 13*(3), 209–223.

Hoffman, M. L. (1970). Conscience, personality, and socialization techniques. *Human Development, 13*, 90–126.

Hofman, P. L., Regan, F., Jackson, W. E., Jefferies, C., Knight, D. B., Robinson, E. M., & Cutfield, W. S. (2004). Premature birth and later insulin resistance. *New England Journal of Medicine, 351*, 2179–2186.

Hogge, W. A. (2003). The clinical use of karyotyping spontaneous abortions. *American Journal of Obstetrics and Gynecology, 189*, 397–402.

Hohmann-Marriott, B. E. (2006). Shared beliefs and the union stability of married and cohabiting couples. *Journal of Marriage and Family, 68*, 1015–1028.

Holden, G. W., & Miller, P. C. (1999). Enduring and different: A meta-analysis of the similarity in parents' child rearing. *Psychological Bulletin, 125*, 223–254.

Holliday, R. (2004). The multiple and irreversible causes of aging. *Journal of Gerontology: Biological Sciences, 59A*, 568–572.

Holmes E. A., James, E. L., Kilford, E. J., & Deeprose, C. (2010). Key steps in developing a cognitive vaccine against traumatic flashbacks: Visuospatial tetris versus verbal pub quiz. *PLoS ONE, 5*(11), e13706. doi:10.1371/journal.pone.0013706

Holmes, J., Powell-Griner, E., Lethbridge-Cejku, M., & Heyman, K. (2009). Aging differently: Physical limitations among adults aged 50 years and over: United States, 2001–2007. *NCHS Data Brief, 20*, 1–8. Hyattsville, MD: National Center for Health Statistics.

Holmes, T. H., & Rahe, R. H. (1976). The social readjustment rating scale. *Journal of Psychosomatic Research, 11*, 213.

Holowka, S., & Petitto, L. A. (2002). Left hemisphere cerebral specialization for babies while babbling. *Science, 297*, 1515.

Holstein, M. B., & Minkler, M. (2003). Self, society, and the "New Gerontology." *Gerontologist, 43*, 787–796.

Holt-Lunstad, J., Birmingham, W., & Jones, B. Q. (2008). Is there something unique about marriage? The relative impact of marital status, relationship quality, and network social support on ambulatory blood pressure and mental health. *Annals of Behavioral Medicine, 35*(2), 239–244.

Holt-Lunstad, J., Smith, T. B., & Layton, J. B. (2010). Social relationships and mortality risk: A meta-analytic review. *PLoS Medicine, 7*(7), e1000316. doi:10.1371/journal.pmed.1000316

Holtzman, N. A., Murphy, P. D., Watson, M. S., & Barr, P. A. (1997). Predictive genetic testing: From basic research to clinical practice. *Science, 278*, 602–605.

Holtzman, R. E., Rebok, G. W., Saczynski, J. S., Kouzis, A. C., Doyle, K. W., & Eaton, W. W. (2004). Social network characteristics and cognition in middle-aged and older adults. *Journal of Gerontology: Psychological Sciences, 59B*, 278–284.

Honein, M. A., Paulozzi, L. J., Mathews, T. J., Erickson, J. D., & Wong, L.-Y. C. (2001). Impact of folic acid fortification of the U.S. food supply on the occurrence of neural tube defects. *Journal of the American Medical Association, 285*, 2981–2986.

Hopkins, B., & Westra, T. (1988). Maternal handling and motor development: An intracultural study. *Genetic, Social and General Psychology Monographs, 14*, 377–420.

Hopkins, B., & Westra, T. (1990). Motor development, maternal expectations and the role of handling. *Infant Behavior and Development, 13*, 117–122.

Horbar, J. D., Wright, E. C., Onstad, L., & the Members of the National Institute of Child Health and Human Development Neonatal Research Network. (1993). Decreasing mortality associated with the introduction of surfactant therapy: An observational study of neonates weighing 601 to 1300 grams at birth. *Pediatrics, 92*, 191–196.

Horn, J. C., & Meer, J. (1987, May). The vintage years. *Psychology Today*, pp. 76–90.

Horn, J. L. (1967). Intelligence—Why it grows, why it declines. *Transaction, 5*(1), 23–31.

Horn, J. L. (1968). Organization of abilities and the development of intelligence. *Psychological Review, 75*, 242–259.

Horn, J. L. (1970). Organization of data on life-span development of human abilities. In L. R. Goulet & P. B. Baltes (Eds.), *Life-span developmental psychology: Theory and research* (pp. 424–466). New York: Academic Press.

Horn, J. L. (1982a). The aging of human abilities. In B. B. Wolman (Ed.), *Handbook of developmental psychology* (pp. 847–870). Englewood Cliffs, NJ: Prentice Hall.

Horn, J. L. (1982b). The theory of fluid and crystallized intelligence in relation to concepts of cognitive psychology and aging in adulthood. In F. I. M. Craik & S. Trehub (Eds.), *Aging and cognitive processes* (pp. 237–278). New York: Plenum Press.

Horn, J. L., & Donaldson, G. (1980). Cognitive development: 2. Adulthood development of human abilities. In O. G. Brim & J. Kagan (Eds.), *Constancy and change in human development.* Cambridge, MA: Harvard University Press.

Horn, J. L., & Hofer, S. M. (1992). Major abilities and development in the adult. In R. J. Sternberg & C. A. Berg (Eds.), *Intellectual development.* New York: Cambridge University Press.

Horn, L., & Berger, R. (2004). *College persistence on the rise? Changes in 5-year completion and postsecondary persistence rates between 1994 and 2000* (NCES 2005-156). Washington, DC: U.S. Department of Education, National Center for Education Statistics.

Horne, J. (2000). Neuroscience: Images of lost sleep. *Nature, 403*, 605–606.

Hornig, M., Briese, T., Buie, T., Bauman, M. L., Lauwers, G., Siemetzki, U., . . . Lipkin, W. I. (2008). Lack of association between measles virus vaccine and autism with enteropathy: A case-control study. *PloS One, 3*(9), e3140. doi:10.1371/journal.pone.0003140

Horowitz, B. N., Neiderhiser, J. M., Ganiban, J. M., Spotts, E. L., Lichtenstein, P., & Reiss, D. (2010). Genetic and environmental influences on global family conflict. *Journal of Family Psychology, 24*(2), 217–220.

Horton, R., & Shweder, R. A. (2004). Ethnic conservatism, psychological well-being, and the downside of mainstreaming: Generational differences. In O. G. Brim, C. D. Ryff, & R. C. Kessler (Eds.), *How healthy are we? A national study of well-being at midlife* (pp. 373–397). Chicago: University of Chicago Press.

Houltberg, B. J., Henry, C. S., & Morris, A. S. (2012). Family interactions, exposure to violence, and emotion regulation: Perceptions of children and early adolescents at risk. *Family Relations, 61*, 283–296. doi: 10.1111/j.1741-3729.2011.00699.x

Howard, K. S., Lefever, J. B., Borkowski, J. G., & Whitman, T. L. (2006). Fathers' influence in the lives of children with adolescent mothers. *Journal of Family Psychology, 20*, 468–476.

Howe, M. L. (2003). Memories from the cradle. *Current Directions in Psychological Science, 12*, 62–65.

Howe, N., Petrakos, H., Rinaldi, C. M., & LeFebvre, R. (2005). "This is a bad dog, you know . . ." : Constructing shared meanings during sibling pretend play. *Child Development, 76*, 783–794.

Howell, R. R. (2006). We need expanded newborn screening. *Pediatrics, 117*, 1800–1805.

Howlett, N., Kirk, E., & Pine, K. J. (2010). Does "wanting the best" create more stress? The link between baby sign classes and maternal anxiety. *Infant and Child Development, 20.* Advance online publication. doi: 10.1002/icd.705

Howson, C. P., Kinney, M. V., & Lawn, J. E. (Eds.). (2012). *Born too soon: The global action report on preterm birth.* Geneva: World Health Organization.

Hoxby, C. M. (2004). *Achievement in charter schools and regular public schools in the United States: Understanding the differences.* Cambridge, MA: Department of Economics, Harvard University.

Hoyer, W. J., & Rybash, J. M. (1994). Characterizing adult cognitive development. *Journal of Adult Development, 1*(1), 7–12.

Hoyert, D. L. (2007). Maternal mortality and related concepts. *Vital and Health Statistics, 3*(33). Hyattsville, MD: National Center for Health Statistics.

Hoyert, D. L., Arias, E., Smith, B. L., Murphy, S. L., & Kochanek, K. D. (2001). Deaths: Final data for 1999. *National Vital Statistics Reports, 49*(8). Hyattsville, MD: National Center for Health Statistics.

Hoyert, D. L., Kochanek, K. D., & Murphy, S. L. (1999). Deaths: Final data for 1997. *National Vital Statistics Reports, 47*(19). Hyattsville, MD: National Center for Health Statistics.

Hoyert, D. L., Mathews, T. J., Menacker, F., Strobino, D. M., & Guyer, B. (2006). Annual summary of vital statistics: 2004. *Pediatrics, 117*, 168–183.

Hoyland, A., Dye, L., & Lawton, C. L. (2009). A systematic review of the effect of breakfast on cognitive performance of children and adolescents. *Nutrition Research, 20*(2), 220–243.

Hsu, L. M., Chung, J., & Langer, E. J. (2010). The influence of age-related cues on health and longevity. *Perspectives on Psychological Science, 5*(6), 632–648.

Hu, F. B., Willett, W. C., Li, T., Stampfer, M. J., Colditz, G. A., & Manson, J. E. (2004). Adiposity as compared with physical activity in predicting mortality among women. *New England Journal of Medicine, 351*, 2694–2703.

Hu, W. (2011, January 4). Math that moves: Schools embrace the iPad. *The New York Times.* Retrieved from http://www.nytimes.com/2011/01/05/education/05tablets.html?ref=education

Hudd, S., Dumlao, J., Erdmann-Sager, D., Murray, D., Phan, E., & Soukas, N. (2000). Stress at college: Effects on health habits, health status and self-esteem. *College Students Journal, 34*(2), 217–227.

Hudson, J. I., Hiripi, E., Pope, H. G., Jr., & Kessler, R. C. (2007). The prevalence and correlates of eating disorders in the National Comorbidity Survey Replication. *Biological Psychiatry, 61*(3), 348–358.

Hudson, V. M., & den Boer, A. M. (2004). *Bare branches: Security implications of Asia's surplus male population.* Cambridge, MA: MIT Press.

Huebner, A. J., Mancini, J. A., Wilcox, R. M., Grass, S. R., & Grass, G. A. (2007). Parental deployment and youth in military families: Exploring uncertainty and ambiguous loss. *Family Relations, 56*(2), 112–122.

Huesmann, R. (2007). The impact of electronic media violence: Scientific theory and research. *Journal of Adolescent Health, 41*, S6–S13.

Huesmann, L. R., & Kirwil, L. (2007). Why observing violence increases the risk of violent behavior in the observer. In D. Flannery, A. Vazinsyi, & I. Waldman (Eds.), *The Cambridge handbook of violent behavior and agression* (pp. 545–570). Cambridge, UK: Cambridge University Press.

Huesmann, L. R., Moise-Titus, J., Podolski, C. L., & Eron, L. (2003). Longitudinal relations between children's exposure to TV violence and their aggressive and violent behavior in young adulthood: 1977–1992. *Developmental Psychology, 39*, 201–221.

Huge payout in U.S. stuttering case. (2007, August 17). *BBC News*. Retrieved from http://news.bbc.co.uk/2/hi/americas/6952446.stm

Hughes, D., Rodriguez, J., Smith, E. P., Johnson, D. J., Stevenson, H. C., & Spicer, P. (2006). Parents' ethnic-racial socialization practices: A review of research and directions for future study. *Developmental Psychology, 42*, 747–770.

Hughes, I. A. (2004). Female development—All by default? *New England Journal of Medicine, 351*, 748–750.

Hughes, K. L., Bailey, T. R., & Mechur, M. J. (2001). *School-to-work: Making a difference in education: A research report to America.* New York: Columbia University, Teachers College, Institute on Education and the Economy.

Hughes, M. E., & Waite, L. J. (2009). Marital biography and health at mid-life. *Journal of Health and Social Behavior, 50*, 344–358.

Hughes, S. M., Harrison, M. A., & Gallup, G. G., Jr. (2007). Sex differences in romantic kissing among college students: An evolutionary perspective. *Evolutionary Psychology, 5*(3), 612–631.

Huizink, A., Robles de Medina, P., Mulder, E., Visser, G., & Buitelaar, J. (2002). Psychological measures of prenatal stress as predictors of infant temperament. *Journal of the American Academy of Child and Adolescent Psychiatry, 41*, 1078–1085.

Hujoel, P. P., Bollen, A.-M., Noonan, C. J., & del Aguila, M. A. (2004). Antepartum dental radiography and infant low birth weight. *Journal of the American Medical Association, 291*, 1987–1993.

Hulley, S., Furberg, C., Barrett-Connor, E., Cauley, J., Grady, D., Haskell, W., . . . Hunninghake, D. (2002). Non-cardiovascular disease outcomes during 6.8 years of hormone therapy. *Journal of the American Medical Association, 288*, 58–66.

Human Rights Watch. (2008). *A violent education: Corporal punishment in U.S. public schools.* Retrieved from www.aclu.org/human-rights-racial-justice/violent-education-corporal-punishment-children-us-public-schools

Hungerford, T. L. (2001). The economic consequences of widowhood on elderly women in the United States and Germany. *Gerontologist, 41*, 103–110.

Hunt, C. E. (1996). Prone sleeping in healthy infants and victims of sudden infant death syndrome. *Journal of Pediatrics, 128*, 594–596.

Huntsinger, C. S., & Jose, P. E. (1995). Chinese American and Caucasian American family interaction patterns in spatial rotation puzzle solutions. *Merrill-Palmer Quarterly, 41*, 471–496.

Huston, A. C., Duncan, G. J., McLoyd, V. C., Crosby, D. A., Ripke, M. N., Weisner, T. S., & Eldred, C. A. (2005). Impacts on children of a policy to promote employment and reduce poverty for low-income parents: New hope after 5 years. *Developmental Psychology, 41*, 902–918.

Huston, A. C., & Wright, J. C. (1983). Childrens' processing of television: The informative functions of formal features. In J. Bryant & D. R. Anderson (Eds.), *Children's understanding of television: Research on attention and comprehension* (pp. 35–68). New York: Academic Press.

Huston, H. C., Duncan, G. J., Granger, R., Bos, J., McLoyd, V., Mistry, R., . . . Ventura, A. (2001). Work-based antipoverty programs for parents can enhance the performance and social behavior of children. *Child Development, 72*(1), 318–336.

Huttenlocher, J. (1998). Language input and language growth. *Preventive Medicine, 27*, 195–199.

Huttenlocher, J., Haight, W., Bryk, A., Seltzer, M., & Lyons, T. (1991). Early vocabulary growth: Relation to language input and gender. *Developmental Psychology, 27*, 236–248.

Huttenlocher, J., Levine, S., & Vevea, J. (1998). Environmental input and cognitive growth: A study using time period comparisons. *Child Development, 69*, 1012–1029.

Huttenlocher, J., Vasilyeva, M., Cymerman, E., & Levine, S. (2002). Language input and child syntax. *Cognitive Psychology, 45*, 337–374.

Huyck, M. H. (1990). Gender differences in aging. In J. E. Birren & K. W. Schaie (Eds.), *Handbook of the psychology of aging* (3rd ed., pp. 124–132). San Diego: Academic Press.

Huyck, M. H. (1995). Marriage and close relationships of the marital kind. In R. Blieszner & V. Hilkevitch (Eds.), *Handbook of aging and the family* (pp. 181–200). Westport, CT: Greenwood Press.

Huyck, M. H. (1999). Gender roles and gender identity in midlife. In S. L. Willis & J. D. Reid (Eds.), *Life in the middle: Psychological and social development in middle age* (pp. 209–232). New York: Academic Press.

Hyde, J., Lindberg, S., Linn, M., Ellis, A., & Williams, C. (2008). Gender similarities characterize math performance. *Science, 321*, 494–495.

Hyde, J. S. (2005). The gender similarity hypothesis. *American Psychologist, 60*, 581–592.

Hyde, J. S., & Mertz, J. E. (2009). Gender, culture, and mathematics performance. *Proceedings of the National Academy of Sciences, 106*(22), 8801–8807.

Hyde, Z., Flicker, L., Hankey, G. J., Almeida, O. P., McCaul, K. A., Chubb, S. A., & Yeap, B. B. (2010). Prevalence of sexual activity and associated factors in men aged 75 to 95 years. *Annals of Internal Medicine, 153*(11), 693–702.

Iacoboni, M. (2008). *Mirroring people: The new science of how we connect with others.* New York: Farrar, Straus, & Giroux.

Iacoboni, M., & Mazziotta, J. C. (2007). Mirror neuron system: Basic findings and clinical applications. *Annals of Neurology, 62*, 213–218.

Ialongo, N. S., Edelsohn, G., & Kellam, S. G. (2001). A further look at the prognostic power of young children's reports of depressed mood and feelings. *Child Development, 72*, 736–747.

Iaria, G., Palermo, L., Committeri, G., & Barton, J. J. S. (2009). Age differences in the formation and use of cognitive maps. *Behavioural Brain Research, 196*(2), 187–191.

Iervolino, A. C., Hines, M., Golombok, S. E., Rust, J., & Plomin, R. (2005). Genetic and environmental influences on sex-types behavior during the preschool years. *Child Development, 76*, 826–840.

Iervolino, A. C., Pike, A., Manke, B., Reiss, D., Hetherington, E. M., & Plomin, R. (2002). Genetic and environmental influences in adolescent peer socialization: Evidence from two genetically sensitive designs. *Child Development, 73*(1), 162–174.

Iglowstein, I., Jenni, O. G., Molinari, L., & Largo, R. H. (2003). Sleep duration from infancy to adolescence: Reference values and generational trends. *Pediatrics, 111*, 302–307.

Ijzerman, H., & Semin, G. R. (2009). The thermometer of social relations: Mapping social proximity on temperature. *Psychological Science, 20*(10), 1214–1220.

Imada, T., Zhang, Y., Cheour, M., Taulu, S., Ahonen, A., & Kuhl, P. (2006). Infant speech perception activates Broca's area: A developmental magnetoencephalography study. *NeuroReport, 17*, 957–962.

Ingersoll, E. W., & Thoman, E. B. (1999). Sleep/wake states of preterm infants: Stability, developmental change, diurnal variation, and relation with care giving activity. *Child Development, 70*, 1–10.

Ingersoll-Dayton, B., Neal, M. B., Ha, J., & Hammer, L. B. (2003). Redressing inequity in parent care among siblings. *Journal of Marriage and Family, 65*, 201–212.

Ingoldsby, B. B. (1995). Mate selection and marriage. In B. B. Ingoldsby & S. Smith (Eds.), *Families in multicultural perspective* (pp. 143–160). New York: Guilford Press.

Ingram, J. L., Stodgell, C. S., Hyman, S. L., Figlewicz, D. A., Weitkamp, L. R., & Rodier, P. M. (2000). Discovery of allelic variants of HOXA1 and HOXB1: Genetic susceptibility to autism spectrum disorders. *Teratology, 62*, 393–406.

Insel, K., Morrow, D., Brewer, B., & Figueredo, A. (2006). Executive function, working memory, and medication adherence among older adults. *Journal of Gerontology, 61*(2, Series B), 102–107.

Institute of Medicine (IOM) National Academy of Sciences. (1993, November). *Assessing genetic risks: Implications for health and social policy.* Washington, DC: National Academy of Sciences.

International Committee for Monitoring Assisted Reproductive Technologies (ICMART). (2006, June). *2002 World report on ART.* Report released at meeting of the European Society of Human Reproduction and Embryology, Prague.

International Human Genome Sequencing Consortium. (2004). Finishing the euchromatic sequence of the human genome. *Nature, 431*, 931–945.

International Longevity Center-USA. (2002). Is there an anti-aging medicine? *ILC Workshop Report.* Retrieved from www.ilcusa.org

Isaacowitz, D. M., & Smith, J. (2003). Positive and negative affect in very old age. *Journal of*

Gerontology: Psychological Sciences, 58B, P143–P152.

Isaacson, W. (2007). *Einstein: His life and universe.* New York: Simon & Schuster.

Isabella, R. A. (1993). Origins of attachment: Maternal interactive behavior across the first year. *Child Development, 64*(2), 605–621.

Ishii, N., Fujii, M., Hartman, P. S., Tsuda, M., Yasuda, K., Senoo-Matsuda, N., . . . Suzuki, K. (1998). A mutation in succinate dehydrogenase cytochrome b causes oxidative stress and ageing in nematodes. *Nature, 394*, 694–697.

Izard, C. E., Porges, S. W., Simons, R. F., Haynes, O. M., & Cohen, B. (1991). Infant cardiac activity: Developmental changes and relations with attachment. *Developmental Psychology, 27*, 432–439.

Jaccard, J., & Dittus, P. J. (2000). Adolescent perceptions of maternal approval of birth control and sexual risk behavior. *American Journal of Public Health, 90*, 1426–1430.

Jackson, K. D., Howie, L. D., & Akinbami, L. J. (2013). *Trends in allergic conditions among children: United States, 1997–2011.* NCHS Data Brief No 121. Hyattsville, MD: National Center for Health Statistics.

Jackson, A. S., Sui, X., Hébert, J. R., Church, T. S., & Blair, S. N. (2009). Role of lifestyle and aging on the longitudinal change in cardiorespiratory fitness. *Archives of Internal Medicine, 169*(19), 1781–1787.

Jackson, R. D., LaCroix, A. Z., Gass, M., Wallace, R. B., Robbins, J., Lewis, C. E., . . . Women's Health Initiative Invesigators. (2006). Calcium plus vitamin D supplementation and the risk of fractures. *New England Journal of Medicine, 354*, 669–683.

Jacobsen, T., & Hofmann, V. (1997). Children's attachment representations: Longitudinal relations to school behavior and academic competency in middle childhood and adolescence. *Developmental Psychology, 33*, 703–710.

Jacobsen, L. A., Mark, M., & Dupuis, G. (2012). Household change in the United States. *Population Bulletin 67*, No. 1. Retrieved from http://www.prb.org/pdf12/us-household-change-2012.pdf

Jacobson, J. L., & Wille, D. E. (1986). The influence of attachment pattern on developmental changes in peer interaction from the toddler to the preschool period. *Child Development, 57*, 338–347.

Jacobson, K. C., & Crockett, L. J. (2000). Parental monitoring and adolescent adjustment: An ecological perspective. *Journal of Research on Adolescence, 10*(1), 65–97.

Jaffari-Bimmel, N., Juffer, F., van IJzendoorn, M. H., Bakermans-Kranenburg, M. J., & Mooijaart, A. (2006). Social development from infancy to adolescence: Longitudinal and concurrent factors in an adoption sample. *Developmental Psychology, 42*, 1143–1153.

Jaffee, S., & Hyde, J. S. (2000). Gender differences in moral orientation: A meta-analysis. *Psychological Bulletin, 126*, 703–726.

Jaffee, S. R., Caspi, A., Moffitt, T. E., Dodge, K. A., Rutter, M., Taylor, A., & Tully, L. A. (2005). Nature x nature: Genetic vulnerabilities interact with physical maltreatment to promote conduct problems. *Developmental Psychopathology, 17*, 67–84.

Jaffee, S. R., Caspi, A., Moffitt, T. E., Polo-Tomas, M., Price, T. S., & Taylor, A. (2004). The limits of child effects: Evidence for genetically mediated child effects on corporal punishment but not on physical maltreatment. *Developmental Psychology, 40*, 1047–1058.

Jagasia, R., Grote, P., Westermann, B., & Conradt, B. (2005). DRP-1-mediated mitochondrial fragmentation during EGL-1-induced cell death in C. elegans. *Nature, 433*, 754–760.

Jakicic, J. M., Marcus, B. H., Gallagher, K. I., Napolitano, M., & Lang, W. (2003). Effect of exercise duration and intensity on weight loss in overweight sedentary women: A randomized trial. *Journal of the American Medical Association, 290*, 1323–1330.

James, J. B., & Lewkowicz, C. J. (1997). Themes of power and affiliation across time. In M. E. Lachman & J. B. James (Eds.), *Multiple paths of midlife development* (pp. 109–143). Chicago: University of Chicago Press.

Jankowiak, W. (1992). Father-child relations in urban China. In B. S. Hewlett (Ed.), *Father-child relations: Cultural and bi-social contexts* (pp. 345–363). New York: de Gruyter.

Jankowski, J. J., Rose, S. A., & Feldman, J. F. (2001). Modifying the distribution of attention in infants. *Child Development, 72*, 339–351.

Janssen, I., Craig, W. M., Boyce, W. F., & Pickett, W. (2004). Associations between overweight and obesity with bullying behaviors in school-aged children. *Pediatrics, 113*, 1187–1194.

Janssen, S., Murre, J., & Meeter, M. (2007). Reminiscence bump in memory for public events. *European Journal of Cognitive Psychology, 20*(4), 738–764. doi: 10.1080/09541440701554409

Jaques, E. (1967). The midlife crisis. In R. Owen (Ed.), *Middle age.* London: BBC.

Javaid, M. K., Crozier, S. R., Harvey, N. C., Gale, C. R., Dennison, E. M., Boucher, B. J., . . . Princess Anne Hospital Study Group. (2006). Maternal vitamin D status during pregnancy and childhood bone mass at age 9 years: A longitudinal study. *Lancet, 367*(9504), 36–43.

Jee, S. H., Sull, J. W., Park, J., Lee, S., Ohrr, H., Guallar, E., & Samet, J. M. (2006). Body-mass index and mortality in Korean men and women. *New England Journal of Medicine, 355*, 779–787.

Jensen, A. R. (1969). How much can we boost IQ and scholastic achievement? *Harvard Educational Review, 39*, 1–123.

Jenson, L. A. (1997). Different worldviews, different morals: America's culture war divide. *Human Development, 40*, 325–344.

Jeynes, W. H., & Littell, S. W. (2000). A meta-analysis of studies examining the effect of whole language instruction on the literacy of low-SES students. *Elementary School Journal, 101*(1), 21–33.

Ji, B. T., Shu, X. O., Linet, M. S., Zheng, W., Wacholder, S., Gao, Y. T., . . . Jin, F. (1997). Paternal cigarette smoking and the risk of childhood cancer among offspring of nonsmoking mothers. *Journal of the National Cancer Institute, 89*, 238–244.

Jia, Y., Way, N., Ling, G., Yoshikawa, H., Chen, X., Hughes, D., . . . Lu, Z. (2009). The influence of student perceptions of school climate on socioemotional and academic adjustment: A comparison of Chinese and American adolescents. *Child Development, 80*(5), 1514–1530.

Jiao, S., Ji, G., & Jing, Q. (1996). Cognitive development of Chinese urban only children and children with siblings. *Child Development, 67*, 387–395.

Jipson, J. L., & Gelman, S. A. (2007). Robots and rodents: Children's inferences about living and nonliving kinds. *Child Development, 78*(6), 1675–1688.

Ji-Yeon, K., McHale, S. M., Crouter, A. C., & Osgood, D. W. (2007). Longitudinal linkages between sibling relationships and adjustment from middle childhood through adolescence. *Developmental Psychology, 43*(4), 960–973.

Jodl, K. M., Michael, A., Malanchuk, O., Eccles, J. S., & Sameroff, A. (2001). Parents' roles in shaping early adolescents' occupational aspirations. *Child Development, 72*(4), 1247–1265.

Joe, S., Baser, R. E., Breeden, G., Neighbors, H. W., & Jackson, J. S. (2006). Prevalence of and risk factors for lifetime suicide attempts among blacks in the United States. *Journal of the American Medical Association, 296*, 2112–2123.

Johansson, B., Hofer, S. M., Allaire, J. C., Maldonado-Molina, M. M., Piccinin, A. M., Berg, S., . . . McClearn, G. E. (2004). Change in cognitive capabilities in the oldest old: The effects of proximity to death in genetically related individuals over a 6-year period. *Psychology and Aging, 19*, 145–156.

Johnson, A. J., Becker, J. A. H., Craig, E. A., Gilchrist, E. S., & Haigh, M. M. (2009). Changes in friendship commitment: Comparing geographically close and long-distance young-adult friendships. *Communication Quarterly, 57*(4), 395–415.

Johnson, C. L. (1995). Cultural diversity in the late-life family. In R. Blieszner & V. Hilkevitch (Eds.), *Handbook of aging and the family* (pp. 307–331). Westport, CT: Greenwood Press.

Johnson, C. L., & Troll, L. E. (1994). Constraints and facilitators to friendships in late late life. *Gerontologist, 34*, 79–87.

Johnson, C. P., Myers, S. M., & the Council on Children with Disabilities. (2007). Identification and evaluation of children with autism spectrum disorders. *Pediatrics, 120*, 1183–1215.

Johnson, D. J., Jaeger, E., Randolph, S. M., Cauce, A. M., Ward, J., & National Institute of Child Health and Human Development Early Child Care Research Network. (2003). Studying the effects of early child care experiences on the development of children of color in the United States: Toward a more inclusive research agenda. *Child Development, 74*, 1227–1244.

Johnson, J. G., Cohen, P., Gould, M. S., Kasen, S., Brown, J., & Brook, J. S. (2002). Childhood adversities, interpersonal difficulties, and risk for suicide attempts during late adolescence and early adulthood. *Archives of General Psychiatry, 59*, 741–749.

Johnson, M. H. (1998). The neural basis of cognitive development. In D. Kuhn & R. S. Siegler (Eds.), *Handbook of child psychology: Vol. 2. Cognition, perception, and language* (5th ed., pp. 1–49). New York: Wiley.

Johnson, R. A., Hoffmann, J. P., & Gerstein, D. R. (1996). *The relationship between family structure and adolescent substance use* (DHHS Publication No. SMA 96–3086). Washington, DC: U.S. Department of Health and Human Services.

Johnson, S. J., & Rybash, J. M. (1993). A cognitive neuroscience perspective on age-related slowing: Developmental changes in the functional architecture. In J. Cerella, J. M. Rybash, W. J. Hoyer, & M. L. Commons (Eds.), *Adult information processing: Limits on loss* (pp. 143–175). San Diego: Academic Press.

Johnson, W., McGue, M., & Krueger, R. F. (2005). Personality stability in late adulthood: A behavioral genetic analysis. *Journal of Personality, 73*(2), 523–552.

Johnston, L. D., O'Malley, P. M., Bachman, J. G., & Schulenberg, J. E. (2006). *Monitoring the Future: National results on adolescent drug use: Overview of key findings, 2005* (NIH Publication No. 06-5882). Bethesda, MD: National Institute on Drug Abuse.

Johnston, L. D., O'Malley, P. M., Bachman, J. G., & Schulenberg, J. E. (2013). *Monitoring the Future: National results on drug use: 2012 Overview, key findings on adolescent drug use.* Ann Arbor: Institute for Social Research, The University of Michigan.

Jones, A. M. (2004). *Review of gap year provisions.* London: Department of Education and Skills.

Jones, C. L., Tepperman, L., & Wilson, S. J. (1995). *The future of the family.* Englewood Cliffs, NJ: Prentice Hall.

Jones, K. M., Whitbourne, S. K., & Skultety, K. M. (2006). Identity processes and the transition to midlife among baby boomers. In S. K. Whitbourne & S. L. Willis (Eds.), *The baby boomers grow up: Contemporary perspectives on midlife* (pp. 149–164). Mahwah, NJ: Erlbaum.

Jones, N. A., Field, T., Fox, N. A., Davalos, M., Lundy, B., & Hart, S. (1998). Newborns of mothers with depressive symptoms are physiologically less developed. *Infant Behavior & Development, 21*(3), 537–541.

Jones, N. A., Field, T., Fox, N. A., Lundy, B., & Davalos, M. (1997). EEG activation in one-month-old infants of depressed mothers. *Development and Psychopathology, 9*, 491–505.

Jopp, D., & Smith, J. (2006). Resources and life management strategies as determinants of successful aging: On the protective effect of selection, optimization, and compensation. *Psychology and Aging, 21*, 253–265.

Jordan, N. C., Kaplan, D., Oláh, L. N., & Locuniak, M. N. (2006). Number sense growth in kindergarten: A longitudinal investigation of children at risk for mathematics difficulties. *Child Development, 77*, 153–175.

Jordan, N. C., Kaplan, D., Raminemi, C., & Locuniak, M. N. (2009). Early math matters: Kindergarten number competence and later mathematics outcomes. *Developmental Psychology, 45*(3), 850–867.

Jose, A., O'Leary, K. D., & Moyer, A. (2010). Does premarital cohabitation predict subsequent marital stability and marital quality? A meta-analysis. *Journal of Marriage and Family, 72*(1), 105–116.

Josselson, R. (2003). Revisions: Processes of development in midlife women. In J. Demick & C. Andreoletti (Eds.), *Handbook of adult development.* New York: Plenum Press.

Jung, C. G. (1933). *Modern man in search of a soul.* New York: Harcourt Brace.

Jung, C. G. (1953). The stages of life. In H. Read, M. Fordham, & G. Adler (Eds.), *Collected works* (Vol. 2). Princeton, NJ: Princeton University Press. (Original work published 1931)

Jung, C. G. (1966). Two essays on analytic psychology. In *Collected works* (Vol. 7). Princeton, NJ: Princeton University Press.

Jung, C. G. (1969). *The structure and dynamics of the psyche.* Princeton, NJ: Princeton University Press.

Jung, C. G. (1971). Aion: Phenomenology of the self (the ego, the shadow, the syzgy: Anima/animus). In J. Campbell (Ed.), *The portable Jung.* New York: Viking Penguin.

Jusczyk, P. W., & Hohne, E. A. (1997). Infants' memory for spoken words. *Science, 277*, 1984–1986.

Juster, F. T., Ono, H., & Stafford, F. P. (2004). *Changing times of American youth: 1981–2003* (Child Development Supplement). Ann Arbor, MI: University of Michigan Institute for Social Research.

Juul-Dam, N., Townsend, J., & Courchesne, E. (2001). Prenatal, perinatal, and neonatal factors in autism, pervasive developmental disorder—Not otherwise specified, and the general population. *Pediatrics, 107*(4), e63.

Just, M. A., Cherkassky, V. L., Keller, T. A., Kana, R. K., & Minshew, N. J. (2007). Functional and anatomical cortical underconnectivity in autism: Evidence from an fMRI study of an executive function task and corpus callosum morphometry. *Cerebral Cortex, 17*(4), 951–961.

Jyhla, M. (2004). Old age and loneliness: Cross-sectional and longitudinal analyses in the Tampere Longitudinal Study on Aging. *Canadian Journal on Aging, 23*(2), 157–168.

Kaczynski, K. J., Lindahl, K. M., Malik, N. M., & Laurenceau, J. (2006). Marital conflict, maternal and paternal parenting, and child adjustment: A test of mediation and moderation. *Journal of Family Psychology, 20*, 199–208.

Kagan, J. (1997). Temperament and the reactions to unfamiliarity. *Child Development, 68*, 139–143.

Kagan, J. (2008). In defense of qualitative changes in development. *Child Development, 79*, 1606–1624.

Kagan, J., & Snidman, N. (2004). *The long shadow of temperament.* Cambridge, MA: Belknap Press.

Kahn, R. L., & Antonucci, T. C. (1980). Convoys over the life course: Attachment, roles, and social support. In P. B. Baltes & O. G. Brim Jr. (Eds.), *Life-span development and behavior* (pp. 253–286). New York: Academic Press.

Kaiser Family Foundation, Hoff, T., Greene, L., & Davis, J. (2003). *National survey of adolescents and young adults: Sexual health knowledge, attitudes and experiences.* Menlo Park, CA: Henry J. Kaiser Foundation.

Kalil, A., & Ziol-Guest, K. M. (2005). Single mothers' employment dynamics and adolescent well-being. *Child Development, 76*, 196–211.

Kalisch, T., Wilimzig, C., Kleibel, N., Tegenthoff, M., & Dinse, H. R. (2006). Age-related attenuation of dominant hand superiority. *PLoS ONE, 1*, 1–9.

Kalmijn, M., & Saraceno, C. (2008). A comparative perspective on intergenerational support: Responsiveness to parental needs in individualistic and familialistic cultures. *European Societies, 10*(3), 479–508.

Kalmuss, D., Davidson, A., & Cushman, L. (1992). Parenting expectations, experiences, and adjustment to parenthood: A test of the violated expectations framework. *Journal of Marriage and Family, 54*(3), 516–526.

Kanaya, T., Scullin, M. H., & Ceci, S. J. (2003). The Flynn effect and U.S. policies: The impact of rising IQ scores on American society via mental retardation diagnoses. *American Psychologist, 58*, 778–790.

Kaneda, T. (2006). *China's concern over population aging and health.* Retrieved from www.prb.org/Articles/2006/ChinasConcernOverPopulationAgingandHealth.aspx

Kanz, F., & Grossschmidt, K. (2006). Head injuries of Roman gladiators. *Forensic Science, 160*, 207–216.

Kaplan, H., & Dove, H. (1987). Infant development among the Ache of East Paraguay. *Developmental Psychology, 23*, 190–198.

Kaplan, M. K., Crespo, C. J., Huguet, N., & Marks, G. (2009). Ethnic/racial homogeneity and sexually transmitted diseases: A study of 77 Chicago Community Areas. *Sexually Transmitted Diseases, 36*(2), 108–111.

Kaplan, R. M., & Kronick, R. G. (2006). Marital status and longevity in the United States population. *Journal of Epidemiological Community Health, 60*, 760–765.

Kaplowitz, P. B. (2008). The link between body fat and the timing of puberty. *Pediatrics, 121* (2, Suppl. 3), S208–S217.

Karafantis, D. M., & Levy, S. R. (2004). The role of children's lay theories about the malleability of human attributes in beliefs about and volunteering for disadvantaged groups. *Child Development, 75*, 236–250.

Karasick, L. B., Tamis-LeMonda, C. S., & Adolph, K. E. (2011). Transition from crawling to walking and infants' actions with objects and people. *Child Development, 82*(4), 1199–1209.

Karney, B. R., & Bradbury, T. N. (1995). The longitudinal course of marital quality and stability: A review of theory, method, and research. *Psychological Bulletin, 118*, 3–34.

Kasper, J. D., Pezzin, L. E., & Rice, J. B. (2010). Stability and changes in living arrangements: Relationship to nursing home admission and timing of placement. *Journals of Gerontology, 65B*(Series B), 783–791.

Katchadourian, H. (1987). *Fifty: Midlife in perspective.* New York: W. H. Freeman.

Katzman, R. (1993). Education and prevalence of Alzheimer's disease. *Neurology, 43*, 13–20.

Kaufman, A. S., & Kaufman, N. L. (1983). *Kaufman Assessment Battery for Children: Administration and scoring manual.* Circle Pines, MN: American Guidance Service.

Kaufman, A. S., & Kaufman, N. L. (2003). *Kaufman Assessment Battery for Children* (2nd ed.). Circle Pines, MN: American Guidance Service.

Kaukinen, C. (2004). Status compatibility, physical violence, and emotional abuse in intimate relationships. *Journal of Marriage and Family, 66*, 452–471.

Kawabata, Y., & Crick, N. (2008). The roles of cross-racial/ethnic friendships in social adjustment. *Developmental Psychology, 44*(4), 1177–1183.

Kaye, E. K., Valencia, A., Baba, N., Spiro, A., Dietrich, T., & Garcia, R. I. (2010). Tooth loss and periodontal disease predict poor cognitive function in older men. *Journal of the American Geriatrics Society, 58*(4), 713–718.

Kazdin, A. E., & Benjet, C. (2003). Spanking children: Evidence and issues. *Current Directions in Psychological Science, 12*, 99–103.

Kearney, M. S., & Levine, P. B. (2014). *Media Influences on Social Outcomes: The Impact of MTV's 16 and Pregnant on Teen Childbearing* (No. w19795). National Bureau of Economic Research.

Kearney, P. M., Whelton, M., Reynolds, K., Muntner, P., Whelton, P. K., & He, J. (2005). Global burden of hypertension: Analysis of worldwide data. *Lancet, 365*, 217–223.

Keegan, C., Gross, S., Fisher, L., & Remez, S. (2004). *Boomers at midlife: The AARP Life Stage Study: Executive summary. Wave 3.* Washington, DC: American Association of Retired Persons.

Keegan, R. T. (1996). *Creativity from childhood to adulthood: A difference of degree and not of kind* (New Directions for Child Development, No. 72, pp. 57–66). San Francisco: Jossey-Bass.

Keel, P. K., & Klump, K. L. (2003). Are eating disorders culture-bound syndromes? Implications for conceptualizing their etiology. *Psychological Bulletin, 129*, 747–769.

Keenan, K., & Shaw, D. (1997). Developmental and social influences on young girls' early problem behavior. *Psychological Bulletin, 121*(1), 95–113.

Kefalas, M., Furstenberg, F., & Napolitano, L. (2005, September). *Marriage is more than being together: The meaning of marriage among young adults in the United States.* Network on Transitions to Adulthood Research Working Paper.

Keijsers, L., Branje, S. J. T., Frijns, T., Finkenauer, C., & Meeus, W. (2010). Gender differences in keeping secrets from parents in adolescence. *Developmental Psychology, 46*(1), 293–298.

Keil, F. C., Lockhart, K. L., & Schlegel, E. (2010). A bump on a bump? Emerging intuitions concerning the relative difficulty of the sciences. *Journal of Experimental Psychology. General, 139*(1), 1–15.

Kellehear, A., Pugh, E., & Atter, L. (2009). Home away from home? A case study of bedside objects in a hospice. *International Journal of Palliative Nursing, 15*(3), 148.

Keller, B. (1999, February 24). *A time and place for teenagers.* Retrieved from www.edweek.org/ew/vol-18/24studen.h18

Kelley, M. L., Smith, T. S., Green, A. P., Berndt, A. E., & Rogers, M. C. (1998). Importance of fathers' parenting to African-American toddlers' social and cognitive development. *Infant Behavior & Development, 21*, 733–744.

Kellman, P. J., & Arterberry, M. E. (1998). *The cradle of knowledge: Development of perception in infancy.* Cambridge, MA: MIT Press.

Kellogg, N., & the Committee on Child Abuse and Neglect. (2005). The evaluation of sexual abuse in children. *Pediatrics, 116*(2), 506–512.

Kellogg, R. (1970). Understanding children's art. In P. Cramer (Ed.), *Readings in developmental psychology today.* Delmar, CA: CRM.

Kelly, A. M., Wall, M., Eisenberg, M., Story, M., & Neumark-Sztainer, D. (2004). High body satisfaction in adolescent girls: Association with demographic, socio-environmental, personal, and behavioral factors. *Journal of Adolescent Health, 34*, 129.

Kelly, J. B., & Emery, R. E. (2003). Children's adjustment following divorce: Risk and resiliency perspectives. *Family Relations, 52*, 352–362.

Kelly, J. R. (1994). Recreation and leisure. In A. Monk (Ed.), *The Columbia retirement handbook* (pp. 489–508). New York: Columbia University Press.

Kellymom Breast Feeding and Parenting. (2006). *Average calorie and fat content of human milk.* Retrieved from http://www.kellymom.com/nutrition/milk/change-milkfat.html

Kemper, S., Thompson, M., & Marquis, J. (2001). Longitudinal change in language production: Effects of aging and dementia on grammatical complexity and propositional content. *Psychology and Aging, 16*, 600–614.

Kensinger, E. A. (2009). How emotion affects older adults' memories for event details. *Memory, 17*(2), 208–219.

Keppel, K. G., Pearcy, J. N., & Wagener, D. K. (2002). Trends in racial and ethnic-specific rates for the health status indicators: United States, 1990–1998. *Statistical Notes,* No. 23. Hyattsville, MD: National Center for Health Statistics.

Kere, J., Hannula-Jouppi, K., Kaminen-Ahola, N., Taipale, M., Eklund, R., Nopola-Hemmi, J., & Kaariainen, H. (2005, October). *Identification of the dyslexia susceptibility gene for DYX5 on chromosone 3.* Paper presented at the meeting of the American Society of Human Genetics, Salt Lake City, UT.

Kern, M. L., & Friedman, H. S. (2008). Do conscientious individuals live longer?: A quantitative review. *Health Psychology, 27*(5), 505–512.

Kerns, K. A., Don, A., Mateer, C. A., & Streissguth, A. P. (1997). Cognitive deficits in nonretarded adults with fetal alcohol syndrome. *Journal of Learning Disabilities, 30*, 685–693.

Kerr, D. C. R., Lopez, N. L., Olson, S. L., & Sameroff, A. J. (2004). Parental discipline and externalizing behavior problems in early childhood: The roles of moral regulation and child gender. *Journal of Abnormal Child Psychology, 32*(4), 369–383.

Kessler, R. C., Berglund, P., Demler, O., Jin, R., Merikangas, K. R., & Walters, E. E. (2005). Lifetime prevalence and age-of-onset distributions of DSM-IV disorders in the National Comorbidity Survey Replication. *Archives of General Psychiatry, 62*, 593–602.

Kestenbaum, R., & Gelman, S. A. (1995). Preschool children's identification and understanding of mixed emotions. *Cognitive Development, 10*, 443–458.

Keyes, C. L. M., & Ryff, C. D. (1998). Generativity in adult lives: Social structural contours and quality of life consequences. In D. P. McAdams & E. de St. Aubin (Eds.), *Generativity and adult development* (pp. 227–263). Washington, DC: American Psychological Association.

Keyes, C. L. M., & Ryff, C. D. (1999). Psychological well-being in midlife. In S. L. Willis & J. D. Reid (Eds.), *Life in the middle* (pp. 161–180). San Diego: Academic Press.

Keyes, C. L. M., & Shapiro, A. D. (2004). Social well-being in the United States: A descriptive epidemiology. In O. G. Brim, C. D. Ryff, & R. C. Kessler (Eds.), *How healthy are we? A national study of well-being at midlife* (pp. 350–372). Chicago: University of Chicago Press.

Keyes, K. M., Grant, B. M., & Hasin, D. S. (2007). Evidence for a closing gender gap in alcohol use, abuse and dependence in the United States population. *Drug and Alcohol Dependence, 93*, 21–29.

Khashan, A. S., Abel, K. M., McNamee, R., Pedersen, M. G., Webb, R. T., Baker, P. N., . . . Mortensen, P. B. (2008). Higher risk of offspring schizophrenia following antenatal maternal exposure to severe adverse life events. *Archives of General Psychiatry, 65*, 146–152.

Khaw, K. T., Wareham, N., Bingham, S., Welch, A., Luben, R., & Day, N. (2008). Combined impact of health behaviours and mortality in men and women: The EPIC-Norfolk Prospective Population Study. *PLoS Medicine, 5*(1), e12. doi: 10.1371/journal.pmed.0050012

Khoury, M. J., McCabe, L. L., & McCabe, E. R. B. (2003). Population screening in the age of genomic medicine. *New England Journal of Medicine, 348*, 50–58.

Kiecolt-Glaser, J. K., & Glaser, R. (2001). Stress and immunity: Age enhances the risks. *Current Directions in Psychological Science, 10*, 18–21.

Kiecolt-Glaser, J. K., & Newton, T. L. (2001). Marriage and health: His and hers. *Psychological Bulletin, 127,* 472–503.

Kiefe, C. I., Williams, O. D., Weissman, N. W., Schreiner, P. J., Sidney, S., & Wallace, D. D. (2000). Changes in U.S. health care access in the 90s: Race and income differences from the CARDIA study. Coronary artery risk development in young adults. *Ethnicity and Disease, 10,* 418–431.

Kiefer, K. M., Summer, L., & Shirey, L. (2001). What are the attitudes of young retirees and older workers? *Data Profiles: Young Retirees and Older Workers,* 5.

Kier, C., & Lewis, C. (1998). Preschool sibling interaction in separated and married families: Are same-sex pairs or older sisters more sociable? *Journal of Child Psychology and Psychiatry, 39,* 191–201.

Kim, J., McHale, S. M., Osgood, D. W., & Crouter, A. C. (2006). Longitudinal course and family correlates of sibling relationships from childhood through adolescence. *Child Development, 77,* 1746–1761.

Kim, J., Peterson, K. E., Scanlon, K. S., Fitzmaurice, G. M., Must, A., Oken, E., . . . Gillman, M. W. (2006). Trends in overweight from 1980 through 2001 among preschool-aged children enrolled in a health maintenance organization. *Obesity, 14*(7), 1107–1112.

Kim, J. E., & Moen, P. (2001). Moving into retirement: Preparation and transitions in late midlife. In M. E. Lachman (Ed.), *Handbook of midlife development* (pp. 487–527). New York: Wiley.

Kim, J. E., & Moen, P. (2002). Retirement transitions, gender, and psychological well-being: A life-course, ecological model. *Journal of Gerontology: Psychological Sciences, 57B,* P212–P222.

Kimball, M. M. (1986). Television and sex-role attitudes. In T. M. Williams (Ed.), *The impact of television: A natural experiment in three communities* (pp. 265–301). Orlando, FL: Academic Press.

Kim-Cohen, J., Caspi, A., Moffitt, T. E., Harrington, H., Milne, B. J., & Poulton, R. (2003). Prior juvenile diagnoses in adults with mental disorder: Developmental follow-back of a prospective-longitudinal cohort. *Archives of General Psychiatry, 60,* 709–717.

Kim-Cohen, J., Moffitt, T. E., Caspi, A., & Taylor, A. (2004). Genetic and environmental processes in young children's resilience and vulnerability to socioeconomic deprivation. *Child Development, 75,* 651–668.

Kimmel, D. (1990). *Adulthood and aging: An interdisciplinary, developmental view.* New York: Wiley.

Kimmel, M. S. (2002). "Gender symmetry" in domestic violence: A substantive and methodological research review. *Violence Against Women, 8,* 1332–1363.

King, B. M. (1996). *Human sexuality today.* Englewood Cliffs, NJ: Prentice Hall.

King, K. M., Meehan, B. T., Trim, R. S., & Chassin, L. (2006). Market or mediator? The effects of adolescent substance use on young adult educational attainment. *Addiction, 101,* 1730–1740.

King, M., & Bartlett, A. (2006). What same sex civil partnerships may mean for health. *Journal of Epidemiology and Community Health, 60,* 188–191.

King, W. J., MacKay, M., Sirnick, A., & The Canadian Shaken Baby Study Group. (2003). Shaken baby syndrome in Canada: Clinical characteristics and outcomes of hospital cases. *Canadian Medical Association Journal, 168,* 155–159.

Kinsella, K., & He, W. (2009). *An aging world: 2008. International Population Reports* (P95/09-1). Washington, DC: U.S. Government Printing. Office.

Kinsella, K., & Phillips, P. (2005, March). Global aging: The challenges of success. *Population Bulletin,* No. 1. Washington, DC: Population Reference Bureau.

Kinsella, K., & Velkoff, V. A. (2001). *An aging world: 2001* (U.S. Census Bureau, Series P95/01-1). Washington, DC: U.S. Government Printing Office.

Kinsley, C. H., & Meyer, E. A. (2010). The construction of the maternal brain: Theoretical comment on Kim et al. (2010). *Behavioral Neuroscience, 124*(5), 710–714.

Kirby, D., & Laris, B. (2009). Effective curriculum-based sex and STD/HIV education programs for adolescents. *Child Development Perspectives, 3,* 21–29.

Kirk, J. K., D'Agostino, R. B., Jr., Bell, R. A., Passmore, L. V., Bonds, D. E., Karter, A. J., & Narayan, K. M. V. (2006). Disparities in HbA1c levels between African-American and Non-Hispanic white adults with diabetes: A meta-analysis. *Diabetes Care, 29*(9), 2130–2136.

Kirkorian, H. L., Wartella, E. A., & Anderson, D. R. (2008). Media and young children's learning. *Future of Children, 18,* 39–61.

Kirschner, P. A., & Karpinski, A. C. (2010). Facebook and academic performance. *Computers in Human Behavior, 26*(6), 1237–1245.

Kirschner, S., & Tomasello, M. (2010). Joint music making promotes prosocial behavior in 4-year-old children. *Evolution and Human Behavior, 31*(5), 354-364. doi: 10.1016/j.evolhumbehav. 2010.04.004

Kisilevsky, B. S., Hains, S. M. J., Lee, K., Xie, X., Huang, H., Ye, H. H., Zhang, K., & Wang, Z. (2003). Effects of experience on fetal voice recognition. *Psychological Science, 14,* 220–224.

Kisilevsky, B. S., & Haines, S. M. J. (2010). Exploring the relationship between fetal heart rate and cognition. *Infant and Child Development, 19,* 60–75.

Kisilevsky, B. S., Haines, S. M., Lee, K., Xie, X., Huang, H., Ye, H. H., Zhang, K., & Wang, Z. (2003). Effects of experience on fetal voice recognition. *Psychological Science, 14*(3), 220–224.

Kisilevsky, B. S., Muir, D. W., & Low, J. A. (1992). Maturation of human fetal responses to vibroacoustic stimulation. *Child Development, 63,* 1497–1508.

Kitzmann, K. M., & Beech, B. (2006). Family-based interventions for pediatric obesity: Methodological and conceptual challenges from family psychology. *Journal of Family Psychology, 20,* 175–189.

Kitzmann, K. M., Dalton, W. T., III, Stanley, C. M., Beech, B. M., Reeves, T. P., Bescemi, J., . . . Midgett, E. L. (2010). Lifestyle interventions for youth who are overweight: A meta-analytic review. *Health Psychology, 29*(1), 91–101.

Kivett, V. R. (1991). Centrality of the grandfather role among older rural black and white men. *Journal of Gerontology: Social Sciences, 46*(5), S250–S258.

Kivett, V. R. (1993). Racial comparisons of the grandmother role: Implications for strengthening the family support system of older black women. *Family Relations, 42,* 165–172.

Kivett, V. R. (1996). The saliency of the grandmother-granddaughter relationship: Predictors of association. *Journal of Women and Aging, 8,* 25–39.

Klar, A. J. S. (1996). A single locus, RGHT, specifies preference for hand utilization in humans. *Cold Spring Harbor Symposia on Quantitative Biology, 61,* 59–65. Cold Spring Harbor, NY: Cold Spring Harbor Laboratory Press.

Klein, J. D., & the American Academy of Pediatrics Committee on Adolescence. (2005). Adolescent pregnancy: Current trends and issues. *Pediatrics, 116,* 281–286.

Klein-Velderman, M., Bakermans-Kranenburg, M. J., Juffer, F., & van IJzendoorn, M. H. (2006). Effects of attachment-based interventions on maternal sensitivity and infant attachment: Differential susceptibility of highly reactive infants. *Journal of Family Psychology, 20,* 266–274.

Klemenc-Ketis, Z., Kersnik, J., & Grmec, S. (2010). The effect of carbon dioxide on near-death experiences in out-of-hospital cardiac arrest survivors: A prospective observational study. *Critical Care, 14*(2), R56.

Klibanoff, R. S., Levine, S. C., Huttenlocher, J., Vasilyeva, M., & Hedges, L. V. (2006). Preschool children's mathematical knowledge: The effect of teacher "math talk." *Developmental Psychology, 42,* 59–69.

Kline, D. W., Kline, T. J. B., Fozard, J. L., Kosnik, W., Schieber, F., & Sekuler, R. (1992). Vision, aging, and driving: The problems of older drivers. *Journal of Gerontology: Psychological Sciences, 47*(1), P27–P34.

Kline, D. W., & Scialfa, C. T. (1996). Visual and auditory aging. In J. E. Birren & K. W. Schaie (Eds.), *Handbook of the psychology of aging* (pp. 191–208). San Diego: Academic Press.

Klohnen, E. C. (1996). Conceptual analysis and measurement of the construct of ego-resiliency. *Journal of Personality and Social Psychology, 70,* 1067–1079.

Klump, K. L., & Culbert, K. M. (2007). Molecular genetic studies of eating disorders: Current status and future directions. *Current Directions in Psychological Science, 16,* 37–41.

Knafo, A., & Plomin, R. (2006). Parental discipline and affection and children's prosocial behavior: Genetic and environmental links. *Journal of Personality and Social Psychology, 90*, 147–164.

Knecht, S., Drager, B., Deppe, M., Bobe, L., Lohmann, H., Floel, A., Ringelstein, E. B., & Henningsen, H. (2000). Handedness and hemispheric language dominance in healthy humans. *Brain: A Journal of Neurology, 123*(12), 2512–2518.

Knickmeyer, R., Baron-Cohen, S., Raggatt, P., & Taylor, K. (2005). Foetal testosterone, social relationships, and restricted interests in children. *Journal of Child Psychology and Psychiatry, 46*, 198–210.

Knickmeyer, R. C., Gouttard, S., Kang, C., Evans, D., Wilber, K., Smith, J. K., . . . Gilmore, J. H. (2008). A structural MRI study of human brain development from birth to 2 years. *Journal of Neuroscience, 28*(47), 12176–12182.

Knochel, K. A., Quam, J. K., & Croghan, C. F. (2011). Are old lesbian and gay people well served? Understanding the perceptions, preparation, and experiences of aging services providers. *Journal of Applied Gerontology, 30*(3), 370–389.

Kochanek, K. D., Murphy, S. L., Anderson, R. N., & Scott, C. (2004). Deaths: Final data for 2002. *National Vital Statistics Reports, 53*(5). Hyattsville, MD: National Center for Health Statistics.

Kochanska, G. (2001). Emotional development in children with different attachment histories: The first three years. *Child Development, 72*, 474–490.

Kochanska, G. (2002). Mutually responsive orientation between mothers and their young children: A context for the early development of conscience. *Current Directions in Psychological Science, 11*, 191–195.

Kochanska, G., & Aksan, N. (1995). Mother-child positive affect, the quality of child compliance to requests and prohibitions, and maternal control as correlates of early internalization. *Child Development, 66*, 236–254.

Kochanska, G., Aksan, N., & Carlson, J. J. (2005). Temperament, relationships, and young children's receptive cooperation with their parents. *Developmental Psychology, 41*, 648–660.

Kochanska, G., Aksan, N., & Joy, M. E. (2007). Children's fearfulness as a moderator of parenting in early socialization: Two longitudinal studies. *Developmental Psychology, 43*, 222–237.

Kochanska, G., Askan, N., Prisco, T. R., & Adams, E. E. (2008). Mother-child and father-child mutually responsive orientation in the first two years and children's outcomes at preschool age: Mechanisms of influence. *Child Development, 79*, 30–44.

Kochanska, G., Aksan, N., Knaack, A., & Rhines, H. M. (2004). Maternal parenting and children's conscience: Early security as moderator. *Child Development, 75*, 1229–1242.

Kochanska, G., Coy, K. C., & Murray, K. T. (2001). The development of self-regulation in the first four years of life. *Child Development, 72*(4), 1091–1111.

Kochanska, G., Friesenborg, A. E., Lange, L. A., & Martel, M. M. (2004). Parents' personality and infants' temperament as contributors to their emerging relationship. *Journal of Personality and Social Psychology, 86*, 744–759.

Kochanska, G., Gross, J. N., Lin, M. H., & Nichols, K. E. (2002). Guilt in young children: Development, determinants, and relations with a broader system of standards. *Child Development, 73*(2), 461–482.

Kochanska, G., Tjebkes, T. L., & Forman, D. R. (1998). Children's emerging regulation of conduct: Restraint, compliance, and internalization from infancy to the second year. *Child Development, 69*(5), 1378–1389.

Koechlin, E., Basso, G., Pietrini, P., Panzer, S., & Grafman, J. (1999). The role of the anterior prefrontal cortex in human cognition. *Nature, 399*, 148–151.

Koenig, L. B., & Vaillant, G. E. (2009). A prospective study of church attendance and health over the lifespan. *Health Psychology, 28*(1), 117–124.

Kogan, M. D., Newacheck, P. W., Honberg, L., & Strickland, B. (2005). Association between underinsurance and access to care among children with special health care needs in the United States. *Pediatrics, 116*, 1162–1169.

Kohlberg, L. (1966). A cognitive-developmental analysis of children's sex role concepts and attitudes. In E. E. Maccoby (Ed.), *The development of sex differences.* Stanford, CA: Stanford University Press.

Kohlberg, L. (1969). Stage and sequence: The cognitive-developmental approach to socialization. In D. A. Goslin (Ed.), *Handbook of socialization theory and research.* Chicago: Rand McNally.

Kohlberg, L. (1973). Continuities in childhood and adult moral development revisited. In P. Baltes & K. W. Schaie (Eds.), *Life-span developmental psychology: Personality and socialization* (pp. 180–207). New York: Academic Press.

Kohlberg, L. (1981). *Essays on moral development.* San Francisco: Harper & Row.

Kohlberg, L., & Ryncarz, R. A. (1990). Beyond justice reasoning: Moral development and consideration of a seventh stage. In C. N. Alexander & E. J. Langer (Eds.), *Higher stages of human development* (pp. 191–207). New York: Oxford University Press.

Kohn, D. B., & Candotti, F. (2009). Gene therapy fulfilling its promise. *New England Journal of Medicine, 360*, 518–521.

Kohn, M. L. (1980). Job complexity and adult personality. In N. J. Smelser & E. H. Erikson (Eds.), *Themes of work and love in adulthood.* Cambridge, MA: Harvard University Press.

Kohn, M. L., & Schooler, C. (1983). The cross-national universality of the interpretive model. In M. L. Kohn & C. Schooler (Eds.), *Work and personality: An inquiry into the impact of social stratification* (pp. 281–295). Norwood, NJ: Ablex.

Koivula, I., Sten, M., & Makela, P. H. (1999). Prognosis after community-acquired pneumonia in the elderly. *Archives of Internal Medicine, 159*, 1550–1555.

Kolata, G. (1999, March 9). Pushing limits of the human life span. *The New York Times.* Retrieved from www.nytimes.com/library/national/science/030999sci-aging.html

Kolata, G. (2010, June 23). Promise seen for detection of Alzheimer's. *The New York Times.* Retrieved from http://www.nytimes.com/2010/06/24/health/research/24scans.html

Kolbert, E. (1994, January 11). Canadians curbing TV violence. *The New York Times,* pp. C15, C19.

Kopp, C. B. (1982). Antecedents of self-regulation. *Developmental Psychology, 18*, 199–214.

Koren, G., Pastuszak, A., & Ito, S. (1998). Drugs in pregnancy. *New England Journal of Medicine, 338*, 1128–1137.

Korner, A. (1996). Reliable individual differences in preterm infants' excitation management. *Child Development, 67*, 1793–1805.

Koropeckyj-Cox, T. (2002). Beyond parental status: Psychological well-being in middle and old age. *Journal of Marriage and Family, 64*, 957–971.

Koropeckyj-Cox, T., Pienta, A. M., & Brown, T. H. (2007). Women of the 1950s and the "normative" life course: The implications of childlessness, fertility timing, and marital status for psychological well-being in late midlife. *International Journal of Aging and Human Development, 64*(4), 299–330.

Kost, K., Henshaw, S., & Carlin, L. (2013). *U.S. teenage pregnancies, births and abortions: National and state trends and trends by race and ethnicity, 2010.* Retrieved from http://www.guttmacher.org/pubs/USTPtrends.pdf

Kosterman, R., Graham, J. W., Hawkins, J. D., Catalano, R. F., & Herrenkohl, T. I. (2001). Childhood risk factors for persistence of violence in the transition to adulthood: A social development perspective. *Violence & Victims. Special Issue: Developmental Perspectives on Violence and Victimization, 16*(4), 355–369.

Kovas, Y., Hayiou-Thomas, M. E., Dale, P. S., Bishop, D. V. M., & Plomin, R. (2005). Genetic influences in different aspects of language development: The etiology of language skills in 4.5-year-old twins. *Child Development, 76*, 632–651.

Kowal, A. K., & Pike, L. B. (2004). Sibling influences on adolescents' attitudes toward safe sex practices. *Family Relations, 53*, 377–384.

Kozlowska, K., & Hanney, L. (1999). Family assessment and intervention using an interactive art exercise. *Australia and New Zealand Journal of Family Therapy, 20*(2), 61–69.

Kramer, A. F., Hahn, S., McAuley, E., Cohen, N. J., Banich, M. T., Harrison, C., . . . Vakil, E. (1999). Ageing, fitness and neurocognitive function. *Nature, 400*, 418–419.

Kramer, A. F., Erickson, K. I., & Colcombe, S. J. (2006). Exercise, cognition and the aging brain. *Journal of Applied Physiology, 101*, 1237–1242.

Kramer, D. A. (2003). The ontogeny of wisdom in its variations. In J. Demick & C. Andreolett (Eds.), *Handbook of adult development* (pp. 131–151). New York: Plenum Press.

Kramer, L. (2010). The essential ingredients of successful sibling relationships: An emerging framework for advancing theory and practice. *Child Development Perspectives, 4*(2), 80–86.

Kramer, L., & Kowal, A. K. (2005). Sibling relationship quality from birth to adolescence: The enduring contributions of friends. *Journal of Family Psychology, 19*, 503–511.

Kramer, M. S., Aboud, F., Mironova, E., Vanilovich, I., Platt, R. W., Matush, L., . . . Shaprio, S., for the Promotion of Breastfeeding Intervention Trial (PROBIT) Study Group. (2008). Breastfeeding and child cognitive development: New evidence from a large randomized trial. *Archives of General Psychiatry, 65*(5), 578–584.

Kramer, M. S., Chalmers, B., Hodnett, E. D., Sevkovskaya, Z., Dzikovich, I., Shapiro, S., . . . for the PROBIT Study Group. (2001). Promotion of Breastfeeding Intervention Trial (PROBIT): A randomized trial in the Republic of Belarus. *Journal of the American Medical Association, 285*, 413–420.

Krashen, S., & McField, G. (2005). What works? Reviewing the latest evidence on bilingual education. *Language Learner 1*(2), 7–10, 34.

Krause, N. (2004a). Common facets of religion, unique facets of religion, and life satisfaction among older African Americans. *Journal of Gerontology: Social Sciences, 59B*, S109–S117.

Krause, N. (2004b). Lifetime trauma, emotional support, and life satisfaction among older adults. *Gerontologist, 44*, 615–623.

Krause, N., & Rook, K. S. (2003). Negative interaction in late life: Issues in the stability and generalizability of conflict across relationships. *Journal of Gerontology: Psychological Sciences, 58B*, P88–P99.

Kraut, R., Kiesler S., Boneva, B., Cummings, J., Helgeson, V., & Crawford, A. (2002). Internet paradox revisited. *Journal of Social Issues, 58*, 49–74.

Kraut, R., Patterson, M., Lunmark, V., Kiesler, S., Mukopadhyay, T., & Scherlis, W. (1998). Internet paradox: A social technology that reduces social involvement and psychological well being? *American Psychologist, 53*, 1017–1031.

Kreider, R. M. (2003). Adopted children and stepchildren: 2000. *Census 2000 Special Reports*. Washington, DC: U.S. Bureau of the Census.

Kreider, R. M. (2005). Number, timing, and duration of marriages and divorces: 2001. *Household Economic Studies* (P70-97). Washington, DC: U.S. Census Bureau.

Kreider, R. M. (2008). Living arrangements of children: 2004. *Current Population Reports* (70-114). Washington, DC: U.S. Census Bureau.

Kreider, R. M. (2010). Increase in opposite-sex cohabiting couples from 2009 to 2010 in the Annual Social and Economic Supplement (ASEC) to the Current Population Survey (CPS). *Housing and Household Eonomic Statistics Working Paper.* Retrieved from http://www.census.gov/population/www/socdemo/Inc-Opp-sex-2009-to-2010.pdf

Kreider, R. M., & Ellis, R. (2011). Living arrangements of children: 2009. *Current Population Reports*, P70-126. Washington, DC: U.S. Census Bureau.

Kreider, R. M., & Fields, J. (2005). Living arrangements of children: 2001. *Current Population Reports* (P70-104). Washington, DC: U.S. Census Bureau.

Kreider, R. M., & Fields, J. M. (2002). Number, timing, and duration of marriages and divorces: Fall 1996. *Current Population Reports* (P70–80). Washington, DC: U.S. Census Bureau.

Kremen, A. M., & Block, J. (1998). The roots of ego-control in young adulthood: Links with parenting in early childhood. *Journal of Personality and Social Psychology, 75*(4), 1062–1075.

Krevans, J., & Gibbs, J. C. (1996). Parents' use of inductive discipline: Relations to children's empathy and prosocial behavior. *Child Development, 67*, 3263–3277.

Krishnamoorthy, J. S., Hart, C., & Jelalian, E. (2006). The epidemic of childhood obesity: Review of research and implications for public policy. *Society for Research in Child Development (SRCD) Social Policy Report, 20*(2).

Kritchevsky, S. B., Nicklas, B. J., Visser, M., Simonsick, E. M., Newman, A. B., Harris, T. B., . . . Pahor, M. (2005). Angiotensin-converting enzyme insertion/deletion genotype, exercise, and physical decline. *Journal of the American Medical Association, 294*, 691–698.

Kroenke, K., & Spitzer, R. L. (1998). Gender differences in the reporting of physical and somatoform symptoms. *Psychosomatic Medicine, 60*, 50–155.

Kroger, J. (1993). Ego identity: An overview. In J. Kroger (Ed.), *Discussions on ego identity* (pp. 1–20). Hillsdale, NJ: Erlbaum.

Kroger, J. (2003). Identity development during adolescence. In G. R. Adams & M. D. Berzonsky (Eds.), *Blackwell handbook of adolescence* (pp. 205–226). Malden, MA: Blackwell.

Kroger, J., & Haslett, S. J. (1991). A comparison of ego identity status transition pathways and change rates across five identity domains. *International Journal of Aging and Human Development, 32*, 303–330.

Kroger, J., Martinussen, M., & Marcia, J. E. (2009). Identity status change during adolescence and young adulthood: A meta-analysis. *Journal of Adolescence, 33*(5), 683–698.

Krueger, A. B. (2003, February). Economic considerations and class size. *Economic Journal, 113,* F34–F63.

Kübler-Ross, E. (1969). *On death and dying.* New York: Macmillan.

Kübler-Ross, E. (1970). *On death and dying* [Paperback]. New York: Macmillan.

Kübler-Ross, E. (Ed.). (1975). *Death: The final stage of growth.* Englewood Cliffs, NJ: Prentice Hall.

Kuczmarski, R. J., Ogden, C. L., Grummer-Strawn, L. M., Flegal, K. M., Guo, S. S., Wei, R., . . . Johnson, C. L. (2000). *CDC growth charts: United States* (Advance Data, No. 314). Washington, DC: Centers for Disease Control and Prevention, U.S. Department of Health and Human Services.

Kuczynski, L., & Kochanska, G. (1995). Function and content of maternal demands: Developmental significance of early demands for competent action. *Child Development, 66*, 616–628.

Kuhl, P., & Rivera-Gaxiola, M. (2008). Neural substrates of language acquisition. *Annual Review of Neuroscience, 31*, 511–534.

Kuhl, P. K. (2004). Early language acquisition: Cracking the speech code. *Nature Reviews Neuroscience, 5*, 831–843.

Kuhl, P. K., Andruski, J. E., Chistovich, I. A., Chistovich, L. A., Kozhevnikova, E. V., Ryskina, V. L., . . . Lacerda, F. (1997). Cross-language analysis of phonetic units in language addressed to infants. *Science, 277*, 684–686.

Kuhl, P. K., Conboy, B. T., Padden, D., Nelson, T., & Pruitt, J. (2005). Early speech perception and later language development: Implications for the "critical period." *Language Learning and Development, 1*, 237–264.

Kuhl, P. K., Williams, K. A., Lacerda, F., Stevens, K. N., & Lindblom, B. (1992). Linguistic experience alters phonetic perception in infants by 6 months of age. *Science, 255*, 606–608.

Kuhn, D. (2006). Do cognitive changes accompany developments in the adolescent brain? *Perspectives on Psychological Science, 1*, 59–67.

Kulmala, J., Viljanen, A., Sipilï, S., Pajala, S., Pärssinen, O., Kauppinen, M., . . . Rantanen, T. (2009). Poor vision accompanied with other sensory impairments as a predictor of falls in older women. *Age and Ageing, 38*(2), 162–167.

Kumwenda, N. I., Hoover, D. R., Mofenson, L. M., Thigpen, M. C., Kafulafula, G., Li, Q., . . . Taha, T. E. (2008). Extended antiretroviral prophylaxis to reduce breast-milk HIV-1 transmission. *New England Journal of Medicine, 359*, 119–129.

Kung, H.-C., Hoyert, D. L., Xu, J., & Murphy, S. L. (2007, September). *Deaths: Preliminary data for 2005* (Health E-Stats). Retrieved from www.cdc.gov/nchs/products/pubs/pubd/hestats/prelimdeaths05/prelimdeaths05.htm

Kung, H.-C., Hoyert, D. L., Xu, J., & Murphy, S. L. (2008). Deaths: Final data for 2005. *National Vital Statistics Reports, 56*(10). Hyattsville, MD: National Center for Health Statistics.

Kuperman, S., Chan, G., Kramer, J. R., Bierut, L., Buckholz, K. K., Fox, L., . . . Schuckit, M. A. (2005). Relationship of age of first drink to child behavioral problems and family psychopathology. *Alcoholism: Clinical and Experimental Research, 29*(10), 1869–1876.

Kupersmidt, J. B., & Coie, J. D. (1990). Preadolescent peer status, aggression, and school adjustment as predictors of externalizing

problems in adolescence. *Child Development, 61,* 1350–1362.
Kurdek, L. A. (2004). Are gay and lesbian cohabiting couples really different from heterosexual married couples? *Journal of Marriage and Family, 66,* 880–900.
Kurdek, L. A. (2005). What do we know about gay and lesbian couples? *Current Directions in Psychological Science, 5,* 251–254.
Kurdek, L. A. (2006). Differences between partners from heterosexual, gay, and lesbian cohabiting couples. *Journal of Marriage and Family, 68,* 509–528.
Kurdek, L. A. (2008). A general model of relationship commitment: Evidence from same-sex partners. *Personal Relationships, 15*(3), 391–405.
Kurjak, A., Kupesic, S., Matijevic, R., Kos, M., & Marton, M. (1999). First trimester malformation screening. *European Journal of Obstetrics & Gynecology and Reproductive Biology, 85*(1), 93–96.
Kuther, T., & McDonald, E. (2004). Early adolescents' experiences with, and views of, Barbie. *Adolescence, 39,* 39–51.
Kushnir, T., Xu, F., & Wellman, H. M. (2010). Young children use statistical sampling to infer the preferences of other people. *Psychological Science, 21,* 1134–1140. doi: 10.1177/0956797610376652
Kusumi, T., Matsuda, K., & Sugimori, E. (2010). The effects of aging on nostalgia in consumers' advertisement processing. *Japanese Psychological Research, 52,* 50–162. doi: 10.1111/j.1468-5884.2010.00431.x
Kutner, M., Greenberg, E., Jin, Y., Boyle, B., Hsu, Y., & Dunleavy, E. (2007). *Literacy in everyday life: Results from the 2003 National Assessment of Adult Literacy* (NCES 2007-480). Washington, DC: U.S. Department of Education, National Center for Education Statistics.
Labarere, J., Gelbert-Baudino, N., Ayral, A. S., Duc, C., Berchotteau, M., Bouchon, N., . . . Pons, J.-C. (2005). Efficacy of breast-feeding support provided by trained clinicians during an early, routine, preventive visit: A prospective, randomized, open trial of 226 mother-infant pairs. *Pediatrics, 115,* e139–e146.
Laberge, L., Tremblay, R. E., Vitaro, F., & Montplaisir, J. (2000). Development of parasomnias from childhood to early adolescence. *Pediatrics, 106,* 67–74.
Labouvie-Vief, G. (1990a). Modes of knowledge and the organization of development. In M. L. Commons, C. Armon, L. Kohlberg, F. Richards, T. Grotzer, & J. Sinnott (Eds.), *Adult development: Vol. 2. Models and methods in the study of adult and adolescent thought* (pp. 43–62). New York: Praeger.
Labouvie-Vief, G. (1990b). Wisdom as integrated thought: Historical and development perspectives. In R. J. Sternberg (Ed.), *Wisdom: Its nature, origins, and development* (pp. 52–83). Cambridge, UK: Cambridge University Press.
Labouvie-Vief, G. (2006). Emerging structures of adult thought. In J. J. Arnett & J. L. Tanner (Eds.), *Emerging adults in America: Coming of age in the 21st century* (pp. 59–84). Washington, DC: American Psychological Association.
Labov, T. (1992). Social and language boundaries among adolescents. *American Speech, 67,* 339–366.
Lacey, J. V., Jr., Mink, P. J., Lubin, J. H., Sherman, M. E., Troisi, R., Hartge, P., . . . Schairer, C. (2002). Menopausal hormone replacement therapy and risk of ovarian cancer. *Journal of the American Medical Association, 288,* 334–341.
Lachman, M. E. (2001). Introduction. In M. E. Lachman (Ed.), *Handbook of midlife development.* New York: Wiley.
Lachman, M. E. (2004). Development in midlife. *Annual Review of Psychology, 55,* 305–331.
Lachman, M. E., & Firth, K. M. P. (2004). The adaptive value of feeling in control during midlife. In O. G. Brim, C. D. Ryff, & R. C. Kessler (Eds.), *How healthy are we? A national study of well-being at midlife* (pp. 320–349). Chicago: University of Chicago Press.
Lachman, M. E., & James, J. B. (1997). Charting the course of midlife development: An overview. In M. E. Lachman & J. B. James (Eds.), *Multiple paths of midlife development* (pp. 1–17). Chicago: University of Chicago Press.
Ladd, G. W., Herald-Brown, S. L., & Reiser, M. (2008). Does chronic classroom peer rejection predict the development of children's classroom participation during the grade school years? *Child Development, 79*(4), 1001–1015.
LaFontana, K. M., & Cillessen, A. H. N. (2002). Children's perceptions of popular and unpopular peers: A multi-method assessment. *Developmental Psychology, 38,* 635–647.
Lagattuta, K. H. (2005). When you shouldn't do what you want to do: Young children's understanding of desires, rules, and emotions. *Child Development, 76,* 713–733.
Lagercrantz, H., & Slotkin, T. A. (1986). The "stress" of being born. *Scientific American, 254*(4), 100–107.
Lahey, B. B. (2009). Public health significance of neuroticism. *American Psychologist, 64*(4), 241–256.
Laible, D. J., & Thompson, R. A. (1998). Attachment and emotional understanding in preschool children. *Developmental Psychology, 34*(5), 1038–1045.
Laird, J., Lew, S., DeBell, M., & Chapman, C. (2006). *Dropout rates in the United States: 2002 and 2003* (NCES 2006-062). Washington, DC: U.S. Department of Education, National Center for Education Statistics.
Laird, R. D., Pettit, G. S., Bates, J. E., & Dodge, K. A. (2003). Parents' monitoring relevant knowledge and adolescents' delinquent behavior: Evidence of correlated developmental changes and reciprocal influences. *Child Development, 74,* 752–768.
Lakatos, K., Nemoda, Z., Toth, I., Ronai, Z., Ney, K., Sasvari-Szekely, M., & Gervai, J. (2002). Further evidence for the role of the dopamine D4 receptor gene (DRD4) in attachment disorganization: Interaction of the exon III 48 bp repeat and the –521 C/T promoter polymorphisms. *Molecular Psychiatry, 7,* 27–31.
Lakatos, K., Toth, I., Nemoda, Z., Ney, K., Sasvari-Szekely, M., & Gervai, J. (2000), Dopamine D4 receptor (DRD4) gene polymorphism is associated with attachment disorganization. *Molecular Psychiatry, 5,* 633–637.
Lalonde, C. E., & Werker, J. F. (1995). Cognitive influences on cross-language speech perception in infancy. *Infant Behavior and Development, 18,* 459–475.
Lamb, M. E. (1981). The development of father-infant relationships. In M. E. Lamb (Ed.), *The role of the father in child development* (2nd ed.). New York: Wiley.
Lamb, M. E., Frodi, A. M., Frodi, M., & Hwang, C. P. (1982). Characteristics of maternal and paternal behavior in traditional and non-traditional Swedish families. *International Journal of Behavior Development, 5,* 131–151.
Lamberts, S. W. J., van den Beld, A. W., & van der Lely, A. (1997). The endocrinology of aging. *Science, 278,* 419–424.
Lambeth, G. S., & Hallett, M. (2002). Promoting healthy decision making in relationships: Developmental interventions with young adults on college and university campuses. In C. L. Juntunen & D. R. Atkinson (Eds.), *Counseling across the lifespan: Prevention and treatment* (pp. 209–226). Thousand Oaks, CA: Sage.
Lamm, C., Zelazo, P. D., & Lewis, M. D. (2006). Neural correlates of cognitive control in childhood and adolescence: Disentangling the contributions of age and executive function. *Neuropsychologia, 44,* 2139–2148.
Landon, M. B., Hauth, J. C., Leveno, K. J., Spong, C. Y., Leindecker, S., Varner, M. W., . . . Gabbe, S. G., for the National Institute of Child Health and Human Development Maternal-Fetal Medicine Units Network. (2004). Maternal and perinatal outcomes associated with a trial of labor after prior cesarean delivery. *New England Journal of Medicine, 351,* 2581–2589.
Landry, S. H., Smith, K. E., Swank, P. R., & Miller-Loncar, C. L. (2000). Early maternal and child influences on children's later independent cognitive and social functioning. *Child Development, 71,* 358–375.
Landy, F. J. (1994, July–August). Mandatory retirement age: Serving the public welfare? *Psychological Science Agenda* (Science Directorate, American Psychological Association), pp. 10–11, 20.
Lang, F. R. (2001). Regulation of social relationships in later adulthood. *Journal of Gerontology: Psychological and Social Sciences, 56B,* P321–P326.
Långström, N., Rahman, Q., Carlström, E., & Lichtenstein, P. (2008). Genetic and environmental effects on same-sex sexual behavior: A population study of twins in Sweden. *Archives of Sexual Behavior.* Retrieved from https://commerce.metapress.com/content/2263646523551487/-resource-secured/?target=fulltext.pdf&sid=ur4ndr55ssgnkk550wsdrbuz&sh=www.springerlink.-com. doi: 10.1007/s10508-008-9386-1

Lankford, A. (2010). Do suicide terrorists exhibit clinically suicidal risk factors? A review of initial evidence and a call for future research. *Aggression and Violent Behavior, 15*(5), 334–340.

Lanphear, B. P., Aligne, C. A., Auinger, P., Weitzman, M., & Byrd, R. S. (2001). Residential exposure associated with asthma in U.S. children. *Pediatrics, 107*, 505–511.

Lansford, J. E. (2009). Parental divorce and children's adjustment. *Perspectives on Psychological Science, 4*(2), 140–152.

Lansford, J. E., Chang, L., Dodge, K. A., Malone, P. S., Oburu, P., Palmérus, K., . . . Quinn, N. (2005). Physical discipline and children's adjustment: Cultural normativeness as a moderator. *Child Development, 76*, 1234–1246.

Lansford, J. E., Criss, M. M., Dodge, K. A., Shaw, D. S., Pettit, G. S., & Bates, J. E. (2009). Trajectories of physical discipline: Early childhood antecedents and developmental outcomes. *Child Development, 80*(5), 1385–1402. doi: 10.1111/j.1467-8624.2009.01340.x

Lansford, J. E., Dodge, K. A., Pettit, G. S., Bates, J. E., Crozier, J., & Kaplow, J. (2002). A 12-year prospective study of the long-term effects of early child physical maltreatment on psychological, behavioral, and academic problems in adolescence. *Archives of Pediatric and Adolescent Medicine, 156*(8), 824–830.

Lanting, C. I., Fidler, V., Huisman, M., Touwen, B. C. L., & Boersma, E. R. (1994). Neurological differences between 9-year-old children fed breastmilk or formula-milk as babies. *Lancet, 334*, 1319–1322.

Laquatra, J., & Chi, P. S. K. (1998, September). *Housing for an aging-in-place society.* Paper presented at the European Network for Housing Research Conference, Cardiff, Wales.

Larsen, D. (1990, December–1991, January). Unplanned parenthood. *Modern Maturity*, pp. 32–36.

Larson, R. (2008). Family mealtimes as a developmental context. *Social Policy Report, 22*(4), 21.

Larson, R., & Seepersad, S. (2003). Adolescents' leisure time in the United States: Partying, sports, and the American experiment. In S. Verma & R. Larson (Eds.), *Examining adolescent leisure time across cultures: Developmental opportunities and risks* (New Directions for Child and Adolescent Development, No. 99, pp. 53–64). San Francisco: Jossey-Bass.

Larson, R., & Wilson, S. (2004). Adolescents across place and time: Globalization and the changing pathways to adulthood. In R. M. Lerner & L. Steinberg (Eds.), *Handbook of adolescent psychology* (2nd ed., pp. 299–331). Hoboken, NJ: Wiley.

Larson, R. W. (1997). The emergence of solitude as a constructive domain of experience in early adolescence. *Child Development, 68*, 80–93.

Larson, R. W., Moneta, G., Richards, M. H., & Wilson, S. (2002). Continuity, stability, and change in daily emotional experience across adolescence. *Child Development, 73*, 1151–1165.

Larson, R. W., & Verma, S. (1999). How children and adolescents spend time across the world: Work, play, and developmental opportunities. *Psychological Bulletin, 125*, 701–736.

Laumann, E. O., Das, W., & Waite, L. J. (2008). Sexual dysfunction among older adults: Prevalence and risk factors from a nationally representative U.S. probability sample of men and women 57–85 years of age. *Journal of Sexual Medicine, 5*(10), 2300–2311.

Laumann, E. O., & Michael, R. T. (Eds.). (2000). *Sex, love, and health in America: Private choices and public policies.* Chicago: University of Chicago Press.

Launer, L. J., Andersen, K., Dewey, M. E., Letenneur, L., Ott, A., Amaducci, L. A., . . . Hofman, A. (1999). Rates and risk factors for dementia and Alzheimer's disease: Results from EURODEM pooled analyses. *Neurology, 52*, 78–84.

Laursen, B. (1996). Closeness and conflict in adolescent peer relationships: Interdependence with friends and romantic partners. In W. M. Bukowski, A. F. Newcomb, & W. W. Hartup (Eds.), *The company they keep: Friendship in childhood and adolescence* (pp. 186–210). New York: Cambridge University Press.

Lautenschlager, N. T., Cox, K. L., Flicker, L., Foster, J. K., van Bockxmeer, F. M., Xiao, J., . . . Almeida, O. P. (2008). Effects of physical activity on cognitive function in older adults at risk for Alzheimer's disease. *Journal of the American Medical Association, 300*(9), 1027–1037.

Lavee, Y., & Ben-Ari, A. (2004). Emotional expressiveness and neuroticism: Do they predict marital quality? *Journal of Marriage and Family, 18*, 620–627.

Lavelli, M., & Fogel, A. (2005). Developmental changes in the relationship between the infant's attention and emotion during early face-to-face communication: The 2-month transition. *Developmental Psychology, 41*, 265–280.

Lavie, C. J., Kuruvanka, T., Milani, R. V., Prasad, A., & Ventura, H. O. (2004). Exercise capacity in adult African-Americans referred for exercise stress testing: Is fitness affected by race? *Chest, 126*, 1962–1968.

Lawler-Row, K. A., & Elliott, J. (2009). The role of religious activity and spirituality in the health and well-being of older adults. *Journal of Health Psychology, 14*(1), 43–52.

Lawn, J. E., Gravett, M. G., Nunes, T. M., Rubens, C. E., Stanton, C., & the Gapps Review Group. (2010). Global report on preterm birth and stillbirth (1 of 7): Definitions, description of the burden and opportunities to improve data. *BMS Pregnancy and Childbirth, 10*(Suppl. 1), S1. doi: 10.1186/1471-2393-10-S1-S1

Lawn, J. E., Cousens, S., & Zupan, J., for the Lancet Neonatal Survival Steering Team. (2005). 4 million neonatal deaths: When? Where? Why? *Lancet, 365*, 891–900.

Lawrence, E., Rothman, A. D., Cobb, R., Rothman, M. T., & Bradbury, T. (2008). Marital satisfaction across the transition to parenthood. *Journal of Family Psychology, 22*(1), 41–50.

Layne, J. E., & Nelson, M. E. (1999). The effects of progressive resistance training on bone density: A review. *Medicine and Science in Sports and Exercise, 31*, 25–30.

Lazarus, R. S., & Folkman, S. (1984). *Stress, appraisal, and coping.* New York: Springer.

Le, H. N. (2000). Never leave your little one alone: Raising an Ifaluk child. In J. S. DeLoache & A. Gottlieb (Eds.), *A world of babies: Imagined childcare guides for seven societies* (pp. 199–201). Cambridge, UK: Cambridge University Press.

Le Bourdais, C., & LaPierre-Adamcyk, E. (2004). Changes in conjugal life in Canada: Is cohabitation progressively replacing marriage? *Journal of Marriage and Family, 66*, 929–942.

Leadbeater, B. J., & Hoglund, W. L. G. (2009). The effects of peer victimization and physical aggression on changes in internalizing from first to third grade. *Child Development, 80*(3), 843–859.

Leaper, C., Anderson, K. J., & Sanders, P. (1998). Moderators of gender effects on parents' talk to their children: A meta-analysis. *Developmental Psychology, 34*(1), 3–27.

Leaper, C., & Smith, T. E. (2004). A meta-analytic review of gender variations in children's language use: Talkativeness, affiliative speech, and assertive speech. *Developmental Psychology, 40*, 993–1027.

Leblanc, M., & Ritchie, M. (2001). A meta-analysis of play therapy outcomes. *Counseling Psychology Quarterly, 14*, 149–163.

Lecanuet, J. P., Granier-Deferre, C., & Busnel, M.-C. (1995). Human fetal auditory perception. In J. P. Lecanuet, W. P. Fifer, N. A. Krasnegor, & W. P. Smotherman (Eds.), *Fetal development: A psychobiological perspective* (pp. 239–262). Hillsdale, NJ: Erlbaum.

Lee, F. R. (2004, July 3). Engineering more sons than daughters: Will it tip the scales toward war? *The New York Times*, pp. A17, A19.

Lee, G. R., Netzer, J. K., & Coward, R. T. (1995). Depression among older parents: The role of intergenerational exchange. *Journal of Marriage and Family, 57*, 823–833.

Lee, I., Djoussé, L., & Sesso, H. D. (2010). Physical activity and weight gain prevention. *Journal of the American Medical Association, 303*(12), 1173–1179.

Lee, J. M., Appugliese, D., Kaciroti, N., Corwyn, R. F., Bradley, R., & Lumeng, J. C. (2007). Weight status in young girls and the onset of puberty. *Pediatrics, 119*, e624–e630.

Lee, R. M., Grotevant, H. D., Hellerstedt, W. L., Gunnar, M. R., & The Minnesota International Adoption Project Team. (2006). Cultural socialization in families with internationally adopted children. *Journal of Family Psychology, 20*(4), 571–580.

Lee, S. J., Ralston, H. J. P., Drey, E. A., Partridge, J. C., & Rosen, M. A. (2005). Fetal pain: A systematic multidisciplinary review of the evidence. *Journal of the American Medical Association, 294*, 947–954.

Leerkes, E. M., Blankson, A. N., & O'Brien, M. (2009). Differential effects of maternal sensitivity to infant distress and nondistress on social-emotional functioning. *Child Development, 80*(3), 762–775.

Lefkowitz, E. S., & Fingerman, K. L. (2003). Positive and negative emotional feelings and behaviors in mother-daughter ties in late life. *Journal of Family Psychology, 17,* 607–617.

Lefkowitz, E. S., & Gillen, M. M. (2006). "Sex is just a normal part of life": Sexuality in emerging adulthood. In J. J. Arnett & J. L. Tanner (Eds.), *Emerging adults in America: Coming of age in the 21st century* (pp. 235–255). Washington, DC: American Psychological Association.

Legerstee, M., & Varghese, J. (2001). The role of maternal affect mirroring on social expectancies in three-month-old infants. *Child Development, 72,* 1301–1313.

Leigh, B. C. (1999). Peril, chance, adventure: Concepts of risk, alcohol use, and risky behavior in young adults. *Addiction, 94*(3), 371–383.

Leman, P. J., Ahmed, S., & Ozarow, L. (2005). Gender, gender relations, and the social dynamics of children's conversations. *Developmental Psychology, 41,* 64–74.

Lemke, M., Miller, D., Johnson, J., Krenze, T., Alvarez-Rojas, L., Kastberg, D., & Jocelyn, L. (2005). *Highlights from the 2003 International Adult Literacy and Lifeskills Survey (ALL) Revised* (NCES 2005-117). Washington, DC: National Center for Education Statistics.

Lemke, M., Sen, A., Pahlke, E., Partelow, L., Miller, D., Williams, T., . . . Jocelyn, L. (2004). *International outomes of learning in mathematics literacy and problem solving: PISA 2003. Results from the U.S. perspective* (NCES 2005-003). Washington, DC: National Center for Education Statistics.

Lenneberg, E. H. (1967). *Biological functions of language.* New York: Wiley.

Lenneberg, E. H. (1969). On explaining language. *Science, 164*(3880), 635–643.

Lenroot, R. K., & Giedd, J. N. (2006). Brain development in children and adolescents: Insights from anatomical magnetic resonance imaging. *Neuroscience and Biobehavioral Reviews, 30*(6), 718–729.

Leone, J. M., Johnson, M. P., Cohan, C. L., & Lloyd, S. E. (2004). Consequences of male partner violence for low-income minority women. *Journal of Marriage and Family, 66,* 472–490.

Lerman, C., Caporaso, N. E., Audrain, J., Main, D., Bowman, E. D., Lockshin, B., . . . Shields, P. G. (1999). Evidence suggesting the role of specific genetic factors in cigarette smoking. *Health Psychology, 18,* 14–20.

Lesch, K. P., Bengel, D., Heils, A., Sabol, S. Z., Greenberg, B. D., Petri, S., . . .Murphy, D. L. (1996). Association of anxiety-related traits with a polymorphism in the serotonin transporter gene regulatory region. *Science, 274,* 1527–1531.

Lesgold, A., Glaser, R., Rubinson, H., Klopfer, D., Feltovich, P., & Wang, Y. (1988). Expertise in a complex skill: Diagnosing X-ray pictures. In M. T. H. Chi, R. Glaser, & M. J. Farr (Eds.), *The nature of expertise* (pp. 311–342). Hillsdale, NJ: Erlbaum.

Leslie, A. M. (1982). The perception of causality in infants. *Perception, 11,* 173–186.

Leslie, A. M. (1984). Spatiotemporal continuity and the perception of causality in infants. *Perception, 13,* 287–305.

Leslie, A. M. (1995). A theory of agency. In D. Sperber, D. Premack, & A. J. Premack (Eds.), *Causal cognition* (pp. 121–149). Oxford: Clarendon Press.

Leslie, L. K., Newman, T. B., Chesney, J., & Perrin, J. M. (2005). The Food and Drug Administration's deliberations on antidepressant use in pediatric patients. *Pediatrics, 116,* 195–204.

Lester, B. M., & Boukydis, C. F. Z. (1985). *Infant crying: Theoretical and research perspectives.* New York: Plenum Press.

LeVay, S. (1991). A difference in hypothalamic structure between heterosexual and homosexual men. *Science, 253,* 1034–1037.

Levenstein, S., Ackerman, S., Kiecolt-Glaser, J. K., & Dubois, A. (1999). Stress and peptic ulcer disease. *Journal of the American Medical Association, 281,* 10–11.

Levine, R. (1980). Adulthood among the Gusii of Kenya. In N. J. Smelser & E. H. Erikson (Eds.), *Themes of work and love in adulthood* (pp. 77–104). Cambridge, MA: Harvard University Press.

LeVine, R. A. (1994). *Child care and culture: Lessons from Africa.* Cambridge, UK: Cambridge University Press.

LeVine, R. A., & LeVine, S. (1998). Fertility and maturity in Africa: Gusii parents in middle adulthood. In R. A. Schweder (Ed.), *Welcome to middle age! (and other cultural fictions)* (pp. 189–207). Chicago: University of Chicago Press.

Levine, L. J., & Edelstein, R. S. (2009). Emotion and memory narrowing: A review and goal-relevance approach. *Cognition and Emotion, 23*(5), 833–875.

Levinson, D. (1978). *The seasons of a man's life.* New York: Knopf.

Levinson, D. (1996). *The seasons of a woman's life.* New York: Knopf.

Levron, J., Aviram, A., Madgar, I., Livshits, A., Raviv, G., Bider, D., . . . Mashiach, S. (1998, October). *High rate of chromosomal aneupoloidies in testicular spermatozoa retrieved from azoospermic patients undergoing testicular sperm extraction for in vitro fertilization.* Paper presented at the 16th World Congress on Fertility and Sterility and the 54th annual meeting of the American Society for Reproductive Medicine, San Francisco.

Levy, B. R. (2003). Mind matters: Cognitive and physical effects of aging self-stereotypes. *Journal of Gerontology: Psychological Sciences, 58B,* P203–P211.

Levy, B., Zonderman, A., Slade, M., & Ferrucci, L. (2009). Age stereotypes held earlier in life predict cardiovascular events in later life. *Psychological Science, 20*(3), 296–298. doi: 10.1111/j.1467-9280.2009.02298.x

Levy-Shiff, R., Zoran, N., & Shulman, S. (1997). International and domestic adoption: Child, parents, and family adjustment. *International Journal of Behavioral Development, 20,* 109–129.

Lewinsohn, P. M., Gotlib, I. H., Lewinsohn, M., Seeley, J. R., & Allen, N. B. (1998). Gender differences in anxiety disorders and anxiety symptoms in adolescence. *Journal of Abnormal Psychology, 107,* 109–117.

Lewis, B. H., Legato, M., & Fisch, H. (2006). Medical implications of the male biological clock. *Journal of the American Medical Association, 19,* 2369–2371.

Lewis, M. (1995). Self-conscious emotions. *American Scientist, 83,* 68–78.

Lewis, M. (1997). The self in self-conscious emotions. In S. G. Snodgrass & R. L. Thompson (Eds.), *The self across psychology: Self-recognition, self-awareness, and the self-concept: Vol. 818.* New York: New York Academy of Sciences.

Lewis, M. (1998). Emotional competence and development. In D. Pushkar, W. Bukowski, A. E. Schwartzman, D. M. Stack, & D. R. White (Eds.), *Improving competence across the lifespan* (pp. 27–36). New York: Plenum Press.

Lewis, M. (2007). Early emotional development. In A. Slater & M. Lewis (Eds.), *Introduction to infant development.* Malden, MA: Blackwell.

Lewis, M., & Brooks, J. (1974). Self, other, and fear: Infants' reaction to people. In H. Lewis & L. Rosenblum (Eds.), *The origins of fear: The origins of behavior* (Vol. 2). New York: Wiley.

Lewis, M. I., & Butler, R. N. (1974). Life-review therapy: Putting memories to work in individual and group psychotherapy. *Geriatrics, 29,* 165–173.

Lewit, E., & Kerrebrock, N. (1997). Population-based growth stunting. *Future of Children, 7*(2), 149–156.

Li, J., Laursen, T. M., Precht, D. H., Olsen, J., & Mortensen, P. B. (2005). Hospitalization for mental illness among parents after the death of a child. *New England Journal of Medicine, 352,* 1190–1196.

Li, J., Precht, D. H., Mortensen, P. B., & Olsen, J. (2003). Mortality in parents after death of a child in Denmark: A nationwide follow-up study. *Lancet, 361,* 363–367.

Li, R., Chase, M., Jung, S., Smith, P. J. S., & Loeken, M. R. (2005). Hypoxic stress in diabetic pregnancy contributes to impaired embryo gene expression and defective development by inducing oxidative stress. *American Journal of Physiology: Endocrinology and Metabolism, 289,* 591–599.

Li, X., Li, S., Ulusoy, E., Chen, W., Srinivasan, S. R., & Berenson, G. S. (2004). Childhood adiposity as a predictor of cardiac mass in adulthood. *Circulation, 110,* 3488–3492.

Li, Y., & Ferraro, K. F. (2005). Volunteering and depression in later life: Social benefit or selection processes? *Journal of Health and Social Behavior, 46*(1), 68–84.

Lickliter, R., & Honeycutt, H. (2003). Developmental dynamics: Toward a biologically plausible evolutionary psychology. *Psychological Bulletin, 129,* 819–835.

Lickona, T. (Ed.). (1976). *Moral development and behavior.* New York: Holt.

Lieberman, M. (1996). *Doors close, doors open: Widows, grieving and growing.* New York: Putnam.

Liebman, B. (1995, June). A meat & potatoes man. *Nutrition Action Health Letter, 22*(5), 6–7.

Light, K. C., Girdler, S. S., Sherwood, A., Bragdon, E. E., Brownley, K. A., West, S. G., & Hinderliter, A. L. (1999). High stress responsivity predicts later blood pressure only in combination with positive family history and high life stress. *Hypertension, 33,* 1458–1464.

Light, S. N., Coan, J. A., Zahn-Waxler, C., Frye, C., Goldsmith, H. H., & Davidson, R. J. (2009). Empathy is associated with dynamic change in prefrontal brain electrical activity during positive emotion in children. *Child Development, 80,* 1210–1231. doi: 10.1111/j.1467-8624.2009.01326.x

Lillard, A., & Curenton, S. (1999). Do young children understand what others feel, want, and know? *Young Children, 54*(5), 52–57.

Lillard, A., & Else-Quest, N. (2006). The early years: Evaluating Montessori education. *Science, 313,* 1893–1894.

Lin, I., Goldman, N., Weinstein, M., Lin, Y., Gorrindo, T., & Seeman, T. (2003). Gender differences in adult childrens' support of their parents in Taiwan. *Journal of Marriage and Family, 65,* 184–200.

Lin, S., Hwang, S. A., Marshall, E. G., & Marion, D. (1998). Does paternal occupational lead exposure increase the risks of low birth weight or prematurity? *American Journal of Epidemiology, 148,* 173–181.

Lin, S. S., & Kelsey, J. L. (2000). Use of race and ethnicity in epidemiological research: Concepts, methodological issues, and suggestions for research. *Epidemiologic Reviews, 22*(2), 187–202.

Lin, Y., Seroude, L., & Benzer, S. (1998). Extended life-span and stress resistance in the Drosophila mutant methuselah. *Science, 282,* 943–946.

Lindau, S. T., Schumm, P., Laumann, E. O., Levinson, W., O'Muircheartaigh, C. A., & Waite, L. J. (2007). A study of sexuality and health among older adults in the United States. *New England Journal of Medicine, 357,* 762–774.

Linder, K. (1990). *Functional literacy projects and project proposals: Selected examples.* Paris: United Nations Educational, Scientific, and Cultural Organization.

Lindsay, R., Gallagher, J. C., Kleerekoper, M., & Pickar, J. H. (2002). Effect of lower doses of conjugated equine estrogens with and without medroxyprogesterone acetate on bone in early postmenopausal women. *Journal of the American Medical Association, 287,* 2668–2676.

Linnet, K. M., Wisborg, K., Obel, C., Secher, N. J., Thomsen, P. H., Agerbo, E., & Henriksen, T. B. (2005). Smoking during pregnancy and the risk of hyperkinetic disorder in offspring. *Pediatrics, 116,* 462–467.

Lippman, L. H., & McIntosh, H. (2010). *The demographics of spirituality and religiosity among youth: International and U. S. patterns (2010–21).* Retrieved from http://www.childtrends.org/Files//Child_Trends-2010_09_27_RB_Spirituality.pdf

Lissau, I., Overpeck, M. D., Ruan, J., Due, P., Holstein, B. E., Hediger, M. L., & Health Behaviours in School-Aged Children Obesity Working Group. (2004). Body mass index and overweight in adolescents in 13 European countries, Israel, and the United States. *Archives of Pediatric and Adolescent Medicine, 158,* 27–33.

Liszkowski, U., Carpenter, M., & Tomasello, M. (2008). Twelve-month-olds communicate helpfully and appropriately for knowledgeable and ignorant partners. *Cognition, 108,* 732–739.

Littleton, H., Breitkopf, C., & Berenson, A. (2006, August 13). *Correlates of anxiety symptoms during pregnancy and association with perinatal outcomes: A meta-analysis.* Presentation at the 114th annual convention of the American Psychological Association, New Orleans.

Litwin, H., & Shiovitz-Ezra, S. (2006). The association between activity and well-being in later life: What really matters? *Aging and Society, 26*(2), 225–242.

Livingston, G., & Parker, K. (2010, September 9). *Since the start of the Great Recession, more children raised by grandparents.* Retrieved from http://pewsocialtrends.org/2010/09/09/since-the-start-of-the-great-recession-more-children-raised-by-grandparents/

Liu, D., Sabbagh, M. A., Gehring, W. J., & Wellman, H. M. (2009). Neural correlates of children's theory of mind development. *Child Development, 80*(2), 318–326.

Liu, J., Raine, A., Venables, P. H., Dalais, C., & Mednick, S. A. (2003). Malnutrition at age 3 years and lower cognitive ability at age 11 years. *Archives of Pediatric and Adolescent Medicine, 157,* 593–600.

Lloyd, J. J., & Anthony, J. C. (2003). Hanging out with the wrong crowd: How much difference can parents make in an urban environment? *Journal of Urban Health, 80,* 383–399.

Lloyd, T., Andon, M. B., Rollings, N., Martel, J. K., Landis, J. R., Demers, L. M., & Kulin, H. E. (1993). Calcium supplementation and bone mineral density in adolescent girls. *Journal of the American Medical Association, 270,* 841–844.

LoBue, V., & DeLoache, J. (2011). Pretty in pink: The early development of gender-stereotyped colour preferences. *British Journal of Developmental Psychology, 29*(3), 656–667. doi: 10.1111/j.2044-835X.2011.02027.x

Lock, A., Young, A., Service, V., & Chandler, P. (1990). Some observations on the origin of the pointing gesture. In V. Volterra & C. J. Erting (Eds.), *From gesture to language in hearing and deaf children.* New York: Springer.

Lock, M. (1994). Menopause in cultural context. *Experimental Gerontology, 29,* 307–317.

Lock, M. (1998). Deconstructing the change: Female maturation in Japan and North America. In R. A. Shweder (Ed.), *Welcome to middle age! (and other cultural fictions)* (pp. 45–74). Chicago: University of Chicago Press.

Lockenhoff, C. E., Terracciano, A., & Costa, P. T. (2009). Five-factor model personality traits and the retirement transition: Longitudinal and cross-sectional associations. *Psychology and Aging, 24*(3), 722–728.

Lohse, N., Hansen, A. E., Pedersen, G., Kronborg, G., Gerstoft, J., Sørensen, H. T., . . . Obel, N. (2007). Survival of persons with and without HIV infection in Denmark, 1995–2005. *Annals of Internal Medicine, 146,* 87–95.

Lonczak, H. S., Abbott, R. D., Hawkins, J. D., Kosterman, R., & Catalano, R. F. (2002). Effects of the Seattle Social Development Project on sexual behavior, pregnancy, birth, and sexually transmitted disease. *Archives of Pediatric and Adolescent Medicine, 156,* 438–447.

Longnecker, M. P., Klebanoff, M. A., Zhou, H., & Brock, J. W. (2001). Association between maternal serum concentration of the DDT metabolite DDE and preterm and small-for-gestational-age babies at birth. *Lancet, 358,* 110–114.

Longo, M. R., & Haggard, P. (2010). An implicit body representation underlying human position sense. *Proceedings of the National Academy of Sciences of the U.S.A., 107*(26), 11727–11732. doi:10.1073/pnas.1003483107

Lonigan, C. J., Burgess, S. R., & Anthony, J. L. (2000). Development of emergent literacy and early reading skills in preschool children: Evidence from a latent-variable longitudinal study. *Developmental Psychology, 36,* 593–613.

Lopatto, E. (2007, May 12). *Marrying smarter, later leading to decline in US divorce rate: Survey shows figure is lowest since 1970.* Retrieved from www.boston.com/news/nation/articles/2007/05/12/marrying_smarter_later_leading_to_decline_in_us_divorce_rate/

Lopes, P. N., Brackett, M. A., Nezlek, J. B., Schütz, A., Sellin, L., & Salovey, P. (2004). Emotional intelligence and social interaction. *Personality and Social Psychology Bulletin, 30,* 1018–1034.

Lopes, P. N., Grewal, D., Kadis, J., Gall, M., & Salovey, P. (2006). Evidence that emotional intelligence is related to job performance and affect and attitudes at work. *Psicothema, 18*(Suppl. 1), 132–138.

Lopes, P. N., Salovey, P., & Straus, R. (2003). Emotional intelligence, personality, and the perceived quality of social relationships. *Personality and Individual Differences, 35,* 641–658.

Lorenz, K. (1957). Comparative study of behavior. In C. H. Schiller (Ed.), *Instinctive behavior.* New York: International Universities Press.

Lorsbach, T. C., & Reimer, J. F. (1997). Developmental changes in the inhibition of previously relevant information. *Journal of Experimental Child Psychology, 64,* 317–342.

Love, J. M., Kisker, E. E., Ross, C., Raikes, H., Constantine, J., Boller, K., . . . Vogel, C. (2005). The effectiveness of Early Head Start for 3-year-old children and their parents: Lessons for policy and programs. *Developmental Psychology, 41,* 885–901.

Love, J. M., Kisker, E. E., Ross, C. M., Schochet, P. Z., Brooks-Gunn, J., Paulsell, D., . . . Brady-Smith, C. (2002). *Making a difference in the lives of infants and toddlers and their families: The impacts of Early Head Start:*

Executive summary. Washington, DC: U.S. Department of Health and Human Services.

Lovelace, E. A. (1990). Basic concepts in cognition and aging. In E. A. Lovelace (Ed.), *Aging and cognition: Mental processes, self-awareness, and interventions* (pp. 1–28). Amsterdam: North-Holland, Elsevier.

Lu, T., Pan, Y., Kao, S.-Y., Li, C., Cohane, I., Chan, J., & Yankner, B. A. (2004). Gene regulation and DNA damage in the ageing human brain. *Nature, 429,* 883–891.

Lubell, K. M., Kegler, S. R., Crosby, A. E., & Karch, M. D. (2007). Suicide trends among youths and young adults aged 10–24 years—United States, 1990–2004. *Morbidity and Mortality Weekly Report, 56*(35), 905–908.

Lubell, K. M., Swahn, M. H., Crosby, A. E., & Kegler, S. R. (2004). Methods of suicide among persons aged 10–19 years—United States, 1992–2001. *Morbidity and Mortality Weekly Report, 53,* 471–474.

Lucas, R. E., & Diener, E. (2009). Personality and subjectivity of well-being. In E. Diener (Ed.), *The science of well-being: The collected works of Ed Diener* (pp. 75–102). New York: Springer.

Lucas, R. E., Clark, A. E., Georgellis, Y., & Diener, E. (2003). Reexamining adaptation and the set point model of happiness: Reactions to changes in marital status. *Journal of Personality and Social Psychology, 84,* 527–539.

Lucas-Thompson, R. G., Goldberg, W. A., & Prause, J. (2010). Maternal work early in the lives of children and its distal associations with achievement and behavior problems: A meta-analysis. *Psychological Bulletin, 136* (6), 915–942.

Lucile Packard Children's Hospital at Stanford. (2009). *Failure to thrive.* Retrieved from www.lpch.org/DiseaseHealthInfo/Health/Library/growth/thrive.html

Luciana, M. (2010). Adolescent brain development: Introduction to the special issue. *Brain and Cognition, 72*(1), 1–5.

Ludwig, D. S. (2007). Childhood obesity—The shape of things to come. *New England Journal of Medicine, 357,* 2325–2327.

Ludwig, J., & Phillips, D. (2007). The benefits and costs of Head Start. *Social Policy Report, 21,* 3–20.

Lugaila, T. A. (2003). A child's day: 2000 (Selected indicators of child well-being). *Current Population Reports* (P70–89). Washington, DC: U.S. Census Bureau.

Luke, B., Mamelle, N., Keith, L., Munoz, F., Minogue, J., Papiernik, E., & Johnson, T. R. B. (1995). The association between occupational factors and preterm birth: A United States nurses' study. *American Journal of Obstetrics and Gynecology, 173,* 849–862.

Luna, B., Garver, K. E., Urban, T. A., Lazar, N. A., & Sweeney, J. A. (2004). Maturation of cognitive processes from late childhood to adulthood. *Child Development, 75,* 1357–1372.

Lund, D. A. (1993a). Caregiving. In R. Kastenbaum (Ed.), *Encyclopedia of adult development* (pp. 57–63). Phoenix, AZ: Oryx Press.

Lund, D. A. (1993b). Widowhood: The coping response. In R. Kastenbaum (Ed.), *Encyclopedia of adult development* (pp. 537–541). Phoenix, AZ: Oryx Press.

Lund, H. D., Reider, B. D., Whiting, A. B., & Prichard, J. R. (2010). Sleep patterns and predictors of disturbed sleep in a large population of college students. *Journal of Adolescent Health, 46*(2), 125–132.

Lundy, B. L. (2003). Father—and mother—infant face-to-face interactions: Differences in mind-related comments and infant attachment? *Infant Behavior and Development, 26*(2), 200–212.

Lundy, B. L., Jones, N. A., Field, T., Nearing, G., Davalos, M., Pietro, P. A., . . . Kuhn, C. (1999). Prenatal depression effects on neonates. *Infant Behavior and Development, 22,* 119–129.

Luo, L., & Craik, F. I. M. (2008). Aging and memory: A cognitive approach. *Canadian Journal of Psychiatry, 53*(6), 346–353.

Lusardi, A., Mitchell, O. S., & Curto, V. (2009). *Financial literacy among the young: Evidence and implications for consumer policy* (No. 15352). Retrieved from http://papers.nber.org/papers/w15352

Lustig, C., & Flegal, K. (2008). Age differences in memory: Demands on cognitive control and association processes. *Advances in Psychology, 139,* 137–149.

Luthar, S. S., & Latendresse, S. J. (2005). Children of the affluent: Challenges to well-being. *Current Directions in Psychological Science, 14,* 49–53.

Lyons-Ruth, K., Alpern, L., & Repacholi, B. (1993). Disorganized infant attachment classification and maternal psychosocial problems as predictors of hostile-aggressive behavior in the preschool classroom. *Child Development, 64,* 572–585.

Lyyra, T., & Heikkinen, R. (2006). Perceived social support and mortality in older people. *Journal of Gerontology: Social Sciences, 61B,* S147–S152.

Maccoby, E. (1980). *Social development.* New York: Harcourt Brace Jovanovich.

Maccoby, E. E. (1984). Middle childhood in the context of the family. In W. A. Collins (Ed.), *Development during middle childhood.* Washington, DC: National Academy.

Maccoby, E. E. (1992). The role of parents in the socialization of children: A historical overview. *Developmental Psychology, 28*(6), 1006–1017.

Maccoby, E. E. (2000). Perspectives on gender development. *International Journal of Behavioral Development, 24*(4), 398–406.

Maccoby, E. E. (2002). Gender and group process: A developmental perspective. *Current Directions in Psychological Science, 11,* 54–58.

Maccoby, E. E., & Jacklin, C. N. (1987). Gender segregation in childhood. *Advances in Child Development and Behavior, 20,* 239–287.

Maccoby, E. E., & Lewis, C. C. (2003). Less day care or different day care? *Child Development, 74,* 1069–1075.

Maccoby, E. E., & Martin, J. A. (1983). Socialization in the context of the family: Parent-child interaction. In P. H. Mussen (Series Ed.) & E. M. Hetherington (Vol. Ed.), *Handbook of child psychology: Vol. 4. Socialization, personality, and social development* (pp. 1–101). New York: Wiley.

MacDonald, K. (1998). Evolution and development. In A. Campbell & S. Muncer (Eds.), *Social development* (pp. 21–49). London: UCL Press.

MacDonald, K. (1998). Evolution and development. In A. Campbell & S. Muncer (Eds.), *Social development* (pp. 21–49). London: UCL Press.

MacDonald, W. L., & DeMaris, A. (1996). Parenting stepchildren and biological children. *Journal of Family Issues, 17,* 5–25.

Macdonald, K., & Hershberger, S. (2005). Theoretical issues in the study of evolution and development. In R. Burgess & K. MacDonald (Eds.), *Evolutionary perspectives on human development* (2nd ed., pp. 21–72). Thousand Oaks, CA: Sage.

MacDorman, M., Declercq, E., & Menacker, F. (2011). Recent trends and patterns in cesarean and vaginal birth after cesarean (VBAC) deliveries in the United States. *Clinical Perinatology, 38*(2), 179–192. doi:10.1016/j.clp.2011.02.007

MacDorman, M. F., & Kirmeyer, S. (2009). Fetal and perinatal mortality, United States, 2005. *National Vital Statistics Reports, 57*(8). Hyattsville, MD: National Center for Health Statistics.

MacDorman, M. F., & Mathews, T. J. (2009). Behind international rankings of infant mortality: How the United States compares with Europe. *NCHS Data Brief, 23.* Hyattsville, MD: National Center for Health Statistics.

MacDorman, M. F., Menacker, F., & Declercq, E. (2010). Trends and characteristics of home and other out-of-hospital births in the United States, 1990–2006. *National Vital Statistics Reports, 58*(11), 1–14, 16.

MacDorman, M. F., Kirmeyer, S. E., & Wilson, E. C. (2012). Fetal and perinatal mortality, United States, 2006. *National Vital Statistics Reports, 60*(8). Hyattsville, MD: National Center for Health Statistics.

Mackenzie, C. S., Scott, T., Mather, A., & Sareen, J. (2008). Older adults' help-seeking attitudes and treatment beliefs concerning mental problems. *American Journal of Geriatric Psychiatry, 16*(12), 1010–1019.

MacKinnon-Lewis, C., Starnes, R., Volling, B., & Johnson, S. (1997). Perceptions of parenting as predictors of boys' sibling and peer relations. *Developmental Psychology, 33,* 1024–1031.

Macmillan, C., Magder, L. S., Brouwers, P., Chase, C., Hittelman, J., Lasky, T., . . . Velez–Borras, J., & for the Women and Infants Transmission Study. (2001). Head growth and neurodevelopment of infants born to HIV-infected drug-using women. *Neurology, 57,* 1402–1411.

MacMillan, H. M., Boyle, M. H., Wong, M. Y.-Y., Duku, E. K., Fleming, J. E., & Walsh, C. A. (1999). Slapping and spanking in childhood and its association with lifetime prevalence of psychiatric disorders in a general population sample. *Canadian Medical Association Journal, 161,* 805–809.

Macmillan, R., McMorris, B. J., & Kruttschnitt, C. (2004). Linked lives: Stability and change in maternal circumstances and trajectories of antisocial behavior in children. *Child Development, 75,* 205–220.

Madden, D. J., & Langley, I. K. (2003). Age-related changes in selective attention and perceptual load during visual search. *Psychology & Aging, 18,* 54–67.

Maestas, N. (2010). *Encouraging work at older ages. Testimony presented before the Senate Finance Committee on July 15, 2010* (CT-350). Rand Corporation. Retrieved from http://finance.senate.gov/imo/media/doc/071510nmtest.pdf

Maestripieri, D., Higley, J., Lindell, S., Newman, T., McCormack, K., & Sanchez, M. (2006). Early maternal rejection affects the development of monoaminergic systems and adult abusive parenting in Rhesus Macaques (Macaca mulatta). *Behavioral Neuroscience, 120*(5), 1017–1024.

Maheshwari, A. (2010). Overweight and obesity in infertility: Cost and consequences. *Human Reproductive Updates, 16*(3), 229–230.

Mahoney, J. L. (2000). School extracurricular activity participation as a moderator in the development of antisocial patterns. *Child Development, 71*(2), 502–516.

Mahoney, J. L., Lord, H., & Carryl, E. (2005). An ecological analysis of after-school program participation and the development of academic performance and motivational attributes for disadvantaged children. *Child Development, 76*(4), 811–825.

Main, M. (1995). Recent studies in attachment: Overview, with selected implications for clinical work. In S. Goldberg, R. Muir, & J. Kerr (Eds.), *Attachment theory: Social, developmental, and clinical perspectives* (pp. 407–470). Hillsdale, NJ: Analytic Press.

Main, M., Kaplan, N., & Cassidy, J. (1985). Security in infancy, childhood and adulthood: A move to the level of representation. In I. Bretherton & E. Waters (Eds.), *Growing points in attachment. Monographs of the Society for Research in Child Development, 50*(1–20), 66–104.

Main, M., & Solomon, J. (1986). Discovery of an insecure, disorganized/disoriented attachment pattern: Procedures, findings, and implications for the classification of behavior. In M. Yogman & T. B. Brazelton (Eds.), *Affective development in infancy.* Norwood, NJ: Ablex.

Maisonet, M., Christensen, K. Y., & Rubin, C., Holmes, A., Flanders, A. H., Heron, J., . . . Ong, K. K. (2010). Role of prenatal characteristics and early growth on pubertal attainment of British girls. *Pediatrics, 126*(3), 591–600.

Makino, M., Tsuboi, K., & Dennerstein, L. (2004). Prevalence of eating disorders: A comparison of Western and non-Western countries. *Medscape General Medicine, 6*(3). Retrieved from www.medscape.com/viewarticle/487413

Makridis, M., Gibson, R. A., McPhee, A. J., Collins, C. T., Davis, P. G., Doyle, L. W., . . . Ryan, P. (2009). Neurodevelopmental outcomes of preterm infants fed high-dose docosahexaenoic acid. *Journal of the American Medical Association, 301,* 175–182.

Malaguzzi, L. (1993). For an education based on relationships. *Young Children, 49*(1), 9–12.

Malaspina, D., Harlap, S., Fennig, S., Heiman, D., Nahon, D., Feldman, D., & Susser, E. S. (2001). Advancing paternal age and the risk of schizophrenia. *Archives of General Psychiatry, 58,* 361–371.

Malik, V. S., Willett, W. C., & Hu, F. B. (2012). Global obesity: Trends, risk factors and policy implications. *Nature Reviews: Endocrinology, 9,* 13–27. doi:10.1038/nrendo.2012.199/

Malloy, M. H. (2008). Impact of Cesarean section on neonatal mortality rates among very preterm infants in the United States, 2000–2003. *Pediatrics, 122,* 285–292.

Malone, F. D., Canick, J. A., Ball, R. H., Nyberg, D. A., Comstock, C. H., Bukowski, R., . . . D'Alton, M. E. (2005). First-trimester or second-trimester screening, or both, for Down's syndrome. *New England Journal of Medicine, 353,* 2001–2011.

Mampe, B., Friederici, A. D., Christophe, A., & Wermke, K. (2009). Newborns' cry melody is shaped by their native language. *Current Biology, 19*(23), 1994–1997. doi: 10.1016/j.cub.2009.09.064

Mancini, A. D., & Bonanno, G. A. (2006). Marital closeness, functional disability, and adjustment in late life. *Psychology and Aging, 21,* 600–610.

Mandara, J., Gaylord-Harden, N. K., Richards, M. H., & Ragsdale, B. L. (2009). The effects of change in racial identity and self-esteem on changes in African American adolescents' mental health. *Child Development, 80*(6), 1660–1675.

Mandler, J. M. (1998). Representation. In D. Kuhn & R. S. Siegler (Eds.), *Handbook of child psychology: Vol. 2. Cognition, perception, and language* (5th ed., pp. 255–308). New York: Wiley.

Mandler, J. M. (2007). On the origins of the conceptual system. *American Psychologist, 62,* 741–751.

Manlove, J., Ryan, S., & Franzetta, K. (2003). Patterns of contraceptive use within teenagers' first sexual relationships. *Perspectives on Sexual and Reproductive Health, 35,* 246–255.

Manning, W. D., Longmore, M. A., & Giodano, P. C. (2007). The changing institution of marriage: Adolescents' expectations to cohabit and to marry. *Journal of Marriage and Family, 69*(3), 559–575.

Mannix, L. J. (2008). Menstrual-related pain conditions: Dysmenorrhea and migraine. *Journal of Women's Health, 17*(5), 879–891. doi:10.1089/jwh.2007.0440

Manson, J. E., Allison, M. A., Rossouw, J. E., Carr, J. J., Langer, R. D., Hsia, J., . . . the WHI and WHI-CACS Investigators. (2007). Estrogen therapy and coronary-artery calcification. *New England Journal of Medicine, 356,* 2591–2602.

Manson, J. E., & Martin, K. A. (2001). Postmenopausal hormone-replacement therapy. *New England Journal of Medicine, 345,* 34–40.

March, J., & the TADS Team. (2007). The Treatment for Adolescents with Depression Study (TADS): Long-term effectiveness and safety outcomes. *Archives of General Psychiatry, 64,* 1132–1143.

March of Dimes Birth Defects Foundation. (1987). *Genetic counseling: A public health information booklet* (Rev. ed.). White Plains, NY: Author.

March of Dimes Birth Defects Foundation. (2004a). *Cocaine use during pregnancy* [Fact sheet]. Retrieved from www.marchofdimes.com/professionals/681_1169.asp

March of Dimes Birth Defects Foundation. (2004b). *Marijuana: What you need to know.* Retrieved from www.marchofdimes.com/pnhec/159_4427.asp

March of Dimes Foundation. (2002). *Toxoplasmosis* [Fact sheet]. Wilkes-Barre, PA: Author.

Marchman, V. A., & Fernald, A. (2008). Speed of word recognition and vocabulary knowledge in infancy predict cognitive and language outcomes in later childhood. *Developmental Science, 11,* F9–16.

Marcia, J. E. (1966). Development and validation of ego identity status. *Journal of Personality and Social Psychology, 3*(5), 551–558.

Marcia, J. E. (1979, June). *Identity status in late adolescence: Description and some clinical implications.* Address given at symposium on identity development, Rijksuniversitat Groningen, Netherlands.

Marcia, J. E. (1993). The relational roots of identity. In J. Kroger (Ed.), *Discussions on ego identity* (pp. 101–120). Hillsdale, NJ: Erlbaum.

Marcoen, A. (1995). Filial maturity of middle-aged adult children in the context of parent care: Model and measures. *Journal of Adult Development, 2,* 125–136.

Marcus, G. F., Vijayan, S., Rao, S. B., & Vishton, P. M. (1999). Rule learning by seven-month-old infants. *Science, 283,* 77–80.

Margolin, S. J., & Abrams, L. (2007). Individual differences in young and older adults' spelling: Do good spellers age better than poor spellers? *Aging, Neuropsychology, and Cognition, 14,* 529–544.

Markel, H. (2007). Is there an autism epidemic? *Medscape Pediatrics.* Retrieved from www.medscape.com/viewarticle/551540

Markoff, J. (1992, October 12). Miscarriages tied to chip factories. *The New York Times,* pp. A1, D2.

Markowitz, S., Friedman, M. A., & Arent, S. M. (2008). Understanding the relation between obesity and depression: Causal mechanisms and duplications for treatment. *Clinical Psychology: Science and Practice, 15,* 1–20.

Marks, H. (2000). Student engagement in instructional activity: Patterns in the elementary, middle, and high school years. *American Education Research Journal, 37,* 153–184.

Marks, N. F. (1996). Caregiving across the life-span: National prevalence and predictors. *Family Relations, 45,* 27–36.

Marks, N. F., Bumpass, L. L., & Jun, H. (2004). Family roles and well-being during the middle life course. In O. G. Brim, C. D. Ryff, & R. C. Kessler (Eds.), *How healthy are we? A national study of well-being at midlife* (pp. 514–549). Chicago: University of Chicago Press.

Marks, N. F., & Lambert, J. D. (1998). Marital status continuity and change among young and midlife adults. *Journal of Family Issues, 19*, 652–686.

Markus, H. R., Ryff, C. D., Curhan, K. B., & Palmersheim, K. A. (2004). In their own words: Well-being at midlife among high school-educated and college-educated adults. In O. G. Brim, C. D. Ryff, & R. C. Kessler (Eds.), *How healthy are we? A national study of well-being at midlife* (pp. 273–319). Chicago: University of Chicago Press.

Marmot, M. G., & Fuhrer, R. (2004). Socioeconomic position and health across midlife. In O. G. Brim, C. D. Ryff, & R. C. Kessler (Eds.), *How healthy are we? A national study of well-being at midlife.* Chicago: University of Chicago Press.

Marshall, N. L. (2004). The quality of early child care and children's development. *Current Directions in Psychological Science, 13*, 165–168.

Martikainen, P., Moustgaard, H., Murphy, M., Einio, E. K., Koskinen, S., Martelin, T., & Noro, A. (2009). Gender, living arrangements, and social circumstances as determinants of entry into and exit from long-term institutional care at older ages: A 6-year follow-up study of older Finns. *The Gerontologist, 49*(1), 34–45.

Martikainen, P., & Valkonen, T. (1996). Mortality after the death of a spouse: Rates and causes of death in a large Finnish cohort. *American Journal of Public Health, 86*, 1087–1093.

Martin, C. L., Eisenbud, L., & Rose, H. (1995). Children's gender-based reasoning about toys. *Child Development, 66*, 1453–1471.

Martin, C. L., & Fabes, R. A. (2001). The stability and consequences of young children's same-sex peer interactions. *Developmental Psychology, 37*, 431–446.

Martin, C. L., & Fabes, R. A. (2001). The stability and consequences of young children's same-sex peer interactions. *Developmental Psychology, 37*(3), 431–446.

Martin, C. L., & Ruble, D. (2004). Children's search for gender cues: Cognitive perspectives on gender development. *Current Directions in Psychological Science, 13*, 67–70.

Martin, C. L., Ruble, D. N., & Szkrybalo, J. (2002). Cognitive theories of early gender development. *Psychological Bulletin, 128*, 903–933.

Martin, J. A., Hamilton B. E., & Osterman, M. J. K. (2012). *Three decades of twin births in the United States, 1980–2009.* NCHS Data Brief No 80. Hyattsville, MD: National Center for Health Statistics.

Martin, J. A., Hamilton, B. E., Sutton, P. D., Ventura, S. J., Mathews, T. J., & Ostermam M. J. K. (2010). Births: Final data for 2008. *National Vital Statistics Reports, 59*(1). Hyattsville, MD: National Center for Health Statistics.

Martin, J. A., Hamilton, B. E., Sutton, P. D., Ventura, S. J., Menacker, F., & Kirmeyer, S. (2006). Births: Final data for 2004. *National Vital Statistics Reports, 55*(1). Hyattsville, MD: National Center for Health Statistics.

Martin, J. A., Hamilton, B. E., Sutton, P. D., Ventura, S. J., Menacker, F., Kirmeyer, S., & Mathews, T. J. (2009). Births: Final data for 2006. *National Vital Statistics Reports, 57*(7). Hyattsville, MD: National Center for Health Statistics.

Martin, J. A., Hamilton, B. E., Sutton, P. D., Ventura, S. J., Menacker, F., Kirmeyer, S., & Munson, M. (2007). Births: Final data for 2005. *National Vital Statistics Reports, 56*(6). Hyattsville, MD: National Center for Health Statistics.

Martin, J. A., Hamilton, B. E., Sutton, P. D., Ventura, S. J., Menacker, F., & Munson, M. L. (2005). Births: Final data for 2003. *National Vital Statistics Reports, 54*(2). Hyattsville, MD: National Center for Health Statistics.

Martin, J. A., Hamilton, B. E., Ventura, S. J., Menacker, F., & Park, M. M. (2002). Births: Final Data for 2000. *National Vital Statistics Reports, 50*(5). Hyattsville, MD: National Center for Health Statistics.

Martin, J. A., Hamilton, B. E., Ventura, S. J., et al. (2011). Births: Final data for 2009. *National Vital Statistics Reports, 60*(1). Hyattsville, MD: National Center for Health Statistics. Retrieved from http://www.cdc.gov/nchs/data/nvsr/nvsr60/nvsr60_01.pdf

Martin, J. A., Hamilton, B. E., Ventura, S. J., et al. (2013). Final data for 2011. *National Vital Statistics Reports, 62*(1). Hyattsville, MD: National Center for Health Statistics.

Martin, J. A., Hamilton, B. E., Ventura, S. J., Osterman, M. J. K., & Mathews, T. J. (2013). Births: final data for 2011. *National Vital Statistics Report, 62*(1).

Martin, J. A., Hamilton, B. E., Ventura, S. J., Osterman, M. J. K., Wilson, E. C., & Mathews, T. J. (2012). Births: Final data for 2010. *National Vital Statistics Report, 61*(1). Hyattsville, MD: National Center for Health Statistics.

Martin, J. A., Kirmeyer, S., Osterman, M., & Shepherd, R. A. (2009). Born a bit too early: Recent trends in late preterm births. *NCHS Data Brief, 24.* Hyattsville, MD: National Center for Health Statistics.

Martin, J. A., Osterman, M. J. K., & Sutton, P. D (2010). Are preterm births on the decline in the United States? Recent data from the National Vital Statistics System. *NCHS Data Brief, 39.* Hyattsville, MD: National Center for Health Statistics.

Martin, L. R., Friedman, H. S., & Schwartz, J. E. (2007). Personality and mortality risk across the life span: The importance of conscientiousness as a biopsychosocial attribute. *Health Psychology, 26*(4), 428–436.

Martin, N., & Montgomery, G. (2002, March 18). *Is having twins, either identical or fraternal, in someone's genes? Is there a way to increase your chances of twins or is having twins just luck?* Retrieved from http://genepi.qimr.edu.au/Scientific American Twins.html

Martin, P., Kliegel, M., Rott, C., Poon, L. W., & Johnson, M. A. (2007). Personality and coping among centenarians. In L. W. Poon & T. T. Perls (Eds.), *Annual review of gerontology and geriatrics, vol. 27: Biopsychosocial approaches to longevity* (pp. 89–106). New York: Springer.

Martin, P., Kliegel, M., Rott, C., Poon, L. W., & Johnson, M. A. (2008). Age differences and changes of coping behavior in three age groups: Findings from the Georgia Centenarian Study. *International Journal of Aging & Human Development, 66*(2), 97–114.

Martin, R., Noyes, J., Wisenbaker, J., & Huttunen, M. (2000). Prediction of early childhood negative emotionality and inhibition from maternal distress during pregnancy. *Merrill-Palmer Quarterly, 45*, 370–391.

Martin, S. P., & Parashar, S. (2006). Women's changing attitudes toward divorce, 1974–2002: Evidence for an educational crossover. *Journal of Marriage and Family, 68*, 29–40.

Martinez, G., Copen, C. E., & Abma, J. C. (2011). Teenagers in the United States: Sexual activity, contraceptive use, and childbearing, 2006–2010. National Survey of Family Growth. National Center for Health Statistics. *Vital Health Statistics 23*(31).

Martorell, S., & Martorell, G. (2006). Bridging uncharted waters: Down syndrome association of Atlanta outreach to Latino/a families. *American Journal of Community Psychology,* 37, 219–225.

Mashburn, A. J., Justice, L. M., Downer, J. T., & Pianta, R. C. (2009). Peer effects on children's language achievement during prekindergarten. *Child Development, 80*(3), 686–702.

Maslow, A. (1968). *Toward a psychology of living.* Princeton, NJ: Van Nostrand Reinhold.

Masse, L. C., & Tremblay, R. E. (1997). Behavior of boys in kindergarten and the onset of substance use during adolescence. *Archives of General Psychiatry, 54,* 62–68.

Masten, A. S., & Coatsworth, J. D. (1998). The development of competence in favorable and unfavorable environments: Lessons from research on successful children. *American Psychologist, 53*, 205–220.

Masters, W. H., & Johnson, V. E. (1966). *Human sexual response.* Boston: Little, Brown.

Mather, M. (2010). *U.S. children in single-mother families.* Washington, DC: Population Reference Bureau.

Mather, M., & Carstensen, L. L. (2003). Aging and attentional biases for emotional faces. *Psychological Science, 14,* 409–415.

Mather, M., & Lavery, D. (2012). *In U.S., proportion married at lowest recorded levels.* Population Reference Bureau. Retrieved from http://www.prb.org/Publications/Articles/2010/

Mathews, T. J., & MacDorman, M. F. (2008). Infant mortality statistics from the 2005 period linked birth/infant death data set. *National Vital Statistics Report, 57*(2). Hyattsville, MD: National Center for Health Statistics.

Mathews, T. J., & MacDorman, M. F. (2010). Infant mortality statistics from the 2006 period linked infant birth/death data set. *National Vital Statistics Reports, 58*(17). Hyattsville, MD: National Center for Health Statistics.

Mathie, A., & Carnozzi, A. (2005). *Qualitative research for tobacco control: A how-to introductory manual for researchers and development practitioners.* Ottawa, Ontario, Canada: International Development Research Centre.

Matsumoto, D., & Juang, L. (2008). *Culture and psychology* (4th ed.). Belmont, CA: Wadsworth, Cengage Learning.

Mattanah, J. F., Ayers, J. F., Brand, B. L., Brooks, L. J., Quimby, J. L., & McNary, S. W. (2010). A social support intervention to ease the college transition: Exploring main effects and moderators. *Journal of College Student Development, 51*(1), 93–108.

Maurer, D., & Lewis, T. L. (1979). Peripheral discrimination by three-month-old infants. *Child Development, 50,* 276–279.

Mayer, J. D., Salovey, P., & Caruso, D. (2002). *The Mayer-Salovey-Caruso Emotional Intelligence Test (MSCEIT).* Toronto, Ontario, Canada: Multi-Health Systems.

Mayo Clinic. (2005, December 7). *Infertility.* Retrieved from www.mayoclinic.com/health/infertility/DS00310

Mayo Foundation for Medical Education and Research. (2009, January). Beyond the human genome: Meet the epigenome. *Mayo Clinic Health Letter, 27*(1), pp. 4–5.

Mazzeo, R. S., Cavanaugh, P., Evans, W. J., Fiatarone, M., Hagberg, J., McAuley, E., & Startzell, J. (1998). ACSM position stand on exercise and physical activity for older adults. *Medicine and Science in Sports and Exercise, 30,* 992–1008.

McAdams, D. (1993). *The stories we live by.* New York: Morrow.

McAdams, D. P. (2001). Generativity in midlife. In M. E. Lachman (Ed.), *Handbook of midlife development* (pp. 395–443). New York: Wiley.

McAdams, D. P. (2006). The redemptive self: Generativity and the stories Americans live by. *Research in Human Development, 3,* 81–100.

McAdams, D. P., & de St. Aubin, E. (1992). A theory of generativity and its assessment through self-report, behavioral acts, and narrative themes in autobiography. *Journal of Personality and Social Psychology, 62,* 1003–1015.

McAdams, D. P., Diamond, A., de St. Aubin, E., & Mansfield, E. (1997). Stories of commitment: The psychosocial construction of generative lives. *Journal of Personality and Social Psychology, 72,* 678–694.

McCall, D. D., & Clifton, R. K. (1999). Infants' means-end search for hidden objects in the absence of visual feedback. *Infant Behavior and Development, 22*(2), 179–195.

McCallum, K. E., & Bruton, J. R. (2003). The continuum of care in the treatment of eating disorders. *Primary Psychiatry, 10*(6), 48–54.

McCartney, N., Hicks, A. L., Martin, J., & Webber, C. E. (1996). A longitudinal trial of weight training in the elderly: Continued improvements in year 2. *Journal of Gerontology: Biological and Medical Sciences, 51,* B425–B433.

McCartt, A. T. (2001). Graduated driver licensing systems: Reducing crashes among teenage drivers. *Journal of the American Medical Association, 286,* 1631–1632.

McCarty, M. E., Clifton, R. K., Ashmead, D. H., Lee, P., & Goubet, N. (2001). How infants use vision for grasping objects. *Child Development, 72,* 973–987.

McClearn, G. E., Johansson, B., Berg, S., Pedersen, N. L., Ahern, F., Petrill, S. A., & Plomin, R. (1997). Substantial genetic influence on cognitive abilities in twins 80 or more years old. *Science, 276,* 1560–1563.

McClintock, M. K., & Herdt, G. (1996). Rethinking puberty: The development of sexual attraction. *Current Directions in Psychological Science, 5*(6), 178–183.

McCrae, R. R. (2002). Cross-cultural research on the five-factor model of personality. In W. J. Lonner, D. L. Dinnel, S. A. Hayes, & D. N. Sattler (Eds.), *Online readings in psychology and culture* (Unit 6, Chapter 1). Bellingham, WA: Center for Cross-Cultural Research, Western Washington University.

McCrae, R. R., & Costa, P. T., Jr. (1984). *Emerging lives, enduring dispositions.* Boston: Little, Brown.

McCrae, R. R., Costa, P. T., Jr., & Busch, C. M. (1986). Evaluating comprehensiveness in personality systems: The California Q-set and the five-factor model. *Journal of Personality, 54,* 430–446.

McCrae, R. R., Costa, P. T., Jr., Ostendorf, F., Angleitner, A., Hebrícková, M., Avia, M. D., . . . Smith, P. B. (2000). Nature over nurture: Temperament, personality, and lifespan development. *Journal of Personality and Social Psychology, 78,* 173–186.

McCrink, K., & Wynn, K. (2004). Large-number addition and subtraction by 9-month-old infants. *Psychological Science, 15,* 776–781.

McCue, J. D. (1995). The naturalness of dying. *Journal of the American Medical Association, 273,* 1039–1043.

McDaniel, M., Paxson, C., & Waldfogel, J. (2006). Racial disparities in childhood asthma in the United States: Evidence from the National Health Interview Survey, 1997 to 2003. *Pediatrics, 117,* 868–877.

McDermott, R., Fowler, J. H., & Christakis, N. A. (2009). *Breaking up is hard to do, unless everyone else is doing it too: Social network effects on divorce in a longitudinal sample followed for 32 years.* Retrieved from http://ssrn.com/abstract=1490708

McDowell, D. J., & Parke, R. (2009). Parental correlates of children's peer relations: An empirical test of a tripartite model. *Developmental Psychology, 45*(1), 224–235.

McDowell, M., Fryar, C., Odgen, C., & Flegal, K. (2008). Anthropometric reference data for children and adults: United States, 2003–2006. *National Health Statistics Report* (No. 10). Hyattsville, MD: National Center for Health Statistics.

McDowell, M. A., Fryar, C. D., & Ogden, C. L. (2009). Anthropometric reference data for children and adults: United States, 1988–1994. National Center for Health Statistics. *Vital Health Statistics, 11*(249).

McElwain, N. L., & Volling, B. L. (2005). Preschool children's interactions with friends and older siblings: Relationship specificity and joint contributions to problem behavior. *Journal of Family Psychology, 19,* 486–496.

McFarland, R. A., Tune, G. B., & Welford, A. (1964). On the driving of automobiles by older people. *Journal of Gerontology, 19,* 190–197.

McGue, M. (1997). The democracy of the genes. *Nature, 388,* 417–418.

McGuffin, P., Owen, M. J., & Farmer, A. E. (1995). Genetic basis of schizophrenia. *Lancet, 346,* 678–682.

McGuffin, P., Riley, B., & Plomin, R. (2001). Toward behavioral genomics. *Science, 291,* 1232–1249.

McGuigan, F., & Salmon, K. (2004). The time to talk: The influence of the timing of adult–child talk on children's event memory. *Child Development, 75*(3), 669–686.

McHale, S. M., & Huston, T. L. (1985). The effect of the transition to parenthood on the marriage relationship. *Journal of Family Issues, 6*(4), 409–433.

McIlvane, J. M., Ajrouch, K. J., & Antonucci, T. C. (2007). Generational structure and social resources in mid-life influences on health and well-being. *Journal of Social Issues, 63,* 759–774.

McKenna, K. Y. A., & Bargh, J. A. (2000). Plan 9 from cyberspace: The implication of the Internet for personality and social psychology. *Personality and Social Psychology Review, 4,* 57–75.

McKusick, V. A. (2001). The anatomy of the human genome. *Journal of the American Medical Association, 286*(18), 2289–2295.

McLaughlin, D., Vagenas, D., Pachana, N. A., Begum, N., & Dobson, A. (2010). Gender differences in social network size and satisfaction in adults in their 70s. *Journal of Health Psychology, 15*(5), 671–679.

McLeod, C. M., Gopie, N., Hourihan, K. L., Neary, K. R., & Ozubko, J. D. (2010). The production effect: Delineation of a phenomenon. *Journal of Experimental Psychology: Learning, Memory, and Cognition, 36*(3), 671–685.

McLeod, R., Boyer, K., Karrison, T., Kasza, K., Swisher, C., Roizen, N., . . . Toxoplamosis Study Group. (2006). Outcome of treatment for congenital toxoplasmosis, 1981–2004: The national collaborative Chicago-based, congenital toxoplasmosis study. *Clinical Infectious Diseases: An Official Publication of the Infectious Diseases Society of America, 42*(10), 1383–1394.

McLoyd, V. C. (1990). The impact of economic hardship on black families and children: Psychological distress, parenting, and socioemotional development. *Child Development, 61,* 311–346.

McLoyd, V. C. (1998). Socioeconomic disadvantage and child development. *American Psychologist, 53,* 185–204.

McLoyd, V. C., & Smith, J. (2002). Physical discipline and behavior problems in African American, European American, and Hispanic children: Emotional support as a moderator. *Journal of Marriage and Family, 64*, 40–53.

McPherson, M., Smith-Lovin, L., & Brashears, M. E. (2006). Social isolation in America: Changes in core discussion networks over two decades. *American Sociological Review, 71*, 353–375.

McQueeny, T., Schweinsburg, B. C., Schweinsburg, A. D., Jacobus, J., Bava, S., Frank, L. R., & Tapert, S. F. (2009). Altered white matter integrity in adolescent binge drinkers. *Alcoholism: Clinical and Experimental Research, 33*(7), 1278–1285.

McQuillan, J., Greil, A. L., White, L., & Jacob, M. C. (2003). Frustrated fertility: Infertility and psychological distress among women. *Journal of Marriage and Family, 65*, 1007–1018.

McTiernan, A., Kooperberg, C., White, E., Wilcox, S., Coates, R., Adams-Campbell, L. L., . . . Ockene, J. (2003). Recreational physical activity and the risk of breast cancer in postmenopausal women: The Women's Health Initiative Cohort Study. *Journal of the American Medical Association, 290*, 1331–1336.

Mears, B. (2005, March 1). *High court: Juvenile death penalty unconstitutional: Slim majority cites "evolving standards" in American society.* Retrieved from http://cnn.com./2005/LAW/03/01/scotus.death.penalty

Medland, S. E., Duffy, D. L., Wright, M. J., Geffen, G. M., Hay, D. A., Levy, F., . . . Boomsma, D. I. (2009). Genetic influences on handedness: Data from 25,732 Australian and Dutch twin families. *Neuropsychologica, 47*(2), 333–337.

Mednick, S. C., Nakayama, K., Cantero, J. L., Atienza, M., Levin, A. A., Pathak, N., & Stickgold, R. (2002). The restorative effect of naps on perceptual deterioration. *Nature Neuroscience, 5*, 677–681.

Meeks, J. J., Weiss, J., & Jameson, J. L. (2003, May). Dax1 is required for testis formation. *Nature Genetics, 34*, 32–33.

Meezan, W., & Rauch, J. (2005). Gay marriage, same-sex parenting, and America's children. *Future of Children, 15*, 97–115.

Meier, D. (1995). *The power of their ideas.* Boston: Beacon Press.

Meier, D. E., Emmons, C.-A., Wallenstein, S., Quill, T., Morrison, R. S., & Cassel, C. (1998). A national survey of physician-assisted suicide and euthanasia in the United States. *New England Journal of Medicine, 338*, 1193–1201.

Meier, R. (1991, January–February). Language acquisition by deaf children. *American Scientist, 79*, 60–70.

Meijer, A. M., & van den Wittenboer, G. L. H. (2007). Contributions of infants' sleep and crying to marital relationship of first-time parent couples in the 1st year after childbirth. *Journal of Family Psychology, 21*, 49–57.

Meins, E. (1998). The effects of security of attachment and maternal attribution of meaning on children's linguistic acquisitional style. *Infant Behavior and Development, 21*, 237–252.

Melby, J., Conger, R., Fang, S., Wickrama, K., & Conger, K. (2008). Adolescent family experiences and educational attainment during early adulthood. *Developmental Psychology, 44*(6), 1519–1536.

Meltzoff, A. N. (2007). "Like me": A foundation for social cognition. *Developmental Science, 10*, 126–134.

Meltzoff, A. N., & Moore, M. K. (1989). Imitation in newborn infants: Exploring the range of gestures imitated and the underlying mechanisms. *Developmental Psychology, 25*, 954–962.

Meltzoff, A. N., & Moore, M. K. (1994). Imitation, memory, and the representation of persons. *Infant Behavior and Development, 17*, 83–99.

Menacker, F., Martin, J. A., MacDorman, M. F., & Ventura, S. J. (2004). Births to 10–14 year-old mothers, 1990–2002: Trends and health outcomes. *National Vital Statistics Reports, 53*(7). Hyattsville, MD: National Center for Health Statistics.

Mendelsohn, M. E., & Karas, R. H. (2007). HRT and the young at heart. *New England Journal of Medicine, 356*, 2639–2643.

Mendle, J., Turkheimer, E., D'Onofrio, B. M., Lynch, S. K., Emery, R. E., Slutske, W. S., & Martin, N. G. (2006). Family structure and age at menarche: A children-of-twins approach. *Developmental Psychology, 42*, 533–542.

Menec, V. H. (2003). The relation between everyday activities and successful aging: A 6-year longitudinal study. *Journal of Gerontology: Social Sciences, 58B*, S74–S82.

Menec, V. H., Shooshtari, S., Nowicki, S., & Fournier, S. (2010). Does the relationship between neighborhood socioeconomic status and health outcomes persist into very old age? A population-based study. *Journal of Aging and Health, 22*(1), 27–47.

Menegaux, F., Baruchel, A., Bertrand, Y., Lescoeur, B., Leverger, G., Nelken, B., . . . Clavel, J. (2006). Household exposure to pesticides and risk of childhood acute leukaemia. *Occupational and Environmental Medicine, 63*(2), 131–134.

Meng, H., Smith, S. D., Hager, K., Held, M., Liu, J., Olson, R. K., . . . Gruen, J. R. (2005, October). *A deletion in DCDC2 on 6p22 is associated with reading disability*. Paper presented at the American Society of Human Genetics meeting, Salt Lake City, UT.

Meng, Y., Lee, J. H., Cheng, R., St. George-Hyslop, P., Mayeux, R., & Farrer, L. A. (2007). Association between SORL1 and Alzheimer's disease in a genome-wide study. *NeuroReport, 18*(17), 1761–1764.

Mennella, J. A., & Beauchamp, G. K. (1996). The early development of human flavor preferences. In E. D. Capaldi (Ed.), *Why we eat what we eat: The psychology of eating* (pp. 83–112). Washington DC: American Psychological Association.

Mennella, J. A., & Beauchamp, G. K. (2002). Flavor experiences during formula feeding are related to preferences during childhood. *Early Human Development, 68*, 71–82.

Mennella, J. A., Jagnow, C. P., & Beauchamp, G. K. (2001). Prenatal and postnatal flavor learning by human infants. *Pediatrics, 107*(6), E88.

Menon, U. (2001). Middle adulthood in cultural perspective: The imagined and the experienced in three cultures. In M. E. Lachman (Ed.), *Handbook of midlife development* (pp. 40–74). New York: Wiley.

Merewood, A., Mehta, S. D., Chamberlain, L. B., Philipp, B. L., & Bauchner, H. (2005). Breastfeeding rates in US baby-friendly hospitals: Results of a national survey. *Pediatrics, 116*, 628–634.

Merikangas, K. D., He, J-P., Brody, D., Fisher, P. W., Bourdon, K., & Koretz, D. S. (2009). Prevalence and treatment of mental disorders among U.S. children in the 2001–2004 NHASES. *Pediatrics, 125*(1), 75–81. doi: 10.1542/peds.2008-2598

Merrell, K., Gueldner, B., Ross, S., & Isava, D. (2008). How effective are school bullying intervention programs? A meta-analysis of intervention research. *School Psychology Quarterly, 23*(1), 26–42.

Merrill, S. S., & Verbrugge, L. M. (1999). Health and disease in midlife. In S. L. Willis & J. D. Reid (Eds.), *Life in the middle: Psychological and social development in middle age* (pp. 78–103). San Diego: Academic Press.

Mesch, G. (2001). Social relationships and Internet use among adolescents in Israel. *Social Science Quarterly, 82*, 329–340.

Messinger, D. S., Bauer, C. R., Das, A., Seifer, R., Lester, B. M., Lagasse, L. L., . . . Poole, W. K. (2004). The maternal lifestyle study: Cognitive, motor, and behavioral outcomes of cocaine-exposed and opiate-exposed infants through three years of age. *Pediatrics, 113*, 1677–1685.

Messinis, L., Krypianidou, A., Maletaki, S., & Papathanasopoulos, P. (2006). Neuropsychological deficits in long-term cannabis users. *Neurology, 66*, 737–739.

Meyer, I. H. (2003). Prejudice, social stress, and mental health in lesbian, gay, and bisexual populations: Conceptual issues and research evidence. *Psychological Bulletin*, 129, 674–697.

Meyer, B. J. F., Russo, C., & Talbot, A. (1995). Discourse comprehension and problem solving: Decisions about the treatment of breast cancer by women across the life-span. *Psychology in Aging, 10*, 84–103.

Miech, R. A., Kumanyika, S. K., Stettler, N., Link, B., Phelan, J. C., & Chang, V. W. (2006). Trends in the association of poverty with overweight among US adolescents, 1971–2004. *Journal of the American Medical Association, 295*, 2385–2393.

Miedzian, M. (1991). *Boys will be boys: Breaking the link between masculinity and violence.* New York: Doubleday.

Migeon, B. R. (2006). The role of X inactivation and cellular mosaicism in women's health and sex-specific disorders. *Journal of the American Medical Association, 295*, 1428–1433.

Migliore, L., & Coppede, F. (2008). Genetics, environmental factors, and the emerging role of epigenetics in neurodegenerative disease. *Mutation Research/Fundamental and Molecular Mechanisms of Mutagenesis, 667*, 82–97.

Mikkola, K., Ritari, N., Tommiska, V., Salokorpi, T., Lehtonen, L., Tammela, O., . . . Fellman, V., for the Finnish ELBW Cohort Study Group. (2005). Neurodevelopmental outcome at 5 years of age of a national cohort of extremely low birth weight infants who were born in 1996–1997. *Pediatrics, 116*, 1391–1400.

Miles, C. L., Matthews, J., Brennan, L., & Mitchell, S. (2010). Changes in the content of children's school lunches across the school week. *Health Promotion Journal of Australia, 21*(3), 196–201.

Milkie, M. A., Mattingly, M. J., Nomaguchi, S. M., Bianchi, S. M., & Robinson, J. P. (2004). The time squeeze: Parental statuses and feelings about time with children. *Journal of Marriage and Family, 66*, 739–761.

Milkie, M. A., & Peltola, P. (1999). Playing all the roles: Gender and the work-family balancing act. *Journal of Marriage and Family, 61*, 476–490.

Miller, G. E., & Blackwell, E. (2006). Turning up the heat. *Current Directions in Psychological Science, 15*, 269–272.

Miller, J. W., Naimi, T. S., Brewer, R. D., & Jones, S. E. (2007). Binge drinking and associated health risk behaviors among high school students. *Pediatrics, 119*, 76–85.

Miller, K., & Kohn, M. (1983). The reciprocal effects of job condition and the intellectuality of leisure-time activities. In M. L. Kohn & C. Schooler (Eds.), *Work and personality: An inquiry into the impact of social stratification* (pp. 217–241). Norwood, NJ: Ablex.

Miller, L. J., Myers, A., Prinzi, L., & Mittenberg, W. (2009). Changes in intellectual functioning associated with normal aging. *Archives of Clinical Neuropsychology*, *24*(7), 681–688. doi: 10.1093/arclin/acp072

Miller, M. A., & Rahe, R. H. (1997). Life changes scaling for the 1990s. *Journal of Psychosomatic Research, 43*, 279–292.

Miller-Kovach, K. (2003). *Childhood and adolescent obesity: A review of the scientific literature* (Weight Watchers International). Unpublished manuscript.

Millman, R. P., Working Group on Sleepiness in Adolescents/Young Adults, & AAP Committee on Adolescents. (2005). Excessive sleepiness in adolescents and young adults: Causes, consequences, and treatment strategies. *Pediatrics, 115*, 1774–1786.

Mindell, J. A., Sadeh, A., Wiegand, B., How, T. H., & Goh, D. Y. T. (2010). Cross-cultural differences in infant and toddler sleep. *Sleep Medicine, 11*, 274–289.

Miner, J. L., & Clarke-Stewart, A. (2009). Trajectories of externalizing behaviors from age 2 to age 9: Relations with gender, temperament, ethnicity, parenting and rater. *Developmental Psychology, 44*(3), 771–786.

Miniño, A. M. (2010). Mortality among teenagers aged 12–19 years: United States, 1999–2006. *NCHS Data Brief, 37*. Hyattsville, MD: National Center for Health Statistics.

Miniño, A. M., Anderson, R. N., Fingerhut, L. A., Boudreault, M. A., & Warner, M. (2006). Deaths: Injuries, 2002. *National Vital Statistics Reports, 54*(10). Hyattsville, MD: National Center for Health Statistics.

Miniño, A. M., Heron, M. P., Murphy, S. L., & Kochanek, K. D. (2007). Deaths: Final data for 2004. *National Vital Statistics Reports, 55*(19). Hyattsville, MD: National Center for Health Statistics.

Miniño, A. M., Xu, J., & Kochanek, K. D. (2010). Deaths: Preliminary data for 2008. *National Vital Statistics Reports, 59*(2). Hyattsville, MD: National Center for Health Statistics.

Mintz, T. H. (2005). Linguistic and conceptual influences on adjective acquisition in 24- to 36-month-olds. *Developmental Psychology, 41*, 17–29.

Mischel, W. (1966). A social learning view of sex differences in behavior. In E. Maccoby (Ed.), *The development of sex differences* (pp. 57–81). Stanford, CA: Stanford University Press.

Mistry, R. S., Vandewater, E. A., Huston, A. C., & McLoyd, V. (2002). Economic well-being and children's social adjustment: The role of family process in an ethnically diverse low income sample. *Child Development, 73*, 935–951.

Mitchell, E. A., Blair, P. S., & L'Hoir, M. P. (2006). Should pacifiers be recommended to prevent sudden infant death syndrome? *Pediatrics, 117*, 1755–1758.

Mitchell, V., & Helson, R. (1990). Women's prime of life: Is it the 50s? *Psychology of Women Quarterly, 16*, 331–347.

Mitnick, D. M., Heyman, R. E., & Slep, A. M. S. (2009). Changes in relationship satisfaction across the transition to parenthood: A meta-analysis. *Journal of Family Psychology, 23*(6), 848–852.

Mix, K. S., Huttenlocher, J., & Levine, S. C. (2002). Multiple cues for quantification in infancy: Is number one of them? *Psychological Bulletin, 128*, 278–294.

Mix, K. S., Levine, S. C., & Huttenlocher, J. (1999). Early fraction calculation ability. *Developmental Psychology, 35*, 164–174.

Miyake, K., Chen, S., & Campos, J. (1985). Infants' temperament, mothers' mode of interaction and attachment in Japan: An interim report. In I. Bretherton & E. Waters (Eds.), *Growing points of attachment theory and research. Monographs of the Society for Research in Child Development, 50*(1–2, Serial No. 109), 276–297.

Mlot, C. (1998). Probing the biology of emotion. *Science, 280*, 1005–1007.

Modzeleski, W., Feucht, T., Rand, M., Hall, J. E., Simon, T. R., Butler, L., . . . Hertz, M. (2008). School-associated student homicides—United States, 1992–2006. *Morbidity and Mortality Weekly Report, 57*(02), 33–36.

Moen, P., Dempster-McClain, D., & Williams, R. M., Jr. (1992). Successful aging: Life-course perspective on women's multiple roles and health. *American Journal of Sociology, 97*, 1612–1638.

Moen, P., & Wethington, E. (1999). Midlife development in a life course context. In S. L. Willis & J. D. Reid (Eds.), *Life in the middle: Psychological and social development in middle age* (pp. 1–23). San Diego: Academic Press.

Mohai, P., Lantz, P. M., Morenoff, J., House, J. S., & Mero, R. P. (2009). Racial and socioeconomic disparities in residential proximity to polluting industrial facilities: Evidence from the Americans' Changing Lives study. *American Journal of Public Health, 99*, S649–S656.

Mojon-Azzi, S., Kunz, A., & Mojon, D. S. (2010). Strabismus and discrimination in children: Are children with strabismus invited to fewer birthday parties? *British Journal of Ophthalmology, 95*(4), 473–476. doi: 10.1136/bjo.2010.185793

Mokdad, A. H., Marks, J. S., Stroup, D. F., & Gerberding, J. L. (2005). Correction: Actual causes of death in the United States, 2000. *Journal of the American Medical Association, 293*, 293–294.

Moline, M. L., & Zendell, S. M. (2000). Evaluating and managing premenstrual syndrome. *Medscape General Medicine, 2*. Retrieved from www. medscape.com/viewarticle/408913_print

Mollenkopf, J., Waters, M. C., Holdaway, J., & Kasinitz, P. (2005). The ever-winding path: Ethnic and racial diversity in the transition to adulthood. In R. A. Settersten Jr., F. F. Furstenberg Jr., & R. G. Rumbaut (Eds.), *On the frontier of adulthood: Theory, research, and public policy* (pp. 454–497). Chicago: University of Chicago Press.

Molofsky, A. V., Slutsky, S. G., Joseph, N. M., He, S., Pardal, R., Krishnamurthy, J., . . . Morrison, S. J. (2006). Increasing p16INK4a expression decreases forebrain progenitors and neurogenesis during ageing. *Nature, 443*, 448–452.

Monahan, K. C., Cauffman, E., & Steinberg, L. (2009). Affiliation with antisocial peers, susceptibility to peer influence, and antisocial behavior during the transition to adulthood. *Developmental Psychology, 45*(6), 1520–1530.

Mondschein, E. R., Adolph, K. E., & Tamis-LeMonda, C. S. (2000). Gender bias in mothers' expectations about infant crawling. *Journal of Experimental Child Psychology* (Special Issue on Gender), *77*, 304–316.

Money, J., Hampson, J. G., & Hampson, J. L. (1955). Hermaphroditism: Recommendations concerning assignment of sex, change of sex and psychologic management. *Bulletin of the Johns Hopkins Hospital, 97*(4), 284–300.

Montague, D. P. F., & Walker-Andrews, A. S. (2001). Peekaboo: A new look at infants' perception of emotion expressions. *Developmental Psychology, 37*, 826–838.

Montenegro, X. P. (2004). *The divorce experience: A study of divorce at midlife and beyond.* Washington, DC: American Association of Retired Persons.

Montessori, M. (with Chattin-McNichogls, J.). (1995). *The absorbent mind.* New York: Holt.
Montgomery, M. J., & Côté, J. E. (2003). College as a transition to adulthood. In G. R. Adams & M. D. Berzonsky (Eds.), *Blackwell handbook of adolescence.* Malden, MA: Blackwell.
Moody, H. R. (2009). *Aging: Concepts and controversies.* Thousand Oaks, CA: Pine Forge/Sage.
Mook-Kanamori, D. O., Steegers, E. A., Eilers, P. H., Raat, H., Hofman, A., & Jaddoe, V. W. (2010). Risk factors and outcomes associated with first-trimester fetal growth restriction. *Journal of the American Medical Association, 303*(6), 527–534. doi: 10.1001/jama.2010.78
Moon, C., & Fifer, W. P. (1990, April). *Newborns prefer a prenatal version of mother's voice.* Paper presented at the biannual meeting of the International Society of Infant Studies, Montreal, Canada.
Mooney-Somers, J., & Golombok, S. (2000). Children of lesbian mothers: From the 1970s to the new millennium. *Sexual and Relationship Therapy, 15*(2), 121–126.
Moore, M. J., Moir, P., & Patrick, M. M. (2004). *The state of aging and health in America 2004.* Washington, DC: Centers for Disease Control and Prevention and Merck Institute of Aging & Health.
Moore, S. E., Cole, T. J., Poskitt, E. M. E., Sonko, B. J., Whitehead, R. G., McGregor, I. A., & Prentice, A. M. (1997). Season of birth predicts mortality in rural Gambia. *Nature, 388,* 434.
Moran, C., & Hughes, L. (2006). Coping with stress: Social work students and humour. *Social Work Education, 25*(5), 501–517.
Morgan, R. A., Dudley, M. E., Wunderlich, J. R., Hughes, M. S., Yang, J. C., Sherry, R. M., . . . Rosenberg, S. A. (2006). Cancer regression in patients mediated by transfer of genetically engineered lymphocytes. *Science, 314*(5796), 126–129.
Morin, C. M., Colecchi, C., Stone, J., Sood, R., & Brink, D. (1999). Behavioral and pharmacological therapies for late-life insomnia: A randomized controlled trial. *Journal of the American Medical Association, 281*, 991–999.
Morin, R. (2009, May 28). *Most middle-aged adults are rethinking retirement plans: The threshold generation.* Retrieved from http://pewresearch.org/pubs/1234/the-threshold-generation
Morin, R. (2013). *Study: Opposition to same sex marriage is likely to be understated in public opinion polls.* Pew Research Center. Retrieved from http://www.pewresearch.org/fact-tank/2013/09/30/opposition-to-same-sex-marriage-may-be-understated-in-public-opinion-polls/
Moretti, F., De Ronchi, D., Bernabel, V., Marchetti, L., Ferrari, B., Forlani, C., . . . Atti, A. R. (2010). Pet therapy in elderly patients with mental illness. *Psychogeriatrics.* Advance online publication. doi: 10.1111/j.1479-8301.2010.00329.x
Morris, M. C. (2004). Diet and Alzheimer's disease: What the evidence shows. *Medscape General Medicine, 6*, 1–5.
Morris, M. S., Jacques, P. F., Rosenberg, I. H., & Selhub, J. (2007). Folate and vitamin B-12 status in relation to anemia, macrocytosis, and cognitive impairment in older Americans in the age of folic acid fortification. *American Journal of Clinical Nutrition, 85*(1), 193–200.
Morrissey, T. W. (2009). Multiple child-care arrangements and young children's behavioral outcomes. *Child Development, 80,* 59–76.
Morrison, J. A., Friedman, L. A., Harlan, W. R., Harlan, L. C., Barton, B. A., Schreiber, G. B., & Klein, D. J. (2005). Development of the metabolic syndrome in black and white adolescent girls. *Pediatrics, 116*, 1178–1182.
Morrow, D. G., Menard, W. W. E., Stine-Morrow, E. A. L., Teller, T., & Bryant, D. (2001). The influence of expertise and task factors on age differences in pilot communication. *Psychology and Aging, 16*, 31–46.
Mortensen, E. L., Michaelson, K. F., Sanders, S. A., & Reinisch, J. M. (2002). The association between duration of breastfeeding and adult intelligence. *Journal of the American Medical Association, 287,* 2365–2371.
Morton, H. (1996). *Becoming Tongan: An ethnography of childhood.* Honolulu: University of Hawaii Press.
Mortimer, J. A., Snowdon, D. A., & Markesbery, W. R. (2002). Head circumference, education, and risk of dementia: Findings from the Nun Study. *Journal of Clinical and Experimental Neuropsychology, 25*, 671–679.
Mosca, L., Collins, P., Harrington, D. M., Mendelsohn, M. E., Pasternak, R. C., Robertson, R. M., . . . Wenger, N. K. (2001). Hormone therapy and cardiovascular disease: A statement for healthcare professionals from the American Heart Association. *Circulation, 104*, 499–503.
Mosconi, L., Tsui, W. H., Herholz, K., Pupi, A., Drzezga, A., Lucignani, G., . . . de Leon, M. J. (2008). Multicenter standardized 18F-FDG PET diagnosis of mild cognitive impairment, Alzheimer's disease, and other dementias. *Journal of Nuclear Medicine, 49,* 390–398.
Moses, L. J., Baldwin, D. A., Rosicky, J. G., & Tidball, G. (2001). Evidence for referential understanding in the emotions domain at twelve and eighteen months. *Child Development, 72*, 718–735.
Mosher, W. D., Chandra, A., & Jones, J. (2005). Sexual behavior and selected health measures: Men and women 15–44 years of age, United States, 2002. *Advance Data from Vital and Health Statistics,* No. 362. Hyattsville, MD: Centers for Disease Control and Prevention, National Center for Health Statistics.
Mosier, C. E., & Rogoff, B. (2003). Privileged treatment of toddlers: Cultural aspects of individual choice and responsibility. *Developmental Psychology, 39*, 1047–1060.
Moskovitz, J., Bar-Noy, S., Williams, W. M., Requena, J., Berlett, B. S., & Stadtman, E. R. (2001). Methionine sulfoxide reductase (MsrA) is a regulator of antioxidant defense and lifespan in mammals. *Proceedings of the National Academy of Sciences, 98*, 12920–12925.
Moss, M. S., & Moss, S. Z. (1989). The death of a parent. In R. A. Kalish (Ed.), *Midlife loss: Coping strategies.* Newbury Park, CA: Sage.
Moster, D., Lie, R. T., & Markestad, T. (2008). Long-term medical and social consequences of preterm birth. *New England Journal of Medicine, 359,* 262–273.
Moulson, M. C., Fox, N. A., Zeanah, C. H., & Nelson, C. A. (2009). Early adverse experiences and the neurobiology of facial emotion processing. *Developmental Psychology, 45,* 17–30.
Mounts, N. S., & Steinberg, L. (1995). An ecological analysis of peer influence on adolescent grade point average and drug use. *Developmental Psychology, 31*, 915–922.
Mouw, T. (2005). Sequences of early adult transition: A look at variability and consequences. In R. A. Settersten Jr., F. F. Furstenberg Jr., & R. G. Rumbaut (Eds.), *On the frontier of adulthood: Theory, research, and public policy* (pp. 256–291). Chicago: University of Chicago Press.
Mroczek, D. K. (2004). Positive and negative affect at midlife. In O. G. Brim, C. D. Ryff, & R. C. Kessler (Eds.), *How healthy are we? A national study of well-being at midlife* (pp. 205–226). Chicago: University of Chicago Press.
Mroczek, D. K., & Kolarz, C. M. (1998). The effect of age on positive and negative affect: A developmental perspective on happiness. *Journal of Personality and Social Psychology, 75*(5), 1333–1349.
Mroczek, D. K., & Spiro, A. (2005). Change in life satisfaction during adulthood: Findings from the Veterans Affairs Normative Aging Study. *Journal of Personality and Social Psychology, 88*, 189–202.
Mroczek, D. K., & Spiro, A., III. (2007). Personality change influences mortality in older men. *Psychological Science, 18*(5), 371–376.
Msall, M. S. E. (2004). Developmental vulnerability and resilience in extremely preterm infants. *Journal of the American Medical Association, 292*, 2399–2401.
MTA Cooperative Group. (1999). A 14-month randomized clinical trial of treatment strategies for attention-deficit/hyperactivity disorder. *Archives of General Psychiatry, 56*, 1073–1986.
MTA Cooperative Group. (2004a). National Institute of Mental Health multimodal treatment study of ADHD follow-up: Changes in effectiveness and growth after the end of treatment. *Pediatrics, 113*, 762–769.
MTA Cooperative Group. (2004b). National Institute of Mental Health multimodal treatment study of ADHD follow-up: 24-month outcomes of treatment strategies for attention-deficit/hyperactivity disorder. *Pediatrics, 113*, 754–769.
Mueller, T. I., Kohn, R., Leventhal, N., Leon, A. C., Solomon, D., Coryell, W., . . . Keller, M. B. (2004). The course of depression in elderly patients. *American Journal of Psychiatry, 12*, 22–29.
Mulford, C., & Giordano, P. (2008). Teen dating violence: A closer look at adolescent romantic relationships. *National Institute of Justice Journal, 261,* 34–41.

Mullan, D., & Currie, C. (2000). Socioeconomic equalities in adolescent health. In C. Currie, K. Hurrelmann, W. Settertobulte, R. Smith, & J. Todd (Eds.), *Health and health behaviour among young people: A WHO cross-national study (HBSC) international report* (pp. 65–72). (WHO Policy Series: Healthy Policy for Children and Adolescents, Series No. 1.) Copenhagen, Denmark: World Health Organization Regional Office for Europe.

Mumme, D. L., & Fernald, A. (2003). The infant as onlooker: Learning from emotional reactions observed in a television scenario. *Child Development, 74*, 221–237.

Munakata, Y., McClelland, J. L., Johnson, M. J., & Siegler, R. S. (1997). Rethinking infant knowledge: Toward an adaptive process account of successes and failures in object permanence tasks. *Psychological Review, 104*, 686–714.

Munk-Olsen, T., Laursen, T. M., Pedersen, C. B., Mors, O., & Mortensen, P. B. (2006). New parents and mental disorders: A population-based register study. *Journal of the American Medical Association, 296*, 2582–2589.

Munson, M. L., & Sutton, P. D. (2004). Births, marriages, divorces, and deaths: Provisional data for November 2003. *National Vital Statistics Reports, 52*(20). Hyattsville, MD: National Center for Health Statistics.

Murachver, T., Pipe, M., Gordon, R., Owens, J. L., & Fivush, R. (1996). Do, show, and tell: Children's event memories acquired through direct experience, observation, and stories. *Child Development, 67*, 3029–3044.

Muraco, A. (2006). Intentional families: Fictive kin ties between cross-gender, different sexual orientation friends. *Journal of Marriage and Family, 68*, 1313–1325.

Muris, P., Merckelbach, H., & Collaris, R. (1997). Common childhood fears and their origins. *Behaviour Research and Therapy, 35*, 929–937.

Murzyn, E. (2008). Do we only dream in colour? A comparison of reported dream colour in younger and older adults with different experiences of black and white media. *Consciousness and Cognition, 17*(4), 1228–1237. doi: 10.1016/j.concog.2008.09.002

Musick, M. A., Herzog, A. R., & House, J. S. (1999). Volunteering and mortality among older adults: Findings from a national sample. *Journal of Gerontology: Psychological Sciences, 54B*, S173–S180.

Mustanski, B. S., DuPree, M. G., Nievergelt, C. M., Bocklandt, S., Schork, N. J., & Hamer, D. H. (2005). A genomewide scan of male sexual orientation. *Human Genetics, 116*, 272–278.

Mustillo, S., Worthman, C., Erkanli, A., Keeler, G., Angold, A., & Costello, E. J. (2003). Obesity and psychiatric disorder: Developmental trajectories. *Pediatrics, 111*, 851–859.

Muter, V., Hulme, C., Snowling, M. J., & Stevenson, J. (2004). Phonemes, rimes, vocabulary, and grammatical skill as foundations of early reading development: Evidence from a longitudinal study. *Developmental Psychology, 40*, 665–681.

Myers, D., & Diener, E. (1995). Who is happy? *Psychological Science, 6*, 10–19.

Myers, D. G. (2000). The funds, friends, and faith of happy people. *American Psychologist, 55*, 56–67.

Myers, D. G., & Diener, E. (1996). The pursuit of happiness. *Scientific American, 274*, 54–56.

Myers, J. E., Madathil, J., & Tingle, L. R. (2005). Marriage satisfaction and wellness in India and the United States: A preliminary comparison of arranged marriages and marriages of choice. *Journal of Counseling and Development, 83*(2), 183–190.

Myers, J. E., & Perrin, N. (1993). Grandparents affected by parental divorce: A population at risk? *Journal of Counseling and Development, 72*, 62–66.

Myers, S. M., Johnson, C. P., & Council on Children with Disabilities. (2007). Management of children with autism spectrum disorders. *Pediatrics, 120*(5), 1162–1182.

Nader, P. R., Bradley, R. H., Houts, R. M., McRitchie, S. L., & O'Brien, M. (2008). Moderate-to-vigorous physical activity from ages 9 to 15 years. *Journal of the American Medical Association, 300*, 295–305.

Nadig, A. S., Ozonoff, S., Young, G. S., Rozga, A., Sigman, M., & Rogers, S. J. (2007). A prospective study of response to name in infants at risk for autism. *Archives of Pediatric and Adolescent Medicine, 161*, 378–383.

Nagaoka, J., & Roderick, M. (2004, April). *Ending social promotion: The effects of retention.* Chicago: Consortium on Chicago School Research.

Nagaraja, J., Menkedick, J., Phelan, K. J., Ashley, P., Zhang, X., & Lanphear, B. P. (2005). Deaths from residential injuries in US children and adolescents, 1985–1997. *Pediatrics, 116*, 454–461.

Najman, J. M., Hayatbakhsh, M. R., Heron, M. A., Bor, W., O'Callaghan, M. J., & Williams, G. M. (2009). The impact of episodic and chronic poverty on child cognitive development. *Journal of Pediatrics, 154*(2), 284–289.

Naveh-Benjamin, M., Brav, T., & Levy, O. (2007). The associative memory deficit of older adults: The role of strategy utilization. *Psychology and Aging, 22*(1), 202–208.

Naito, M., & Miura, H. (2001). Japanese childrens' numerical competencies: Age and school-related influences on the development of number concepts and addition skills. *Developmental Psychology, 37*, 217–230.

Naito, T., & Geilen, U. P. (2005). The changing Japanese family: A psychological portrait. In J. L. Roopnarine & U. P. Gielen (Eds.), *Families in global perspective* (pp. 63–84). Boston, MA: Allyn & Bacon.

Nansel, T. R., Overpeck, M., Pilla, R. S., Ruan, W. J., Simons-Morton, B., & Scheidt, P. (2001). Bullying behaviors among U.S. youth: Prevalence and association with psychosocial adjustment. *Journal of the American Medical Association, 285*, 2094–2100.

Napier, J. L., & Jost, J. T. (2008). Why are conservatives happier than liberals? *Psychological Science, 19*(6), 565–572. doi: 10.1111/j.1467-9280.2008.02124.x

Naquin, C., Kurtzberg, T., & Belkin, L. (2010). The finer points of lying online: E-mail versus pen and paper. *Journal of Applied Psychology, 95*(2), 387–394 doi: 10.1037/a0018627

Natenshon, A. (2006). *Parental influence takes precedence over Barbie and the media.* Retrieved from www.empoweredparents.com/1prevention/prevention_09.htm

Nathanielsz, P. W. (1995). The role of basic science in preventing low birth weight. *Future of Our Children, 5*(1), 57–70.

National Assessment of Educational Progress: The Nation's Report Card. (2004). *America's charter schools: Results from the NAEP 2003 pilot study* (NCES 2005-456). Jessup, MD: U.S. Department of Education.

National Association for Gifted Children (NAGC). (n.d.). *Frequently asked questions.* Retrieved from www.nagc.org/index.aspx?id=548

National Association of Child Care Resource and Referral Agencies (NACCRRA). (2010). *Parents and the high cost of child care: 2010 update.* Retrieved from http://www.naccrra.org/docs/High_Cost_Report_2010_One_Pager_072910a-final.pdf

National Association of State Boards of Education. (2000). *Fit, healthy, and ready to learn: A school health policy guide.* Alexandria, VA: Author.

National Center for Complementary and Alternative Medicine (NCCAM). (2008). *Get the facts: Menopausal symptoms and complementary health practices.* Retrieved from http://nccam.nih.gov/sites/nccam.nih.gov/files/Get_The_Facts_Menopause_09-19-2013.pdf

National Center for Education Statistics (NCES). (2001). *The condition of education 2001* (NCES 2001-072). Washington, DC: U.S. Government Printing Office.

National Center for Education Statistics (NCES). (2003). *The condition of education, 2003* (NCES 2003-067). Washington, DC: Author.

National Center for Education Statistics (NCES). (2004). *The condition of education 2004* (NCES 2004-077). Washington, DC: U.S. Government Printing Office.

National Center for Education Statistics (NCES). (2005a). *Children born in 2001—First results from the base year of Early Childhood Longitudinal Study, Birth Cohort* (ECLS-B). Retrieved from http://nces.ed.gov/pubs2005/children/index.asp

National Center for Education Statistics (NCES). (2005b). *The condition of education 2005* (NCES 2005-094). Washington, DC: U.S. Government Printing Office.

National Center for Education Statistics (NCES). (2005c). *Trends in educational equity of girls & women 2004.* Retrieved from http://nces.ed.gov/pubsearch/pubsinfo.asp?pubid=2005016

National Center for Education Statistics (NCES). (2006a). *Calories in, calories out: Food and*

exercise in public elementary schools, 2005 (NCES 2006-057). Washington, DC: Author.
National Center for Education Statistics (NCES). (2006b). *The condition of education 2006* (NCES 2006-071). Washington, DC: U.S. Government Printing Office.
National Center for Education Statistics (NCES). (2006c). *National Assessment of Adult Literacy (NAAL): A first look at the literacy of America's adults in the 21st century* (NCES 2006-470). Washington, DC: Author.
National Center for Education Statistics (NCES). (2007a). *College enrollment rate of recent high school completers, by sex: 1960 through 2006. Table 191* [Digest of Education Statistics]. Retrieved from http://nces.ed.gov/programs/digest/d07/tables/dt07_191.asp
National Center for Education Statistics (NCES). (2007b). *The condition of education 2007* (NCES 2007-064). Washington, DC: Author.
National Center for Education Statistics (NCES). (2007c). *The Nation's Report Card: Mathematics 2007* (NCES 2007-494). Washington, DC: Author.
National Center for Education Statistics (NCES). (2007d). *The Nation's Report Card: Reading 2007* (NCES 2007-496). Washington, DC: Author.
National Center for Education Statistics (NCES). (2007e). *The reading literacy of U.S. fourth-grade students in an international context: Results from the 2001 and 2006 Progress in International Reading Literacy Study (PIRLS)* (NCES 2008-017). Washington, DC: Author.
National Center for Education Statistics (NCES). (2008). *1.5 million homeschooled students in the United States in 2007* (NCES 2009-030). Washington, DC: Author.
National Center for Education Statistics (NCES). (2009a). *Bachelor's degrees conferred by degree-granting institutions, by race/ethnicity and sex of student: Selected years, 1976–77 through 2006–07. Table 284* [Digest of Education Statistics: 2008]. Retrieved from http://nces.ed.gov/programs/digest/d08/tables/dt08_284.asp?referrer=report
National Center for Education Statistics (NCES). (2009b). *The condition of education 2009* (NCES 2009-081). Washington, DC: Author.
National Center for Education Statistics (NCES). (2012a). *The condition of education 2012.* (NCES 2012-045), Table A-47-2.
National Center for Education Statistics (NCES). (2012b). *Digest of education statistics, 2011* (NCES 2012-001), Chapter 3.
National Center for Education Statistics (NCES). (2013). *The condition of education 2013* (NCES 2013-037). Immediate Transition to College.
National Center for Elder Abuse. (2014). *Statistics/data.* Retrieved from http://www.ncea.aoa.gov/Library/Data/index.aspx#abuser
National Center for Health Statistics (NCHS). (1999). *Abstract adapted from Births: Final Data for 1999 by Mid-Atlantic Parents of Multiples.* Retrieved from www.orgsites.com/va/mapom/_pgg1.php3
National Center for Health Statistics (NCHS). (2004). *Health, United States, 2004 with chartbook on trends in the health of Americans* (DHHS Publication No. 2004-1232). Hyattsville, MD: Author.
National Center for Health Statistics (NCHS). (2005). *Health, United States, 2005* (DHHS Publication No. 2005-1232). Hyattsville, MD: Author.
National Center for Health Statistics (NCHS). (2006). *Health, United States, 2006.* Hyattsville, MD: Author.
National Center for Health Statistics (NCHS). (2007). *Health, United States, 2007 with chartbook on trends in the health of Americans.* Hyattsville, MD: Author.
National Center for Health Statistics (NCHS). (2008). *Health, United States, 2008, with chartbook.* Retrieved from http://www.cdc.gov/nchs/data/hus/hus08.pdf
National Center for Health Statistics (NCHS). (2009a). Distribution of teen births by age, 2007. *Vital Statistics Reports.* Hyattsville, MD: Author.
National Center for Health Statistics (NCHS). (2009b). Divorce rates by state: 1990, 1995, 1996–2007. *Division of Vital Statistics.* Retrieved from http://www.cdc.gov/nchs/data/nvss/Divorce%20Rates%2090%2095%20and%2099-07.pdf
National Center for Health Statistics (NCHS). (2010). Table 68. Hypertension and elevated blood pressure among persons 20 years of age and over, by selected characteristics: United States, 1988-1994, 1999-2002, and 2003-2006. *Health, United States, 2009: With special feature on medical technology* (DHHS Publication No. 2010-1232). Hyattsville, MD: Author. Retrieved from http://www.cdc.gov/nchs/data/hus/hus09.pdf#068
National Center for Health Statistics (NCHS). (2013). *Health, United States, 2012: With special feature on emergency care.* Hyattsville, MD: Author.
National Center for Learning Disabilities. (2004a). *Dyslexia: Learning disabilities in reading* [Fact sheet]. Retrieved from www.ld.org/LDInfoZone/InfoZone_FactSheet_Dyslexia.cfm
National Center for Learning Disabilities (2004b). *LD at a glance* [Fact sheet]. Retrieved from www.ld.org/LDInfoZone/InfoZone_FactSheet_LD.cfm
National Center on Addiction and Substance Abuse (CASA). (2006, September). *The importance of family dinners III.* New York: Columbia University.
National Center on Addiction and Substance Abuse (CASA). (2007, September). *The importance of family dinners IV* . Retrieved from www.casacolumbia.org/
National Center on Elder Abuse & Westat, Inc. (1998). *National Elder Abuse Incidence Study: Executive summary.* Washington, DC: American Public Human Services Association.
National Center on Shaken Baby Syndrome. (2000). *SBS questions.* Retrieved from www.dontshake.com/sbsquestions.html
National Clearinghouse on Child Abuse and Neglect Information (NCCANI). (2004). *Long-term consequences of child abuse and neglect.* Retrieved from http://nccanch.acf.hhs.gov/pubs/factsheets/longtermconsequences.cfm
National Coalition for the Homeless. (2006). *Education of homeless children and youth* (NCH Fact Sheet No. 10). Washington, DC: Author.
National Coalition for the Homeless. (2009). *Why are people homeless?* [NCH fact sheet #1]. Retrieved from www.nationalhomeless.org/factsheets/why.html
National Council on Aging. (2002). *American perceptions of aging in the 21st century: The NCOA's Continuing Study of the Myths and Realities of Aging (2002 update).* Washington, DC: Author.
National Diabetes Education Program. (2008). *Overview of diabetes in children and adolescents. A fact sheet from the National Diabetes Education Program.* Retrieved from http://ndep.nih.gov/media/diabetes/youth/youth_FS.htm
National Diabetes Information Clearinghouse (NDIC). (2007). *National diabetes statistics.* Retrieved from http://diabetes.niddk.nih.gov/DM/PUBS/statistics/#allages
National Fatherhood Initiative. (2013). *The father factor: Data on the consequences of father absence.* Retrieved from http://www.fatherhood.org/media/consequences-of-father-absence-statistics
National Forum on Early Childhood Policy and Programs (2010). *Understanding the Head Start Impact Study.* Retrieved from http://www.developingchild.harvard.edu/
National Healthy Marriage Resource Center. (n.d.). *Marriage trends in Western culture: A fact sheet.* Retrieved from http://www.healthymarriageinfo.org/docs/MarriageTrendsinWesternCulture.pdf
National Highway Traffic Safety Administration. (2009). *Traffic safety facts research note.* Washington, DC: Author.
National Institute of Child Health and Development. (2008). *Facts about Down syndrome.* Retrieved from www.nichd.nih gov/publications/pubs/downsyndrome.cfm
National Institute of Child Health and Human Development (NICHD). (2010). *Phenylketonuria (PKU).* Retrieved from www.nichd.nih.gov/health/topics/phenylketonuria.cfm
National Institute of Mental Health (NIMH). (1999, April). *Suicide facts.* Retrieved from www.nimh.nih.gov/research/suifact.htm
National Institute of Mental Health (NIMH). (2001a). *Helping children and adolescents cope with violence and disasters: Fact sheet* (NIH Publication No. 01-3518). Bethesda, MD: Author.
National Institute of Mental Health (NIMH). (2001b). *Teenage brain: A work in progress.* Retrieved from www.nimh.gov/publicat/teen-brain.cfm
National Institute of Mental Health (NIMH). (2002). *Preventive sessions after divorce protect children into teens.* Retrieved from www.nimh.nih.gov

National Institute of Neurological Disorders and Stroke (NINDS). (2006, January 25). *NINDS shaken baby syndrome information page.* Retrieved from www.ninds.nih.gov/disorders/shakenbaby/shakenbaby.htm

National Institute of Neurological Disorders and Stroke (NINDS). (2007). *NINDS asperger syndrome information page.* Retrieved from www.ninds.nih.gov/disorders/asperger/asperger.htm

National Institute on Aging (NIA). (1980). *Senility: Myth or madness.* Washington, DC: U.S. Government Printing Office.

National Institute on Aging (NIA). (1993). *Bound for good health: A collection of age pages.* Washington, DC: U.S. Government Printing Office.

National Institute on Aging (NIA). (2011). *Global health and aging.* Retrieved from http://www.nia.nih.gov/sites/default/files/nia-who_report_booklet_oct-2011_a4__1-12-12_5.pdf

National Institute on Alcohol Abuse and Alcoholism (NIAAA). (1996, July). *Alcohol alert* (No. 33-1996 [PH 366]). Bethesda, MD: Author.

National Insitute on Alcohol Abuse and Alcoholism (NIAAA). (2010). *Alcohol use and older adults.* Retrieved from http://nihseniorhealth.gov/alcoholuse/alcoholandaging/01.html

National Insitute on Alcohol Abuse and Alcoholism (NIAAA). (n.d.). *Rethinking drinking: Alcohol and your health.* Retrieved from http://rethinkingdrinking.niaaa.nih.gov/default.asp

National Institute on Drug Abuse (NIDA). (2008). *Quarterly report: Potency Monitoring Project* (Report 100, December 16, 2007 thru March 15, 2008). University, MS: National Center for Natural Products Research, University of Mississippi.

National Institutes of Health (NIH). (1992, December 7–9). Impotence. *NIH Consensus Statement, 10*(4). Washington, DC: U.S. Government Printing Office.

National Institutes of Health (NIH). (2003). The low-down on osteoporosis: What we know and what we don't. *Word on health.* Bethesda, MD: Author.

National Institutes of Health (NIH). (2005). NIH state-of-the-science conference statement: Management of menopause-related symptoms. *Annals of Internal Medicine, 142*(12, Pt.1), 1003–1013.

National Institutes of Health (NIH). (2010a, February 4). *NIH scientists identify maternal and fetal genes that increase preterm birth risk* [Press release]. Retrieved from http://www.nih.gov/news/health/feb2010/nichd-04.htm

National Institutes of Health (NIH). (2010b, March 8–10). *Consensus Development Conference on Vaginal Birth after Cesarean: New insights.* Bethesda, MD: Author. Retrieved from http://consensus.nih.gov/2010/vbac.htm

National Institutes of Health (NIH) Consensus Development Panel. (2001). National Institutes of Health Consensus Development conference statement: Phenyl-ketonuria screening and management. October 16–18, 2000. *Pediatrics, 108*(4), 972–982.

National Institutes of Health (NIH) Consensus Development Panel on Osteoporosis Prevention, Diagnosis, and Therapy. (2001). Osteoporosis prevention, diagnosis, and therapy. *Journal of the American Medical Association, 285,* 785–794.

National Institutes of Health/National Institute on Aging. (1993, May). *In search of the secrets of aging* (NIH Publication No. 93-2756). Washington, DC: National Institutes of Health.

National Library of Medicine. (2003). *Medical encyclopedia: Conduct disorder.* Retrieved from www.nlm.nih.gov/medlineplus/ency/article/000919.htm

National Library of Medicine. (2004). *Medical encyclopedia: Oppositional defiant disorder.* Retrieved from www.nlm.nih.gov/medlineplus/ency/article/001537.htm

National Mental Health Association. (n.d.). *Coping with loss—bereavement and grief* [Fact sheet]. Alexandria, VA: Author.

National Parents' Resource Institute for Drug Education. (1999, September 8). *PRIDE surveys, 1998–99 national summary: Grades 6–12.* Bowling Green, KY: Author.

National Reading Panel. (2000). *Report of the National Reading Panel. Teaching children to read: An evidence-based assessment of the scientific research literature on reading and its implications for reading instruction: Reports of the subgroups.* Washington, DC: National Institute of Child Health and Human Development.

National Research Council (NRC). (1993a). *Losing generations: Adolescents in high risk settings.* Washington, DC: National Academy Press.

National Research Council (NRC). (1993b). *Understanding child abuse and neglect.* Washington, DC: National Academy Press.

National Research Council (NRC). (2006). *Food insecurity and hunger in the United States: An assessment of the measure.* Washington, DC: National Academies Press.

National Scientific Council on the Developing Child. (2010). *Persistent fear and anxiety can affect young children's learning and development: Working paper #9.* Retrieved from http://www.developingchild.net

National Sleep Foundation. (2001). *2001 Sleep in America poll.* Retrieved from www.sleepfoundation.org/publications/2001poll.html

National Sleep Foundation. (2004). *Sleep in America.* Washington, DC: Author.

National Survey on Drug Use and Health (NSDUH). (2009, September 17). *Suicidal thoughts and behaviors among adults.* Retreived from http://www.oas.samhsa.gov/2k9/165/Suicide.htm

National Survey on Drug Use and Health (NSDUH). (2012). *Results from the 2011 national survey on drug use and health: Mental health findings.* NSDUH Series H-45. HHS Publication No. (SMA) 12-4725. Rockville, MD: Substance Abuse and Mental Health Services Administration. Retrieved from http://www.samhsa.gov/data/NSDUH/2k11MH_FindingsandDetTables/2K11MHFR/NSDUHmhfr2011.htm

Neale, B. M., Lasky-Su., J., Anney, R., Franke, B., Zhou, K., Maller, J. B., . . . Faraone, S. V. (2008). Genome-wide association scan of attention deficit hyperactivity disorder. *American Journal of Medical Genetics Part B: Neuropsychiatric Genetics, 147B* (8), 1337–1344.

Nedrow, A., Miller, J., Walker, M., Nygren, P., Huffman, L. H., & Nelson, H. D. (2006). Complementary and alternative therapies for the management of menopause-related symptoms. *Archives of Internal Medicine, 166,* 1453–1465.

The need is real. (n.d.) Retrieved from www.organdonor.gov

Nef, S., Verma-Kurvari, S., Merenmies, J., Vassallt, J.-D., Efstratiadis, A., Accili, D., & Parada, L. F. (2003). Testis determination requires insulin receptor family function in mice. *Nature, 426,* 291–295.

Neidorf, S., & Morin, R. (2011). *Four-in-ten Americans have close friends or relatives who are gay.* Retrieved from http://pewresearch.org/pubs/485/friends-who-are-gay

Neimeyer, R. A., & Currier, J. M. (2009). Grief therapy: Evidence of efficacy and emerging directions. *Current Directions in Psychological Science, 18*(6), 352–356.

Neisser, U., Boodoo, G., Bouchard, T. J., Jr., Boykin, A. W., Brody, N., Ceci, S. J., . . . Urbina, S. (1996). Intelligence: Knowns and unknowns. *American Psychologist, 51*(2), 77–101.

Neitzel, C., & Stright, A. D. (2003). Relations between parents' scaffolding and children's academic self-regulation: Establishing a foundation of self-regulatory competence. *Journal of Family Psychology, 17,* 147–159.

Nelson, C. A. (1995). The ontogeny of human memory: A cognitive neuroscience perspective. *Developmental Psychology, 31,* 723–738.

Nelson, C. A. (2008). A neurobiological perspective on early human deprivation. *Child Development Perspectives, 1,* 13–18.

Nelson, C. A., Monk, C. S., Lin, J., Carver, L. J., Thomas, K. M., & Truwit, C. L. (2000). Functional neuroanatomy of spatial working memory in children. *Developmental Psychology, 36,* 109–116.

Nelson, C. A., Thomas, K. M., & deHaan, M. (2006). Neural bases of cognitive development. In W. Damon & R. Lerner (Eds.), *Handbook of child psychology* (6th ed.). Hoboken, NJ: Wiley.

Nelson, H. D., Vescon, K. K., Haney, E., Fu, R., Nedrow, A., Miller, J., . . . Humphrey, L. (2006). Nonhormonal therapies for menopausal hot flashes: Systematic review and meta-analysis. *Journal of the American Medical Association, 295,* 2057–2071.

Nelson, K. (1993). The psychological and social origins of autobiographical memory. *Psychological Science, 47,* 7–14.

Nelson, K. (2005). Evolution and development of human memory systems. In B. J. Ellis & D. F. Bjorklund (Eds.), *Origins of the social mind: Evolutionary psychology and child development* (pp. 319–345). New York: Guilford Press.

Nelson, K., & Fivush, R. (2004). The emergence of autobiographical memory: A social cultural developmental theory. *Psychological Bulletin, 111*, 486–511.

Nelson, K. B., Dambrosia, J. M., Ting, T. Y., & Grether, J. K. (1996). Uncertain value of electronic fetal monitoring in predicting cerebral palsy. *New England Journal of Medicine, 334*, 613–618.

Nelson, M. C., & Gordon-Larsen, P. (2006). Physical activity and sedentary behavior patterns are associated with selected adolescent risk behaviors. *Pediatrics, 117*, 1281–1290.

Ness, J., Ahmed, A., & Aronow, W. S. (2004). Demographics and payment characteristics of nursing home residents in the United States: A 23-year trend. *Journal of Gerontology: Medical Sciences, 59A*, 1213–1217.

Netz, Y., Wu, M., Becker, B. J., & Tenenbaum, G. (2005). Physical activity and psychological well-being in advanced age: A meta-analysis of intervention studies. *Psychology and Aging, 20*, 272–284.

Neugarten, B. L. (1967). The awareness of middle age. In R. Owen (Ed.), *Middle age.* London: BBC.

Neugarten, B. L. (1968). Adult personality: Toward a psychology of the life cycle. In B. Neugarten (Ed.), *Middle age and aging.* Chicago: University of Chicago Press.

Neugarten, B. L. (1977). Personality and aging. In J. E. Birren & K. W. Schaie (Eds.), *Handbook of the psychology of aging and the social sciences.* New York: Van Nostrand Reinhold.

Neugarten, B. L., Havighurst, R., & Tobin, S. (1968). Personality and patterns of aging. In B. Neugarten (Ed.), *Middle age and aging.* Chicago: University of Chicago Press.

Neugarten, B. L., Moore, J. W., & Lowe, J. C. (1965). Age norms, age constraints, and adult socialization. *American Journal of Sociology, 70*, 710–717.

Neugarten, B. L., & Neugarten, D. A. (1987, May). The changing meanings of age. *Psychology Today,* pp. 29–33.

Neumark, D. (2008). *Reassessing the age discrimination in employment act* (Research Report No. 2008-09). Washington, DC: AARP Public Policy Institute. Retrieved from http://www.socsci.uci.edu/~dneumark/2008_09_adea.pdf

Neumark-Sztainer, D., Wall, M., Haines, J., Story, M., Sherwood, N. E., & van den Berg, P. A. (2007). Shared risk and protective factors for overweight and disordered eating in adolescents. *American Journal of Preventive Medicine, 33*, 359–369.

Neupert, S. D., Almeida, D. M., Mroczek, D. K., & Spiro, A. (2006). Daily stressors and memory failures in a naturalistic setting; Findings from the VA Normative Aging Study. *Psychology and Aging, 21*, 424–429.

Neville, A. (n.d.). *The emotional and psychological effects of miscarriage.* Retrieved from www.opendoors.com.au/EffectsMiscarriage/EffectsMiscarriage.htm

Neville, H. J., & Bavelier, D. (1998). Neural organization and plasticity of language. *Current Opinion in Neurobiology, 8*(2), 254–258.

Newcomb, A. F., & Bagwell, C. L. (1995). Children's friendship relations: A meta-analytic review. *Psychological Bulletin, 117*(2), 306–347.

Newman, A. B., Simonsick, E. M., Naydeck, B. L., Boudreau, R. M., Kritchevsky, S. B., Nevitt, M. C., . . . Harris, T. B. (2006). Association of long-distance corridor walk performance with mortality, cardiovascular disease, mobility limitation, and disability. *Journal of the American Medical Association, 295*, 2018–2026.

Newman, D. L., Caspi, A., Moffitt, T. E., & Silva, P. A. (1997). Antecedents of adult interpersonal functioning: Effects of individual differences in age 3 temperament. *Developmental Psychology, 33*, 206–217.

Newman, K., & Aptekar, S. (2007). Sticking around: Delayed departure from the parental nest in Western Europe. In S. Danziger & C. Rouse (Eds.), *The price of independence: The economics of early adulthood* (pp. 207–230). New York: Russell Sage Foundation.

Newman, R. S. (2005). The cocktail party effect in infants revisited: Listening to one's name in noise. *Developmental Psychology, 41*, 352–362.

Newman, S. (2003). The living conditions of elderly Americans. *Gerontologist, 43,* 99–109.

Newport, E. L. (1991). Contrasting conceptions of the critical period for language. In S. Carey & R. Gelman (Eds.), *The epigenesis of mind: Essays on biology and cognition.* Hillsdale, NJ: Erlbaum.

Newport, E. L., Bavelier, D., & Neville, H. J. (2001). Critical thinking about critical periods: Perspectives on a critical period for language acquisition. In E. Dupoux (Ed.), *Language, brain, and cognitive development: Essays in honor of Jacques Mehler* (pp. 481–502). Cambridge, MA: MIT Press.

Newton, K. M., Reed, S. D., LaCroix, A. Z., Grothaus, L. C., Ehrlich, K., & Guiltinan, J. (2006). Treatment of vasomotor symptoms of menopause with black cohosh, multibotanicals, soy, hormone therapy, or placebo: A randomized trial. *Annals of Internal Medicine, 145*(12), 869–879.

Neyer, F. J., & Lehnart, J. (2007). Relationships matter in personality development: Evidence from an 8-year longitudinal study across young adulthood. *Journal of Personality, 75*(3), 535–568.

NICHD Early Child Care Research Network. (1996). Characteristics of infant child care: Factors contributing to positive caregiving. *Early Childhood Research Quarterly, 11*, 269–306.

NICHD Early Child Care Research Network. (1997). The effects of infant child care on infant-mother attachment security: Results of the NICHD Study of Early Child Care. *Child Development*, 860–879.

NICHD Early Child Care Research Network. (1999a). Child outcomes when child care center classes meet recommended standards for quality. *American Journal of Public Health, 89*, 1072–1077.

NICHD Early Child Care Research Network. (1999b). Chronicity of maternal depressive symptoms, maternal sensitivity, and child functioning at 36 months. *Developmental Psychology, 35*, 1297–1310.

NICHD Early Child Care Research Network. (2000). The relation of child care to cognitive and language development. *Child Development, 71*, 960–980.

NICHD Early Child Care Research Network. (2002). Child-care structure, process, and outcome: Direct and indirect effects of child-care quality on young children's development. *Psychological Science, 13*, 199–206.

NICHD Early Child Care Research Network. (2003). Does amount of time spent in child care predict socioemotional adjustment during the transition to kindergarten? *Child Development, 74*, 976–1005.

NICHD Early Child Care Research Network. (2004a). Are child developmental outcomes related to before- and afterschool care arrangement? Results from the NICHD Study of Early Child Care. *Child Development 75,* 280–295.

NICHD Early Child Care Research Network. (2004b). Does class size in first grade relate to children's academic and social performance or observed classroom processes? *Developmental Psychology, 40*, 651–664.

NICHD Early Child Care Research Network. (2005a). Duration and developmental timing of poverty and children's cognitive and social development from birth through third grade. *Child Development, 76*, 795–810.

NICHD Early Child Care Research Network. (2005b). Pathways to reading: The role of oral language in the transition to reading. *Developmental Psychology, 41*, 428–442.

NICHD Early Child Care Research Network. (2005c). Predicting individual differences in attention, memory, and planning in first graders from experiences at home, child care, and school. *Developmental Psychology, 41*, 99–114.

Nickerson, A. B., & Nagel, R. J. (2005). Parent and peer attachment in late childhood and early adolescence. *Journal of Early Adolescence, 25*, 223–249.

Nie, N. H. (2001). Socialability, interpersonal relations and the Internet: Reconciling conflicting findings. *American Behavioral Scientist, 45*, 420–435.

Nielsen, M., Dissanayake, C., & Kashima, Y. (2003). A longitudinal investigation of self-other discrimination and the emergence of mirror self-recognition. *Infant Behavior & Development, 26*, 213–226.

Nielsen, M., Suddendorf, T., & Slaughter, V. (2006). Mirror self-recognition beyond the face. *Child Development, 77*, 176–185.

Nielsen, M., & Tomaselli, K. (2010). Overimitation in Kalahari Bushman children and the origins of human cultural cognition. *Psychological Science, 21*(5), 729–736.

Nihtilä, E., & Martikainen, P. (2008). Why older people living with a spouse are less likely to be institutionalized: The role of socioeconomic factors and health characteristics. *Scandinavian Journal of Public Health, 36*, 35–43.

Nilsen, E. S., & Graham, S. A. (2009). The relations between children's communicative perspective-taking and executive functioning. *Cognitive Psychology, 58*, 220–249.

Nirmala, A., Reddy, B. M., & Reddy, P. P. (2008). Genetics of human obesity: An overview. *International Journal of Human Genetics, 8*, 217–226.

Nisbett, R. E. (2005). Heredity, environment, and race differences in IQ: A commentary on Rushton and Jensen (2005). *Psychology, Public Policy, and Law, 11*, 302–310.

Nix, R. L., Pinderhughes, E. E., Dodge, K. A., Bates, J. E., Pettit, G. S., & McFadyen-Ketchum, S. A. (1999). The relation between mothers' hostile attribution tendencies and children's externalizing behavior problems: The mediating role of mothers' harsh discipline practices. *Child Development, 70*(4), 896–909.

Njajou, O. T., Hsueh, W., Blackburn, E. H., Newman, A. B., Wu, S., Li, R., . . . Cawthon, R. M. (2009). Association between telomere length, specific causes of death, and years of healthy life in health, aging, and body composition, a population-based cohort study. *Journals of Gerontology. Series A, 64A*(8), 860–864.

Nobes, G., Panagiotaki, G., & Pawson, C. (2009). The influence of negligence, intentions and outcome on children's moral judgments. *Journal of Experimental Child Psychology, 104*(4), 382–397.

Nock, M. K., Borges, G., Bromet, E. J., Alonso, J., Angermeyer, M., Beautrais, A., . . . Williams, D. (2008). Cross-national prevalence and risk factors for suicidal ideation, plans and attempts. *British Journal of Psychiatry, 192*, 98–105.

Noël, P. H., Williams, J. W., Unutzer, J., Worchel, J., Lee, S., Cornell, J., . . . Hunkeler, E. (2004). Depression and comorbid illness in elderly primary care patients: Impact on multiple domains of health status and well-being. *Annals of Family Medicine, 2*, 555–562.

Nord, M., Andrews, A., & Carlson, S. (2008). *Household food security in the United States, 2007* (ERR-66). Retrieved from www.ers.usda.gov/publications/err66

Noriuchi, M., Kikuchi, Y., & Senoo, A. (2008). The functional neuroanatomy of maternal love: Mother's response to infant's attachment behaviors. *Biological Psychiatry, 63*, 415–423.

Norton, A. J., & Moorman, J. E. (1987). Current trends in marriage and divorce among American women. *Journal of Marriage and the Family, 49*(1), 3–14.

Nucci, L., Hasebe, Y., & Lins-Dyer, M. T. (2005). Adolescent psychological well-being and parental control. In J. Smetana (Ed.), *Changing boundaries of parental authority during adolescence* (New Directions for Child and Adolescent Development, No. 108, pp. 17–30). San Francisco: Jossey-Bass.

Nugent, J. K., Lester, B. M., Greene, S. M., Wieczorek-Deering, D., & O'Mahony, P. (1996). The effects of maternal alcohol consumption and cigarette smoking during pregnancy on acoustic cry analysis. *Child Development, 67*, 1806–1815.

Nurnberg, H. G., Hensley, P. L., Gelenberg, A. J., Fava, M., Lauriello, J., & Paine, S. (2003). Treatment of antidepressant-associated sexual dysfunction with sildenafil. *Journal of the American Medical Association, 289*, 56–64.

Nussbaum, R. L. (1998). Putting the parkin into Parkinson's. *Nature, 392*, 544–545.

Ober, C., Tan, Z., Sun, Y., Possick, J. D., Pan, L., Nicolae, R., . . . Chupp, G. L. (2008). Effect of variation in CH13L1 on serum YKL-40 level, risk of asthma, and lung function. *New England Journal of Medicine, 358*, 1682–1691.

Oberman, L. M., & Ramachandran, V. S. (2007). The simulating social mind: The role of the mirror neuron system and simulation in the social and communicative deficits of autism spectrum disorders. *Psychological Bulletin, 133*, 310–327.

Obradovic, J., Stamperdahl, J., Bush, N. R., Adler, N. E., & Boyce, W. T. (2010). Biological sensitivity to context: The interactive effects of stress reactivity and family adversity on socio-emotional behavior and school readiness. *Child Development, 81*, 270–289.

O'Brien, C. M., & Jeffery, H. E. (2002). Sleep deprivation, disorganization and fragmentation during opiate withdrawal in newborns. *Pediatric Child Health, 38*, 66–71.

O'Connor, T., Heron, J., Golding, J., Beveridge, M., & Glover, V. (2002). Maternal antenatal anxiety and children's behavioural/emotional problems at 4 years. *British Journal of Psychiatry, 180*, 502–508.

Odgers, C., Caspi, A., Nagin, D., Piquero, A., Slutske, W., Milne, B., . . . Moffitt, T. E. (2008). Is it important to prevent early exposure to drugs and alcohol among adolescents? *Psychological Science, 19*(10), 1037–1044.

O'Donnell, K. (2006). *Adult education participation in 2004–06* (NCES 2006-077). Washington, DC: National Center for Education Statistics.

O'Donnell, K., Badrick, E., Kumari, M., & Steptoe, A. (2008). Psychological coping styles and cortisol over the day in healthy older adults. *Psychoneuroendocrinology, 33*(5), 601–611.

O'Flynn O'Brien, K. L., Varghese, A. C., & Agarwal, A. (2010). The genetic causes of male factor infertility: A review. *Fertility and Sterility, 93*, 1–12.

Offer, D., & Church, R. B. (1991). Generation gap. In R. M. Lerner, A. C. Petersen, & J. Brooks-Gunn (Eds.), *Encyclopedia of adolescence* (pp. 397–399). New York: Garland.

Offer, D., Kaiz, M., Ostrov, E., & Albert, D. B. (2002). Continuity in family constellation. *Adolescent and Family Health, 3*, 3–8.

Offer, D., Offer, M. K., & Ostrov, E. (2004). *Regular guys: 34 years beyond adolescence.* Dordrecht, The Netherlands: Kluwer-Academic.

Office of Management and Budget. (2011). *Fiscal year 2012 budget of the U.S. government.* Washington, DC: Executive Office of the President.

Office of Minority Health, Centers for Disease Control and Prevention. (2005). Health disparities experienced by Black or African Americans—United States. *Morbidity and Mortality Weekly Report, 54*, 1–3.

Office of National Drug Control Policy. (2004). *The economic costs of drug abuse in the United States, 1992–2002* (No. 207303). Washington, DC: Executive Office of the President.

Office of National Drug Control Policy. (2008). *Teen marijuana use worsens depression: An analysis of recent data shows "self-medicating" could actually make things worse.* Washington, DC: Executive Office of the President.

Office on Smoking and Health, Centers for Disease Control and Prevention. (2006). *The health consequences of involuntary exposure to tobacco smoke: A report of the surgeon-general* (No. 017-024-01685-3). Washington, DC: U.S. Department of Health and Human Services.

Offit, P. A., Quarles, J., Gerber, M. A., Hackett, C. J., Marcuse, E. K., Kollman, T. R., . . . Landry, S. (2002). Addressing parents' concerns: Do multiple vaccines overwhelm or weaken the infant's immune system? *Pediatrics, 109*, 124–129.

Ofori, B., Oraichi, D., Blais, L., Rey, E., & Berard, A. (2006). Risk of congenital anomalies in pregnant users of non-steroidal anti-inflammatory drugs: A nested case-control study. *Birth Defects Research Part B: Developmental and Reproductive Toxicology, 77*(4), 268–279.

Ogden, C. L., Carroll, M. D., Curtin, L. R., Lamb, M. M., & Flegal, K. M. (2010). Prevalence of high body mass index in U.S. children and adolescents, 2007–2008. *Journal of the American Medical Association, 303*(3), 242–249.

Ogden, C. L., Carroll, M. D., Curtin, L. R., McDowell, M. A., Tabak, C. J., & Flegal, K. M. (2006). Prevalence of overweight and obesity in the United States, 1999–2004. *Journal of the American Medical Association, 295*, 1549–1555.

Ogden, C. L., Carroll, M. D., & Flegal, K. M. (2008). High body mass index for age among US children and adolescents, 2003–2006. *Journal of the American Medical Association, 299*, 2401–2405.

Ogden, C. L., Carroll, M. D., McDowell, M. A., & Flegal, K. M. (2007). Obesity among adults in the United States: No change since 2003–2004. *NCHS Data Brief.* Hyattsville, MD: National Center for Health Statistics.

Okamoto, K., & Tanaka, Y. (2004). Subjective usefulness and 6-year mortality risks among elderly persons in Japan. *Journal of Gerontology: Psychological Sciences, 59B*, P246–P249.

Olds, S. W. (1989). *The working parents' survival guide.* Rocklin, CA: Prima.

Olfson, M., Blanco, C., Liu, L., Moreno, C., & Laje, G. (2006). National trends in the outpatient treatment of children and adolescents with antipsychotic drugs. *Archives of General Psychiatry, 63*, 679–685.

Olfson, M., Crystal, S., Huang, C., & Gerhard, T. (2010). Trends in antipsychotic drug use by very young, privately insured children. *Journal of Child and Adolescent Psychiatry, 49*(1), 13–23.

Olinto, P., Beegle, K., Sobrado, C., & Uematsu, H. (2013). The state of the poor: Where are the poor, where is extreme poverty harder to end, and what is the current profile of the world's poor? *Economic Premise*, 125. Washington, DC: World Bank.

Ollendick, T. H., Yang, B., King, N. J., Dong, Q., & Akande, A. (1996). Fears in American, Australian, Chinese, and Nigerian children and adolescents: A cross-cultural study. *Journal of Child Psychology and Psychiatry, 37*, 213–220.

Olshansky, S. J., Hayflick, L., & Carnes, B. A. (2002a). No truth to the fountain of youth. *Scientific American, 286*, 92–95.

Olshansky, S. J., Hayflick, L., & Perls, T. T. (2004). Anti-aging medicine: The hype and the reality—Part I. *Journal of Gerontology: Biological Sciences, 59A*, 513–514.

Olshansky, S. J., Passaro, D. J., Hershow, R. C., Layden, J., Carnes, B. A., Brody, J., . . . Ludwig, D. S. (2005). A potential decline in life expectancy in the United States in the 21st century. *New England Journal of Medicine, 352*, 1138–1145.

Olson, K., & Shaw, A. (2010). "No fair, copycat!": What children's response to plagiarism tells us about their understanding of ideas. *Developmental Science, 14*(2), 431–439. doi: 10.1111/j.1467-7687.2010.00993.x

Olson, K. R., & Spelke, E. S. (2008). Foundations of cooperation in young children. *Cognition, 108*, 222–231.

Olthof, T., Schouten, A., Kuiper, H., Stegge, H., & Jennekens-Schinkel, A. (2000). Shame and guilt in children: Differential situational antecedents and experiential correlates. *British Journal of Developmental Psychology, 18*, 51–64.

Olweus, D. (1995). Bullying or peer abuse at school: Facts and intervention. *Current Directions in Psychological Science, 4*, 196–200.

Omodei, D., & Fontana, L. (2011). Calorie restriction and prevention of age-associated chronic disease. *FEBS Letters, 585*(11), 1537–1542.

O'Neill, G., Summer, L., & Shirey, L. (1999). *Hearing loss: A growing problem that affects quality of life*. Washington, DC: National Academy on an Aging Society.

Orathinkal, J., & Vansteenwegen, A. (2007). Do demographics affect marital satisfaction? *Journal of Sex & Marital Therapy, 33*(1), 73–85.

Orbuch, T. L., House, J. S., Mero, R. P., & Webster, P. S. (1996). Marital quality over the life course. *Social Psychology Quarterly, 59*, 162–171.

Oregon Health Authority. (n.d.). *Death with Dignity Act.* Retrieved from http://public.health.oregon.gov/ProviderPartnerResources/EvaluationResearch/DeathwithDignityAct/Pages/index.aspx

Orenstein, P. (2002, April 21). Mourning my miscarriage. *The New York Times*. Retrieved from www.NYTimes.com

Orentlicher, D. (1996). The legalization of physician-assisted suicide. *New England Journal of Medicine, 335*, 663–667.

Organization for Economic Cooperation and Development (OCED). (2004). Education at a glance: OECD indicators—2004. *Education & Skills, 2004*(14), 1–456.

Organisation for Economic Cooperation and Development (OECD). (2008). *Education at a glance.* Paris, France: Author.

Orr, W. C., & Sohal, R. S. (1994). Extension of life-span by overexpression of superoxide dimutase and catylase in Drosphila melanogaster. *Science, 263*, 1128–1130.

Orth, U., Trzesniewski, K. H., & Robins, R. W. (2010). Self-esteem development from young adulthood to old age: A cohort-sequential longitudinal study. *Journal of Personality and Social Psychology, 98*, 645–658. doi: 10.1037/a0018769

Osborne, C., Manning, W. D., & Smock, P. J. (2007). Married and cohabiting parents' relationship stability: A focus on race and ethnicity. *Journal of Marriage and Family, 69*(5), 1345–1366.

Osgood, D. W., Ruth, G., Eccles, J., Jacobs, J., & Barber, B. (2005). Six paths to adulthood: Fast starters, parents without careers, educated partners, educated singles, working singles, and slow starters. In R. A. Settersten Jr., F. F. Furstenberg Jr., & R. G. Rumbaut (Eds.), *On the frontier of adulthood: Theory, research, and public policy* (pp. 320–355). Chicago: University of Chicago Press.

Ossorio, P., & Duster, T. (2005). Race and genetics: Controversies in biomedical, behavioral, and forensic sciences. *American Psychologist, 60*, 115–128.

Ostfeld, B. M., Esposity, L., Perl, H., & Hegyl, T. (2010). Concurrent risks in sudden infant death syndrome. *Pediatrics, 125*(3), 447–453.

Ostir, G. V., Ottenbacher, K. J., & Markides, K. S. (2004). Onset of frailty in older adults and the protective role of positive affect. *Psychology and Aging, 19*, 402–408.

Otsuka, R., Watanabe, H., Hirata, K., Tokai, K., Muro, T., Yoshiyama, M., Takeuchi, K., & Yoshikawa, J. (2001). Acute effects of passive smoking on the coronary circulation in healthy young adults. *Journal of the American Medical Association, 286*, 436–441.

Ott, M. G., Schmidt, M., Schwarzwaelder, K., Stein, S., Siler, U., Koehl, U., . . . Grez, M. (2006). Correction of X-linked chronic granulomatous disease by gene therapy, augmented by insertional activation of MDS1-EVI1, PRDM16 or SETBP1. *Nature Medicine, 12*, 401–409.

Ouellette, G. P., & Sénéchal, M. (2008). A window into early literacy: Exploring the cognitive and linguistic underpinnings of invented spelling. *Scientific Studies of Reading, 12*(2), 195–219.

Out of sight, out of mind: Hidden cost of neglected tropical diseases. (2010, November 25). *The Guardian*. Retrieved from http://www.guardian.co.uk/science/blog/2010/nov/25/neglected-tropical-diseases

Over, H., & Carpenter, M. (2009). Eighteen-month-old infants show increased helping following priming with affiliation. *Psychological Science, 20*(10), 1189–1193.

Overbeek, G., Stattin, H., Vermulst, A., Ha, T., & Engels, R. C. M. E. (2007). Parent-child relationships, partner relationships, and emotional adjustment: A birth-to-maturity prospective study. *Developmental Psychology, 43*, 429–437.

Owen, C. G., Whincup, P. H., Odoki, K., Gilg, J. A., & Cook, D. G. (2002). Infant feeding and blood cholesterol: A study in adolescents and a systematic review. *Pediatrics, 110*, 597–608.

Owens, R. E. (1996). *Language development* (4th ed.). Boston: Allyn & Bacon.

Padilla, A. M., Lindholm, K. J., Chen, A., Duran, R., Hakuta, K., Lambert, W., & Tucker, G. R. (1991). The English-only movement: Myths, reality, and implications for psychology. *American Psychologist, 46*(2), 120–130.

Paley, B., & O'Connor, M. J. (2011). Behavioral interventions for children and adolescents with Fetal Alcohol Spectrum Disorders. *Alcohol Research and Health, 34*, 64–75.

Pamuk, E., Makuc, D., Heck, K., Reuben, C., & Lochner, K. (1998). Socioeconomic status and health chartbook. In *Health, United States, 1998.* Hyattsville, MD: National Center for Health Statistics.

Pan, B. A., Rowe, M. L., Singer, J. D., & Snow, C. E. (2005). Maternal correlates of growth in toddler vocabulary production in low-income families. *Child Development, 76*, 763–782.

Pan, S. Y., Ugnat, A. M., Mao, Y., & Canadian Cancer Registries Epidemiology Research Group. (2005). Physical activity and the risk of ovarian cancer: A case-control study in Canada. *International Journal of Cancer, 117*, 300–307.

Panigrahy, A., Filiano, J., Sleeper, L. A., Mandell, F., Valdes-Dapena, M., Krous, H. F., . . . Kinney, H. C. (2000). Decreased serotonergic receptor binding in rhombic lip-derived regions of the medulla oblongata in the sudden infant death syndrome. *Journal of Neuropathology and Experimental Neurology, 59*, 377–384.

Papadatou-Pastou, M., Martin, M., Munafo, M., & Jones, G. (2008). Sex differences in left-handedness: A meta-analysis of 144 studies. *American Psychological Association Bulletin, 134*(5), 677–699.

Papernow, P. (1993). *Becoming a stepfamily: Patterns of development in remarried families.* San Francisco: Jossey-Bass.

Park, D., & Gutchess, A. (2006). The cognitive neuroscience of aging and culture. *Current Directions in Psychological Science, 15*, 105–108.

Park, D. C., & Gutchess, A. H. (2005). Long-term memory and aging: A cognitive neuroscience perspective. In R. Cabeza, L. Nyberg, & D. C. Park (Eds.), *Cognitive neuroscience of aging: linking cognitive and cerebral aging* (pp. 218–245). New York: Oxford University Press.

Park, D. C., & Reuter-Lorenz, P. (2009). The adaptive brain: Aging and neurocognitive scaffolding. *Annual Review of Psychology, 60*(1), 173–176.

Park, M. J., Mulye, T. P., Adams, S. H., Brindis, C. D., & Irwin, C. E. (2006). The health status of young adults in the United States. *Journal of Adolescent Health, 39*, 305–317.

Park, Y., & Killen, M. (2010). When is peer rejection justifiable? Children's understanding across two cultures. *Cognitive Development, 25*(3), 290–301. doi: 10.1016/j.cogdev.2009.10.004

Park, S., Belsky, J., Putnam, S., & Crnic, K. (1997). Infant emotionality, parenting, and 3-year inhibition: Exploring stability and lawful discontinuity in a male sample. *Developmental Psychology, 33*, 218–227.

Park, J. M., Metraux, S., & Culhane, D. P. (2010). Behavioral health services use among heads of homeless and housed poor families. *Journal of Health Care for the Poor and Underserved, 21*(2), 582–590.

Parke, R. D. (2004a). Development in the family. *Annual Review of Psychology, 55*, 365–399.

Parke, R. D. (2004b). The Society for Research in Child Development at 70: Progress and promise. *Child Development, 75*, 1–24.

Parke, R. D., & Buriel, R. (1998). Socialization in the family: Ethnic and ecological perspectives. In W. Damon (Series Ed.) & N. Eisenberg (Vol. Ed.), *Handbook of child psychology: Vol. 3. Social, emotional, and personality development* (5th ed., pp. 463–552). New York: Wiley.

Parke, R. D., Grossman, K., & Tinsley, R. (1981). Father-mother-infant interaction in the newborn period: A German-American comparison. In T. M. Field, A. M. Sostek, P. Viete, & P. H. Leideman (Eds.), *Culture and early interaction*. Hillsdale, NJ: Erlbaum.

Parker, J. D., Woodruff, T. J., Basu, R., & Schoendorf, K. C. (2005). Air pollution and birth weight among term infants in California. *Pediatrics, 115*, 121–128.

Parker, K. (2009a). *End-of-life decisions: How Americans cope*. Retrieved from www.pewresearch.org/

Parker, K. (2009b). *The harried life of the working mother*. Retrieved from http://pewsocialtrends.org/2009/10/01/the-harried-life-of-the-working-mother/

Parker, L., Pearce, M. S., Dickinson, H. O., Aitkin, M., & Craft, A. W. (1999). Stillbirths among offspring of male radiation workers at Sellafield Nuclear Reprocessing Plant. *Lancet, 354*, 1407–1414.

Parkes, T. L., Elia, A. J., Dickinson, D., Hilliker, A. J., Phillips, J. P., & Boulianne, G. L. (1998). Extension of Drosophila lifespan by overexpression of human SOD1 in motorneurons. *Nature Genetics, 19*, 171–174.

Parry, W. (2010, August 29). Bring it: Boys make benefit from aggressive play. *Today Health*. Retrieved from http://today.msnbc.msn.com/id/38882665/ns/health-kids_and_parenting/

Parten, M. B. (1932). Social play among preschool children. *Journal of Abnormal and Social Psychology, 27*, 243–269.

Partridge, L. (2010). The new biology of ageing. *Philosophical Transactions, 365*(1537), 147–154.

Pascarella, E. T., Edison, M. I., Nora, A., Hagedorn, L. S., & Terenzini, P. T. (1998). Does work inhibit cognitive development during college? *Educational Evaluation and Policy Analysis, 20*, 75–93.

Pascual-Leone, A., Amedi, A., Fregni, F., & Merabet, L. B. (2005). The plastic human brain cortex. *Annual Review of Neuroscience, 28*, 377–401.

Pastor, P. N., & Reuben, C. A. (2008). Diagnosed attention deficit hyperactivity disorder and learning disability, United States, 2004–2006. *Vital and Health Statistics, 10*(237). Hyattsville, MD: National Center for Health Statistics.

Pasupathi, M., Staudinger, U. M., & Baltes, P. B. (2001). Seeds of wisdom: Adolescents' knowledge and judgment about difficult life problems. *Developmental Psychology, 37*(3), 351–361.

Patel, H., Rosengren, A., & Ekman, I. (2004). Symptoms in acute coronary syndromes: Does sex make a difference? *American Heart Journal, 148*, 27–33.

Patel, K. V., Coppin, A. K., Manini, T. M., Lauretani, F., Bandinelli, S., Ferrucci, L., & Guralnik, J. M. (2006, August 10). Midlife physical activity and mobility in older age: The InCHIANTI Study. *American Journal of Preventive Medicine, 31*(3), 217–224.

Patenaude, A. F., Guttmacher, A. E., & Collins, F. S. (2002). Genetic testing and psychology: New roles, new responsibilities. *American Psychologist, 57*, 271–282.

Paterson, D. S., Trachtenberg, F. L., Thompson, E. G., Belliveau, R. A., Beggs, A. H., Darnell, R., . . . Kinney, H. C. (2006). Multiple serotogenic brainstem abnormalities in sudden infant death syndrome. *Journal of the American Medical Association, 296*, 2124–2132.

Patrick, K., Norman, G. J., Calfas, K. J., Sallis, J. F., Zabinski, M. F., Rupp, J., & Cella, J. (2004). Diet, physical activity, and sedentary behaviors as risk factors for overweight in adolescence. *Archives of Pediatric Adolescent Medicine, 158*, 385–390.

Patterson, C. J. (1992). Children of lesbian and gay parents. *Child Development, 63*, 1025–1042.

Patterson, C. J. (1995a). Lesbian mothers, gay fathers, and their children. In A. R. D'Augelli & C. J. Patterson (Eds.), *Lesbian, gay, and bisexual identities over the lifespan: Psychological perspectives* (pp. 293–320). New York: Oxford University Press.

Patterson, C. J. (1995b). Sexual orientation and human development: An overview. *Developmental Psychology, 31*, 3–11.

Patterson, G. R., DeBaryshe, B. D., & Ramsey, E. (1989). A developmental perspective on antisocial behavior. *American Psychologist, 44*(2), 329–335.

Pauen, S. (2002). Evidence for knowledge-based category discrimination in infancy. *Child Development, 73*, 1016–1033.

Paul, E. L. (1997). A longitudinal analysis of midlife interpersonal relationships and well-being. In M. E. Lachman & J. B. James (Eds.), *Multiple paths of midlife development* (pp. 171–206). Chicago: University of Chicago Press.

Pawelski, J. G., Perrin, E. C., Foy, J. M., Allen, C. E., Crawford, J. E., Del Monte, M., . . . Vickers, D. L. (2006). The effects of marriage, civil union, and domestic partnership laws on the health and well-being of children. *Pediatrics, 118*, 349–364.

Pearson, J. D., Morell, C. H., Gordon-Salant, S., Brant, L. J., Metter, E. J., Klein, L., & Fozard, J. L. (1995). Gender differences in a longitudinal study of age-associated hearing loss. *Journal of the Acoustical Society of America, 97*, 1196–1205.

Pearson, H. (2002, February 12). Study refines breast cancer risks. *Nature Science Update*. Retrieved from www.nature.com/nsu/020211/020211-8.html

Peeters, A., Barendregt, J. J., Willekens, F., Mackenbach, J. P., Al Mamun, A., & Bonneux, L., for NEDCOM, the Netherlands Epidemiology and Demography Compression of Morbidity Research Group. (2003). Obesity in adulthood and its consequences for life expectancy. *Annals of Internal Medicine, 138*, 24–32.

Pellegrini, A. D., & Archer, J. (2005). Sex differences in competitive and aggressive behavior: A view from sexual selection theory. In B. J. Ellis & D. F. Bjorklund (Eds.), *Origins of the social mind: Evolutionary psychology and child development* (pp. 219–244). New York: Guilford Press.

Pellegrini, A. D., Kato, K., Blatchford, P., & Baines, E. (2002). A short-term longitudinal study of children's playground games across the first year of school: Implications for social competence and adjustment to school. *American Educational Research Journal, 39*, 991–1015.

Pellegrini, A. D., & Long, J. D. (2002). A longitudinal study of bullying, dominance, and victimization during the transition from primary school through secondary school. *British Journal of Developmental Psychology, 20*, 259–280.

Pennington, B. F., Moon, J., Edgin, J., Stedron, J., & Nadel, L. (2003). The neuropsychology of Down syndrome: Evidence for hippocampal dysfunction. *Child Development, 74*, 75–93.

Pennisi, E. (1998). Single gene controls fruit fly life-span. *Science, 282*, 856.

Pepper, S. C. (1942). *World hypotheses*. Berkeley: University of California Press.

Pepper, S. C. (1961). *World hypotheses*. Berkeley: University of California Press.

Pereira, M. A., Kartashov, A. I., Ebbeling, C. B., Van Horn, L., Slattery, M. L., Jacobs, D. R., Jr., & Ludwig, D. S. (2005). Fast-food habits, weight gain, and insulin resistance (the CARDIA study): 15-year prospective analysis. *Lancet, 365*, 36–42.

Perera, F. P., Rauh, V., Whyatt, R. M., Tsai, W. Y., Bernert, J. T., Tu, Y.-H., . . . Tang, D. (2004).

Molecular evidence of an interaction between prenatal environmental exposures and birth outcomes in a multiethnic population. *Environmental Health Perspectives, 112*, 626–630.

Perera, F., Tang, W-y., Herbstman, J., Tang, D., Levin, L., Miller, R., & Ho, S.-m. (2009). Relation of DNA methylation of 5'-CpG island of *ACSL3* to transplacental exposure to airborne polycyclic aromatic hydrocarbons and childhood asthma. *PloS ONE, 4*, e44–e48.

Pérez-Stable, E. J., Herrera, B., Jacob, P., III, & Benowitz, N. L. (1998). Nicotine metabolism and intake in black and white smokers. *Journal of the American Medical Association, 280*, 152–156.

Perls, T., Kunkel, L. M., & Puca, A. (2002a). The genetics of aging. *Current Opinion in Genetics and Development, 12*, 362–369.

Perls, T., Kunkel, L. M., & Puca, A. A. (2002b). The genetics of exceptional human longevity. *Journal of the American Geriatric Society, 50*, 359–368.

Perls, T. T., Alpert, L., & Fretts, R. C. (1997). Middle-aged mothers live longer. *Nature, 389*, 133.

Perls, T. T., Hutter-Silver, M., & Lauerman, J. F. (1999). *Living to 100: Lessons in living to your maximum potential at any age.* New York: Basic Books.

Perrin, E. C., & AAP Committee on Psychosocial Aspects of Child and Family Health. (2002). Technical report: Coparent or second-parent adoption by same-sex parents. *Pediatrics, 109*(2), 341–344.

Perrin, E. M., Finkle, J. P., & Benjamin, J. T. (2007). Obesity prevention and the primary care pediatrician's office. *Current Opinion in Pediatrics, 19*(3), 354–361.

Perry, W. G. (1970). *Forms of intellectual and ethical development in the college years.* New York: Holt.

Pesonen, A., Raïkkönen, K., Keltikangas-Järvinen, L., Strandberg, T., & Järvenpää, A. (2003). Parental perception of infant temperament: Does parents' joint attachment matter? *Infant Behavior and Development, 26*, 167–182.

Peter, K., & Horn, L. (2005). *Gender differences in participation and completion of undergraduate education and how they have changed over time* (NCES 2005-169). Washington, DC: U.S. Government Printing Office.

Peters, E., Hess, T. M., Västfjäll, D., & Auman, C. (2007). Adult age differences in dual information processes: Implications for the role of affective and deliberative processes in older adults' decision making. *Perspectives on Psychological Science, 2*(1), 1–23.

Peters, R., Peters, J., Warner, J., Beckett, N., & Bulpitt, C. (2008). Alcohol, dementia and cognitive decline in the elderly: A systematic review. *Age and ageing, 37*(5), 505–512.

Petersen, A. C. (1993). Presidential address: Creating adolescents: The role of context and process in developmental transitions. *Journal of Research on Adolescents, 3*(1), 1–18.

Petersen, A. C., Compas, B. E., Brooks-Gunn, J., Stemmler, M., Ey, S., & Grant, K. E. (1993). Depression in adolescence. *American Psychologist, 48*(2), 155–168.

Petersen, R. C., Roberts, R. O., Knopman, D. S., Geda, Y. E., Cha, R. H., Pankratz, V. S., . . . Rocca, W. A. (2010). Prevalence of mild cognitive impairment is higher in men: The Mayo Clinic Study of Aging. *Neurology, 75*(10), 889–897. doi: 10.1212/WNL.0b013e3181f11d85

Peterson, B. E. (2002). Longitudinal analysis of midlife generativity, intergenerational roles, and caregiving. *Psychology and Aging, 17*, 161–168.

Peterson, B. E., & Duncan, L. E. (2007). Midlife women's generativity and authoritarianism: Marriage, motherhood and 10 years of aging. *Psychology and Aging, 22*(3), 411–419.

Petit, D., Touchette, E., Tremblay, R. E., Boivin, M., & Montplaisir, J. (2007). Dyssomnias and parasomnias in early childhoold. *Pediatrics, 119*(5), e1016–e1025.

Petitti, D. B. (2002). Hormone replacement therapy for prevention: More evidence, more pessimism. *Journal of the American Medical Association, 288*, 99–101.

Petitto, L. A., Holowka, S., Sergio, L., & Ostry, D. (2001). Language rhythms in babies' hand movements. *Nature, 413*, 35–36.

Petitto, L. A., Katerelos, M., Levy, B., Gauna, K., Tetrault, K., & Ferraro, V. (2001). Bilingual signed and spoken language acquisition from birth: Implications for mechanisms underlying bilingual language acquisition. *Journal of Child Language, 28*, 1–44.

Petitto, L. A., & Kovelman, I. (2003). The bilingual paradox: How signing-speaking bilingual children help us to resolve it and teach us about the brain's mechanisms underlying all language acquisition. *Learning Languages, 8*, 5–18.

Petitto, L. A., & Marentette, P. F. (1991). Babbling in the manual mode: Evidence for the ontogeny of language. *Science, 251*, 1493–1495.

Petrill, S. A., Lipton, P. A., Hewitt, J. K., Plomin, R., Cherny, S. S., Corley, R., & DeFries, J. C. (2004). Genetic and environmental contributions to general cognitive ability through the first 16 years of life. *Developmental Psychology, 40*, 805–812.

Pettit, G. S., Bates, J. E., & Dodge, K. A. (1997). Supportive parenting, ecological context, and children's adjustment: A seven-year longitudinal study. *Child Development, 68*, 908–923.

Pew Research Center. (2007a). *As marriage and parenthood drift apart, public is concerned about social impact.* Retrieved from http://pewsocialtrends.org/2007/07/01/as-marriage-and-parenthood-drift-apart-public-is-concerned-about-social-impact/

Pew Research Center. (2007b). *Modern marriage.* Retrieved from http://pewsocialtrends.org/2007/07/18/modern-marriage/

Pew Research Center. (2009a). *Growing old in America: Expectations vs. reality*. Retrieved from http://pewsocialtrends.org/2009/06/29/growing-old-in-america-expectations-vs-reality/

Pew Research Center. (2010a). *The millennials: Confident. Connected. Open to change.* Retrieved from http://pewresearch.org/pubs/1501/millennials-new-survey-generational-personality-upbeat-open-new-ideas-technology-bound

Pew Research Center. (2010b). *The return of the multi-generational family household.* Retrieved from http://pewsocialtrends.org/2010/03/18/the-return-of-the-multi-generational-family-household/

Pew Research Center. (2011). *How millennial are you? The quiz.* Retrieved from http://pewresearch.org/millennials/quiz/

Pew Research Center. (2012). *More support for gun rights, gay marriage, than in 2008 or 2004.* Retrieved from http://www.people-press.org/2012/04/25/more-support-for-gun-rights-gay-marriage-than-in-2008-or-2004/

Pew Research Center. (2013). *Gay marriage around the world.* Retrieved from http://www.pewforum.org/2013/12/19/gay-marriage-around-the-world-2013/

Phelan, E. A., Williams, B., Penninx, B. W. J. H., LoGerfo, J. P., & Leveille, S. G. (2004). Activities of daily living function and disability in older adults in a randomized trial of the Health Enhancement Program. *Journal of Geronotology: Medical Sciences, 59A*, 838–843.

Philippe, F. L., & Vallerand, R. J. (2008). Actual environments do affect motivation and psychological adjustment: A test of self-determination theory in a natural setting. *Motivation and Emotion, 32*(2), 81–89.

Phillips, J. A., & Sweeney, M. M. (2005). Premarital cohabitation and marital disruption among white, black, and Mexican American women. *Journal of Marriage and Family, 67*, 296–314.

Phinney, J. S. (1989). Stages of ethnic identity development in minority group of adolescents. *Journal of Early Adolescence, 9*, 34–49.

Phinney, J. S. (1998). Stages of ethnic identity development in minority group adolescents. In R. E. Muuss & H. D. Porton (Eds.), *Adolescent behavior and society: A book of readings* (pp. 271–280). Boston: McGraw-Hill.

Phinney, J. S. (2003). Ethnic identity and acculturation. In K. Chun, P. B. Organista, & G. Marin (Eds.), *Acculturation: Advances in theory, measurement, and applied research* (pp. 63–81). Washington DC: American Psychological Association.

Phinney, J. S. (2006). Ethnic identity exploration in emerging adulthood. In J. J. Arnett & J. L. Tanner (Eds.), *Emerging adults in America: Coming of age in the 21st century* (pp. 117–134). Washington, DC: American Psychological Association.

Phinney, J. S., Ferguson, D. L., & Tate, J. D. (1997). Intergroup attitudes among ethnic minorities. *Child Development, 68*(3), 955–969.

Phinney, J. S., Jacoby, B., & Silva, C. (2007). Positive intergroup attitudes: The role of ethnic identity. *International Journal of Behavioral Development, 31*(5), 478–490.

Piaget, J. (1929). *The child's conception of the world.* New York: Harcourt Brace.

Piaget, J. (1932). *The moral judgment of the child.* New York: Harcourt Brace.

Piaget, J. (1952). *The origins of intelligence in children.* New York: International Universities Press. (Original work published 1936)

Piaget, J. (1962). *The language and thought of the child* (M. Gabain, Trans.). Cleveland, OH: Meridian. (Original work published 1923)

Piaget, J. (1964). *Six psychological studies.* New York: Vintage Books.

Piaget, J. (1969). *The child's conception of time* (A. J. Pomerans, Trans.). London: Routledge & Kegan Paul.

Piaget, J. (1972). Intellectual evolution from adolescence to adulthood. *Human Development, 15,* 1–12.

Piaget, J., & Inhelder, B. (1967). *The child's conception of space.* New York: Norton.

Piaget, J., & Inhelder, B. (1969). *The psychology of the child.* New York: Basic Books.

Pianezza, M. L., Sellers, E. M., & Tyndale, R. F. (1998). Nicotine metabolism defect reduces smoking. *Nature, 393,* 750.

Picker, J. (2005). The role of genetic and environmental factors in the development of schizophrenia. *Psychiatric Times, 22,* 1–9.

Pierce, K. M., Hamm, J. V., & Vandell, D. L. (1999). Experiences in afterschool programs and children's adjustment in first-grade classrooms. *Child Development, 70*(3), 756–767.

Piernas, C., & Popkin, B. M. (2010). Trends in snacking among U.S. children. *Health Affairs, 29*(3), 398–404.

Pike, A., Coldwell, J., & Dunn, J. F. (2005). Sibling relationships in early/middle childhood: Links with individual adjustment. *Journal of Family Psychology, 19,* 523–532.

Pillemer, K., & Suitor, J. J. (1991). "Will I ever escape my child's problems?" Effects of adult children's problems on elderly parents. *Journal of Marriage and Family, 53,* 585–594.

Pillow, B. H. (2002). Children's and adult's evaluation of the certainty of deductive inferences, inductive inferences and guesses. *Child Development, 73*(3), 779–792.

Pillow, B. H., & Henrichon, A. J. (1996). There's more to the picture than meets the eye: Young children's difficulty understanding biased interpretation. *Child Development, 67,* 803–819.

Pimentel, E. E., & Liu, J. (2004). Exploring nonnormative coresidence in urban China: Living with wives' parents. *Journal of Marriage and Family, 66,* 821–836.

Pines, M. (1981). The civilizing of Genie. *Psychology Today, 15*(9), 28–34.

Pinquart, M., & Sörensen, S. (2006). Gender differences in caregiver stressors, social resources, and health: An updated meta-analysis. *Journal of Gerontology: Psychological and Social Sciences, 61B,* P33–P45.

Pinquart, M., & Sörensen, S. (2007). Correlates of physical health of informal caregivers: A meta-analysis. *Journal of Gerontology: Psychological and Social Sciences, 62B,* P126–P137.

Plant, L. D., Bowers, P. N., Liu, Q., Morgan, T., Zhang, T., State, M. W., . . . Goldstein, S. A. (2006). A common cardiac sodium channel variant associated with sudden infant death in African Americans, SCN5A S1103Y. *Journal of Clinical Investigation, 116*(2), 430–435.

Plassman, B. L., Langa, K. M., Fisher, G. G., Heeringa, S. G., Weir, D. R., Ofstedal, M. B., . . . Wallace, R. B. (2007). Prevalence of dementia in the United States: The Aging, Demographics, and Memory Study. *Neuroepidemiology, 29,* 125–132.

Plassman, B. L., Langa, K. M., Fisher, G. G., Heeringa, S. G., Weir, D. R., Ofstedal, M. B., . . . Wallace, R. B. (2008). Prevalence of cognitive impairment without dementia in the United States. *Annals of Internal Medicine, 14*(6), 427–434.

Pleck, J. H. (1997). Paternal involvement: Levels, sources, and consequences. In M. E. Lamb (Ed.), *The role of the father in child development* (3rd ed., pp. 66–103). New York: Wiley.

Pleis, J. R., & Lucas, J. W. (2009). Summary health statistics for U.S. adults: National health interview survey 2007. *Vital Health Statistics, 10*(240). Hyattsville, MD: National Center for Health Statistics.

Plomin, R. (1996). Nature and nurture. In M. R. Merrens & G. G. Brannigan (Eds.), *The developmental psychologist: Research adventures across the life span* (pp. 3–19). New York: McGraw-Hill.

Plomin, R. (2004). Genetics and developmental psychology. *Merrill-Palmer Quarterly, 50,* 341–352.

Plomin, R., & Daniels, D. (1987). Why are children in the same family so different from one another? *Behavioral and Brain Sciences, 10,* 1–16.

Plomin, R., & DeFries, J. C. (1999). The genetics of cognitive abilities and disabilities. In S. J. Ceci & W. M. Williams (Eds.), *The nature-nurture debate: The essential readings* (pp. 178–195). Malden, MA: Blackwell.

Plomin, R., & Daniels, D. (2011). Why are children in the same family so different from one another? *International Journal of Epidemiology, 40*(3), 563–582.

Plomin, R., & Kovas, Y. (2005). Generalist genes and learning disabilities. *Psychological Bulletin, 131,* 592–617.

Plomin, R., Owen, M. J., & McGuffin, P. (1994). The genetic bases of behavior. *Science, 264,* 1733–1739.

Plomin, R., & Rutter, M. (1998). Child development, molecular genetics, and what to do with genes once they are found. *Child Development, 69*(4), 1223–1242.

Plomin, R., & Thompson, L. A. (1993). Genetics and high cognitive ability. *Ciba Foundation Symposium, 178,* 67–79.

Pogarsky, G., Thornberry, T. P., & Lizotte, A. J. (2006). Developmental outcomes for children of young mothers. *Journal of Marriage and Family, 68,* 332–344.

Pogash, C. (2014). Suicides mounting, golden gate looks to add a safety net. Retrieved May 14, 2014, from http://www.nytimes.com/2014/03/27/us/suicides-mounting-golden-gate-looks-to-add-a-safety-net.html?_r=0

Pomerantz, E. M., Qin, L., Wang, Q., & Chen, H. (2009). *Child Development, 80*(1), 792–807.

Pomerantz, E. M., & Saxon, J. L. (2001). Conceptions of ability as stable and self-evaluative processes: A longitudinal examination. *Child Development, 72,* 152–173.

Pomerantz, E. M., & Wang, Q. (2009). The role of parental control in children's development in Western and Asian countries. *Current Directions in Psychological Science, 18*(5), 285–289.

Pomery, E. A., Gibbons, F. X., Gerrard, M., Cleveland, M. J., Brody, G. H., & Wills, T. A. (2005). Families and risk: Prospective analyses of familial and social influences on adolescent substance use. *Journal of Family Psychology, 19,* 560–570.

Pong, S., Dronkers, J., & Hampden-Thompson, G. (2003). Family policies and children's school achievement in single- versus two-parent families. *Journal of Marriage and the Family, 65,* 681–699.

Pope, A. L., Murray, C. E., & Mobley, A. K. (2010). Personal, relational, and contextual resources and relationship satisfaction in same-sex couples. *Family Journal, 18,* 163–168.

Popenoe, D., & Whitehead, B. D. (2003). *The state of our unions 2003: The social health of marriage in America.* Piscataway, NJ: National Marriage Project.

Popenoe, D., & Whitehead, B. D. (Eds.). (2004). *The state of our unions 2004: The social health of marriage in America.* Piscataway, NJ: National Marriage Project, Rutgers University.

Porcino, J. (1993, April–May). Designs for living. *Modern Maturity,* pp. 24–33.

Porter, P. (2008). "Westernizing" women's risks? Breast cancer in lower-income countries. *New England Journal of Medicine, 358,* 213–216.

Portes, P. R., Dunham, R., & Del Castillo, K. (2000). Identity formation and status across cultures: Exploring the cultural validity of Eriksonian Theory. In A. L. Communian & U. Geilen (Eds.), *International perspectives on human development* (pp. 449–460). Berlin: abst Science.

Posada, G., Gao, Y., Wu, F., Posada, R., Tascon, M., Schoelmerich, A., . . . Synnevaag, B. (1995). The secure-base phenomenon across cultures: Children's behavior, mothers' preferences, and experts' concepts. In E. Waters, B. E. Vaughn, G. Posada, & K. Kondo-Ikemura (Eds.), *Caregiving, cultural, and cognitive perspectives on secure-base behavior and working models: New growing points of attachment theory and research* (pp. 27–48). *Monographs of the Society for Research in Child Development, 60*(2–3, Serial No. 244).

Posthuma, D., & de Geus, E. J. C. (2006). Progress in the molecular-genetic study of intelligence. *Current Directions in Psychological Science, 15*(4), 151–155.

Povinelli, D. J., & Giambrone, S. (2001). Reasoning about beliefs: A human specialization? *Child Development, 72,* 691–695.

Powell, L. H., Calvin, J. E., III, & Calvin, J. E., Jr. (2007). Effective obesity treatments. *American Psychologist, 62,* 234–246.

Powell, L. H., Shahabi, L., & Thoresen, C. E. (2003). Religion and spirituality: Linkages to

physical health. *American Psychologist, 58,* 36–52.
Powell, M. B., & Thomson, D. M. (1996). Children's memory of an occurrence of a repeated event: Effects of age, repetition, and retention interval across three question types. *Child Development, 67,* 1988–2004.
Power, T. G., & Chapieski, M. L. (1986). Childrearing and impulse control in toddlers: A naturalistic investigation. *Developmental Psychology, 22,* 271–275.
Powlishta, K. K., Serbin, L. A., Doyle, A. B., & White, D. R. (1994). Gender, ethnic, and body type biases: The generality of prejudice in childhood. *Developmental Psychology, 30,* 526–536.
Pratt, L. A., Dey, A. N., & Cohen, A. J. (2007). Characteristics of adults with serious psychological distress as measured by the K6 Scale: United States, 2001–04. *Advance Data from Health and Vital Statistics, No. 382.* Hyattsville, MD: National Center for Health Statistics.
Prechtl, H. F. R., & Beintema, D. J. (1964). The neurological examination of the full-term newborn infant. *Clinics in Developmental Medicine* (No. 12). London: Heinemann.
Preissler, M., & Bloom, P. (2007). Two-year-olds appreciate the dual nature of pictures. *Psychological Science, 18*(1), 1–2.
Pressley, J. C., Barlow, B., Kendig, T., & Paneth-Pollak, R. (2007). Twenty-year trends in fatal injuries to very young children: The persistence of racial disparities. *Pediatrics, 119,* 875–884.
Preston, S. H. (2005). Deadweight? The influence of obesity on longevity. *New England Journal of Medicine, 352,* 1135–1137.
Previti, D., & Amato, P. R. (2003). Why stay married? Rewards, barriers, and marital stability. *Journal of Marriage and Family, 65,* 561–573.
Price, T. S., Grosser, T., Plomin, R., & Jaffee, S. R. (2010). Fetal genotype for the xenobiotic metabolizing enzyme NQO1 influences intrauterine growth among infants whose mothers smoked during pregnancy. *Child Development, 81*(1), 101–114.
Price, T. S., Simonoff, E., Waldman, I., Asherson, P., & Plomin, R. (2001). Hyperactivity in preschool children is highly heritable. *Journal of the American Academy of Child and Adolescent Psychiatry, 40*(12), 1362–1364.
Prockop, D. J. (1998). The genetic trail of osteoporosis. *New England Journal of Medicine, 338,* 1061–1062.
Profet, M. (1992). Pregnancy sickness as adaptation: A deterrent to maternal ingestion of teratogens. In L. Cosmides, J. Tooby, & J. H. Barkov (Eds.), *The adapted mind* (pp. 327–366). New York: Oxford University Press.
Pruchno, R., & Johnson, K. W. (1996). Research on grandparenting: Current studies and future needs. *Generations, 20*(1), 65–70.
Pruden, S. M., Hirsch-Pasek, K., Golinkoff, R. M., & Hennon, E. A. (2006). The birth of words: Ten-month-olds learn words through perceptual salience. *Child Development, 77,* 266–280.
Puca, A. A., Daly, M. J., Brewster, S. J., Matise, T. C., Barrett, J., Shea-Drinkwater, M., . . . Perls, T. (2001). A genomewide scan for linkage to human exceptional longevity identifies a locus on chromosome 4. *Proceedings of the National Academy of Science, 28,* 10505–10508.
Pudrovska, T., Schieman, S., & Carr, D. (2006). Strains of singlehood in later life: Do race and gender matter? *Journal of Gerontology: Social Sciences, 61B,* S315–S322.
Pulkkinen, L. (1996). Female and male personality styles: A typological and developmental analysis. *Journal of Personality and Social Psychology, 70,* 1288–1306.
Puma, M., Bell, S., Cook, R., Heid, C., Broene, P., Jenkins, F., . . . Downer, J. (2012). *Third grade follow-up to the Head Start impact study: Final report.* OPRE Report 2012-45. Administration for Children & Families.
Purcell, P. J. (2002). Older workers: Employment and retirement trends. *Congressional Research Service Report for Congress.* Washington, DC: Congressional Research Service.
Pushkar, D., Chaikelson, J., Conway, M., Etezadi, J., Giannopoulus, C., Li, K., & Wrosch, C. (2009). Testing continuity and activity variables as predictors of positive and negative affect in retirement. *Journals of Gerontology, 65*(1), 42–49.
Pushkar, D., Chaikelson, J., Conway, M., Etezadi, J., Giannopoulus, C., Li, K., & Wrosch, C. (2010). Testing continuity and activity variables as predictors of positive and negative affect in retirement. *Journals of Gerontology Series B: Psychological Sciences and Social Sciences, 65*(1), 42–49.
Putallaz, M., & Bierman, K. L. (Eds.). (2004). *Aggression, antisocial behavior, and violence among girls: A developmental perspective.* New York: Guilford Press.
Putney, N. M., & Bengtson, V. L. (2001). Families, intergenerational relationships, and kin-keeping in midlife. In M. E. Lachman (Ed.), *Handbook of midlife development* (pp. 528–570). New York: Wiley.
Quamie, L. (2010, February 2). *Paid family leave funding included in budget.* Retrieved from http://www.clasp.org/issues/in_focus?type=work_life_and_job_quality&id=0009
Quattrin, T., Liu, E., Shaw, N., Shine, B., & Chiang, E. (2005). Obese children who are referred to the pediatric oncologist: Characteristics and outcome. *Pediatrics, 115,* 348–351.
Quigley, H. A., & Broman, A. T. (2006). The number of people with glaucoma worldwide in 2010 and 2020. *British Journal of Ophthalmology, 90,* 262–267.
Quill, T. E., Lo, B., & Brock, D. W. (1997). Palliative options of the last resort. *Journal of the American Medical Association, 278,* 2099–2104.
Quinn, P. C., Westerlund, A., & Nelson, C. A. (2006). Neural markers of categorization in 6-month-old infants. *Psychological Science, 17,* 59–66.
Rabbitt, P., Watson, P., Donlan, C., McInnes, L., Horan, M., Pendleton, N., & Clague, J. (2002). Effects of death within 11 years on cognitive performance in old age. *Psychology and Aging, 17,* 468–481.
Racz, S. J., & McMahon, R. J. (2011). The relationship between parental knowledge and monitoring and child and adolescent conduct: A 10-year update. *Clinical Child and Family Psychology Review, 14*(4), 377–398.
Raikes, H., Pan, B. A., Luze, G., Tamis-LeMonda, C. S., Brooks-Gunn, J., Constantine, J., . . . Rodriguez, E. T. (2006). Mother-child bookreading in low-income families: Correlates and outcomes during three years of life. *Child Development, 77,* 924–953.
Raine, A., Mellingen, K., Liu, J., Venables, P., & Mednick, S. (2003). Effects of environmental enrichment at ages 3–5 years in schizotypal personality and antisocial behavior at ages 17 and 23 years. *American Journal of Psychiatry, 160,* 1627–1635.
Raizada, R., Richards, T., Meltzoff, A., & Kuhl, P. (2008). Socioeconomic status predicts hemispheric specialisation of the left inferior frontal gyrus in young children. *NeuroImage, 40*(3), 1392–1401. doi: 10.1016/j.neuroimage.2008.01.021
Rakison, D. H. (2005). Infant perception and cognition. In B. J. Ellis & D. F. Bjorklund (Eds.), *Origins of the social mind* (pp. 317–353). New York: Guilford Press.
Rakoczy, H., Tomasello, M., & Striano, T. (2004). Young children know that trying is not pretending: A test of the "behaving-as-if" construal of children's early concept of pretense. *Developmental Psychology, 40,* 388–399.
Rakyan, V., & Beck., S. (2006). Epigenetic inheritance and variation in mammals. *Current Opinion in Genetics and Development, 16*(6), 573–577.
Ram, A., & Ross, H. S. (2001). Problem solving, contention, and struggle: How siblings resolve a conflict of interests. *Child Development, 72,* 1710–1722.
Ramey, C. T., & Ramey, S. L. (1998a). Early intervention and early experience. *American Psychologist, 53,* 109–120.
Ramey, C. T., & Ramey, S. L. (1998b). Prevention of intellectual disabilities: Early interventions to improve cognitive development. *Preventive Medicine, 21,* 224–232.
Ramey, C. T., & Ramey, S. L. (2003, May). *Preparing America's children for success in school.* Paper prepared for an invited address at the White House Early Childhood Summit on Ready to Read, Ready to Learn, Denver, CO.
Ramey, C. T., & Ramey, S. L. (2004). Early learning and school readiness: Can early intervention make a difference? *Merrill-Palmer Quarterly, 50*(4), 471–491.
Ramey, G., & Ramey, V. (2010). The rug rat race. In D. H. Romer & J. Wolfers (Eds.), *Brookings papers on economic activity* (pp. 129–200). Washington, DC: Brookings Institution.
Ramey, S. L., & Ramey, C. T. (1992). Early educational intervention with disadvantaged children—To what effect? *Applied and Preventive Psychology, 1,* 131–140.

Ramoz, N., Reichert, J. G., Smith, C. J., Silverman, J. M., Bespalova, I. N., Davis, K. L., & Buxbaum, J. D. (2004). Linkage and association of the mitochondrial aspartate/glutamate carrier SLC25A12 gene with autism. *American Journal of Psychiatry, 161*, 662–669.

Rampey, B. D., Dion, G. S., & Donahue, P. L. (2009). *The nation's report card: Trends in academic progress in reading and mathematics 2008.* Retrieved from http://nces.ed.gov/nationsreportcard/pubs/main2008/2009479.asp

Ramsey, P. G., & Lasquade, C. (1996). Preschool children's entry attempts. *Journal of Applied Developmental Psychology, 17*, 135–150.

Rapoport, J. L., Addington, A. M., & Frangou, S. (2005). The neurodevelopmental model of schizophrenia: Update 2005. *Molecular Psychiatry, 10*, 434–449.

Rapp, S. R., Espeland, M. A., Shumaker, S. A., Henderson, V. W., Brunner, R. L., Manson, J. E., . . . Bowen, D., for the WHIMIS Investigators. (2003). Effects of estrogen plus progestin on global cognitive function in postmenopausal women: The Women's Health Initiative Memory Study: A randomized controlled trial. *Journal of the American Medical Association, 289*(20), 2663–2672.

Rask-Nissilä, L., Jokinen, E., Terho, P., Tammi, A., Lapinleimu, H., Ronnemaa, T., . . . Simell, O. (2000). Neurological development of 5-year-old children receiving a low saturated fat, low cholesterol diet since infancy. *Journal of the American Medical Association, 284*(8), 993–1000.

Rasmussen, K. M., Yaktine, A. L. (Eds.), & Institute of Medicine and National Research Council. (2009). *Weight gain during pregnancy: Reexamining the guidelines.* Washington, DC: National Academies Press.

Rathbun, A., West, J., & Germino-Hausken, E. (2004). *From kindergarten through third grade: Children's beginning school experiences* (NCES 2004-007). Washington, DC: National Center for Education Statistics.

Rauh, V. A., Whyatt, R. M., Garfinkel, R., Andrews, H., Hoepner, L., Reyes, A., . . . Perera, F. P. (2004). Developmental effects of exposure to environmental tobacco smoke and material hardship among inner-city children. *Neurotoxicology and Teratology, 26*, 373–385.

Raver, C. C. (2002). Emotions matter: Making the case for the role of young children's emotional development for early school readiness. *Social Policy Report, 16*(3).

Ray, O. (2004). How the mind hurts and heals the body. *American Psychologist, 59*, 29–40.

Ray, S., Brischgi, M., Herbert, C., Takeda-Uchimura, Y., Boxer, A., Blennow, K., . . . Coray-Wyss, T. (2007). Classification and prediction of clinical Alzheimer's diagnosis based on plasma signaling proteins. *Nature Medicine, 13*, 1359–1362.

Reaney, P. (2006, June 21). Three million babies born after fertility treatment. *Medscape.* Retrieved from www.medscape.com/viewarticle/537128

Recchia, H. E., & Howe, N. (2009). Associations between social understanding, sibling relationship quality, and siblings' conflict strategies and outcomes. *Child Development, 80*(5), 1564–1578.

Redman, L. M., & Ravussin, E. (2009). Endocrine alterations in response to calorie restriction in humans. *Molecular and Cellular Endocrinology, 299*(1), 129–136.

Reed, T., Dick, D. M., Uniacke, S. K., Foroud, T., & Nichols, W. C. (2004). Genomewide scan for a healthy aging phenotype provides support for a locus near D4S1564 promoting healthy aging. *Journal of Gerontology: Biological Sciences, 59A*, 227–232.

Reef, S. E., Strebel, P., Dabbagh, A., Gacic-Dobo, M., & Cochi, S. (2011). Progress toward control of rubella and prevention of congenital rubella syndrome—worldwide, 2009. *Journal of Infectious Diseases, 204*(1), 24–27.

Reese, E. (1995). Predicting children's literacy from mother-child conversations. *Cognitive Development, 10*, 381–405.

Reese, E., & Cox, A. (1999). Quality of adult book reading affects children's emergent literacy. *Developmental Psychology, 35*, 20–28.

Reese, E., & Newcombe, R. (2007). Training mothers in elaborative reminiscing enhances children's autobiographical memory and narrative. *Child Development, 78*(4), 1153–1170.

Reichenberg, A., Gross, R., Weiser, M., Bresnahan, M., Silverman, J., Harlap, S., . . . Susser, E. (2006). Advancing paternal age and autism. *Archives of General Psychiatry, 63*(9), 1026–1032.

Reichstadt, J., Sengupta, G., Depp, C. A., Palinkas, L. A., & Jeste, D. V. (2010). Older adults' perspectives on successful aging: Qualitative interviews. *American Journal of Geriatric Psychiatry, 18*(7), 567–575.

Reid, J. D. (1995). Development in late life: Older lesbian and gay life. In A. R. D'Augelli & C. J. Patterson (Eds.), *Lesbian, gay, and bisexual identities over the lifespan: Psychological perspectives* (pp. 215–240). New York: Oxford University Press.

Reid, J. D., & Willis, S. K. (1999). Middle age: New thoughts, new directions. In S. L. Willis & J. D. Reid (Eds.), *Life in the middle* (pp. 272–289). San Diego: Academic Press.

Reijo, R., Alagappan, R. K., Patrizio, P., & Page, D. C. (1996). Severe oligozoospermia resulting from deletions of azoospermia factor gene on Y chromosome. *Lancet, 347*, 1290–1293.

Reiner, W. G., & Gearhart, J. P. (2004). Discordant sexual identity in some genetic males with cloacal exstrophy assigned to female sex at birth. *New England Journal of Medicine, 350*(4), 333–341.

Reisberg, B., Doody, R., Stöffler, A., Schmitt, F., Ferris, S., & Möbius, H. J. (2006). A 24-week open-label extension study of memantine in moderate to severe Alzheimer disease. *Archives of Neurology, 63*, 49–54.

Reiss, A. L., Abrams, M. T., Singer, H. S., Ross, J. L., & Denckla, M. B. (1996). Brain development, gender and IQ in children: A volumetric imaging study. *Brain, 119*, 1763–1774.

Reitzes, D. C., & Mutran, E. J. (2004). Grandparenthood: Factors influencing frequency of grandparent-grandchildren contact and role satisfaction. *Journal of Gerontology: Social Sciences, 59*, S9–S16.

Remez, L. (2000). Oral sex among adolescents: Is it sex or is it abstinence? *Family Planning Perspectives, 32*, 298–304.

Rende, R., Slomkowski, C., Lloyd-Richardson, E., & Niaura, R. (2005). Sibling effects on substance use in adolescence: Social contagion and genetic relatedness. *Journal of Family Psychology, 19*, 611–618.

Repetti, R. L., Taylor, S. E., & Seeman, T. S. (2002). Risky families: Family social environments and the mental and physical health of the offspring. *Psychological Bulletin, 128*(2), 330–366.

Resnick, L. B. (1989). Developing mathematical knowledge. *American Psychologist, 44*, 162–169.

Reuter, M., Roth, S., Holve, K., & Hennig, J. (2006). Identification of first candidate genes for creativity: A pilot study. *Brain Research, 1069*, 190–197.

Reuter-Lorenz, P. A., Jonides, J., Smith, E. E., Hartley, A., Miller, A., Marshuetz, C., & Koeppe, R. A. (2000). Age differences in the frontal lateralization of verbal and spatial working memory revealed by PET. *Journal of Cognitive Neuroscience, 12*, 174–187.

Reuter-Lorenz, P. A., Stanczak, L., & Miller, A. (1999). Neural recruitment and cognitive aging: Two hemispheres are better than one especially as you age. *Psychological Science, 10*, 494–500.

Reynolds, A. J., & Temple, J. A. (1998). Extended early childhood intervention and school achievement: Age thirteen findings from the Chicago Longitudinal Study. *Child Development, 69*, 231–246.

Reynolds, A. J., Temple, J. A., Robertson, D. L., & Mann, E. A. (2001). Long-term effects of an early childhood intervention on educational achievement and juvenile arrest: A 15-year follow-up of low-income children in public schools. *Journal of the American Medical Association, 285*(18), 2339–2346.

Reynolds, C. F., III, Buysse, D. J., & Kupfer, D. J. (1999). Treating insomnia in older adults: Taking a long-term view. *Journal of the American Medical Association, 281*, 1034–1035.

Rhee, S. H., & Waldman, I. D. (2002). Genetic and environmental influences on antisocial behavior: A meta-analysis of twin and adoption studies. *Psychological Bulletin, 128*, 490–529.

Ricciuti, H. N. (1999). Single parenthood and school readiness in white, black, and Hispanic 6- and 7-year-olds. *Journal of Family Psychology, 13*, 450–465.

Ricciuti, H. N. (2004). Single parenthood, achievement, and problem behavior in white, black, and Hispanic children. *Journal of Educational Research, 97*, 196–206.

Rice, M. L. (1982). Child language: What children know and how. In T. M. Field, A. Hudson, H. C. Quay, L. Troll, & G. E. Finley (Eds.), *Review of human development research.* New York: Wiley.

Rice, M. L. (1989). Children's language acquisition. *American Psychologist, 44*(2), 149–156.

Rice, M. L., Huston, A. C., Truglio, R., & Wright, J. (1990). Words from "Sesame Street": Learning vocabulary while viewing. *Developmental Psychology, 26*, 421–428.

Rice, M. L., Taylor, C. L., & Zubrick, S. R. (2008). Language outcomes of 7-year-old children with or without a history of late language emergence at 24 months. *Journal of Speech, Language, and Hearing Research, 51*, 394–407.

Rice, K. G., & Van Arsdale, A. C. (2010). Perfectionism, perceived stress, drinking to cope, and alcohol-related problems among college students. *Journal of Counseling Psychology, 57*(4), 439–450. doi: 10.1037/a00200221

Richardson, C. R., Kriska, A. M., Lantz, P. M., & Hayward, R. A. (2004). Physical activity and mortality across cardiovascular disease risk groups. *Medicine and Science in Sports and Exercise, 36*, 1923–1929.

Richardson, J. (1995). *Achieving gender equality in families: The role of males* (Innocenti Global Seminar, Summary Report). Florence, Italy: UNICEF International Child Development Centre, Spedale degli Innocenti.

Richman, L. S., Kubzansky, L., Maselko, J., Kawachi, I., Choo, P., & Bauer, M. (2005). Positive emotion and health: Going beyond the negative. *Health Psychology, 24*, 422–429.

Rideout, V. J., Vandewater, E. A., & Wartella, E. A. (2003). *Zero to six: Electronic media in the lives of infants, toddlers and preschoolers.* Menlo Park, CA: Kaiser Family Foundation.

Rideout, V. J., Foehr, U. G., & Roberts, D. F. (2010). *Generation M^2: Media in the lives of 8- to 18-year-olds.* Menlo Park, CA: Henry J. Kaiser Family Foundation.

Riemann, M. K., & Kanstrup Hansen, I. L. (2000). Effects on the fetus of exercise in pregnancy. *Scandinavian Journal of Medicine & Science in Sports, 10*(1), 12–19.

Ries, L. A. G., Melbert, D., Krapcho, M., Mariotto, A., Miller, B. A., Feuer, E. J., . . . Edwards, B. K. (Eds.). (2007). *SEER cancer statistics review, 1975–2004.* Bethesda, MD: National Cancer Institute.

Rifkin, J. (1998, May 5). Creating the "perfect" human. *Chicago Sun-Times*, p. 29.

Riggle, E. D. B., Rotosky, S. S., & Riggle, S. G. (2010). Psychological distress, well-being and legal recognition in same-sex couple relationships. *Journal of Family Psychology, 24*(1), 82–86.

Riley, K. P., Snowdon, D. A., Desrosiers, M. F., & Markesbery, W. R. (2005). Early life linguistic ability, late life cognitive function, and neuropathology: Findings from the Nun Study. *Neurobiology of Aging, 26*, 341–347.

Rimm-Kaufman, S. E., Curby, T. W., Grimm, K. J., Nathanson, L., & Brock, L. L. (2009). The contribution of children's self-regulation and classroom quality to children's adaptive behaviors in the kindergarten classroom. *Developmental Psychology, 45*(4), 958–972.

Ritchie, L., Crawford, P., Woodward-Lopez, G., Ivey, S., Masch, M., & Ikeda, J. (2001). *Prevention of childhood overweight: What should be done?* Berkeley: Center for Weight and Health, University of California, Berkeley.

Rittenour, C. E., Myers, S. A., & Brann, M. (2007). Commitment and emotional closeness in the sibling relationship. *Southern Communication Journal, 72*(2), 169–183.

Ritter, J. (1999, November 23). Scientists close in on DNA code. *Chicago Sun-Times*, p. 7.

Rivera, J. A., Sotres-Alvarez, D., Habicht, J.-P., Shamah, T., & Villalpando, S. (2004). Impact of the Mexican Program for Education, Health and Nutrition (Progresa) on rates of growth and anemia in infants and young children. *Journal of the American Medical Association, 291*, 2563–2570.

Rivera, S. M., Wakeley, A., & Langer, J. (1999). The drawbridge phenomenon: Representational reasoning or perceptual preference? *Developmental Psychology, 35*(2), 427–435.

Robbins, A., & Wilner, A. (Eds.). (2001). *Quarterlife crisis: The unique challenges of life in your twenties.* New York: Putnam.

Roberts, B. W., Caspi, A., & Moffitt, T. E. (2003). Work experiences and personality development in young adulthood. *Journal of Personality and Social Psychology, 84*, 582–593.

Roberts, B., & Mzoczek, D. (2008). Personality trait change in adulthood. *Current Directions in Psychological Science, 17*(1), 31–35.

Roberts, B. W., & Del Vecchio, W. F. (2000). The rank-order consistency of personality traits from childhood to old age: A quantitative review of longitudinal studies. *Psychological Bulletin, 126*, 3–25.

Roberts, B. W., Walton, K. E., & Viechtbauer, W. (2006a). Patterns of mean-level change in personality traits across the life course: A meta-analysis of longitudinal studies. *Psychological Bulletin, 132*, 1–25.

Roberts, B. W., Walton, K. E., & Viechtbauer, W. (2006b). Personality traits change in adulthood: Reply to Costa and McCrae (2006). *Psychological Bulletin, 132*, 29–32.

Robin, D. J., Berthier, N. E., & Clifton, R. K. (1996). Infants' predictive reaching for moving objects in the dark. *Developmental Psychology, 32*, 824–835.

Robins, R. W., John, O. P., Caspi, A., Moffitt, T. E., & Stouthamer-Loeber, M. (1996). Resilient, overcontrolled, and undercontrolled boys: Three replicable personality types. *Journal of Personality and Social Psychology, 70*, 157–171.

Robins, R. W., & Trzesniewski, K. H. (2005). Self-esteem development across the life-span. *Current Directions in Psychological Science, 14*(3), 158–162.

Robinson M., Thiel, M. M., Backus, M. M., & Meyer, E. C. (2006). Matters of spirituality at the end of life in the pediatric intensive care unit. *Pediatrics, 118*, 719–729.

Robinson, S. D., Rosenberg, H. J., & Farrell, M. P. (1999). The midlife crisis revisited. In S. L. Willis & J. D. Reid (Eds.), *Life in the middle: Psychological and social development in middle age* (pp. 47–77). San Diego: Academic Press.

Rochat, P., Querido, J. G., & Striano, T. (1999). Emerging sensitivity to the timing and structure of proto conversations in early infancy. *Developmental Psychology, 35*, 950–957.

Rochat, P., & Striano, T. (2002). Who's in the mirror? Self-other discrimination in specular images by 4- and 9-month-old infants. *Child Development, 73*, 35–46.

Rocke, C., & Lachman, M. E. (2008). Perceived trajectories of life satisfaction across past, present and future: Profiles and correlates of subjective change in young, middle-aged, and older adults. *Psychology and Aging, 23*(4), 833–847.

Rodier, P. M. (2000, February). The early origins of autism. *Scientific American*, pp. 56–63.

Rodin, J., & Ickovics, J. (1990). Women's health: Review and research agenda as we approach the 21st century. *American Psychologist, 45*, 1018–1034.

Rodriguez, C., Patel, A. V., Calle, E. E., Jacob, E. J., & Thun, M. J. (2001). Estrogen replacement therapy and ovarian cancer mortality in a large prospective study of U.S. women. *Journal of the American Medical Association, 285*, 1460–1465.

Rogaeva, E., Meng, Y., Lee, J. H., Gu, Y., Kawarai, T., Zou, F., . . . St George-Hyslop, P. (2006). The neuronal sortilin-related receptor SORL1 is genetically associated with Alzheimer disease. *Nature Genetics, 39*, 168–177.

Rogers, C. R. (1961). *On becoming a person.* Boston: Houghton Mifflin.

Rogers, S. J. (2004). Dollars, dependency, and divorce: Four perspectives on the role of wives' income. *Journal of Marriage and Family, 66*, 59–74.

Rogler, L. H. (2002). Historical generations and psychology: The case of the Great Depression and World War II. *American Psychologist, 57*(12), 1013–1023.

Rogoff, B., Mistry, J., Göncü, A., & Mosier, C. (1993). Guided participation in cultural activity by toddlers and caregivers. *Monographs of the Society for Research in Child Development, 58*(8, Serial No. 236).

Rogoff, B., & Morelli, G. (1989). Perspectives on children's development from cultural psychology. *American Psychologist, 44*, 343–348.

Roisman, G. I., Clausell, E., Holland, A., Fortuna, K., & Elieff, C. (2008). Adult romantic relationships as contexts of human development: A multimethod comparison of same-sex couples with opposite-sex dating, engaged, and married dyads. *Developmental Psychology, 44*, 91–101.

Roisman, G. I., Masten, A. S., Coatsworth, J. D., & Tellegen, A. (2004). Salient and emerging developmental tasks in the transition to adulthood. *Child Development, 75*, 123–133.

Rolls, B. J., Engell, D., & Birch, L. L. (2000). Serving portion size influences 5-year-old but not 3-year-old children's food intake. *Journal of the American Dietetic Association, 100*, 232–234.

Romano, E., Tremblay, R. E., Boulerice, B., & Swisher, R. (2005). Multi-level correlates of childhood physical aggression and prosocial behavior. *Journal of Abnormal Child Psychology, 33*(5), 565–578.

Roopnarine, J., & Honig, A. S. (1985, September). The unpopular child. *Young Children*, pp. 59–64.

Roopnarine, J. L., Hooper, F. H., Ahmeduzzaman, M., & Pollack, B. (1993). Gentle play partners: Mother-child and father-child play in New Delhi, India. In K. MacDonald (Ed.), *Parent-child play* (pp. 287–304). Albany: State University of New York Press.

Roopnarine, J. L., Talokder, E., Jain, D., Josh, P., & Srivastav, P. (1992). Personal well-being, kinship ties, and mother-infant and father-infant interactions in single-wage and dual-wage families in New Delhi, India. *Journal of Marriage and Family, 54*, 293–301.

Roosa, M. W., Deng, S., Ryu, E., Burrell, G. L., Tein, J., Jones, S., Lopez, V., & Crowder, S. (2005). Family and child characteristics linking neighborhood context and child externalizing behavior. *Journal of Marriage and Family, 667*, 515–529.

Rosamond, W., Flegal, K., Furie, K., Go, A., Greenlund, K., Haase, N., . . . Hong, Y. (2008). Heart disease and stroke statistics—2008 update: A report from the American Heart Association Statistics Committee and Stroke Statistics Subcommittee. *Circulation, 117*(4), e25–e146.

Rosamond, W. D., Chambless, L. E., Folsom, A. R., Cooper, L. S., Conwill, D. E., Clegg, L., . . . Heiss, G. (1998). Trends in the incidence of myocardial infarction and in mortality due to coronary heart disease, 1987 to 1994. *New England Journal of Medicine, 339*, 861–867.

Rose, S. A., & Feldman, J. F. (1995). Prediction of IQ and specific cognitive abilities at 11 years from infancy measures. *Developmental Psychology, 31*, 685–696.

Rose, S. A., & Feldman, J. F. (1997). Memory and speed: Their role in the relation of infant information processing to later IQ. *Child Development, 68*, 630–641.

Rose, S. A., Feldman, J. F., & Jankowski, J. J. (2002). Processing speed in the 1st year of life: A longitudinal study of preterm and full-term infants. *Developmental Psychology, 38*, 895–902.

Rose, S., Jankowski, J., & Feldman, J. (2002). Speed of processing and face recognition at 7 and 12 months. *Infancy, 3*(4), 435–455.

Rosenbaum, J. E. (2009). Patient teenagers? A comparison of the sexual behavior of virginity pledgers and matched nonpledgers. *Pediatrics, 123*, e110–e120.

Rosenberg, S. D., Rosenberg, H. J., & Farrell, M. P. (1999). The midlife crisis revisited. In S. L. Willis & J. D. Reid (Eds.), *Life in the middle* (pp. 47–73). San Diego: Academic Press.

Rosenblum, G. D., & Lewis, M. (1999). The relations among body image, physical attractiveness, and body mass in adolescence. *Child Development, 70*, 50–64.

Rosenbluth, S. C., & Steil, J. M. (1995). Predictors of intimacy for women in heterosexual and homosexual couples. *Journal of Social and Personal Relationships, 12*(2), 163–175.

Rosenfeld, D. (1999). Identity work among lesbian and gay elderly. *Journal of Aging Studies, 13*, 121–144.

Ross, H. S. (1996). Negotiating principles of entitlement in sibling property disputes. *Developmental Psychology, 32*, 90–101.

Rossi, A. S. (2004). The menopausal transition and aging process. In O. G. Brim, C. D. Ryff, & R. C. Kessler (Eds.), *How healthy are we? A national study of well-being at midlife.* Chicago: University of Chicago Press.

Rossi, R. (1996, August 30). Small schools under microscope. *Chicago Sun-Times*, p. 24.

Roth, G., Assor, A., Niemiec, C. P., Ryan, R. M., & Deci, E. L. (2009). The emotional and academic consequences of parental conditional regard: Comparing conditional positive regard, conditional negative regard, and autonomy supports as parenting practices. *Developmental Psychology, 45*(4), 1119–1142.

Rothbart, M. K., Ahadi, S. A., & Evans, D. E. (2000). Temperament and personality: Origins and outcomes. *Journal of Personality and Social Psychology, 78*, 122–135.

Rothbart, M. K., Ahadi, S. A., Hershey, K. L., & Fisher, P. (2001). Investigations of temperament at three to seven years: The Children's Behavior Questionnaire. *Child Development*, *72*(5), 1394–1408.

Rothermund, K., & Brandtstädter, J. (2003). Coping with deficits and losses in later life: From compensatory action to accommodation. *Psychology and Aging, 18*, 896–905.

Rouse, C., Brooks-Gunn, J., & McLanahan, S. (2005). Introducing the issue. *Future of Children, 15*(1), 5–14.

Roussotte, F. F., Bramen, J. E., Nunez, C., Quandt, L. C., Smith, L., O'Connor, M. J., . . . Sowell, E. R. (2011). Abnormal brain activation during working memory in children with prenatal exposure to drugs of abuse: The effects of methamphetamine, alcohol, and polydrug exposure. *NeuroImage, 54*(4), 3067–3075.

Rovee-Collier, C. (1996). Shifting the focus from what to why. *Infant Behavior and Development, 19*, 385–400.

Rovee-Collier, C. (1999). The development of infant memory. *Current Directions in Psychological Science, 8*, 80–85.

Rowe, J. W., & Kahn, R. L. (1997). Successful aging. *Gerontologist, 37*, 433–440.

Rubin, D. H., Krasilnikoff, P. A., Leventhal, J. M., Weile, B., & Berget, A. (1986, August 23). Effect of passive smoking on birth weight. *Lancet,* 415–417.

Rubin, K. H., Bukowski, W., & Parker, J. G. (1998). Peer interactions, relationships, and groups. In W. Damon (Series Ed.) & N. Eisenberg (Vol. Ed.), *Handbook of child psychology: Vol. 3. Social, emotional, and personality development* (5th ed., pp. 619–700). New York: Wiley.

Rubin, K. H., Burgess, K. B., Dwyer K. M., & Hastings, P. D. (2003). Predicting preschoolers' externalizing behavior from toddler temperament, conflict, and maternal negativity. *Developmental Psychology, 39*(1), 164–176.

Rubin, K. H., Burgess, K. B., & Hastings, P. D. (2002). Stability and social-behavioral consequences of toddlers' inhibited temperament and parenting behaviors. *Child Development, 73*(2), 483–495.

Ruble, D. N., & Dweck, C. S. (1995). Self-conceptions, person conceptions, and their development. In N. Eisenberg (Ed.), *Social development: Review of personality and social psychology* (pp. 109–139). Thousand Oaks, CA: Sage.

Ruble, D. N., & Martin, C. L. (1998). Gender development. In W. Damon (Series Ed.) & N. Eisenberg (Vol. Ed.), *Handbook of child psychology: Vol. 3. Social, emotional, and personality development* (5th ed., pp. 933–1016). New York: Wiley.

Ruble, D. N., Martin, C. L., & Berenbaum, S. A. (2006). Gender development. In W. Damon & R. M. Lerner (Series Eds.) & D. Kuhn & R. S. Seigler (Vol. Eds.), *Handbook of child psychology: Vol 2. Cognition, perception, and language* (pp. 858–932). Hoboken: NJ: Wiley.

Rudolph, K. D., Lambert, S. F., Clark, A. G., & Kurlakowsky, K. D. (2001). Negotiating the transition to middle school: The role of self-regulatory processes. *Child Development, 72*(3), 929–946.

Rudy, D., & Grusec, J. E. (2006). Authoritarian parenting in individualistic and collectivistic groups: Associations with maternal emotion and cognition and children's self-esteem. *Journal of Family Psychology, 20*, 68–78.

Rueda, M. R., & Rothbart, M. K. (2009). The influence of temperament on the development of coping: The role of maturation and experience. *New Directions for Child and Adolescent Development, 124*, 19–31.

Rueter, M. A., & Conger, R. D. (1995). Antecedents of parent-adolescent disagreements. *Journal of Marriage and Family, 57*, 435–448.

Rueter, M. A., & Koerner, A. F. (2009). The effect of family communication patterns on adopted adolescent adjustment. *Journal of Marriage and Family, 70*(3), 715–727.

Ruitenberg, A., van Swieten, J. C., Witteman, J. C., Mehta, K. M., van Duijn, C. M., Hofman, A., & Breteler, M. M. (2002). Alcohol consumption and risk of dementia: The Rotterdam Study. *Lancet, 359*, 281–286.

Rushton, J. P., & Jensen, A. R. (2005). Thirty years of research on race differences in cognitive ability. *Psychology, Public Policy, and Law, 11*, 235–294.

Rutledge, T., Reis, S. T., Olson, M., Owens, J., Kelsey, S. F., Pepine, C. J., . . . Matthews, K. A. (2004). Social networks are associated with lower mortality rates among women with suspected coronary disease: The National Heart,

Lung, and Blood Institute-sponsored Women's Ischemia Syndrome Evaluation Study. *Psychosomatic Medicine, 66*, 882–888.

Rutter, M. (2002). Nature, nurture, and development: From evangelism through science toward policy and practice. *Child Development, 73*, 1–21.

Rutter, M. (2007). Gene-environment interdependence. *Developmental Science, 10*, 12–18.

Rutter, M., O'Connor, T. G., & English & Romanian Adoptees (ERA) Study Team. (2004). Are there biological programming effects for psychological development? Findings from a study of Romanian adoptees. *Developmental Psychology, 40*, 81–94.

Ryan, A. S., Wenjun, Z., & Acosta, A. (2002). Breastfeeding continues to increase into the new millennium. *Pediatrics, 110*, 1103–1109.

Ryan, V., & Needham, C. (2001). Nondirective play therapy with children experiencing psychic trauma. *Clinical Child Psychology and Psychiatry, 6*(Special issue), 437–453.

Ryff, C. D. (1995). Psychological well-being in adult life. *Current Directions in Psychological Science, 4*, 99–104.

Ryff, C. D., & Keyes, C. L. M. (1995). The structure of psychological well-being revisited. *Journal of Personality and Social Psychology, 69*, 719–727.

Ryff, C. D., Keyes, C. L., & Hughes, D. L. (2004). Psychological well-being in MIDUS: Profiles of ethnic/racial diversity and life-course uniformity. In O. G. Brim, C. D. Ryff, & R. C. Kessler (Eds.), *How healthy are we? A national study of well-being at midlife* (pp. 398–424). Chicago: University of Chicago Press.

Ryff, C. D., & Seltzer, M. M. (1995). Family relations and individual development in adulthood and aging. In R. Blieszner & V. Hilkevitch (Eds.), *Handbook of aging and the family* (pp. 95–113). Westport, CT: Greenwood Press.

Ryff, C. D., & Singer, B. (1998). Middle age and well-being. *Encyclopedia of Mental Health, 2*, 707–719.

Ryff, C. D., Singer, B. H., & Palmersheim, K. A. (2004). Social inequalities in health and well-being: The role of relational and religious protective factors. In O. G. Brim, C. D. Ryff, & R. C. Kessler (Eds.), *How healthy are we? A national study of well-being at midlife.* Chicago: University of Chicago Press.

Rymer, R. (1993). *An abused child: Flight from silence.* New York: HarperCollins.

Saarni, C., Campos, J. J., Camras, A., & Witherington, D. (2006). Emotional development: Action, communication, and understanding. In N. Eisenberg, W. Damon, & R. Lerner (Eds.), *Handbook of child psychology: Vol. 3, Social, emotional and personality development* (6th ed., pp. 226–299). Hoboken, NJ: Wiley.

Saarni, C., Mumme, D. L., & Campos, J. J. (1998). Emotional development: Action, communication, and understanding. In W. Damon (Series Ed.) & N. Eisenberg (Vol. Ed.), *Handbook of child psychology: Vol. 3. Social, emotional, and personality development* (5th ed., pp. 237–309). New York: Wiley.

Sabol, S. Z., Nelson, M. L., Fisher, C., Gunzerath, L., Brody, C. L., Hu, S., . . . Hamer, D. H. (1999). A genetic association for cigarette smoking behavior. *Health Psychology, 18*, 7–13.

Sadeh, A., Raviv, A., & Gruber, R. (2000). Sleep patterns and sleep disruptions in school age children. *Developmental Psychology, 36*(3), 291–301.

Saffran, J. R., Pollak, S. D., Seibel, R. L., & Shkolnik, A. (2007). Dog is a dog is a dog: Infant rule learning is not specific to language. *Cognition, 105*(3), 669–680.

Sahin, E., & DePinho, R. A. (2010). Linking functional decline of telomeres, mitochondria and stem cells during ageing. *Nature*, 464, 271–278.

Saigal, S., Hoult, L. A., Streiner, D. L., Stoskopf, B. L., & Rosenbaum, P. L. (2000). School difficulties at adolescence in a regional cohort of children who were extremely low birth weight. *Pediatrics, 105*, 325–331.

Saigal, S., Stoskopf, B., Streiner, D., Boyle, M., Pinelli, J., Paneth, N., & Goddeeris, J. (2006). Transition of extremely low-birth-weight infants from adolescence to young adulthood: Comparison with normal birth-weight controls. *Journal of the American Medical Association, 295*, 667–675.

Salkind, N. J. (Ed.). (2005). Smiling. *The encyclopedia of human development.* Thousand Oaks, CA: Sage.

Sallmen, M., Sandler, D. P., Hoppin, J. A., Blair, A., & Day, D. (2006). Reduced fertility among overweight and obese men. *Epidemiology, 17*(5), 520–523.

Salmela-Aro, K., Aunola, K., & Nurmi, J. (2007). Personal goals during emerging adulthood: A 10-year follow up. *Journal of Adolescent Research, 22*(6), 690–715.

Salmela-Aro, K., Tynkkynen, L., & Vuori, J. (2010). Parents' work burnout and adolescents' school burnout: Are they shared? *European Journal of Developmental Psychology, 8*(2), 215–227. doi: 10.1080/17405620903578060

Salovey, P., & Mayer, J. D. (1990). Emotional intelligence. *Imagination, Cognition, and Personality, 9*, 185–211.

Salovey, P., Rothman, A. J., Detweiler, J. B., & Steward, W. T. (2000). Emotional states and physical health. *American Psychologist, 55*, 110–121.

Salthouse, T. A. (1991). *Theoretical perspectives on cognitive aging.* Hillsdale, NJ: Erlbaum.

Salthouse, T. A., & Maurer, T. J. (1996). Aging, job performance, and career development. In J. E. Birren & K. W. Schaie (Eds.), *Handbook of the psychology of aging* (pp. 353–364). San Diego: Academic Press.

Salzman, C. (2008). Pharmacologic treatment of disturbed sleep in the elderly. *Harvard Review of Psychiatry, 16*(5), 271–278.

Samara, M., Marlow, N., Wolke, D. for the EPICure Study Group. (2008). Pervasive behavior problems at 6 years of age in a total-population sample of children born at 25 weeks of gestation. *Pediatrics, 122*, 562–573.

Samdal, O., & Dür, W. (2000). The school environment and the health of adolescents. In C. Currie, K. Hurrelmann, W. Settertobulte, R. Smith, & J. Todd (Eds.), *Health and health behaviour among young people: A WHO cross-national study (HBSC) international report* (pp. 49–64). (WHO Policy Series: Health Policy for Children and Adolescents, Series No. 1.) Copenhagen, Denmark: World Health Organization Regional Office for Europe.

Sampson, R. J. (1997). The embeddedness of child and adolescent development: A community-level perspective on urban violence. In J. McCord (Ed.), *Violence and childhood in the inner city* (pp. 31–77). Cambridge, UK: Cambridge University Press.

Samuelsson, M., Radestad, I., & Segesten, K. (2001). A waste of life: Fathers' experience of losing a child before birth. *Birth, 28*, 124–130.

Sandefur, G., Eggerling-Boeck, J., & Park, H. (2005). Off to a good start? Postsecondary education and early adult life. In R. A. Settersten Jr., F. F. Furstenberg Jr., & R. G. Rumbaut (Eds.), *On the frontier of adulthood: Theory, research, and public policy* (pp. 292–319). (John D. and Catherine T. MacArthur Foundation Series on Mental Health and Development, Research Network on Transitions to Adulthood and Public Policy.) Chicago: University of Chicago Press.

Sanders, A., Stone, R., Meador, R., & Parker, V. (2010). Aging in place partnerships: A training program for family caregivers of residents living in affordable senior housing. *Cityscape: A Journal of Policy Development and Research, 12*(2), 85–104.

Sandnabba, H. K., & Ahlberg, C. (1999). Parents' attitudes and expectations about children's cross-gender behavior. *Sex Roles, 40*, 249–263.

Sando, S. B., Melquist, S., Cannon, A., Hutton, M., Sletvold, O., Saltvedt, I., . . . Aasly, J. (2008). Risk-reducing effect of education in Alzheimer's disease. *International Journal of Geriatric Psychiatry, 23*(11), 1156–1162.

Sandstrom, M. J., & Coie, J. D. (1999). A developmental perspective on peer rejection: Mechanisms of stability and change. *Child Development, 70*(4), 955–966.

Santelli, J., Carter, M., Orr, M., & Dittus, P. (2007). Trends in sexual risk behaviors, by nonsexual risk behavior involvement. *Journal of Adolescent Health, 44*(4), 372–379.

Santos, I. S., Victora, C. G., Huttly, S., & Carvalhal, J. B. (1998). Caffeine intake and low birthweight: A population-based case-control study. *American Journal of Epidemiology, 147*, 620–627.

Sapienza, C. (1990, October). Parental imprinting of genes. *Scientific American*, pp. 52–60.

Sapolsky, R. M. (1992). Stress and neuroendocrine changes during aging. *Generations, 16*(4), 35–38.

Sapp, F., Lee, K., & Muir, D. (2000). Three-year-olds' difficulty with the appearance-reality distinction: Is it real or apparent? *Developmental Psychology, 36*, 547–560.

Sargent, J. D., & Dalton, M. (2001). Does parental disapproval of smoking prevent adolescents from becoming established smokers? *Pediatrics, 108*(6), 1256–1262.

Sarnecka, B. W., & Carey, S. (2007). How counting represents number: What children must learn and when they learn it. *Cognition, 108*(3), 662–674.

Satcher, D. (2001). *Women and smoking: A report of the surgeon general.* Washington, DC: Department of Health and Human Services.

Savage, J. S., Fisher, J. O., & Birch, L. L. (2007). Parental influence on eating behavior: Conception to adolescence. *Journal of Law, Medicine, and Ethics, 35*(1), 22–34.

Savic, I., Berglund, H., & Lindström, P. (2005). Brain response to putative pheromones in homosexual men. *Proceedings of the National Academy of Sciences, 102*, 7356–7361.

Savic, I., Berglund, H., & Lindström, P. (2006). Brain response to putative pheromones. *Proceedings of the National Academy of Sciences, 102*(20), 7356–7361.

Savic, I., & Lindström, P. (2008). PET and MRI show differences in cerebral asymmetry and functional connectivity between homo- and heterosexual subjects. *Proceedings of the National Academy of Sciences, USA, 105*, 9403–9408. doi: 10.1073/pnas.0801566105

Savin-Williams, R. C. (2006). Who's gay? Does it matter? *Current Directions in Psychological Science, 15*, 40–44.

Sawicki, M. B. (2005, March 16). *Collision course: The Bush budget and Social Security* (EPI Briefing Paper No. 156). Retrieved from www.epinet.org/content.cfm/bp156

Saxe, R., & Carey, S. (2006). The perception of causality in infancy. *Acta Psychologica,123*, 144–165.

Saxe, R., Tenenbaum, J. B., & Carey, S. (2005). Secret agents: Inferences about hidden causes by 10- and 12-month old infants. *Psychological Science, 16*, 995–1001.

Saxe, R., Tzelnic, T., & Carey, S. (2007). Knowing who dunnit: Infants identify the causal agent in an unseen causal interaction. *Developmental Psychology, 43*, 149–158.

Scarr, S. (1992). Developmental theories for the 1990s: Development and individual differences. *Child Development, 63*, 1–19.

Scarr, S. (1998). American child care today. *American Psychologist, 53*, 95–108.

Scarr, S., & McCartney, K. (1983). How people make their own environments: A theory of genotype-environment effects. *Child Development, 54*, 424–435.

Schaie, K. W. (1977-1978). Toward a stage theory of adult cognitive development. *Journal of Aging and Human Development, 8*(2), 129–138.

Schaie, K. W. (1984). Midlife influences upon intellectual functioning in old age. *International Journal of Behavioral Development, 7*, 463–478.

Schaie, K. W. (1990). Intellectual development in adulthood. In J. E. Birren & K. W. Schaie (Eds.), *Handbook of the psychology of aging* (pp. 291–309). San Diego: Academic Press.

Schaie, K. W. (1994). The course of adult intellectual development. *American Psychologist, 49*(4), 304–313.

Schaie, K. W. (1996a). Intellectual development in adulthood. In J. E. Birren & K. W. Schaie (Eds.), *Handbook of the psychology of aging* (4th ed., pp. 266–286). San Diego: Academic Press.

Schaie, K. W. (1996b). *Intellectual development in adulthood: The Seattle Longitudinal Study.* Cambridge, UK: Cambridge University Press.

Schaie, K. W. (2005). *Developmental influences on adult intelligence: The Seattle Longitudinal Study.* New York: Oxford University Press.

Schaie, K. W., & Willis, S. L. (1996). Psychometric intelligence and aging. In F. Blanchard-Fields & T. M. Hess (Eds.), *Perspectives on cognitive change in adulthood and aging* (pp. 293–322). New York: McGraw-Hill.

Schaie, K. W., & Willis, S. L. (2000). A stage theory model of adult cognitive development revisited. In B. Rubinstein, M. Moss, & M. Kleban (Eds.), *The many dimensions of aging: Essays in honor of M. Powell Lawton* (pp. 173–191). New York: Springer.

Schardt, D. (1995, June). For men only. *Nutrition Action Health Letter, 22*(5), 4–7.

Scharf, M., Mayseless, O., & Kivenson-Baron, I. (2004). Adolescents' attachment representations and developmental tasks in emerging adulthood. *Developmental Psychology, 40*, 430–444.

Scharlach, A. E., & Fredriksen, K. I. (1993). Reactions to the death of a parent during midlife. *Omega, 27*, 307–319.

Schaumberg, D. A., Mendes, F., Balaram, M., Dana, M. R., Sparrow, D., & Hu, H. (2004). Accumulated lead exposure and risk of age-related cataract in men. *Journal of the American Medical Association, 292*, 2750–2754.

Scher, A., Epstein, R., & Tirosh, E. (2004). Stability and changes in sleep regulation: A longitudinal study from 3 months to 3 years. *International Journal of Behavioral Development, 28*(3), 268–274.

Scheers, N. J., Rutherford, G. W., & Kemp, J. S. (2003). Where should infants sleep? A comparison of risk for suffocation of infants sleeping in cribs, adult beds, and other sleeping locations. *Pediatrics, 112*, 883–889.

Scheidt, P., Overpeck, M. D., Whatt, W., & Aszmann, A. (2000). Adolescents' general health and wellbeing. In C. Currie, K. Hurrelmann, W. Settertobulte, R. Smith, & J. Todd (Eds.), *Health and health behaviour among young people: A WHO cross-national study (HBSC) international report* (pp. 24–38). (WHO Policy Series: Healthy Policy for Children and Adolescents, Series No. 1.) Copenhagen, Denmark: World Health Organization Regional Office for Europe.

Schemo, D. J. (2004, August 19). Charter schools lagging behind, test scores show. *The New York Times*, pp. A1, A16.

Scher, M. S., Richardson, G. A., & Day, N. L. (2000). Effects of prenatal crack/cocaine and other drug exposure on electroencephalographic sleep studies at birth and one year. *Pediatrics, 105*, 39–48.

Schetter, C. D. (2009). Stress processes in pregnancy and preterm birth. *Current Directions in Psychological Science, 18*(4), 205–209.

Schiller, J. S., & Bernadel, L. (2004). Summary health statistics for the U.S. population: National Health Interview Survey, 2002. *Vital and Health Statistics, 10*(220). Hyattsville, MD: National Center for Health Statistics.

Schlenker, E. D. (2010). Healthy aging: Nutrition concepts for older adults. In T. Wilson, N. J. Temple, G. A. Bray, & M. B. Struble (Eds.), *Nutrition guide for physicians* (pp. 215–226). New York: Humana Press.

Schlotz, W., Jones, A., Phillips, D. I. W., Gale, C. R., Robinson, S. M., & Godrey, K. M. (2009). Lower maternal folate status in early pregnancy is associated with childhood hyperactivity and peer problems in offspring. *Journal of Child Psychology and Psychiatry, 51*(5), 594–602. doi: 10.1111/j.1469-7610.2009.02182.x

Schmidt, P. J., Nieman, L. K., Danaceau, M. A., Adams, L. F., & Rubinow, D. R. (1998). Differential behavioral effects of gonadal steroids in women with and in those without premenstrual syndrome. *New England Journal of Medicine, 338*, 209–216.

Schmidt, M. E., Rich, M., Rifas-Shiman, S., Oken, E., & Taveras, E. (2009). Television viewing in infancy and child cognition at 3 years of age in a U.S. cohort. *Pediatrics, 123*(3), e370–375.

Schmitt, D. P., Realo, A., Voracek, M., & Allik, J. (2008). Why can't a man be more like a woman? Sex differences in big five personality traits across 55 cultures. *Journal of Personality and Social Psychology, 94*(1), 168–182.

Schmitt, M., Kliegel, M., & Shapiro, A. (2007). Marital interaction in middle and old age: A predictor of marital satisfaction? *International Journal of Aging & Human Development, 65*(4), 283–300.

Schmitt, S. A., Simpson, A. M., & Friend, M. (2011). A longitudinal assessment of the home literacy environment and early language. *Infant and Child Development, 20*(6), 409–431.

Schmitz, S., Saudino, K. J., Plomin, R., Fulker, D. W., & DeFries, J. C. (1996). Genetic and environmental influences on temperament in middle childhood: Analyses of teacher and tester ratings. *Child Development, 67*, 409–422.

Schnaas, L., Rothenberg, S. J., Flores, M., Martinez, S., Hernandez, C., Osorio, E., . . . Perroni, E. (2006). Reduced intellectual development in children with prenatal lead exposure. *Environmental Health Perspectives, 114*(5), 791–797.

Schneider, B. H., Atkinson, L., & Tardif, C. (2001). Child-parent attachment and children's peer relations: A quantitative review. *Developmental Psychology, 37*, 86–100.

Schneider, E. L. (1992). Biological theories of aging. *Generations, 16*(4), 7–10.

Schneider, M. (2002). *Do school facilities affect academic outcomes?* Washington, DC: National Clearinghouse for Educational Facilities.

Schoenborn, C. A. (2004). Marital status and health: United States, 1999–2002. *Advance Data from Vital and Health Statistics, No. 351.* Hyattsville, MD: National Center for Health Statistics.

Schoenborn, C. A., & Heyman, K. M. (2009). Health characteristics of adults aged 55 years and older: United States, 2004–2007. *National Health Statistics Reports, 16,* 1–31. Hyattsville, MD: National Center for Health Statistics.

Schoenborn, C. A., Vickerie, J. L., & Powell-Griner, E. (2006). Health characteristics of adults 55 years of age and over: United States, 2000–2003. *Advance Data from Vital and Health Statistics, No. 370.* Hyattsville, MD: National Center for Health Statistics.

Schoeni, R., & Ross, K. (2005). Maternal assistance from families during the transition to adulthood. In R. A. Settersten Jr., F. F. Furstenberg Jr., & R. G. Rumbaut (Eds.), *On the frontier of adulthood: Theory, research, and public policy* (pp. 396–416). Chicago: University of Chicago Press.

Scholten, C. M. (1985). *Childbearing in American society: 1650–1850.* New York: New York University Press.

Schooler, C. (1990). Psychosocial factors and effective cognitive functioning in adulthood. In J. E. Burren & K. W. Schaie (Eds.), *The handbook of aging* (pp. 347–358). San Diego: Academic Press.

Schooler, C., Revell, A. J., & Caplan, L. J. (2007). Parental practices and willingness to ask for children's help later in life. *Journal of Gerontology Psychological and Social Sciences, 57B,* S3–S13.

Schore, A. N. (1994). *Affect regulation and the origin of the self: The neurobiology of emotional development.* Hillsdale, NJ: Erlbaum.

Schulenberg, J., O'Malley, P., Backman, J., & Johnston, L. (2005). Early adult transitions and their relation to well-being and substance use. In R. A. Settersten Jr., F. F. Furstenberg Jr., & R. G. Rumbaut (Eds.), *On the frontier of adulthood: Theory, research, and public policy* (pp. 417–453). Chicago: University of Chicago Press.

Schulenberg, J. E., & Zarrett, N. R. (2006). Mental health during emerging adulthood: Continuity and discontinuity in courses, causes, and functions. In J. J. Arnett & J. L. Tanner (Eds.), *Emerging adults in America: Coming of age in the 21st century* (pp. 135–172). Washington, DC: American Psychological Association.

Schulting, A. B., Malone, P. S., & Dodge, K. A. (2005). The effect of school-based kindergarten transition policies and practices on child academic outcomes. *Developmental Psychology, 41,* 860–871.

Schulz, M. S., Cowan, C. P., & Cowan, P. A. (2006). Promoting healthy beginnings: A randomized controlled trial of a preventive intervention to preserve marital quality during the transition to parenthood. *Journal of Consulting and Clinical Psychology, 74,* 20–31.

Schulz, M. S., Cowan, P. A., Cowan, C. P., & Brennan, R. T. (2004). Coming home upset: Gender, marital satisfaction, and the daily spillover of workday experience into couple interactions. *Journal of Family Psychology, 18,* 250–263.

Schulz, R. (1978). *A psychology of death, dying, and bereavement.* Reading, MA: Addison-Wesley.

Schulz, R., & Martire, L. M. (2004). Family caregiving of persons with dementia: Prevalence, health effects, and support strategies. *American Journal of Geriatric Psychiatry, 12,* 240–249.

Schumann, C. M., & Amaral, D. G. (2006). Stereological analysis of amygdala neuron number in autism. *Journal of Neuroscience, 26*(29), 7674–7679.

Schumann, J. (1997). The view from elsewhere: Why there can be no best method for teaching a second language. *Clarion: Magazine of the European Second Language Acquisition, 3*(1), 23–24.

Schuur, M., Ikram, M. A., vanSwietan, J. C., Isaacs, A., Vergeer-Drop, J. M., Hofman, A., . . . van Duijn, C. M. (2009). Cathepsin D and the risk of Alzheimer's disease: A population-based study and meta-analysis. *Neurobiology and Aging.* Published online. doi: 10.1016/j.neurobiolaging.2009.10.011

Schwartz, B. L. (2008). Working memory load differentially affects tip-of-the-tongue states and feeling-of-knowing judgments. *Memory & Cognition, 36*(1), 9–19.

Schwartz, D., Chang, L., & Farver, J. M. (2001). Correlates of victimization in Chinese children's peer groups. *Developmental Psychology, 37*(4), 520–532.

Schwartz, D., Dodge, K. A., Pettit, G. S., Bates, J. E., & Conduct Problems Prevention Research Group. (2000). Friendship as a moderating factor in the pathway between early harsh home environment and later victimization in the peer group. *Developmental Psychology, 36,* 646–662.

Schwartz, D., McFadyen-Ketchum, S. A., Dodge, K. A., Pettit, G. S., & Bates, J. E. (1998). Peer group victimization as a predictor of children's behavior problems at home and in school. *Development and Psychopathology, 10,* 87–99.

Schwartz, L. L. (2003). A nightmare for King Solomon: The new reproductive technologies. *Journal of Family Psychology, 17,* 229–237.

Schweinhart, L. J. (2007). Crime prevention by the High/Scope Perry preschool program. *Victims & Offenders, 2*(2), 141–160.

Schweinhart, L. J., Barnes, H. V., & Weikart, D. P. (1993). *Significant benefits: The High/Scope Perry Preschool Study through age 27* (Monographs of the High/Scope Educational Research Foundation No. 10). Ypsilanti, MI: High/Scope.

Scola, C., & Vauclair, J. (2010). Infant holding side biases displayed by fathers in maternity hospitals. *Journal of Reproductive and Infant Psychology, 28*(1), 3–10.

Scott, J. (1998). Changing attitudes to sexual morality: A cross-national comparison. *Sociology, 32,* 815–845.

Scott, R. M., & Baillargeon, R. (2009). Which penguin is this? Attributing false beliefs about object identity at 18 months. *Child Development, 80*(4), 1172–1196.

Scott, M. E., Booth, A., King, V., & Johnson, D. R. (2007). Postdivorce father-adolescent closeness. *Journal of Marriage and Family, 69*(5), 1194–1209.

Seblega, B. K., Zhang, N. J., Unruh, L. Y., Breen, G. M., Paek, S. C., & Wan, T. T. (2010). Changes in nursing home staffing levels, 1997 to 2007. *Medical Care Research and Review, 67*(2), 232–246.

Sedlak, A. J., & Broadhurst, D. D. (1996). *Executive summary of the third national incidence study of child abuse and neglect* (NIS-3). Washington, DC: U.S. Department of Health and Human Services.

Seeman, T. E., Merkin, S. S., Crimmins, E. M., & Karlamangla, A. (2009). Disability trends among older Americans: National health and nutrition examination surveys, 1988–1994 and 1999–2004. *American Journal of Public Health, 100*(1), 100–107.

Segerstrom, S. C., & Miller, G. E. (2004). Psychological stress and the human immune system: A meta-analytic study of 30 years of inquiry. *Psychological Bulletin, 130,* 601–630.

Seider, B. H., Shiota, M. N., Whalen, P., & Levenson, R. W. (2010). Greater sadness reactivity in late life. *Social Cognitive and Affective Neuroscience, 6*(2), 186–194. doi: 10.1093/scan/nsq069

Seidler, A., Neinhaus, A., Bernhardt, T., Kauppinen, T., Elo, A. L., & Frolich, L. (2004). Psychosocial work factors and dementia. *Occupational and Environmental Medicine, 61,* 962–971.

Seifer, R., Schiller, M., Sameroff, A. J., Resnick, S., & Riordan, K. (1996). Attachment, maternal sensitivity, and infant temperament during the first year of life. *Developmental Psychology, 32,* 12–25.

Seiner, S. H., & Gelfand, D. M. (1995). Effects of mother's simulated withdrawal and depressed affect on mother-toddler interactions. *Child Development, 60,* 1519–1528.

Sellers, E. M. (1998). Pharmacogenetics and ethnoracial differences in smoking. *Journal of the American Medical Association, 280,* 179–180.

Selman, R. L. (1980). *The growth of interpersonal understanding: Developmental and clinical analyses.* New York: Academic Press.

Selman, R. L., & Selman, A. P. (1979, April). Children's ideas about friendship: A new theory. *Psychology Today,* pp. 71–80.

Seltzer, J. A. (2000). Families formed outside of marriage. *Journal of Marriage and Family, 62,* 1247–1268.

Seltzer, J. A. (2004). Cohabitation in the United States and Britain: Demography, kinship, and the future. *Journal of Marriage and Family, 66,* 921–928.

Sen, A., Partelow, L., & Miller, D. C. (2005). *Comparative indicators of education in the United States and other G8 countries: 2004* (NCES 2005–021). Washington, DC: National Center for Education Statistics.

Serbin, L., Poulin-Dubois, D., Colburne, K. A., Sen, M., & Eichstedt, J. A. (2001). Gender stereotyping in infancy: Visual preferences for knowledge of gender-stereotyped toys in the second year. *International Journal of Behavioral Development, 25*, 7–15.

Sethi, A., Mischel, W., Aber, J. L., Shoda, Y., & Rodriguez, M. L. (2000). The role of strategic attention deployment in development of self-regulation: Predicting preschoolers' delay of gratification from mother-toddler interactions. *Developmental Psychology, 36*, 767–777.

Settersten, R. A., Jr. (2005). Social policy and the transition to adulthood: Toward stronger institutions and individual capacities. In R. A. Settersten Jr., F. F. Furstenberg Jr., & R. G. Rumbaut (Eds.), *On the frontier of adulthood: Theory, research, and public policy* (pp. 534–560). Chicago: University of Chicago Press.

Seybold, K. S., & Hill, P. C. (2001). The role of religion and spirituality in mental and physical health. *Current Directions in Psychological Science, 10*, 21–24.

Shafto, M. A., Burke, D. M., Stamatakis, E. A., Tam, P. P., & Tyler, L. K. (2007). On the tip-of-the-tongue: Neural correlates of increased word-finding failures in normal aging. *Journal of Cognitive Neuroscience, 19*(2), 2060–2070.

Shah, T., Sullivan, K., & Carter, J. (2006). Sudden infant death syndrome and reported maternal smoking during pregnancy. *American Journal of Public Health, 96*(10), 1757–1759.

Shanahan, M., Porfeli, E., & Mortimer, J. (2005). Subjective age identity and the transition to adulthood: When do adolescents become adults? In R. A. Settersten Jr., F. F. Furstenberg Jr., & R. G. Rumbaut (Eds.), *On the frontier of adulthood: Theory, research, and public policy* (pp. 225–255). Chicago: University of Chicago Press.

Shankaran, S., Das, A., Bauer, C. R., Bada, H. S., Lester, B., Wright, L. L., & Smeriglio, V. (2004). Association between patterns of maternal substance use and infant birth weight, length, and head circumference. *Pediatrics, 114*, e226–e234.

Shannon, J. D., Tamis-LeMonda, C. S., London, K., & Cabrera, N. (2002). Beyond rough and tumble: Low income fathers' interactions and children's cognitive development at 24 months. *Parenting: Science & Practice, 2*(2), 77–104.

Shapiro, A., & Cooney, T. M. (2007). Interpersonal relations across the life course. *Advances in Life Course Research, 12*, 191–219.

Shapiro, P. (1994, November). My house is your house: Advance planning can ease the way when parents move in with adult kids. *AARP Bulletin*, p. 2.

Sharma, A. R., McGue, M. K., & Benson, P. L. (1996a). The emotional and behavioral adjustment of United States adopted adolescents, Part I: An overview. *Children and Youth Services Review, 18*, 83–100.

Sharma, A. R., McGue, M. K., & Benson, P. L. (1996b). The emotional and behavioral adjustment of United States adopted adolescents, Part II: Age at adoption. *Children and Youth Services Review, 18*, 101–114.

Sharon, T., & DeLoache, J. S. (2003). The role of perseveration in children's symbolic understanding and skill. *Developmental Science, 6*(3), 289–296.

Sharp, E. S., Reynolds, C. A., Pedersen, N. L., & Gatz, M. (2010). Cognitive engagement and cognitive aging: Is openness protective? *Psychology and Aging, 25*(1), 60–73.

Shatz, M., & Gelman, R. (1973). The development of communication skills: Modifications in the speech of young children as a function of listener. *Monographs of the Society for Research in Child Development, 38*(5, Serial No. 152).

Shaw, B. A., Krause, N., Liang, J., & Bennett, J. (2007). Tracking changes in social relations throughout late life. *Journal of Gerontology: Social Sciences, 62B*, S90–S99.

Shaw, P., Gornick, M., Lerch, J., Addington, A., Seal, J., Greenstein, D., . . . Rapoport, J. L. (2007). Polymorphisms of the dopamine D_4 receptor, clinical outcome, and cortical structure in attention-deficit/hyperactivity disorder. *Archives of General Psychiatry, 64*, 921–931.

Shaw, P., Greenstein, D., Lerch, J., Clasen, L., Lenroot, R., Gogtay, N., . . . Giedd, J. (2006). Intellectual ability and cortical development in children and adolescents. *Nature, 440*, 676–679.

Shayer, M., Ginsburg, D., & Coe, R. (2007). Thirty years on—A large anti-Flynn effect? The Piagetian Test Volume & Heaviness norms 1975–2003. *British Journal of Educational Psychology, 77*(1), 25–41.

Shaywitz, S. (2003). *Overcoming dyslexia: A new and complete science-based program for overcoming reading problems at any level.* New York: Knopf.

Shaywitz, S. E. (1998). Current concepts: Dyslexia. *New England Journal of Medicine, 338*, 307–312.

Shaywitz, S. E., Mody, M., & Shaywitz, B. A. (2006). Neural mechanisms in dyslexia. *Current Directions in Psychological Science, 15*, 278–281.

Shea, K. M., Little, R. E., & the ALSPAC Study Team. (1997). Is there an association between preconceptual paternal X-ray exposure and birth outcome? *American Journal of Epidemiology, 145*, 546–551.

Shea, S., Basch, C. E., Stein, A. D., Contento, I. R., Irigoyen, M., & Zybert, P. (1993). Is there a relationship between dietary fat and stature or growth in children 3 to 5 years of age? *Pediatrics, 92*, 579–586.

Shedlock, D. J., & Cornelius, S. W. (2003). Psychological approaches to wisdom and its development. In J. Demick & C. Andreoletti (Eds.), *Handbook of adult development* (pp. 153–167). New York: Plenum Press.

Sheldon, K. M., & Kasser, T. (2001). Getting older, getting better? Personal strivings and psychological maturity across the life span. *Developmental Psychology, 37*, 491–501.

Shepherd, J. (2010, September 1). Girls think they are cleverer than boys from age four, study finds. *The Guardian*. Retrieved from http://www.guardian.co.uk/education/2010/sep/01/girls-boys-schools-gender-gap

Sherman, E. (1993). Mental health and successful adaptation in late life. *Generations, 17*(1), 43–46.

Shiffman, S., Brockwell, S., Pillitteri, J., & Gitchell, J. (2008). Use of smoking-cessation treatments in the United States. *American Journal of Preventive Medicine, 34*(2), 102–111.

Shields, M. K., & Behrman, R. E. (2004). Children of immigrant families: Analysis and recommendations. *Future of Children, 14*(2), 4–15. Retrieved from www.futureofchildren.org

Shin, M., Besser, L. M., Kucik, J. E., Lu, C., Siffel, C., Correa, A., & the Congenital Anomaly Multistate Prevalence and Survival (CAMPS) Collaborative. (2009). Prevalence of Down syndrome among children and adolescents in 10 regions of the United States. *Pediatrics, 124*(6), 1565–1571.

Shiono, P. H., & Behrman, R. E. (1995). Low birth weight: Analysis and recommendations. *Future of Children, 5*(1), 4–18.

Shoghi-Jadid, K., Small, G. W., Agdeppa, E. D., Kepe, V., Ercoli, L. M., Siddarth, P., . . . Barrio, J. R. (2002). Localization of neurofibrillary tangles and beta-amyloid plaques in the brains of living patients with Alzheimer disease. *American Journal of Geriatric Psychiatry, 10*, 24–35.

Shonkoff, J., & Phillips, D. (2000). Growing up in child care. In I. Shonkoff & D. Phillips (Eds.), *From neurons to neighborhoods* (pp. 297–327). Washington, DC: National Research Council/Institute of Medicine.

Shook, N. J., & Fazio, R. H. (2008). Interracial roommate relationships: An experimental field test of the contact hypothesis. *Psychological Science 19*(7), 717–723.

Shuey, K., & Hardy, M. A. (2003). Assistance to aging parents and parents-in-law: Does lineage affect family allocation decisions? *Journal of Marriage and Family, 65*, 418–431.

Shulman, S., Scharf, M., Lumer, D., & Maurer, O. (2001). Parental divorce and young adult children's romantic relationships: Resolution of the divorce experience. *American Journal of Orthopsychiatry, 71*, 473–478.

Shumaker, S. A., Legault, C., Kuller, L., Rapp, S. R., Thal, L., Lane, D. S., . . . Coker, L. H., for the Women's Health Initiative Memory Study Investigators. (2004). Conjugated equine estrogens and incidence of probable dementia and mild cognitive impairment in postmenopausal women: Women's Health Initiative Memory Study. *Journal of the American Medical Association, 291*, 2947–2958.

Shwe, H. I., & Markman, E. M. (1997). Young children's appreciation of the mental impact of their communicative signals. *Developmental Psychology, 33*(4), 630–636.

Shweder, R. A., Goodnow, J., Hatano, G., Levine, R. A., Markus, H., & Miller, P. (2006). The cultural psychology of development: One mind, many mentalities. In W. Damon (Ed.), *Handbook of child development* (pp. 865–937). New York: Wiley.

Siedlecki, K., Tucker-Drop, E. M., Oishi, S., & Salthouse, T. A. (2008). Life satisfaction across adulthood: Different determinants at different ages? *Journal of Positive Psychology, 3*(3), 153–164.

Seiffge-Krenke, I. (2006). Coping with relationship stressors: The impact of different working models of attachment and links to adaptation. *Journal of Youth and Adolescence, 35*(1), 25–39.

Siegel, M. B., Tanwar, K. L., & Wood, K. S. (2011). Electronic cigarettes as a smoking-cessation tool: Results from an online survey. *American Journal of Preventive Medicine*. doi: 10.1016/j.amepre.2010.12.006

Siegler, I. C. (1997). Promoting health and minimizing stress in midlife. In M. E. Lachman & J. B. James (Eds.), *Multiple paths of midlife development* (pp. 241–255). Chicago: University of Chicago Press.

Siegler, I. C., & Brummett, B. H. (2000). Associations among NEO personality assessments and well-being at midlife: Facet-level analyses. *Psychology and Aging, 15*, 710–714.

Siegler, R. S. (1998). *Children's thinking* (3rd ed.). Upper Saddle River, NJ: Prentice Hall.

Siegler, R. S. (2000). The rebirth of children's learning. *Child Development, 71*(1), 26–35.

Siegler, R. S. (2009). Improving the numerical understanding of children from low-income families. *Child Development Perspectives, 3*(2), 118–124.

Siegler, R. S., & Booth, J. L. (2004). Development of numerical estimation in young children. *Child Development, 75*, 428–444.

Siegler, R. S., & Opfer, J. E. (2003). The development of numerical estimation: Evidence for multiple representations of numerical quantity. *Psychological Science, 14*, 237–243.

Siegler, R. S., & Richards, D. (1982). The development of intelligence. In R. Sternberg (Ed.), *Handbook of human intelligence*. London: Cambridge University Press.

Sieving, R. E., McNeely, C. S., & Blum, R. W. (2000). Maternal expectations, mother-child connectedness, and adolescent sexual debut. *Archives of Pediatric & Adolescent Medicine, 154*, 809–816.

Sieving, R. E., Oliphant, J. A., & Blum, R. W. (2002). Adolescent sexual behavior and sexual health. *Pediatrics in Review, 23*, 407–416.

Sigman, M., Cohen, S. E., & Beckwith, L. (1997). Why does infant attention predict adolescent intelligence? *Infant Behavior and Development, 20*, 133–140.

Silveira, M. J., Kim, S. Y. H., & Langa, K. M. (2010). Advance directives and outcomes of surrogate decision making before death. *New England Journal of Medicine, 362*, 1211–1218.

Silver, M. H., Bubrick, E., Jilinskaia, E., & Perls, T. T. (1998, August). *Is there a centenarian personality?* Paper presented at the annual meeting of the American Psychological Association, San Francisco.

Silverberg, S. B. (1996). Parents' well-being as their children transition to adolescence. In C. Ryff & M. M. Seltzer (Eds.), *The parental experience in midlife* (pp. 215–254). Chicago: University of Chicago Press.

Silverman, W. K., La Greca, A. M., & Wasserstein, S. (1995). What do children worry about? Worries and their relation to anxiety. *Child Development, 66*, 671–686.

Silverstein, M., & Bengtson, V. L. (1997). Intergenerational solidarity and the structure of adult child-parent relationships in American families. *American Journal of Sociology, 103*, 429–460.

Silverstein, M., Cong, Z., & Li, S. (2006). Intergenerational transfers and living arrangements of older people in rural China: Consequences for psychological well-being. *Journal of Gerontology: Social Sciences, 61B*, S256–S266.

Simmons, R. G., Blyth, D. A., & McKinney, K. L. (1983). The social and psychological effect of puberty on white females. In J. Brooks-Gunn & A. C. Petersen (Eds.), *Girls at puberty: Biological and psychological perspectives*. New York: Plenum Press.

Simon, G. E. (2006). The antidepressant quandary—Considering suicide risk when treating adolescent depression. *New England Journal of Medicine, 355*, 2722–2723.

Simon, G. E., Savarino, J., Operskalski, B., & Wang, P. S. (2006). Suicide risk during antidepressant treatment. *American Journal of Psychiatry, 163*, 41–47.

Simon, M., Smoller, J. W., McNamara, K. L., Maser, R. S., Zalta, A. K., Pollack, M. H., . . . Wong, K-K. (2006). Telomere shortening and mood disorders: Preliminary support for a chronic stress model of accelerated aging. *Biological Psychiatry, 60*, 432–435.

Simons, M. (1993, February 10). Dutch parliament approves law permitting euthanasia. *The New York Times*, p. A10.

Simons, R. L., Chao, W., Conger, R. D. B., & Elder, G. H. (2001). Quality of parenting as mediator of the effect of childhood defiance on adolescent friendship choices and delinquency: A growth curve analysis. *Journal of Marriage and Family, 63*, 63–79.

Simonton, D. K. (1989). The swan-song phenomenon: Last-works effects for 172 classical composers. *Psychology and Aging, 4*, 42–47.

Simonton, D. K. (1990). Creativity and wisdom in aging. In J. E. Birren & K. W. Schaie (Eds.), *Handbook of the psychology of aging* (pp. 320–329). New York: Academic Press.

Simonton, D. K. (2000). Creativity: Cognitive, personal, developmental, and social aspects. *American Psychologist, 55*, 151–158.

Simpson, J. A., Collins, A., Tran, S., & Haydon, K. C. (2007). Attachment and the experience and expression of emotions in romantic relationships: A developmental perspective. *Journal of Personality and Social Psychology, 92*, 355–367.

Simpson, K. H. (1996). Alternatives to physician-assisted suicide. *Humanistic Judaism, 24*(4), 21–23.

Sines, E., Syed, U., Wall, S., & Worley, H. (2007). Postnatal care: A critical opportunity to save mothers and newborns. *Policy Perspectives on Newborn Health*. Washington, DC: Save the Children and Population Reference Bureau.

Singer, D. G., & Singer, J. L. (1990). *The house of make-believe: Play and the developing imagination*. Cambridge, MA: Harvard University Press.

Singer, J. L. (2004). Narrative identity and meaning-making across the adult lifespan. *Journal of Personality, 72*, 437–459.

Singer, J. L., & Singer, D. G. (1998). Barney & Friends as entertainment and education: Evaluating the quality and effectiveness of a television series for preschool children. In J. K. Asamen & G. L. Berry (Eds.), *Research paradigms, television, and social behavior* (pp. 305–367). Thousand Oaks, CA: Sage.

Singer, L. T., Minnes, S., Short, E., Arendt, K., Farkas, K., Lewis, B., . . . Kirchner, H. L. (2004). Cognitive outcomes of preschool children with prenatal cocaine exposure. *Journal of the American Medical Association, 291*, 2448–2456.

Singer, T., Verhaeghen, P., Ghisletta, P., Lindenberger, U., & Baltes, P. B. (2003). The fate of cognition in very old age: Six-year longitudinal findings in the Berlin Aging Study (BASE). *Psychology and Aging, 18*, 318–331.

Singer-Freeman, K. E., & Goswami, U. (2001). Does half a pizza equal half a box of chocolates?: Proportional matching in an analogy task. *Cognitive Development, 16*(3), 811–829.

Singhal, A., Cole, T. J., Fewtrell, M., & Lucas, A. (2004). Breastmilk feeding and lipoprotein profile in adolescents born preterm: Follow-up of a prospective randomised study. *Lancet, 363*, 1571–1578.

Singh-Manoux, A., Hillsdon, M., Brunner, E., & Marmot, M. (2005). Effects of physical activity on cognitive functioning in middle age: Evidence from the Whitehall II Prospective Cohort Study. *American Journal of Public Health, 95*, 2252–2258.

Sinnott, J. (1996). The developmental approach: Postformal thought as adaptive intelligence. In F. Blanchard-Fields & T. M. Hess (Eds.), *Perspectives on cognitive change in adulthood and aging* (pp. 358–386). New York: McGraw-Hill.

Sinnott, J. D. (2003). Postformal thought and adult development. In J. Demick & C. Andreoletti (Eds.), *Handbook of adult development*. New York: Plenum Press.

Sipos, A., Rasmussen, F., Harrison, G., Tynelius, P., Lewis, G., Leon, D. A., et al. (2004). Paternal age and schizophrenia: A population based cohort study. *British Medical Journal, 329*, 1070–1073.

Siris, E. S., Miller, P. D., Barrett-Connor, E., Faulkner, K. G., Wehren, L. E., Abbott, T. A., Berger, M. L., . . . Sherwood, L. M. (2001). Identification and fracture outcomes of undiagnosed low bone mineral density in postmenopausal women: Results from the National Osteoporosis Risk Assessment. *Journal of the American Medical Association, 286*, 2815–2822.

Sisson, S. B., Broyles, S. T., Newton, R. L., Baker, B. L., & Chernausek, S. D. (2011). TVs in the bedrooms of children: Does it impact health and behavior? *Preventive Medicine, 52*(2), 104–108.

Sitzer, D. I., Twamley, E. W., & Jeste, D. V. (2006). Cognitive training in Alzheimer's disease: A meta-analysis of the literature. *Acta Psychiatrica Scandinavica, 114*(2), 75–90.

Skadberg, B. T., Morild, I., & Markestad, T. (1998). Abandoning prone sleeping: Effects on the risk of sudden infant death syndrome. *Journal of Pediatrics, 132,* 234–239.

Skaff, M. M. (2006). The view from the driver's seat: Sense of control in the baby boomers at midlife. In S. K. Whitbourne & S. L. Willis (Eds.), *The baby boomers grow up: Contemporary perspectives on midlife* (pp. 185–204). Mahwah, NJ: Erlbaum.

Skinner, B. F. (1957). *Verbal behavior.* New York: Appleton-Century-Crofts.

Skinner, D. (1989). The socialization of gender identity: Observations from Nepal. In J. Valsiner (Ed.), *Child development in cultural context* (pp. 181–192). Toronto, Canada: Hogrefe & Huber.

Skirbekk, V. (2008). Age and productivity capacity: Descriptions, causes and policy options. *Ageing Horizons, 8*(4), 12.

Skolnick Weisberg, D., & Bloom, P. (2009). Young children separate multiple pretend worlds. *Developmental Science, 12*(5), 699–705. doi: 10.1111/j.1467-7687.2009.00819.x

Skulachev, V. P., Anisimov, V. N., Antonenko, Y. N., Bakeeva, L. E., Chernyak, B. V., Erichev, V. P., . . . Zorov, D. B. (2009). An attempt to prevent senescence: A mitochondrial approach. *Biochimica et biophysica acta, 1787*(5), 437–461.

Slobin, D. (1971). Universals of grammatical development in children. In W. Levitt & G. B. Flores d' Arcais (Eds.), *Advances in psycholinguistic research.* Amsterdam: New Holland.

Slobin, D. (1973). Cognitive prerequisites for the acquisition of language. In C. Ferguson & D. Slobin (Eds.), *Studies of child language development.* New York: Holt, Rinehart & Winston.

Slobin, D. (1983). Universal and particular in the acquisition of grammar. In E. Wanner & L. Gleitman (Eds.), *Language acquisition: The state of the art.* Cambridge, UK: Cambridge University Press.

Slobin, D. (1990). The development from child speaker to native speaker. In J. W. Stigler, R. A. Schweder, & G. H. Herdt (Eds.), *Cultural psychology: Essays on comparative human development* (pp. 233–258). New York: Cambridge University Press.

Sly, R. M. (2000). Decreases in asthma mortality in the United States. *Annals of Allergy, Asthma, and Immunology, 85,* 121–127.

Slyper, A. H. (2006). The pubertal timing controversy in the USA, and a review of possible causative factors for the advance in timing of onset of puberty. *Clinical Endocrinology, 65,* 1–8.

Small, B. J., Fratiglioni, L., von Strauss, E., & Bäckman, L. (2003). Terminal decline and cognitive performance in very old age: Does cause of death matter? *Psychology and Aging, 18,* 193–202.

Small, G. W., Kepe, V., Ercoli, L. M., Siddarth, P., Bookheimer, S. Y., Miller, K. J., . . . Barrio, J. R. (2006). PET of brain amyloid and tau in mild cognitive impairment. *New England Journal of Medicine, 355,* 2652–2663.

Small, G. W., Moody, T. D., Siddarth, P., & Bookheimer, S. Y. (2009). Your brain on Google: Patterns of cerebral activation during Internet searching. *American Journal of Geriatric Psychiatry, 17*(2), 116–126. doi: 10.1097/JGP.0b013e3181953a02

Smedley, A., & Smedley, B. D. (2005). Race as biology is fiction, racism as a social problem is real: Anthropological and historical perspectives on the social construction of race. *American Psychologist, 60,* 16–26.

Smedley, B. D., Stith, A. Y., & Nelson, A. R. (Eds.). (2002). *Unequal treatment: Confronting racial and ethnic disparities in health care.* Washington, DC: National Academy Press.

Smetana, J., Crean, H., & Campione-Barr, N. (2005). Adolescents' and parents' changing conceptions of parental authority. In J. Smetana (Ed.), *Changing boundaries of parental authority during adolescence* (New Directions for Child and Adolescent Development, No. 108, pp. 31–46). San Francisco: Jossey-Bass.

Smetana, J. G., Metzger, A., Gettman, D. C., & Campione-Barr, N. (2006). Disclosure and secrecy in adolescent-parent relationships. *Child Development, 77,* 201–217.

Smilansky, S. (1968). *The effects of sociodramatic play on disadvantaged preschool children.* New York: Wiley.

Smith, A. P. (2009). Chewing gum, stress, and health. *Stress and Health, 5*(5), 445–451.

Smith, C. D., Chebrolu, H., Wekstein, D. R., Schmitt, F. A., Jicha, G. A., Cooper, G., & Markesbery, W. R. (2007). Brain structural alterations before mild cognitive impairment. *Neurology, 68,* 1268–1273.

Smith, C. D., Walton, A., Loveland, A. D., Umberger, G. H., Kryscio, R. J., & Gash, D. M. (2005). Memories that last in old age: Motor skill learning and memory preservation. *Neurobiology of Aging, 26*(6), 883–890.

Smith, E. A. (2001). The role of tacit and explicit knowledge in the workplace. *Journal of Knowledge Management, 5,* 311–321.

Smith, E. E., Geva, A., Jonides, J., Miller, A., Reuter-Lorenz, P., & Koeppe, R. A. (2001). The neural basis of task-switching in working memory: Effects of performance and aging. *Proceedings of the National Academy of Science USA, 98,* 2095–2100.

Smith, G. C. S., Pell, J. P., Cameron, A. D., & Dobbie, R. (2002). Risk of perinatal death associated with labor after previous cesarean delivery in uncomplicated term pregnancies. *Journal of the American Medical Association, 287,* 2684–2690.

Smith, J., & Baltes, P. B. (1990). Wisdom-related knowledge: Age/cohort differences in response to life planning problems. *Developmental Psychology, 26*(3), 494–505.

Smith, L. B., & Thelen, E. (2003). Development as a dynamic system. *Trends in Cognitive Sciences, 7,* 343–348.

Smith, L. M., LaGasse, L. L., Derauf, C., Grant, P., Shah, R., Arria, A., . . . Lester, B. M. (2006). The infant development, environment, and lifestyle study: Effects of prenatal methamphetamine exposure, polydrug exposure, and poverty on intrauterine growth. *Pediatrics, 118,* 1149–1156.

Smith, P. K. (2005a). Play: Types and functions in human development. In A. D. Pellegrini & P. K. Smith (Eds.), *The nature of play* (pp. 271–291). New York: Guilford Press.

Smith, P. K. (2005b). Social and pretend play in children. In A. D. Pellegrini & P. K. Smith (Eds.), *The nature of play* (pp. 173–209). New York: Guilford Press.

Smith, S. L., Pieper, K. M., Granados, A., & Choueiti, M. (2010). Assessing gender-related portrayals in top-grossing G-rated films. *Sex Roles, 62,* 774–786. doi: 10-1007/s11199-009-9736z

Smith, T. W. (2003). *American sexual behavior: Trends, socio-demographic differences, and risk behavior* (GSS Topical Report No. 25). Chicago: National Opinion Research Center, University of Chicago.

Smith, T. W. (2005). Generation gaps in attitudes and values from the 1970s to the 1990s. In R. A. Settersten Jr., F. F. Furstenberg Jr., & R. G. Rumbaut (Eds.), *On the frontier of adulthood: Theory, research, and public policy* (pp. 177–221). Chicago: University of Chicago Press.

Smith, T. W. (2006). Personality as risk and resilience in physical health. *Current Directions in Psychological Science, 15,* 227–231.

Smith-Khuri, E., Iachan, R., Scheidt, P. C., Overpeck, M. D., Gabhainn, S. N., Pickett, W., & Harel, Y. (2004). A cross-national study of violence-related behaviors in adolescents. *Archives of Pediatrics and Adolescent Medicine, 158,* 539–544.

Smock, P. J., Manning, W. D., & Porter, M. (2005). "Everything's there except money"; How money shapes decisions to marry among cohabitors. *Journal of Marriage and Family, 67,* 680–696.

Smotherman, W. P., & Robinson, S. R. (1996). The development of behavior before birth. *Developmental Psychology, 32,* 425–434.

Snow, C. E. (1993). Families as social contexts for literacy development. In C. Daiute (Ed.), *The development of literacy through social interaction* (New Directions for Child Development, No. 61, pp. 11–24). San Francisco: Jossey-Bass.

Snow, C. E., & Beals, D. E. (2006). Mealtime talk that supports literacy development. In R. W. Larson, A. R. Wiley, & K. R. Branscomb (Eds.), *Family mealtime as a context of development and socialization* (New Directions for Child and Adolescent Development, No. 111, pp. 51–66). San Francisco: Jossey-Bass.

Snow, M. E., Jacklin, C. N., & Maccoby, E. E. (1983). Sex-of-child differences in father-child interaction at one year of age. *Child Development, 54,* 227–232.

Snowdon, D. A., Kemper, S. J., Mortimer, J. A., Greiner, L. H., Wekstein, D. R., & Markesbery, W. R. (1996). Linguistic ability in early life and cognitive function and Alzheimer's disease in late life: Findings from the Nun Study. *JAMA, 275*(7), 528–532.

Snyder, E. E., Walts, B., Perusse, L., Chagnon, Y. C., Weisnagel, S. J., Raniken, T., & Bouchard, C. (2004). The human obesity gene map. *Obesity Research, 12*, 369–439.

Snyder, J., Bank, L., & Burraston, B. (2005). The consequences of antisocial behavior in older male siblings for younger brothers and sisters. *Journal of Family Psychology, 19*, 643–653.

Snyder, J., Cramer, A., Afrank, J., & Patterson, G. R. (2005). The contributions of ineffective discipline and parental hostile attributions of child misbehavior to the development of conduct problems at home and school. *Developmental Psychology, 41*, 30–41.

Snyder, J., West, L., Stockemer, V., Gibbons, S., & Almquist-Parks, L. (1996). A social learning model of peer choice in the natural environment. *Journal of Applied Developmental Psychology, 17*, 215–237.

Sobolewski, J. M., & Amato, P. J. (2005). Economic hardship in the family of origin and children's psychological well-being in adulthood. *Journal of Marriage and Family, 67*, 141–156.

Sobolewski, J. M., & King, V. (2005). The importance of the coparental relationship for nonresident fathers' ties to children. *Journal of Marriage and Family, 67*, 1196–1212.

Social Security Administration. (2013). *Fact sheet.* Retrieved from http://www.ssa.gov/pressoffice/basicfact.htm

Society for Assisted Reproductive Technology & American Society for Reproductive Medicine. (2002). Assisted reproductive technology in the United States: 1998 results generated from the American Society for Reproductive Medicine/Society for Assisted Reproductive Technology Registry. *Fertility & Sterility, 77*(1), 18–31.

Society for Neuroscience. (2008). Neural disorders: Advances and challenges. In *Brain facts: A primer on the brain and nervous system* (pp. 36–54). Washington, DC: Author.

Society for Research in Child Development (SRCD). (2007). *Ethical standards for research with children.* (Updated by SRCD Governing Council, March 2007.) Retrieved from www.srcd.org/ethicalstandards.html

Soenens, B., Vansteenkiste, M., Luyckx, K., & Goossens, L. (2006). Parenting and adolescent problem behavior: An integrated model with adolescent self-disclosure and perceived parental knowledge as intervening variables. *Developmental Psychology, 42*, 305–318.

Sokol, R. J., Delaney-Black, V., & Nordstrom, B. (2003). Fetal alcohol spectrum disorder. *Journal of the American Medical Association, 209*, 2996–2999.

Sokol, R. Z., Kraft, P., Fowler, I. M., Mamet, R., Kim, E., & Berhane, K. T. (2006). Exposure to environmental ozone alters semen quality. *Environmental Health Perspectives, 114*(3), 360–365.

Soldz, S., & Vaillant, G. E. (1998). A 50-year longitudinal study of defense use among inner city men: A validation of the DSM-IV defense axis. *Journal of Nervous and Mental Disease, 186*, 104–111.

Solomon, B., & Frenkel, D. (2010). Immunotherapy for Alzheimer's disease. *Neuropharmacology, 59*(4–5), 303–309.

Sommer, B., Avis, N., Meyer, P., Ory, M., Madden, T., Kagawa-Singer, M., . . . Adler, S. (1999). Attitudes toward menopause and aging across ethnic/racial groups. *Psychosomatic Medicine, 61*, 868–875.

Sood, B., Delaney-Black, V., Covington, C., Nordstrom-Klee, B., Ager, J., Templin, T., . . . Sokol, R. J. (2001). Prenatal alcohol exposure and childhood behavior at age 6 to 7 years: I. Dose-response effect. *Pediatrics, 108*(8), e461–e462.

Sophian, C., Garyantes, D., & Chang, C. (1997). When three is less than two: Early developments in children's understanding of fractional quantities. *Developmental Psychology, 33*, 731–744.

Sophian, C., & Wood, A. (1997). Proportional reasoning in young children: The parts and the whole of it. *Journal of Educational Psychology, 89*, 309–317.

Sophian, C., Wood, A., & Vong, K. I. (1995). Making numbers count: The early development of numerical inferences. *Developmental Psychology, 31*, 263–273.

Sorof, J. M., Lai, D., Turner, J., Poffenbarger, T., & Portman, R. J. (2004). Overweight, ethnicity, and the prevalence of hypertension in school-aged children. *Pediatrics, 113*, 475–482.

Span, P. (2010, December 13). Getting to know you. *The New York Times*. Retrieved from http://newoldage.blogs.nytimes.com/2010/12/13/getting-to-know-you/?ref=elderly

Speece, M. W., & Brent, S. B. (1984). Children's understanding of death: A review of three components of a death concept. *Child Development, 55*, 1671–1686.

Spelke, E. (1994). Initial knowledge: Six suggestions. *Cognition, 50*, 431–445.

Spelke, E. S. (1998). Nativism, empiricism, and the origins of knowledge. *Infant Behavior and Development, 21*(2), 181–200.

Spelke, E. S. (2005). Sex differences in intrinsic aptitude for mathematics and science? A critical review. *American Psychologist, 60*, 950–958.

Spencer, J. P., Clearfield, M., Corbetta, D., Ulrich, B., Buchanan, P., & Schöner, G. (2006). Moving toward a grand theory of development: In memory of Esther Thelen. *Child Development, 77*, 1521–1538.

Sperling, M. A. (2004). Prematurity—A window of opportunity? *New England Journal of Medicine, 351*, 2229–2231.

Spinath, F. M., Price, T. S., Dale, P. S., & Plomin, R. (2004). The genetic and environmental origins of language disability and ability. *Child Development, 75*, 445–454.

Spinrad, T. L., Eisenberg, N., Harris, E., Hanish, L., Fabes, R. A., Kupanoff, K., . . . Holmes, J. (2004). The relation of children's everyday nonsocial peer play behavior to their emotionality, regulation, and social functioning. *Developmental Psychology, 40*, 67–80.

Spira, E. G., Brachen, S. S., & Fischel, J. E. (2005). Predicting improvement after first-grade reading difficulties: The effects of oral language, emergent literacy, and behavior skills. *Developmental Psychology, 41*, 225–234.

Spirduso, W. W., & MacRae, P. G. (1990). Motor performance and aging. In J. E. Birren & K. W. Schaie (Eds.), *Psychology of aging* (3rd ed., pp. 183–200). New York: Academic Press.

Spiro, A., III. (2001). Health in midlife: Toward a life-span view. In M. E. Lachman (Ed.), *Handbook of midlife development* (pp. 156–187). New York: Wiley.

Spitz, R. A. (1945). Hospitalism: An inquiry into the genesis of psychiatric conditioning in early childhood. In D. Fenschel et al. (Eds.), *Psychoanalytic studies of the child* (Vol. 1, pp. 53–74). New York: International Universities Press.

Spitz, R. A. (1946). Hospitalism: A follow-up report. In D. Fenschel et al. (Eds.), *Psychoanalytic studies of the child* (Vol. 1, pp. 113–117). New York: International Universities Press.

Spitze, G., & Trent, K. (2006). Gender differences in adult sibling relations in two-child families. *Journal of Marriage and Family, 68*, 977–992.

Spohr, H. L., Willms, J., & Steinhausen, H.-C. (1993). Prenatal alcohol exposure and long-term developmental consequences. *Lancet, 341*, 907–910.

Spraggins, C. E. (2003). Women and men in the United States: March 2002. *Current Population Reports* (P20-544). Washington, DC: U.S. Census Bureau.

Springer, M. V., McIntosh, A. R., Winocur, G., & Grady, C. L. (2005). The relation between brain activity during memory tasks and years of education in young and older adults. *Neuropsychology, 19*, 181–192.

Sroufe, L. A. (1979). Socioemotional development. In J. Osofsky (Ed.), *Handbook of infant development* (pp. 462–516). New York: Wiley.

Sroufe, L. A. (1997). *Emotional development.* Cambridge, UK: Cambridge University Press.

Sroufe, L. A., Carlson, E., & Shulman, S. (1993). Individuals in relationships: Development from infancy through adolescence. In D. C. Funder, R. D. Parke, C. Tomlinson-Keasey, & K. Widaman (Eds.), *Studying lives through time: Personality and development* (pp. 315–342). Washington, DC: American Psychological Association.

Sroufe, L. A., Coffino, B., & Carlson, E. A. (2010). Conceptualizing the role of early experience: Lessons from the Minnesota Longitudinal Study. *Developmental Review, 30*(1), 36–51.

Sroufe, L. A., Egeland, B., Carlson, E. A., & Collins, W. A. (2005). *The development of the person: The Minnesota study of risk and adaptation from birth to adulthood.* New York: Guilford Press.

St. Clair, D., Xu, M., Wang, P., Yu, Y., Fang, Y., Zhang, F., . . . He, L. (2005). Rates of adult schizophrenia following prenatal exposure to the Chinese famine of 1959–1961. *Journal of the American Medical Association, 294*, 557–562.

Stadtman, E. R. (1992). Protein oxidation and aging. *Science, 257*, 1220–1224.

Staff, J., Mortimer, J. T., & Uggen, C. (2004). Work and leisure in adolescence. In R. M. Lerner & L. Steinberg (Eds.), *Handbook of adolescent development* (2nd ed., pp. 429–450). Hoboken, NJ: Wiley.

Stanley, S. M., Amato, P. R., Johnson, C. A., & Markman, H. J. (2006). Premarital education, marital quality, and marital stability: Findings from a large, random household survey. *Journal of Family Psychology, 20*, 117–126.

Starr, J. M., Deary, I. J., Lemmon, H., & Whalley, L. J. (2000). Mental ability age 11 years and health status age 77 years. *Age and Ageing, 29*, 523–528.

Staub, E. (1996). Cultural-societal roots of violence: The examples of genocidal violence and of contemporary youth violence in the United States. *American Psychologist, 51*, 117–132.

Stauder, J. E. A., Molenaar, P. C. M., & Van der Molen, M. W. (1993). Scalp topography of event-related brain potentials and cognitive transition during childhood. *Child Development, 64*, 769–788.

Staudinger, U. M., & Baltes, P. B. (1996). Interactive minds: A facilitative setting for wisdom-related performance? *Journal of Personality and Social Psychology, 71*, 746–762.

Staudinger, U. M., & Bluck, S. (2001). A view of midlife development from life-span theory. In M. E. Lachman (Ed.), *Handbook of midlife development* (pp. 3–39). New York: Wiley.

Staudinger, U. M., Fleeson, W., & Baltes, P. B. (1999). Predictors of subjective physical health and global well-being: Similarities and differences between the United States and Germany. *Journal of Personality and Social Psychology, 76*, 305–319.

Staudinger, U. M., Smith, J., & Baltes, P. B. (1992). Wisdom-related knowledge in a life review task: Age differences and the role of professional specialization. *Psychology and Aging, 7*, 271–281.

Steffen, L. M., Kroenke, C. H., Yu, X., Pereira, M. A., Slattery, M. L., Van Horn, L., . . . Jacobs, D. R., Jr. (2005). Associations of plant food, dairy product, and meat intakes with 15-y incidence of elevated blood pressure in young black and white adults: The Coronary Artery Risk Development in Young Adults (CARDIA) Study. *American Journal of Clinical Nutrition, 82*, 1169–1177.

Steinbach, U. (1992). Social networks, institutionalization, and mortality among elderly people in the United States. *Journal of Gerontology: Social Sciences, 47*(4), S183–S190.

Steinberg, L. (2005). Psychological control: Style or substance? In J. Smetana (Ed.), *Changing boundaries of parental authority during adolescence* (New Directions for Child and Adolescent Development, No. 108, pp. 71–78). San Francisco: Jossey-Bass.

Steinberg, L. (2007). Risk taking in adolescence: New perspectives from brain and behavioral science. *Current Directions in Psychological Science, 16*, 55–59.

Steinberg, L., & Darling, N. (1994). The broader context of social influence in adolescence. In R. Silberstein & E. Todt (Eds.), *Adolescence in context.* New York: Springer.

Steinberg, L., Dornbusch, S. M., & Brown, B. B. (1992). Ethnic differences in adolescent achievement: An ecological perspective. *American Psychologist, 47*, 723–729.

Steinberg, L., Eisengard, B., & Cauffman, E. (2006). Patterns of competence and adjustment among adolescents from authoritative, authoritarian, indulgent, and neglectful homes: A replication in a sample of serious juvenile offenders. *Journal of Research on Adolescence, 16*(1), 47–58.

Steinberg, L., & Scott, E. S. (2003). Less guilty by reason of adolescence: Developmental immaturity, diminished responsibility, and the juvenile death penalty. *American Psychologist, 58*, 1009–1018.

Steinbrook, R. (2008). Physician-assisted death—From Oregon to Washington state. *New England Journal of Medicine, 35*(24), 2513–2515.

Steinhagen-Thiessen, E., & Borchelt, M. (1993). Health differences in advanced old age. *Ageing and Society, 13*, 619–655.

Steinhausen, H. C. (2002). The outcome of anorexia nervosa in the 20th century. *American Journal of Psychiatry, 159*,1284–1293.

Stennes, L. M., Burch, M. M., Sen, M. G., & Bauer, P. J. (2005). A longitudinal study of gendered vocabulary and communicative action in young children. *Developmental Psychology, 41*, 75–88.

Stephan, Y., Sutin, A. R., & Terracciano, A. (2013). Physical activity and personality development across adulthood and old age: Evidence from two longitudinal studies. *Journal of Research in Personality.* doi: http://dx.doi.org/10/1016/j.jrp.2013.12.003

Stern, Y. (2009). Cognitive reserve. *Neuropsychologia, 47*(10), 2015–2028.

Sternberg, R. J. (1985). *Beyond IQ: A triarchic theory of human intelligence.* New York: Cambridge University Press.

Sternberg, R. J. (1986). A triangular theory of love. *Psychological Review, 93*, 119–135.

Sternberg, R. J. (1987, September 23). The use and misuse of intelligence testing: Misunderstanding meaning, users over-rely on scores. *Education Week*, pp. 22, 28.

Sternberg, R. J. (1993). *Sternberg Triarchic Abilities Test.* Unpublished manuscript.

Sternberg, R. J. (1995). Love as a story. *Journal of Social and Personal Relationships, 12*(4), 541–546.

Sternberg, R. J. (1997). The concept of intelligence and its role in lifelong learning and success. *American Psychologist, 52*, 1030–1037.

Sternberg, R. J. (1998a). *Cupid's arrow.* New York: Cambridge University Press.

Sternberg, R. J. (1998b). *Love is a story: A new theory of relationships.* New York: Oxford University Press.

Sternberg, R. J. (2004). Culture and intelligence. *American Psychologist, 59*, 325–338.

Sternberg, R. J. (2005). There are no public policy implications: A reply to Rushton and Jensen (2005). *Psychology, Public Policy, and Law, 11*, 295–301.

Sternberg, R. J. (2006). A duplex theory of love. In R. J. Sternberg & K. Weis (Eds.), *The new psychology of love* (pp. 184–199). New Haven, CT: Yale University Press.

Sternberg, R. J., & Clinkenbeard, P. (1995). A triarchic view of identifying, teaching, and assessing gifted children. *Roeper Review, 17*, 255–260.

Sternberg, R. J., Forsythe, G. B., Hedlund, J., Horvath, J. A., Wagner, R. K., Williams, W. M., . . . Grigorenko, E. L. (2000). *Practical intelligence in everyday life.* New York: Cambridge University Press.

Sternberg, R. J., Grigorenko, E. L., & Kidd, K. K. (2005). Intelligence, race, and genetics. *American Psychologist, 60*, 46–59.

Sternberg, R. J., Grigorenko, E. L., & Oh, S. (2001). The development of intelligence at midlife. In M. E. Lachman (Ed.), *Handbook of midlife development* (pp. 217–247). New York: Wiley.

Sternberg, R. J., & Horvath, J. A. (1998). Cognitive conceptions of expertise and their relations to giftedness. In R. C. Friedman & K. B. Rogers (Eds.), *Talent in context: Historical and social perspectives on giftedness* (pp. 177–191). Washington, DC: American Psychological Association.

Sternberg, R. J., & Lubart, T. I. (1995). *Defying the crowd: Cultivating creativity in a culture of conformity.* New York: Free Press.

Sternberg, R. J., Wagner, R. K., Williams, W. M., & Horvath, J. A. (1995). Testing common sense. *American Psychologist, 50*, 912–927.

Sterns, H. L. (2010). New and old thoughts about aging and work in the present and future. *The Gerontologist, 50*(4), 568–571.

Sterns, H. L., & Huyck, M. H. (2001). The role of work in midlife. In M. E. Lachman (Ed.), *Handbook of midlife development* (pp. 447–486). New York: Wiley.

Stevens, J. C., Cain, W. S., Demarque, A., & Ruthruff, A. M. (1991). On the discrimination of missing ingredients: Aging and salt flavor. *Appetite, 16*, 129–140.

Stevens, J. C., Cruz, L. A., Hoffman, J. M., & Patterson, M. Q. (1995). Taste sensitivity and aging: High incidence of decline revealed by repeated threshold measures. *Chemical Senses, 20*, 451–459.

Stevens, J. H., & Bakeman, R. (1985). A factor analytic study of the HOME scale for infants. *Developmental Psychology, 21*, 1106–1203.

Stevens, W. D., Hasher, L., Chiew, K. S., & Grady, C. L. (2008). A neural mechanism underlying memory failure in older adults. *Journal of Neuroscience, 28*(48), 12820–12824.

Stevenson, D. G., & Grabowski, D. C. (2010). Sizing up the market for assisted living. *Health Affairs, 29*(1), 35–43.

Stevenson, H. W. (1995). Mathematics achievement of American students: First in the world by the year 2000? In C. A. Nelson (Ed.), *The Minnesota Symposia on Child Psychology: Vol. 28. Basic and applied perspectives on learning, cognition, and development* (pp. 131–149). Mahwah, NJ: Erlbaum.

Stevenson-Hinde, J., & Shouldice, A. (1996). Fearfulness: Developmental consistency. In A. J. Sameroff & M. M. Haith (Eds.), *The five- to seven-year shift: The age of reason and responsibility* (pp. 237–252). Chicago: University of Chicago Press.

Stewart, A. J., & Ostrove, J. M. (1998). Women's personality in middle age: Gender, history, and midcourse correction. *American Psychologist, 53*, 1185–1194.

Stewart, A. J., & Vandewater, E. A. (1998). The course of generativity. In D. P. McAdams & D. de St. Aubin (Eds.), *Generativity and adult development: How and why we care for the next generation.* Washington, DC: American Psychological Association.

Stewart, A. J., & Vandewater, E. A. (1999). "If I had to do it over again": Midlife review, midlife corrections, and women's well-being in midlife. *Journal of Personality and Social Psychology, 76*, 270–283.

Stice, E., & Bearman, K. (2001). Body image and eating disturbances prospectively predict increases in depressive symptoms in adolescent girls: A growth curve analysis. *Developmental Psychology, 37*(5), 597–607.

Stice, E., Presnell, K., Shaw, H., & Rohde, P. (2005). Psychological and behavioral risk factors for obesity onset in adolescent girls: A prospective study. *Journal of Consulting and Clinical Psychology, 73*, 195–202.

Stillwell, R., & Sable, J. (2013). *Public school graduates and dropouts from the common core of data: School year 2009–10: First look (provisional data).* NCES 2013-309. Washington, DC: National Center for Education Statistics. Retrieved from http://nces.ed.gov/pubsearch

Stipek, D. J., Gralinski, H., & Kopp, C. B. (1990). Self-concept development in the toddler years. *Developmental Psychology, 26*, 972–977.

Stock, G., & Callahan, D. (2004). Point-counterpoint: Would doubling the human life span be a net positive or negative for us either as individuals or as a society? *Journal of Gerontology: Biological Sciences, 59A*, 554–559.

Stoelhorst, M. S. J., Rijken, M., Martens, S. E., Brand, R., den Ouden, A. L., Wit, J.-M., & Veen, S., on behalf of the Leiden Follow-up Project on Prematurity. (2005). Changes in neonatology: Comparison of two cohorts of very preterm infants (gestational age <32 weeks): The Project on Preterm and Small for Gestational Age Infants 1983 and the Leiden Follow-up Project on Prematurity 1996–1997. *Pediatrics, 115*, 396–405.

Stoll, B. J., Hansen, N. I., Adams-Chapman, I., Fanaroff, A. A., Hintz, S. R., Vohr, B., & Higgins, R. D., for the National Institute of Child Health and Human Development Neonatal Research Network. (2004). Neurodevelopmental and growth impairment among extremely low-birth-weight infants with neonatal infection. *Journal of the American Medical Association, 292*, 2357–2365.

Stone, A. A., Schwartz, J. E., Broderick, J. E., & Deaton, A. (2010). A snapshot of the age distribution of psychological well-being in the United States. *Proceedings of the National Academy of Sciences of the U.S.A., 107*(22), 9985–9990.

Stone, W. L., McMahon, C. R., Yoder, P. J., & Walden, T. A. (2007). Early social-communicative and cognitive development of younger siblings of children with autism spectrum disorders. *Archives of Pediatric and Adolescent Medicine, 161*, 384–390.

Stones, M. J., & Kozma, A. (1996). Activity, exercise, and behavior. In J. E. Birren & K. W. Schaie (Eds.), *Handbook of the psychology of aging* (4th ed., pp. 338–352). San Diego: Academic Press.

Stothard, K. J., Tennant, P. W. G., Bell, R., & Rankin, J. (2009). Maternal overweight and obesity and the risk of congenital anomalies: A systematic review and meta-analysis. *Journal of the American Medical Association, 301*, 636–650.

Straus, M. A. (1994). *Beating the devil out of them: Corporal punishment in American families.* San Francisco: Jossey-Bass.

Straus, M. A. (1999). The benefits of avoiding corporal punishment: New and more definitive evidence. Submitted for publication in K. C. Blaine (Ed.), *Raising America's children.*

Straus, M. A., & Stewart, J. H. (1999). Corporal punishment by American parents: National data on prevalence, chronicity, severity, and duration, in relation to child and family characteristics. *Clinical Child and Family Psychology Review, 2*(21), 55–70.

Strayer, D., & Drews, F. (2004). Profiles in driver distraction: Effects of cell phone conversations on younger and older drivers. *Human Factors, 4*(4), 640–649.

Strayer, D. L., Drews, F. A., & Crouch, D. J. (2006). A comparison of the cell phone driver and the drunk driver. *Human Factors, 48*(2), 381–391.

Strayer, D. L., & Drews, F. A. (2007). Cell-phone–induced driver distraction. *Current Directions in Psychological Science, 16*(3), 128–131.

Streissguth, A. P., Aase, J. M., Clarren, S. K., Randels, S. P., LaDue, R. A., & Smith, D. F. (1991). Fetal alcohol syndrome in adolescents and adults. *Journal of the American Medical Association, 265*, 1961–1967.

Streissguth, A. P., Bookstein, F. L., Barr, H. M., Sampson, P. D., O'Malley, K., & Young, J. K. (2004). Risk factors for adverse life outcomes in fetal alcohol syndrome and fetal alcohol effects. *Journal of Developmental and Behavioral Pediatrics, 25*, 228–238.

Strenze, T. (2007). Intelligence and socioeconomic success: A meta-analytic review of longitudinal research. *Intelligence, 35*(5), 401–426.

Striegel-Moore, R. H., & Bulik, C. (2007). Risk factors for eating disorders. *American Psychologist, 62*, 181–198.

Stright, A. D., Gallagher, K. C., & Kelley, K. (2008). Infant temperament moderates relations between maternal parenting in early childhood and children's adjustment in first grade. *Child Development, 79*, 186–200.

Stringhini, S., Sabia, S., Shipley, M., Brunner, E., Nabi, H., Kivimaki, M., & Singh-Manoux, A. (2010). Association of socioeconomic position with health behaviors and mortality. *Journal of the American Medical Association, 303*(12), 1159–1166.

Stroebe, M., Gergen, M. M., Gergen, K. J., & Stroebe, W. (1992). Broken hearts or broken bonds: Love and death in historical perspective. *American Psychologist, 47*(10), 1205–1212.

Stroebe, M., Schut, H., & Stroebe, W. (2007). Health outcomes of bereavement. *Lancet, 370*, 1960–1973.

Stroebe, W. (2010). The graying of academia: Will it reduce scientific productivity? *American Psychologist, 65*, 660–673.

Strohschein, L. (2005). Parental divorce and child mental health trajectories. *Journal of Marriage and Family, 67*, 1286–1300.

Strömland, K., & Hellström, A. (1996). Fetal alcohol syndrome—An ophthalmological and socioeducational prospective study. *Pediatrics, 97*, 845–850.

Stromwall, L. A., Granhag, P. A., & Landstrom, S. (2007). Children's prepared and unprepared lies: Can adults see through their strategies? *Applied Cognitive Psychology, 21*, 457–471.

Stuck, A. E., Egger, M., Hammer, A., Minder, C. E., & Beck, J. C. (2002). Home visits to prevent nursing home admission and functional decline in elderly people: Systematic review and meta-regression analysis. *Journal of the American Medical Association, 287*, 1022–1028.

Stueve, A., & O'Donnell, L. N. (2005). Early alcohol initiation and subsequent sexual and alcohol risk behaviors among urban youths. *American Journal of Public Health, 95*, 887–893.

Stutzer, A., & Frey, B. S. (2006). Does marriage make people happy, or do happy people get married? *Journal of Socioeconomics, 35*(2), 326–347.

Subrahmanyam, K., Reich, S. M., Waecheter, N., & Espinoza, G. (2008). Online and offline social networks: Use of social networking sites by emerging adults. *Journal of Applied Developmental Psychology, 29*(6), 420–433.

Substance Abuse and Mental Health Services Administration (SAMHSA). (2004a, October 22). Alcohol dependence or abuse and age at first use. *The NSDUH Report.* Retrieved from http://oas.samhsa.gov/2k4/ageDependence/ageDependence.htm

Substance Abuse and Mental Health Services Administration (SAMHSA). (2004b). *Results from the 2003 National Survey on Drug Use & Health: National findings* (Office of Applied

Studies, NSDUH Series H-25, DHHS Publication No. SMA 04-3964). Rockville, MD: U.S. Department of Health and Human Services.

Substance Abuse and Mental Health Services Administration (SAMHSA), Office of Applied Studies. (2006a). Academic performance and substance use among students aged 12 to 17: 2002, 2003, and 2004. *NSDUH Report* (Issue 18). Rockville, MD: Author.

Substance Abuse and Mental Health Services Administration (SAMHSA), Office of Applied Studies. (2007a). *Results from the 2006 National Survey on Drug Use and Health: National findings* (NSDUH Series H-32, DHHS Publication No. SMA 07-4293). Rockville, MD: Author.

Substance Abuse and Mental Health Services Administration (SAMHSA), Office of Applied Studies. (2007b, March 30). Sexually transmitted diseases and substance use. *NSDUH Report.* Rockville, MD: Author.

Substance Abuse and Mental Health Services Administration (SAMHSA), Office of Applied Studies. (2008, April 18). State estimates of persons aged 18 or older driving under the influence of alcohol or illicit drugs. *NSDUH Report.* Rockville, MD: Author.

Substance Abuse and Mental Health Services Administration (SAMHSA). (2009a). *Results from the 2008 National Survey on Drug Use and Health: National findings* (Office of Applied Studies, NSDUH Series H-36, HHS Publication No. SMA 09-4434). Rockville, MD: Author.

Substance Abuse and Mental Health Services Administration (SAMHSA). (2013). *Behavioral health, United States, 2012.* HHS Publication No. (SMA) 13-4797. Rockville, MD: Substance Abuse and Mental Health Services Administration.

Substance Abuse and Mental Health Services Administration (SAMHSA). (2013). *Results from the 2012 national survey on drug use and health: Mental health findings.* NSDUH Series H-47, HHS Publication No. (SMA) 13-4805. Rockville, MD: Author. Retrieved from http://www.samhsa.gov/data/NSDUH/2k12MH_FindingsandDetTables/2K12MHF/NSDUHmhfr2012.htm#fig3-2

Substance Abuse and Mental Health Services Administration (SAMHSA). (2013). *Results from the 2012 national survey on drug use and health: Summary of national findings.* NSDUH Series H-46, HHS Publication No. (SMA) 13-4795. Rockville, MD: Author.

Suetta, C., Andersen, J. L., Dalgas, U., Berget, J., Koskinen, S., Aagaard, P., Magnusson, S. P., & Kjaer, M. (2008). Resistance training induces qualitative changes in muscle morphology, muscle architecture, and muscle function in elderly postoperative patients. *Journal of Applied Physiology, 105*(1), 180–186.

Suicide—Part I. (1996, November). *Harvard Mental Health Letter,* pp. 1–5.

Suitor, J. J., & Pillemer, K. (1993). Support and interpersonal stress in the social networks of married daughters caring for parents with dementia. *Journal of Gerontology: Social Sciences, 41*(1), S1–S8.

Suitor, J. J., Pillemer, K., Keeton, S., & Robison, J. (1995). Aged parents and aging children: Determinants of relationship quality. In R. Blieszner & V. Hilkevitch (Eds.), *Handbook of aging and the family* (pp. 223–242). Westport, CT: Greenwood Press.

Suitor, J. J., Seechrist, J., Plikuhn, M., & Pillemer, K. (2008). Within-family differences in parent-child relations across the life course. *Current Directions in Psychological Science, 17*(5), 334–338.

Sullivan, M. W., Bennett, D. S., Carpenter, K., & Lewis, M. (2007). *Emotion knowledge in young maltreated children.* Manuscript submitted for publication.

Sullivan, K. T., Pasch, L. A., Johnson, M. D., & Bradbury, T. N. (2010). Social support, problem solving, and the longitudinal course of newlywed marriage. *Journal of Personality and Social Psychology, 98*(4), 631–644.

Sulloway, F. J., & Zweigenhaft, R. L. (2010). Birth order and risk taking in athletics: A meta-analysis and study of major league baseball. *Personality and Social Psychology Review, 14*(4), 402–416. doi: 10.1177/1088868310361241

Sun, Y. (2001). Family environment and adolescents' well-being before and after parents' marital disruption. *Journal of Marriage and Family, 63*, 697–713.

Sundet, J., Barlaug, D., & Torjussen, T. (2004). The end of the Flynn Effect? A study of secular trends in mean intelligence test scores of Norwegian conscripts during half a century. *Intelligence, 32*, 349–362.

Suomi, S., & Harlow, H. (1972). Social rehabilitation of isolate-reared monkeys. *Developmental Psychology, 6*, 487–496.

SUPPORT Principal Investigators. (1995). A controlled trial to improve care for seriously ill hospitalized patients: The Study to Understand Prognoses and Preferences for Outcomes and Risks of Treatments (SUPPORT). *Journal of the American Medical Association, 274*, 1591–1598.

Surkan, P. J., Stephansson, O., Dickman, P. W., & Cnattingius, S. (2004). Previous preterm and small-for-gestational-age births and the subsequent risk of stillbirth. *New England Journal of Medicine, 350*, 777–785.

Susman, E. J., & Rogol, A. (2004). Puberty and psychological development. In R. M. Lerner & L. Steinberg (Eds.), *Handbook of adolescent psychology* (2nd ed., pp. 15–44). Hoboken, NJ: Wiley.

Susser, E. S., & Lin, S. P. (1992). Schizophrenia after prenatal exposure to the Dutch hunger winter of 1944–1945. *Archives of General Psychiatry, 49*, 983–988.

Swain, I., Zelano, P., & Clifton, R. (1993). Newborn infants' memory for speech sounds retained over 24 hours. *Developmental Psychology, 29*, 312–323.

Swain, J. E., Tasgin, E., Mayes, L. C., Feldman, R., Constable, R. T., & Leckman, J. F. (2008). Maternal brain response to own baby cry is affected by cesarean section delivery. *Journal of Child Psychology and Psychiatry, 49*, 1042–1052.

Swallen, K. C., Reither, E. N., Haas, S. A., & Meier, A. M. (2005). Overweight, obesity, and health-related quality of life among adolescents: The National Longitudinal Study of Adolescent Health. *Pediatrics, 115*, 340–347.

Swamy, G. K., Ostbye, T., & Skjaerven, R. (2008). Association of preterm birth with long-term survival, reproduction, and next-generation preterm birth. *Journal of the American Medical Association, 299*,1429–1436.

Swan, S. H., Kruse, R. L., Liu, F., Barr, D. B., Drobnis, E. Z., Redmon, J. B., . . . Study for Future Families Research Group. (2003). Semen quality in relation to biomarkers of pesticide exposure. *Environmental Health Perspectives, 111*, 1478–1484.

Swanston, H. Y., Tebbutt, J. S., O'Toole, B. I., & Oates, R. K. (1997). Sexually abused children 5 years after presentation: A case-control study. *Pediatrics, 100*, 600–608.

Sweeney, M. M., & Phillips, J. A. (2004). Understanding racial differences in marital disruption: Recent trends and explanations. *Journal of Marriage and Family, 66*, 639–650.

Swingley, D. (2008). The roots of the early vocabulary in infants' learning from speech. *Current Directions in Psychological Science, 17*, 308–312.

Swingley, D., & Fernald, A. (2002). Recognition of words referring to present and absent objects by 24-month-olds. *Journal of Memory and Language, 46*, 39–56.

Szatmari, P., Paterson, A. D., Zwaigenbaum, L., Roberts, W., Brian, J., Liu, X.-Q., . . . Shih, A. (2007). Mapping autism risk loci using genetic linkage and chromosomal rearrangements. *Nature Genetics, 39*, 319–328.

Tackett, J. L., Krueger, R. F., Iacono, W. G., & McGue, M. (2005). Symptom-based subfactors of DSM-defined conduct disorder: Evidence for etiologic distinctions. *Journal of Abnormal Psychology, 114*, 483–487.

Tajfel, H. (1981). *Human groups and social categories.* Cambridge, UK: Cambridge University Press.

Takachi, R., Inoue, M., Ishihara, J., Kurahashi, N., Iwasaki, M., Sasazuki, S., . . . Tsugane, S. (2007). Fruit and vegetable intake and risk of total cancer and cardiovascular disease: Japan Public Health Center-based Prospective Study. *American Journal of Epidemiology, 167*(1), 59–70.

Tal-Or, N. (2010). Direct and indirect self-promotion in the eyes of the perceivers. *Social Influence, 5*(2), 87–100. doi: 10.1080/15534510903306489

Tallent-Runnels, M., Thomas, J. A., Lan, W. Y., Cooper, S., Ahern, T. C., Shaw, S. M., & Liu, X. (2006). Teaching courses online: A review of the research. *Review of Educational Research, 76*(1), 93–135.

Tamis-LeMonda, C. S., Bornstein, M. H., & Baumwell, L. (2001). Maternal responsiveness and children's achievement of language milestones. *Child Development, 72*(3), 748–767.

Tamis-LeMonda, C. S., Shannon, J. D., Cabrera, N. J., & Lamb, M. E. (2004). Fathers and mothers at play with their 2- and 3-year-olds: Contributions to language and cognitive development. *Child Development, 75*, 1806–1820.

Tanner, J. L. (2006). Recentering during emerging adulthood: A critical turning point in life span human development. In J. J. Arnett & J. L. Tanner (Eds.), *Emerging adults in America: Coming of age in the 21st century* (pp. 21–55). Washington DC: American Psychological Association.

Tao, K.-T. (1998). An overview of only child family mental health in China. *Psychiatry and Clinical Neurosciences, 52*(Suppl.), S206–S211.

Taveras, E. M., Capra, A. M., Braveman, P. A., Jensvold, N. G., Escobar, G. J., & Lieu, T. A. (2003). Clinician support and psychosocial risk factors associated with breastfeeding discontinuation. *Pediatrics, 112*, 108–115.

Taylor, C. A., Lee, S. J., Guterman, N. B., & Rice, J. C. (2010). Use of spanking for 3-year-old children and associated intimate partner aggression or violence. *Pediatrics, 126*(3), 415–424. doi: 10.1542/peds.2010-0314

Taylor, D. J., Lichstein, K. L., Durrence, H. H., Reidel, B. W., & Bush, A. J. (2005). Epidemiology of insomnia, depression and anxiety. *Sleep, 28*(11), 1457–1464.

Taylor, J. G. (2007). Psychosocial and moral development of PTSD-diagnosed combat veterans. *Journal of Counseling and Development, 85*(3), 364–369.

Taylor, M., & Carlson, S. M. (1997). The relation between individual differences in fantasy and theory of mind. *Child Development, 68*, 436–455.

Taylor, M., Cartwright, B. S., & Carlson, S. M. (1993). A developmental investigation of children's imaginary companions. *Developmental Psychology, 28*, 276–285.

Taylor, P., & Wang, W. (2010). *The fading glory of the television and telephone*. Retrieved from http://pewsocialtrends.org/2010/08/19/the-fading-glory-of-the-television-and-telephone/

Taylor, R. D., & Roberts, D. (1995). Kinship support in maternal and adolescent well-being in economically disadvantaged African-American families. *Child Development, 66*, 1585–1597.

Taylor, S. E. (2006). Tend and befriend: Biobehavioral bases of affiliation under stress. *Current Directions in Psychological Science, 15*, 273–276.

Taylor, S. E., Lehman, B. J., Kiefe, C. I., & Seeman, T. E. (2006). Relationship of early life stress and psychological functioning to adult C-reactive protein in the coronary artery risk development in young adults study. *Biological Psychiatry, 60*(8), 819–824.

Teachers Resisting Unhealthy Children's Entertainment (TRUCE). (2008). *Media action guide*. Retrieved from www.truceteachers.org/mediaviolence.html

Teachman, J. (2003). Premarital sex, premarital cohabitation, and the risk of subsequent marital dissolution among women. *Journal of Marriage and Family, 65*, 444–455.

Teachman, J. D., Tedrow, L. M., & Crowder, K. D. (2000). The changing demography of America's families. *Journal of Marriage and Family, 62*, 1234–1246.

Teasdale, T. W., & Owen, D. R. (2008). Secular declines in cognitive test scores: A reversal of the Flynn effect. *Intelligence, 36*, 121–126.

Tejada-Vera, B., & Sutton, P. D. (2009). Births, marriages, divorces, and deaths: Provisional data for 2008. *National Vital Statistics Reports, 57*(19). Hyattsville, MD: National Center for Health Statistics. Retrieved from http://www.cdc.g/nchs/data/nvsr/nvsr57/nvsr57_19.pdf

Telzer, E. H., & Fuligni, A. J. (2009). Daily family assistance and the psychological well-being of adolescents from Latin American, Asian and European backgrounds. *Developmental Psychology, 45*(4), 1177–1189.

Temel, J. S., Greer, J. A., Muzikanskym, A., Gallagher, E. R., Admane, S., Jackson, V. A., . . . Lynch, T. J. (2010). Early palliative care for patients with metastatic non-small-cell lung cancer. *New England Journal of Medicine, 363*(8), 733–742.

Temple, J. A., Reynolds, A. J., & Miedel, W. T. (2000). Can early intervention prevent high school dropout? Evidence from the Chicago Child-Parent Centers. *Urban Education, 35*(1), 31–57.

Tenenbaum, H., & Leaper, C. (2002). Are parents' gender schemas related to their children's gender-related cognitions? A meta-analysis. *Developmental Psychology, 38*(4), 615–630.

Terracio, A., McCrae, R., & Costa, P. (2009). Intra-individual change in personality stability and age. *Journal of Research in Personality, 44*(1), 31–37.

Tester, D. J., Carturan, E., Dura, M., Reiken, S., Wronska, A., Marks, A. R., & Ackerman, M. J. (2006, May). *Molecular and functional characterization of novel RyR2-encoded cardiac ryanodine receptor/calcium release channel mutations in sudden infant death syndrome.* Presentation at Heart Rhythm 2006, the 27th Annual Scientific Sessions of the Heart Rhythm Society, Boston.

Teti, D. M., & Ablard, K. E. (1989). Security of attachment and infant-sibling relationships: A laboratory study. *Child Development, 60*, 1519–1528.

Teti, D. M., Bo-Ram, K., Mayer, G., & Countermine, M. (2010). Maternal emotional availability at bedtime predicts infant sleep quality. *Journal of Family Psychology, 24*(3), 307–315.

Teti, D. M., Gelfand, D. M., Messinger, D. S., & Isabella, R. (1995). Maternal depression and the quality of early attachment: An examination of infants, preschoolers, and their mothers. *Developmental Psychology, 31*, 364–376.

Thabes, V. (1997). A survey analysis of women's long-term, postdivorce adjustment. *Journal of Divorce & Remarriage, 27*, 163–175.

Thapar, A., Fowler, T., Rice, F., Scourfield, J., van den Bree, M., Thomas, H., Harold, G., & Hay, D. (2003). Maternal smoking during pregnancy and attention deficit hyperactivity disorder symptoms in offspring. *American Journal of Psychiatry, 160*, 1985–1989.

Thelen, E. (1995). Motor development: A new synthesis. *American Psychologist, 50*(2), 79–95.

Thelen, E., & Fisher, D. M. (1982). Newborn stepping: An explanation for a "disappearing" reflex. *Developmental Psychology, 18*, 760–775.

Thelen, E., & Fisher, D. M. (1983). The organization of spontaneous leg movements in newborn infants. *Journal of Motor Behavior, 15*, 353–377.

Thomas, A., & Chess, S. (1977). *Temperament and development.* New York: Brunner/Mazel.

Thomas, A., & Chess, S. (1984). Genesis and evolution of behavioral disorders: From infancy to early adult life. *American Journal of Orthopsychiatry, 141*(1), 1–9.

Thomas, A., Chess, S., & Birch, H. G. (1968). *Temperament and behavior disorders in children.* New York: New York University Press.

Thomas, P. A. (2010). Is it better to give or to receive? Social support and the well-being of older adults. *Journals of Gerontology Series B: Psychological Sciences and Social Sciences, 65*(3), 351–357.

Thomas, S. P. (1997). Psychosocial correlates of women's self-rated physical health in middle adulthood. In M. E. Lachman & J. B. James (Eds.), *Multiple paths of midlife development* (pp. 257–291). Chicago: University of Chicago Press.

Thomas, W. P., & Collier, V. P. (1998). Two languages are better than one. *Educational Leadership, 55*(4), 23–28.

Thompson, L. A., Goodman, D. C., Chang, C-H., & Stukel, T. A. (2005). Regional variation in rates of low birth weight. *Pediatrics, 116*, 1114–1121.

Thompson, P. M., Cannon, T. D., Narr, K. L., van Erp, T., Poutanen, V., Huttunen, M., . . . Toga, A. W. (2001). Genetic influences on brain structure. *Nature Neuroscience, 4*, 1253–1258.

Thompson, P. M., Giedd, J. N., Woods, R. P., MacDonald, D., Evans, A. C., & Toga, A. W. (2000). Growth patterns in the developing brain detected by using continuum mechanical tensor maps. *Nature, 404*, 190–193.

Thompson, R. A. (1991). Emotional regulation and emotional development. *Educational Psychology Review, 3*, 269–307.

Thompson, R. A. (2011). Emotion and emotion regulation: Two sides of the developing coin. *Emotion Review, 3*(1), 53–61.

Thompson, W. W., Price, C., Goodson, B., Shay, D. K., Benson, P., Hinrichsen, V. L., . . . DeStefano, F., for the Vaccine Safety Datalink Team. (2007). Early thimerosal exposure and neuropsychological outcomes at 7 to 10 years. *New England Journal of Medicine, 357*, 1281–1292.

Thomson, E., Mosley, J., Hanson, T. L., & McLanahan, S. S. (2001). Remarriage, cohabitation, and changes in mothering behavior. *Journal of Marriage and Family, 63*, 370–380.

Thorne, A., & Michaelieu, Q. (1996). Situating adolescent gender and self-esteem with personal memories. *Child Development, 67*, 1374–1390.

Thornton, W. J. L., & Dumke, H. A. (2005). Age differences in everyday problem-solving and decision-making effectiveness: A meta-analytic review. *Psychology and Aging, 20*, 85–99.

Thorvaldsson, V., Hofer, S. M., Berg, S., Skoog, I., Sacuiu, S., & Johansson, B. (2008). Onset of terminal decline in cognitive abilities in individuals without dementia. *Neurology.* Advance online publication. doi: 10.1212/01.wnl.0000312379.02302.ba

Tidwell, L. C., & Walther, J. B. (2002). Computer-mediated communication effects on disclosure, impressions, and interpersonal evaluations: Getting to know one another a bit at a time. *Human Communication Research, 28*, 317–348.

Tilvis, R. S., Kahonen-Vare, M. H., Jolkkonen, J., Valvanne, J., Pitkala, K. H., & Stradnberg, T. E. (2004). Predictors of cognitive decline and mortality of aged people over a 10-year period. *Journal of Gerontology: Medical Sciences, 59A*, 268–274.

Tincoff, R., & Jusczyk, P. W. (1999). Some beginnings of word comprehension in 6-month-olds. *Psychological Science, 10*, 172–177.

Tindle, H. A., Chang, Y., Kuller, L. H., Manson, J. E., Robinson, J. G., Rosal, M. C., . . . Matthews, K. A. (2009). Optimism, cynical hostility and incident coronary heart disease and mortality in the women's health initiative. *Circulation, 120*(8), 656–662.

Tisdale, S. (1988). The mother. *Hippocrates, 2*(3) 64–72.

Tither, J., & Ellis, B. (2008). Impact of fathers on daughter's age at menarche: A genetically and environmentally controlled sibling study. *Developmental Psychology, 44*(5), 1409–1420.

Tjaden, P., & Thoennes, N. (2000). *Extent, nature, and consequences of intimate partner violence: Findings from the National Violence Against Women Survey.* Washington, DC: National Institute of Justice and Centers for Disease Control and Prevention.

Toga, A., & Thompson, P. M. (2005). Genetics of brain structure and intelligence. *Annual Review of Neurology, 28*, 1–23.

Toga, A. W., Thompson, P. M., & Sowell, E. R. (2006). Mapping brain maturation. *Trends in Neurosciences, 29*(3), 148–159.

Tolan, P. H., Gorman-Smith, D., & Henry, D. B. (2003). The developmental ecology of urban males' youth violence. *Developmental Psychology, 39*, 274–291.

Toma, C. L., Hancock, J. T., & Ellison, N. B. (2008). Separating fact from fiction: An examination of deceptive self-presentation in online dating profiles. *Personality and Social Psychology Bulletin, 34*(8), 1023–1036.

Tomasello, M. (2007). Cooperation and communication in the 2nd year of life. *Child Development Perspectives, 1*, 8–12.

Tomashek, K. M., Hsia, J., & Iyasu, S. (2003). Trends in postneonatal mortality attributable to injury, United States, 1988–1998. *Pediatrics, 111*, 1215–1218.

Torrance, E. P. (1974). *The Torrance Tests of Creative Thinking: Technical norms manual.* Bensonville, IL: Scholastic Testing Service.

Torrance, E. P. (1988). The nature of creativity as manifest in its testing. In R. J. Sternberg (Ed.), *The nature of creativity: Contemporary psychological perspectives* (pp. 43–75). Cambridge, UK: Cambridge University Press.

Torrance, E. P., & Ball, O. E. (1984). *Torrance Tests of Creative Thinking: Streamlined (revised) manual, Figural A and B.* Bensonville, IL: Scholastic Testing Service.

Totsika, V., & Sylva, K. (2004). The Home Observation for Measurement of the Environment revisited. *Child and Adolescent Mental Health, 9*, 25–35.

Towfighi, A., Zheng, L., & Ovbiagele, B. (2009). Sex-specific trends in midlife coronary heart disease risk and prevalence. *Archives of Internal Medicine, 169*(19), 1762–1766.

Townsend, N. W. (1997). Men, migration, and households in Botswana: An exploration of connections over time and space. *Journal of Southern African Studies, 23*, 405–420.

Trautner, H. M., Ruble, D. N., Cyphers, L., Kirsten, B., Behrendt, R., & Hartmann, P. (2005). Rigidity and flexibility of gender stereotypes in childhood: Developmental or differential? *Infant and Child Development, 14*(4), 365–381.

Tremblay, R. E., Nagin, D. S., Séguin, J. R., Zoccolillo, M., Zelazo, P. D., Boivin, M., . . . Japel, C. (2004). Physical aggression during early childhood: Trajectories and predictors. *Pediatrics, 114*(1), e43–e50.

Trenholm, C., Devaney, B., Fortson, K., Quay, L., Wheeler, J., & Clark, M. (2007). *Impacts of four Title V, Section 510 abstinence education programs: Final report.* Princeton, NJ: Mathematica Policy Research.

Trimble, C. L., Genkinger, J. M., Burke, A. E., Helzlsouer, K. J., Diener-West, M., Comstock, G. W., & Alberg, A. J. (2005). Active and passive cigarette smoking and the risk of cervical neoplasia. *Obstetrics & Gynecology, 105*, 174–181.

Trionfi, G., & Reese, E. (2009). A good story: Children with imaginary companions create richer narratives. *Child Development, 80*(4), 1301–1313.

Troll, L. E. (1985). *Early and middle adulthood* (2nd ed.). Monterey, CA: Brooks/Cole.

Troll, L. E., & Fingerman, K. L. (1996). Connections between parents and their adult children. In C. Magai & S. H. McFadden (Eds.), *Handbook of emotion, adult development, and aging* (pp. 185–205). San Diego: Academic Press.

Tronick, E. (1972). Stimulus control and the growth of the infant's visual field. *Perception and Psychophysics, 11*, 373–375.

Tronick, E. Z. (1989). Emotions and emotional communication in infants. *American Psychologist, 44*(2), 112–119.

Tronick, E. Z., Morelli, G. A., & Ivey, P. (1992). The Efe forager infant and toddler's pattern of social relationships: Multiple and simultaneous. *Developmental Psychology, 28*, 568–577.

Troseth, G. L., & DeLoache, J. S. (1998). The medium can obscure the message: Young children's understanding of video. *Child Development, 69*, 950–965.

Troseth, G. L., Saylor, M. M., & Archer, A. H. (2006). Young children's use of video as a source of socially relevant information. *Child Development, 77*, 786–799.

Trotter, R. J. (1986, August). Profile: Robert J. Sternberg: Three heads are better than one. *Psychology Today,* pp. 56–62.

Trudel, G., Villeneuve, V., Anderson, A., & Pilon, G. (2008). Sexual and marital aspects of old age: An update. *Sexual and Relationship Therapy, 23*(2), 161–169.

Tsao, F. M., Liu, H. M., & Kuhl, P. K. (2004). Speech perception in infancy predicts language development in the second year of life: A longitudinal study. *Child Development, 75*, 1067–1084.

Tsuchiya, K., Matsumoto, K., Miyachi, T., Tsujii, M., Nakamura, K., Takagai, S., . . . Takei, N. (2008). Paternal age at birth and high-functioning autistic-spectrum disorder in offspring. *British Journal of Psychiatry, 193*, 316–321.

Tucker, M. B., Taylor, R. J., & Mitchell-Kernan, C. (1993). Marriage and romantic involvement among aged African Americans. *Journal of Gerontology: Social Sciences, 48*, S123–S132.

Turati, C., Simion, F., Milani, I., & Umilta, C. (2002). Newborns' preference for faces: What is crucial? *Developmental Psychology, 38*, 875–882.

Turkheimer, E., Haley, A., Waldron, J., D'Onofrio, B., & Gottesman, I. I. (2003). Socioeconomic status modifies heritability of IQ in young children. *Psychological Science, 14*, 623–628.

Turkle, S. (2011). *Alone together: Why we expect more from technology and less from each other.* New York: Basic Books.

Turner, C. F., Ku, L., Rogers, S. M., Lindberg, L. D., Pleck, J. H., & Sonenstein, F. L. (1998). Adolescent sexual behavior, drug use, and violence: Increased reporting with computer survey technology. *Science, 280*, 867–873.

Turner, P. J., & Gervai, J. (1995). A multidimensional study of gender typing in preschool children and their parents: Personality, attitudes, preferences, behavior, and cultural differences. *Developmental Psychology, 31*, 759–772.

Turrisi, R., Wiersman, K. A., & Hughes, K. K. (2000). Binge-drinking-related consequences in college students: Role of drinking beliefs and mother-teen communication. *Psychology of Addictive Behaviors, 14*(4), 342–345.

Twenge, J. M. (2000). The age of anxiety? Birth cohort change in anxiety and neuroticism, 1952–1993. *Journal of Personality and Social Psychology, 79*, 1007–1021.

Twenge, J. M., Campbell, W. K., & Foster, C. A. (2003). Parenthood and marital satisfaction: A meta-analytic review. *Journal of Marriage and Family, 65*, 574–583.

Tyas, S. L., Salazar, J. C., Snowdon, D. A., Desrosiers, M. F., Riley, K. P., Mendiondo,

M. S., & Kryscio, R. J. (2007). Transitions to mild cognitive impairments, dementia, and death: Findings from the Nun Study. *American Journal of Epidemiology, 165*(11), 1231–1238.

Uitterlinden, A. G., Burger, H., Huang, Q., Yue, F., McGuigan, F. E. A., Grant, S. F. A., . . . Ralston, S. H. (1998). Relation of alleles of the collagen type Iα1 gene to bone density and the risk of osteoporitic fractures in postmenopausal women. *New England Journal of Medicine, 33*, 1016–1021.

Umana-Taylor, A. J., Gonzalez-Backen, M. A., & Guimond, A. B. (2009). Latino adolescents' ethnic identity: Is there a developmental progression and does growth in ethnic identity predict growth in self-esteem? *Child Development, 80*(2), 391–405.

Umana-Taylor, A. J., & Updegraff, K. A. (2006). Latino adolescents' mental health: Exploring the interrelationships among discrimination, ethnic identity, cultural orientation, self-esteem and depressive symptoms. *Journal of Adolescence, 30*(4), 549–567.

Umberson, D., Williams, K., Powers, D. A., Liu, H., & Needham, B. (2006). You make me sick: Marital quality and health over the life course. *Journal of Health and Social Behavior, 47*, 1–16.

UNAIDS/WHO Joint United Nations Programme on HIV/AIDS and World Health Organization. (2004). *AIDS epidemic update* (Publication No. UNAIDS/04.45E). Geneva: Author.

UNAIDS. (2013). *UNAIDS report on the global AIDS epidemic.* Retrieved from http://www.unaids.org/en/media/unaids/contentassets/documents/epidemiology/2013/gr2013/UNAIDS_Global_Report_2013_en.pdf

UNICEF. (2013). *Improving child nutrition: The achievable imperative for global progress.* Retrieved from http://www.unicef.org/media/files/nutrition_report_2013.pdf

United Nations. (2007, April). An ageing world poses new challenges for development strategists. *DESA (Department of Economic and Social Affairs) News, 11*(4). Retrieved from www.un.org/esa/desa/desaNews/v11n04/feature.html

United Nations. (2009). *Rethinking poverty: Report on the world social situation* (No. E.09. IV.10). Retrieved from http://www.un.org/esa/socdev/rwss/docs/2010/fullreport.pdf

United Nations Children's Fund (UNICEF). (2007). *The state of the world's children 2008: Child survival.* New York: Author.

United Nations Children's Fund (UNICEF). (2008). *State of the world's children 2009: Maternal and newborn health.* New York: Author.

United Nations Children's Fund (UNICEF). (2009). *Worldwide deaths of children under five decline, continuing positive trend.* Retrieved from www.unicef.org/childsurvival/index_51095.html

United Nations Children's Fund (UNICEF) and World Health Organization (WHO). (2004). *Low birthweight: Country, regional and global estimates.* New York: UNICEF.

United Nations Educational, Scientific, and Cultural Organization (UNESCO). (2004). *Education for All Global Monitoring Report 2005—The quality imperative.* Retrieved from www.unesco.org/education/GMR2005/press

United Nations Educational, Scientific, and Cultural Organization (UNESCO). (2007). *Literacy portal: United Nations Literacy Decade: Why the Literacy Decade?* Retrieved from http://portal.unesco.org/education/en/ev.php-URL_ID=53899&URL_DO=DO_TOPIC&URL_SECTION=201.htm

United Nations High Commissioner for Human Rights. (1989, November 20). *Convention on the Rights of the Child.* General Assembly Resolution 44/25.

United Nations Statistics Division. (2007). *Population and vital statistics report: Series A.* Table 3: Live births, deaths, and infant deaths, latest available year. Retrieved from http://unstats.un.org/unsd/demographic/products/vitstats/seriesa2.htm

United States Breastfeeding Committee. (2002). *Benefits of breastfeeding.* Raleigh, NC: Author.

Urasaki, E., Tokimura, T., Kumai, J., & Yokota, A. (1992). Preserved spinal dorsal horn potentials in a brain dead patient with Lazarus sign. Case report. *Journal of Neurosurgery, 77*(5), 823–824.

U.S. Bureau of Labor Statistics. (2008a, May 30). *Employment characteristics of families in 2007* [News release]. Washington, DC: U.S. Department of Labor.

U.S. Bureau of Labor Statistics. (2008b). *Spotlight on statistics. Older workers.* Washington, DC: Author. Retrieved from http://stats.bls.gov/spotlight/2008/older_workers/

U.S. Bureau of Labor Statistics. (2012, April 26). Employment characteristics of families in 2011. [News release]. Washington, DC: U.S. Department of Labor. Retrieved from http://www.bls.gov/news.release/famee.nr0.htm

U.S. Bureau of the Census. (1991a). *Household and family characteristics, March 1991* (Publication No. AP-20–458). Washington, DC: U.S. Government Printing Office.

U.S. Bureau of the Census. (1991b). *1990 census of population and housing.* Washington, DC: Data User Service Division.

U.S. Bureau of the Census. (1992). *Marital status and living arrangements: March 1991* (Current Population Reports, Series P-20-461). Washington, DC: U.S. Government Printing Office.

U.S. Bureau of the Census. (1993). *Sixty-five plus in America.* Washington, DC: U.S. Government Printing Office.

U.S. Census Bureau. (2000, November). *Resident population estimates of the United States by age and sex.* Washington, DC: Author.

U.S. Census Bureau. (2004). *Global population profile, 2002. International population reports WP/02.* Washington, DC: U.S. Government Printing Office.

U.S. Census Bureau. (2006). Educational attainment in the United States, 2006. Data from *2006 Current Population Survey's Social and Economic Supplement.* Washington, DC: Author.

U.S. Census Bureau. (2007a, March 15). *Earnings gap highlighted by Census Bureau data on educational attainment* [Press release]. Retrieved from www.census.gov/Press-Release/www/releases/archives/education/009749.html

U.S. Census Bureau. (2007b). *The population profile of the United States: Dynamic version.* Retrieved from www.census.gov/population/www/pop-profile/profiledynamic.html

U.S. Census Bureau. (2008a). *Population profile of the United States.* Retrieved from www.census.gov/population/www/pop-profile/profiledynamic.html

U.S. Census Bureau. (2008b). *Who's minding the kids? Child care arrangements: Spring 2005.* Washington, DC: U.S. Census Bureau, Housing and Household Economic Statistics Division, Fertility & Family Statistics Branch.

U.S. Census Bureau. (2009a). *Births, deaths, and life expectancy by country or area, Table 3.* Washington, DC: U.S. Census Bureau, International Data Base. Retrieved from www.census.gov/compendia/statab/2010/tables/10s1303.xls

U.S. Census Bureau. (2009b). School enrollment in the United States, 2007, Table 1: Enrollment status of the population 3 years old and over, by sex, age, race, Hispanic origin, foreign born, and foreign-born parentage: October 2007, Hispanic. *School enrollment—Social and economic characteristics of students: October 2007.* Washington, DC: Author.

U.S. Census Bureau. (2009c). School enrollment in the United States, 2007, Table 3. Nursery and primary school enrollment of people 3 to 6 years old, by control of school, attendance status, age, race, Hispanic origin, mother's labor force status and education, and family income. *School enrollment—Social and economic chracteristics of students: October 2007.* Washington, DC: Author.

U.S. Census Bureau. (2009d). *Census bureau estimates nearly half of children under age 5 are minorities.* Retrieved from http://www.census.gov/newsroom/releases/archives/population/cb09-75.html

U.S. Census Bureau. (2010a). *America's families and living arrangements: 2010.* Retrieved from http://www.census.gov/population/www/socdemo/hh-fam/cps2010.html

U.S. Census Bureau. (2010b). *Poverty. Highlights.* Retrieved from http://www.census.gov/hhes/www/poverty/about/overview/index.html

U.S. Department of Agriculture (USDA). (2010). *Dietary guidelines.* Retrieved from http://www.cnpp.usda.gov/Publications/DietaryGuidelines/2010/PolicyDoc/ExecSumm.pdf

U.S. Department of Agriculture Economic Research Service. (2011). *Food security in the United States.* Retrieved from http://www.ers.usda.gov/topics/food-nutrition-assistance/food-security-in-the-us/key-statistics-graphics.aspx#

U.S. Department of Energy Office of Science, Office of Biological and Environmental Research, Human Genome Program. (2008a).

Human genome project information: Gene testing. Retrieved from www.ornl.gov/sci/techresources/Human_Genome/medicine/genetest.shtml

U.S. Department of Energy Office of Science, Office of Biological and Environmental Research, Human Genome Program. (2008b). *Human genome project information: Gene therapy.* Retrieved from www.ornl.gov/sci/techresources/Human_Genome/medicine/genetherapy.shtml

U.S. Department of Health and Human Services (USDHHS). (1992). *Health, United States, 1991, and Prevention Profile* (DHHS Publication No. PHS 92–1232). Washington, DC: U.S. Government Printing Office.

U.S. Department of Health and Human Services (USDHHS). (1996). *Health, United States, 1995* (DHHS Publication No. PHS 96-1232). Washington, DC: U.S. Government Printing Office.

U.S. Department of Health and Human Services (USDHHS). (1999a). *Blending perspectives and building common ground: A report to Congress on substance abuse and child protection.* Washington, DC: U.S. Government Printing Office.

U.S. Department of Health and Human Services (USDHHS). (1999b). *Mental health: A report of the surgeon general.* Rockville, MD: U.S. Department of Health and Human Services, Substance Abuse and Mental Health Services Administration, National Institutes of Health, National Institute of Mental Health.

U.S. Department of Health and Human Services (USDHHS). (2004). *Child maltreatment 2002.* Retrieved from www.acf.hhs.gov/programs/cb/publications/cm02/index.htm

U.S. Department of Health and Human Services (USDHHS). (2010). *How tobacco smoke causes disease: The biology and behavioral basis for smoking-attributable disease.* A Report of the Surgeon General. Atlanta, GA: U.S. Department of Health and Human Services, Centers for Disease Control and Prevention, National Center for Chronic Disease Prevention and Health Promotion, Office on Smoking and Health.

U.S. Department of Health and Human Services (USDHHS). (2012). Youth risk behavior surveillance: United States 2011. *MMWR Surveillance Summaries, 61*(4): Table 65. Retrieved from http://www.cdc.gov/mmwr/pdf/ss/ss6104.pdf

U.S. Department of Health and Human Services (USDHHS), Administration on Children, Youth, and Families. (2006). *Child maltreatment 2004.* Washington, DC: U.S. Government Printing Office.

U.S. Department of Health and Human Services (USDHHS), Administration on Children, Youth and Families. (2008). *Child maltreatment 2006.* Washington, DC: U.S. Government Printing Office.

U.S. Department of Health and Human Services, Administration on Children, Youth, and Families. (2012). *Child maltreatment 2011.* Retrieved from http://www.acf.hhs.gov/programs/cb/research-data-technology/statistics-research/child-maltreatment

U.S. Department of Health and Human Services (USDHHS), Health Resources and Services Administration, Maternal and Child Health Bureau. (2008). *Child health USA 2007.* Rockville, MD: U.S. Department of Health and Human Services, 2008.

U.S. Preventive Services Task Force. (2002). *Screening for breast cancer: Recommendations and rationale.* Rockville, MD: Agency for Healthcare Research and Quality. Retrieved from www.ahrq.gov/clinic/3rduspstf/breastcancer/brcanrr.htm

U.S. Preventive Services Task Force. (2006). Screening for speech and language delay in preschool children: Recommendation statement. *Pediatrics, 117*, 497–501.

U.S. Preventive Services Task Force. (2010). Screening for obesity in children and adolescents: Recommendation statement. *Pediatrics, 125*(2), 361–367. doi: 10.1542/peds.2009-2037

Utiger, R. D. (1998). A pill for impotence. *New England Journal of Medicine, 338*, 1458–1459.

Vaccarino, V., Parsons, L., Peterson, E. D., Rogers, W. J., Kiefe, C. I., & Canto, J. (2009). Sex differences in mortality after acute myocardial infarction: Changes from 1994 to 2006. *Archives of Internal Medicine, 169*(19), 1767–1774.

Vaillant, G. E. (1977). *Adaptation to life.* Boston: Little, Brown.

Vaillant, G. E. (1989). The evolution of defense mechanisms during the middle years. In J. M. Oldman & R. S. Liebert (Eds.), *The middle years.* New Haven, CT: Yale University Press.

Vaillant, G. E. (1993). *The wisdom of the ego.* Cambridge, MA: Harvard University Press.

Vaillant, G. E. (2000). Adaptive mental mechanisms: Their role in a positive psychology. *American Psychologist, 55*, 89–98.

Vainio, S., Heikkiia, M., Kispert, A., Chin, N., & McMahon, A. P. (1999). Female development in mammals is regulated by Wnt-4 signaling. *Nature, 397*, 405–409.

Valkenburg, P., & Peter, J. (2009). Social consequences of the Internet for adolescents: A decade of research. *Current Directions in Psychological Science, 18*(11), 1–5.

Valkenburg, P. M., & Peter, J. (2007). Preadolescents and adolescents' online communication and their closeness to friends. *Developmental Psychology, 43*, 267–277.

Valladares, S., & Moore, K. A. (2009). *The strengths of the poor families* (Research Brief #2009-26). Retrieved from http://www.childtrends.org/Files/Child_Trends-2009_5_14_poorfamstrengths.pdf

Van, P. (2001). Breaking the silence of African American women: Healing after pregnancy loss. *Health Care Women International, 22*, 229–243.

Van Cleave, J., Gortmaker, S. L., & Perrin, J. M. (2010). Dynamics of obesity and chronic health conditions among children and youth. *Journal of the American Medical Association, 303*(7), 623–630.

Van den Boom, D. C. (1989). Neonatal irritability and the development of attachment. In G. A. Kohnstamm, J. E. Bates, & M. K. Rothbart (Eds.), *Temperament in childhood* (pp. 299–318). Chichester, UK: Wiley.

Van den Boom, D. C. (1994). The influence of temperament and mothering on attachment and exploration: An experimental manipulation of sensitive responsiveness among lower-class mothers with irritable infants. *Child Development, 65*, 1457–1477.

van der Heide, A., Deliens, L., Faisst, K., Nilstun, T., Norup, M., Paci, E., . . . van der Maas, P. J., on behalf of the EURELD consortium. (2003). End-of-life decision making in six European countries: Descriptive study. *Lancet, 362*, 345–350.

van der Heide, A., Onwuteaka-Philipsen, B. D., Rurup, M. L., Buiting, H. M., van Delden, J. J. M., Hanssen-de Wolf, J. E., . . . van der Wal, G. (2007). End-of-life practices in the Netherlands under the Euthanasia Act. *New England Journal of Medicine, 356*, 1957–1965.

Van Dongen, H. P. A., Maislin, G., Mullington, J. M., & Dinges, D. F. (2003). The cumulative cost of additional wakefulness: Dose-response effects on neurobehavioral functions and sleep physiology from chronic sleep restriction and total sleep deprivation. *Sleep, 26*, 117–126.

van Dyk, D. (2005, January 24). Parlez-vous twixter? *Time*, p. 50.

van Gelder, B. M., Tijhuis, M. A. R., Kalmijn, S., Giampaoli, S., Nissinen, A., & Krombout, D. (2004). Physical activity in relation to cognitive decline in elderly men. *American Academy of Neurology, 63*, 2316–2321.

van Goozen, S., Fairchild, G., Snoek, H., & Harold, G. (2007). The evidence for a neurobiological model of childhood antisocial behavior. *Psychological Bulletin, 133*, 149–182.

Van Heuvelen, M. J., Kempen, G. I., Ormel, J., & Rispens, P. (1998). Physical fitness related to age and physical activity in older persons. *Medicine and Science in Sports and Exercise, 30*, 434–441.

van Hooren, S. A. H., Valentijn, S. A. M., Bosma, H., Ponds, R. W. H. M., van Boxtel, M. P. J., & Jolles, J. (2005). Relation between health status and cognitive functioning: A 6-year follow-up of the Maastricht Aging Study. *Journal of Gerontology: Psychological Sciences, 60B*, P57–P60.

van IJzendoorn, M. H., & Bakermans-Kranenburg, M. J. (2006). DRD47-repeat polymorphism moderates the association between maternal unresolved loss or trauma and infant disorganization. *Attachment & Human Development, 8*(4), 291–307.

van IJzendoorn, M. H., & Kroonenberg, P. M. (1988). Cross-cultural patterns of attachment: A meta-analysis of the Strange Situation. *Child Development, 59*, 147–156.

van IJzendoorn, M. H., & Sagi, A. (1999). Cross-cultural patterns of attachment: Universal and contextual dimensions. In J. Cassidy & P. R. Shaver (Eds.), *Handbook of attachment: Theory, research, and clinical applications* (pp. 713–734). New York: Guilford Press.

van IJzendoorn, M. H., Schuengel, C., & Bakermans-Kranenburg, M. J. (1999). Disorganized attachment in early childhood: Meta-analysis of precursors, concomitants, and sequelae. *Development and Psychopathology, 11*, 225–250.

van Lieshout, C. F. M., Haselager, G. J. T., Riksen-Walraven, J. M., & van Aken, M. A. G. (1995, April). Personality development in middle childhood. In D. Hart (Chair), *The contribution of childhood personality to adolescent competence: Insights from longitudinal studies from three societies*. Symposium conducted at the biennial meeting of the Society for Research in Child Development, Indianapolis, IN.

van Lommel, P., van Wees, R., Meyers, V., & Efferich, I. (2001). Near-death experiences in survivors of cardiac arrest: A prospective study in the Netherlands. *The Lancet, 358*, 2039–2045.

van Noord-Zaadstra, B. M., Looman, C. W., Alsbach, H., Habbema, J. D., te Velde, E. R., & Karbaat, J. (1991). Delayed childbearing: Effect of age on fecundity and outcome of pregnancy. *British Medical Journal, 302*, 1361–1365.

van Praag, H., Schinder, A. F., Christie, B. R., Toni, N., Palmer, T. D., & Gage, F. H. (2002). Functional neurogenesis in the adult hippocampus. *Nature, 415*, 1030–1034.

van Solinge, H., & Henkens, K. (2005). Couples' adjustment to retirement: A multi-actor panel study. *Journal of Gerontology: Social Sciences, 60B*, S11–S20.

Van Voorhis, B. J. (2007). In vitro fertilization. *New England Journal of Medicine, 356*, 379–386.

Vance, D. E., Webb, N. M., Marceaux, J. C., Viamonte, S. M., Foote, A. W., & Ball, K. K. (2008). Mental stimulation, neural plasticity, and aging: Directions for nursing research and practice. *Journal of Neuroscience Nursing, 40*(4), 241–249.

Vandell, D. L., & Bailey, M. D. (1992). Conflicts between siblings. In C. U. Shantz & W. W. Hartup (Eds.), *Conflict in child and adolescent development* (pp. 242–269). New York: Cambridge University Press.

Vandell, D. L., Belsky, J., Burchinal, M., Steinberg, L., Vandergrift, N., & NICHD Early Child Care Research Network. (2010). Do effects of early child care extend to age 15 years? Results from the NICHD study of early child care and youth development. *Child Development, 81*, 737–756. doi: 10.1111/j.1467-8624.2010.01431.x

Vandewater, E. A., Rideout, V. J., Wartella, E. A., Huang, X., Lee, J. H., & Shim, M.-S. (2007). Digital childhood: Electronic media and technology use among infants, toddlers, and preschoolers. *Pediatrics, 119*, e1006–e1015.

Vasilyeva, M., & Huttenlocher, J. (2004). Early development of scaling ability. *Developmental Psychology, 40*, 682–690.

Vasilyeva, M., Huttenlocher, J., & Waterfall, H. (2006). Effects of language intervention on syntactic skill levels in preschoolers. *Developmental Psychology, 42*, 164–174.

Vaupel, J. W., Carey, J. R., Christensen, K., Johnson, T. E., Yashin, A. I., Holm, N. V., . . . Curtsinger, J. W. (1998). Biodemographic trajectories of longevity. *Science, 280*, 855–860.

Veenstra, R., Lindenberg, S., Oldehinkel, A. J., De Winter, A. F., Verhulst, F. C., & Ormel, J. (2005). Bullying and victimization in elementary schools: A comparison of bullies, victims, bully/victims, and uninvolved preadolescents. *Developmental Psychology, 41*, 672–682.

Ventura, S. J., Mathews, T. J., & Hamilton, B. E. (2001). Births to teenagers in the United States, 1940–2000. *National Vital Statistics Reports, 49*(10). Hyattsville, MD: National Center for Health Statistics.

Ventura, A. K., & Mennella, J. A. (2011). Innate and learned preferences for sweet taste during childhood. *Current Opinion in Clinical Nutrition and Metabolic Care, 14*(4), 379–384.

Vercruyssen, M. (1997). Movement control and speed of behavior. In A. D. Fisk & W. A. Rogers (Eds.), *Handbook of human factors and the older adult* (pp. 55–86). San Diego: Academic Press.

Vereecken, C., & Maes, L. (2000). Eating habits, dental care and dieting. In C. Currie, K. Hurrelmann, W. Settertobulte, R. Smith, & J. Todd (Eds.), *Health and health behaviour among young people: A WHO cross-national study (HBSC) international report* (pp. 83–96). WHO Policy Series: Healthy Policy for Children and Adolescents, Series No. 1. Copenhagen, Denmark: World Health Organization Regional Office for Europe.

Verlinsky, Y., Rechitsky, S., Verlinsky, O., Masciangelo, C., Lederer, K., & Kuliev, A. (2002). Preimplantation diagnosis for early-onset Alzheimer disease caused by V717L mutation. *Journal of the American Medical Association, 287*, 1018–1021.

Verma, S., & Larson, R. (2003). Editors' notes. In S. Verma & R. Larson (Eds.), Chromosomal congenital anomalies and residence near hazardous waste landfill sites. *Lancet, 359*, 320–322.

Verschueren, K., Buyck, P., & Marcoen, A. (2001). Self-representations and socioemotional competence in young children: A 3-year longitudinal study. *Developmental Psychology, 37*, 126–134.

Verschueren, K., Marcoen, A., & Schoefs, V. (1996). The internal working model of the self, attachment, and competence in five-year-olds. *Child Development, 67*, 2493–2511.

Verschuren, W. M. M., Jacobs, D. R., Bloemberg, B. P. M., Kromhout, D., Menotti, A., Aravanis, C., . . . Toshima, H. (1995). Serum total cholesterol and long-term coronary heart disease mortality in different cultures. *Journal of the American Medical Association, 274*, 131–136.

Vespa, J., Lewis, J. M., & Kreider, R. M. (2013). *America's families and living arrangements: 2012. Current Population Reports,* P20-570. Washington, DC: U.S. Census Bureau.

Vgontzas, A. N., & Kales, A. (1999). Sleep and its disorders. *Annual Review of Medicine, 50*, 387–400.

Vieno, A., Nation, M., Pastore, M., & Santinello, M. (2009). *Developmental Psychology, 45*(6), 1509–1519.

Viner, R. M., & Cole, T. J. (2005). Television viewing in early childhood predicts adult body mass index. *Journal of Pediatrics, 147*, 429–435

Vita, A. J., Terry, R. B., Hubert, H. B., & Fries, J. F. (1998). Aging, health risk, and cumulative disability. *New England Journal of Medicine, 338*, 1035–1041.

Vitalian, P. P., Zhang, J., & Scanlan, J. M. (2003). Is caregiving hazardous to one's physical health? A meta-analysis. *Psychological Bulletin, 129*, 946–972.

Vittone, M. (2010, June 16). *Drowning doesn't look like drowning*. Retrieved from http://gcaptain.com/maritime/blog/drowning/?10981

Vlad, S. C., Miller, D. R., Kowall, N. W., & Felson, D. T. (2008). Protective effects of NSAIDs on the development of Alzheimer disease. *Neurology, 70*, 1672–1677.

Vohr, B. R., Wright, L. L., Poole, K., & McDonald, S. A., for the NICHD Neonatal Research Network Follow-up Study. (2005). Neurodevelopmental outcomes of extremely low birth weight infants <30 weeks' gestation between 1993 and 1998. *Pediatrics, 116*, 635–643.

Volkow, N. D., Wang, G. J., Newcorn, J., Telang, F., Solanto, M. V., Fowler, J. S., . . . & Swanson, J. M. (2007). Depressed dopamine activity in caudate and preliminary evidence of limbic involvement in adults with attention-deficit/hyperactivity disorder. *Archives of general psychiatry, 64*(8), 932–940.

von Hippel, W. (2007). Aging, executive functioning, and social control. *Current Directions in Psychological Science, 16*(5), 240–244.

von Hofsten, C. (2004). An action perspective on motor development. *Cognitive Sciences, 8*(1), 266–272.

Von Korff, L., Grotevant, H. D., & McRoy, R. G. (2006). Openness arrangements and psychological adjustment in adolescent adoptees. *Journal of Family Psychology, 20*, 531–534.

Vondra, J. I., & Barnett, D. (1999). A typical attachment in infancy and early childhood among children at developmental risk. *Monographs of the Society for Research in Child Development, 64*(3, Serial No. 258).

Votruba-Drzal, E., Li-Grining, C. R., & Maldonado-Carreno, C. (2008). A developmental perspective on full- versus part-day kindergarten and children's academic trajectories through fifth grade. *Child Development, 79*, 957–978.

Vrijenhoek, T., Buizer-Voskamp, J. E., van der Stelt, I., Strengman, E., Sabatti, C., van Kessel, A. G., . . . Veltman, J. A. (2008). Recurrent CNVs disrupt three candidate genes in schizophrenia patients. *American Journal of Human Genetics, 83*, 504–510.

Voydanoff, P. (2004). The effects of work demands and resources on work-to-family conflict and facilitation. *Journal of Marriage and Family, 66*, 398–412.

Vrijheld, M., Dolk, H., Armstrong, B., Abramsky, L., Bianchi, F., Fazarinc, I., . . . Tenconi, R. (2002). Chromosomal congenital anomalies and residence near hazardous waste landfill sites. *Lancet, 359*(9303), 320–322.

Vu, T., Liu, T., Garside, D. B., & Daviglus, M. L. (2009). Unhealthy lifestyle choices in older age and subsequent health-related quality of life: The Chicago Heart Association Detection Project. *Circulation, 120*, S482–S483.

Vuchinich, S., Angelelli, J., & Gatherum, A. (1996). Context and development in family problem solving with preadolescent children. *Child Development, 67*, 1276–1288.

Vuoksimaa, E., Koskenvuo, M., Rose, R. J., & Kaprio, J. (2009). Origins of handedness: A nationwide study of 30,161 adults. *Neuropsychologia, 47*(5), 1294–1301.

Vygotsky, L. S. (1962). *Thought and language.* Cambridge, MA: MIT Press. (Original work published 1934)

Vuori, L., Christiansen, N., Clement, J., Mora, J., Wagner, M., & Herrera, M. (1979). Nutritional supplementation and the outcome of pregnancy: 2. Visual habitation at 15 days. *Journal of Clinical Nutrition, 32,* 463–469.

Vygotsky, L. S. (1978). *Mind in society: The development of higher psychological processes.* Cambridge, MA: Harvard University Press.

Wadsworth, M. E., Raviv, T., Reinhard, C., Wolff, B., Santiago, C. D., & Einhorn, L. (2008). An indirect effects model of the association between poverty and child functioning: The role of children's poverty related stress. *Journal of Loss and Trauma: International Perspectives on Stress and Coping, 13*(2–3), 156–185.

Wahlbeck, K., Forsen, T., Osmond, C., Barker, D. J. P., & Erikkson, J. G. (2001). Association of schizophrenia with low maternal body mass index, small size at birth, and thinness during childhood. *Archives of General Psychiatry, 58,* 48–55.

Wainright, J. L., Russell, S. T., & Patterson, C. J. (2004). Psychosocial adjustment, school outcomes, and romantic relationships of adolescents with same-sex parents. *Child Development, 75*, 1886–1898.

Waite, L. J., & Joyner, K. (2000). Emotional and physical satisfaction with sex in married, cohabiting, and dating sexual unions: Do men and women differ? In E. O. Laumann & R. T. Michael (Eds.), *Sex, love, and health in America: Private choices and public policies* (pp. 239–269). Chicago: University of Chicago Press.

Waite, L. J., Luo, Y., & Lewin, A. C. (2009). Marital happiness and marital stability: Consequences for psychological well-being. *Social Science Research, 38*(1), 201–212.

Waknine, Y. (2006). Highlights from MMWR: Prevalence of U.S. birth defects and more. *Medscape*. Retrieved from www.medscape.com/viewarticle/521056

Wald, N. J. (2004). Folic acid and the prevention of neural-tube defects. *New England Journal of Medicine, 350,* 101–103.

Waldman, I. D. (1996). Aggressive boys' hostile perceptual and response biases: The role of attention and impulsivity. *Child Development, 67*, 1015–1033.

Walk, R. D., & Gibson, E. J. (1961). A comparative and analytical study of visual depth perception. *Psychology Monographs, 75*(15).

Walker, L. (1995). Sexism in Kohlberg's moral psychology? In W. M. Kurtines & J. L. Gewirtz (Eds.), *Moral development: An introduction* (pp. 83–107). Boston: Allyn & Bacon.

Walker, L. E. (1999). Psychology and domestic violence around the world. *American Psychologist, 54*, 21–29.

Walker, M. P., Brakefield, T., Morgan, A., Hobson, J. A., & Stickgold, R. (2002). Practice with sleep makes perfect: Sleep-dependent motor skill learning. *Neuron, 35*, 205–211.

Walker, W. R., Skowronski, J. J., & Thompson, C. P. (2003). Life is pleasant—And memory helps to keep it that way! *Review of General Psychology, 7*, 203–210.

Wallace, D. C. (1992). Mitochondrial genetics: A paradigm for aging and degenerative diseases? *Science, 256*, 628–632.

Wallace, J. M., Bachman, J. G., O'Malley, P. M., Johnson, L. D., Schulenberg, J. E., & Cooper, S. M. (2005). Tobacco, alcohol and illicit drug use: Racial and ethnic differences among U.S. high school seniors 1976-2000. *Public Health Reports, 117*, S67–S75.

Wallace, P. M., & Gotlib, I. H. (1990). Marital adjustment during the transition to parenthood: Stability and predictors of change. *Journal of Marriage and the Family, 52*, 21–29.

Waller, M. W., Hallfors, D. D., Halpern, C. T., Iritani, B., Ford, C. A., & Guo, G. (2006). Gender differences in associations between depressive symptoms and patterns of substance use and risky sexual behavior among a nationally representative sample of U.S. adolescents. *Archives of Women's Mental Health, 9*, 139–150.

Waller, N. G., Kojetin, B. A., Bouchard, T. J. Jr., Lykken, D. T., & Tellegen, A. (1990). Genetic and environmental influences on religious interests, attitudes, and values: A study of twins reared apart and together. *Psychological Science, 1*(2), 138–142.

Wallerstein, J. S., Lewis, J. M., & Blakeslee, S. (2000). *The unexpected legacy of divorce: A 25-year landmark study.* New York: Hyperion.

Wallhagen, M. I., Strawbridge, W. J., Cohen, R. D., & Kaplan, G. A. (1997). An increasing prevalence of hearing impairment and associated risk factors over three decades of the Alameda County Study. *American Journal of Public Health, 87*, 440–442.

Wallhagen, M. I., Strawbridge, W. J., Shema, S. J., & Kaplan, G. A. (2004). Impact of self-assessed hearing loss on a spouse: A longitudinal analysis of couples. *Journal of Gerontology: Social Sciences, 59*, S190–S196.

Walma van der Molen, J. (2004). Violence and suffering in television news: Toward a broader conception of harmful television content for children. *Pediatrics, 113*, 1771–1775.

Walsh, T., McClellan, J. M., McCarthy, S. E., Addington, A. M., Pierce, S. B., Cooper, G. M., . . . Sebat, J. (2008). Rare structural variants disrupt multiple genes in neurodevelopmental pathways in schizophrenia. *Science, 320,* 539–543.

Walston, J. T., & West, J. (2004). *Full-day and half-day kindergarten in the United States: Findings from the Early Childhood Longitudinal Study, Kindergarten Class of 1998-99* (NCES 2004-078). Washington, DC: National Center for Education Statistics.

Wang, D. W., Desai, R. R., Crotti, L., Arnestad, M., Insolia, R., Pedrazzini, M., . . . George, A. L. (2007). Cardiac sodium channel dysfunction in sudden infant death syndrome. *Circulation, 115*, 368–376.

Wang, H. X., Karp, A., Herlitz, A., Crowe, M., Kåreholt, I., Winblad, B., & Fratiglioni, L. (2009). Personality and lifestyle in relation to dementia incidence. *Neurology, 72*(3), 253–259.

Wang, L., Wang, X., Wang, W., Chen, C., Ronnennberg, A. G., Guang, W., . . . Xu, X. (2004). Stress and dysmenorrhea: A population-based prospective study. *Occupational and Environmental Medicine, 61*, 1021–1026.

Wang, M., & Shultz, K. A. (2009). Employee retirement: A review and recommendations for future investigation. *Journal of Management, 36,* 172–206.

Wang, W., & Morin, R. (2009, November 24). *Recession brings many young people back to the nest: Home for the holidays . . . and every other day.* Retrieved from http://pewresearch.org/pubs/1423/home-for-the-holidays-boomeranged-parents

Wannamethee, S. G., Shaper, A. G., Whincup, P. H., & Walker, M. (1995). Smoking cessation and the risk of stroke in middle-aged men. *Journal of the American Medical Association, 274,* 155–160.

Wansink, B. (2010). *Mindless eating.* New York: Bantam.

Wardle, J., Robb, K. A., Johnson, F., Griffith, J., Brunner, E., Power, C., & TovÈe, M. (2004). Socioeconomic variation in attitudes to eating and weight in female adolescents. *Health Psychology, 23*, 275–282.

Warneken, F., & Tomasello, M. (2006). Altruistic helping in human infants and young chimpanzees. *Science, 311*, 1301–1303.

Warneken, F., & Tomasello, M. (2008). Extrinsic rewards undermine altruistic tendencies in 20-month-olds. *Developmental Psychology, 44,* 1785–1788.

Warner, J. (2008, January 3). Domestic disturbances. *The New York Times.* Retrieved from http://warner.blogs.nytimes.com/2008/01/03/outsourced-wombs/

Warren, J. A., & Johnson, P. J. (1995). The impact of workplace support on work-family role strain. *Family Relations, 44*, 163–169.

Wasik, B. H., Ramey, C. T., Bryant, D. M., & Sparling, J. J. (1990). A longitudinal study of two early intervention strategies: Project CARE. *Child Development, 61,* 1682–1696.

Wass, S., Porayska-Pomsta, K., & Johnson, M. (2011). Training attentional control in infancy. *Current Biology.* doi:10.1016/j.cub.2011.08.00

Wasserman, D. (2006). *Depression: The facts.* Oxford, UK: Oxford University Press.

Wassertheil-Smoller, S., Hendrix, S. L., Limacher, M., Heiss, G., Kooperberg, C., Baird, A., . . . Mysiw, W. J., for the WHI Investigators. (2003). Effects of estrogen plus progestin on stroke in post-menopausal women: The Women's Health Initiative: A randomized trial. *Journal of the American Medical Association, 289*, 2673–2684.

Watamura, S. E., Donzella, B., Alwin, J., & Gunnar, M. R. (2003). Morning-to-afternoon increases in cortisol concentrations for infants and toddlers at child care: Age differences and behavioral correlates. *Child Development, 74*, 1006–1020.

Watanabe, C. (2007, October 15). Land of the rising sons: Number of elderly Japanese climbing Everest mounts. *Chicago Sun-Times*, p. 28.

Waters, E., & Deane, K. E. (1985). Defining and assessing individual differences in attachment relationships: Q-methodology and the organization of behavior in infancy and early childhood. *Monographs of the Society for Research in Child Development, 50*, 41–65.

Waters, E., Wippman, J., & Sroufe, L. A. (1979). Attachment, positive affect, and competence in the peer group: Two studies in construct validation. *Child Development, 50*, 821–829.

Watson, A. C., Nixon, C. L., Wilson, A., & Capage, L. (1999). Social interaction skills and theory of mind in young children. *Developmental Psychology, 35*(2), 386–391.

Watson, J. B., & Rayner, R. (1920). Conditioned emotional reactions. *Journal of Experimental Psychology, 3*, 1–14.

Wayne, J., Musisca, N., & Fleeson, W. (2004). Considering the role of personality in the work–family experience: Relationships of the big five to work–family conflict and facilitation. *Journal of Vocational Behavior, 64*(1), 108–130.

Weatherbee, S. R., & Allaire, J. C. (2008). Everyday cognition and mortality: Performance differences and predictive utility of the everyday cognition battery. *Psychology and Aging, 23*(1), 216–221.

Weese-Mayer, D. E., Berry-Kravis, E. M., Zhou, L., Maher, B. S., Curran, M. E., Silvestri, J. M., & Marazita, M. L. (2004). Sudden infant death syndrome: Case-control frequency differences at genes pertinent to autonomic nervous system embryological development. *Pediatric Research, 56*, 391–395.

Weg, R. B. (1989). Sensuality/sexuality of the middle years. In S. Hunter & M. Sundel (Eds.), *Midlife myths.* Newbury Park, CA: Sage.

Wegienka, G., Johnson, C. C., Havstad, S., Ownby, D. R., Nicholas, C., & Zoratti, E. M. (2011). Lifetime dog and cat exposure and dog- and cat-specific sensitization at age 18 years. *Clinical & Experimental Allergy, 41*(7), 979–986.

Weinberger, D. R. (2001, March 10). A brain too young for good judgment. *The New York Times.* Retrieved from www.nytimes.com/2001/03/10/opinion/10WEIN.html?ex_985250309&ei_1&en_995bc03f7a8c7207

Weinberger, J. (1999, May 18). Enlightening conversation [Letter to the editor]. *The New York Times*, p. F3.

Weinraub, M. (1978). The effects of height on infants' social responses to unfamiliar persons. *Child Development, 49*(3), 598–603.

Weinreb, L., Wehler, C., Perloff, J., Scott, R., Hosmer, D., Sagor, L., & Gundersen, C. (2002). Hunger: Its impact on children's health and mental health. *Pediatrics, 110*, 816.

Weinstein, A. R., Sesso, H. D., Lee, I. M., Cook, N. R., Manson, J. E., Buring, J. E., & Gaziano, J. M. (2004). Relationship of physical activity vs body mass index with type 2 diabetes in women. *Journal of the American Medical Association, 292*, 1188–1194.

Weinstock, H., Berman, S., & Cates, W., Jr. (2004). Sexually transmitted diseases among American youth: Incidence and prevalence estimates, 2000. *Perspectives on Sexual and Reproductive Health, 36*, 6–10.

Weinstock, H., et al. (2004). Sexually transmitted diseases among American youth: Incidence and prevalence estimates, 2000. *Perspectives on Sexual and Reproductive Health, 36*(1), 6–10.

Weisner, T. S. (1993). Ethnographic and ecocultural perspectives on sibling relationships. In Z. Stoneman & P. W. Berman (Eds.), *The effects of mental retardation, visibility, and illness on sibling relationships* (pp. 51–83). Baltimore, MD: Brooks.

Weiss, A., Bates, T. C., & Luciano, M. (2008). Happiness is a personal(ity) thing. The genetics of personality and well-being in a representative sample. *Psychological Science, 19*, 205–210.

Weiss, B., Amler, S., & Amler, R. W. (2004). Pesticides. *Pediatrics, 113*, 1030–1036.

Weiss, B., Dodge, K. A., Bates, J. E., & Pettit, G. S. (1992). Some consequences of early harsh discipline: Child aggression and a maladaptive social information processing style. *Child Development, 63*, 1321–1335.

Weiss, R. B., Baker, T. B., Cannon, D. S., vonNeiderhausern, A., Dunn, D. M., Matsunami, N., . . . Leppert, M. F. (2008). A candidate gene approach identifies the CHRNA5-A3 B4 region as a risk factor for age dependent nicotine addiction. *Public Library of Science, 4*(7), e1000125.

Weissman, M. M., Warner, V., Wickramaratne, P. J., & Kandel, D. B. (1999). Maternal smoking during pregnancy and psychopathology in offspring followed to adulthood. *Journal of the American Academy of Child and Adolescent Psychiatry, 38*, 892–899.

Weisz, J. R., McCarty, C. A., & Valeri, S. M. (2006). Effects of psychotherapy for depression in children and adolescents: A meta-analysis. *Psychological Bulletin, 132*, 132–149.

Weisz, J. R., Weiss, B., Han, S. S., Granger, D. A., & Morton, T. (1995). Effects of psychotherapy with children and adolescents revisited: A meta-analysis of treatment outcome studies. *Psychological Bulletin, 117*(3), 450–468.

Welch-Ross, M. K., & Schmidt, C. R. (1996). Gender-schema development and children's story memory: Evidence for a developmental model. *Child Development, 67*, 820–835.

Wellman, H. M., Cross, D., & Watson, J. (2001). Meta-analysis of theory-of-mind development: The truth about false belief. *Child Development, 72*, 655–684.

Wellman, H. M., & Liu, D. (2004). Scaling theory-of-mind tasks. *Child Development, 75*, 523–541.

Wellman, H. M., Lopez-Duran, S., LaBounty, J., & Hamilton, B. (2008). Infant attention to intentional action predicts preschool theory of mind. *Developmental Psychology, 44*, 618–623.

Wellman, H. M., & Woolley, J. D. (1990). From simple desires to ordinary beliefs: The early development of everyday psychology. *Cognition, 35*, 245–275.

Wells, J., & Lewis, L. (2006). *Internet access in the U.S. public schools and classrooms: 1990–2005* (NCES 2007-020). Washington, DC: National Center for Education Statistics.

Welt, C. K. (2008). Primary ovarian insufficiency: A more accurate term for premature ovarian failure. *Clinical Endocrinology, 68*(4), 499–509.

Welton, A. J., Vickers, M. R., Kim, J., Ford, D., Lawton, B. A., MacLennan, A. H., . . . Meade, T. W. for the WISDOM team. (2008). Health related quality of life after combined hormone replacement therapy: Randomised controlled trial. *British Medical Journal, 337*, a1190.

Wen, X., Wen, S. W., Fleming, N., Demissie, K., Rhoads, G. G., & Walker, M. (2007). Teenage pregnancy and adverse birth outcomes: A large population based retrospective cohort study. *International Journal of Epidemiology, 36*(2), 368–373.

Weng, X., Odouli, R., & Li, D.-K. (2008). Maternal caffeine consumption during pregnancy and the risk of miscarriage: A prospective cohort study. *American Journal of Obstetrics and Gynecology, 198*(3), 279.e1–279.e8.

Wentworth, N., Benson, J. B., & Haith, M. M. (2000). The development of infants' reaches for stationary and moving targets. *Child Development, 71*, 576–601.

Wentzel, K. R. (2002). Are effective teachers like good parents? Teaching styles and student adjustment in early adolescence. *Child Development, 73*, 287–301.

Weon, M. W., & Je, J. H. (2009). Theoretical estimation of maximum human lifespan. *Biogerontology, 10*(1), 65–71. doi: 10.1007/s10522-008-9156-4

Werker, J. F., Pegg, J. E., & McLeod, P. J. (1994). A cross-language investigation of infant preference for infant-directed communication. *Infant Behavior and Development, 17*, 323–333.

Werner, E., Bierman, L., French, F. E., Simonian, K., Connor, A., Smith, R., & Campbell, M. (1968). Reproductive and environmental casualties: A report on the 10-year follow-up of the children of the Kauai pregnancy study. *Pediatrics, 42*, 112–127.

Werner, E., & Smith, R. S. (2001). *Journeys from childhood to midlife.* Ithaca, NY: Cornell University Press.

Werner, E. E. (1985). Stress and protective factors in children's lives. In A. R. Nichol (Ed.),

Longitudinal studies in child psychology and psychiatry. New York: Wiley.

Werner, E. E. (1987, July 15). *Vulnerability and resiliency: A longitudinal study of Asian Americans from birth to age 30.* Invited address at the ninth biennial meeting of the International Society for the Study of Behavioral Development, Tokyo, Japan.

Werner, E. E. (1989). Children of the garden island. *Scientific American, 260*(4), 106–111.

Werner, E. E. (1993). Risk and resilience in individuals with learning disabilities: Lessons learned from the Kauai longitudinal study. *Learning Disabilities Research and Practice, 8*, 28–34.

Werner, E. E. (1995). Resilience in development. *Current Directions in Psychological Science, 4*(3), 81–85.

Westby, E. L., & Dawson, V. L. (1995). Creativity: Asset or burden in the classroom. *Creativity Research Journal, 8*(1), 1–10.

Westen, D. (1998). The scientific legacy of Sigmund Freud: Toward a psychodynamically informed psychological science. *Psychological Bulletin, 124*, 333–371.

Wethington, E., Kessler, R. C., & Pixley, J. E. (2004). Turning points in adulthood. In O. G. Brim, C. D. Ryff, & R. C. Kessler (Eds.), *How healthy are we? A national study of well-being at midlife* (pp. 586–613). Chicago: University of Chicago Press.

Weuve, J., Kang, J. H., Manson, J. E., Breteler, M. M. B., Ware, J. H., & Grodstein, F. (2004). Physical activity, including walking, and cognitive function in older women. *Journal of the American Medical Association, 292*, 1454–1461.

Wexler, A. (2008, August 12). Groundbreaking genetic non-discrimination bill signed into law. *HemOnc Today: Clinical News in Oncology and Hematology.* Retrieved from www/hemonctoday.com/article.aspx?rid=30268

Wexler, I. D., Branski, D., & Kerem, E. (2006). War and children. *Journal of the American Medical Association, 296*, 579–581.

Whalley, L. J., & Deary, I. J. (2001). Longitudinal cohort study of childhood IQ and survival up to age 76. *British Medical Journal, 322*, 819.

Whalley, L. J., Starr, J. M., Athawes, R., Hunter, D., Pattie, A., & Deary, I. J. (2000). Childhood mental ability and dementia. *Neurology, 55*, 1455–1459.

Whisman, M. A., Uebelacker, L. A., Tolejko, N., Chatav, Y., & McKelvie, M. (2006). Marital discord and well-being in older adults: Is the association confounded by personality? *Psychology and Aging, 21*, 626–631.

Whitaker, R. C., Wright, J. A., Pepe, M. S., Seidel, K. D., & Dietz, W. H. (1997). Predicting obesity in young adulthood from childhood and parental obesity. *New England Journal of Medicine, 337*, 869–873.

Whitbourne, S. K. (1987). Personality development in adulthood and old age: Relationships among identity style, health, and well-being. In K. W. Schaie (Ed.), *Annual review of gerontology and geriatrics* (pp. 189–216). New York: Springer.

Whitbourne, S. K. (1996). *The aging individual: Physical and psychological perspectives.* New York: Springer.

Whitbourne, S. K. (1999). Physical changes. In J. C. Cavanaugh & S. K. Whitbourne (Eds.), *Gerontology: An interdisciplinary perspective* (pp. 91–122). New York: Oxford University Press.

Whitbourne, S. K. (2001). The physical aging process in midlife: Interactions with psychological and sociocultural factors. In M. E. Lachman (Ed.), *Handbook of midlife development* (pp. 109–155). New York: Wiley.

Whitbourne, S. K., & Connolly, L. A. (1999). The developing self in midlife. In S. L. Willis & J. D. Reid (Eds.), *Life in the middle: Psychological and social development in middle age* (pp. 25–45). San Diego: Academic Press.

Whitbourne, S. K., Sneed, J. R., & Sayer, S. (2009). Psychosocial development from college through midlife: A 34-year sequential study. *Developmental Psychology, 45*(5), 1328–1340.

White, A. (2001). *Alcohol and adolescent brain development.* Retrieved from www.duke.edu/~amwhite/alc_adik_pf.html

White, B. L. (1971, October). *Fundamental early environmental influences on the development of competence.* Paper presented at the third Western Symposium on Learning: Cognitive Learning, Western Washington State College, Bellingham, WA.

White, B. L., Kaban, B., & Attanucci, J. (1979). *The origins of human competence.* Lexington, MA: Heath.

White, H. R., McMorris, B. J., Catalano, R. F., Fleming, C. B., Haggerty, K .P., & Abbott, R. D. (2006). Increases in alcohol and marijuana use during the transition out of high school into emerging adulthood: The effects of leaving home, going to college, and high school protective factors. *Journal of Studies on Alcohol, 67*(6), 810–822.

Whitehead, B. D., & Poponoe, D. (2003). *The social health of marriage in America 2003. Essay: Marriage and children: Coming together again?* Piscataway, NJ: The National Marriage Project, Rutgers University.

Whitehurst, G. J., Falco, F. L., Lonigan, C. J., Fischel, J. E., DeBaryshe, B. D., Valdez-Menchaca, M. D., & Caulfield, M. (1988). Accelerating language development through picture book reading. *Developmental Psychology, 24*, 552–559.

Whitehurst, G. J., & Lonigan, C. J. (1998). Child development and emergent literacy. *Child Development, 69*, 848–872.

Whitehurst, G. J., & Lonigan, C. J. (2001). Emergent literacy: Development from prereaders to readers. In S. B. Neuman & D. K. Dickinson (Eds.), *Handbook of early literacy research* (pp. 11–29). New York: Guilford Press.

Whitwell, J. L., Przybelski, S. A., Weigand, S. D., Knopman, D. S., Boeve, B. F., Petersen, R. C., & Jack, C. R., Jr. (2007). 3D maps from multiple MRI illustrate changing atrophy patterns as subjects progress from mild cognitive impairment to Alzheimer's disease. *Brain, 130*(7), 1777–1786.

Whyatt, R. M., Rauh, V., Barr, D. B., Camann, D. E., Andrews, H. F., Garfinkel, R., . . . Perera, F. P. (2004). Prenatal insecticide exposures and birth weight and length among an urban minority cohort. *Environmental Health Perspectives, 112*(110), 1125–1132.

Widaman, K. F. (2009). Phenylketonuria in children and mothers: Genes, environment, behavior. *Current Directions in Psychological Science, 18*(1), 48–52.

Wijngaards-de Meij, L., Stroebe, M., Schut, H., Stroebe, W., van den Bout, J., van der Heijden, P., & Dijkstra, I. (2005). Couples at risk following the death of their child: Predictors of grief versus depression. *Journal of Consulting and Clinical Psychology, 73*, 617–623.

Wilcox, A. J., Dunson, D., & Baird, D. D. (2000). The timing of the "fertile window" in the menstrual cycle: Day specific estimates from a prospective study. *British Medical Journal, 321*, 1259–1262.

Wilcox, W. B., & Wolfinger, N. H. (2007). Then comes marriage? Religion, race, and marriage in urban America. *Social Science Research, 36*(2), 569–589.

Wilcox, W. B., & Nock, S. L. (2006). What's love got to do with it? Equality, equity, commitment and women's marital quality. *Social Forces, 84*, 1321–1345.

Wildsmith, E., Schelar, E., Peterson, K., & Manlove, J. (2010). *Sexually transmitted diseases among young adults: Prevalence, perceived risk and risk-taking behaviors* (2010-21). Retrieved from http://www.childtrends.org/Files/Child_Trends-2010_05_01_RB_STD.pdf

Willard, N. E. (2006). *Cyberbullying and cyberthreats.* Eugene, OR: Center for Safe and Responsible Internet Use.

Willcox, B. J., Donlon, T. A., He, Q., Chen, R., Grove, J. S., Yano, K., . . . Curb, J. D. (2008). FOXO3A genotype is strongly associated with human longevity. *Proceedings of the National Academy of Sciences of the United States of America, 105*(37), 13987–13992.

Willett, W. C., Colditz, G., & Stampfer, M. (2000). Postmenopausal estrogens—Opposed, unopposed, or none of the above. *Journal of the American Medical Association, 283*, 534–535.

Williams, J., Wake, M., Hesketh, K., Maher, E., & Waters, E. (2005). Health-related quality of life of overweight and obese children. *Journal of the American Medical Association, 293*, 70–76.

Williams, K. (2004). The transition to widowhood and the social regulation of health: Consequences for health and health risk behavior. *Journal of Gerontology: Social Sciences, 59B*, S343–S349.

Williams, K., & Dunne-Bryant, A. (2006). Divorce and adult psychological well-being: Clarifying the role of gender and child age. *Journal of Marriage and Family, 68*, 1178–1196.

Willinger, M., Hoffman, H. T., & Hartford, R. B. (1994). Infant sleep position and risk for sudden infant death syndrome: Report of meeting held January 13 and 14, 1994. *Pediatrics, 93*, 814–819.

Willingham, D. T. (2004). Reframing the mind. *Education Next, 4*, 19–24.

Willis, S. L., & Reid, J. D. (1999). *Life in the middle.* San Diego: Academic Press.

Willis, S. L., & Schaie, K. W. (1999). Intellectual functioning in midlife. In S. L. Willis & J. D. Reid (Eds.), *Life in the middle: Psychological and social development in middle age* (pp. 233–247). San Diego: Academic Press.

Willis, S. L., & Schaie, K. W. (2005). Cognitive trajectories in midlife and cognitive functioning in old age. In S. L. Willis & M. Martin (Eds.), *Middle adulthood: A lifespan perspective* (pp. 243–276). Thousand Oaks, CA: Sage.

Willis, S. L., & Schaie, K. W. (2006). Cognitive functioning in the baby boomers: Longitudinal and cohort effects. In S. K. Whitbourne & S. L. Willis (Eds.), *The baby boomers grow up: Contemporary perspectives on midlife* (pp. 205–234). Mahwah, NJ: Erlbaum.

Willson, A. E., Shuey, K. M., & Elder, G. H. (2003). Ambivalence in the relationship of adult children to aging parents and in-laws. *Journal of Marriage and Family, 65*, 1055–1072.

Wilmoth, J., & Koso, G. (2002). Does marital history count? Marital status and wealth outcomes among preretirement adults. *Journal of Marriage and Family, 64*, 254–268.

Wilmoth, J. R. (2000). Demography of longevity: Past, present, and future trends. *Experimental Gerontology, 35*, 1111–1129.

Wilmoth, J. R., Deegan, L. J., Lundstrom, H., & Horiuchi, S. (2000). Increase of maximum life-span in Sweden, 1861–1999. *Science, 289*, 2366–2368.

Wilson, B. J. (2008). Media and children's aggression, fear, and altruism. *Future of Children, 18*, 87–118.

Wilson, E. O. (1975). *Sociobiology: The new synthesis.* Cambridge, MA: Belknap Press of Harvard University Press.

Wilson, G. T., Grilo, C. M., & Vitousek, K. M. (2007). Psychological treatment of eating disorders. *American Psychologist, 62*, 199–216.

Wilson, R. S., & Bennett, D. A. (2003). Cognitive activity and risk of Alzheimer's disease. *Current Directions in Psychological Science, 12*, 87–91.

Wilson, R. S., Scherr, P. A., Schneider, J. A., Tang, Y., & Bennett, D. A. (2007). Relation of cognitive ability to risk of developing Alzheimer disease. *Neurology, 69*, 1911–1920.

Wilson, R. S., Schneider, J. A., Arnold, S. E., Bienias, J. L., & Bennett, D. A. (2007). Conscientiousness and the incidence of Alzheimer disease and mild cognitive impairment. *Archives of General Psychiatry, 64*, 1204–1212.

Wilson-Costello, D., Friedman, H., Minich, N., Siner, B., Taylor, G., Schluchter, M., & Hack, M. (2007). Improved neurodevelopmental outcomes for extremely low birth weight infants in 2000–2002. *Pediatrics, 119*, 37–45.

Wingfield, A., & Stine, E. A. L. (1989). Modeling memory processes: Research and theory on memory and aging. In G. C. Gilmore, P. J. Whitehouse, & M. L. Wykle (Eds.), *Memory, aging, and dementia: Theory, assessment, and treatment* (pp. 4–40). New York: Springer.

Winner, E. (1997). Exceptionally high intelligence and schooling. *American Psychologist, 52*(10), 1070–1081.

Winner, E. (2000). The origins and ends of giftedness. *American Psychologist, 55*, 159–169.

Wisner, K. L., Chambers, C., & Sit, D. K. Y. (2006). Postpartum depression: A major public health problem. *Journal of the American Medical Association, 296*, 2616–2618.

Wisner, K. L., Parry, B. L., & Piontek, C. M. (2002). Postpartum depression. *New England Journal of Medicine, 347*(3), 194–199.

Wittstein, I. S., Thiemann, D. R., Lima, J. A. C., Baughman, K. L., Schulman, S. P., Gerstenblith, G., . . . Champion, H. C. (2005). Neurohumoral features of myocardial stunning due to sudden emotional stress. *New England Journal of Medicine, 352*, 539–548.

Woerlee, G. M. (2005). *Mortal minds: The biology of the near-death experience.* New York: Prometheus Books.

Wolchik, S. A., Sandler, I. N., Millsap, R. E., Plummer, B. A., Greene, S. M., Anderson, E. R., . . . Haine, R. A. (2002). Six-year follow-up of a randomized, controlled trial of preventive interventions for children of divorce. *Journal of the American Medical Association, 288*, 1874–1881.

Wolf, M. (1968). *The house of Lim.* Englewood Cliffs, NJ: Prentice Hall.

Wolfe, L. (2004). Should parents speak with a dying child about impending death? *New England Journal of Medicine, 351*, 1251–1253.

Wolff, M. S., & IJzendoorn, M. H. (1997). Sensitivity and attachment: A meta-analysis on parental antecedents of infant attachment. *Child Development, 68*(4), 571–591.

Wolff, J. L., & Agree, E. M. (2004). Depression among recipients of informal care: The effects of reciprocity, respect, and adequacy of support. *Journal of Gerontology: Psychological Sciences, 59B*, S173–S180.

Wolff, P. H. (1966). The causes, controls, and organizations of behavior in the newborn. *Psychological Issues, 5*(1, Whole No. 17), 1–105.

Wolff, P. H. (1969). The natural history of crying and other vocalizations in early infancy. In B. M. Foss (Ed.), *Determinants of infant behavior* (Vol. 4). London: Methuen.

Wolfson, A. R., Carskadon, M. A., Mindell, J. A., & Drake, C. (2006). *The National Sleep Foundation: Sleep in America poll.* Retrieved from http://www.sleepfoundation.org/sites/default/files/2006_summary_of_findings.pdf

Wolf-Maier, K., Cooper, R. S., Banegas, J. R., Giampaoli, S., Hense, H., Joffres, M., . . . Vescio, F. (2003). Hypertension prevalence and blood pressure levels in 6 European countries, Canada, and the United States. *Journal of the American Medical Association, 289*, 2363–2369.

Wolraich, M. L., Wibbelsman, C. J., Brown, T. E., Evans, S. W., Gotlieb, E. M., Knight, J. R., Ross, C., . . . Wilens, T. (2005). Attention-deficit/hyperactivity disorder among adolescents: A review of the diagnosis, treatment, and clinical implications. *Pediatrics, 115*, 1734–1746.

Wong, C. A., Scavone, B. M., Peaceman, A. M., McCarthy, R. J., Sullivan, J. T., Diaz, N. T., . . . Grouper, S. (2005). The risk of cesarean delivery with neuraxial analgesia given early versus late in labor. *New England Journal of Medicine, 352*, 655–665.

Wong, H., Gottesman, I., & Petronis, A. (2005). Phenotypic differences in genetically identical organisms: The epigenetic perspective. *Human Molecular Genetics, 14*(Review Issue 1), R11–R18.

Wong, M. M., Nigg, J. T., Zucker, R. A., Puttler, L. I., Fitzgerald, H. E., Jester, J. M., . . . Adams, K. (2006). Behavioral control and resiliency in the onset of alcohol and illicit drug use: A prospective study from preschool to adolescence. *Child Development, 77*, 1016–1033.

Wood, D. (1980). Teaching the young child: Some relationships between social interaction, language, and thought. In D. Olson (Ed.), *The social foundations of language and thought* (pp. 280–296). New York: Norton.

Wood, D., Bruner, J., & Ross, G. (1976). The role of tutoring in problem solving. *Journal of Child Psychiatry and Psychology, 17*, 89–100.

Wood, R. M., & Gustafson, G. E. (2001). Infant crying and adults' anticipated caregiving responses: Acoustic and contextual influences. *Child Development, 72*, 1287–1300.

Wood, W., & Eagly, A. (2002). A cross-cultural analysis of the behavior of women and men: Implications for the origins of sex differences. *Psychological Bulletin, 128*, 699–727.

Woodruff, T. J., Axelrad, D. A., Kyle, A. D., Nweke, O., Miller, G. G., & Hurley, B. J. (2004). Trends in environmentally related childhood illnesses. *Pediatrics, 113*, 1133–1140.

Woodward, A. L., Markman, E. M., & Fitzsimmons, C. M. (1994). Rapid word learning in 13- and 18-month olds. *Development Psychology, 30*, 553–566.

Woolley, J. D. (1997). Thinking about fantasy: Are children fundamentally different thinkers and believers from adults? *Child Development, 68*(6), 991–1011.

Woolley, J. D., & Boerger, E. A. (2002). Development of beliefs about the origins and controllability of dreams. *Developmental Psychology, 38*(1), 24–41.

Woolley, J. D., Phelps, K. E., Davis, D. L., & Mandell, D. J. (1999). Where theories of mind meet magic: The development of children's beliefs about wishing. *Child Development, 70*, 571–587.

World Bank. (2006). *Repositioning nutrition as central to development.* Washington, DC: Author.

World Bank. (n.d.). *Life expectancy at birth, total (years).* Retrieved from http://data.worldbank.org/indicator/SP.DYN.LE00.IN

World Cancer Research Fund. (2007, November). *Food, nutrition, physical activity, and the prevention of cancer: A global perspective.* London: Author.

World Health Organization (WHO). (2000, June 4). *WHO issues new healthy life expectancy rankings: Japan number one in new "healthy life" system* [Press release]. Washington, DC: Author.

World Health Organization (WHO). (2003). *The world health report—Shaping the future.* Retrieved from www.who.int/wrh/2003/chapter1en/index2.html

World Health Organization (WHO). (2005). *WHO multi-country study on women's health and domestic violence against women: Summary report of initial results of prevalence, health outcomes and women's responses.* Geneva: Author.

World Health Organization (WHO). (2007a). *Neonatal and perinatal mortality: Country, regional and global estimates 2004.* Geneva: Author.

World Health Organization (WHO). (2007b). *World health statistics 2007.* Geneva: Author.

World Health Organization (WHO). (2008). *Preventable injuries kill 2000 children every day.* Retrieved from www.who.int/mediacentre/news/releases/2008/pr46/en/print.html

World Health Organization (WHO). (2010). *Causes of child mortality.* Retrieved from http://www.who.int/gho/child_health/mortality/causes/en/index.html

World Health Organization. (2011). *World health statistics 2011.* Geneva: Author.

World Health Organization (WHO). (2012). *Trends in maternal mortality: 1990–2010.* Retrieved from http://whqlibdoc.who.int/publications/2012/9789241503631_eng.pdf

World Health Organization (WHO). (2013). *Levels and trends in child mortality.* Retrieved from http://www.who.int/maternal_child_adolescent/documents/levels_trends_child_mortality_2013

World Health Organization (WHO). (n.d.). *Global health observatory: Life expectancy.* Retrieved from http://www.who.int/gho/mortality_burden_disease/life_tables/situation_trends/en/

Worth, K., Gibson, J., Chambers, M. S., Nassau, D., Balvinder, K., Rakhra, A. B., & Sargent, J. (2008). Exposure of U.S. adolescents to extremely violent movies. *Pediatrics, 122*(2), 306–312.

Wortman, C. B., & Silver, R. C. (1989). The myths of coping with loss. *Journal of Consulting and Clinical Psychology, 57*(3), 349–357.

Wozniak, R. H. (1991). *Childhood: A viewer's guide.* New York: WNET.

Wright, J. D., Hirsch, R., & Wang, C. (2009). One-third of adults embraced most heart healthy behaviors in 1999–2002. *NCHS Data Brief, 17.* Hyattsville, MD: National Center for Health Statistics.

Wright, V. C., Chang, J., Jeng, G., & Macaluso, M. (2006). Assisted reproduction technology surveillance—United States, 2003. *Morbidity and Mortality Weekly Report (Surveillance Summaries), 55*(SS04), 1–22.

Wright, V. C., Chang, J., Jeng, G., & Macaluso, M. (2008, June 20). Assisted reproductive technology surveillance—United States, 2005. *Morbidity and Mortality Weekly Report, 57*(SS05), 1–23.

Writing Group for the Women's Health Initiative Investigators. (2002). Risks and benefits of estrogen plus progestin in healthy postmenopausal women: Principal results from the Women's Health Initiative randomized controlled trial. *Journal of the American Medical Association, 288,* 321–333.

Wu, T., Mendola, P., & Buck, G. M. (2002). Ethnic differences in the presence of secondary sex characteristics and menarche among U.S. girls: The Third National Health and Nutrition Survey, 1988–1994. *Pediatrics, 11,* 752–757.

Wu, Z., & Hart, R. (2002). The effects of marital and nonmarital union transition on health. *Journal of Marriage and Family, 64,* 420–432.

Wu, Z., Hou, F., & Schimmele, C. M. (2008). Family structure and children's psychosocial outcomes. *Journal of Family Issues, 29,* 1600–1624.

Wulczyn, F. (2004). Family reunification. In David and Lucile Packard Foundation, Children, families, and foster care. *Future of Children, 14*(1). Retrieved from www.futureofchildren.org

Wykle, M. L., & Musil, C. M. (1993). Mental health of older persons: Social and cultural factors. *Generations, 17*(1), 7–12.

Wynn, K. (1990). Children's understanding of counting. *Cognition, 36,* 155–193.

Wynn, K. (1992). Evidence against empiricist accounts of the origins of numerical knowledge. *Mind and Language, 7,* 315–332.

Wyrobek, A. J., Eskenazi, B., Young, S., Arnheim, N., Tiemann-Boege, I., Jabs, E. W., . . . & Evenson, D. (2006). Advancing age has differential effects on DNA damage, chromatin integrity, gene mutations, and aneuploidies in sperm. *Proceedings of the National Academy of Sciences, 103*(25), 9601–9606.

Xu, J. Q., Kochanek, K. D., Murphy, S. L., & Tejada-Vera, B. (2010). Deaths: Final data for 2007. *National Vital Statistics Report, 58*(19). Hyattsville, MD: National Center for Health Statistics.

Xu, X., Hudspeth, C. D., & Bartkowski, J. P. (2006). The role of cohabitation in remarriage. *Journal of Marriage and Family, 68,* 261–274.

Yamada, H. (2004). Japanese mothers' views of young children's areas of personal discretion. *Child Development, 75,* 164–179.

Yamazaki, J. N., & Schull, W. J. (1990). Perinatal loss and neurological abnormalities among children of the atomic bomb. *Journal of the American Medical Association, 264,* 605–609.

Yan, L. L., Daviglus, M. L., Liu, K., Stamler, J., Wang, R., Pirzada, A., . . . Greenland, P. (2006). Midlife body mass index and hospitalization and mortality in older age. *Journal of the American Medical Association, 295,* 190–198.

Yan, L. L., Liu, K., Matthews, K. A., Daviglus, M. L., Ferguson, T. F., & Kiefe, C. I. (2003). Psychosocial factors and risk of hypertension: The Coronary Artery Risk Development in Young Adults (CARDIA) study. *Journal of the American Medical Association, 290,* 2138.

Yang, B., Ollendick, T. H., Dong, Q., Xia, Y., & Lin, L. (1995). Only children and children with siblings in the People's Republic of China: Levels of fear, anxiety, and depression. *Child Development, 66,* 1301–1311.

Yang, Y. (2008). Social inequalities in happiness in the United States, 1972 to 2004: An age-period-cohort analysis. *American Sociological Review, 73,* 204–226.

Yarkoni, T. (2010). Personality in 100,000 words: A large-scale analysis of personality and word use among bloggers. *Journal of Research in Personality, 44*(33), 363–373.

Yau, J. P., Tausopoulos-Chan, M., & Smetana, J. G. (2009). Disclosure to parents about everyday activities among American adolescents from Mexican, Chinese and European backgrounds. *Child Development, 80*(5), 1481–1498.

Yeh, H., Lorenz, F. O., Wickrama, K. A. S., Conger, R. D., & Elder, G. H. (2006). Relationships among sexual satisfaction, marital quality, and marital instability at midlife. *Journal of Family Psychology, 20,* 339–343.

Yeung, W. J., Sandberg, J. F., Davis-Kean, P. E., & Hofferth, S. L. (2001). Children's time with fathers in intact families. *Journal of Marriage and Family, 63,* 136–154.

Yip, T., Seaton, E. K., & Sellers, R. M. (2006). African American racial identity across the lifespan: Identity status, identity content, and depressive symptoms. *Child Development, 77,* 1504–1517.

Yokota, F., & Thompson, K. M. (2000). Violence in G-rated animated films. *Journal of the American Medical Association, 283,* 2716–2720.

Yoshikawa, H. (1994). Prevention as cumulative protection: Effects of early family support and education on chronic delinquency and its risks. *Psychological Bulletin, 115*(1), 28–54.

Yoshikawa, H., Weisner, T. S., Kalil, A., & Way, N. (2008). Mixing qualitative and quantitative research in developmental science: Uses and methodological choices. *Developmental Psychology, 44,* 344–354.

Young, K. A., Holcomb, L. A., Bonkale, W. L., Hicks, P. B., Yazdani, U., & German, D. C. (2007). 5HTTLPR polymorphism and enlargement of the pulvinar: Unlocking the backdoor to the limbic system. *Biological Psychiatry, 61*(1), 813–818.

Youngblade, L. M., & Belsky, J. (1992). Parent-child antecedents of 5-year-olds' close friendships: A longitudinal analysis. *Developmental Psychology, 28,* 700–713.

Youngblade, L. M., Theokas, C., Schulenberg, J., Curry, L., Huang, I-C., & Novak, M. (2007). Risk and promotive factors in families, schools, and communities: A contextual model of positive youth development in adolescence. *Pediatrics, 119,* 47–53.

Youth violence: A report of the surgeon general (2001, January). Retrieved from www.surgeongeneral.gov/library/youthviolence/default.htm

Yu, S. M., Huang, Z. J., & Singh, G. K. (2004). Health status and health services utilization among U.S. Chinese, Asian Indian, Filipino, and other Asian/Pacific Islander children. *Pediatrics, 113*(1), 101–107.

Yu, T., & Adler-Baeder, F. (2007). The intergenerational transmission of relationship quality: The effect of parental remarriage quality on young adults relationships. *Journal of Divorce and Remarriage, 3–4,* 87–102.

Yunger, J. L., Carver, P. R., & Perry, D. G. (2004). Does gender identity influence children's psychological well-being? *Developmental Psychology, 40,* 572–582.

Yurgelun-Todd, D. (2002). *Inside the teen brain.* Retrieved from www.pbs.org/wgbh/pages/frontline/shows/teenbrain/interviews/todd.html

Zadik, Y., Bechor, R., Galor, S., & Levin, L. (2010). Periodontal disease might be associated even with impaired fasting glucose. *British Dental Journal, 208*(10), E20–E20.

Zahn-Waxler, C., Friedman, R. J., Cole, P. M., Mizuta, I., & Hiruma, N. (1996). Japanese and U.S. preschool children's responses to conflict and distress. *Child Development, 67,* 2462–2477.

Zahn-Waxler, C., Radke-Yarrow, M., Wagner, E., & Chapman, M. (1992). Development of concern for others. *Developmental Psychology, 28,* 126–136.

Zajonc, R. B., Adelmann, P. K., Murphy, S. T., & Niedenthal, P. M. (1987). Convergence in the physical appearance of spouses. *Motivation and Emotion, 11*(4), 335–346.

Zametkin, A. J., & Ernst, M. (1999). Problems in the management of attention-deficit-hyperactivity disorder. *New England Journal of Medicine, 340,* 40–46.

Zanardo, V., Svegliado, G., Cavallin, F., Giustardi, A., Cosmi, E., Litta, P., & Trevisanuto, D. (2010). Elective cesarean delivery: Does it have a negative effect on breastfeeding? *Birth, 37*(4), 275–279.

Zandi, P. P., Anthony, J. C., Hayden, K. M., Mehta, K., Mayer, L., & Breitner, J. C. S. (2002). Reduced incidence of AD with NSAID but no H_2 receptor antagonists. *Neurology, 59,* 880–886.

Zeiger, J. S., Beaty, T. H., & Liang, K. (2005). Oral clefts, maternal smoking, and TGFA: A meta-analysis of gene-environment interaction. *The Cleft Palate-Craniofacial Journal, 42*(1) 58–63.

Zelazo, P. D., & Müller, U. (2002). Executive function in typical and atypical development. In U. Goswami (Ed.), *Handbook of childhood cognitive development* (pp. 445–469). Oxford: Blackwell.

Zelazo, P. D., Müller, U., Frye, D., & Marcovitch, S. (2003). The development of executive function in early childhood. *Monographs of the Society for Research in Child Development, 68*(3, Serial No. 274).

Zelazo, P. R., Kearsley, R. B., & Stack, D. M. (1995). Mental representations for visual sequences: Increased speed of central processing from 22 to 32 months. *Intelligence, 20,* 41–63.

Zhang, Q. F. (2004). Economic transition and new patterns of parent-adult child coresidence in China. *Journal of Marriage and Family, 66,* 1232–1245.

Zhang, Z. (2006). Marital history and the burden of cardiovascular disease in midlife. *Gerontologist, 46,* 266–270.

Zhang, X., Huang, C. T., Chen, J., Pankratz, M. T., Xi, J., Li, J., . . . Zhang, S-U. (2010). Pax6 is a human neuroectoderm cell fate determinant. *Cell Stem Cell, 7*(1), 90–100.

Zhang, W., Johnson, T. J., Seltzer, T., & Bichard, S. L. (2010). The revolution will be networked: The influence of social networking sites on political attitudes and behavior. *Social Science Computer Review, 28,* 75–92. doi: 10.1177/0894439309335162

Zhao, D., Zhang, Q., Fu, M., Tang, Y., & Zhao, Y. (2010). Effects of physical positions on sleep architectures and post-nap functions among habitual nappers. *Biological Psychology, 83*(3), 207–213. doi: 10.1016/j.biopsycho.2009.12.008

Zhao, Y. (2002, May 29). Cultural divide over parental discipline. *The New York Times.* Retreived from www.nytimes.com/2002/05/29/nyregion/29DISC.html?ex

Zigler, E., & Styfco, S. J. (2001). Extended childhood intervention prepares children for school and beyond. *Journal of the American Medical Association, 285,* 2378–2380.

Zigler, E., Taussig, C., & Black, K. (1992). Early childhood intervention: A promising preventative for juvenile delinquency. *American Psychologist, 47,* 997–1006.

Zimmerman, B. J., Bandura, A., & Martinez-Pons, M. (1992). Self-motivation for academic attainment: The role of self-efficacy beliefs and personal goal setting. *American Educational Research Journal, 29,* 663–676.

Zimmerman, F. J., & Christakis, D. A. (2005). Children's television viewing and cognitive outcomes: A longitudinal analysis of national data. *Archives of Pediatrics & Adolescent Medicine, 159*(7), 619–625.

Zimmerman, F. J., Christakis, D. A., & Meltzoff, A. N. (2007). Associations between media viewing and language development in children under age 2 years. *Journal of Pediatrics, 151*(4), 364–368.

Zizza, C., Siega-Riz, A. M., & Popkin, B. M. (2001). Significant increase in young adults' snacking between 1977–1978 and 1994–1996 represents a cause for concern! *Preventive Medicine, 32,* 303–310.

Zosuls, K. M., Ruble, D. N., Tamis-LeMonda, C. S., Shrout, P. E., Bornstein, M. H., & Greulich, F. K. (2009). The acquisition of gender labels in infancy: Implications for gender-typed play. *Developmental Psychology, 45*(3), 688–701. doi: 10.1037/a0014053

Zucker, A. N., Ostrove, J. M., & Stewart, A. J. (2002). College-educated women's personality development in adulthood: Perceptions and age differences. *Psychology and Aging, 17,* 236–244.

Zuckerman, B. S., & Beardslee, W. R. (1987). Maternal depression: A concern for pediatricians. *Pediatrics, 79,* 110–117.

Zylke, J., & DeAngelis, C. (2007). Pediatric chronic diseases—Stealing childhood. *Journal of the American Medical Association, 297*(24), 2765–2766.

credits

TEXT AND LINE ART CREDITS

Chapter 1

Figure 2: From Diane E. Papalia and Ruth Duskin Feldman, *A Child's World: Infancy through Adolescence*, 12th ed., p. 11, Figure 1.1 a & b. Copyright © 2011 by the McGraw-Hill Companies, Inc. Reprinted with permission.

Chapter 2

Figure 2: From Gabriela Martorell, Diane Papalia and Ruth Feldman, *A Child's World: Infancy through Adolescence*, 13th ed. Copyright © 2013 by The McGraw-Hill Companies, Inc. Reprinted with permission; Table 1: From Gabriela Martorell, Diane Papalia and Ruth Feldman, *A Child's World: Infancy through Adolescence*, 13th ed. Copyright © 2013 by The McGraw-Hill Companies, Inc. Reprinted with permission; Figure 3: From Gabriela Martorell, Diane Papalia and Ruth Feldman, *A Child's World: Infancy through Adolescence*, 13th ed. Copyright © 2013 by The McGraw-Hill Companies, Inc. Reprinted with permission; Figure 4: From Gabriela Martorell, Diane Papalia and Ruth Feldman, *A Child's World: Infancy through Adolescence*, 13th ed. Copyright © 2013 by The McGraw-Hill Companies, Inc. Reprinted with permission.

Chapter 3

Figure 4: From Diane E. Papalia and Ruth Duskin Feldman, *A Child's World: Infancy through Adolescence*, 12th ed., p. 67, Figure 3.4. Copyright © 2011 by The McGraw-Hill Companies, Inc. Reprinted with permission; Figure 7: From Diane E. Papalia and Ruth Duskin Feldman, *A Child's World: Infancy through Adolescence*, 8th ed. Copyright © 1999 by The McGraw-Hill Companies, Inc. Reprinted with permission. Figure 8: Art by Patricia J. Wynne from H. Lagercrantz and T. A. Slotkin, *"The stress of being born,"* Scientific American 254(4), 1986, pp. 100–107. Reprinted by permission of Patricia J. Wynne.

Chapter 4

Figure 1: From Diane E. Papalia and Ruth Duskin Feldman, *A Child's World: Infancy through Adolescence*, 12th ed., p. 109, Figure 5.1. Copyright © 2011 by The McGraw-Hill Companies, Inc. Reprinted with permission; Figure 4: From Diane E. Papalia and Ruth Duskin Feldman, *A Child's World: Infancy through Adolescence*, 12th ed., p. 121, Figure 5.4. Copyright © 2011 by The McGraw-Hill Companies, Inc. Reprinted with permission; Figure 6: From Diane E. Papalia and Ruth Duskin Feldman, A Child's World: Infacy through Adolescence, 11th ed., Figure 6.8. Copyright © 2008 by The McGraw-Hill Companies, Inc. Reprinted with permission; Figure 10: From Diane E. Papalia and Ruth Duskin Feldman, *A Child's World: Infancy through Adolescence*, 13th ed. Copyright © 2011 by the McGraw-Hill Companies, Inc. Reprinted with permission.

Chapter 5

Table 1: From Diane E. Papalia, Sally Wendkos Olds, and Ruth Duskin Feldman, *A Child's World: Infancy through Adolescence*, 11th ed. Copyright © 2008 by The McGraw-Hill Companies, Inc. Reprinted with permission; Figure 2: From Gabriela Martorell, Diane Papalia and Ruth Feldman, *A Child's World: Infancy through Adolescence*, 13th ed. Copyright © 2013 by The McGraw-Hill Companies, Inc. Reprinted with permission.

Chapter 6

Figure 2: From Papalia, *Experience Human Development*, 12th ed. Copyright © 2011. Reprinted by permission of The McGraw-Hill Companies, Inc.; Table 4: From Diane E. Papalia, Sally Wendkos Olds, and Ruth Duskin Feldman, *A Child's World: Infancy through Adolescence*, 11th ed. Copyright © 2008 by The McGraw-Hill Companies, Inc. Reprinted with permission.

Chapter 7

Table 1: From Diane E. Papalia, Sally Wendkos Olds, and Ruth Duskin Feldman, *A Child's World: Infancy through Adolescence*, 9th ed., p. 213. Copyright © 2002 by The McGraw-Hill Copmanies, Inc. Reprinted with permission; Figure 2: From Rhoda Kellogg, *Analyzing Children's Art*. Mountain View, CA: Mayfield Publishing Company, 1970. Copyright © 1969, 1970 by Rhoda Kellogg. Reprinted by permission of The McGraw-Hill Companies, Inc.; Table 5: From Diane E. Papalia, Sally Wendkos Olds, and Ruth Duskin Feldman, *A Child's World: Infancy through Adolescence*, 9th ed., p. 237. Copyright © 2002 by The McGraw-Hill Companies, Inc. Reprinted with permission; Figure 4: From Martorell, Child: *From Birth to Adolescence*. Copyright © 2012. Reprinted by permission of The McGraw-Hill Companies, Inc.; Table 6: From Diane E. Papalia, Sally Wendkos Olds, and Ruth Duskin Feldman, *A Child's World: Infancy through Adolescence*, 9th ed., p. 241. Copyright © 2002 by The McGraw-Hill Companies, Inc. Reprinted with permission.

Chapter 10

Figure 1: From Gabriela Martorell, Diane Papalia and Ruth Feldman, *A Child's World: Infancy through Adolescence*, 13th ed. Copyright © 2013 by The McGraw-Hill Companies, Inc. Reprinted with permission;

Chapter 11

Table 1: From Diane E. Papalia and Ruth Duskin Feldman, *A Child's World: Infancy through Adolescence*, 12th ed., p. 407, Table 15.3. Copyright © 2011 by The McGraw-Hill Companies, Inc. Reprinted with permission.

Chapter 14

Table 1: Sternberg, R.J. "A Triangular Theory of Love." *Psychological Review*, 93, 119–135 (1986). Reprinted with permission of Robert J. Sternberg.

Chapter 16

Figure 1: Source: Wethington, E., Kessler, R. C., & Pixley, J. E. (2004). Turning points in adulthood. In O. G. Brim, C. D. Ryff , & R. C. Kessler, (Eds.), *How Healthy Are We? A National Study of Well-Being at Midlife*, Figure 3, p. 600. © 2004 by The University of Chicago. Reprinted by permission of The University of Chicago Press.

PHOTOS

Image Researcher:
Toni Michaels/PhotoFind, L.L.C.

Front Matter

Page vi(top): © Alistair Berg/Getty Images RF; p. vi(bottom): © Corbis RF; p. viii: © Laura Dwight; p. ix: © Moodboard/age fotostock RF; p. x: © moodboard/Alamy RF; p. xi(top): © Image Source/Getty Images RF; p. xi(bottom): © 2009, Mike Watson Images Limited/Glow Images RF; p. xii: © Blend Images/Getty Images RF; p. xiii: © Con Tanasiuk/Design Pics/age fotostock RF.

Chapter 1

Opener: © Alistair Berg/Getty Images RF; p. 4: © Living Art Enterprises, LLC/Science Source; p. 5: © Ariel Skelley/Blend Images RF; p. 9: © Blend Images/Alamy RF; p. 12: © SWNS.com; p. 14: © Digital Archive Japan/Alamy RF; p. 15: © Nina Leen/TimePix/Getty Images.

Chapter 2

Opener: © Sean Locke/Getty Images RF; p. 25: © Imagno/Getty Images; p. 27: © Bettmann/Corbis; p. 29: © Ron Nickel/Design Pics/age fotostock; p. 30: © Bill Anderson/Science Source; p. 31: © Sovfoto/UIG/Getty Images; p. 38: © Lawrence Migdale/Science Source; p. 39: © WDCN/University College London/Science Source.

Chapter 3

Opener: © Corbis RF; p. 49: © Pascal Goetgheluck/Science Source; p. 54(top left): © Plush Studios/Blend Images RF; p. 54(top right): © Ariel Skelley/Blend Images RF; p. 54(left): © Glow Images RF; p. 54(center left): © Sean Justice/Corbis RF; p. 54(center right): © Glow Images RF; p. 54(right): © Pixtal/AGE Fotostock RF; p. 54(bottom): © Rubberball/Getty Images RF; p. 55: © Pat Sullivan/AP Images; p. 56: © Science

Photo Library RF/Getty Images RF; p. 59: © Stockbyte/Veer RF; p. 63: © T.K. Wanstal/The Image Works; p. 66: © Corbis RF; p. 68: © Digital Vision/ PunchStock RF; p. 74: © Jose Luis Pelaez/Blend Images/Alamy RF; p. 77: © BSIP/UIG/Getty Images; p. 70(1 mo.): © Petit Format/Nestle/Science Source; p. 70(3 mo.): © Science Pictures Ltd./Science Source; p. 70(4 mo.): © Tissuepix/Science Source; p. 70(5 mo.): © James Stevenson/Science Source; p. 70(7 wks.): © Petit Format/Nestle/Science Source; p. 71(6 mo.): © Anatomical Travelogue/Science Source; p. 71(7 mo.): © Petit Format/Nestle/Science Source; p. 71(8 mo.): © Petit Format/Nestle/Science Source; p. 71(9 mo.): © Jennie Hart/Alamy.

Chapter 4

Opener: © Maya Barnes Johansen/The Image Works; p. 92: © Brand X Pictures/Jupiterimages RF; p. 97: © Chris Harvey/Getty Images; p. 98: © Charles Thatcher/Getty Images; p. 100: © U.S. Air Force photo by Staff Sgt. Marcus McDonald; p. 105: © Mark Thomas/SPL/Science Source; p. 108: © Jose Luis Pelaez Inc./Blend Images RF; p. 109: © Dennis MacDonald/PhotoEdit; p. 115(top left): © Laura Dwight; p. 115(top center): © Lew Merrim/Science Source; p. 115(top right): © Laura Dwight; p. 115(bottom left): © Elizabeth Crews; p. 115(bottom center): © Astier/Science Source; p. 115(bottom right): © BSIP/UIG/Getty Images; p. 118(left): © Erika Stone; p. 118(center): © Elizabeth Crews; p. 118(right): © Jennie Woodcock/Corbis Images; p. 121: © Mark Richards/PhotoEdit; p. 122: © Sue Bennett/Alamy.

Chapter 5

Opener: © UpperCut Images/Superstock RF; p. 128: © Rajesh Kumar Singh/AP Images; p. 129: © Bananastock/PictureQuest RF; p. 131(top): © Corbis RF; p. 131(bottom): © Glow Images RF; p. 137: © Doug Goodman/Science Source; p. 138: © Albert Mollon/Flickr/Getty Images; p. 144: © Laura Dwight; p. 151: © PhotoDisc/Getty Images RF; p. 154: © Jani Bryson/Getty Images; p. 156: © Uniquely India/Getty Images RF; p. 157: © Keith Brofsky/Blend Images RF.

Chapter 6

Opener: © Bob Lewine/Tetra Images/Corbis RF; p. 162: © Bananastock/PictureQuest RF; p. 163(top): © Frare/Davis Photography/Brand X/Corbis RF; p. 163(center): © Amos Morgan/Getty Images RF; p. 163(bottom): © Comstock Images RF; p. 164: Courtesy of Primo Pelczynski; p. 167: © Camille Tokerud/Getty Images; p. 169: Harlow Primate Laboratory, University of Wisconsin; p. 170: © Brand X Pictures/Jupiterimages RF; p. 172: Courtesy Jonathan Finlay; p. 175: © Michael Newman/PhotoEdit; p. 179(top): © Laura Dwight; p. 179(bottom): © Steve Wisbauer/Getty Images RF; p. 184: © Eastcott/The Image Works.

Chapter 7

Opener: © Laura Dwight; p. 196: © Laura Dwight; p. 199(left): © Laura Dwight; p. 199(center): © Ariel Skelley/Blend Images/Getty Images; p. 199(right): © Kid Stock/Blend Images/Getty Images; p. 201: © Jose Luis Pelaez Inc./Getty Images; p. 206: © Tony Freeman/PhotoEdit; p. 209: © Erika Stone; p. 214: © Tony Freeman/PhotoEdit; p. 217: © Don Hammond/DesignPics RF; p. 220: © Rubberball/PictureQuest RF; p. 223: © Bernhard Classen/Alamy.

Chapter 8

Opener: © Masterfile; p. 231: © Phoebe Dunn/Stock Connection Distribution/Alamy; p. 233: © Nancy Richmond/The Image Works; p. 235: © Leanna Rathkelly/Getty Images; p. 244: © Sean Justice/Corbis RF; p. 246: © Pixtal/age fotostock RF; p. 250: © Laura Dwight; p. 252: © Randy Faris/Corbis; p. 253: © Dave Umberger/AP Images; p. 255: Courtesy, Gabriela Martorell.

Chapter 9

Opener: © Moodboard/age fotostock RF; p. 262: © Blue Jean Images/Corbis; p. 265: © Ingram Publishing/Superstock RF; p. 270: © Laura Dwight; p. 273: © Evan Vucci/AP Images; p. 276: © Image 100 Ltd. RF; p. 279: © Juan Silva 2010/Getty Images; p. 283: © Blend Images/Getty Images RF; p. 285: © Digital Vision RF; p. 289: © Brian Mitchell/Corbis.

Chapter 10

Opener: © Juice Images/Getty Images RF; p. 296: © Michael Justice/The Image Works; p. 298: © Jose Luis Pelaez Inc./Getty Images RF; p. 299: © Ariel Skelley/Blend Images RF; p. 302: © Laura Dwight/PhotoEdit; p. 304: © Fancy Photography/Veer RF; p. 306: © Roberto/Schmidt/AFP/Getty Images; p. 309: © Erika Stone; p. 310: © Don Hammond/Design Pics Inc./Alamy RF; p. 312: © Jonathan Nourok/PhotoEdit; p. 316: © Michael Newman/PhotoEdit.

Chapter 11

Opener: © moodboard/Alamy RF; p. 324: © Enric Marti/AP Images; p. 327: © Mary Kate Denny/PhotoEdit; p. 331: © Corbis RF; p. 334: © Richard Nowitz/Science Source; p. 337: © Doug Menuez/Getty Images RF; p. 339: © Fancy Collection/Superstock RF; p. 348: © Purestock/Getty Images RF; p. 353: © Peter Arkell/Imagestate Media Partners Ltd./Impact Photos/Alamy.

Chapter 12

Opener: © Red Chopsticks/Photolibrary RF; p. 358: © Michael Pole/Corbis; p. 362: © Ryan McVay/Getty Images RF; p. 368: MTV/Photofest © MTV; p. 370: © Erika Stone; p. 375: © Design Pics/Kristy-Anne Glubish/Getty Images; p. 376: © Pixtal/age fotostock RF; p. 381: © Rubberball/Getty Images RF.

Chapter 13

Opener: © Image Source/Getty Images RF; p. 386: © Digital Vision/Getty Images RF; p. 389: © Ulrich Baumgarten/vario images GmbH & Co.KG/Alamy; p. 390: © Ryan McVay/Getty Images RF; p. 392: © David Wells//The Image Works; p. 393: © Royalty-Free/Corbis RF; p. 397: © Minot Daily News/AP Images; p. 406: © Doug Menuez/Getty Images RF; p. 408: © Spencer Grant/Getty Images.

Chapter 14

Opener: © Sam Edwards/age fotostock RF; p. 414: © Mike Kemp/Rubberball/Getty Images RF; p. 416: © Jupiterimages/Thinkstock/Alamy RF; p. 418: © Mark Scott/Getty Images; p. 423: © 2009 Jupiterimages Corporation; p. 425: © Fiona Goodall/Getty Images; p. 429: © Aman Sharma/AP Images; p. 432: © Image100/Corbis RF.

Chapter 15

Opener: © 2009, Mike Watson Images Limited/Glow Images RF; p. 441: © Rene Macura/AP Images; p. 443: © Ronnie Kaufman/Blend Images RF; p. 446: © Ty Milford/Aurora Open/Getty Images RF; p. 452: © Ron Chapple/Getty Images; p. 453(left): © Susumu Nishinaga/Science Source; p. 453(right): © Steve Gschmeissner/Science Source; p. 454: © Rhoda Baer/National Cancer Institute (NCI); p. 455: © BananaStock/Alamy RF; p. 456: © Brian Yarvin/The Image Works; p. 462: © Corbis RF; p. 463: © Lester Cohen/WireImage/Getty Images.

Chapter 16

Opener: © Picturenet/Blend Images/age fotostock RF; p. 472: © Getty Images RF; p. 475: © Laura Dwight; p. 477: © AP Images; p. 479: © Las Cruces Sun-News, Norm Dettlaff/AP Images; p. 485: © Lars A. Niki RF; p. 489: © Hero/Corbis/Glow Images RF; p. 492: © Cameramann/The Image Works.

Chapter 17

Opener: © Blend Images/Getty Images RF; p. 497: © Noel Vasquez/Getty Images; p. 502: © Digital Vision/PunchStock RF; p. 505: © Kyodo/AP Images; p. 508(both): National Eye Institute, National Institutes of Health; p. 513: © Boiffin-Vivierre/Explorer/Science Source; p. 517(both): Artwork by Esther Lipman Rosenthal. Photos courtesy Linda Lee Goldman; p. 518: © Dr. Robert Friedland/Science Photo Library/Science Source; p. 523: © Blend Images/Granger Wootz/Getty Images.

Chapter 18

Opener: © Joselito Briones/Getty Images; p. 529: © Carolyn Kaster/AP Images; p. 530: © Skip O'Rourke/The Image Works; p. 533: © Mukhtar Khan/AP Images; p. 535: © Steve Mason/Getty Images RF; p. 539: © Jim West/Alamy; p. 542: © Journal-Courier/Clayton Stalter/The Image Works; p. 547: © Stockbyte/Getty Images RF; p. 550: © Thinkstock RF; p. 553: © Matthew Jordan Smith.

Chapter 19

Opener: © Con Tanasiuk/Design Pics/age fotostock RF; p. 558: © Ron Nickel/Design Pics/Corbis; p. 560: © Mark Gibbons/Alamy RF; p. 561: © Spohn Matthieu/Getty Images RF; p. 565: © John Lund/Tiffany Schoepp/Blend Images RF; p. 566: © Colin Paterson/Getty Images RF; p. 570: © Jose Luis Pelaez, Inc./Corbis Images; p. 576: © Royalty-Free/Corbis RF.

name index

subject index

Page numbers in **boldface** indicate key terms. Page numbers followed by *t* indicate tables; page numbers followed by *f* indicate figures.

$$(.5)(-.5) + (-1.5)(-3) + (3.5)(-14) + (-2.5)(-7.5)$$

$$\frac{(-.25) + (4.5) + (-49) + (18.75)}{3}$$

$$-8.5$$